Unifying Causality and Psychology

Gerald Young

Unifying Causality and Psychology

Being, Brain, and Behavior

Springer

Gerald Young
Toronto, ON, Canada

ISBN 978-3-319-24092-3 ISBN 978-3-319-24094-7 (eBook)
DOI 10.1007/978-3-319-24094-7

Library of Congress Control Number: 2016936102

Printed on acid-free paper

This Springer imprint is published by Springer Nature
The registered company is Springer International Publishing AG Switzerland

Preface

We are all born with this basic curiosity about understanding our origins and heritage. We all want to understand not only what happens, what people are like, and what things are interesting but also why things happen; why people behave, think, and feel like they do; and why things work and how. This book is about the causes of behavior considered broadly. It examines behavior both in terms of actions and its mental content, such as cognition, motivation, and emotion. It examines behavior that is considered abnormal as well as normal. It adopts an approach to the causes of behavior that respects the extreme positions that they are all biological (Nature) or environmental (Nurture) by creating an inclusive interactional model. Moreover, the model addresses the role of personal or self-factors in development, such as free will and self-control.

I have written on the topic of causality in behavior in development (*Development and Causality: Neo-Piagetian Perspectives*, Springer Science + Business Media, 2011) and psychological injury (*Causality of Psychological Injury: Presenting Evidence in Court*, Springer Science + Business Media, 2007) and expanded these endeavors in subsequent publications (e.g., *Malingering, Feigning, and Response Bias in Psychiatric/Psychological Injury: Implications for Practice and Court*, Springer Science + Business Media, 2014). This new book on the topic greatly expands these initial endeavors in understanding causality in behavior. It provides comprehensive chapters ranging from genetics and epigenetics, to the brain and stress response in adversity, to the role of development and the environment. It deals with topics as diverse as free will and psychopathology. It presents new models related to behavioral causality; reworks other models, such as the renowned Maslow model of motivation; and generally puts together a comprehensive understanding of behavior and its causes.

My career in psychology began with studying facial expressions in infants from an evolutionary perspective (publishing an article in *American Behavior* in 1977). Then I edited a book on brain development (*Manual Specialization and the Developing Brain*, Academic Press, 1983). Next, I wrote a book on adult development (*Adult Development, Therapy, and Culture: A Postmodern Synthesis*, Plenum, 1997). Also, I began my externship to become a clinical psychologist about that time. It led to my work on psychological injury and law, for which I founded the first journal and first society dedicated to the topic [*Psychological Injury and Law* (PIL; www.springer.com) and *Association of Scientific Advancement in Psychological Injury and Law* (ASAPIL; www.asapil.net)]. Many colleagues have helped in these multiple endeavors (e.g., see the PIL masthead for the board members). We all share an abiding and deep interest in studying the causes of behavior, and this book is a culmination of a long voyage in that study. Its broad scope is the only way to tackle the intricacies of the question and to present new ideas toward stimulating further work on it. Please take the challenge.

Toronto, ON, Canada Gerald Young

Acknowledgments

The constant encouragement and support of the editorial and production team at the publishers has been instrumental toward completing this book, in particular. I owe so much thanks to Sharon Panulla and Sylvana Ruggirello in the editorial office and Project Manager Ramya Prakash, Project Coordinator Alamelu Damodharan, and their production team. My staffs has been responsible for the onerous task of typing and keeping track of the manuscript as it has been written. Jenny X. Wang especially has worked at it and kept it organized, with Joyce Chan helping diligently as well and I am so thankful for that. My colleagues at Glendon College at York University have always supported my work as well as my teachers over the years. Finally, this book has been inspired by the need to have students see the big picture in psychology, and I thank mine for all their probing questions over the years.

Evidence-supported practice in psychology is important to the field, as it is in medicine, and I hope that this book contributes to that trend and the respect that science deserves. This book reflects the nature of science, its proponents, and its hardworking and insightful researchers who produce replicable results and refined theory. In this regard, this is my third massive book in the last few years having an integrative scientific theme (also see Young (2011) and Young (2014)). Finally, the book is dedicated to our grandchildren and to our daughters.

Brief Biography

Gerald Young, Ph.D., C. Psych., is an associate professor in the Department of Psychology at Glendon College, York University, Toronto, ON, Canada, who has just been elected as a Fellow of the American Psychological Association. He has just received an award for outstanding lifetime contributions for his trauma research from the Canadian Psychological Association. In addition, he is a practicing psychologist. He is the sole author or senior editor/coauthor of seven books, including one on malingering (*Malingering, Feigning, and Response Bias in Psychiatric/Psychological Injury: Implications for Practice and Court* published by Springer SBM, New York, 2014). For the area of psychological injury and law, he is the first to have organized (a) a scientific association (www.asapil.net), and (b) an academic journal [*Psychological Injury and Law* (PIL; www.springer.com)], and (c) he has written integrative articles in multiple journals on the topic. His other areas of research include child development (*Development and Causality: Neo-Piagetian Perspectives*, Springer SBM, 2011) and the DSM-5 (he coedited two PIL special issues on the topic, in 2010 and 2013). His most recent work is on revising the ethics code of the American Psychological Association (articles in 2014 and 2016). He has successfully testified in a case involving the Supreme Court of Canada on the rights of injured workers.

Contents

Part VI The Neo-Piagetian/Neo-Eriksonian Model

Part I

Core Causality in Behavior: Foundations and Models

Brief Book Description and Book Assumptions

1

Chapter Introduction

Goal

Introduction The major goal of the present book is to meet the challenge presented by its title: *Unifying Causality and Psychology: Being, Brain, and Behavior*. First in this regard, the book constitutes a project on unifying psychology. It does not provide an answer for the project but, rather, presents a path or process toward the integration of psychology. Second, the book deals with the related project of integrating causality. The primary assumption of the book is that by integrating knowledge on the causality of behavior we can proceed toward the integration of psychology. In this regard, the book also attempts to integrate different concepts related to the etiology of disordered behavior. Third, the book examines the multiple causes of behavior, both normal and abnormal. Further, it adapts an approach that is constructivist rather than reductionist. In this regard, it allows for the emergence of factors that influence behavioral causation such as self and . In the end, it adds these "personal" components to the standard argument that Nature and Nurture interact in determining behavior. Finally, it expands the concept of free will to include freedom in being, freeing the brain, and so on. Also, it expands the concept of the self to include the causal self. Indeed, the book proposes that humans are unique in their search for understanding causality of behavior and should be called *Homo Causa*.

Psychology studies both the description (or structure) of behavior and its causes or processes. Much of psychology is concerned with the latter and establishing the "why" or "how" of behavior. However, there is no general book in psychology explicitly devoted to causality, causation, origins, and determinants. Therefore, a major goal of the present book is to promote leading-edge conceptualization on the topic of causality or causation that integrates psychological research and knowledge with interdisciplinary scholarship. How do multiple proximal, or immediate, and distal, or more remote or removed, causal streams combine in their impact or influence on a particular behavior or on a behavior set in a particular situation? When do the influences include only proximal ones, such as present context, and when are there more distal ones, too, not only in genetic influences but also in the environment, such as deriving from one's past, one's development, or one's early unconscious influences that had been repressed? To what extent do immediate influences include room for free will, especially in terms of the effects of believing in it? More specifically, does having a belief in free will alter the options considered in a particular situation and the one eventually chosen? Or, are we simply a deterministic product of our genes and environment without an active say in our own development and life course and, therefore, any construction or model of behavior that includes any role for free

G. Young, *Unifying Causality and Psychology*, DOI 10.1007/978-3-319-24094-7_1

will is inconsistent with the science in the matter? The present book is dedicated to answering questions such as these, toward an integration of not only the area of causality in behavioral study but also the integration of psychology, itself.

To review, the study of causality in psychology rarely is a central topic that is integrated across its separate components. The two goals of the present book concern the integration of causality in psychology and, indeed, movement toward the integration of psychology. In this regard, this book represents the first wide-ranging integration of causality in psychology. As well, it emphasizes that causality has the potential to be a unifying concept in psychological science. Finally, the book promotes the concept of , freedom in being as one that can help fulfill its two primary goals. First, freedom in being is considered an essential driving force in the causality of behavior. Second, the concept of freedom in being can help integrate psychology because it describes the epitome of what it means to be human.

Probability Is causality a sufficient focus to integrate psychology even though it is a ubiquitous aspect even if an underemphasized one of behavioral study? In its present status, in the field, it does not have that potential. To repeat, it needs integration itself before that goal can be accomplished. Moreover, in and of itself, it cannot help unify the field, but only point to directions in this regard.

That being said, the directions toward its integration that the field of psychology needs to take through the medium of causality are clear. On the one hand, having causality as a focus as an integrating concept in psychology enables consideration of its multifactorial nature and the ramifications of such a differentiated process in the determination of both normal and abnormal behavior. On the other hand, with causality as a focus toward integrating psychology both older and newer concepts in the field can serve the task, as long as they are relevant to it and they fit the conceptual construction involved and the empirical directions that are needed to support its validity.

In this regard, the present work is founded both in a comprehensive review of the current literature for its conceptual and empirical contributions and in integration of prior theories to that review that still have value in cohering psychology as a unified discipline in the present context. However, my approach to these traditional models has been to update them to the current context of conceptual and empirical study in psychology, so that I end of presenting revised models for them, e.g., Neo-Maslovian, Neo-Eriksonian, and Neo-Piagetian, and this makes them more foundational than traditional. Moreover, at many junctures in the present book, I show how the different foundational models can be integrated themselves, especially after I have arrived at their revision, and moreover, they can even be integrated with newer models, such as embodiment, the biopsychosocial model, and systems theory.

Certainty That being said, there is no one umbrella model yet in psychology that can serve to integrate it, and perhaps accomplishing that task is impossible. In this regard, we might be able to better integrate the various theories in the field, but none hold promise to be the axis in this regard. The integration has to take place at a different level, in which science is placed at the top of the hierarchy of needs in the integrative task, which automatically places causality as a prime focus, aside from the reliable and valid description of behavior and its organization, per se. The theoretical models have to follow that lead and, in the end, a co-existential model of how each of them contributes to the whole in the field would be sufficient.

The theories in psychology form an integrated system that develops just as the subject matter of the theories develops—that is, we constitute ever-changing systems, especially in terms of all the complexities and causal forces impinging on us, and perhaps that perspective constitutes the best axis for integrating psychology, holding more than any other axis, including that of any one theory about human behavior. We are causal beings both in how we grow and change and in how we think, feel, and act. Perhaps that is the only certainty about ourselves, and perhaps that constitutes the best axis on which to have psychology integrate.

Outline

This first chapter of the present work emphasizes its central assumption of the primacy of causality in psychology and explicates the tens of other assumptions that have guided the book's construction. The chapter after this one describes the book in depth, especially chapter by chapter. The next chapter that follows, the third one of the book, describes the starting point of the book, that is, the ideas on causality presented in Young (2011) and the beginnings of how these ideas have been expanded. That chapter discusses aspects of three major axes in the study of causality in psychology (Young, 2011)—free will, mechanism, and causal graph modeling—as well as providing some new perspectives on the topic, including on the major theme of the book, that of freedom in being. , The remaining 30+ chapters in the book together especially provide a comprehensive review of causality in psychology and related disciplines, before proceeding to a last series of chapters on my personal contributions to understanding causality.

Axes

The number of axes on causality in psychology considered in the book has expanded from three to tens of them, and the book expounds on many of them, while keeping the three primary ones in central focus. That is, despite expanding well beyond them in the present work, the three major axes of the book on causality—of mechanism, free will, and graphic modeling approaches—together still stand as the primary ones toward understanding the causality of behavior. Finally, consistent with the title of the book, I note that free will constitutes a central axis behavioral causality, as well as associated personal/self factors in the determination of behavior.

In this regard, whenever discussing free will in the present book, I maintain that we develop toward and remain people who can create, choose from among, and act on options, thereby doing otherwise than prior and present factors might dictate based uniquely on our biology and our environment. We ourselves constitute the central impetus in the causality of our behavior, everything else being equal. The book explores novel concepts in this regard that I have developed, including, among others: , freedom in being; having a sense of free will; free will working models (which concern the quite-studied concept of free will belief, as well as having a sense of free will); psychotherapeutic questions based on promoting free will; a model of maturity that puts responsibility and free will at its fulcrum, and a free will questionnaire.

Unifying Causality and Psychology: Being, Brain, and Behavior

Preamble: The Causal Self, Freedom in Being, Stages, and Unifying Psychology

Introduction

This preamble introduces critical terms and concepts related to the present book. Specifically, it addresses factors related to causality, free will, a unified psychology, and stage and change models applicable to psychology.

The Causal Self

Model The causal self connotes the central nature of causality to our psychological identity. The self concerns the personal representation that we have cognitively and affectively of our subjective sense and of the personhood that we project or display to others. In this present book, I argue that the self is causal because much of what we do, think, and feel relates to causality. We perceive phenomena causally. We try to decipher the causes of events, people's actions, natural phenomena, and so on. We learn about causality and reason causally. We are motivated to gain causal control of events, people, phenomena, and so on. Overall, we strive to become active causal agents of our behavior that supercedes the passive influences on us of biology and of environment. The world is a causal one, and we want to take our place in the world not merely as effects of the forces that create the universe but as effects, in part, in at least part of that creation.

Comment The concept of the causal self is the last one that I developed for the book, when looking back at what it all means. Therefore, I have introduced the concept at this juncture, and, in Chap. 35, I will integrate material in the present book on what it teaches about the causal self. For example, for the chapter on revising Maslow's concept of a hierarchy of needs, I refer to a tripartite distinction in the self of the self-definitional self, the relatedness self, and the competence/environmental/ecological self. This distinction can be seen to replace the classic Jamesian distinction of the "I" and the "me," the subjective and the objective self, and so on.

Freedom in Being

Model The concept of Freedom in Being borrows heavily from Heidegger's (1927/1962) conception of *Dasein*, which I described as a critical one for understanding adult development (Young, 1997; also see Han-Pile, 2013). *Dasein* translates as Being-in-the-World, and in Young (1997) I expanded the concept to Being-Becoming-World/World-Becoming-Being (see Fig. 1.1). Similarly, Freedom in Being is really a multiple, dialectical concept reflective of how we continue to become and to be dialectically. It encapsulates the *product*, or state, of Freedom in (and of) Being (or being fully in the moment), as well as the *process* of becoming or developing toward Freedom in and of Being. Becoming is a trajectory more than an end-state, and we never really get to full Freedom in Being (or Being Freedom), and so on, because of the constraints both in ourselves and in the world, no matter how conducive toward full mature growth that they might be.

Therefore, the concept of Freedom in Being as applied in the present work is quite like Heidegger's understanding of *Dasien* (Han-Pile, 2013), and also quite like other concepts related to it, such as Freedom of Being (Frazier, 2012). Because it is a concept of becoming, as found in my understanding of *Dasein* as Being-Becoming-World/World-Becoming-Being (Young, 1997), the term of Freedom in Being could be expanded to denote a multiplicity of meanings and, in this regard, could be referred to as "Freedom Becoming Being" or even "Freedom Becoming Being/Being Becoming Freedom." However, even if these latter terms capture better the essence of the underlying concept, they are unwieldy and I refrain from pursuing their use.

The term Freedom in Being might connote to some a being in freedom, in which the word "being" is a noun. Instead of this meaning for the term, I prefer to associate it with the meaning of freedom of the person in *becoming*, as mentioned, so that, in this context, the word "being" in the term Freedom in Being is a gerund as much as a noun. In this regard, all of us are beings who are always in process or, said in another way, we are people on *pathways to* stations rather than individuals *living at* stations. In this sense, beings continually engage in being and do not stand still; they do not always just be (or exist as they are) without dynamically changing. Rather, they live in the processes of change and of becoming, or at least having that potential.

The concept of Freedom in Being is important to the book, but in terms of the amount of work devoted to it in the book, there is not much relative to the question of behavioral causality, in general. In this sense, the particular concept of Freedom in Being exists as a guide to the book and, in contrast, the work on causality, in general, provides much of its substance.

As presently conceived, the concept of Freedom in Being has multiple components and can dynamically change in the person. In particular, the present conceptualization of Freedom in Being has two major components—free will belief and having a sense of free will (see Fig. 1.1). The concept of having a sense of free will is a new one, much like the case for the overarching concept in which it is embedded. However, the concept of belief in free will is becoming well-known and well-received (e.g., Baumeister, 2008, 2014). In this regard, when the present book deals with the topic of free will, or Freedom in Being, it is mostly in terms of the work on belief in free will and its effects.

A Parallel From a conceptual point of view, the psychology of free will belief is not a uniquely unitary construct but exists as part of a complex of related subcomponents, and any free will

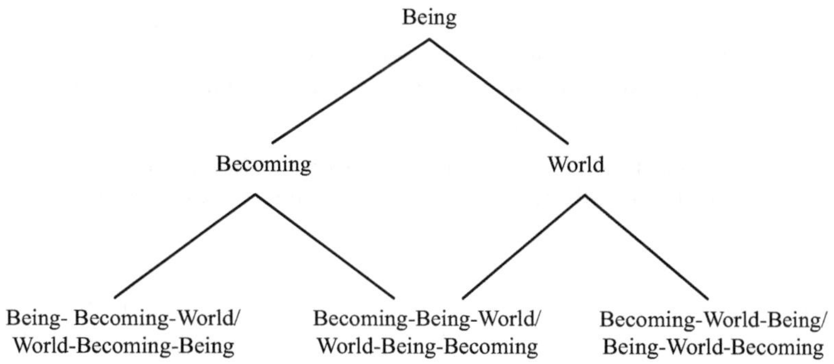

Fig. 1.1 Dasein as being-becoming-world/world-becoming-being. *Dasein* is dynamic potential. "it is a mode of being … which is never static, always moving forward toward new potentialities … '*Dasein* is in every case what it can be, and in the way it is its possibility'" (Heidegger, 1927/1962, p. 143). Mind and related concepts may be characterized, in particular, as "becoming being-in-world/world-in-being," or more simply "being-becoming-world/world-becoming-being." When defined at this level, the separate body and mind do not seem to exist. Nor do the separate self-defined-as-distinct-from--other and other-defined-as-distinct-from-self. Implicated in this concept of mind as a shared relation is that it must be activity in the Vygotskian sense of the word. Its ethos is ethics; its action is moral practice; its agency is communal; its communion is agentic. If Freud described mature life as work and love, I would qualify it as world work and world love. The meaning of life is the life of meaning, especially as constituted in togetherness. At this level, work and love become orders of magnitude more vibrant, more authentic, and more enduring. Adopted with permission of Springer Science + Business Media. Young, G. (1997). *Adult Development, therapy, and culture: A postmodern synthesis*. New York: Plenum; with kind permission from Springer Science + Business Media B. V. [Figure 11.1, Page 256]

questionnaire should be broad enough to cover these components. In particular, free will belief is the cognitive component of a broader construct of the psychology of free will, in that behavior, by definition, is colored and influenced by emotions, the social context, self-factors, broad meanings and acting on the beliefs involved, where possible. This multifactorial approach to free will belief is consistent with the model of the person (Blatt, 2008) that includes a self-definitional and relatedness component. It is consistent with the research relating it to the desire to punish transgressions by others. Finally, it enables it to fit into a broader biopsychosocial view of its causes.

As for the fit with Blatt's (2008) work on a self-definitional and relatedness self as per Young (2011), it would be appropriate to assign free will belief to the self-definitional component. About the relatedness component of the self, up to this point in the present work, I have been using having a sense of free will in parallel with the term of free will belief. It would be appropriate to juxtapose having a sense of free will and free will belief, and relate the former to the relatedness self (while relating the latter to the self-definitional one). Therefore, having a sense of free will becomes specified as both (a) the manner in which one behaves in relationships and social exchange to convey that one has less constraints on behavior than is the norm, or even that one can overcome or bypass such constraints and, therefore, think, choose, decide, act, and relate in a manner reflecting that one is behaving freely despite the constraints, and (b) actually demonstrating in behavior that this is indeed the case.

Comment Note that it is beyond the scope of the present work to examine in depth the concept of *Dasein* (see Wrathall, 2013), not only because the book is more about psychology than philosophy but also because the concept of Freedom in Being that animates the book is different from the concept of *Dasein* and takes on its own meaning relative to its precursors. To conclude, this book is about Freedom in and of Being, and honors the transcendence inherent in the concept of *Dasein* from which it emanates, but it has meanings distinct from related concepts. Moreover, I have presented it in a way that keeps it grounded and amenable to study in empirical science, with testable predictions.

About the other component of the book title involving brain, I refer to "freeing the brain," which is an approach consistent with new paradigms of understanding the brain (e.g., Friston, 2010). The concept of freeing the brain indicates: the constructivist nature of brain activity; its lack of reductionistic, deterministic functioning; and its potentially emergent and free functioning from lower-order levels. Also, the term is consistent with network approaches to the brain, which highlight that the brain functions as a predictive and probability-related entity to reduce "surprise" and unexpected and nonoptimal energy expenditure. Several parts of the book describe in depth this new approach to brain function. Note that it is quite linked to the one of nonlinear dynamical systems theory (NLDST), in that both consider emergence as possible if not inevitable in behavior. Therefore, both are quite consistent with, and speak to, the notion of free will as an emergent force in, or driver, in behavioral causality.

Stages

Model Throughout the book, I refer to the concept of stages in development. The manner in which I use the term is a soft and radical one, and not a hard and traditional one. In the latter framework, a stage is a qualitatively different organization of the components of a system, and one that will appear universally in a sequence if there are a number of them that apply to the population at hand. There is little room for flexibility and individual difference in the stage structure that applies and, moreover, the manner in which the system at issue can reorganize at a higher-order level remains a puzzle and seemingly impossible, but some sort of internal program might be attributed to the process. Further, in this view, the various acquisitions in the system should manifest their new properties more or less simultaneously and, if not, the décalages in the sequencing can be readily explained by task or contextual and other external factors rather than internal ones.

In developing the opposing soft approach to stages, I remove all the rigidities associated with the concept. In this regard, stages are neither universal (necessarily manifesting in the same sequence for everybody) nor do they appear as abruptly as contended, everything else being equal. Moreover, there are mechanisms that can be used to explain their qualitative transitioning.

(a) First, stages are not universal because everyone develops individually in context to adapt to the contingencies in the context at hand and, if there are commonalities from one person to the next, it is only because the solutions in context found by the various individuals in the population at hand in the development that takes place are common ones.
(b) Second, the order in the development of successive stages might seem universal for the same reasons but, once more, the commonalities in individual solutions to the adaptive challenges in development lead to the perception of a universal program that applies to all, when none really exists.
(c) Third, development is especially individual and contextual, which clearly allows for exceptions to the rule that passage through a sequence of stages that seem like the best adaptive route to functionality in context should be found universally.
(d) Fourth, the same logic applies to the variations in acquisitions associated with a stage at issue. There should be no hard and fast rule that all should be acquired at the same time or close to it, or else exceptions to the rule explained away when it does not happen only because of task and contextual variations. Each actor passing through the stage sequence at issue will have internal as well as external factors that serve to disrupt smooth passage through the system, finding the modal solutions involved, and so on.
(e) Fifth, these fundamental attributes of the radical stage conception that I am proposing apply to the proposed substages in any applicable stage model.
(f) Sixth, another confounding factor for traditional stage models is that they contend that once the individual arrives at a new stage or substage, it incorporates the prior one for the acquisition at hand, and it is no longer available. Moreover, the new qualitative advance

spreads throughout the system involved, bootstrapping the whole system to its more advanced level. However, it is more likely that as new advanced levels are constructed in the system, they do not necessarily replace the prior ones, but can co-exist with them. For example, there is no reason to presume that lower-order sensorimotor thinking processes cannot co-exist with higher-order abstract ones, and even supplement them as they work together in solving a problem. In Young (2011), I referred to the process of using simultaneously lower- and higher-order thought processes as yoking. Moreover, they come together locally to solve the problem at hand, can drop out, reappear, bring in intermediate forms, and so on. That is, the components of the wider cognitive system constituted in stage models function in an ongoing, adaptive, soft-assembly manner.

(g) Seventh, the mechanisms that allow for the emergence of qualitatively different levels in any system are being elucidated, and they apply to stage modeling, as well, in particular, systems theory refers to—emergence; the whole being greater than the sum of the parts; new states in the system being unpredictable from knowledge of the parts and their properties; self-organization; complexity; different levels within the system from lower to higher; circular causality (which I have called causal circular emergence); being far from equilibrium, or at the edge of order and disorder, or of stability and change, perhaps with a minor perturbation nonlinearly and dynamically enabling system change (e.g., bifurcating to a new state, basin, or regime; the butterfly effect).

Comment Given these premises of how stages function in a highly adaptive, ongoing, and flexible way, the rigidities associated with traditional models of stages in psychology have been obviated and, therefore, stage conceptions should not be seen as inexact, misleading, unable to explain the data, and failures. Rather, the new conception allows for a rereading of the data that applies to any stage model and also it suggests new empirical directions to test them. That being said, in using the terms of stages or substages in the present book, often I take them from the context in which they were presented without this qualifier of how they can be changed according to the present version.

Unifying Psychology

Introduction Counterintuitively, I maintain that psychology cannot be unified. However, psychology can adopt the project of attempting to unify itself. The unification of psychology is more of a process or a pathway than a product or a unified model. There are many contributions in this present book to this unification of psychology project. However, at the same time, I admit and even fully endorse that the project will never be complete, nor should it be.

Models Sternberg and Grigorenko (2001) described that unified psychology should be multiparadigmatic, multidisciplinary, and integrated through converging operations such as learning and memory as a focus of study from multiple points of view. They described that Staats (1983, 1991, 1993, 1999) argued for a unified empirical positivistic approach to help unify psychology over its different hierarchical levels. Sternberg and Grigorenko (2001) noted some similarity with Staats's approach and that of system theory (e.g., Thelen & Smith, 1994, 1998).

The first book that has attempted unification of psychology is published in 2011 by Henriques, and he called the book "A New Unified Theory of Psychology." He argued that unification of the scientific discipline of psychology should approach more folk psychology. In this regard, he related human exceptionality to our capacity for symbolic language. And, languages are especially useful for social justification, that is, for explaining one's behavior in terms of what is socially legitimate. Further, human self-consciousness exists to function as a system of justification. Therefore, humans are justifying both to themselves and others their behavior. Ultimately, they formulate justification narratives, which provide meaning to their behaviors, and that make sense their world and their place in it.

Finally, humans develop cultures that are especially justification focused. Cultures are constituted by social constructions that are large scale collective systems of justification aimed that coordinating people, for example, in its laws, norms, values, and religions.

He had three more frames that constituted his unified theory of psychology and, as with the justification hypothesis he created these frames himself. The broadest frame is the tree of knowledge system, which is based on the work of Chaisson (2001). This work serves the present book in its efforts at unification, as well. That is, its "big history" approach and emphasis on energy and thermodynamics give a broad picture of not only human evolution and behavior but also the evolution and behavior of the universe. Another important frame in Henriques's (2011) unified theory of psychology is behavioral investment theory. It, too, concerns energy and evolution, but also it concerns genetics, neurocomputational control, learning, and development. These principles of the theory are related to Tinbergen, four questions, as discussed in Chap. 3. The last component of Henriques's model is the influence matrix. It presents various motivations and emotions along three major axes: power, love, and freedom. In the present book, I deal with these various aspects of behavior in Chap. 34, in which I present a modified Neo-Maslovian model.

In 2013, the journal, *Review of General Psychology* published a special issue on unifying psychology. Aside from Henriques's (2013) outline of the concepts in his 2011, it included other articles, many of which I have integrated into the present book (e.g., Chemero, 2013). Marsh and Boag (2014) attempted to integrate these articles along a "continuum of practical assumptions," and placed the Henriques's paper on the risk end because of its experimental predictions. An example of work at the metaphysical end involves Petocz and Mackay (2013; on situational realism).

Green (2015) maintained that psychology cannot become unified because of its lack of clear boundaries. He referred to the development of "super sub-disciplines" as one way to give psychology some coherence (at least within each).

The central tenet of the present work is that any continuum that arranges approaches to unifying psychology can be conceived in terms of concepts such as causality and free will, as illustrated in my approach to a unifying project for psychology. Also, any discipline, super, sub, or moderate in size, in psychology or a neighboring discipline, such as psychiatry, will find commonality with others related to it through a focus on causality and free will and similar concepts, as evidenced in the present work.

Comment Although I respect the desire of Sternberg and Grigorenko, Staats, and Henriques, as well as others striving to integrate or unifying psychology, I believe that, by definition, any one answer, no matter how intellectually cohesive and nuanced, will be limited and not arrive at the goal. Recall that I consider the unification of psychology more of a process than a product. It is a project that we need to adopt, knowing from the beginning that it will never be complete. Just as any area of psychology keeps evolving and science, itself, keeps evolving, psychology can never be fully integrated and unified into one answer, model, theory, or paradigm. At the end of the present book, in Chap. 36, I elaborate this idea of how the pathway toward unifying psychology can proceed, yet without indicating its absolute final status in this regard, which is impossible, and thankfully so.

Introduction

This book is the first comprehensive one on the topic of the causality of behavior in psychology and related disciplines. Also, it is only the second book on the unification of psychology, and it is much broader in scope of the first one (Henriques, 2011). By placing causality as a central axis on which the integration of psychology can be built, the book will speak to all the subareas of psychology, and of related disciplines, as well. It offers multiple ways that causality can constitute an integrating concept in psychology and related disciplines. Moreover, it integrates the study of causality in psychology not just by showing its undeniable breadth but also by offering ways causality as a construct can, itself, be cohered or integrated. It reviews many theoretical models on causality or related topics and also conducts an extensive literature review of contemporary empirical research on or related to the topic. It includes many new concepts that I have developed, especially related to free will, but also others. The latter include new concepts about causality, in general. In addition, I present revised models related to major figures in psychology, especially Piaget, Erikson, Maslow, and Kuhn. Finally, at the applied level, I present a reworked definition of mental disorder, I rework several disorders in the DSM-5 (Diagnostic and Statistical Manual of Mental Disorders, Fifth Edition; American Psychiatric Association), and I present a workable approach toward revising the DSM-5.

If there is one simple concept that covers much of the integrated nature of behavioral causality covered in the present book, it is the one of the biopsychosocial model. The book adopts a biopsychosocial perspective in that behavior is considered influenced not only by Nature and Nurture but also by the self. As humans develop, we become increasingly the primary active agents of our behavior and are not simply the passive outcomes of biology and environment. Behavior is not simply deterministic in nature, or shaped by the past and present context. Rather, we have an element of free will in the choices on which we focus and the decisions that we make. In this regard, the book considers an important aspect of self/personal influence on behavior—freedom in being, which develops in the person through its major components of believing in free will and having a sense of free will.

With these prefatory comments that help grasp the nature of the present book, I proceed to describe its major parts, or groups of chapters, and then its assumptions. A more detailed description of each chapter can be found in the next chapter.

Book Parts

Parts

The first part of the book gives a general overview in the study of behavioral causality. It includes a chapter on philosophy and others on models. The second part of the book examines the brain, especially in terms of neuronal networks and hemispheric and manual specialization (lateralization). There are three chapters on genetics and related topics. The part concludes with a chapter on evolution. The third part of the book considers development as well as free will. The last chapter in this part is on self-control and its depletion, in particular. The fourth part of the book is applied. It deals with the use of free will in psychotherapy, posttraumatic stress disorder (PTSD) and the DSM-5 (American Psychiatric Association, 2013), including on etiology. It presents an integrated top-down/bottom-up model of the etiology of mental disorder. The fifth part of the book presents my personal conceptualizations and innovations, for example, for the area of psychological injury and law. Also, I present a revised model of Stimulus-Organism-Response (S-O-R) and new terms that I have created. A model that I developed to represent the contents of the book is called the Co-existential Causal Intraactive model. The part includes a chapter on change mechanisms. The last part of the book reviews my Neo-Piagetian/Neo-Eriksonian developmental model (Young, 2011, also in Young, 2014), I apply the model to revising Maslow's and Kuhn's, and to develop a generic change model. The book concludes with a process model of behavioral causality.

Comment

Overall, the present book stands out by its comprehensive integration on the topic of causality of behavior and by attempting to place the concept of causality as a unifying construct for the field. Also, the present book has concrete and practical applications, such as dealing with psychopathology, the DSM-5, and new questionnaires, including ones related to free will. Lastly, it places the self—and especially free will—as an emergent important aspect of behavioral determination, emphasizing that we have the ultimate role in establishing the causality of our own behavior. In many ways, the book deals with human exceptionalism, and what makes us unique as a species. In this regard, I hope that by acquiring a better understanding of the causes of our behavior through this book, other sources, and scientific investigation, we can better facilitate that our advanced capacities are used for the benefit of all species and the planet.

The Broader Context

Integrations

Human scholarship aims to understand human behavior in all its pulses and origins, and psychology constitutes a critical field of endeavor in this regard. Psychology is an integrative science that borrows from and contributes to disparate fields, such as genetics, anthropology, evolution, and sociology. It shares their concern for rigorous study, testable conceptualization, empirical support, and replicable research using reliable and valid methods. It is an offshoot of philosophy and, historically, the latter field has been more concerned with conceptualization in its approach, although oriented to empirical verification questions to a degree. That being said, philosophy is now gravitating to the experimental front.

Disciplines in the social sciences might lack unified principles that help to coalesce them into coherent bodies of conceptualization and study. They migrate in multiple, disparate directions, and presently appear to lack the need for and search for integrative, overarching concepts across the whole field. Consilience (Wilson, 1999) is the endeavor to find common ground in scholarship, and, as with philosophy, among other disciplines, psychology is becoming more concerned with broad theoretical and empirical issues and with unifying models. Workers such as Chemero (2013) and Clark (2013a, 2013b) are making inroads on these regards, but we still need broad, meta-theoretical models (Overton, 2015).

Moreover, other areas of social and humanistic studies are further along than psychology in its cross-disciplinary and integrative efforts, for example, especially history, with its concept of "Big History" (Chaisson, 2010, 2011). The latter explores history in terms of antecedents that shaped human evolution, from the Big Bang onwards. In this regard, psychology might want to consider its role in this perspective and adopt a "Big Psychology" viewpoint. This suggestion might justify developing unifying ideas in psychology related to critical factors and models that have potential unifying power, such as dynamical, thermodynamic, and emergent systems modeling of behavior, embodiment modeling, the superordinate meta-model of relationism, and so on. However, the present work opts for two other potential unifying modeling foci for psychology—behavioral causality and the role of free will compared to determinism in behavior, along with models that are related to or that encompass them (e.g., the biopsychosocial model). I have addressed above the import of free will and related concepts and, in the following, I turn to the centrality that causality could have as a unifying force in psychology.

Causality

Unification Causality can serve as a unifying force in psychology but, before disciplinary integration such as this can take place, the work on the topic itself needs to be integrated. Moreover, causality would appear to be central not only to psychology but to any field of scholarship, especially science.

Aside from more clearly embedding itself in other scientific and scholarly approaches to understanding human behavior and its origins, psychology should address in more depth questions that are common to all related disciplines. In this regard, whatever the discipline, prominent questions for students and academics relate to the "wh" questions. These can be simplified to understanding the "what" or description of the phenomena at issue, and their "why" or how, which concerns causality and causation. The present work attempts to address this larger picture in psychology, dealing with both the phenomenological description of behavior and its causal origins. Only by tackling in concert both of these major foci, might we obtain an appreciation of the study of causality as one unifying force in psychology, placing it at the forefront of our activities in scholarship in the field.

Even if it is not a unifying factor in present scholarship, despite appearances to the contrary, causality does constitute the central question in scholarly investigation, especially in science. Because of its ubiquity in scientific/scholarly investigation, in and of itself, most would argue that it does not seem to be a topic of predominant focus. However, it is an undercurrent in every area of research, and the ultimate question to which each one is addressed.

Doubt about the centrality of causality in research appears to apply to social science, in particular, perhaps because often it is difficult to undertake strict experimental studies in its disciplines. Relative to correlational research, controlled experimental research allows the investigator to better grasp causality. However, when dealing with human populations, ethical issues impose limitations on the experimental manipulations needed to address directly the matter of causality of behavior.

Also, in the social sciences, strict positivism, or empiricism, is being challenged by approaches that are more constructivist, relational, hermeneutical (interpretative), relativistic, dialectical, and so on. Therefore, the foundations of the disciplines in social science are challenged at every turn in terms of the "established" facts, information, empirical output, data, and so on. Because these disciplines are still focused on establishing the conceptual grounds for their research and on describing the phenomena that comprise the field of study, the investigation of their associated causes often is left behind and, even if undertaken, left uncertain. However, alternative ways of addressing causality in behavior are bearing fruit, as shall be shown in this present work.

Other Books Of the books with causality, causation, cause, or causal in the title, none have been integrative across psychology. I mention and review all the books having these terms in the title for psychology and related disciplines as the present work proceeds. Much work in the area is on statistical methodology and causal graph modeling, but we can only give a flavor here (e.g., Pearl, 2009). Other books emphasize the application of this latter approach to psychology (e.g., Sloman, 2005).

Recently, Shrout (2011) edited a book that focused on epidemiology and psychopathology, in particular. Psychology deals with mental illness, and all advances in the field related to its etiology are welcome. Markus and Borsboom (2013) wrote a book on testing and causality, which I review in Chap. 6. Mikulincer and Shaver (2014) edited a work on social connection, which I review in Chap. 15. Corrigan (2014) edited a work on the causes of disability and stigma. Relative to present purposes, it is too specific for me to give it more than a brief mention, but it illustrates that there is an evident increasing focus on causation in psychology.

The books that have been written earlier on the topic also had been quite specific in focus. They include ones by Rodin, Schaie, and Schooler (1990) on self-directedness, Ouimette and Brown (2003) [updated in Ouimette and Read (2013)] on trauma and substance abuse, and Haynes (1992) on psychopathology. The latter book is classic to the field, having investigated causality in psychopathology both conceptually and statistically. My own books have been on causality in psychological injury and development (Young, Kane, & Nicholson, 2007; Young, 2011, respectively). With Young, Kane, and Nicholson (2006), the former book helped coalesce this relatively new field in psychology (also see Young, 2008). The 2011 Young book is a precursor to the present one, and it is entitled Development and Causality. In some senses, the present book could be entitled its inverse—Causality and Development.

Conclusion The present work considers causality as a potentially core, unifying focus in psychology. Every behavior of interest requires not only careful elucidation of its objective characteristics but also incisive clarification of its causality, and especially in terms of mechanisms. Also, the quest to elaborate the descriptive phenomenology of behavior should not be considered separate from search for its causal origins; the streams of seeking to know the "what" and the "why" of behavior should be integrated at every turn; each of the two informs the other and provides information that reciprocally innervates the study and understanding of the other. Describing behavior gives the product of the processes involved while, at the same time, the processes provide ground on the particular product (behavior) at hand, so that in psychology product and process constitute a unified intrinsic interrelation. Note that at several junctures in the book, I refer to the "what" and the "why" of behavior at product and process, respectively.

Limitations

The present work covers a large portion of the conceptualization and research investigation of causality in psychology. In addition, it explores the topic in several related disciplines, such as philosophy, psychiatry, ecology, epidemiology, evolution, neuroscience, law, statistics, and network modeling. The causality concepts in these latter disciplines are rich and complex, and the empirical findings are dense and burgeoning, so that it is becoming exponentially more difficult to seize the essence of the area of causality in any one of them, let alone over all of them. Nevertheless, the goal of the present work is to conduct a partial survey of how causality is considered in these various disciplines, especially in how it relates to psychology.

Given that there was so much material to cover in order to understand the causality of behavior, much of the book involves description of critical concepts and empirical research on the topic. As I delved into the topic, my approach was to learn from every article, chapter, or book. As I read them, I considered each of them as independent "data" that had to be described carefully before I proceeded to comment on them. The reader will notice that many times there are headings in the book related to models, evidence, and commentary, or similar ones. This approach of describing the work of others directly before commenting on them permitted me to have a large fund of material related to causality written by many others before arriving at constructed integrations in the field. [Of course, please understand that in describing the extant research, many times it was impossible to give all the pertinent details, especially methodological ones]. Nevertheless, this approach has limitations in that often it leads to description of one article after another in a particular section without ongoing integrative efforts taking place.

In the next part of the chapter, I describe some basic premises and concepts that guided my understanding of causality as I proceeded in my attempt to summarize all the relevant material and integrate it. In the chapters that follow, often I return to these themes. There are 30 of these foundational assumptions to the present book, and they are organized into common themes.

Assumptions

In this description of the 30 fundamental assumptions underlying present work, I present in an accessible way the basic notions that conditioned my approach to the study of causality in psychology. The assumptions range from the importance of being inclusive to understanding causality to placing it centrally in the efforts to find an integrative concept in psychology. The assumptions and constructs involved will be described with more precision and in depth as the work proceeds. They are divided into six major groups of five assumptions.

General

1. Causality is central to the study of psychology, but despite its ubiquity it has not been given sufficient prominence in the field as a distinct focus. For example, in psychology, there are very few books with the words causality, causation, cause, or causal in the title.
2. Causality is one of the two major arms of psychological study, the other being the description of behavior. The study of the "what" and the "why" of a system go hand in hand, and knowledge of the why could alter understanding of the what, as much as the inverse applies. Indeed, trying to define the "what" in a system should always mean trying to define the "why," as well. Both of these foci of behavior—the "what" and "why," product and process, and phenomenological description and causal

explanation—need to be investigated in psychological research and practice. The descriptive "what" of a discipline cannot be well understood separately from a good grasp of its causal why or how; approaches to description and explanation reciprocally inform each other. As one example, the nosological manuals of psychiatric disease are into their next generation (DSM-5; American Psychiatric Association, 2013; International Classification of Diseases, ICD-11, World Health Organization, 2017), but despite what the manuals proffer as the causal bases underlying the categories in the manuals (i.e., etiology), often the categories involved are presented in the manuals only as symptom-based and without reference to underlying causes, which are still being differentiated in the literature. As the latter effort progresses, the psychiatric phenotypes proposed by the manuals are qualified or changed with each new edition. Where there is little causal understanding, the danger is that new categories could proliferate in new editions. Generally, the manuals have too many categories, and ones that are not necessarily reliable and valid. By working from cause to disorder, and back, the quagmires and conundrums in these regards might demonstrate progress or resolve more quickly.

3. Causality requires integrated concepts in psychology. At the heuristic level, variants of the biopsychosocial model can capture its major constituents. For example, these would include genetic/neuronal, personality/self, and family/cultural factors, respectively. However, this type of model needs to be expanded to cover all possible contingencies in causal analysis. In this regard, one model that can help to understand the "what" and the "why" of behavior is the biopersonalsocial one (Young, 2011), a label that is a variant of the biopsychosocial model. I changed the terminology of the model in this way to indicate that, in behavior, we have an active say in our growth, and behavioral causality is not just about "nature" and "nurture" but also about ourselves. Moreover, referring to a personal component in the causality of behavior directly in the name of the model allows me to include under its rubric work on free will as an essential aspect of the personal component in the causality of human behavior.
4. Causality in psychology requires sophisticated statistical approaches that can tease apart the confounder variables inherent in research designs that are not strictly experimental. There is much progress being made in this regard, and whole disciplines exist in which only observational and correlational data can be gathered (e.g., epidemiology, astronomy), yet causality is addressed nonetheless.
5. Much of behavior reflects biological influences. It is so complex that only isolated components might seem totally environmental. As a whole, its biological, genetic, and evolutionary bases need to be explicated in order to understand what it is and its causal why and how. That being said, the present work is neither nativistic nor especially biological in nature. To the contrary, it adopts an interactive approach in its biopsychosocial emphasis, but adds the personal component to the interaction.

Specifics

6. The integrated concepts needed in the study of causality in psychology, and the methods, as well, should be broad enough to cover behavior in any species, at any age, and in any context. If we are to understand behavioral causality in humans, we need an integrative approach that incorporates evolutionary, developmental, and contextual (e.g., cultural) foundations and variations.
7. The organisms of the species studied in psychology and related disciplines should not be considered static entities. Even if apparently static in nature, a state never exists as a state without change. A state in equilibrium exists in dynamic tension among it constituents and with its context, and so is changing in the sense that it keeps adjusting to the changes in its constituents/context in order to preserve its ongoing state characteristics.

8. Behavior takes place over multiple time frames, from the micro- to macro-, from the immediate and over the lifespan, and from within the lifespan to across it over generations [and prior to it in its influences from our ancestral past]. The models developed on causality should integrate these multiple time frames, from the milliseconds in neuronal firing, to the ongoing micro-attunements to context, to the macro changes in development, and to the cross-generational transitions from one generation to the next, if not over the paleontological epochs in evolution.
9. The causal models developed should avoid isolating organism from context, stimulus from response, action from perception (and appraisal), mind from brain, and so on. The phenomena in psychology exist in a relational matrix in which it is difficult to isolate complementarities that exist reciprocally. We might be tempted to consider as linear the stream of behavior and its effects and outcomes and to consider its evident organizational tiers simply as reflections of ones lower in the hierarchy that is revealed for an area. However, although positivism and reductionism might be needed to help in understanding at one level the issues at hand, their use might mask the depth needed to fully understand them.
10. Behavior exists in systems, functions as part of them and, indeed, reflects them. Causality is as much about systems as particular behaviors. From a dynamical systems perspective, it is impossible to separate the "what" and the "why" in a system. Cause resides in system pattern configurations, and these re-arrange through self-organization. Moreover, system change could include emergent patterns that are unpredictable from full knowledge of the elements (and their characteristics) involved.

Biopsychosocial

11. Behavior is always about the brain (and related central and peripheral nervous system agents). This does not deny that there are multiple levels in behavioral organization that do not include the brain. Nevertheless, in one way or another, brain structure, function, connectivity, networking, specialization, and properties are involved in all behavior. Moreover, these various system levels are complicated in their relation and, as mentioned, they even allow for emergence, e.g., through reciprocal circular causality in bottom-up and top-down influences. Therefore, although behavior is always about the brain, the relationship between brain and behavior is complex, with multiple mediators and moderators that are involved, and even emergent properties not predicted the components that constitute them.
12. Behavior is always about the person. It is more than the effect of genes/biology/brain and culture/group/family influences, because the person has a say in her or his own growth. Each person is unique even if there are universals that provide scaffolds on which one's uniqueness is molded.
13. Self-regulation is essential for behavior that is adaptive environmentally. It leads to efficient and effective behavioral control and execution. However, it can become problematic, for example, due to early adversity/maltreatment (especially when biological vulnerability factors also present). Also, self-control can be depleted by context and the sequences involved in behavioral adaptation.
14. Behavior is about both (a) commonalities or universals and (b) individual or group differences. To understand causality in full, we need to understand both of these aspects of behavior. However, in this regard, the study of behavior at times is more about the individual and group differences among people more than the normative averages collated from the individual and group differences expressed. Individual differences include group differences, such as those related to age, sex, and culture. To understand the causality of behavior, psychology needs to conceptualize and study both universal and individual differences in behavior.

15. Behavior in the present is always stochastic and probabilistic. It is never fully specified or determined by priors or pre-existing states/factors, whether biological, personal, or environmental. This does not make it any less deterministic at a global level. General patterns might involve attractors, for example, in which system states inevitably gravitate to powerful basins in their state space despite momentary, ongoing deviations from them (although attractor regimes are subject to change).

Change

16. Psychology needs to elucidate general change mechanisms in behavior. Because transformation in organisms is ubiquitous and constant (as argued above, even stasis in behavior involves a type of ongoing change to ongoing system variability toward the homeostatic target), causal modeling needs to account for both change and preservation of the status quo without apparent change. The concepts of causality in behavior need to be generic enough to account both for any types of change and their resistance.
17. Part of the general change mechanisms in behavior should be able to accommodate qualitative transformation (to new, quite different states), in that change is not always quantitative and accretional. In developmental psychology, stage models, such as those of Piaget and Erikson, reflect conceptualization of development as qualitative and step-like. Change models need to account for stage transitions that are qualitative as much as accounting for quantitative change and general change.
18. The change mechanisms developed in the field should be able to accommodate regressions, problematic behavior, the effect of adversities, and so on, and not just change in an increasingly adaptive, adjusting, and progressive direction. Behavior can go awry, become disturbed, or even grossly psychotic and criminal. The root causes are multiple. Models of behavioral causality need to be generic in this sense, as well.
19. At the same time, therapeutic interventions can help when behavior becomes problematic. The generic change mechanisms described in a generic change model need to be general enough to cover change through psychotherapeutic interventions and treatment. Moreover, often the latter tackle common undercurrents to disorders, or have shared transdiagnostic or cross-disorder commonalities, including in stages of change. Models of change processes in psychotherapy should be general enough to accommodate to factors such as these so that the models of therapeutic change fit the generic change models that are developed as much as the case for any other area.
20. The change models and mechanisms proposed even should be general enough to apply to change processes in nonliving systems. For example, nonlinear dynamical systems theory (NLDST) applies to the rapid and radical transformations that can take place in multiple types of systems, including nonliving ones. The so-called chaos of change is a misnomer. Chaotic change in NLDST really is about orderly change, for example, in the processes that take place at the cusp of change.

Systems and Axes

21. The systems structures hypothesized to characterize behavior should be sufficiently flexible to accommodate multiple levels and their arrangements, for example, both in vertical and hierarchical interactions. Moreover, multiple system levels can express both bottom-up and top-down processes. This could happen both within and across them. Systems are constituted by elements and their interrelations, and reflect the dictum that the whole is greater than the sum of the parts. Moreover, how much is there correspondence over levels in systems due to fractalization processes? For example, behavior cannot be uniformly reduced to physiological or brain processes,

or mind to stimulus–response connections. Indeed, factors in behavioral causality at the personal level exist independent as emergent phenomena of these more basic levels in the behavioral system. This applies to the influence of free will on our behavior. The proposition that it is important to behavioral causality has validity only to the extent that conceptually we agree that it reflects a higher-order level of behavior distinct from lower levels and capable of influencing them as much as they influence it. Fractalization permits propagation of kernels of behavioral causality throughout the behavioral system as self-similar expressions over levels.

22. The behavior to which causal explanations are aimed should vary from the most simple to the most complex, and the relationships over the levels in the full system at issue acknowledged, despite any emergence that might take place in the system being examined. For example, in terms of simplicity, what are the causal mechanisms in the simplest neuronal firings for the simplest newborn behaviors? Do they exhibit the complexities evident in other levels in their system? At the other extreme, in terms of complexity, how does the emergent property of free will in the personal level of the system relate to the simplest neuronal firings in the newborn? Are there common properties to different levels of a behavior system despite any intermediary emergence that appears to differentiate their basic characteristics? Similarly, relative to the development of the simplest of behaviors in the person, how do the most complex develop in groups of people or in their institutions; for example, how does scientific thought itself develop? How do scientific paradigms that govern the frameworks in which scientific thought evolve function to evolve themselves? How do societies organize into superordinate structures from the collection of individuals involved?
23. Most areas of psychology witness an increasing differentiation and integration in concepts, terminology, and definition as the areas evolve. However, the study of causality as a unique or distinct focus in psychology is nascent. It needs to respect extant terms but also create novel ones reflective of and also instigative of new ideas and fresh directions. Granted, the topic of causality is ubiquitous in psychology, and the dictum that correlation does not mean causation is present pervasively. However, innovations conceptually can spur work in the area, and allow for cohering of its disparate directions. In this regard, one concept that I promote is that humans are *Homo Causa*. .It is not just that we consider causality important to discover. Rather, discovering causality is the essence of who we are and how we behave.
24. The search for causality in the different areas of psychology should constitute its primary axis of integration. In a certain sense, how causality is studied defines a field. Psychology needs an integrated approach to this question. As the study of causality matures in psychology, it should come to inform, influence, and even transform and dictate to other areas of psychology. Granted, psychology has distinct fields or domains of inquiry and it is separated into major areas that might not have much cross-talk. However, ways should be found to allow for better integration over its separate fields or domains. Also, the value in a movement to integrate the fields or domains of psychology applies equally to other disciplines and also to their relationships with psychology (e.g., with neuroscience). In this regard, by placing causality as a central axis in psychological study, it can help cohere it, on the one hand, over its fields and domains, and on the other hand, over its links to their disciplines.
25. As the study of causality matures, it will also continue to grow, transform, change, differentiate, and integrate. Indeed, it could become center stage in the study of behavior as it does so. Yet, it never should be considered to have evolved to a final understanding, and having reached a plateau of knowledge. Rather, as with other areas of psychology specifically and science and scholarship generally, the study of causality and change in behavior should constantly change and improve.

Integration, Exceptionalism, and Essence

26. One fruitful avenue toward the study of causality in behavior lies in my own work (e.g., Young, 2011, 2014). The last portion of the present work explores further how my ideas in my prior books have contributed to the study of causality in psychology and how they can be further expanded. I unabashedly support a stage model of change, one that can even be applied to nonliving systems. In this regard, I have developed a Neo-Piagetian/Neo-Eriksonian lifespan model of development and sought its general characteristics so that its proposed underlying change process can be applied even to nonliving systems. Other concepts that I have developed can help in the study of causality. For example, the concept of activation/inhibition coordination across the diverse levels of the behavioral, brain, neuronal network, development, and social relational systems could prove helpful in this regard.
27. Causality generally considered involves normal and abnormal behavior. However, for abnormal behavior alone, causality refers to etiology. A broad understanding of behavioral causality needs to include concepts that are applicable to etiology. In both cases, the integration of top-down and bottom-up processes over different levels of the system involved would be important.
28. Behavior is about human exceptionalism. What makes us a distinct species? Is it our superordinate abstract thought, our apparent free will, the choices that we make for ourselves and our children, our capacity to teach them formally and have them learn greatly from our endeavors, our capacity to construct cities and other collective and cultural institutions, and so on? Perhaps part of the answer lies in causality, in that we appear to be the only species that can affect the course of our behavior and also our environment. Moreover, perhaps one aspect of human causality contributes especially to our exceptionalism—that related to free will.
29. Causality is not only the essence of psychology but also causality is psychology, and vice versa. Without understanding the origins of what we describe as behavior, we can never be certain that the descriptions are accurate. That is, we have seen that we need to understand the "why" and "how" of behavior to truly understand the "what" of behavior. Further, because every field or domain of psychology seeks causal understanding, concepts about causality in each of them need to have shared characteristics over them in order to facilitate communicative exchange and integration. As much as causality is potentially central to psychology, its present state of dispersion detracts from its potentially integrative role. In this regard, a book such as the present one can help the causality project that I am advocating for psychology, for example, through its collection of the diverse elements in its study into one source, its innovations, and the models that I have created.
30. Psychology, in general, struggles with integration and differentiation. On the one hand, I have come across efforts to integrate it. Also, it is more seamless in many ways than the cut and dry nature of its distinctions imply. This is true, for example, for stimulus vs. response, organism vs. context, mind vs. brain, gene vs. environment, and even "what" vs. "why" and "how." However, on the other hand, it is very difficult for these efforts toward integrating psychology to have much impact despite their promise. It could be argued that it is either premature to undertake this type of integration, given the early nature in the development of the discipline relative to some others, or that, indeed, the task itself is impossible. Nevertheless, the fundamental assumption of the present book is that causality can be the unifying force in psychology, especially if its ideas advance further enough and are integrated themselves. To help along this causality project, that causality can take its central, unifying place in psychology and also that its center can be understood better, some of the

disjunctive divisions in psychology that have been mentioned, themselves, need better conceptualization and integration toward being unified. That is, the higher-order goal of placing causality as a central axis in psychology to address some of its divisiveness can be achieved only if some of its lower-order separations can be congealed. Psychology needs to create a superordinate system of behavioral understanding and research, as well as a system that is multidisciplinary in this regard, with the aim to conceptualize better behavioral causality and the consequences of its causes, including normatively and psychopathologically.

Chapter Conclusions

The present book is about the causality of behavior, for which free will is considered a cardinal factor. One major focus of the present work is the concept of "free being," which I explain further in the next chapters. Other chapters in the book deal more in depth on free will in behavior. The last chapter of the book includes a more integrative model of the causal origins of free being.

To conclude this introduction to the first chapter of the present work, another guiding concept has been the biopsychosocial model, which I have modified and labeled the biopersonalsocial model. It reflects that the causes of behavior are multiple and interactive in dynamic ways over the whole behavioral system. Behavior can become dysfunctional, disturbed, and so on, and the biopsychosocial model constitutes a unifying one for understanding normal and abnormal behavior, as well as how to deal with the latter. Yet one model is insufficient to capture conceptually the state of affairs in psychology at present. Other integrative models that appear throughout the book include the ones of NLDST, networks, and embodiment, among others.

There are many other theoretical and conceptual sources to the present work that will become evident as it unfolds. However, I emphasize that the study of causality in psychology and related disciplines could help lead to a paradigm shift in its understanding and in how to help children, people in need, and society, in general. Causality could be the superordinate unifying concept to the disparate models in the field, given its potential central axis in the study of behavior generally.

To conclude this introduction to the present book, it underscores the potential unifying role for psychology of understanding the causality of behavior, both normal and abnormal and how it needs to be unified itself before it can have a unifying role in psychology. Moreover, the study of causality in behavior can help us understand our own place in the determination of our behavior—at the apex of its influences, and hopefully as a free being that seeks to be free in helpful actions both for the self and others.

References

American Psychiatric Association. (2013). *Diagnostic and statistical manual of mental disorders: DSM-5* (5th ed.). Washington, DC: Author.

Baumeister, R. F. (2008). Free will in scientific psychology. *Perspectives on Psychological Science, 3*, 14–19.

Baumeister, R. F. (2014). Constructing a scientific theory of free will. In W. Sinnott-Armstrong (Ed.), *Moral psychology: Free will and moral responsibility* (Vol. 4, pp. 235–255). Cambridge, MA: MIT Press.

Blatt, S. J. (2008). *Polarities of experience: Relatedness and self-definition in personality development, psychopathology, and the therapeutic process.* Washington: American Psychological Association.

Chaisson, E. J. (2001). *Cosmic evolutions: The rise of complexity in nature.* Cambridge, MA: Harvard University Press.

Chaisson, E. J. (2010). Energy rate density as a complexity metric and evolutionary driver. *Complexity, 16*, 27–40.

Chaisson, E. J. (2011). Energy rate density. II. Probing further a new complexity metric. *Complexity, 17*, 44–63.

Chemero, A. (2013). Radical embodied cognitive science. *Review of General Psychology, 17*, 145–150.

Clark, A. (2013a). Whatever next? Predictive brains, situated agents, and the future of cognitive science. *Behavioral and Brain Sciences, 36*, 1–24.

Clark, A. (2013b). Are we predictive engines? Perils, prospects, and the puzzle of the porous perceiver. *Behavior and Brain Sciences, 36*, 53–64.

Corrigan, P. W. (2014). *The stigma of disease and disability: Understanding causes and overcoming injustices.* Washington, DC: American Psychological Association.

Frazier, J. (2012). *The freedom of being: At ease with what is.* Newburyport, MA: Weiser.

Friston, K. (2010). The free-energy principle: A unified brain theory? *Nature Reviews Neuroscience, 11*, 127–138.

Green, C. D. (2015). Why psychology isn't unified, and probably never will be. *Review of General Psychology, 19*, 207–214.

Han-Pile, B. (2013). Freedom and the "choice to choose oneself" in being and time. In M. A. Wrathall (Ed.), *The Cambridge companion to Heidegger's being and time* (pp. 291–319). New York: Cambridge University Press.

Haynes, S. N. (1992). *Models of causality in psychopathology: Toward dynamic, synthetic and nonlinear models of behavior disorders*. New York: Macmillan.

Heidegger, M. (1927/1962). *Being and time* (J. Macquarrie & E. Robinson, Trans.). Oxford, UK: Blackwell. (Original work published 1927)

Henriques, G. (2011). *A new unified theory of psychology*. New York: Springer Science + Business Media.

Henriques, G. (2013). Evolving from methodological to conceptual unification. *Review of General Psychology, 17*, 168–173.

Markus, K. A., & Borsboom, D. (2013). *Frontiers of test validity theory: Measurement, causation, and meaning*. New York: Routledge.

Marsh, T., & Boag, S. (2014). Unifying psychology: Shared ontology and the continuum of practical assumptions. *Review of General Psychology, 18*, 49–59.

Mikulincer, M., & Shaver, P. R. (2014). *Mechanisms of social connection: From brain to group*. Washington, DC: American Psychological Association.

Ouimette, P., & Brown, P. J. (2003). *Trauma and substance abuse: Causes, consequences, and treatment of comorbid disorders* (1st ed.). Washington, DC: American Psychological Association.

Ouimette, P., & Read, J. P. (2013). *Trauma and substance abuse: Causes, consequences, and treatment of comorbid disorders* (2nd ed.). Washington, DC: American Psychological Association.

Overton, W. F. (2015). Relational developmental systems and developmental science. In R. M. Lerner, W. F. Overton, & P. C. Molenaar (Eds.), *Handbook of child psychology and developmental science: Vol. 1. Theory and method* (7th ed., pp. 9–62). Hoboken, NJ: Wiley.

Pearl, J. (2009). *Causality: Models, reasoning, and inference* (2nd ed.). New York: Cambridge University Press.

Petocz, A., & Mackay, N. (2013). Unifying psychology through situational realism. *Review of General Psychology, 17*, 216–223.

Rodin, J., Schaie, K. W., & Schooler, C. (1990). *Self-directedness: Cause and effects throughout the life course*. Hillsdale, NJ: Erlbaum.

Shrout, P. E. (2011). Integrating causal analysis into psychopathology research. In P. E. Shrout, K. M. Keyes, & K. Ornstein (Eds.), *Causality and psychopathology: Finding the determinants of disorders and their cures* (pp. 3–24). New York: Oxford University Press.

Sloman, S. (2005). *Causal models: How people think about the world and its alternatives*. New York: Oxford University Press.

Staats, A. W. (1983). *Psychology's crisis of disunity: Philosophy and method for a unified science*. New York: Praeger.

Staats, A. W. (1991). Unified positivism and unification psychology: Fad or new field? *American Psychologist, 46*, 899–912.

Staats, A. W. (1993). Separattism and unification. In H. V. Rappard, P. J. Van Strien, L. P. Mos, & W. J. Baker (Eds.), *Annals of theoretical psychology* (Vol. 9, pp. 155–164). New York: Plenum.

Staats, A. W. (1999). Unifying psychology requires new infrastructure, theory, method, and a research agenda. *Review of General Psychology, 3*, 3–13.

Sternberg, R. J., & Grigorenko, E. L. (2001). Unified psychology. *American Psychologist, 56*, 1069–1079.

Thelen, E., & Smith, L. B. (1994). *A dynamic systems approach to the development of cognition and action*. Cambridge, MA: MIT Press.

Thelen, E., & Smith, L. B. (1998). Dynamic systems theories. In W. Damon (Series Ed.) & R. M. Lerner (Vol. Ed.), *Handbook of child psychology* (5th ed., Vol. 1, pp. 563–634). New York: Wiley.

Wilson, E. O. (1999). *Consilience: The unity of knowledge*. New York: First Vintage Books.

World Health Organization. (2017). *International Classification of Disease*, 11th Revision.

Wrathall, M. A. (2013). *The Cambridge companion to Heidegger's being and time*. New York: Cambridge University Press.

Young, G. (1997). *Adult development, therapy, and culture: A postmodern synthesis*. New York: Plenum.

Young, G. (2008). Causality and causation in law, medicine, psychiatry, and psychology: Progression or regression? *Psychological Injury and Law, 1*, 161–181.

Young, G. (2011). *Development and causality: Neo-Piagetian perspectives*. New York: Springer Science + Business Media.

Young, G. (2014). *Malingering, feigning, and response bias in psychiatric/psychological injury: Implications for practice and court*. Dordrecht, Netherlands: Springer Science + Business Media.

Young, G., Kane, A. W., & Nicholson, K. (Eds.). (2006). *Psychological knowledge in court: PTSD, pain, and TBI*. New York: Springer Science + Business Media.

Young, G., Kane, A. W., & Nicholson, K. (Eds.). (2007). *Causality of psychological injury: Presenting evidence in court*. New York: Springer Science + Business Media.

2 Overview of Book Parts and Chapter by Chapter Overview

Chapter Introduction

This overview chapter of the book, its second, includes description of each of its chapters. This chapter informs the scope of the book and its basic concepts and conclusions. This is the first integrative book on the causality of behavior in the field of psychology, but it will be useful to related disciplines, such as psychiatry. It focuses on influences on behavior not only in terms of Nature and Nurture but also for those related to the self, such as those involving free will.

The book presents many innovations to help integrate the study of causality in behavior. Aside from those related to free will and causality that I have developed (e.g., the concept of Freedom in Being; humans as *Homo Causa*, respectively), others that are central to the present enterprise include ones related to my developmental Neo-Piagetian/Neo-Eriksonian (sub)stage model and also a revision of Maslow's classic hierarchical model based on this model. In addition, I have created a generic change model based on the developmental one (Neo-Piagetian/Neo-Eriksonian). Further, based on these models, I have developed a Neo-Kuhnian model of paradigmatic change in the sciences (and also in any scholarly activity). Finally, the present work has practical applications related to presentation and critique of the DSM-5 (Diagnostic and Statistical Manual of Mental Disorders, Fifth Edition; American Psychiatric Association, 2013), and it includes many recommendations to improve it, as well as making psychotherapeutic suggestions. Also, it offers several new questionnaires, including on the topic of free will.

Parts of the Book

Introduction

This book is based on a comprehensive literature review in multiple areas of causality in the discipline of psychology, while touching some related disciplines that deal with behavioral causality. It examines the classic influences on behavior of Nature and Nurture, and their interaction, as well as the powerful forces in behavioral causality related to the self (e.g., free will); hence the book's title. The book is comprised of six parts, each with five to seven chapters.

Parts

The first part of the book presents the core of conceptualization and research on the causality of behavior. It considers foundations and assumptions underlying the study of behavioral causality, and then it elaborates the biological portion in psychological causality, especially with respect to genes, the brain, and evolution. It addresses the revolutions that are taking place in the study of behavioral causation, including the work on epigenesis and differential susceptibility.

G. Young, *Unifying Causality and Psychology*, DOI 10.1007/978-3-319-24094-7_2

The second part of the book deals both with development and free will. As well, it considers abnormal behavior/psychopathology and its diagnosis in the DSM-5 (American Psychiatric Association, 2013). This applied portion of the book includes concrete applications, such as a new free will questionnaire and recommendations for the DSM-5.

The third part of the book presents my personal contributions to the study of and conceptualization of behavioral causality. First, I present models related to the causes of psychological injury, and then new models and terms related to stimulus–response relations, and their relations to the organism, networks, and the brain (the "neurome"). The last part of the book concludes with description and extension of my Neo-Piagetian/Neo-Eriksonian lifespan developmental model (Young, 2011; and extended in Young, 2014) and its applications and extensions for understanding behavioral causality. This includes a generic change model, a revised model of Maslow's hierarchy of needs, and a revised model of Kuhn's paradigmatic approach to scientific change.

Conclusion

The present book is comprehensive and massive, but only an approach such as this can do justice to the topic of the causality of behavior. It will test your patience but improve your knowledge as you work through it. It might inspire you to adopt its major goals—of trying to unify psychology, unify the study of causality, and include free will as central to both endeavors, while considering my models as contributory in these regards.

Part I: Core Causality in Behavior: Foundations and Models

The first part of the book deals with the causality of behavior from the smallest of genes and their molecular constituents to the largest complex systems in which behavior resides. The first part of this book serves as an introduction to the basics in causality modeling, in particular. Also, it provides a philosophical discussion not only on causality but also for psychology, in general. The integrative models that it considers include the biopsychosocial, embodiment, and network models. It seeks organizational principles across brain and behavior, including in nonlinear dynamical systems theory (NLDST) and the concept of activation/inhibition coordination.

The study of causality of behavior exists in dynamic tension between more statistical, methodological, empirical approaches and more theoretical, modeling, philosophical ones. For example, at the statistical level, experimentation is considered crucial in causal determination, and randomized control trials, in particular, are considered the sine qua non in establishing causality in the clinical domain. However, psychology and psychiatry often are limited ethically in the ability to conduct experiments, and have to resort to quasi-experiments, longitudinal designs using statistical controls, and advanced statistical procedures. The last chapter in this part reviews statistical approaches to causality. It includes network and graphing approaches, which are becoming increasingly important.

Part II: Biology and Revolutions

The basic models presented in the first part of the book continue to appear in the later parts, and they are interweaved as the book unfolds. For example, in the second part of the book, I present the biological bases of behavior, in particular. I start with two chapters on the brain, and both reflect the increasing influence of the network approach to conceptualizing behavior. The next three chapters are on genetics and the genetic revolution. Genes no longer are considered only for their direct effects on behavior; rather, their intricate interaction with the environment predominates in understanding their influence on behavior. The study of the interaction of genes and environment (G×E) includes the burgeoning area of epigenetics, as well as the areas of cultural neuroscience and social genomics. These areas further stamp the study of the genetic influence on behavior as complex and intimately entwined with the environment. At the same time, the ability of genes to affect the environment is indicated in the phenomenon of correlated G×E interactions. The phenomenon of the interaction of G by E presents a challenge not only to understanding genetic effects on behavior but also environmental ones. The last chapter of this part of the book deals with evolution. Darwinian influences on behavior have expanded to include concepts relating genes and culture.

Part III: Normal and Abnormal Development and Free Will: Normal Development and Free Will

This third part of the book shifts to the topics of developmental and social psychology. For development, I focus on the early years, in particular, to determine to what extent behavior seems core and "prepared," e.g., in empathy and prosocial behavior. For social psychology, I focus on the study of free will in behavior. The part begins with a chapter on the evolution of behavior from a developmental perspective, and the fascinating model of differential susceptibility to the environment. This model integrates evolution, genetics, development, life history, resilience, vulnerability, social buffering, and positive as well as negative outcomes, such as antisocial behavior. It is a lifespan perspective. The next chapter continues with a lifespan approach to development and its positive as well as negative outcomes, by considering the effects of early adversity, fetal programming, and the enduring effects model, among others.

The environment no longer can be considered according to the classic model, or as an independent entity that impacts people who, in turn, are considered to stand as separate from the environment. Rather, in contemporary thought, the environment "gets under the skin" not only in phenomena such as epigenetics and cultural genomics but also in its early effects in differential susceptibility and from early adversity. In this sense, just as there are genetic and, generally, biological revolutions in the study of behavior (e.g., brain network concepts), so are there environmental revolutions.

As the same time, in keeping in mind the major focus of the present book on Freedom in Being, another revolution in behavioral understanding seems evident. From the point of view of the biopsychosocial model that I espouse as a crux in understanding the causality of behavior, there are not only biological (genetic) and environmental revolutions in behavioral study, there are also revolutions in understanding the person's contribution to his/her own development and behavior. People have different personalities, coping skills/resiliencies, directions in self-development, and other factors that contribute to how their development unfolds and how their behavior is expressed in their contexts. In this regard, believing in and having a sense of free will is especially important in freeing the person from being passive before the biological and environmental influences on her or him. Living in freedom of being can help the person to construct actively at least to some degree aspects of her or his development and behavior so that it is more probabilistic and emergent instead of being fully deterministic and reductionist. Keep in mind that themes like this about behavior being the product or output of more than the combined effects of Nature and Nurture, given the additional influences of personal or self factors in this regard, have powerful antecedent historical antecedents, such as found in humanism's third force and Piaget's tertium (third) quid.

The third part of the book shifts from chapters on development to presentation of ones on concepts and empirical research related to free will. These include the belief in free will and its consequences, and it should be noted that this belief in free will is quite widespread and quite consequential. The last chapter in this part of the book considers the related topic of "ego" or resource depletion and its effects on self-control. After reviewing the literature on the topic, the chapter presents an integrated biopsychosocial model of depletion effects, specifically (and of self-control, generally). This chapter concludes with a new questionnaire on free will, after cogent analysis of extant ones. Also, I describe another questionnaire on depletion.

Part IV: Abnormalities in Development and the DSM-5

The fourth part of the present work considers applied aspects related to the causality of behavior. For the causality of abnormal behavior or disorder, often one refers to etiology rather than causality, in general.

The first chapter of this part shows how free will can be used in psychotherapy, which might be especially useful for addictions. Next, the part considers the origins of posttraumatic stress disorder (PTSD), especially in terms of endophenotypes, or the pathway from genes to disease.

The remaining four chapters of this part deal with the DSM-5 (American Psychiatric Association, 2013). This diagnostic manual of mental disorders is a compendium developed by workgroups, and its major goal is to be clinically useful, while considering current research. However, as does medicine more generally, it has difficulty attaining its stated goal of finding specific etiological causes leading to each specific disorder, and then finding specific treatments to help or to cure them. The first chapter of the four in the series describes the changes in the DSM-5 in relation to the DSM-IV-TR (Diagnostic and Statistical Manual of Mental Disorders, Fourth Edition, Text Revised; American Psychiatric Association, 2000) and the views of the critics of the DSM-5. The second and third chapters in this four-part series on the DSM-5 concentrate on the basic psychological injuries (PTSD, chronic pain, mild traumatic brain injury (TBI)), given that psychological injuries are the primary focus of my clinical work. I review how they are treated in the DSM-5 and review criticisms in this regard, leading to recommendations on how to improve their diagnostic criteria. The last mentioned chapter on the DSM also considers the Research Domain of Criteria (RDoC) project, which seeks a more biologically (neuroscientifically) informed understanding of psychopathology. For both the DSM-5 and the RDoC, I recommend a more biopsychosocial approach. This last chapter of the four on the DSM-5 in this part also considers recommendations for the DSM, in general, including with respect to causality and etiology. In particular for the latter, I present an integrated top-down/bottom-up model of how mental disorder and symptoms causally relate to each other.

Part V: Personal Contributions to the Study of Causality in Behavior: New Models

The biopsychosocial model can help explain much of the nature of causality of the psychological injuries. However, PTSD, chronic pain, and mild TBI are all contentious diagnoses and are difficult to discern in assessment because of the potential for evaluees to express secondary gain, exaggeration, and even malingering. Therefore, in this area, an astute forensic perspective helps in arriving at equitable determinations. However, the person is not the only source possible bias, given the negative effects of the insurance/legal process (and even medical process, referred to as iatrogenesis). Because of these complicating factors, establishing, the etiology of psychological injuries and indeed, the whole assessment process of these disorders, needs careful evaluation. I note that the best manner of achieving these goals is to assess complainants from a comprehensive, impartial, and scientific perspective from the point of referral, and throughout the assessment, right to offering conclusions in reports or in testimony to court. In the next chapters in this part, I leave the topic of psychological injury and refer to a host of new models related to causality in psychology, in general. First, I consider options to the classic model of stimuli (S) leading to response (R), in which these components are considered as separate entities. Rather, the organism/processor needs to be considered in the S-R relationship and, in so doing, it becomes evident that they are not separable, distinct components in behavioral causality. In this regard, to conclude the part, I expand upon an integrated cross-network model of behavior and also present many other novel terms and concepts, such as that of the neurome. Another new terminology that I created on causality is "Coexistential Causal Intraactionism." Finally, the part examines change mechanisms, for example, related to activation/inhibition coordination and readiness for change.

Part VI: The Neo-Piagetian/Neo-Eriksonian Model

The last part of the present book elaborates my Neo-Piagetian/Neo-Eriksonian (sub)stage model of 25 steps in lifespan development, as well as its applications and implications. The first chapter focuses on its socioemotional component, in particular, as described in Young (2011). The next one examines its cognitive extensions, especially as presented in Young (2014). The third chapter presents a generic change model of five steps based on the model. I show how it can be applied to multiple phenomena, including in normal and abnormal behavior.

The last three chapters of the book present more innovations for the study and conceptualization of behavioral causality. First, it presents a Neo-Maslovian model based on my Neo-Piagetian/Neo-Eriksonian one. It is a revision of the one presented in Young (2011). The second last chapter of the book also is based on my 2011 model, and it presents a revised Kuhnian model of paradigms in scientific change. In this regard, it considers Overton's (2013, 2014) examination of the Kuhnian model in terms relationism, and shows how my Neo-Kuhnian model is consistent with that view. Also, the latter model that I created would appear to be applicable to any area of scholarship, not just scientific ones. Finally, the book concludes with a chapter on new directions for the study of behavioral causality. Most of the models presented in this concluding chapter elaborate the present overall perspective, for example, in its consideration of free will, which is central focus of the present work.

Conclusion

The factual description of the parts of the present book that has just been presented belies the complexity in the study of psychology as well as some of its raging debates, controversies, and issues. In this regard, note that there is no contradiction (a) in espousing a view of behavioral causality that includes emergence and aspects of free will as part of a self-agent acting in its own best interest in an active way and, in doing so, countering passive deterministic impacts of biology and environment and (b) maintaining that the integrative model being espoused is not Cartesian, dualistic, and separative of mind and body. That is, in a behavioral system such as the one being described, emergent properties are still contained within and reflect the system, are part of it, and do not stand out of it. They are hierarchically arranged within it, perhaps at a superordinate level, and can act top-down on these levels, but are still constitutively derived elements of the system and its component interactions, aside from being subject themselves to lower-order influences in the system. The mind does not stand as distinct from the body even if it is more than the body. The unity of both might be captured by concepts such as embodiment, in which higher-order, more abstract psychological (mental) structures still maintain integral components, linkages, and dynamics involving more grounded, sensorimotor and related structures and, indeed, reflect and are empowered by them.

Also, there is no contradiction (a) in referring to free will as part of the apex of self forces that behave actively in generating free choice, decisions, and actions and (b) in maintaining that free will as being described for present purposes (free being, as per the book title), might not be an active component much of the time in the life of the person. First in this regard, many unconscious processes are involved in behavioral production and, second, even if it is active in conscious ways at times, free will aspects might not be predominant, the arbiter of final choices, decisions, and actions, and so on. That being said, free will has the potential to be the ultimate contributor to behavioral guidance at any one moment. Moreover, in terms of setting long-term life goals, moral values, and so on, it could be the supreme guide, setting the agenda even if not involved directly in building behavior in any or every moment.

Finally, there is no contradiction (a) in referring to free will (and its aspects) as an emergent, higher-order phenomenon and (b) in considering that it is grounded, participatory, developmental, and related to lower-order phenomena. That is, free will is embodied in and constituted by elements of lower-order phenomena, in a systems perspective. In this sense, free will in psychology should be considered as "embodied free will" and, similarly in this regard, the apex in psychological growth "free being," should be considered an embodied product of an embodied process, or as "embodied free being." Further, the hypothesized major constituents of free being—free will belief and having a sense of free will—should be considered "embodied free will belief" and the "embodied sense of having free will," respectively.

The present line of thought leads to a complex understanding of emergence as an embodied process producing an embodied product. Emergence in a system does not lead to higher-order, superordinate, top-down levels distinct from, divorced from, or separate from lower levels of the system involved, but ones intimately related to them, as are all levels of any system in their hierarchical and integrative relationship. In this sense, any emergent phenomena or level in a system is always embodied or linked to any lower-order level(s) and reflective of them. Therefore, it might be best to refer to any emergence as "embodied emergence" and any of its related products as embodied, as well, as should be the process producing them (i.e., embodied X and its embodied or embodying process, respectively).

Human free will is part of our causality engine. Free will is part of our personal contributions to our behavioral causality and stands at the apex in this regard. I chose the title for the book as "The Unifying Psychology and Causality Project: Freedom in Being, Brain, Self, and Behavior" because of my emphasis on the psychology of free will in psychological causation. I look forward to further work on the study of causation of behavior; on free will as an essential focus in this regard; and perhaps with my own modeling serving as relevant axes in this pursuit.

Chapter Descriptions

In the following, I provide brief chapter descriptions with the goal of showing exciting developments in the field of psychology pertaining to causality. Rather than describing in depth each chapter for its specific contents, I take a step back and indicate the novel findings and modeling in each one that are altering the field. The reader should refer to the chapter introductions and summaries for a comprehensive description of their contents.

Part I: Core Causality in Behavior: Foundations and Models

Chapter 1: Brief Book Description and Book Assumptions Psychology is a field growing rapidly, and also it is developing links to many other areas of study, such as psychiatry, genetics, neuroscience, evolutionary modeling, law, and philosophy. Therefore, it is difficult to perceive it in its entirety, or grasp fundamental unifying conceptions that could tie it together and give it a coherent, practical sense. Each subarea in psychology believes that it has developed a central axis that could help integrate psychology into a cohesive field. Moreover, as soon as a new focus develops in a subarea, new ones materialize and spread rapidly even beyond the subarea involved.

As I approached the task of promoting causality as central to psychology and a possible unifying axis for it, I realized the vast nature of the task. Only a book as elaborate as the present one can give the topic justice. In this regard, this first chapter of the book begins the process of championing causality as a cardinal, unifying concept for psychology. It indicates the book's multidisciplinary nature and its underlying assumptions. Also, I present 30 assumptions that are fundamental toward integrating causality as a unifying concept in psychology and also I emphasize the need to explain better the multifactorial nature of causality in psychology. Some of the models that help toward this end include the biopsychosocial model, NLDST, and the model of embodiment. As well, the assumptions that underlie the present book underscore the importance of evolutionary processes, genetics, brain networks, development, and free will in the causation of behavior (and they mention my own work on stage/step models in development).

Chapter 2: Part Overview and Chapter by Chapter Overview The present chapter provides an overview of the parts and chapters of the book. It does not go into depth in describing the chapters; rather, it focuses on the critical concepts, innovations, and modeling that informed and that emerged from the present book.

I wrote this present chapter to serve as a general accessible introduction that shows both the vigor of the field and my excitement and integrative efforts in dealing with it. Above all, this chapter emphasizes the book's critical content and major concepts and models, including of the centrality of causality in psychology and also the centrality of ourselves as active, emergent agents in determining our own psychology (and the role of our "free will" in this regard). Also, in writing this chapter description, I created new terms relevant to the major themes of the book, for example, embodied free being, as well as embodied free will belief and an embodied sense of having free will. Also, at a different point in the chapter, I refer to the concept of "causality engine" in behavior, for example, of which our free will beliefs are prime drivers. We are indeed *Homo Causa*.

Chapter 3: Causality in Psychology This chapter of the present book further elaborates the triadic axis model of causality in the study in psychology, as presented in Young (2011). Although, it describes the scope of the study of causality across multiple disciplines, it still considers the primary axes in this regard as being free will, mechanism, and causal graph modeling. In this chapter, I elaborate further on these three axes in the study of causality in psychology.

This chapter is especially based on the details of my approach to causality as described in Young (2011). I have taken the kernel arguments related to causality in that book and summarized them. Of note, I introduce the following concepts related to causality as central to psychology: the causal landscape and causal streams; hot vs. cold causality; and dimensions in causality study. Also in Young (2011), as summarized in this third chapter of the present book, I was developing models to help in the study of behavioral causality, such as one integrating the concepts of reaction range with the model of differential susceptibility. The chapter also presents other critical models that help in understanding better the causality of behavior. These include NLDST, a stage or step approach to both evolution and development, and the concept of activation/inhibition coordination.

The next part of the chapter gives new material about the three major axes in the study of behavioral causality. (a) Specifically, for the topic of free will, it presents more material on free being, which concerns: having a belief in free will and also having a sense of free will. (b) As for mechanism, I especially present work on energy dynamics as sources of causality throughout the universe and its evolution over time. Inevitably, this concept applies to psychology, as well, for example, in NLDST. (c) Finally, I give new material on explaining causal graph/network modeling. This relates to the work of Sloman (2005), which I use to help structure a better understanding of behavioral causality.

Chapter 4: Causality in Philosophy; Philosophy in Psychology This chapter of the book on philosophy deals with philosophy, in general, as it relates to psychology, and also it deals more specifically with key topics in philosophy in relation to causality and to free will. Some of the positions broached include the distinctions between reductionism and constructivism, causalism and acausalism, and determinism and compatibilism (also libertarian and semi-compatibilist views). Some of the particular, intermediate, or integrative positions considered include eliminative reductionism, elemental constructivism, criterial causation, and probabilistic determinism. The opposition between positivism and relationism is treated toward the end of the chapter. The smorgasbord of philosophical viewpoints continues with discussion of ones for reductionism (moderate, constitutive, neo), constructivism (emergent, situated, neo), dualism (property), positivism (neo), determinism (hard, soft), compatibilism (semi), and dispositionalism. The chapter explores brain-based research related to free will, including intrinsic networks. It presents a model termed "apparent" mental causation.

As for my contributions to the study of philosophy in relation to psychology, I have formulated the integrative concepts of neoreductio constructivism, co-existentialism, dialectical semi-compatibilism, quantum neoepistemology, and Neo-Kuhnianism. In addition, for the development of emergent psychological maturity, which might permit free will to manifest psychologically, as mentioned, at many points in the present book I describe the concept of Free Being. For me, mental causation is as real as biological and social causation.

Chapter 5: Models and Systems of Causality of Behavior This chapter reviews three major models in psychology relevant to the present work—the biopsychosocial model, complexity/NLDST, and embodiment. In Young (2011), I reviewed in depth the first two of these models. All three models are considered wide-ranging, integrative ones.

However, each of the models includes limitations—for example, each possesses properties that make it difficult to apply clearly to the domains that have been considered under its scope.

In this regard, the biopsychosocial model suffers from a lack of precise mechanisms in how its major components might interact to produce a behavior at issue (e.g., illness, psychopathology) or how the treatments under its guise might work. Also, the NLDST approach provides a generic approach to describing system states and their change, as well as the processes that might bring about the change, but it has not made the widespread inroads in psychology predicted for it. Part of the reason might lie in the different approaches that are espoused under its umbrella (as well as its complex mathematics and its different approach to variability in behavior, which is considered "noise" in many of the standard approaches in psychology but the primary subject matter in this approach to psychology).

Finally, the embodied approach is only beginning to prosper as a potentially unifying one in psychology, and it too needs to work on specific mechanisms than entrain development and change, or else it will be considered simply as a redescription of behavioral phenomena rather than a model with sufficient explanatory transformative acumen. Certainly, this present work is dedicated to integrating these various integrative models in psychology and providing them with a reliable and valid suite of change mechanisms that can help explain stability/instability and gradual/abrupt changes in behavior.

As for key terms in this chapter, there are a few for the biopsychosocial approach, given its prevalence throughout the present book. I refer to the psychological component of this model as the "personal" one because all three components are involved in the psychology or behavior and it makes no sense to consider one of the components of the term as especially psychological when, in essence, all three are psychological in nature. It is important to note that the three components involved in the model are not as distinct as their separate presentation might indicate.

Some examples of the biological, psychological (personal), and social components of the model included in the present book follow. These examples are taken from throughout the book and not uniquely from Chap. 5 that is being summarized here.

For the biological component of the biopsychosocial model, among others, the present work examines the influence on behavior of genes/epigenetics; Gene × Environment (G × E) interactions and correlated G × E (rGE); the brain and brain networks (the Connectome, structural and functional); lateralization and hemispheric specialization; evolution, life history theory, and differential susceptibility; as well as the stress response and its major physiological systems (hypothalamic pituitary adrenal (HPA) axis; sympathetic adrenal medullary (SAM) system), and critical molecular biochemicals and neurotransmitter components (cortisol, norepinephrine, glucocorticoid receptors) and their action on neurons and the brain.

For the psychological (personal) component of the biopsychosocial model, among others, the book examines aspects of the self; self-control/regulation (cognitive, emotional); executive function; relevant cognitive acquisitions, including belief; resilience and coping; personality and temperament; motivation and attention; and free will and resource (ego) depletion.

For the social component of the biopsychosocial model, among others, the book explores cultural and societal influences; socioeconomic status (SES), minority status, and other demographics; prenatal influences, early adversity, early life experiences; parenting, parenting style, and schooling; maltreatment, abuse; buffering the environment, etc.

Clearly, free will is a major anchor of the present book. Another component to the personal agency in behavioral causation that I introduce in this chapter concerns passion. I review the definition of passion and also the questionnaire currently in use in evaluating it and, in both regards, develop better ones.

As for the complexity and NLDST, they especially refer, in particular, respectively, (a) to complex adaptive systems, networks, and agents, and (b) to attractors, self-organization, emergence, fractals, and circular causality. They also refer to collective autocatalytic sets and to complexity pyramids, as well as to control and order parameters, respectively.

The key terms and concepts in the embodiment model of behavior are proliferating. The embodiment model has been differentiated into strong, secondary, hybrid, and radical versions. A similar model is that of radical enactivism. It has been applied to cognition, affect, the brain (e.g., the mirror system), and even the extended mind, inter-brain, embodied attunement, and conjoined people (through joint attractors). It incorporates extended concepts of behavior, such as body-becoming-mind and the brain-body-environment landscape, yet also quite basic ones, such as chemosignals in intersubjectivity and force dynamics in language and sociality. Some of its concepts are rarified, such as having a hypergrip on affordances and also hermeneutic realism. As for my contributions to the area of embodiment, I develop the concepts of embodied causation or etiology and of causal or etiological embodiment. Also, I refer to the human species as *Homo Causa* in this chapter and to the causalization process as inimical to who we are and how we become.

Chapter 6: Statistical Concepts and Networks in Causality The present chapter focuses on more statistical approaches to causality, including network approaches. It examines test validity models (reflective, formative, mutualistic) and causal models in testing (regularity, counterfactual, process). Test validity involves two major approaches—behavior domain theory and causal theory of measurement.

Statistical approaches to causality are important, but classic experimental approaches to causality need to be supplemented by other means when the classic approaches cannot be applied, for example, due to ethical considerations in setting up certain experimental manipulations. The classical causal model involving experimentation gives validity (and generalizability) cardinal importance, and these are difficult to target in nonexperimental designs but, through their statistical innovations, they are narrowing their limits in these regards. The supplementary statistical approaches in the study of behavioral causality include the potential outcomes model and the directed acyclic graphs (DAGs) model. The former includes a basis in hypothetical outcomes that cannot be ascertained directly, involving the SUTVA (stable unit treatment value assumption), and the latter includes the equivalent of experimental manipulations in its graph surgery/"do" operators (interventions), causal descendants, and counterfactuals. A variation of this latter approach is the ICA (integrated counterfactual approach). Some of the new approaches to statistical mediation analysis include: average causal mediation effect; left-out variables error method; latent growth curve modeling; state space modeling; and the ignorability-based approach.

Some of the philosophical precursors to statistical and related causality not only concern interventionist/counterfactual accounts but also concepts such as NESS and INUS. The former is defined as necessary element for the sufficiency of a sufficient set and the latter as insufficient but necessary components of unnecessary but sufficient causes. These are complex concepts that inform but to not direct statistical approaches to causality in psychology. Aristotle's concept of four causes still has currency today (material, efficient, formal, final), with efficient causes considered as the equivalent of mechanisms.

Baye's theorem is an emerging approach in the statistical approach to causality. It is subjective rather than classically frequentist. It deals with concepts such as priors, precision, likelihood, posteriors, and credibility instead of confidence intervals, and it stands in opposition to the classic approach to testing null vs. experimental hypotheses.

Other portions of the chapter deal with FACCDs (Functional Analytic Clinical Case Diagram), ecology, Granger Causality (GC), and networks. The latter is explored in much more detail in subsequent chapters on the brain, in particular. Among the notable aspects of networks discussed in the present chapter include measures of centrality and betweenness.

The chapter also covers epidemiology, with its emphasis on temporality (e.g., predisposing, precipitating, perpetuating factors), and causal webs or pies. The chapter includes new models of statistics and causality, such as the decision theoretic approach, minimal causal models, dynamic causal modeling, and convergent cross-mapping.

The chapter includes a section on PTSD because McNally et al. (2015) related it to the concept of networks. For this area of research, the authors contrasted network modeling with the approach of latent variable/constructs. Some of the network concepts applied to the data include: networks of association, concentration, and relative importance. The key measures used also related to centrality and betweenness.

Part II: Biology and Revolutions

Chapter 7: Brain: The Neuronal Network Revolution This chapter deals with a central concept in causality in psychology and related disciplines—that of networks, and especially as the concept is applied to the brain. On the one hand, it deals with the Connectome, in general, as applied to brain networks and, on the other hand, it describes intrinsic or core brain networks. The concept of the Connectome is part of the burgeoning field of connectomics, which also involves pathoconnectomics. Brain connectivities might be structural, functional, or effective. Connections are established by connection matrices, which include graphs, nodes, edges, hubs, cores, and paths. The connectivities might evidence rich clubs or small worlds. The measures include ones of centrality and betweenness.

The field has determined up to 14 brain networks, but three generally are considered primary—the salience network, the central executive network, and the default mode network. Another one referred to in the chapter is the frontoparietal network.

A major theory cutting across networks involves a Bayesian model of the brain acting to reduce its free energy or surprise by minimizing prediction errors and otherwise functioning thermodynamically (Friston, 2010). This work is important enough to have been emphasized in the title of the book, when I refer to freeing the brain. Other concepts in this model include the ones of local and global dynamics, inference machines, meta-stability/quasi-stability, and hidden causes and econiches.

The chapter refers to other causality-related terms, such as causal flow. One article discusses network organization in terms of "cacti." The work on networks incorporates the perspective on NLDST, and the chapter is replete with terminology from this model and related ones. For example, it refers to "criticality," which is the region in state space of a system that facilitates state change, including to "chaotic" regimes. Also, the chapter refers to state space "viscosity," a concept not traditionally encountered in NLDST.

The chapter examines systems at the micro level, that is, neuronal networks and even the networked nature of concept cells and of astrocytes. Finally, wherever one looks in research and conceptualization about the brain, one finds evidence supporting the present model of activation/inhibition coordination as being a common metric within each of and across brain and behavior, and in this chapter I point out areas where this concept applies.

As for the application of network models to more behavioral phenomena, the chapter describes a network causal system model that treats items or symptoms of mental disorder. It is contrasted to the latent variable/construct model. Causality inheres in linkages across symptoms themselves rather than to underlying constructs relating them or central constructs that they address.

Chapter 8: Lateralization and Specialization of the Brain The second chapter in the present book on the brain is on cerebral hemispheric specialization and the associated topic of behavioral lateralization. As with other areas of brain study, the concept of networks is making inroads in this area. The findings in this regard reinforce the left-hemisphere as differentially specialized for its skills relative to the right. Although each hemisphere has its specializations, the left hemisphere has been called dominant and, in this regard, the network approach is touting its efficiency and also its more centrally organized characteristics. Moreover, the findings show that even neonates possess this type of left hemisphere specialization. These findings on the differential networking in the hemispheres are consistent with the present model that the left hemisphere possesses better activation/inhibition coordination skills compared to the right hemisphere, which has other inhibitory skills.

Aspects of manual behavior reflect the differential skills of the left and right hemispheres, and so reflect a manual specialization that reflects its underlying hemispheric specialization. Handedness is not as clearly related to hemispheric specialization as are other manual behaviors. Most often, language abilities are associated with the left hemisphere, which is why it is called the dominant hemisphere, but each hemisphere has its skill set (e.g., certain spatial skills in the right hemisphere) and, moreover, the advantages that each hemisphere possesses are relative rather than absolute ones. Research is showing that the left hemisphere is associated with certain cognitive skills, as well. The hemispheres work in concert in adaptation to context, problem-solving, and so on. Interhemispheric communication is important in this regard.

As for how the chapter is organized as it reviews the research on hemispheric specialization, manual specialization, and behavioral lateralities, and their relationship to handedness, language development, cognitive achievement, and so on, it considers each age period separately from preconception into childhood, in particular. For each age period under review, first, results of research related to manual lateralities are presented. Then, for each age period, other results related to the brain are presented. Finally, aside from considering the developmental origins of specialization/lateralization, the chapter considers evolutionary ones.

Chapter 9: The Genetics Revolution The study of causality of behavior is marked by fields undergoing rapid expansion, including the one of genetics. The genetic revolution has witnessed the classic model of genotype ⟶ transcription ⟶ protein ⟶ phenotype evolve to become a supercomplex one of multiple "-omics" (genomics, epigenomics, etc.). The research on candidate genes that aims to find simple gene–behavior associations has been supplemented by genome-wide association studies and genome-wide complex trait analysis (GWAS, GCTA, respectively). The classic search for the heritability in behavioral variation explanation has been supplemented for a search of "missing" heritability. Instead of straightforward genetic main effects, researchers also look for Gene × Environment interaction. These include *MAOA* × Maltreatment interaction in antisocial behavior outcome.

Aside from considering G × E influences on behavior, one needs to consider multiple genes interacting with E and also multiple environmental factors in interaction beyond their interaction with G (G × G × E and G × E × E, respectively), as well as all these types of interactions with D (development). Also, there are correlated G × E findings (rGE), which lie more on the genetic than the environmental side of behavioral causal influence (e.g., phenotypes underlain by certain genotypes lead to behaviors that influence the environment, rather than vice versa). In addition, research is demonstrating epigenetic effects (gene silencing) on genes, which lies more on the environmental side relative to the genetic side of behavioral causal influence.

These examples illustrate that even in the area of genetics of behavior the dividing line between genes and environment are fuzzy and interactive.

There are numerous key genetic terms in the chapter, given its genetic focus. They include CNVs (copy number variations), VNTRs (variable number of random repeats), and LPR (length polymorphism in *MAOA* promoter region). Among the genetic polymorphisms in the chapter, one will find *5-HTTLPR* (serotonin transporter polymorphism), *COMT* (catechol-*O*-methyltransferase), *DRD4* (dopamine receptor D4), and *MAOA* (monoamine oxidase A).

The chapter considers broader phenomena related to genes, such as biointelligence, evolvability, versatility, and polygenetic scores. As for my contributions to the field, I suggest investigation of the "phenome" to better understand the disparate and sometimes conflicting or nonreplicated results on the genome (not to mention my concept of the "loveome").

Chapter 10: Gene × Environment Interaction: The Environmental Revolution The phenomenon of Genetic × Environmental (G × E) interaction illustrates not only the genetic revolution but also the environmental one. Neither genes nor environment is considered as separate and additive causal factors in development. Rather, now they are each considered multifactorial, as is their interaction. The current chapter especially presents a detailed literature review of the effects of G × E on behavior. Some of the polymorphisms involved include those related to *MAOA*, *5-HTTLPR*, *OXTR* (oxytocin receptor), *CRHR1* (corticotropin releasing hormone receptor 1), *BDNF* (brain-derived neurotrophic factor), *NET* (norepinephrine transporter; *SLC6A2*; solute carrier family 6 member 2), and *DAT1* (dopamine active transporter gene). The outcomes include antisocial behavior, anger, depression, ADHD (attention deficit hyperactivity disorder), educational attainment, etc. Generally, the psychopathological effects can be qualified as internalizing and externalizing. The environments involved include child abuse, early adversity, and multiple aspects of parenting. The findings are complex, including differential effects according to age, gene, environment, and outcome. Moreover, the qualifications G × G × E, G × E × E, and G × E × D interactions reveal the complexities in behavioral genetics research. The chapter examines other genetic processes, such as epigenetics, differential susceptibility, and NLDST.

Some of the most striking findings in the chapter relate to the longitudinal associations found. Clearly, just as the environment early in life is now considered as having an enduring impact so, too, should the effects of genes; they are not overwhelmed in their causal impact on behavior by environmental impacts. Once more, the interaction of genes and environment in behavioral causality stands out according to the empirical research.

Chapter 11: Genes and Environment: The Person Revolution Whereas the introductions to the two prior chapters on genetics and behavior have addressed the fast-pace changes in the field, the present chapter accelerates in this progression. It considers in detail epigenetics, correlated Gene × Environment (rGE) interactions, and cultural neuroscience. Moreover, in doing so, it illustrates further the difficulty in separating genes, environments, and the person as distinct entities. Finally, it includes other models pertinent to the present work, such as differential susceptibility. The genes, environment, and person form a complex causal behavioral system, which includes developmental, learning, evolutionary, and contextual factors. Moreover, the interplay among these diverse factors in behavioral causality is so intricate that only the refined types of conceptualization and empirical study as described in the chapter can elucidate the complexity involved.

In epigenesis, among other processes, DNA methylation helps silence genes in their promoter regions. Moreover, the effects can be transmitted over generations through epigenetic marks. The chapter refers to the "methylome" in this regard. [There are other epigenetic processes related to histones and micro-RNA, in particular]. Epigenetic effects could take place prenatally, such as through maternal distress. They could influence development through their genetically-modified alterations in critical neurogenetic processes, including in brain regions and related functions, such as in the stress-mediating HPA axis.

Overall, it is argued that the best metaphorical formula to describe the causes of behavior is not Nature or Nurture or Nature and Nurture but Nature *is* Nurture, given the apparent Lamarkian-like effects of epigenesis. Some of the epigenesis-susceptible gene polymorphisms involved include *NR3C1* (nuclear receptor subfamily 3, group C, member 1), *OXTR*, *BDNF*, and *COX2* (cytochrome c oxidase subunit II). The work on epigenesis shows how it can lead to either internalization or externalization behavioral difficulties. As for rGE, some of the genetic polymorphisms involved include *5-HTTLPR* and D2 (*TaqIAI* allele). For cultural neuroscience, they include *5-HTTLPR*, *OXTR*, and *DRD4*.

If rGE illustrates that genes influence environment, for example, through their evocative active effects, cultural neuroscience illustrates how environment (through culture) alters gene expression through genetic susceptibility to differential cultural effects. That being said, in the present book, the person stands as the ultimate influence in behavioral causation. Genes and environment are both passive players relative to our own potential to be in control of our own behavior.

Chapter 12: Nature and Nurture: Evolution and Complexities Evolutionary psychology has been presented as a unifying force in psychology. In this chapter, I emphasize that, in adapting a systems perspective in which evolution is considered as one primary factor, a pathway can be laid down toward the unification of psychology. Tinbergen's four questions are still seminal for the field (adaptive function, phylogeny, ontogeny, mechanism). They can serve to create an integrative meta-model of behavioral causality along with the biopsychosocial model, NLDST, and related models. The NLDST gives one axis of integration in these regards through its related concept of complexity.

A more integrated process of evolution with other models would consider the influence of niche, culture, development, and person. As emphasized in the approach of niche construction, organisms are active, casual agents in their own evolution.

Life history theory indicates that evolution constructs each developmental period as adaptive. This model is consistent with the notions that development affords flexibility and that evolution is informed by optimization.

Social genomics indicates that the genome is fluid, and that it is a metagenome. The socioaffective environment gets "under the skin," as in epigenetics; but more so—it gets "onto the genome." For example, social rejection can create social signals of even a short-term immediate nature that have long-lasting molecular imprints that affect health through effects on the HPA axis and also on inflammatory responses.

Overall, the concept of evolution is evolving, as is the concept of genetic influence on behavior. Both need to adopt a broader framework in which the environment is included in a systems framework. For example, the field needs to integrate social genomics with evolution, and ask how social genomics has influenced evolution. Already, epigenesis has been shown to have transgenerational effects and the same might be true of social genomics, for example, through epigenetic and related processes. Similarly, if there might be transgenerational effects through epigenesis and perhaps through social genomics, one could ask to what extent the field of evolution should consider better how the environment has gotten in our forebears under their skin and onto their genome (and subsequently ours).

Part III: Normal and Abnormal Development and Free Will: Normal Development and Free Will

Chapter 13: Differential Susceptibility: Orchids, Dandelions, and the Flowering of Developmental Psychology The chapter on developmental evolutionary models especially concerns differential susceptibility. Comparable models include biological sensitivity to context and adaptive calibration. These interactive models involving polyphenotypic options are distinct from unilateral uniphenotypic ones of combined vulnerabilities and adversities (diathesis-stress, allostatic load). They are evolutionary through the concepts of bet hedging, conditional adaptation, and stochastic developmental switch. They offer accounts of differential life history strategies (slow, less risky; fast, risky), in psychological acceleration, depending on early environment quality. The former is fashioned by predictable early environments and the latter by unpredictable ones, for example. Therefore, forecasting based on early environmental sampling appears a mechanism in life history strategy.

Another aspect of the model of differential susceptibility concerns certain polymorphisms having susceptibility to environment impacts relative to others and, furthermore, in ways that could be more positive for supportive environments with a susceptibility allele present but more negative for nonsupportive environments with the same allele present. Some of the alleles in this regard include those related to *5-HTTLPR*, *DRD4*, *DAT1*, *BDNF*, *OXTR*, and *MAOA*, with polygenetic combinations also involved. Some of the early stressors in this research include maternal emotionality/sensitivity. The negative outcomes involved in early adversity include externalizing (e.g., conduct disorder) and internalizing (e.g., depression) ones. The mediators in the relationships include stress-response physiology. The mechanisms affecting the genes involved appear to be epigenetic.

Chapter 14: Early Adversity, Fetal Programming, and Getting Under the Skin Early adversity affects long-term physical and mental health, but in interaction with and mediation by many factors. Related models refer to fetal programming and enduring effects. The environment is considered to "get under the skin" even prenatally. The pathways are multiple and include hypo- and hyperactivation of cortisol and, generally, effects on the HPA axis and the SAM axis. The early adversities described in this chapter include: prenatal substance abuse/depression/anxiety; abuse/neglect, low SES; poverty; and maternal factors (depression, caregiver sensitivity/attachment style promotion). The genes involved in the interaction include *5-HTTLPR*, *COMT*, *NR2C1* (nuclear receptor subfamily 2, group c, member 1), *DAT1*, and *DRD4*. The effects include on disease/mortality; telomere length/inflammatory markers; depression/neuroticism; delinquency/other externalization behavior; and working memory/academic attainment. The mediating effect of epigenesis (environmentally-induced gene-silence) appears a prominent intermediate mechanism in the relations described.

Chapter 15: Connecting the Social Dots The chapter emphasizes the distinctiveness in humans of our extreme social skills and/or organization. It investigates the evolutionary and developmental origins of these skills. For example, are they innate, prepared, and core, or do they depend on gradual learning, for example, in imitation? The chapter includes work on social neuroscience, and emphasizes the frontalization process, as well as the mirror neuron system and the somatic marker hypothesis. Also, it refers to biobehavioral synchrony and physiological attunement that happens in the neonatal-parental embodied dance or intersubjectivity. Other more biological topics include the perception–action mechanism and supramodal perception. Generally, the models presented are quite biopsychosocial, including the "SOCIAL" model and ones of stress contagion and shared embodiment.

Other models in the chapter include the empirical/nativist enactivism one, and one involving an affective sharing device. In addition, the chapter includes the goal alignment and social normative models, as well as the prosocial construal and partner choice ones.

About evolution, the concepts reviewed include superorganism, cultural evolution, group selection, and cultural group selection, as well as gene–culture co-evolution. Some of the terms indicating the complexity of human social behavior include group mindedness, collective morality, collective intentionality, and hypercollaboration.

The proximal mechanisms involved in early social learning include not only imitation and parental practice but also factors such as emulation and overimitation. The most intriguing research is with infants, and this includes work on biobehavioral synchrony, even in heart rate coordination, and work with puppets who are helpers or hinderers/mean or nice, and infants responding to them (e.g., preferring not only helpers but hinderers of hinderers). The chapter spans the full developmental range, and for adults, it refers to narrative/self-autobiography/identity, as well as the public good/political ideology. Also, it includes research not only on humans but also nonhuman primates. In this chapter on connecting the social dots, clearly, I had to consider many dots to connect.

Chapter 16: Causal Learning: Understanding the World This chapter focuses heavily on empirical research on whether causal learning is evident very early in life as an associative or as a primitive inferential, abstract fashion. The current predominant view is that it is Bayesian, statistical, probabilistic, computational, and so on, and not governed by either innate preformed abstraction-ready modules or associative, nonrepresentational mechanisms. The Bayesian point of view in this chapter is complemented by the interventionist and causal mapping ones. In working in this area, the traditional Piagetian perspective on mental schemas still appears useful, and it is much cited. However, others dismiss its utility. In my compromise position, I show how a modified, integrative Neo-Piagetian view can be informative.

The associative point of view is promoted by theorists who argue that too much is read into studies of very young infants in terms of their early abstractive abilities. Rather than being little logicians, young children are intuitive statisticians. A view that accommodates to the opposition of the fast minimal nativist and slow constructivist points of view on early causal learning concerns the middle-of-the-road one of rational constructivism.

Early cognitive structures in the associationist camp have been referred to as intuitive and nontheoretical, with motor resonance involved. Yet the field also encounters contrary concepts, such as infants possessing an abstract framework and the blessing of abstraction. In a nativist-friendly approach, neonates might even understand physical causation/Michottian launching events. Yet, in the contrary view, only older children might develop a full theory of mind, which has been referred to as a "theory" theory. Aside from innate factors, the chapter refers to natural pedagogy, and observational causal learning/interventionist, causality-informative behavior. For some of the intriguing methods used in the research, they include "blicket" detectors, sticky mittens, everted rabbits, and win-stay/lose-shift strategies. Other concepts in the chapter include causal, higher-order relational cognition and the quantum probability model of causal reasoning.

Chapter 17: Developing the Mind, Minding Development This chapter bridges the next ones on free will, reviewing (a) the development of executive function, which includes self-control and inhibition, and (b) developmental versions of models that have informed the present work (biopsychosocial, embodiment, NLDST). It bridges the previous chapter by presenting views on development of theory of mind. In all these spheres, a primary issue concerns the nativist vs. learning perspectives and the speed of development in the different domains. For example, is early theory of mind/false belief understanding best considered as being (a) implicit, rule-based, and emergent-expressive or (b) explicit reasoning, and mentalizing based, including in usage-base? In these acquisitions, are biologically-based systems, such as mirror neuronal systems, or environmentally-based ones, such as parenting and rapid cultural learning, more involved? Integrative models, of course, would argue that all these factors are involved in the multifactorial complexity of behavioral causality. Finally, the chapter considers that Piagetian concepts have much to offer the needed integration in the field.

Chapter 18: Free Will in Behavior: Believing Makes It So Free will is not an illusion, and its belief is widespread and has important consequences, for example, in self-control. The research findings apparently show that the intention to move follows rather than precedes movement (Libet), but this type of research has not been undertaken with ecological validity. Questionnaires have been developed to measure free will, and the results indicate relevant associations, such as with personality attributes and motivation. That free will is relevant to psychological function does not deny that unconscious influences are important in behavior. They provide the automaticity for much of our daily actions. However, conscious causation appears to play a superordinate, deliberative role. Much of the chapter deals with the neuronal and brain bases thought to underlie free decision making, which appears emergent and not uniquely reductionist. There are enough bases in the chapter to enable further conceptual work on free will in psychology, such as through my own concept on free being.

Chapter 19: An Integrated Model of "Free Will" and New Free Will Questionnaires The question of free will is related closely to that of self-control and its depletion. Self-control can be depleted in successive relevant self-control tasks in the laboratory in which the first one serves to degrade self-control in the second. The phenomenon has been termed ego-depletion, and it has been related to physiological depletion in available glucose. This model is a resource one, and other models have been developed for self-control depletion that are inclusive of motivational and social factors. In this chapter, I present an integrated biopsychosocial model of self-control, across these various factors thought to affect self-control, which helps explain the depletion effect. Also, I present a biopsychosocial concept of free will. Further, I develop a new free will questionnaire that is consistent with the biopsychosocial approach to free will. The chapter also deals with dual process cognitive models, which I integrate into the general theme of the chapter. Finally, the chapter integrates some of my other work on activation/ inhibition coordination and cognitive stages in development.

Part IV: Abnormalities in Development and the DSM-5

Chapter 20: Free Will in Psychotherapy: Helping People Believe This chapter takes the work on free will in psychology and translates it in a module on the use of free will in psychotherapy. Sample questions that one could use in this regard include the following:

(a) For free will in everyday life: "Think of several ways in your daily life that you show you have a sense of free will. Then, think of several ways your sense of free will can be improved, e.g., in helping you reach desired goals and outcomes. How can you help yourself increase your sense of free will in your everyday life? Think of several ways."
(b) For self-regulation: "Delay of gratification is important to everyday life. List several benefits in waiting for better choices later on rather than seeking immediate gratification. How can you improve this skill?"
(c) For conscious causation: "Writing about or talking about past events that need reworking, such as traumas, improves the ability to move forward."
(d) For mechanisms in motivation: "I might feel that I should act impulsively, but I can get back on target and control that."
(e) For meaning making: "Whenever you think that free will does not exist for you, how can you bring it back as a part of you?"
(f) For promoting logic: "How have you used automatic thought, intuition, or fast responding without thinking through first, and it helped? When did it not? How could you have handled it differently?"
(g) For the change process: "Growth happens by exchanging ideas, talking, reflecting on the exchanges and ideas, etc. How can you keep it going so that change for the better continues or is maintained despite ups and downs over time?"
(h) For addictions: "Belief that addiction can be controlled begins with the belief that it is a condition for which such control is possible; it is not only medical and biological but also psychological and social."

The chapter develops some novel concepts related to free will in psychotherapy. These include free will working schemata. Also, we develop asymptotically in free will growth. Further, we endure a paradoxical loss of free will to do anything that we want when we mature and take on our responsibilities.

Chapter 21: PTSD: Traumatic Causation The causality of abnormal or disordered behavior is referred to as etiology. The various versions of the DSM diagnostic manual are based on the medical model, which seeks clear, specific relationships among etiology, disorder category, and treatment. A major approach to understanding etiology involves the search for endophenotypes that lie between genes and disorders. This chapter reviews current conceptualization and research on PTSD, focusing on the biological markers of the disorder that might constitute endophenotypes. The search for candidate endophenotypes in PTSD must begin with determining its genetic bases, as well as the effects of epigenesis on their expression. However, establishing the endophenotype of PTSD is confounded by the uncertainty of which model best conceives it and the factor structure of its symptoms, let alone that both the number of its symptoms and their arrangement in clusters change from one version of the DSM to the next.

The chapter is heavily biological and is too dense to summarize in detail in this regard. Some of the candidate genes for the endophenotype for PTSD mentioned in the chapter include: *SLC6A39* (dopamine transporter gene polymorphism, allele 9), *FKBP5* (glucocorticoid receptor co-chaperone protein 5), *COMT*, *RGS2* (regulator of G-protein signaling 2), *5-HTTLPR*, *BDNF*, *NR3C1*, and *DRD2* (dopamine receptor D2). Some of the brain areas involved in PTSD include: the hippocampus, the amygdala, the anterior cingulate, the insula, the orbitofrontal region, and the medial prefrontal cortex. As for neurotransmitters, they include: prefrontal cortex alpha 2c (PFC α 2c); alpha, noradrenergic (noradrenergic α); dopamine type 1 (*DA1*); serotonin type 2 receptor (*5HT2R*); dehydroepiandrosterone, or its sulfated derivative (*DHEA (S)*); cannabinoid type 1 receptor (*CB1R*); alpha 2c noradrenergic receptor polymorphism (α2cDel1322-325); gamma-aminobutyric acid (GABA); (allo)pregnanolone (*ALLO*); neuropeptide Y (*NPY*), catecholamines, serotonin, cortisol, corticotrophin-releasing factor (*CRF*), dehydroepiandrostorone, (allo)pregnalolone, and immune factors. The general message of the chapter is that progress is being made in determining the pathway to disorder for PTSD. However, as with the many disorders in the DSM, effort to establish the endophenotype of PTSD needs to consider the biopsychosocial model. A strict biological emphasis on the origins of PTSD will confound understanding of its causality (etiology).

Chapter 22: DSM-5: Basics and Critics The next four chapters of the present work review the DSM-5 (American Psychiatric Association, 2013), in general, and particular DSM categories, especially PTSD. It gives voice to critics of the DSM-5, and ends with recommendations. The first chapter of the four in this series begins with an overview of the DSM-5 and the assumptions that are needed to revise it. It examines etiology and also the biopsychosocial model. Then, it gives the major specific changes incorporated in the DSM-5.

The critique of the DSM-5 has focused on deficits in its utility, reliability, and validity. In addition, often it sets a bar too low, and exposes both vulnerable people and normal ones to the risks of overdiagnosis and of pathologizing normal conditions.

Further, apparently the DSM-5 workgroups were compromised ethically. Also, the field trials for the DSM-5 used a draft version that was changed for the final version. Finally, I compared the draft and final version, and found that any mention of the term biopsychosocial was removed.

My contributions to the field in this chapter include developing a better definition of mental disorder. I underscore the need to adopt the biopsychosocial approach in psychiatry, generally, and for revising the DSM-5, specifically. To conclude, I note that using the DSM-5 might induce in the users the humorously entitled DSM-5 Confusion Disorder.

Chapter 23: The DSM-5 and the RDoC Grand Designs and Grander Problems The two great projects in psychiatry concern the psychiatric diagnostic manual DSM-5 (American Psychiatric Association, 2013) and the neuroscientific-based psychiatric research project RDoC (Insel et al., 2010; Insel & Lieberman, 2013). Insel et al. (2010) had considered the latter as a step in improving psychiatric understanding of mental disorder and eventually as a key for a new approach to psychiatric diagnosis. More recently, he considered the two projects as collaborative and mutually-informing (Insel & Lieberman, 2013). This chapter first examines the multiple criticisms of the RDoC project, which are eerily similar to those applicable to the DSM-5. Both projects appear insular and focused on the neurobiology of mental disorder, in particular, despite protestations to the contrary.

Next, the chapter describes once more PTSD, but this time as treated in the DSM-5. I review its criteria, its factor structure, and so on, and present recent research and criticisms related to it. I describe my own research on PTSD, including on the excessive symptom combinations possible because of its polythetic structure, especially when possible comorbidities are considered (Young, Lareau, & Pierre, 2014). It would appear that simplifying the approach to symptom organization for PTSD makes sense, and the same message applies to many DSM-5 disorders.

Chapter 24: The Disordered DSM-5 Disorders As much as PTSD was presented in the DSM-5 (American Psychiatric Association, 2013), it is open to criticism. Other disorders in the DSM-5 have been subject to even more negative evaluations of their conceptualization and symptom criteria. For example, Neurocognitive Disorder (NCD) has specifiers for Mild and Major but not Moderate. Many patients with TBI diagnosed using this system will find that the bar has been set too high for their moderate condition, and they will be assigned a mild level of TBI. As for patients with chronic pain, they will be given a diagnosis of somatic symptom disorder (SSD), with pain as a specifier, instead of Pain Disorder, which is a category in the prior DSM manual (DSM-IV-TR; American Psychiatric Association, 2000).

Other disorders were changed so much by the working groups in charge of revising the DSM-IV-TR that they were consigned to the DSM-5's appendix section for further study, given the outcry about their lack of clinical clarity and utility (e.g., personality disorders). Finally, other categories in the DSM-IV-TR that had been roundly criticized and even ignored (e.g., malingering) have remained relatively unchanged in the DSM-5.

In this chapter, I review these various categories in the DSM-5, how they had been treated in the DSM-IV, the criticisms raised about them, including my own, and the recommendations made to revise them for the DSM-5. In particular, I present a revision of SSD and label it Chronic Pain Complications Disorder. It takes the best of the criteria for SSD, revises them, and adds others, while maintaining chronic pain as a focus in the disorder and also dealing with the criticisms of the category applied to it in the DSM-IV. Another recommendation that I make for the DSM-5 is how to better define malingering.

Chapter 25: DSM-5: Recommendations The fourth chapter on the DSM-5 (American Psychiatric Association, 2013) in the present work reviews the psychiatric approaches to etiology and endophenotype. Then, it proceeds to make recommendations for revising in psychiatry the approach to both assessment and diagnosis. For etiology, I highlight Kendler's models on emergence and mechanism, and other work indicating the multifactorial, fuzzy nature of psychiatric symptoms and disorders, including the network approach. I argue for an inclusive biopsychosocial model not only for etiology but also for the related concept of endophenotypes. Further, I propose a reciprocally dynamic causal model of mental disorder that considers its relation to symptoms in an integrated top-down/bottom-up fashion.

As for recommendations to revise the extant DSM nosology system and assessments related to it, I propose the following: (a) a manner to integrate categorical and dimensional approaches, and (b) use of a range of assessment dimensions.

Note that all the DSM chapters in the present work consider forensic factors, given the import of the DSMs in forensic work and the problems raised in using them this way.

Part V: Personal Contributions to the Study of Causality in Behavior: New Models

Chapter 26: Causality in Psychological Injury & Law: Basics and Critics In the next two chapters of the present work, I turn to an area of psychology in which I have helped place causality as a central concept (psychological injury and law; e.g., Young, 2014, 2015; Young & Drogin, 2014). Psychological injuries concern contentious conditions, especially PTSD, chronic pain, and mild TBI. The chapter considers causation both in civil law and in terms of *mens rea* in criminal law. I propose new terms that might help disambiguate some of the confusion in the field (e.g., biopsychosocial causation). The biopsychosocial model serves as a central focus in the area of psychological injury and law (along with forensic considerations).

Chapter 27: Causality in Psychological Injury & Law: Models In the second chapter in the present book on causality in the area of psychological injury and law, I present a new model that includes iatrogenesis among the various influences on individuals with psychological injuries. Much of the chapter deals with iatrogenesis, which has not been a central topic in psychology despite its importance in the medical field. I review other models in the area of psychological injury and law that include iatrogenesis, as well as the many terms related to it. This chapter and the prior one emphasize the need to conduct comprehensive assessments that are impartial and scientifically informed in order to evaluate effectively psychological injury determinations and their causality.

Chapter 28: Stimulus–Organism–Response Model: SORing to New Heights This chapter begins a series of nine chapters in which I present major innovations that I have proposed about the causality of behavior. The first of these chapters is on a model on stimulus–organism–response (S-O-R) relations. The next two are on new concepts and terms for the field. The last of these three chapters introduces applications in understanding behavioral causality in terms of my 25-step Neo-Piagetian/Neo-Eriksonian developmental model, a process that especially takes up most of the last six chapters of the present book.

The revised S-O-R model that I propose is based on the interrelational quality of the components of the model, wherein each of stimulus, organism, and response are considered "fuzzy" and probabilistic, or without distinct boundaries (or even standard order in their sequencing; e.g., does S always enter the organism independently without the effects of feedback/forward mechanisms?). Free will plays a role in the model through free will belief and its effects on behavior. Just as genes can evoke active effects in the environment (gene–environment correlations), I propose that free will belief engaged in the person can do the same ("free will/environment correlations").

Chapter 29: Networked Causal Terms This chapter proposes integrative models of behavioral causality, notably an Integrated Cross Network model and a GEODS (Genes, Environment, Organism, Development, Systems) model. In addition, it presents some catchy terms meant to promote further interest in the study of behavioral causation, given its disparate focus in psychology. These new terms include not only simpler ones, such as embodied causation, but also more thought-provoking ones, such as humans constituting a species of *Homo Causa* and also the universe being comprised of cause–effect relations, or of "causicles." The most important new term that I created is meant to capture the broad approach that I took in it with respect to behavioral causality, and it is called "Coexistential Causal Intraactionism." The first and last of the components if this term indicate, respectively, (a) that opposite concepts might be really complementary and (b) phenomena exist not as interactions among their components but in the interactions themselves, or their intraactive interactions.

Chapter 30: Change Mechanisms This chapter presents review of the critical change mechanism of activation/inhibition coordination and it gives details of two conceptual innovations that I have proposed in the book, those of neuromal networks and readiness for change in terms of my 25-step (5 stage × 5 substage) developmental model. The neuromal network model is a developmentally-tuned one that helps explain behavioral acquisitions. The readiness for change model is one that helps explain behavioral changes, in general. The chapter also describes dimensions involved in change.

Part VI: The Neo-Piagetian/Neo-Eriksonian Model

Chapter 31: A Neo-Piagetian/Neo-Eriksonian 25-Step (Sub)Stage Model This chapter presents the Neo-Piagetian/Neo-Eriksonian developmental model that I have developed and expanded (Young, 2011, 2014). The model is a lifespan one that is not only consistent with and integrates the prior models on which it is based but also integrates and often explains better the data that had been used in building the prior models. In Young (2011), I explicated how the current 25-step model that I created accounts for the data used by both Fischer and Case in their Neo-Piagetian models and is comprehensive to the point that it fills in gaps in their (sub)stage sequences. Presentation of these arguments is beyond the scope of the present work.

In this first chapter of five devoted to my model, I integrate prior material to show that the model includes descriptions of biological, personal (psychological, self), and environmental/social components at each step. For example, at the biological level, it gives the presumed evolutionary phase in which the step might have evolved and the presumed brain organization that might subserve it. At the personal/psychological/self level, it refers to the cognitive (mis)perception of the other that develops at each step. As for the environmental/social side, I give the social self-working schemata that might develop in response to the social environment.

The chapter considers some cognitive applications of the model especially in terms of the growth in two more advanced cognitions. Specifically, from Young (2014), it looks at the growth of free will belief and of ethical thought. Both emerge and continue to develop in the adolescent and adult periods, and so start with single abstract acquisitions and then superordinate ones.

Chapter 32: Further Expansions of the Present Stage Model This chapter explains more the socioaffective correspondences to the cognitive ones in the present 25-step model of development. It especially describes how a Neo-Eriksonian developmental sequence corresponds to the Neo-Piagetian one. It shows how a modified Neo-Maslovian sequence fits it, as well. It indicates how other acquisitions, such as theory of mind and having a sense of responsibility, fit it, too. It looks at correspondences across cognitive steps and both therapeutic advances and dysfunctional regressions (in pain patients). It even explores broader changes, such as might take place with controversies as processed in thought and how they might resolve. The chapter also considers the growth of scientific thought (e.g., Darwin), in that I show that the model of individual development that I have proposed can be applied to other developmental phenomena. Indeed, it would be interesting to analyze current, psychological theorizing along these lines in its effort to create a unifying concept for the discipline.

Chapter 33: Generic Change Model This chapter presents a generic change model based on the Neo-Piagetian/Neo-Eriksonian one that I have developed. It helps in understanding other step models of various psychological phenomena by showing their consistency with this one. It helps by indicating generic change processes applicable even to nonliving systems. Some of the topics referred to in this chapter with respect to the present generic change model include readiness for change, information processing, discovery learning, open-ended change, executive function, psychotherapy, education, evolution, social drivers, and causality itself (e.g., genes/epigenesis, causal graphs).

Chapter 34: Revising Maslow This chapter focuses on revising my Neo-Maslovian model (Young, 2011) by incorporating social psychology conceptualization on moral and other motives (Forbes, Haidt, and Janoff-Bulman and colleagues). My first Maslovian model revision in Young (2011) had divided his well-known triangular model of hierarchical needs into two halves—one on self-definition and one on relatedness (after Blatt, 2008). The current revision adds a third component to the triangular model, related to environmental mastery/competence. Like the other two aspects of the self in the revised model, I show how it develops in five stages that are consistent with the five levels in the model on hierarchical needs. Moreover, my reworking of Maslow in this way allowed me to revisit the work of Forbes, Haidt, and Janoff-Bulman and colleagues and show how their models need to be revised in light of my own. In particular, I developed a model of foundational moral motives based on Haidt's work on foundational motives and Janoff-Bulman's on moral motives.

Finally, I added a superordinate sublevel to Maslow's one of self-actualization and related concepts, such as generativity, that involves "psychological completeness." At the same time, I referred to the process of becoming psychologically complete or "psychological completing." These concepts could complement other concepts related to adult psychological maturity, such as psychological integrity or wisdom.

Chapter 35: Staging Revolutions and Paradigms Kuhn's concept of paradigm shift is a prominent one in science. This chapter describes a revision of the model by showing that the changes that take place in paradigms fit the present five-step generic change model. First, I present and rework Overton's revision of Kuhn's work. I refer to his concept of relationism as one central to my own work, too. The chapter covers broad topics of interest, such as unifying psychology and presenting a co-existential philosophical model. Overall, the chapter continues the work in this last part of the book of revising critical theorists in the behavioral sciences (Maslow, Kuhn) and integrating causality as central to the unification needed in the field (as well, perhaps, using my own models in this regard). The chapter concludes with how the concept of the causal self can help unify psychology.

Chapter 36: New Directions in Psychological Causality The prior chapters in this last portion of the book have shown the value of the development and generic change models that I have created. In the last chapter of the book, I create a different generic model on behavioral causality that is not step-based. It covers distal, proximal, and triggering causes in behavior. I apply it to rework the three models that helped in creating them (on neuroticism, action/self-control, and self-definition/relatedness). Then, I show its value in helping to understand the origins of free will (free being, believing in free will, having a sense of free will), depletion in self-control, and PTSD. Potentially, the model has wide applicability in indicating the multifactorial causation in behavior, in general, and how it could be conceptualized and researched.

To close the last chapter and the book, I present further modeling of behavioral causality, this time returning to my generic change model for the most part. I apply it to free will, in particular, but also to growth in modeling and change mechanisms.

Chapter 37: Epilogue The epilogue examines the most recent literature on behavior and causality, including on genes and environment, development, free will, and psychopathology (posttraumatic stress disorder, PTSD). Next, it examines recent work on critical models, including the relational, Piagetian/Neo-Piagetian, network (e.g., in neurocircuitry), and nonlinear dynamical systems theory (NLDST), as well as ones related to causality (e.g., top-down processes). Then, it presents three models that I created having the common theme of top-down/bottom up coordination in multilevel hierarchical systems (for symptom-construct relations, the nature of cognitive stages, and multiple emotional intelligences). Conclusions value the need to place causality as central to psychology and its unification, while considering both as ongoing dynamic projects.

Chapter Conclusions

This general overview and specific chapter description of the present book on behavioral causality in psychology and related disciplines underscores the massive nature of its scope. Moreover, work in the area is accelerating in multiple, disparate directions that defy unifying them. Nevertheless, the concept of causality itself could serve as a unifying focus in psychology and related disciplines once it gains some conceptual and methodological clarity. In this regard, I present models, both extant ones and new ones that I have developed, that can help unify the study of behavioral causality and point to directions in unifying psychology itself.

References

American Psychiatric Association. (2000). *Diagnostic and statistical manual of mental disorders: DSM-IV-TR* (4th ed., text rev.). Washington, DC: Author.

American Psychiatric Association. (2013). *Diagnostic and statistical manual of mental disorders: DSM-5* (5th ed.). Washington, DC: Author.

Blatt, S. J. (2008). *Polarities of experience: Relatedness and self-definition in personality development, psychopathology, and the therapeutic process*. Washington, DC: American Psychological Association.

Friston, K. (2010). The free-energy principle: A unified brain theory? *Nature Reviews Neuroscience, 11*, 127–138.

Insel, T. R., Cuthbert, B. N., Garvey, M. A., Heinssen, R. K., Pine, D. S., Quinn, K. J., et al. (2010). Research domain criteria (RDoC): Toward a new classification framework for research on mental disorders. *American Journal of Psychiatry, 167*, 748–751.

Insel, T. R., & Lieberman, J. A. (2013). DSM-5 and RDoC: Shared interests. The National Institute of Mental Health. www.nimh.nih.gov

McNally, R. J., Robinaugh, D. J., Wu, G. W. Y., Wang, L., Deserno, M. K., & Borsboom, D. (2015). Mental disorders as causal systems: A network approach to posttraumatic stress disorder. *Clinical Psychological Science, 3*, 836–849.

Overton, W. F. (2013). Relationism and relational developmental systems: A paradigm for developmental science in the post-cartesian era. In R. M. Lerner & J. B. Benson (Eds.), *Advances in child development and behavior. Embodiment and epigenesis: Theoretical and methodological issues in understanding the role of biology within the relational developmental system. Part A: Philosophical, theoretical, and biological dimensions* (Vol. 44, pp. 21–64). Oxford, UK: Elsevier.

Overton, W. F. (2014). The process-relational paradigm and relational-developmental-systems metamodel as context. *Research in Human Development, 11*, 323–331.

Sloman, S. (2005). *Causal models: How people think about the world and its alternatives*. New York: Oxford University Press.

Young, G. (2011). *Development and causality: Neo-Piagetian perspectives*. New York: Springer Science + Business Media.

Young, G. (2014). *Malingering, feigning, and response bias in psychiatric/psychological injury: Implications for practice and court*. Dordrecht, Netherlands: Springer Science + Business Media.

Young, G. (2015). Causality in civil disability and criminal forensic cases: Legal and psychological comparison. *International Journal of Law and Psychiatry, 42–43*, 114–120.

Young, G., & Drogin, E. (2014). Psychological injury and law I: Causality, malingering, and PTSD. *Mental Health Law & Policy Journal, 3*, 373–417.

Young, G., Lareau, C., & Pierre, B. (2014). One quintillion ways to have PTSD comorbidity: Recommendations for the disordered DSM-5. *Psychological Injury and Law, 7*, 61–74.

3 Introducing Causality in Psychology

Chapter Introduction

This chapter looks both back and forward. It presents material from my recent book on development and causality (Young, 2011) that served as a springboard for the present book, while presenting some new material related to the topic of the book that prepares the way for the present much expanded tome on causality in psychology, as described in the remainder of the book, which goes way beyond my effort on the topic in the 2011 book. In particular, this chapter expands my original model of the axes of causality relevant to psychology from the three primary ones that I had considered as crucial in Young (2011) to over 20 of them (still keeping the three primary ones central). In this regard, the three primary axes in the study of causality concern mechanism, causal mapping/learning, and free will. Specifically, the major foci in the study of causality number: (a) causal learning/mapping, which includes the counterfactual argument; (b) mechanisms, which include systems modeling, brain-behavior processes, epigenetics, development, and evolution; and (c) free will/consciousness, which includes consequences for having belief in free will (Baumeister, 2008; Young, 2011).

In this chapter, I organize the material taken from Young (2011) for purposes of this present chapter in terms of these three axes, while adding to their description, such as by presenting the work of Sloman (2005) on causal graph modeling and the work of Chaisson (2010, 2011) on thermodynamics in the universe as a mechanistic driving force in Big History. I elaborate these three causality axes in psychology, in particular, indicating their hierarchical and coordinated nature, and show how they relate to recent work on concepts that I have developed—on freedom in being, the biopersonalsocial model, and cross-network models, in particular.

Content-wise, (a) mechanism remains the primary focus of the present book on causality, as it must be. From this perspective, I review material on genetics, epigenesis, neural networks and neurons, the brain, and so on. (b) At the same time, free will remains the center of advanced development and thought in human behavior (e.g., belief in free will). It represents the epitome of the causal force at the apogee of influences in the causality of behavior, that of the self, or the person him/herself, and one's emergence as an active contributor beyond Nature and Nurture to one's growth.

By reviewing and extending the material in Young (2011) on these themes, I prepare the way for what follows in the book in the 30+ chapters remaining, which give a comprehensive review of the literature on behavioral causality and also the new conceptualizations that I propose for understanding the causality of behavior. (c) The work on causal graph modeling is making inroads in causality conceptualization and research, and it appears throughout the book, as well as in this chapter through the work of Sloman (2005), in particular.

G. Young, *Unifying Causality and Psychology*, DOI 10.1007/978-3-319-24094-7_3

Although, generally, psychology has adapted a nuanced nature–nurture interaction perspective on behavioral causality, or a biological–environmental interface perspective, in understanding the "why" of behavior, the discipline of psychology lacks an overriding theoretical focus. Toward rectifying this lack, the present book promotes an integrated biopsychosocial model of causality situated in nonlinear dynamical system theory (NLDST; with multiple levels, e.g., distal, proximal, immediate sequentially; higher-order, such as free will belief, lower order, such as brain mechanisms), and other potentially unifying models (e.g., networks, embodiment). The model of nonlinear dynamical systems, among others, appears at many junctures in the book, because concepts related to nonlinear dynamical systems, as well as the related construct of networks, have gained increasing currency and even primacy in psychology.

The book supports the notion that the person her- or himself has an active say in her/his development with the psychological or personal/self component of the person including possibility of influence of believing in free will on behavior. If it is properly elaborated in a nuanced integrative fashion, the construct of causality has the potential to stand as a unifying one in psychology and, indeed, in the social sciences and also the sciences generally.

The study of causality/causation is found widespread in psychology, even if its study is dispersed. For example, the basic tenet that correlation does not mean causation is one of the overriding themes in psychology. However, despite its ubiquity, it is not considered a central focus, and not even close to a unifying force in psychology. Recently, its conceptualization and study have increased quickly, but consideration of the integrative nature of causality in areas in which its study is accelerating is elusive and, as a focus of study, it remains disparate and unintegrated. Therefore, in this book, I expand the description of causality in psychology, and include others areas of scholarship for which the topic of causality, potentially is central, such as those of epidemiology, ecology, and law.

Throughout the book, I present up-to-date literature reviews and integrative concepts, such as on stimulus–response relations, gene–environment interactions, endophenotypes, activation/inhibition coordination, and emergent circular causality. That said, the major focus of the present book involves highlighting free will as a central concept in the study of causality in behavior, as per the title of the book. In this regard, the book consistently reviews the work of Baumeister (e.g., 2008), in particular, for example, on the consequences of believing in free will, and considers its implications and applications. In particular, for the latter, I develop a developmental model of free will, a questionnaire on free will, and also therapeutic modules that can be used to promote it with patients.

To summarize, the present chapter examines key terms and concepts in the study of causality, as well as integrative models. It describes the work of Young (2011) that served as a starting point for the book. It presents a figure showing the multiple areas of psychological study of causality beyond the three major ones of mechanism, graphic modeling, and free will. The study of behavioral causality is expanding exponentially, but it needs a coherent focus and, in this regard, the present book offers one way of arriving at this necessary anchor for the field of psychology and related disciplines.

Causality in Psychology

Introduction

The study of causality in psychology is widespread but has been very limited as a distinct focus, for example, in books devoted to the topic. Aside from recent ones by Young (Young, 2011; Young, Kane, & Nicholson, 2007), there have been only a handful of books in psychology with the terms causality or causation in the title (e.g., Shrout, Keyes, & Ornstein, 2011). But the importance of causality in the sciences is gaining traction in the field, as illustrated by a "manifesto" of why one should study causality in the sciences (Illari, Russo, & Williamson, 2011a, 2011b).

The classic issue in science concerning causality relates to the distinction between correlation and causation, and it still permeates the field. Philosophers, psychologists, and other scientists are expanding this work in several ways (such as in the work on causal mappings and learning; Beebee, Hitchcock, & Menzies, 2009; Gopnik & Schulz, 2007; Illari et al., 2011a, 2011b; Markus, 2011; Pearl, 2000, 2009; Russo, 2009; Sloman, 2005; etc.). However, they have been more concerned with immediate, proximal causal processes, as represented by causal graph and their mathematical underpinnings, and they have ignored other approaches, such as answering to Tinbergen's (1963) four questions about causation, which cover longer term causal processes, including evolution and development. In this regard, toward its beginning, the present book examines in depth these latter fields, as well as that of genetics. In addition, as mentioned, an important axis in the study of causality relates to free will and consciousness (Baumeister, 2008; Baumeister, Crescioni, & Alquist, 2011), and later portions of the book deal in depth with this aspect. In Young (2011), I concentrated on the question of mechanism pertaining to causality (e.g., Gene × Environment (G × E) interaction, epigenetics), but there is room for integrating the diverse approaches on causality (e.g., genes, environment, evolution, brain, development, psychopathology, free will, mechanism), and the book is dedicated to undertaking this task in depth for each area considered.

Causal Reasoning Skills Training

Introduction Layne, Steinberg, and Steinberg (2014) argued that causal reasoning skills should be central in training mental health professionals. Causal reasoning is "pervasive and indispensable" in clinical decision-making and practice. It should be part of core competency training. For example, clinicians assemble causally-relevant information related to patient issues and their treatment. Causal reasoning can help elucidate a patient's causal matrix, including precursors, mechanisms, pathways, and consequences. Causal reasoning skills training should involve five curricular modules.

Modules In the first module, students should learn about the important domains of clinical practice in which making causal inferences is crucial. These include understanding etiology, formulating an assessment plan, determining whether clinically significant distress/impairment is present, creating an intervention plan, and monitoring therapeutic progress and responding to the information. Also, causal reasoning is important in understanding the research in the field and integrating one's clinical experience with it.

In the second module, students should learn critical causal concepts. Also, they should learn common errors in causal reasoning.

In the third module, they should learn about both internal and external validity. The former is about the research allows for causal inferences and the former is about generalizability of results in research.

In module four, students should learn how to formulate and evaluate working theories about the determinants of patients' presenting problems and how they are maintained. In this regard, the students should consider the "ecopathology" and "ecoresilience" of patients.

In the last module, causal reasoning skill training should focus on planning, targeting, and evaluating interventions. Diagrams might be helpful in this regard to generate causal hypotheses.

Layne et al. (2014) concluded that causal modeling can help in case conceptualization, intervention planning, and prioritizing target foci in interventions. Causal modeling in clinical practice helps in generating causal hypotheses with patients, implementing causal experiments in therapy, and monitoring and evaluating outcomes of interventions.

History

There are several major academic streams in the study of causality, and its origins have a venerable history in philosophy. The topic has been important in philosophy, and Arisotle's approach to the four causes still marks the field. Moreover, Aristotle's views have influenced psychology.

However, the study of causality has not emerged as a distinct field of study, despite its ubiquity as an underlying theme in multiple disciplines, including psychology. Aside from a lack of a unifying structure for the study of causality, there is even a philosophical point of view of acausalism (promoted by Hume and Russell, in particular), which minimizes the importance of seeking causality, or even denies its existence.

Critical Terms

Introduction Part of the difficulty in the study of causality in psychology is that the terms used in the field are at times not clearly defined. Young (Young, 2008; Young et al., 2007; Young & Shore, 2007) found this to be true for the study of causality in the area of psychological injury and law. For example, there is misconception about terms such as causality and causation, and related ones. In the following, I provide definitions related to the two terms. Moreover, I add others from the list of critical terms related to causality that had been noted by Layne et al. (2014).

Terms

(a) *Causality*. Defined as the principle of causal relation; the relationship between cause and effect (Garner, 2009, p. 249). Layne et al. (2014) defined it as the relation between two conditions/events in which the antecedent one determines in whole or part the consequent one. Garner noted the equivalence of the term "causation" and "causality." Pearl (2009) noted that although the concept of causality is fundamental to human thought, it is embedded in mystery and controversy, given the difficulty in establishing when agents genuinely cause effects.

(b) *Causation*. Garner described that causation refers to causality, and defined it as the causing or producing of an effect (Garner, 2009). I add that the effect must be produced by an agent, act, or process. Garner (2009) noted that, in law, for causation what matters is liability. Is the causative source proximate or dominant, or at least contributory, substantive, or material, and not tangential or "de minimus." Establishing the material contribution of an event at claim might be more relevant to it than invoking the "but-for" test (Douglas, Huss, Murdoch, Washington, & Koch, 1999). The latter argument indicates that the psychological condition at issue would not have existed "but for" the occurrence of the index event (Cocchiarella & Lord, 2001). This term reflects the counterfactual condition, which is so important to causal graph modeling approaches (Pearl, 2009), and philosophical related approaches.

(c) Layne et al. (2014) elaborated that a cause could be partial/contributory or sole. It could be conjunctive or disjunctive. It could be necessary or sufficient. It could be complex through reciprocal effects or through multi-step chains. It could involve a moderator that is a vulnerability factor, protective, facilitative, or inhibitory. It could involve a mediator that is partial, or full. It might involve a risk marker, or even one that is causal.

(d) *General causation* refers to whether the event at claim legally is capable of inducing the alleged harm. General causation is compared to *specific causation*, for which the event at issue had "actually caused" the alleged harm (Young & Shore, 2007).

Comment Young et al. (2007) distinguished causality and causation in terms of the distinction between product and process although, in practice, the terms are used interchangeably. Causation is associated more with product and causality is associated more with process.

Moreover, it would seem that in the hierarchy of explanatory terms, mechanism is more specific; mechanisms serve the unfolding of causal principles. Much of the present book attempts to discern critical mechanisms in producing behavior.

Critical Concepts

Reducing Reductionism

Some major approaches in science and psychology are deterministic, reductionistic, and passive with respect to the role of the person himself/herself in causality (e.g., behaviorism). Typically, they understand behavior or events as the product of unalterable influences in the past and present, so that factors such as free will and self, agency and autonomy, and consciousness cannot influence behavior.

In this predominant approach in the sciences about behavior and its influences, behavior is considered the product of the chain of biological and environmental influences in a deterministic fashion; it is considered the outcome of a passive causality. Rather than perceiving the individual as having an active voice in the direction and path of choices that could be made, behavior and choice are viewed as reflections of internal and external constraints. Free will is relegated to illusory status and, at best, consciousness to a reductionist epiphenomenon.

(a) However, basically, behavior can be considered the result of more than biology and environment because people themselves are involved in their own development. (b) Also, behavior should be considered the expression of system factors that include emergence beyond the influences involved. (c) Third, part of behavior includes the possibility of belief in free will, which has major consequences in how people behave (independent of the philosophical question of whether it exists; Baumeister, 2008).

Hot vs. Cold Causality

One way of distinguishing a passive versus active approach to causality is to refer to the concept of "hot" or "cold" causality. This distinction allows for individual differences in the influence of the person as agent in behavioral determination. "Hot" causality refers to when people themselves buffer influences on them, such as environmental adversity. They serve as their own buttresses in their development. Individuals are buffeted by powerful influences and immersed in complex life scenarios but, nevertheless, could strive to achieve an assertive, active stance in which they can evaluate prudently their options, and even act to create better ones, in order to adapt better to the environment and alter it for the better.

In contrast, "cold" causality refers to an absence of or fundamentally compromised hot causality. That is, the individual cannot rationally take charge of the self and the situation, even in a simpler one, and ends up choosing not at all or poorly from among the choices that might be available (Young, 2011).

Causal Streams and Three Major Causality Axes

In Young (2011), I addressed the disparate study of causality and causation as a predominant topic in psychology by referring to three areas of its study—as mechanism, in causal mapping/learning, and in free will (see Fig. 3.1). In the following, I elaborate the approach taken in Young (2011) with respect to these axes, adding new material related to them.

Causal Mapping and Learning Contemporary study in this approach to causality began with the work of the philosophers, Spirtes, Glymour, and Scheines (2001) and the computer scientist-statistician, Pearl (2000, 2009), in particular. Sloman (2005) and Gopnik and Schulz (2007) have written books extending the approach into the psychological domain. It is consistent with the counterfactual approach to causality. Woodward (2007) explained that counterfactual theories in philosophy are about difference-making and typal accounts of cause, whereas the causal process approach to causation eschews the general for particular or individual accounts of

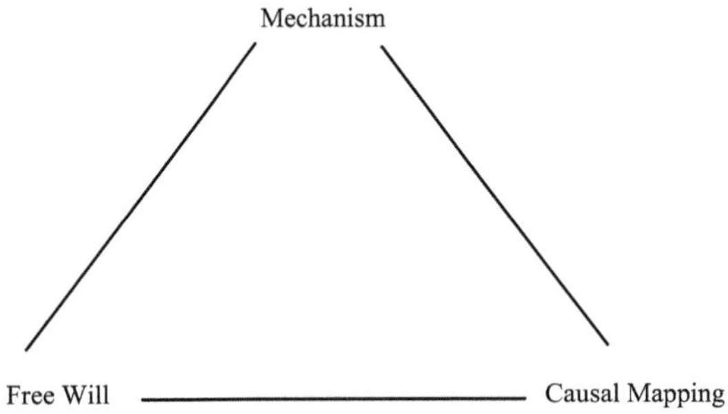

Fig. 3.1 Causality landscape. The three major axes in conceptualizing the causality of behavior include mechanism, causal graph modeling, and free will. The present books builds on this model presented in Young (2011), and elaborates many more axes while considering these three as fundamental. Adopted with permission of Springer Science + Business Media. Young, G. (2011). *Development and causality: Neo-Piagetian perspectives*. New York: Springer Science + Business Media; with kind permission from Springer Science + Business Media B. V. [Figure 35.5, Page 835]

cause. In this regard, one way used in this approach in order to support the validity of the causal sequence described is to apply "interventions" that could alter it in predictable ways (e.g., "graph surgery"). This type of approach is consistent with the counterfactual or but-for argument.

Free Will A third locus in the study of causality in psychology concerns free will and consciousness. Free will can never be proven outright, but on average people believe they have free will, which affects their behavior (Baumeister, 2008). Baumeister maintained that we have evolved a form of action-control involving self-control and rational choice, which corresponds to popular notions of free will. Therefore, free will involves: personal responsibility, conscious deliberation, abstract rules and principles in guiding behavior, autonomous initiative, and resisting urges. This approach reflects the active view of behavior, that we have voice or agency in determining our behavior beyond any biological or environmental influences.

Baumeister et al. (2011) elaborated that free will evolved to meet the demands of "enlightened self-interest" in cultural context. This view is consistent with the present one that behavior evolved through steps of increasing gene co-option through individual-level natural selection, as described below.

Given that free will is related to consciousness, Young (2011) examined briefly how it develops. Zelazo (2004; Zelazo, Carlson, & Kesek, 2008), Carlson (2010) noted that, first, consciousness is considered minimally present, and, then, more deliberate action develops. Next, conscious control develops, in which action is formulated based on explicit rule systems. Berger (2011) presented a skill-based model of self-regulation, labeling it the self-regulatory strength model.

Mechanism

In the following, I review briefly the topics covered in Young (2011) that are related to mechanism. They concern the processes of epigenetics, evolution, development, hemispheric specialization, and nonlinear dynamics.

Genetics/Epigenetics

Introduction The research in the area of gene–environment interaction and epigenesis is remarkable and is revolutionizing our understanding of psychology and the biological influences on behavior. Genetic × Environment (G × E) interaction research is indicating the complexities involved, such as complex interactions involving G × E1 × E2. The research also indicates G × G and multi-gene x multi-environment modeling (G × G × E × E interactions). The developmental pathways prescribed by how these interactions unfold are neither nativist nor empiricist. For example, in social genomics, social-environmental influences (e.g., perceived loneliness) can affect the immune system response, and even survival. One conclusion is that modern study of genetics needs to be "environmentally conscious."

Caspi et al. (2002) examined the functional polymorphism related to the promoter region of the monoamine oxidase A (*MAOA*) gene. In particular, they found a functional polymorphism in the gene that encodes *MAOA*, which is a neurotransmitter-metabolizing enzyme. Their results showed that the functional polymorphism moderated the effects of maltreatment. Specifically, male adolescents who carried the allele that conferred high levels of *MAOA* expression were less likely to develop anti-social behavioral problems had they been exposed to childhood maltreatment.

To their credit, Belsky and Pluess (2009a, 2009b) noticed other major findings in the results of Caspi et al. (2002). Participants who were most susceptible genetically to adverse effects of childhood maltreatment but who had not been exposed to childhood maltreatment obtained the lowest scores on the study's measures of anti-social behavior. Belsky and Pluess (2009a, 2009b) posited that particular alleles could heighten vulnerability to a wide range of environments. In particular, for *MAOA*, supportive and risky environments promote positive and negative child outcomes, respectively. Through their astute analysis, Belsky and Pluess have developed a differential susceptibility model of genes. It resembles Ellis and Boyce's (2008) concept of biological sensitivity to context.

Caspi et al. (2003) presented similar results for the influence of the serotonin transporter gene, *5-HTT*. Individuals carrying the short allele, relative to being homozygous for the long one, were found to experience a greater influence of stressful life events on depression (its symptoms and diagnosis, as well as suicidality).

Caspi, Hariri, Holmes, Uher, and Moffitt (2010) indicated that there are at least four types of evidence for the involvement of the *5-HTT* gene in stress sensitivity. A recent meta-analysis supported the reliability of the research, with strong evidence found that *5-HTTLPR* moderates the relationship between stress and depression (Karg, Shedden, Burmeister, & Sen, 2011).

Reaction Range Dick (2011) argued that the most appropriate manner of representing gene–environment interactions is by a "cross-over" graph rather than a "fan"-shaped graph. The fan-shaped interaction represents the traditional diathesis-stress framework and is consistent with the concept of "vulnerability" genes, whereas the cross-over interaction graph is consistent with Belsky and Pluess's differential susceptibility model of genes ("plasticity genes").

Epigenetics Recent epigenetic research is confirming a role for genetic polymorphisms in interaction with environmental vulnerability factors for behaviors that are associated with self-control. Epigenetics concerns how environmental factors such as adversity can alter gene expression, e.g., silencing them at promoter regions due to DNA methylation. Carver, Johnson, Joormann, Kim, and Nam (2011) found that a polymorphism (*s*, short allele) in the promoter region of serotonin transporter gene, *5-HTTLPR*, is linked to measures of impulsive reactions to emotions in students who reported early childhood adversity (e.g., in care received, abuse). In a prospective study, Dick et al. (2011) reported an association between the gene *CHRM2* (codes for the cholinergic muscarinic 2 receptor) and adolescent externalizing behavior as measured by standardized instruments, but particularly in the context of low parental monitoring, as measured by a questionnaire.

Figure 3.2 presents a model representing the concept of epigenetics in a general fashion. The figure presents a model indicating how epigenetic effects can have either more negative or positive behaviorally adaptive outcomes, depending on individual and environmental differences. In epigenetics, the outcome is not necessarily negative in cases of susceptible alleles affecting behavioral adaptation. Belsky and Pluess (2009a, 2009b) have posited that when genes are silenced in promoter regions involved in behavioral reactivity, the outcome could involve more resilience, and not only more behavioral difficulties, at least when the environment is supportive rather than adverse. Moreover, the figure shows that the effects might accentuate with development. Also, epigenetic changes are known to be transmitted over generations, creating a dynamic trajectory of increased or decreased adaptation in individual lines.

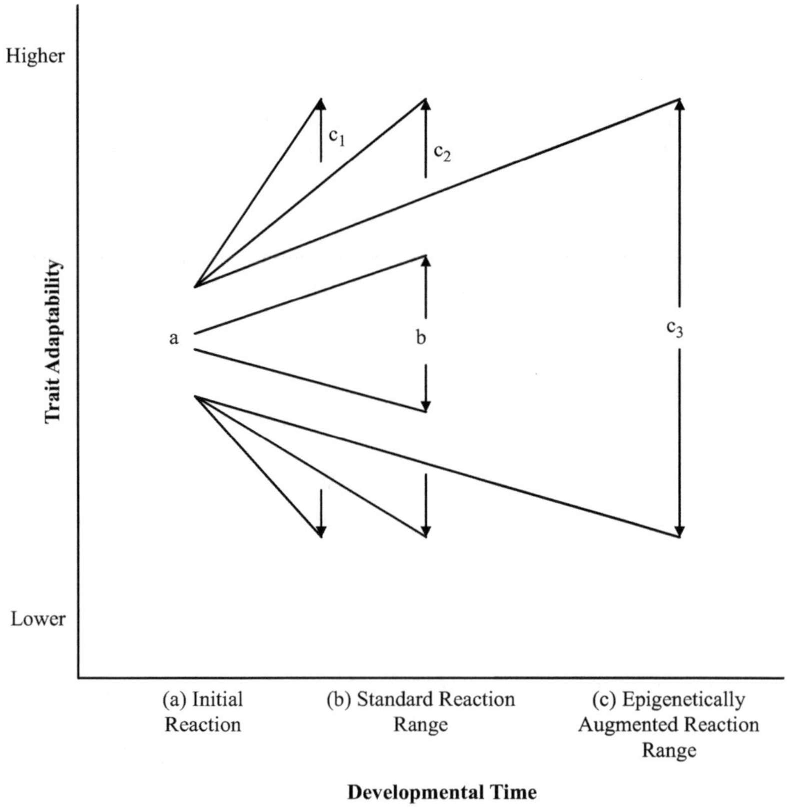

Fig. 3.2 Environmental action leads to increased reaction range in gene expression for certain alleles. Epigenetic processes act to increase reaction range, or degree of gene-mediated susceptibility to environmental influence, and in which the reaction can be either adaptive or not in the long term. Adopted with permission of Springer Science + Business Media. Young, G. (2011). *Development and causality: Neo-Piagetian perspectives*. New York: Springer Science + Business Media; with kind permission from Springer Science + Business Media B. V. [Figure 30.5, Page 699]

Evolution

Life History The life history approach to biological evolution offers a developmental perspective that informs the present approach (Simpson & Belsky, 2008). In this evolutionary model, due to competing pressures and options for alternate lifestyles, each developmental stage and its prominent acquisitions have been selected for their ongoing and immediate contribution to survival (permitting eventual reproduction). They are not pre-adaptations that serve, in a teleological fashion, later adaptations, but they are primed to function concurrently in the equivalent of the niche in which they had evolved.

Eusociality Nowak, Tarnita, and Wilson (2010) presented a new interpretation of the evolution of eusociality, which occurs when some individuals of a species reduce their own reproductive potential over their lifetime in order to raise the offspring of others. In the social insects, eusociality is demonstrated by sterile worker castes helping to raise offspring of the queen and creating a colony, or a "super-organism." The traditional explanation of eusociality involves kin selection, which is based on the concept of inclusive fitness. Nowak et al. argued that standard natural selection theory is sufficient to explain the evolution of eusociality, and that it is a genuine "gene-centered" approach, unlike the one of inclusive fitness.

In Novak et al.'s model, eusociality evolved in five steps. (a) First, groups formed in freely mixing populations. They built and occupied defensible nests, and the behavior arose because of "individual-level" selection. (b) In the second phase, the groups more tightly formed. (c) Next, actual eusocial alleles originated, either by mutation or recombination. (d) Most likely, the fourth phase involved evolution of ecologically-adaptive behaviors related to the nest, such as fierce defense against predators, parasites, and rival colonies. These behaviors had been shaped through "natural selection by environmental forces." (e) Finally, in the fifth phase, the more advanced eusocial species evolved very specialized, elaborate social systems. In contrast to the other steps, this one involved multilevel selection, which includes group selection as well as natural selection. It served to help drive changes in the colony behavior to more elaborate extremes.

Development

Stages The Neo-Piagetian stage model in Young (2011) consists of 25 steps (5 stages × 5 substages), and it includes parallel cognitive and socio-affective acquisitions. The stages are named: (a) reflexive, (b) sensorimotor, (c) perioperational (representational; preoperational and concrete operational), (d) abstract, and (e) collective intelligence. The cyclically-recurring substages are labeled: (a) coordination, (b) hierarchization, (c) systematization, (d) multiplication, and (e) integration. The corresponding 25 Neo-Eriksonian steps in the model are built around the original eight Eriksonian stages (at the second and fourth substages of each of the last four stages of the model), with 17 other steps created to complete the sequence.

The combined Neo-Piagetian/Neo-Eriksonian model helps understand multiple areas of development. For example, Maslow's model of a hierarchy of needs consists of five levels, and Young (2011) showed how they can be reworked to relate to the five developmental stages of the present model. Other examples relate to a reworking of the concept of internal working models in attachment theory in terms of their development through the steps of the present model, and also reworking of the steps in the development of theory of mind and multiple intelligences in terms of the steps of the present model.

Activation/Inhibition Coordination Young (e.g., Young, 2011; Young & Gagnon, 1990) presented a model of hemispheric specialization in which the cerebral hemispheres are differentially specialized for inhibition. In particular, the left hemisphere is considered the primary site of inhibitory control, specializing in a sophisticated interweaving of activation and inhibitory skills. Activation/inhibition coordination particularly involves the suppression of interference due to inappropriate alternative behavior, both when selecting adaptive goal-directed activity and during its (movement) transitions. Through this skill, the left hemisphere controls the subtle, refined sequences in both language and fine motor activities. Moreover, successful unfolding of these functions requires not only activation/inhibition inter-coordination within the left hemisphere but also activation/inhibition coordination over the hemispheres.

In contrast to the left hemisphere, the right hemisphere appears specialized for less dynamic inhibition, such as general damping of activity over time, or activation/inhibition coordination instantaneously or for a short time period. The latter capacity would be conducive to spatial processes. In summary, the hemispheres seem to have complementary, cooperative specializations for inhibition.

Vauclair and Imbault (2009) found that 10- to 40-month-olds pointed with their right hand even if they were left-handers or ambidextrous. The results showed that the correlation between manual preference and pointing preference was strongest during the development of vocabulary spurt and the development of syntactic capacity. Their results support the argument that, in the left cerebral hemisphere, there are dual systems for controlling communicative gesture and language, on the one hand, and pure motor functions, such as object manipulation, on the other hand. According to Vauclair and Imbault, the left hemisphere expresses a hyper-mobilization during critical periods of language acquisition because of a "better facilitatory/inhibitory" system within the left hemisphere. This hypothesis is quite consistent with Young's about the left hemisphere's superior activation/inhibition coordination skills.

Nonlinear Dynamical Systems

Systems theory helps understand not only the contents of development, through examination of how components of wholes cohere, but also its change mechanisms (e.g., Kauffman, 1993; Thelen & Smith, 2006, respectively). Dynamical systems are capable of autonomously generating self-organizing emergent forms. Self-organization proceeds in the system's moment-to-moment adaptive, contextual transitioning. In emergence, new system states would not be predictable uniquely from knowing the pre-existing state of the system in its context. New forms of the state could be discontinuous, being very different than its preceding form-state. For example, systems might evolve into attractor forms. Attractors are viewed as system trajectories that gravitate repeatedly to the same attractor basins, or fixed values, despite their initial values or ongoing perturbations.

Systems are reworked constantly, even if in equilibrium, because of perturbations. Systems might change abruptly, for example, at bifurcations points. Perturbations move systems to change state. In the butterfly effect, quite minor inputs to the system can elicit system change because of sensitivities to initial conditions. Lower-level interactions in systems constitute "bottom-up" processes, and higher-level interactions are considered "top-down" processes.

In fractals, one finds that a system is self-similar across different levels. Fractal organization facilitates multiple-level system change toward complexity. In complexity theory, systems tend to hover on the edge of order and disorder, or on the cusp of change. In this regard, systems are considered at the edge of chaos, which is not chaotic at all in the colloquial sense of the word.

Dimensions

Dimensions involve continua with oppositions or poles, and they should cover major components of behavior for the topic of causality. In this regard, the ones that are emphasized in the present work concern: time, the person, control, and nonlinear dynamical systems.

1. Understanding causality as an integration in its time line—from evolutionary time right to immediate neuronal firing in synaptic time. The time line stretches from millions of years ago to nano-seconds ago. It even includes the future, in terms of anticipations and expectations that guide behavior.
2. Appreciating that the multiple factors involved can be grouped into biological, environmental, and personal (psychological) ones, and that they interact. Causality is exquisitely contextual and relational; the environment is not an independent player acting without personal perception/appraisal/filtering, nor is the person able to function without the reciprocity of participation in the environment. That is, causality does not reside in the person alone nor his/her biology, but how the person and environment reciprocally, causally influence each other in their interaction—it is emergent in that process, and the process defines it as much as the product. As Young (2011) has written, biology predisposes, the environment disposes, but the individual composes.
3. Studying causality from the perspective of control: ranging from determinism/unconscious influences, and so on, to autonomous, free will, probabilistic, compatibilist approaches.
4. NLDST describes emergent, self-organizing properties of systems, their top-down and bottom-up influences, and their fractal nature, in particular.

One manner of presenting the dimensions in behavior involved in causality is offered in Table 3.1. The table organizes major themes in causality into a dimensional framework. As per the dimensions in causality just presented, it considers the acquisition of a sense of free will as cardinal in development (Baumeister, 2008). It indicates that (a) time can vary in the immediate or longer terms (evolution, development); (b) the person evolves and develops as a biopsychosocial entity; (c) part of what develops is a sense of

Table 3.1 Development, causality, and free will: dimensions

Area	Axes	Poles, components
Time	Immediate	Distal (before moment) Proximal (at moment)
	Development (steps, other)	Normative (universal, average) Individual (unique)
	Evolution	Adaptation (selective advantage) Speciation (evolutionary tree/bush)
Person	Biological	Brain, hemispheres Physiology, body, epigenetics
	Social	Sociocultural, general Context, specific
	Personal	Cognition, appraisal Affect, mood
Control	Free will in self	Free/flexible action to perceive/create/act on choices (defined as "hot" causality) Determined/unconscious/fixed action ("cold" causality)
	Its perception in other	Same
	Direction, value	Positive, moral, responsible Negative, immoral, irresponsible
Mechanism	Organization	Emergent, self-organizing Random, perceived chaos
	Level	Macrolevel, top-down Microlevel, bottom-up
	Nonlinear dynamics	Deterministic globally (in attractors) Probabilistic in particular trajectory

Adopted with permission of Springer Science + Business Media. Young, G. (2011). *Development and causality: Neo-Piagetian perspectives*. New York: Springer Science + Business Media; with kind permission from Springer Science + Business Media B. V. [Table 35.9, Page 835]

one's personal control, including in liberty of action, and the perception of the same in the other; and (d) nonlinear dynamical system processes, such as emergence and self-organization, can help explain the mechanisms of development.

Note that an overarching theme that could explain multiple levels of any behavioral system is activation/inhibition coordination, which could be a common metric that could help explain multiple frames in behavior. This dynamic is apparent at multiple levels of behavior and its control, from neurons and the brain to society and its agents/institutions.

In their dynamic neural field theory, Spencer, Austin, and Schutte (2012) illustrated and modeled the interplay of activation and inhibition in neurons in their dynamic neural field theory modeling of their functioning. Specifically, layers of excitatory neurons couple with layers of inhibitory interneurons. The model includes a Hebbian layer (or of cell assemblies).

The concept of activation/inhibition coordination seems to apply at multiple points in causality study. For example, this dynamic helps to understanding organization of both brain and behavior, including in the processes that facilitate the acquisition of a sense of free will.

Further Elaboration of the Three Major Axes in Causality Study

Dimensional Causality Model

Figure 3.3 presents an integrated causality model of behavior that is based on the dimensions of causality presented in Table 3.1. The model combines several graphic devices. Time is indicated on the

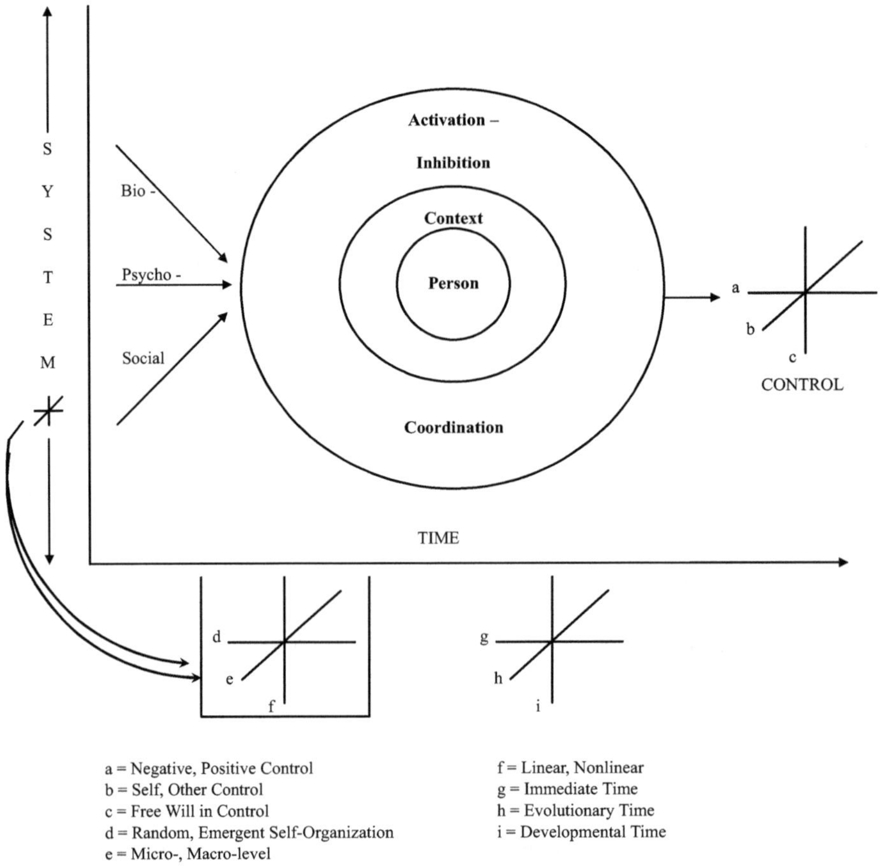

Fig. 3.3 Dimensions in causality. The figure indicates central components to consider in modeling causality in psychology. The causality system over time involves biopsychosocial influences processed in context, leading to behavioral control variations, including in the influence of free will belief

X-axis and system organization on the *Y*-axis. Time concerns behavior in the immediate context, over developmental time, or as inherited evolutionarily. Systems exist at hierarchical levels, are either linear or nonlinear, and are either self-organized or random, with emergence associated with the former. The person behaving in context is illustrated in the concentric circle model. The components of the biopsychosocial complex (interaction of biology, personal psychology, sociocultural factors) influence behavior, as indicated by the arrows leading from the components to the person-in-context representation.

The central focus of the outcome of the model is control, and it emphasizes that control concerns having a sense of free will. Baumeister (2008) has described the psychological components that contribute to the development and maintenance of a sense of having free will, and Young (2011) describes a developmental model of free will and its components based on the Neo-Piagetian stage model that he described. The figure indicates that the dimension of free will vs. unconsciousness can be applied positively or negatively, and to the perception of the self or the other.

The construct of activation/inhibition coordination is highlighted as surrounding the person and context. Young (2011) proposed that activation/inhibition coordination characterizes both elements of the person and context. For example, for the person, both the brain and behavior can be described in terms of the ebb and flow of activation and inhibition and their coordination. Similarly, the environment presents to the person as the waxing and waning of activations and inhibitions in relationship.

In this regard, control processes, being the focus output of the person in the figure, are also considered the effect of activation/inhibition coordination. Ideally, in this regard, the person activates positives capacities, such as good will, sense of responsibilities, moral imperatives, psychological maturity, rational thinking, creating and thinking through options, choosing effectively from among them, and so on, associated with optimally mature human activity. Simultaneously, the person inhibits interfering tendencies, temptations, search for immediate gratification, short term but ineffective solutions, irrational thinking, irresponsible behavior, and immature and immoral behavior, so that planned, directed, and free will guided behavioral output obtains.

The Causality Landscape

Introduction

For the most part, the three major topics in the study of causality in psychology being discussed (causal mapping/learning, mechanism, free will) are studied separately. Causality is studied from quite different perspectives and needs an integrating landscape. Developing a causality landscape requires steps toward developing an integrative model.

Figure 3.4 lists other axes in its study of causality beyond the three core ones. The central triangular portion of the figure indicates that the study of causal learning/mapping, mechanism, and free will stand as the major axes in the area.

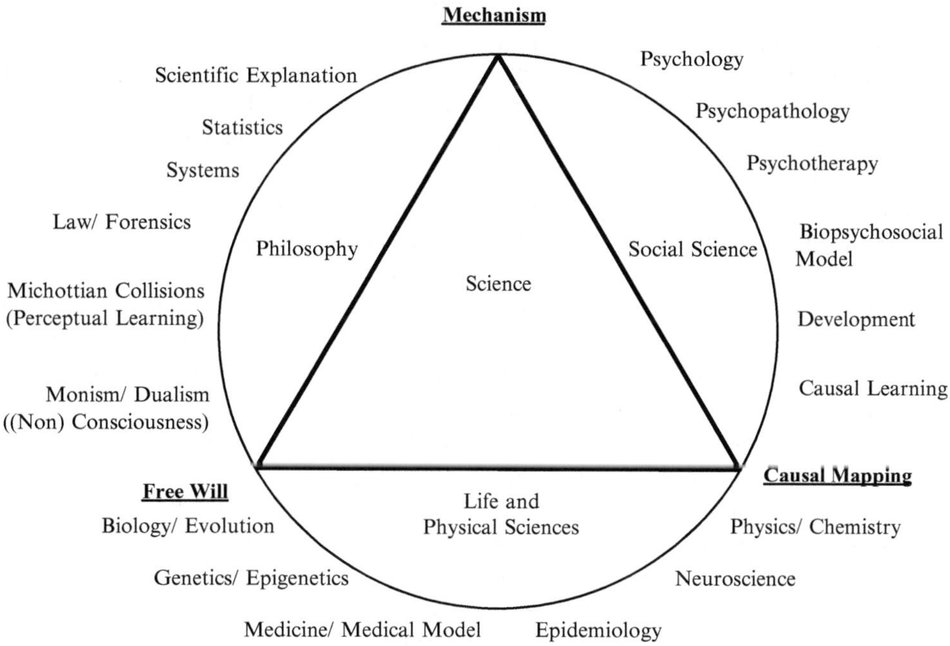

Fig. 3.4 Causality landscape: causality axes coming together. *Note*. Aside from all the areas mentiond, this figure from Young (2014) also could mention, among others, the disciplines of ecology, engineering, political science, sociology, and history, and the notion of interdisciplinary. The three major axes in conceptualizing causality concern (**a**) elaboration of causal maps and learning using Bayesian probabilities and counterfactual argumentation, (**b**) as well as mechanisms, such as in development, and (**c**) free will. A more integrative approach would keep these axes as fundamental, but include others. The present book elaborates many of the varying degrees of study mentioned in the figure, seeking an integrated framework for the study of the causality of behavior. It considers free will as the apex of behavioral causation, in the sense that we develop to the degree possible to arrive at making self-determined free choices among the behavioral options in any one situation, while escaping the deterministic influences of biology and environment. Adapted from Young (2014)

The figure includes 24 components or areas in the study of causality and causation related to psychology and related disciplines.

Model

The discipline of science is placed at the center of the figure, in that science stands as the umbrella discipline for all the other areas in terms of the study of causality and causation. Other areas of science consider and investigate causality (e.g., the social sciences, the life sciences, and the physical sciences), and often have concepts and models similar to those in psychology (e.g., the value of experimentation, statistics). The roots of the study of causality lie in classical Greek philosophical theories, especially that of Aristotle and his concept of four types of causes. Implicit in one of them resides the notion that mechanism is critical to understanding cause. Mechanism lies at the heart of any scientific explanation of cause, and it typically takes the form of—some combination of genetic and environmental contributions at the distal level; brain and networks at the intermediate level; and factors such as stimuli, stress, and situation at the proximal level, but within a transactional model that includes individual differences in perceptions, or appraisal of the input involved.

Psychological and philosophical models [for example, the counterfactual model] consider that causes are evident by the changes effected by the event at issue and the corresponding realization that, absent the event, there would be none of changes in state that had transpired. This argument takes the form of the "but-for" test in law (e.g., "but for the accident, the patient would not be expressing…"). Both the philosophical and psychological approaches to causality include an interventionist component in some ways, as in experimentation. However, the study of causality is not restricted to such accounts and procedures.

Some models in the field of causality are quite restricted in scope, as in the medical model. The field of medicine takes a classic biological, physiological, and reductionist approach to physical disease and mental health. However, psychiatry and psychology are expanding its understanding of disease to include a biopsychosocial model, in which multiple factors interact [although in medicine, traditional approaches still have much influence, as in the DSM (Diagnostic and Statistical Manual of Mental Disorders) and RDoC (Research Domain Criteria) projects]. In many ways, the new field of psychiatric genetics is leading the way in studying the causality of behavior, as with the concepts of gene by environment interactions and epigenetics. In epigenesis, environmental factors can help "silence" genes involved in the regulation of behavior, and the effects can be transmitted intergenerationally. The study of evolution also is undergoing change, in that group selection is now considered a complementary process to natural selection.

The field of epidemiology is another one studying causality and causation from disparate perspectives. Hill's criteria help, but statistical and causal mapping approaches are becoming important. Causal mapping includes not only mapping graphical causal linkages in events and their effects but also mapping the altered outcomes that arise after interventions. When studied developmentally, interesting experiments reveal that 2- to 3-year-olds and even infants appreciate (perceive) causality and engage in causal learning. Causal perception has a storied past in the research of Michotte. A systems perspective of causality and causation offers a transdisciplinary approach that might help simplify the plethora of concepts and approaches in the field. The study of the brain is being marked increasingly by systems concepts, such as networks, and the subfield of Connectomes is emerging rapidly in neuroscience in this regard. The concepts of causality and causation are central to the areas of psychopathology and psychotherapy, through the associated concept of etiology. There are controversies in the field, and the most significant relate to free will, and the (un)consciousness, and their link to action. Libet's research, which showed an unconscious preparation of movement before it takes place and before the person expresses an intention to move, leads to question about free will. However, Baumeister and others maintain that although we can never ascertain truly whether behavior is genuinely free or deterministic, there are important consequences in believing that one has free will relative to those who do not. The study of individual differences in belief in free will is increasing. The field needs more integrative models of causality and causation in psychology and related disciplines.

Comment

Clearly, the study of causality in psychology and related sciences is expanding rapidly, but without a cohering framework. Like in the model of the inflationary expansion of the universe, the disparate areas in its study risk losing contact with each other and working in their separate clusters of study. The present book attempts to provide coherence to the field in this regard, but still with the three axes that are highlighted in the book as a central focus in this pursuit.

As for expanding these three axes in the present chapter, for each I take a broader view. (a) For free will, I consider the integrative concept of Freedom in Being. (b) For mechanism, I discuss causal modeling in terms of thermodynamics. (c) For causal graph modeling, I present a good introduction in the work of Sloman (2005).

Free Will

Concept

In my view, free will is a psychological phenomenon that does not manifest universally but is conditional on reducing control of, and eliminating, constraints to its constitutive application. As a corollary, then, free will (or being) is exquisitely individual and varies with not only psychological immaturity but also with developmental progression and adaptation, motivation and emotion, energy and effort, temperament and personality, rationality and reflectivity, self-control and self-regulation, context and constraint, opportunity and invitation, openness and possibility, and so on.

The basic premises of the present work are the following that (a) we have an active, causal say in our behavior beyond the influences of biology and environment. (b) We cause our behavior as much as any other factor. (c) Behaving as if we were free, toward being free, and in being free characterizes the human will and the human way. This is referred to as "free being." (d) Free will is neither free nor will. It is hard-earned rather than being "free" and it more than will. Rather, will provides the starting point for the behavior at issue, but it is up to us to implement it. (e) We never reach full free will in the sense of belief and sense. However, we can keep moving in that direction. Integration along these lines is as much a path as a state. (f) Not having free will is an illusion. Most people believe it and act as if they feel free. (g) Free being is as much cultural, collective, and interpersonal as it is individual, interior, and intrapersonal.

In short, as we grow in and toward psychological maturity, experiencing being free or having a free being is facilitated. In turn, this helps to be free in all phases of behavior, from selecting input, creating and choosing from options, deciding, and acting upon decisions.

There are both cognitive and social affective components of free being, which are termed free will belief and having a sense of free will. These components exist in dynamic relation and constitute an integrated, inseparable whole. Free being grows asymptotically to full freedom, but rarely gets there, given the constraints on and limitations in the development of each of us. In this sense, the model is an asymptotic one. It is also paradoxical in the sense that, as we grow toward and into free being, we inevitably opt to choose to undertake responsibilities, which acts to constrain being free in the more primitive sense of acting with freedom on anything we wish to do.

Comment

The general message for the causality of behavior is that free will is an emergent force that ends up participating in defining our essence and also in defining the causes of our behavior through its position at the apex of maturity in behavior. It could be involved, as well, when behavior goes awry in disturbances and abnormality in behavior, for example, in addictions.

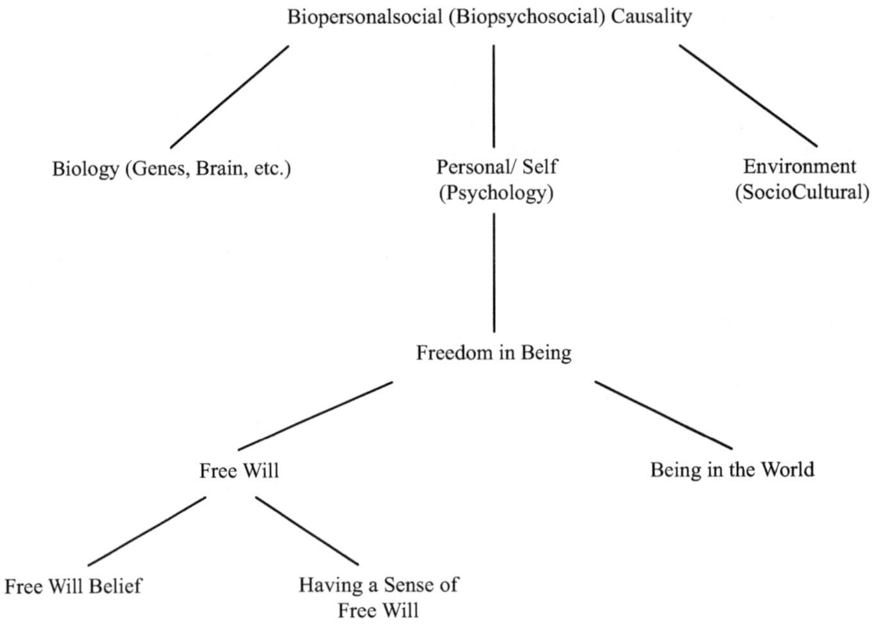

Fig. 3.5 Freedom in being as central to the causality of psychology. Free will is constituted by a cognitive component and by an affective component (free will belief, sense of free will, respectively). Freedom of being is a superordinate concept that includes free will and being in the world. Freedom in Being stands at the apex of the suite of concepts on free will. Free will is an essential component of the personal, self-determined psychological forces in the causality of behavior, which are part of the multifactorial biopsychosocial (biopersonalsocial) influences on behavior

Freedom in Being

Figure 3.5 clarifies the relationship of free will to the overall perspective of the present work. It indicates that behavioral causality should be considered as influenced by biopsychosocial (biopersonalsocial) factors, and that free will is a critical aspect of the psychological (personal) component of the model, through the concept of Freedom in Being. In addition, the figure incorporates Heidegger's concept of *Dasein*, or being in the world (Heidegger, 1927/1962), which is the root of the concept of freedom of being as used in the present work. That is, Freedom in Being should be considered as deriving from and being encapsulated in participatory, dialogic, co-actional, constitutive relations in the world.

Biopsychosocial Causality

A systems approach would seem beneficial for viewing the broad, multifactorial perspective involved in how free will participates in the causality of behavior. In this regard, consider modeling causality with both (a) a vertical axis in which there are multiple interacting components that have more or less equal effect and (b) a horizontal axis for which each of the multifactorial components has a series of increasing complex levels. Therefore, on the one hand, behavioral causality concerns a broad array of interacting factors, as in the biopsychosocial model. On the other hand, each of these factors is constituted by both simpler and more complex processes. The more complex ones might be emergent, or deriving from lower-order levels in a way that is more than additive and reductionistic. Figure 3.6 illustrates a model in this regard that considers the place of free will in a broad behavioral causality system-type model.

The figure indicates that not only free will but also other important components involving freedom stand at the apex of the biological, psychological (personal), and social influences on behavior. Freedom in being implies not only a psychological maturity that actively drives behavior but also a brain free of more passive

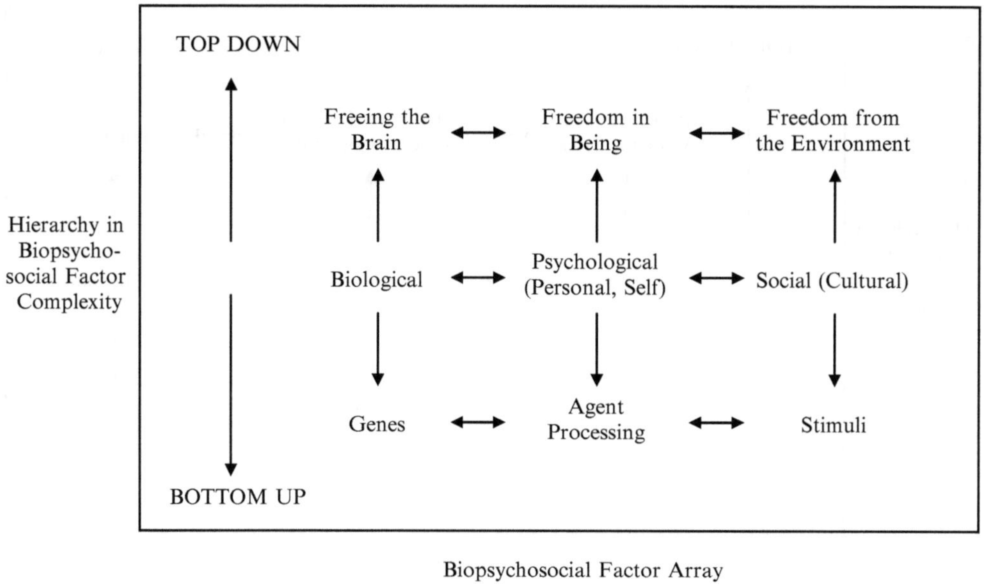

Fig. 3.6 Biopsychosocial causality: a broad vertical/horizontal systems model. The figure models causality in behavior to vary (**a**) horizontally in terms of its multifactorial (biopsychosocial, biopersonalsocial) influences and (**b**) vertically in terms of the hierarchical arrangement of its different levels of complexity. At the apex of all three major causal influences on behavior stand constructs related to free will and freedom. Behavioral causality is much more than reaction to lower-order levels in the various interactive causal forces on behavior, such as genes and stimuli producing passive response. Rather, behavior is actively emergent in a system, with self forces involved psychologically as causal factors

influences, such as physiological and environmental ones, and an environment that is not in active of the person; rather, the person has developed to the point of expressing freedom from capture by the environment.

In the following, I turn to expanding description of mechanism in behavioral causation. After that, I extend work on causal graph modeling, the third of the three major axes on causality in the present work.

Mechanism

Model

Introduction In the next part of this chapter, I show how a vertical–horizontal systems perspective, as presented in Fig. 3.7, can help understand the mechanism component to causality. Mechanism relates to causality through the specific causal processes that it describes for the products of the system. Systems can be defined in terms of their components and their interacting relationships but also in terms of the factors that promote state changes in their configurations. The latter provide impetus to change, depending on their degree of distance from equilibrium (and also depending on how the system handles incoming energy, information. See Fig. 3.7).

In my approach to mechanism in the present work, I try to avoid reductionistic, biology-based conceptualizations that are only lower-level in complexity. For example, a reductionistic explanation of having cancer might dismiss smoking as a cause, and also societal influences encouraging smoking, and only seek physiological change mechanisms coupled with genetic risk ones. However, a hierarchical, multilevel conceptualization of causality in behavior would recognize that both lower-order and higher-order levels arranged in a hierarchical model help explain the link between smoking and lung cancer. Moreover, by acknowledging a biopsychosocial model even for cancer, and that mechanism can reside in any of the components of the biopsychosocial model,

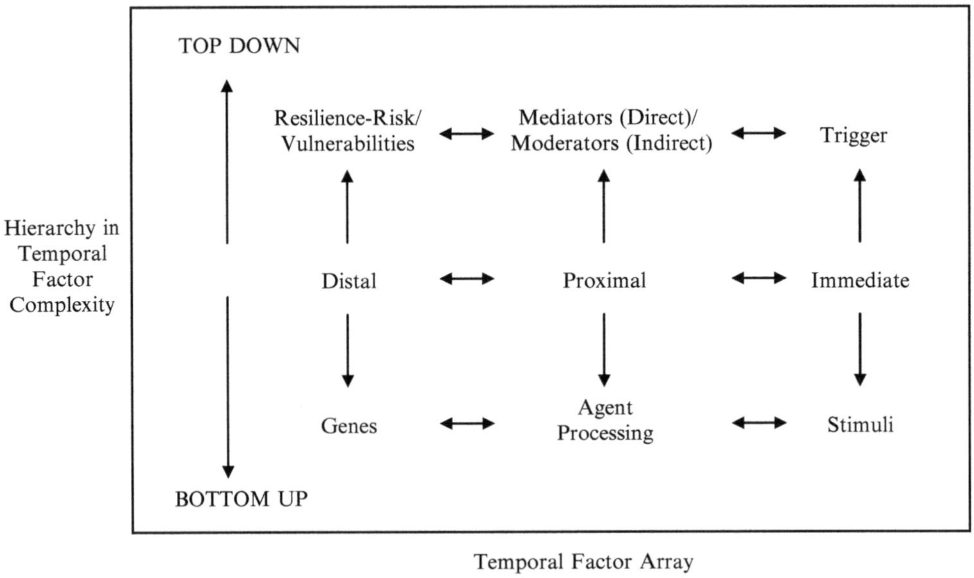

Fig. 3.7 Temporal behavioral causality: a broad vertical/horizontal systems model. Temporality in the causality of behavior does not proceed simply at the basic level from stimulus to response, or from genes leading to agent processing passively and then to outcome. That is, distal and proximal influences on behavior are not fully deterministic of behavior, nor are immediate triggers that apparently precede it. Instead, more inclusively, there are higher-order factors in behavioral causation, including mediators coming from the person him- or herself, that are more active, dynamic, emergent, and altering of all other causal factors in behavior and the temporal sequences that precede it

then mechanism cannot be considered either reductionisticly, linearly from genes upward to behavior, or unifactorially.

Model In this regard, I constructed a hierarchical horizontal/vertical model of causality related to temporality of putative cause and effect. Events, situations, triggers, and stimuli do not automatically lead to responses, behavior, and outcome. The agent processing the incoming material does not perceive it passively but rather, adds an adaptive filtration, an anticipation, a future-oriented element, and so on. Often, in human behavior, one thinks of agent as a passive perceptual system and a brain reacting passively to the impact of the environment. However, the person has a say in her or his psychology even at this level. The environment does not just exist at a lower level in terms of its physical, quantitative properties in how it impacts the person. Rather, at a higher level, the person serves as a qualitative, active intermediary between environment and behavior.

Conclusion In the end, when examining the temporality of causal factors in behavior, sequences are never what they seem because they are embedded in larger systems in which they function. A birds-eye view of causality focuses too strictly on sequences, apparent cause and effect, and so on. But a wider eagle-eye view will see that causality does not lie in any one level, in any one mechanism, in any one cause–effect sequence, and so on. Rather, causality lies in the whole behavioral system. In this sense, the component of free will belief (and associated free will factors) has an equal if not superordinate role to play in behavioral causality.

In the following, I look at mechanism from the perspective of the widest system possible, that of the universe. Chaisson (2010, 2011) describes Big History in terms of the origins of behavior since the Big Bang. He emerges with a model that integrates living and non-living systems, which is a goal of the present work, as well. Perhaps his work will lead to a Big Psychology perspective.

Big History

Introduction Chaisson (2010, 2011) has presented a model of Big History that is mechanism-driven in terms of energy, evolution, and culture, in particular. The search for mechanism is basic to the present work.

Model Chaisson's (2010, 2011) model unifies evolutionary causation of diverse natural phenomena in the physical, biological, and cultural realms. He begins with cosmic evolution and ends with contemporary phenomena, such as computers. Whatever the realm, he perceives them as products of energy rate density, which is a complexity metric, or an evolutionary "driver." In this regard, the concept of energy rate density has more general applicability toward unifying evolutionary causation compared to other concepts, such as those based on information or entropy. Energy rate density is a mass-normalized (free) energy flow, represented by Φm.

Chaisson (2010, 2011) considered "indisputable" that, on a grand scale, in the course of evolution, complexity inexorably increases. Energy flow provides the basis for establishing a unifying metric across all complex living and nonliving systems, helping to explain their origin, maintenance, and complexification. Generally, whether living or nonliving, complex systems are open, ordered, nonequilibrated entities in which energy is important. In complex systems, energy is acquired, stored, and expressed in the systems.

According to Chaisson, natural selection works in tandem with energy evolution as biological systems evolve. Life forms are open to resource flow exchange and, from a systems point of view, are selected partly for their capacity to "command" energy. Systems adapt more effectively if they undertake the latter. If not, they are selected out. Moreover, energy appears to "drive" systems beyond equilibrium. If advantageously adaptive, the emergent, more complex forms that are constructed in the process are selected. That is, the capacity of a system to reach normalized energy flow (in terms of managing the increased energy flow after system perturbation per unit mass) indicates its survivability in the competition of natural selection, as well as its reproductive success.

Chaisson (2010) explained that at critical energies or thresholds, after departure from equilibrium, when there is availability of optimal energy, systems can draw the power of the energy to construct structures or functions needed to adaptively "engage" the energies. If they cannot, they risk deterioration, destruction, or loss in competition. In this sense, the most successful regimes remain dynamic steady states after energy influx, and they have the capacity to create the pathways needed to arrive at equilibrium, with other options selected out.

Conclusion Chaisson (2010) concluded that energy flow is a universal process in evolution, from the Big Bang to galaxies to humans, and it can be represented in the way indicated. Ultimately, appropriate energy flow helps to control a system's dissipation to disorder (in entropy). It helps construct increasingly ordered, localized systems having to deal with the increasingly disordered wider environment.

Chaisson (2011) added that culture has accelerated human evolution, taking it beyond the results of Darwinian natural selection. Culture functions in accompanying the effects of natural selection with its own intergenerational adaptive transmissions, bringing it into the realms of Lamarckian processes. Chaisson qualified that natural selection and cultural selection are processes that are reciprocally interrelated as adjacent evolutionary influences. The products of culture help deal with the limitations in the environment impeding evolution by selection. Humans are even capable of challenging the environment. Through its innovations, human culture can work in tandem with energy to catalyze human evolution.

Mapping

Model

According to Sloman (2005), the study of causality is important from a psychological point of view because we are agents who have goals and

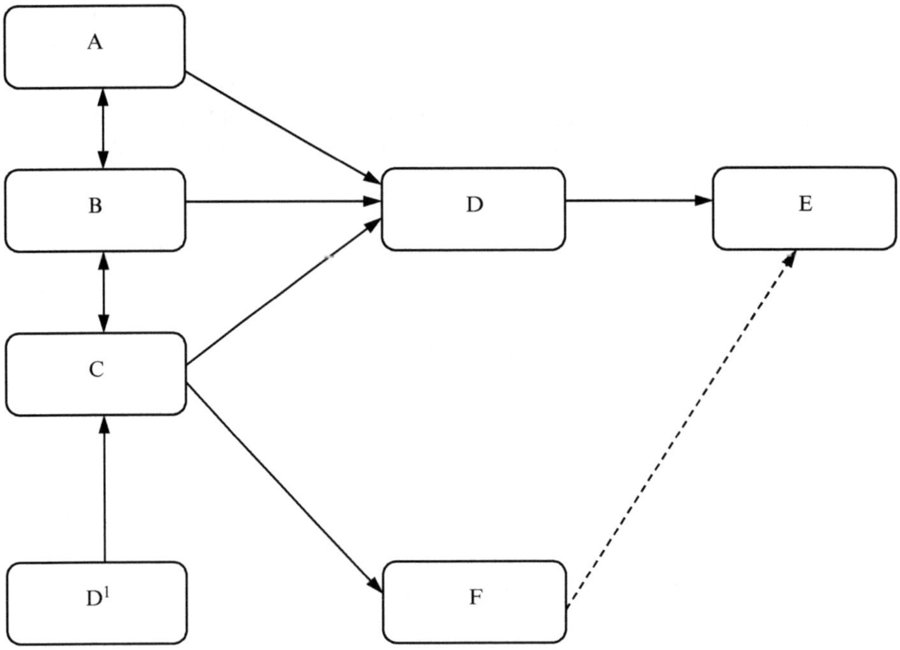

A = Causal Mapping/ Learning

B = Mechanisms (Biopsychosocial)

C = Free Will/ Consciousness

D^1=Causality Study, General

D = Integrating Causality Areas

E = Causality Centralizing in Sciences

F = Causality Centralizing in Psychology

Fig. 3.8 A causal Bayes network. The figure indicates how different areas in the study of causality and causation in psychology need to coalesce toward an integrated science of causality in which causality is promoted as its central construct. At the same time, the figure serves double duty because it uses the causal Bayes network or causal mapping/graphing approach to illustrate the area of study of causality. For examples with specific event sequences, see Sloman (2005)

act as if we have free will. Moreover, understanding causation is central in trying to understand the world. Agency refers to the ability to intervene on the environment and change it, beyond anything it might mean with respect to consciousness and intentionality. Moreover, people attempt to represent their ability to act on the world and change it. Often, knowledge that we acquire is about causal mechanisms that bring about effects, or their "why." Moreover, causal knowledge includes statements about counterfactuals (belief statements about possibilities other than the one of concern; which effects would follow had the causes been different or absent). Therefore, agency involves thinking about how things might be otherwise should the correct intervention be implemented, or about representing interventions, both real and imagined (see Fig. 3.8).

Sloman (2005) continued that understanding of causal systems depends on our cognition, or construals. We construct causal frames in order to help understand the mechanisms that have produced the world as we know it and how it might be otherwise in different circumstances and with different mechanisms.

The approach of developing causal maps based on Bayesian networks is consistent with this approach to causality, because it allows us to represent in graphical form both real and imagined actions and their effects. Moreover, they speak to the diversity of causal relations, whether probabilistic or deterministic, necessary or sufficient, weak or strong, direct or indirect, or actual or background.

Causal models, maps, or networks are created to represent causal relations found in invariants in information. Individuals establish invariants in the world by using psychological capacities, such as selective attention. Indeed, the critical focus of reasoning and learning relates to the invariance of causal structure. Sloman maintained that causal relations function or hold "across space, time, and *individuals*" (italics mine, added for emphasis; p. 20). Consistent with this line of argument, Sloman continued that the logic of causality is the guide that people use for prediction, explanation, and action, and that "people are designed to learn and to reason with causal models" (p. 20).

Comment

Note that I agree with Sloman that seeking and understanding causality is central to everything that we do, think, [and emote]. However, I would argue that individual selective attention, perception, understanding, interpretation, prediction, and control are crucial elements of the individual's appraisal of context and world. Appraisal is individual and personal and is involved in establishing informational invariants for the person alone; they are not universal causal structures that cut across individuals. That is, we construct our world individually at each moment, and although we are influenced by cultural norms in these regards, as well as our past constructions, each moment is uniquely created and highly individual, and greatly related to the immediate and individual adaptation needed in the world.

Model

Sloman (2005) proceeded to explain the relationship between causal relations and mechanisms. For him, cause involves "change over time" and causal relations are "enacted" over time. Causal relations imply that a mechanism "unfolds" over time to produce an effect, "using" the cause. Time could be immediate (e.g., a shadow is created) or extensive (e.g., the continually inflating universe since the Big Bang). Therefore, mechanisms are any type of "process" that "takes" causes to produce effects. Mechanisms are at a lower level in the hierarchy of a system compared to principles that might govern it. Nevertheless, the most valuable appraisals that we can make are about mechanisms.

Experiments are good ways of establishing cause, because potential causes (independent variables) are manipulated to determine potential effects (on independent variables). Correlations cannot establish causation because, at best, they describe associations and cannot specify counterfactuals, or possible worlds, which experiments, in particular, can help ascertain.

Comment

I would add that, although cause involves change, as Sloman emphasized, cause could also involve stability without change in a system. Each moment in the life of a system brings the possibility of change, but often the system gravitates to stability and keeps its equilibrium. Moreover, this might happen even if the system is far from equilibrium and even if a perturbation of the system is major. Systems have conserving as well as change tendencies. This being said, even the maintenance of stability can be viewed as change, because the inputs into the system and its contextual ground change unceasingly overt time, but the whole that is the system and its surround preserves a constancy despite the erstwhile changes in the surround and the inputs into it.

Model

Sloman (2005) continued that causes could be enabling or disabling, and he added that, in a certain sense, everything can be a cause. Events could have alternate causes that can act together or separately (conjunctively or disjunctively). They can create chains of causal links. Each link is local, autonomous, and stable. The nature of the links is subject to the counterfactual argument—links are considered part of the chain when it can be established that had they not occurred, other links and the ultimate effect at issue would not have occurred.

In terms of probabilities that are central to the causal modeling framework, Sloman indicated that patterns of probability involving dependence and independence derive from particular causal structures. Causal structures can be inferred from dependencies based on two assumptions. In the causal Markov condition, the direct causes of a variable, or its "parents," render the variable "probabilistically independent of" or "screened off" from other variables, such as indirect ones [except for its effects], at least when the "parent" values are "fixed." The second assumption is that of stability or "faithfulness," which specifies that probabilistic independencies in a data set are due to causal structure and not due to chance or coincidence. Or, independence in a system is neither due to chance nor is incidental, because it arises in the absence of causal relatedness.

Of course, the task becomes to specify all relevant variables such that there is no error or chance that can be invoked in establishing cause. Theoretically, this is possible—prediction is deterministically-based in systems under the assumption that all relevant variables and parameters can be specified. Practically, "noise" is part and parcel of any system under real-world investigation. Our powers at specifying the full range of variables and parameters in a system often are limited, at best, to all major ones.

Sloman indicated this by noting that when we cannot identify a unique causal structure, we can still limit the set of possible causal structures. Causal networks are constructed as best fits to the data, and their arrows are acyclic, characterizing causal relations forward in time, and not back. Moreover, once we graph a causal model, we can act on it, intervene, or conduct a "do" operation on it (conduct "graphic surgery"; Pearl, 2009). These types of graphic modeling concern creating imagined outcomes as interventional probabilities rather than conditional ones (e.g., the counterfactual: "If we eliminate the peptic ulcer, what is the probability of gut pain?"). In conclusion, for Sloman, the power of the causal modeling framework lies in its synergy of causal links, mechanisms, and interventions [and I would add—the counterfactual reasoning and imaginary actions that it permits].

Comment

Danks (2014) proposed that causal graph modeling can be used as a common framework for understanding and reinterpreting many areas of cognition (not only causal learning). He described his approach as one that affords a unified understanding of mind.

Danks (2014) makes the bold statement that his version of representations of graphical models actually represents how we think and navigate the world successfully. Different cognitions have a seamless, common store of cognitive representations that are structured as representational graphic models. His concept reduces the importance of modular domains in cognition and helps explain its flexibility, that which permits "free-ranging" cognition. Different cognitive domains vary in the "operations" they conduct on the core models. [Not all domains can be graphed this way, though, e.g., perceptual causation.]

Not only does each of us have a common representational graphical model, which can differentiate to for different domains but also our shared cognitive representations are structured this way.

Conclusion

The causal graph modeling approach (Pearl, 2000, 2009) is an influential one in psychology.

Its concept of interventions and "graph surgery" as indicative of causal relations is an important one. (a) However, it is not the only graphical model that has gained currency in psychology. For example, network modeling is increasing in scope and has found application in research in psychology and beyond (neuroscience; see Chap. 7). (b) Also, at the clinical level, Haynes, O'Brien, and Kaholokula (2011) described functional analytic clinical case diagrams that are perceptive (see Chap. 6). I refer to my own network model as an Integrative Cross-Network one (see Chap. 29). A complementary perspective in graphical modeling of behavior involves NLDST, which I described in depth in Young (2011) and to which refer to quite often in the present work (e.g., about emergence). Figure 3.9 organizes these different causal graphing models into a framework according to their complexity and focus.

NLDST graphs phenomena in terms of attractors, which can shift in basins according to both internal dynamics (e.g., tension due to far-from-equilibrium state) and external ones (e.g., even minor perturbations can produce chaotic effects).

I refer to these various models as top-down or bottom-up, depending on whether system parameters can influence their behavior (top-down) or whether the behavior of the elements creates patterns that exert relatively minor influence relative to the component activity themselves. In this sense, NLDST belongs with casual graph modeling theory as higher-order top-down ones, along with my cross-network model.

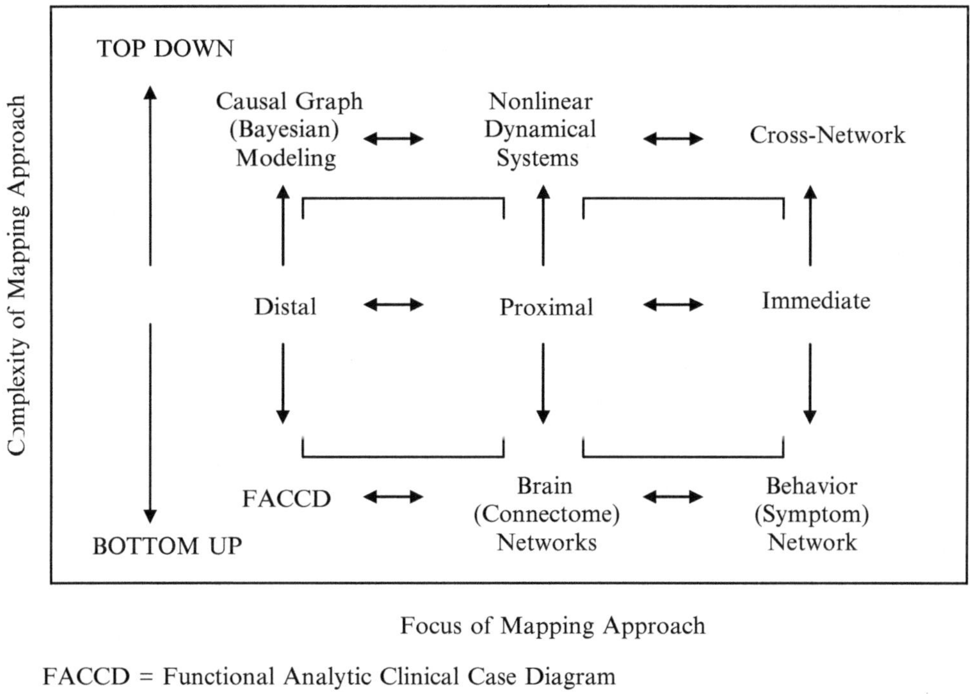

Fig. 3.9 Conceptual flow map of causal mapping approaches. Network approaches to causal model are burgeoning. They have been applied to the brain (Connectome; Sporns, 2011, 2012) and symptoms (Borsboom & Cramer, 2014; McNally et al., 2015). They are concerned more with proximal/immediate causal antecedents rather than distal ones. The proposed integrated cross-network approach (see Chap. 29) takes a broader network perspective (including on development) in understanding causality. Other mapping approaches to causality vary in whether they tackle lower-order or higher-order system organization. For example, FACCD (Haynes et al., 2011) are about patient patterns and constitute a lower-order approach while DAGs (Directed Acyclic Graphs)/causal graph modeling (e.g., Pearl, 2000, 2009) are more generic and constitute a higher-order one

Chapter Conclusions

In particular, the present chapter examines critical terms in the field and describes the three axes in the study of causality (causal mapping/learning, mechanisms, free will) that were emphasized in Young (2011). Then, it presents integrative models that expand the focus of behavioral causality study, yet still emphasizes these three areas as central to understanding behavioral causality.

Causality is an increasing focus in some aspects of psychology (for example, in psychological injury and law; Young, 2008, 2014, 2015). Also, for training in psychology, Layne et al. (2014) has recommended that it takes a more central stage. However, in psychology, in general, causality is more of a background consideration rather than a key focus.

The chapter illustrates the general approach of the present book to consider (a) causality as central to the study of behavior and (b) free will and related aspects as an important component in the causality of behavior. As with all behavior, individual differences are critical in the expression of causality-related behavior, such as happens with free will belief. In this regard, despite general models related to universally present factors, the causality of behavior never expresses itself universally in the same way for everyone, so that it is marked normatively by extensive individual differences.

Key terms introduced in the chapter related to causality include systems, emergence, mechanisms, free will, causal mapping/learning, control, dimensions, and activation/inhibition coordination, as well as the areas of development, genetics, evolution, and the brain. The remainder of the present book expands on these concepts and areas, while introducing others as it progresses. Causality can stand as the central unifying construct in psychology, and the book's extensive study of it and effort to integrate it are dedicated to that proposition.

References

Baumeister, R. F. (2008). Free will in scientific psychology. *Perspectives on Psychological Science, 3*, 14–19.

Baumeister, R. F., Crescioni, A. W., & Alquist, J. L. (2011). Free will as advanced action control for human social life and culture. *Neuroethics, 4*, 1–11.

Beebee, H., Hitchcock, C., & Menzies, P. (2009). *The Oxford handbook of causation*. New York: Oxford University Press.

Belsky, J., & Pluess, M. (2009a). Beyond diathesis stress: Differential susceptibility to environmental influences. *Psychological Bulletin, 135*, 885–908.

Belsky, J., & Pluess, M. (2009b). The nature (and nurture?) of plasticity in early human development. *Perspectives on Psychological Science, 4*, 345–351.

Berger, A. (2011). *Self-regulation: Brain, cognition, and development*. Washington: American Psychological Association.

Borsboom, D., & Cramer, A. O. J. (2014). Network analysis: An integrative approach to the structure of psychopathology. *Annual Review of Clinical Psychology, 9*, 91–121.

Carlson, S. M. (2010). Development of conscious control and imagination. In R. F. Baumeister, A. R. Mele, & K. D. Vohs (Eds.), *Free will and consciousness: How might they work?* (pp. 135–152). New York: Oxford University Press.

Carver, C. S., Johnson, S. L., Joormann, J., Kim, Y., & Nam, J. Y. (2011). Serotonin transporter polymorphism interacts with childhood adversity to predict aspects of impulsivity. *Psychological Science, 22*, 589–595.

Caspi, A., Hariri, A. R., Holmes, A., Uher, R., & Moffitt, T. E. (2010). Genetic sensitivity to the environment: The case of the serotonin transporter gene and its implications for studying complex diseases and traits. *American Journal of Psychiatry, 167*, 509–527.

Caspi, A., McClay, J., Moffitt, T. E., Mill, J., Martin, J., Craig, I. W., Taylor, A., & Poulton, R. (2002). Role of genotype in the cycle of violence in maltreated children. *Science, 297*, 851–854.

Caspi, A., Sugden, K., Moffitt, T. E., Taylor, A., Craig, I. W., Harrington, H., et al. (2003). Influence of life stress on depression: Moderation by a polymorphism in the 5-HTT gene. *Science, 301*, 386–389.

Chaisson, E. J. (2010). Energy rate density as a complexity metric and evolutionary driver. *Complexity, 16*, 27–40.

Chaisson, E. J. (2011). Energy rate density. II. Probing further a new complexity metric. *Complexity, 17*, 44–63.

Cocchiarella, L., & Lord, S. J. (Eds.). (2001). *Master the AMA guides fifth* (5th ed., pp. 327–341). Chicago: American Medical Association.

Danks, D. (2014). *Unifying the mind: Cognitive representations as graphical models*. Cambridge, MA: The MIT Press.

Dick, D. M. (2011). Gene-environment interaction in psychological traits and disorders. *Annual Review of Clinical Psychology, 7*, 383–409.

Dick, D. M., Meyers, J. L., Latendresse, S. J., Creemers, H. E., Lansford, J. E., Pettit, G. S., et al. (2011). *CHRM2*, parental monitoring, and adolescent externalizing behavior: Evidence for gene-environment interaction. *Psychological Science, 22*, 481–489.

Douglas, K. S., Huss, M. T., Murdoch, L. L., Washington, D. O., & Koch, W. J. (1999). Posttraumatic stress disorder stemming from motor vehicle accidents: Legal issues in Canada and the United States. In E. J. Hickling & E. B. Blanchard (Eds.), *The international handbook of road traffic accidents and psychological trauma: Current understanding, treatment and law* (pp. 271–289). New York: Elsevier.

Ellis, B. J., & Boyce, W. T. (2008). Biological sensitivity to context. *Current Directions in Psychological Science, 17*, 183–187.

Garner, B. A. (Ed.). (2009). *Black's law dictionary* (9th ed.). St. Paul, MN: West.

Gopnik, A., & Schulz, L. (2007). *Causal learning: Psychology, philosophy, and computation*. New York: Oxford University Press.

Haynes, S. N., O'Brien, W. H., & Kaholokula, J. K. (2011). *Behavioral assessment and case formulation*. Hoboken, NJ: Wiley.

Heidegger, M. (1927/1962). *Being in time*. London, UK: SCM.

Illari, P. M., Russo, F., & Williamson, J. (Eds.). (2011a). *Causality in the sciences*. New York: Oxford University Press.

Illari, P. M., Russo, F., & Williamson, J. (2011b). Why look at causality in the sciences? A manifesto. In P. M. Illari, F. Russo, & J. Williamson (Eds.), *Causality in the sciences* (pp. 3–22). New York: Oxford University Press.

Karg, K., Shedden, K., Burmeister, M., & Sen, S. (2011). The serotonin transporter promoter variant (*5-HTTLPR*), stress, and depression meta-analysis revisited: Evidence of genetic moderation. *Archives of General Psychiatry, 68*, 444–454.

Kauffman, S. (1993). *The origins of order: Self-organization and selection in evolution*. New York: Oxford University Press.

Layne, C. M., Steinberg, J. R., & Steinberg, A. M. (2014). Causal reasoning skills training for mental health practitioners: Promoting sound clinical judgment in evidence-based practice. *Training and Education in Professional Psychology*. doi:10.1037/tep0000037.

Markus, K. A. (2011). Real causes and ideal manipulations: Pearl's theory of causal inference from the point of view of psychological research methods. In P. M. Illari, F. Russo, & J. Williamson (Eds.), *Causality in the sciences* (pp. 240–269). New York: Oxford University Press.

McNally, R. J., Robinaugh, D. J., Wu, G. W. Y., Wang, L., Deserno, M. K., & Borsboom, D. (2015). Mental disorders as causal systems: A network approach to posttraumatic stress disorder. *Clinical Psychological Science 3*, 836–849.

Nowak, M. A., Tarnita, C. E., & Wilson, E. O. (2010). The evolution of eusociality. *Nature, 466*, 1057–1062.

Pearl, J. (2000). *Causality: Models, reasoning, and inference*. New York: Cambridge University Press.

Pearl, J. (2009). *Causality: Models, reasoning, and inference* (2nd ed.). New York: Cambridge University Press.

Russo, F. (2009). *Causality and causal modeling in the social sciences: Measuring variations*. New York: Springer Science + Business Media.

Shrout, P. E., Keyes, K. M., & Ornstein, K. (Eds.). (2011). *Causality and psychopathology: Finding the determinants of disorders and their cures*. New York: Oxford University Press.

Simpson, J. A., & Belsky, J. (2008). Attachment theory within a modern evolutionary framework. In J. Cassidy & P. R. Shaver (Eds.), *Handbook of attachment: Theory, research, and clinical applications* (pp. 131–157). New York: Guilford Press.

Sloman, S. (2005). *Causal models: How people think about the world and its alternatives*. New York: Oxford University Press.

Spencer, J. P., Austin, A., & Schutte, A. R. (2012). Contributions of dynamic systems theory to cognitive development. *Cognitive Development, 27*, 401–418.

Spirtes, P., Glymour, C., & Scheines, R. (2001). *Causation, prediction, and search*. Cambridge, MA: MIT Press.

Sporns, O. (2011). *Networks of the brain*. Cambridge, MA: MIT Press.

Sporns, O. (2012). *Discovering the human connectome*. Cambridge, MA: MIT Press.

Thelen, E., & Smith, L. B. (2006). Dynamic systems theories. In W. Damon & R. M. Lerner (Eds.), *Handbook of child psychology: Vol. 1. Theoretical models of human development* (6th ed., pp. 258–312). Hoboken, NJ: Wiley.

Tinbergen, N. (1963). On aims and methods in ethology. *Zeitschrift für Tierpsychologie, 20*, 410–433.

Vauclair, J., & Imbault, J. (2009). Relationship between manual preferences for object manipulation and pointing gestures for infants and toddlers. *Developmental Science, 12*, 1060–1069.

Woodward, J. (2007). Interventionist theories of causation in psychological perspective. In A. Gopnik & L. Schulz (Eds.), *Causal learning: Psychology, philosophy, and computation* (pp. 19–36). New York: Oxford University Press.

Young, G. (2008). Causality and causation in law, medicine, psychiatry, and psychology: Progression or regression? *Psychological Injury and Law, 1*, 161–181.

Young, G. (2011). *Development and causality: Neo-Piagetian perspectives*. New York: Springer Science + Business Media.

Young, G. (2014). *Malingering, feigning, and response bias in psychiatric/psychological injury: Implications for practice and court*. Dordrecht, Netherlands: Springer Science + Business Media.

Young, G. (2015). Causality in civil disability and criminal forensic cases: Legal and psychological comparison. *International Journal of Law and Psychiatry, 37*.

Young, G., & Gagnon, M. (1990). Neonatal laterality, birth stress, familial sinistrality, and left brain inhibition. *Developmental Neuropsychology, 6*, 127–150.

Young, G., Kane, A. W., & Nicholson, K. (2007). *Causality of psychological injury: Presenting evidence in court*. New York: Springer Science + Business Media.

Young, G., & Shore, R. (2007). Dictionary of terms related to causality, causation, law, and psychology. In G. Young, A. W. Kane, & K. Nicholson (Eds.), *Causality of psychological injury: Presenting evidence in court* (pp. 87–135). New York: Springer Science + Business Media.

Zelazo, P. D. (2004). The development of conscious control in childhood. *Trends in Cognitive Sciences, 8*, 12–17.

Zelazo, P. D., Carlson, S. M., & Kesek, A. (2008). The development of executive function in childhood. In C. Nelson & M. Luciana (Eds.), *Handbook of developmental cognitive neuroscience* (2nd ed., pp. 553–574). Cambridge, MA: MIT Press.

4 Causality in Philosophy; Philosophy in Psychology

Chapter Introduction

Philosophical concepts of mind, brain, behavior, and their relationships, including on causality and free will, provide essential intellectual foreground in the psychological study of these concepts. The present book deals with the complexity of the causes of behavior, and has been informed by the philosophical work in the area. This chapter of the present work reviews critical philosophical issues in the field related to behavior and its causation, and it proposes concepts that might help bridge the philosophical and psychological constructs in the area.

The first part of the chapter explores the relation of psychology and philosophy from the psychological perspective. It concentrates on schools of thought such as reductionism and constructionism. Lilienfeld (2012a, 2012b) proposed an integrated model of "constitutive reductionism." It allows for emergence of higher-order levels in behavior, a concept that lends itself to viable models of free will in human behavior. Newcombe (2011a, 2011b) proposed an integrative model of "neoconstructivism," and Allen and Bickhard (2011, 2013a, 2013b) proposed an "emergent constructivist" one. In other work in this chapter, Seligman, Railton, Baumeister, and Sripada (2013) and Sripada, Railton, Baumeister, and Seligman (2013) argued for a model of causation that is probabilistic and appears adeterministic.

Note that in Chap. 35, I present a philosophical model related to the ones under discussion, referred to as a "co-existential" model for epistemology. It combines different viewpoints on positivistic reality and its social construction. This prior philosophical work of mine illustrates how different philosophical positions can be combined into superordinate ones involving a dialectical integration of the constituents. Later in the present chapter, I develop an equivalent integrative philosophical model of "neoreductio-constructivism." It serves to create an interdialogue of predominant themes on the philosophical discourse about psychology, and also it applies quite well to the issue at hand of the causality of behavior. That is, by proposing a hierarchical model subsuming the philosophical extremes on the question of the nature of reality and its causality, none predominate to muddy the discourse. Moreover, the constitutive emergence of the whole that they create allows for a more rational debate on the question in which all sides are respected for their contributions to understanding behavior and its origins.

The work of Barrett and colleagues (e.g., Lindquist & Barrett, 2012) on a constructivist approach to psychological constructs places the brain and its networks at the heart of understanding psychological "primitives." The neuronal network approach is an important one in the present book, and helps keep the philosophical debates grounded in "hard" science.

G. Young, *Unifying Causality and Psychology*, DOI 10.1007/978-3-319-24094-7_4

At the same time, philosophers are venturing into neuroscientific study and conceptualization, and this is quite evident in the section of the chapter on the philosophy of free will.

Philosophers deal with free will in terms of the axis of determinism or its lack in behavior and the issue of compatibilism of free will and determinism. Compromise stances include semi-compatibilist ones. In the chapter, I propose a semi-compatibilist model that is based on the construct of "free being" rather than free will.

The chapter concludes with presentation of the integrated approach of relationism, which is a metatheoretical/worldview approach that is heavily developmental. Also, it refers to Kuhn's (1962, 1970) philosophy of science concept of paradigms in science, and their shifts to new paradigms once the inertia of change reaches the tipping point. In a chapter toward the end of the book, I return to the topics of relationism and paradigms in psychology. I develop an integrated model of paradigms and their changes based on the work of Overton (2013, 2014a, 2015), showing how my generic model of the change process (Young, 2011) can be used to elaborate Overton's work, and consequently Kuhn's. Indeed, much of the latter part of the book is based on applications of my change model and its corresponding model of Neo-Piagetian/Neo-Eriksonian development over the lifespan (Young, 2011, 2012, 2014).

The Constitution and Construction of Reality

The great debate in psychology as well as philosophy about the nature of behavior is whether it can be reduced to biochemical and physical processes in body and brain or whether it can be more than that and even constructed (including by mind) at levels beyond reductionistic influences. The following section of the chapter delves into these thorny issues, and terminates by presenting my own co-existential model on the question.

Reductionism and Constructivism

Lilienfeld (2012a) characterized the predominant view in psychology as "constitutive reductionism." In this view, mental phenomena are considered material products of brain and other central nervous system activity [I would add in interaction with the peripheral nervous system]. A more extreme version of reductionism is "eliminative reductionism," which is a neurocentric perspective. In this view, neuroscience leads the way in translating all behavior, emotion, and thought into neural activity (which is also called "greedy reductionism"; Dennett, 1995).

Lilienfeld (2012a) noted that an extreme reductionist point of view discounts that behavior and psychology can be analyzed at several levels. However, constitutive reductionism allows for the "emergence" of higher-order properties that derive from the interaction of lower-order elements at different levels of the behavioral system, and cannot be reduced entirely to the lower-order constituents involved. Lilienfeld gave the example of traffic jams as an emergent phenomenon. He noted that, in the end, the concept of emergence might not be supported. Nevertheless, that would not deny the validity of a hierarchical model of behavior in which neuroscience and psychology function at different valid levels.

Lilienfeld (2012b) continued that constitutive reductionism disavows the proposition of "substance dualism," which considers that mind and body are fundamentally distinct, or composed of different "stuff." Instead, it accepts that mind and brain comprise different levels of analysis of psychological phenomena, a viewpoint that he termed "property dualism."

Lilienfeld (2012b) addressed causality of behavior, indicating that psychology is studying critical variables in this regard as well as "rough outlines" of their "directional pathways." He argued that the field should clarify the precise steps linking relevant causal variables into integrated etiological explanations.

He responded to Tryon (2012a), who criticized the biopsychosocial model as providing simply a list of contributing factors without explaining how causal connections work, or what are the mechanisms involved, thereby promoting only an "illusion of understanding." Lilienfeld (2012b) agreed that the biopsychosocial model is unfalsifiable, without much explanatory power. [However, I have developed a modified biopsychosocial model terms "biopersonalsocial," that could have more relevance to psychological science (Young, 2011).]

Tryon (2012a) favored the connectionist model as one that circumvents these lacunae in psychological theory construction. However, in another exchange on the philosophical roots of behavioral study, Newcombe (2011a, 2011b) devalued the connectionist model as applied to developmental psychology. Before delving into that issue, I examine Tryon's informative presentation on cause and mechanism.

Tryon (2009) referred to Kazdin (2008), who distinguished mechanism and causation. Mechanism refers to the processes that explain why things (e.g., therapy) work and how they produce change. For example, at the causal level, it is well-known that cigarettes cause cancer but the precise main mechanism involves mediation by DNA mutation induced by nicotine exposure. However, in psychology, causal modeling is often approached using "box-and-arrow schematic diagrams" as explanations, but these lack information on mechanisms. They might identify mediators (more direct causal influences) and moderators (more indirect ones), but these are at a level removed from establishing mechanism.

Tryon (2012a) continued that psychology is infused with three major explanatory problems. First, it is comprised of separate mini-theories, schools, or camps that lack integration. Second, often the problem in this regard relates to the use of distinct terminology in each mini-theory/school/camp. Third, the various approaches lack in precise mechanistic explanations and, instead, they rely too heavily on functional ones. Tryon defined mechanism as a sequence of causal events that are necessary or sufficient to bring about a result at issue as it operates. For Tryon (2012b), psychological phenomena can be emergent, or not predictable from the constituents involved. Just as wetness cannot be predicted from knowledge of the atoms constituting water, so the properties of neural networks cannot be predicted from knowledge of their constituent neurons.

Neoconstructivism

Newcombe (2011a, 2011b) noted that Piaget bridged or reconciled the nativism–empiricism split in cognitive development by adopting a constructivist stance. An emerging neoconstructivist viewpoint extends the constructivist model; it advocates that minds are biologically prepared at the outset and that they interact in biologically-evolved ways within their varying but expectable environments. The environment provides rich structures, redundancies, and correlations that serve like Gibsonian (Gibson, 1979) affordances and support experience-expectant learning (Bahrick, Lickliter, & Flom, 2004; Greenough, Black, & Wallace, 1987).

Neoconstructivism cuts across nativist and empirical perspectives and, moreover, it views both learning and development, including of reasoning, as probabilistic, statistical, and Bayesian (Gopnik & Tenenbaum, 2007). It is both quantitative and qualitative, depending on the granularity of the lens used.

Neoconstructivism also integrates (a) development with (b) neural, (c) evolutionary, and (d) ecological (current state) approaches. This perspective cuts across all four of Aristotle's view of causes: (a) formal, (b) material, (c) final, and (d) efficient, respectively. Finally, it is an umbrella term that covers other views, such as dynamic systems theory/emergence models (Thelen & Smith, 1994) and stage (e.g., Young, 2011) and wave (e.g., Siegler, 2006) models.

Allen and Bickhard (2011, 2013a, 2013b) proposed an "emergent constructivist" model. They explained that both the nativist and empiricist points of view of the starting point of cognitive development in infancy are "foundational." That is, they proposed that further learning takes place because of the presence of givens in "core knowledge" or perceptual skills ("feature"), respectively. The two points of view disallow any possibility of emergence. Further, both empirical and nativist models are passive ontological models of the developing person, concerning environment or innate factors, respectively. Even if models try to combine empirical and nativist approaches, they just attempt to bridge the divide and not transcend it. Only a "third way" can do that, which Piaget termed "tertium quid." In Allen and Bickhard's model of cognitive development, called representational emergence, action systems are constructed, and representations emerge from the pragmatic, functional, interactive activity involved. Their model, therefore, allows for emergent constructivism in new knowledge learning. The model is quite Piagetian (Piaget, 1954), in that Piaget had posited that the starting point of cognitive development involves goal-oriented sensorimotor activity on which emergence can take place. Allen and Bickhard (2013a) added that their version of this action-based model especially concerns anticipations. Allen and Bickhard (2011) noted, "New constructions can emerge from variations of an internally organized emergence base" (p. 165). Development takes place on the basis of emergence out of action, which is an (inter)action perspective.

Newcombe (2011b) concluded that empiricism might be best referred to as a bottom-up theory. She placed dynamic systems theory among the bottom-up theories, as per Thelen and Smith's (1994) description of it.

Determinism and Indeterminism

The exchange by Seligman and colleagues and Fukukura and colleagues in 2013 tackles the role of determinism in psychological behavior and causation. Seligman et al. (2013) championed prospection as a central process to frame behavior, mind, and brain. It focuses on future orientation, allowing probabilistic elements to interpose in strict determination of present from past. Humans are considered as active agents who are constantly constructing alternative possibilities, evaluating them, and electing which ones to follow.

Causality derives from prospective processes. However, at the metaphysical level, the concept of prospection is agnostic about determinism. The authors also make the strong claim that the scientific method and even fundamental scientific principles do not inevitably stand on or require determinism, given that natural science theorizing now involves "probabilistic elements."

Fukukura, Helzer, and Ferguson (2013) commented that Seligman et al. (2013) are incorrect to dismiss determinism in science. By definition, science implicates a "deterministic understanding" of human behavior and thought. Sripada et al. (2013) replied that determinism should not be considered inviolate but simply an empirical thesis about the types of laws in nature (the universe). Sripada et al. (2013) then presented the contrasting view of a quantum universe, which is fundamentally "stochastic" and marked by physical laws that yield a distribution of probabilities in outcome. Beyond quantum phenomena, natural ones, including psychological ones, are understood best in terms of statistical generalizations on laws rather than deterministic ones.

In another example, work in political science indicates that causality in this area is not deterministic (Acemoglu & Robinson, 2012; Fukuyama, 2011). As for particular major (macrolevel) areas related to psychology, no firm conclusions can be drawn yet whether probabilistic causation explains operation (e.g., neurons, brain). The same applies to the particular area of free will.

Co-Existentialism

One manner of describing the metatheoretical approach to the question of determinism in psychology, as presented in Seligman et al. (2013) and Sripada et al. (2013), is to term it a "probabilistic adeterministic" one. Another possibility is that the label of "probabilisticism" best captures their approach to reality construction and determinism. In this regard, the authors also refer to the concept of prospection that they consider important in human cognition as being "agnostic" about determinism. I would add that the concept of emergence as a possible outcome in the probabilistic universe of behavior solidifies the construct that human behavior is probabilistic and adeterministic.

In this regard, especially considering that philosophical debates about the role of determinism in human behavior cannot end with definitive answers, a combined, pluralistic view that acknowledges multiple possibilities and realities in the causal construction of behavior might be an appropriate blended approach. Evidence might be found supporting either extremes of the continuum of determinism and probabilism in human behavior causation but, more likely, evidence might be lacking, be ambiguous, or be interpretable in different ways, taking different quantum faces depending on the observer.

One way of accommodating the various approaches to reductionism, constructivism, determinism, adeterminism, causalism, acausalism, probabilism, and any "fixism" in understanding the external world and its reality is to suggest they can co-exist epistemologically, in one metaview of reality. The co-existence could reflect that some aspects of reality are already reduced or reducible, cannot be constructed de novo, etc., while others can be personally or socially constructed.

Also, some aspects of reality could be wholly determined by preceding factors, deriving from either immediate proximally preceding antecedents or, rather, quite distal ones, for example, even ones that are evolutionarily, intergenerationally, genetically, or post-conceptually distal in origin. In contrast, other aspects of reality could be wholly probabilistic, even emergent, and utterly unpredictable from prior states, events, stimuli, or conditions/contexts, and so on.

Finally, it is conceivable that some aspects of reality are indeed totally random and without cause, with no probabilistic element. They might not even reflect in any way extant system elements, their configurations, and system inputs. This type of reality might be deemed acausal. However, most if not all reality should reflect causal processes at work in its initiation and maintenance.

This combined point of view of the nature of reality is a neo-epistemological one, and because it recommends viewing different epistemological stances as co-existential and not mutually incompatible, despite what they might advocate at their intellectual origins, it is a quantum one. Perhaps it is best to refer to the proposed blended epistemological model as a co-existential epistemological one, but another way of capturing its intricacy is to refer to it as one involving quantum neo-epistemology. The model being proposed allows integration of Lilienfeld's (2012a, 2012b) concept of constitutive reductionism, Newcombe's (2011a, 2011b) concept of neoconstructivism, Allen and Bickhard's (2011) concept of emergent constructivism, and Seligman et al.'s (2013)/Sripada et al.'s (2013) approach that I have labeled "probabilisticism" or probabilistic adeterminism. In this regard, the combined model of reality and causal elucidation that I am proposing could be termed "neo-reductioconstructivism." Specifically, the model accepts that reality at once is reductionist and constructionist, deterministic and adeterministic, and causal but perhaps with some aspects acausal. Emergence can mark it, but within the constraints offered at any and all levels involved by pre-existing factors, present context, and prospection. The perception of reality is influenced by positivistic factors in the present but, in the end, in the human case, it is influenced, as well, by perceptions of projected reality into the future based on past and present context and even the goal to alter it in order to allow for better adaptation.

Comment

The integrated, synthetic, co-existential model that I have developed on the construction of reality and the empirical influences that impact that construction speaks to my dialectical, constructivist, yet realistic, positivistic approach to other similar philosophical questions, such as whether free will exists or is an illusion and whether causality exists or is a figment of behavioral perception and interpretation. In the following, I turn to the latter two philosophical questions, dealing first with free will and then causality. In both cases, I support the pertinence of the study of and reflection on the matter—first, free will exists and can influence behavior, partly through its emergent and constructed qualities; and, second, causality not only exists but is central to understanding behavior, including through free will as a primary factor in these regards and the mechanisms that allow for it and other aspects of behavior.

Free Will, Causality Modeling, and Philosophy

The present model of epistemology is consistent with the psychological and neuroscientific literature. For example, it fits the view that people can express free will belief, which in turn influences their behavior (Baumeister, 2008). Russell and Deery (2013) showed how the classic debates about the question of whether free will exists (and influences behavior) have evolved into more nuanced and integrated approaches. Nevertheless, the great divide in the issues, such as determinism/indeterminism, compatibilism/incompatibilism, and the matter of responsibility remain cogent in contemporary philosophy.

For other recent philosophical work on causality, the reader should consult Gibb, Lowe, and Ingthorsson (2013), Lawson (2013), Markus (2012), Reiss (2015), Mumford and Anjum (2013), Paul and Hall (2013), and Reutlinger (2013). Balaguer (2014) has written an accessible philosophical book on free will, as did Mele (2014a, 2014b). Castellani and Quitterer (2007) edited a philosophy book to help decipher the relationship between agency and causation. It includes chapters on free will (e.g., Mele, 2007). For example, Reiss (2015) explained the relationship among causation, evidence, and inference. He described the historical roots of causality scholarship, and the recent approaches related to regularity, probability, process, counterfactuals, interventions, radical causal pluralism, and power theory, while developing his inferentialist philosophical theory of causation. Review of these books is beyond the scope of the present work.

Philosophers increasingly are not adverse to broaching neuroscientific and experimental work, and this is especially true for the topic of free will. They examine both the classic neuroscientific studies in the area, their methodological drawbacks, and their implications for understanding free will in autonomous acting agents, or its lack in this regard. Therefore, in the following, I review the work on brain and networks in causality, as presented by Tse (2013) philosophically in terms of the concept of emergence and Lindquist and Barrett (2012) psychologically in terms of the concept of constructionism at the level of networks. A later chapter in the present book that is fully on free will (see Chap. 18) explores further the philosophical and neuroscientific bases involved.

Neurophilosophy and Free Will

Emergence

Tse (2013) adopted a more pragmatic approach to the question of free will by examining its neural basis. Neuronal circuits exhibit "emergent" spatiotemporal properties that are not found in any single neuron. Circuits need to exhibit precise timing and interplay over activation ("excitation") and also inhibition, in cascades of activity involving the whole network and without a "command" neuron. An example of emergence in behavior relative to neurons underpinning the behavior is that we can engage in swimming even though no one neuron encodes for it.

According to Tse (2013), in this approach to neurons, in terms of input, the energy involved also is spatiotemporal in pattern. The patterns are higher-order and emergent but this does not mean that they are beyond physical laws. They exert "downward" causal influences and have a degree of independence, but they do not do the "causal work" in and of themselves. Rather, meeting thresholds of neural activation does the causal work involved.

Tse (2013) pointed out that input patterns could genuinely cause behavior only if neurons detect them at the necessary threshold levels, and thereby change the body and brain. It's not just energy transfer or amount that is causal in neural activity, but energy patterns meeting thresholds that trigger a neuronal response.

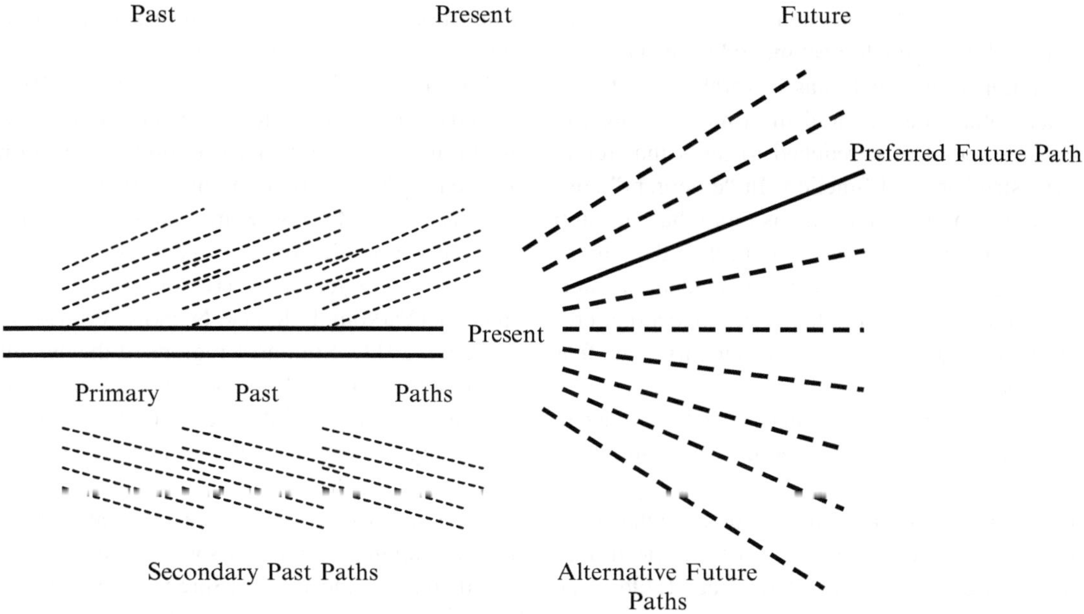

Fig. 4.1 An actual and several possible paths. In the case of causation among neurons, criteria on neuronal input realize possible paths that are also links in informational causal chains, as indicated by the *solid line*. The *dashed lines* indicate possible paths that would not be part of any informational causal chain. There is downward causation by threshold-released detectors of input spatiotemporal patterns. Adapted from Tse (2013)

Tse (2013) presented much detail of how neurons work. In this regard, he maintained that free will is especially "about the future." In particular, free will relates to "the next cycle in iterative information processing loops" (p. 15). Specially, the way free will works in causation is through "criterial causation." Figure 4.1 presents Tse's (2013) model of criterial causation. In the model, the path actually followed from among possibilities in neuronal activity indicates downward causation by criterially-released detectors of spatiotemporal input patterns that are involved "in informational causal chains." Therefore, for the neural basis of free will, Tse (2013) supported a model of downward influence on neural activity due to "criterial" thresholds of input toward neural activity causation. Neuronal criterial causation is a model that is compatible with the philosophical positions of both determinism and indeterminism.

Runyan (2014) presented a philosophically-based analysis of human agency in terms of factors that cannot be reduced to neural causes. Specifically, he considered humans as "emergent" voluntary agents who, at the macro/whole level, are capable of voluntary, purposive choice in deliberating, moving, and refraining to move. The emergentist view acknowledges superordinate, top-down functioning levels in hierarchical organization of behavior, but does not deny that we are partly constituted by lower-order, bottom-up processes, such as neural activities.

For further neuroscientific work related to free will, refer to Pockett, Banks, and Gallagher (2006). For example, they discussed the work of Libet (1994) and Wegner (2002), who essentially deny the validity of considering free will in behavior.

Networks

Lindquist and Barrett (2012) adopted a constructionist approach to understanding basic human faculties, such as emotions, cognitions, and perception. As their starting point, they took the functional networks being described in cognitive neuroscience, and proposed that they can be described as lower-level, basic psychological operations that interact to produce the typical modular categories associated with a "faculty" approach to psychological mental state. The constructionist approach has several variants. In "elemental" constructionism, a mental state can be disassembled or reduced to units that retain their structure and function. In "emergent" constructionism, a mental state is more than the sum of its parts, just as bread is more than the sum of its ingredients. Third, context-dependent or "situated" constructionism allows for conceptual creation of specific instances of a category (e.g., fear of snakes vs. falling).

The neuronal network analyses taking place in the research inform these models. Neuroimaging research supports the utility of examining neuronal networks as platforms for the articulation of psychologically meaningful yet basic primitives in constructing mental state (see Table 4.1). Lindquist and Barrett's (2012) review of the literature supports multiple networks (seven, after Yeo et al., 2011) as important in psychological operations. These include the three core ones emphasized by Menon (2011, 2012)—salience, the executive, and the default model—as well as four others related to the limbic system, attention, and perception. The authors referred to the psychological operations in the salience network as body-directed attention, those in the executive one as executive control, and those in the default one as conceptualization. The limbic system concerns core affect generation, the attention one visuospatial attention, and the perceptual ones exteroceptive perception (auditory/tactile visual).

To show that the networks involved function both cross-categorically yet specific to instances of categories, Lindquist and Barrett (2012) referred to the literature on these networks and emotions. In this regard, meaning-making under executive control is associated with multiple neuronal networks and is involved in creation of all mental states. For example, the brain regions associated with emotional experiences also are associated with other mental phenomena, as per a review of meta-analyses. These findings are consistent with a model that brain regions are enabling ("implementing") basic pan-mental state (more than pan-emotional or specific emotional) psychological operations.

Specifically, Lindquist and Barrett (2012) related emotional experience/perception processing brain-region activation to similar activation by memory/theory of mind/navigation/prospection (Spreng, Mar, & Kim, 2009), semantics (Binder, Desai, Graves, & Conant, 2009), moral decision-making/empathy (Bzdok et al., 2012), and pain (Yarkoni, Poldrack, Nichols, Van Essen, & Wager, 2011). Similarly, regions of the default network are activated not only in emotions but also in empathy (Bzdok et al., 2012), semantic processing (Binder et al., 2009), moral judgments (Bzdok et al., 2012), mentalizing about other people (Bzdok et al., 2012; Spreng et al., 2009), autobiographical memory (Spreng et al., 2009), and imagining the future (Spreng et al., 2009). The authors provided similar data about other networks, including the limbic one.

Lindquist and Barrett (2012) concluded that networks are broadly-distributed, flexible assemblies that fire together in probabilistic ways. Psychological operations "emerge" from neuronal interplay, although the exact emergentic mechanism has not been elucidated. The authors' constructionist approach calls for abandoning naïve realism that psychological faculties/categories, such as emotions, reveal understanding of causal mechanisms in the brain. It is more accurate to seek psychological "primitives" in these regards, and even the ones mentioned still might be further decomposable.

Note that Hamann (2012) adopted an approach to neural networks quite similar to that of Lindquist and Barrett (2012). However, he based his work on Kober et al. (2008), who found six primary, functionally distributed groups that help serve in the generation of emotional states.

Kelly, Biswal, Craddock, Castellanos, and Milham (2012) referred to the complete set of intrinsic functional connections in the brain as the "functional connectome." They cautioned that functional maps such as these need to consider individual differences and variations in functional zones in relation to variations in behavior.

Table 4.1 Intrinsic networks and their functional description in the constructionist framework

Network name(s)	Brain regions included	Psychological operation in a constructionist ontology
"Limbic" (Yeo et al., 2011)	Medial temporal lobe, subgenual anterior cingulated cortex, medial, and lateral orbitofrontal cortex[a]	**Core affect generation:** representing visceromotor states from prior experience or engaging visceromotor control of the body to create the core affective tone (pleasure or displeasure with some degree of arousal) that is a basic feature of all conscious experience and that directs basic approach/withdrawal behaviors.
"Salience network" (Seeley et al., 2007) "Ventral attention network" (Yeo et al., 2011) "Cingulo-opercular network" (Vincent, Kahn, Snyder, Raichle, & Buckner, 2008) Network # 8 (Smith et al., 2009)	Anterior midcingulate cortex (aMCC), bilateral dorsal anterior insula, and frontal operculum	**Body-directed attention:** using representations from the body to guide attention and behavior. This process might use changes in the homeostatic state of the body to signal salient events in the environment and regulate behavioral responses. Likely, this network can be decomposed further into aspects that represent bodily states (a ventral anterior insula network) and use bodily states to drive attention and behavior (a dorsal anterior insula network) (Touroutoglou, Hollenbeck, Dickerson, & Feldman Barrett, 2012)
"Default network" (Yeo et al., 2011) Network # 4 (Smith et al., 2009)	Medial prefrontal cortex, retrosplenial area, posterior cingulate cortex/precuneus, medial temporal lobe (hippocampus, entorhinal cortex), bilateral superior temporal sulcus	**Conceptualization:** representing prior experiences (i.e., memory or category knowledge). During autobiographical memory or representation of concept knowledge, this process simulates prior sensory-motor experiences. During perception of objects, this process helps to make meaning of sensations from the world in a context-specific manner. During emotion, this process helps to make meaning of sensations from the body in a context-specific manner.
"Frontoparietal network" (Yeo et al., 2011) "Executive control network" (Seeley et al., 2007) Network # 9 (Smith et al., 2009)	Bilateral dorsolateral prefrontal cortex, inferior parietal lobe, inferior parietal sulcus, precuneus, and middle cingulated cortex (mCC)	**Executive control:** modulating activity in other networks to create a unified conscious field during the construction of a mental state (e.g., selecting some conceptual content when meaning is made of sensations and inhibiting other content; selecting some sensations for conscious awareness and inhibiting others).
"Dorsal attention network" (Yeo et al., 2011) Network # 9 (Smith et al., 2009)	Bilateral frontal eye fields, dorsal posterior parietal cortex, fusiform gyrus, area MT+	**Visuospatial attention:** modulating activity in exteroceptive sensory regions (e.g., selecting which visual sensation is selected for conscious awareness and inhibiting others). This process may be specific to visual sensations given the importance of these sensations in human evolution.
"Sensorimotor" (Yeo et al., 2011)	Precentral and postcentral gyri (sensorimotor cortex), Heschl's gyrus (primary auditory cortex) cortex, posterior insula	**Exteroceptive sensory perception:** representing auditory and tactile sensations
"Visual" (Yeo et al., 2011)	Occipital lobe	**Exteroceptive sensory perception:** representing visual sensations

[a]Although Yeo et al. (2011) did not include subcortical structures in their analysis, we include subcortical structures in this network based on their known anatomical connections. We include the nuclei of the basal ganglia, which are involved in orchestrating effortful behavior and motor control (Wager et al., 2008). We also hypothesize that the central nucleus of the amygdale, which is involved in producing autonomic responses (Wager et al., 2008), and the midbrain periaqueductal gray, which is involved in coordinating coherent physiological and behavioral responses (Wager et al., 2008), are part of this network. The basal ganglia, the amygdale, and the periaqueductal gray all project to the ventromedial prefrontal cortex (vmPFC), the major cortical site in Yeo et al.'s (2011) limbic network

Adopted with permission of Elsevier. Reprinted from *Trends in Cognitive Sciences,* Vol. 16, Lindquist, K. A., & Barrett, L. F., A functional architecture of the human brain: Emerging insights from the science of emotion, Pages 533–540, Copyright 2012; with kind permission from Elsevier. [Table 1, Page 536]

Comment

The danger of focusing on the brain and its workings in the philosophical context is that behavior is reduced to biochemical and physical processes. However, the positions that I have described in this section related to free will adhere to a constructionist, emergentist account of behavior both philosophically and psychologically. That being said, as in any area of philosophy, and in any discipline for that matter, when contemplating the question of free will, there always will be a dynamic tension between more liberal and conservative views about its existence and its differentiation from the biophysical bases that constitute the brain and body.

The next part of the discussion of philosophical points of view related to causality and free will leaves the neuroscientific, constructionist approach for more classical philosophical debates on the question. The models discussed lead to a semi-compatibilistic one that I have developed for the issue.

Philosophy and Free Will

Schools

Kane (2011a, 2011b) noted that determinism also is referred to as a doctrine of "conditional necessity," and that it constitutes a "threat" to free will. Determinism can be referred to as conditional necessity because, given determining conditions, the occurrence of an event inevitably is determined. Determinism poses a threat to free will, as mentioned, because, typically, we view ourselves as agents having free will and capable of influencing the world. There are open alternatives from which we can choose and it is up to us to choose them so that, although we choose one option, we could have acted otherwise. We have control over the sources of our action.

Compatibilists argue that determinism does not really pose a threat to free will. For example, there might be "contextual emergence," in which higher-level phenomena mentally self-organize in novel ways from lower-level phenomena. There are not only "classic" compatibilists but also "new" compatibilists, who argue that free will is a type of "dispositional power." In the latter approach, concepts such as reflective self-control are important.

In semi-compatibilism (e.g., Fischer, 1994; Fischer & Ravizza, 1998; Ravizza, 1994), moral responsibility but not free will is compatible with determinism. The former is compatible with it because it does not require the power to do otherwise. However, freedom is not because it does require this power, and, essentially, semi-compatibilists maintain that this is impossible.

From a libertarian framework, Doyle (2010) developed a theory that seems like a semi-compatibilistic one. In his model, there is, first, an indeterministic stage involving factors that might influence choice. Then, there is a second stage that is deterministic and in which the actor exercises control about the choice made in light of the factors considered in the first step.

Kane (2011c) developed a libertarian view of free will that focuses on indeterminism in choices and decisions themselves. He emphasized "ultimate responsibility," involving actors having free will as the ultimate source of their actions or their wills in performing the actions.

Kane (2011a) noted that the philosopher William James (1956) had distinguished "hard" and "soft" determinism. Only the latter is compatibilist. There is also a point of view called "hard" incompatibilism. He continued that Smilansky (2002) has taken an "unusual" view of free will, in that Smilansky argued that "we can and should be both incompatibilists and compatibilists about freedom and responsibility" (p. 26). That is, "certain forms of moral responsibility, desert, and blame require libertarian free will, whereas other forms can be sustained without it" (p. 26). It would appear that this is a semi-compatibilist position in which hard determinism and compatibilism exist simultaneously, or co-exist in one understanding of "truth."

A Compatible Semi-Compatibilism

Introduction Note that I am attracted to the semi-compatibilist position not only because it appears to reflect better psychological "truth" compared to other philosophical positions on free will but also because it admits to ambiguity and uncertainty in understanding that "truth." Moreover, it allows for constructive integration of the diverse positions, even if the term is somewhat ambiguous and uncertain. This might be a better approach than strongly advocating for one position rather than another and falling toward a possible morass of philosophical squabbles and incoherent chaos. In this sense, one possible label to capture the essence of my argument is that a good way to describe the present semi-compatibilist position is that it is a "dialectical semi-compatibilism."

Perhaps it is best to accept that there is not only quantum-level entanglement at the micro level but also entanglement at the macrolevel of philosophy. Entanglement might one day be shown to involve the macrolevel of our physical selves (Lvovsky, Ghobadi, Chandra, Prasad, & Simon, 2013), so why not also the macrolevel of our abstract mental ideas? Another way of saying this is that an understanding of free will should be continuously dialectical, indeterminate (but also determinate), unfolding, discursive, and hermeneutical in process, and one in which we all should engage. However, at the psychological level, research is showing that, despite the philosophical uncertainty about the status of free will, whether we believe in it or not has profound consequences (Baumeister, 2008).

Evidence In this regard, the experimental philosophers Nichols and Knobe (2013) showed that in abstract conditions, participants tend toward incompatibilism about moral responsibility, but in concrete, affective ones, they are more compatibilistic. Nahmias, Morris, Nadelhoffer, and Turner (2013) found that, after imagining a difficult choice to make, participants then chose a compatibilist compared to an incompatibilist description of the ability to do otherwise as a description reflecting their previously imagined experience.

Similar Models Vihvelin (2013) has written a philosophical treatise on causality and free will that represents very well the present position. She argued that the folk psychological view of free will and moral responsibility reflects common sense, and that should return to the center stage in philosophy. The common sense view of causality, free will, and moral responsibility minimizes a role of determinism in understanding behavior because we still have free will even if all our behavior is predictable from the laws of nature (no matter how uncertainly established might be the laws at present). For Vihvelin (2013) determinism cannot be used as a basis to deny that we have free will, even though we are governed by natural laws. In contrast, maintains that we have free will, being free to choose from alternative options, so that we are morally responsible for our behavior. That responsibility could be undermined for any one individual at any one time, but not by any blanket reason, such as determinism.

Part of the reason that a deterministic world cannot negate the possibility of free will is that at least some of the fundamental laws in the world are not all-encompassing but are probabilistic. The world, therefore, is partly indeterministic and probabilistic rather than solely deterministic without room for free will. Quantum physics informs us about this indeterminate nature of the world. Nevertheless, Vihvelin (2013) maintained that, in her view, both moral responsibility and free will are compatible with determinism. However, she also argued that our ability to act and to choose is compatible not only with determinism but also with indeterminism.

Berofsky (2012) is another philosopher who maintained that determinism does not "preclude" free will. Because we are "decision-makers," we can determine, in part, the laws that govern us. Psychological laws are "autonomous" and not reducible to the physical. They are autonomous when they are created without coercion but by rationally stepping back, weighing, reflecting on, and choosing in an independent way that is based on deepest desires or values. Psychological laws are facilitated by "emotional maturity." We are active beings determining our own self, our world, and our destiny, including accepting responsibility. This is a compatibilist view in which free will is conceived of as self-determination, "self-control," or "self-regulation."

In the compatibility mind frame, determinism exists as well as free will. As Berofsky (2012) explained, free will is not a facet of being that is enabled only in an indeterministic world. To the contrary, a genuinely active agent with personhood who is making decisions does not passively wait for a breach in the deterministic world, otherwise remaining impotent. Governance is self-directed and freedoms can flourish through free will, but freedoms are meaningless without being accompanied by having decision-making powers and moral responsibility for decisions taken. In behaving at this level, we participate with free will in the deterministic world about us and within which we must live.

The Illusion of No Free Will Others have weighed in with the criticism of the approach that free will is an "illusion." For example, Mele (2003, 2009, 2010, 2011) described the limits of the views of Libet and Wagner for understanding consciousness and unconsciousness. Freeman (2006) described a view of consciousness, intentionality, and causality that is based on circular causality. In this nonlinear, dynamical model of causality, intentionality and awareness emerge as the result of self-organizing neuronal processes that include feedback and "enslavement," serving to enhance coherence. He related his model to standard concepts in nonlinear dynamical system theory, such as attractors and control of chaos.

In contrast, Harris (2012) is a neuroscientist who ended up denying that free will exists. He maintained that, in order to actually have free will, we need to be aware of all the factors that determine our behavior and have complete control over them. However, there are many factors of which we are unaware that are behind our behavior, including unconscious ones. Moreover, we have a sense of freedom only because of our "moment-to-moment ignorance" of the prior causes of our behavior. The next choice we make in our behavior will emerge from "the darkness of prior causes" that we did not have at hand. We cannot decide what we will decide to do even though we can decide to do what we have decided. Even though there are choices, efforts, intentions, and reasoning that influence us, they are all part of a chain of causes outside of conscious awareness and over which we have no control. Harris (2012) concluded that, "the illusion of free will is itself an illusion."

Comment The question of whether free will is an illusion will not be resolved either by philosophical debate or empirical investigation. What matters is that its belief and related psychological phenomena have psychological consequences (Baumeister, 2008), which can be rigorously investigated (e.g., Alquist, Ainsworth, Baumeister, Daly, & Stillman, 2015). Moreover, the philosophical positions either denying it or advocating its existence can be nuanced by intermediate stances, as well, such as in semi-compatibilism.

A New Semi-Compatibilism Model

Model The compatibilistic view and the pragmatic " neuroemergence" view together suggest that we can be active, autonomous agents in decision-making. In this regard, as mentioned, Berofsky (2012) took a more psychological view and indicated that behaving in this autonomous way requires emotional maturity. Similarly, I maintain that free will is a psychological function that develops with increasing psychological maturity, in a model that I refer to as the paradoxical, asymptotic model of free will (i.e., being mature for one's age leads us to choose responsibilities that reduce freedom of action).

The model that I present is a semi-compatibilistic model in that, for me, free will does not always exist compatibly in a deterministic world because whether it is present or not depends on the person's psychology. That is, free will is emergent when the person develops to the threshold of psychological maturity for one's age and, therefore, is capable of living at or beyond that threshold so that the person voluntarily and consciously chooses the best adaptive options in all the steps in giving attention, selecting action, and deploying action in behavior. Free will is more than "will" and more than "free" because it is all of being in a process of being free or functioning as a "free being."

Note that this semi-compatibilistic psychology model of free will is different from the philosophical approach to semi-compatibilism in free will scholarship. For example, the latter might mean that free will does not exist in a deterministic world but that moral responsibility still does exist (e.g., Fischer, 1994; Haji, 2009). Reading between the lines of this approach, free will is taken as a universal that marks each of us in the deterministic world that we inhabit. However, from a psychological point of view, free will, or, as we are defining it—free being—is something that develops, is gained with difficulty, and not necessarily in all of us, or even at all times in all of us who have it.

Table 4.2 presents different philosophical positions about free will and moral responsibility in relationship to determinism and indeterminism. It also includes the traditional philosophical semi-compatibilist approach and my version of dialectical semi-compatibilism. The table indicates that traditional semi-compatibilism admits to determinism, but my approach entails a dialectical engagement between determinism and indeterminism.

Free Will Development The implication of my dialectical semi-compatibilist model on the question of free will is that free will might not develop in individuals who do not grow toward psychological maturity, e.g., in terms of Erikson's concept of generativity. Moreover, even if one enters this phase, there will always be distractions and depletions impeding full psychological maturity and, therefore, lapses in free will. In this regard, the model that I am proposing for free will growth is an asymptotic one in that we never fully arrive at full psychological maturity and constant deployment of free will. Moreover, the model is a paradoxical one in that in developing psychological maturity and being able to dispose our free will freely in such development, we especially opt for behaviors related to generativity, e.g., caring for others, family, children, society, and/or the environment, and going beyond our personal (and selfish) needs (Young, 2014).

Philosophically, my position is consistent with that of Lévinas (1985), who considered that Responsibility constitutes a critical human activity (Morgan, 2011). In my model that I developed based on the work of Lévinas, I refer to the human imperative as one involving Re-Responsibilities rather than Responsibility. This is because to be engaged responsibly, we must constantly re-dedicate ourselves and do so to each of our multiple responsibilities (see Chap. 32 for further presentation of this model).

Table 4.2 Philosophical positions that relate Free Will (FW) and Moral Responsibility (MR) to determinism

Philosophical position		
Determinism	Indeterminism	Stance on Free Will/Moral Responsibility
Compatibilism	Libertarianism (Incompatibilist)	Present
Hard determinism	Hard incompatibilism	Absent
Traditional semi-compatibilism (Philosophical)		Only MR, not FW
Dialectic semi-compatibilism (Young, present volume)		As we mature psychologically, we grow asymptotically toward free will and, also, paradoxically, we accept the constraints of responsibility (including MR)

Compatibilism maintains that FW and MR are compatible with determinism. Incompatibilism does not accept this view: Hard determinists are incompatibilists who think that determinism is true and that we do not have free will. Libertarians maintain that determinism is false and that we have free will. Hard incompatibilists believe that FW and MR are impossible, independently of whether (in)determinism is true, both being incompatible with either option. "Semi-compatibilism" accepts that MR is possible in a deterministic universe even if FW is not [Note that Bertelsen (2011) adds that hard libertarianism allows for free will and rejects that it is compatible with scientific methods of explanation. In soft libertarianism, the person is seen to relate with his/her own self-construction of the world]
Adapted from Roskies (2012) and Bertelsen (2011)

Comment Having pondered the most difficult question of free will, responsibility, and morality, I have arrived at an intermediate position about whether it can exist in a deterministic world. Essentially, free will develops and might not reach the critical threshold of making a difference in behavior if it is ephemeral, transient, at risk, or otherwise compromised through genetics, biology (brain), environment (including family or culture), developmental program, and so on. In this regard, the model that I espouse is a dialectical, semi-compatibilistic one. Moreover, the model allows for rectification by the environment of less than optimal support for having free will in behavior, as in psychotherapy. For direct application of free will concepts in psychotherapy, refer to Chap. 20.

The next part of this philosophical chapter of this book on causality considers directly the topic of causality in philosophy. Overall, just as one finds with free will that there are deniers of its existence, so too for causality there are its deniers. That school of thought began with Hume, and though it is still current, I am not the one to think that causality is an illusion.

Causality in Philosophy

Introduction

Allen and Stoneham (2011a, 2011b) provided a historical perspective on the philosophy of causation, describing that past issues are still unresolved. Aristotle's four causes (material, formal, efficient, final) have informed philosophical debate on causation. For example, in the seventeenth century, scholarship on causation shifted from an emphasis on final causes (e.g., purpose) to efficient ones (e.g., mechanism). Another issue that bedevils philosophical study of causation relates to whether causes can be independent of their effects or are mutually related to them.

Blasimme, Maugeri, and Germain (2013) specified that explanatory frameworks are superordinate to mechanistic models. The explanatory and mechanistic levels are dynamically related. As explanatory frameworks change, their subsumed mechanisms can be seen or interpreted in novel ways, and also openings are provided to discovery of new mechanisms that might apply.

Interventionism

Menzies (2012) supported the interventionist approach to causation. By extending it into a "structural equations" framework, he indicated that it provides a clear account of the "causal structure of mechanisms" (citing Craver, 2007).

Claveau (2012) supported the interventionist approach in helping to determine causation. He referred to it as the "counterfactual-manipulationist" account of causality. Extensions of the approach include Pearl's (2009) causal mapping work ("graph surgery" = intervention) and Rubin's (1974, 1990) potential outcomes framework.

In this approach of manipulationist counterfactuals, for two "disjoint" variables (*X*, *Y*), *X* causes *Y* only if there is an "ideal" manipulation of *X* that alters *Y*'s value, or its probability distribution. The counterfactual component refers to "what if" manipulative, interventionist scenarios (the present value of *Y* would not exist absent the current value of *X*).

Kerry, Eriksen, Lie, Mumford, and Anjum (2012) considered causation in evidence-based practice (EBP), which often is based on epidemiological evidence. Whereas randomized controlled trials (RCTs) provide clearer evidence of causation relative to epidemiology research (observational study; Broadbent, 2011), the regularities found in the latter type of study could be revealing. More important, although RCTs are consistent with an interventionist-counterfactual approach to causality, both the latter approach to causality and the one of observational regularity might be limited to indicating the "symptoms" of causality rather than being "constitutive" of it.

Dispositionalism

Mumford and Anjum (2011; as cited in Blasimme et al., 2013) provided an account of causation that is "dispositional." For these authors, causation is a "primitive" that cannot be reduced to "non-causal" facts, including any counterfactual or regularity. In dispositionalism, a cause does not necessarily effect an outcome but it only "tends" toward doing so. For example, smoking tends toward cancer. Further, the approach considers cause and effect as "partners" rather than discrete events. In this regard, in causal dispositionalism, as applied to health, the patient is of utmost importance.

In dispositionalism, causality is individualized, probabilistic, context-sensitive, and complex. It is not simply a population-level phenomenon but is rich at the individual level, with the same putative universal cause potentially having different effects. Causation is not distantly statistical and without variance but is embedded in the patient's activity and is proximal. Tendency is less than necessity because of causal multiplicity and also because of nonlinear interactions. In this perspective, interventions are just one more causal factor to consider in the tendencies involved in causal dispositions. The real nature of causation can be found in the single case.

Note that in the area of psychology and law, we make a distinction between general and specific causation, or population-level and individual-level causation, respectively. The concept of dispositionalism is kindred in spirit to this distinction.

Mechanism

Chao, Chen, and Millstein (2013) explored the relationship between causality and mechanism in philosophy. They described the various approaches to both, and the complexities in relating them. In the end, they supported Darden (2013), who noted that the concept of mechanism is much more detailed and specific than that of causality.

Some of the earliest books on causality in psychology related to development, and in one philosophy had been considered. Butterworth and Bryant (1990) edited a volume on causes of development. They covered biological and social/cultural topics, as well as cognitive ones. In this volume, Hopkins and Butterworth (1990) related Aristotle's conception of four types of causes to Piagetian theory (Piaget, 1971). The authors equated Aristotle's material, formal, efficient, and final causes with biology, cognitive structure, environment, and equilibration, respectively [Material: something is produced from …; efficient: something is initiated from …; formal: something is done according to …; final: something is done for the sake of …]. They concluded that in order to understand developmental causation, we need to consider differentially all the organism–environment relationships at each juncture in development.

Comment

The philosophy of causality includes approaches that are differentiated in its support, as has been shown, and others that even deny its existence (e.g., Russell, 1919, on acausalism). The present book maintains a view that supports the differentiating models, including those on interventionism/counterfactuals, mechanisms, and free will (reviewed above), as axes in the study of causality, including philosophically. One point of view that affords integration among these diverse points of view in causality study is that of relationism. Aside from the description below, Chap. 35 considers an elaboration of relationism from the point of view of Kuhn's (1962) model of scientific paradigms, and shows how relationism and Kuhnianism can be redescribed in terms of the model in the present work on stages in change and generic change.

Relationism

Model

Overton (2014a) elaborated that relational developmental systems theory fits into the relational tradition of metatheory, scientific pursuit, and methodology rather than the more conventional Cartesian, reductionist, neopositivist one. At the psychological level, in this worldview, individuals are active, embodied in activity, open, adaptive, contextual, complex, systemic, self-organizing, subject to emergence, plastic, individualized, and so on.

For reductionism, causal explanation lies especially in mechanisms (Aristotle's efficient cause). However, in relationism, all four of Aristotle's causes are considered. For example, at the psychological level, material cause refers to the substance of inquiry (e.g., the neuron) and efficient cause to the forces in causation (e.g., the neuron firing). Formal cause refers to the organization of the resultant activity. In relational developmental systems, mechanisms are critical, and they refer to structure (architecture)—function (activity) relations. The latter can develop into novel structural forms or relations, as in Piaget's theory (1952, 1985).

Overton (2014a) elaborated the relational developmental systems perspective in terms of methodology (the set of guiding principles for establishing particular methods). Methodology serves to complement metatheory in the discourses in scientific research programs/paradigms. Metatheories vary in terms of worldviews, and relationism is opposed to the Cartesian neopositivistic/instrumental view in this regard.

In the Cartesian view, methodology moves from description/reduction, to explanations and their antecedent mechanisms (causes), to induction of hypothesis/theory/"law." In the methodology associated with relationism, the reductionist turn is replaced by relational analysis. Explanation is replaced by seeking relational action patterns. Finally, induction (and deduction) is replaced by cyclical "abductive" (retroductive) logic (explanation derives from observation–background integration as complementary polarities).

As for causality, Overton (2014a) maintained that the methodology of relationism dictates a radical stance about causes. That is, because system and activity are dynamically joined, understanding causation in terms of "conditions" associated with behavior should be the foci, in that they serve as assets/resources for "intraindividual" changes that might take place. Genes and environment are not causes in this view, but conditions that facilitate growth.

For Overton (2014a), if causes are "best understood" as conditions in this view, the determinants of behavioral change remains an open question. He referred to "mechanism" as the source of behavioral change, but only as defined with respect to the relational perspective. In this regard, a mechanism is an active "process" inherent in the "structure–function" relations serving to "identify" action patterns.

According to Overton (2014a), all living systems are relational and developmental ones. They actively function, organize structures and processes, and undergo "directed" sequences of "emergent" change in their organization, involving new relations in structure–function. The models of Piaget (stages in cognitive development) and Bowlby (attachment) are relational developmental models that fit the relational worldview (and its methodology).

About Piaget, Overton (2014a) concluded that he adopted a "person" standpoint (as actor) rather than a biological or cultural one (although the latter are relevant resources or conditions). In this regard, both Overton's (2014a) emphasis on the person as focus and agent in development and Piaget's equivalent focus place mechanism as having priority over any domain of understanding related to causality in behavior. However, for both, mechanism lies in active processes in dynamic relations that can produce emergent, contextualized, increasingly complex change at the individual level.

Supporting Work

The relational systems perspective is quite biopsychosocial in nature, but it adds a developmental component (Aldwin, 2014). In this view, adult development is considered "purposive." We have the potential to make conscious decisions to change aspects of ourselves (Aldwin, 2007). Overton (2014b) concurred that behavior can attain purposive attributes in behavior. In this regard, according to Aldwin (2014), free will/agency (Baumeister, 2008) involves a developmental process in which individuation from context enables deployment of free will. Development is about increasing freedom from social and biological influences. Therefore, it appears to me that development in a relational systems framework allows for stages in development (qualitative discontinuities; Lerner, Agans, DeSouza, & Hershberg, 2014), as per my own work (Young, 2011).

Greenberg (2014a, 2014b) underscored the importance of emergence, self-organization, relational systems, the biopsychosocial approach, and holism in development. There might be room for a "moderate reductionism" in science as long as it does not ignore the possibility of emergence.

Witherington (2014) considered self-organization as part of top-down and bottom-up reciprocal effects both between and within system levels and the system as a whole (parts-to-whole and whole-to-parts influences). The bottom-up component is embedded in a broader framework of circular causality that affords emergence or organic development. Overton and Lerner (2014) considered concepts that fit the meta-theoretical approach of "relationism."

Comment

Overall, the present chapter so far has demonstrated that philosophy has much to offer to psychology and related disciplines in understanding behavior, including at the levels of comprehending what are reality, free will, and causality. Nevertheless, the field needs an overarching perspective that coheres the diverse philosophical positions on these various topics. One prominent position in this regard is that of relationism, which contrasts with realism, for example. Later in the book, in Chap. 35, I show how relationism can be incorporated into a growing process in philosophical and psychological thought that is consistent with and explained by the present framework on stages and steps in development and change. I applied the same modeling to Kuhn's (1962) philosophy of science concept of paradigm change, which I review and comment on below.

Kuhnian Paradigms

Timmins (2013) examined the "Kuhnian" concept of paradigms in science and its applicability to historiography. Specifically, he focused on understanding of the Second World War (WWII) of 1939–1945 in terms of the evolution of the conceptualization of its nature. He noted that Kuhn's (1962) work was formulated for the sciences, but it has been applied widely in the social sciences.

Kuhn's (1962) concept of paradigm depends on a dominant consensus in a field of study. Timmins (2013) argued that the historiography of WWII consisted of three periods—the orthodox thesis, the revisionist one, and then the post-revisionist one. Paradigms might shift due to factors internal to a discipline or external to it (social, political). In his model of historiography, the new and old formulations exist in an essential tension. Moreover, there is not an abrupt transition but more of a gradual one. Finally, the factors leading to change in historiography are more internal than external.

Later in the present work, as mentioned, I present a revised Neo-Kuhnian model of paradigm. It allows for evolution in any field of scholarship and not just that of science, which is consistent with the approach of Timmins (2013).

Chapter Conclusions

Psychologists are both inspired by philosophy and tackle it with trepidation. The present chapter mostly deals with the relationship of psychology and philosophy from the point of view of psychologists making it more tangible. It includes mention of experimental philosophy and the brain (as well as neurons and networks), providing further familiarity. Moreover, the integrated concepts proposed by psychologists in the areas involved (related to behavior, brain, mind, free will, causality) are based on combined reductionist, positivistic and constructivist, relationist approaches, and so are inviting readers to persist.

My own contributions to the area are about: (a) integrating differing views of epistemology on realism/constructivism and compatibilism/incompatibilism; and (b) creating the concept of "free being" (an integrated psychological construct of free will belief and having a sense of free will). Baumeister (2008) has been important in arguing that the philosophical debate of whether free will exists is an intractable one, but believing in free will is quite prevalent and has psychological consequences. My proposal of the concept of free being can carry that logic farther in understanding the human proclivity to believe in free will and to act on it.

References

Acemoglu, D., & Robinson, J. (2012). *Why nations fail: The origins of power, prosperity, and poverty*. New York: Crown.

Aldwin, C. M. (2007). *Stress, coping, and development: An integrative approach* (2nd ed.). New York: Guilford Press.

Aldwin, C. M. (2014). Rethinking developmental science. *Research in Human Development, 11*, 247–254.

Allen, J. W. P., & Bickhard, M. H. (2011). Emergent constructivism. *Child Development Perspectives, 5*, 164–165.

Allen, J. W. P., & Bickhard, M. H. (2013a). Stepping of the pendulum: Why only an action-based approach can transcend the nativist-empiricist debate. *Cognitive Development, 28*, 96–133.

Allen, J. W. P., & Bickhard, M. H. (2013b). The pendulum still swings. *Cognitive Development, 28*, 164–174.

Allen, K., & Stoneham, T. (2011a). *Causation and modern philosophy*. New York: Taylor & Francis.

Allen, K., & Stoneham, T. (2011b). Introduction. In K. Allen & T. Stoneham (Eds.), *Causation and modern philosophy* (pp. 1–12). New York: Taylor & Francis.

Alquist, J. L., Ainsworth, S., Baumeister, R., Daly, M., & Stillman, T. (2015). The making of might-have-beens: Effects of free will belief on counterfactual thinking. *Personality and Social Psychology Bulletin, 41*, 268–283.

Bahrick, L. E., Lickliter, R., & Flom, R. (2004). Intersensory redundancy guides infants' selective attention, perceptual, and cognitive development. *Current Directions in Psychological Science, 13*, 99–102.

Balaguer, M. (2014). *Free will*. Cambridge, MA: MIT Press.

Baumeister, R. F. (2008). Free will in scientific psychology. *Perspectives on Psychological Science, 3*, 14–19.

Berofsky, B. (2012). *Nature's challenge to free will*. New York: Oxford University Press.

Bertelsen, P. (2011). Intentional activity and free will as core concepts in criminal law and psychology. *Theory & Psychology, 22*, 46–66.

Binder, J. R., Desai, R. H., Graves, W. W., & Conant, L. L. (2009). Where is the semantic system? A critical review and meta-analysis of 120 functional neuroimaging studies. *Cerebral Cortex, 19*, 2767–2796.

Blasimme, A., Maugeri, P., & Germain, P. L. (2013). What mechanisms can't do: Explanatory frameworks and the function of the p53 gene in molecular oncology. *Studies in History and Philosophy of Biological and Biomedical Sciences, 44*, 374–384.

Broadbent, A. (2011). *Epidemiology, risk and causation*. Cambridge, UK: PHG Foundation.

Butterworth, G., & Bryant, P. (1990). *Causes of development: Interdisciplinary perspectives*. Hertfordshire, UK: Harvester Wheatsheaf.

Bzdok, D., Schilbach, L., Vogeley, K., Schneider, K., Laird, A. R., Langner, R., et al. (2012). Parsing the neural correlates of moral cognition: ALE meta-analysis on morality, theory of mind and empathy. *Brain Structure and Function, 217*, 783–796.

Castellani, F., & Quitterer, J. (2007). *Agency and causation in the human sciences*. Paderborn, Germany: Mentis.

Chao, H.-K., Chen, S.-T., & Millstein, R. L. (2013). *Mechanism and causality in biology and economics*. Dordrecht, Netherlands: Springer Science + Business Media.

Claveau, F. (2012). The Russo-Williamson these in the social sciences: Causal inference drawing on two types of evidence. *Studies in History and Philosophy of Biological and Biomedical Sciences, 43*, 806–813.

Craver, C. (2007). *Explaining the brain: Mechanisms and the mosaic unity of neuroscience*. New York: Oxford University Press.

Darden, L. (2013). Mechanisms versus causes in biology and medicine. In H.-K. Chao, S.-T. Chen, & R. L. Millstein (Eds.), *Mechanism and causality in biology and economics* (pp. 19–34). Dordrecht, Netherlands: Springer Science + Business Media.

Dennett, D. C. (1995). *Darwin's dangerous idea*. New York: Simon & Schuster.

Doyle, B. (2010). Jamesian free will: The two-stage model of William James. *William James Studies, 5*, 25–50.

Fischer, J. M. (1994). *The metaphysics of free will*. Oxford, UK: Blackwell.

Fischer, J. M., & Ravizza, M. S. J. (1998). *Responsibility and control: A theory of moral responsibility*. Cambridge, UK: Cambridge University Press.

Freeman, W. J. (2006). Consciousness, intentionality, and causality. In S. Pockett, W. P. Banks, & S. Gallagher (Eds.), *Does consciousness cause behavior?* (pp. 73–105). Cambridge, MA: MIT Press.

Fukukura, J., Helzer, E. G., & Ferguson, M. J. (2013). Prospection by any other name? A response to Seligman et al. (2003). *Perspectives on Psychological Science, 8*, 146–150.

Fukuyama, F. (2011). *The origins of political order: From prehuman times to the French revolution*. New York: Farrah, Straus and Giroux.

Gibb, S. C., Lowe, E. J., & Ingthorsson, R. D. (2013). *Mental causation and ontology*. Oxford, UK: Oxford University Press.

Gibson, J. J. (1979/1986). *The ecological approach to visual perception*. Boston: Houghton Mifflin.

Gopnik, A., & Tenenbaum, J. B. (2007). Bayesian networks, Bayesian learning and cognitive development. *Developmental Science, 10*, 281–287.

Greenberg, G. (2014a). Emergence, self-organization, and developmental science: Introduction. *Research in Human Development, 11*, 1–4.

Greenberg, G. (2014b). How new ideas in physics and biology influence developmental science. *Research in Human Development, 11*, 5–21.

Greenough, W. T., Black, J. E., & Wallace, C. S. (1987). Experience and brain development. *Child Development, 58*, 539–559.

Haji, I. (2009). *Incompatibilism's allure: Principal arguments for incompatibilism*. Peterborough, ON: Broadview Press.

Hamann, S. (2012). Mapping discrete and dimensional emotions onto the brain: Controversies and consensus. *Trends in Cognitive Sciences, 16*, 458–466.

Harris, S. (2012). *Free will*. New York: Free Press.

Hopkins, B., & Butterworth, G. E. (1990). Concepts of causality in explanations of development. In G. Butterworth & P. Bryant (Eds.), *Causes of development: Interdisciplinary perspectives* (pp. 3–32). Hove, UK: Erlbaum.

James, W. (1956). The dilemma of determinism. In W. James (Ed.), *The will to believe and other essays in popular philosophy* (pp. 145–184). New York: Dover.

Kane, R. (2011a). Introduction: The contours of contemporary free-will debates (part 2). In R. Kane (Ed.), *The Oxford handbook of free will* (2nd ed., pp. 3–35). New York: Oxford University Press.

Kane, R. (2011b). *The Oxford handbook of free will* (2nd ed.). New York: Oxford University Press.

Kane, R. (2011c). Rethinking free will: New perspectives on an ancient problem. In R. Kane (Ed.), *The Oxford handbook of free will* (2nd ed., pp. 381–400). New York: Oxford University Press.

Kazdin, A. E. (2008). Evidence-based treatment and practice: New opportunities to bridge clinical research and practice, enhance the knowledge base, and improve patient care. *American Psychologist, 63*, 146–159.

Kelly, C., Biswal, B. B., Craddock, R. C., Castellanos, F. X., & Milham, M. P. (2012). Characterizing variation in the functional connectome: Promise and pitfalls. *Trends in Cognitive Sciences, 16*, 181–188.

Kerry, R., Eriksen, T. E., Lie, A. N., Mumford, S., & Anjum, R. L. (2012). Causation and evidence-based practice: An ontological review. *Journal of Evaluation in Clinical Practice, 18*, 1006–1012.

Kober, H., Barrett, L. F., Joseph, J., Bliss-Moreau, E., Lindquist, K., & Wager, T. D. (2008). Functional grouping and cortical-subcortical interactions in emotion: A meta-analysis of neuroimaging studies. *NeuroImage, 42*, 998–1031.

Kuhn, T. S. (1962). *The structure of scientific revolutions*. Chicago, IL: University of Chicago Press.

Kuhn, T. S. (1970). *The structure of scientific revolutions* (2nd ed.). Chicago, IL: University of Chicago Press.

Lawson, T. (2013). Emergence and morphogenesis: Causal reduction and downward causation? In M. S. Archer (Ed.), *Social morphogenesis* (pp. 61–84). New York: Springer Science + Business Media.

Lévinas, E. (1985). *Ethics and infinity*. Pittsburgh: Duquesne University Press.

Lerner, R. M., Agans, J. P., DeSouza, L. M., & Hershberg, R. M. (2014). Developmental science in 2025: A predictive review. *Research in Human Development, 11*, 255–272.

Libet, B. (1994). A testable field theory of mind-brain interaction. *Journal of Consciousness Studies, 1*, 119–126.

Lilienfeld, S. O. (2012a). Public skepticism of psychology: Why many people perceive the study of human behavior as unscientific. *American Psychologist, 67*, 111–129.

Lilienfeld, S. O. (2012b). Further sources of our field's embattled public reputation. *American Psychologist, 67*, 808–809.

Lindquist, K. A., & Barrett, L. F. (2012). A functional architecture of the human brain: Emerging insights from the science of emotion. *Trends in Cognitive Sciences, 16*, 533–540.

Lvovsky, A. I., Ghobadi, R., Chandra, A., Prasad, A. S., & Simon, C. (2013). Observation of micro–macro entanglement of light. *Nature Physics, 9*, 541–544.

Markus, K. A. (2012). A review of bias and causation: Models and judgment for valid comparison. *Journal of Educational and Behavioral Statistics, 37*, 475–476.

Mele, A. (2003). *Motivation and agency*. New York: Oxford University Press.

Mele, A. (2007). Free action, moral responsibility, and alternative possibilities: Frankfurt style cases revisited. In F. Castellani & J. Quitterer (Eds.), *Agency and causation in the human sciences* (pp. 125–140). Paderborn, Germany: Mentis.

Mele, A. (2009). *Efficacious intentions*. Oxford, UK: Oxford University Press.

Mele, A. R. (2010). Conscious deciding and the science of free will. In R. F. Baumeister, A. R. Mele, & K. D. Vohs (Eds.), *Free will and consciousness: How might they work?* (pp. 43–65). New York: Oxford University Press.

Mele, A. R. (2011). Free will and science. In R. Kane (Ed.), *The Oxford handbook of free will* (2nd ed., pp. 499–514). Oxford, UK: Oxford University Press.

Mele, A. R. (2014a). *A dialogue on free will and science*. New York: Oxford University Press.

Mele, A. R. (2014b). *Free: Why science hasn't disproved free will*. New York: Oxford University Press.

Menon, V. (2011). Large-scale brain networks and psychopathology: A unifying triple network model. *Trends in Cognitive Sciences, 15*, 483–506.

Menon, V. (2012). Functional connectivity, neurocognitive networks, and brain dynamics. In M. I. Rabinovich, K. J. Friston, & P. Varona (Eds.), *Principles of brain dynamics: Global state interactions* (pp. 27–47). Cambridge, MA: MIT Press.

Menzies, P. (2012). The causal structure of mechanisms. *Studies in History and Philosophy of Biological and Biomedical Sciences, 43*, 796–805.

Morgan, M. L. (2011). *The Cambridge introduction to Emmanuel Lévinas*. Cambridge, MA: Cambridge University Press.

Mumford, S. D., & Anjum, R. L. (2011). *Getting causes from powers*. New York: Oxford University Press.

Mumford, S., & Anjum, R. L. (2013). *Causation: A very short introduction*. Oxford, UK: Oxford University Press.

Nahmias, E., Morris, S., Nadelhoffer, T., & Turner, J. (2013). The phenomenology of free will. In P. Russell & O. Deery (Eds.), *The philosophy of free will: Essential readings from the contemporary debates* (pp. 486–505). New York: Oxford University Press.

Newcombe, N. S. (2011a). What is neoconstructivism? *Child Development Perspectives, 5*, 157–160.

Newcombe, N. S. (2011b). Three families of isms. *Child Development Perspectives, 5*, 171–172.

Nichols, S., & Knobe, J. (2013). Moral responsibility and determinism: The cognitive science of folk intuitions. In P. Russell & O. Deery (Eds.), *The philosophy of free will: Essential readings from the contemporary debates* (pp. 506–529). New York: Oxford University Press.

Overton, W. F. (2013). Relationism and relational developmental systems: A paradigm for developmental science in the post-cartesian era. In R. M. Lerner & J. B. Benson (Eds.), *Advances in child development and behavior. Embodiment and epigenesis: Theoretical and methodological issues in understanding the role of biology within the relational developmental system. Part A: Philosophical, theoretical, and biological dimensions* (Vol. 44, pp. 21–64). Oxford, UK: Elsevier.

Overton, W. F. (2014a). Relational developmental systems and developmental science. In P. C. M. Molenaar, R. M. Lerner, & K. M. Newell (Eds.), *Handbook of developmental systems theory and methodology* (pp. 19–65). New York: Guilford Press.

Overton, W. F. (2014b). The process-relational paradigm and relational-developmental-systems metamodel as context. *Research in Human Development, 11*, 323–331.

Overton, W. F. (2015). Relational developmental systems and developmental science. In R. M. Lerner, W. F. Overton, & P. C. Molenaar (Eds.), *Handbook of child psychology and developmental science, Vol. 1: Theory and method* (7th ed., pp. 9–62). Hoboken, NJ: Wiley.

Overton, W. F., & Lerner, R. M. (2014). Fundamental concepts and methods in developmental science: A relational perspective. *Research in Human Development, 11*, 63–73.

Paul, L. A., & Hall, N. (2013). *Causation: A user's guide*. Oxford, UK: Oxford University Press.

Pearl, J. (2009). *Causality: Models, reasoning, and inference* (2nd ed.). New York: Cambridge University Press.

Piaget, J. (1952). *The origins of intelligence in children*. Oxford, UK: International Universities Press.

Piaget, J. (1954). *The construction of reality in the child*. New York: Basic.

Piaget, J. (1971). *Biology and knowledge*. Edinburgh, UK: Edinburgh University Press.

Piaget, J. (1985). *The equilibration of cognitive structures*. Chicago, IL: University of Chicago Press.

Pockett, S., Banks, W. P., & Gallagher, S. (2006). *Does consciousness cause behavior?* Cambridge, MA: MIT Press.

Ravizza, M. (1994). Semi-compatibilism and the transfer of non-responsibility. *Philosophical Studies, 75*, 61–93.

Reiss, J. (2015). *Causation, evidence, and inference*. New York: Routledge.

Reutlinger, A. (2013). *A theory of causation in the social and biological science*. New York: Palgrave Macmillan.

Roskies, A. L. (2012). How does the neuroscience of decision making bear on our understanding of moral responsibility and free will? *Current Opinion in Neurobiology, 22*, 1022–1026.

Rubin, D. B. (1974). Estimating causal effects of treatments in randomized and non-randomized studies. *Journal of Educational Psychology, 66*, 688–701.

Rubin, D. B. (1990). Formal modes of statistical inference for causal effects. *Journal of Statistical Planning and Inference, 25*, 279–292.

Runyan, J. D. (2014). *Human agency and neural causes: Philosophy of action and the neuroscience of voluntary agency*. London, UK: Palgrave Macmillan.

Russell, B. (1919). *Introduction to mathematical philosophy*. London, UK: George Allen and Unwin.

Russell, P., & Deery, O. (2013). *The philosophy of free will: Essential readings from the contemporary debates*. New York: Oxford University Press.

Seeley, W. W., Menon, V., Schatzberg, A. F., Keller, J., Glover, G. H., Kenna, H., et al. (2007). Dissociable intrinsic connectivity networks for salience processing and executive control. *Journal of Neuroscience: The Official Journal of the Society for Neuroscience, 27*, 2349–2356.

Seligman, M. E. P., Railton, P., Baumeister, R. F., & Sripada, C. (2013). Navigating into the future or driven by the past. *Perspectives on Psychological Science, 8*, 119–141.

Siegler, R. S. (2006). Microgenetic analyses of learning. In W. Damon, R. M. Lerner, D. Kuhn, & R. S. Siegler (Eds.), *Handbook of child psychology: Cognition, perception, and language* (6th ed., Vol. 2, pp. 464–510). New York: Wiley.

Smilansky, S. (2002). *Free will, fundamental dualism, and the centrality of illusion*. Retrieved from http://evans-experientialism.freewebspace.com/smilansky.htm

Smith, S. M., Fox, P. T., Miller, K. L., Glahn, D. C., Fox, P. M., Mackay, C. E., et al. (2009). Correspondence of the brain's functional architecture during activation and rest. *Proceedings of the National Academy of Sciences of the United States of America, 106*, 13040–13045.

Spreng, R. N., Mar, R. A., & Kim, A. S. (2009). The common neural basis of autobiographical memory, prospection, navigation, theory of mind, and the default mode: A quantitative meta-analysis. *Journal of Cognitive Neuroscience, 21*, 489–510.

Sripada, C., Railton, P., Baumeister, R. F., & Seligman, M. E. P. (2013). Reply to comment. *Perspectives on Psychological Science, 8*, 151–154.

Thelen, E., & Smith, L. B. (1994). *A dynamic systems approach to the development of cognition and action*. Cambridge, MA: MIT Press.

Timmins, A. (2013). Kuhnian consensus & historiography. *Journal of the Philosophy of History, 7*, 82–105.

Touroutoglou, A., Hollenbeck, M., Dickerson, B. C., & Feldman Barrett, L. (2012). Dissociable large-scale networks anchored in the right anterior insula subserve affective experience and attention. *NeuroImage, 60*, 1947–1958.

Tryon, W. W. (2009). Missing mechanism information. *American Psychologist, 64*, 273–274.

Tryon, W. W. (2012a). A connectionist network approach to psychological science: Core and corollary principles. *Review of General Psychology, 16*, 305–317.

Tryon, W. W. (2012b). Emergence vs. reductionism. *American Psychologist, 67*, 806–807.

Tse, P. U. (2013). *The neural basis of free will: Criterial causation*. Cambridge, MA: MIT Press.

Vihvelin, K. (2013). *Causes, laws, and free will: Why determinism doesn't matter*. New York: Oxford University Press.

Vincent, J. L., Kahn, I., Snyder, A. Z., Raichle, M. E., & Buckner, R. L. (2008). Evidence for a frontoparietal control system revealed by intrinsic functional connectivity. *Journal of Neurophysiology, 100*, 3328–3342.

Wager, T. D., Barrett, L. F., Bliss-Moreau, E., Lindquist, K., Duncan, S., Kober, H., et al. (2008). The neuroimaging of emotion. In M. Lewis, J. M. Haviland-Jones, & L. F. Barrett (Eds.), *The handbook of emotions* (3rd ed., pp. 249–271). New York: Guilford Press.

Wegner, D. M. (2002). *The illusion of conscious will*. Cambridge, MA: MIT Press.

Witherington, D. C. (2014). Self-organization and explanatory pluralism: Avoiding the snares of reductionism in developmental science. *Research in Human Development, 11*, 22–36.

Yarkoni, T., Poldrack, R. A., Nichols, T. E., Van Essen, D. C., & Wager, T. D. (2011). Large-scale automated synthesis of human functional neuroimaging data. *Nature Methods, 8*, 665–670.

Yeo, B. T., Krienen, F. M., Sepulcre, J., Sabuncu, M. R., Lashkari, D., Hollinshead, M., et al. (2011). The organization of the human cerebral cortex estimated by intrinsic functional connectivity. *Journal of Neurophysiology, 106*, 1125–1165.

Young, G. (2011). *Development and causality: Neo-Piagetian perspectives*. New York: Springer Science + Business Media.

Young, G. (2012). A unitary Neo-Piagetian/Neo-Eriksonian model of development: Fundamental assumptions and meta-issues. *New Ideas in Psychology, 30*, 241–249.

Young, G. (2014). *Malingering, feigning, and response bias in psychiatric/psychological injury: Implications for practice and court*. Dordrecht, Netherlands: Springer Science + Business Media.

Models and Systems of Causality of Behavior

5

Chapter Introduction

Models in science range from metatheoretical worldviews, to theories and mini-theories, to local models on reduced subject matter, to straightforward empirical-centered hypotheses in research. The present chapter considers three major models in psychology that are more theories than mini-theories or larger worldviews—biopsychosocial, embodiment, and systems theory.

The biopsychosocial model was developed originally to help explain the origins of disordered behavior, psychosomatic conditions, vulnerabilities to psychopathology, etc. (Melchert, 2015; Sperry, 2009), but also it has been applied to development and other areas of psychology (Overton, 2015; Young, 2011). It allows for a multifactorial consideration of each of the causal factors underlying behavior, its expression and, if applicable, its treatment. As such, it stands as a fundamental model undergirding the present work. I consider the psychological portion of the biopsychosocial model as "personal" in nature. For example, it includes free will as a factor. This topic is one of the central ones in the book.

The view of embodiment in behavior has been applied especially to the area of cognition, but it is gaining widespread currency as a potential unifying model in psychology (Chemero, 2013). The research undertaken and the findings are emerging in the area are intriguing.

Dynamical systems theory and other systems approaches (related to complexity) offer the potential to explain both the structure and causal origins of behavior (Thelen & Smith, 1994; Young, 2011). Moreover, the models are general enough to apply to nonliving systems, as well. The work in this area includes key concepts for the present book, such as emergence, self-organization, attractors, and circular causality.

Along with other newer models in the field of psychology and related disciplines, such as network modeling and differential susceptibility, the present work has a broad theoretical basis with which to work and to attempt to integrate toward a unifying model for psychology.

Introduction

The biopsychosocial model, by definition, attempts to be an integrative one. Originally, it was developed in the medical and illness context to indicate the multifactorial nature of health and disease. It has been applied to other areas of psychology, including psychotherapy and development. With modification, it can stand as an integrative model in many domains of psychology. However, it is more descriptive of behavior and its causes than offering insight in exact mechanisms of its origins. The model of embodiment discussed in the present chapter also might suffer from this lack. The systems model considers the

G. Young, *Unifying Causality and Psychology*, DOI 10.1007/978-3-319-24094-7_5

multiplicity of factors that are involved in behavior, like the biopsychosocial model, but, in addition, it includes plausible mechanisms of behavioral expression and change through its concepts of self-organization, emergence, attractors, being on the cusp of change at far from equilibrium, the butterfly effect, and so on.

Together, the three models discussed in this chapter are central to the task of understanding of behavioral causality. Each offers conceptual, methodological, and empirical foundations that themselves should be integrated into a unified model of behavioral causality, along with other relevant models. Moreover, they allow room for free will as one factor in the array of factors that influence behavior, and so fit the framework that the present work promotes.

In the following section, I present in depth the biopsychosocial model and then turn to the embodiment and systems models. Because I have presented in great depth the biopsychosocial model and the systems model in Young (2011), the chapter presents less material on these models relative to the one of embodiment. The latter model is a fascinating one, and the evidence for its validity is growing. Nevertheless, it can be seen as one more way of combining biopsychosocial influences in behavioral causality. That being said, I have developed in this chapter concepts related to embodiment that might be quite relevant (e.g., embodied causation; causal embodiment).

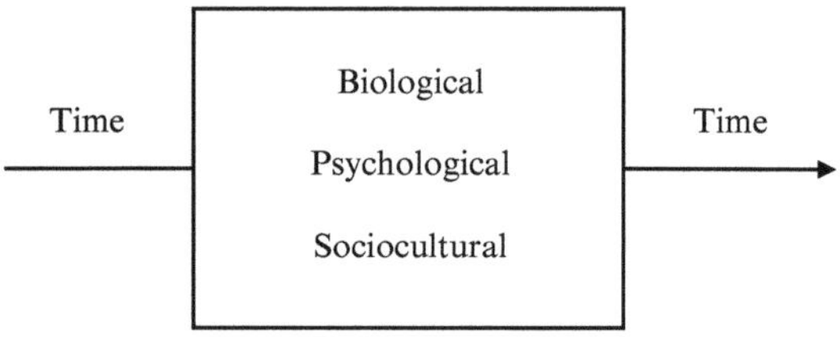

Fig. 5.1 The biopsychosocial metatheoretical approach. Human psychology is explained by the interactions among the three inextricably intertwined biopsychosocial dimensions across time. Adapted from Melchert (2011)

Biopsychosocial Model

Model

Health Melchert (2015) proposed a unifying concept for psychology and behavioral health care in terms of the biopsychosocial model that he labeled as biopsychosocial practice. According to Melchert, biological, psychological, and sociocultural influences, along with developmental ones, are "inextricably intertwined" in behavior (see Fig. 5.1). A science-based psychological approach provides a unified perspective on psychological practice. It can lead the field into a paradigmatic phase (Kuhn, 1962). According to Melchert (2015), the biopsychosocial approach is a metatheoretical one (although I disagree; it is more of a theoretical-level model than a metatheoretical one). For Melchert (2015) the biopsychosocial model not only is "not" a theoretical approach, but it is also not an eclectic, practice one. It needs to work in concert with an ethical stance in effective psychotherapeutic practice. Schools of thought about psychotherapy should be relegated under its umbrella.

Behavioral heath care should consider the following areas: (a) biological—general medical history, childhood health history, medications, health habits/behaviors; (b) psychological—history of presenting problems, level of psychological function, individual psychological history, substance use/addictions, suicidal ideation/risk assessment, individual development history, childhood abuse/neglect history, other trauma, mental status exam, personality style/characteristics; and (c) sociocultural—relationships/support system, current living situation, family history, education, employment, financial resources, legal/criminal issues, military record, activities/interests/hobbies, religion/spirituality, and (multi) cultural issues.

Magnavita and Anchin (2014) also supported the value of the biopsychosocial model in psychotherapy. Like Melchert (2015), they considered it a unifying construct. They contrasted the holistic and reductionistic approaches to science, referring to the latter as insufficient. For Magnavita and Anchin (2014), the two approaches are complementary and stand in a dialectical relationship. In terms of paradigm, the biopsychosocial model is a systems metatheory that is a holistic system one. In this sense, it should be called biopsychosocial systems theory. This approach potentially provides unifying principles for psychotherapy and accommodates to the limits in the field that are evident at present.

Note, as with my disagreement with Melchert (2015), I cannot support the notion that a biopsychosocial model is a metatheory. It is just not in the same camp as schools of thought such as relationism. Even referring to it as a biopsychosocial systems theory does not elevate it to meta-theoretical status.

Peterson, Goodie, and Andrasik (2015) described clinical health psychology in terms of the biopsychosocial model (see Fig. 5.2, based on the work of Belar & Deardorff, 2009, 2015). They elaborated the factor of the psychological component to include behavioral, emotional, and cognitive domains. They considered each of the factors (biological, psychological, social) as varying from minimal to significant.

McEwen and Getz (2013) illustrated how the medical model needs to incorporate psychosocial aspects. In the context of personalized medicine, they advocated that the person encompasses both biological and "biographical" components. In medicine, bio-molecular aspects of the person need to be informed by sociocultural ones, especially if the goal is to promote healthy brains and bodies, as well as healthy society. Human experience becomes "inscribed" in the developing person, for example, in epigenetics. Also, human experience can work either favorably or unfavorably [especially in cases of differentially susceptible genes having either protective resilient or reactive, potentially damaging alleles, depending on the presence of adverse or supportive environments, respectively, in a Gene × Environment interaction]. In adverse environments, stressors can create an "allostasis" overload that is chronically unbuffered, leading to pathogenesis and disease.

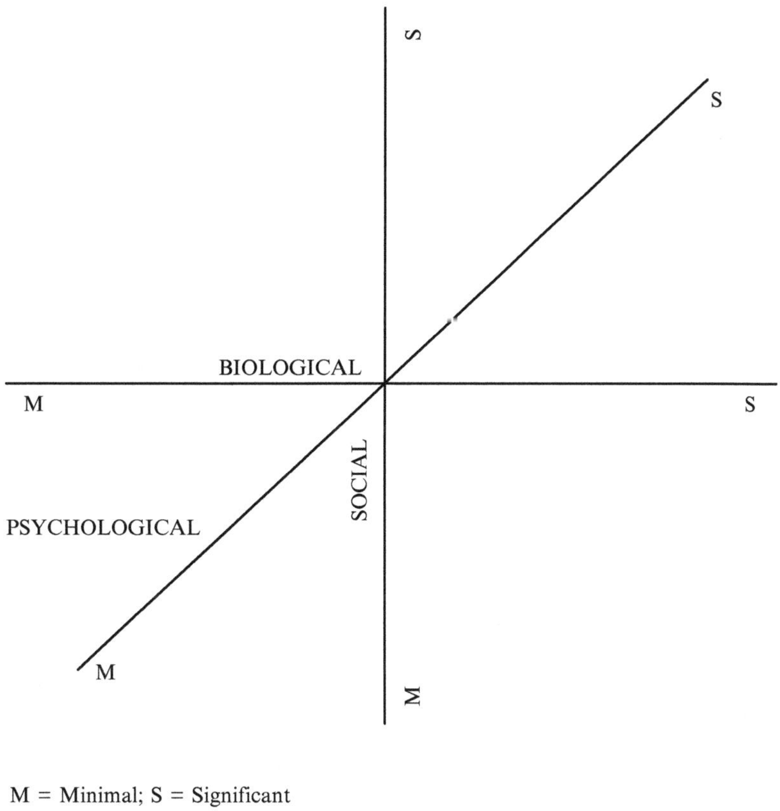

Fig. 5.2 A domain and intensity biopsychosocial model. The factors in the biopsychosocial model include different domains, and they vary in intensity toward their contributions to clinical psychological health. Adapted from Peterson et al. (2015)

McEwen and Getz (2013) indicated that protection and damage in health involves networked, interacting, nonlinearly dynamic mediators that can affect all body organs, including the brain. The brain is plastic, early life experiences mark it, and the social context (gradient, e.g., socioeconomic status, SES) has a major role to play in individual and public health.

Both Helmchen (2013) and Stier (2014) supported a biopsychosocial model of mental illness. At the same time, it needs to specify better how its major components interact and operate, so that it is integrative rather than arbitrary.

Wiggins and Monk (2013) presented an integrated model of psychopathology that speaks to the biopsychosocial model (see Fig. 5.3). It includes changes in developmental disorder manifestation with context and genetic variation. The different levels are interactive, and in ways that differ depending on developmental period.

Livneh, Chan, and Kaya (2014) presented models of disability that encapsulate causation of stigma. These include the moral, biomedical, functional, social, and biopsychosocial models (e.g., Schultz & Stewart, 2008). As for specific origins (determinants) of stigma, the authors developed a two-dimensional model that varies along the phylogenetic ontogenetic continuum and whether sources are internally or externally derived (e.g., inner needs, socioculture, respectively). Livneh et al. (2014) concluded by presenting relevant attitude change strategies.

Pain The primary model of pain experience is that it is biopsychosocial (Gatchel, McGeary, McGeary, & Lippe, 2014; Jensen & Turk, 2014). Flor (2014) noted there is a brain–body interaction, involving neurophysiological characteristics of pain. Treatment should not only be pharmacological but also psychological.

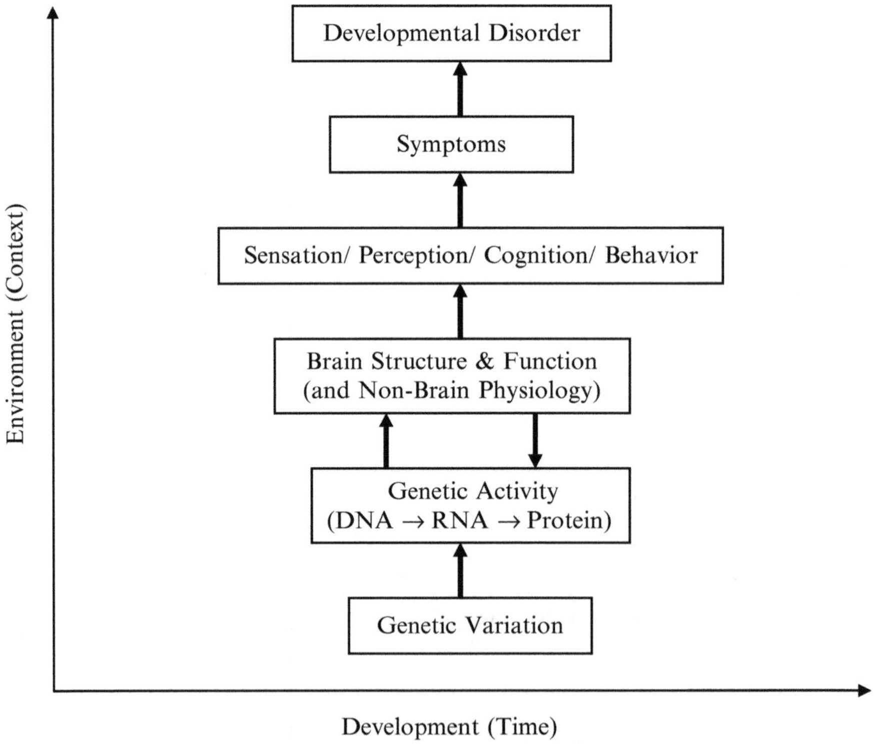

Fig. 5.3 The translational development neuroscience framework. The figure indicates the generic pathway from genetic variation to disorder. Genes prescribe protein activity that leads to the construction of neural structure and function. Psychological activity derives from brain function in context. In unsupportive rather than supportive environments, brain, psychological processes, development, and behavior can become disordered. Adapted from Wiggins and Monk (2013)

Psychological interventions can have effects on "somatic" processes, in general. The biopsychosocial model of pain also has considered its positive consequences (Bastian, Jetten, Hornsey, & Leknes, 2014). Generally, biopsychosocial models of somatic-related disorders should consider predisposing, precipitating, and perpetuating factors (Lievesley, Rimes, & Chalder, 2014).

Two studies recently explored the relationship between pain and cognition. Schoth, Nunes, and Liossi (2012) studied the role of attentional bias in the causation and maintenance of chronic pain. It leads to focusing on pain-related information, especially in both initial orienting of attention and in maintained, later attention, findings that are consistent with a role for rumination in perpetuating pain. This attentional bias could affect negatively more general cognitive performance.

Wager and Atlas (2013) reviewed neuroimaging research to show that pain can be manipulated psychologically because it is influenced by social-cognitive processes. Even placebos constitute cognitive interventions that can produce real changes in the processing of pain. Pain experience is intimately linked to megamaps in working memory, emotion, and physical pain in the brain that partially overlap, and also pain is related to the opioid system. According to Wager and Atlas (2013), biology, cognition, emotion, and social processes interact in pain experience, indicating that mental events are more than localized brain patterns.

Comment Weidig and Michaux (2015) proposed an integrative framework for the biopsychosocial model. They noted an absence of relationship understanding explicit means of relating between biological and psychological processes. Essentially, their model referred to the domain of memory as an integrative ground. In this regard, they referred to confined and communicative memories. The former are associative, motor, and sensory memories, and the latter concern cultural memes.

Carey, Mansell, and Tai (2014) argued that the biopsychosocial model is missing a mechanism underlying it, and, in this regard, they proposed a negative feedback one. Negative feedback serves to keep systems at equilibrium after environmental perturbations. In the broadest sense, it includes feed forward (damage prevention) mechanisms. Understanding individuals as biopsychosocial entities under the influence of negative feedback provides one common embodied process for understanding behavior. In this vein, action is not the result of a trigger that activates a chain leading to it, but an effort to reinstate disturbed states due to environmental impact to their reference levels. I note that any perspective on adaptive, flexible, and changing behavior should offer opportunities for functional change in state, or adaptive new references, as well as their return to a reference point.

Conclusion My approach to the question of the value of the biopsychosocial model and the mechanisms involved is to refer to the full array of personal psychological processes that mediate interaction among biology (body), psychology (e.g., mind), and the social (environment) in determining behavior outcome, including in development or of illness or abnormal behavior. The personal processes involved include appraisals, beliefs, attitude, motivation, and so on. The grand question is how these multifactorial contributions to behavior interact over time in the specific micromoments of their transactions as they create the longitudinal course of development and behavioral change.

In addition, mechanism does not just lie in a biophysical process or location, such as the brain, but in a process that is more general and covers all aspects of the biopsychosocial system. In this sense, in the biopsychosocial model, one can speak of biopsychosocial inputs, biopsychosocial processes, and biopsychosocial outputs (with the processes including biopsychosocial therapy), while acknowledging that the distinctions between these levels are not as clearly cut as presented.

Further, the common metric that could describe both the behavioral structure and the mechanisms involved in its undergirding and change must be general enough to cover each of the biological, personal/psychological, and social components of the model. Systems theory does afford the necessary language in these regards, in that it describes systems in terms of constituents that adopt patterns of organization, which, in and of itself, is sufficient to lead to organizational preservation or change, e.g., depending on whether the system involved has gravitated to the pressure point of being too far from equilibrium. Embodiment theory might help, too, in that body, brain, behavior, and mind, and so on, are not really separate entities but ones that constitutively help compose and reflect each other, so that stability and change processes for one necessarily entail stability and change processes for the others.

However, it might be best to find the underlying common metric to mechanistic processes across the biological, personal/psychological, and social, as well as cultural/contextual components involved in establishing behavioral stability and instability. The one that I find pertinent in this regard concerns activation/inhibition coordination (Young, 2011). In this regard, behavior as well as brain processes can be redescribed quite well in this type of language. For example, I developed this concept while watching the baby reach, noticing how interfering movements are controlled better in the right arm and hand (and the left hemisphere) relative to the opposite sides involved (Young & Gagnon, 1990). Social behavior can be described in terms of activation/inhibition coordination, as well. Moreover, psychotherapy can be conceived as attempts to better structure behavioral activation/inhibition coordinations in patients (and in the underlying brain processes involved). Similarly, throughout the present work, wherever I find evidence of it, I indicate how the brain is involved in activation/inhibition coordination. Later in the book (see Chap. 31), I pursue this line of thought and show how a model of activation/inhibition coordination provides a powerful mechanism for preserving behavioral statis and for effecting its change.

Interim Conclusions

The present book focuses on the free will as an influential force in the causality of behavior, and it embeds easily in the biopsychosocial framework. The personal contributions we bring to our own growth and change in behavior are based on our positioning as selves at least somewhat free of biology and environment, which are passive influences compared to our active, agentic selves, and its elements related to free will, for example.

The next section of the chapter examines the model of embodiment, which relates cognition, in particular, to body-centric processes rather than merely fully abstract, representational ones. Models generally emphasize their special contributions in silos to underscore their uniqueness, and then they begin to differentiate and integrate other conceptions under their umbrellas. This is happening to the embodiment model, as it moves to a more active, agentic formulation of behavioral expression, for example. In this sense, its unifying potential in psychology holds promise, as it maintains. Nevertheless, all the major models in psychology need the type of integration toward unification being promoted in the present work, and there is not one by itself that should be privileged.

The Embodiment Model

Cognition Embodied

Model

Foglia and Wilson (2013) noted that the construct of embodied cognition is providing new perspectives on mind–body reductionism. This approach underscores the role of sensory and motor functions in cognitive activity. The mind is considered anchored in sensory and motor groundings. The boundaries between cognition, body, and context are blurred ("no fracture"). Therefore, the agent's body constrains, regulates, and fashions the nature of cognition. This happens not necessarily through direct intrinsic control but through experiential reenactment in perceptual-action systems moderated by the brain. Information is not just represented abstractly and nonmodally. Knowledge is not just symbolic, representational, and propositional. Activity is not simply the result of representational instructions.

Among other mechanisms, mirror neurons subserve embodied cognition. They activate in observing/understanding another's action and, moreover, they are activated when the body acts the same way (Rizzolatti & Craighero, 2004). Therefore, in understanding/mentalizing about the other, mirror neurons ensure that the necessary body/motor systems are intrinsically involved. This network provides the foundation for complex social life, social coordination, empathic emotion, learning by imitation, and communication by language. Single-cell research in humans has provided the first evidence of neurons responding to both the observation and execution of grasping actions (Mukamel, Ekstrom, Kaplan, Iacoboni, & Fried, 2010), so that even individual neurons are now being detected with "mirror-like properties."

For Foglia and Wilson (2013), the implications of embodied cognition include cognition being "body-scaled" even if it is "disconnected" from the environment. Second, the body is involved in cognition not only directly (in online embodiment) but also indirectly (in neural simulation, offline embodiment). Third, embodied online activity can be stored for use later in offline processing. Fourth, embodied cognition requires certain advances in evolutionary thresholds, but because species' bodies are different, their embodied cognition is different.

As for the roles or functions of embodied cognition, it serves as constraint and distributor. For the former, the body functions to cognitively constrain, e.g., talking/thinking about objects engages specific bodily activity patterns. For the latter, the body "spreads" cognitive activity over neural and nonneural structures, helping partially in realizing mentation. That is, the body does not just simply transduce perceptual input into cognition, in preparation to produce behavioral output from internal cognitive processing; but, rather, the body is an active control agent in perception and action.

Foglia and Wilson (2013) concluded that embodied cognition addresses the traditional divide between considering the psychological as autonomous and the mind as reducible to the body (brain). An integrated perspective based on embodied cognition would acknowledge that cognition is body-grounded but also not wholly determined in this way, thereby allowing for autonomy of a "kind" to psychological processing.

Philosophy

Slife and Christensen (2013) presented a philosophical approach to psychology that is compatible with the embodied one, called "hermeneutic realism." The focus in psychology should be not on "self-contained objects" but, rather, on "contextually-constituted" meanings. Moreover, the meanings are neither purely relativistic nor subjective, but are "grounded in the reality of the world." Objects form relationships of which their "betweenness" is more relevant to understanding behavior than are the objects themselves. In this view, free will exists but not in isolation from mechanistic forces. Rather, it exists as a range of possibilities involving constraints and opportunities.

Tonneau (2013) also presented a philosophical view compatible with embodied cognition. In "neorealism," cognition and environment are unified. The contents of cognition reflect parts of the environment. In this regard, consciousness emanates from the relationship between knower and known.

Embodied Cognition

Views

There are different points of view on the degree that embodiment characterizes cognition. In general, I have promoted the embodied cognition view, but there are dissenters. At the other extreme, there are radical versions in which the essence of behavior, brain, and all their manifestations are embodied.

Skepticism According to Wellsby and Pexman (2014), although embodied cognition is a powerful concept (e.g., Glenberg & Gallese, 2012), some argue that the converse concept of disembodied cognition is still relevant (see Meteyard, Cuadrado, Bahrami, & Viglicco, 2012). A "strong" embodied cognition model maintains that cognition is constituted in sensorimotor processing and action, recreating direct sensory experiences. "Secondary" embodiment models maintain that cognitive processing activates, as a by-product, sensorimotor brain areas. A "weak" embodiment model suggests that cognitive concepts derive partially from sensorimotor experience/information, but end up as independent organization.

Wilson and Golonka (2013) argued that embodied cognition is not merely about how body states modify mind states. Rather, disembodied cognition does not exist, and embodiment occupies the center in the organism's effort to resolve any problem or tasks.

Radicalism A combined, hybrid, or "pluralist" embodied model allows for more embodiment processing for concrete concepts and less so for abstract ones, which might even be disembodied (e.g., Dove, 2011). In this regard, Chemero (2013) presented the notion of a "radical embodied cognitive science." It integrates phenomenological, ecological, and dynamical systems approaches to psychology. For example, in this view, mental representations are "action-oriented" (Clark, 1997). Representations are geared to an organism's "not-neutral" affordant perceptions of the environment (Gibson, 1979), as are the actions involved. The approach is consistent with a computational one, at least if one broadens the scope and refers to a "wide computationalism." In the latter perspective, computational system representations span body, brain, and context.

Hutto (2013) proposed a similar approach to radical embodied cognitive science, which he labeled "radical enactivism". In this approach, mental activity is considered embodied activity. It contrasts with the approach of traditional cognitivism, which focuses on internalism, intellectualism, and individualism. Cognition is not hands-off (off-stage, behind-the-scenes) but a hands-on engagement of the organism with features of the environment in specific ways. Cognition is self-organizing, contextualized, messily interactive, and "without representing, reasoning, or thinking" about the contextual world in ways involving content ("contentful ways"). That being said, meaning-making emerges from shared linguistic practices and narration, so that the mind is socially scaffolded.

Finally, Kiverstein and Miller (2015) presented an updated version of radical embodied cognitive neuroscience. They included the notion that emotions and cognitions are inseparable and that both are deeply dependent on the living body. They promoted an ecological and dynamical approach to cognitive neuroscience that builds on the work of Chemero (2009) and Barrett (2011), among others.

Comment

In the embodied point of view, I find an unresolved tension between its Gibsonian anti-representational stance and its valuation of action-oriented representations. The model is both "skeptical" of representations yet accentuates an embodied perspective on them. For Gibson, the thinker is embedded in the world, and does not "causally impinge" on it. Rather, the person interacts dynamically with it, and does not have to form representations to do so. However, although this argument might apply to perception and perceptual learning, which were the focus of Gibson's work, it applies less readily to the cognitive sphere. A more dynamical model of environment, body, and mind might argue that abstract representations can form beyond the effects of the environment on the person, but they are still environmentally mediated and constitutive of interaction with the environment. That is, neither the extreme embodiment view nor the extreme non-embodiment view of cognition seems adequate in explaining cognition.

Social/Emotional

The concept of extended mind is one of an embodied cognition or an enactive mind (Robinson, 2013). The mind interacts with body and world, and these interactions are constitutive of and inseparable from thought. Mind participates in material events and, as it does so, feels or experiences phenomenologically. Therefore, mind arises out of affect and conation standing as intermediaries between the physical movements of the body and the qualities of mind. For Robinson (2013), "affective-becoming-conative sociality" is the primary extension of "body-becoming-mind."

[Similarly, Voestermans and Verheggen (2013) have applied the concept of embodiment to culture.]

McGann, De Jaegher, and Di Paolo (2013) provided insight into the dynamical and enactive nature of mind. It does not inhere in the person but is dynamically emergent in individual–context interaction. We make sense of the world by coupling, coordinating, and dynamically adapting to its constraints (e.g., Kelso, 2009). Cognition is relational and the brain is interactive and mediating. When disorder arises, it's not localized in the individual but resides in the engagements of the individual in the constitutive context. In this perspective, the "incorporated" is considered environmental rather than external.

In the embodied view of social cognition (Winkielman & Kavanagh, 2013), information processing is shaped by specific body and nervous system "forms," along with interactions in the physical environment. Therefore, thinking involves, in part, the reproduction or "simulation" of motor and experiential states "presented" when the individual engages with the focus of perception.

Fuchs and Koch (2014) extended the embodiment concept into the emotional realm. They referred to "embodied affectivity," personal bodily resonance, inter-affectivity, interbodily resonance, movement/vitality rhythms/contours, and the relevance of these concepts for psychopathology and therapy.

Similarly, Gapenne (2014) proposed an embodied concept of the self. The self and world (exterior) are co-constituted in action and in proprioception coupling. He referred to this concept as applying to even the simplest of life forms. In this vein, Soliman, Gibson, and Glenberg (2013) proposed that the ground of culture influences the embodiment of sensorimotor mechanisms in the constitution of thoughts. The mechanism of embodiment can serve the cognitive, social, and cultural levels. Therefore, sensorimotor processes can help unify psychology. Bodily mechanisms might reflect a foundational principle in the structural and functional organization of the brain.

Also, Kyselo and Tschacher (2014) developed a joint enactive model of dyadic relationships that is based on dynamical systems theory (e.g., joint attractors developing over self and other). This conceptualization is not an embodied one, per se, but stems from it in that individuation is conceived as both a person-centered cognitive embodiment and a social, networked one. Similarly, Gallotti (2013) referred to a second-personal plural approach to social cognition, or the "we" mode.

Evidence

Cognitive

Glenberg, Witt, and Metcalfe (2013) provided a range of studies demonstrating the importance of embodiment in cognition. First, they reminded that in the embodied cognition view, action shapes cognition; thinking is strongly influenced by body; cognition reflects a dynamic interplay of brain, bodily action, and perception; the body in action fashions the self and language; cognition and perception exist in order to permit and guide bodily movement; action intention influences perception; emotions exist also to underpin action, and so on.

Some findings in support of this model follow. Glenberg et al. (2013) reviewed that Casasanto (2011) found that right- and left-handers' thinking about action verbs used different regions of the brain. Havas, Glenberg, Gutowski, Lucarelli, and Davidson (2010) showed that inhibiting frowning by blocking the corrugator muscle with botox slows sentence processing for descriptions of sad and angry events but not happy ones. These studies revealed that thinking appears "grounded" in the "sensorimotor system."

Perception appears similarly grounded in the action system. Gibson's (1979) concept of affordances is consistent with this notion. Self-locomotion is instrumental in perception (Held & Hein, 1963, in a kitten study). Action is essential for learning how to perceive (Campos et al., 2000; in an infant study).

With adults, Brockmole, Davoli, Abrams, and Witt (2013) found that having participants place their hands next to the visual display in studies influences their visual attention, detection, search, and inhibition processes. Also, variations in apparent size of participants' bodies in virtual reality research affect the perceived distance to objects and their size (Linkenauger, Mohler, & Bülthoff, 2011). The hand is used to scale the size of objects that are graspable (Linkenauger, Witt, & Proffitt, 2011).

Mechanisms exist for coordinating discourse by aligning speaker rate, word choice, and syntax (Pickering & Garrod, 2013). Memory is enhanced when it is amenable to actions by the self, or when "self involvement" otherwise is involved (e.g., Engelcamp, 1995). Hearing action words, such as "pick," involving the hand, activates regions of the brain controlling hand movements (Hauk, Johnsrude, & Pulvemüller, 2004). Understanding emotion-relevant language engages emotion-related neural systems (Havas et al., 2010). Inclusion of action facilitates learning to read, solving mathematical problems, etc. (e.g., Glenberg, Willford, Gibson, Goldberg, & Zhu, 2012).

Glenberg et al. (2013) have integrated a wide-ranging literature related to embodied cognition. They have shown its importance in basic processes, such as perception, and the role of the sensorimotor system even in more advanced cognitive activities, such as language and education.

Chemical

Semin and de Groot (2013) related human sociality to "shared bodily state." People respond to other's chemosignals, and it usually takes place outside of "verbal awareness," or automatically. We are capable of distinguishing another's sweat depending on the state in which it was collected. Sociality has a chemical basis that leads us to simulate the signals received in chemosensory perception so that we "reproduce" the other's emotional state. Communication is "grounded" and "vicariously" reconstituted.

Oxytocin is being used for social enhancement (Farah, 2012). It is given intravenously or in inhaled doses to alter behavior (e.g., trust, generosity). Stallen, De Dreu, Shalvi, Smidts, and Sanfey (2012) investigated the degree to which it stimulates in-group conformity. The results showed that it can influence subjective preferences in context.

In general, chemosignals are better understood as being important in human emotions (de Groot, Smeets, Kaldewaij, Duijndam, & Semin, 2012). The signals are outside of conscious access but have emotion-specific effects. In this study, fear chemosignals generated facial expressions of fear (medial frontal is activity in EMG recording) and increased sniff magnitude/eye scanning (fear sensory acquisition). In contrast, disgust chemosignals generated disgust-related facial expressions (in levator labii activity). de Groot et al. (2012) concluded that their work supports an embodied social-communication model (Semin, 2007).

Brain

Aspell et al. (2013) provided evidence that self-consciousness and the body self form integrated cortical systems for bodily self-consciousness. Embodied cognition extends into consciousness and self-cognition. Integration includes signals from inside and outside the body (interoceptive and exteroceptive signals, respectively), which are associated with distinct anatomical systems. Consult their fascinating study on heartbeat, projected ("virtual") bodies, and their synchronization in "cardio-visual" signals.

Pulvermüller (2013) presented evidence on the brain mechanisms involved in "embodied" semantics, as well as abstract-symbolic general-meaning semantics. The embodied mechanisms are anchored in sensorimotor neural systems, in contrast to the non-embodied ones, which are anchored in multimodal convergence zones (e.g., prefrontal, posterior parietal, temporal cortex). Pulvermüller noted that the "semantic hubs" in the brain seem to express differential semantic contributions. There are semantic category effects. For example, the left inferior frontal cortex (iFC) and bilateral frontocentral motor systems are most strongly active when processing action-related phrases and words. However, at the supramarginal gyrus, the left iFC is most strongly activated by spatial language. The temporal cortex is more involved in sounds, names, color/form words, and emotional terms. Pulvermüller (2013) presented multiple findings relating the making of meaning to neuronal activity, including in sensory and motor areas of the cortex.

The currents toward an integrated rather than isolationist view of person, brain, and environment include the work of Schilbach et al. (2013; and commentaries). Schilbach et al. (2013) referred to a second-person neuroscience, which they contrasted with a "spectator" view of cognition. Rather than using detached inference-making in social knowing, we immediately experience, interact, engage with, and know the other through the engagement. The world is not "ready-made" or out there, and passively construed; rather, it is embodied actively in our situated, embedded, coupled cognition. Understanding of the world is facilitated by emotional engagement and leads to interaction dynamics that are emergent, and reflective of "inter-brain" effects on relational activity.

Froese, Iizuka, and Ikegami (2013) referred to the "brain-body-environment-body-brain" system in order to illustrate the dynamical, situated, embodied, constituted, coupled social interactional approach as a second-person neuroscience (see Fig. 5.4).

Overall, we can conclude that the embodiment approach provides a rich source of ideas conducive to integrating diverse areas of psychology, and the brain constitutes a primary focus in this regard.

Extensions

Introduction

In the following, I indicate how models of embodiment are being integrated with other models and being extended by this integration. In particular, there is work relating it to the biopsychosocial model, Gibsonian affordances, networks, and systems theory.

Biopsychosocial

The concept of embodiment provides one possible cohering mechanism to the biopsychosocial model. Zhang and Risen (2014) referred to embodied motivation to understand goal activation. For example, sometimes physical and social

Actor/ Agent 1 Interacting with Actor/ Agent 2

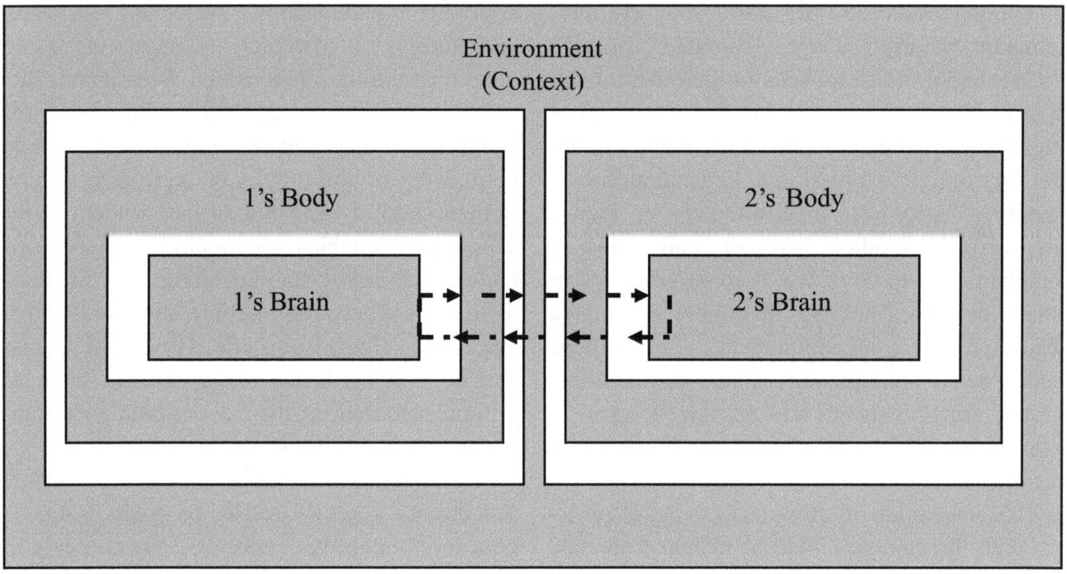

Fig. 5.4 Dynamical perspective on the interaction between two situated, embodied agents/actors. Not only does the person live an embodied brain-behavior relationship, for interacting people do, as well, which complicates understanding of dyadic and group processes. The influence of environmental context on the reciprocal, multiple embodiments that take place in human interaction complicate even more any understanding of behavior. Adapted from Froese et al. (2013)

warmth correlate positively, but they might correlate negatively, too, depending on context.

Clearly, biological influences become embodied in brain and behavior. But embodiment can also influence reciprocally brain and behavior. Also, it can affect social and affective processes, but in turn these can affect embodiment. Ultimately, the person is the seat of embodiment, and can influence it, in turn, thereby affecting its influence on biology, brain, behavior, and him- or herself as an acting agent.

Affordances

McGann (2014) extended the construct of radical embodied cognition (Chemero, 2009) by supporting its alignment with an intentional theory of Gibsonian ecological affordances (Gibson, 1986; Heft, 1989). The mind is world-involving, situated, embedded, and participatory, and so on; the person is agentic and active; and the environment offers affordances of place that are joint. However, affordance-promoted actions cannot be understood without considering the embodied motivations and intentions in the dynamical, relational nature of affordances.

Bruineberg and Rietveld (2014) also attempted an embodied-focused integration of several predominant theories. They elaborated Gibson's (1979) model of affordances in the environment to include solicitations in a landscape or field of affordances in the econiche. Individuals in context, for example, expressing skilled intentionality, acquire a "grip" on the affordances or even a "hypergrip." Another way of understanding solicitations is to conceive them as gradients or prediction errors helping in attunement to the environment (or disattunement). Solicitations lead to active anticipatory patterns that facilitate optimal grip. Organisms are "selectively open" to affordances that are relevant to their particular circumstance.

This conception of affordances is quite consistent with the emerging field of radical embodied cognitive neuroscience (Chemero, 2009). For example, affordances function in a brain–body landscape and a brain–body–environment system.

Networks

Bruineberg and Rietveld (2014) attempted to integrate the free energy principle approach to the brain and also dynamical systems theory (especially in the concept of self-organization) into their embodiment theory. In the free energy principle (Friston, 2010, 2011, 2012, 2013), surprisal is a measure of the unexpectedness of an event, and free energy is the upper bound in surprisal that might obtain in some data, such that it is the sum of prediction errors or difference between anticipated and actual sensory input. Organisms strive to minimize free energy, for example, by using their "anticipating" brain. Perception and action subserve this principle, and, in consequence, reflect the nature of the environment (that is, the niche "implies" an organism's structure). The organism is an agent that "infers" the causal structure of the environment (not at the cognitive level, but in a generic adaptive sense, to reduce surprise).

Systems

As for dynamical systems theory, according to Bruineberg and Rietveld (2014), circular causality refers to intra-organismic, cross-level constraining relationships, whereas secondary circularity refers to organism-environment, mutually constraining relationships. Self-organization refers to the internal dynamics of a system that adapt to its components and context. System component might couple, or seek meta-stability in their coupling and in their independent action. This regime enables systems to be poised at the edge of stability–instability so that they are ready to transition between multiple attractors in their state space (Davids, Araújo, Hristovski, Passos, & Chow, 2012; Kelso, 2012). Just as there are optimal affordances, there are optimal metastable distances or environmental attunement.

The authors concluded that skilled activity reflects not a set of desires or goals. Rather, it concerns adaptive, coupled, dynamic self-organizing systems that allow for adequate interaction, or embodied attunement and anticipation involving organism in environment.

Favela (2014) expanded the radical embodied cognition model of Chemero (2009, 2013) to the area of neuroscience. In doing so, the author gave less importance to the Gibsonian model of affordances (e.g., Gibson, 1966/1979, 1973/1983) and gave more importance to the concept of self-organized criticality (e.g., Bak, Tang, & Wiesenfeld, 1987, 1988). Both views of radical cognitive embodiment highlight systems theory as central in efforts to unify psychology (e.g., Thelen & Smith, 1994, 2006). This approach is consistent with that of the present work.

Kugler, Kelso, and Turvey (1980) had already proposed that action is not a product of an inner agent using sensory representations to develop motor ones. Rather, human behavior is dynamically self-organizing and nondecomposable with the environment.

Siegel (2012) adopted a systems perspective in defining the mind as an embodied and relational process that regulates energy and information flow. It does so both within and between brains. The mind is a process that is emergent from brain, body, and relational activity. Mind, brain, and relationships are not independent entities but, rather, are three components of energy/information flow. They are three faces of "one reality."

Comment

Theorists in embodiment are leading the way in efforts to integrate theoretical work over different integrative models, by specifying linkages with their models and other leading ones, such as the biopsychosocial model and dynamical systems theory. At the same time, these extensions may be broadening the base of theoretical integration, but they are missing the theoretical glue that would make them genuinely integrated and interactive. I have argued already that integrative theoretical work in psychology needs to focus on mechanism, such as afforded by the concept of activation/inhibition coordination that cuts across both efforts to characterize the "what" of behavior and the "why." In this regard, in the next section of the chapter, I examine the embodiment model from the point of view of causation.

Causation

Wolff (2008) reviewed the major approaches to understanding causation. For Hume (1975), all that people can observe is spatial–temporal contiguity, successive events, and covariation, but not force, necessary connection, causal power, and energy (Dowe, 2000). Therefore, conjectures of causality do not relate to "reality." Causality is "invisible" and, therefore, in contemporary psychology, approaches adhering to this tradition study causality only in terms of observables and their frequencies.

Another Humean-type approach to causation concerns Bayesian probability network models (e.g., Pearl, 2000; Sloman, 2005). However, these theories involve statistical dependencies of the visible/observable and so also are limited in efforts to understand the intrinsic processes in causality.

Wolff (2008) added that Michotte's (1946/1963) model of causality in collisions does not address representation of force and energy mechanisms. Rather, it concerns perceptions, possible innate mechanisms, and perceptual illusions of causality more than casual understanding, per se.

Aside from Humean models of causation, physicalist models allow for partial isomorphism between representations and reality. Causal concepts can represent physical quantities in the real world, such as force and energy exchange or transmission (Dowe, 2000). However, according to Wolff (2008), physicalist models cannot differentiate causation from other events involving energy transfer.

Wolff (2008) referred to his force dynamics model as a physicalist model. However, instead of emphasizing energy transfer, it examines patterns of forces and end-states represented by position vectors. The vectors are (a) qualitative; (b) concern the variables of cause, "enable," and prevent; (c) apply equally to sociopsychological and physical causation; and (d) are represented as tendency, concordance, and the end state approached (result). The studies conducted in support of the model (Wolff, 2007) suggest that a person's causal concepts are formulated in terms of force configurations.

Wolff (2008) concluded that event dynamics are central to causal conceptualization and indicate that we are grounded to the real world as we try to represent causality. Finally, the model helps appreciate that "causation might be experienced in our own bodies."

Interim Conclusions

A concept that I created to encapsulate both causality and embodied cognition is compatible with the dynamic force approach to understanding causality. The concept that makes sense in this context is "embodied causation." It refers to the grounded "body-centric" origin of causal understanding. It is consistent with the Piagetian approach to understanding causality as a sensorimotor acquisition (Young, 2011) and also with the recent research on the development in infancy of causal understanding (e.g., Gopnik & Wellman, 2012).

The concept of embodied causation is consistent with the physicalist model of causality. Causality understanding develops from a participation in the environment in an active way that promotes better adaptation to the environment. In addition, the participation is heavily organism-centric from early in life, with the person's body constraining the nature of causal activity and shaping its understanding.

Finally, I propose that the developing embodied cognition that results from active grounding in the environment is marked by the centrality of causal search and understanding, given the importance of understanding causality for survival. Embodied cognition, therefore, includes embodied causation and, furthermore, exists in order to foster an exquisite and sensitive adaptivity in the environment. Cognition, in general, (as well as embodied cognition, in particular) is an adaptive function that exists especially to seek and explain causality because, without its proper understanding, adaptation to the environment cannot take place. The increasing emphasis on social cognition fits this perspective, as well. Without proper understanding of the complex vicissitudes of social causality, adaptation cannot take place effectively.

In all these senses, although I have been describing "embodied causation," the primary concept that covers the multifaceted cognition, embodiment, and causality search and understanding in behavior concerns "causal embodiment." We engage and embroil in the complexity and chaos of the physical and social worlds as active agents whom are physically and socially grounded in order to explore and create causal understanding so that we can relate appropriately to that environment, survive in it, and ultimately reproduce. It is not that we engage in cognition including on causality, through embodiment; rather, we live embodiment and cognition, including on causality, and causality is central to that project. In these regards, causal embodiment constitutes the quintessential modality of human behavior and its relational adaptation to the reality of the physical and social worlds.

In terms of mental illness and psychopathology, the concepts that I have proposed of embodied causality and causal embodiment subsume the equivalent concepts that also seem appropriate to propose—those of "embodied etiology" and "etiological embodiment." When behavior is disturbed or disordered, it is imperative to understand its psychiatric origins and, inevitably, that will be developmental and also sourced from the body. When deep understanding of behavior is sought, causality must be considered its central axis, including in mental disorder.

This discussion of embodied causation/etiology and causal/etiological embodiment concludes the section of the chapter on embodiment. In the next section, I move to presentation of work on systems theory. The reader will be familiar with some of its major concepts because of their discussion in the embodiment section. I value this theory greatly, viewing its concepts of emergence, self-organization, circular causality, the cusp of change, and so on, as ones that are applicable not only to my work on behavioral causality but also on integrating psychology.

Systems Models and Causality

Introduction

Systems models come in two major types. One concerns complex adaptive systems (CAS) and agent-based modeling, and the like, and the other nonlinear dynamical systems, and the like.

The latter approach comes in two varieties, as well, depending on whether the systems involved are soft-assembled from the bottom or ground up or might include some form of top-down influence, as well. Either way, causality is understood to reside in the system as a whole through the interactions among its components and their organization, its inputs and how they are processed in the system, and the contexts in which they dynamically reside and change or resist change.

Complex Adaptive Systems

Model

The major approaches to complexity in science reside in the approaches of Holland (2012) and Kauffman (1993, 2013). Holland (2012) described an approach to CAS that differs from Kauffman's (1993) approach. The latter is concerned with self-organization, order, emergence, far-from-equilibrium (the edge of chaos), criticality, landscapes, attractors, evolution, Boolean networks, and so on. Holland (2012) considered agents, networks and flows, control, autonomy, boundaries, signals and their processing, adaptation and evolution, emergence, and so on (see Fig. 5.5). Holland's approach is important to current network approaches and Kauffman's is important in nonlinear dynamical systems work.

Kauffman (2013) described how Darwinian natural selection and complexification could work synergistically in evolution. "Collective autocatalytic sets" can emerge spontaneously at system phase transitions. Indeed, their emergence is "expected." Moreover, because the "law" applies to any type of system amenable to phase transitions, it is generalizable beyond particular materials and processes. The sets can become webbed, linked, or cross-coupled, and transformed themselves. In becoming "generalized (collective) autocatalytic sets," they can "jointly cause … continued co-creativity" from one to the other(s), even in terms of creating new niches for each other. Kauffman (2013) concluded with the example of stars forming a galaxy that outlives (some of) them and also gives birth to new ones.

Lineweaver, Davies, and Ruse (2013a) collected workers in the hard and soft sciences and in philosophy to consider the role of complexity in evolution. Lineweaver, Davies, and Ruse (2013b) noted the difficulty in reaching a common understanding of complexity. About the thesis on the directionality of evolution toward increasing complexity, Gould (1996) had noted that there is no evolutionary driving force toward increasing complexity. However, complexity emerges in evolution in the sense of increasing diversity (e.g., McShea & Brandon, 2010) "by the simple accumulation of accidents." Others have noted that new niches provide the context for the survivability of increasing accidents/complexity and that "free energy" is needed to "generate" or "transfer" any increasing complexity. In this regard, Chaisson (2013) maintained that specific free energy flow/energy rate density is important in understanding increasing complexity in the universe and life. Lineweaver et al. (2013b) continued that there appears to be a complexity pyramid, and that free energy might be oriented to keep increasing the complexity of the most complex objects in the pyramid. This local complexification process affects other regions of the pyramid.

Applications

Based on the work of Wilson and Holt (2001), Merbitz, Merbitz, and Ripsch (2012) applied the concept of CAS to rehabilitation (see Tables 5.1 and 5.2). The upshot of the model for illness and health is that they are neither predictable nor amenable to modeling in simple cause-effect ways. Individuals are interconnected so that the systems that they form alter the predictability afforded by any one aspect of the system involved.

The integrated nature of illness and health is indicated in the complex model of coping, stress, and care giving in multiple sclerosis (Pakenham, 2012; see Fig. 5.6). Stressors are impacted by all of internal factors, context, treatment, perception/appraisal, and coping strategies and resources, which lead to adjustment outcome.

Walton (2014) viewed social problems as complex and multicaused. They are complex systems with dynamic, recursive trajectories, in

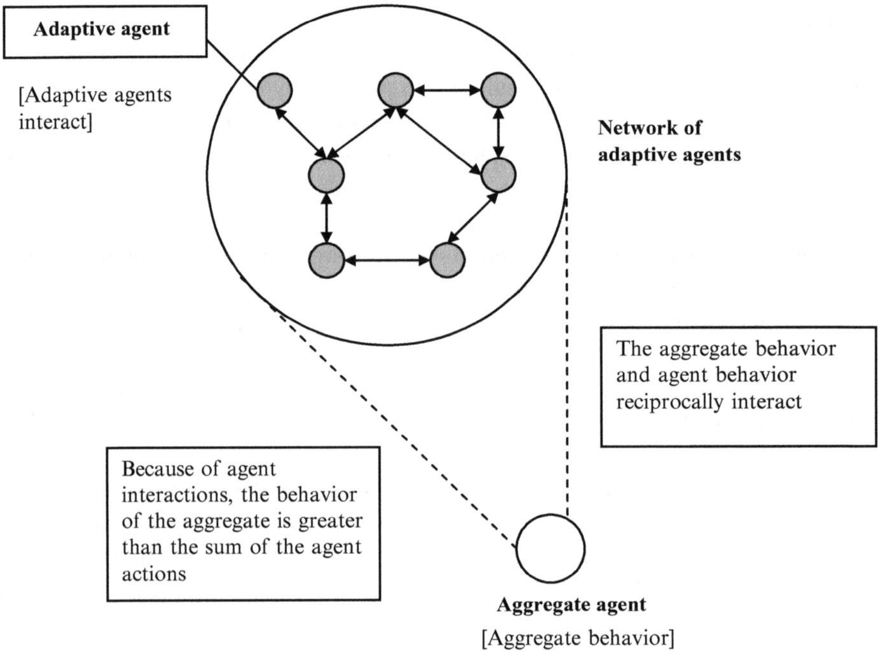

Fig. 5.5 Complex adaptive systems. A complex adaptive system is comprised of interacting network agents creating aggregate agents/behaviors greater than the sum of agent actions. One interesting variation of dynamical systems has been described by Holland (2012), complex adaptive systems (*cas*), in general, are characterized by subtle hierarchal arrangements of boundaries and signals. Nodes represent bounded entities (species, neurons, organelles); and internodal connections represent the signal flow. Agents are bounded (sub)systems capable of internal processing. They might be organized hierarchically. In other systems, the aggregate behavior depends on local interactions in distributed control. Learning can take place in such *autonomous systems*, for they are not driven alone by current ongoing stimuli. Hierarchies could result, of enclosing semi-permeable boundaries, with matching signals at each level.

The components of a *cas* are bounded subsystems (agents) that adapt or learn as they interact. The agents "accept" some signals and ignore others, with "programs" inside the boundary present for processing/sending signals. Also, there are and mechanisms in place for changing (adapting) a program in response to learning/experience.

Emergence comes from patterns or properties that appear under the constraints imposed by the rules of combination in a system. In *cas*, emergent properties could occur when coevolving signals and boundaries generate new levels in hierarchical organization. Similarly, emergence is generated by combining building blocks, which contrasts with the view of emergence as a holistic phenomenon. In the latter, the emergent phenomenon cannot be reduced to an interaction of components. However, the building block approach allows for reduction. That being said, the reduction involved surpasses the traditional reduction in which "the whole is equal to the sum of its parts." The interactions between signals and boundaries in a *cas* cannot be simply added together. When these conditional interactions are included, reduction is understood as part of a system's emergent properties in signal/boundary relations. Adapted from Holland (2012)

which interventions can be short-term yet "wise," having long-term downstream consequences. By targeting relevant psychological processes in complex systems, key levers or drivers of system dysregulation can be addressed with timely interventions.

Sturmberg, O'Halloran, and Martin (2012) applied the concept of CAS to the health system. They referred to the opposition of people-centered and financial-centered attractors in the system.

Hollenstein and Lougheed (2013) applied the concept of CAS to adolescence. In the CAS perspective, constant, dynamic interaction moment-by-moment both within and between people causally produces behavior and also provides explanatory mechanisms of behavioral change, including in adolescents.

Table 5.1 Properties of system in rehabilitation

Level	Explanation
1	The body has multiple interacting/self-regulating physiological systems, including biochemical/neuroendocrine feedback loops
2	Behavior is determined both by an internal set of rules based and responses to new stimuli
3	Individuals are embedded within social relationships and within social, political, and cultural systems. These can influence outcomes in entirely novel/unpredictable ways
4	A small change in the system could lead to a much larger change through nonlinear
5	Therefore, behavior, including illness is not predictable and it cannot be reflected in a simple cause and effect approach

Adapted from Wilson and Holt (2001)

Table 5.2 Properties of complex adaptive systems (CAS) in rehabilitation

	Explanation
Adaptable elements	System element can change themselves. Under the right conditions, change can happen from within
Simple rules	Complex outcomes can develop from a few simple rules applied locally
Emergent behavior, novelty	Continual creativity is a natural state of the system
Unpredictable in detail	Prediction takes place globally not in locally. For example, detailed, accurate long-range weather forecasting is essentially impossible
Self-organization	Systems can appear ordered despite not having central control. Self-organization takes place inherently
Co-evolution	A *cas* evolves through constant tension and balance (e.g., certainty vs. uncertainty)

Adapted from Wilson and Holt (2001)

Systems

Model

Urban, Osgood, and Mabry (2011) noted that there are three major scientific "methodologies" associated with systems, although I prefer to call them frameworks or models. The approaches involve: system dynamics, agent-based modeling, and network analysis. In the above, I have reviewed Holland's (2012) approach to agent-based modeling. As for the construct of networks, the next chapter examines it in more detail. This section of the chapter is concerned with systems. The value of these approaches is that they integrate multiple levels of analysis (from cells to behavior to society) in attempting to understand development.

DiDonato, England, Martin, and Amazeen (2013) provided a tutorial on nonlinear dynamical systems theory (Thelen & Smith, 1994, 2006). Nonlinearity is indicated in the example of a horse's gallop style shifting to a running style at a certain speed threshold. In their review, DiDonato et al. (2013) referred to self-organization, emergence, attractors, fractals, and so on. When control parameters reach threshold, the order parameter governing system behavior shifts, moving the system to a different attractor configuration; moreover, the change might be abrupt. Energy entering the system provides "escapement," e.g., as evidenced in oscillations across two attractors regions. As for fractals, DiDonato et al. (2013) found fractal patterns in nested patterns of change in behavior over days, weeks, and months.

Vallacher, Van Geert, and Nowak (2015) argued that, in psychology, the dynamic approach of nonlinear dynamical systems theory (NLDST; Thelen & Smith, 1996) is a promising "integrative paradigm" over its diverse landscape of topics. Rather than considering psychological processes only in terms of external cause and related effects, it considers them, as well, as reflective of internal, intrinsic dynamical mechanisms, and also their interaction with new system input. In NLDST, variability within the person's behavior over time might be more important than any average in understanding behavior. The sequence of system states leading to the present also is important.

A system is comprised of a set of interconnected elements that try to find balance over iterations, or "mutual coherence." As elements adjust to one another, they are self-organizing in

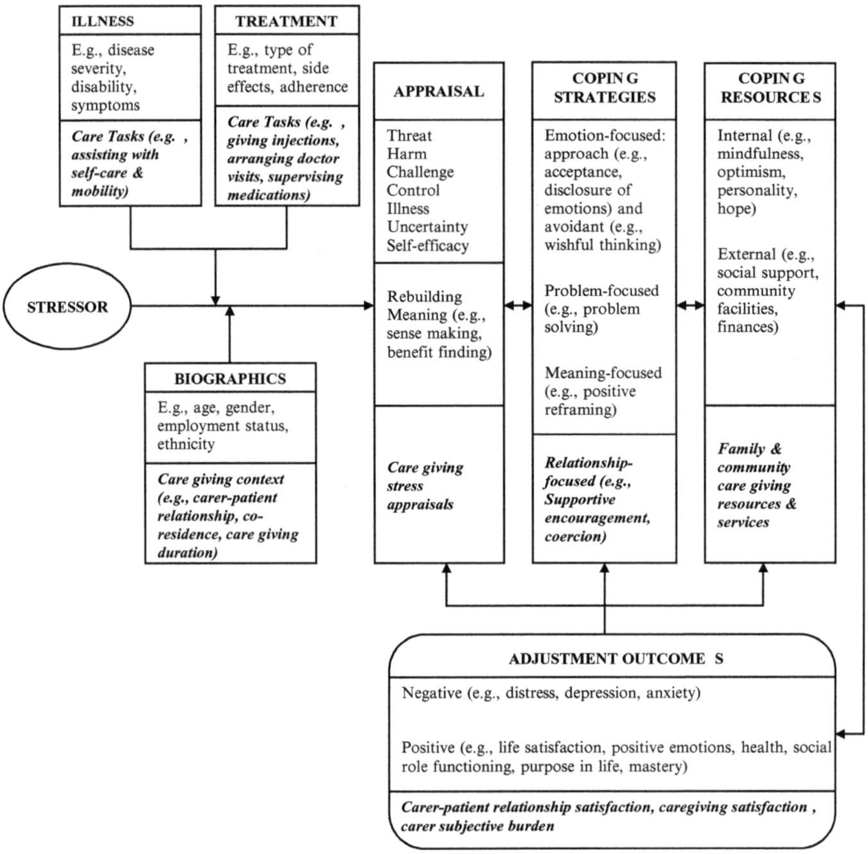

Fig. 5.6 Summary of a stress and coping framework for assessing and intervening in the coping processes that shape adjustment to multiple sclerosis and the care giving role. Key generic variables applicable to both the person with MS and caregiver are depicted by regular font; and variables specific to care giving are denoted by the *bolded* and *shaded italics*. Adapted from Pakenham (2012)

a bottom-up fashion. Self-organization allows for the emergence of higher-order pattern from elemental interaction. As systems stabilize, they constrain system behavior toward their patterns, and new input "evolves" toward them even if they are initially discrepant with them. Stable systems are referred to as attractors, and there might be more than one attractor in any one system Attractors are state convergence loci in the system. External influences might perturb or disrupt a system's stability; in response, the system might damp these influences over time, or lead to system change.

Attractors might owe their stability to control parameters, and critical thresholds in the latter might lead to change in system organization. The system might resist change until pushed to its limits, and then undergo nonlinear "dramatic" change (self-organized criticality at a critical value; Bak, 1996). Therefore, systems express both stability and flexibility, depending on context. Finally, a system's temporal patterns might behave fractally, with similar patterns over different time-scales (short, long).

To conclude, Vallacher et al. (2015) noted that external forces have their effects on behavior through the intrinsic dynamics mediating them in the systems that they engage. Ignoring system dynamics in determining causal factors will lead to an "incomplete and potentially misleading" understanding of behavior.

Afraimovich, Rabinovich, and Varona (2012) presented a tutorial on nonlinear dynamical systems theory. They indicated that dynamical systems are mathematical models that represent deterministic processes. In a dynamic system, a state is any point in time ($t>0$) that is determined solely by its initial state. A collection of variables x describes a state. The set of a system's states describes its phase space of states. States in a system change in time according to the system's set of evolution operators (ϕ^t, $t>0$) that expresses the mathematical law that governs system state change (at initial point x_0 to point x_i at point in time t). Formulaically, the set of operators satisfies the "group identity":

$$\phi^{t1+t2}x_0 = \phi^{t2}\left(\phi^{t1}x_0\right)$$

As states follow trajectories in phase space, they follow an attractor regime if they gravitate to preferred states, or their basins. The attractors can take many forms—from point ones, to limit ones, to "strange" or chaotic ones.

Freeman (2006) described circular causality in terms of macroscopic, top-down and microscopic, bottom-up mutual influences, such that there are no simple, direct cause-effect relations within a system but only "second-order perturbations" having "higher-order capacities." Macroscopic "back flow" by upper level "order parameters" helps regulate behavior by the circular causality entailed in "holding or releasing" lower levels (e.g., subsystems). Microscopic fluctuations might also have effects by initiating state phase transitions. Circular causality is divorced from agency, which resides in the self-organization of the system dynamics in toto.

Applications

Spencer, Austin, and Schutte (2012) noted that, in systems theory, qualitative change takes place when either the number of or the type of attractor changes (Thelen & Smith, 1994). The changes in attractor organization during qualitative change occur at bifurcation points. The qualitative shifts might even transpire after gradual quantitative changes in one particular aspect of a system. For example, horses shift from walking to running at a transition in quantitative speed after which their gait shifts qualitatively to the new regime.

Spencer et al. (2012) also noted that, in systems, soft assembly governs the process of system patterning. The organism constructs behavior from moment to moment from among multiple interacting components that combine "freely" according to context, the task at hand, and developmental history.

Stanton and Welsh (2012) have applied systems theory to therapy with couples and family. They were influenced by the work of Lunkenheimer and Dishion (2009) and colleagues (e.g., Granic, Hollenstein, Dishion, & Patterson, 2003). In systems, collective variables are the equivalent of dependent variables and control parameters are the equivalent of independent variables. Systems express patterns represented as attractors (e.g., a couple gravitates easily during conflict to a "violence" attractor). Attractors can be mapped in time, and critical transition points can be identified (phase transitions). These periods are amenable to psychotherapeutic intervention (e.g., moving to cooperative rather than hostile state space regions).

Langer, Cohen, and Djikic (2012) applied the concept of attractors to mindfulness. They considered mindfulness as a psychological attractor, and that people expressing it are considered more "attractive". Dolcos, Iordan, and Dolcos (2011) reminded that cognition involves emotion and the two are reciprocally related in complex dynamical behavior.

Cabell and Valsiner (2014a, 2014b) presented a catalytic model of mental activity, which is similar to a systems approach. It is grounded in semiosis. It considers all of Aristotle's four causes—material, formal, efficient, and final. Typically, psychology engages in the study mostly of the third one, which concerns the system in which the cause operates. For the authors, Aristotle's other three types of causes are equally relevant for psychology. Also, we need to study how a phenomenon emerges, develops, and disappears; what form it takes and why; and what is its purpose, goal, or intention.

In semiotic cultural psychology, mediating processes are viewed as changing the relationship between cause and effect, stimulus–response, or two associated phenomena. Semiotic regulators have a direct impact on effects, but semiotic catalyzers are noninvasive interventions. Valsiner (2014) explained that catalysis is a concept derived from chemistry. Toomela (2014) considered the model preliminary, e.g., about its proposals for how downward and upward causation relate. Rather, for Toomela, parts of a system change qualitatively as the whole emerges.

Brain

Rolls (2010) described neuronal networks in attractor terms (see Fig. 5.7). He considered attractor neural networks as interconnections that settle into stable firing patterns (e.g., in the

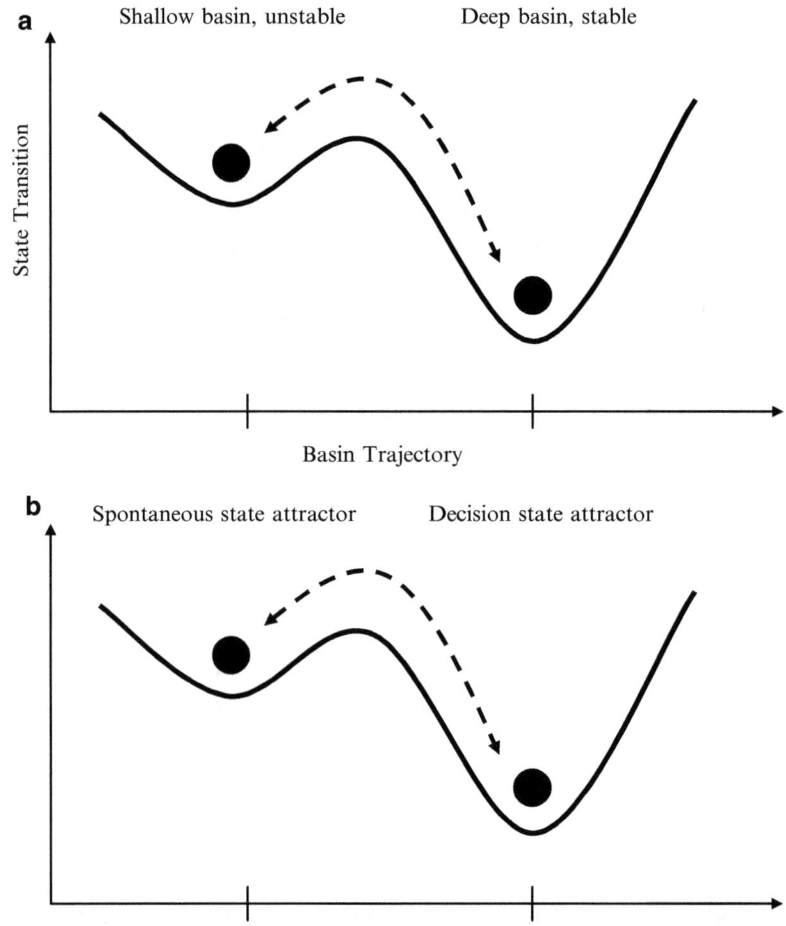

Fig. 5.7 State transitions through basin trajectories. (**a**) Attractor dynamics can be depicted by state transition trajectories in effective energy landscapes, which indicate the basins of attraction by valleys. Attractor states (or fixed points) are depicted as balls moving over the landscape, e.g., captured at the *bottom* of valleys. The stability of an attractor is indicated by the average time in which the system stays in a basin, resisting of noise, which can instigate movement to other attractor basins (and states). Two factors determine the stability of an attractor. First, if the depth of an attractor basin is shallow (as in the *left* compared to the *right* valley), less force is needed to move an attractor (ball) from the shallow valley to another. Second, a high level of noise adds to the possibility that a system will jump over an energy boundary from one state to another. For neural functioning, as depicted in the figure, the noise in the network caused by random spiking means that, on some trials of measurement, for given inputs, the neurons in the first attractor are more likely to fire and, on other trials, the neurons in the second attractor are more likely to fire. This makes the decision-making in neural firing probabilistic. In (**b**), for example, the noise involved influences when the neural system will jump out of the spontaneously firing, stable (low energy) state, and into the high-firing state for one "decision" or another. Adapted from Rolls (2010)

hippocampus, a seat of memory). The interconnections are excitatory. Firing rates vary, and those that are persistent could reflect a particular memory. When incoming information is partial, attractors can complete it. Attractors can vary in stability and reactivity to input. The "decision-making" of competing attractors is "probabilistic." Attractors can be held "online," allowing powerful computations.

Mustafa et al. (2012) hypothesized that the cerebral cortex is akin to a fractal structure. It is constituted by parts that reflect similarities with the whole. Its cortical fractal structure lies especially in the irregularity of the external cortical surface, and in white matter complexity, which can be represented mathematically as a fractal dimension (FD). In their research, they found that FD was associated with fluid intellectual abilities. They referred to environmental influence on brain structure as the mediating variable in their findings. Similarly, Im et al. (2006) had found that cortical surface FD related to intelligence and years of education.

Bassett and Gazzaniga (2011) considered the brain as a site of complexity organization. Complex network theory is quite applicable to its study. It is characterized by emergent phenomena in "bidirectional" causation and complementarity over top-down and bottom-up processes, with the former feeding back to the latter in downward causation. Emergence is "upward," that is, it takes place as a higher-order emergence deriving from a lower level in the system involved. The mind and brain constitute an interface with "conditional causation" (causes are neither necessary nor sufficient in all relevant contingencies).

According to Bassett and Gazzaniga (2011), the mind is not reducible in that components have "causal power" in systems, such as the mind–brain system (referred to as "nonfundamental causality" as distinct from "determinism"). Therefore, Bassett and Gazzaniga (2011) considered "mind-brain emergence" as a "strong" emergence, as opposed to "weak" ones (e.g., substance, conjunction, property, function, living emergence).

van der Helm (2012) introduced the concept of "transparallel processing" to help explain how "hyperstring-like" neural assemblies are formed. He referred to the latter as "gnosons."

I conclude that any concept of memory and its representation, as well as its underpinning in neurons, assemblies, and attractors, need to consider multilevel modeling in which motivation, affect, emotions, and the general architecture and integration of the "emergent" mind works top-down reciprocally along with bottom-up influences.

Integrating the Models

In the following, I show how various developmental models are being integrated with a focus on systems theory.

Lickliter and Honeycutt (2013) presented the metatheoretical assumptions in the developmental evolutionary approach. They maintained that development unfolds within a hierarchical organization of embedded, reciprocally-influencing relational systems. Control of developmental processes takes place in a distributed fashion. The innate and acquired cannot be separated in their integrated multilevel interaction, which begins the moment of conception. Developmental changes are the product of self-organization. Developmental changes provide the phenotypic variation on which evolutionary forces can act. The variations arise in organismic-environmental transactions. A developmental evolutionary framework allows for a "causal analysis" of behavior, "unpacking" developmental dynamics over multiple levels.

Michel (2013) described the similar developmental psychobiological approach. It offers explanations both of species-typical behavior and individual differences. It explores the causal mechanisms behind developmental trajectories. It asks what are the mechanisms leading to developmental behaviors and what are the ones that account for their individual differences.

The approach uses the concepts in the dynamical systems approach. System elements are interdependent and express periodic ("punctuated") phase transitions (e.g., stages) in development, with these reorganizations resulting in the emergence of "new," stable behaviors after the instability preceding the shifts. Perturbations that effect transitions might be small or large, and they help define individual vulnerability/resilience.

As for the relational developmental view, Lerner, Agans, DeSouza, and Gasca (2013) referred to the mutually-influential, bidirectional, reciprocal, synergistic, and fused relations over the multiple levels in development, including of the individual in context achieving adaptive developmental regulation. Gene-context relations afford developmental plasticity and within-individual change. Diversity is substantive in development and cannot be reduced to genetic mechanisms alone.

Chapter Conclusions

Efforts to create more inclusive models in psychology have focused on the ones mentioned in the present chapter. In later chapters, I show how they apply to the area of development. All these models help understand behavior and its change. They consider causality to a degree. However, causality could be one axis that serves to integrate them. The biopsychosocial model considers its major components as interactional. The embodiment model considers them as constitutive. The systems model considers them as primed for change. Together, the models offer positive portents of a more integrative model than each of them allows by itself, despite their increasing outreach. As argued throughout the present work, causality could be the interstitial glue that functions to cohere putative integrating psychological models into a unifying structure. At the same time, causality could be the essentializing psychological characteristic of the human species. Perhaps we adapt especially in terms of deciphering the causal influences around us, reasoning about and with causality, and becoming causal influences in our own right.

Notions of causality that we develop should not be uniquely abstract, but also related to the participation that we engage in life, including the cosocial and, therefore, causality is best conceived as emergent from and dialectical with context. That being said, causality is actively lived and conceived. The physicalist notion of causality acknowledges some degree of isomorphism between its "psycholization" and its reality, but one that includes ourselves as participatory agents, for example, through the activity of the self of ourselves and of aspects of free will. This approach suggests a continual interaction between the organism, agent, or individual and the environment or context in terms of seeking and understanding causality. Given the primacy of causality in our psychology that I am suggesting, it is as if we should be designated, as a species, as "*Homo Causa*" (or *Homo Humanus Causa*).

In this view, the human focus on causality means that we continually "causalize," or seek and propose causal understanding. Moreover, we continually act for the causal outcomes involved and the world is filtered for what it contributes to causal understanding and causal action. Therefore, one could argue that, as much is the case for our internal world, the external world exists only through its causal relations, or cause-effect co-ordinations. Not only our mental activity but also our relations with things, people, and events are defined by their causal history and participation in causal co-ordinations.

To summarize briefly, reality is imbued by causality and humans are causalizing agents. In this regard, the psychological models that we develop should place causality at the forefront both as an integrating concept and as the product and process of what we do, of who we are, and of what distinguishes us as exceptional. The models should cover individual (and group) differences in this regard and, as well, the change mechanisms involved as we change (hopefully for the better both for ourselves and others).

References

Afraimovich, V. S., Rabinovich, M. I., & Varona, P. (2012). Short guide to modern nonlinear dynamics. In M. I. Rabinovich, K. J. Friston, & P. Varona (Eds.), *Principles of brain dynamics: Global state interactions* (pp. 313–338). Cambridge, MA: MIT Press.

Aspell, J. E., Heydrich, L., Marillier, G., Lavanchy, T., Herbelin, B., & Blanke, O. (2013). Turning body and self inside out: Visualized heartbeat alter bodily self-consciousness and tactile perception. *Psychological Science, 24*, 2445–2453.

Bak, P. (1996). *How nature works: The science of self-organized criticality*. New York: Springer.

Bak, P., Tang, C., & Wiesenfeld, K. (1987). Self-organized criticality: An explanation of 1/*f* noise. *Physical Review Letters, 59*, 381–384.

Bak, P., Tang, C., & Wiesenfeld, K. (1988). Self-organized criticality. *Physical Review A, 38*, 364–375.

Barrett, L. (2011). *Beyond the Brain: How Body and Environment Shape Animal and Human Minds*. Princeton, NJ: Princeton University Press.

Bassett, D. S., & Gazzaniga, M. S. (2011). Understanding complexity in the human brain. *Trends in Cognitive Sciences, 15*, 200–209.

Bastian, B., Jetten, J., Hornsey, M. J., & Leknes, S. (2014). The positive consequence of pain: A biopsychosocial approach. *Personality and Social Psychology Review, 18*, 256–279.

Belar, C. D., & Deardorff, W. W. (2009). *Clinical health psychology in medical settings: A practitioner's guidebook* (2nd ed.). Washington, DC: American Psychological Association.

Belar, C. D., & Deardorff, W. W. (2015). Fundamentals of assessment in clinical health psychology. In F. Andrasik, J. L. Goodie, & A. L. Peterson (Eds.), *Biopsychosocial assessment in clinical health psychology* (pp. 8–20). New York: The Guilford Press.

Brockmole, J. R., Davoli, C. C., Abrams, R. A., & Witt, J. K. (2013). The world within reach: Effects of hand posture and tool-use on visual cognition. *Current Directions in Psychological Science, 22*, 38–44.

Bruineberg, J., & Rietveld, E. (2014). Self-organization, free energy minimization, and optimal grip on a field of affordances. *Frontiers in Human Neuroscience, 8*, 599. doi:10.3389/fnhum.2014.00599.

Cabell, K. R., & Valsiner, J. (2014a). *The catalyzing mind: Beyond models of causality*. New York: Springer Science + Business Media.

Cabell, K. R., & Valsiner, J. (2014b). Systematic systemics: Causality, catalysis, and developmental cybernetics. In K. R. Cabell & J. Valsiner (Eds.), *The catalyzing mind: Beyond models of causality* (pp. 3–13). New York: Springer Science + Business Media.

Campos, J. J., Anderson, D. I., Barbu-Roth, M. A., Hubbard, E. M., Hertenstein, M. J., & Witherington, D. (2000). Travel broadens the mind. *Infancy, 1*, 149–219.

Carey, T. A., Mansell, W., & Tai, S. J. (2014). A biopsychosocial model based on negative feedback and control. *Frontiers in Human Neuroscience, 8*, 94. doi:10.3389/fnhum.2014.00094.

Casasanto, D. (2011). Different bodies, different minds: The body specificity of language and thought. *Current Directions in Psychological Science, 20*, 378–383.

Chaisson, E. J. (2013). Using complexity science to search for unity in the natural sciences. In C. H. Lineweaver, P. C. W. Davies, & M. Ruse (Eds.), *Complexity and the arrow of time* (pp. 68–79). New York: Cambridge University Press.

Chemero, A. (2009). *Radical embodied cognitive science*. Cambridge, MA: MIT Press.

Chemero, A. (2013). Radical embodied cognitive science. *Review of General Psychology, 17*, 145–150.

Clark, A. (1997). *Being there: Putting brain, body, and world together again*. Cambridge, MA: MIT Press.

Davids, K., Araújo, D., Hristovski, R., Passos, P., & Chow, J. Y. (2012). Ecological dynamics and motor learning design in sport. In N. H. Mark Williams (Ed.), *Skill acquisition in sport: Research, theory, and practice* (2nd ed., pp. 112–130). London: Routledge.

de Groot, J. H. B., Smeets, M. A. M., Kaldewaij, A., Duijndam, M. J. A., & Semin, G. R. (2012). Chemosignals communicates human emotions. *Psychological Science, 23*, 1417–1424.

DiDonato, M. D., England, D., Martin, C. L., & Amazeen, P. G. (2013). Dynamical analysis for developmental science: A primer for intrigued scientists. *Human Development, 56*, 59–75.

Dolcos, F., Iordan, A. D., & Dolcos, S. (2011). Neural correlates of emotion-cognition interactions: A review of evidence from brain imaging investigations. *Journal of Cognitive Psychology, 23*, 669–694.

Dove, G. (2011). On the need for embodied and disembodied cognition. *Frontiers in Psychology, 1*, 242. doi:10.3389/fpsyg.2010.00242.

Dowe, P. (2000). *Physical causation*. Cambridge, UK: Cambridge University Press.

Engelcamp, J. (1995). Visual imagery and enactment of actions in memory. *British Journal of Psychology, 86*, 227–240.

Farah, M. J. (2012). Neuroethics: The ethical, legal, and societal impact of neuroscience. *Annual Review of Psychology, 63*, 571–591.

Favela, L. H. (2014). Radical embodied cognitive neuroscience: Addressing "grand challenges" of the mind sciences. *Frontiers in Human Neuroscience, 8*, 796. doi:10.3389/fnhum.2014.00796.

Flor, H. (2014). Psychological pain interventions and neurophysiology: Implications for a mechanism-based approach. *American Psychologist, 69*, 188–196.

Foglia, L., & Wilson, R. A. (2013). Embodied cognition. *Wiley Interdisciplinary Reviews: Cognitive Science, 4*, 319–325.

Freeman, W. J. (2006). Consciousness, intentionality, and causality. In S. Pockett, W. P. Banks, & S. Gallagher (Eds.), *Does consciousness cause behavior?* (pp. 73–105). Cambridge, MA: MIT Press.

Friston, K. (2010). The free-energy principle: A unified brain theory? *Nature Reviews Neuroscience, 11*, 127–138.

Friston, K. (2011). Embodied inference: Or 'I think therefore I am, if I am what I think.'. In W. Tschacher & C. Bergomi (Eds.), *The implications of embodiment (cognition and communication)* (pp. 89–125). Exeter, UK: Imprint Academic.

Friston, K. (2012). A free energy principle for biological systems. *Entropy, 14*, 2100–2121.

Friston, K. (2013). Active inference and free energy. *Behavioral and Brain Sciences, 36*, 212–213.

Froese, T., Iizuka, H., & Ikegami, T. (2013). From synthetic modeling of social interaction to dynamic theories of brain-body-environment-body-brain systems. *Behavioral and Brain Sciences, 36*, 420–421.

Fuchs, T., & Koch, S. C. (2014). Embodied affectivity: On moving and being moved. *Frontiers in Psychology, 5*, 508. doi:10.3389/fpsyg.2014.00508.

Gallotti, M. (2013). Why not the first-person plural in social cognition? *Behavioral and Brain Sciences, 36*, 422–423.

Gapenne, O. (2014). The co-constitution of the self and the world: Action and proprioceptive coupling. *Frontiers in Psychology, 5*, 594. doi:10.3389/fpsyg.2014.00594.

Gatchel, R. J., McGeary, D. D., McGeary, C. A., & Lippe, B. (2014). Interdisciplinary chronic pain management: Past, present, and future. *American Psychologist, 69*, 119–130.

Gibson, J. J. (1966/1979). *The ecological approach to visual perception*. Boston: Houghton Mifflin.

Gibson, J. J. (1973/1983). *The senses considered as perceptual systems*. Westport, CT: Greenwood Press.

Gibson, J. J. (1979). *The ecological approach to visual perception*. Boston: Houghton Mifflin.

Gibson, J. J. (1986). *The ecological approach to visual perception*. New York: Psychology Press.

Glenberg, A. M., & Gallese, V. (2012). Action-based language: A theory of language acquisition, comprehension, and production. *Cortex, 48*, 905–922.

Glenberg, A. M., Willford, J., Gibson, B., Goldberg, A., & Zhu, X. (2012). Improving reading to improve math. *Scientific Studies of Reading, 16*, 316–340.

Glenberg, A. M., Witt, J. K., & Metcalfe, J. (2013). From the revolution to embodiment: 25 years of cognitive psychology. *Perspectives on Psychological Science, 8*, 573–585.

Gopnik, A., & Wellman, H. M. (2012). Reconstructing constructivism: Causal models, Bayesian learning mechanisms, and the theory. *Psychological Bulletin, 138*, 1085–1108.

Gould, S. J. (1996). *Full house: The spread of excellence from Plato to Darwin*. New York: Harmony Books.

Granic, I., Hollenstein, T., Dishion, T. J., & Patterson, G. R. (2003). Longitudinal analysis of flexibility and reorganization in early adolescence: A dynamic systems study of family interactions. *Developmental Psychology, 39*, 606–617.

Hauk, O., Johnsrude, I., & Pulvemüller, F. (2004). Somatotopic representation of action words in human motor and premotor cortex. *Neuron, 41*, 301–307.

Havas, D. A., Glenberg, A. M., Gutowski, K. A., Lucarelli, M. J., & Davidson, R. J. (2010). Cosmetic use of botulinum toxin-A affects processing of emotional language. *Psychological Science, 21*, 895–900.

Heft, H. (1989). Affordances and the body: An intentional analysis of Gibson's ecological approach to visual perception. *Journal of the Theory of Social Behavior, 19*, 1–30.

Held, R., & Hein, A. (1963). Movement-produced simulation in the development of visually guided behavior. *Journal of Comparative and Physiological Psychology, 56*, 872–876.

Helmchen, H. (2013). Different conceptions of mental illness: Consequences for the association with patients. *Frontiers in Psychology, 4*, 269. doi:10.3389/fpsyg.2013.00269.

Holland, J. H. (2012). *Signals and boundaries: Building blocks for complex adaptive systems*. Cambridge, MA: MIT Press.

Hollenstein, T., & Lougheed, J. P. (2013). Beyond storm and stress: Typically, transactions, timing, and temperament to account for adolescent change. *American Psychologist, 68*, 444–454.

Hume, D. (1975). In L. A. Selby-Bigge & P. H. Nidditch (Eds.), *Enquiry concerning human understanding and concerning in principles of morals* (3rd ed.). New York: Oxford University Press. (Original work published 1748).

Hutto, D. D. (2013). Psychology unified: From folk psychology to radical enactivism. *Review of General Psychology, 17*, 174–178.

Im, K., Lee, J. M., Yoon, U., Shin, Y. W., Hong, S. B., Kim, I. Y., et al. (2006). Fractal dimension in human cortical surface: Multiple regression analysis with cortical thickness, sulcal depth, and folding area. *Human Brain Mapping, 27*, 994–1003.

Jensen, M. P., & Turk, D. C. (2014). Contributions of psychology to the understanding and treatment of people with chronic pain. *American Psychologist, 69*, 105–118.

Kauffman, S. A. (1993). *The origins of order: Self-organization and selection in evolution*. New York: Oxford University Press.

Kauffman, S. A. (2013). Evolution beyond Newton, Darwin, and entailing law: The origins of complexity in the evolving biosphere. In C. H. Lineweaver, P. C. W. Davies, & M. Ruse (Eds.), *Complexity and the arrow of time* (pp. 162–190). New York: Cambridge University Press.

Kelso, J. A. S. (2009). Coordination dynamics. In R. A. Meyers (Ed.), *Encyclopedia of complexity and system science* (pp. 1537–1564). Heidelberg, Germany: Springer Science + Business Media.

Kelso, J. A. S. (2012). Multistability and metastability: Understanding dynamic coordination in the brain. *Philosophical Transactions of the Royal Society, B: Biological Sciences, 367*, 906–918.

Kiverstein, J., & Miller, M. (2015). The embodied brain: Towards a radical embodied cognitive neuroscience. *Frontiers in Human Neuroscience, 9*, 237. doi:10.3389/fnhum.2015.00237.

Kugler, P. N., Kelso, J. A. S., & Turvey, M. T. (1980). Coordinative structures as dissipative structures: I. Theoretical lines of convergence. In G. E. Stelmach & J. Requin (Eds.), *Tutorials in motor behavior* (pp. 3–47). Amsterdam, Netherlands: North-Holland.

Kuhn, T. S. (1962). *The structure of scientific revolutions* (3rd ed.). Chicago: University of Chicago Press.

Kyselo, M., & Tschacher, W. (2014). An enactive and dynamical systems theory account of dyadic relationships. *Frontiers in Psychology, 5*, 452. doi:10.3389/fpsyg.2014.00452.

Langer, E. J., Cohen, M., & Djikic, M. (2012). Mindfulness as a psychological attractor: The effect on children.

Journal of Applied Social Psychology, 42, 1114–1122.
Lerner, R. M., Agans, J. P., DeSouza, L. M., & Gasca, S. (2013). Describing, explaining, and optimizing within-individual change across the life span: A relational developmental systems perspective. *Review of General Psychology, 17*, 179–183.
Lickliter, R., & Honeycutt, H. (2013). A developmental evolutionary framework for psychology. *Review of General Psychology, 17*, 184–189.
Lievesley, K., Rimes, K., & Chalder, T. (2014). A review of the predisposing, precipitating and perpetuating factors in Chronic Fatigue Syndrome in children and adolescents. *Clinical Psychology Review, 34*, 233–248.
Lineweaver, C. H., Davies, P. C. W., & Ruse, M. (2013a). *Complexity and the arrow of time*. New York: Cambridge University Press.
Lineweaver, C. H., Davies, P. C. W., & Ruse, M. (2013b). What is complexity? Is it increasing? In C. H. Lineweaver, P. C. W. Davies, & M. Ruse (Eds.), *Complexity and the arrow of time* (pp. 3–16). New York: Cambridge University Press.
Linkenauger, S. A., Mohler, B. J., & Bülthoff, H. H. (2011, May). *Welcome to wonderland: The apparent size of the self-representing avatar's hands and arms influences perceived size and shape in virtual environments*. Poster presented at the 10th Annual meeting of the Vision Sciences Society, Tampa, FL.
Linkenauger, S. A., Witt, J. K., & Proffitt, D. R. (2011). Taking a hands-on approach: Apparent grasping ability scales the perception of object size. *Journal of Experimental Psychology: Human Perception and Performance, 37*, 1432–1441.
Livneh, H., Chan, F., & Kaya, C. (2014). Stigma related to physical and sensory disabilities. In P. W. Corrigan (Ed.), *The stigma of disease and disability: Understanding causes and overcoming injustices* (pp. 93–120). Washington, DC: American Psychological Association.
Lunkenheimer, E. S., & Dishion, T. J. (2009). Developmental psychopathology: Maladaptive and adaptive attractors in children's close relationships. In S. J. Guastello, M. Koopmans, & D. Pincus (Eds.), *Chaos and complexity in psychology: The theory of nonlinear dynamical system* (pp. 282–306). New York: Cambridge University Press.
Magnavita, J. J., & Anchin, J. C. (2014). The emergence of a unifying paradigm for psychotherapy. In J. J. Magnavita & J. C. Anchin (Eds.), *Unifying psychotherapy: Principles, methods, and evidence from clinical science* (pp. 3–34). New York: Springer Publishing Company.
McEwen, B. S., & Getz, L. (2013). Lifetime experiences, the brain and personalized medicine: An integrative perspective. *Metabolism Clinical and Experimental, 62*, S20–S26.
McGann, M. (2014). Enacting a social ecology: Radically embodied intersubjectivity. *Frontiers in Psychology, 5*, 1321. doi:10.3389/fpsyg.2014.01321.
McGann, M., De Jaegher, H., & Di Paolo, E. (2013). Enaction and psychology. *Review of General Psychology, 17*, 203–209.
McShea, D. W., & Brandon, R. N. (2010). *Biology's first law*. Chicago: University of Chicago Press.
Melchert, T. P. (2011). *Foundations of professional psychology: The end of theoretical orientations and the emergence of the biopsychosocial approach*. London, ON: Elsevier.
Melchert, T. P. (2015). *Biopsychosocial practice: A science-based framework for behavioral health care*. Washington, DC: American Psychological Association.
Merbitz, N. H., Merbitz, C. T., & Ripsch, J. P. (2012). Rehabilitation outcomes and assessment: Toward a model of complex adaptive rehabilitation. In P. Kennedy (Ed.), *The oxford handbook of rehabilitation psychology* (pp. 96–127). New York: Oxford University Press.
Meteyard, L., Cuadrado, S. R., Bahrami, B., & Viglicco, G. (2012). Coming of age: A review of embodiment and the neuroscience of semantics. *Cortex, 48*, 788–804.
Michel, G. F. (2013). The role of developmental psychobiology in the unification of psychology. *Review of General Psychology, 17*, 210–215.
Michotte, A. E. (1946/1963). *The perception of causality*. New York: Basic Books.
Mukamel, R., Ekstrom, A. D., Kaplan, J., Iacoboni, M., & Fried, I. (2010). Single-neuron responses in humans during execution and observation of actions. *Current Biology, 20*, 750–756.
Mustafa, N., Ahearn, T. S., Waiter, G. D., Murray, A. D., Whalley, L. J., & Staff, R. T. (2012). Brain structural complexity and life course cognitive change. *NeuroImage, 61*, 694–701.
Overton, W. F. (2015). Relational developmental systems and developmental science. In R. M. Lerner, W. F. Overton, & P. C. Molenaar (Eds.), *Handbook of child psychology and developmental science, Vol. 1: Theory and method* (7th ed., pp. 9–62). Hoboken, NJ: Wiley.
Pakenham, K. I. (2012). Multiple sclerosis. In P. Kennedy (Ed.), *The Oxford handbook of rehabilitation psychology* (pp. 211–234). New York: Oxford University Press.
Pearl, J. (2000). *Causality: Models, reasoning, and inference*. Cambridge, MA: Cambridge University Press.
Peterson, A. L., Goodie, J. L., & Andrasik, F. (2015). Introduction to biopsychosocial assessment in clinical health psychology. In F. Andrasik, J. L. Goodie, & A. L. Peterson (Eds.), *Biopsychosocial assessment in clinical health psychology* (pp. 3–7). New York: The Guilford Press.
Pickering, M., & Garrod, S. (2013). An integrated view of language production and comprehension. *Behavioral & Brain Sciences, 36*, 329–347.
Pulvermüller, F. (2013). How neurons make meaning: Brain mechanisms for embodied and abstract-symbolic semantics. *Trends in Cognitive Sciences, 17*, 458–470.

Rizzolatti, G., & Craighero, K. (2004). The mirror-neuron system. *Annual Review of Neuroscience, 27*, 169–192.
Robinson, D. (2013). *Feeling extended: Sociality as extended body-becoming-mind*. Cambridge, MA: MIT Press.
Rolls, E. T. (2010). Attractor networks. *Wiley Interdisciplinary Reviews: Cognitive Science, 1*, 119–134.
Schilbach, L., Timmermans, B., Reddy, V., Costall, A., Bente, G., Schlicht, T., et al. (2013). Toward a second-person neuroscience. *Behavioral and Brain Sciences, 36*, 393–462.
Schoth, D. E., Nunes, V. D., & Liossi, C. (2012). Attentional bias toward pain-related information in chronic pain; a meta-analysis of visual-probe investigations. *Clinical Psychology Review, 32*, 13–25.
Schultz, I. Z., & Stewart, A. M. (2008). Disentangling disability quagmire in psychological injury and law. Part II. Evolution of disability models: Conceptual, methodological and forensic issues. *Psychological Injury and Law, 1*, 103–121.
Semin, G. R. (2007). Grounding communication: Synchrony. In A. W. Kruglanski & E. T. Higgins (Eds.), *Social psychology: Handbook of basic principles* (2nd ed., pp. 630–649). New York: Guilford Press.
Semin, G. R., & de Groot, J. H. B. (2013). The chemical bases of human sociality. *Trends in Cognitive Sciences, 17*, 427–429.
Siegel, D. J. (2012). *The developing mind: How relationships and the brain interact to shape who we are* (2nd ed.). New York: The Guilford Press.
Slife, B. D., & Christensen, T. R. (2013). Hermeneutic realism: Toward a truly meaningful psychology. *Review of General Psychology, 17*, 230–236.
Sloman, S. (2005). *Causal models: How people think about the world and its alternatives*. New York: Oxford University Press.
Soliman, T., Gibson, A., & Glenberg, A. M. (2013). Sensory motor mechanisms unify psychology: The embodiment of culture. *Frontiers in Psychology, 4*, 885. doi:10.3389/fpsyg.2013.00885.
Spencer, J. P., Austin, A., & Schutte, A. R. (2012). Contributions of dynamic systems theory to cognitive development. *Cognitive Development, 27*, 401–418.
Sperry, L. (2009). *Treatment of chronic medical conditions: Cognitive-behavioral therapy strategies and integrative treatment protocols*. Washington, DC: American Psychological Association.
Stallen, M., De Dreu, C. K. W., Shalvi, S., Smidts, A., & Sanfey, A. G. (2012). The herding hormone: Oxytocin stimulates in-group conformity. *Psychological Science, 23*, 1288–1292.
Stanton, M., & Welsh, R. (2012). Systemic thinking in couple and family psychology research and practice. *Couple and Family Psychology: Research and Practice, 1*, 14–30.
Stier, M. (2014). The biopsychosocial model between biologism and arbitrariness. A commentary to H. Helmchen. *Frontiers in Psychology, 5*, 126. doi:10.3389/fpsyg.2014.00126.
Sturmberg, J. P., O'Halloran, D. M., & Martin, C. M. (2012). Understanding health system reform – A complex adaptive systems perspective. *Journal of Evaluation in Clinical Practice, 18*, 202–208.
Thelen, E., & Smith, L. B. (1994). *A dynamic systems approach to the development of cognition and action*. Cambridge, MA: MIT Press.
Thelen, E., & Smith, L. B. (1996). *A dynamic systems approach to the development of cognition and action*. Cambridge, MA: MIT Press/Bradford Books.
Thelen, E., & Smith, L. B. (2006). Dynamic systems theories. In R. M. Lerner (Ed.), *Handbook of child psychology: Theoretical models of human development* (Vol. 1, pp. 258–312). Hoboken, NJ: Wiley.
Tonneau, F. (2013). Neorealism: Unifying cognition and environment. *Review of General Psychology, 17*, 237–242.
Toomela, A. (2014). A structural systemic theory of causality and catalysis. In K. R. Cabell & J. Valsiner (Eds.), *The catalyzing mind: Beyond models of causality* (pp. 271–292). New York: Springer Science + Business Media.
Urban, J. B., Osgood, N. D., & Mabry, P. L. (2011). Developmental systems science: Exploring the application of systems science methods to developmental science questions. *Research in Human Development, 8*, 1–25.
Vallacher, R. R., Van Geert, P., & Nowak, A. (2015). The intrinsic dynamics of psychological process. *Current Directions in Psychological Science, 24*, 58–64.
Vallerand, R. J., Mageau, G. A., Ratelle, C., Léonard, M., Blanchard, C., Koestner, R., et al. (2003). Les passions de l'âme: On obsessive and harmonious passion. *Journal of Personality and Social Psychology, 85*, 756–767.
Valsiner, J. (2014). Breaking the arrows of causality: The idea of catalysis in its making. In K. R. Cabell & J. Valsiner (Eds.), *The catalyzing mind: Beyond models of causality* (pp. 17–32). New York: Springer Science + Business Media.
van der Helm, P. A. (2012). Cognitive architecture of perceptual organization: From neurons to gnosons. *Cognitive Process, 13*, 13–40.
Voestermans, P., & Verheggen, T. (2013). *Culture as embodiment: The social turning of behavior*. West Sussex, UK: Wiley-Blackwell.
Wager, T. D., & Atlas, L. Y. (2013). How is pain influenced by cognition? Neuroimaging weighs in. *Perspectives on Psychological Science, 8*, 91–97.
Walton, G. M. (2014). The new science of wise psychological interventions. *Current Directions in Psychological Science, 23*, 73–82.
Weidig, T., & Michaux, G. (2015). How the tower of information leads to an integrated framework for biopsychosocial ideas. *New Ideas in Psychology, 36*, 25–29.
Wellsby, M., & Pexman, P. M. (2014). Developing embodied cognition: Insights from children's concepts and language processing. *Frontiers in Psychology, 5*, 506. doi:10.3389/fpsyg.2014.00506.

Wiggins, J. L., & Monk, C. S. (2013). A translational neuroscience framework for the development of socioemotional functioning in health and psychopathology. *Development and Psychopathology, 25*, 1293–1309.

Wilson, A. D., & Golonka, S. (2013). Embodied cognition is not what you think it is. *Frontiers in Psychology, 4*, 58. doi:10.3389/fpsyg.2013.00058.

Wilson, T., & Holt, T. (2001). Complexity science: Complexity and clinical care. *British Medical Journal, 323*, 685–688.

Winkielman, P., & Kavanagh, L. C. (2013). The embodied perspective on cognition-emotion interactions. In M. D. Robinson, E. R. Watkins, & E. Harmon-Jones (Eds.), *Handbook of cognition and emotion* (pp. 213–230). New York: Guilford Press.

Wolff, P. (2007). Representing causation. *Journal of Experimental Psychology: General, 136*, 82–111.

Wolff, P. (2008). Dynamics and the perception of causal events. In T. Shipley & J. Zacks (Eds.), *Understanding events: How humans see, represent, and act on events*. New York: Oxford University Press.

Young, G. (2011). *Development and causality: Neo-Piagetian perspectives*. New York: Springer Science + Business Media.

Young, G., & Gagnon, M. (1990). Neonatal laterality, birth stress, familial sinistrality, and left brain inhibition. *Developmental Neuropsychology, 6*, 127–150.

Zhang, Y., & Risen, J. L. (2014). Embodied motivation: Using a goal systems framework to understand the preference for social and physical warmth. *Journal of Personality and Social Psychology, 107*, 965–977.

6 Statistical Concepts and Networks in Causality

Chapter Introduction

This chapter focuses on statistical concepts and applications in the study of causality over a range of topics in psychology and related disciplines. It shows that even classic designs related to uncovering causal influences (controlled studies, randomized control trials) can be complemented statistically by informative approaches. In addition, the chapter introduces the concept of networks in psychology and related disciplines, which is a cardinal concept in several chapters and one that permits the type of integration in psychology being sought in the book. The work in networks brings with it a new set of concepts in how components of networks relate to each other. Also, this work is heavily statistical, for example, in calculating the concepts of efficiency and betweenness in networks.

The first part of the chapter looks at causal modeling in psychological testing theory, for which Markus and Borsboom (2013) covered a range of theories and issues. For example, for testing, they considered reflective, formative, and mutualistic models and, for causation, they considered regularity, counterfactual, and process theories.

Shadish and Sullivan (2012) explored in depth three major approaches to statistical causal models. There is much overlap in their review and that of Markus and Borsboom (2013). They compared and contrasted the classic causal model (Campbell) with those of Rubin and Pearl. The former model is related to potential outcomes and the latter model to counterfactuals (directed acyclic graphs, DAGs). The chapter refers to Pearl's (2014a) updating of his important work (Pearl, 2000, 2009).

Epidemiology is an observational science and so it is highly dependent on statistical techniques for inferring causality. In this present chapter, Shrout, Keyes, and Ornstein (2011), in particular, present the various statistical approaches in epidemiology. The works of Rubin and of Pearl are central in this discipline, too, but chapters in Shrout et al. (2011) show how they are being revised.

The Bayesian approach constitutes a major advance in the field and is becoming increasingly important and prevalent. I review the accessible summary of the Bayesian approach provided by van der Schoot et al. (2013).

Other work elaborates methods in statistics that help elucidate causal inference. In particular, in this regard in this chapter, I review the work of Berzuini, Dawid, and Bernardinelli (2012a, 2012b) on approaches to this question. It is noteworthy that the work of Rubin and Pearl is involved (and updated). The book by Berzuini et al. includes a chapter by Rutter (2012) on relevant design.

The next section of the chapter provides examples of psychological study in which causality has been a central focus. Often, these designs are longitudinal and consider possible reverse causation (e.g., pre-existing factors can account for patterns imputed to a putative intervening variable). Generally, in this type of research, confounders,

G. Young, *Unifying Causality and Psychology*, DOI 10.1007/978-3-319-24094-7_6

moderating, and mediating influences need to be considered.

In the area of psychopathology, Haynes has been a leader in the field in explaining how causality can be determined. He has augmented his classic 1992 work with another (Haynes, O'Brien, & Kaholokula, 2011), which I review.

Friston, Moran, and Seth (2013) described the techniques that are used to establish neuronal connectivity in brain research, such as in fMRI (functional magnetic resonance imaging). The dynamic approach has been complemented by the newer Granger Causality (GC) approach. The latter originated in economics but has been applied to multiple disciplines.

GC has been applied to ecology, as well. The next portion of the chapter presents work in the area of ecology related to causality involving GC and other approaches. This work could have import for psychopathology (e.g., bipolarity), given the effort to map tonic and phasic activity in ecological systems.

The chapter terminates with an in-depth presentation of the concepts of networks in psychology. Borsboom and colleagues have been leaders in the field in network modeling of psychological disorder, and I describe their work on PTSD (posttraumatic stress disorder), in particular (McNally et al., 2015). The major types of networks in psychological phenomena relate to centrality compared to various measures of dispersion. McNally et al. (2015) investigated the symptom structure in PTSD with respect to their dynamical linkages. They indicated that their approach is superior to the standard latent construct model of psychological disorder. Other workers have investigated PTSD in ways that speak to networks, and this research includes research on biomarkers and the brain. However, I argue for a more integrated approach to networks in psychopathology, consistent with a more transdiagnostic approach, for example, and one that determines core symptoms of disorder, as well. Note that the concept of networks is explored in more depth in the ensuing chapters on the brain and its lateralization. As well, it surfaces in the chapters on the DSM-5 (Diagnostic and Statistical Manual of Mental Disorder, Fifth Edition; American Psychiatric Association, 2013).

Testing and Causality

Introduction

The two fields of statistics (and mathematics) and conceptions of reality are fields of inquiry that influence each other. Statistical scholarship involves more than methodological tools, because statistical methods reflect naturally present concepts that they are meant to represent. At the same time, proposals of naturally present concepts might be bereft of the subtleties that mathematics allow, and so they can be complemented and fleshed out by translation into mathematics, where possible. That being said, statistics and mathematics cannot propose by themselves the concepts needed to understand nature. They might emanate from and reflect them, but conceptual modeling can take place independently from them. However, statistics and mathematics can be so far advanced that they actually create the natural concepts that we seek. They are languages in their own right that verbal representations of nature might find hard to grasp. Truly, science needs statistics and mathematics to stand at the frontlines of its conceptual endeavors, and not just its empirical ones.

Testing

Markus and Borsboom (2013) offered a view of test validity theorizing in which causation is central. Their points of view are indicated by the following questions. Do latent constructs act to cause test score values, as in latent variable models? Or, do behavioral/test item indices act to cause latent constructs? Or, rather, is there no causal relationship involved, merely empirical ones? The latent variable argument maintains that individual difference in (item) response probabilities are "caused" by individual differences in the latent variable, aside from other item factors. The other views deny this classic version of test theory.

Markus and Borsboom elaborated that, in models governing testing statistics, behavior domain theory (BDT) conceptualizes item responses as samples from behavior domains, which is one way of conceptualizing constructs.

In the causal theory of measurement (CTM), constructs represent common causes that underlie sets of item responses. The former model requires generalization from item to domain, and is "agnostic" about causation, while the latter is "generic" about causal inference.

These theoretical test models relate to the psychometric models of reflective and formative test construction, respectively. In the former model, standard statistical clustering approaches are used (e.g., factor analysis); individual item scores are decomposed into a common latent variable and a unique score. In the latter model, newer statistical methods are used (e.g., principle components analysis); a composite variable is modeled as a weighted summation of item scores. These contrasting positions (BDT, CTM) can be combined into a compatibilist model within the reflective approach by considering items as causally homogenous behavior domains. They reflect "attributes" that cause item scores. They lead to domain scores that supervene over item scores.

As for causality in measurement, Markus and Borsboom (2013) returned to the difference between reflective and formative models. In the former model, test scores are modeled as effects of the construct. It implies that item responses have local independence. In the latter model, test scores are modeled as causes of the construct. It denies local independence of item responses. The reflective model has a step in its working that tests whether the composite score calculated is an estimate of the attribute, unlike the case for the formative model.

Markus and Borsboom (2013) proposed that it is difficult to establish unifactorial models, such as "*g*" for intelligence, because there are usually multiple underlying latent variables or causes involved. Even when, statistically, one factor seems predominant, simply, it could be through shared multiple "bonds." A similar model has been proposed, the watershed model, in which there are downstream phenotypes and upstream influences, which are more distal, such as genes, and with intermediate influences along the pathway, such as cerebral volume and neural plasticity.

An alternate model of intelligence considers its subtests as positively intercorrelated, or "mutualistic" (Van der Maas et al., 2006). This concept is conducive to a network model, such as in directed acyclic graph (DAG) causal modeling (Pearl, 2009). In this model, if there are no feedback loops, conditional independence relations between the variables in the network can be found (which is not the case for latent variable models). However, generally, in the psychological sphere, network nodes are connected and reciprocal. The authors noted that the model needs further work for effective application psychometrically.

To conclude, for traits such as found in personality, one can take the stance that they reflect constructs, or that they, simply, are pragmatic synthesizing descriptions. Further work is needed to integrate these approaches, and, in this regard, variations of network modeling might be the avenue to take.

Causality

Markus and Borsboom (2013) considered three major theories of causation. (a) In regularity theory, causation is found in basic regularities in nature, actual states, and empirical reductionist variables. (b) Counterfactual theories attempt to reduce causation to counterfactuals (such as "but-for" evidence), and are quite popular today (e.g., Pearl, 2009; Rubin, 1974). (c) Process theories concern mechanisms, or the assumptions underlying the theories.

Regularity theory is not much more than "probability" theory about regularities in actual events. Counterfactuals examine "unrealized possibilities." Process theories are about the causal processes that "sustain" causal relationships.

About interpretation, regularity theory does not go much beyond the evidence. Counterfactual theory seeks evidence about possible dependencies. Process theories seek evidence beyond dependencies.

Markus and Borsboom (2013) ended their book with work on causal interpretations in measurement models. In regularity causation, models are robust when control variables are "inert." It seeks generalization to new populations and situations ("transfer over inert variables"). In counterfactual causation, interventions are applied, and it seeks support for causal links that are robust against changing control variables. In process causation, causal models remain robust to interventions that do not change the response process. It seeks evidence that the mechanism is responsible for the relevant causal link.

Markus and Borsboom (2013) have presented a work at the frontier of test validity theory. I have left aside their mathematical work, concepts on validity, and so on. However, the authors are to be complemented for placing causation at the forefront in test construction and modeling.

Statistical Causal Modeling

Introduction

Shadish and Sullivan (2012) compared and contrasted three primary statistical causal models in psychological science: Campbell's Causal Model (CCM); Rubin's Causal Model (RCM); and Pearl's Causal Model (PCM). The first model was developed by Campbell (1957) and then extended (e.g., Shadish, Cook, & Campbell, 2002). The second model is attributed to a group of workers headed by Rubin (e.g., Holland, 1986; Rubin, 2004a, 2004b, 2010; and also Rubin & Thomas, 1992). The third model is based on the work of Pearl and colleagues (e.g., Pearl, 2000, 2009; Tian & Pearl, 2000). CCM is based on validity typology, RCM on estimating potential outcomes, with its core assumption of stable-unit-treatment-value assumption (SUTVA); and PCM on path models based on DAGs.

Models

CCM begins with the distinction between internal and external validity, or representativeness and generalizability (the latter is considered the most important type of validity). It adds statistical conclusion validity (the validity of inferences about the correlation/covariation between treatment and outcome) and, as well, construct validity, which is a mainstay of psychological science (inferring validity from a study's operations to the theoretical constructs that they supposedly represent). CCM gives importance to threats to validity, and these should be minimized by appropriate study design.

In RCM, Y represents the outcome measure. The independent variable is W. $Y(1)$ represents the potential outcome if the unit/participant is exposed to the treatment level of $W(1)$. $Y(0)$ represents the potential outcome if there is no such exposure ($W=0$). Given these parameters, the potential individual causal effect is the difference between $Y(1)$ and $Y(0)$. Once treatment begins, depending on which is administered, potential outcomes become measurable. Therefore, the difficulty in RCM is estimating missing, nonobserved potential outcomes, which are sometimes referred to as counterfactuals.

In PCM, causal inference is established by a set of statistical rules, including nonparametric structural equation models (SEM) and path analysis. DAGs resemble diagrams but include graph theory and elements from logic study. They are Markovian (acyclic). Being nonparametric in SEMs, they do not specify whether links between nodes are linear, quadratic, cubic, etc. Nodes are represented by single solid dots in DAGs. Also, arrows represent "edges," which indicate the link between variables (e.g., X, Y). When arrows are "directed," or are going in one direction, they indicate the presumed causal effect or relationship. Edges could be bidirectional, could form path sequences, etc. Statistically independent variables are considered "d" separated (directional separation). The mathematical operator $do(x)$ helps model causal effects and counterfactuals.

Shadish and Sullivan (2012) noted that PCM differs from CCM and RCM by emphasizing explanatory compared to descriptive causation (respectively, addressing the causal model within which X and Y are embedded; did X cause Y?). The explanations sought provide the basis for more general causal claims (the necessary and sufficient conditions that allow for generalized descriptive causal relations).

Also, Shadish and Sullivan (2012) pointed out that PCM's definition of causal effect depends on solving an equation set that represents a DAG in order to estimate the effect of X ($X=x$) on Y, using the *do(x)* operator (usually by calculating a regression coefficient). Another approach is in relation to the difference in the effect involving *X* as *x*1 and *x*2.

According to Shadish and Sullivan (2012), critics of the PCM note that cause-probing studies in field settings cannot lead to accurate DAGs (e.g., due to selection biases). PCM is an inductivist approach and both CCM and RCM require good research design and deduction.

Comment

Shadish and Sullivan concluded that the three models are beginning to cross-reference each other, and this portends a truly integrated theory of causation in the social sciences. Similarly, Gelman (2011) noted that PCM "do" operators are like interventions. The "causality-as-intervention" perspective needs to be complemented by a "system-variable" perspective.

Pearl (2014a) furthered his work on statistical modeling by developing notions and mathematics related to the interpretation and identification of causal mediation. According to Pearl (2014a), the modeling presented could facilitate real-world causal scenario understanding.

Epidemiology

Introduction

Gerstman (2013) presented the epidemiological view of causality. Disease is induced by causal interactions, some of the components of which must necessarily be present. Other factors are contributing. Causal complements complete the set of needed components for a disease. Causes are arrayed in a causal web, some of which are direct, downstream, or proximal and others of which are indirect, upstream, or distal. Direct causes usually are found at the microlevel, and indirect ones at the macrolevel. Deciding the presence of causality in a system demands causal inference, given the observational, nonexperimental nature of epidemiology.

Hill's (1965) framework is the classic one in arriving at decisions about causal inference in epidemiology. For example, in temporality, exposure to the causal factor precedes disease onset in a reasonable amount of time. Causality decision making is a process of judgment. Biological interaction refers to the relationship of the causal components in disease. Statistical interaction is not equivalent to this—it refers to the joint effects of different exposures.

Bracken (2013) referred to the ultimate cause as equivalent to Aristotle's final one. It is the necessary and sufficient cause, the tipping cause that produces a disease, notwithstanding risk factors that are proximal in the core of causation.

Rabins (2013) developed a causal epidemiological model that refers to predisposing (vulnerability) and precipitating (triggering) cause [Generally, there is also perpetuating cause that accompanies the other two]. For Rabins, two other causes in epidemiology concern programmatic cause and purposive cause. Programmatic cause refers to systemic, interactional factors and purposive cause to the why an event occurred (e.g., natural selection). The four levels in this model were derived from the Aristotelian concepts of material, efficient, formal, and final cause, respectively.

Statistical Models

Shrout et al. (2011) co-edited a book on the topic of epidemiological study of psychopathology, and it covers a range of topics conceptually and methodologically related to the question. The difficulty that this area of study needs to confront with respect to causality concerns making causal inferences from observational data. The contributors presented both conceptual and methodological advances that removed some of the uncertainties inevitably associated with the question. The book deals with the models by Rubin and Pearl and colleagues, but gives insight beyond them, too.

In the book's introduction, Shrout (2011) presented several outstanding themes in causal analysis. Rubin (1974, 1978) pioneered work on making strong causal inferences even in nonexperimental studies by using a "potential outcomes approach." The approach asks to consider the differential effects of causes A vs. B as they might influence a given individual, even though the person cannot experience both causes/conditions. Only one treatment, for example, can be administered to an individual for a given outcome measurement.

Shrout (2011) pointed out that although individual causal effects cannot be known in this area of study, the average causal effects can be estimated in appropriate research designs. In particular, between-individual information can be used to estimate the within-person treatment counterfactual potential outcome causal effects. However, in this type of research, the subjects must be equivalent on all relevant parameters, or be interchangeable. Rubin (1980, 1990) referred to this assumption as SUTVA, as mentioned.

In experiments with actual clinical trials, methodological confounders relate to nonadherence to treatment, missing data, and confounding variables, which serve to create bias in the causal effect. Participants might be dealt with in terms of intent to treat (ITT). As for nonexperimental observational studies, the alleged causal effects might be overstated without consideration of all confounding variables. Given the difficulties in designing randomized controlled trials (RCTs) for many of the topics in psychopathology, alternate designs, such as quasi-experimental ones, might be used.

However, analytic approaches have been developed to deal with confounding variables. Pearl's (2000, 2009) work on DAGs is the most noteworthy in this regard. DAGs constitute explicit statements of assumed causal paths. They include concepts such as "do" operators, causal "descendents," and "control" variables.

Shrout (2011) noted that DAGs tend to emphasize causal relations as if they had their effects simultaneously, without due consideration of temporal patterns. For example, outcome might be unstable and change over time. Also, Shrout (2011) noted the difference in mediation and moderation of causal effects. Mediators might fully or partially explain causal effects, and are considered involved in indirect causal paths. Moreover, even if moderators (influences) and mediators are fully established in a mediation analysis of a causal dynamic, the next step of determining the meaning of the data might not be clear. Causality is heterogeneous in scope and effects are individualized (e.g., to intervention).

Schwartz, Gatto, and Campbell (2011) presented a variation of the counterfactual approach and its emphasis on causal intervention or manipulation. It involves two preliminary steps—causal identification and causal explanation. The former concerns identifying whether an exposure/treatment had caused an outcome, while the latter concerns how the exposure/treatment caused it. Causation is multiply determined and can be established through manipulation.

Schwartz et al. (2011) contended that manipulation in experiments or hypotheticals constitute ideal cases that do not necessarily apply to the real world. A study might have internal validity but not external validity, lacking real-world generalization. Therefore, Schwartz et al. (2011) developed their model of an integrated counterfactual approach (ICA). In step 1, causal identification is undertaken, following Mackie's (1965, 1974) concept of INUS (insufficient but necessary components of unnecessary but sufficient causes) and Rothman's (1976) "causal pies." The upshot of the approach is that causality is multi-determined.

Schwartz et al. (2011) contrasted the ICA model with the traditional potential outcomes approach (see Table 6.1). Whereas in the former, the goal is to establish effects of causes, in the latter, the goal is to establish causes of effects. The former's quantitative approach can inform the latter, which remains a qualitative one. Moreover, in ICA any factor can be a cause, even if it is not manipulable. In interpretation, the former model expects inconsistencies but not the latter.

About causal explanation, it involves traditional concepts of validity (construct, and external). What ingredients and pathways are involved and can the results be generalized?

As for causal manipulation, Schwartz et al. (2011) contended that the interpretative approach should involve dynamic complexity theory and systems analysis. This promotes an integrated causal understanding that can account for feedback loops. It facilitates appropriate policy and therapeutic decisions. In this step, the focus is on prediction and on the mediators, moderators, and other

Table 6.1 Comparison of the potential outcomes model and the integrated counterfactual approach

	Potential outcomes model	Integrated counterfactual approach
Goal	Estimates true causal effects • Estimate • Quantitative • Effects of causes	Identifies true causes • Identify • Qualitative • Causes of effects
Mean	Compares two potential outcomes • Entire population under two exposures • Manipulable causes • Stable Unit Treatment Value Assumption (SUTVA) • Mimics random assignment	Compares a fact with a counterfactual • Exposed under two conditions • Any factor • Construct validity • Mimics assignment of exposed
Interpretation	Potential outcome in future • Consistency expected	Causal effect of past • Inconsistency expected

Adopted by permission of Oxford University Press. Schwartz et al. (2011). What would have been is not what would be: Counterfactuals of the past and potential outcomes of the future. In P. E. Shrout, K. M. Keyes, & K. Ornstein (Eds.), *Causality and psychopathology: Finding the determinants of disorders and their cures* (pp. 25–46). New York: Oxford University Press. Reprinted by permission of Oxford University Press, USA. [Table 2.1, Page 39]

nodes in the system. The authors concluded that the methods for this level in their model are not yet fully developed.

Comment

Kendler (2011) advocated for the interventionist/counterfactual approach for psychiatry. Psychopathology is ill-suited to the deductive-nomological and mechanistic approaches to causality, in that these approaches are reductive. In contrast, DAG/interventionist/counterfactual approaches can account for the "extraordinary" complexity of psychiatric disorders and their causes. The approach is practical, empirical, atheoretical, and causality-oriented ("optimal").

Bayesian Approach

Introduction

According to van der Schoot et al. (2013), the Bayesian approach to statistical analysis offers an alternative to traditional approaches and might allow for better understanding of psychological phenomena. The contrasting approach, the predominant one in psychological science, is referred to as null hypothesis significance testing (NHST; in it Ho is contrasted to the experimental hypothesis H1). The main advantage of Bayesian analysis (BA) is that it permits the incorporation of background knowledge into statistical testing, instead of setting aside lessons from past studies. The major statistical underpinnings to BA compared to NHST relate to that, in the latter, the paradigm is "frequentist," whereas, for the former, it is "subjective."

Models

In the NHST frequentist approach, the base of calculations depends on "long run" frequency, such as in an infinite coin toss. For this example, the probability p of head and tail outcomes is enumerated in a "sample space" of possibilities. In the BA subjective approach, probability is interpreted as "the subjective experience of uncertainty." The paradigmatic example for this statistical approach to probability is "placing a bet." This approach allows for learning from experience, such as from prior information and using personal judgment. Once the outcome is established, it leads to appropriate revision of priors. The ingredients of the BA approach, therefore, include the following core factors.

They help contrast the BA approach from the frequentist one:

(a) Background knowledge of the parameters of the model being tested. This ingredient is "captured" in the distribution of priors, or "prior distribution," which might take the form of a normal distribution. The uncertainty parameter is expressed by the variance in the prior distribution, the inverse of which is referred to as "precision."

(b) The second BA ingredient is constituted by the information contained in the sample data. This "observed" evidence is expressed by the "likelihood function" of the sample data in light of the model parameters.

(c) The third ingredient in BA reflects a combination of the prior two. It is referred to as the "posterior inference."

Together, these three fundamentals constitute a working version of Bayes' theorem (BT). Specifically BT states that an updated understanding of parameters of interest, given observed data, depends on prior knowledge about these parameters weighted by the current evidence, as based on the parameters.

The knowledge and empirical base in any area of study might not allow for enough prior information to help in elaborating posterior inferences. In the BA approach, this state of affairs can still be captured into statistical specification. Quantifying "ignorance" is as important as quantifying cumulative understanding in an area. If the prior distribution cannot be estimated with confidence, different prior specifications are compared for outcomes according to their influence, in a process of prior "sensitivity analysis." If there is none of relevant prior data, accumulated knowledge, or meta-analyses, the prior distribution is referred to as "noninformative" and, in this regard, it parallels the NHST and its frequentist approach of letting the data speak for themselves.

However, often, informative expected prior distributions can be estimated and, in such cases, the parameters involved are referred to as "hyperparameters." They might refer to an estimated prior mean or average and the associated prior precision. If the precision estimate is low (the associated prior variance is high), the prior distribution is considered "low-informative." Every parameter in an applicable model requires specification of its associated prior distribution. These become more accurate estimates with appropriate specification of inclusion/exclusion criteria. Priors need to be determined before examination of obtained data.

According to BT, prior distributions and current data are employed in combination to form the posterior distribution. In most cases, a simulation process using Markovian chain Monte Carlo methods specifies the posterior distribution. It uses an iterative procedure to estimate parameters instead of traditional analysis for "point estimates."

In the traditional approach, confidence intervals (CIs; e.g., 95 %) specify the certainty of the range of possible values associated with a result obtained statistically (or, better, the degree to which the true parameter is captured under Ho). The equivalent BA calculation to this frequentist approach is referred to as "posterior probabilities intervals" (PPIs). This "credibility" interval refers to the probability (e.g., 95 %) in the population at hand that the parameter at issue lays between the two specified values. Although classical CIs are interpreted this way, that is mistaken, for they are really reflections of how well replications of the same study will capture the fixed yet unknown parameter at issue, assuming that the alternative hypothesis about the parameter is "true." Thus, PPIs appear "easier" to communicate than NHST CIs. Moreover, the more priors are accurate estimates, the more Bayesian PPIs are lower than equivalent NHST CIs; that is, one can be "more certain" about the obtained statistical results.

Model fitting is a statistical process in BA accomplished with the chi-square statistic. It contrasts with traditional frequentist approaches, e.g., SEM, which evaluate an entire model rather than a single hypothesis. Model fitting in BA involves assessing model predictive accuracy via posterior "predictive checking." The better the model fits, the less the data are discrepant, and the BA process inherently functions toward arriving at this end because of BA's capacity to adjust priors in light of accrued knowledge. Chi-square is used in cases in which model fit is quantified by computing Bayesian posterior predictive *p* values (*ppp*s). The *ppp* value is calculated as the proportion of chi-square values obtained in simulated data relevant to the problem that are in excess of the actual data, so that models that fit well have *ppp* values of around 0.50.

Conclusion

According to van der Schoot et al. (2013), even when there are large sample sizes and all parameters are normally distributed, BA might represent a better approach than NHST because of its advantages in interpretation (even though in such cases the specific results would be quite comparable). First, the results in BA are more "intuitive," being focused on predictive accuracy. Second, BA incorporates background knowledge via a prior distribution. Also, it specifies when there is a lack or ignorance of such knowledge. When the latter is present, they might influence results. Third, the BA procedure allows for updating knowledge, instead of engaging in repeated null hypothesis testing in an area. Practically, in particular, there is less worry about small sample sizes and about non-normal distributions of parameters.

The authors concluded that Bayesian methods could be applied fruitfully to psychological study. They contrasted frequentist and Bayesian statistics in the following way. (a) For definition of *p* value, traditionally, *p* refers to the probability of obtaining the same or more extreme data in the population, assuming Ho is true. In BA, *p* value is the probability of H0, or "the (null) hypothesis." (b) For sample sizes, the NHST approach requires large ones when normal theory-based measures are used and, in BA, this is "not necessarily" the case. (c) For inclusion of prior knowledge, the contrast lies in the fact that it is not part of the statistical procedure in NHST, but it is possible in BA. (d) For nature of model parameters, in NHST, they are "unknown but fixed," whereas in BA they are "unknown and therefore random." (e) For population parameters, "one true value" in NHST is contrasted with "a distribution of values reflecting certainty" in BA. (f) For defining certainty, compare "the sampling distribution" based on the notion of "infinite repeated sampling" in NHST with "probability distribution for the population parameter" in BA. (g) For estimated intervals, CI in NHST is contrasted with credibility interval in BA. van der Schoot et al. (2013) referred the interested reader to the online version of the article, which includes demonstrations of applicable statistical programs (e.g., Mplus; Muthén & Asparouhov, 2012).

Indeed, even the brain can be described in attributes related to freedom. The Bayesian model has been applied to brain theory (De Ridder, Vanneste, & Freeman, 2014). A Bayesian brain is like a "probability machine" aimed at reducing the perception of uncertainty, prediction error, and "free energy" (Friston, 2009, 2010).

Bayesian models of behavior are important to the present work on causality of behavior. The indeterminacy of causal influences and their subjective appraisals are evident in this approach. Therefore, it is consistent with a model of behavioral causality that de-emphasizes the inevitable one-to-one correspondence between (a) biological and social/environmental influences on behavior, and their interaction and (b) behavioral outcome.

Methods

Introduction

The statistical study of causality is an essential component to its scientific study. Berzuini et al. (2012a) described approaches in the field. In the following, I focus on background and material accessible to psychology.

Berzuini et al. (2012b) noted that before the field began to mature (Fisher, 1935), epidemiology and biostatistics were cautious about causality. Studies had to be "secure" and did not rely on any special assumptions pertaining to the nature of any "uncontrolled variation." Only through randomization in experimental studies could security be achieved, in that any pre-existing group differences in treatment groups are controlled by randomization.

The classic epidemiological approach to causality is based on Hill's (1965) criteria (see Table 6.2). They allow for inference about causality in the absence of critical experimentation and solely on observational data (see Chen & Cao, 2012).

Hill's (1965) criteria for establishing causation in observational studies constituted an

Table 6.2 Hill's criteria for causation

Criteria	Explanation
Strength of association	The stronger the more likely causal
Consistency	The observed association repeatable in different populations at different times
Temporal relationship	The cause precedes the effect
Biological gradient	Dose–response relationship
Plausibility	Must make sense biologically
Coherence	The observation should not conflict with existing knowledge
Experimental evidence	A controlled study firmly supports causation
Specificity	Associated with only one outcome
Analogy	Can be applied to similar case

Adapted from Hill (1965)

advance in the area. He proposed a list of guidelines to support inferences about causal interpretation in such studies.

At the philosophical level, Berzuini et al. (2012b) referred to Mackie's (1965) INUS model and Wright's (1988) NESS one. The latter refers to "necessary element for the sufficiency of a sufficient set" and the former, as mentioned, to "an insufficient but necessary part of a necessary but sufficient condition."

As reviewed above, cause-effect relations were also studied through potential outcomes (Rubin, 1974) and graphical representation (e.g., Non Parametric Structural Equation Models, NPSEMs; Pearl, 2000; also called DAGs) approaches. The decision theoretic approach (Dawid, 2012) developed as an alternative and is considered superordinate to these latter approaches.

Berzuini et al. (2012b) remarked that studies based on randomization might be secure but do little to unravel mechanism. They described that there are different approaches to the concept of mechanism, each having different statistical approaches. For example, one could ask if a treatment causally affects an outcome directly or indirectly (via mediators and moderators, respectively; Baron & Kenny, 1986).

Berzuini et al. (2012b) continued that causality is dynamic and its elucidation requires synthesis of multiple streams of evidence. Moreover, it applies as much to establishing causal relations in individual cases (which is important legally, for example), as to the population level. In this regard, they make the distinction between "scientific" causality, which is interested in the "effects of causes," and "legal" causality, which is concerned with the "causes of effects."

Sauce and Matzel (2013) distinguished between the normative causation of behavior and the causes of individual differences in behavior. The former might be only an ideal in that systemic variation in behavior is the norm. Moreover, individual differences result from an interaction of causes. Sauce and Matzel (2013) concluded that, in this sense, correlational methods are quite relevant to the study of causality.

Designs

Rutter (2012) examined "natural" or "quasi" experiments, or the research designs available other than randomization ones, such as in behavior genetics. He found that causal inferences could be established with natural experiments (Cook & Campbell, 1979; Shadish et al., 2002). Beyond genetically sensitive designs (twin, adoptee, migration studies), one could examine discordant sibling pairs, the children of twins, offspring of assisted reproductive technology applications, adoption involving radical change in environment (Romanian orphanage studies), universal introduction of risk (WWII famine studies), and universal removal of risk (stopping use of putatively dangerous environmental variables). To rule out reverse causation, designs could include Mendelian randomization and study of early puberty. To deal with unmeasured confounders, one approach is to use regression discontinuity design. Rutter (2012) concluded that no design is free of limitations. Emsley and Dunn (2012) noted the potential mediators in randomized control trials involving psychotherapy.

Donofrino, Class, Lahey, and Larsson (2014) suggested that family-based, quasi-experimental designs can be used carefully to test the causal link between early risk factors and later psychopathological outcomes independent of confounding factors. These techniques include design features that can act to "rule out" confounding influences and, therefore, are more powerful in this regard than statistical techniques involving the control of relevant covariates. Similar to Rutter (2012), Donofrino et al. (2014) noted the utility of family-based quasi-experimental designs, which include sibling comparison, cotwin control, offspring of siblings/twins, adoption at birth, and in vitro fertilization.

Statistical Strategies

McLanahan, Tach, and Schneider (2013) reviewed the multiple methodological strategies being used to ascertain causal effects when questions arise about variable bias and reverse causality. The topic they addressed concerned the effects of father absence. The studies reviewed use innovations such as lagged dependent variable (LDV) models, growth curve models, individual fixed effects models, sibling fixed effects models, propensity score matching models, and natural experiments. Each approach was considered to have limitations as well as advantages, with the LDV and growth curve models tending to find "stronger" evidence for some outcome variables.

Duncan and Magnuson (2012) indicated how components of socioeconomic status (SES) could be causally related to cognitive functioning even without the possibility of studying global SES in experimental designs. For example, quasi-experimental or natural experiments could take place (e.g., increased income available through change in income tax policies) in ongoing research on children's cognitive function. Or, actual early intervention programs can be studied experimentally in random assignment designs in which aspects of cognitive function are measured.

To move from correlates to causes, Jaffee, Strait, and Odgers (2011) suggested using quasi-experimental and twin research designs. Statistically, the authors recommended propensity score approaches (e.g., Rosenbaum & Rubin, 1985) and group-based trajectory modeling combined with them. To conclude, to help ascertain causal chains, Jaffee et al. (2011) recommended the use of longitudinal research with measurement burst designs. This allows capturing short-term finer-grained change at critical developmental junctions. Also, within-individual changes allow children to serve as their own control in the more elaborate statistical procedures available (e.g., regression discontinuity).

Causal Mediation

Introduction

Shpitser (2012) described "compromise" approaches to potential outcome (e.g., Rubin's) and Non-Parametric Structural Equation Models (NPSEM; e.g., Pearl's) approaches. They include minimal causal models (MCMs, Robins & Richardson, 2011) and using covariate adjustment in NPSEMs for identifying causal effects (Shpitser, VanderWeele, & Robins, 2010). Both Dawid (2012) and Greenland (2012) have noted that there is no formal explication of statistical causality that could satisfy the different approaches.

Statistical Strategies

MacKinnon and Pirlott (2015) examined statistical approaches for enhancing causal interpretation in statistical mediation methods. They presented new statistical methods to help infer mediator variables (*M*) as indicators of causes or psychological processes underlying outcome (dependent) variables (*Y*) at issue (independent of independent variables, *X*) in research. The first approach might be to reduce the effect of confounder bias and the second to address their possible influences. Confounder bias severely limits the capacity to infer causation of the mediator for the dependent outcome variable. Randomization research can deal with confounders, at least for the relationship of *X* to *M* and *X* to *Y*, but not of the *M* to *Y* mediation (the "b" effect in regression), where "a" and "c" represent the estimated *X* to *M* and *X* to *Y* relations).

To control for confounder bias, in sensitivity analysis, counterfactual/potential outcomes modeling can be used. This type of modeling is needed because there is no randomization experiment and, in the typical case, individuals participate in only one condition. The strategy in this approach is to estimate outcome by asking the counterfactual "what might their behavior be otherwise?" Practically, one could determine how large a confounder effect on the *M* to *Y* relation must exist in order to compromise causal interpretation. MacKinnon and Pirlott (2015) referred to this method under the rubric of "average causal mediation effect" (ACME). A second approach was developed by VanderWeele (2010), and is beyond the scope of the present paper. A third approach is the left-out variables error method (LOVE). It calculates correlations using a hypothesized confounder (for the confounder with *Y* and with *M*), making an observed mediation effect zero (MacKinnon, Cox, Miocevic, & Kisbu-Sakarya, 2012).

As for statistical methods to improve causal conclusions from mediation data, new approaches to address violations of assumptions about confounder bias have been formulated. They involve: (a) comprehensive structural equation models (Bollen, 1989); (b) instrumental variable methods (Holland, 1988; Sobel, 2008); (c) principal stratification (Frangakis & Rubin, 2002; Jo, 2008); and (d) inverse probability weighting (Robins, Hernán, & Brumback, 2000). In (a), the researcher attempts to measure all possible confounders; in (b), a randomized *X* predicts *M* and then the predicted values of *M* predict *Y*. The coefficient related *M* predicted to *Y* can stand as the causal estimator of b (under certain conditions); in (c), investigators identity hypothetical subsets of subjects on the basis of how *M* might change in response to experimental manipulation *X* or control (an approach applicable to categorical mediators); and in (d), investigators use observed covariates to measure confounder effects and then to adjust analyses to remove any confounder bias.

Mediation analyses are designed to extract information about causal mechanism(s) through which a predictor variable affects an outcome or outcomes. Preacher (2015) reviewed current approaches to statistical mediation analysis. They include mediation analysis in: (a) longitudinal research; (b) in causal inferences; (c) for discrete/nonnormal variables; and (d) in multilevel designs.

For longitudinal mediation analyses, there are three major types: the approaches of (a) cross-lagged panel modeling (CLPM); (b) latent growth curve modeling (LGM); and (c) latent change scores (LCS). Even better models are emerging in this regard, such as state-space modeling (SSM), and continuous time modeling (CTM). For example, the former recognizes explicitly that mediation is a "within-person" process; it uses either a single individual's multivariate time series or those of multiple people.

For the section of causal inference for indirect effects, Preacher (2015) referred to the Campbell approach (e.g., Campbell & Stanley, 1963), which is a design-based one, and model-based traditions (e.g., Rubin, 1974, 2004a). These approaches had been compared in Shadish and Sullivan (2012), as reviewed above. Other approaches in this regard include Pearl's (2009) DAGs approach. Imai, Jo, and Stuart (2011) and Imai, Tingley, and Yamamoto (2013) have developed an approach that borrows the strength of each of these approaches, especially the design- and model-based approaches.

Categorical/nonnormal variables in mediation modeling include generalized linear mediation models (GLMs). For mediation in multilevel designs, Preacher (2015) referred to multilevel modeling strategies and multilevel structural equation modeling. He concluded that there is not one correct way to implement mediation analysis of data.

Pearl (2014a, 2014b) reviewed the foundations of mediation analysis, building on his earlier work (e.g., Pearl, 2000). Part of his goal was to compare his approach that of Imai and colleagues (e.g., Imai, Keele, & Tingley, 2010; Imai, Keele, Tingley, & Yamamoto, 2014), who used an "ignorability"-based approach. Pearl's approach is based on DAGs, as we have seen, which he deems essential in judging/interpreting plausibility because, for identification analysis, it enables researchers to "mechanize" choices made of relevant covariates. His approach focuses on the "natural" mediated effect, which concerns the expected output change when letting the mediator change "as if" the input changed. Pearl concluded that, for proper definition, the concept of mediation requires counterfactual conditionals rather than Bayes ones.

Comment

This concludes a complex sojourn into the statistical basis in the study of causality, and work in epidemiology has led the field. The classic approach of establishing validity as best one can has been supplemented by the approaches of potential outcomes and DAGs, and these, in turn, have been revised. Moreover, other models have been developed. In addition, meditational analyses have taken center stage, and the tests that can be used are becoming too complex for simple presentation in a brief review, so that the reader should consult the original sources mentioned. That said, population-level research needs to establish with rigor causality in order that it can be applied effectively to individuals, such as in the health professional-patient context.

In research on causality in psychology, Stephen Haynes has been a leader in the field. For population research, he refers to classical statistics, but for work with patients he uses diagrams. In the following, I switch course from advanced statistics to see how causality might be treated classically at the statistical level, given that this approach still predominates. After in this section, I examine Haynes' diagrammatic approach to patients.

Once Hayne's work is reviewed, I look at other areas in psychology in which statistics are relevant to establishing causality. Then, I consider it in neuroscience, ecology, and other nonpsychological areas. To close the chapter, I return to the causality of psychology by considering networks in PTSD.

Applications

Psychopathology

Populations Haynes, O'Brien, Kaholokula, and Witteman (2012) analyzed concepts of causality in psychopathology, extending Hayne's work (1992; Haynes et al., 2011). They argued that clinicians need a firm understanding of causality for psychological assessment, case formulation, and functional analysis.

According to Haynes et al. (2012), causes can be sufficient, necessary, insufficient, and immediate (proximal). A sufficient cause does not have to be exclusive in eliciting the indicated outcome. A necessary cause can still occur without the outcome taking place. An insufficient cause implies that multiple causative factors need to be present in order to induce the outcome, including the one at issue. An immediate or proximal cause is indicated by temporal contiguity, but practically, it is hard to determine if intervening causes are indeed excluded in the chain. Distal causes precede proximal ones, such as in the case of medication noncompliance eventually leading to more proximal complications.

In order to infer a causal relationship, Haynes et al. (2011) described that four necessary conditions need to be present: covariation, temporal precedence, alternative explanation exclusion, and logical connection. Each presents challenges. For example, for covariation, measurement error must be controlled. For temporal precedence, a third variable might be involved. For alternative explanation exclusion, controlled experiments are not always possible nor might they give definitive answers. As for logical connection, the variables should be at the same level so that mechanism (mediating variables) can be imputed. For example, the construct of frustration should be broken down to explain how specific types of aggression might be caused by it.

According to Haynes et al. (2011), in psychopathology the causal relations involved might change over time or exhibit dynamic features. States at a point in time exhibit patterns over time (phases), so that appreciation of state dynamic phase functions can accommodate to the changing nature of causality. Also, in a process of reciprocal determinism or circular causation, environment influences state. These might include positive feedback loops, include more complex (e.g., triadic) relations, and so on.

The statistical approaches to establishing causality in nonexperimental designs are varied, dynamically changing, and expanding, but they still cannot ascertain with enough precision the causality involved in this type of research relative to research based on experimental designs.

That said, methods in the latter vein, such as RCTs, have their own problems, including relative to ecological validity. For example, RCTs on the effectiveness of psychotherapies conducted in controlled lab settings with ideal, selected patients might not emerge with results that are generalizable to the real world of messy clinics with messy patients.

Patients In the FACCDs (Haynes et al., 2011) model, functional analysis concerns the identification of important, controllable functional relationships in specified behaviors of individuals, whether causal or noncausal. Functional analysis leads to dynamic modeling of patient symptoms, goals, and relationships, with FACCD graphic representations used to diagram the patient maps of her/his difficulties. Therefore, the FACCD procedure individualizes causality in relation to psychological difficulties in immediate contexts of patients.

Figures 6.1 and 6.2 together offer pertinent details of the functional approach to behavioral assessment and to case formulation (Haynes et al., 2011), including of FACCDs. The first figure of the two (Fig. 6.1) documents the problems faced by a family in terms of relations, and their importance, causes, and modifiability. The second figure of the two (Fig. 6.2) explains the symbols in the diagram.

Other Areas

Landolt, Ystrom, Stene-Larsen, Holmstrøm, and Vollrath (2013) demonstrated the value of using SEM in exploring causal pathways of child behavior (internalizing) and maternal mental health (distress) in families having a child with congenital heart disease. Their longitudinal study between 6 and 36 months in child age found that both individual and family-based (shared) factors contributed to risk for mental health problems. Also, it found that a mutual influence mechanism model proved useful in understanding the data.

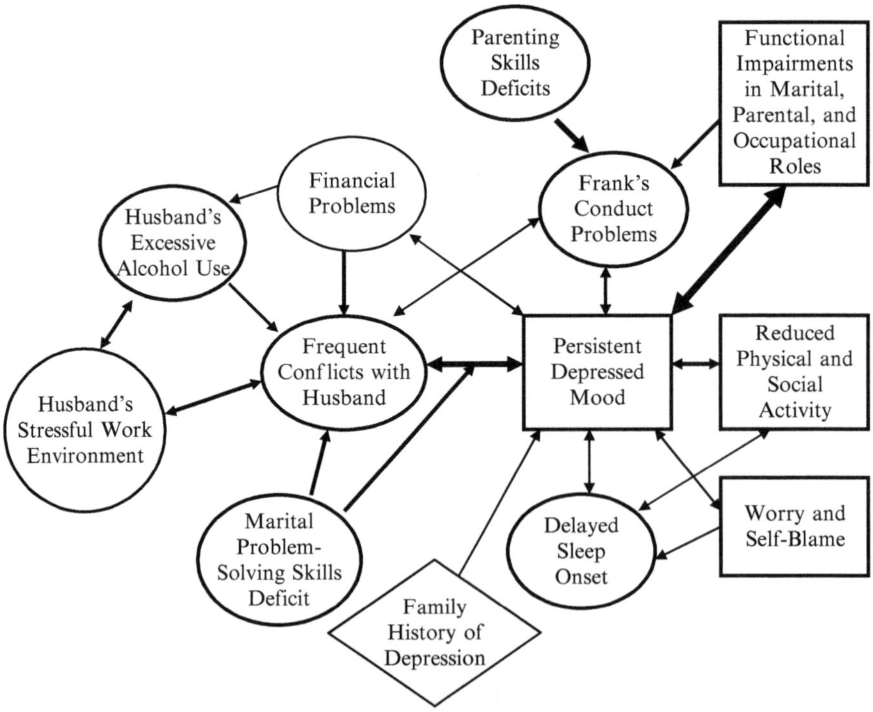

Fig. 6.1 Functional Analytic Clinical Case Diagram (FACCD). FACCD illustrates several behavior problems with different levels of importance, their functional relations, multiple causal variables with different degrees of modifiability, and functional relations between causal variables and behavior problems. Adapted from Haynes, Yoshioka, Kloezeman, and Bello (2009)

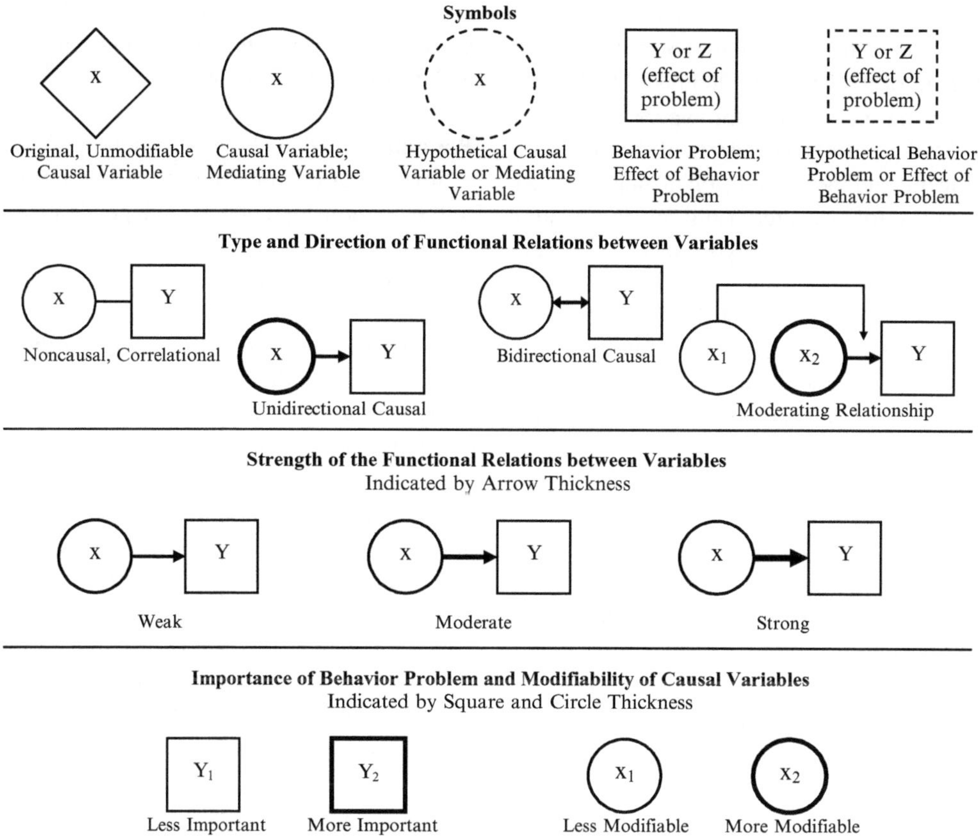

Fig. 6.2 Symbols used in FACCDs. *FACCD* Functional Analytic Clinical Case Diagram. Adopted with permission of John Wiley & Sons. Haynes et al. (2011). *Behavioral assessment and case formulation*. Hoboken, NJ: Wiley. Copyright © 2011 and John Wiley & Sons, Inc. Reproduced with permission of John Wiley & Sons, Inc. [Figure 2.2, Page 53]

Van Bockstaele et al. (2013) analyzed research and causation criteria to determine the temporal primacy of attentional bias toward threatening stimuli in the manifestation of fear/anxiety. The authors noted that causality refers not only to "strict" linear cause-effect relations (etiology) but also to roles for vulnerability, maintaining, and exacerbating factors. The research on the topic investigates strength of relation, consistency, dose–response curve, plausibility, temporality, prospective studies, experimental evidence, and analogy (Hill, 1965).

Van Bockstaele et al. (2013) arrived at a conclusion of reciprocal (bidirectional, mutually reinforcing, circular) causality in the relationship of attentional bias and fear/anxiety, rather than a unique causal impact of the bias on the emotions. The experimental research that they reviewed provided the strongest evidence for the association.

For the case of antisocial behavior, Jaffee et al. (2011) queried the types of research and statistics that can be used to identify better the causes of behavior that are not amenable to experimental manipulation. Risk factors might appear causative but a third variable might be involved, or, evocative or active gene-environment correlation might be involved (the former is also called reverse causation). Or, the risk factor might appear as a correlated feature. That being said, the ideal solution of controlled experimentation, such as using randomized control trials, have their own limitations, such as possible low external validity.

Marshall, Parker, Ciarrochi, and Heaven (2013) queried whether self-esteem is a "cause or consequence" of social support. They investigated longitudinally 961 adolescents (mean of 13.4 at the start) across five time points over 4 years. By using more of the latter time points in their study and the same measures at the waves, they could better test the causal antecedents of the outcomes. Self-esteem and perceived social support (network, size) were measured using self-report questionnaires, respectively, by Rosenberg (1979) and a revised version of a questionnaire by Ciarrochi, Chan, and Bajgar (2001; 4 items). Covariates were measured on the self-esteem questionnaire. Item parcels were created for latent variable analysis, given the scale's large number of items (10). SEM was used with a latent variables approach, analyzed with Mplus. Chi-square and other fit indices were calculated.

The results showed that causal priority lied with self-esteem rather than perceived support. Self-esteem was found to predict increasing levels of social support (quality, in particular, also size). The study illustrates the classical manner in which SEM analysis can discern causal relations.

Comment

Individuals In determining causality in psychology, population-level research has difficulty transferring its conclusions to clinical situations in which one patient at a time is assessed and treated. Epidemiology provides odds ratios about the influence of risk factors on health outcomes. As documented in Young (2014), I was involved in a case that has gone and that is going again to the Supreme Court of Canada in which I had to review the population-level research on work stress and depression/disability relative to other stressors and also relative to the outcome of PTSD instead of depression. Even here, there was confusion in the court present in the testimony by the "dueling" epidemiologists relative to the odds ratios involved, and I had to clarify. Statistical work of the population-level research offers a powerful pathway to causal understanding, but clinical work also needs astute observational and clinical skills. In this regard, use of the scientific approach in information gathering in an individual assessment, then in the interpretation of psychological test results, and finally in using scientific reasoning in arriving at justifiable conclusions constitutes the best strategy in causality and disability determination for court.

Populations The classic distinction in causality estimation of deciphering more direct mediators of the relationship between independent variable/risk factors and dependent variable/outcomes and more indirect, moderating influences on the relationships involved still remains a fruitful one to consider in establishing causality, but the statistics based on this distinction are changing. Moreover, alternative approaches in establishing causality based on alternative methods related to Rubin's potential outcomes and Pearl's DAGs hold promise, but they too are lacking in some ways according to the literature review, most likely due to the inherent difficulty with establishing causation in nonexperimental research. Psychology and other behavior-based disciplines have come a long way from shying away from tackling causality issues when observations and correlations are the methods and statistics used. Developmental research is limited ethically in using RCTs, but longitudinal research, for example, using prospective designs, to some degree, have their advantages toward establishing causality. Nevertheless, everything considered, the limits of statistics in establishing causality need to be recognized. That said, the area constitutes a dynamically evolving field, and psychology needs to keep abreast of the developments in it.

Brain

Granger Causality

Friston et al. (2013) examined statistical approaches to analyzing functional integration (directed connectivity) in neuronal macrocircuits. The neuronal information might be acquired by electroencephalography (EEG) or by fMRI. The two approaches compared concern Granger Causality (GC) and Dynamic Causal Modeling (DCM).

In DCM, causality lies in the "form" of the model, and inferred "hidden" or unobservable neuronal states are taken to fluctuate and thereby "cause changes" in other hidden neuronal states. In DCM, causal interactions are "mediated" by the hidden neural dynamics. It is a multi-input, multi-output model, with augmented "forward" observation modeling of mapped neural activity and observed responses. The model is "fully" generative, with key outputs including "posterior parameter estimates" of the best data-fitting model with respect to intra brain-region coupling.

DCM can estimate coupling between brain regions in fMRI for a particular modeled architecture using Bayesian methods. It helps account for "directed" brain region connections, disambiguating neural "drivers" of neuronal events/signal propagation. It can be used after GC to elucidate more mechanistic characterization of the system involved (i.e., with respect to specific models/hypotheses). The DCM models hidden neuronal state coupling that could generate the observations made. It attempts to get beneath the data surface structure in order to understand the "how" of their generation. To conclude, Friston et al. (2013) considered the newer GC "complementary" to approaches in analyzing neural connectivity for its causality.

Hu and Liang (2012) proposed a revision of GC as applied to spectral GC in the frequency domain. They showed that spectral GC analysis as presently constituted leads to "misleading" results. Their model speaks to the need for better tools in causality analysis of neural connectivity.

Other workers have modified GC approaches. For example, von Eye, Wiedermann, and Mun (2013) incorporated configural frequency analysis into it for categorical data, and showed the approach applied to determining which changes in adolescent aggressive impulses led to changes in peer aggression.

Friston et al. (2014) elaborated GC methodology for analysis of biological time series. They demonstrated that GC analyses can be unreliable when there is measurement noise, whether the analyses are based on autoregressive models or nonparametric measures. They "finessed" the problem by deriving spectral causality measures from "Volterra kernels," which were estimated using the approach of DCM rather than based on GC, per se. DCM uses a Bayesian state-space model with "hidden" states in generating data in continuous time.

Comment

In the next section, I review in more depth GC in the ecological field. As with brain research, the review of ecology shows that GC is an important in statistical parameterization, yet is being complemented by other approaches.

Ecology

Interventions

Raerinne (2011) offered an account of causal mechanism in ecology that considers the relative lack of ecological laws in the discipline. Raerinne argued that ecological generalizations can be explanatory as long as they are invariant even if they are not lawlike. Generalizations can be demonstrated as invariant if they are maintained in "interventions" that change the value of the variables involved. The philosophical stance by Woodward (2000, 2001, 2003) on causality has gained wide application, including in psychology (Gopnik & Wellman, 2012), and here it is extended to ecology.

Raerinne (2011) noted that interventions can demonstrate whether causes are "difference makers" in that the variable altered leads to consequences in the system (e.g., the intervention of reducing habitat has the effect of lowering species diversity). In "simple" causality chains, there might be an invariant relationship, but no known or proposed mechanisms to account for it. In mechanistic explanations, the internal causal structure in the phenomena is discerned, and interventions can contribute to their elucidation.

Granger Causality

Establishing causality in time-dependent transformations existing in systems such as ecological ones (that cannot be manipulated experimentally) presents formidable challenges. In order to identify causation, given the problems with correlation for imputing causation, Granger (1969) developed an approach, now referred to as GC, which was based on prediction in time-series variables. In Granger modeling, a critical requirement is that information pertaining to a putative causal factor is independent and unique to that variable (e.g., on predator effects) so that it can be removed or eliminated from the model involving time series (e.g., on prey). However, in ecological systems, variable separability might not obtain, nor would coupling be strongly coupled or synchronized, which is another condition for GC.

Detto et al. (2012) presented a revision of the GC approach in ecology that is nonparametric and spectral (frequency-based). The approach is termed "conditional" GC. It can accommodate or untangle oscillatory, external, time-dependent, periodic drivers overlapping self-sustaining, endogenous, natural, signature dynamics, and the direct and feedback relationships involved. This permits the approach to map any early effects or state variable on later outcomes or other state variables, indicating the "directionality" in coupling inherent in ecological causality. Also, it can establish associated variable couplings related to any external drivers, compared to the endogenous structure of the core ecological system or network.

Convergent Cross-Mapping

Sugihara et al. (2012) faced the difficulty in establishing causality in complex systems for which observational data had been collected. Correlations change in complex ecosystems, as variables might be coupled positively, negatively, or not at all, depending on time of observation and extant system state (state-dependent behavior). The system expresses "radically different dynamic control regimes," either top-down or bottom-up, thereby altering correlational dynamics (e.g., in predator–prey relations). A system having properties such as this is considered nonlinear dynamical and complex. The altering correlational profile is considered ephemeral or "mirage," which is a common finding in even the simplest of nonlinear dynamical systems. The variables alter their coupling to even become decoupled or "anti-correlated," and this might happen "spontaneously."

In order to detect causality in complex ecosystems in which GC might not apply, Sugihara et al. (2012) developed a convergent cross-mapping (CC-M) approach. It is a method based on nonlinear state-space reconstruction in time-series variables. It calculates to what degree the historical record of *Y* values can estimate reliably states of *X* values. The model tests for correspondence between attractor "shadow" manifolds, which are constructed using "lagged" coordinate embeddings of *X* and *Y*. The authors concluded that the CC-M avoids the problem of mirage correlations, changes in threshold in regimes, and also the ubiquity of nonlinear dynamical systems in nature acting to confound the determination of causality.

Comment

GC has been applied to mental health research especially in the area of neuroscience. GC (Granger, 1969, 1988) originated in the field of econometrics, but it has been applied to multiple disciplines, including neuroscience. It helps detect phenomena due to effects laying in prior causes in time, which other approaches, such as SEM, cannot do. Also, "G"-causality can distinguish unidirectional and bidirectional couplings, as well as accommodate colinearity, unlike path analysis or other SEM approaches. The conditional G-causality approach helps decompose and analyze causal relations as a function of spectral frequency (e.g., diurnal, seasonal) rather than using correlations over time. As for mechanisms that might be involved, these would have to be inferred from the data. To conclude, even though experiments are not readily applicable to some fields, such as ecology, by using refined statistical approaches, to a degree, causality still can be determined.

Aside from its application to neuroscience and to ecology, GC has much potential for application to development. von Eye and Wiedermann (2015) developed a taxonomy of GC models applicable to developmental research. They argued that Granger models help interpret causally the relations between variables. But different models imply different causal theories of the relations. In their taxonomy, the authors help structure existing models and allow for derivation of new ones. The classification includes models based on considering: (a) order effects; (b) type of contemporaneous effects; (c) the a priori assumptions applicable to the status of variables as explanatory causes or outcome effects; and (d) the sectioning of a dependent series that is predicted from an independent one.

PTSD Networks

Concept

McNally Et al McNally et al. (2015) developed a network approach to the symptoms of PTSD, imputing causality to the functional interacting symptom linkages themselves (while refuting the notion that an underlying latent construct can explain the configuration of symptoms in the disorder). The McNally et al. work on PTSD is based heavily on the approach of Borsboom and colleagues on the network approach to psychopathology and network calculation (respectively, Borsboom & Cramer, 2014; Epskamp, Cramer, Waldorp, Schmittmann, & Borsboom, 2012).

In the network approach, symptoms covary or couple variably, and through their constitutive relationship (rather than due to a presumed underlying latent construct of disease). Symptoms in this sense are directly constitutive of mental disorder and there are no intermediates causally in their relationship to disorder, such as underlying disease entities. Symptoms affect each other through feedback loops, homeostatic relations, and so on, and they are not conditionally independent of the stressors that might lead to them.

The symptom network view affords and exquisite sensitivity to individual differences in symptom expression and their causality, unlike the contrasting model of common cause/latent variable approach to mental disorder. In this network view, diagnostic symptoms are not caused by or are reflective of a latent entity or entities; rather, they are constitutive of them.

In this network view, ontologically, a diagnostic attribution is neither an essentialist, carved-at-the-joint category nor a socially-constructed, convenient DSM (Diagnostic and Statistical Manual of Mental Disorders) category, but a realist entity carved by the causality among the system dynamics themselves. For example, an episode of a disorder follows a course as symptom nodes in the network "turn on" and "transmit activation" to nodes connected to them.

To test their model, McNally et al. conducted a questionnaire study of a 2008 Chinese earthquake, with over 360 survivors. They used a translated version of the PCL (Posttraumatic Checklist—Civilian; Weathers, Litz, Herman, Huska, & Keane, 1993; Mandarin Chinese version; Li et al., 2010). The questionnaire is keyed to the DSM-IV (Diagnostic and Statistical Manual of Mental Disorders, Fourth Edition; American Psychiatric Association, 1994). Among the survivors, the questionnaire indicated that 38 % met the criteria for probable PTSD (5 years after the earthquake when the data were gathered).

Data analysis included search for common network properties. In "association" networks, each edge represents the correlations between symptoms, from zero-order to larger, with magnitude indicated by edge thickness in the diagrams (not direction). A more restricted association network (involving only links for which $r \leq 0.30$) was also calculated. In "concentration" networks, edges indicate partial correlations, controlling for all other correlations in the network with the symptom pair at hand. In "relative importance" networks, each edge indicates the relative significance of a symptom as a predictor of another symptom (both for magnitude and direction). As for symptom centrality, the authors calculated node strength, closeness, and betweenness. Degree refers to the number of links to a node, but strength refers to the sum of correlation magnitudes (weights) of each edge linked to a node. The variable of closeness is indicated by the mean distance to all other nodes from the node of concern. Betweenness refers to the amount of times a node lies on the shortest path between two other nodes.

The results showed that the 17 DSM-IV PTSD symptoms are highly interconnected in the population studied. When results with $r \leq 0.30$ are excluded in the association network calculated, strong associations become more evident. They included the symptoms of hypervigilance and startle and also avoidance of thoughts and activities (about the trauma and associated with it, respectively). Numbing and dissociation symptoms were strongly linked (loss of interest in enjoyable activities; feeling distance from others, respectively). Finally, nightmares, flashbacks, and intrusive memories related to the trauma were tightly linked. The authors noted that these various symptom linkages appear related to the three DSM-IV symptom clusters of hyperarousal, avoidance/numbing, and re-experiencing, respectively. However, other symptom linkages did not conform to these DSM clusters—those of startle-concentration problems and anger-concentration problems.

Other results accentuated these findings. For example, the concentration network showed that two re-experiencing symptoms were not connected to the others (physiological reactivity, feeling upset at reminders), but quite connected to each other. Centrality calculations showed that perceiving the future as foreshortened is highly central. Overall, the authors concluded that hypervigilance, future foreshortening, and sleep appear predominant symptoms in PTSD symptom network analysis, with multiple symptom linkages involved, including some not previously considered.

Others Sadeh, Spielberg, Warren, Miller, and Heller (2014) conducted a neural connectivity study during an emotional processing task in trauma-exposed adults. The participants were assessed for PTSD symptoms using the SCID-IV-TR (Structured Clinical Interview for DSM-IV-TR; First, Spitzer, Gibbon, & Williams, 2002). Emotional processing was evaluated on an emotion-word Stroop task. Both reaction time and error frequency were scored. The participants were subject to fMRI functional data acquisition.

PTSD symptom severity (especially hyperarousal) moderated amygdala medial-prefrontal cortex (mPFC) coupling during unpleasant word processing. Also, re-experiencing severity moderated insula/putamen hippocampus connectivity during both pleasant and unpleasant word stimuli.

The authors concluded that different PTSD symptoms moderate different functional neural connectivities during emotional interference. There appears to be separable components of dysfunctional inhibitory control in PTSD during affective processing. Therefore, I conclude that network modeling at the central level in PTSD highlights mechanisms different than network modeling at the symptomatic level.

Lehrner and Yehuda (2014) noted that PTSD is a complex phenomenon so that no one single biomarker can be isolated to indicate it. They argued that PTSD symptoms should be conceptualized as emergent characteristics of dynamic networks rather than uniquely as outcomes only of core biological processes. Their model is a multifaceted one, with risk as well as illness networks, and with possible biomarkers for each of diagnosis/severity, risk factor/predictors, trauma exposure susceptibility, recovery (prediction, verification), and subtyping.

Comment

The network approach to symptom linkages in mental disorder is a novel one and it adds incremental findings to the field. However, first, it needs to be supplemented by work in mental disorder development, course, and comorbidity (e.g., PTSD mutually maintained with chronic pain). Moreover, network analysis can be performed on risk factors before mental illness onset and also on therapeutic response after it. The core symptoms in both cases might be different than during the active onset phase.

Second, the symptom network approach should not readily dismiss other avenues of conceptualization and empirical investigation of mental disorder. For example, confirmatory factor analysis is suggesting apparently valid multiple-factor models of PTSD. Moreover, the latent variable approach could be modified to help explain better some of the core symptoms that emerge in network research. McNally et al. (2015) themselves showed the value of a modified latent variable approach to PTSD in this regard by referring to the model of PTSD that describes it as a syndrome involving continued impending threat (Ehlers & Clark, 2000) when they explained the centrality of the symptom of hypervigilance in their findings.

Therefore, the authors might have to prematurely dismissed the approaches of Barlow, Sauer-Zavala, Carl, Bullis, and Ellard (2014) and of Caspi et al. (2014) on general factors in psychopathology. I am not suggesting that the latter approaches are more powerful than network ones, but they could be complementary. There is room for both bottom-up (network) and top-down (latent variable) concepts of psychopathology in an integrated hierarchical multilevel multicausal model. Symptom linkages express causal relations but so might other factors facilitative of their cohering.

Finally, any multilevel, multifactorial combined hierarchical model, as being suggested could justify combining network and latent entity approaches by explaining that both are needed to understand how individual differences in causality of symptom expression and connection might scaffold on general tendencies in behavioral configuration that are promoted by causal biological and environmental factors. Overall, the supplemental research on networks and related aspects of PTSD cited in this section indicates that the application of network conceptualization to PTSD is burgeoning but should integrate to the degree possible other relevant work.

Related Research

This section of the chapter on networks in PTSD considers related concepts such as biomarkers and other aspects of brain function. Genetics takes its place, as well.

Biomarkers Schmidt, Faltwasser, and Wotjak (2013) reviewed the research on potential biomarkers in PTSD. They differentiated between possible biomarkers of risk, disorder expression, and therapeutic response. In the following, I review the most consistent findings among the biological findings (for the illness markers only), and exclude the research cited on possible cognitive and related markers of PTSD. For PTSD susceptibility, Schmidt et al. (2013) referred to, elevated sensitivity of leukocytes of glucocorticoid receptors (GR) in peripheral blood monocytes prior to deployment (in trauma-exposed Dutch soldiers). Other evidence indicated molecular regulators of the hypothalamus-pituitary-adrenal (HPA) axis activity, especially for GR and associated molecules, as predictive of PTSD (e.g., in this military sample; Geuze et al., 2012; van Zuiden, Geuze, et al., 2012; van Zuiden et al., 2011; van Zuiden, Heijnen, et al., 2012).

Epigenetic effects also seem involved (in another military sample). In individuals with and without PTSD post-deployment, the genomic repetitive elements *LINE-1* and *Alu* were differentially methylated pre-deployment. Genetic polymorphisms associated with PTSD susceptibility include *FKBP5* (*FK506* binding protein 5), *COMT* (catechol-*O*-methyltransferase), and the dopamine transporter and receptor genes (Wu et al., 2013).

As for PTSD disease markers, Schmidt et al. (2013) referred to the HPA axis (dysregulation; attenuation) and the sympathetic adrenomedullary system (overdrive) (Pitman et al., 2012; Yehuda, 2002, respectively). Note that biomarkers are not necessarily endophenotypes (part of a chain in causation leading back to genes).

Brain Scott et al. (2015) conducted a meta-analysis of neurocognitive function in PTSD, involving 60 studies. Their review found deficits in PTSD for attention, verbal memory, and speed of information processing, in particular. However, the analysis could not differentiate whether the cognitive deficits related to the disorder itself or to pre-existing factors. Also, in terms of possible confounders, the 60 studies rarely screened using symptom validity testing or urine toxicology/breathalyzer methods. Nevertheless, according to Scott et al. (2015), the results found by their meta-analysis support a view of PTSD as involving dysregulation of frontolimbic circuitry.

As for neuroendocrine abnormalities in PTSD, Zoladz and Diamond (2013) referred to studies on cortisol and abnormal HPA axis function, among others. Neurobiological abnormalities focused on amygdala hyperresponsivity, reduced prefrontal cortex (PFC) activity, and possibly small hippocampal size/function, although the amygdala and hippocampal findings especially might concern pre-existing factors.

Genes Zoladz and Diamond (2013) conducted a similar review of genetic factors in PTSD susceptibility. Their list of possible genetic factors in PTSD was quite extensive: *FK506*-binding protein (*FKP5*), neuropeptide Y (*NPY*), dopamine beta-hydroxylase (DBH), *COMT*, dopamine receptor D2 (*DRD2*), dopamine transporter (*DAT*), solute carrier family 6, member 4 (*SLC6A4*), serotonin 2A receptor (*5-HTR2A*), gamma-aminobutyric acid receptor alpha 2 (*GABARA2*), regulator of G-protein signaling 2 (*RGS2*), and brain-derived neurotrophic factor (*BDNF*) (e.g., Digangi, Guffanti, McLaughlin, & Koenen, 2013; Klengel et al., 2013; Skelton, Ressler, Norrholm, Jovanovic, & Bradley-Davino, 2012).

Zoladz and Diamond (2013) concluded that there might be different biomarker profiles for different PTSD subtypes. PTSD is the result of a complex interaction among genetic, neurobiological, endocrine, immunological, and developmental factors. It does not appear to be a single disorder, but multiple ones, with each having different biomarker "signatures."

Transdiagnostics The studies in this section do not pertain to PTSD, per se. But they have implications for determining both the common and unique characteristics of DSM disorders.

Wigman et al. (2015) used the network approach to differentiate the symptom dynamics of individuals ($N=599$) with depression, with psychotic disorder, and as controls. The participants filled in a structured self-report diary at quasi-random moments 10 times in the day over most of a week (when signaled; this is the ESM, experience sampling method). They reported on their thoughts, affect, context, and appraisals, but five item adjectives were selected for the study (cheerful, insecure, content, down, suspicious; filled in on a 7-point Likert scale).

The results indicated that having a diagnosis of depression, in particular, was associated more strongly with connected moment-to-moment network structures over momentary mental states (that were reported in the sampling). Also, there were elevated interconnections between positive and negative mental states in the participants in this group. The authors considered results of confirmatory factor analysis, as well. They concluded that the network approach might be useful to map transdiagnostic processes.

Hong and Cheung (2015) investigated the common core cognitive vulnerabilities to depression and anxiety. They conducted a meta-analytic review over 73 relevant articles and found that six cognitive vulnerabilities (e.g., for depression, rumination; for anxiety, uncertainty tolerance) were moderately to strongly correlated. They found that a single latent-factor model best fit the data (e.g., "common core vulnerability;" repetitive negative thinking with uncertainty/uncontrollability present, along with cognitive distortions). The authors concluded that the findings are consistent with a transdiagnostic etiological process underpinning emotional disorder (e.g., Barlow et al., 2014).

Lane and Sher (2015) found that, in Alcohol Use Disorder (AUD; in the DSM-5; American Psychiatric Association, 2013), the assumptions of equal criterion severity and strict additivity of criteria combinations are questionable. The DSM uses a polythetic format that is problematic ("highly fallible") not just for AUD but also for all disorders subject to this format. The authors recommended a dimensional approach to symptom criteria, with graded severity of each symptom in any one disorder instead of the present 0–1/present–absent categorical approach. They noted that different causes may be involved in a mild compared to a more severe symptom in a disorder. Using such an approach to the etiology of mental disorders might help find unique, transdiagnostic etiological processes across disorders.

Comment

The predominant model in psychopathology is the medical one, in which disorders typically are considered categories. The extant diagnostic manuals have hundreds of separate disorders in their nosological tomes. Moreover, in them, each category is considered as associated with or potentially associated with a particular cause or etiology and a particular cure or helpful treatment. However, the transdiagnostic approach seeks common and differential symptoms across and within disorders, respectively, so has the advantage of being amenable to network modeling, aside from the simplicity it could create for clinicians in the field.

The conceptual distinction between markers of risk, disease expression, and therapeutic response is a welcome one. However, research on biomarkers, in general, as well as on risk and therapeutic response, might not address directly the related question of endophenotypes. Endophenotypes are thought to represent pathways from gene to disease expression.

Given its spreading influence, the study of networks might introduce a new way of studying endophenotypes in PTSD. Network modeling could isolate the core, essential components of each disorder, as well as causal relations among them.

However, the research on PTSD endophenotypes even from a network perspective might be limited by focus on linear modeling. On the one hand, the amount of variance explained in behavior by any one gene or even one gene complex is limited. Moreover, epigenetic and other environmental factors need to be considered in a full biopsychosocial model of endophenotypes for PTSD. Finally, network concepts both neurally and symptomatically can refine understanding of the biological factors involved in PTSD and how they dynamically interact with the genes involved, the environment involved, and the personal (self) vulnerability and resilience factors involved.

Chapter Conclusions

This chapter shows the centrality of statistics for the study of and elucidation of causality in disciplines such as psychology, epidemiology, and ecology. In psychology, it covers material related to psychological tests and psychopathology, as well as the brain and development. Many other examples could be provided. Essentially, with appropriate design and statistics, causality is amenable to inference in scientific study even when the ideal designs are impossible to use. However, these methods and concepts are in flux and keep being refined, so that causal inference in any discipline requires the care for which science often is exemplary.

The chapter hints at the difference between population estimates of causality and causality in individual cases (e.g., legal ones). This refers to the distinction between general and specific causation. I deal with this aspect of causal conceptualization and study in two later chapters on psychological injury (e.g., due to negligence in legal cases).

The most important and fastest growing area of statistical applications to the study of causality of behavior relates to networks. I have described the basics in this area, especially as it applies to PTSD. Later chapters in the present work consider network analysis for brain connectivity and also for the causality of psychopathology.

References

American Psychiatric Association. (1994). *Diagnostic and statistical manual of mental disorders: DSM-IV* (4th ed.). Washington, DC: Author.

American Psychiatric Association. (2013). *Diagnostic and statistical manual of mental disorders: DSM-5* (5th ed.). Washington, DC: Author.

Barlow, D. H., Sauer-Zavala, S., Carl, J. R., Bullis, J. R., & Ellard, K. K. (2014). The nature, diagnosis, and treatment of neuroticism: Back to the future. *Clinical Psychological Science, 2*, 344–365.

Baron, R. M., & Kenny, D. A. (1986). The moderator-mediator variable distinction in social psychological research: Conceptual, strategic and statistical considerations. *Journal of Personality and Social Psychology, 51*, 1173–1182.

Berzuini, C., Dawid, P., & Bernardinelli, L. (2012a). *Causality: Statistical perspectives and applications*. West Sussex, UK: Wiley.

Berzuini, C., Dawid, P., & Bernardinelli, L. (2012b). An overview of statistical causality. In C. Berzuini, P. Dawid, & L. Bernardinelli (Eds.), *Causality: Statistical perspectives and applications* (pp. 1–4). West Sussex, UK: Wiley.

Bollen, K. A. (1989). *Structural equations with latent variables*. New York: Wiley.

Borsboom, D., & Cramer, A. O. J. (2014). Network analysis: An integrative approach to the structure of psychopathology. *Annual Review of Clinical Psychology, 9*, 91–121.

Bracken, M. B. (2013). *Risk, chance, and causation: Investigating the origins and treatment of disease*. New Haven, CT: Yale University Press.

Campbell, D. T. (1957). Factors relevant to the validity of experiments in social settings. *Psychological Bulletin, 54*, 297–312.

Campbell, D. T., & Stanley, J. C. (1963). Experimental and quasi-experimental designs for research on teaching. In N. L. Gage (Ed.), *Handbook of research methods for studying daily life* (pp. 171–246). Chicago: Rand McNally.

Caspi, A., Houts, R. M., Belsky, D. W., Goldman-Mellor, S. J., Harrington, H., Israel, S., et al. (2014). The p factor: One general psychopathology factor in the structure of psychiatric disorders? *Clinical Psychological Science, 2*, 119–137.

Chen, Y., & Cao, Y. (2012). Epidemiological context and concerns. In P. Kennedy (Ed.), *The Oxford handbook of rehabilitation psychology* (pp. 88–95). New York: Oxford University Press.

Ciarrochi, J., Chan, A. Y. C., & Bajgar, J. (2001). Measuring emotional intelligence in adolescents. *Personality and Individual Differences, 31*, 1105–1119.

Cook, T. D., & Campbell, D. T. (1979). *Quasi-experimentation: Design and analysis issues for field settings*. Chicago: Rand McNally.

Dawid, P. (2012). The decision-theoretic approach to causal inference. In C. Berzuini, P. Dawid, & L. Bernardinelli (Eds.), *Causality: Statistical perspectives and applications* (pp. 25–42). West Sussex, UK: Wiley.

De Ridder, D., Vanneste, S., & Freeman, W. (2014). The Bayesian brain: Phantom percepts resolve sensory uncertainty. *Neuroscience and Biobehavioral Reviews, 44*, 4–15.

Detto, M., Molini, A., Katul, G., Stoy, P., Palmroth, S., & Baldocchi, D. (2012). Causality and persistence in ecological systems: A nonparametric spectral Granger causality approach. *The American Naturalist, 179*, 524–535.

Digangi, J., Guffanti, G., McLaughlin, K. A., & Koenen, K. C. (2013). Considering trauma exposure in the context of genetics studies of posttraumatic stress disorder: A systematic review. *Biology of Mood and Anxiety Disorders, 3*, 1–12.

Donofrino, B., Class, Q., Lahey, B., & Larsson, H. (2014). Testing the developmental origins of health and disease hypothesis for psychopathology using family-based, quasi-experimental designs. *Child Development Perspectives, 8*, 151–157.

Duncan, G. J., & Magnuson, K. (2012). Socioeconomic status and cognitive functioning: Moving from correlation to causation. *Wiley Interdisciplinary Reviews: Cognitive Science, 3*, 377–386.

Ehlers, A., & Clark, D. M. (2000). A cognitive model of posttraumatic stress disorder. *Behavior Research and Therapy, 38*, 319–345.

Emsley, R., & Dunn, G. (2012). Evaluation of potential mediators in randomized trials of complex interventions (psychotherapies). In C. Berzuini, P. Dawid, & L. Bernardinelli (Eds.), *Causality: Statistical perspectives and applications* (pp. 290–326). West Sussex, UK: Wiley.

Epskamp, S., Cramer, A. O. J., Waldorp, L. J., Schmittmann, V. D., & Borsboom, D. (2012). qgraph: Network visualization of relationships in psychometric data. *Journal of Statistical Software, 48*, 1018.

First, M., Spitzer, R., Gibbon, M., & Williams, J. (2002). *Structural clinical interview for DSM-IV-TR, Research Version, Nonpatient Edition*. New York: New York State Psychiatric Institute, Biometric Research.

Fisher, R. A. (1935). *Statistical methods for research workers*. Edinburgh, UK: Oliver and Boyd.

Frangakis, C. E., & Rubin, D. B. (2002). Principal stratification in causal inference. *Biometrics, 58*, 21–29.

Friston, K. (2009). The free-energy principle: A rough guide to the brain? *Trends in Cognitive Sciences, 13*, 293–301.

Friston, K. (2010). The free-energy principle: A unified brain theory? *Nature Reviews Neuroscience, 11*, 127–138.

Friston, K. J., Bastos, A. M., Oswal, A., van Wijk, B., Richter, C., & Litvak, V. (2014). Granger causality revisited. *NeuroImage, 101*, 796–808.

Friston, K., Moran, R., & Seth, A. K. (2013). Analysing connectivity with Granger causality and dynamic causal modeling. *Current Opinion in Neurobiology, 23*, 172–178.

Gelman, A. (2011). Causality and statistical learning. *American Journal of Sociology, 117*, 955–966.

Gerstman, B. B. (2013). *Epidemiology kept simple: An introduction to traditional and modern epidemiology*. Oxford, UK: Wiley-Blackwell.

Geuze, E., van Wingen, G. A., van Zuiden, M., Rademaker, A. R., Vermetten, E., Kavelaars, A., et al. (2012). Glucocorticoid receptor number predicts increase in amygdala activity after severe stress. *Psychoneuroendocrinology, 37*, 1837–1844.

Gopnik, A., & Wellman, H. M. (2012). Reconstructing constructivism: Causal models, Bayesian learning mechanisms, and the theory. *Psychological Bulletin, 138*, 1085–1108.

Granger, C. W. J. (1969). Investigating causal relations by econometric models and cross-spectral methods. *Econometrica: Journal of the Econometric Society, 37*, 424–438.

Granger, C. W. J. (1988). Some recent developments in the concept of causality. *Journal of Econometrics, 39*, 199–211.

Greenland, S. (2012). Causal inference as a prediction problem: Assumptions, identification and evidence synthesis. In C. Berzuini, P. Dawid, & L. Bernardinelli (Eds.), *Causality: Statistical perspectives and applications* (pp. 43–58). West Sussex, UK: Wiley.

Haynes, S. N. (1992). *Models of causality in psychopathology: Toward synthetic, dynamic and nonlinear models of causality in psychopathology*. Des Moines, IA: Allyn & Bacon.

Haynes, S. N., O'Brien, W. H., Kaholokula, J. K., & Witteman, C. (2012). Concepts of causality in psychopathology: Applications in clinical assessment, clinical case formulation and functional analysis. *Journal of Unified Psychotherapy and Clinical Science, 1*, 87–103.

Haynes, S. N., O'Brien, W. H., & Kaholokula, J. K. (2011). *Behavioral assessment and case formulation*. Hoboken, NJ: Wiley.

Haynes, S. N., Yoshioka, D., Kloezeman, K., & Bello, I. (2009). Clinical applications of behavioral assessment: Identifying and explaining behavior problems in clinical assessment. In J. Butcher (Ed.), *Oxford handbook of clinical assessment* (pp. 226–249). Oxford, UK: Oxford University Press.

Hill, A. B. (1965). The environment and disease: Association or causation? *Proceedings of the Royal Society of Medicine, 58*, 295–300.

Holland, P. W. (1986). Statistics and causal inference. *Journal of the American Statistical Association, 81*, 945–970.

Holland, P. W. (1988). Causal inference, path analysis, and recursive structural equation models. *Sociological Methodology, 18*, 449–484.

Hong, R. Y., & Cheung, M. W.-L. (2015). The structure of cognitive vulnerabilities to depression and anxiety: Evidence for a common core etiologic process based on a meta-analytic review. *Clinical Psychological Science, 3*, 892–912.

Hu, S., & Liang, H. (2012). Causality analysis of neural connectivity: New tool and limitations of spectral Granger causality. *Neurocomputing, 76*, 44–47.

Imai, K., Jo, B., & Stuart, E. A. (2011). Commentary: Using potential outcomes to understand causal mediation analysis. *Multivariate Behavioral Research, 46*, 861–873.

Imai, K., Keele, L., Tingley, D., & Yamamoto, T. (2014). Comment on Pearl: Practical implications of theoretical results for causal mediation analysis. *Psychological Methods, 19*, 482–487.

Imai, K., Keele, L., & Tingley, D. (2010). A general approach to causal mediation analysis. *Psychological Methods, 15*, 309–334.

Imai, K., Tingley, D., & Yamamoto, T. (2013). Experimental designs for identifying causal mechanisms. *Journal of the Royal Statistical Society, 176*, 5–51.

Jaffee, S. R., Strait, L. B., & Odgers, C. L. (2011). From correlates to causes: Can quasi-experimental studies and statistical innovations bring us closer to identifying the causes of antisocial behavior? *Psychological Bulletin, 138*, 272–295.

Jo, B. (2008). Causal inference in randomized experiments with meditational processes. *Psychological Methods, 13*, 314–336.

Kendler, K. S. (2011). Causal thinking in psychiatry: A genetic and manipulationist perspective. In P. E. Shrout, K. M. Keyes, & K. Ornstein (Eds.), *Causality and psychopathology: Finding the determinants of disorders and their cures* (pp. 66–78). New York: Oxford University Press.

Klengel, T., Mehta, D., Anacker, C., Rex-Haffner, M., Pruessner, J. C., Pariante, C. M., et al. (2013). Allele-specific FKBP5 DNA demethylation mediates gene-childhood trauma interactions. *Nature Neuroscience, 16*, 33–41.

Landolt, M. A., Ystrom, E., Stene-Larsen, K., Holmstrøm, H., & Vollrath, M. E. (2013). Exploring causal pathways of child behavior and maternal mental health in families with a child with congenital heart disease: A longitudinal study. *Psychological Medicine, 44*, 3421–3433.

Lane, S. P., & Sher, K. J. (2015). Limits of current approaches to diagnosis severity based on criterion counts: An example with DSM-5 alcohol use disorder. *Clinical Psychological Science, 3*, 819–835.

Lehrner, A., & Yehuda, R. (2014). Biomarkers of PTSD: Military applications and considerations. *European Journal of Psychotraumatology, 5*, 1–11.

Li, H., Wang, L., Shi, Z., Zhang, Y., Wu, K., & Liu, P. (2010). Diagnostic utility of the PTSD Checklist in detecting PTSD in Chinese earthquake victims. *Psychological Reports, 107*, 733–739.

Mackie, J. L. (1965). Causes and conditions. *American Philosophical Quarterly, 4*, 245–264.

Mackie, J. L. (1974). *Cement of the universe: A study of causation*. Oxford, UK: Oxford University Press.

MacKinnon, D. P., Cox, M. G., Miocevic, M., & Kisbu-Sakarya, Y. (2012, March). *Methods to assess confounder bias applied to an anabolic steroid prevention program*. Paper presented at the Frontiers in Causal Inference Conference, Harvard University, Cambridge, MA.

MacKinnon, D. P., & Pirlott, A. G. (2015). Statistical approaches for enhancing causal interpretation of the M to Y relation in mediation analysis. *Personality and Social Psychology Review, 19*, 30–43.

Markus, K. A., & Borsboom, D. (2013). *Frontiers of test validity theory: Measurement, causation, and meaning*. New York: Routledge.

Marshall, S. L., Parker, P. D., Ciarrochi, J., & Heaven, P. C. L. (2013). Is self-esteem a cause of consequence of social support? A 4-year longitudinal study. *Child Development, 85*, 1275–1291.

McLanahan, S., Tach, L., & Schneider, D. (2013). The causal effects of father absence. *Annual Review of Sociology, 39*, 399–427.

McNally, R. J., Robinaugh, D. J., Wu, G. W. Y., Wang, L., Deserno, M. K., & Borsboom, D. (2015). Mental disorders as causal systems: A network approach to posttraumatic stress disorder. *Clinical Psychological Science, 3*, 836–849.

Muthén, B., & Asparouhov, T. (2012). Bayesian SEM: A more flexible representation of substantive theory. *Psychological Methods, 17*, 313–335.

Pearl, J. (2000). *Causality: Models, reasoning, and inference*. New York: Cambridge University Press.
Pearl, J. (2009). *Causality: Models, reasoning, and inference* (2nd ed.). New York: Cambridge University Press.
Pearl, J. (2014a). Interpretation and identification of causal mediation. *Psychological Methods, 19*, 459–481.
Pearl, J. (2014b). Reply to commentary by Imai, Keele, Tingley, and Yamamoto concerning causal mediation analysis. *Psychological Methods, 19*, 488–492.
Pitman, R. K., Rasmusson, A. M., Koenen, K. C., Shin, L. M., Orr, S. P., Gilbertson, M. W., et al. (2012). Biological studies of post-traumatic stress disorder. *Nature Reviews Neuroscience, 13*, 769–787.
Preacher, K. J. (2015). Advances in mediation analysis: A survey and synthesis of new developments. *Annual Review of Psychology, 66*, 825–852.
Rabins, P. (2013). *The why of things: Causality in science, medicine, and life*. New York: Columbia University Press.
Raerinne, J. (2011). Causal and mechanistic explanations in ecology. *Acta Briotheoretica, 59*, 251–271.
Robins, J. M., Hernán, M. A., & Brumback, B. (2000). Marginal structural models and causal inference in epidemiology. *Epidemiology, 11*, 550–560.
Robins, J. M., & Richardson, T. S. (2011). Alternative graphical causal models and the identification of direct effects. In P. E. Shrout, K. M. Keyes, & K. Ornstein (Eds.), *Causality and psychopathology: Finding the determinants of disorders and their cures* (pp. 103–158). New York: Oxford University Press.
Rosenbaum, P. R., & Rubin, D. B. (1985). Constructing a control group using multivariate matched sampling methods that incorporate the propensity score. *The American Statistician, 39*, 33–38.
Rosenberg, M. (1979). *Conceiving the self*. New York: Basic Books.
Rothman, K. J. (1976). Reviews and commentary: Causes. *American Journal of Epidemiology, 104*, 587–592.
Rubin, D. B. (1974). Estimating causal effects of treatments in randomized and non-randomized studies. *Journal of Educational Psychology, 66*, 688–701.
Rubin, D. B. (1978). Bayesian inference for causal effects: The role of randomization. *Annals of Statistics, 6*, 34–58.
Rubin, D. B. (1980). Discussion of "Randomization analysis of experimental data in the Fisher randomization test", by D. Basu. *Journal of the American Statistical Association, 75*, 591–593.
Rubin, D. B. (1990). Formal models of statistical inference for causal effects. *Journal of Statistical Planning and Inference, 25*, 279–292.
Rubin, D. B. (2004a). Direct and indirect causal effects via potential outcomes. *Scandinavian Journal of Statistics, 31*, 161–170.
Rubin, D. B. (2004b). Teaching statistical inference for causal effects in experiments and observational studies. *Journal of Educational and Behavioral Statistics, 29*, 343–367.
Rubin, D. B. (2010). Reflections stimulated by the comments of Shadish (2010) and West and Thoemmes (2010). *Psychological Methods, 15*, 38–46.
Rubin, D. B., & Thomas, N. (1992). Characterizing the effect of matching using linear propensity score methods with normal covariates. *Biometrika, 79*, 797–809.
Rutter, M. (2012). "Natural experiments" as a means of testing causal inferences. In C. Berzuini, P. Dawid, & L. Bernardinelli (Eds.), *Causality: Statistical perspectives and applications* (pp. 253–272). West Sussex, UK: Wiley.
Sadeh, N., Spielberg, J. M., Warren, S. L., Miller, G. A., & Heller, W. (2014). Aberrant neural connectivity during emotional processing associated with posttraumatic stress. *Clinical Psychological Science, 2*, 748–755.
Sauce, B., & Matzel, L. D. (2013). The causes of variation in learning and behavior: Why individual differences matter. *Frontiers in Psychology, 4*, 395. doi:10.3389/fpsyg.2013.00395.
Schmidt, U., Faltwasser, S. F., & Wotjak, C. T. (2013). Biomarkers in posttraumatic stress disorder: Overview and implications for future research. *Disease Markers, 35*, 43–54.
Schwartz, S., Gatto, N. M., & Campbell, U. B. (2011). What would have been is not what would be: Counterfactuals of the past and potential outcomes of the future. In P. E. Shrout, K. M. Keyes, & K. Ornstein (Eds.), *Causality and psychopathology: Finding the determinants of disorders and their cures* (pp. 25–46). New York: Oxford University Press.
Scott, J. C., Matt, G. E., Wrocklage, K. M., Crnich, C., Jordan, J., Southwick, S. M., et al. (2015). A quantitative meta-analysis of neurocognitive functioning in posttraumatic stress disorder. *Psychological Bulletin, 141*, 105–140.
Shadish, W. R., Cook, T. D., & Campbell, D. T. (2002). *Experimental and quasi-experimental design for generalized casual inference*. Boston: Houghton Mifflin.
Shadish, W. R., & Sullivan, K. J. (2012). Theories of causation in psychological science. In H. Copper, P. M. Camic, D. L. Long, A. T. Panter, D. Rindskopf, & K. J. Sher (Eds.), *APA handbook of research methods in psychology, Vol 1: Foundations, planning, measures, and psychometrics* (pp. 23–52). Washington: American Psychological Association.
Shpitser, I. (2012). Structural equations, graphs, and interventions. In C. Berzuini, P. Dawid, & L. Bernardinelli (Eds.), *Causality: Statistical perspectives and applications* (pp. 15–24). West Sussex, UK: Wiley.
Shpitser, I., VanderWeele, T., & Robins, J. M. (2010). On the validity of covariate adjustment for estimating causal effects. *Proceedings of the 26th Conference of Uncertainty and Artificial Intelligence* (pp. 527–536). Corvallis, WA: AUAI Press.
Shrout, P. E. (2011). Integrating causal analysis into psychopathology research. In P. E. Shrout, K. M. Keyes, & K. Ornstein (Eds.), *Causality and psychopathology: Finding the determinants of disorders and their cures* (pp. 3–24). New York: Oxford University Press.

Shrout, P. E., Keyes, K. M., & Ornstein, K. (Eds.). (2011). *Causality and psychopathology: Finding the determinants of disorders and their cures*. New York: Oxford University Press.

Skelton, K., Ressler, K. J., Norrholm, S. D., Jovanovic, T., & Bradley-Davino, B. (2012). PTSD and gene variants: New pathways and new thinking. *Neuropharmacology, 62*, 628–637.

Sobel, M. E. (2008). Identification of causal parameters in randomized studies with mediating variables. *Journal of Educational and Behavioral Statistics, 33*, 230–251.

Sugihara, G., May, R., Ye, H., Hsieh, C.-H., Deyle, E., Fogarty, M., et al. (2012). Detecting causality in complex ecosystem. *Science, 338*, 496–500.

Tian, J., & Pearl, J. (2000). Probabilities of causation: Bounds and identification. In C. Boutilier & M. Goldszmidt (Eds.), *Proceedings of the conference on uncertainty in artificial intelligence* (pp. 589–598). San Francisco, CA: Morgan Kaufmann.

Van Bockstaele, B., Verschuere, B., Tibboel, H., De Houwer, J., Crombez, G., & Koster, E. H. W. (2013). A review of current evidence for the causal impact of attentional bias on fear and anxiety. *Psychological Bulletin, 140*, 682–721.

Van der Maas, H. L. J., Dolan, C. V., Grasman, R. P. P. P., Wichertz, J. M., Huizenga, H. M., & Raijmakers, M. E. J. (2006). A dynamical model of general intelligence: The positive manifold of intelligence by mutualism. *Psychological Review, 113*, 842–861.

van der Schoot, R., Denissen, J., Neyer, F. J., Kaplan, D., Asendorpf, J. B., & van Aken, M. A. G. (2013). A gentle introduction to Bayesian analysis: Applications to developmental research. *Child Development, 85*, 842–860.

van Zuiden, M., Geuze, E., Willemen, H. L. D. M., Vermetten, E., Maas, M., Amarouchi, K., et al. (2012). Glucocorticoid receptor pathway components predict posttraumatic stress disorder symptom development: A prospective study. *Biological Psychiatry, 71*, 309–316.

van Zuiden, M., Geuze, E., Willemen, H. L. D. M., Vermetten, E., Maas, M., Heijnen, C. J., et al. (2011). Pre-existing high glucocorticoid receptor number predicting development of posttraumatic stress symptoms after military deployment. *American Journal of Psychiatry, 168*, 89–96.

van Zuiden, M., Heijnen, C. J., Maas, M., Amarouchi, K., Vermetten, E., Geuze, E., et al. (2012). Glucocorticoid sensitivity of leukocytes predicts PTSD, depressive and fatigue symptoms after military deployment: A prospective study. *Psychoneuroendocrinology, 37*, 1822–1836.

VanderWeele, T. J. (2010). Bias formulas for sensitivity analysis for direct and indirect effects. *Epidemiology, 21*(540), 551.

von Eye, A., & Wiedermann, W. (2015). Manifest variable Granger causality models for developmental research: A taxonomy. *Applied Developmental Science, 19*, 183–195.

von Eye, A., Wiedermann, W., & Mun, E.-Y. (2013). Granger causality – Statistical analysis under a configural perspective. *Integrative Psychological and Behavioral Science, 48*, 79–99.

Weathers, F. W., Litz, B. T., Herman, D. S., Huska, J. A., & Keane, T. M. (1993, October). *The PTSD Checklist (PCL): Reliability, validity, and diagnostic utility*. Paper presented at the meeting of the International Society for Traumatic Stress Studies, San Antonio, TX.

Wigman, J. T. W., van Os, J., Borsboom, D., Wardenaar, K. J., Epskamp, S., Klippel, A., et al. (2015). Exploring the underlying structure of mental disorders: Cross-diagnostic differences and similarities from a network perspective using both a top-down and a bottom-up approach. *Psychological Medicine*. doi:10.1017/S0033291715000331.

Woodward, J. (2000). Explanation and invariance in the special sciences. *British Journal of Philosophy, 51*, 197–254.

Woodward, J. (2001). Law and explanation in biology: Invariance is the kind of stability that matters. *Philosophical Science, 68*, 1–20.

Woodward, J. (2003). *Making things happen: A theory of causal explanation*. New York: Oxford University Press.

Wright, R. W. (1988). Causation, responsibility, risk, probability, naked statistics, and proof: Pruning the bramble bush by clarifying the concepts. *Iowa Law Review, 73*, 1001–1077.

Wu, G., Feder, A., Cohen, H., Kim, J. J., Calderon, S., Charney, D. S., et al. (2013). Understanding resilience. *Frontiers in Behavioral Neuroscience, 7*, 10. doi:10.3389/fnbeh.2013.00010.

Yehuda, R. (2002). Current status of cortisol findings in post-traumatic stress disorder. *Psychiatric Clinics of North America, 25*, 341–368.

Young, G. (2014). *Malingering, feigning, and response bias in psychiatric/psychological injury: Implications for practice and court*. Dordrecht, Netherlands: Springer Science + Business Media.

Zoladz, P. R., & Diamond, D. M. (2013). Current status on behavioral and biological markers of PTSD: A search for clarity in a conflicting literature. *Neuroscience and Biobehavioral Reviews, 37*, 860–895.

Part II

Biology and Revolutions

7 Brain: The Neuronal Network Revolution

Chapter Introduction

Network concepts are being applied to many disciplines, including neuroscience and psychology. The present chapter reviews the work involving the brain, in particular. The prototypical construct in network science as applied to the brain is the connectome (e.g., Sporns, 2012). The intricacies of neuronal linkages and patterns are acquiring their own language, such as hubs. Researchers are finding core networks in the brain, involving, in particular, three major ones—central executive, salience, and default (resting state) networks.

Concepts involving brain networks include those emphasized in Friston's (2010, 2012) work on entropy, "free energy," and "surprise." In this approach, the brain is described in thermodynamic terms, and functions as if it seeks to minimize the descent into disorder. As with many systems treated as nonlinear dynamical ones, in this view, the brain functions optimally when it is held between order and disorder. As well, in Friston's view, perception (and action) aims to improve accuracy of perception and predictability. In this regard, brain function is Bayesian in its process.

The chapter also reviews work on networks at the cellular level. Cells in the brain also function in dynamic complexity. For example, "concept" cells code and fire in order when they are registering response to specific people or places, including famous people. Also, in this regard, astrocytes integrate with neurons to form dynamic systems.

As for psychological networks, Schmittmann et al. (2013) expound that the reflective and formative models of the relationship between items and constructs should be replaced by network ones. As happens with other network models, this one allows for nonlinear dynamical emergence in the causality of behavior.

Introduction

Some topics in science are obtuse, unobservable, enigmatic, and downright dry. The brain stands at the opposite ends in all these regards. We hunger for news on it, views of it, scans of its activations, ideas on its inner workings, and so on. Yet there are dangers in brain science, as well, to which we can fall prey. We might believe that if a brain region "lights up" on a scan while a person is resolving one task or the next, it means that the brain region involved is "responsible" uniquely for the behavior. We might believe that if a scan for a criminal indicates abnormalities relative to norms, then the person should be absolved of responsibility for the crime at issue. Clearly, there is more to behavior than just the brain regions associated with it. Moreover, there is more to the causality of behavior than all things neurological and neuronal. The concepts driving neuroscience are proliferating exponentially, and

G. Young, *Unifying Causality and Psychology*, DOI 10.1007/978-3-319-24094-7_7

the present chapter examines networks in this regard. However, the reader should be aware of the limitations of their capacity to explain behavior, as is presently being argued. I am enamored of the brain, like all of you. However, I perceive it as just one more part of the puzzle of what we do and why in our behavior. In the end, as I tell my patients, the brain does not control us. Rather, we should place ourselves in position where we control it, at least to the degree possible.

Networks

Introduction

Brandes, Robins, McCranie, and Wasserman (2013), who founded the journal *Network Science*, indicated the increasing importance of networks in science. Network models consider networked phenomena, and develop network concepts, including representations, leading to network explanations of the data. Network theory assumes that any of a cause, an effect, or an association can be represented as a network, even in complex cases. It asks for specification of the constituents in a relation, the strength of their ties, and so on.

Brain

Byrge, Sporns, and Smith (2014) applied the concept of brain networks to development. Structural brain networks consist of anatomical connections between distinct cortical and subcortical brain areas. Functional networks involve inter-regional connections that reflect statistical dependencies in neural activity temporal patterns, either in neural activity during tasks (evoked) or intrinsically at rest (spontaneous). In the longer-term, structural networks evidence some change. However, even in the short term, functional networks can change continuously, although they might stabilize. Structural and functional networks interact both in the short term and long term, in a reciprocal shaping/constraining process for the former and in the generation of and modulating process for the latter (in patterns of behavior and learning; see Table 7.1).

Developmentally, changing physical bodies and their activities modify the statistical inputs to the brain, molding brain networks. In turn, the latter promote further changes in input and behavior. Brain networks extend from the brain into the environment; development emerges at the level of process from extended networks involving brain, body, and behavior. These extended networks actively select and even create information, which in turn modifies the brain's networks and their dynamics. Developmental change, therefore, is neither maturational nor universal.

Brain regions cooperate and coactivate, yet are mutually constrained. They manifest individual activity differences that are associated with differences in cognitive and behavioral performance (Kanai & Rees, 2011; Koyama et al., 2011; Zatorre, Fields, & Johansen-Berg, 2012). Connectivity is not passive, but generates complex, system-wide dynamics. External inputs are not received passively. Instead, their perturbations have widespread effects. Therefore, an individual's cumulative history of input perturbations leaves a map of the past in changing connectivities, and this varies over individuals. Connectivity involves constant dialogue over multiple parameters of network systems and their inputs and outputs. Therefore, brain networks are adaptive, online systems that are dynamically co-evolving over multiple time scales (Gross & Blasius, 2008). The process is circular and cascading, and changes with development.

Byrge et al. (2014) concluded that network connectivity and dynamics can lead to both continuous and discontinuous (qualitatively different) change both in the input patterns affected by behavior and in neural system coupling. Brain networks develop dynamically and their changes have widespread effects. We need to consider the extended brain–body–behavior network in development. This gives us a more mechanistic view of development, resituating the developing brain in the developing organism. However, at the same time, the model gives a "less deterministic" comprehension of the process of development.

Table 7.1 Common social network measures and concepts

Level of analysis	Network measure	Definition
Individual	Degree centrality	Count of an actor's total number of social ties. *Indegree* refers to incoming ties, and *outdegree* refers to outgoing ones
	Betweenness centrality	A node could lie between or connects two nodes that would not otherwise be connect; its extent
	Closeness centrality	A node could be close to all other nodes in the network; its extent
	Structural equivalence	A node could play a similar role within a network; its extent
Group or subgroup	Modularity	A network could divide into modules; its strength. High modularity means a network has dense connections between the nodes within modules but sparse connections between nodes in different modules
	Clique	A *clique* has every individual directly tied to every other individual in a subgroup
	Transitivity	Two nodes could be are connected to a same third node and also connected to each other; the extent
Network	Density	The proportion of pairs of nodes that have ties of a given type (existing ties in a network/all possible ties in the network)
	Reciprocity	The proportion of all directional ties that are reciprocated
	Centralization	A network could revolve around one or a few nodes; the extent
	Diameter	Geodesics (paths between two nodes); the longest
	Clustering	A network has clumps (small subgroups within the network with close ties to each other); the extent
Core concepts	Stocks	An accumulation representing a system's memory or state (e.g., in infant behavior)
	Flows	Stocks change because of associated flow dynamics connecting stocks (outflow to inflow at rates)
	Feedback	A structural feature causing cascades in other factors when it affects a stock (positive or negative; could be in balance)
	Systems structure/Causal loop diagrams	Illustrate system reinforcing feedbacks, polarities involves, whether vicious or virtuous cycles develop
	Agent-based modeling (ABMS)	Dynamic modeling of system states that includes parameters, rules, environments, emergence, complexity, etc.

Adapted from Urban, Osgood, Okamoto, Mabry, and Lich in Molenaar, Lerner, and Newell (2014)

That is, the multiple influences and constraints on behavior and brain development are exquisitely complex and involve biological, physical, and cultural factors that yield modal similarities, yet reveal deep individual, unique variation both in moment-to-moment expression and in developmental path.

Comment

The work of Byrge et al. (2014) and that of others, such as Urban, Osgood, Okamoto, Mabry, and Lich (2014), illustrate the growing research of network modeling (e.g., Sporns, 2011, 2012) that is being applied increasingly to behavior.

A lot of the concepts that they describe reflect general network concepts, but some are unique to the particular applied context, such as development or the social situation. Other workers who are informed by network analysis (e.g., Borsboom, 2008, on psychopathology) use comparable language. Generally, network modeling is consistent with other modeling approaches, such as dynamical systems theory (e.g., Thelen & Smith, 1994) and causal graph modeling (e.g., Pearl, 2009).

Connectome

Model

Sporns (2011, 2012) is leading the way in specifying the brain as a "Connectome," which refers to the way neurons and brain regions are interconnected. Sporns indicated that, generally, biological systems are organized as networks having components connected in complex patterns. Moreover, biological systems function well globally because they coordinate the action of networks. Figure 7.1 presents a map of levels of organization in biological systems and the brain—moving from molecules; to synapses and neurons; to networks, maps, and systems; to behavior (Fig. 7.1a). In this perspective, the nervous system is considered a hierarchy of networks that are multi-scalar and, also, the connectome is considered to involve network scales operating between the cellular and social levels (Fig. 7.1b).

Networks of the brain are mapped at three modality levels, or in terms of: (a) structural connectivity across regions, or physical linkages (synapses, pathways); (b) functional connectivity, or mutual information/coherence as indicated by statistical dependencies; and (c) effective connectivity, which involves causal relations among collections of nodes (Jirsa & McIntosh, 2007). Therefore, networks are not metaphors but actual representations of empirical, neuroscientific data that are mathematically formulated.

Terms

Sporns (2011, 2012) provided detailed definitions and explanations of critical terms and concepts in brain network research. In the following, I enumerate them.

A graph or network is an abstract depiction of a set of interconnected elements (nodes and edges) representing the system at hand. A simple graph is composed of a set of nodes and edges. A node (vertex) is a fundamental element of a system (e.g., a neuron, a person). An edge connects pairs of nodes. An edge can be either directed (e.g., synaptic link, causal effect) from origin to destination, or undirected (representing a symmetrical relationship). It can be binary (0, 1) or weighted (fractional; positive or negative). Most neuroscientific work has been on binary, undirected graphs, usually with binary graphs resulting when a cut-off is used with continuous data. An example of a directed graph (or digraph) would involve chemical synaptic connections.

Topology refers to the geometric relation between nodes. An adjacency matrix (or connection matrix) defines graph topology in rows and columns in matrix format. Node neighbors are a node's set of connected links. The degree of a node is its number of incoming and outgoing edges, and they can be mapped in a degree distribution for a system. Strength is a concept similar to degree. Degree constitutes the most fundamental attribute of a graph. Assortivity refers to the correlation between the degrees of connected or neighboring node pairs.

A path is a series of unique edges that connect node pairs. Path length involves the number or sum of its edges (weights). Characteristic path length is constituted by the mean of the finite distances in a network. A path is an ordered sequence of unique edges and intermediate nodes. A cyclic path connects a node to itself, or it loops. Distance is the shortest topological path in a node pair, with diameter being the maximum distance possible in a node pair. Distance matrices

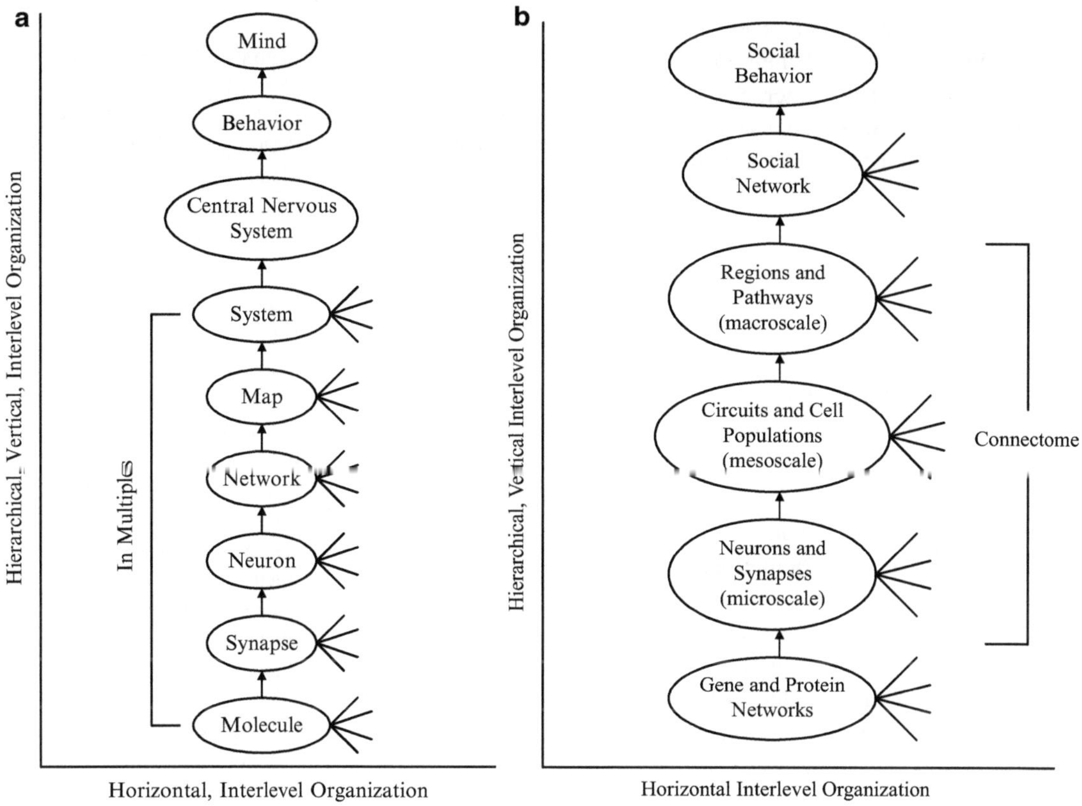

Fig. 7.1 The vertical and horizontal organization underlying the connectome. The first part of the figure (**a**) illustrates the progression from biochemical constituents of cells to cells and their networks/maps to larger systems and behavior. I added a horizontal diversifying component to the original model, as indicated by the *lines* to the right. Adapted from Churchland and Sejnowski (1992). The second part of the figure (**b**) illustrates the basic levels of the connectome in terms of the output of social networks/behavior. Adapted from Sporns (2012)

complement connection matrices in describing network communication patterns.

Other network properties include the clustering coefficient, or the fraction of connections connecting node neighbors (representing network neighborhood "cliquishness"). Connectivity refers to the set of node connections. Modules are communities of strongly interconnected nodes, having connection patterns and "partitions."

A core is a coherent, highly and mutually interconnected node set. A hub is a node that is influentially important, or central to network interconnectivity. Connector hubs function to link nodes over modules. Provincial hubs link constituent nodes in a module. A motif is a reduced subset of network nodes and edges, or a subgraph.

A rich club is a set of high-degree nodes, a term related to the core. A random network has stochastic interconnections; in the simplest case, its edges between nodes are randomly assigned with fixed and uniform probabilities. In a scale-free network, its degree distribution follows a power law. A small world network combines high clustering (as in a regular lattice network) and short characteristic path length (as in a random network). Global efficiency is a distance measure, and centrality is a node or edge measure. Generally, graph measures involve segregation, integration, or influence.

The work of Sporns (2011, 2012) can be consulted for the massive details of the connectome. Two conclusions in Sporns (2012) that I found important relate to intrinsic brain networks and intermediate endophenotypes. For the former, Raichle (2011) has found seven major resting-state brain networks and their interconnections (see Table 7.2). For the latter, Sporns postulated that the connectome will serve an integral mediator in understanding genetic-behavioral linkages.

Systems

Sporns (2011) explained the value of network thinking in brain theory and research. It allows an integrative look at brain function from a complex connectivity perspective. It incorporates complexity science as a framework for understanding element coupling and interconnections. Networks create dynamical patterns of interrelationships that are not reducible to parts. Brain networks have multiple scales in their arrangements, from cells to the social networks that they allow. These levels are interrelated, with the patterns of each critically dependent on processes that unfold at lower and at higher levels. In this hierarchy, there are no privileged level, with neither full-scale reduction to lower levels nor inclusive top-down influences from higher levels. In this type of modeling, connectivity permits neurons to act in both independent and collective ways. Connectivity permits brain integration. In other words, the brain functions like any network in complex systems.

Sporns (2011) noted that network models run counter to both the doctrine of the centrality of the neuron and the mechanistic functional localization of the brain. Rather, they help explain how neurons and regions work and also how they are interconnected. In this regard, Sporns (2011) described various neuroanatomical pathways and linkages in terms of "connectomal fingerprints," such as connectional fingerprints, connectional families, hierarchical fingerprints, and motif fingerprints.

"Connectomics" means that two brains from different individuals are never exactly the same. Despite these individual differences, their brains

Table 7.2 Seven resting-state brain networks/systems and their interconnections

Resting-state brain network/system	Central regions of interest (According to BOLD, blood-oxygen-level dependent values)
Default mode (DMN)	Posterior cingulate/precuneus
	Medial prefrontal
	L lateral parietal
	R lateral parietal
	L inferior temporal
	R inferior temporal
	Medial dorsal thalamus
	R posterior cerebellum
Dorsal attentional (DAN)	L posterior cerebellum
	L frontal eye field
	R frontal eye field
	L posterior inferior parietal sulcus
	R posterior inferior parietal sulcus
	L anterior inferior parietal sulcus
	R posterior inferior parietal sulcus
	L middle temporal area
	R middle temporal area
Executive control (ECN)	Dorsal medial prefrontal cortex
	L anterior prefrontal cortex
	R anterior prefrontal cortex
	L superior parietal
	R superior parietal
Salience (SN)	Dorsal anterior cingulate
	L anterior prefrontal cortex
	R anterior prefrontal cortex
	L insula
	R insula
	L lateral parietal
	R lateral parietal
Sensorimotor (SS)	L motor cortex
	R motor cortex
	Supplementary motor area
Auditory (AS)	L auditory area
	R auditory area
Visual (VS)	R visual area 1
	L visual area 1

Adapted from Raichle (2011)
Note: *L*=left, *R*=right, *N*=network, *S*=system

still express functional homeostasis, or common activity in outcome, at least to a certain degree. In this perspective, the functional localization approach of the brain comes closer to a distributionist approach to the brain. Local specialization should be seen as the result of patterned and distributed interactions involving individual and collective elements. Therefore, the brain should be considered an integrative system with emergent and complex properties. In this regard, Fair et al. (2009) found that functional networks seem to progress from local/segregated to distributed/integrated organizational modes.

Sporns (2011) also examined brain networks from the perspective of dynamics, which allows for integration of stability and change and diversity in systems. Systems express a multi-scale, nested hierarchical structure that is neither entirely stable nor unstable but, instead, is "metastable." System trajectories travel in manifolds with attractor "pockets" that slow or entrap them, creating intermittent, "quasi-stable," temporal behavior. The wells or indentations into which the systems fall are visited repeatedly, in a process of chaotic itinerancy, or itinerant roaming motion. The flow is turbulent because, although the system elements are globally coupled, they are far-from-equilibrium. The system trajectories alternate between order and transition, losing their coupling coherence within the movement between attractor "ruins."

Systems might contain "saddle point" chains that both attract and repel trajectories, creating the meta-stable dynamic. Also, network connection facilitates creation of "collector" variables that "enslave" lower levels, reducing their degrees of freedom, thereby adding to stabilization tendencies. But, as system order moves toward disorder, in the critical region or at the "edge of chaos," emergence of novelty and complex system modes become favored (Bak, Tang, & Wiesenfeld, 1987).

Criticality might be a property favored in the dynamic regime of systems, given the inherent tradeoff of randomness and regularity in environments. Connectivity could promote stability and diversity by collecting system behavior into superordinate variables and reducing degrees of freedom, and so "contracting" the regions of space accessible to systems [but without denying movement to the cusp of change and emergence of new regimes and meta-stability] (e.g., Kello, Beltz, Holden, & Van Orden, 2008). It appears that brains are primed to inhabit this state space of order and disorder, facilitating phase transitions marked by variable stability, instability, and meta-stability.

Evidence

Sporns and van den Heuvel (2013) statistically analyzed weighted projections among different cortical regions in healthy volunteers (van den Heuvel, Kahn, Goñi, & Sporns, 2012; van den Heuvel & Sporns, 2011). Their model includes network "hubs," defined in terms of high-degree node connectivity. They posed the question whether hubs themselves, proportionately, are highly mutually connected, in what is called a "rich club."

The results revealed a rich club core involving portions of the following brain regions: superior frontal cortex, superior parietal cortex, precuneus, cingulate cortex, and insula. These areas are midline focused, with a rich club set found in each hemisphere. The work of Sporns and van den Heuvel (2013) showed that rich club brain connectives constitute central communication cores of global information. They are widely distributed, and often their connections span relatively long distances. According to the authors, longer connection lengths are "costly," but the advantages of having core communicating hubs involving them comprise a communicative "backbone" in the brain.

van den Heuvel and Sporns (2013) expanded on the role of hubs in brain networks. For example, the interaction of frontal hubs and distributed cortical regions increase in development. The hubs and their connections are critical in information integration and in efficient neural signaling/communication in the brain.

Conclusions

Sporns (2011) concluded that complexity is a central design feature of the brain, allowing it to adapt to variable and partly predictable environments. The organism becomes autonomous because it is part of a rich dynamic web of person, brain, mind, and environment in which the organism is not controlled by any algorithm or blueprint but is expressed in the full network system.

I would add that a full network understanding of the brain, its networks, and the person in context considers emergent properties of mind, such as free will. Emergent concepts such as these allow escapement from network constraints and dictates, and inform bidirectionally development of networks so that they actively function beyond the influences of biology and environment. A crucial element in this regard is the emergent sense of freedom from internal or external constraint or control that the person can develop and use, at least partially, to direct and determine behavior. Behavior is never fully free nor is it the complete product of free will. However, believing in it and having a sense of free will give us some freedom of action (Baumeister, 2008), and that is the best system we, and our brains, along with their networks, can hope to and happen to have.

Core Networks

Model

Menon (2012) investigated neurocognitive networks in brain dynamics as evidenced by intrinsic functional connectivity. During cognitive tasks, brain areas that are engaged appear to form coherent global networks. Shirer, Ryali, Rykhlevskaia, Menon, and Greicius (2012) have identified 14 intrinsic connectivity networks in resting-state functional MRI neuroimaging data. They are important not only in sensory processing but also in higher cognitive functions. According to Menon (2012), among these 14 networks, three appear "core" neurocognitive networks. They are termed the central executive network (CEN), the salience network (SN), and the default mode network (DMN). The salience network is involved in dynamic switching to the other two (DMN, CEN), which are focused on endogenously-mediated/self-referential mental activity and exogenously driven/cognitively-demanding mental activity, respectively (see Fig. 7.2).

The CEN is especially comprised of interconnectivity of the dorsolateral prefrontal cortex (DLPFC) and posterior parietal cortex (PPC). The SN is anchored in the anterior insula (AI), the adjoining fronto-insular cortex (FIC), and the anterior cingulate cortex (ACC). The DMN is focused in the posterior cingulate cortex (PCC), medial prefrontal cortex (mPFC), medial temporal lobe (MTL), and angular gyrus (AG). These three networks are considered core because they can be involved in a very broad array of cognitive tasks and they are reciprocally related and dynamically engaged and disengaged (Greicius & Menon, 2004; Raichle et al., 2001; Sridharan, Levitin, & Menon, 2008).

Network analysis of temporal dynamics reveals "causal flow" over core networks. In both auditory and visual tasks, the right hemisphere FIC had the highest number of causal outflow connections (out-degree) and the lowest number of inflow, in-degree ones, as well as the shortest path length of measured regions (also ACC, rDLPFC, rPPC, VMPFC, PCC). These results combine to give the rFIC the highest net causal outflow to inflow ratio (out-in degree), making it a causal outflow "hub" in the SN to which it is anchored.

The AI, in general, is considered the integral hub of the SN. As a dynamic switching mechanism to endogenous and exogenous stimuli, the SN includes bottom-up and top-down interactions that underpin attentional control. Bottom-up stimulus-detection signals (in CPS, cycles per second) are transmitted to brain regions that include the AI, which amplifies them, thereby triggering a strong ACC response. The ACC generates a top-down control signal, including to the CEN. Premotor cortical and temporoparietal areas respond. Response mediation also takes place in other areas (e.g., supplementary motor cortex).

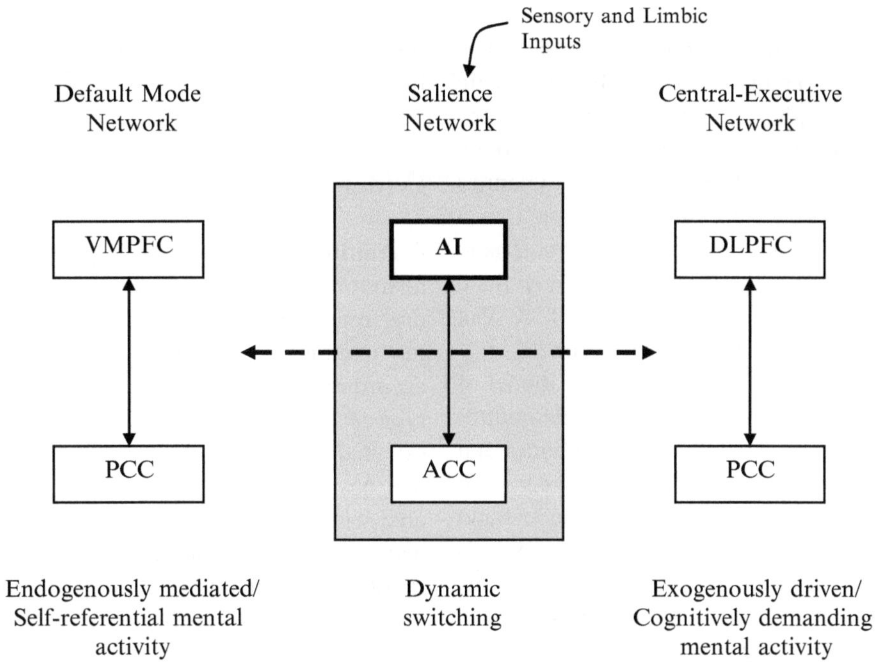

Fig. 7.2 Multinetwork switching initiated by the salience network. The SN (salience network) is hypothesized to initiate dynamic switching between the CEN (central-executive network) and DNM (default mode network) and to mediate between attention to endogenous and exogenous events. In this model, sensory and limbic inputs are processed by the anterior insula (AI), which detects salient events and initiates appropriate control signals to regulate behavior via the anterior cingulate cortex (ACC) and homeostatic state via the mid and posterior insular cortex. Key nodes of the SN: AI and ACC. Key nodes of the DMN: ventral medial prefrontal cortex (VMPFC) and posterior cingulate cortex (PCC). Key nodes of the CEN: dorsolateral prefrontal cortex (DLPFC) and the posterior parietal cortex (PPC). Adapted from Menon (2012), based on Bressler and Menon (2010), original from Uddin and Menon (2009). Adopted with permission of Elsevier. Reprinted from *Neuroscience and Behavioral Reviews,* Vol. 33, Uddin, L. Q., & Menon, V., The anterior insula in autism: Under-connected and under-examined, Pages 1198–1203, Copyright 2009; with kind permission from Elsevier. [Figure 2, Page 1202]

Menon (2013) described six emerging principles of developmental pathways for functional brain networks. Among them are the development of "small-world," hierarchical organization and hubs, segregation of functional circuits, their pruning and reconfiguration, and a balance in excitation/inhibition in underpinning physiology in neurotransmitters (impacting local circuits and large-scale connectivity).

Rubinov and Bullmore (2013) indicated that, in psychiatric disorder, there might be "pathoconnectomics" at work. However, at present, the evidence for specific relationships between disorder and such pathology is inconclusive.

Systems

Singer (2013) described cortical networks as dynamic, nonlinear, self-organized, and complex. Their organization allows support of "high dimensional" states and the binding of local processors into highly interconnected coherent global states. The organization constitutes a "dense connectome" that permits essentially "unconstrained" interactions between any pair of neurons in the cortical mantle. The couplings can be modified very quickly by inhibition in synchronized oscillating cell circuits at the correct phase.

The connectome varies between randomness and regularity so that its complexity and dimensionality is neither excessively stochastic (independent, highly dimensional) nor synchronized (low dimensionality), but is intermediate along this continuum. The resting-state dynamics of cortical networks appear to function like a self-organized critical system, a characteristic that is favorable for computations (Deco & Jirsa, 2012; Priesemann, Valderrama, Wibral, & Van Quyen, 2013; Wang, Hilgetag, & Zhou, 2011).

Ruths and Ruths (2014) proposed a model of complex networks that included multiple control nodes. Networks consist of branching nodes and "dilation" points; also, each "stem" in the system has a control mechanism. We need to understand the configuration and causal origin of a network's minimal control points to grasp it better. Stems have buds and cycles, and are referred to as "cacti." Biological neural and social networks are not top-down driven; rather, they are source-dominated in control, allowing uncorrelated behavior and distributed processing.

Moretti and Muñoz (2013) have modified the criticality model of complex systems by specifying that operating at the edge of chaos (in the critical region) is not simply a borderline or singular point between organization and disorganization but a whole extended region around it. The existence of such a "stretched" criticality (called Griffith phases, GPs) facilitates self-organization toward criticality. Brain networks that are hierarchical and modular (as in the connectome) appear to function in this way, facilitating their adaptive functionality.

Hilgetag and Hütt (2014) pointed out that criticality allows for adaptation because a small change in an external control parameter can lead to disproportionately large reconfiguration in system state organization. Stretching criticality in hierarchical modular brain connectivity takes place through regional mixtures of sub- and super-critical behavior in the GPs. The concept of stretched criticality in brain networks could be applied to "dysfunctional" functional networks (e.g., for depression, see Sombataro, Wolf, Pennuto, Vasic, & Wolf, 2014; van Tol et al., 2014). Similarly, Pessoa (2014) took a network view of brain architecture, and related it to an integrated emotion-cognitive perspective of the brain.

Evidence

Cognition Zanto and Gazzaley (2013) reviewed a study by Cole et al. (2013) demonstrating that the fronto-parietal network (FPN) is altered in its functional connections with other networks according to task goals. The FPN is a control-type network compared to others that are process-oriented. It involves the lateral prefrontal cortex and posterior parietal cortex areas. It is associated with cognitive control abilities in initiation and modulation. Control networks are flexible, rapid, and dynamic compared to processing networks, which are relatively task-specific, modular, and static.

The authors concluded that dynamic multi-network interactions that appear to take place in cognition denote a flexible hub model of connectome activity. Task resolution flexibility leads not only to intra-neural network reorganization but also inter-network reorganization in a synchronous fashion. Harmelech and Malach (2013) examined the spontaneous activity in the resting brain (no overt task). They found that spontaneous fluctuations in this default mode revealed by BOLD-fMRI (blood-oxygen-level dependent functional magnetic resonance imaging) readings seem to reflect the person's profile of prior neuronal connectivity and cognitive biases. The latter serve to influence "synaptic efficacies" in cortical networks. As such, they can be remodeled. Therefore, their current state offers a window into their past states (priors), inner (cortical) world, pathologies, cognitive biases and traits, and personality traits/tendencies (e.g., Adelstein et al., 2011).

Reinhart and Woodman (2013) demonstrated the online dynamic reorganization in oscillatory coupling of large-scale neuronal networks in relation to changing phases and task demands of a search task lasting several seconds in which participants had to locate target objects in cluttered visual scenes. The task phases tapped reward encoding, working memory, and attentional processes. The reward cue indicated the monetary value of the trial in process. The target cue was presented briefly (100 ms), so that information retention in working memory was needed in relation to the attentional phase. The final search phase lasted 2 s. Recordings that indicated oscillatory coupling involved cross-frequency coupling analyses of participant EEG oscillations, in search of fast rhythmic temporal correlations of neuronal activity.

The results showed that each cognitive operation led to formation and dissolution of functional connectivity between different brain areas. In particular, in large reward conditions, initial/task phase theta and beta oscillations over prefrontal brain regions realized a distributed network as defined by the coupling of these frequencies. In the next task phase of working memory, the theta and alpha oscillations across frontoparietal areas formed a neuronal network, which was distinct in dynamic relative to the one in the first task phase. Next, in the target search phase, theta and alpha oscillations over frontotemporal areas formed another distinct network. Other results showed that networks could form quickly, and they predict even better than either local oscillations or ERPs (event-related potentials) subsequent network strength and actual behavioral response (speed and accuracy) that takes place seconds later.

The authors concluded that the results support a dynamic or transient stimulus coding model. Also, large-scale neuronal network activity constitutes an intermediate organization level between circuit-level computation and higher-order behavior/experience.

Matsumoto and Kakigi (2013) noted that the dynamic balance of left frontal and temporal cortical regions can be primed by subliminal unconscious semantic cues. In their study, subliminal semantic priming induced significant modulation of alpha band activity in the left inferior frontal cortex and of gamma band activity in left inferior temporal regions. The influence of the priming extended beyond local brain regions to online dynamics that were over them.

Applied Using voxel-based lesion-symptom mapping in focal brain-injury patients, Barbey, Colom, and Grafman (2014) demonstrated that a common neural network is engaged in executive, social, and emotional processes. Specifically, a broadly distributed neural network of frontal, temporal, and parietal regions is shared or convergent with not only general intelligence but also with emotional intelligence and personality. The authors concluded that behavior is orchestrated in multiple brain regions that aggregate in function supporting intellectual and affective processes. The broad neural network architecture involved is coordinated, integrated, interactive, intersecting, connective, and collaborative, rather than being localized, selective, or distinct.

Barch (2013) examined brain network interactions, as well. He focused on the research of Palaniyappan, Simmonite, White, Liddle, and Liddle (2013), which showed that deficits in reciprocal causal interactions across the salience and CENs are implicated in schizophrenia. In particular, they focused on interactions involving the insula (part of the salience system) and the DLPFC (part of the CEN). The deficits involved difficulties related to inhibition of the DLPFC and excitations into it (both findings in relation to the insula).

Sex Ingalhalikar et al. (2014) illustrated in the research the value of studying whole-brain connectome networks. They studied sex differences in the structural connectome in 8- to 22-year-olds. In all supratentorial regions, males showed greater within-hemisphere connectivity, with connections extending front to back. In contrast, females showed greater between-hemisphere connectivity. Males also differed by their enhanced modularity/transitivity, compared to females who, in contrast, were more cross-module in connectivity.

The authors concluded that the results reflect fundamental cerebral functional differences in males and females. The former have brains structured to facilitate connection between perception and coordinated action. In contrast, females have a brain organization conducive to communication between analytic and intuitive processing modalities. Finally, the male difference emerges earlier than the female one.

Comment

Network modeling provides a rich conceptual network and vocabulary that greatly expands our understanding of brain and behavior. In systems, we can now determine the degree of centrality and distribution, efficiency and dispersion, pathways and functions, and so on. The work on brain networks has focused on core ones, such as those relating to salience and attention, executive function, and resting state. Network concepts are greatly intertwined with those of systems theory, such as emergence, criticality, attractors, and the cusp of change. The marriage is fortified by the development of new systems concepts, such as stretched criticality. I note that the research in the area refers to activations and inhibitions.

This latter point is consistent with my proposal that a common metric that crosses brain and behavior is activation/inhibition coordination. As networks self-organize into adaptive patterns to support the behavior of the organism, it does not happen without an implicit economical process that accounts for system stretching to the edge of change after perturbation. In this regard, the construct of activation/inhibition coordination should be added into the network lexicon and rework some of its terms while adding new ones. In addition, the construct applies equally well not only to internal dynamics of brain and behavior but also to interactive ones of individuals with one or more others.

For example, do network betweenness, centrality, efficiency, or small world and rich club characteristics develop because certain nodes and edges in network pathways are inhibited while others are activated, and how does this happen through intrinsic dynamics? Can psychological activation/inhibition coordination dynamics feed into neural network ones and create characteristics parallel to them, or vice versa, and how might this happen reciprocally between brain and behavior? In this regard, to what extent are activation/inhibition coordinations superordinate to rather than reflective of brain networks and behavioral networks both within and between people? Are they the constitutive stuff of brain, behavior, and their networks, the defining attributes of their interactions, in what I have referred to as the intraactive interactional dynamics that constitute the essence of phenomena more than the components of the interactions themselves?

In the next section of the chapter, I elaborate the construct of free energy in the brain that has already been introduced because of its importance to the book and its understanding of behavioral causality. I have supported a role of free will in behavior and this concept of free energy related to brain function is consistent with it. However, the relationship between free will and free energy appears to be an inverse one. Free energy in the brain might compromise free will in behavior because it reflects disorder more than order and the brain works to diminish it. In this regard, the more the brain is successful in the task, the more there should be degrees of freedom available in its functioning to implement free will (in choosing and deciding and so on), so that freedom of being obtains.

Free Energy and Surprise

Model

As described by Friston (2010), organisms and their brains function according to adaptive resistance toward disruptive disorder. In order to maintain equilibrium in its environment, any biological entity or agent needs to self-organizationally minimize its free energy. In resisting tendency to disorder, a small range of adaptive states is entered into (the entity, phenotypic expression), which means it has low "entropy." "Surprise" refers to the average entropic state (mathematically, the negative log-probability of an outcome). By keeping surprise low, which is the biological equivalent of the second law of thermodynamics, the principle of a natural decline in disorder and also increase in entropy (the "fluctuation" theorem) is violated "constructively" by the adapting biological entities/agents.

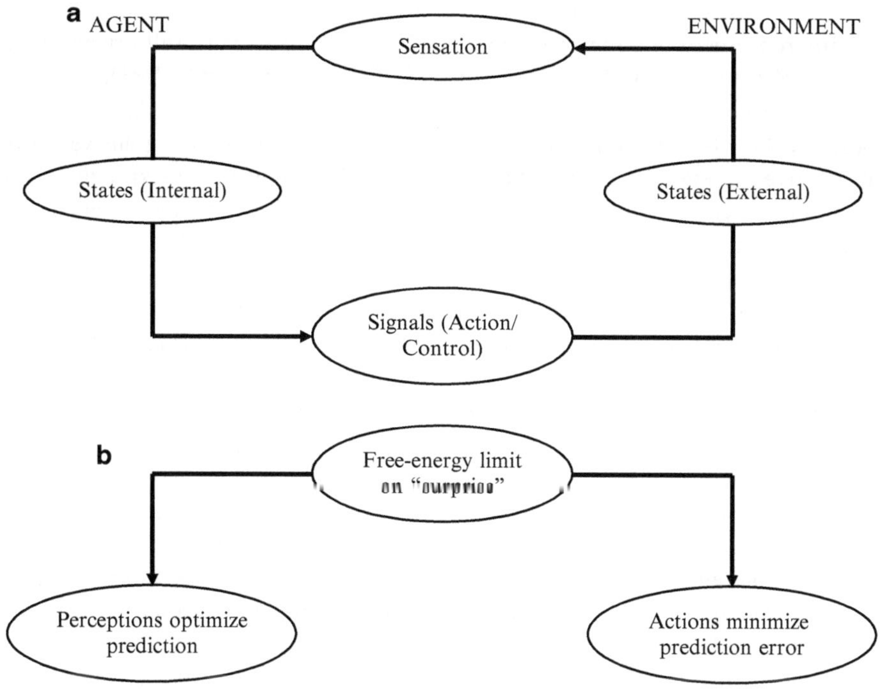

Fig. 7.3 Principle of free energy. Part (**a**) of the figure indicates the elements among the factors that define free energy. These include the internal states of the brain and its exchange with the environment, which involves sensory signals leading to action. Sensory input includes hidden states, parameters, and precisions. Internal brain states and action serve to minimize free energy, and it involves, the "recognition density" that is encoded by internal states. The free energy depends on two probability densities—the one of recognition and the one that generates sensory samples (and their causes). The latter is akin to a probabilistic generative model. Part (**b**) of the figure indicates that free energy minimization involves action reducing it by increasing accuracy (i.e., by selectively sampling predicted data). Conversely, the optimization of brain states constructs the "representation" of "approximate conditional density" of "causes" of sensorial inputs. This process allows action to avoid sensory encounters that are surprising. Adapted from Friston (2010)

Free energy regulation optimizes movements from one state to another, thereby minimizing surprise and keeping the state movements within a small set of adaptive states, referred to as a global random "attractor." Surprise is an information "theoric quantity" and not an energetic thermodynamic one. The agent entity can regulate it as a function of sensory state and "recognition density," which refers to factors such as neuronal activity and connection strength (for the brain). It is defined as an approximate probability distribution of the causes of data (e.g., sensory input).

The figure presenting Friston's model (Fig. 7.3) shows that external states might produce action or control signals, but only by way of sensations and internal states. The environment can be represented mathematically in equations that specify its "hidden states." Therefore, the "causes of sensory input" include such hidden states. Moreover, brain states function to minimize free energy either by increasing or optimizing "accuracy," or by minimizing prediction errors (e.g., selectively sampling data that are predicted).

According to a more formal description of the model, in optimization, the entity/agent implicitly represents or infers the causes behind its sensory data in a "Bayes-optimal" manner. By changing sensory input, either by acting on the environment or by changing an internal state, an entity/organism can self-organize appropriately to avoid excessive surprise. "Bayesian surprise" refers to the difference between a prior recognition density, e.g., about beliefs about the state of the environment before assimilation of sensory data, and posterior beliefs. The entity/agent acts to formulate "active" inferences about anticipations/expectations and tries to confirm them.

In the Bayesian brain hypothesis (Knill & Pouget, 2004), by using sensory inputs or information, or updated posterior beliefs, the brain optimally uses probability theory to form optimized, constructed perceptions. In the Bayesian brain model, the brain is construed as an inference machine or engine that actively optimizes probabilistic representations of the causes of sensory input, using them simultaneously. It actively predicts and explains sensations, using predictive coding. The predictions enable testing of sensory samples to help update belief about their causes. Generative models help facilitate mapping probabilistic likelihoods and priors, and their inversions, so that adaptive perception results from sensory input. Hierarchical generative models help explain how prior beliefs are formed and are consistent with the hierarchical architecture of cortical areas.

Systems

Friston (2012) further described his "free energy" model of global brain dynamics (see Table 7.3). To review, it includes concepts such as "surprise" and "hidden causes." The model helps explicate self-organized neuronal activity in relation to brain activity. The neuronal dynamics involved are framed in terms of "optimization" (e.g., function minimization). The brain functions to model sensorial input, including with free energy minimization and consideration of Bayesian priors.

Friston (2012) continued that the brain is not equally distributed in energy and potential states, but gravitates to a small number. As a biological agent, it maintains a distribution of low entropy (high order) among the states it could occupy. In this regard, entropy is the average "surprise" (or negative log probability) of an agent being in a specific state. The agent involved seeks to minimize average surprise or unexpected events. Friston (2012) maintained that self-organization is insufficient to explain how biological agents can avoid surprise in an indefinite fashion.

For Friston (2012), the answer to this conundrum lies in agents maximizing evidence for their models of sensory exchanges with the world. Our brains or its agents are model optimizers, or inference machines, based on statistical engines with reference to sensory data available to us. In Bayesian brain models, the brain makes inferences about its sensations. The brain becomes a dynamic model of its collective environmental "econiches." Moreover, surprise is minimized in this model by creating free-energy "bounds." Therefore, in the Bayesian brain hypothesis, minimizing variational free energy entails "Bayes-optimal" perception, or reducing prediction errors. Further, to minimize prediction error, either perception or action can be altered; with the latter giving us agency to act on the world in order to ensure that predictions arise as they should. Moreover, prior expectations produce "policies" that are followed. State spaces are characterized by "viscosity," which can be negative, with a slowing friction, or which can be positive. Agents wander in state space to find spaces equivalent to priors to which they had gravitated and, at this point, viscosity switches from positive to negative. If the priors are rewarding and low-cost, they are "exploited" and populated. Stability prevails and disorder is resisted, unless rewards and costs determine otherwise.

Neurons

Deco, Jirsa, and Friston (2012) explicated the systemic nature of local and global network dynamics in brain activity. They examined (a) integrate-and-fire spiking neurons at the local level and (b) large-scale anatomical connectivity matrices of local nodes over distributed brain areas at the global level. The global dynamics included functional integration and effective connectivity across segregated, interacting, and mutually influencing brain areas. They were found to emerge from the local ones of each brain area.

Table 7.3 Generic variables and quantities in the free-energy formation of active inference under Laplace assumption (i.e., generalized predictive coding)

Variable	Description
Generative model or agent	In the free-energy formulation, each agent or system is taken to be a model of the environment in which it is immersed. It corresponds to the form (e.g., degrees of freedom) of a model entailed by an agent, which is used to predict sensory signals
Action	These variables are states of the world that correspond to the movement or configuration of an agent (i.e., its effectors)
Sensory signals	These generalized sensory signals or samples comprise the sensory states, their velocity, acceleration, and temporal derivatives to high order. In other words, they correspond to the trajectory of an agent's sensations
Surprise	This is a scalar function of sensory samples and reports the improbability of sampling some signals under a generative model of how those signals were caused. It is sometimes called (sensory) surprisal or self-information. In statistics, it is known as the negative log-evidence of the model
Entropy	Sensory entropy is, under ergodic assumptions, proportional to the long-term time average of surprise
Gibbs energy	The negative log of the density specified by the generative model; namely, surprise about the joint occurrence of sensory samples and their causes
Free energy	A scalar function of sensory samples and a proposal density, which upper bounds surprise. It is called free energy because it is the expected Gibbs energy minus the entropy of the proposal density. Under a Gaussian (Laplace) assumption about the form of the proposal density, free energy reduces to the simple function of Gibbs energy shown
Free action	A scalar function of sensory samples and a proposal density, which upper bounds the entropy of sensory signals. It is the time or path integral of free energy
Proposal density	Also known as a variational ensemble or recognition density. It becomes (approximates) the conditional density over hidden causes of sensory samples when free-energy is minimized. Under the Laplace assumption, it is specified by its conditional expectation and covariance
True and hidden causes	Quantities that cause sensory signals. The true quantities exist in the environment, and the hidden homologues are those assumed by the generative model of the environment. Both are partitioned into time-dependent variables and time-invariant parameters
Hidden parameters	Parameters of the mapping (e.g., equations of motion) that constitute the deterministic part of a generative model
Log-precisions	Parameters that control the precision (inverse variance) of fluctuations that constitute the random part of a generative model
Hidden states	Hidden variables that encode the hierarchical states in a generative model of dynamics in the world
Hidden causes	Hidden variables that link different levels of a hierarchical generative model
Deterministic mappings	Equations at the *i*th level of a hierarchical generative model that map from states at one level to another and map hidden states to their motion within each level. They specify the deterministic part of a generative model
Random fluctuations	These relate to hidden causes and the motion of hidden states. Gaussian assumptions about these fluctuations furnish the probabilistic part of a generative model
Precision matrices	The inverse covariances among (generalized) random fluctuations on the hidden causes and motion of hidden states
Roughness matrices	The inverse of a matrix encoding serial correlations among (generalized) random fluctuations on the hidden causes and motion of hidden states
Prediction errors	The prediction errors on the hidden causes and motion of hidden states evaluated at their current conditional expectation
Precision-weighted predic tion errors	The prediction errors weighted by their respective precisions

Adopted by permission of The MIT Press. Rabinovich, Mikhail I., Karl J. Friston, and Pablo Varona, eds., *Principles of Brain Dynamics: Global State Interactions*, Table 12.1, pp. 13, pp. 264–265, © 2012 Massachusetts Institute of Technology, by permission of The MIT Press. [Table 12.1, Pages. 264–265]

Reciprocally, the global level constrains or couples with local activity. Also, the whole system expresses self-organization. The interaction of the levels can be described in terms of the concept of circular causality, attractors, functioning in critical regimes that power phase transitions, and other dynamical system concepts. Self-organization occurs through enslavement of neuronal populations within a specific brain area by large-scale intercortical dynamics.

The dynamical approach is consistent with the computational neuroscience one in which this approach is embedded. The computational neuroscience approach attempts to describe the dynamics of neuronal and synaptic networks with realistic models to reproduce "emergent" characteristics, or to predict neurophysiological data and associated behavior. The concept of attractor dynamics has been applied to represent neural computations related to attention, memory, and decision-making in cognitive functions (e.g., Brunel & Wang, 2001).

Attractor networks of spiking neurons are hypothesized to consist of fixed-point attractors representing local networks. The network consists of excitatory and inhibitory neural populations (see Fig. 7.4). Dynamical equations can be used to describe the activity of each neuron, which settle into particular regions of their state space to which they are consistently pulled. The excitatory and inhibitory neurons influence each other through coupling and connectivity.

Specifically, spikes arriving at a given synapse constitute input to the neuron, leading to postsynaptic excitatory or inhibitory firing potentials at postsynaptic receptors. In the present case, the total synaptic current is an expression of glutamatergic (excitatory) and GABAergic (inhibitory) transmitters deriving from reciprocally modulated excitatory pyramidal cells and inhibitory interneurons.

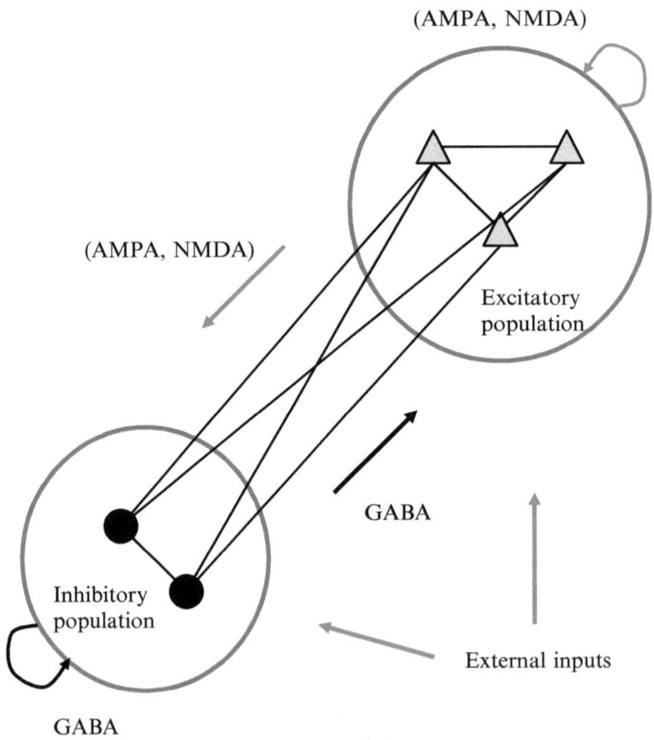

Fig. 7.4 A local network. The network consists of spiking neurons with realistic AMPA (α-Amino-3-hydroxy-5-methyl-4-isoxazolepropionic acid), NMDA (*N*-methyl-D-aspartate receptor), and GABA (gamma-Aminobutyric acid) synaptic dynamics. The network contains excitatory pyramidal cells and inhibitory interneurons. Adopted by permission of The MIT Press. Rabinovich, Mikhail I., Karl J. Friston, and Pablo Varona, eds., *Principles of Brain Dynamics: Global State Interactions*, Figure 1.1, pp. 13, pp. 13, © 2012 Massachusetts Institute of Technology, by permission of The MIT Press. [Figure 1.1, Page 13]

Connectome

As for the global level of brain organization, Deco et al. (2012) referred to the concept of the connectome (e.g., Jirsa, Sporns, Breakspear, Deco, & McIntosh, 2010). The authors continued that, as a whole, the brain is not passive, nor is it driven by information but, in contrast, the brain actively generates predictions and, in its resting state, networks participate in priming it for predictivity. The global attractor landscape is conditioned by global inter-area coupling strength that emerges in form as multi-stable, dispersed fixed-point areal attractors under optimal intermediate global coupling. Real brain dynamics adopt this pattern; otherwise, there is mostly either inhibitory neuronal firing or excitatory (epileptic) neuronal firing. Moreover, the brain does not have a central pattern generator orchestrating this real-world dynamics, but it is inherently self-organizing and settles into attractor landscape regions near phase transition bifurcations so that it can function toward an itinerant or wandering (chaotic) dynamic that facilitates adaptivity. This type of model has been applied to whole brain and to neocortical connectivity (Sporns, 2011; Buice & Cowan, 2009; respectively).

Comment

The work by Friston on free energy in the brain is consistent with the thermodynamic approach of systems theory to system organization and its drivers. The emphasis on the brain as a predictive organ trying to reduce surprise or unpredictability is a Bayesian concept that indicates the brain is a probability-regulating machine trying to adapt to the landscape of probabilities possible in the environment and also that are involved in the present context and in future courses of action. The brain is rendered the ideal adaptive learner in having these properties, because it builds on priors, or its past states that have led it to its present organization.

When Bayesian concepts are applied to the thinking process, they allow for intuitive knowledge and guessing, given that full knowledge of both prior states and predictions of the future (state, environment, best adaptive response, etc.) is impossible. At the same time, Bayesian thinking that is probability-governed and contextual needs higher-order thought and reflection to guide the pathways to optimization in thought and subsequent action. This brings free will into the picture of the Bayesian brain, because conscious reflective thought enables distancing from the context so that a fuller picture of the options, choices that can be made, and aware decision-making, and so on, can be formulated. Because the brain is Bayesian, so is behavior and so can free will in behavior exist. Difficulty in engaging in efficient probability processes in brain and thinking processes complicate the ability to engage in free will. Said another way, an unadaptive amount of free energy complicates the stability needed for free will to manifest and be used effectively. The more free energy present, then, the less there is free will.

In the following, I examine to what extent cells are governed by network models, in particular, the so-called "concept" cells and astrocytes. In both of these cases, network and systems model concepts apply, and we learn that we can no longer consider cells as straight-through avenues of signal detection and conduction. The cell assemblies and interlockings that they form are plastic and environmental-responsive. This makes them psychological at their core.

Cells

Concept Cells

"Concept cells" in the medial temporal lobe (MTL) appear crucial to declarative memory functions (Quiroga, 2012). One avenue of research demonstrating the firing of these cells involves patients who are suffering from intractable epilepsy. The hippocampus portion of the MTL appears especially open to encoding the "meaning" of a stimulus. Meaning is subjective and the cells fire explicitly to the conscious perception of the stimulus. The cells are "remarkably" selective in firing, and had once been

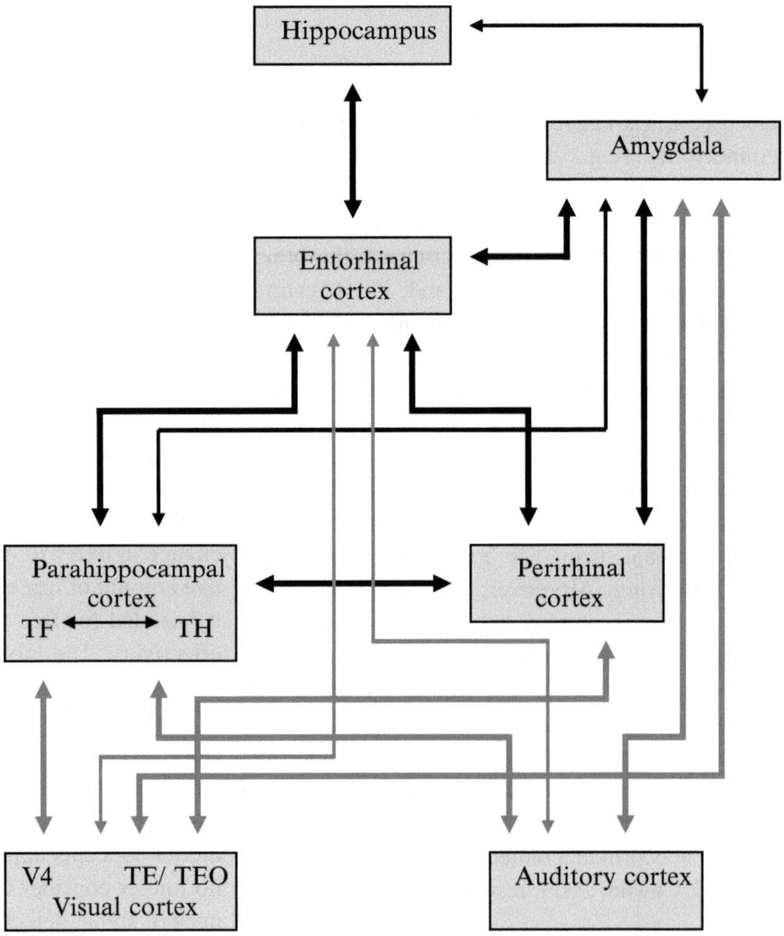

Fig. 7.5 Hierarchical processing in the human medial temporal lobe. The medial temporal lobe consists of the hippocampus, entorhinal cortex, parahippocampal cortex, perirhinal cortex, and amygdala. "Concept cells"—that is, neurons that encode the meaning of the stimulus—mostly are located in these areas: *TE* temporal area, *TE/TEO* temporal occipital area, *TF* temporal area, *TH* temporal area. Adopted from Quiroga (2012), original from Quiroga, Kraskov, Koch, and Fried (2009). Adapted with permission of Elsevier. Reprinted from *Current Biology*, Vol. 19, Quiroga, R. Q., Kraskov, A., Koch, C., & Fried, I., Explicit encoding of multimodal percepts by single neurons in the human brain, Pages 1308–1313, Copyright 2009; with kind permission from Elsevier. [Figure 4, Page 1312]

labeled "Jennifer Aniston" neurons. Other famous celebrities have been shown to be involved in single neurons (e.g., Brad Pitt). Both pictures and written names can elicit their firing, and even just thinking of the person can elicit their firing.

Quiroga (2012) proposed that concept cell firing is embedded within related facts and circumstances, facilitating semantic representation, associations, and flow of consciousness, aside from memory. The processing permitting this undertaking takes place hierarchically in the MTL (see Fig. 7.5).

In this model, cells could form abstract specificities, could become interlinked in "cell assemblies," could fire sequentially, etc. (see Fig. 7.5). Quiroga (2012) gave the example of Star Wars and a Luke Skywalker cell assembly (What about "Brangelina?"). The details encoded in the cells are "sparse," so that the learning and specification happens rapidly, and could happen even after single exposures. The cells are organized non-topographically. They appear to constitute "attractors," or networks of neural representations. I note that this concept of concept cells opens them to investigation in terms of far-from-equilibrium state transitions (e.g., can "Brangelina" cells bifurcate if the couple splits?).

Suthana and Fried (2012) presented an account of concept cells similar to that of Quiroga (2012). They noted that the cells might respond to landmarks (such as the Sydney Opera House) as well as people. The representations are not coded in a single cell alone. They help transform novel stimuli to representations available for later conscious retrieval as episodic memories.

The authors noted that stimulation of specific neural networks might be the way to "unlock" memories, moving from correlation to causation. For example, Liu et al. (2012) used optogenetic stimulation of specific hippocampal neurons to reactivate fear memory recall.

Smith, Smith, Branco, and Häusser (2013) found that cortical pyramidal neurons also engage in in vivo computational activities. In a mouse study, they found that dendritic spikes that are triggered by visually evoked sensory input serve to enhance stimulus orientation selectivity in the visual cortex.

Astrocytes

De Pittà et al. (2012) described the conceptual revolution taking place in understanding brain communication. It appears that information is transmitted and processed not only in neuronal circuitry but also in an expanded network of neuronal–glial cell interactions. In particular, glial cell astrocytes engage in synaptic interactions by means of calcium signaling and setting the basal physiological tone of synaptic transmission. The synapse needs to be considered as a tripartite entity that includes astrocytes modulating synaptic release and contributing to its plasticity.

Astrocytes possess the properties of not only sensing neighboring neuronal activity but also releasing neuroactive agents, which are called gliotransmitters. They form a complex signaling network that even regulates synapses. They influence presynaptic and postsynaptic terminals and are influenced themselves by synaptic cleft activity. In addition, they are modulated further downstream by other input/output pathways. The synapses and astrocytes are intrinsically coupled and mutually influence each other. They maintain both feedforward and feedback relationships.

Astrocyte signaling derivatives can facilitate either increase or decrease in neurotransmitter release. Their activity can promote or inhibit, thereby activating or inactivating synaptic activity. Aside from modulating synapses tonically and diffusely, evidence is accumulating that they engage in more focused, constrained, and precise communications with synapses. For example, they organize functionally similar to cortical neurons. In this regard, in the ferret, visual cortical astrocytes respond to visual stimuli, expressing distinct spatial receptive fields and sharp tuning to features of visual stimuli (e.g., orientation, spatial frequency; Schummers, Yu, & Sur, 2008). The findings of astrocyte participation in synaptic function have profound implications for brain and behavior.

Comment

I find it interesting that researchers in neuronal, synaptic, and astrocyte coordination are referring to aspects such as causality. Moreover, if a particular neuronal cell can register an item in memory that can be recalled easily enough, such as a famous person, the implication is that there are many cells that are concept ones and that register significant others in our lives, significant objects/landmarks, and so on. Research should continue to specify the role of these cellular structures not only in memory but even socially, e.g., in the mirror system. It could be that the linkages from stimuli, to registration, to action proceed as much through these cells as the more frequent more generic ones and that they are reciprocally altered by them, once they become committed. Also notable is the mention of activation and inhibition in astrocyte complexes, which is consistent with my activation/inhibition coordination model of brain and behavior. No doubt, the molecular interactions in calcium channel workings and other related functions in neuronal and glial cell functioning, as well as synaptic cleft and related activity involving neurotransmitters found in intercellular neuronal activity should evidence this type of coordination.

In the following, I switch from considering networks and related concepts in the micro-firings of neuronal cells to the networks in the macro-activity in behavior. Network concepts would appear to be translatable across different levels of human activity and, indeed, the broader biosphere.

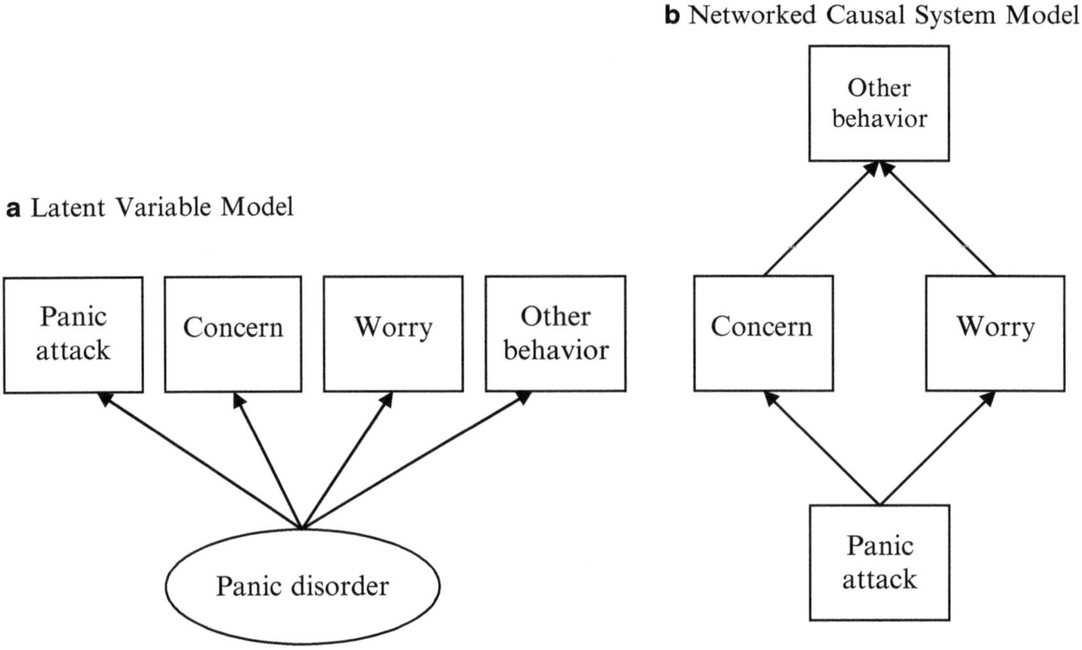

Fig. 7.6 Latent variable and networked causal models. Panel "a" depicts the relation between panic disorder and its symptoms. Panel "b" depicts these symptoms as a networked causal system. Adapted from Borsboom (2008)

Psychological Networks

Borsboom and colleagues have developed network models of relationships between observable variables that challenge more traditional models and that address the question of causality. Schmittmann et al. (2013) presented a network model on the relationship between psychological attributes (e.g., neuroticism) and observed variables (e.g., jittery, worried). In their model, attributes are considered network systems of causally-coupled or directly related observable variables (see Fig. 7.6).

The model of these authors is distinct from the two prevalent ones in the field. In the first common model in the field, the reflective model, an attribute is conceptualized as a common cause of obtained scores. For example, neuroticism might emerge as the best label in a factor analysis for a particular factor. Of the items loading on the factor, the construct of neuroticism is viewed as the attribute that serves as the common cause of observed scores and their variation. In another example, the construct of depression is a construct that causes depression's observable symptoms. As for Fig. 7.7 that presents the models involved, the authors represent the component or construct of the reflective model by placing the attribute in the center of a circle, with outward-directed arrows varying in relation to the strength of the items (scores, observables) involved.

The second prevailing viewpoint on the relationship between psychological attributes and observables is termed the formative model (see Fig. 7.8). In this approach, observed scores are understood as contributors to the attribute, defining or determining it as a composite score. Latent composite variables are modeled as an attribute existing as a function of the indicators, or items, involved. For example, socioeconomic status (SES) is viewed as a composite of other variables. Therefore, in terms of diagramming the formative model, for the example of neuroticism, it can be mapped in relation to items as a central component with inward arrows pointing to it from the surrounding items involved (with different arrow strengths indicative of item contribution to the composite score).

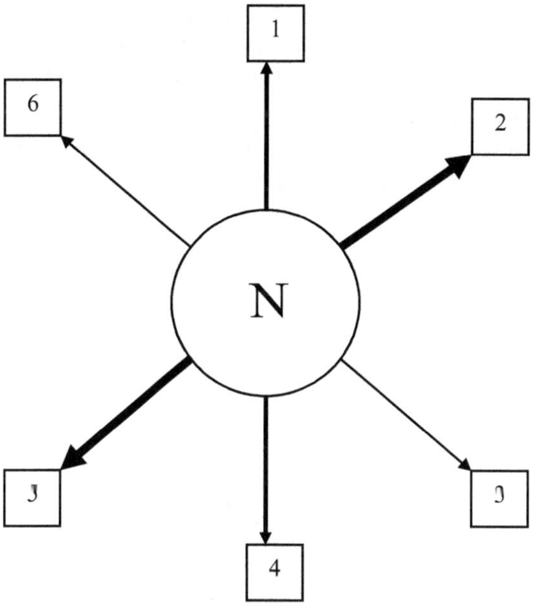

Fig. 7.7 Reflective model of neuroticism items. In the reflective model, one underlying factor determines the variation in the items. The thicker the arrow is from the factor to an item, the higher is the factor loading. Residual variances are not represented. Adapted from Schmittmann et al. (2013), slightly modified

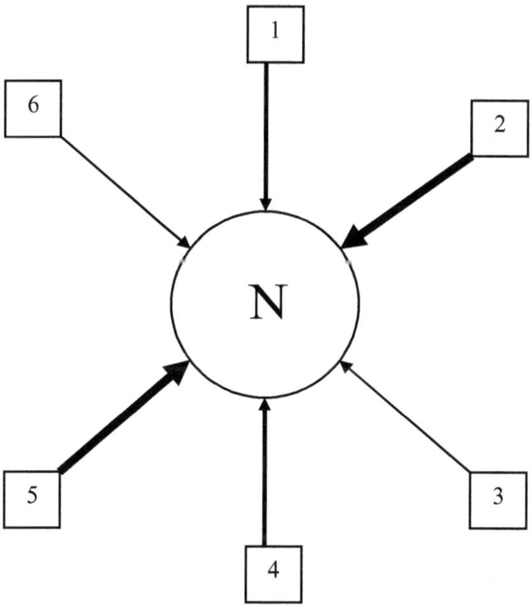

Fig. 7.8 Formative model of neuroticism items. In the formative model, arrows point from the items to the composite variable (*circle*). The thicker is the arrow, the higher is the contribution of the item to the composite score. Correlations between items are not represented. Adapted from Schmittmann et al. (2013), slightly modified

Schmittmann et al. (2013) concluded that both the reflective and formative models are "extremely problematic" for addressing causal relations. They noted three difficulties in these prior models leading to this latter conclusion. First, the models lack a temporal dimension, thereby compromising the understanding of causality. Typical causality models involve causes that temporally precede effects. Second, the models do not lend themselves to breaking down causal relations into precise mechanisms underlying them. For example, although smoking generally causes lung cancer, specific physiological pathways constitute precise mechanisms and, in contemporary research in cancer, these are being elucidated. In contrast to fuller causal modeling, the reflective and formative models of causal relationships rarely advance to this process level of causality. For example, we do not really know in these models how neuroticism causes worry. Third, the reflective and formative models entirely exclude seeking causal relations between (among) the observed indicators involved.

These three criticisms of prior models led Schmittmann et al. (2013) to develop their network perspective. In this model, observables are considered autonomous causal entities in dynamical relations. The observables are autonomous in the sense of being active causal connectors, and their underlying linkage processes can be studied or are known. The observables have functions in the network (e.g., some are more dominant in strength of relations with other variables). This dynamical network model of the relationship between psychological attributes and observables does not place any attribute as privileged as the center of a nexus. Rather, the mapping of the network uses algorithms that place more dominant observables as nodes toward the center and also place the relationship between nodes as edges indicating the empirical statistics involved (e.g., correlations). Strongly correlated sets of items are clustered together (see Fig. 7.9).

According to Schmittmann et al. (2013), the changing nature of interconnected network variables can be formalized by dynamical system theory equations (Van der Maas & Molenaar, 1992). The system's state is represented by the set of interrelations among the variables.

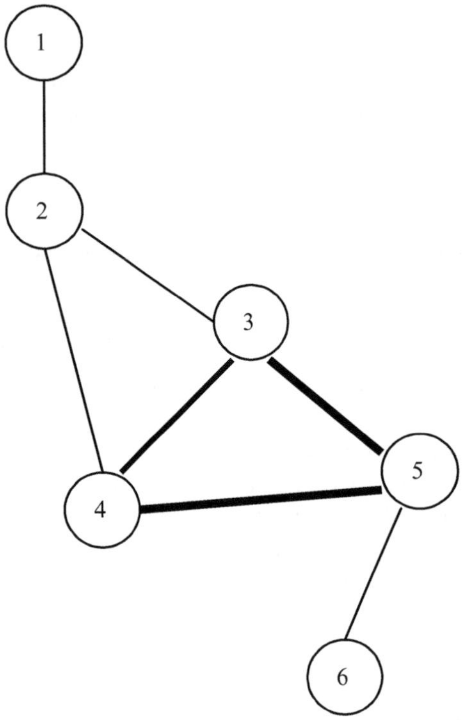

Fig. 7.9 A network of neuroticism items. *Nodes* represent items: *Edges* represent the empirical correlations between items. Numbers in nodes refer to items. A stronger correlation is represented by a *thicker* and *darker edge*. Adapted from Schmittmann et al. (2013) based on Epskamp, Cramer, Waldorp, Schmitmann, and Borsboom (2011), slightly modified

State changes depend on how variables influence each other, as represented by equations describing prior and present state dependencies. If the system gravitates to an attractor state, its dynamical path converges on it (globally, despite probabilistic variations) and might stay in equilibrium in it. State transitions are regulated by parameters. Transition to new attractors indicates qualitative change in the system. For example, there might be different system attractors indexing depression and mental equilibrium, and the two might alternate in the system's (person's) state space. In the network model of psychological phenomena proposed by Schmittmann et al. (2013), networks are considered systems that can come to interrelate themselves. For example, psychiatric comorbidity reflects such network intercoordination.

As proposed, the network model helps explain emergent phenomena because they are governed by nonlinear dynamical system properties. Moreover, causality does not reside in the overall state of the network but might depend on only a few of its elements, in particular.

Comment

Although a powerful model, the network approach to psychological attributes might have engaged in oversimplification of behavioral item (and symptom) networking in explaining causality and their relationship to higher-order attributes. For example, the authors integrate systems theory in their modeling, but do not consider, as might happen in systems generally, that a higher-order level (e.g., the attribute level) can develop in systems from lower-order ones (such as at item/symptom levels) and interact with the lower-order levels, with the various levels reciprocally shaping each other through their interactions. Moreover, the higher-order levels in any system might be emergent in ways that are unpredictable from knowing the lower-order levels, and be quite informative of the full system picture. A more inclusive network model relative to the ones proposed by the authors would allow for both reflective-type and formative-processes in the interactions over different levels of the system as it forms its networks. That is, the differences in the various models involved in the present context might not be in opposition, but might be offering complementary perspectives of a larger system.

Chapter Conclusions

The concept of networks is revolutionizing the understanding of brain and behavior because network approaches are integrating hierarchical multi-level analysis of brain and behavior with subtle within-level dynamical analysis. They reveal the dynamical nature of millisecond-by-millisecond brain activity and micro-relations in ongoing behavior within and across people, while enabling macro-level functioning. They translate into reframing psychological constructs, such as depression and neuroticism, not just as symptom clusters relating to broader terms but also especially as symptom systems that change dynamically, jump to different states, hover on the edge of order–disorder bifurcations, and so on. They collapse cause and effect into trackable systems instead of intractable concepts. That being said, I offer ways to integrate the models that neuronal network ones are dismissing into more integrated perspectives.

References

Adelstein, J. S., Shehzad, Z., Mennes, M., DeYoung, C. G., Zuo, Z.-N., Kelly, C., et al. (2011). Personality is reflected in the brain's intrinsic functional architecture. *PLoS One, 6*(11), e27633. doi:10.1371/journal.pone.0027633.

Bak, P., Tang, C., & Wiesenfeld, K. (1987). Self-organized criticality: An explanation of the 1/f noise. *Physical Review Letters, 59*, 381–384.

Barbey, A. K., Colom, R., & Grafman, J. (2014). Distributed neural system for emotional intelligence revealed by lesion mapping. *Social Cognitive and Affective Neuroscience, 9*, 265–272.

Barch, D. M. (2013). Brain network interactions in health and disease. *Trends in Cognitive Sciences, 17*, 603–605.

Baumeister, R. F. (2008). Free will in scientific psychology. *Perspectives on Psychological Science, 3*, 14–19.

Borsboom, D. (2008). Psychometric perspectives on diagnostic systems. *Journal of Clinical Psychology, 64*, 1089–1108.

Brandes, U., Robins, G., McCranie, A., & Wasserman, S. (2013). What is network science? *Network Science, 1*, 1–15.

Bressler, S. L., & Menon, V. (2010). Large-scale brain networks in cognition: Emerging methods and principles. *Trends in Cognitive Sciences, 14*, 277–290.

Brunel, N., & Wang, X. J. (2001). Effects of neuromodulation in a cortical network model of object working memory dominated by recurrent inhibition. *Journal of Computational Neuroscience, 11*, 63–85.

Buice, M. A., & Cowan, J. D. (2009). Statistical mechanics of the neocortex. *Progress in Biophysics and Molecular Biology, 99*, 53–86.

Byrge, L., Sporns, O., & Smith, L. B. (2014). Developmental process emerges from extended brain-body-behavior networks. *Trends in Cognitive Sciences, 18*, 395–403.

Churchland, P. S., & Sejnowski, T. J. (1992). *The computational brain*. Cambridge, MA: MIT Press.

Cole, M. W., Reynolds, J. R., Power, J. D., Repovs, G., Anticevic, A., & Braver, T. S. (2013). Multi-task connectivity reveals flexible hubs for adaptive task control. *Nature Neuroscience, 16*, 1348–1355.

Deco, G., & Jirsa, V. K. (2012). Ongoing cortical activity at rest: Criticality, multistability, and ghost attractors. *Journal of Neuroscience, 32*, 3366–3375.

Deco, G., Jirsa, V., & Friston, K. J. (2012). The dynamical and structural basis of brain activity. In M. I. Rabinovich, K. J. Friston, & P. Varona (Eds.), *Principles of brain dynamics: Global state interactions* (pp. 9–25). Cambridge, MA: MIT Press.

De Pittà, M., Volman, V., Berry, H., Parpura, V., Volterra, A., & Ben-Jacob, E. (2012). Computational quest for understanding the role of astrocyte signaling in synaptic transmission and plasticity. *Frontiers in Computational Neuroscience, 6*, 98. doi:10.3389/fncom.2012.00098.

Epskamp, S., Cramer, A. O. J., Waldorp, L. J., Schmitmann, V. D., & Borsboom, D. (2011). Qgraph: Network representations of relationships in data. R package version 0.4.10. Available from http://CRAN.R-project.org/package=qgraph

Fair, D. A., Cohen, A. L., Power, J. D., Dosenbach, N. U. F., Church, J. A., Miezin, F. M., et al. (2009). Functional brain networks develop from a "local to distributed" organization. *PLoS Computational Biology, 5*, e1000381. doi:10.1371/journal.pcbi.1000381.

Friston, K. (2010). The free-energy principle: A unified brain theory? *Nature Reviews Neuroscience, 11*, 127–138.

Friston, K. (2012). A free energy principle for biological systems. *Entropy, 14*, 2100–2121.

Greicius, M. D., & Menon, V. (2004). Default-mode activity during a passive sensory task: Uncoupled from deactivation but impacting activation. *Journal of Cognitive Neuroscience, 16*, 1484–1492.

Gross, T., & Blasius, B. (2008). Adaptive coevolutionary networks: A review. *Journal of the Royal Society Interface, 5*, 259–271.

Harmelech, T., & Malach, R. (2013). Neurocognitive biases and the patterns of spontaneous correlations in the human cortex. *Trends in Cognitive Sciences, 17*, 606–615.

Hilgetag, C. C., & Hütt, M.-T. (2014). Hierarchical modular brain connectivity is a stretch for criticality. *Trends in Cognitive Sciences, 18*, 114–115.

Ingalhalikar, M., Smith, A., Parker, D., Satterthwaite, T. D., Elliott, M. A., Ruparel, K., et al. (2014). Sex differences in the structural connectome of the human brain. *Proceedings of the National Academy of Sciences, USA, 111*, 823–828.

Jirsa, V. K., & McIntosh, A. R. (2007). *Handbook of brain connectivity*. New York: Springer Science+Business Media.

Jirsa, V. K., Sporns, O., Breakspear, M., Deco, G., & McIntosh, A. R. (2010). Towards the virtual brain: Network modeling of the intact and the damaged brain. *Archives Italiennes de Biologie, 148*, 189–205.

Kanai, R., & Rees, G. (2011). The structural basis of inter-individual differences in human behavior and cognition. *Nature Reviews Neuroscience, 12*, 231–242.

Kello, C. T., Beltz, B. C., Holden, J. G., & Van Orden, G. C. (2008). The pervasiveness of 1/f scaling in speech reflects the metastable basis of cognition. *Cognitive Science, 32*, 1217–1231.

Knill, D. C., & Pouget, A. (2004). The Bayesian brain: The role of uncertainty in neural coding and computation. *Trends in Neuroscience, 27*, 712–719.

Koyama, M. S., Di Martino, A., Zuo, X. N., Kelly, C., Mennes, M., Jutagir, D. R., et al. (2011). Resting-state functional connectivity indexes reading competence in children and adults. *Journal of Neuroscience, 31*, 8617–8624.

Liu, X., Ramirez, S., Pang, P. T., Puryear, C. B., Govindarajan, A., Deisseroth, K., et al. (2012). Optogenetic stimulation of a hippocampal engram activates fear memory recall. *Nature, 484*, 381–385.

Matsumoto, A., & Kakigi, R. (2013). Subliminal semantic priming changes the dynamic causal influence between the left frontal and temporal cortex. *Journal of Cognitive Neuroscience, 26*, 165–174.

Menon, V. (2012). Functional connectivity, neurocognitive networks, and brain dynamics. In M. I. Rabinovich, K. J. Friston, & P. Varona (Eds.), *Principles of brain dynamics: Global state interactions* (pp. 27–47). Cambridge, MA: MIT Press.

Menon, V. (2013). Developmental pathways to functional brain networks: Emerging principles. *Trends in Cognitive Sciences, 17*, 627–640.

Moretti, P., & Muñoz, M. A. (2013). Griffiths phases and the stretching of criticality in brain networks. *Nature Communications, 4*, 1–10.

Palaniyappan, L., Simmonite, M., White, T. P., Liddle, E. B., & Liddle, P. F. (2013). Neural primacy of the salience processing system in schizophrenia. *Neuron, 79*, 814–828.

Pearl, J. (2009). *Causality: Models, reasoning, and inference* (2nd ed.). New York: Cambridge University Press.

Pessoa, L. (2014). Précis of the cognitive-emotional brain. *Behavioral and Brain Sciences, 10*, 1–66.

Priesemann, V., Valderrama, M., Wibral, M., & Van Quyen, M. L. (2013). Neuronal avalanches differ from wakefulness to deep sleep – Evidence from intracranial depth recordings in humans. *PLoS Computational Biology, 9*, e1002985. doi:10.1371/journal.pcbi.1002985.

Quiroga, R. Q. (2012). Concept cells: The building blocks of declarative memory functions. *Nature Reviews Neuroscience, 13*, 587–597.

Quiroga, R. Q., Kraskov, A., Koch, C., & Fried, I. (2009). Explicit encoding of multimodal percepts by single neurons in the human brain. *Current Biology, 19*, 1308–1313.

Raichle, M. E. (2011). The restless brain. *Brain Connectivity, 1*, 3–12.

Raichle, M. E., MacLeod, A. M., Snyder, A. Z., Powers, W. J., Gusnard, D. A., & Shulman, G. L. (2001). A default mode of brain function. *Proceedings of the National Academy of Sciences, USA, 98*, 676–682.

Reinhart, R. M. G., & Woodman, G. F. (2013). Oscillatory coupling reveals the dynamic reorganization of large-scale neural networks as cognitive demands change. *Journal of Cognitive Neuroscience, 26*, 175–188.

Rubinov, M., & Bullmore, E. (2013). Fledgling pathoconnectomics of psychiatric disorder. *Trends in Cognitive Sciences, 17*, 641–647.

Ruths, J., & Ruths, D. (2014). Control profiles of complex networks. *Science, 343*, 1373–1376.

Schmittmann, V. D., Cramer, A. O. J., Waldorp, L. J., Epskamp, S., Kievit, R. A., & Borsboom, D. (2013). Deconstructing the construct: A network perspective on psychological phenomena. *New Ideas in Psychology, 31*, 43–53.

Schummers, J., Yu, H., & Sur, M. (2008). Tuned responses of astrocytes and their influence on hemodynamic signals in the visual cortex. *Science, 320*, 1638–1843.

Shirer, W. R., Ryali, S., Rykhlevskaia, E., Menon, V., & Greicius, M. D. (2012). Decoding subject-driven cognitive states with whole-brain connectivity patterns. *Cerebral Cortex, 22*, 158–165.

Singer, W. (2013). Cortical dynamics revisited. *Trends in Cognitive Sciences, 17*, 616–626.

Smith, S. L., Smith, I. T., Branco, T., & Häusser, M. (2013). Dendritic spikes enhance stimulus selectivity in cortical neurons in vivo. *Nature, 503*, 115–120.

Sombataro, F., Wolf, N. D., Pennuto, M., Vasic, N., & Wolf, R. C. (2014). Revisiting default mode network function in major depression: Evidence for disrupted subsystem connectivity. *Psychological Medicine, 44*, 2041–2051.

Sporns, O. (2011). *Networks of the brain*. Cambridge, MA: MIT Press.

Sporns, O. (2012). *Discovering the human connectome*. Cambridge, MA: MIT Press.

Sporns, O., & van den Heuvel, M. P. (2013). Network maps of the human brain's rich club. *Network Science, 1*, 248–250.

Sridharan, D., Levitin, D. J., & Menon, V. (2008). A critical role for the right fronto-insular cortex in switching between central-executive and default-mode networks. *Proceedings of the National Academy of Sciences, USA, 105*, 12569–12574.

Suthana, N., & Fried, I. (2012). Percepts to recollections: Insights from single neuron recordings in the human brain. *Trends in Cognitive Sciences, 16*, 427–436.

Thelen, E., & Smith, L. B. (1994). *A dynamic systems approach to the development of cognition and action*. Cambridge, MA: MIT Press.

Uddin, L. Q., & Menon, V. (2009). The anterior insula in autism: Under-connected and under-examined. *Neuroscience and Biobehavioral Reviews, 33*, 1198–1203.

Urban, J. B., Osgood, N., Okamoto, J., Mabry, P., & Lich, K. H. (2014). Developmental systems science:

Extending developmental science with systems science methodologies. In M. Molenaar, R. M. Lerner, & K. M. Newell (Eds.), *Handbook of developmental systems theory and methodology* (pp. 95–127). New York: Guildford Press.

van den Heuvel, M. P., Kahn, R. S., Goñi, J., & Sporns, O. (2012). A high-cost, high-capacity backbone for global brain communication. *Proceedings of the National Academy of Sciences, USA, 109*, 11372–11377.

van den Heuvel, M. P., & Sporns, O. (2011). Rich-club organization of the human connectome. *Journal of Neuroscience, 31*, 15775–15786.

van den Heuvel, M. P., & Sporns, O. (2013). Network hubs in the human brain. *Trends in Cognitive Sciences, 17*, 683–696.

Van der Maas, H. L. J., & Molenaar, P. C. M. (1992). Stagewise cognitive development: An application of catastrophe theory. *Psychological Review, 113*, 842–861.

van Tol, M.-J., Li, M., Metzger, C. D., Hailla, N., Horn, D. I., Li, W., et al. (2014). Local cortical thinning links to resting-state disconnectivity in major depressive disorder. *Psychological Medicine, 44*, 2053–2065.

Wang, S.-J., Hilgetag, C. C., & Zhou, C. (2011). Sustained activity in hierarchical modular neural networks: Self-organized criticality and oscillations. *Frontiers in Computational Neuroscience, 5*, 30. doi:10.3389/fncom.2011.00030.

Zanto, T. P., & Gazzaley, A. (2013). Fronto-parietal network: Flexible hub of cognitive control. *Trends in Cognitive Sciences, 17*, 602–603.

Zatorre, R. J., Fields, D. R., & Johansen-Berg, H. (2012). Plasticity in gray and white: Neuroimaging changes in brain structure during learning. *Nature Neuroscience, 15*, 528–536.

Lateralization and Specialization of the Brain

8

Chapter Introduction

This chapter focuses on manual lateralization and the related area of hemispheric specialization, as well as on early handedness and hemispheric dominance for language. These are areas that had considered that the preferred sides involved either (a) acquire their shifts gradually in an equipotential and then progressively shifting model early in life or (b) that they are acquired rapidly and innately, with the patterns involved reflecting early on the characteristics of the later emerging adult model in these regards.

Generally, the research is quite supportive of latter the rapid, innate model of early manual lateralization and hemispheric specialization. In particular, it points to early right-hand manual lateralization and a corresponding underlying early left-hemisphere specialization, respectively (the relationship of manual lateralization to corresponding control by the hemispheres is cross-hemispheric). That is, the left hemisphere appears specialized for its functions (verbal/language; fine motor) from early in life onward and the right hemisphere for its skills (e.g., spatial) also early in life. Therefore, the selection of appropriate tasks of manual lateralization, such as grasping and spatial-related ones, respectively, for the functions of the left and right hemispheres, will give results corresponding to the manual lateralization's associated hemispheric specialization function.

However, about the fundamental nature of differential hemispheric function, there has not been one accepted model of the distinctive, unique and underlying, integrative nature of each hemisphere, with the model capturing the full range of behaviors and skills with which each hemisphere (and cross-lateralized manual behavior) is associated. Various models refer to differences in the left and right hemispheres related to: language/fine motor versus spatial function; analysis versus synthesis/holistic function; and so on. Of course, for proper adaptivity, the hemispheres need to work together effectively with their differential functions, skills, and associated behaviors.

Note that the research in the area does not necessarily support the connection between all lateralized manual behavior and all verbal/spatial behavior that are putatively associated with the hemispheres. In particular, notable exceptions in these regards involve handedness as an index of hemispheric dominance and also language disorders as problems deriving from uniquely a left-hemisphere difficulty. This is especially the case for early phases in the development of these various behaviors and problems. That is, early handedness is not as distinct as later handedness and correlates minimally with hemispheric specialization, in general. Also, advances in early language skills, or problems in this regard, do not relate unequivocally with left-hemisphere function.

The development of manual lateralization and corresponding hemispheric specialization/differentiation of hemispheric architecture appears to

G. Young, *Unifying Causality and Psychology*, DOI 10.1007/978-3-319-24094-7_8

being prenatally (Hepper, 2013), but both are more plastic early in life compared to later on. The chapter reviews the development of manual lateralization and hemispheric specialization together at each age period from the fetal and neonatal periods onward, through the various infancy ages to childhood. The chapter reviews the patterns in right–left manual lateralization of behavior on many types of tasks, such as reaching, grasping, and even tool use. It reviews associated hemispheric specialization function and corresponding structural differences across the hemispheres.

Early hemispheric specialization also reflects early motivational/emotional lateralization differences, with the left hemisphere being related to approach and to positive emotions relative to the right one, which is more associated with withdrawal/negative emotions. The left-hemisphere specialization for positive emotions is consistent with its apparently more advanced functions and its ability to weave together activation and inhibition, a process that is implicit in positive social and emotional behavior of a continual interacting type.

The left-hemisphere advantage translates not only into advances in language development but also in cognitive development to a degree. This chapter reviews the literature on those varied topics, including data showing that the left hemisphere is associated with some general cognitive advances.

I have proposed a model as critical in differentiating the underlying functions of the left and right hemispheres. It refers to the left hemisphere expressing a refined specialization for activation–inhibition coordination, in particular (Young, 2011; Young & Gagnon, 1990). Reciprocally, the right hemisphere is specialized for less complex inhibition skills. [Keep in mind that manual and hemispheric left-right side differences are found in a relative sense and they are plastic to a degree. Also, the patterns are present better in the typical right-hander compared to in the typical left-hander]. As a general model of hemispheric function and corresponding manual lateralization differences, when the literature is supportive of it, the chapter points out the role of activation/inhibition coordination as a mechanism in the development of brain and of behavior.

The chapter also considers the evolutionary origins of lateralization and specialization in behavior and in the brain. It shows some fascinating links across lateralization/specialization models and those of differential susceptibility and neuronal networks. For example, for the network research on the topic, right from birth, the left hemisphere appears specialized for intraregional integration and segregation in the interconnection among its various regions and also for "betweenness centrality." Network wise, the left hemisphere presents as more efficient. This work is consistent with description of the left hemisphere's functional advantages and, as well, especially in terms of the model that these advantages relate to its better capacity for activation/inhibition coordination.

Lateralization and Specialization Development by Age Period

Prenatal

Manual Behavior Hepper (2013) described his prior research on fetal laterality, before presenting a further study. Hepper, Shahidullah, and White (1991) had found right thumb sucking in the fetus. This research was followed by their study on fetal right head turning (Hepper, McCartney, & Shannon, 1998). McCartney and Hepper (1999) found that right arm movement preference was consistently displayed in the fetal period (also see Ververs, de Vries, van Geijn, & Hopkins, 1994; Kurjak et al., 2002; in contrast, see de Vries, Wimmers, Ververs, Hopkins, Savelsbergh, & van Geijn, 2001). Hepper, Wells, and Lynch (2005) showed that right thumb sucking in the fetus predicted right-handedness in 10- to 12-year-olds. Hepper (2013) replicated the finding of more right arm reaching in the fetus, but the preference decreased as the fetal period progressed (from 24 to 36 weeks; although the author indicated using a small sample size).

Hepper (2013) noted that although structural hemispheric differences are being found fetally, their relationship to any manual lateralities is unknown (e.g., Habas et al., 2012; Kasprian et al. 2011; Kivilevitch, Achiron, & Zalel, 2010).

Reissland, Francis, Aydin, Mason, and Exley (2014) examined prenatal mouth opening movements using scan technology. The scans took place between 24- to 36-weeks gestation. The mouth movements were upper lip raisers and mouth stretches. The results showed greater left lateralization in mouth opening movements.

Although not a manual lateralization study, it is worth noting that Van Dongen et al. (2014) investigated asymmetry in limbic bones at 10- to 20-weeks of gestation. Already at this age, the right side appears larger than the left side for several bones of both the upper and lower limbs. The authors related the findings to the influence of internal asymmetric organ positioning. The developmental process involved might include asymmetric gene expression acting in concert with differential mechanical loading.

Brain The hemispheric differences appear to develop at the structural level even prenatally, with first cortical signs favoring the left hemisphere in the superior temporal sulci (more frequent sulcal pits; Im et al., 2010). For white matter, the arcuate fasciculus and corticospinal tract seem involved (Dubois et al., 2009).

Kasprian et al. (2011) demonstrated the prenatal origin of cerebral lateralization in an in vivo, in utero neuroimaging investigation. First, they described the research of Sun et al. (2005) that referred to early asymmetry of gene transcription (as early as 12 weeks gestational age, GW) in the cerebral cortices. In their neuroimaging study, in a large sample between 18 and 37 gestational weeks of age, Kasprian et al. (2011) found temporal lobe asymmetry. The asymmetry favored a larger temporal lobe on the left side. Also, they found an earlier appearance of the right superior temporal sulcus by 23 GW.

Comment Overall, the results in the various investigations reviewed for the prenatal period indicate that, in some senses, the hemispheres are structurally programmed in this period already like in the adult. There might be continued anchoring and embedding of the relative skills of the hemispheres as development proceeds but the concept of equipotentiality in early hemispheric specialization does not appear valid today, and even the notion of progressive lateralization is difficult to establish for behaviors and functions that are age-appropriate, and this obtains in the prenatal period, as well.

Neonates

Manual Behavior Nagy, Pal, and Orvos (2014) demonstrated that neonates could imitate modeled gestures involving the index finger, and two- and three-finger movements. In addition, the first study of the series investigated manual laterality. The infants were about 2 days old. There were two conditions—baseline and modeling (finger raise). Gestures were made about every 12 s and they lasted about 2 s. As for the results, the left hand proved more accurate and also quicker. According to the authors, the results suggest a lateralized neural network involved in neonatal gestural imitation. In this regard, there might be an early sensitive period, in that older neonates (8+ days) typically do not imitate gesturally.

Nagy et al. (2014) related these results to the mirror neuron system, and also elsewhere (e.g., the inferior frontal gyrus, the inferoparietal lobule). These areas have been implicated in early interaction and intersubjectivity.

The authors did not relate left-hand preference for early neonatal imitation to models of developing lateralization. Nagy et al.'s (2014) findings on imitation patterns of finger movements to demonstrated models should be analyzed for whether they are more related to underlying functions involving left- or right-hemisphere skills. In this regard, imitating finger postures and movements appears more space-related and holistic rather than verbal and sequential, as described in Young (2011). The results are consistent with Young and Gagnon (1990), who found that, in 2-day-olds, the left hemisphere relative to the right appears specialized for speech relative to musical stimulus processing. That is, already at this age, the right hemisphere appears specialized in its turn for spatial-related functions, or less complex ones relative to speech ones that are associated with the left hemisphere.

To conclude, the results on early neonatal imitation of finger movements found by Nagy et al. (2014) are consistent with other research on early hemispheric specialization, which has found that the left hemisphere is "prepared" from birth for specializations related to speech and fine motor coordinations, such as reaching and hand-opening, and the right hemisphere is specialized for spatial skills and exploration. In the following, I examine whether this trend is evident both in research directly on the brain in this age period and also in later ages.

Brain Streri and de Hevia (2015) reviewed research on newborns tested for cross-modal transfer of shape from touch to vision using the habituation paradigm (Streri & Gentaz, 2004). They were habituated to an object haptically and then were presented visually with it or a novel shape. The participants showed visual recognition if they were habituated to the familiar object with the right hand, but not the left one. Generally, 2-month-olds retain better object shape information with their left hand. Also, young infants detect object contour changes better with the left hand, but object detail ones better with the left hand (Streri, 2002). Overall, the results are consistent with the differential analytic vs. global distinction of left- and right-hemisphere function, respectively, even for the period after birth. In a longitudinal study, Li et al. (2014) mapped structural hemispheric asymmetries at birth, 1 year of age, and 2 years of age. They used surface-based morphometry of MRIs (magnetic resonance imaging). They found that the left planum temporale was larger and deeper than the right at all three time points. Also, the right superior temporal sulcus (STS) and the right parieto-occipito sulcus were larger and deeper than the corresponding left-side regions.

These longitudinal, postnatal results are consistent with other findings, such as by Habas et al. (2012) and Kasprian et al. (2011), who studied asymmetries in in utero fetal MRIs, and by Hill et al. (2010) and Glasel et al. (2011), who obtained similar results postnatally, with the latter three studies all showing findings related to a right-side advantage in asymmetry for the STS.

Ratnarajah et al. (2014) investigated asymmetry in structural brain connectivity in the neonatal brain. They used diffusion tensor imaging (DTI) deterministic tractography and structural network analysis based on graph theory. They tracked white-matter axonal pathways characterizing interregional connections in 32 defined cortical and subcortical regions.

Both cerebral hemispheres revealed a connectivity marked by "small world" properties, which means that regions are tightly connected (and with shorter paths; any one region is only a few paths away from any other region within a hemisphere). As for efficiency in structural connectivity, the left hemisphere already proved more efficient than the right at birth. That is, the neonatal left hemisphere evidences better intraregional integration and segregation in their interconnection. Moreover, this takes place in regions known to develop later on functional specializations in motor, language, and memory functions. Further, the left-hemisphere advantage in efficiency manifested at both local and global levels. This suggests that shorter circuit paths in the left hemisphere facilitate speedier information transfer and flow. Other findings implicated leftward asymmetries in the connectivity measure of "betweenness centrality." Overall, the results support an early specialization of the hemispheres consistent with the adult model.

Cheng, Lee, Chen, Wang, and Decety (2012) showed that neonates within the first few days of life already appear to have a neural mechanism responsible for emotional vocalization discrimination. In particular, the neonates demonstrated a mismatch in electroencephalographic response over the right hemisphere when exposed to emotionally-laden stimuli (happy or fearful compared to neutral syllables).

Using DTI, Dubois et al. (2009) demonstrated leftward asymmetries in microstructure, in particular, in the arcuate fasciculus and in the cortico-spinal tract. The participants were 1–4 months of age, with results already evident at 1 month. The two tracts are in white-matter networks, and the former is associated with language development whereas the latter is a sensorimotor one.

Comment Studies of neonatal manual lateralization and hemispheric specialization have demonstrated the left- and right-side advantages that are associated with adults, and they have shown that the left hemisphere already possesses network properties that are consistent with its advantages. Moreover, the differential structural properties of the hemispheres at birth already are of the type that is consistent with the adult model. The early presence of hemispheric specialization and its associated manual lateralizations speak to the evolutionary significance of the structural differences across the hemispheres and the functional and behavioral differences that are associated with these cerebral differences.

First Year

Manual Behavior Morange-Majoux, Lemoine, and Dellatolas (2013) found that, in the 20- to 30-week age period, in a task in which an object was placed to the left or right, the average latency time to approach was shorter for the left hand and the average latency time to grasping it was shorter with the right hand. The results are consistent with a hemispheric specialization view of manual lateralization in which the left hemisphere is specialized for fine motor activity and the right spatial activity, as argued in Young (2011).

Morange-Majoux and Devouche (2014) examined spontaneous manual preference in 6-month-olds to mid-line positioned figurines on a table placed within reaching distance. A minority of the infants exhibited a manual preference, but when they did the ratio of right to left-hand preference was about 2:1.

Michel, Babik, Shue, and Campbell (2013) followed infants from 6 to 14 months of age in object acquisition behavior (lift, move toy). Right-hand preference was evident in most infants (38 % clearly, 48 % trend, left 14 %). The groups differed in developmental trajectory. The authors found a right-shift from a continuous distribution, which is consistent with Annett's (2002) genetic model. Follow-up studies from this research group confirm these findings, Campbell, Marcinowski, Babik, and Michel (2015) and Campbell, Marcinowski, Latta, and Michel (2015) examined manual preferences in samples studied monthly to 14 months of age, beginning from 6 and 8 months of age, respectively. The tasks in the latter study required acquiring objects and, although the study was not aimed at establishing which hand is preferred, a cascading model from acquisition behavior to unimanual manipulation fits the data. The tasks in the former study required manipulative behavior mostly, and it showed a right-hand preference mostly, although not to the degree of the adult.

Rönnqvist and Domellöf (2006) studied 6- to 36-month-olds. They related infants' early right-handed reaching preference to their capacity to reach straighter with the right arm.

That handedness is not co-lateralized with other lateralizations is indicated by the results of the study by Babik, Campbell, and Michel (2013). They investigated the influence of postural constraints on the longitudinal development of reaching from 6 to 14 months of age, as well asymmetric bimanual coordination for object acquisition. The results showed a weak right-side advantage for lateralized infants, and the laterality developed further in the first year, only to decrease later on.

Jacquet, Esseily, Rider, and Fagard (2012) followed 8- to 20-month-olds in grasping and declarative pointing, and found them "loosely" correlated. The left-hemisphere superiority for language dominance appears relatively independent of lateralization related to grasping (and pointing should be related to that).

Brain Aslin, Shukla, and Emberson (2015) reported a right-hemisphere advantage for face processing in 4- to 8-month-old infants over five studies (Grossmann et al., 2008; Grossmann, Parise, & Friederici, 2010; Lloyd-Fox et al., 2009; Nakato, Otsuka, Kanazawa, Yamaguchi, & Kakigi, 2011; Otsuka et al., 2007). However, the left hemisphere appeared involved, as well. For example, this was evident in a mutual gaze face paradigm [for the left fronto-polar cortex and the left prefrontal channel in 4- and 5-month-olds, respectively (Grossmann et al. 2008, 2010, respectively)] and for videos of faces [the left posterior temporal area (Lloyd-Fox et al., 2009)].

Maternal synchrony (coordination of maternal social behavior with infant signal) was associated with greater left nucleus accumbens activation. Further, maternal intrusiveness was related to right amygdala activation (Atzil, Hendler, & Feldman, 2011).

Missana and Grossmann (2014) measured frontal electroencephalographic (EEG) alpha asymmetry in response to dynamic "happy" body expressions and also "fearful" ones in 4- and 8-month-old infants (stimuli either upright or inverted). The 8-month-olds exhibited the expected left frontal activation to the upright happy stimuli and right frontal activation to the fearful ones (but not the 4-month-olds).

The next two studies described relate to brain function, but were based on behavioral results (non-manual). Smith, Gibilisco, Meisinger, and Hankey (2013) found that 5- to 8-month-old infants focused on a talker's right eye as she produced infant-directed speech stimuli. The results are consistent with the approach-withdrawal (motivation) and positive–negative (valence) emotion models of left-hemisphere cerebral lateralization (which includes that the right hemisphere is specialized for withdrawal/negative emotions; Davidson, Ekman, Saron, & Senulius, 1990; Davidson & Fox, 1982). The results could reflect an early specialization for left-hemisphere language processing, as well (at least for infant-directed speech, Zangl & Mills, 2007).

Holowka and Petitto (2002) found that 5- and 12-month-old infants expressed right-mouth side asymmetries while babbling, but left-side ones when smiling. The results are consistent with a left-hemisphere cerebral specialization for language and a right one for expressiveness and related processes.

One Year

Manual Behavior Corbetta, Friedman, and Bell (2014) found that 12-month-olds reached for small toys with the right hand to grasp them, but only if they were experienced walkers compared to novice or non-walkers. They related their results to arm coupling practiced during early walking.

Sacrey, Arnold, Whishaw, and Gonzales (2013) studied reach-to-eat compared to reach-to-grasp movement in 1- to 5-year-olds. The latter behavior was right lateralized at 1 year of age, but the former only at 4 years of age.

Vauclair and Cochet (2013) studied pointing gesture in the age range of 12–30 months of age. The infants were tested with pictures and toys. They demonstrated a right-hand pointing preference as early as 12 months of age. Moreover, for infants with a developmental quotient (DQ) for language above 100, the more they were right-handed for pointing, the more their DQ increased.

Brain Gander and Buchheim (2015) reviewed research on attachment classification in relation to frontal lobe EEG asymmetry. For example, securely attached infants showed greater right frontal activity when their nondepressed mothers walked to the door, in contrast to those of depressed mothers, who showed greater left-hemisphere activation (e.g., Dawson et al., 2001).

Comment The range of methods and behaviors studied in relation to manual laterality and hemispheric specialization increases in the first year of life. The studies involve behaviors such as hand to mouth behavior and accuracy in reaching, and various indices of emotional and social differences associated with the hemispheres. Nevertheless, the same pattern of results is found as with earlier and later ages, and they indicate that the adult model of hemispheric specialization and its functional and behavioral consequences are present from early in life onward.

Year Two

Manual Behavior Esseily, Jacquet, and Fagard (2011) found a right-side grasping and pointing preference in 14-month-olds, with the right-side pointing laterality related to word production. Cochet and Vauclair (2010) showed that toddlers (15 months and older) used the right hand more in "informative pointing" gestures. They found similar results with 11- to 38-month-olds in natural observations (Cochet & Vauclair, 2010).

Cochet (2012) also argued that different left-hemisphere cerebral networks control object-directed action and pointing gestures. She studied 15-month-olds longitudinally to 25 months, and found a right-sided preference for the two behaviors but little relationship between them.

Rat-Fischer, O'Regan, and Fagard (2013) examined toddler manual preference tool use. The children had to use a rake to get a toy that was out of reach. Even the 16-month-olds preferred to grasp the rake with the right hand.

Wilbourn, Gottfried, and Kee (2011) found an interesting relationship between consistency in 18- to 42-month manual drawing preference in girls (almost all ended up right-handed), but not boys, and the participants' 10- to 17-year-old verbal intelligence and reading achievement. The authors related their results to early left-hemisphere specialization maturation in the consistent girls, as well as early exposure to reading (frequency, intensity). Björk, Brus, Osika, and Montgomery (2012) found a relationship between results on a test of left-side hand control and lower scholastic test scores, and they related their results to possible "suboptimal" hemispheric specialization.

Using motion-capture technology, Kahrs, Jung, and Lockman (2014) filmed right-handed toddlers hammering a peg into a pegboard. The toddlers were 19–25 months of age. Only the older ones used more distally (wrist) controlled movements, but the findings were limited to the right hand. Wrist specialization might be uniquely human and, moreover, as a lateralized phenomenon, it follows in development for that of reaching and bimanual coordination.

Brain Fagard, Sirri, and Rämä (2014) investigated N400 event-related potential in a semantic primary task in infants who were 18- to 24-months old. Only infants who were 24 months of age had a more pronounced N400 effect over the right parietal-occipital recording sites. However, this was found only if they were right-handers in grasping and had a significantly higher vocabulary size. Aside from the laterality findings, according to the authors, the results do not support a general causal relationship between handedness and language lateralization.

The research on early prosociality supports the view that consists of relatively independent and heterogeneous behaviors that are often placed under one umbrella. For example, Paulus, Kühn-Popp, Licata, Sodian, and Meinhardt (2013) found that empathic responding/comforting in the second year of life was associated with left frontal hemispheric activation, which stands in contrast to a right-centered temporal lobe asymmetry for instrumental helping. Note that Dunfield (2014) also argued for different and separate modalities in early prosocial-related behavior (helping, sharing, comforting).

Comment The range of behaviors studies for manual lateralization in the second year has expanded to include raking and wrist movements. The results in these studies are indicating the long-term relations between early lateralization/specialization and much later language/cognitive development. This speaks to the stability of the former and also to their importance for development.

Children

Manual Behavior Michel, Babik, Nelson, Campbell, and Marcinowski (2013) supported an embodied view of the development of handedness in relation to language development and its left-hemisphere specialization. Manual skills develop as sensorimotor acquisitions through pre-reach, reach, grasping, manipulating, and object use, leading eventually to imitation and to differentiate bimanual manipulation. Arbib (2006) had also postulated a sensorimotor basis for the development of language—from actions to speech gestures to (proto) speech. According to Michel et al. (2013), sensorimotor manual skills might help promote speech processing by influencing the development of "tool-using and object management" skills. The mediation of the two trajectories might take place through elaboration and development of "proprioceptive maps."

Nelson, Campbell, and Michel (2013) found that, in bimanual manipulation, the majority of children were right-handed. In their longitudinal study, those who were bilateral earlier ended up right-sided.

Gonzalez, Li, Mills, Rosen, and Gibb (2014) related manual preference in "grasp-to-mouth" feeding movements of small food items to articulatory differentiation of the "sh" and "s" sounds. The children were 4–5 years of age. The more that they were right lateralized in their grasping, the more enhanced was their articulatory discrimination for these two sounds. The comparison condition of "grasp to construct" did not show this relationship.

Gonzalez et al. (2014) found a relationship in 5- to 6-year-olds and 9- to 10-year-olds between greater right-hand grasping and higher scores on executive function (EF), as per indicators on the BRIEF (Behavioral Rating Inventory of Executive Function; Gioia, Isquith, Guy, & Kenworthy, 2000). The authors related the results to a greater structural efficiency in the left hemisphere, which supports enhanced EF. As mentioned, Ratnarajah et al. (2014) had found this advantage in greater structural efficiency for the left hemisphere already present in the neonate brain.

Brain Kikuchi et al. (2011) found that, in preschoolers, left-hemisphere dominance in parietotemporal coherence of theta band activity was associated with better performance on language-related tasks (but not nonverbal cognitive ones). For language/cognitive testing, the Kaufman was used (Kaufman Assessment Battery for Children, Kaufman & Kaufman, 1983). The authors concluded that left-lateralized connectivity via theta band (6–8 Hz) oscillation resulted in better semantic processing performance due to a phase-locked connectivity (long distance; temporal and parietal regions). The frontotemporal coherence did not provide similar results, but the authors stated that their frontal placement of the sensors in this magnetoencephalographic (MEG) study might be one reason.

Cheyne, Jobst, Tesan, Crain, and Johnson (2014) studied self-initiated right or left index finger movements generated in a video game-type task in right-handed 3- to 4-year-olds. According to pediatric MEG, all the children showed activation of the right superior temporal gyrus.

Berl et al. (2014) examined the relationship between core language skills in 4- to 12-year-olds and lateralization in the distributed language network. The core language skills were correlated with greater right lateralization in the cerebellum.

Yu et al. (2014) used MEG to investigate sex differences in language lateralization in children (4–18 years of age). Boys manifested the expected left-hemisphere lateralization (in the frontal and temporal regions) according to low-gamma event-related desynchrony during an overt visual verb generation task. However, girls evidenced a more bilateral pattern, especially in the frontal regions. These differential lateralization and sex of child results were especially found in the younger age period.

Kurth, Mayer, Toga, Thompson, and Luders (2013) found that, in 170 healthy children and adolescents, better pegboard task performance with the right (dominant) hand was associated with greater callosal thickness (isthmus and posterior mid-body). Given the role of the corpus callosum in interhemispheric communication, the results suggested to the authors that there is more influence of the left hemisphere compared to the right in interhemispheric inhibition.

Sheridan, Kharitonova, Martin, Chatterjee, and Gabrieli (2014) studied cognitive conflict detection and resolution in 5- to 10-year-olds, using fMRI, during a blocked spatial response incompatibility task. Among other results, the right prefrontal cortex activated more during incompatible experimental conditions relative to compatible ones.

Yaakoby-Rotem and Geva (2014) studied 5- to 6-year-olds in their alerting efficiency to targets displayed in the left (L) and right (R) visual fields (VF). They found a right-hemisphere advantage in alerting-attention, in that there was a higher alerting efficiency for stimulus targets displayed in the LVF.

MacDonald, Ganjavi, Collins, Evans, and Karama (2014) studied 6- to 18-year-olds (mean 11) on a measure of IQ (intelligence quotient; Wechsler Abbreviated Scale of Intelligence, Wechsler, 1999) in relation to striatal volume (caudate nucleus and putamen), as determined by

MRI. They found a positive correlation between IQ and left striatal volume. The findings have import for the lateralization of general higher-order cognitive function and ability.

Hemisphere lateralization has functional consequences, especially for language and motor functions. Barber et al. (2012) found that 8- to 12-year-old right-handed children, who had demonstrated in a scanner left-hemisphere lateralization of intrinsic, resting state functional motor circuit connectivity, performed better motorically on a battery (PANESS, Denckla, 1985).

Comment As with the prior ages reviewed for research findings on manual behavior and hemispheric function that are sided one way or the other, the present section on children reveals an increasing range of behavior studies, more refined central findings, and more associations between the cerebral hemispheric specialization and language and cognitive consequences. Results related to sex differences are emerging, too. However, it must be kept in mind that the differences between the left and right sides of the body and brain in terms of structure, function, and behavior are relative, and the same applies for any interactions in these regards with respect to gender differences.

Other Developmental Topics

Networks

Hervé, Zago, Petit, Mazoyer, and Tzourio-Mazoyer (2013) conducted a review of neuroimaging research on hemispheric specialization and its development. This research allows for in vivo macroscopic, fine-grained description of the physiological basis of hemispheric asymmetry. For example, the right hemisphere appears more efficiently organized, having greater interregional connectivity. In contrast, the left hemisphere contains more "crucial" network hub regions (Iturria-Medina et al., 2011). This distinction in networking enables the different specialization of the two hemispheres (L: highly demanding, e.g., language; R: broader, e.g., visuospatial integration).

Functionally, the shift to the left hemisphere takes place progressively (Friederici, Brauer, & Lohmann, 2011). There are individual differences associated with degree of leftward asymmetry/activation (e.g., for verbal IQ, Everts et al., 2009; and for syntactic verbal performance/skills, respectively, Lebel & Beaulieu, 2009; Nuñez et al., 2011).

According to Hervé et al. (2013), Turken and Dronkers (2011) described a left-hemisphere brain network critical in sentence comprehension. It includes temporo-parietal and IFG (inferior frontal gyrus) regions connected by the inferior occipitofrontal arcuate, and middle/inferior longitudinal fasciculi. Also, Morillon et al. (2010) found leftward asymmetries in a core network of intrinsic connectivities combining auditory, somatosensory motor, and inferior parietal cortices. In contrast, an attentional network has been found for the right hemisphere.

Barbey et al. (2012) found that patients having focal brain damage, as assessed by voxel-based lesion-symptom mapping, had impaired performance on a measure of *g* (general intelligence; using the WAIS; Wechsler Adult Intelligence Test; Wechsler, 1997) and of executive function (using the Delis–Kaplan Executive Function System; Delis, Kaplan, & Kramer, 2001). Specifically, they implicated damage to a distributed network of left-lateralized brain areas (white matter, including the superior longitudinal/arcuate fasciculus, which connects the frontal and parietal cortices).

I note that some of these results in the last two are mixed with respect to the predominant patterns in the literature that are being described. For example, the right hemisphere seems more efficient and hemispheric specialization seems to take place progressively in development according to some of the findings.

Differential Susceptibility

Fortier et al. (2014) related the two areas of (a) hemispheric specialization for emotions/motivation and (b) biological sensitivity context (the orchids/dandelion hypothesis). Greater right frontal lobe EEG resting state activity (RSA) has been associated with a predisposition to experience negative emotions or behavioral withdrawal (Davidson, 2000; Fox, 1991; Schmidt, 1999). In contrast, left frontal asymmetry (LFA) is associated with positive emotions and motivation (Harmon-Jones, Gable, & Peterson, 2010; Schmidt, Shahinfar, & Fox, 1996). At the same time, the emotions specialized in the left hemisphere might be negative but with an approach motivation (e.g., anger).

In their study, Fortier et al. (2014) studied the effects of extremely low birth weight (ELBW; <1 kg) compared to normal birth weight (NBW; >2.5 kg). Birth weight was a critical variable in their hypothesis, representing the quality of the intrauterine environment. Specifically, ELBW stood as a proxy for developmental insults. It was hypothesized that ELBW would have a negative impact developmentally, but only in interaction with FA. That is, ELBW could lead to differential outcomes, depending on the pattern of frontal lobe alpha-activation asymmetry. In this regard, the authors posited that LFA constitutes a biological or differential sensitivity/susceptibility factor (and its proxy measure of BW), leading to either positive or negative outcome depending on environmental quality (Belsky & Pluess, 2009; Pluess & Belsky, 2013; Ellis, Boyce, Belsky, Bakermans-Kranenburg, & van IJzendoorn, 2011).

Although suggestive of relationship between differential sensitivity/susceptibility and differential hemispheric specialization for emotion/motivation, the research did not include genetic variables typically used in this kind of research. However, Christou et al. (2015) studied variations in the single nucleotide promoter polymorphic region of the serotonin transporter gene (*5-HTTLPR*) in relation to differential frontal hemispheric EEG asymmetries in 4- to 6-year-olds. Children who were homozygous for the short (*s*) allele exhibited rightward alpha band asymmetries (the *s* allele is associated with lower basal genetic activity/protein production) and those homozygous for those long (*l*) allele exhibited leftward asymmetries, with heterozygous exhibiting equal left and right frontal activation. The controlled condition (activity viewing nonsocial clips compared to social ones) did not show these patterns (readings from the parietal; and results for the catechol-*O*-methyltransferase (*COMT*) Val^{158}Met polymorphism). The authors also studied whether the genetic and hemispheric differences in the groups were related to internalizing and externalizing symptomology, but these results were not significant. I conclude that this exciting area of research relating differential sensitivity/susceptibility, differential hemispheric specialization, and effects on behavior is beginning and will further show the importance of lateralization/specialization of behavior and brain.

As for the results of the study, Fortier et al. (2014) found that ELBW LFA adults had the highest scores on measures of attention problems and of withdrawn behavior (see Fig. 8.1), while NBW LFA adults had the lowest scores. This pattern of results represents a statistical interaction effect. Further analysis revealed that RFA adults had moderate problem behavior scores irrespective of birth weight. Behavior problems were measured using the Young Adult Self-Report (YSR; Achenbach, 1991), a questionnaire filled in when the participants were 30–35 years of age.

The authors concluded that LFA is associated with developmental susceptibility/sensitivity to context. Furthermore, the results support a motivational (e.g., approach-withdrawal) rather than a valence (i.e., positive–negative) view of differential frontal lobe specialization with respect to resting EEG.

Language Development

Corballis, Badzakova-Trajkov, and Häberling (2012) noted that there are genetic models of human handedness (e.g., Annett, 2002; McManus, 2002), but that epigenetic models also have been proposed (Crow, 2010; Klar, 2004). However, handedness and manual praxis appear to depend on different lateralized systems, with the latter more closely linked to language lateralization than the former. This conclusion is similar to the one of Bishop (2013).

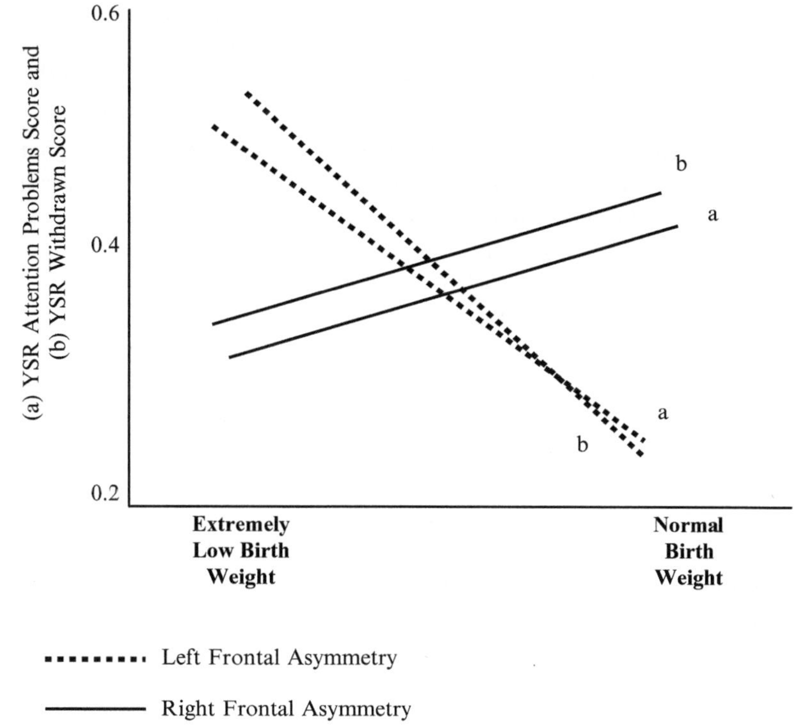

Fig. 8.1 The association between birth weight and YSR subscale scores. Average scores on (*a*) the attention problems subscales, and (*b*) the withdrawn subscale of the Young Adult Self-Report (YSR; Achenbach, 1991) as a function of birth weight and frontal alpha-activation asymmetry. Adapted from Fortier et al. (2014)

Bishop (2013) proposed that the relationship between cerebral asymmetry and language development might be best explained in a way opposite to traditional explanations. Traditionally, the research shows that left-side language lateralization typically is reduced in specific language impairment, which suggests that reduced cerebral asymmetry might be a mediating endophenotype between genes involved in cerebral asymmetry and outcomes in language development. However, according to Bishop (2013), the research does not support that genes clearly affect individual differences in cerebral lateralization. Instead of genetic influence being predominant, nongenetic, experience-dependent language learning might be especially responsible for the development of cerebral asymmetry.

Bishop (2013) acknowledged the presence of early prenatal differences in this regard, but the evidence is that reduced cerebral lateralization is not clearly related to language impairments. More likely, poor language development is a cause rather than a consequence of atypical cerebral asymmetry. Granted, research has found a relationship between structural and functional brain lateralization and vocabulary in children (receptive vocabulary, vocabulary score, respectively) in studies by Lebel and Beaulieu (2009) and Groen, Whitehouse, Badcock, and Bishop (2012), respectively (on laterality of the arcuate fasciculus measured by diffuse tensor imaging and in using FTCD (functional transcranial Doppler ultrasound), respectively). However, the results of these studies did not preclude normal or better language development with atypical lateralization.

Bishop (2013) concluded that, for cerebral lateralization to develop normally, the child has to engage lateralized systems for language learning and analysis (Minagawa-Kawai, Cristià, & Dupoux, 2011). In addition, cerebral asymmetry might not be a unitary trait in development, but a multidimensional one that changes as development proceeds.

Comment

The work on differential susceptibility in emotion-related aspects of behavior and of language development in relation to hemispheric specialization illustrates that not all lateralized phenomena or behaviors that express a side preference are related in a straightforward manner to hemispheric specialization. There are too many variables involved both in the behaviors at issue and in the cerebral hemispheres as they develop to expect clear brain–behavior relationships for all behaviors and functions. The behaviors that show the best correspondences in this regard are behaviors that reflect the basic or fundamental functional specializations of the hemispheres. In this vein, note that I have argued that the left hemisphere is specialized for activation–inhibition coordination and that the right hemisphere is specialized for less complex inhibitions. The following sections of the chapter address the research on inhibition in brain and in behavior from a lateralized point of view.

Inhibition in Children

Left Houdé et al. (2011) used functional magnetic resonance imaging (fMRI) during conservation of number task performance (Piaget, 1942/1952) in 5- to 6-year-olds and 9- to 10-year-olds. The control condition involved determining whether the two rows of objects had the same color. The results showed that both for younger and older children, but especially for the latter, task success was related to bilateral parietofrontal network activity, which is known to be involved in numerical and executive (e.g., working memory) functions. The network found included the bilateral intraparietal sulcus and the bilateral inferior frontal gyri, the latter of which is also associated with inhibition (Aron, Robbins, & Poldrack, 2004). There was also associated left hemisphere and bilateral activity in the cingulate, insula, and thalamus.

In the study of lateralized brain activation, Heitzeg et al. (2014) investigated inhibitory errors in 9- to 12-year-old children (primarily male) in a Go/No-Go task as they underwent a functional MRI scan. In addition, they examined activation in correct inhibition. The go/no-go task requires inhibition of a prepotent response when infrequent "no go" signals occur in relation to frequent "go" signals. Participants could display inhibition successfully on a no-go trial or fail in inhibition on a no-go trial. Specifically, the children were given instructions to respond to target stimuli (letters other than X) by pressing a button (the go trials) or by not pressing it to nontarget stimuli (X letters, no-go trials). Stimuli lasted ½ second and were followed by 3 s of fixation. Both reaction time (RT) and accuracy were measured.

The study was a longitudinal one in which the relationship of inhibition, laterality, and later substance use was determined. Externalizing difficulties were measured at ages 3–8, 9–12, and 11–13 years. Drug use/problem alcohol use was determined at age 13–16.

The results indicated no difference in activation during correct inhibition in relation to baseline. However, the user/problem group in relation to matched controls demonstrated blunted activation during failed inhibition in the left middle frontal gyrus (MFG). The at-risk group developed more externalizing problems at ages 11–13. By applying logistic regression, left MFG activation during inhibition errors was found to predict group membership, and even after statistical control of externalizing problems and RT.

Heitzeg et al. (2014) concluded that early teenage substance abuse and increased risk of substance abuse disorder (SUD) might derive from under-controlled behavior associated with blunted left MFG activation for required inhibitory self-control. In this regard, they found that left MFG activation to inhibitory errors on the no-go task was inversely correlated with degree of externalizing difficulties.

The Heitzeg et al. (2014) study is relevant to the present model that the left hemisphere is specialized for more complex activation/inhibition coordination and the right for less complex inhibition functions, such as stopping outright (or quite short-term activation–inhibition coordination). That is, in an ongoing task in children, when inhibition was called for, the left hemisphere (the MFG) was associated with the inhibitory skill of actively suppressing erroneous inhibition. Not only does the study support the activation/inhibition model of left-hemisphere specialization and its differential inhibitory function relative to the right, it indicates its developmental presence, as per Young (2011).

Neither Dempster and Brainerd (1995) had emphasized the importance of inhibition for succeeding in conservation. For example, successful conservation involves suppressing the first response on conservation tasks in order to consider variations in the two dimensions that are typically involved on these problems. Aside from parietal and frontal regions, the insula also is involved in inhibition (Houdé, Rossi, Lubin, & Joliot, 2010). Therefore, it appears that the brain network found to be associated with number conservation includes widespread inhibition functions (i.e., parietal, frontal, insula areas, the activation of which leads to inhibitory functioning).

Borst, Poirel, Pineau, Cassotti, and Houdé (2013) extended the research group's analysis of inhibitory skills required in Piagetian tasks to class inclusion (for example, one asks "Are there more green squares than squares?" after seeing a series with many green and some other colored squares), although they did not consider hemispheric specialization in this regard. The authors made a distinction between inhibiting content and inhibiting strategy (i.e., misleadingly focusing on subordinate classes in this task; e.g., green vs. other colored squares). The study showed that not only 10-year-olds but also 20-year-olds needed inhibitory skills to solve the task. The study did not address side differences, as mentioned, but it illustrates the importance of inhibition for the tasks involved.

Inhibition in Adults

Model

Both Grimshaw and Carmel (2014) presented a model of hemispheric specialization of emotions that focused on inhibition. First, mechanisms in the left dorsolateral prefrontal cortex (DLPFC) inhibit negative distractors, while those in the right inhibit positive distractors. That is, the left PFC subserves inhibition of withdrawal rather than being an instrument of approach. Also, the right PFC subserves inhibition of approach rather than withdrawal, per se. In this regard, the model puts EF front and center in the differential understanding of the hemispheres, with its inhibition component being primary. Grimshaw and Carmel (2014) also noted that, in EEG and neuroimaging research, left-hemisphere lateralization of inhibition of negative stimuli is "stronger" than that of the right for positive stimuli, given that inhibiting negative stimuli (words, faces) is more "taxing" than inhibiting positive ones.

Sainburg's (2014) model of handedness and brain lateralization is consistent with the one in the present work. He argued that, for motor control processes, the left hemisphere is specialized for behavior that predicts the effects of body/environment dynamics. The left-hemisphere function allows it to account for predicable dynamic conditions, facilitating mechanical and energetic efficiency (as in precise trajectory and coordinated patterns, e.g., at the end of a movement). In contrast, the right hemisphere is specialized for "impedance" control processing in order to contain possible errors in unexpected "mechanical" events and conditions, which together constitute a process that serves to obtain steady-state postures (equilibrium). The right-hemisphere function leads to positional and velocity stability, allowing greater flexibility and robustness in situations of unpredictability and instability.

Sainburg (2014) argued that his dynamic dominance hypothesis of motor lateralization is consistent with the general model of lateralization proposed by Rogers, Zucca, and Vallortigara (2004). They had maintained that the left hemisphere is specialized for well-established behavior patterns performed in environments that are familiar, and the right hemisphere functions in response to unforeseen events in the environment.

Comment Both the Grimshaw and Carmel (2014) and Sainburg (2014) models are consistent with my own model of activation/inhibition coordination (Young, 2011), in which the left hemisphere is specialized for subtle, dynamic activation/inhibition coordination and the right for less nuanced inhibition processes (e.g., short-term coordination in this regard, or more full-scale inhibition by itself). For example, Sainburg's emphasis on left-hemisphere acuity in efficiency, precision, and coordination fits the activation–inhibition coordination model, with the left hemisphere doing this more proficiently.

The research supports that the hemispheres developed their specializations independently and that the right hemisphere did not take on its functions only because the left hemisphere had already been specialized for language (e.g., Rosch, Bishop, & Badcock, 2012). Also, although the lateralizations of language and manual skills are co-lateralized in the left hemisphere, to a degree, handedness appears independent of this complex (Vingerhoets et al., 2012). The left hemisphere would appear to have (some of) its advantages due to a superior inter-hemispheric inhibition capacity (Talelli, Ewas, Waddingham, Rothwell, & Ward, 2008).

Concepts Consistent with the Present Model

Left The work of Caeyenberghs and Leemans (2014) revealed a topological organization in structural brain networks consistent with an advantage of the left hemisphere in efficiency in organization. They used fiber tractography to build ("reconstruct") the networks, considering 45 nodes in each hemisphere in doing so.

The results showed that the left hemisphere is structured to be more efficient than the right. In contrast, the right hemisphere demonstrates more "small world" properties and "betweenness centrality." This occurred especially in brain regions associated with typical left- and right-hemisphere specializations (for language/motor actions; memory/visuospatial attention, respectively).

The authors concluded that the left hemisphere is more optimal for information processing compared to the right. Its efficiency is found both for global and local levels. The left hemisphere is integrated better in its interconnections. In contrast, the right hemisphere compensates for its "reduced efficiency" in its capacity in "parallel information transfer" by having more focal betweenness centrality.

The results of Caeyenberghs and Leemans (2014) speak to the present work's emphasis on the specialization of the left hemisphere for activation–inhibition coordination. In showing that the left hemisphere is more efficient and integrated both locally and globally in its networked interconnections over regions, a structural basis appears evident for the suggested activation–inhibition coordination in the left hemisphere.

Marinsek, Turner, Gazzaniga, and Miller (2014) reviewed the research on split-brain and brain-damaged patients, in particular. They argued that, in inferential reasoning strategies, the left hemisphere appears to create explanations, make inferences, and bridge information gaps. In contrast, the right hemisphere appears to detect conflicts, update beliefs, facilitate shifts in mental sets, and monitor and inhibit ("brake") behavior. As a summary model, they conjectured that the left hemisphere appears to create hypotheses and "represent causality." In contrast, the right hemisphere appears to evaluate hypotheses and reject evidence-evident implausible/inconsistent ones. Finally, for Marinsek et al. (2014), the left hemisphere functions to reduce uncertainty and the right to resolve inconsistency.

Marinsek et al. (2014) related their model of hemispheric specialization to other lateralization theories. For example, Bowden, Jung-Beeman, Fleck, and Kounios (2005) considered that the left hemisphere is more finely-tuned, and Braun (2007) considered that the right is more inhibitory (to "freeze and recoup") in a process of "effortful inhibition" (Aron et al., 2014).

About causality, Marinsek et al. (2014) continued that the left hemisphere appears superior in making judgments about causal structure. In contrast, the right hemisphere has its own causality skills (in making perceptual and possible social causal judgments and influences).

The authors concluded that the left hemisphere may be especially recruited for creativity and "liberal" inference making. In contrast, the right hemisphere is recruited for caution and conservative reasoning. Overall, the emphasis on the left hemisphere in reducing uncertainty and more expansive inference making, in contrast to the right one's skill in more temperate influences, is consistent with the present emphasis on left-hemisphere skill in activation–inhibition coordination.

Shobe (2014) presented a model of left- and right-hemisphere specialization for emotional processing that is quite consistent with the present model of left-hemisphere superiority for complex tasks, such as activation–inhibition coordination, as in sociality and in positive emotions. Shobe's (2014) model emphasizes the independent yet collaborative contributions of the two hemispheres. At the same time, he supported that the left hemisphere has a higher-order role in this duality. For Shobe (2014), the research indicates that the right hemisphere's pulvinar-amygdala-superior colliculus pathway deals with fast, course, and unconscious processing of emotional stimuli. Its subcortical connections provide additional processing capacity of emotional stimuli.

Overall, then, the right hemisphere mediates directly the identification/comprehension of emotional stimuli, whether positive or negative in valence. It is the seat of subjective feelings. This happens in steps; first, it comprehends/processes the valence of emotional stimuli, and then it generates the feeling that fits the interpretation. So it is the perceptual and experiential locus of emotional processing.

The role of the left hemisphere appears far more complex in emotional processing and it occurs later in the process compared to the role for the right hemisphere, although the hemispheres communicate via the corpus callosum. The left hemisphere is involved in a secondary, additional emotional interpretation after it receives the right-hemisphere information.

That is, for Shobe (2014), the left hemisphere gives a verbal, propositional (semantic, linguistic, meaningful) code to the emotional information (and the brain regions activated during emotional processing in the left hemisphere are language-related). It directs our conscious interpretation of and also our interaction with emotional stimuli. It is involved with emotional regulation (e.g., attenuating/reinterpreting the negative; problem solving), executive function (e.g., planning, decision-making), knowledge representation, social regulation/well-being, and self-preservation/adaptation, all of which concern higher-level emotional processing. It is detached and transformative, and integrates the information received from the right hemisphere into higher-level cognitions. The left hemisphere is limited by a positivity bias, so that both hemispheres are needed in processing negatively-valenced emotional information.

Left Different models and tasks have associated inhibition functions more with one hemisphere or the other (e.g., right hemisphere, Bourgeois, Chica, Milgliaccio, Thiebaut de Schotten, & Bartolomeo, 2012; Wright & Hardie, 2011; left hemisphere, Kurth et al., 2013), with age differences also evident (e.g., Vidal, Mills, Pang, & Taylor, 2012). Reid and Serrien (2012) presented a model consistent with the present one that the left hemisphere, in particular, is specialized for activation–inhibition coordination (Young, 2011). On a bimanual task, right-handers but not left-handers evidenced increased inhibitory processing that "favored" left-hemisphere control. Specifically, right-handers appeared to express intra- and interhemispheric inhibitory asymmetries or enhanced within- and cross-hemisphere inhibitory processing.

These models are consistent with Gazzaniga (2013) who referred to the left hemisphere as having a facility in interpretation. It generates narratives or stories explaining what we do and why, through a dedicated "special module." In this regard, Mackey, Whitaker, and Bunge (2012) found data in support of left-hemisphere specialization for "reasoning" (also Krawczyk, 2012). As well, it might achieve its superiority in reasoning by efficiently recruiting homologous right-hemisphere cortex areas, especially for complex reasoning.

Evidence

Right Aron et al. (2014) considered the right inferior frontal cortex (rIFC) as an inhibitory pausing device or brake and not just for outright stopping. It functions accordingly along with one or more fronto-basal-ganglia networks. I note that these studies are differentiating the types of tasks, techniques, inhibitory skills, areas of the brain and subareas, and developmental trends in behavior control.

Dambacher et al. (2014) examined adult ability to inhibit responses in action restraint and action cancellation (as indexed in a go/no-go task and a stop signal task, respectively). They used fMRI data and response to continuous theta burst brain stimulation. Action restraint was associated with right anterior insula (AI) and right superior frontal gyrus activation, among others, while action cancellation was associated with the right AI and the right MFG, among others. The brain stimulation acts to disrupt targeted regions. This technique found the right AI had been disrupted in both tasks used. For the right superior frontal gyrus, only the restraint task had inhibition interrupted.

Bourgeois, Chica, Valero-Cabré, and Bartolomeo (2013) conducted a study of cortical control of inhibition of return (IOR) in adults, which demonstrated that the right hemisphere is involved in less complex inhibitory function. This type of inhibition involves inspection of spatial locations. Ones already inspected generate longer response times relative to those that have not yet been inspected. The research demonstrates right parietal cortex involvement in the inhibition, but not left.

Similarly, O'Connor, Upton, Moore, and Hester (2014) demonstrated with a go/no-go task that enhanced action withholding especially is associated with the right inferior frontal junction (and precentral gyrus). This area is involved not only with "outright stopping" (Aron et al., 2014) but also with "pausing" and "braking" responses, in general. The authors related their results to impulse control disorders, such as SUD.

Shackman, McMenamin, Maxwell, Greischar, and Davidson (2009) found that higher self-reported behavioral inhibition was associated with greater tonic (resting) high-resolution EEG in the right dorsolateral prefrontal cortex. These series of studies are confirming a role for the right hemisphere in inhibition functions, but I note that the type of inhibitions involved do not reflect the type of activation/inhibition coordination that I suggest is central to left-hemisphere functioning.

Left Serrien and Sovijävi-Spapé (2013) determined a relationship between hemispheric specialization and inhibition. Inhibition is important for successful goal-directed behavior, for example, of irrelevant information or to sudden changes in the environment. Habitual responses that could interfere with task completion need to be contained.

To measure response inhibition, a common task that is used in the laboratory is the Go/No-Go or Go/Stop task. Participants must either, respectively, withhold or discontinue a prepared response to target cues. Distinct inhibitory processes are involved in the two conditions—action restraint and action cancellation, respectively. If the behavior itself needs to be altered, this is referred to as "switching."

In their research, the authors used EEG coherence as an index of functional connectivity. Inhibition has been related to a widespread brain network, with differential left- and right-hemisphere involvement depending on inhibition demand characteristics of the task used.

As for the methods of their study, Serrien and Sovijävi-Spapé (2013) tested right and left-handed young adults. The task involved reaction time to visually-presented stimuli. In the Go condition, participants had to fixate a cross that was presented for 1 s. Then, a preparation cue (L or R) was presented for 400 ms. This procedure allowed participants to prepare a response with either the left or right index finger, as cued. Interstimulus intervals lasted for 1 s ± 200 ms (random). During these intervals, the screen was blank. Then, the target cue, a colored square, was presented for 920 ms. The square was either green in color (Go) or red (No-Go). If the square was blue, the participants had to switch index finger used. Training trials were used to encourage rapid response or inhibition/change, as required.

With respect to EEG, measurements took place in the alpha band (8–12 Hz), which captures both response excitation and inhibition.

Coherence was established over the regions of interest chosen, which corresponded to dorsal, prefrontal, premotor, primary motor, and superior parietal areas.

The results for EEG coherence revealed strengthening of interregional coupling in the alpha band following presentation of target cues, with an association with fronto-medial circuitry. Also, parietal areas appeared to be involved in response switching. The relationship between behavioral response and EEG measures indicated a functional significance of left-side hemispheric regions for successful response inhibition and response switching. For both right- and left-handers, the left hemisphere appeared specialized for goal-directed activity or higher-order aspects of action, with its inhibitory function (e.g., response selection, response withholding) critical to success.

The authors analyzed the temporal patterns in the inhibition that was evident. Early coupling started within ≤ 100 ms in the No-Go condition, implying attentional control. Between 100 and 200 ms, the coupling that took place appeared to involve decision to withhold/regulation. Next, coupling after 200 ms appeared to reflect actual deployment of inhibition and potential conflict monitoring. The interval related to decision-making was the one more related to left-sided frontal region coupling. Note that although Go/No-Go comparisons yielded results implicating left-hemisphere control for inhibition, the switching tasks yielded bilateral associations, but the authors did implicate the left hemisphere in switching, too (p. 288). Note that the research in the field supports that stopping is a right-hemisphere function (Rubia et al., 2001). Overall, the data support Young's (2011) model that the left hemisphere is specialized for activation (excitation)/inhibition coordination and the right hemisphere for less complex inhibitions (e.g., stopping).

Nee et al. (2012) conducted a meta-analysis to determine the "operations" that contribute to working memory (WM). The four component executive functions central to WM involve: (a) controlling external distraction (distractor resistance); (b) controlling intrusion by irrelevant memories; (c) shifting attention within WM; and (d) updating WM contents. The review revealed a broad network of medial and lateral frontal and parietal regions involved in WM executive processing.

Some of the main results indicated laterality effects. The midlateral prefrontal cortex was involved in nonspatial content and reflected a left lateralization. The more dorsal caudal superior frontal sulcus appeared sensitive to spatial content. The results reflect a dual selection model (focused on "what" and "where" functions, respectively). Inhibitory functions (intrusion resistance) appeared right-lateralized in the inferior frontal sulcus, but other functions related to inhibition (distractor resistance) were more left lateralized.

Ocklenburg, Ness, Güntürkün, Suchan, and Beste (2013) conducted a study consistent with the model that the initial processing of verbal stimuli takes place in the left hemisphere and leads to more efficient response inhibition in that hemisphere. Using a facial go/no-go task, they found an equivalent inhibitory advantage in these regards for the right hemisphere.

Cerutti (2013) reported in his research that stimulating the left prefrontal cortex by anodal stimulation improves a verbal task performance with EF (memory load) demand. Similarly, using inhibitory cathodal stimulation of the corresponding region in the right hemisphere improved performance on a verbal task of semantic organization. The results show how facilitatory and inhibitory links function in inter- and intra-regional neuronal connectivity.

Balconi, Finocchiaro, and Canavesio (2014) examined lateralized cortical frontal alpha band oscillation modulation in relation to Iowa Gambling Task performance in both an SUD group and controls. They administered a questionnaire on the Behavioral Activation and Behavior Inhibition Systems (BAS and BIS, respectively). The SUD group revealed a pattern on the gambling task favoring the choice for immediate reward and also an increase in left-hemisphere activation in response to the choice associated with immediate reward.

The authors concluded that the SUD group could have a higher left-hemisphere mediated BAS trait relative to controls [who would have a more left (BAS)—right (BIS) balance; note that in the latter description I added the BIS function to the right hemisphere].

Evolution

Cochet and Byrne (2013) noted that there might be evolutionary continuity in the origins of manual laterality and hemispheric specialization. In this regard, they considered possible drivers in skilled manipulative activity (tool use), gestural communication, organization complexity in action (hierarchical structure), and goal-directed, intentional action for manual lateralization and associated hemispheric specialization. They referred to a possible "association" of hemispheric dominance of language and specific characteristics that cut across the typical right-sided laterality in manual tasks.

MacNeilage (2014) presented a model of the evolution of human handedness as a right-favoring adaptation in the context of an earlier evolved left-handedness. Specifically, the left hand was specialized by prosimians for postural support in their arboreal habitat. Later, simians evolved right-side adaptations for each of the behaviors of: manipulation; lead hand in bimanual coordination; throwing; and manual communication. Humans cemented the right-hand bias through an evolved "superstructure" related to tool-use and language.

Doubts

Not all results reveal a clear lateralization effect in children's manual or hemispheric specialization. Scharoun and Bryden (2014) indicated controversy on the age of emergence of hand preference and hand performance abilities. Johansson, Domellöf, and Rönnqvist (2014) found that only full-term (compared to preterm) birthed children showed side differences in goal-directed movements. Yu et al. (2014) investigated spatiotemporal patterns of language lateralization using MEG, and found age-related sex differences on a visual verb generation task.

Part of the reasons for the conflicting results in the field related to the disjoint in lateralization of the brain, related manual skills, and handedness. The latter might reflect environmental influences more than the other lateralities, in that handedness is an expression of multifactorial genetic and environmental influences (Ocklenburg, Beste, & Güntürkün, 2013).

The research on the relationship of lateralization and the expression of autism in children generally reveals little conclusive findings (e.g., Dennis & Thompson, 2013; Preslar, Kushner, Marino, & Pearce, 2014). However, Joseph et al. (2014) examined structural asymmetries in relation to language function in 4- to 7-year-old children with autism spectrum disorder (ASD) and matched controls. They used structural MRI and magnetic resonance DTI tractography.

The researchers found no gray matter differences between the groups, but did find white-matter differences. The ASD group was less left-lateralized than controls both in the volume and radial diffusivity of the arcuate fasciculus (AF). Also, within the ASD group, decreased left-side/increased right-side asymmetry of the pars opercularis was associated both with an earlier language onset and with a greater ability in language.

To conclude, the area of the neurodevelopment of lateralities and how it becomes affected in disturbances in development holds much promise. However, as well, it illustrates the complexities in lateralization development.

Chapter Conclusions

The study of laterality of behavior and specialization of the brain should be considered a core area in development because of the implications of this area of research for the brain, networks, developmental abnormalities, developmental adversity and differential susceptibility, underpinning to motivation/emotion, and general overarching models of brain and behavior (such as activation–inhibition coordination). The research on the evolution of laterality in behavior and hemispheric specialization in the brain reveals its origins in basic protomammalian brain–behavior relations, and not just in nonhuman primates and their ancestors. Indeed, it stretches earlier into our evolution and stands as an important building block in our evolutionary heritage. The model of neuronal networks has led to research that the left hemisphere congenitally is more efficient in connectivity. This fits Young's (2011) model that it is specialized for activation–inhibition coordination. Lateralization might be prevalent in animal species, but its evolution to its current state in humans might address aspects of human exceptionality and their underpinning basis in the brain.

References

Achenbach, T. M. (1991). *Manual for the adult self-report and 1991 profile*. Burlington, VT: University of Vermont, Department of Psychiatry.

Annett, M. (2002). *Handedness and brain asymmetry: The right shift theory*. Hove, UK: Psychology Press.

Arbib, M. A. (2006). The mirror system hypothesis on the linkage of action and languages. In M. A. Arbib (Ed.), *Action to language via the mirror neuron system* (pp. 3–47). New York: Cambridge University Press.

Aron, A. R., Robbins, T. W., & Poldrack, R. A. (2004). Inhibition and the right inferior frontal cortex. *Trends in Cognitive Sciences, 8*, 170–177.

Aron, A. R., Robbins, T. W., & Poldrack, R. A. (2014). Inhibition and the right inferior frontal cortex: One decade on. *Trends in Cognitive Sciences, 18*, 177–185.

Aslin, R. N., Shukla, M., & Emberson, L. L. (2015). Hemodynamic correlates of cognition in human infants. *Annual Review of Psychology, 66*, 349–379.

Atzil, S., Hendler, T., & Feldman, R. (2011). Specifying the neurobiological basis of human attachment: Brain, hormones, and behavior in synchronous and intrusive mothers. *Neuropsychopharmacology, 36*, 2603–2615.

Babik, I., Campbell, J. M., & Michel, G. F. (2013). Postural influences on the development of infant lateralized and symmetric hand-use. *Child Development, 85*, 294–307.

Balconi, M., Finocchiaro, R., & Canavesio, Y. (2014). Reward-system effect (BAS rating), left hemispheric "unbalance" (alpha band oscillations) and decision impairments in drug addiction. *Addictive Behaviors, 39*, 1026–1032.

Barber, A. D., Srinivasan, P., Joel, S. E., Caffo, B. S., Pekar, J. J., & Mostofsky, S. H. (2012). Motor "dexterity"? Evidence that left hemisphere lateralization of motor circuit connectivity is associated with better motor performance in children. *Cerebral Cortex, 22*, 51–59.

Barbey, A. K., Colom, R., Solomon, J., Krueger, F., Forbes, C., & Grafman, J. (2012). An integrative architecture for general intelligence and executive function revealed by lesion mapping. *Brain, 135*, 1154–1164.

Belsky, J., & Pluess, M. (2009). The nature (and nurture?) of plasticity in early human development. *Perspectives on Psychological Science, 4*, 345–351.

Berl, M. M., Mayo, J., Parks, E. N., Rosenberger, L. R., VanMeter, J., Ratner, N. B., et al. (2014). Regional differences in the developmental trajectory of lateralization of the language network. *Human Brain Mapping, 35*, 270–284.

Bishop, D. V. M. (2013). Cerebral asymmetry and language development: Cause, correlate, or consequence? *Science, 340*, 6138. doi:10.1126/science.1230531.

Björk, T., Brus, O., Osika, W., & Montgomery, S. (2012). Laterality, hand control and scholastic performance: A British birth cohort study. *British Medical Journal Open, 2*, e000314. doi:10.1136/bmjopen-2011-000314.

Borst, G., Poirel, N., Pineau, A., Cassotti, M., & Houdé, O. (2013). Inhibitory control efficiency in a Piaget-like class-inclusion task in school-age children and adults: A developmental negative priming study. *Developmental Psychology, 49*, 1366–1374.

Bourgeois, A., Chica, A. B., Migliaccio, R., Thiebaut de Schotten, M., & Bartolomeo, P. (2012). Cortical control of inhibition of return: Evidence from patients with inferior parietal damage and visual neglect. *Neuropsychologia, 50*, 800–809.

Bourgeois, A., Chica, A. B., Valero-Cabré, A., & Bartolomeo, P. (2013). Cortical control of inhibition of return: Exploring the causal contributions of the left parietal cortex. *Cortex, 49*, 2927–2934.

Bowden, E. M., Jung-Beeman, M., Fleck, J., & Kounios, J. (2005). New approaches to demystifying insight. *Trends in Cognitive Science, 9*, 322–328.

Braun, C. M. J. (2007). Evolution of hemispheric specialisation of antagonistic systems of management of the body's energy resources. *Laterality, 12*, 397–427.

Caeyenberghs, K., & Leemans, A. (2014). Hemispheric lateralization of topological organization in structural brain networks. *Human Brain Mapping, 35*, 4944–4957.

Campbell, J. M., Marcinowski, E. C., Babik, I., & Michel, G. F. (2015). The influence of a hand preference for acquiring objects on the development of a hand preference for unimanual manipulation from 6 to 14 months. *Infant Behavior and Development, 39*, 107–117.

Campbell, J. M., Marcinowski, E. C., Latta, J., & Michel, G. F. (2015). Different assessment tasks produce different estimates of handedness stability during the eight to 14 month age period. *Infant Behavior and Development, 39*, 67–80.

Cerutti, C. (2013). Building a functional multiple intelligence theory to advance educational neuroscience.

Frontiers in Psychology, 4, 950. doi:10.3389/fpsyg.2013.00950.
Cheng, Y., Lee, S. Y., Chen, H. Y., Wang, P., & Decety, J. (2012). Voice and emotion processing in the human neonatal brain. *Journal of Cognitive Neuroscience, 24*, 1411–1419.
Cheyne, D., Jobst, C., Tesan, G., Crain, S., & Johnson, B. (2014). Movement-related neuromagnetic fields in preschool age children. *Human Brain Mapping, 35*, 4858–4875.
Christou, A. I., Endo, S., Wallis, Y., Bair, H., Zeggers, M. P., & McCleery, J. P. (2015). Variation in serotonin transporter linked polymorphic region (5-HTTLPR) short/long genotype modulates resting frontal electroencephalography asymmetries in children. *Development and Psychopathology*, 1–12. doi:10.1017/S0954579415000413.
Cochet, H. (2012). Development of hand preference for object-directed actions and pointing gestures: A longitudinal study between 15 and 25 months of age. *Developmental Psychobiology, 54*, 105–111.
Cochet, H., & Byrne, R. W. (2013). Evolutionary origins of human handedness: Evaluating contrasting hypotheses. *Animal Cognition, 16*, 531–542.
Cochet, H., & Vauclair, J. (2010). Pointing gestures produced by toddlers from 15 to 30 months: Different functions, hand shapes and laterality patterns. *Infant Behavior and Development, 33*, 431–441.
Corballis, M. C., Badzakova-Trajkov, G., & Häberling, I. S. (2012). Right hand, left brain: Genetic and evolutionary bases of cerebral asymmetries for language and manual action. *Wiley Interdisciplinary Reviews: Cognitive Science, 3*, 1–17.
Corbetta, D., Friedman, D. R., & Bell, M. A. (2014). Brain reorganization as a function of walking experience in 12-month-old infants: Implications for the development of manual laterality. *Frontiers in Psychology, 5*, 245. doi:10.3389/fpsyg.2014.00245.
Crow, T. J. (2010). A theory of origin of cerebral asymmetry: Epigenetic variation superimposed on a fixed right-shift. *Laterality, 15*, 289–303.
Dambacher, F., Sack, A. T., Lobbestael, J., Arntz, A., Brugmann, S., & Schuhmann, T. (2014). The role of right prefrontal and medial cortex in response inhibition: Interfering with action restraint and action cancellation using transcranial magnetic brain stimulation. *Journal of Cognitive Neuroscience, 26*, 1775–1784.
Davidson, R. J. (2000). Affective style, psychopathology, and resilience: Brain mechanisms and plasticity. *American Psychologist, 55*, 1196–1214.
Davidson, R. J., Ekman, P., Saron, C. D., & Senulius, J. A. (1990). Approach-withdrawal and cerebral asymmetry: Emotional express and brain physiology. *International Journal of Personality and Social Psychology, 58*, 330–341.
Davidson, R. J., & Fox, N. A. (1982). Asymmetrical brain activity discriminates between positive and negative affective stimuli in human infants. *Science, 218*, 1235–1237.
Dawson, G., Ashman, S. B., Hessl, D., Spieker, S., Frey, K., Panagiotides, H., et al. (2001). Autonomic and brain electrical activity in securely- and insecurely-attached infants of depressed mothers. *Infant Behavior and Development, 24*, 135–149.
de Vries, J. I. P., Wimmers, R. H., Ververs, I. A. P., Hopkins, B., Savelsbergh, G. J. P., & van Geijn, H. P. (2001). Fetal handedness and head position preference: A developmental study. *Developmental Psychobiology, 39*, 171–178.
Delis, D. C., Kaplan, E., & Kramer, J. H. (2001). *Delis Kaplan executive function system*. San Antonio, TX: The Psychological Corporation.
Dempster, F., & Brainerd, C. (Eds.). (1995). *Interference and inhibition in cognition*. San Diego, CA: Academic.
Denckla, M. B. (1985). Revised PANESS. *Psychopharmacology Bulletin, 21*, 773–800.
Dennis, E. L., & Thompson, P. M. (2013). Mapping connectivity in the developing brain. *International Journal of Developmental Neuroscience, 31*, 525–542.
Dubois, J., Hertz-Pannier, L., Cachia, A., Mangin, J. F., Le Bihan, D., & Dehaene-Lambertz, G. (2009). Structural asymmetries in the infant language and sensori-motor networks. *Cerebral Cortex, 19*, 414–423.
Dunfield, K. A. (2014). A construct divided: Prosocial behavior as helping, sharing, and comforting subtypes. *Frontiers in Psychology, 5*, 958. doi:10.3389/fpsyg.2014.00958.
Ellis, B. J., Boyce, W. T., Belsky, J., Bakermans-Kranenburg, M. J., & van IJzendoorn, M. H. (2011). Differential susceptibility to the environment: An evolutionary-neurodevelopmental theory. *Development and Psychopathology, 23*, 7–28.
Esseily, R., Jacquet, A.-Y., & Fagard, J. (2011). Handedness for grasping objects and pointing and the development of language in 14-month-old infants. *Laterality, 16*, 565–585.
Everts, R., Lidzba, K., Wilke, M., Kiefer, C., Mordasini, M., Schroth, G., et al. (2009). Strengthening of laterality of verbal and visuospatial functions during childhood and adolescence. *Human Brain Mapping, 30*, 473–483.
Fagard, J., Sirri, L., & Rämä, P. (2014). Effect of handedness on the occurrence of semantic N400 priming effect in 18- and 24-month-old children. *Frontiers in Psychology, 5*, 355. doi:10.3389/fpsyg.2014.00355.
Fortier, P., Van Lieshout, R. J., Waxman, J. A., Boyle, M. H., Saigal, S., & Schmidt, L. A. (2014). Are orchids left and dandelions right? Frontal brain activation asymmetry and its sensitivity to developmental context. *Psychological Science, 25*, 1526–1533.
Fox, N. A. (1991). If it's not left, it's right: Electroencephalograph asymmetry and the development of emotion. *American Psychologist, 46*, 863–872.
Friederici, A. D., Brauer, J., & Lohmann, G. (2011). Maturation of the language network: from inter-to

intrahemispheric connectivities. *PLoS ONE, 6*, e20726. doi:10.1371/journal.pone.0020726.

Gander, M., & Buchheim, A. (2015). Attachment classification, psychophysiology and frontal EEG asymmetry across the lifespan: A review. *Frontiers in Human Neuroscience, 9*, 79. doi:10.3389/fnhum.2015.00079.

Gazzaniga, M. S. (2013). Shifting gears: Seeking new approaches for mind/brain mechanisms. *Annual Review of Psychology, 64*, 1–20.

Gioia, G. A., Isquith, P. K., Guy, S. C., & Kenworthy, L. (2000). *Behavior rating inventory of executive function (BRIEF)*. Odessa, FL: Psychological Assessment Resources.

Glasel, H., Leroy, F., Dubois, J., Hertz-Pannier, L., Mangin, J. F., & Dehaene-Lambertz, G. (2011). A robust cerebral asymmetry in the infant brain: The rightward superior temporal sulcus. *NeuroImage, 58*, 716–723.

Gonzalez, C. L. R., Li, F., Mills, K. J., Rosen, N., & Gibb, R. L. (2014). Speech in action: Degree of hand preference for grasping predicts speech articulation competence in children. *Frontiers in Psychology, 5*, 1267. doi:10.3389/fpsyg.2014.01267.

Gonzalez, C. L. R., Mills, K. J., Genee, I., Li, F., Piquette, N., Rosen, N., et al. (2014). Getting the right grasp on executive function. *Frontiers in Psychology, 5*, 285. doi:10.3389/fpsyg.2014.00285.

Grimshaw, G. M., & Carmel, D. (2014). An asymmetric inhibition model of hemispheric differences in emotional processing. *Frontiers in Psychology, 5*, 489. doi:10.3389/fpsyg.2014.00489.

Groen, M. A., Whitehouse, A. J., Badcock, N. A., & Bishop, D. V. (2012). Does cerebral lateralization develop? A study using functional transcranial Doppler ultrasound assessing lateralization for language production and visuospatial memory. *Brain and Behavior, 2*, 256–296.

Grossmann, T., Johnson, M. H., Lloyd-Fox, S., Blasi, A., Deligianni, F., Elwell, C., et al. (2008). Early cortical specialization for face-to-face communication in human infants. *Proceedings of the Royal Society B: Biological Sciences, 275*, 2803–2811.

Grossmann, T., Parise, E., & Friederici, A. D. (2010). The detection of communicative signals directed at the self in infant prefrontal cortex. *Frontiers in Human Neuroscience, 4*, 201. doi:10.3389/fnhum.2010.00201.

Habas, P. A., Scott, J. A., Roosta, A., Rajagopalan, V., Kim, K., Rousseau, F., et al. (2012). Early folding patterns and asymmetries of the normal human brain detected from in utero MRI. *Cerebral Cortex, 22*, 13–25.

Harmon-Jones, E., Gable, P. A., & Peterson, C. K. (2010). The role of asymmetric frontal cortical activity in emotion-related phenomena: A review and update. *Biological Psychology, 84*, 451–462.

Heitzeg, M. M., Nigg, J. T., Hardee, J. E., Soules, M., Steinberg, D., Zubieta, J-K., et al. (2014). Left middle frontal gyrus response to inhibitory errors in children prospectively predicts early problem substance use. *Drug and Alcohol Dependence, 141*, 51–57.

Hepper, P. G. (2013). The developmental origins of laterality: Fetal handedness. *Developmental Psychobiology, 55*, 588–595.

Hepper, P. G., McCartney, G. R., & Shannon, E. A. (1998). Lateralised behavior in first trimester human fetuses. *Neuropsychologia, 36*, 531–534.

Hepper, P. G., Shahidullah, S., & White, R. (1991). Handedness in human fetus. *Neuropsychologia, 29*, 1107–1111.

Hepper, P. G., Wells, D. K., & Lynch, C. (2005). Prenatal thumb sucking is related to postnatal handedness. *Neuropsychologia, 43*, 313–315.

Hervé, P. Y., Zago, L., Petit, L., Mazoyer, B., & Tzourio-Mazoyer, N. (2013). Revisiting human hemispheric specialization with neuroimaging. *Trends in Cognitive Sciences, 17*, 69–80.

Hill, J., Dierker, D., Neil, J., Inder, T., Knutsen, A., Harwell, J., et al. (2010). A surface-based analysis of hemispheric asymmetries and folding of cerebral cortex in term-born human infants. *Journal of Neuroscience, 30*, 2268–2276.

Holowka, S., & Petitto, L. A. (2002). Left hemisphere cerebral specialization for babies while babbling. *Science, 297*, 1515. doi:10.1126/science.1074941.

Houdé, O., Pineau, A., Leroux, G., Poirel, N., Perchey, G., Lanoë, C., et al. (2011). Functional magnetic resonance imaging study of Piaget's conservation-of-number task in preschool and school-age children: A neo-Piagetian approach. *Journal of Experimental Child Psychology, 110*, 332–346.

Houdé, O., Rossi, S., Lubin, A., & Joliot, M. (2010). Mapping numerical procession, reading, and executive functions in the developing brain: An fMRI meta-analysis on 52 studies including 842 children. *Developmental Science, 13*, 876–885.

Im, K., Jo, H. J., Mangin, J. F., Evans, A. C., Kim, S. I., & Lee, J. M. (2010). Spatial distribution of deep sulcal landmarks and hemispherical asymmetry on the cortical surface. *NeuroImage, 58*, 716–723.

Iturria-Medina, Y., Pérez Fernández, A., Morris, D. M., Canales-Rodríguez, E. J., Haroon, H. A., García Pentón, L., et al. (2011). Brain hemispheric structural efficiency and interconnectivity rightward asymmetry in human and nonhuman primates. *Cerebral Cortex, 21*, 56–67.

Jacquet, A.-Y., Esseily, R., Rider, D., & Fagard, J. (2012). Handedness for grasping objects and declarative pointing: A longitudinal study. *Developmental Psychobiology, 54*, 36–46.

Johansson, A.-M., Domellöf, E., & Rönnqvist, L. (2014). Long-term influences of a preterm birth on movement organization and side specialization in children at 4–8 years of age. *Developmental Psychobiology, 56*, 1263–1277.

Joseph, R. M., Fricker, Z., Fenoglio, A., Lindgren, K. A., Knaus, T. A., & Tager-Flusberg, H. (2014). Structural asymmetries of language-related gray and white matter and their relationship to language function in young children with ASD. *Brain Imaging and Behavior, 8*, 60–72.

Kahrs, B. A., Jung, W. P., & Lockman, J. J. (2014). When does tool use become distinctively human? Hammering in young children. *Child Development, 85*, 1050–1061.

Kasprian, G., Langs, G., Brugger, P. C., Bittner, M., Weber, M., Arantes, M., et al. (2011). The prenatal origin of hemispheric asymmetry: An in utero neuroimaging study. *Cerebral Cortex, 21*, 1076–1083.

Kaufman, A., & Kaufman, N. (1983). *Kaufman assessment battery for children: Administration and scoring manual*. Circle Pines, MN: American Guidance Service.

Kikuchi, M., Shitamichi, K., Yoshimura, Y., Ueno, S., Remijn, G. B., Hirosawa, T., et al. (2011). Lateralized theta wave connectivity and language performance in 2- to 5-year-old children. *Journal of Neuroscience, 31*, 14984–14988.

Kivilevitch, Z., Achiron, R., & Zalel, Y. (2010). Fetal brain asymmetry: In utero sonographic findings. *American Journal of Obstetrics and Gynecology, 202*, 359.e1–e8.

Klar, A. (2004). An epigenetic hypothesis for human brain laterality, handedness, and psychosis development. *Cold Spring Harbor Symposia Quantitative Biology, 69*, 499–506.

Krawczyk, D. C. (2012). The cognition and neuroscience of relational reasoning. *Brain Research, 1428*, 13–23.

Kurjak, A., Vecek, N., Hafner, T., Bozek, T., Funduk-Kirjak, B., & Ujevic, B. (2002). Prenatal diagnosis: What does four-dimensional ultrasound add? *Journal of Perinatal Medicine, 30*, 57–62.

Kurth, F., Mayer, E. A., Toga, A. W., Thompson, P. M., & Luders, E. (2013). The right inhibition? Callosal correlates of hand performance in healthy children and adolescents callosal correlates of hand performance. *Human Brain Mapping, 34*, 2259–2265.

Lebel, C., & Beaulieu, C. (2009). Lateralization of arcuate fasciculus from childhood to adulthood and its relation to cognitive abilities in children. *Human Brain Mapping, 30*, 3563–3573.

Li, G., Nie, J., Li, W., Shi, F., Lyan, A. E., Lin, W., et al. (2014). Mapping longitudinal hemispheric structural asymmetries of the human cerebral cortex from birth to 2 years of age. *Cerebral Cortex, 24*, 1289–1300.

Lloyd-Fox, S., Blasi, A., Volein, A., Everdell, N., Elwell, C. E., & Johnson, M. H. (2009). Social perception in infancy: A near infrared spectroscopy study. *Child Development, 80*, 986–999.

MacDonald, P. A., Ganjavi, H., Collins, D. L., Evans, A. C., & Karama, S. (2014). Investigating the relation between striatal volume and IQ. *Brain Imaging and Behavior, 8*, 52–59.

Mackey, A. P., Whitaker, K. J., & Bunge, S. A. (2012). Experience-dependent plasticity in white matter microstructure: Reasoning training alters structural connectivity. *Frontiers in Neuroanatomy, 6*, 32. doi:10.3389/fnana.2012.00032.

MacNeilage, P. F. (2014). Evolution of the strongest vertebrate rightward action asymmetries: Marine mammal sidedness and human handedness. *Psychological Bulletin, 140*, 587–609.

Marinsek, N., Turner, B. O., Gazzaniga, M., & Miller, M. B. (2014). Divergent hemispheric reasoning strategies: Reducing uncertainty versus resolving inconsistency. *Frontiers in Human Neuroscience, 8*, 839. doi:10.3389/fnhum.2014.00839.

McCartney, G., & Hepper, P. G. (1999). Developmental of lateralised behavior in the human fetus from 12 to 27 weeks' gestation. *Developmental Medicine and Child Neurology, 41*, 83–86.

McManus, C. (2002). *Right hand, left hand*. London: Weidenfeld & Nicolson.

Michel, G. F., Babik, I., Nelson, E. L., Campbell, J. M., & Marcinowski, E. C. (2013). How the development of handedness could contribute to the development of language. *Developmental Psychobiology, 55*, 608–620.

Michel, G. F., Babik, I., Shue, C.-F., & Campbell, J. M. (2013). Latent classes in the developmental trajectories of infant handedness. *Developmental Psychology, 50*, 349–359.

Minagawa-Kawai, Y., Cristià, A., & Dupoux, E. (2011). Cerebral lateralization and early speech acquisition: A developmental scenario. *Developmental Cognitive Neuroscience, 1*, 217–232.

Missana, M., & Grossmann, T. (2014). Infants' emerging sensitivity to emotional body expressions: Insights from asymmetrical frontal brain activity. *Developmental Psychology, 51*, 151–160.

Morange-Majoux, F., & Devouche, E. (2014). Social encouragement can influence manual preference in 6 month-old-infants. *Frontiers in Psychology, 5*, 1225. doi:10.3389/fpsyg.2014.01225.

Morange-Majoux, F., Lemoine, C., & Dellatolas, G. (2013). Early manifestations of manual specialization in infants: A longitudinal study from 20 to 30 weeks. *Laterality, 18*, 231–250.

Morillon, B., Lehongre, K., Frackowiak, R. S., Ducorps, A., Kleinschmidt, A., Poeppel, D., et al. (2010). Neurophysiological origin of human brain asymmetry for speech and language. *Proceedings of the National Academy of Sciences USA, 107*, 18688–18693.

Nagy, E., Pal, A., & Orvos, H. (2014). Learning to imitate individual finger movements by the human neonate. *Developmental Science, 17*, 841–857.

Nakato, E., Otsuka, Y., Kanazawa, S., Yamaguchi, M. K., & Kakigi, R. (2011). Distinct differences in the pattern of hemodynamic response to happy and angry facial expressions in infants—a near-infrared spectroscopic study. *NeuroImage, 54*, 1600–1606.

Nee, D. E., Brown, J. W., Askren, M. K., Berman, M. G., Demiralp, E., Krawitz, A., et al. (2012). A meta-analysis of executive components of working memory. *Cerebral Cortex, 23*, 264–282.

Nelson, E. L., Campbell, J. M., & Michel, G. F. (2013). Unimanual to bimanual: Tracking the development of handedness from 6 to 24 months. *Infant Behavior and Development, 36*, 181–188.

Nuñez, S. C., Dapretto, M., Katzir, T., Starr, A., Bramen, J., Kan, E., et al. (2011). fMRI of syntactic processing in typically developing children: Structural correlates in the inferior frontal gyrus. *Developmental Cognitive Neuroscience, 1*, 313–323.

O'Connor, D. A., Upton, D. J., Moore, J., & Hester, R. (2014). Motivationally significant self-control: Enhanced action withholding involves the right inferior frontal junction. *Journal of Cognitive Neuroscience, 27*, 112–123.

Ocklenburg, S., Beste, C., & Güntürkün, O. (2013). Handedness: A neurogenetic shift of perspective. *Neuroscience and Biobehavioral Reviews, 37*, 2788–2793.

Ocklenburg, S., Ness, V., Güntürkün, O., Suchan, B., & Beste, C. (2013). Response inhibition is modulated by functional cerebral asymmetries for facial expression perception. *Frontiers in Psychology, 4*, 879. doi:10.3389/fpsyg.2013.00879.

Otsuka, Y., Nakato, E., Kanazawas, S., Yamaguchi, M. K., Watanabe, S., & Kakigi, R. (2007). Neural activation to upright and inverted faces in infants measured by near infrared spectroscopy. *NeuroImage, 34*, 399–406.

Paulus, M., Kühn-Popp, M., Licata, M., Sodian, B., & Meinhardt, J. (2013). Neural correlates of prosocial behavior in infancy: Different neurophysiological mechanisms support the emergence of helping and comforting. *NeuroImage, 66*, 522–530.

Piaget, J. (1941/1952). *The child's conception of number*. London: Kegan Paul, Trench, & Trubner.

Pluess, M., & Belsky, J. (2013). Vantage sensitivity: Individual differences in response to positive experiences. *Psychological Bulletin, 139*, 901–916.

Preslar, J., Kushner, H. I., Marino, L., & Pearce, B. (2014). Autism, lateralization, and handedness: A review of the literature and meta-analysis. *Laterality, 19*, 64–95.

Rat-Fischer, L., O'Regan, J. K., & Fagard, J. (2013). Handedness in infants' tool use. *Developmental Psychobiology, 55*, 860–868.

Ratnarajah, N., Rifkin-Graboi, A., Fortier, M. V., Chong, Y. S., Kwek, K., Saw, S. M., et al. (2014). Structural connectivity asymmetry in the neonatal brain. *NeuroImage, 75*, 187–194.

Reid, C. S., & Serrien, D. J. (2012). Handedness and the excitability of cortical inhibitory circuits. *Behavioral Brain Research, 230*, 144–148.

Reissland, N., Francis, B., Aydin, E., Mason, J., & Exley, K. (2014). Development of prenatal lateralization: Evidence from fetal mouth movements. *Physiology & Behavior, 131*, 160–163.

Rogers, L. J., Zucca, P., & Vallortigara, G. (2004). Advantages of having a lateralized brain. *Proceedings of the Royal Society B: Biological Science, 271*, S420–S422.

Rönnqvist, L., & Domellöf, E. (2006). Quantitative assessment of right and left reaching movements in infants: A longitudinal study from 6 to 36 months. *Developmental Psychobiology, 48*, 444–459.

Rosch, R. E., Bishop, D. V., & Badcock, N. A. (2012). Lateralised visual attention is unrelated to language lateralisation, and not influenced by task difficulty–a functional transcranial Doppler study. *Neuropsychologia, 50*, 810–815.

Rubia, K., Russell, T., Overmeyer, S., Brammer, M. J., Bullmore, E. T., Sharma, T., et al. (2001). Mapping motor inhibition: Conjunctive brain activations across different versions of go/no-go and stop tasks. *NeuroImage, 13*, 250–261.

Sacrey, L-A., Arnold, B., Whishaw, I. Q., & Gonzales, C. L. (2013). Precocious hand use preference in reach-to-eat behavior versus manual construction in 1- to 5-year-old children. *Developmental Psychobiology, 55*, 902–911.

Sainburg, R. L. (2014). Convergent models of handedness and brain lateralization. *Frontiers in Psychology, 5*, 1092. doi:10.3389/fpsyg.2014.01092.

Scharoun, S. M., & Bryden, P. J. (2014). Hand preference, performance abilities, and hand selection in children. *Frontiers in Psychology, 5*, 82. doi:10.3389/fpsyg.2014.00082.

Schmidt, L. A. (1999). Frontal brain electrical activity in shyness and sociability. *Psychological Science, 10*, 316–320.

Schmidt, L. A., Shahinfar, A., & Fox, N. A. (1996). Regional brain electrical activity (EEG) in toddlers' externalizing problems. *Infant Behavior and Development, 19*, 75.

Serrien, D. J., & Sovijävi-Spapé, M. M. (2013). Cognitive control of response inhibition and switching: Hemispheric lateralization and hand preference. *Brain and Cognition, 82*, 283–290.

Shackman, A. J., McMenamin, B. W., Maxwell, J. S., Greischar, L. L., & Davidson, R. J. (2009). Right dorsolateral prefrontal cortical activity and behavioral inhibition. *Psychological Science, 20*, 1500–1506.

Sheridan, M., Kharitonova, M., Martin, R. E., Chatterjee, A., & Gabrieli, J. D. E. (2014). Neural substrates of the development of cognitive control in children ages 5–10 years. *Journal of Cognitive Neuroscience, 26*, 1840–1850.

Shobe, E. R. (2014). Independent and collaborative contributions of the cerebral hemispheres to emotional processing. *Frontiers in Human Neuroscience, 8*, 230. doi:10.3389/fnhum.2014.00230.

Smith, N. A., Gibilisco, C. R., Meisinger, R. E., & Hankey, M. (2013). Asymmetry in infants' selective attention to facial features during visual processing of infant-directed speech. *Frontiers in Psychology, 4*, 601. doi:10.3389/fpsyg.2013.00601.

Streri, A. (2002). Hand preference in 4-month-old infants: Global or local processing of objects in the haptic mode. *Current Psychology Letters, 7*, 39–50.

Streri, A., & de Hevia, M. D. (2015). Manual lateralization in infancy. *Frontiers in Psychology, 5*, 1575. doi:10.3389/fpsyg.2014.01575.

Streri, A., & Gentaz, E. (2004). Crossmodal recognition of shape from hand to eyes and handedness in human newborns. *Neuropsychologia, 42*, 1365–1369.

Sun, T., Patoine, C., Abu-Khalil, A., Visvader, J., Sum, E., Cherry, T. J., et al. (2005). Early asymmetry of gene transcription in embryonic human left and right cerebral cortex. *Science, 308*, 1794–1798.

Talelli, P., Ewas, A., Waddingham, W., Rothwell, J. C., & Ward, N. S. (2008). Neuro correlates of age-related changes in cortical neurophysiology. *NeuroImage, 40*, 1772–1781.

Turken, A. U., & Dronkers, N. F. (2011). The neural architecture of the language comprehension network: Converging evidence from lesion and connectivity analyses. *Frontiers in Systems Neuroscience, 5*, 1. doi:10.3389/fnsys.2011.00001.

Van Dongen, S., Galis, F., Broek, C. T., Heikinheimo, K., Wijnaendts, L. C. D., Delen, S., et al. (2014). When right differs from left: Human limb directional asymmetry emerges during very early development. *Laterality, 19*, 591–601.

Vauclair, J., & Cochet, H. (2013). Hand preference for pointing and language development in toddlers. *Developmental Psychobiology, 55*, 757–765.

Ververs, I. A. P., de Vries, J. I. P., van Geijn, H. P., & Hopkins, B. (1994). Prenatal head position from 12 to 38 weeks. 1. Developmental aspects. *Early Human Development, 39*, 83–91.

Vidal, J., Mills, T., Pang, E. W., & Taylor, M. J. (2012). Response inhibition in adults and teenagers: Spatiotemporal differences in prefrontal cortex. *Brain and Cognition, 79*, 49–59.

Vingerhoets, G., Acke, F., Alderweireldt, A. S., Nys, J., Vandemaele, P., & Achten, E. (2012). Cerebral lateralization of praxis in right- and left-handedness: Same pattern, different strength. *Human Brain Mapping, 33*, 763–777.

Wechsler, D. (1997). *Wechsler Adult Intelligence Test administration and scoring manual*. San Antonio, TX: The Psychological Corporation.

Wechsler, D. (1999). *Wechsler Abbreviated Scale of Intelligence (WASI)*. San Antonio, TX: The Psychological Corporation.

Wilbourn, M. P., Gottfried, A. W., & Kee, D. W. (2011). Consistency of hand-preference across the early years: Long-term relationship to verbal intelligence and reading achievement in girls. *Developmental Psychology, 47*, 931–942.

Wright, L., & Hardie, S. M. (2011). "Not ready to sort it yet": Revised reinforcement sensitivity theory (rRST) predicts left-handed behavioral inhibition during a manual sorting task. *Laterality, 16*, 753–767.

Yaakoby-Rotem, S., & Geva, R. (2014). Asymmetric attention networks: The case of children. *Journal of the International Neuropsychological Society, 20*, 434–443.

Young, G. (2011). *Development and causality: Neo-Piagetian perspectives*. New York: Springer Science+Business Media.

Young, G., & Gagnon, M. (1990). Neonatal laterality, birth stress, familial sinistrality, and left brain inhibition. *Developmental Neuropsychology, 6*, 127–150.

Yu, V. Y., MacDonald, M. J., Oh, A., Hua, G. N., De Nil, L. F., & Pang, E. W. (2014). Age-related sex differences in language lateralization: A magnetoencephalography study in children. *Developmental Psychology, 50*, 2276–2284.

Zangl, R., & Mills, D. L. (2007). Increased brain activity to infant-directed speech in 6- and 13-month-old infants. *Infancy, 11*, 31–62.

The Genetics Revolution 9

Chapter Introduction

The area of genetic research is evolving at a dizzying speed and differentiating into multiple -omics (including genomics and epigenomics). The search for candidate genes to help explain the origins of specific disorders has given way to multifactorial approaches in the genes studied and in the disorders investigated in any one study. Some of the research methods include GWAS and GCTA. A central concern in the area is the "missing heritability" problem, which the chapter addresses for intelligence, in particular.

The classic approach of Nature interacting with Nurture, and even the behavioral genetic approach of seeking Gene × Environment (G × E) interactions, are approaches that are rapidly being replaced by more nuanced ones that are consistent with the complexity of genetic influences on behavior. In this regard, to complement the search for the genome, I suggest that behavioral geneticists search for each species their "phenome," or the collection of phenotypes characterizing any one species. The relationship between the genome and the proposed phenome for a species will be mapped better as the burgeoning research in the field continues to expand. To conclude the chapter, I refer to the importance of evolvability and versatility.

Introduction

Genes are expanses on our DNA that regulate protein production, leading to the construction of our body and brain. However, genes do not construct our mind. Moreover, the environment has much influence in how our genes regulate the production of our morphology, including our brain. Factors such as the newly-discovered epigenesis, let alone what we know about early present toxins, radiation, and other negative influences that affect early brain development, affect the genetic program so that we are not merely reflections uniquely of its straightforward unfolding. However, both genes and environment are passive controls in the causality of our behavior and, as we develop, we can take an increasing active, agentic role in determining who we are and what we want to become. Nevertheless, our causality lies in the grounding of both our genes and the environment, and knowledge of their role in our behavioral causality is important in order to help us find our place as agents beyond them in the determination of our behavior.

G. Young, *Unifying Causality and Psychology*, DOI 10.1007/978-3-319-24094-7_9

Neogenomics and G × E

Introduction

Boyce and Kobor (2015) indicated that gene–environment interplay is comprised of at least three types of processes: Gene × Environment (G × E) interaction, gene–environment correlation (rGE), and epigenesis. The present chapter gives the background to delve into these topics.

Charney (2012) examined behavior genetics in the contexts of postgenomics and the paradigm shift that is taking place in genetics. Standard dogmas in genetics refer to DNA (deoxyribonucleic acid) as (a) the unchanging template of heredity; (b) identical in all cells/tissues; and (c) the sole agent in inheritance.

However, contemporary research has established that (a) as a template, DNA is subject to environmentally-induced change; (b) .somatic mosaicism characterizes cells/tissues (there are different genomes in different cells/tissues of the individual); and (c) the epigenome can be inherited via the germline, so that DNA is now understood as just one and not the only agent of inheritance. (In this regard, there is extranuclear mitochondrial DNA maternal, or non-Mendelian, transmission.) DNA is not fixed or sequenced at the time of conception. Rather, it is dynamic and altered by rearrangements, insertions, and deletions.

For example, in embryogenesis, retrotransposons, the putative "jumping genes," duplicate and insert themselves in a mobile way within the DNA sequence involved. About the epigenome, which is the system that regulates gene expression, and which is "highly environmental responsive," it can turn genes on and off and modify their "transcribability" and heritability, and also their intergenerational transmission, without affecting the DNA involved, per se. Because these new findings about epigenesis indicate that the phenotypic changes that they induce can be passed on intergenerationally, the process has been referred to as "Neo-Lamarckian" (e.g., Gissis & Jablonka, 2001) but without Lamarck.

Charney (2012) addressed the implications of these contemporary developments in genetics for the field of behavior genetics. He referred to the shifts in the field as "neogenetics" or "neogenomics" and not only "postgenomics." He stated that the major implication of this new area involves the "blurring" between genes and environment.

Terms

Charney (2012) provided some basic definitions worth noting. Genes are DNA segments that code for the production of RNA/proteins. Transcription allows for the translation of DNA into messenger RNA (mRNA) and then proteins. Copies of genes are called alleles, and normally they come in pairs, one maternal and one paternal. Paired alleles might be identical or might differ by as little as one nucleotide, with the subunits comprising the DNA molecule. If in the population an allele is rare (less than 1 %), it is considered a mutation. Otherwise, it is considered a polymorphism. When paired alleles are identical, we call them homozygous. Otherwise, they are heterozygous.

Mendelian inheritance refers to classic individual allele inheritance and also to the dominance–recessive relationship that they might express in phenotypes. Most psychological traits are multiallelic or polygenetic in biological origin, and so are not inherited in a classical Mendelian manner (with notable exceptions in monogenetic disorders).

Heritability is defined as the proportion of phenotypic variance that is attributable to genotypic variance in a particular population at a given time. [Note it is a population statistic, not an individual one, so the total genotypic and non-genetic variance involved can be additive. In this regard, at the individual level, we do not consider that genetic and environmental contributions to the phenotype are additive; rather, we consider them multiplicative, e.g., Nature × Nurture.]

Behavior Genetics

In behavior genetics, studies typically examine biological twins, adoptees, and families for phenotypic concordances and discordances between/among subjects in relation to their presumed degree of genetic similarity/dissimilarity. The commonest modeling technique for V_P, the total phenotypic variation for a trait, partitions it into additive contributions from genetic (genotypic) and environmental variation (V_C and V_E, respectively). It is acknowledged that the model is a simplification—there are non-additive genetic effects, e.g., dominance–recessive interactions among alleles at a single locus; epistatic interactions across alleles at a different locus; and gene–environment interactions between alleles and the environment (G×E). G×E interactions are central to the study of behavior genetics. Aside from heritability research, the field has proliferated with gene or GWAS, which investigate whether single nucleotide polymorphisms (SNPs) differ in individuals with and without a trait of interest.

Charney (2012) continued that germline inheritance concerns genetic information transmission through sexual reproduction but, in contrast, somatic inheritance takes place postconception when changes in non-gametic DNA are passed on via mitosis. The genome includes up to 50 % of transposable jumping genes, most of which are retrotransposons. They have a critical influence on the transcriptome, or transcription output of the genome.

SNPs and CNVs

DNA variation is marked by SNPs. However, structural variations (SVs) increasingly are being given prominence in the literature. They are changes in the chromosomal architecture due to deletions, insertions, duplications, and inversions, in particular. CNVs are submicroscopic "copy number variations." They consist of at least 1000 consecutive base pairs in DNA that are either deleted or multiply copied. Many are polymorphic, and are referred to as "copy number polymorphisms." Sometimes they consist of multiple deletions or copies of whole genes, which average up to 60,000 base pairs (CNVs average 250,000 base pairs). CNVs constitute a major force in intraindividual and interindividual variation and in phylogenetic evolution. CNVs have been identified as potential causal elements in several behavior disorders (autism spectrum disorder, schizophrenia, and ADHD; among others, the former two mentioned have been associated with mitochondrial DNA, as well).

Epigenetics

Charney (2012) proceeded to discuss the epigenome. He defined epigenetics in terms of heritable changes that take place without alteration of DNA sequences, e.g., by gene silencing, so that the genes are not transcribed. Epigenetic modifications can be environmentally contingent, responding to environmental input. The term "environmental epigenomics" has been created to reflect the constant interplay between the epigenome and the environment. Note that the environment might be exogenous (external) or endogenous (i.e., internal, e.g., hormonal).

The most studied epigenetic mechanisms are DNA methylation, histone modification, and expression of non-coding micro RNAs (see Table 9.1). It is worthwhile to consider Charney's (2012) detailed but accessible description of epigenetic mechanisms. Nuclear DNA, as opposed to mitochondrial DNA, wrap around a core of histone proteins. Their tails or strands wrap around the DNA molecule. In the process of histone modification, the processes of acetylation, methylation, and phosphorylation are the primary modes in the chemical modifications involved. They alter the histone structure to either facilitate or inhibit access of the DNA to transcription factors. In DNA methylation, a methyl group is added to cystine–guanine (C–G) dinucleotides, thereby barring transcriptional activity. Noncoding (including micro RNA) epigenetic modification does not concern transcription, but regulates gene silencing, nonetheless, by binding to messenger RNA post-transcriptionally. Behavioral epigenetic studies have shown that epigenetic modifications contribute to abnormal gene expression in neuropsychiatric disorders, such as in people with autism and schizophrenia.

As shown by Charney (2012; see Fig. 9.1), epigenetic stamps or marks even can lead to activated/silenced genetic/epigenetic differences in

Table 9.1 Primary epigenetic modifications and pathways

Mechanism	Description
DNA methylation	DNA is wrapped around histone proteins for packaging in the nucleus. Methyl groups are added to cytosines on DNA by way of DNA methyltransferases (DNMTs), and the subsequent binding of methyl-CpG-binding protein 2 (*MeCP2*) can either recruit histone deacetylases (*HDAC*s) or other corepressors to repress transcription or transcription factors like *CREB1* to promote transcription
Histone modification	Posttranslational modifications to histone H3 include lysine (K) acetylation and methylation (for clarity, only lysines and their modifications discussed). Histone acetyltransferases (HATs) facilitate gene activation by adding acetyl groups, which loosen chromatin packaging to allow for transcription factors to bind. HDACs remove acetyl groups, and therefore repress transcription and silence a gene. Histone methyltransferases (HMTs) and histone demethylases (HDMs) catalyze lysine methylation and demethylation, respectively, and their effects on gene transcription or suppression depend upon which basic residue is targeted and the degree of methylation
MicroRNA processing	The binding of microRNAs (miRNAs) to target mRNA can induce gene silencing. The molecular cascade of events that leads to gene silencing begins with the presence of a primary miRNA (pri-miRNA) transcript, which is cleaved in the nucleus by a microprocessor complex containing the Rnase III Drosha and the RNA-binding protein DGCR8 (DiGeorge critical region 8). The binding of DGCR8 and cleaving action of Drosha in the nucleus are critical in the initiation of miRNA biogenesis, and malfunction of either of these proteins interferes with the generation of mature miRNAs. After processing in the nucleus, the immature pre-miRNA is transported to the cytoplasm via the Exportin-5 (Exp5) pathway, in which the Exp5, in combination with its cofactor Ran-GTP, binds the pre-miRNA and induces nuclear export. In the cytoplasm, the Rnase III Dicer cleaves the pre-miRNA into a mature miRNA duplex, and deletion of Dicer decreases and even eliminates mature and functional miRNAs produced in the cytoplasm. After cleavage by Dicer, the newly mature miRNA duplex is loaded into an Argonaute (Ago) protein of the RNA-induced silencing complex (RISC). Once loaded, the RISC binds to the target mRNA, facilitating gene silencing via mRNA degradation, destabilization, or translational inhibition

Adopted with permission of John Wiley & Sons. Blaze, J., & Roth, T. L. (2013). Epigenetic mechanisms in learning and memory. *Wiley Interdisciplinary Reviews: Cognitive Science*, *4*, 105–115. Copyright © 2013 and John Wiley & Sons, Inc. Reproduced with permission of John Wiley & Sons, Inc. [Excerpt from Figure 1 Text, Page 107]

monozygotic co-twins. All of the various components of the neogenome—retroposons, CNVs, mitochondrial DNA, epigenetics, and aneuploidy (i.e., other than the typical diploidy)—indicate that although it constitutes a distinct class of "heritable agents," it does not concern specifically either G (genes) or E (environment) alone, or their G×E interaction. Therefore, heritability studies that seek heritability estimates, G×E interactions, etc., might not constitute valid approaches.

Programming

Prenatal programming is an important area of study in the field. For example, prenatal stress has developmental consequences, and research is revealing that, in animal models, first-trimester stress is associated with hypermethylation of the glucocorticoid receptor (GR) promoter in the hypothalamus, with reduced methylation of the corticotrophin releasing factor (CRF) promoter in the amygdala, and so on.

GWAS

Charney (2012) returned to the assumptions underlying gene association studies, and found them wanting. Because of three factors, in particular, ((a) somatic mosaicism, (b) epigenesis, and (c) a lack of specific allele-specific protein production relations), GWAS studies are not as productive as first hoped. [In this regard, Chabris et al. (2012) found that most reported genetic associations with general intelligence (*g*) were not replicated in data sets taken from three major studies involving almost 10,000 subjects.]

About the latter of the three points, genes in humans might contain several DNA sequences coding for amino acids (exons) that are interspersed with noncoding regions (introns).

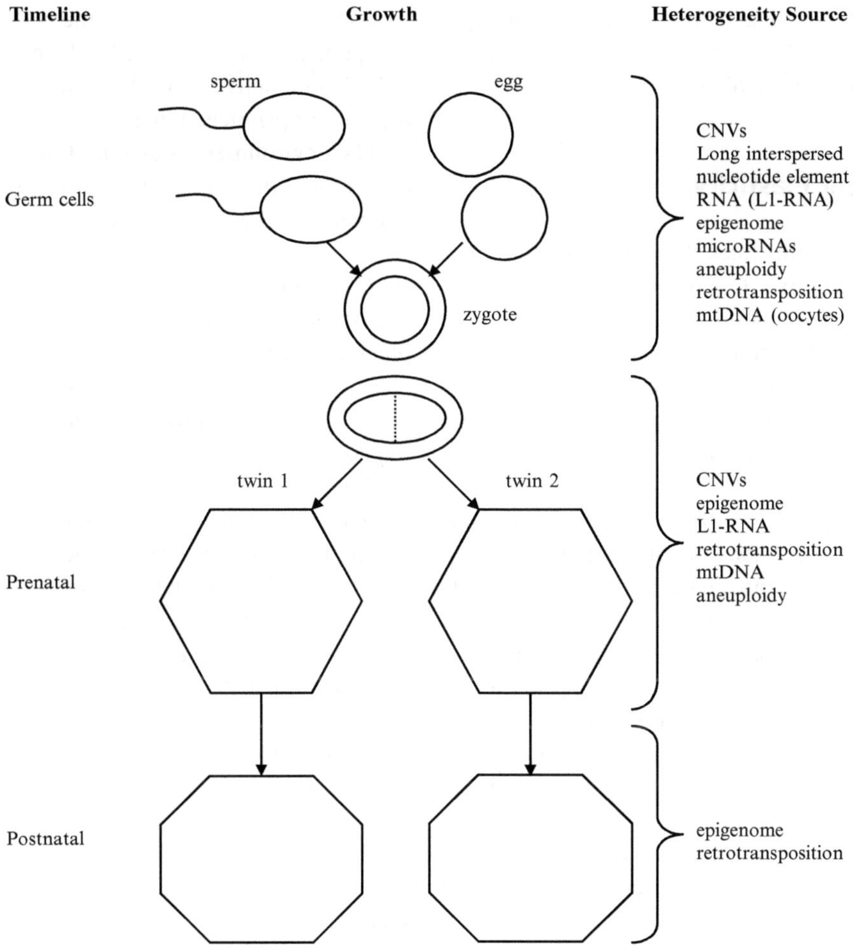

Fig. 9.1 Overview of several sources of genetic and epigenetic heterogeneity between germ cells of the same two individuals and between monozygotic co-twins. Germ cells: spermatocytes exhibit interindividual variation in L1-RNA, copy number variations (CNVs), epigenetic profiles, and microRNAs (miRNAs) (as well as smaller differences in aneuploidy). Oocytes exhibit interindividual variation in L1-RNA, CNVs, epigenetic profiles, and miRNAs, as well as significant differences in mitochondrial DNA (mtDNA) and aneuploidy. Environmental inputs influencing germ cell variation may include maternal stress, activity, diet, and environmental toxins. Prenatal environment: splitting of the zygote into two (monozygotic twins): CNVs, aneuploidy, mtDNA partitioning and heteroplasmy, L1 retrotransposition, and the epigenome develop non-identically in the two twin embryos. Prenatal environmental inputs that may affect any of these phenomena in the prenatal environment may include maternal stress, anxiety, depression, diet, activity, (prenatal) environmental toxins, intrauterine position effects, and chorion effects. Postnatal environment: intertwin discordance due to difference epigenomes and differences in ongoing retrotransposition resulting from neurogenesis in the hippocampus. The epigenomes of the twins are depicted as being substantially different due to differences in life experiences and environments. Adopted with permission of Cambridge University Press. Charney, E. (2012). Behavior genetics and postgenomics. *Behavioral and Brain Sciences*, *35*, 331–410; with kind permission from Cambridge University Press. [Figure 2, Page 343]

In the process of gene transcription, first, pre-messenger RNA is copied. When pre-mRNA exons combine in different ways to form different proteins, the process is referred to as "alternate splicing." Therefore, as understood now, a single particular gene can potentially code for multiple rather than one protein, indicating protein diversity and molecular plasticity, e.g., in the brain. Moreover, even monogenetic disorders do not simply express one phenotype, because they are complex traits, although the phenotypic differences involved do not mean that there are different diseases involved.

Phenotypic Plasticity

This example illustrates the prevalence of "phenotypic plasticity." Organisms inherit not only genes but also ecological niches that optimize developmental, life-course adaptive (survival and reproductive) strategies (Pigliucci, 2010). Developmental plasticity is fostered by "maternal programming," as happens in "intergenerationally-transmitted epigenetic modifications." The mother is capable of adjusting offspring phenotype in response to the environment, transmitting to them adaptive information, for example, differentially expressing one epigenetic pathway to best match a particular ongoing environmental condition and passing on that information adaptively to offspring because, normally, the particular environmental condition should continue in the next generation. Parental investment itself might be compromised in harsh environments, so that instead of high-quality parenting, as might obtain in supportive environments and reduced reproduction rate, the adaptive strategy involved leads to quantitative reproductive strategies, or accelerated mating, which epigenetically might be programmed in offspring as per differential life history models (e.g., Ellis, 2004).

Causality

In the last section of his informative article, Charney (2012) considered postgenomics and causation. There are both bottom-up and top-down influences in biological systems that are evident (respectively, related to the molecular level, and all other levels, from the cellular to the organism and environment) (Noble, 2010; Shapiro, 2009; Srividhya, Li, & Pomerening, 2011). The influences are reciprocally causal, and pervade the different levels of the hierarchical system involved through feedback and feed-forward loops. The genome is a critical component of this "exceedingly complex, integrated, interactive, multilevel process," but not the only or privileged one.

The environment is essential, too, in the various -omics in neogenetics. In the postgenomic perspective, the environment functions as a carrier/transmitter of information at the DNA sequence in terms of shaping both phenotypes and information that can help predict specific phenotypes. Gene expression varies greatly stochastically, and genetic "hyperdiversity" might be the rule that allows an adaptive phenotypic hyperdiversity.

Similarly, epigenomic function also is highly stochastic, in that gene promoters can vary greatly in epigenetic state, to the point that quantum mechanical models are being used in the context of probability landscape models of epigenetic states. They are considered as stochastic networks that are not simply modeled by computational approaches. To conclude, Charney (2012) noted that these types of genetic and epigenetic stochastic processes might have served rapid evolution (Feinberg & Irizarry, 2010).

Comment

Charney (2012) has provided an essential introduction to the field of the new area of neogenomics. It gives the tools for understanding the basics in gene expression, epigenetics, the effects of the environment on genes, and the complex system involved in phenotypic expression and plasticity. Monogenetic control of behavior is rare and does not apply to complex psychological behavior.

Chabris, Lee, Cesarini, Benjamin, and Laibson (2015) noted that GWAS studies allow for explanation of the genetics underlying behavior, but that any behavioral trait associated with genes does so through many genetic variants. Furthermore, each of them accounts for only a minimal percentage of the behavioral variability involved. Chabris et al. (2015) referred to this effect as the fourth law of behavior genetics.

Genetics and Behavior

Introduction

Berger (2011) provided a tutorial on genetics. DNA is a molecule that includes genes, which are DNA portions that code for the production of protein (after transcription). Codons are trinucleotide units that genetically code for an amino acid; amino acids are constituents of proteins. The nucleotides in a codon consist of guanine, adenine, thymine, and cytosine (G, A, T, C). DNA consists of a chain of paired molecules that typically take the form of a double-stranded helix. G, A, T, and C form the bases of the strands and are paired in exclusive complementary pairs—A–T and C–G. The particular sequence of bases along DNA strands provides the code for transcribing particular proteins. In transcription/translation, DNA leads to the synthesis of messenger ribonucleic acid (mRNA), which leads to the production of polypeptides and proteins. The coding region of a gene begins with the initiation codon (usually ATG) and ends with a termination codon (TAA, TAG, or TGA).

Human DNA consists of 23 pairs of chromosomes, 22 of which are autosomes and one pair of which is constituted by the sex chromosomes X and Y. A chromosome has a central centromere and four arms—the short pair is designated *p* and the long arm *q*. The genes' cytogenetic location on the arms refers to the band it occupies on an arm. In the standardized format for representing genes, the first alphanumeric code indicates the chromosome number involved, the second indicates the arm, and the third and fourth indicate the specific position on the arm, that is, designating a region and the band itself, with increased numbering indicating increased distance from the centromere involved (e.g., *7q21*). There might be a decimal place and more digits if there is a sub-band involved.

[As mentioned previously, typically, genes are divided into exon and intron regions, with only the former found in mRNA transcripts. Genes vary in form, consisting of different alleles. Variation is determined by a number of factors, including the number of repetitions (variable number of random repeats, VNTR).]

Dopamine Genes

Berger (2011) examined several dopamine genes related to self-regulation. The dopamine D4 receptor (*DRD4* gene) is located on chromosome 11 at 11p15. Dopamine constitutes an important neurotransmitter. The *DRD4* polymorphism most studied is in exon III, in which the base pair sequence represents a VNTR, and for which the most frequent allelic variations are the 4-repeat and the 7-repeat alleles. The polymorphism is involved in dopamine receptor function.

The 7-repeat allele has been associated with particular behavioral tendencies related to self-regulation from early after birth onward. In particular, studies of diverse selected and executive attention skills have shown an association in self-regulation and the *DRD4* 7-repeat allele (e.g., Posner, Rothbart, & Sheese, 2007; using the Attention Network Task, ANT). The allele also has been associated with disorganized attachment, and especially in conjunction with the −521 C/T polymorphism in the regulatory region of the gene (Lakatos et al., 2000, 2002).

Another dopamine gene related to self-regulation via attention is catechol-*O*-methyltransferase (*COMT*). It codes in the process of clearing dopamine from extracellular space after the release of this neurotransmitter into synaptic space. The *COMT* enzyme involved appears to work especially in the prefrontal cortex (PFC). Its location is in 22q11. A variation in the G/A base pair at codon 158 of the gene allows dopamine to stay longer in extracellular space, especially in the PFC, and another, the valine allele, has been associated with effects on attention (positive and negative, respectively).

Another dopamine gene for which variants have been related to self-regulation is the *DAT1*; it codes for the dopamine transporter. The risk allele involved is 480-bp (also called 10R), a VNTR at 5p15.3. The gene is expressed especially in the basal ganglia.

Finally, the monoamine oxidase (*MAOA*) gene is located on chromosome X at Xp11. It codes for enzymes involved in catalyzation of biogenic amines, including dopamine, serotonin, and another neurotransmitter, norepinephrine. Research has specified several *MAOA* polymorphisms involved in attention (e.g., C vs. T; 4-repeat length polymorphism in *MAOA* promoter region (LPR), vs. 3-repeat).

G×G

Gene–gene (G×G) interactions are also important to consider in self-regulation. Berger (2011) specified that interactions involving the serotonin transporter gene (*5-HTT*) and different dopamine genes affect self-regulation related behavior. In particular, the allelic variation involved is *5-HTTLPR*, which could be short (*s*) or long (*l*). It is a repetition in the promoter regulatory region of the gene. Schmidt, Fox, and Hamer (2007) reported that 7-year-olds scoring higher on a checklist that measures internalizing and externalizing behavior had long *DRD4* alleles and one or more risk *5-HTT* alleles.

G×E

Moreover, G×E interactions are ones that are relevant to understanding self-regulation. Bakermans-Kranenburg and van IJzendoorn (2006) and Sheese, Voelker, Rothbart, and Posner (2007) found that externalizing/temperament (sensation seeking) in children was affected by maternal sensitivity/parenting quality and also the presence of the 7-repeat allele of *DRD4*. Other G×E interactions have been shown for *MAOA* (Caspi et al., 2002) and *5-HTT* (Caspi et al., 2003; Fox et al., 2005).

Attention and Genes

Ristic and Enns (2015) promoted a dynamic view of attention in development, in that it is taken to both influence and be influenced by interactions between the individual and environment. Attention mediates between environment and behavior by influencing and being influenced by sensory cues and by the person, factors that include goals and consciousness, respectively.

The dynamic attentional model is consistent with the one of Johnson et al. (2005) of interactive specialization. In the latter model, the environment facilitates brain development through person–environment interactions. Brain regions supportive of the behavior involved continually mature in these interactions along with the relevant interregional connections (through their reorganization). This point of view contrasts with the traditional one in which developing behavioral function is mapped onto developing brain structure.

Consistent with Berger (2011), who referred to the importance of attentional mechanisms, Posner, Rothbart, Sheese, and Voelker (2012) provided evidence for a neural control network in early development related to attentional processes. In particular, they highlighted an infant brain network underlying attentional orienting to sensory events, and including areas of the superior and inferior parietal lobe and also the frontal eye fields. The proposed network "provides the chief means" of infant self-regulation. The network appears moderated by the nicotinic cholinergic system based in the nucleus basalis.

With development, by 3–4 years of age, the executive network takes over in control and other neuromodulators are involved. Specifically, executive attentional control of cognition and emotion in self-regulation becomes focused in the brain network that includes areas of the anterior cingulate gyrus, anterior insula, and basal ganglia, as well as parts of the PFC and connections of the network to more remote brain areas. The executive attention network is neuromodulated primarily by the dopaminergic system based in the ventral tegmental area.

A third network is involved in attention, the alerting network. It is modulated by the norepinephrine system. The orienting network is related to the frontoparietal network. The executive network shares brain regions with the cingulo-opercular network according to resting state fMRI studies (functional magnetic resonance imaging; Fair, Dosenbach, Petersen, & Schlagger, 2012; Gao et al., 2009). Intranetwork connectivity is sparse in the neonate and rapidly expands by 2 years of age, and later.

The authors discussed genetic underpinnings to the executive control system. They concern the *DRD4* gene and the *COMT* gene for the dopamine system and the *CHRNA4* (cholinergic receptor, nicotinic, alpha 4) gene for the cholinergic modulation. These links are not exclusive, and also environmental (parental) practices are involved according to the research (e.g., in the positive sense, perhaps by parents presenting objects and reading to young infants). The research undertaken by Posner et al. (2012) supported the notion of transition in attentional control networks early in life. Relevant longitudinal correlations on the measures used were found across the ages of 6–7 months and 4 years.

Reward and Genes

Berger (2011) had focused on genes regulating neurotransmitters in terms of attention. Others relate them to more downstream processes, such as reward. For example, Nikolova, Bogdan, and Hariri (2013) examined dopamine-related genes in terms of reward processing from a neurogenetic or a genetic/neuroimaging approach. Reward processing refers to collecting, storing, and utilizing information about the appetitive value of stimuli to promote survival and well-being. The brain regions involved form a distributed mesocorticostriatal circuitry critically regulated by dopamine, which is a neurotransmitter functioning as a mediator in the system. They described the dopamine signaling and metabolic activity of various polymorphisms that differentially affect areas of the reward processing neural circuitry (see Fig. 9.2).

Comment

Much of the remaining section of this portion of the chapter on genetics takes the same approach as Berger (2011) on the genetics of behavior. The research in the area is booming. As I describe the empirical literature, often I repeat for the reader

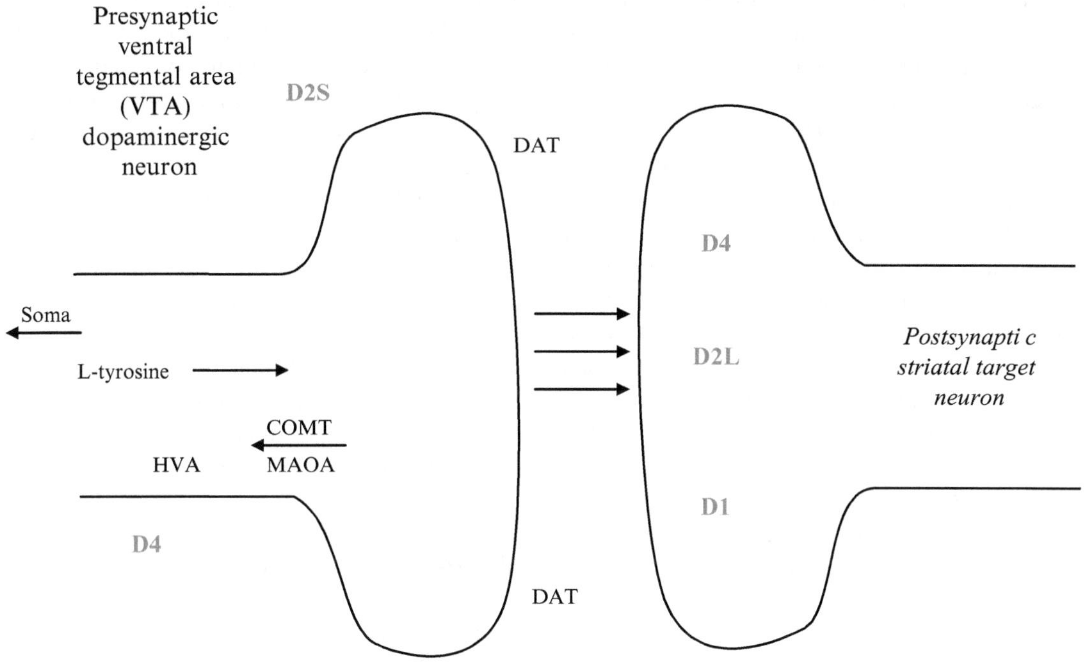

Fig. 9.2 Schematic representation of a dopaminergic synapse and the genes involved. The figure illustrates the multiple genes involved in the functioning of the dopamine neurotransmitter at the level of interneuronal synapses. *COMT*, catechol-*O*-methyltransferase; *D1*, *D2*, *D3*, *D4*, dopamine receptors; *D2L*, dopamine *D2* receptor long (postsynaptic) isoform; *D2S*, dopamine *D2* receptor short (presynaptic) isoform; *DAT*, dopamine transporter; *HVA*, homovanillic acid; *MAOA*, monoamine oxidase A. Adapted from Nikolova, Bogdan, and Hariri (2013)

that full name of the genes involved and their normative effects, before getting to either interactions with the environment, the behavioral difficulties with which they might be associated, and so on.

Applications

Introduction

This section of the present work contrasts (a) search for particular genes associated with particular psychiatric conditions with (b) search for multiple genes implicated in multiple conditions. The two approaches in genomic research should be considered complementary.

ADHD

The work on neural endophenotypes is bringing psychiatry closer to a genetically-mediated neurochemical and neuroanatomical basis for understanding psychiatric conditions. del Campo, Müller, and Sahakian (2012) focused on neuroimaging techniques in studies of ADHD. These measures provide data on ADHD that is more proximal to the susceptibility genes that might underpin the disorder. The two gene loci most associated with ADHD are the dopamine (DA) receptor type 4 (*DRD4*) and the DA transporter gene (*DAT1*) (e.g., Brookes et al., 2006). The neural circuitry often associated with ADHD involves (a) the distributed fronto-striato-cerebellar circuits, which are implicated in top-down cognitive control processes, and (b) the meso-cortico-limbic network, which appears to underlie motivational processes. These circuits are neuromodulated by catecholamines. Research is showing that, in adult ADHD, there appears to be decreased DAT as well as D_2/D_3 receptor availability in select subcortical regions of the left hemisphere.

ASC

Lombardo, Baron-Cohen, Belmonte, and Chakrabarti (2011) examined possible neural endophenotypes in autism spectrum conditions (ASC), specifically related to social behavior. According to the neuroimaging research, the dorsomedial prefrontal cortex (dMPFC) appears hypoactivated during theory of mind tasks in ASC. As well, other areas show similar hypoactivation in ASC social cognition and they comprise a complex neural circuit, including the ventral MPFC (vMPFC). Another circuit appears affected in ASC for face processing (e.g., including the amygdala). For the authors, the circuits reflect neural endophenotypes in ASC that index specific social impairments, with the vMPFC serving as a hub. Because of the hypoactivations discovered, other regions might compensate with hyperactivations (e.g., involved in nonsocial cognitive strategies).

As for the gene polymorphisms associated with neuroimaging results related to facial processing circuitry in ASC, they include the serotonin transporter gene (*SLC6A4*), the arginine vasopressin receptor 1A gene (*AVPR1A*), and the cannabinoid receptor, type 1 gene (*CNR1*).

Chakrabarti et al. (2009) studied genetic associations related to empathy in Asperger's syndrome, and 27 genes were discerned, falling into three classes: (a) social emotional responsivity related, i.e., genes coding for oxytocin and its receptor (*OXT*, *OXTR*); (b) neural growth and connectivity; and (c) sex steroid related. Given the deficits in social cognition in ASC, these genetic underpinnings to facial processing and empathy underscore its downstream, genetic base, and also its upstream neuroendophenotypic (intermediary to phenotypic expression) base.

Although the search for specific gene loci associated with specific disorders continues, others are taking a wider perspective. They seek multiple genes that might be simultaneously associated with multiple disorders.

Missing Heritability

Methodology Explains

Manuck and McCaffery (2014) noted that, despite much research on genetic variants in relation to behavioral phenotypes, only a small portion of its heritable variation has been accounted for (the missing heritability problem, as mentioned). One plausible explanation of the missing heritability problem lies in G×E interaction effects. Heritability estimates reflect the proportion of phenotypic variation attributable to individual genetic differences in a population (specific in time and (range of) environment).

Behavioral genetics uses linkage analysis to study gene–effect relations. It seeks variants in DNA sequence (potential markers) found in association with disease/disorder in pedigreed families having both affected and unaffected members. The method is limited in detecting variants with other than large effects. Diseases/disorders might involve multiple genetic variants each with small effects.

In the candidate gene method of study in molecular genetics, specific target genes considered associated with the disease/disorder can be studied outside of pedigreed families. Usually, in behavioral research, the genes relate to components of neurotransmission, neuroendocrine function, or other cellular processes in the pathway to disease/disorder. Either known allelic variants of gene polymorphisms or multiple polymorphisms are studied within the same gene (haplotypes). However, many candidate genes in putative relations with disease/disorder might be published with much fanfare, but they do not stand up to replication research.

GWAS uses probe for SNPs tagging common genetic variation. It can detect small genetic effects, but only with very large samples. GWAS research is often replicated well. GWAS that looks at common genetic contributions to major diseases/disorders (studied simultaneously) have accounted for up to 6 % of the variance in behavior disorders (Smoller, Kendler, & Craddock, 2013).

However, twin studies often find results with up to 50 % of individual differences in behavioral traits accounted for by genetic influences (but without being specific about the polymorphisms involved). This gap between the percentage of heritable differences explained by family research and GWAS research (the "missing heritability" problem) needs better research and explication.

That said, research is reducing the missing component in the knowledge about heritability for mental disease/disorder. For example, the technique of "genomewide complex trait analysis" (GCTA) has been applied to schizophrenia (Visscher, Goddard, Derks, & Wray, 2012), major depression (Lubke et al., 2012), intelligence (Chabris et al., 2012), and personality traits (e.g., Verweij et al., 2012). Respectively, the genetic variation estimated in the research explained up to 40 % of the variance in schizophrenia, 30 % in depression, 50 % in intelligence, and 12 % in personality. These percentages are approaching the heritability estimates associated with the behaviors/conditions.

Despite these improved results, there are still confounds in this type of research. For example, G×E interaction effects could "dilute" genetic main effects. G×E interaction involves genotype-dependent variation in phenotypic reaction to variations in conditions in the environment. The problem might not be with missing heritability but with missing the right questions to ask—main effect questions related to heritability, by definition, do not account for G by E interactions.

Hypercomplexity Explains

Introduction Richardson (2013) explored the possible reasons for "missing heritability"in relation to intelligence research. In behavior genetics, for intelligence, the "missing heritability" problem has remained intractable.

The heritability findings for intelligence based on twin studies and standard statistics (analysis of variance) suggest that over 50 % of normal variation in intelligence in the population can be attributed to genetic factors. Nevertheless, the search for the genetic substrate for the heritability of intelligence has been elusive, and Richardson (2013) suggested heritability has been eclipsed.

GWAS have sought variations in specific gene alleles and related variations in measure of intelligence, or IQ (intelligent quotient) scores. In GWAS, DNA is scanned at the level of SNPs. But despite early promise and hopes, molecular genetics has failed to identify reliably genetic underpinning that could explain the high heritability estimates for variation in IQ scores (Davis et al., 2010; Deary, Penke, & Johnson, 2010; Turkheimer, 2011).

Standard explanations for the missing heritability problem concern (a) the large number of genetic loci that must underly the noted variations, and also (b) the resultant massive research undertaken required to detect their cumulative effects (Plomin & Davis, 2009). However, explanations also range into ones that the high heritabilities involved are "phantom" and do not exist, e.g., are artifacts of twin studies or the approach in genetics to the matter (Zuk, Hechter, Sunyaeva, & Lander, 2012).

Richardson (2013) invoked the notion that the search for "missing heritability" in IQ research might be misplaced because of new approaches to understanding genetics, environment, and intelligence. In each case, the systems involved are considered complex and interdependent, with independent agency residing in neither genes nor environment.

Biointelligence Indeed, at the molecular level, Richardson (2013) referred to a "biointelligence." For example, cells in multicellular organisms encounter "storms" of signals from other cells and constantly adapt. Richardson termed the environment as providing "structure in experience" or "information in structure" even at the cellular level, thereby providing "structure-for-predictability" in complex environments. Cells negotiate their environments by abstracting underlying patterns and self-organizing ongoing states based on them. Remarkably, Richardson (2013) described cells as exhibiting "emergent" properties, such as highly-processed novel signal integration, feedback loops, and metabolic and developmental pathways (Hlavecek & Faeder, 2009; López-Maury, Marguerat, & Bähler, 2008).

Richardson (2013) continued that cells respond to these signals through pathways involving genes, but not as independent agents or predetermined codes/commands. The traditional model of gene transcription—having a complementary RNA copy of the relevant strand of DNA functioning as a messenger template in protein production—no longer applies. Rather, the transcription process can be radically altered by the environment, as happens through epigenetics. The process is highly fluid and dynamic, and is multi-regulatory and cooperative, so that phenotypic variation might appear to be majorly genetic in origin but "really is environmental" (e.g., Bell, Tiwari, Thomä, & Schübeler, 2012; Feil & Fraga, 2012).

These epigenetic and related processes lead to continuous "rewiring" of the network of genes as they respond to environmental change. New gene expressions are created allowing new adaptabilities. The intensity, speed, and novelty of the multiple processes involved in this cross-talk of multiple "-omic" levels (genomic, epigenomic, transcriptomic, etc.) are "unlikely" to be the products of linear deterministic processes. Rather, cells are maintained in "far-from-equilibrium" states in which nonlinear dynamics in molecular networks create "criticality," or edge-of-change movements, that might cascade into novel states in response to even minor perturbations.

Richardson (2013) concluded that this logic of metabolism extends into the different developmental levels of the organism. Therefore, self-organized system conceptualizations are suggesting "radical" changes in understanding nature, genes, and phenotypic variation. Offspring inherit not autonomous gene command centers but whole dynamic, emergent developmental systems.

With respect to the question of "missing heritability," its traditional conceptualization leads to it being "hidden." In dynamic, biointelligence conceptions of cells, genes, and environment (as well as in upper levels in the network of relevant systems, such as in nervous systems), traditional accounts of heritability do not apply, and for the best of evolutionary reasons.

Physiological systems are now described as "homeodynamic" rather than homeostatic (Yates, 2008). At one level, nervous systems are comprised of emergent networks that modulate cell activity in the context of environmental information. Animals respond not to external stimuli but to activity patterns within relevant brain structures that they engender, as created by emergent, intelligent, nonlinear dynamics (see Freeman, 2000; who used mice olfactory bulb responsiveness as an example).

As for cognitive intelligence, for Richardson (2013), it is also emergent and self-organized, being generated from its own activity. Piaget (1988) referred to this process as "reflective abstraction." Artificial neural networks (ANNs) demonstrate the same properties (e.g., Ciszac, Montina, & Arecchi, 2009; Hollis, Kloos, & Van Orden, 2009). Network ensembles are activated and yoked together, demonstrating emergent properties, including hierarchically-organized, progressively developing (toward increased abstraction) "attractor" states. According to Richardson (2010, 2013), this cognitive differentiation and lifelong development in cognitive speed, efficacy, and creativity in responding allow organisms to better predict, to anticipate, and to even "make" the future, a concept that is similar to Seligman, Railton, Baumeister, and Sripada's (2013) one of "prospection."

Richardson (2013) next examined evolution and culture in his work on the foundations of intelligence. The emergent, self-organized, and dynamical cognitive systems that could develop have fueled evolutionary change in an evolutionary spiral co-activated by the social cooperativity enabled by the intelligence (and the underlying larger network capacity and brains). The social cooperativity involved needed refined attentions and actions, which could only be achieved through interindividual "epicognitive" regulation (e.g., as in language, tools, rules) or culture. As dynamical brains interact, they too can form emerging hierarchies of nested attractors that manifest reflective abstraction. Through socioeconomic processes such as this, which includes the scientific enterprise, humans have gone beyond an intelligence of adapting to the environment to one of adapting the environment to themselves. [I would add that both adaptive aspects are involved in each of individual and group intelligent environmental adaptation.]

Conclusion In Richardson (2013), Turkheimer (2011) is given the last word. He argued that "complex human behavior emerges out of a hypercomplex developmental network" (p. 600). Genes and environment constitute inputs to the system. They have no direct "causal effects," in that any are "lost" in the hypercomplex developmental network. Complex differences in human behavior cannot be explained causally in either individual genes or environments (in the same way that geographical planetary plate tectonics cannot be explained in properties of individual rocks).

The work by Richardson (2013) on the missing heritability problem illustrates the fast-changing landscape in the study of genetics in behavior. The issue is not only whether the search for specific gene—specific outcome—is appropriate compared to broader searches, including pleiotropy, but just how central is the question of direct genetic influences on behavior either way. Although, the work of Richardson suggests that the missing heritability problem is artifactual, novel genetic approaches are suggesting otherwise.

GCTA Resolves

Introduction Plomin, Haworth, et al. (2013) addressed the "missing heritability" problem through empirical investigation. Their research has moved the field toward resolving the problem. Moreover, they based their study on a novel genome-wide approach consistent with the much used but often criticized GWAS approach. As mentioned, the missing heritability problem refers to the disjoint in the behavioral genetic research that twin and adoption studies have shown that heritability estimate for general cognitive ability is about 0.50, or substantial (Plomin, DeFries, Knopik, & Neiderhiser, 2013), yet GWAS investigations have not yet found the genetic variants that might account for the heritability (Davies et al., 2011). Plomin, Haworth, et al. (2013) noted that GWAS have investigated associations without much success perhaps because the typical study excludes rare DNA variants among the SNPs typically researched.

Plomin, Haworth, et al. (2013) addressed the problem of missing heritability by using a new method that is population- rather than family-based. In GCTA, all the SNPs genotyped in a sample can be used, not just those from genetically-related individuals (twins, families, or adoptees). Therefore, to estimate the genetic variance of these individuals, whose genetic similarity might range only from 0.00 to 0.02, SNPs are compared pair-wise to decipher phenotypic similarity for each pair of individuals in a sample based on their total SNP similarity.

Evidence The GCTA investigation of the genetic variants that might account for heritability of cognitive abilities conducted by Plomin, Haworth, et al. (2013) was based on over 3000 12-year-old co-twins. The methods included measures of language (verbal, nonverbal) and general intelligence. The variants investigated were common only, not rare. Note that the nature of the GCTA method does not allow for identification of which SNPs might contribute to the total heritability estimate captured by DNA markers.

The results showed that tagged DNA markers accounted for, on average, 0.66 of the estimated twin heritability, or that common genetic variants can account for two thirds of the putative missing heritability in cognitive ability, with the results for general cognitive ability being the highest (although all were significant).

Conclusion The authors concluded that GCTA provides a powerful technique in genome–behavior association research because, in terms of genetic influences, it is much harder to dispute evidence that is DNA-based relative to findings from twin and adoption studies. They argued that the GCTA method could "mark the beginning of the end of the nature-nurture controversy" about a role for genetics in cognitive ability, although the specific SNPs and nucleotides involved require further research.

I would add that the amount of variance explained by any one collection of SNPs in the overall variance explanation attributable to genetics is bound to be moderate, even if significant. The approach taken by Plomin, Haworth, et al. (2013) might be the way to salvage not only the concept of missing heritability but also the fundamental assumptions of behavioral genetics, in particular. In this regard, it is worth noting that in twin concordance studies, the rate usually is moderate or perhaps high for behavioral phenotypes, including for intelligence and personality traits, but does not approach 100 %, as found in more physical and physiological traits (e.g., Mash & Wolfe, 2015). As workers in the field emphasize, this leaves ample room for understanding phenotypic expression as an interaction of genetic and environmental influences.

Commonalities and Pleiotropy in Psychopathology

Explanation

Introduction The Psychiatric Genomics Consortium, which has the largest psychiatric GWAS data set currently available, studied the genetic relatedness of five major psychiatric disorders (Cross-Disorder Group of the Psychiatric Genomics Consortium, 2013). This psychiatric genomics consortium headed by Smoller, Kendler, et al. (2013) studied risk loci, or specific allelic variants on genes having or underlying shared genetic effects, on ASD, ADHD, bipolar disorder, major depressive disorder, and schizophrenia. These five major psychiatric disorders (child and adult onset) have been studied singly and in various combinations for risk loci, but never together until this GWAS (Cross-Disorder Group of the Psychiatric Genomics Consortium, 2013).

Evidence The consortium calculated the estimate of the total variance in liability for disorder explained together by common genetic polymorphisms (such as SNPs) for the disorders. The authors analyzed genome-wide genotype data from the Consortium database both for cases and controls. The consortium analyzed SNPs in over 60,000 cases and controls, mostly of European ancestry. The methods included search for allelic effects of each disorder and cross-disorder effects.

The results of the study revealed that the genetic contribution of common SNPs to the five major psychiatric disorder studied is important. SNPs "explained" 17–29 % of the variance in liability for disorder. Four SNPs met criteria for cross-disorder effects on multiple or all disorders, and they especially involved ones in voltage-gated calcium-channel signaling.

Specifically, for four of the five disorders studied, cut-off was exceeded for genome-wide significance in the primary (e.g., fixed-effects) meta-analysis. The common risk loci involved SNPs at regions on chromosomes 3p21 and 10q24 andSNPs in two L-type voltage-gated calcium-channel subunits—*CACNA1C* and *CACNB2*, introns of brain-expressed genes. The *CACNA1C* polymorphism has been termed a "susceptibility gene," in that its variants have effects on a range of structural and functional brain genotypes, e.g., circuitry involved in emotions, executive function, attention, and memory.

Conclusion The authors concluded that genetic risk factors are shared among the major neuropsychiatric disorders studied, having broad phenotypic effects, or pleiotropic effects, on at least two of the five disorders studied. There appears to be a sharing of genetic risk across key psychiatric disorders, as found in the study, and with results uncontaminated by environment because of the distant genetic relatedness among individuals in the sample studied.

Individual and aggregate molecular genetic risk factors were shown to be shared among the five common psychiatric disorders studied even though they are treated separately in psychiatric diagnostic systems. Psychiatric nosology needs to move beyond diagnostic categories that are descriptive to a classification system informed by causation of conditions.

The authors maintained that diagnostic manuals, such as those of the DSM-5 (Diagnostic Statistical Manual of Mental Disorder, Fifth Edition; American Psychiatric Association, 2013) and the upcoming ICD-11 (International Classification of Diseases, 11th Edition; World Health Organization, 2017), need to move beyond constructing syndromes descriptively toward a classification system informed by etiology. By seeking shared cause at a molecular level, the task of describing psychiatric disorder and determining cause is facilitated. Some loci will evidence diagnostic specificity but others a more common thread, with both individual and aggregate molecular genetic risk factors involved. The widespread pleiotropy that seems involved could help explain the frequent comorbidities in use of traditional nosology and also inform valid approaches to psychopharmacological treatment.

In this regard, for the authors, as in other medical fields, there might be broad pleiotropy of genetic risk factors cutting across descriptive DSM boundaries and also the vulnerabilities of the disorders. The results speak to a shared genetic etiology and pathophysiology underlying these disorders. Further, the mechanism at work in broad risk pleiotropy might relate to gene loci involved in brain-located calcium-channel activity, in general, and its alterations.

Aside from genetic research calling into question the splitting of psychiatric disorder in separate categories that might not have validity because of lacunae in addressing their etiology, other research is arriving at the same conclusions using symptom clustering techniques. For example, as shown next, there might be a common *p* (psychopathology) factor to multiple disorders.

General *p* Factor

Introduction Caspi et al. (2014) conducted a revealing study of psychopathology that calls into question the standard paradigm that the field should focus on individual disorders or psychiatric categories. In intelligence research, not only are specific ability factors found (e.g., verbal, visuospatial, working memory, processing speed) but also a general *g* factor emerges (Deary, 2001). Similarly, Caspi et al. (2014) asked the provocative question whether their results support the existence of a general *p* factor of psychopathology in the structure of psychiatric disorders, indicative of a common etiological (developmental) pathway to disorders.

Evidence Caspi et al. (2014) tested participants in the Dunedin Multidisciplinary Health and Development Study ($N=1037$ to begin, with 95 % tested of the 1007 participants still alive in the last wave). Assessments took place at ages 3, 5, 7, 9, 11, 13, 15, 18, 21, 26, 32, and 38. Mental disorders were investigated longitudinally over 20 years from adolescence onward. To accomplish this, interviews were included in the assessment, and they asked about past-year psychopathology. Gaps were queried using a life history calendar. The interviews included the Diagnostic Interview Schedule (Robins, Cottler, Bucholz, & Compton, 1995) in the last five waves. Prevalence rates for the disorders investigated (common ones, 11 disorders or clusters) that were found in this research study were similar to those in the extant literature.

Caspi et al. (2014) reviewed the literature on factor structure of psychopathology and different models have been proposed. The literature supports a two-factor structure to common mental disorders—internalizing and externalizing (e.g., for children, young adults, and adults, respectively, Achenbach & Edelbrock, 1981; Forbush & Watson, 2013; Krueger, Caspi, Moffitt, & Silva, 1998). Other research adds a third factor of thought disorder. Lahey et al. (2012) proposed that mental disorders might reflect one common underlying factor, in addition to internalizing and externalizing ones.

Caspi et al. (2014) used confirmatory factor analysis to test the various multiple, bi-, and unifactor approaches to symptom structure. They used multitrait-multimethod models, seeking significant polychoric correlations. Their three-factor model fits the data well, and its intercorrelations were all positive. Their bifactor model had to be adjusted, however, but ended up fitting the data, as well, and slightly more parsimoniously. Further analyses suggested that the p factor model fits well the data, but that the internalizing and externalizing dimensions added information beyond p. However, all three individual factors were highly correlated with p. Also, higher p scores were associated with relevant risk factors related to life impairment, familiarity, developmental history, and early brain function.

Conclusion Caspi et al. (2014) interpreted their range of findings as supportive of a general p factor in psychopathology. The existence of a general psychopathology factor in the structure of mental disorder suggests a general risk to develop "any and all forms" of common mental disorders. The p dimension seems to lie in "neurological roots," or in dynamic developmental processes. It suggests that all disorders are "united," with a "single unitary cause." There should be a pleiotropic genetic liability involved. That genetic variants have been found to be linked to multiple diagnoses fits this conjecture (Smoller, Craddock, et al., 2013; also Cross-Disorder Group of the Psychiatric Genomics Consortium, 2013).

Caspi et al. (2014) examined the implications of their findings for understanding causality of single disorders. These would seem difficult to identify. Not only are disorders often comorbid but also they share common risk factors and correlates. The authors' results suggest that the attempt to find biomarkers, genetic underpinnings, and distinct cause in single disorders is misplaced.

Other research is consistent with the approach of Caspi et al. (2014) toward the existence of a general psychopathological factor. I note that the authors discussed the etiology or causality of psychopathology in these terms and the import of their findings for psychiatric classification and its general splitting rather than lumping approach to mental disorder.

Generalist Genes

Introduction Rhee, Lahey, and Waldman (2014) reviewed the literature showing significant common genetic influences in all psychiatric disorders but, in contrast, nonshared environmental influences on specific disorders (Cosgrove et al., 2011; Lahey, Van Hulle, Singh, Waldman, & Rathouz, 2011). The results support the "generalist gene and specialist environments" model of psychopathology (Eley, 1997; Kendler et al., 2011). The common underlying feature to psychopathology might be a pervasive disposition toward experiencing unpleasant affective state (Lilienfeld, 2003) or negative emotionality/neuroticism (Lahey & Waldman, 2003).

Evidence Rhee et al. (2014) noted that studies have found common genetic influences involving neuroticism and externalizing/internalizing disorders and related aspects, e.g., negative emotionality and externalizing behavior (Kendler, Gardner, Gatz, & Pedersen, 2007; Taylor, Allan, Mikolajewski, & Hart, 2013, respectively). Twin studies have indicated that negative emotionality/

neuroticism is a heritable common feature underlying the overlap between internalizing and externalizing disorders in children (Hink et al., 2013; Mikolajewski, Allan, Hart, Lonigan, & Taylor, 2013; Tackett et al., 2013). Other studies have revealed that SNPs help explain a significant proportion of variance for disorders (internalizing, externalizing) and for neuroticism, which relate to them (respectively, Lubke et al., 2012; Vinkhuyzen et al., 2012; Vrieze et al., 2014).

Conclusion The authors concluded that a hierarchical model fits the data (Lahey et al., 2011). That is, some genes influence risk, generally, for psychopathology, and others are specific to certain dimensions.

Similarly, Chow, Ho, Wong, Waye, and Bishop (2013) studied nonverbal, cognitive, language, and reading abilities in 3- to 11-year-old Chinese co-twins, as part of a larger cognitive ability battery. The results indicated shared genetic origins for the three areas involved, although distinct genetic influences were found for verbal skills. They concluded that the "generalist" gene hypotheses could be universal in different languages, such that the same set of genes "largely" influences diverse cognitive abilities, as per Plomin and Kovas (2005).

Others

Despite these findings of general gene effects on behavior, other studies show very specific genetic effects. For example, Avinun et al. (2011) found that the arginine vasopressin receptor 1A (*AVPR1A*) gene is associated with adult altruistic behavior, especially the specific 327 bp allele of one of its promoter region polymorphisms (*R53*). Their research found that, in contrast, for 3-year-old twin preschoolers the target allele was associated with less altruistic type behavior. The age difference could reflect either environmental or developmental influences, still to be discovered.

Molecular analysis for genetic risk is conducted not only for shared risk over disorders by multiple genetic alleles but also in the more traditional way of finding single (candidate) genes that might affect psychological disorder. The success in finding such associations is rare, but one attempt that has succeeded relates to speech and language disorder. Nudel and Newbury (2013) have reviewed the forkhead box P2 gene (*FOXP2*) in relation to the disorder. The *FOXP2* gene functions as a transcription factor that "represses the expression of neural targets," especially in brain circuits involved in vocal learning/communication. The gene was found originally in one human family. It should not be confused with the genetic array found in specific language impairment, which is polygenetic, not monogenetic.

Comment

The Smoller–Kendler–Craddock research, the Caspi team study, and others' work is important for both researchers of psychiatric disorders and practitioners. It calls into question the very nature of the category-dominated approach of the DSM enterprise and points to important general etiological considerations. At the same time, it might serve to entrench a biological rather than more inclusive biopsychosocial understanding of the etiology, expression, and treatment of psychiatric disorder. Workers in the field should be wary of falling into this one-sided position.

Child Genomics

Grigorenko and Dozier (2013) edited a special issue on genomics and child development. Genomics concerns the science of the genome's structure and function. The Human Genome Project had sequenced the full human genome and has led to GWAS, to remind, which attempt to match DNA variants with particular disorders. The underlying rationale for this kind of research is the common disease-common variant (CD-CV) hypothesis; that is, specific allelescause specific diseases. In the special issue, in an interesting innovation, Connolly, Glessner, and Hakonarson (2013) showed that specific polymorphisms, SNPs, were related to items on assessment instruments, in this case, on ASDs [the usual search is for SNP–phenotype associations]. GWAS and related studies continue to proliferate and include such innovations because the initial hope that it would clarify genetic underpinnings to disease has not been met.

As mentioned, in the "missing heritability" problem, genetic variance does not account for an estimated heritability (Plomin, 2013). However, Grigorenko and Dozier (2013) indicated that ongoing conceptualization and research might clarify the problem. New approaches include the common disease-rare variant (CD-RV) hypothesis.

Moreover, Grigorenko and Dozier (2013) explained that the research is now focusing on epigenetics and epigenomics, which lead to the genome changing across the life span, e.g., through gene silencing. Unlike for genomic research, it would not be possible to find a single reference epigenome, although it might be possible to specify a minimum epigenome of importance. Future research should seek to find the causal roots of clinical diseases and disorders in common genomic and epigenomic factors. That is, the CD-CV and CD-RV hypotheses could be elaborated into a common CD-GE hypothesis.

As for the transcriptome, involved in the RNA-based translation/transcription of the genome to proteins, Naumova, Lee, Rychkov, Vlasova, and Grigorenko (2013) examined the brain transcriptome. It permits focusing on the whole system involved as "causative change" agents, rather than just focusing on causative genes, and on patterns of gene regulation and expression. Similarly, Hu (2013) reviewed the area of ASD and concluded that findings need to be integrated systematically over the different "omic" sciences (genomics, epigenomics, transcriptomics, proteomics, interactomics) for better understanding of the disorder.

Reaction Range

Model

Manuck and McCaffery (2014) have described a model relating genotype and phenotype in the context of models important to the present book. Figure 9.3 in Manuck and McCaffery (2014)

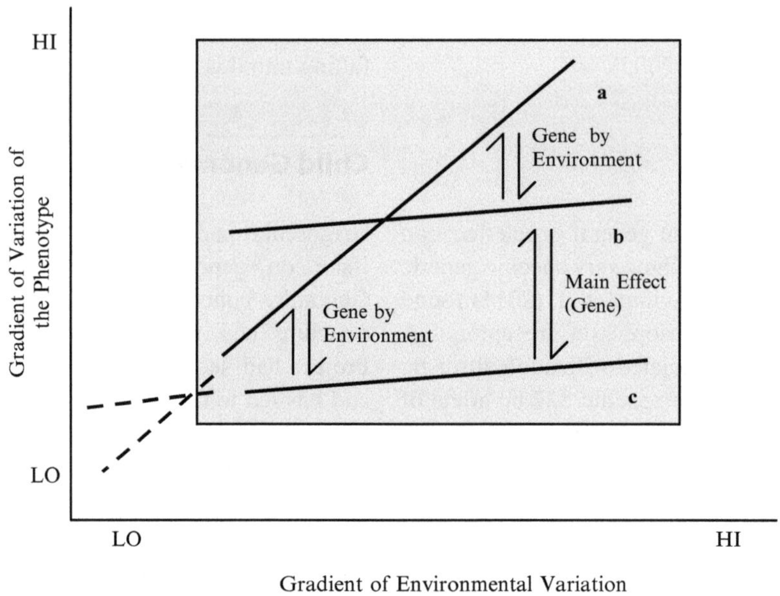

Fig. 9.3 Hypothetical reaction ranges (variations in possible phenotypes) for genotypes/variations in environment. The possible reaction ranges are for gradients of variability related to the phenotypes and the environment. Slope angle indicates degree of variability. $a = G \times E$; $b = G$; $c = G \times E$ but, for the latter, at a different environmental variability than in "a." *Dashed lines* indicate possible extensions of the reaction norms for *a* and *c*. The differential susceptibility model is represented in the mid-range of the environmental gradient, while the diathesis-stress one is represented at the end portions. Adapted from Manuck (2010)

presents Manuck's (2010) model of a "reaction norm" perspective on phenotypic variation in relation to environmental variation. A reaction norm refers to the range of variation in phenotypes observable over different environments found in individuals having the same genotype.

In the figure, the slopes of the lines depicting the model indicate whether there is greater or lesser plasticity in producing a broad range of phenotypic expressions across the gradient of variation in the environment. The parallel lines in the slopes represent an absence of G×E interaction, whereas the lines with different slopes represent interaction. In the latter, different phenotypes (in the same environmental range) serve to yield different phenotypic responses.

Note that, according to the authors, the a–b interaction exemplifies the diathesis-stress [vulnerability×stress] model of psychopathology (e.g., Caspi et al., 2002, 2003) and the a–c one the differential susceptibility model (Belsky & Pluess, 2009). [In the latter model, certain allelic variations in concert with positive or negative environments are sensitive to context and lead to phenotypically positive or negative phenotypes, respectively.] In terms of the model of reaction norm or range in the figure, differential susceptibility effects are captured mid-range in the environmental gradient and those of (vulnerability) diathesis-stress are captured at either end (also called the vantage sensitivity model).

Parenthetically, I note that the diatheses-stress model is not quite equivalent to the genetic by environmental (G×E) model, unlike the contention of the authors, and Caspi's research should not be an example that is in line with it. The diatheses-stress model is about cumulative vulnerabilities, in particular, and not the vulnerability afforded by certain alleles, which is the case for the G×E model.

Evidence

As for recent research in support of the various models cited by Manuck and McCaffery (2014), for the diathesis-stress model, Byrd and Manuck (2014) conducted a meta-analysis of the childhood maltreatment×*MAOA* (low vs. high activity allele) interaction effect that has been found for later male aggressive and antisocial behavior outcomes. For the differential susceptibility model, Hankin et al. (2011) found variations in the gene *5-HTTLPR* and affectivity in both supportive and unsupportive parenting/environments (but did not find the association with alternate genotypes).

Manuck and McCaffery (2014) presented research illustrating what the environment does and to what the E refers in G×E. For the former, they showed how stress (recent widowhood) leads to inflammation, but only in carriers of an allele (G, not C) of an SNP labeled *IL6 174G/C* (Schultze-Florey et al., 2012). The mechanism implicated is a genotype-dependent stressor effect on inflammatory responses (involving interleukin-6, *It6*). For the former, rGE indicates that variables in G×E research are not necessarily genetic or environmental (rGE=correlated gene by environment effects, e.g., heritable predispositions influence activity in or evocation of the environment; Plomin, DeFries, McClearn, & McGuffin, 2008). Only experimentally-manipulated environmental exposures can address rGE confounds.

Conclusion

As an overall conclusion, the authors noted that the field should adopt the broader term of "G×E expression," or gene×environmental exposure interactions, which would include "complexly" determined experiences, dispositions, abilities, attitudes, and affective states.

I note that the conclusions offered by Manuck and McCaffery (2014) on genotype–phenotype relations cover the range of topics reviewed in the book, including—development, psychopathology, genes, and environment. The models covered include diathesis-stress compared to differential susceptibility and G×E and rGE in the genetic area. The concept of reaction range is used to integrate much of this work. In Young (2011), I also used this concept to help explain epigenesis.

Genes/Causality

Wahlsten (2013) elaborated definitions related to gene function (see Fig. 9.4), which I present as a reminding tutorial. (a) The figure indicates that any one gene can alter several phenotypes. This is termed pleiotropy. (b) Also, genes could interact with each other (epistasis). (c) In heterogeneity, multiple pathways to outcome can take place, depending on which genes are implicated. In gene–environment interaction, the strength of influence of a particular gene and a particular environment become evident only when both are present simultaneously.

Wahlsten (2013) emphasized how genes form networks and do not function in isolation. They interact with each other and also with the environment. At a larger-scale, when gene interactions involve thousands of genes, workers now refer to the "interactome" (Li et al., 2004).

Krimsky (2013) added that genetic components act nonlinearly so that genetic causation is complex. Causation is multiple, involving not only genes but also epigenetic effects, the environment in interaction, and so on. In this regard, Turkheimer (2011) referred to the "hyper-complex developmental network." Landrigan, Lambertini, and Birnbaum (2012) referred to the "causal tree."

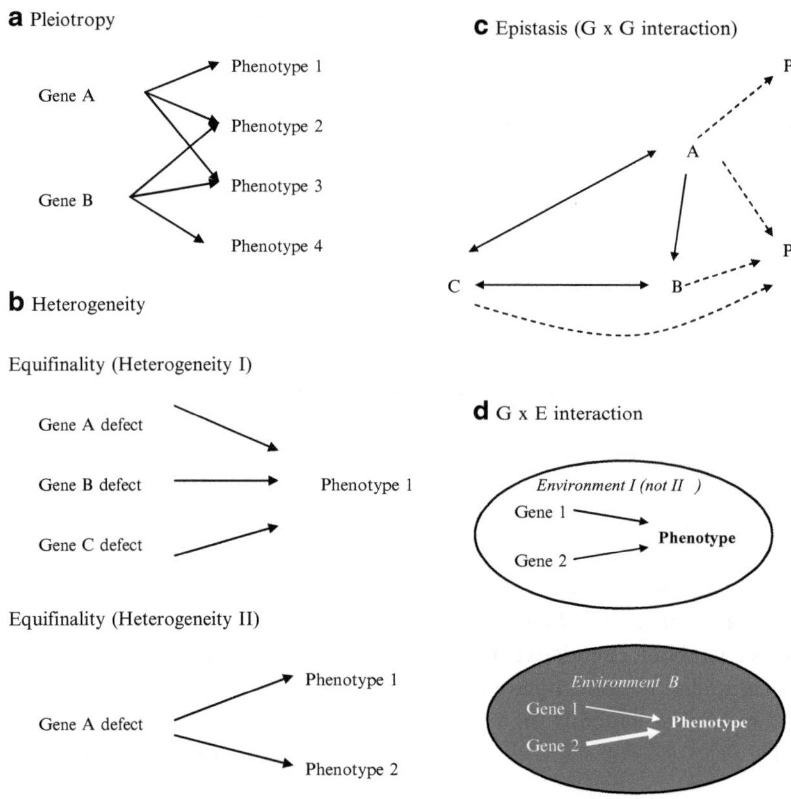

Fig. 9.4 Pleiotropy, heterogeneity, epistasis, and G × E in genetic influence. (a) A specific gene could influence more than one phenotype, and most phenotypes, in turn, are influenced by different genes. Any one gene does not simply code for one particular phenotype, despite the name that might be given to the gene. (b) Different genetic defects could result in the same disease. Conversely, one defect could lead to different disease. (c) Genes function in networks in which genes influence each other. Interactions might be unidirectional or bidirectional. (d) The influence of a gene on a phenotype depends on the organism's environment, and the allele of the gene itself. The strength of the influence, therefore, is determined jointly by two factors, and their influences cannot be separated statistically. Adapted from Wahlsten (2013)

Chapter Conclusions

Phenome

One -ome that has not been considered in the various publications just reviewed is the "phenome," a term that I coined to indicate the collection of phenotypes in a species. Moreover, phenotypes within the individual are multiple, and infinitely varied, especially in the human case. Multiple species are endowed with the capacity for phenotypic plasticity that enables rapid online adaptation and that promotes not just survival and well-being, but also, in a different, more prolonged time frame, Darwinian adaptation and even speciation in appropriate contexts. The system-wide "omic" integrations that characterize phenotypes appear to work together to maximize robust phenotypic adaptation in both the online and evolutionary sense and also the ability to flexibly resist or meet environmental or niche challenges.

Evolvability

Two more terms that I find important in order to understand the concept of the "phenome" are evolvability and versatility. Evolvability does not just relate to genetic variations and alterations that promote adaptive heritable phenotypes, but also system-wide genomic and related -omics, including epigenetic ones, that function in these regards.

Versatility

As for the concept of versatility as it applies to evolutionary thought, evolution appears to be especially about versatility in an active way rather than in only a passive type of flexibility or plasticity that might be required for environmental or niche challenges. This is not to say there is an active "design" to evolution in a teleological sense. Rather, evolutionary systems, in general, are poised at the "cusp of change," to use Kauffman's (1993) nonlinear dynamical systems theory (NLDST) term, in order to maximize flexibility in adaptive response. Being ready for change permits systems to optimize variations and adaptability within and across in each of the cases of (a) intra-agent systems, (b) whole individual agent (phenotypic) systems, and, as applicable, (c) multiple inter-agent (e.g., over individuals, radiation over a niche/niches) systems.

By taking a systems approach to the phenome and its context, some of the complexities and contradictions in the genetic and molecular genetic research on behavior might be demystified. In studying the genetics of behavior, as with many aspects in the study of behavior, one needs to take a step backwards, at times, in order to try to see the whole, or the forest between the trees.

Loveome

Aside from establishing a species' genome and phenome and their interactions, researchers should work toward establishing the range of environmental factors that can affect each of the genome and phenome. In the human case, one aspect in this regard could be called the "loveome" (or "lovome"). How that interacts to produce the range of human behavior expressed in the human phenome should deserve the same scrutiny being applied to the case of the genome. The best in human outcomes requires the best in supportive environments. A too great focus on genetics could place this issue in the background, along with the biopsychosocial model within which it fits.

References

Achenbach, T. M., & Edelbrock, C. (1981). Behavioral problems and competencies reported by parents of normal and disturbed children aged 4 through 16. *Monographs of the Society for Research in Child Development, 46*, 1–82.

American Psychiatric Association. (2013). *Diagnostic and statistical manual of mental disorders: DSM-5* (5th ed.). Washington, DC: Author.

Avinun, R., Israel, S., Shalev, I., Gritsenko, I., Bornstein, G., Ebstein, R. P., et al. (2011). AVPR1A variant associated with preschoolers' lower altruistic behavior. *PLoS One, 6*, e25274. doi:10.1371/journal.pone.0025274.

Bakermans-Kranenburg, M. J., & van IJzendoorn, M. H. (2006). Gene-environment interaction of the dopamine D4 receptor (DRD4) and observed maternal insensitivity predicting externalizing behavior in preschoolers. *Developmental Psychobiology, 48*, 406–409.

Bell, O., Tiwari, V. K., Thomä, N. H., & Schübeler, D. (2012). Determinants and dynamics of genome accessibility. *Nature Reviews Genetics, 12*, 554–564.

Belsky, J., & Pluess, M. (2009). The nature (and nurture?) of plasticity in early human development. *Perspectives on Psychological Science, 4*, 345–351.

Berger, A. (2011). *Self-regulation: Brain, cognition, and development.* Washington, DC: American Psychological Association.

Blaze, J., & Roth, T. L. (2013). Epigenetic mechanisms in learning and memory. *Wiley Interdisciplinary Reviews: Cognitive Science, 4*, 105–115.

Boyce, W. T., & Kobor, M. S. (2015). Development and the epigenome: The "synapse" of gene-environment interplay. *Developmental Science, 18*, 1–23.

Brookes, K., Xu, X., Chen, W., Zhou, K., Neale, B., Lowe, N., et al. (2006). The analysis of 51 genes in DSM-IV combined type attention deficit hyperactivity disorder: Association signals in DRD4, DAT1 and 16 other genes. *Molecular Psychiatry, 11*, 934–953.

Byrd, A. L., & Manuck, S. B. (2014). MAOA, childhood maltreatment and antisocial behavior: Meta-analysis of a gene-environment interaction. *Biological Psychiatry, 75*, 9–17.

Caspi, A., Houts, R. M., Belsky, D. W., Goldman-Mellor, S. J., Harrington, H., Israel, S., et al. (2014). The p factor: One general psychopathology factor in the structure of psychiatric disorders? *Clinical Psychological Science, 2*, 119–137.

Caspi, A., McClay, J., Moffitt, T. E., Mill, J., Martin, J., Craig, I. W., et al. (2002). Role of genotype in the cycle of violence in maltreated children. *Science, 297*, 851–854.

Caspi, A., Sugden, K., Moffitt, T. E., Taylor, A., Craig, I. W., Harrington, H., et al. (2003). Influence of life stress on depression: Moderation by a polymorphism in the 5-HTT gene. *Science, 301*, 386–389.

Chabris, C. F., Hebert, B. M., Benjamin, D. J., Beauchamp, J., Cesarini, D., van der Loos, M., et al. (2012). Most reported genetic associations with general intelligence are probably false positives. *Psychological Science, 23*, 1314–1323.

Chabris, C. F., Lee, J. J., Cesarini, D., Benjamin, D. J., & Laibson, D. I. (2015). The fourth law of behavior genetics. *Current Directions in Psychological Science, 24*, 304–312.

Chakrabarti, B., Dudbridge, F., Kent, L., Wheelwright, S., Hill-Cawthorne, G., Allison, C., et al. (2009). Genes related to sex-steroids, neural growth, and social-emotional behavior are associated with autistic traits, empathy, and Asperger syndrome. *Autism Research, 2*, 157–177.

Charney, E. (2012). Behavior genetics and postgenomics. *Behavioral and Brain Sciences, 35*, 331–410.

Chow, B. W.-Y., Ho, C. S.-H., Wong, S. W.-L., Waye, M. M. Y., & Bishop, D. V. M. (2013). Generalist genes and cognitive abilities in Chinese twins. *Developmental Science, 16*, 260–268.

Ciszac, M., Montina, A., & Arecchi, F. T. (2009). Control of transient synchronization with external stimuli. *Chaos, 19*, 015104. doi:10.1063/1.3080195.

Connolly, J. J., Glessner, J. T., & Hakonarson, H. (2013). A genome-wide association study of autism incorporating ADI-R, ADOS, and SRS. *Child Development, 84*, 17–33.

Cosgrove, V. E., Rhee, S. H., Gelhorn, H. L., Boeldt, D., Corely, R. C., Ehringer, M. A., et al. (2011). Structure and etiology of co-occurring internalizing and externalizing disorders in adolescents. *Journal of Abnormal Psychology, 39*, 109–123.

Cross-Disorder Group of the Psychiatric Genomics Consortium. (2013). Genetic relationship between five psychiatric disorders estimated from genome-wide SNPs. *Nature Genetics, 45*, 984–994.

Davies, G., Tenesa, A., Payton, A., Yang, J., Harris, S. E., Liewald, D., et al. (2011). Genome-wide association studies establish that human intelligence is highly heritable and polygenic. *Molecular Psychiatry, 16*, 996–1005.

Davis, O. S., Butcher, L. M., Docherty, S. J., Meaburn, E. L., Curtis, C. J., Simpson, M. A., et al. (2010). A three-stage genome-wide association study of general cognitive ability: Hunting the small effects. *Behavior Genetics, 40*, 759–767.

Deary, I. J. (2001). *Intelligence, a very short introduction.* Oxford, UK: Oxford University Press.

Deary, I. J., Penke, L., & Johnson, W. (2010). The neuroscience of human intelligence differences. *Nature Reviews Neuroscience, 11*, 201–211.

del Campo, N., Müller, U., & Sahakian, B. J. (2012). Neural and behavioral endophenotypes in ADHD. *Current Topics in Behavioral Neurosciences, 11*, 65–91.

Eley, T. (1997). General genes: A new theme in developmental psychopathology. *Current Directions in Psychological Science, 6*, 90–95.

Ellis, B. J. (2004). Timing of pubertal maturation in girls: An integrated life history approach. *Psychological Bulletin, 130*, 920–958.

Fair, D. A., Dosenbach, N. U. F., Petersen, S. E., & Schlagger, B. L. (2012). Resting state studies on the development of control systems. In M. I. Posner (Ed.), *Cognitive neuroscience of attention* (2nd ed., pp. 291–311). New York: Guilford Press.

Feil, R., & Fraga, M. F. (2012). Epigenetics and the environment: Emerging patterns and implications. *Nature Reviews Genetics, 13*, 97–109.

Feinberg, A. P., & Irizarry, R. A. (2010). Stochastic epigenetic variation as a driving force of development, evolutionary adaptation & disease. *Proceedings of the National Academy of Sciences of the United States of America, 107*, 1757–1764.

Forbush, K. T., & Watson, D. (2013). The structure of common and uncommon mental disorders. *Psychological Medicine, 43*, 97–108.

Fox, N. A., Nichols, K. E., Henderson, H. A., Rubin, K., Schmidt, L., Hamer, D., et al. (2005). Evidence for a gene-environment interaction in predicting behavioral inhibition in middle childhood. *Psychological Science, 16*, 921–926.

Freeman, W. (2000). Brains create macroscopic order from microscopic disorder by neurodynamics in perception. In P. Århem, C. Blomberg, & H. Liljenström (Eds.), *Disorder versus order in brain function: Essays in theoretical neurobiology* (pp. 205–219). Singapore: World Scientific.

Gao, W., Zhu, H., Giovanello, K. S., Smith, J. K., Shen, D., Gilmore, J. H., et al. (2009). Evidence on the emergence of the brain's default network from 2-week-old to 2-year-old healthy pediatric subjects. *Proceedings of the National Academy of Sciences of the United States of America, 106*, 6790–6795.

Gissis, S. B., & Jablonka, E. (Eds.). (2001). *Transformations of Lamarckism: From subtle fluids to molecular biology*. Cambridge, MA: Cambridge University Press.

Grigorenko, E. L., & Dozier, E. (2013). Introduction to the special section on genomics. *Child Development, 84*, 6–16.

Hankin, B. L., Nederhof, E., Oppenheimer, C. W., Jenness, J., Young, J. F., Abela, J. R., et al. (2011). Differential susceptibility in youth: Evidence that 5-HTTLPR x positive parenting is associated with positive affect "for better and worse.". *Translational Psychiatry, 4*, e44. doi:10.1038/tp.2011.44.

Hink, L. K., Rhee, S. H., Corley, R. P., Cosgrove, V. E., Hewitt, J. K., Schulz-Heik, R., et al. (2013). Personality dimensions as common and broadband-specific features for internalizing and externalizing disorders. *Journal of Abnormal Child Psychology, 41*, 939–957.

Hlavecek, W. S., & Faeder, J. R. (2009). The complexity of cell signaling and the need for a new mechanic. *Science Signaling, 2*, pe46. doi:10.1126/scisignal.281pe46.

Hollis, G., Kloos, H., & Van Orden, G. C. (2009). Origins of order in cognitive activity. In S. J. Guastello, M. Koopmans, & D. Pincus (Eds.), *Chaos and complexity in psychology: The theory of nonlinear dynamical systems* (pp. 206–241). Cambridge, MA: Cambridge University Press.

Hu, V. W. (2013). From genes to environment: Using integrative genomics to build a "systems-level" understanding of autism spectrum disorders. *Child Development, 84*, 89–103.

Johnson, M. H., Griffin, R., Csibra, G., Halit, H., Farroni, T., De Haan, M., et al. (2005). The emergence of the social brain network: Evidence from typical and atypical development. *Development and Psychopathology, 17*, 599–619.

Kauffman, S. (1993). *The origins of order: Self-organization and selection in evolution*. New York: Oxford University Press.

Kendler, K. S., Aggen, S. H., Knudsen, G. P., Røysamb, E., Neale, M. C., & Reichborn-Kjennerud, T. (2011). The structure of genetic and environmental risk factors for syndromal and subsyndromal common DSM-IV Axis I and Axis II disorders. *American Journal of Psychiatry, 168*, 29–39.

Kendler, K. S., Gardner, C. O., Gatz, M., & Pedersen, N. L. (2007). The sources of co-morbidity between major depression and generalized anxiety disorders in the Swedish national twin sample. *Psychological Medicine, 37*, 453–462.

Krimsky, S. (2013). Genetic causation: A cross disciplinary inquiry. In R. M. Lerner & J. B. Benson (Eds.), *Advances in child development and behavior. Embodiment and epigenesis: Theoretical and methodological issues in understanding the role of biology within the relational development system. Part A: Philosophical, theoretical, and biological dimensions* (Vol. 44, pp. 307–323). Waltham, MA: Academic Press.

Krueger, R. F., Caspi, A., Moffitt, T. E., & Silva, P. A. (1998). The structure and stability of common mental disorders (DSM-III-R): A longitudinal-epidemiological study. *Journal of Abnormal Psychology, 107*, 216–227.

Lahey, B. B., Applegate, B., Hakes, J. K., Zald, D. H., Hariri, A. R., & Rathouz, P. J. (2012). Is there a general factor of prevalent psychopathology during adulthood? *Journal of Abnormal Psychology, 121*, 971–977.

Lahey, B. B., Van Hulle, C. A., Singh, A. L., Waldman, I. D., & Rathouz, P. J. (2011). Higher-order genetic and environmental structure of prevalent forms of child and adolescent psychopathology. *Archives of General Psychiatry, 68*, 181–189.

Lahey, B. B., & Waldman, I. D. (2003). A developmental propensity model of the origins of conduct problems during childhood and adolescence. In B. B. Lahey, T. E. Moffit, & A. Caspi (Eds.), *Causes of conduct disorder and juvenile delinquency* (pp. 76–117). New York: Guilford Press.

Lakatos, K., Nemoda, Z., Toth, I., Ronai, Z., Ney, K., Sasvari-Szekely, M., et al. (2002). Further evidence for the role of the dopamine D4 receptor (DRD4) gene in attachment disorganization: Interaction of exon III 48-bp repeat and the −521 C/T promoter polymorphisms. *Molecular Psychiatry, 7*, 27–31.

Lakatos, K., Toth, I., Nemoda, Z., Ney, K., Sasvari-Szekely, M., & Gervai, J. (2000). Dopamine D4 receptor (DRD4) gene polymorphism is associated with attachment disorganization in infants. *Molecular Psychiatry, 5*, 633–637.

Landrigan, P., Lambertini, L., & Birnbaum, L. S. (2012). A research strategy to discover the environmental causes of autism and neurodevelopmental disabilities. *Environmental Health Perspectives, 120*, A258–A260.

Li, S., Armstrong, C. M., Bertin, N., Ge, H., Milstein, S., Boxem, M., et al. (2004). A map of the interactome network of the metazoan. *Science, 303*, 540–543.

Lilienfeld, S. O. (2003). Comorbidity between and within childhood externalizing and internalizing disorders: Reflections and directions. *Journal of Abnormal Child Psychology, 31*, 285–291.

Lombardo, M. V., Baron-Cohen, S., Belmonte, M. K., & Chakrabarti, B. (2011). Neural endophenotypes of social behavior in autism spectrum conditions. In J. T. Cacioppo & J. Decety (Eds.), *The Oxford handbook of social neuroscience* (pp. 830–847). New York: Oxford University Press.
López-Maury, L., Marguerat, S., & Bähler, J. (2008). Tuning gene expression to changing environments. *Nature Reviews Genetics, 9*, 583–594.
Lubke, G. H., Hottenga, J. J., Walters, R., Laurin, C., de Geus, E. J., Willemsen, G., et al. (2012). Estimating the genetic variance of major depressive disorder due to all single nucleotide polymorphisms. *Biological Psychiatry, 72*, 707–709.
Manuck, S. B. (2010). The reaction norm in gene x environment interaction. *Molecular Psychiatry, 15*, 881–882.
Manuck, S. B., & McCaffery, J. M. (2014). Gene-environment interaction. *Annual Review of Psychology, 65*, 41–70.
Mash, E. J., & Wolfe, D. A. (2015). *Abnormal child psychology* (6th ed.). Boston: Cengage Learning.
Mikolajewski, A. J., Allan, N. P., Hart, S. A., Lonigan, C. J., & Taylor, J. (2013). Negative affect shares genetic and environmental influences with symptoms of childhood internalizing and externalizing disorders. *Journal of Abnormal Child Psychology, 41*, 411–423.
Naumova, O. Y., Lee, M., Rychkov, S. Y., Vlasova, N. V., & Grigorenko, E. L. (2013). Gene expression in the human brain: The current state of the study of specificity and spatiotemporal dynamics. *Child Development, 84*, 76–88.
Nikolova, Y. S., Bogdan, R., & Hariri, A. R. (2013). Neurogenetics approach: Insights from studies of dopamine signaling and reward processing. In M. D. Robinson, E. R. Watkins, & E. Harmon-Jones (Eds.), *Handbook of cognition and emotion* (pp. 19–34). New York: Guilford Press.
Noble, D. (2010). Biophysics and systems biology. *Philosophical Transactions of the Royal Society A: Mathematical, Physical and Engineering Sciences, 368*, 1125–1139.
Nudel, R., & Newbury, D. F. (2013). FOXP2. *Wiley Interdisciplinary Reviews: Cognitive Science, 4*, 547–560.
Piaget, J. (1988). Piaget's theory. In K. Richardson & S. Sheldon (Eds.), *Cognitive development to adolescence*. Hove, UK: Erlbaum.
Pigliucci, M. (2010). Phenotypic plasticity. In M. Piliucci & G. B. Müller (Eds.), *Evolution: The extended synthesis* (pp. 355–378). Cambridge, MA: MIT Press.
Plomin, R. (2013). Child development and molecular genetics: 13 years later. *Child Development, 84*, 104–120.
Plomin, R., & Davis, O. S. (2009). The future of genetics in psychology and psychiatry: Microarrays, genome-wide association, and non-coding RNA. *Journal of Child Psychology and Psychiatry, 50*, 63–71.
Plomin, R., DeFries, J. C., Knopik, V. S., & Neiderhiser, J. M. (2013). *Behavioral genetics* (6th ed.). New York: Worth.
Plomin, R., DeFries, J. C., McClearn, G. E., & McGuffin, P. (2008). *Behavioral genetics* (5th ed.). New York: Worth.
Plomin, R., & Kovas, Y. (2005). Generalist genes and learning disabilities. *Psychological Bulletin, 131*, 592–617.
Plomin, R., Haworth, C. M. A., Meaburn, E. L., Price, T. S., Wellcome Trust Case Control Consortium 2, & Davis, O. S. P. (2013). Common DNA markers can account for more than half of the genetic influence on cognitive abilities. *Psychological Science, 24*, 562–568.
Posner, M. I., Rothbart, M. K., Sheese, B. E., & Voelker, P. (2012). Control networks and neuromodulators of early development. *Developmental Psychology, 48*, 827–835.
Posner, M. I., Rothbart, M. K., & Sheese, B. E. (2007). Attention genes. *Developmental Science, 10*, 24–29.
Rhee, S. H., Lahey, B. B., & Waldman, I. D. (2014). Comorbidity among dimensions of childhood psychopathology: Converging evidence from behavior genetics. *Child Development Perspectives, 9*, 26–31.
Richardson, K. (2010). *The evolution of intelligent systems: How molecules became minds*. Basingstoke, UK: Palgrave.
Richardson, K. (2013). The eclipse of heritability and the foundations of intelligence. *New Ideas in Psychology, 31*, 122–129.
Ristic, J., & Enns, J. T. (2015). The changing face of attentional development. *Current Directions in Psychological Science, 24*, 24–31.
Robins, L. N., Cottler, L., Bucholz, K. K., & Compton, W. (1995). *Diagnostic Interview Schedule for DSM-IV*. St. Louis, MO: Washington University School of Medicine.
Schmidt, L. A., Fox, N. A., & Hamer, D. H. (2007). Evidence for a gene-gene interaction in predicting children's behavior problems: Association of serotonin transporter short and dopamine receptor D4 long genotypes with internalizing and externalizing behaviors in typically developing 7-year-olds. *Development and Psychopathology, 19*, 1105–1116.
Schultze-Florey, C. R., Martinex-Maza, O., Magpantay, L., Breen, E. C., Irwin, M. R., Gündel, H., et al. (2012). When grief makes you sick: Bereavement induced systemic inflammation is a question of genotype. *Brain, Behavior, and Immunity, 26*, 1066–1071.
Seligman, M. E. P., Railton, P., Baumeister, R. F., & Sripada, C. (2013). Navigating into the future or driven by the past. *Perspectives on Psychological Science, 8*, 119–141.
Shapiro, L. (2009). Making sense of mirror neurons. *Syntheses, 167*, 439–456.
Sheese, B. E., Voelker, P. M., Rothbart, M. K., & Posner, M. I. (2007). Parenting quality interacts with genetic variation in dopamine receptor D4 to influence temperament in early childhood. *Developmental Psychopathology, 19*, 1039–1046.
Smoller, J. W., Craddock, N., Kendler, K., Lee, P. H., Neale, B. M., Nurnberger, J. L., et al. (2013). Identification of risk loci with shared effects on five major psychiatric disorders: A genome-wide analysis. *Lancet, 381*, 1371–1379.

Smoller, J. W., Kendler, K., & Craddock, N. (2013). Identification of risk loci with shared effects on five major psychiatric disorders: A genome-wide analysis. *Lancet, 381*, 1371–1379.

Srividhya, J., Li, Y., & Pomerening, J. R. (2011). Open cascades as simple solutions to providing ultrasensitivity and adaptation in cellular signaling. *Physiology & Behavior, 8*, 046005. doi:10.1088/1478-3975/8/4/046005.

Tackett, J. L., Lahey, B. B., Van Hulle, C., Waldman, I., Krueger, R. F., & Rathouz, P. J. (2013). Common genetic influences on negative emotionality and a general psychopathology factor in childhood and adolescence. *Journal of Abnormal Psychology, 122*, 1142–1153.

Taylor, J., Allan, N., Mikolajewski, A. J., & Hart, S. A. (2013). Common genetic and nonshared environmental factors contribute to the association between socioemotional dispositions and the externalizing factor in children. *Journal of Child Psychology and Psychiatry, and Allied Disciplines, 54*, 67–76.

Turkheimer, E. (2011). Commentary: Variation and causation in the environment and genome. *International Journal of Epidemiology, 40*, 598–601.

Verweij, K. J., Yang, J., Lahti, J., Veijola, J., Hintsanen, M., Pulkki-Råback, L., et al. (2012). Maintenance of genetic variation in human personality: Testing evolutionary models by estimating heritability due to common causal variants and investigating the effect of distant inbreeding. *Evolution, 66*, 3238–3251.

Vinkhuyzen, A. A. E., Pedersen, N. L., Yang, J., Lee, S. H., Magnusson, P. K. E., Iacono, W. G., et al. (2012). Common SNPs explain some of the variation in the personality dimensions of neuroticism and extraversion. *Translational Psychiatry, 2*, e102. doi:10.1038/tp.2012.49.

Visscher, P. M., Goddard, M. E., Derks, E. M., & Wray, N. R. (2012). Evidence-based psychiatric genetics, AKA the false dichotomy between common and rare variant hypothesis. *Molecular Psychiatry, 17*, 474–485.

Vrieze, S. I., Feng, S., Miller, M. B., Hicks, B. M., Pankratz, N., Abecasis, G. R., et al. (2014). Rare nonsynonymous exonic variants in addiction and behavioral disinhibition. *Biological Psychiatry, 75*, 783–789.

Wahlsten, D. (2013). A contemporary view of genes and behavior: Complex systems and interactions. In R. M. Lerner & J. B. Benson (Eds.), *Advances in child development and behavior. Embodiment and epigenesis: Theoretical and methodological issues in understanding the role of biology within the relational developmental system. Part A: Philosophical, theoretical, and biological dimensions* (Vol. 44, pp. 285–306). Waltham, MA: Academic Press.

World Health Organization. (2017). *International Classification of Disease, 11th Revision*.

Yates, F. E. (2008). Homeokinetics/homeodynamics: A physical heuristic for life and complexity. *Ecological Psychology, 20*, 148–179.

Young, G. (2011). *Development and causality: Neo-Piagetian perspectives*. New York: Springer Science+Business Media.

Zuk, O., Hechter, E., Sunyaeva, S. R., & Lander, E. S. (2012). The mystery of missing heritability. *Proceedings of the National Academy of Sciences of the United States of America, 109*, 1193–1198.

Gene × Environment Interaction: The Environmental Revolution

10

Chapter Introduction

Gene × Environment (G × E) interaction is a crucial aspect of behavior genetics, and the extent of and types of research in the area continues to accelerate. The present chapter reviews the differentiation that is taking place on the question. The chapter reviews the different ways that the field addresses G × E (Rutter, 2011). Notably, there is debate about the replicability of critical findings in the area (Duncan, Pollastri, & Smoller, 2014), yet most of the research is supportive.

Most of the chapter reviews recent research supporting G × E effects in genes, which, for the most part are related to neurotransmitters (especially *5-HTTLPR*, *MAOA*, *DRD4*). The review is divided into the G × E effects on externalizing and internalizing outcomes. Some of the research is becoming quite nuanced in methodology, for example, on the one hand, combining genetic analyses, or, on the other hand, differentiating types of adverse (e.g., parental) environments that lead to negative outcomes in the presence of certain alleles. Also, the area is complicated by interactions beyond G × E, such as G × G and G × E × D. Finally, lack of replication is found in some studies of certain G × E effects, so that large-scale and cross-genomic studies are beginning to proliferate, and sometimes with novel results.

The G × E Model

Candidate Genes

Introduction Duncan et al. (2014) reviewed the psychiatric genetic and psychological science approaches to Gene × Environment (G × E) interaction, noting a "growing divide" in these two approaches to the question. The first studies in behavioral genetics focused on heritability without considering molecular genetics. Typically, these studies examine family constellations, especially in twins, to estimate the proportionate contributions of genetic and environmental factors. This research has established a robust contribution of genetic factors to disorders such as schizophrenia, for which heritability appears to exceed 70 % (Sullivan, Daly, & O'Donovan, 2012). Also, heritability approaches 30–40 % for the heritability of internalizing disorders (depression, anxiety). However, unlike the case for psychiatric genetics, behavior genetics does not specify specific genetic risk factors.

Psychiatric genetics is riding the exponential growth in knowledge and also application of polymorphic genetic loci as risk factors in psychiatric disorder. The first wave of studies in the area could deal with only a few hundred genetic loci of the millions of polymorphic loci in the human genome. The techniques involved linkage analysis

G. Young, *Unifying Causality and Psychology*, DOI 10.1007/978-3-319-24094-7_10

and candidate gene studies. The former examined chromosome regions among family members sharing an illness and the latter examined candidate genes (cG) that could elucidate pathways to disorder (usually involving neurotransmitters). According to Duncan et al. (2014), these were "low throughput" approaches to genetic studies, and failures to replicate were more common than expected in the candidate gene studies.

As technology advanced, phenotypic expression could be studied in relation to millions of common genetic allele variants over the whole genome, in an approach referred to as genome-wide association study (GWAS). Because of the multiple statistical tests involved in any one study, the alpha or p value of significance in results has been established at $p < 0.00000005$, which is far stricter than the typical value in psychological science (usually, $p < 0.05$, 0.01, or 0.001).

In general, GWAS results are changing understanding of psychiatric genetics. Not only are candidate gene findings not being replicated but also the effect sizes for any one gene loci are exceedingly small even if significant. Also, GWAS findings are leading to surprising results, for example, related to gene loci associated with psychiatric disorder not even in the protein-coding portion of genes. That is, the gene loci being underscored are in intergenic and introgenic regions of the genome rather than within exons, which had been the focus in cG research.

A field related to psychiatric genetics is neurogenetics (Hyde, 2015). For example, it describes Imaging Gene × Environment interaction (IG × E). It describes how G × E affects brain and behavior, and I have cited some research in this book in this regard. The new field is finding linkages in common genetic polymorphisms to variations in brain structure, function, and connectivity. For example, Glaser et al. (2014) found the pathway from genotype (corticotropin-releasing hormone receptor 1 gene) [CRHR1] to neural reactivity (right ventral–lateral prefrontal cortex) and then to negative emotionality was moderated by childhood stress in the link from genotype to neural reactivity.

Evidence Duncan et al. (2014) reviewed the research in the field of psychiatry in the first decade (2000–2009) of cG investigation related to G × E interactions (referred to as cG × E). They found 103 studies in 98 publications that met their inclusion criteria. The field flourished with the studies by Caspi et al. (2002, 2003). The former found that childhood maltreatment was associated with antisocial behavior, but only in the presence of a functional polymorphism in the gene encoding monoamine oxidase A (*MAOA*). The latter found that stressful life events were associated with depression, but only for one allele for *5-HTTLPR*, a serotonin-related locus (serotonin transporter linked polymorphic region).

The Duncan et al. (2014) review of the literature found 14 studies similar to Caspi et al. (2002) and 32 similar to Caspi et al. (2003) (with over 50 other studies). The subsequent research involving these two Caspi team studies did not offer unequivocal support for the original findings. Indeed, of the two Caspi et al. studies, only the one in 2002 has found some positive support. For example, in a very similar study, Fergusson, Horwood, Miller, and Kennedy (2011) did not replicate the 2003 study.

Aside from the Caspi and colleagues research, the field has investigated to a sufficient degree four other cG × Es (at least two replication attempts). These include three others involving *5-HTTLPR*—Kaufman et al. (2004) on social support and depression; Kaufman et al. (2007) on adverse life events in predicting alcohol use/abuse; and Kendler, Kuhn, Vittum, Prescott, and Riley (2005) on adverse life events in predicting anxiety—as well as Bradley et al. (2008) on adverse life events and depression for *CRHR1*. The two Kaufman studies have not been confirmed, as was found for Caspi et al. (2003), while results for the other two are mixed, as was found for Caspi et al. (2002).

Conclusion Duncan et al. (2014) concluded that cG × E research in psychiatry has investigated six major interactions, of which only three have received "preliminary" support in the literature. In addition, the variant G × E hypothesis of "differential susceptibility" (Ellis, Boyce, Belsky, Bakermans-Kranenburg, & van IJzendoorn, 2011) has not received empirical support at the stringent research significance levels that are now the norm in psychiatric genetics. It still needs to be shown to an acceptable rigorous statistical standard that some genetic alleles are more impervious to environmental effects while others vary extremely toward negative or positive outcome, depending on the quality of the environment (hardship or the "right" environment, respectively). The authors advocated for a "biopsychosocial" etiology of mental health disorder.

Comment

Duncan et al. (2014) reviewed the literature from 2002 to 2009, and their conclusions seem premature that there are only three cG×Es with some evidence in their support. In the 5 years since the year of the last studies that they reviewed, the field has published relevant G×E research in an exponential fashion and the conclusions offered by Duncan et al. (2014) no longer apply, despite their recent vintage. In the following, I trace some of the critical concepts and empirical research since 2009 in the field in order to buttress this conclusion.

That being said, the work of Dick et al. (2015) cautioned that candidate Gene×Environment research (cG×E) has problems with replicability. They referred to the use of small *N*'s, low power, publication bias, and so on. Even in studies in which *N*'s are large and candidate disorders are associated with genetic contributions (e.g., schizophrenia), there still is lack of statistical power to detect genotype-relative risks that are < 1.1. Typically, the effect size in this research is small. The "false discovery" rate might be "unacceptably high." In the methodology, genes, environment, and even the scale and statistical model used might be chosen inappropriately. It is impossible to control for all covariates and confounders in cG×E research. Nevertheless, the literature presents a fast-developing field converging on certain genes as especially important as influences on behavior, development, disorder, and so on.

Complexities

Introduction In the following, first, I discuss some complexity in the genetics of G×E approaches and, then, do the same with respect to the environmental aspect. G×E is not a straightforward interaction of independent factors.

Genes Uher (2011a) reviewed the major G×E interactions that have been found for mental health outcomes (see Table 10.1). He noted that none involve a direct genetic effect independent of the interactions involved. The table lists nine genes relevant to mental health. For the environment, the exposures range from child abuse to parenting rules. The outcomes include antisocial behavior, depression, psychosis, attention deficit/hyperactive disorder (ADHD), alcohol use, and posttraumatic stress disorder (PTSD). The research started with the work of Caspi et al. (2002), but has burgeoned. Uher (2011a) appears more positive about the work and validity of the Caspi group findings compared to Duncan et al. (2014).

Caspi, Hariri, Holmes, Uher, and Moffitt (2011) noted that the serotonin transporter gene, the *5-HTTLPR* gene, that is involved in G×E interactions or genetic sensitivities to the environment that promotes stress sensitivities, has had its effects replicated in multiple studies and, moreover, intermediate pathways are being investigated. The research considers areas as diverse as bullying, PTSD, aggression, and regulation of negative affect. The brain regions apparently involved include the amygdala and the medial prefrontal cortex (PFC), as well as increased hypothalamic pituitary adrenal (HPA) axis reactivity.

For *5-HTTLPR*, Fig. 10.1, taken from Caspi et al. (2011), indicates that short allele (*s*) carriers, who are more susceptible, have up to five brain regions/neural circuitry affected in their response to threat/stress in the environment. It appears the variant is related to a more general personality trait involving negative affect or neuroticism (instability), rather than to a more specific mood, such as depression.

Table 10.1 Gene–environment interactions on mental health outcomes reported in the literature

			Direct first-order effects				
Gene	Exposure	Outcome	Genotype	Exposure	Reference	Replicated	Reviewed
MAOA	Child abuse	Antisocial behavior	No	Yes	Caspi et al. (2002)	Yes	Taylor and Kim-Cohen (2007)
SERT	Child abuse/life events	Depression	No	Yes	Caspi et al. (2003)	Yes	Uher and McGuffin (2008) Brown and Harris (2008) Munafo, Durrant, Lewis, and Flint (2009) Risch et al. (2009)
CRHR1	Child abuse	Depression	No	Yes	Bradley et al. (2008)	Yes	
FKBP5	Child abuse	Posttraumatic stress disorder	No	Yes	Binder et al. (2008)		
COMT	Cannabis	Psychosis	No	Yes	Caspi et al. (2005)		
DRD4	Season of birth	Attention-deficit hyperactivity disorder (ADHD)	No	Yes	Seeger, Schloss, Schmidt, Ruter-Jungfleisch, and Henn (2004)		
DRD4	Parenting	ADHD	No	Yes	Sheese, Voelker, Rothbart, and Posner (2007)	Yes	Thapar, Langley, Owen, and O'Donovan (2007)
DRD2	Parenting (rules)	Alcohol use	No	Yes	van der Zwaluw et al. (2010)		
DAT1	Mother alcohol use in pregnancy	ADHD	No	Yes	Brookes et al. (2006)		

Adopted by permission of Oxford University Press. Uher, R. (2011a). Gene-environment interactions. In K. S. Kendler, S. R. Jaffee, & D. Romer (Eds.), *The dynamic genome and mental health: The role of genes and environments in youth development* (pp. 29–58). New York: Oxford University Press. Reprinted by permission of Oxford University Press, USA. [Table 2.1, Page 38]

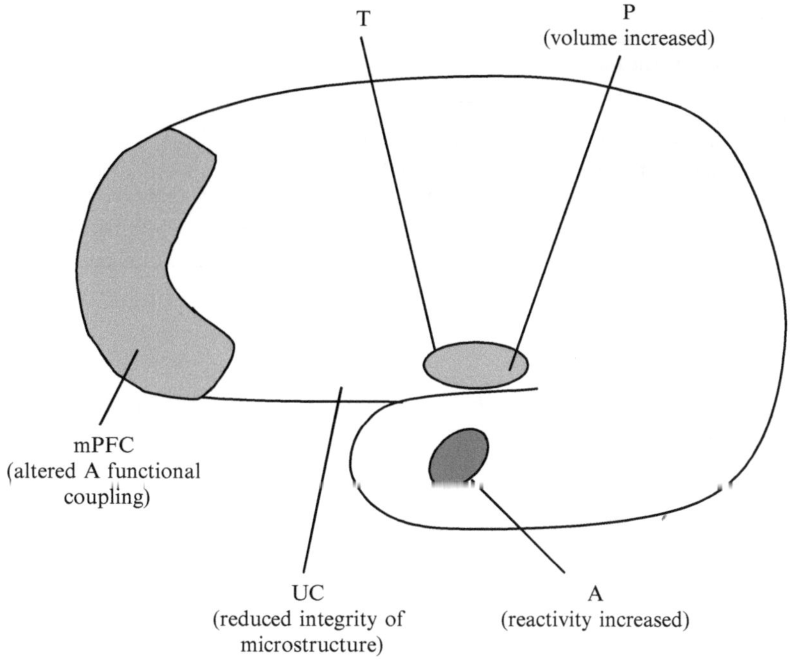

Fig. 10.1 The 5-HTTLPR S (Short) polymorphism affects the neural circuitry for responding to stress and threat in the environment (as implicated in humans and nonhuman primates). *Abbreviation*: *T*=thalamus, *P*=pulvinar, *mPFC*=medial prefrontal cortex, *UC*=urcinate fasciculus, *A*=amygdala. *Note*. Increases in *s* carriers: conditioned fear; startle (auditory); sympathetic nervous system reactivity; hypothalamic pituitary adrenal (HPA) reactivity; attention to threat bias; retrograde amnesia (emotionally induced); financial risk aversion, blushing (socially). Adapted from Caspi, Hariri, Holmes, Uher, and Moffitt (2011), slightly modified

Qualifications Kendler (2011) noted that geneticists understand environment as everything that is not genetic. For social scientists, it refers to what is "outside the skin." In its extreme, the geneticists' definition of environment includes measurement error. Also, Kendler noted that genetics and environment are considered interrelated both statistically and biologically, or in terms of how environment influences gene expression. Biologically, it refers to how genes and environment work together in creating phenotype. Statistically, it refers to the effect of certain combinations of allelic variants of genes and certain environments relevant to the functional activity of the genes. I note that these are quite different conceptions, with the latter limiting outcomes to a simultaneous presence of specific components of two factors (genetic, environmental) and the former expansively allowing any type of additive interactions over multiple variants of both factors.

Kendler (2011) queried the impact of G×E interactions, and the extent to which they have been surpassed by other genetic phenomena. For Kendler, the G×E interaction might be ephemeral. In contrast, gene–environment correlation (rGE) is much "firmer" (e.g., genetic risk factors for disease also increase the probability of exposure to the environmental stressor). The concept of rGE "flips" the causal relationship from humans as passive recipients of the environment to active environmental "creators" outside the skin (see Fig. 10.2).

Development adds complexity to gene–environment effects. Genetic influence might be delayed and a new genetic variation could impact the phenotype later on. Genetic attenuation is when it has less of an effect later on. Developmental homotypy is when genes influence the phenotype the same way over time. In developmental heterotypy, the genes express different phenotypes at different developmental periods. For Kendler (2011), this illustrates the dynamic nature of development and that the boundary between genes and environment is more porous and less clear than it seems.

Rutter (2011) also noted the distinction between statistical and phenomenal interaction in G×E. He discussed whether G×E interactions reflect statistical/mathematical manipulations only, or also whether they address underlying psychological, developmental, and biological

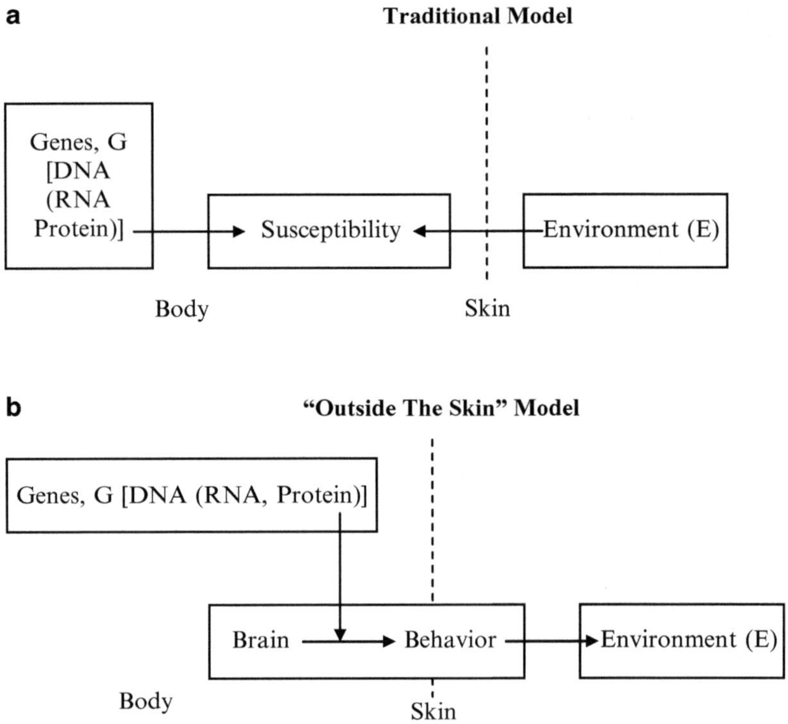

Fig. 10.2 Disease etiology in relation to environment. The top model (traditional) shows disease susceptibility resulting from genetic pathways and the environment, with the latter effect due solely from the environment to the organism. The bottom model presents an outside-the-skin pathway—genetic factors influence the brain and behavior, so that the organism can alter the environment. Adapted from Kendler (2011)

mediation of the outcomes involved. Statistically significant interactions should be discussed in the context of theory and of postulated mechanisms and not just abstract statistical technicalities. Moreover, in the latter, there is no firm or best approach, i.e., in neither the approach of analysis of variance (ANOVA) statistical nor that of regression.

Environment Shanahan and Bauldry (2011) noted that G × E interaction research typically uses measures of environmental markers, such as stressors. They advocated for a systems approach, which organizes environmental features (or candidates) into interrelated interactive networks of risk, or coalesced associations. Environmental candidates accumulate in risk and could become nonlinear in mechanism, and their temporal history must be considered (e.g., sensitive periods or programming), including for history prior to events at issue. Risks are contextually and personally influenced, too (e.g., prior vulnerabilities/protective-resilience factors, subjective meaning ascribed, role-social support at time).

Burt (2011) noted that in gene–environment interplay in genetics, protective factors might "deactivate" genetic influences. Adverse environments might "diminish" the importance of genetic factors. Risky environments might not accentuate but, rather, "obviate" the potential influence of genetic risk, reducing their consequences. She referred to this phenomenon as "G × E protection." In Burt (2015), she added that in "bioecological" G × E environments that are deleterious function to amplify environmental influences on the behavioral outcomes involved. Further, G × E vary in their effects across development.

Dickens, Turkheimer, and Beam (2011) presented a reciprocal effects model of cognitive ability that makes an interesting distinction between endogenous and exogenous environments (see Fig. 10.3). The former are aspects of the environment affected by individual ability, whereas the latter are not. Genetic influences on exogenous environments could become magnified in the process of rGE by the feedback, multiplier process between cognitive ability and endogenous environment.

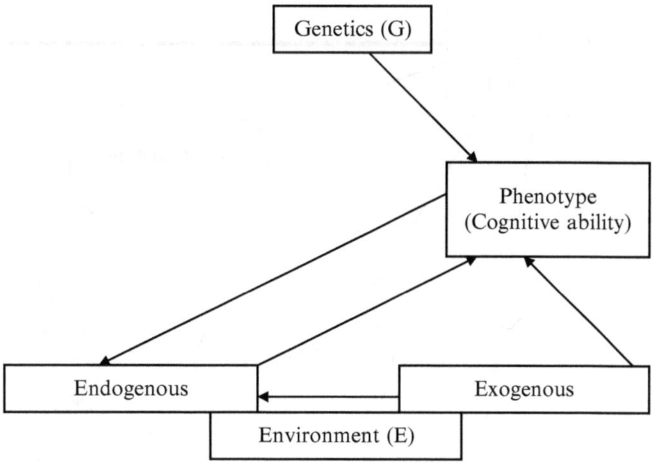

Fig. 10.3 Reciprocal effects model of cognitive ability. Differentiation of the environment in influence on behavior (e.g., cognitive ability) includes its endogenous (internal) and exogenous (external) components. Adapted from Dickens, Turkheimer, & Beam (2011)

Mill (2011) noted that epigenetic changes could serve as pathways to mediate G×E interactions. Moreover, epigenetic programming can be reversed. This might allow for therapeutic intervention, and some psychopharmacological agents might work due to epigenetic programming effects. This illustrates further the dynamic nature of the genome and epigenome.

Rutter and Dodge (2011) specified that environmental stress is more adverse when chronic, constituting "the main causal mechanism" in G×E sensitivities. Moreover, because other people are involved, it is necessary to "separate cause and consequence" pertaining to the individual's own role in the matter. Moreover, interpersonal risk processes typically are reciprocal or relational, so their separation and causal role might be difficult to differentiate.

Rutter and Dodge (2011) added that environmental risk factors might be proximal or distal, and which one is causal in a chain might not be clear. For example, if it is distal, the proximal one only operates noncausally as a by-product of the distal one.

Most important, Rutter and Dodge (2011) noted that true environmental effects might relate to only how the environment is perceived by the individual, or the meaning ascribed. That is, objective environmental features might not be the relevant ones in a particular G×E interaction.

Uher (2011b) described that G×E effects indicate that genes do not directly cause mental illness; rather, mental illness is multiply causative or etiological heterogeneous. In the case of *5-HTTLPR*, the short (*s*) allele renders carriers more vulnerable to depression following childhood adversity, but the long (*l*) allele might lead to depression because of other challenges, such as hormonal changes in pregnancy (Doornbos et al., 2009).

Also, Uher (2011b) pointed out that factors that cause and then perpetuate depression might differ (see Fig. 10.4). Proximal factors seem more involved in the former and distal factors in the latter (e.g., stressful event, childhood abuse, respectively) (Brown, Craig, & Harris, 2008). However, distal factors might have their influence through epigenetic stamps (see Fig. 10.5) that accumulate from the early adversity effects, leading to induction of the illness later on after further epigenetic modifications.

Kaufman and Perephetchikova (2011) noted that, in the case of *5-HTTLPR* and of maltreated children, there might be a G×G (gene by gene interaction) in expression of gene–environment sensitivities toward depression (with the G×G interaction taking place with the brain-derived neurotrophic factor gene, *BDNF*; Kaufman et al., 2006). However, the researchers also found a moderation of this effect with positive social support, indicating a G×G×E×E 4-way interaction effect! The supportive environmental appears to affect epigenetic marks on glucocorticoid receptor gene promoter activity in the hippocampus (McGowan et al., 2009; Weaver et al., 2004).

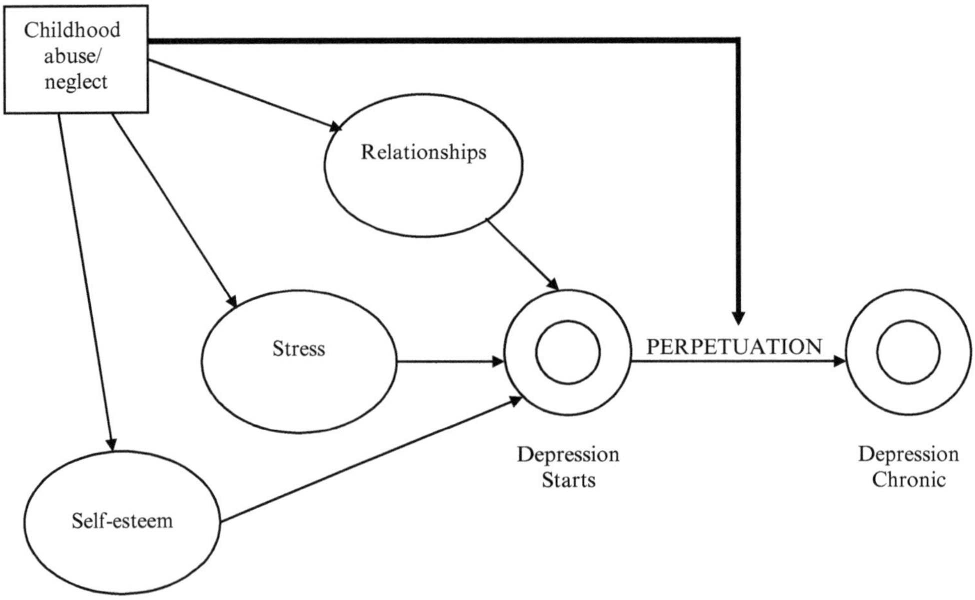

Fig. 10.4 Child abuse/neglect affects onset/maintenance of depression. Child abuse/neglect is associated with depression onset. Proximal factors, including stressful life events, quality of intimate relationships, and low self-esteem, help explain it. Childhood abuse/neglect can also act directly to maintain depression. Adapted from Uher (2011b), modified with data from Brown, Craig, and Harris (2008)

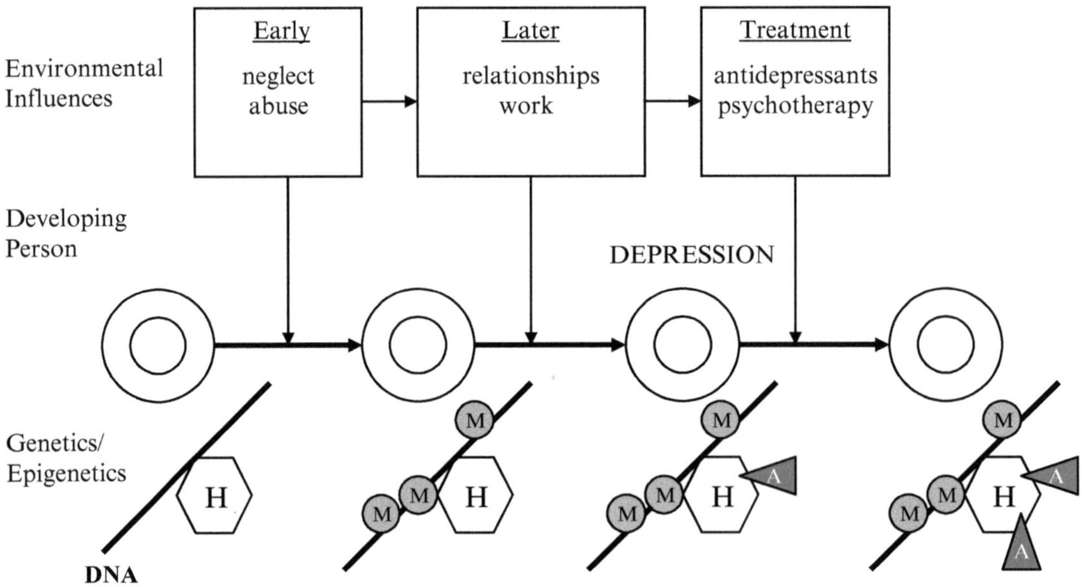

Fig. 10.5 Developmental model of depression etiology and treatment. Genetic script modified by epigenetic stamps (e.g., DNA methylation, "M"), early environmental factors. Environment in adolescence/adulthood leads to further changes (e.g., histone [H] modifications, "A"), depression triggered. Pharmacological/psychosocial treatments counterbalance. Adopted with permission of Guilford Press. Genes, environment, and personalized treatment for depression by Uher, R. in *Gene-environment interactions in developmental psychopathology* by K. A. Dodge & M. Rutter, Copyright 2011, reproduced with permission of Guilford Press. [Figure 8.2, Page 145]

Comment

The concepts qualifying the nature of G×E interactions and the nature of the environment in the interactions point to the complexity of the phenomenon and the difficulty in separating genetic and environmental effects on behavior. Statistically, it is possible to establish main effects and environmental ones on outcome, as well as interaction effects, but, systemically, the factors work together and without the clear boundaries defining them that are assumed in statistical research. For genes, statistically, the complexities include G×G interaction effects, and the same type of complicating interaction occurs with E (E×E). Moreover, the interactions involved might be over genes and over environmental factors together. Furthermore, the research points to G×E×D (development) interactions. These types of interactions at the statistical level narrow the range of what is involved in obtaining outcomes at issue because of the multiple factors involved. However, at the phenomenological level, the complexities in the types of multifactorial interactions that might be at play for any one person are even more complex, and expand the range of factors to consider in understanding outcome and its causation or etiology.

In order to understand all the facets of causality genetically and its interaction with the environment, science needs to meet practice, and emerge with workable formula that consider statistical interactions in the population level research but also factorial interaction at the individual level. This will help in elaborating the appropriate protective and supportive environments, including in psychotherapy, which would lead to controlled or even cured psychopathological outcomes. Just as there are generalist genes that might be involved transdiagnostically in psychopathology, there might be "generalist environments" (e.g., transdiagnostic therapeutic approaches) as well as specific ones to help individuals who suffer disorder and psychological conditions.

Recent Empirical Research

The following section examines research on G×E in psychological science. It examines extensions of the work of Caspi et al. (2002) on child maltreatment and antisocial behavior. It continues with other externalizing behavior. Then, it turns to G×E in internalizing behavior, such as depression.

Externalizing

MAOA Cicchetti, Rogosch, and Thibodeau (2012) have conducted a study illustrating G×E interactions in child maltreatment. They conducted the first multigenic investigation of the question. They considered three candidate genes as moderators—ones related to tryptophan hydroxylase, serotonin transporter, and monoamine oxidase A (*TPH1*, *5-HTT*, and *MAOA*, respectively). All are involved in the regulation of the neurotransmitter serotonin, and all have been shown to be linked to the suite of aggression, violence, and other antisocial behavior, beginning with the breakthrough research of Caspi et al. (2002) with *MAOA*. The authors investigated 10- to 12-year-olds from low-income homes (in prior research, older participants usually have been investigated). They used multiple measures and multiple informants (self, peer, adult camp counselor) in a prospective study with a large sample. Maltreatment was evaluated comprehensively. There was a control group. In the statistical treatment of the data, covariates were used, as well as Bonferroni adjustments to reduce Type I error.

Cicchetti et al. (2012) described in depth the study by Caspi et al. (2002). These latter researchers had found that negative effects of child maltreatment in a longitudinal study of males were significantly less if participants had high compared to low *MAOA* activity, as moderated by the *MAOA* upstream variable number tandem repeat (u-VNTR) polymorphism. They examined four indices of violent behavior (conduct disorder diagnosis, violent crime conviction, disposition to violence, antisocial personality disorder symptoms). The Caspi et al. (2002) results indicated that low *MAOA* activity could not serve as a buffer to maltreatment in its effects on violence indicators due to a concomitant effect on neurotransmitter systems (norepinephrine, serotonin, dopamine).

Cicchetti et al. (2012) noted that a meta-analysis by Kim-Cohen et al. (2006) supported the findings of Caspi et al. (2002) and replications have been conducted since (e.g., Åslund et al., 2011; Fergusson, Boden, Horwood, Miller, & Kennedy 2011; Weder et al., 2009; for adults, adolescents, and children, respectively; although not all studies replicate).

According to Cicchetti et al. (2012), there have not been reported G × E studies involving *TPH1*. There have been two with *5-HTT*, but the polymorphism involved (*5-HTTLPR*) moderated antisocial behavior in girls, not boys (Douglas et al., 2011; Li & Lee, 2010).

As for the results of the Cicchetti et al. (2012) study, child maltreatment variables demonstrated strong main effects on antisocial behavior outcome. Genetic effects were clearly G × E ones, in particular. For nonmaltreated children, genetic variation did not affect indicators of antisocial behavior. In contrast, for maltreated children, specific polymorphisms for each of the three candidate genes were related to heightened antisocial behavior, as indicated by self-report (Pittsburgh Youth Survey; Loeber, Farrington, Stouthamer-Loeber, & Van Kammen, 1998). For *MAOA*, this referred to the low activity variant of the gene and self-report both for lifetime and past 6-month behavior, but only for boys (see Fig. 10.6). [Multiple findings related to *TPH1* and *5-HTTLPR*, but these are not reported here].

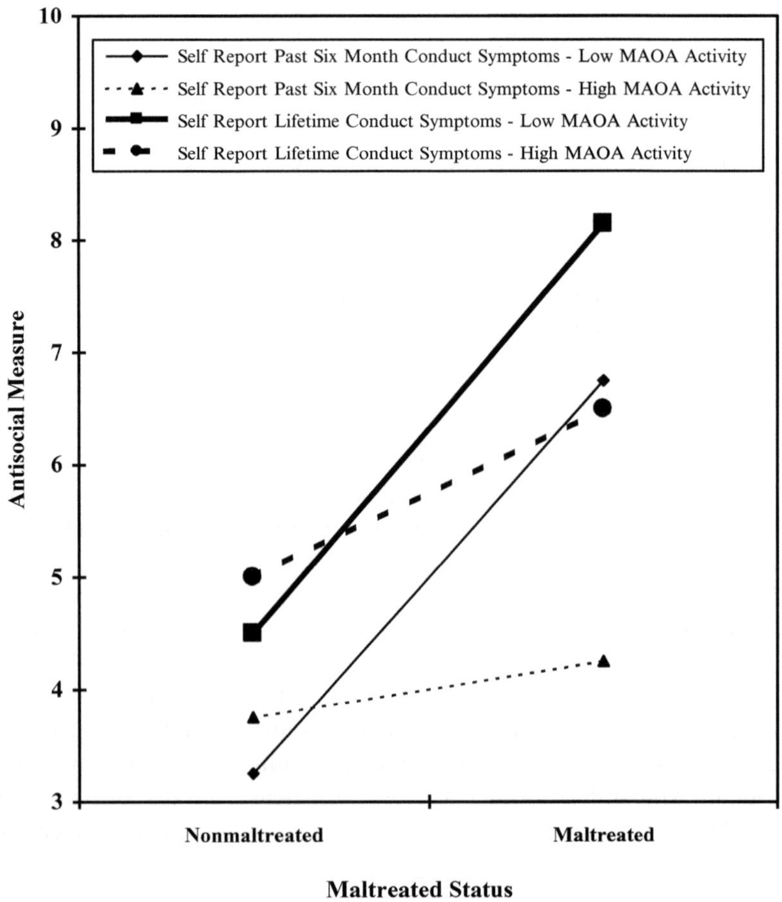

Fig. 10.6 Monoamine Oxidase A (MAOA) and maltreatment status predict antisocial behavior for boys only. The figure indicates that *MAOA* interacts with maltreatment experience in predicting later antisocial behavior in the boys studied. The antisocial measure involved self-reported conduct symptoms in either the past 6 months or over the lifetime. The robust findings and similar pattern in maltreated and nonmaltreated participants speak to the replicability and generalizability of the results. Adapted from Cicchetti, Rogosch, and Thibodeau (2012)

Cicchetti et al. (2012) concluded that there is a genetic moderation of the linkage between child maltreatment and antisocial behavior that involves polymorphisms of genes related to serotonin. Moreover, the genetic moderation in this case is multigenic. Neither direct effect of genes nor rGE effects were found that could account for antisocial behavior in the population studied.

MAOA Other Research Choe, Shaw, Hyde, and Forbes (2014) conducted a longitudinal study of low-income males over 20 years on early punitive discipline and later antisocial behavior. Early punitive discipline at 1.5–5 years was related to antisocial behavior at 15–20 years, but only in those participants with low-activity *MAOA* genotypes. [As mentioned, Caspi et al. (2002) had originally shown a G×E interaction in relation to childhood maltreatment and later anti-social behavior by examining physical abuse and neglect in conjunction with *MAOA*].

The Choe et al. (2014) study expanded the scope of the Caspi et al. findings by extending them to measures of harsh parenting. The measure involved punitive discipline. An early parenting coding system was applied during laboratory tasks (e.g., scoring—too strict, demanding). Mothers' behavior had an earlier effect in these regards compared to that of fathers, with the effects more visible in toddlerhood for mothers and starting in late adolescence for fathers. The results did not differ according to race (Caucasian, African American). The authors concluded that the genetic vulnerability to harsh environments includes an effect of punitive discipline on later antisocial behavior.

Denson, Dobson-Stone, Ronay, von Hippel, and Schira (2014) explained that individuals with the low-risk allele in the promoter region of this gene (high expression allele, *MAOA-H*, 4 variable number tandem repeat allele; uVNTR) are less at risk for increased aggression compared to those having the high-risk allele (low expression *MAOA-L*, 3-repeat; Caspi et al., 2002; Kuepper, Grant, Wielpuetz, & Hennig, 2013). In a laboratory study, Denson et al. (2014) investigated the relationship of anger-control to an insult, and neural activation in the dorsal anterior cingulate (dACC) and also in the amygdala cortex (involved in anger regulation and arousal, respectively) as a function of *MAOA* genotype.

Denson et al. (2014) found that men possessing the high-risk allele of the *MAOA*-uVNTR polymorphism expressed greater neural activity in the indicated regions compared to the low-risk allele (men were tested because the gene is X-linked). The low-risk allele was associated with functional decoupling of the dACC and the amygdala, indicating top-down disengagement of the dACC in anger control when bottom-up amygdala pull is involved, but only for this functional polymorphism.

In G×E research, other studies are examining externalizing behavior different than antisocial behavior, and also related behavior, in conjunction with environmental interactions. Calkins, Propper, and Mills-Koonce (2013) reported G×E interactions involving parenting behavior and developmental psychopathology. For example, Enoch, Steer, Newman, Gibson, and Goldman (2010) found that the low activity allele of *MAOA-LPR* (length promoter region, a 30-base pair repeat in the promoter region) was associated with hyperactivity for 4- and 7-year-old girls who had been exposed to more stressful life events in the period 0.5–3.5 years of age. For boys, the relationship involved 0.5–2.5-year adversity and 7-year hyperactivity. Willoughby, Mills-Koonce, Propper, and Waschbusch (2013) found that harsh and intrusive maternal parenting behavior interacted with the methionine allele of the *BDNF* gene in 3-year-olds expressing oppositional and callous unemotional behavior. Calkins et al. (2013) concluded that this line of research needs to consider G×G interactions, as per Sulik et al. (2012).

5-HTTLPR Davies and Cicchetti (2014) investigated mechanisms that are more proximal in the interaction of early maternal unresponsiveness and the *5-HTTLPR* genotype, and ultimately function as precursors to later disruptive behavioral problems. They postulated that exposure to adversity early in life leads to negative emotional reactions when serotonergic function is compromised, as with the *5-HTTLPR s* allele, and then it leads to externalizing problems (see Fig. 10.7).

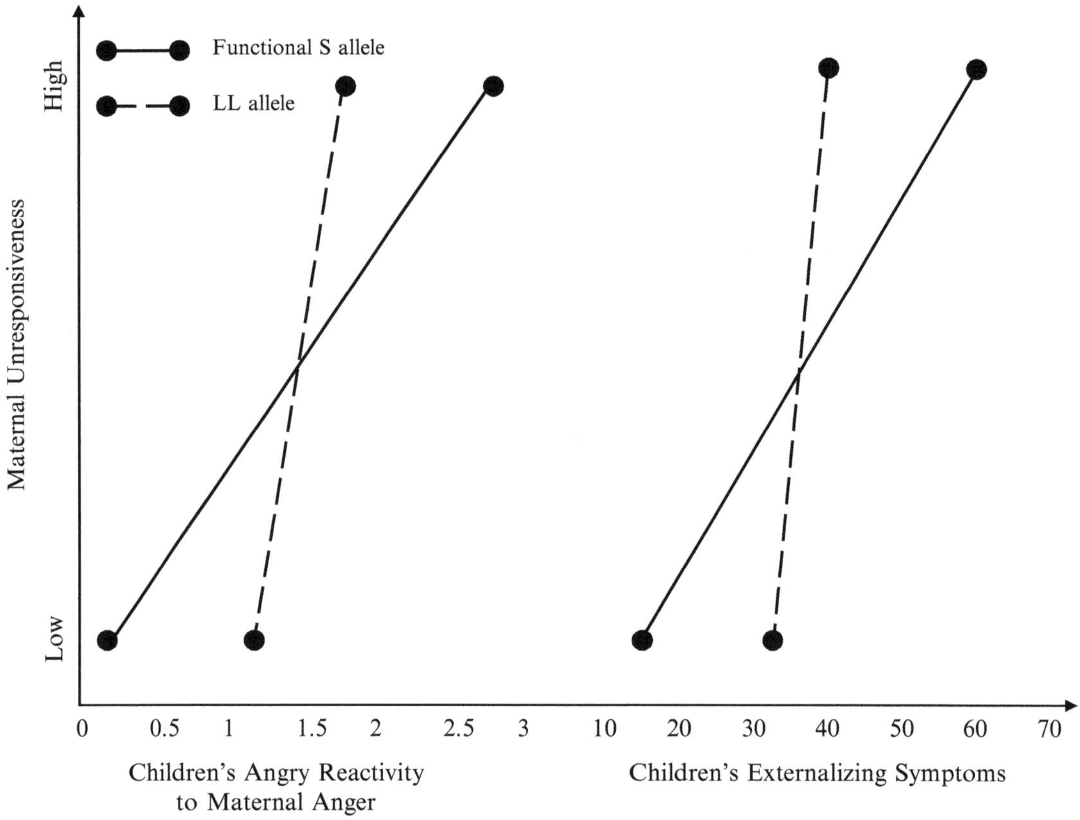

Fig. 10.7 The interaction between maternal unresponsiveness and the 5-HTTLPR gene in children's anger reactivity and children's externalizing symptoms. A G × E interaction is apparent in degree of maternal responsive and the gene *5-HTTLPR* in the outcome measure of the child's angry reactions to maternal anger, as well as in the child's symptoms of externalization. The particular functional alleles involves are S, L. The outcome measure was taken over 2 years in the latter case and at 1 year in the former case. Adapted from Davies and Cicchetti (2014)

The *s* allele appears to magnify the association between early maternal unresponsiveness and later externalization by increasing emotional reactivity in children confronted by stressful parental events. However, the authors posited possible racial differences, in that, for American Black preschoolers, maternal unresponsiveness predicted later externalization if they carried the *5-HTTLPR ll* genotype (e.g., after Anderson & Mayes, 2010).

The sample tested consisted of disadvantaged Black 2-year-olds and their mothers. Two years after initial testing, early maternal unresponsiveness did indeed predict later externalizing symptoms for those having the *ll* genotype. The results further revealed that these carriers evidenced the association by virtue of their tendency to manifest a heightened irritability in response to maternal negativity.

Beaver, Ratchford, and Ferguson (2009) investigated the mediating effect of the *5-HTTLPR* polymorphism on the relationship between exposure to delinquent peers and degree of self-control. The study found that measures of level of self-control in adolescence and young adulthood over 7 years was related to delinquent peer affiliation in adolescence.

Brody et al. (2014) found a genetic moderation involving *5-HTTLPR* serotonin transporter promoter gene (*SLC6A4*) in the longitudinal relationship between age-11 harsh parenting experience and age-19 health. The latter was measured using three indicators (C Reactive protein, CRP, a biomarker of chronic inflammation; self-reported health problems; and depression, as measured by the Center for Epidemiologic Studies Depression scale (CES-D; Radloff, 1977). The teenagers were African American youths living in the rural south. Also, they had their degree of anger measured at ages 16–18 using the State-Trait Anger Expression Inventory (STAEI; Spielberger, Jacobs, Russell, & Crane, 1983).

The results showed that elevated levels of anger forecast 19-year health, but only for *s*-allele carriers of *5-HTTLPR*. That is, *ll* carriers were conferred buffering against poorer health outcomes by early harsh parenting.

OXTR Smearman, Winiarski, Brennan, Najman, and Johnson (2014) conducted a G × E study on the oxytocin receptor gene (*OXTR*) and antisocial behavior. They argued that the study is interesting because oxytocin is called the love or cuddle hormone. However, rather than being uniquely a positive outcome associated hormone, it might generally heighten the salience of either socially positive or negative stimuli. Genetically, the G relative to the A allele of the *rs53576* polymorphism of the *OXTR* gene might be associated with giving more attention to salient social cues rather than being associated with prosocial behavior only. The authors studied these possibilities in high risk youth (exposed to early maternal depression).

In the study, report measures included the YSR (Youth Self-Report; Achenbach, 1991) and the CBCL (Child Behavior Checklist; Achenbach & Edelbrock 1981) for age 15 youth conduct problems. Interviews were used to rate conduct disorder (KSADS-E; Schedule for Affective Disorders and Schizophrenia for School-Aged Children, Epidemiological Version; Orvaschel, 1995). For reported age-20 antisocial behavior, the study used the ASR (Adult Self-Report; Achenbach & Rescorla 2003) and ABCL (Adult Behavior Checklist; Achenbach & Rescorla 2003). Antisocial behavior was rated using the SCID-II (Structured Clinical Interview for DSM-IV Axis II disorders; First, Gibbon, Spitzer, Williams, & Benjamin, 1997). Social stress at both ages was measured by the UCLA Life Stress Interview (UCLALSI; Adrian & Hammen, 1993; Rao, Hammen, & Daley, 1999). In this longitudinal study, early life adversity was scored in the pregnancy, birth, 6-month, and 5-year assessments.

Smearman et al. (2014) found that the G allele participants who had experienced high social stress showed higher age-20 antisocial behavior. Also, they also found an age-15 main effect for G allele participants, which was associated with more conduct problems. The authors concluded that their G × E results concerned polymorphisms of *rs53576* in interaction with high social stress, which together influence social salience, leading to antisocial behavior outcomes.

DRD4 Boyce and Kobor (2015) noted that Zohsel et al. (2014) found an interaction of maternal report of prenatal stress and the 7-repeat allele of *DRD4* (the dopamine D4 receptor gene) for predicting the outcome of conduct/oppositional defiant disorder in early adolescence. Smith, Kryski, Sheikh, Singh, & Hayden (2013) found interplay between parenting behavior and genetic factors in predicting effortful control, which is a self-regulatory ability. It concerns inhibiting a dominant response option so as to produce, instead, a subdominant one. It is associated with a brain region network involving executive attention and having dopamine D4 receptors, regulated in part by the *DRD4* gene.

The *DRD4* 7-repeat variant of the exon III VNTR (variable number tandem repeat) is associated with decreased signal transduction efficiency, decreased RNA stability, and decreased protein folding efficiency. These alterations appear to affect signaling and functioning of neural circuits involved in effortful control. In addition, research has established its association with behavioral conditions that relate to effortful control (e.g., poorer inhibitory control; Congdon, Lesch, & Canli, 2008). However, at times, the research yields contradictory findings (e.g., Kramer et al. 2009; linking the gene to greater inhibitory control). This suggests straightforward genetic models might be only part of the understanding of *DRD4* in relation to effortful control.

In this regard, the research demonstrates that parenting is a primary social experience that shapes effortful control (Karreman, van Tuijl, van Aken, & Dekovic, 2006, 2008). However,

G × E interaction effects have been found in that positive and negative parenting behavior might affect certain children more than others, in a differential susceptibility model (Belsky & Pluess, 2009). For example, the 7-repeat *DRD4* polymorphic variant seems to increase differential susceptibility to parenting effects (Bakermans-Kranenburg & van IJzendoorn 2011). Similarly, Sheese, Rothbart, Voelker, and Posner (2012) found this type of interaction in work with children's effortful control.

Li et al. (2016) found results concerning the dopamine transporter gene in relation to effortful control in children and to their mother's observed parenting quality. The data in the study fit the diathesis-stress model and not the differential susceptibility model. The children were studied longitudinally between 30 and 54 months. Effortful control was measured behaviorally, for example, by latency to touch a gift bag. Maternal parenting quality was assessed from videotaped free play and instructional situations at 30 months, with the behavior measured involving maternal warmth, sensitivity, and intrusiveness. The dopamine transporter gene (*SLC6A3*) variants measured involved single nucleotide polymorphisms (SNPs) and variable number tandem repeats (VNTR), as well as haplotypes of these variants. The VNTRs involved in the results serve to reduce gene expression and so lower dopamine function. These variants specifically concerned Intron 8-A/Intron 13-G, Intron 8-A3′-VTR VNTR-10, and Intron 13-G/3′-UTR VNTR-10 haplotypes. As for the direction of the results, children without these VNTR haplotypes were susceptible to maternal quality effects on the effortful control tasks, being less reactive/sensitive to varying levels of maternal parenting quality. Also, these children performed better on effortful control tasks in the context of less supportive maternal parenting. There were many other results, but we do not discuss them here.

Smith et al. (2013) found that negative parenting interacted with the *DRD4* 7-repeat variant in predicting laboratory-measured effortful control in preschoolers. They focused on inhibitory control (IC), which concerns inhibiting impulsive behavior in relation to social/contextual motivation.

Preschoolers who averaged 40 months of age were tested in the laboratory on two IC tasks. In the tower of patience task, the experimenter and child took turns in building a cardboard block tower. The experimenter waited in increasing delays before placing her blocks, forcing the child to wait longer each time. In the snack delay task, the child had to wait for a bell to ring before being allowed to get a candy that was in view under an upside down transparent cup. Once more, the child was forced to wait up to 30 s.

The results showed a main effect for negative parenting on IC. In addition, positive parenting interacted with the participants' *DRD4* 7-repeat status in predicting IC. Specifically, having the allele was associated with lower IC, but in conjunction with less positive parenting. As for the positive parenting behaviors involved, they concerned supportive presence and engagement. Smith et al. (2013) concluded that further research could specify which aspects of effortful control are more sensitive to influence of parenting and genetic variation.

Polygenic Salvatore et al. (2015) showed the power of polygenic scores as predictors in developmental psychopathology. They developed scores based on weights of SNPs used in GWAS with adults. The scores were found to predict in 14-year-olds and in 20-year-olds externalizing disorder score composites and related measures (subclinical externalizing behavior, impulsivity-related traits), including after accounting for relevant confounders. At the same time, parental monitoring, in particular, moderated the relationships found. The authors concluded that polygenic scores help reveal G × D (Gene × Development) and G × E effects related to risk for externalizing disorder and related behavior.

Internalizing

5-HTTLPR G × E research has investigated internalizing outcomes, and not only externalizing ones. For example, Vrshek-Schallhorn et al. (2014) undertook a study that helps specify the environmental contribution to G × E interactions in major depression. Recall that Caspi et al. (2003) had found an interaction between the *5-HTTLPR* and stressful life events (SLEs) in the onset of major depressive episodes (MDEs). Meta-analytic studies have confirmed the outcome of more depression under the load of stress increases when carrying the *s* allele (Karg, Burmeister, Shedden, & Sen, 2011), especially when stress is measured in interview.

Vrshek-Schallhorn et al. (2014) extended this line of research by examining, in particular, interpersonal major SLEs relative to non-interpersonal ones in relation to *5-HTTLPR*. They measured life stress using the UCLA Life Stress Interview (LSI, Hammen, 1991). The participants were high school juniors oversampled for high neuroticism. They were followed annually for 5 years, including using the SCID/NP (Structured Clinical Interview for DSM-IV Axis I Disorders, nonpatient edition; First, Spitzer, Gibbon, & Williams, 2001). The authors found that, among major SLEs, only interpersonal ones contributed significantly to the G×E interaction with *5-HTTLPR*. Chronic family stress also appeared involved in the results. Vrshek-Schallhorn et al. (2014) concluded that, just as genetic studies seek candidate genes, they should study candidate environments.

Banducci et al. (2014) examined the relationship between childhood emotional abuse and later depressive symptoms in 10- to 12-year-olds. They explored the mediation by (or G×E interactions of) the *5-HTTLPR* gene. The behavioral data was collected using scales: the Emotional Abuse subscale of the Childhood Trauma Questionnaire (CTQ; Fink, Bertstein, Handelsman, Foote, & Lovejoy 1995) and the Revised Child Anxiety and Depression Scale (RCADS; Chorpita, Moffitt, & Gray, 2005).

Caspi et al. (2003) had shown an association in adults of this variant and depression, but only if trauma/abuse had been experienced. The results addressed neither the adolescence period nor sex differences. Later research has done so (e.g., Åslund et al., 2009; Benjet, Thompson, & Gotlib 2010), but the studies have not examined specific subtypes of abuse, such as childhood emotional abuse. Banducci et al. (2014) found that, for girls only, each copy of the s allele of *5-HTTLPR* was associated with an increase in symptoms of depression, but only if they had experienced childhood emotional abuse. The authors concluded that 10- to 12-year-old girls might be especially sensitive to the negative effects of early childhood emotional abuse, but only if they have the s allele of *5-HTTLPR*.

Starr, Hammen, Conway, Raposa, and Brennan (2014) conducted a study on the sensitizing effect of early adversity (EA) on depressive reactions to later (proximal) stress (PS) in a 20-year longitudinal investigation. Their results showed a G×E×E (Gene×Environment×Environment) interaction (involving EA×PS and *5-HTTLPR* s alleles and also *CRHR1* A alleles (*rs110402*)). These polymorphisms in serotonin transporter and corticotropin-releasing hormone receptor genes moderated the relationship between depression and recent (proximal) chronic stress in the context of EA through stress sensitization (resulting in stronger associations between depression and PS).

In youth from at-risk families, Willner, Morris, McCoy, and Adam (2014) investigated the effect cumulative risk exposure on a measure of HPA axis activity (diurnal cortisol rhythms over 2 days), but as moderated by the presence of allelic variants considered more at-risk in the promoter region of the *5-HTTLPR*. For the results of concern to the present section, they found that for *ll* allelic variants, greater cumulative risk exposure was associated with lower average cortisol output. They concluded that dysregulated diurnal cortical rhythms, especially for cortisol waking levels, constitute a risk for psychopathology, but in relation to *5-HTTLPR* as a risk factor.

COMT Hygen, Guzey, Belsky, Berg-Nielsen, and Wichstrøm (2014) showed that different styles of parent-oriented behavior in children with disorganized attachment might be related to genetic underpinnings rather than to presumed parental behavior. In particular, disorganized attachment is associated with two styles of parent-oriented behavior—controlling-punitive (e.g., harsh, threatening, or physical) parent-oriented behavior and controlling/caregiving (proactively being cheery, polite, or helpful, as if wanting to prevent the parent from becoming upset) parent-oriented behavior.

In their prospective, longitudinal study from 4- to 6-years of age ($N=704$; Norwegians), Hygen et al. (2014) examined the effect of the catechol-*O*-methyltransferase (*COMT*) $Val^{158}Met$ genotype in moderating the effect of disorganized attachment on parental report (mothers overrepresented) of aggressive behavior (according to the Children's Behavior Checklist, (CBCL; Achenbach, 1991) and social skills (as per the Social Skills Rating System, SSRS; Gresham & Elliot, 1990). Attachment style was measured using the MCAST (Manchester Child Attachment Story Task; Green, Stanley, Smith, & Goldwyn, 2000), which is a dimensional measure.

The *COMT* gene carries a SNP located at codon 158 ($Val^{158}Met$) that varies in whether it transcribes (instructs) for the enzyme *COMT* the amino acid valine or methionine. This enzyme breaks down the neurotransmitters (especially dopamine) in the prefrontal cortex (PFC). The Val/Val (homozygous for the valine allele) expresses four times as much *COMT* enzyme activity in the PFC compared to Met/Met (methionine allele homozygosity), rendering it a more at-risk allele. However, the facilitation of its risk depends on the presence of childhood adversity.

Specifically, for the results in the Hygen et al. (2014) study, the behavioral measures used stood as proxies for the two types of attachment styles, and gave data significant in the predicted direction. Highly attachment-disorganized preschoolers who were Val/Val in alleles for *COMT* became more aggressive over 2 years and also reduced their positive self-oriented social skills (self-regulation, assertiveness). In Met/Met carriers who were highly disorganized in attachment, over time, aggressive behavior increased and other-oriented social skills (cooperation, responsibility) decreased. The authors concluded that the *COMT* genotype interacts over time in young children with attachment disorganization status and degree in behavioral change (aggression, social skill). Alleles allowing for higher dopamine function in the PFC may favor a less spontaneous/more deliberate behavioral style in dealing with threatening environments, such as in aggressive/frightening, unpredictable parental behavior.

As for origins of internalizing difficulties related to caregiving, Lavigne et al. (2013) undertook a methodologically differentiated study of G×E interactions in 4-year-old children examined for behavioral difficulties and parenting risk factors. The three target candidate genes examined were the serotonin transporter gene, *5-HTT*, also termed *SLC6A4*, the *DRD4*, and the *MAOA*. The risk factors measured were wide-ranging and included socioeconomic status (SES), life stress, caregiver depression, caregiver support, caregiver hostility, and their scaffolding skills.

In contrast to results with adults for *5-HTTLPR*, in which the short (*s*) allele expresses environmental sensitivity, the long (*l*) allele of the serotonin transporter gene was associated with increased symptoms of oppositional defiance in interaction with family stress and also with greater increases in depression/anxiety symptoms in interaction with caretaker depression/family conflict/SES. Other interaction results were found for boys for *MAOA*. The *DRD4* results were limited. There were no rGE effects.

HTR2A Fraley, Roisman, Booth-LaForce, Owen, and Holland (2013) investigated the relationship between early antecedents of long-term consequences in attachment in terms of genetic and interpersonal origins. Because their study was longitudinal, they could determine the relative weight of early compared to later influences and their changes over developmental time. Although early antecedents were found, changes in the effect of variables constituted the most important influences. The authors concluded that the developmental trajectories involved are nuanced and changing, with associations being relatively small.

The sample studied was taken from National Institute of Child Health and Human Development study of Early Child Care and Youth Development ($N=707$, followed from age 1 month to age 18 years). Attachment was measured globally by the Relationships Scales Questionnaire (Griffin & Bartholomew, 1994), which examines attachment-related avoidance and anxiety. Romantic attachment styles were assessed using the Experiences in Close Relationships-Revised Questionnaire (Fraley, Waller, & Brennan, 2000). Maternal sensitivity was assessed in mother–child interactions using developmentally appropriate tasks eliciting engagement (at 6 months, 15 months, 24 months, 36 months, 54 months, grade 1, grade 3, grade 5, and age 15). Maternal depression was assessed using the Center for Epidemiological Studies Depression Scale (Radloff, 1977). Father absence was scored on a binary scale at each wave. Social competence was assessed using the Social Skills Questionnaire (Gresham & Elliot, 1990). Friendship quality was scored on the Friendship Quality Questionnaire (Parker & Asher, 1993). Early (54 months) temperament was assessed with the Children's Behavior Questionnaire (Rothbart, Ahadi, Hershey, & Fisher, 2001).

As for the results, after controlling for confounds, attachment avoidance was associated more with changes in maternal sensitivity, as well as social competence and friendship relations. For anxiety, the results involved maternal depression and social competence. Temperament had little influence. Genetically, there were significant findings only for one polymorphism of interest. Individuals homozygous for the C allele of the serotonin reception gene *HTR2A* (*rsb313*) scored higher in global attachment-related anxiety relative to those with the TT or TC alleles. A G×E interaction was found—TT carriers of the gene exhibited a greater negative association between maternal sensitivity increase and avoidant attachment. These results partially replicate those of Salo, Jokela, Lehtimäki, and Keltikangas-Järvinen (2011).

Other Hostinar, Cicchetti, and Rogosch (2014) investigated the interaction of maltreatment, perceived social support, and presence of the SNP in the oxytocin receptor gene (*OXTR*; *rs53576*) in low SES (socioeconomic status) 13- to 15-year olds. The G-G homozygote genotype was associated with a perception of lower social support (on the NRI, Network of Relationships Inventory; Furman & Buhrmester, 1992) relative to A-carriers who had been maltreated. The former youth also reported more internalizing problems (on the YSR, Youth Self-Report, Achenbach, 1991) than the A-carriers, despite expressing an equivalent type, duration, and intensity of maltreatment (on the MCS; Maltreatment Classification System, Barnett, Manly, & Cicchetti, 1993). The G-G variant might confer sensitivity to negative social experiences, such as maltreatment in the family, so that carriers are more attuned to it and affected by it.

In a study of individual vulnerability to the effects of prenatal anxiety on later developing child internalizing symptoms up to 15 years of age, O'Donnell, Glover, Holbrook, and O'Connor (2014) found a role for *BDNF* polymorphisms (*rs11030121*, *rs7124442*) in G×E interactions. The results showed that there are individual differences in prenatal programming, which acts to set the body's response, e.g., in the stress response, as development proceeds, because of the adaptive advantage of predicting and setting response to future challenges.

Comment

The research that has followed upon Caspi et al.'s (2002) findings of a (G×E) Maltreatment×Genetic interaction in the outcome of antisocial and related behavior is differentiating both the genetic and environmental sides of the findings. On the one hand, multiple polymorphisms seem to be involved. On the other hand, the parenting behaviors associated with maltreatment are being differentiated. These findings are at the specific level of the interaction. At the same time, at the broader level, the polymorphism involved is not associated only with antisocial behavior. Moreover, child maltreatment does not only lead to antisocial and related behavior. The range of Genetic× Environmental interactions that have been studies now includes not only externalizing-related disorders and behavior but also internalizing ones.

Overall, genes involved in regulating neurotransmitters still seem primary in gene–environment interactions, but this candidate gene approach is being complemented by studies examining multiple genes with large study *N*s, and integrating polygenic measures that do not specify particular genes. Candidate genes might be found to be significant in the research on

Gene × Environment interactions, and we do need to know which ones they are and there locations and mechanisms of action in the brain, but the movement in the field is toward ascertaining genetic influence together across genes, and as well, in concert with broad environmental measures, and not just early maltreatment. Moreover, the question of G × E differences for the same gene–environment combinations at different ages or developmental epochs (G × E × D) complicates facile understanding of G × E and related genetic influences in the causality of behavior, as shown next.

(G × E) × Development

Model Vrieze, Iacono, and McGue (2012) argued for the importance of psychological theory about etiology in guiding research on genes, environment, development, and their interaction. In this regard, they referred to G × E × D interaction, noting that developmental factors can modify G × E interaction. They advocated for G × D studies [and rG × D ones; rG = correlated gene (environment)]. Moreover, to improve theoretical and empirical accuracy, they suggested use of increasingly refined endophenotypes.

Vrieze et al. (2012) provided a useful diagram illustrating human DNA structure and variability (see Fig. 10.8). It gives an example of an autosomal segment of chromosomal DNA. There are several major types or sources of genetic variation with SNPs, constituting a major such source in humans. Genetic research has focused on common SNPs (e.g., the Val^{158}Met (*rs4680*) polymorphism is *COMT*). Other relevant genetic variants for psychology include insertions/deletions (indels), VNTRs, and copy number variants (CNVs).

In behavioral genetic research, the search for relationships between genes and behavior has been too broad. GWAS studies are computational intensive, without theory and, behaviorally, the phenotypes examined are far removed from proximal genetic influence. For example, DSM (Diagnostic and Statistical Manual of Mental Disorders, Text Revision; American Psychiatric Association, 2000) categories generally are "not grounded in biology" (p. 1201), being too heterogeneous and complex for discovering gene-phenotypic associations.

Instead of using behavioral phenotypes in this type of research, Vrieze et al. (2012) called for using endophenotypes related to underlying brain processes. They would be more proximal to the effect of genes, more homogeneous, and more heritable. For Vrieze et al., endophenotypes are developmental in their nature. For example, Iacono and Malone (2011) found that for genetic risk of substance abuse and related disorders, a promising developmental endophenotype relates to reduced amplitude of the P300 event-related potential (ERP) as found on an "oddball" task.

Partridge (2011) explored an integration of developmental behavioral genetics and nonlinear dynamical systems theory. The author presented a heuristic phase-space model of variance in developmental history that graphed corresponding variance in genetic background and environmental context. The structure of the graph resembles a "butterfly," and I graphed it simpler than in the original (see Fig. 10.9). Each point of the figure in the phase portrait represents a phenotypic possibility within the organism's hypothetical ecology. At the midpoint in the figure, even minor, seemingly trivial variations in the biology or ecology of the organism can lead to major, large-scale, radical phenotypic change, with phenotype A or B favored, depending on phenotypic place or history in the phase portrait (the midpoint region is referred to as the "separatrix"). However, generally, there is little variation biologically and ecologically outside of normative ranges, so one phenotype or the other dominates phenotypic dynamics, which gives the illusion of strong genetic control (or reduced reaction range). When phase portraits incorporate time, evolution can be plotted within the model. When regions are less explored, the system evidences more compactness, canalization, resistance to change, inflexibility, and vulnerability. Systems theory allows for concepts such as hierarchy, levels, self-organization, and emergence, and it can inform G × E approaches from a relational developmental systems perspective.

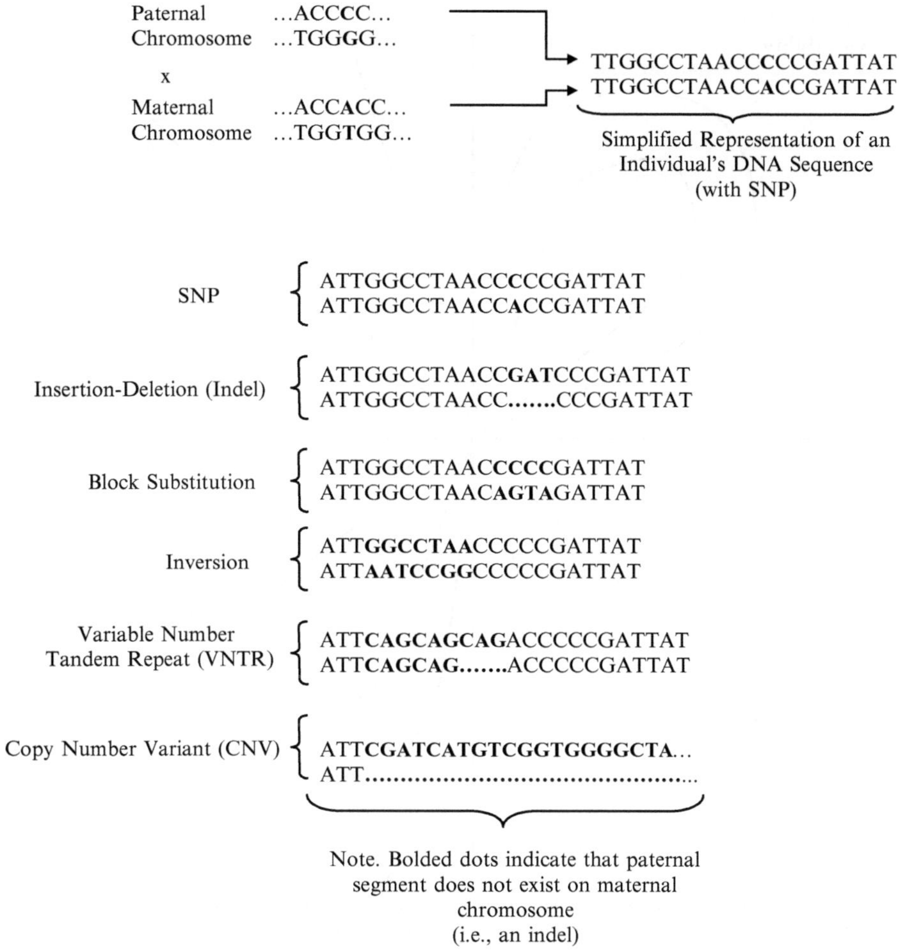

Fig. 10.8 Common forms of DNA variation in genetics, with chromosome sources. Humans have two chromosomes, one inherited from the biological father (paternal, Y or X) and one from the biological mother (maternal, X). The DNA sequences involved are represented by two rows of bases: (adenine (A) with thymine (T); cytosine (C) with guanine (G). The CA single nucleotide polymorphism (SNP) represents the only difference between the maternal and paternal autosomal segments. The figure indicated the SNP as well as several common types of structural variation, which is not necessarily all within any one person. For example, the individual person diagrammed is heterozygous for the SNP, but other individuals may be homozygous CC or homozygous AA. Adapted from Vrieze, Iacono, and McGue (2012)

Overton (2011) concluded the special issue on G×E interplay edited by Wanke and Spittel (2011) by considering the cohesion afforded by integrating relational developmental systems models and behavior genetics. The former concentrates on causal patterns in the development of intraindividual variation, or in differences within the individual, and this approach can inform the quantitative and population approach of behavior genetics, which focuses on interindividual variation, or individual differences.

Belsky and Hartman (2014) argued that a systems level genetic approach is needed in G×E research. They referred to Belsky and Pluess (2009, 2013), who have shown that G×E interactions involve susceptibility genes (carriers of certain genes respond for better or worse, depending on the quality of the environment experienced). There is evidence for a domain-general plasticity in this regard. For example, in a meta-analysis of child and adolescent G×E research, for *5-HTTLPR*, in Caucasian children under 18 years

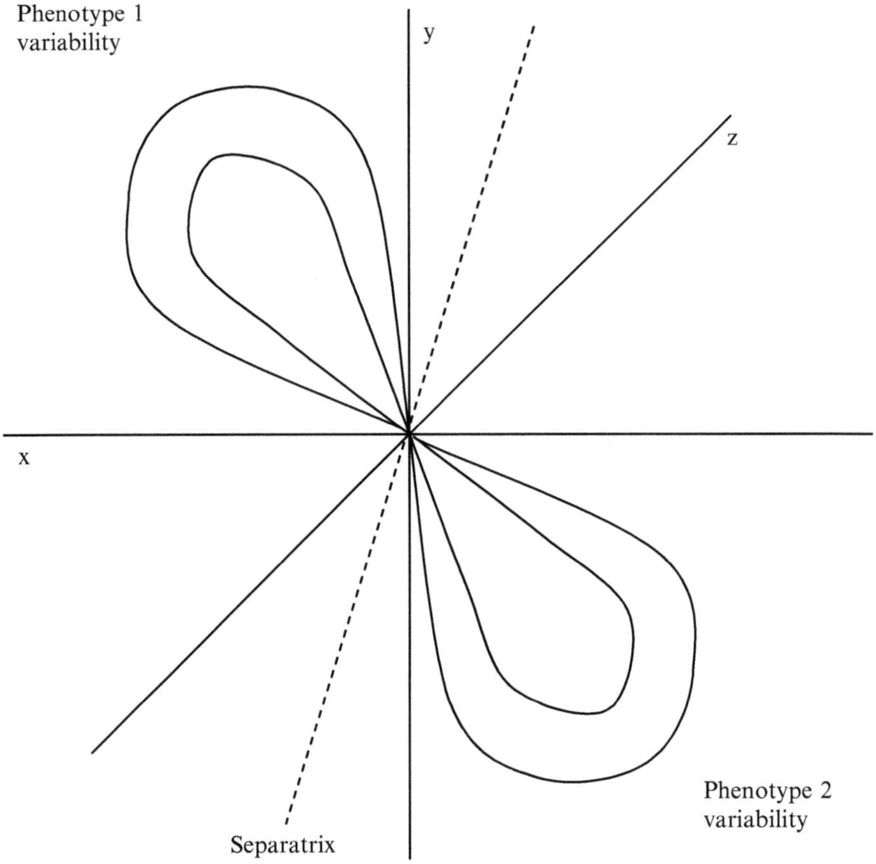

Fig. 10.9 Heuristic phase-space model (**a**) The *x*-axis refers to genetic background variance. (**b**) The *y*-axis refers to environmental context variance. (**c**) The *z*-axis refers to variance in developmental history. Adapted from Partridge (2011)

of age, *s* compared to *l* allele carriers proved more susceptible to both positive and negative developmental experiences (van IJzendoorn, Belsky, & Bakermans-Kranenburg, 2012).

Evidence Cicchetti and Rogosch (2014) conducted a study of genetic moderation of child maltreatment on depression/internalizing symptoms that illustrates the complexity of gene effects on behavior. Not only did they find main effects for maltreatment but also they found various genetic effects, none of which were straightforward. That is they found G×E, and G×G×E interactions, and also effects of developmental timing (D). Moreover, they examined the gene-outcome relationships across four gene polymorphisms related in the literature to depression/internalizing problems.

The four candidate genes studied included:

(a) *5-HTTLPR*. Differences in the promoter region of the serotonin transporter linked polymorphic region of the *5-HTT* gene have been related to stress-vulnerability (Caspi et al., 2003; Cutuli, Raby, Cicchetti, Englund, & Egeland, 2013; McGrath, Weill, Robinson, Macrae, & Smoller, 2012).
(b) A second candidate gene that has been studied in relation to depression/internalization concerns *BDNF* (Gunnar et al., 2012). This gene is involved actively in neurogenesis, and is especially distributed in the cerebral cortex, hippocampus, and basal forebrain.
(c) Another gene implicated in this type of research is *CRHR1* (corticotropin-releasing hormone receptor 1; Bradley et al.,

2008). *CRHR1* serves in the activation of the HPA axis. It binds to receptors involved in initiating the stress response, leading to the release of cortisol from the adrenal cortex.

(d) Fourth, the *NET (SLC6A2)* SNP is located on the gene that encodes for the norepinephrine (NE) transporter (T). These transporters are located on noradrenergic neurons.

The participants in the study involved 7- to 12-year-old African American children ($N = 1096$, maltreated and nonmaltreated). Measures included the Children's Depression Inventory (CDI; Kovacs, 1992), and the Teacher Report Form (TRF; Achenbach, 1991, filled in by camp counselors).

The findings showed that maltreatment was consistently associated with both outcome measures of depression/internalization. For the CDI, a G×E interaction was found (*BDNF*×maltreatment). The G×G×E findings concerned: *BDNF* and triallelic *5-HTTLPR* both in interaction with maltreatment. For the TRF, maltreatment was moderated by triallelic *5-HTTLPR*, with the effects elaborated based on developmental timing of the maltreatment. Another G×G×E interaction involved *NET* moderating the G×E of maltreatment×*5-HTTLPR*. This G×G×E was extended in terms of variation of maltreatment subtype. Another G×G×E involved the genes *BDNF* and *CRHR1*.

As for the particular findings of interest related to the G×G×E interactions, maltreated children having the *s/s* genotype of *5-HTTLPR* and either of the G genotype (AG, GG) of *BDNF* scored significantly higher on self-reported depression compared to controls. Also, maltreated children with the s/*l* genotype and the AA genotype of *5-HTTLPR* and *BDNF*, respectively, had significantly higher self-reported depression than equivalent controls. The results showed a similar pattern for maltreatment in conjunction with the *l/l* and AA alleles of the respective gene polymorphisms involved. Overall, the multigenetic approach adopted to understand the origins of depression/internalization proved necessary and fruitful.

Comment

By definition, genes and environment begin to have their effects on behavior with conception, if not before (think epigenesis and cross-generational transmission, as well as the effects of the environment on the health of the pre-pregnant mother). That is, in this sense, gene–environment interactions always are developmental (never are *not* developmental). Evolutionary concepts, as well, are gravitating to a central role for development (e.g., life history strategy, differential susceptibility, evo-devo). Nevertheless, as with the previous discussion of G×E, in general, there are statistical and conceptual differences in the construct, and G×E×D could be a narrowing one for effects on outcomes given the three-way interaction involved. Nevertheless, these types of findings illustrate both the nuances in development and its hypercomplexity genetically and environmentally. They allow for a more comprehensive understanding of the multifactorial interactions in psychopathological outcome that could help in establishing differentiated and even individualized treatments for the child.

Chapter Conclusions

The recent research on the topic of G×E is moving quickly in new directions. At the same time, the phenomenon is not always replicated and, moreover, the research also finds that straightforward direct influences of environment or of genetics on behavior could occur. For example, Musci et al. (2016) conducted a study on the course of internalizing symptoms from late childhood to late adolescence. They used the major depressive disorder "polygenic" score, which was a significant predictor of the outcome involved. Also, the early childhood stressor divorce or death was involved in the predictions. Finally, no G×E interaction was found as predictor in the results.

As for studies with G×E findings moving in new directions, Rietveld et al. (2014) undertook a large-scale GWAS on education attainment as an outcome. They replicated prior findings involving three SNPs in educational attainment. Moreover, they had created "polygenic" scores as combined indices of the SNPs, and also replicated the relationship between these scores and educational attainment. They noted the small effect sizes of the individual SNPs involved, which works against finding them as statistically significant in small-scale studies. Although the topic of the research (educational attainment, and its SNPs) is not the focus of the present work, the general message—that candidate gene studies have some value; large-N studies can help replicate results from candidate gene research; GWAS is a powerful approach to the question; and polygenic scores add much value to it—are worth nothing.

However, in examining the range of research on G×E, the results are not always consistent or even replicated. For example, Pluess et al. (2011) found that the effects of maternal anxiety during pregnancy on offspring 6-month temperament was moderated by the serotonin transporter polymorphism *5-HTTLPR*. Specifically, short (*s*) allele carriers were more susceptible to adverse behavioral profiles in interaction with maternal antenatal anxiety. However, Braithwaite et al. (2013) did not replicate these findings for boys aged 6 months. Moreover, the results did not extend in their longitudinal sample into the 13-year age reviewed. The studies appear to differ methodologically on critical variables, and could use measures that provide more than a snapshot before the phenomenon at issue is tested fully.

Bastiaansen et al. (2014) illustrated the variability in findings on candidate genes and outcome. In this case, they investigated the relationship between the *5-HTTLPR* and amygdala activation. Hariri et al. (2002) had shown that carriers of the short (*s*) allele exhibit an increased amygdalar response to negative emotional stimuli. A meta-analysis replicated the findings (Murphy et al., 2013). Therefore, it appears to be a genetic risk factor for affective disorder.

However, as described in their paper, Bastiaansen et al. (2014) not only failed to replicate the past findings in their own study but also their meta-analysis failed to support them. The authors concluded that the association between *5-HTTLPR* and amygdala activation might be attenuated, conditional, or even non-existent, with publication bias a probable confound.

Just as the original thrust in genetic research on behavior moved from monogenetic studies to polygenetic ones, and also from genetic ones to G×E ones, the research continues to evolve in complexity as its conceptual base evolves. For example, one finds G×G, G×E×D (development), and related extensions.

In the field of G×E research, it is too early to pronounce definitely which genes are associated with which outcomes, how the environment modifies the relationships, and how exactly they lead to negative outcomes, such as antisocial and other externalizing behaviors and also to depression and other internalizing behaviors. Moreover, genes and environment themselves are not separable components that independently contribute to their interaction. Their boundaries could be fuzzy, as in correlated gene–environment interactions in which genetic predispositions actively influence the environment.

References

Achenbach, T. M. (1991). *Integrative guide for the 1991 CBCL/4-18, YSR, and TRF profiles*. Burlington, VT: University of Vermont, Department of Psychiatry.

Achenbach, T. M., & Edelbrock, C. (1981). Behavioral problems and competencies reported by parents of normal and disturbed children aged 4 through 16. *Monographs of the Society for Research in Child Development, 46*, 1–82.

Achenbach, T. M., & Rescorla, L. A. (2003). *Manual for the ASEBA school-age forms and profiles*. Burlington, VT: University of Vermont, Research Center for Children, Youth, and Families.

Adrian, C., & Hammen, C. (1993). Stress exposure and stress generation in children of depressed mothers. *Journal of Consulting and Clinical Psychology, 61*, 354–359.

American Psychiatric Association. (2000). *Diagnostic and statistical manual of mental disorders: DSM-IV-TR* (4th ed., text rev.). Washington, DC: Author.

Anderson, E. R., & Mayes, L. C. (2010). Race/ethnicity and internalizing disorders in youth: A review. *Clinical Psychology Review, 30*, 338–348.

Åslund, C., Leppert, J., Comasco, E., Nordquist, N., Oreland, L., & Nilsson, K. W. (2009). Impact of the interaction between the 5HTTLPR polymorphism and maltreatment on adolescent depression. A population-based study. *Behavior Genetics, 39*, 524–531.

Åslund, C., Nordquist, N., Comasco, E., Leppert, J., Oreland, L., & Nilsson, K. W. (2011). Maltreatment, *MAOA*, and delinquency: Sex differences in gene-environment interaction in a large population-based cohort of adolescents. *Behavior Genetics, 41*, 262–272.

Bakermans-Kranenburg, M. J., & van IJzendoorn, M. H. (2011). Differential susceptibility to rearing environment depending on dopamine-related genes: New evidence and a meta-analysis. *Development and Psychopathology*, *23*, 39–52.

Banducci, A. N., Gomes, M., MacPherson, L., Lejuez, C. W., Potenza, M. N., Gelernter, et al. (2014). A preliminary examination of the relationship between the *5-HTTLPR* and childhood emotional abuse on depressive symptoms in 10-12-year-old youth. *Psychological Trauma: Theory, Research, Practice, and Policy, 6*, 1–7.

Barnett, D., Manly, J. T., & Cicchetti, D. (1993). Defining child maltreatment: The interface between policy and research. In D. Cicchetti & S. L. Toth (Eds.), *Child abuse, child development, and social policy* (pp. 7–73). Norwood, NJ: Ablex.

Bastiaansen, J. A., Servaas, M. N., Bernard, J., Marsman, C., Ormel, J., Nolte, I. M., et al. (2014). Filling the gap: Relationship between the serotonin-transporter-linked polymorphic region and amygdala activation. *Psychological Science, 25*, 2058–2066.

Beaver, K. M., Ratchford, M., & Ferguson, C. J. (2009). Evidence of genetic and environmental effects on the development of low self-control. *Criminal Justice and Behavior, 36*, 1158–1172.

Belsky, J., & Hartman, S. (2014). Gene-environment interaction in evolutionary perspective: Differential susceptibility to environmental influences. *World Psychiatry, 13*, 87–89.

Belsky, J., & Pluess, M. (2009). Beyond diathesis stress: Differential susceptibility to environmental influences. *Psychological Bulletin, 135*, 885–908.

Belsky, J., & Pluess, M. (2013). Beyond risk, resilience and dysregulation: Phenotypic plasticity and human development. *Development and Psychopathology, 25*, 1243–1261.

Benjet, C., Thompson, R. J., & Gotlib, I. H. (2010). 5-HTTLPR moderates the effect of relational peer victimization on depressive symptoms in adolescent girls. *Journal of Child Psychology and Psychiatry, 51*, 173–179.

Binder, E. B., Bradley, R. G., Liu, W., Epstein, M. P., Deveau, T. C., Mercer, K. B., et al. (2008). Association of FKBP5 polymorphisms and childhood abuse with risk of posttraumatic stress disorder symptoms in adults. *JAMA: The Journal of the American Medical Association*, *299*, 1291–1305.

Boyce, W. T., & Kobor, M. S. (2015). Development and the epigenome: The "synapse" of gene-environment interplay. *Developmental Science, 18*, 1–23.

Bradley, R. G., Binder, E. B., Epstein, M. P., Tang, Y., Nair, H. P., Liu, W., et al. (2008). Influence of child abuse on adult depression: Moderation by the corticotrophin-releasing hormone receptor gene. *Archives of General Psychiatry*, *65*, 190–200.

Braithwaite, E. C., Ramchandani, P. G., O'Connor, T. G., van IJzendoorn, M. H., Bakermans-Kranenburg, M. J., Glover, V., et al. (2013). No moderating effect of 5-HTTLPR on associations between antenatal anxiety and infant behavior. *Journal of the American Academy of Child and Adolescent Psychiatry, 52*, 519–526.

Brody, G. H., Yu, T., Beach, S. R. H., Kogan, S. M., Windle, M., & Philibert, R. A. (2014). Harsh parenting and adolescent health: A longitudinal analysis with genetic moderation. *Health Psychology, 33*, 401–409.

Brookes, K. J., Mill, J., Guindalini, C., Curran, S., Xu, X., Knight, J., et al. (2006). A common haplotype of the dopamine transporter gene associated with attention-deficit/hyperactivity disorder and interacting with maternal use of alcohol during pregnancy. *Archives of General Psychiatry*, *63*, 74–81.

Brown, G. W., Craig, T. K., & Harris, T. O. (2008). Parental maltreatment and proximal risk factors using the childhood experience of care & abuse (CECA) instrument: A life-course study of adult chronic depression-5. *Journal of Affective Disorders, 110*, 222–233.

Brown, G. W., & Harris, T. O. (2008). Depression and serotonin transporter 5-HTTLPR polymorphism: A review and a hypothesis concerning gene-environment interaction. *Journal of Affective Disorders, 111*, 1–12.

Burt, A. (2011). Some key issues in the study of gene-environment interplay: Activation, deactivation, and the role of development. *Research in Human Development, 8*, 192–210.

Burt, A. (2015). Evidence that the gene-environment interactions underlying youth conduct problems vary across development. *Child Development Perspectives, 9*, 217–221.

Calkins, S. D., Propper, C., & Mills-Koonce, W. R. (2013). A biopsychosocial perspective on parenting and developmental psychopathology. *Development and Psychopathology, 25*, 1399–1414.

Caspi, A., Hariri, A. R., Holmes, A., Uher, R., & Moffitt, T. E. (2011). Genetic sensitivity to the environment: The case of the serotonin transporter gene and its implications for studying complex diseases and traits. In K. A. Dodge & M. Rutter (Eds.), *Gene-environment interactions in developmental psychopathology* (pp. 18–58). New York: Guilford Press.

Caspi, A., McClay, J., Moffitt, T. E., Mill, J., Martin, J., Craig, I. W., et al. (2002). Role of genotype in the cycle of violence in maltreated children. *Science, 297*, 851–854.

Caspi, A., Moffitt, T. E., Cannon, M., McClay, J., Murray, R., Harrington, H., et al. (2005). Moderation of the effect of adolescent-onset cannabis use on adult psychosis by a functional polymorphism in the catechol-O-methyltransferase gene: Longitudinal evidence of a gene × environment interaction. *Biological Psychiatry, 57*, 1117–1127.

Caspi, A., Sugden, K., Moffitt, T. E., Taylor, A., Craig, I. W., Harrington, H., et al. (2003). Influence of life stress on depression: Moderation by a polymorphism in the 5-HTT gene. *Science, 301*, 386–389.

Choe, D. E., Shaw, D. S., Hyde, L. W., & Forbes, E. E. (2014). Interactions between monoamine oxidase A and punitive discipline in African American and Caucasian men's antisocial behavior. *Clinical Psychological Science, 2*, 591–601.

Chorpita, B. F., Moffitt, C. E., & Gray, J. (2005). Psychometric properties of the revised child anxiety and depression scale in a clinical sample. *Behavior Research and Therapy, 43*, 309–322.

Cicchetti, D., & Rogosch, F. A. (2014). Genetic moderation of child maltreatment effects on depression and internalizing symptoms by serotonin transporter linked polymorphic region (*5-HTTLPR*), brain-derived neurotrophic factor (*BDNF*), norepinephrine transporter (*NET*), and corticotrophin releasing hormone receptor 1 (*CRHR1*) genes in African American children. *Development and Psychopathology, 26*, 1219–1239.

Cicchetti, D., Rogosch, F. A., & Thibodeau, E. L. (2012). The effects of child maltreatment on early signs of antisocial behavior: Genetic moderation by tryptophan hydroxylase, serotonin transporter, and monoamine oxidase A genes. *Development and Psychopathology, 24*, 907–928.

Congdon, E., Lesch, K. P., & Canli, T. (2008). Analysis of *DRD4* and DAY polymorphisms and behavioral inhibition in healthy adults: Implications for impulsivity. *American Journal of Medical Genetics Part B: Neuropsychiatric Genetics, 147*, 27–32.

Cutuli, J. J., Raby, K. L., Cicchetti, D., Englund, M. M., & Egeland, B. (2013). Contributions of maltreatment and serotonin transporter genotype to depression in childhood, adolescence, and early adulthood. *Journal of Affective Disorders, 149*, 30–37.

Davies, P. T., & Cicchetti, D. (2014). How and why does the 5-HTTLPR gene moderate associated between maternal unresponsiveness and children's disruptive problems? *Child Development, 85*, 484–500.

Denson, T. F., Dobson-Stone, C., Ronay, R., von Hippel, W., & Schira, M. M. (2014). A functional polymorphism of the MAOA gene is associated with neural responses to induced anger control. *Journal of Cognitive Neuroscience, 26*, 1418–1427.

Dick, D. M., Agrawal, A., Keller, M. C., Adkins, A., Aliev, F., Monroe, S., et al. (2015). Candidate gene-environment interaction research: Reflections and recommendations. *Perspectives on Psychological Science, 10*, 37–59.

Dickens, W. T., Turkheimer, E., & Beam, C. (2011). The social dynamics of the expression of genes for cognitive ability. In K. S. Kendler, S. R. Jaffee, & D. Romer (Eds.), *The dynamic genome and mental health: The role of genes and environments in youth development* (pp. 103–127). New York: Oxford University Press.

Doornbos, B., Dijck-Brouwer, D. A., Kema, I. P., Tanke, M. A., van Goor, S. A., Muskiet, F. A., et al. (2009). The development of peripartum depressive symptoms is associated with gene polymorphisms of MAOA, 5-HTT and COMT. *Progress in Neuropsychopharmacology and Biological Psychiatry, 33*, 1250–1254.

Douglas, K., Chan, G., Gelernter, J., Arias, A. J., Anton, R. F., Poling, J., et al. (2011). *5-HTTLPR* as a potential moderator of the effects of adverse childhood experiences on risk of antisocial personality disorder. *Psychiatry Genetics, 21*, 240–248.

Duncan, L. E., Pollastri, A. R., & Smoller, J. W. (2014). Why many geneticists and psychological scientists have discrepant view about gene-environment interaction (G×E) research. *American Psychologist, 69*, 249–268.

Ellis, B. J., Boyce, W. T., Belsky, J., Bakermans-Kranenburg, M. J., & van IJzendoorn, M. H. (2011). Differential susceptibility to the environment: An evolutionary-neurodevelopmental theory. *Development and Psychopathology, 23*, 7–28.

Enoch, M. A., Steer, C. D., Newman, T. K., Gibson, N. N., & Goldman, D. D. (2010). Early life stress, MAOA and gene-environment interactions predict behavioral disinhibition in children. *Genes, Brain and Behavior, 9*, 65–74.

Fergusson, D. M., Boden, J. M., Horwood, L. J., Miller, A. L., & Kennedy, M. A. (2011). MAOA, abuse exposure and antisocial behavior: 30-year longitudinal study. *British Journal of Psychiatry, 198*, 457–463.

Fergusson, D. M., Horwood, L. J., Miller, A. L., & Kennedy, M. A. (2011). Life stress, 5-HTTLPR and mental disorder: Findings from a 30-year longitudinal study. *The British Journal of Psychiatry, 198*, 129–135.

Fink, L. A., Bertstein, D., Handelsman, L., Foote, J., & Lovejoy, M. (1995). Initial reliability and validity of the childhood trauma interview: A new multidimensional measure of childhood interpersonal trauma. *American Journal of Psychiatry, 152*, 1329–1335.

First, M., Gibbon, M., Spitzer, R. L., Williams, J. B. W., & Benjamin, L. S. (1997). *Structured clinical interview for DSM-IV Axis II personality disorders (SCID-II)*. Washington, DC: American Psychiatric Press.

First, M., Spitzer, R., Gibbon, M., & Williams, J. (2001). *Structured clinical interview for DSM-IV-TR Axis I disorders—non-patient edition*. New York: Biometrics Research Department, New York State Psychiatric Institute.

Fraley, R. C., Roisman, G. I., Booth-LaForce, C., Owen, M. T., & Holland, A. S. (2013). Interpersonal and genetic origins of adult attachment styles: A longitudinal study from infancy to early adulthood. *Journal of Personality and Social Psychology, 104*, 817–838.

Fraley, R. C., Waller, N. G., & Brennan, K. A. (2000). An item response theory analysis of self-report measures of adult attachment. *Journal of Personality and Social Psychology, 78*, 350–365.

Furman, W., & Buhrmester, D. (1992). Age and sex differences in perceptions of networks of personal relationships. *Child Development, 63*, 103–115.

Glaser, Y. G., Zubieta, J-K., Hsu, D. T., Villafuerte, S., Mickey, B. J., Trucco, E. M., et al. (2014). Indirect effect of corticotrophin-releasing hormone receptor 1 gene variation on negative emotionality and alcohol use via right ventrolateral prefrontal cortex. *Journal of Neuroscience, 34*, 4099–4107.

Green, J. M., Stanley, C., Smith, V., & Goldwyn, R. (2000). A new method of evaluating attachment representations on young school age children—The Manchester Child Attachment Story Task. *Attachment and Human Development, 2*, 48–70.

Gresham, F. M., & Elliot, S. N. (1990). *Social skills rating system manual.* Circle Pines, MN: American Guidance Service.

Griffin, D., & Bartholomew, K. (1994). Metaphysics of measurement: The case of adult attachment. In K. Bartholomew & D. Perlman (Eds.), *Advances in personal relationships: Vol. 5. Attachment processes in adulthood* (pp. 17–52). London, UK: Jessica Kingsley.

Gunnar, M. R., Wenner, J. A., Thomas, K. M., Glatt, C. E., McKenna, M. C., & Clark, A. G. (2012). The brain-derived neurotrophic factor Val66Met polymorphism moderates early deprivation effects on attention problems. *Development and Psychopathology, 24*, 1215–1223.

Hammen, C. (1991). Generation of stress in the course of unipolar depression. *Journal of Abnormal Psychology, 100*, 555–561.

Hariri, A. R., Mattay, V. S., Tessitore, A., Kolachana, B., Fera, F., Goldman, D., et al. (2002). Serotonin transporter genetic variation and the response of the human amygdala. *Science, 297*, 400–403.

Hostinar, C. E., Cicchetti, D., & Rogosch, F. A. (2014). Oxytocin receptor gene polymorphism, perceived social support, and psychological symptoms in maltreated adolescents. *Development and Psychopathology, 26*, 465–477.

Hyde, L. W. (2015). Developmental psychopathology in an era of molecular genetics and neuroimaging: A development neurogenetics approach. *Development and Psychopathology, 27*, 587–613.

Hygen, B. W., Guzey, I. C., Belsky, J., Berg-Nielsen, T. S., & Wichstrøm, L. (2014). Catechol-O-methyltransferase Val158Met genotype moderates the effect of disorganized attachment on social development in young children. *Development and Psychopathology, 26*, 947–961.

Iacono, W. G., & Malone, S. M. (2011). Developmental endophenotypes: Indexing genetic risk for substance abuse with the P300 brain event-related potential. *Child Development Perspectives, 5*, 239–247.

Karg, K., Burmeister, M., Shedden, K., & Sen, S. (2011). The serotonin transporter promoter variant (5-HTTLPR), stress, and depression meta-analysis revisited: Evidence of genetic moderation. *Archives of General Psychiatry, 68*, 444–454.

Karreman, A., van Tuijl, C., van Aken, M. A. G., & Dekovic, M. (2006). Parenting and self-regulation in preschoolers: A meta-analysis. *Infant and Child Development, 15*, 561–579.

Karreman, A., van Tuijl, C., van Aken, M. A. G., & Dekovic, M. (2008). Parenting, coparenting, and effortful control in preschoolers. *Journal of Family Psychology, 22*, 30–40.

Kaufman, J., & Perephetchikova, F. (2011). Promoting resilience in maltreated children. In K. A. Dodge & M. Rutter (Eds.), *Gene-environment interactions in developmental psychopathology* (pp. 159–188). New York: Guilford Press.

Kaufman, J., Yang, B-Z., Douglas-Palumberi, H., Crouse-Artus, M., Lipschitz, D., Krystal, J. H., et al. (2007). Genetic and environmental predictors of early alcohol use. *Biological Psychiatry, 61*, 1228–1234.

Kaufman, J., Yang, B. Z., Douglas-Palumberi, H., Grasso, D., Lipschitz, D., Houshyar, S., et al. (2006). Brain-derived neurotrophic factor-5-HTTLPR gene interactions and environmental modifiers of depression in children. *Biological Psychiatry, 59*, 673–680.

Kaufman, J., Yang, B-Z., Douglas-Palumberi, H., Houshyar, S., Lipschitz, D., Krystal, J. H., et al. (2004). Social supports and serotonin transporter gene moderate depression in maltreated children. *Proceedings of the National Academy of Sciences, USA, 101*, 17316–17321.

Kendler, K. S. (2011). A conceptual overview of gene-environment interaction and correlation in a developmental context. In K. S. Kendler, S. R. Jaffee, & D. Romer (Eds.), *The dynamic genome and mental health: The role of genes and environments in youth development* (pp. 5–28). New York: Oxford University Press.

Kendler, K. S., Kuhn, J. W., Vittum, J., Prescott, C. A., & Riley, B. (2005). The interaction of stressful life events and a serotonin transporter polymorphism in the prediction of episodes of major depression: A replication. *Archives of General Psychiatry, 62*, 529–535.

Kim-Cohen, J., Caspi, A., Taylor, A., Williams, B., Newcombe, R., Craig, I. W., et al. (2006). MAOA, maltreatment, and gene-environment interaction predicting children's mental health: New evidence and a meta-analysis. *Molecular Psychiatry, 11*, 903–913.

Kovacs, M. (1992). *Children's depression inventory manual.* North Tonawanda, NY: Multi-Health Systems.

Kramer, U. M., Rojo, N., Schule, R., Cunillera, T., Schöls, L., Marco-Pallarés, J., et al. (2009). ADHD candidate gene (*DRD4 exon III*) affects inhibitory control in a healthy sample. *BMC Neuroscience, 10*, 150. doi:10.1186/1471-2202-10-150.

Kuepper, Y., Grant, P., Wielpuetz, C., & Hennig, J. (2013). MAOA-uVNTR genotype predicts interindividual differences in experimental aggressiveness as a function of the degree of provocation. *Behavioral Brain Research, 247*, 73–78.

Lavigne, J. V., Herzing, L. B. K., Cook, E. H., LeBailly, S. A., Gouze, K. R., Hopkins, J., et al. (2013). Gene × Environment effects of serotonin transporter, dopamine receptor D4, and monoamine oxidase A genes with contextual and parenting risk factors on symptoms of oppositional defiant disorder, anxiety, and depression in a community sample of 4-year-old children. *Development and Psychopathology, 25*, 555–575.

Li, J. J., & Lee, S. S. (2010). Latent class analysis of antisocial behavior. Interaction of serotonin transporter genotype and maltreatment. *Journal of Abnormal Child Psychology, 38*, 789–801.

Li, Y., Sulik, M. J., Eisenberg, N., Spinrad, T. L., Lemery-Chalfant, K., Stover, D. A., et al. (2016). Predicting childhood effortful control from interactions between early parenting quality and children's dopamine transporter gene haplotypes. *Development and Psychopathology, 28*, 199–212.

Loeber, R., Farrington, D. P., Stouthamer-Loeber, M., & Van Kammen, W. B. (1998). Multiple risk factors for multiproblem boys: Co-occurrence of delinquency, substance use, attention deficit, conduct problems, physical aggression, covert behavior, depressed mood, and shy/withdrawn behavior. In R. Jessor (Ed.), *New perspectives on adolescent risk behavior* (pp. 90–149). New York: Cambridge University Press.

McGowan, P. O., Sasaki, A., D'Alessio, A. C., Dymov, S., Labonté, B., Szyf, M., et al. (2009). Epigenetic regulation of the glucocorticoid receptor in human brain associates with childhood abuse. *Nature Neuroscience, 12*, 342–348.

McGrath, L. M., Weill, S., Robinson, E. B., Macrae, R., & Smoller, J. W. (2012). Bringing a developmental perspective to anxiety genetics. *Development and Psychopathology, 24*, 1179–1193.

Mill, J. (2011). Epigenetic effects on gene function and their role in mediating gene-environment interactions. In K. S. Kendler, S. R. Jaffee, & D. Romer (Eds.), *The dynamic genome and mental health: The role of genes and environments in youth development* (pp. 145–171). New York: Oxford University Press.

Munafo, M. R., Durrant, C., Lewis, G., & Flint, J. (2009). Gene × environment interactions at the serotonin transporter locus. *Biological Psychiatry, 65*, 211–219.

Murphy, S. E., Nobury, R., Godlewska, B. R., Cowen, P. J., Mannic, Z. M., Harmer, C. J., et al. (2013). The effect of the serotonin transporter polymorphism (5-HTTLPR) on amygdala function: A meta-analysis. *Molecular Psychiatry, 18*, 512–520.

Musci, R. J., Masyn, K. E., Benke, K., Maher, B., Uhl, G., & Ialongo, N. S. (2016). The effects of the interplay of genetics and early environmental risk on the course of internalizing symptoms form late childhood through adolescence. *Development and Psychopathology, 28*, 225–237.

O'Donnell, K. J., Glover, V., Holbrook, J. D., & O'Connor, T. G. (2014). Maternal prenatal anxiety and child brain-derived neurotrophic factor (BDNF) genotype: Effects on internalizing symptoms from 4 to 15 years of age. *Development and Psychopathology, 26*, 1255–1266.

Orvaschel, H. (1995). *The schedule for affective disorders and schizophrenia for school-age children—epidemiologic version 5 (K-SADS-E-5)*. Fort Lauderdale, FL: Author.

Overton, W. F. (2011). Relational developmental systems and quantitative behavior genetics: Alternative or parallel methodologies? *Research in Human Development, 8*, 258–263.

Parker, J. G., & Asher, S. R. (1993). Friendship and friendship quality in middle childhood: Links with peer group acceptance and feelings of loneliness and social dissatisfaction. *Developmental Psychology, 29*, 611–621.

Partridge, T. Y. (2011). Methodological advances toward a dynamic developmental behavioral genetics: Bridging the gap. *Research in Human Development, 8*, 242–257.

Pluess, M., Velders, F. P., Belsky, J., van IJzendoorn, M. H., Bakermans-Kranenburg, M. J., Jaddoe, V. W., et al. (2011). Serotonin transporter polymorphism moderates effects of prenatal maternal anxiety on infant negative emotionality. *Biological Psychiatry, 69*, 520–525.

Radloff, L. S. (1977). The CES-D scale: A self-report depression scale for research in the general population. *Applied Psychological Measurement, 1*, 385–401.

Rao, U. M. A., Hammen, C., & Daley, S. E. (1999). Continuity of depression during the transition to adulthood: A 5-year longitudinal study of young women. *Journal of the American Academy of Child & Adolescent Psychiatry, 38*, 908–915.

Rietveld, C. A., Conley, D., Eriksson, N., Esko, T., Medland, S. E., Vinkhuyzen, A. A. E., et al. (2014). Replicability and robustness of genome-wide-association studies for behavioral traits. *Psychological Science, 25*, 1975–1986.

Risch, N., Herrell, R., Lehner, T., Liang, K. Y., Eaves, L., Hoh, J., et al. (2009). Interaction between the serotonin transporter gene (5-HTTLPR), stressful life events, and risk of depression: A meta-analysis. *Journal of the American Medical Association, 301*, 2462–2471.

Rothbart, M. K., Ahadi, S. A., Hershey, K., & Fisher, P. (2001). Investigations of temperament at three to seven years: The children's behavior questionnaire. *Child Development, 72*, 1394–1408.

Rutter, M. (2011). Gene-environment interplay: Scientific issues and challenges. In K. A. Dodge & M. Rutter (Eds.), *Gene-environment interactions in developmental psychopathology* (pp. 3–17). New York: Guilford Press.

Rutter, M., & Dodge, K. A. (2011). Gene-environment interactions: State of the science. In K. A. Dodge & M. Rutter (Eds.), *Gene-environment interactions in developmental psychopathology* (pp. 87–101). New York: Guilford Press.

Salo, J., Jokela, M., Lehtimäki, T., & Keltikangas-Järvinen, L. (2011). Serotonin receptor 2A gene moderates the effect of childhood maternal nurturance on adulthood social attachment. *Genes, Brain and Behavior, 10*, 702–709.

Salvatore, J. E., Aliev, F., Bucholz, K., Agrawal, A., Hesselbrock, V., Hesselbrock, M., et al. (2015). Polygenic risk for externalizing disorders: Gene-by-development and gene-by-environment effects in adolescents and young adults. *Clinical Psychological Science, 3*, 189–201.

Seeger, G., Schloss, P., Schmidt, M. H., Ruter-Jungfleisch, A., & Henn, F. A. (2004). Gene-environment interaction in hyperkinetic conduct disorder (HD+CD) as indicated by season of birth variations in dopamine receptor (DRD4) gene polymorphism. *Neuroscience Letters, 366*, 282–286.

Shanahan, M. J., & Bauldry, S. (2011). Improving environmental markers in gene-environment research: Insights from life-course sociology. In K. S. Kendler, S. R. Jaffee, & D. Romer (Eds.), *The dynamic genome and mental health: The role of genes and environments in youth development* (pp. 59–78). New York: Oxford University Press.

Sheese, B. E., Rothbart, M. K., Voelker, P. M., & Posner, M. I. (2012). The dopamine receptor D4 gene 7-repeat allele interacts with parenting quality to predict effortful control in four-year-old children. *Child DevelopmentResearch*,1–6.doi:10.1155/2012/863242.

Sheese, B. E., Voelker, P. M., Rothbart, M. K., & Posner, M. I. (2007). Parenting quality interacts with genetic variation in dopamine receptor D4 to influence temperament in early childhood. *Developmental Psychopathology, 19*, 1039–1046.

Smearman, E. L., Winiarski, D. A., Brennan, P. A., Najman, J., & Johnson, K. C. (2014). Social stress and the oxytocin receptor gene interact to predict antisocial behavior in an at-risk cohort. *Development and Psychopathology, 27*, 309–318.

Smith, H. J., Kryski, K. R., Sheikh, H. I., Singh, S. M., & Hayden. E, P. (2013). The role of parenting and dopamine D4 receptor gene polymorphisms in children's inhibitory control. *Developmental Science, 10*, 313–330.

Spielberger, C. D., Jacobs, G., Russell, S., & Crane, R. S. (1983). Assessment of anger: The State-Trait Anger Scale. In J. N. Butcher & C. D., Spielberger (Eds.) *Advances in personality assessment* (pp. 159–187). Hillsdale, NJ: Erlbaum.

Starr, L. R., Hammen, C., Conway, C. C., Raposa, E., & Brennan, P. A. (2014). Sensitizing effect of early adversity on depressive reactions to later proximal stress: Moderation by polymorphisms in serotonin transporter and corticotrophin releasing hormone receptor genes in a 20-year longitudinal study. *Developmental and Psychopathology, 26*, 1241–1254.

Sulik, M. J., Eisenberg, N., Lemery-Chalfant, K., Spinrad, T. L., Silva, K. M., Eggum, N. D., et al. (2012). Interactions between serotonin transporter gene haplotypes and quality of mothers' parenting predict the development of children's noncompliance. *Developmental Psychology, 48*, 740–754.

Sullivan, P. F., Daly, M. J., & O'Donovan, M. (2012). Genetic architectures of psychiatric disorders: The emerging picture and its implications. *Nature Reviews Genetics, 13*, 537–551.

Taylor, A., & Kim-Cohen, J. (2007). Meta-analysis of gene-environment interactions in developmental psychopathology. *Developmental Psychopathology, 19*, 1029–1037.

Thapar, A., Langley, K., Owen, M. J., & O'Donovan, M. C. (2007). Advances in genetic findings on attention deficit hyperactivity disorder. *Psychological Medicine, 37*, 1681–1692.

Uher, R. (2011a). Gene-environment interactions. In K. S. Kendler, S. R. Jaffee, & D. Romer (Eds.), *The dynamic genome and mental health: The role of genes and environments in youth development* (pp. 29–58). New York: Oxford University Press.

Uher, R. (2011b). Genes, environment, and personalized treatment for depression. In K. A. Dodge & M. Rutter (Eds.), *Gene-environment interactions in developmental psychopathology* (pp. 140–158). New York: Guilford Press.

Uher, R., & McGuffin, P. (2008). The moderation by the serotonin transporter gene of environmental adversity in the aetiology of mental illness: Review and methodological analysis. *Molecular Psychiatry, 13*, 131–146.

van der Zwaluw, C. S., Engels, R. C., Vermulst, A. A., Rose, R. J., Verkes, R. J., Buitelaar, J., Franke, B., & Scholte, R. H. (2010). A serotonin transporter polymorphism (5-HTTLPR) predicts the development of adolescent alcohol use. *Drug and Alcohol Dependence, 112*, 134–139.

van IJzendoorn, M. H., Belsky, J., & Bakermans-Kranenburg, M. J. (2012). Serotonin transporter genotype 5HTTLPR as a marker of differential susceptibility? A meta-analysis of child and adolescent gene-by-environment studies. *Translational Psychiatry, 7*, e147. doi:10.1038/tp.2012.73.

Vrieze, S. I., Iacono, W. G., & McGue, M. (2012). Confluence of genes, environment, development, and behavior in a post Genome-Wide Association Study world. *Development and Psychopathology, 24*, 1195–1214.

Vrshek-Schallhorn, S., Mineka, S., Zinbarg, R. E., Craske, M. G., Griffith, J. W., Sutton, J., et al. (2014). Refining the candidate environment: Interpersonal stress, the serotonin transporter polymorphism, and gene-environment interactions in major depression. *Clinical Psychological Science, 2*, 235–248.

Wanke, K. L., & Spittel, M. L. (2011). Advancing research in gene-environment interplay: Can developmental science lead the way? *Research in Human Development, 8*, 165–172.

Weaver, I. C., Cervoni, N., Champagne, F. A., D'Alessio, A. C., Sharma, S., Seckl, J. R., et al. (2004). Epigenetic programming by maternal behavior. *Nature Neuroscience, 7*, 847–854.

Weder, N., Yang, B. Z., Douglas-Palumberi, H., Massey, J., Krystal, J. H., Gelernter, J., et al. (2009). *MAOA* genotype, maltreatment, and aggressive behavior: The changing impact of genotype at varying levels of trauma. *Biological Psychiatry, 65*, 417–424.

Willner, C. J., Morris, P. A., McCoy, D. C., & Adam, E. K. (2014). Erratum. Diurnal cortisol rhythms in youth from risky families: Effects of cumulative risk exposure and variation in the serotonin transporter linked polymorphic region gene. *Development and Psychopathology, 26*, 1185–1188.

Willoughby, M. T., Mills-Koonce, W. R., Propper, C. B., & Waschbusch, D. A. (2013). Observed parenting behaviors interact with a polymorphism of the brain derived neurotrophic factor gene to predict the emergence of oppositional-defiant and callous-unemotional behaviors at age 3 years. *Development and Psychopathology, 25*, 903–917.

Zohsel, K., Buchmann, A. F., Blomeyer, D., Hohm, E., Schmidt, M. H., Esser, G., et al. (2014). Mothers' prenatal stress and their children's antisocial outcomes – A moderating role for the Dopamine D4 Receptor (DRD4) gene. *Journal of Child Psychology and Psychiatry, 55*, 69–76.

Genes and Environments: The Person Revolution

11

Chapter Introduction

The present chapter examines three rapidly emerging areas in behavior-genetic studies—epigenetics, correlated Gene × Environment interactions (rGE), and cultural neuroscience. The research in the areas is nothing short of astounding and revolutionary. Epigenetics is showing how the environment can "silence" genes (turn off their promoter regions, e.g., by DNA methylation), in a frank challenge to classic genetics. Moreover, the altered functionality of the genes can be maintained in subsequent generations because the epigenetic stamps that are involved are passed on as much as are the genes themselves.

As for rGE, the evocative and active types, in particular, suggest that genes elicit corresponding environmental effects via the phenotypic characteristics that they help promote. Moreover, genes might even lead the promoted phenotypes to seek environmental opportunities (or niches) that are consistent with their characteristics (also called niche construction).

Finally, in cultural neuroscience, a strong interaction among genes, environment, and phenotype (including brain) is indicated, including in the selection of different alleles of polymorphisms in different cultures, or the same allele having quite different effects in different cultures. Some of the brain regions involved in cultural neuroscience includes the medial prefrontal cortex (mPFC) and the temporoparietal junction.

The chapter concludes by calling for conceptualization related to "G × E × P" (person) interaction. Behavioral causality lies not only in genes, environment, and their interaction, but also in ourselves as active agents beyond the passive influence of biology and environment.

Epigenetics

DNA Methylation

Nikolova and Hariri (2015) noted that epigenesis concerns a non-DNA sequence-based source of variability in the genome and, together, epigenetic effects refer to the epigenome. Epigenetic modifications do not alter the underlying nucleotide sequence; for example, they alter gene promoter regions and subsequent gene expression. There are several types of epigenetic processes, with the most widespread concerning DNA methylation. Specifically in the epigenetic mechanism of DNA methylation, a methyl group (-CH3) is added at the 5-carbon position in the cytosine carbon ring, most often, within a CpG (cytosine-guanine dinucleotide) site, to form 5-methylcytosine (5-MC), which itself might be further hydroxylated (to 5-MC). When the DNA methylation takes place in CpG-rich regions near the starting (initiation) site of transcription of a gene (its promoter region, i.e., at CpG islands), the process tends toward repression of gene expression (full gene silencing or relatively reduced gene transcription).

G. Young, *Unifying Causality and Psychology*, DOI 10.1007/978-3-319-24094-7_11

Zovkic, Meadows, Kaas, and Sweatt (2013) noted that DNA is methylated initially at the 5′ position of the cytosine-pyrimidine (5mc) ring by the *de novo* DNA methyltransferase enzymes *DNMT3a* and *DNMT3b*. The mark can be demethylated, for example, in response to environmental stimuli. Therefore, cycling of epigenetic modification and return to the original state in neuronal elements is normal.

According to Baker-Andresen, Ratnu, and Bredy (2013), DNA methylation is mediated by DNA methyltransferases, with different ones at different developmental periods and others at any time in development. In this regard, *DNMT3a* and *DNM3b* active in embryonic neurogenesis, *DNMT3a* is active in early postnatal neuronal maturation, and *DNMT3a* (3b?) active in synaptic plasticity. *DNMT1*, like the *de novo DNMT3a*, is active throughout development.

Effects

Szyf and Bick (2013) pointed out that, in epigenetics, DNA methylation markings early in life take place system-wide, and the epigenetic adaptations due to early social adversity could even affect the T-cells of the immune system. For example, McGowan et al. (2011) had indicated that chemical, social, and biosphere activity dynamically interrelates in signal pathways affecting target DNA methylation and demethylation enzymes for multiple targets in the genome. Szyf and Bick (2013) continued that the phenotype is altered dynamically by and reciprocally with, DNA (de)methylation induced by the environment. The resultant DNA methylation matrix dynamically and reciprocally "defines" the phenotype's relationship with the environment. Specifically, the research by McGowan et al. (2011) with rats and Suderman, McGowan, Hallett, Meaney, and Szyf (2012) with humans indicates that variations in maternal care and childhood abuse, respectively, affect DNA methylation across relevant gene clusters and beyond, broadly throughout the genome. In the human case, results apply to the genomic region involving the 6.5 million base-pair region at the glucocorticoid receptor (GR; *NR3C1*) gene in the hippocampus of the brain.

Boyce and Kobor (2015) explained that DNA methylation is a relatively stable epigenetic tag. It involves catalyzation by a group of enzymes referred to as DNA methyltransferases (DNMTs). In the methylation, a direct covalent chemical modification takes place of a cytosine base positioned next to a guanine base that is adjacent to it (referred to as CpG dinucleotides). CpG "islands" are areas in the genome with relatively high CpG presence, being notable because, comparatively, CpG dinucleotides generally are infrequent in the genome comparatively. The islands are hypomethylated and express about 70 % of gene promoters. These are the regulatory, transcription control, noncoding portions of genes. Promoter region DNA methylation yielding epigenetic marks often takes place in these predisposed CpG islands.

Boyce and Kobor (2015) also noted the epigenetic "paradox." In early embryogenesis, epigenesis functions in histological differentiation such that cellular pathways are stabilized toward specific ends despite their generic genetic instructions. Epigenesis narrows the genes involved to a genetic "singularity," a genetic "tabula rasa," thus finely-tuning the genome for purposes of ontogenetic stability. In contrast, as has been discussed throughout, epigenesis also functions in the elicitation of dynamic variation in transcriptional activity in response to the effects of environmental cues and contexts. Epigenesis is ubiquitous in brain function and can lead to not only normal brain development, but also problems and pathologies therein. As this process becomes increasingly known, it has generated much enthusiasm for the potential of epigenesis to help explain many pertinent psychological phenomena.

However, as noted by Mill and Heijmans (2013), the application of epigenesis to understanding epidemiology is fraught with statistical and conceptual conundra and errors. Nevertheless, despite this caution, Boyce and Kobor (2015) maintained that the field is developing a molecular account of the interplay of genes and environment.

Baker-Andresen et al. (2013) referred to DNA methylation as dynamic and affording genomic plasticity in support of behavioral adaptation. Moreover, "the methylome" is regulated "dynamically" throughout the lifespan. Further, "the neuronal methylome" is part of a complex epigenetic process of many marker types that interact synergetically. In so doing, the epigenetic modifications construct an "epigenetic code" that permits and regulates synaptic plasticity. The genome is "metaplastic" yet enduring because of epigenesis. For example, "learning-induced" transcriptions are encoded epigenetically, and these experience-dependent marks help prime (a) the transcriptional response to later occurring stimuli that are learning-related, as well as (b) associated neuronal re-activation.

Applications

Monk, Spicer, and Champagne (2012) reviewed the research linking prenatal maternal adversity to infant development, pointing to a role for epigenetic pathways. Prenatal maternal distress can affect not only fetal development but also postnatal development, although a prenatal–postnatal interplay and also postnatal experiences can moderate outcome. In terms of mechanism and its locus for epigenetic effects, the placenta appears to be highly susceptible to the effects of maternal distress and epigenetic dysregulation (see Fig. 11.1).

Oberlander et al. (2008) studied the impact of prenatal maternal depression/anxiety in the third trimester on infant stress response and epigenetic dysregulation. They found a correlation of maternal distress (as indicated by a questionnaire) and epigenetic effect, or degree of DNA methylation within the glucocorticoid receptor gene as measured in fetal cord blood (specifically nuclear receptor subfamily 3, group C, member 1 [*NR3C1*]). Further, at 3 months postnatally, the epigenetic effect predicted an increase in a salivary-derived measure of cortisol stress response in the HPA axis on a habituation information-processing task. Similarly, Radtke et al. (2011) found that maternal distress (due to intimate partner violence) in pregnancy was associated with the same epigenetic effect in 10- to 19-year-olds. McGowan et al. (2009) helped specify the brain regions involved in human epigenetic effects due to stress. They examined postmortem hippocampal tissue in cases of childhood abuse (leading to suicide), finding decreased expression of the *NR3C1* gene, and increased

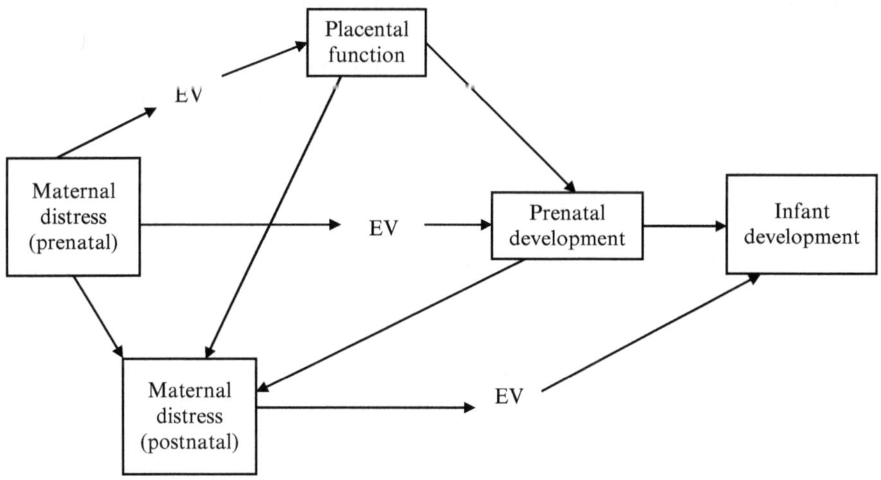

Fig. 11.1 Epigenetic variation (EV) influences infant behavior. Both direct/indirect pathways of epigenetic modification influence infant development (in conjunction with prenatal maternal distress). Also, postnatal maternal distress and placental function are important. Adapted from Monk, Spicer, & Champagne (2012)

epigenetic DNA methylation within the gene's regulatory region. That is, early adversity has been shown to increase risk for later psychopathology by epigenetic effects. In this regard, in further research on adult suicide completers, compared to completers without an abuse history, ones having a history of childhood abuse showed different hippocampal GR DNA methylation of *NR3C1* (the GR gene) and also ribosomal RNA genes (Labonté, Yerko et al., 2012). Roth (2013) described that Tyrka, Price, Marsit, Walters, and Carpenter (2012) showed that parental loss, childhood maltreatment, and parental care disruption were associated with increased *NR3C1* promoter DNA methylation. Similarly, Tyrka et al. (2015) found that, in preschool-aged children, methylation of exons 1D and 1F of the GR gene promoter region was associated with composite measure of adversity. Severe abuse could affect hundreds of gene promoter regions in hippocampal DNA (Labonté, Suderman et al., 2012).

Boyce and Kobor (2015) noted that early social adversity gets embedded by epigenesis in the genome and can have long-term effects. Oberlander et al. (2008) found increased *NR3C1*, GR gene methylation in infants of mothers who had experienced high depressive symptoms in the last trimester of pregnancy.

For another polymorphism, Ouellet-Morin et al. (2013) reported more epigenetic stamping by DNA methylation of the serotonin transporter gene (*5-HTTLPR*) in bullied relative to non-bullied monozygotic co-twins.

Longitudinal research extending into adolescence and adulthood is finding associations involving: (a) childhood disadvantage and genome-wide promoter methylation at mid-life (Borghol et al., 2012); (b) parental stress during infancy and later adolescent differential DNA methylation (Essex et al. 2013); and (c) early SES (socioeconomic status) and later upregulated inflammatory gene expression in the leukocyte transcriptome (Powell et al., 2013). Methylation of the *5HTT* serotonin transporter gene, along with the *s* allele of the gene, has been associated with adolescent depression (Olsson et al. 2010). This type of research speaks to the long-term physical (and mental) consequences that might accompany early epigenesis due to adversity.

As for the apparent target of prenatal epigenetic imprints, Monk et al. (2012) described that epigenetic marks can affect gene transcription within the placenta. The genes involved are termed "imprinted genes," given their capacity to be "silenced" by epigenetic stamps, producing epigenetic variations in gene expression. In humans, heightened maternal anxiety in pregnancy correlated negatively with placental messenger RNA levels (mRNA of the enzyme 11β-hydroxysteroid dehydrogenase 2 gene), which leads to enzymic inactivation of glucocorticoids, so normally reducing circulating maternal stress hormones.

Extensions

van IJzendoorn, Bakermans-Kranenburg, and Ebstein (2011) presented a modified G × E model of behavioral genetics that included the epigenetic process of DNA methylation as a factor that influences development. They depicted their model as G × M × E, in which M represents methylation status (see Fig. 11.2; van IJzendoorn, Caspers, Bakermans-Kranenburg, Beach, & Philibert, 2010). Due to the pervasiveness of epigenetic stamps deriving from experience that silence genes or otherwise alter their expression in context, the authors described the epigenome as dynamic and they recommended that child development be reconceptualized as experiences sculpting the individual's DNA through methylation (and presumably other epigenetic change mechanisms).

Epigenesis even affects differentially the genetic expression of genes in monozygotic co-twins, and the effect increases with age (epigenetic drift; Fraga et al., 2005; Martin, 2005). Epigenesis begins to work its effect in utero, but it continues throughout development (Meaney, 2010).

According to van IJzendoorn et al. (2011), methyl binding proteins that bind to the promoter regions of genes are caps that impede access to the gene for the transcription process leading

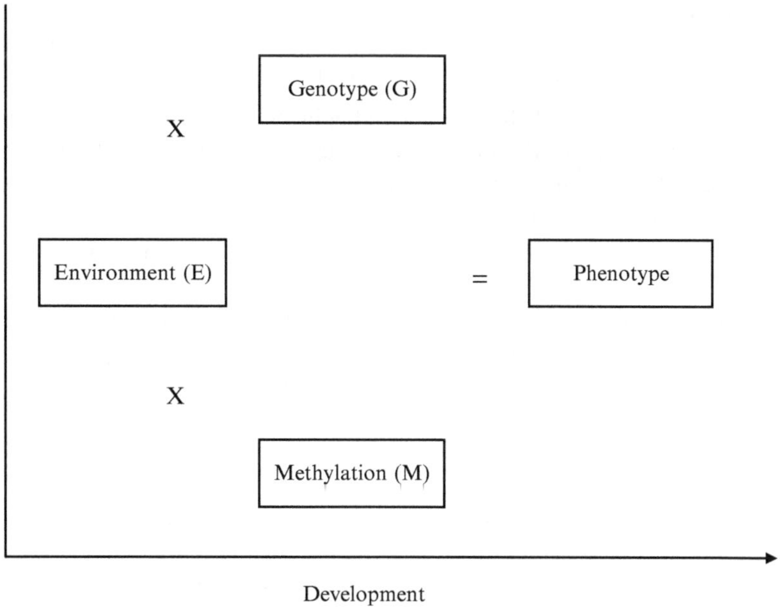

Fig. 11.2 The influences on the phenotype, including epigenesis (methylation). *Note.* I added the developmental component. The influence of the environment on the phenotype is moderated by genes and by epigenesis (methylation, M; Phenotype = G × M × E). Adapted from van IJzendoorn, Bakermans-Kranenburg, and Ebstein (2011)

to mRNA and eventual protein production. In embryogenesis, the process of epigenesis acts paradoxically, as has been shown, and could involve activation as well as gene silencing. At the level of activation, it constitutes the mechanism that differentiates body cells having the same DNA sequence by gene expression into cells with specialized functions. [Epigenesis is also involved in sexually-differentiated phenotypic expression.] Therefore, the environmentally-mediated epigenesis related to gene-expression in phenotypic development is based on a naturally-occurring widespread genetic-related process rather than a totally novel adaptation, allowing the flexible responses to environmental change and challenge that it permits across the lifespan.

van IJzendoorn et al. (2011) examined their model in relation to the differential genetic susceptibility model of Belsky and colleagues (e.g., Belsky, Bakermans-Kranenburg, & van IJzendoorn, 2007). It concerns the different susceptibility availed by certain allelic variations to either positive or negative environments in a style that is for better or worse. For example, children having less efficient dopamine-related genes fared worse in negative environments compared to controls and, moreover, if in positive environments, they profited most (Bakermans-Kranenburg & van IJzendoorn, 2011).

van IJzendoorn et al. (2011) asked in what way could DNA methylation fit into the differential genetic susceptibility model. They suggested that a possible mechanism involves prenatal methylation leading to prenatal programming that renders the affected individuals more liable to respond negatively to environmental challenge/adversity (Oberlander et al., 2008). [The authors noted that positive postnatal environments still could lead to demethylation and better development.]

The authors concluded that epigenesis suggests that, in contradistinction to the typical "nature or nurture" or "nature and nurture" formula of biological–environmental (interactional) promotion of development, to a clear degree, "nature is nurture." Epigenetic products rather than genes alone contribute to the canalization of development. Epigenesis allows the environment to become "embodied" in the developing individual's epigenome.

Comment

I would add that the manner in which van IJzendoorn et al. (2011) have described epigenesis and their G×M×E model clearly suggests that each of us are unique products of our genetic and environmental histories in which neither G or E, G×E, or any combination with other terms (G×E×D, G×M×E) prescribe constants in development applicable across our life histories. At best, G×E, epigenesis, and so on, provide scaffolds and their interstices are fitted with personal experiences, including one's activities sought and promoted by our active selves.

In the following, I examine the role of epigenesis in both externalizing and internalizing behavior and disorders. Genes do not act alone in psychopathology, as we have seen in the last chapters. Moreover, environmental effects can silence them in epigenesis. At the same time, these epigenetic effects can be reversed through the new psychopharmacologies being developed. These are exciting times for psychiatry in that influences on genes that lead to psychopathology can be targeted and even reversed.

Externalizing

Recent research implicates a role for DNA methylation epigenetic effects of the gene encoding the serotonin transporter in cases of antisocial behavior in childhood sexual abuse. This was reported by Beach, Brody, Todorov, Gunter, and Philibert (2011), Vijayendran, Beach, Plume, Brody, and Philibert (2012).

Dadds et al. (2014) found greater methylation of the *OXTR* (oxytocin receptor) gene for two promoter region CpG nucleotide and guanine nucleotide phosphate-linked sites in adolescent males expressing oppositional-defiant or conduct disorder and having higher levels of callous-unemotional traits (CUs), as well as child conduct problems (CPs). The authors concluded that epigenetic changes might be contributing to the demonstrated behavioral outcomes.

In another study by Dadds et al. (2014), in two samples having CPs, high CU trait was associated with the single nucleotide polymorphism *rs1042778* in the 3′ untranslated region of the *OXTR*, in particular. The authors concluded that the OXT system might serve as a developmental antecedent to psychopathology.

Internalizing

For changes in DNA methylation as a function of prenatal environment, Roth (2013) described the work of Oberlander and colleagues. Infants born to mothers who had reported increased depression and anxiety in the third pregnancy trimester expressed increased methylation of the *NR3C1* promoter in cord blood cells (Oberlander et al., 2008). The gene encoding the serotonin transporter (*SLC6A4*) also seemed involved in a similar effect (Devlin, Brain, Austin, & Oberlander, 2010).

Weder et al. (2014) found that epigenetic marks in conjunction with child abuse in 10-year olds (range 5–14) predicted dimensional ratings of depression. The maltreated children had been removed from their homes; they were compared to healthy controls. Psychiatric diagnosis was accomplished using the Schedule for Affective Disorders and Schizophrenia (K-SADS-PL; Kaufman et al., 1997); the Child Behavior Checklist (CBCL; Achenbach & Rescorla, 2001); the Child Dissociative Checklist (CDC; Putnam, Helmers, & Trickett, 1993); the Teachers Report Form (TRF, a teacher version of the parent-scored CBCL; Achenbach & Rescorla, 2001); and the Posttraumatic Stress Disorder Checklist (PTSD-CL; Amaya-Jackson, Newman, & Lipschitz, 2000). A questionnaire was used to establish depression (The Mood and Feelings Questionnaire, MFQ; Costello & Angold, 1988).

The results concerned methylation values in three genes (CpG sites) that were significant genome-wide in predicting depression—DNA-Binding Protein Inhibitor ID-3 (*ID3*); Glutamate Receptor, Ionotropic *N*-methyl-D-aspartate (NMDA) 1 (*GRIN1*); and Tubulin Polymerization Promoting Protein (*TPPP*). *ID3* is associated with the stress response, *GR1NI* with neuroplasticity, and *TPPP* in neurocircuitry development.

The action of methylation of three genes appeared to act independently in affecting depression. Lower depression was associated with greater epigenetic methylation at the CpG sites within each of the three genes.

The authors concluded that epigenetic changes to genes due to early environmental adversity lead to pathophysiological impacts and psychiatric illness. However, that the pathways involve epigenesis speaks to their reversibility and that the window of opportunity is wider than previously believed [also see Nemeroff and Binder (2014)].

Kaliman et al. (2014) studied expert meditators who participated in intense meditation using mindfulness meditation (Kabat-Zinn, 1982), compared to a control group who participated in leisure activities. They found that the meditation group evidenced apparent epigenetic effects on genes related to inflammatory processes. In particular, the meditation group expressed reduced activation of histone deacetylase genes (*HDAC* 2, 3, 9), altered global modification of histones (*H4ac*, *H3K4me3*), and decreased expression of pro-inflammatory genes (*RIPK2*, *COX2*). Also, in both groups, lower level of *RIPK2* and *HDAC2* predicted better recovery of cortisol level in a social stress test.

As for other stress-related research, epigenetic effects in cases of adversity measures and PTSD-related measures were found by Koenen et al. (2011) for *SLC6A4* and Uddin et al. (2011) for *MAN2C1*. In terms of changes in DNA methylation in relation to events later in life, Unternaehrer et al. (2012) found that adults who had experienced war adversity, and who were tested on a social stress test, evidenced stress-evoked DNA methylation effects on two stress-related genes—oxytocin receptors and the brain-derived neurotrophic factor gene (*BDNF*).

Comment

Despite the rapid advance in understanding the impact of epigenesis on behavior, McGowan and Roth (2015) maintained that it provides only a beginning toward understanding better how nature and nurture relate to each other.

Correlated Gene × Environment

Psychopathology and rGE

Introduction Knafo and Jaffee (2013) and Jaffee and Price (2012) reviewed the importance of gene–environment correlation (rGE) in developmental psychopathology. It is studied much less than G × E interactions, but could have much more impact. Although both concepts involve genes and environment, rGE might reflect more genetic influence than G × E because, in the phenomenon, genes affect the environment. In a certain sense, this balances the influence of epigenesis in developmental psychopathology, in which the environment can alter gene expression (e.g., in gene silencing).

"rGE" refers to the process through which the genotype influences or is associated with an individual's exposure to the environment resulting in attendant genetic differences in exposure to particular environments. Plomin, DeFries, and Loehlin (1977) described three main ways rGE functions in behavior genetics. (a) First, in passive rGE, genetic relatedness between offspring and parent accounts for statistical relations between partially heritable (behavioral) traits and the offspring's environment (e.g., a parent possesses and transmits a genetic risk for aggression that increases both her/his use of physical discipline and the offspring's display of aggression). (b) In evocative (or reactive) rGE, the environment reacts to the partially heritable (behavioral) traits involved and an association is evident between an offspring's genetically-influenced behavior and others' reactions to it. (c) In active rGE, through their own actions, offspring actively select or create environments or niches that fit a partially heritable (behavioral) trait.

Figures 11.3 and 11.4 specify how rGE leads to more differentiated understanding of causality in developmental psychopathology. For Knafo and Jaffee (2013), passive and evocative rGE imply reciprocal causality between parent and offspring. Given the feedback involved, minor individual differences earlier in life can become magnified over development.

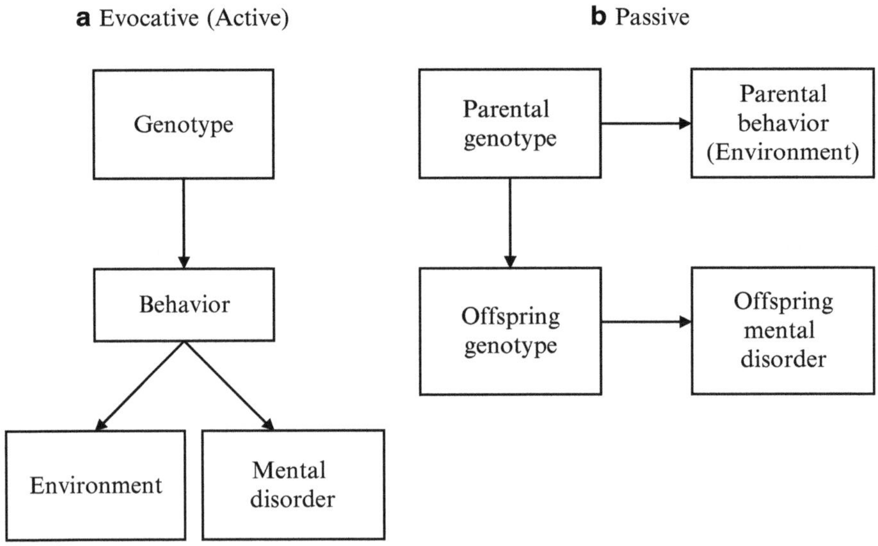

Fig. 11.3 Types of genotype-environment correlation (rG × E). In active/evocative genotype-environment correlation (rGE) (**a**), genotype confounds the relationship between environment and behavior. For example, genes predispose to sensation-seeking/seeking out deviant peers/substance use. In passive rGE (**b**), parental genotype confounds the relationship between family environment and child behavior. For example, genes predispose the parent to use harsh/physical discipline and also predispose the child to manifest aggressive behavior. Adapted from Jaffee (2011)

Parenting Recent research demonstrates rGE. Pener-Tessler et al. (2013) found that mothers modified their parenting behavior based on their 3-year-old boys' ability for self-control. Moreover, the child's *5-HTTLPR* genotype affected the positive parenting behavior involved, in an association driven by the child's genotype (evocative rGE). The boys' self-control mediated the genotype effect (*5-HTTLPR*) on parenting behavior. That is, the genotype affects self-control, which in turn affects positive parenting. In conclusion, the results show that a simple causal model (parenting ⟶ offspring behavior) in this area is being supplanted by one that starts with the offspring's genetic makeup.

Jaffee, Price, and Reyes (2013) noted that Hicks et al. (2013) found that lower scores related to following rules/endorsing conventional norms in 11-year-old twins were associated with higher levels of contextual risk later on in their adolescence. The relationship appeared accounted for by genetic factors as well as shared environmental ones common to both constructs.

Avinun and Knafo (2014) conducted a meta-analysis of 32 "children-as twin" studies (M2-D2 child twin research) in order to investigate causality in child outcomes. They distinguished parenting as a factor and whether the child's genetic influences "affect and shape" parental behavior through rGE, in this case "evocative" rGE, or responses evoked in the environment by genetically-influenced characteristics. The parental behaviors examined were parental positivity and negativity.

The main results of the research found a heritability estimate of 23 % for parental behavior (especially in parental report), supporting a child evocative effect on parenting that is genetically influenced. The shared and nonshared environmental components in the research accounted for higher percentages of the variance than the rGE one, suggesting the presence of both parenting consistency and differential sibling treatment within the family. The shared and nonshared environmental influences at play included culture/SES and intrauterine environment/friend differences, respectively.

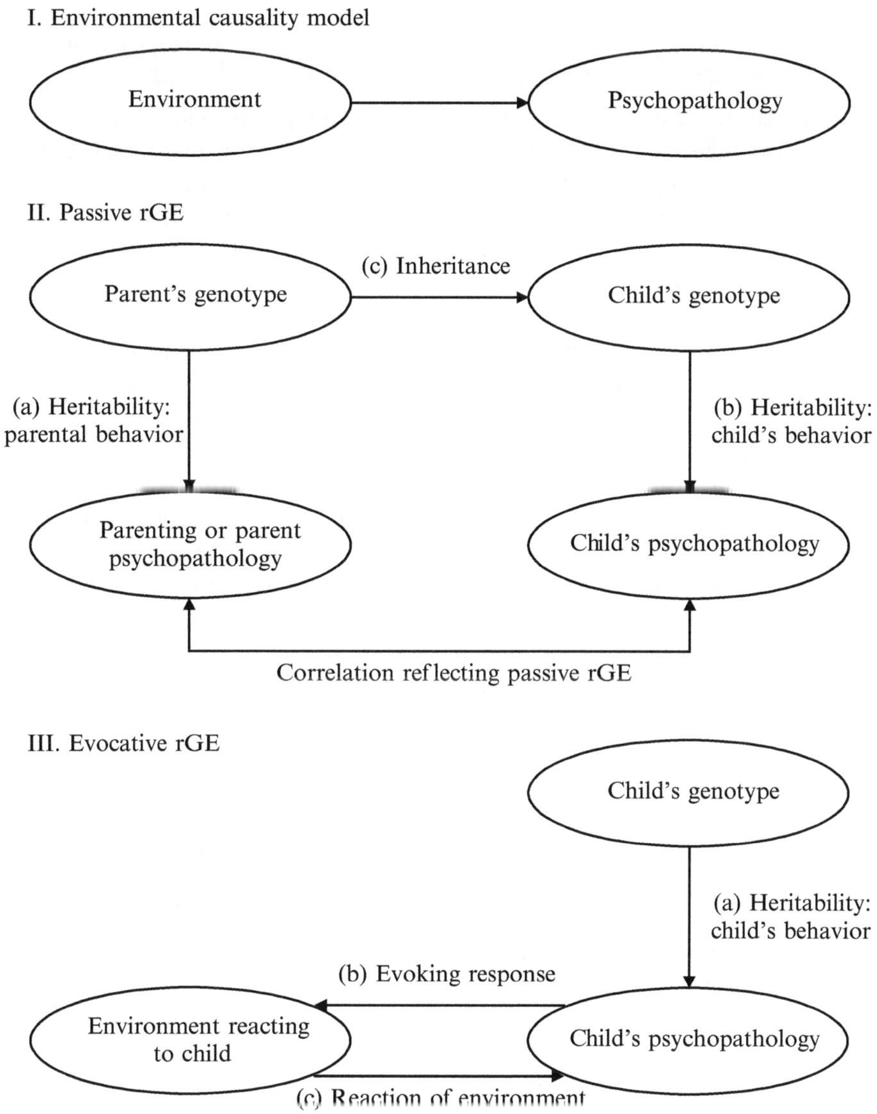

Fig. 11.4 Environmental causality model, passive gene-environment correlation, and evocative gene-environment correlation. The top panel shows how experience in the environment plays a causal role in increasing risk for psychopathology. The middle and bottom panels show how the association between the environment and psychopathology is confounded or initiated by genotype. Adopted with permission of Cambridge University Press. Knafo, A., & Jaffee, S. R. (2013). Gene-environment correlation in developmental psychopathology. *Development and Psychopathology*, *25*, 1–6; with kind permission from Cambridge University Press. [Figure 1, Page 2]

The authors concluded that genetically-influenced child behavior, as evidenced in their rGE data of the evocative type (responses elicited by genetically-influenced characteristics) can influence parenting and that parenting is not the sole factor in child outcome. Children's genotypes can causally lead to "meaningful" effects in parenting. The study is noteworthy by showing that twin studies, or quantitative genetic methods, can still provide rich data in the genomic era. Recent molecular genetic studies complement the children-as-twin paradigm by showing that the *Taq* I A1 allele of the dopamine receptor D2 is related to greater negative mood during parent–

child interactions (Mills-Koonce et al., 2007; also see Pener-Tessler et al., 2013).

In rGE, genetically-influenced child characteristics elicit parental responses tailored to them, so that these genetic influences are "child driven." In a twin study, Klahr, Thomas, Hopwood, Klump, and Burt (2013) investigated rGE using a task in which mother–child interactions were rated in real time and according to the interpersonal dimensions of warmth and control.

The results showed that maternal control was especially influenced by rGE processes. In particular, genetic influences on maternal control were a function of genetic influences on the control-oriented behavior of the children. To be more specific, the children varied in their dominant/submissive behavior, which was partially a function of their genetic predispositions, and the mothers responded online to the variations, thereby indirectly responding to the children's control-oriented genetic predispositions. To conclude, in the study, a driver of maternal behavior appeared based to a degree in the genetic predisposition of the children.

Marceau et al. (2013) investigated the associations between parental negativity and adolescent externalizing problems using a novel experimental design that allowed them to determine whether rGE could help explain the results. The standard model is unidirectional in mechanism—parental negativity contributes to adolescent behavior. Other theories are transactional or bidirectional. The twin study design used by Marceau et al. (2013) allowed them to combine (a) twin parents and their adolescents and (b) adolescent twins, their siblings, and their parents. The study allowed them to investigate a third hypothesis on the matter—the genes of adolescents contribute to both their externalizing problems and their parents' negative behavior toward them.

The results of the study indicated that parental negativity was associated with adolescent externalizing problems. Moreover, the best explanation involved evocative rGE rather than passive rGE or direct environmental effects. In evocative rGE, parenting behavior style is a response to adolescent externalizing behavior. This implicates parental negativity toward the adolescents' genetically-influenced externalizing problems. The literature also indicates that child-based genetic effects on parenting alter dynamically over development and, in considering parent–child relationships, in general, both parent and child genes hold influence.

Genetic research is nuancing understanding of typical etiological mechanisms proposed for common behavioral difficulties and psychiatric disorders. Barnes et al. (2013) found genetic influence on early childhood externalizing behavior problems (EBP). Specifically, they examined the relationship in spanking, self-regulation, and EBP, especially in a twin subsample. Typically, EBP has been considered either the result of low self-regulation or corporal punishment (leading to imitation). However, an alternative causal model is that rGEs are involved, both passive and evocative (i.e., children shape their environments according to their personal characteristics).

The results of the study supported the latter hypothesis; the major variables showed bidirectional relationships and, moreover, genetic influences accounted for some variance for each of the three measures. It even accounted for some of the covariance among them. The authors concluded that the causal relationship involved might reflect the sequence of genetic risk factors → self-regulation → EBP.

SES Tucker-Drob and Briley (2013) presented the concept of Gene × SES interaction in cognitive development. They argued that, although behavior genetic and molecular genetic studies support that genes account for 50–70 % of the variation in cognition, i.e., cognition is heritable at this level, the environment has an important role to play in cognition. Indeed, genetic effects in cognition result from the accumulation of environmental effects encountered. Specifically, genetic influences on cognition increase in higher SES. With increased environmental opportunity, individual differences that are genetically underpinned increasingly can manifest, and this might include selection of environments that are conducive. Therefore, early, slight individual differences become magnified with development in appropriate context.

The model described by Tucker-Drob and Briley (2014) is a transactional one. It is based on rGE, in which genes influence environmental experience, constituting a "key mechanism" in cognitive development. The transactional model is bidirectional with positive feedback loops. Selected environments have causal effects, in turn, on cognition, thereby reinforcing the initial genetically-underpinned behavior that led to their selection.

Research supports the Gene × SES model in cognition. For low-SES children, heritability of cognition "approaches zero" (e.g., Harden, Turkheimer, & Loehlin, 2007), whereas for high SES, the variance accounted for (individual differences explained) is toward 80 %.

Cultural Neuroscience

Chiao, Cheon, Pornpattananangkul, Mrazek, and Blizinsky (2013) presented an interdigitational model of culture, genes, development, and mind/behavior. Cultural neuroscience is an interdisciplinary field that explains how neurobiological processes contribute to the development of differential cultural behaviors, values, beliefs, and practices and, in turn, how culture conditions such neurobiological processes, with the time scales involved in the reciprocal causation both at the micro and macro levels. Culture stands as a dynamical system with looping effects and with neurocultural interactions [Also see Chiao and Immordino-Yang (2013); Han et al. (2013), and Sasaki (2013)].

Culture can be differentiated in neurobiological processes related to genes and behavior; for example, cognitive variation has been found in brain function across cultures (Han & Northoff, 2008). Other relevant findings concern cultural influences on neural representation of self/identity (Vogeley & Roepstorff, 2009). Culturally-patterned neuronal activities facilitate social survival and reproductive success (Kitayama & Uskul, 2011), indicative of culture-gene (neurobiological) co-evolution. Core cognitive and neural architecture might culturally differentiate in structure and function due to the interaction of environmental factors/cultural selection and evolutionary processes, which in turn cause their further refinement for storage/transmission of adaptive cultural attributes. Moreover, the latter might be represented in domain-specific modules (see Fig. 11.5). The situation/ontogeny/phylogeny triangularization mutually affects the reciprocal relations among genes, brain, behavior, mind, and culture. Work on Gene × Culture interactions (Sasaki, 2013) underscores the complexity in this system.

5-HTTLPR

In support of the model of cultural neuroscience, Chiao and Blizinsky (2010) examined culture-gene co-evolution of the cultural values of individualism–collectivism and its relation to the serotonin transporter gene (*SLC6A4*). They mapped the degree of individualism–collectivism in multiple countries in relation to the percent of the population expressing the short (*s*) allele of the polymorphism *5-HTTLPR* (relative to the long, *l*, allele). The results revealed that nations expressing more collectivism also showed a greater percentage of *s* allele carriers. The *s* allele was also associated with nations manifesting less anxiety/mood disorders, in a relationship mediated by an increased prevalence of collectivism.

Finally, in a fascinating result, nations with more pathogen presence exhibited more collectivism, in a relationship mediated by the *s* allele of the *5-HTTLPR* gene. Chiao and Blizinsky (2010) interpreted the findings in terms of collectivist values serving antipathogen functions, i.e., preference for in-group compared to out-group members. In addition, collectivism serves an anti-psychopathological function. The pattern of results was attributed to cultural and genetic selection, e.g., of alleles of the serotonin transporter gene.

Another cultural difference that expresses gene-culture co-evolution is societal tightness/looseness, which refers to the degree to which a nation is sensitive to compliance/violation of social norms (Gelfand et al., 2011). Mrazek, Chiao, Blizinsky, Lun, and Gelfand (2013) found

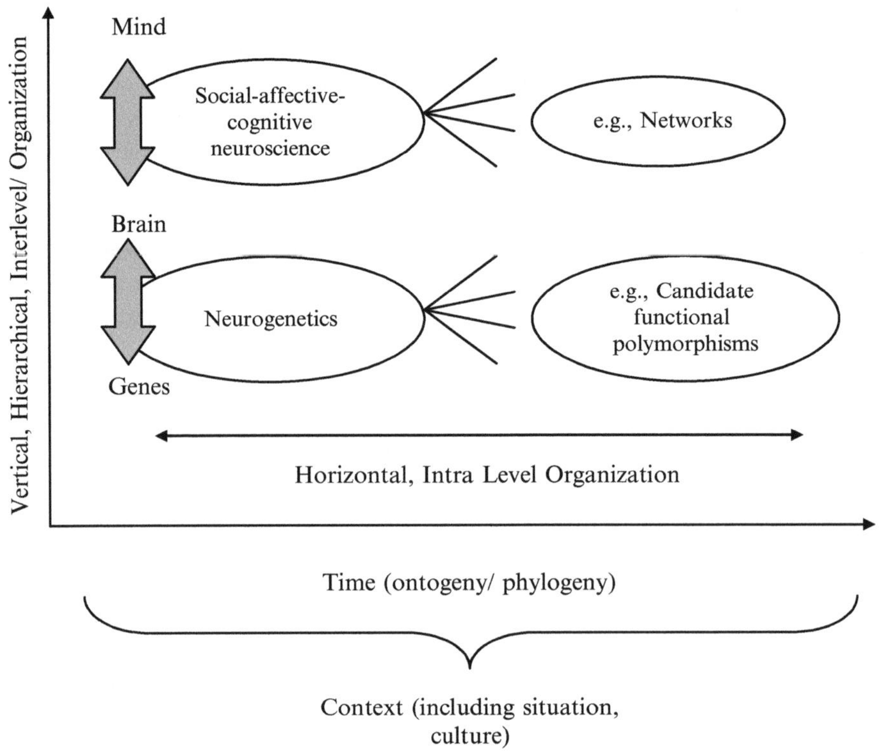

Fig. 11.5 Framework of cultural neuroscience. Cultural neuroscience integrates theory and methods in cultural psychology, social-affective-cognitive neuroscience, and neurogenetics across research in multiple time scales—specifically, situational, ontogenetic, and phylogenetic. Note that I modified the figure by placing culture as part of context. In the original figure, culture was placed at a higher level than mind. On the one hand, mind and culture are reciprocally constitutive. On the other hand, context is not independent of culture. In the original figure, ontogeny and phylogeny were considered different time scales. For this figure, I removed situation from time scales, and considered it as part of overall context. Adapted from Chiao, Cheon, Pornpattananangkul, Mrazek, & Blizinsky (2013), based on Chiao & Ambady (2007), Chiao (2009), and Chiao (2011)

that cultural tightness/looseness co-evolved with the serotonin transporter gene in the production of moral behavior (justification of things like taxes and cheating). Ecological threat was determined in 21 nations, and it predicted tightness/looseness due to the *s* allele variation; also, the latter predicted moral behavior justifiability due to tightness/looseness.

Chiao and Blizinsky (2010) concluded that tight-nation populations express greater social norm sensitivity as a function of greater presence of the *s* allele, whereas looser nations are associated with social norm violation tolerance as a function of carrying the *l* allele. The former allele has been associated with sensitivity/vigilance to negative affective cues, unlike the latter allele, which has been associated with sensitivity to positive affective cues. Chiao and Blizinsky (2010) linked their results to culture-gene co-evolution.

Similarly, countries ranked high in power distance (preference for social hierarchy), which is related to social hierarchy, have more *5-HTTLPR s* allele carriers (Chiao, 2010). Social dominance might be another area implicated in gene-cultural co-evolution involving *5-HTTLPR s* and *l* alleles. Chiao et al. (2009) found that people living in the USA or Japan scoring as individualistic expressed increased neural response within the mPFC to self-statements that were general (e.g., I am…) compared to contextual ones (e.g., when talking to my mother, I am…). In contrast, individuals who were more collectivist expressed mPFC increases to contextual compared to general statements. The results showed that cultural values more than nationality/race are involved in the modulation of neural response in the mPFC during self-processing.

Cheon et al. (2011) found that populations living in countries that express social hierarchies, such as Korea, manifest increased empathic neural response within the left temporoparietal junction (L-TPJ) when viewing in-group members in painful compared to neutral scenarios. The social hierarchic populations manifested this pattern more than egalitarian ones, such as the USA. There appears to be cultural influences in the empathic brain.

Kim and Sasaki (2014) presented a model of cultural neuroscience (see Fig. 11.6) that illustrates its multiple strands of study. The approach underscores that an individual's biological and psychological processes are conditioned within cultural context. Evolution also is crucial for understanding the person [and I add that developmental processes are equally important]. Some of the links in understanding behavior from a cultural neuroscience perspective include gene-culture co-evolution (theory of dual inheritance), G×E interaction, gene–culture interaction, and cultural shaping/moderation of brain structure/function.

In the macrolevel interplay between genes and culture in co-evolution, cultural selection is both influenced by and influences genetic selection (also called niche construction). G×E study is exemplified by Caspi's research (Caspi et al., 2002, 2003) on allelic variations in interaction with predisposing environments to produce later psychopathologies or problems in behavior. Kim and Sasaki (2014) described a paper by Ishii, Kim, Sasaki, Shinada, and Kusumi (2014) on whether differential alleles of *5-HTTLPR* modulate cultural differences in perceiving changes in

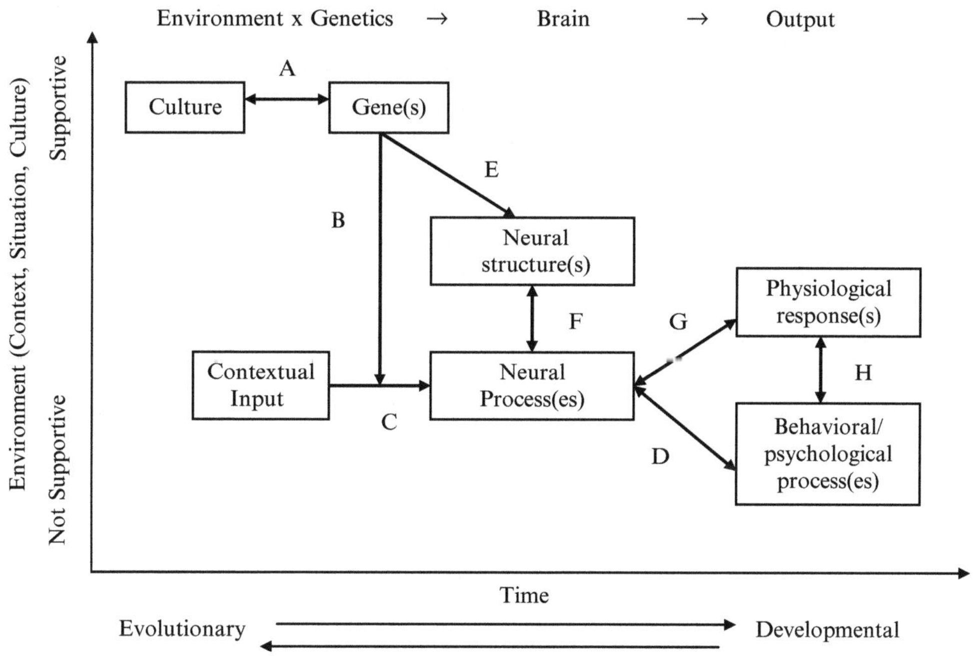

Fig. 11.6 Framework of cultural neuroscience: evolutionary, developmental, and environmental context. The model indicates the contextual, environmental, development, and evolutionary processes at work in gene-culture interplay for: (*A*) gene-culture co-evolution; (*B*→*C*→*D*) gene-culture interaction; (*C*, *D*) neural correlates/structural change; (*E*) gene-culture shaping brain structure; (*F*) culture-specific neural activities; (*C*, *G*) cultural moderation of situational cue response; and (*H*) resultant physiological response as correlates of psychological behavioral outcomes. Adapted from Kim & Sasaki (2014)

facial expression. Japanese people judged the disappearing point of a smile on videos quicker than Americans; and American Asians functioned like the latter and not the former. But the Japanese with the *ss* genotype excelled in the task compared to those with the *sl* and *ll* genotype. The *ss* genotype has been related to greater susceptibility to environmental input. Americans did not show this genetic effect.

OXTR

Other research groups are finding relevant results for cultural neuroscience. Kim et al. (2010) examined high psychological distress in Americans and Koreans and their emotional support seeking. The polymorphism examined concerned the G or A allele of *OXTR rs53576*, and whether individuals carried one or two copies of G compared to being homozygous for A. Having the G allele was associated with increased emotional support-seeking in both cultures. Kim et al. (2010) concluded that culture and the *OXTR* gene interact in producing psychological well-being. Moreover, the A allele is associated with emotional suppression in Koreans but, in Americans, it is the G allele that is so associated (Kim et al., 2011).

Sasaki, Kim, and Xu (2011) undertook work on religiosity, *OXTR*, and psychological well-being. In G×E (culture) results, Koreans who expressed greater religiosity and who were homozygous for G reported greater psychological well-being, but Caucasian Americans with the same characteristics reported reduced psychological well-being.

DRD4

Sasaki et al. (2013) also found that priming/heightening temporarily a belief in religion served to modulate prosocial behavior/altruism, but only for the Dopamine D4 receptor gene (*DRD4*) allele carrier. This happened both for Caucasian and Asian Americans living in the USA. The results were not found without priming. Sasaki (2013) explained her results in terms of Gene×Culture interaction. A particular genetic predisposition can lead to different outcomes, depending on cultural norms. Similarly, culture might influence people differentially, depending on genetic predispositions.

Kitayama et al. (2014) studied whether the *DRD4* moderated cultural differences in interdependent vs. independent social orientation. In this regard, they examined European Americans and Asian-born Asians (who had spent 7–10 years in the USA after puberty) on six scales (Independent subscale, of the Self-Construal Scale, Singelis, 1994; General Self-Efficacy Scale, Schwarzer et al. 1999; Self-Esteem Scale, Rosenberg, 1965; Value of Expression Questionnaire; Kim & Sherman, 2007; Interdependent subscale in Singelis, 1994; and the Analysis-Holism Scale; Choi, Koo, & Choi, 2007). A composite measure was derived from the scales.

The results revealed a Gene×Culture (G×C) interaction. Specifically, the expected cultural difference was found for only 1- or 2-repeat *DRD4* alleles. The alleles are part of the variable-number tandem repeat (VNTR) polymorphism of *DRD4* (Wang et al., 2004). The most common forms have 2, 4, and 7 repeats (2R, 4R, 7R allele, respectively). The 7R allele is more common in Western societies, with the 2R more common in Asian ones. Both are associated with reduced dopamine feedback inhibition. This leads to increased dopamine signaling capacity.

The two variants appear to be plasticity alleles, responding with flourishing outcomes in supportive environments and problematic ones in adverse environments (Belsky & Pluess, 2009; Sasaki et al., 2013). The variants could serve in cultural learning by accentuating reward and reinforcement. Normatively, behaviors that are consistent with cultural expectations are more likely to be reinforced.

Therefore, if cultures have different or even opposing cultural norms, the learning involved still could be mediated in the same way by downstream activities related to the *DRD4* allele variants. Given this understanding of how the gene might function, it makes sense that Kitayama et al. (2014) found that carriers of the 7R and 2R allelic *DRD4* variants exhibited different but still dominant social orientations culturally, compared to noncarriers (interdependence for Asians, independence for European Americans). The *DRD4* R allele is not as sensitive in the way indicated to cultural learning.

However, this assumes that the general environment for the study participants was generally favorable for their socialization (e.g., careful guidance and scaffolding of culturally-sanctioned or desirable behaviors by relevant socializing agents, such as parents, teachers). In unfavorable social conditions/adversity, deviant behaviors might eventuate instead (e.g., delinquency, risk taking). Kitayama et al. (2014) related their study to the co-evolution of genes and culture, as well as research in the field of cultural neuroscience.

Comments

Causadias (2013) described the work of Tamis-LeMonda et al. (2008) on individualism–collectivism and culture. Also, he presented the work of Juang, Syed, Cookston, Wang, and Kim (2012) on an ecological model (Bronfenbrenner, 1994) that inverted the placement of culture in the series of concentric circles in the model, with culture at the center. By doing so, the pervasive influence of culture on development is indicated. Nevertheless, Causadias (2013) took pains to emphasize the link between biology and culture in development, by referring to cultural neuroscience (Chiao et al., 2009), gene–culture interplay (Chiao & Blizinsky, 2010), gene–culture interaction (Dressler, Balieiro, Ribeiro, & Santos, 2008), and cultural epigenetics (Franklin et al., 2010).

For further reading on genomic science and development, refer to Grigorenko and Cicchetti (2012). The special issue that they edited includes articles on rGE (Jaffee & Price, 2012; Propper, Shanahan, Russo, & Mills-Koonce, 2012) that are worth noting. Also, two articles examined structural variation in the genome in relation to development (Gill, 2012; Rucker & McGuffin, 2012). Naples, Katz, and Grigorenko (2012) explored to good effect neuroendophenotypes in psychiatric illness. Also, refer to Knopik, Maccani, Francazio, and McGeary (2012) on epigenetic mechanisms, including in fetal programming.

The research in the field of genomics and other -omics is burgeoning. However, to understand better development, a refined understanding of the components in G × E and related (e.g., epigenesis) research is required. Moreover, G × E should be examined under the umbrella of the biopsychosocial model, or one that no longer parses its constituents into distinct components, so that likewise G, E, and their interactions no longer are considered as ones involving separable entities.

Chapter Conclusions

To conclude, the areas of epigenesis, rGE, and cultural neuroscience have shaken the foundations of genetics, evolution, and brain study. The complex interactive web in the causation of behavior no longer readily separates its components into independent areas and, also, no longer can the influences of genes, environment, and person be considered as separate (and interacting factors). The phenomenon of epigenesis belies the view that genes are distinct from the environment and inviolately biological in nature. Similarly, rGE belies the view that the environment is distinct from biology and influences behavioral causality on its own terms. Finally, the area of cultural neuroscience brings to the fore concepts such as G × C (culture), G × SES, and gene-culture co-evolution. Whether examining humans as they are or humans as they had evolved, in a general sense, in order to understand behavioral causality, different cultural influences have become as much indispensable as are different genetic, neuronal, and other environmental ones.

The nature of the indissociability of biology and environment in the genesis of behavior and its evolution point not only to the revolution taking place about genetics, the brain, and aspects of the environment, including the social and cultural, but also to the needed revolution in the field about the person, to a degree, as an independently active agent in generating her or his own behavior.

The genetic revolution has blurred the boundaries of genes and environment and has elaborated intricate concepts of their interaction that includes development (G×E×D), epistatis (G×G×E), and nested environmental effects)(G×E×E) but, in this emerging conceptualization of the role of biology and environment in behavioral causality, there is no interaction described involving the person (and the attributes of the person) that allows for distancing from and active control of genetic and environmental influences on behavior; in this regard, we need to consider and create the "G×E×P" (person) interaction. Much of the book is dedicated to this premise, that the person him or herself can actively influence instead of passively react to genetic and environmental influences on behavior and, consequently, choose, decide, and act freely instead of deterministically toward adaptive ends, everything else being equal, including having supportive environments toward that end and the development toward the maturity needed to effect this aspect of self (and other) control.

For example, future research could examine not only candidate genes in relation to maltreatment but also the degree of belief in free will as a factor, in interaction with these other factors, in antisocial behavior outcome. Or, gene-culture co-evolution could examine the role of personal (self, free will) factors that mitigate the influence of genes and culture on the evolution of behavior. Culture is not monolithic, and individual differences abound in attitude and behavior within cultures, so that one could ask to what degree these types of differences are individually determined through personal choices toward various freedoms and toward actively choosing, deciding, and behaving beyond the influences of genes and environment (culture). Moreover, it would seem relevant to determine how has this triune influence of heredity, environment (culture), and a personally active being had functioned in the evolution of humans, especially in the recent past epochs in our evolution in which personal factors had more of a chance to be pertinent and involved.

To conclude these chapters on the genetic and environmental influences on behavior, the exponential increase in conceptualization and empirical findings is changing the understanding of development and its causality in complex ways. Some research might emphasize the influence of parenting (e.g., Sulik, Blair, Berry, Mills-Koonce, & Greenberg 2015; on early parenting effects on developing executive function) and some the influence of epigenetics and genetics on behavior (e.g., Dadds, Moul, Hawes, Diaz, & Brennan, 2015; on epigenetic modification of CpG sites in the NR3C1 promoter region 1 F in 4- to 16-year olds with comorbid externalizing and anxiety problems). Thus, the complexity of development demands a broad approach in which causality is examined multifactorially and in novel ways seeking novel concepts.

References

Achenbach, T. M., & Rescorla, L. (2001). *Manual for the ASEBA school-age forms & profiles*. Burlington, VT: University of Vermont, Research Center for Children, Youth, & Families.

Amaya-Jackson, L., Newman, E., & Lipschitz, D. S. (2000, October). *The child PTSD checklist*. Paper presented at annual meeting of the American Academy of Child and Adolescent Psychiatry, New York.

Avinun, R., & Knafo, A. (2014). Parenting as a reaction evoked by children's genotype: A meta-analysis of children-as-twins studies. *Personality and Social Psychology Review, 18*, 87–102.

Baker-Andresen, D., Ratnu, V. S., & Bredy, T. W. (2013). Dynamic DNA methylation: A prime candidate for genomic metaplasticity and behavioral adaptation. *Trends in Neuroscience, 36*, 3–13.

Bakermans-Kranenburg, M. J., & van IJzendoorn, M. H. (2011). Differential susceptibility to rearing environment depending on dopamine-related genes: New evidence and a meta-analysis. *Development and Psychopathology, 23*, 39–52.

Barnes, J. C., Boutwell, B. B., Beaver, K. M., & Gibson, C. L. (2013). Analyzing the origins of childhood externalizing behavioral problems. *Developmental Psychology, 49*, 2272–2284.

Beach, S. R. H., Brody, G. H., Todorov, A. A., Gunter, T. D., & Philibert, R. A. (2011). Methylation at *5HTT* mediates the impact of child sex abuse on women's antisocial behavior: An examination of the Iowa adoptee sample. *Psychosomatic Medicine, 73*, 83–87.

Belsky, J., Bakermans-Kranenburg, M. J., & van IJzendoorn, M. H. (2007). For better and for worse: Differential susceptibility to environmental influences. *Current Directions in Psychological Science, 16*, 300–304.

Belsky, J., & Pluess, M. (2009). The nature (and nurture?) of plasticity in early human development. *Perspectives on Psychological Science, 4*, 345–351.

Borghol, N., Suderman, M., McArdle, W., Racine, A., Hallett, M., Pembrey, M., et al. (2012). Association with early life socio-economic position in adult DNA methylation. *International Journal of Epidemiology, 41*, 62–74.

Boyce, W. T., & Kobor, M. S. (2015). Development and the epigenome: The "synapse" of gene-environment interplay. *Developmental Science, 18*, 1–23.

Bronfenbrenner, U. (1994). Ecological models of human development. In T. Husten & T. N. Postlethwaite (Eds.), *International encyclopedia of education* (2nd ed., Vol. 3, pp. 1643–1647). New York: Elsevier Science.

Caspi, A., McClay, J., Moffitt, T. E., Mill, J., Martin, J., Craig, I. W., et al. (2002). Role of genotype in the cycle of violence in maltreated children. *Science, 297*, 851–854.

Caspi, A., Sugden, K., Moffitt, T. E., Taylor, A., Craig, I. W., Harrington, H., et al. (2003). Influence of life stress on depression: Moderation by a polymorphism in the 5-HTT gene. *Science, 301*, 386–389.

Causadias, J. M. (2013). A roadmap for the integration of culture into developmental psychopathology. *Development and Psychopathology, 25*, 1375–1398.

Cheon, B. K., Im, D., Harada, T., Kim, J., Mathur, V. A., Scimeca, J. M., et al. (2011). Cultural influences on neural basis of intergroup empathy. *NeuroImage, 57*, 642–650.

Chiao, J. Y. (2009). Cultural neuroscience: A once and future discipline. *Progress in Brain Research, 178*, 287–304.

Chiao, J. Y. (2010). Neural basis of social status hierarchy across species. *Current Opinion in Neurobiology, 20*, 803–809.

Chiao, J. Y. (2011). Cultural neuroscience: Visualizing culture-gene influences on brain function. In J. Decety & J. Cacioppo (Eds.), *The Oxford handbook of social neuroscience* (pp. 742–762). New York: Oxford University Press.

Chiao, J. Y., & Ambady, N. (2007). Cultural neuroscience: Parsing universality and diversity across levels of analysis. In S. Kitayama & D. Cohen (Eds.), *Handbook of cultural psychology*. New York: Guilford Press.

Chiao, J. Y., & Blizinsky, K. D. (2010). Culture-gene coevolution of individualism-collectivism and the serotonin transporter gene (5-HTTLPR). *Proceedings of the Royal Society B: Biological Sciences, 277*, 529–537.

Chiao, J. Y., Cheon, B. K., Pornpattananangkul, N., Mrazek, A. J., & Blizinsky, K. D. (2013). Cultural neuroscience: Progress and promise. *Psychological Inquiry, 24*, 1–19.

Chiao, J. Y., Harada, T., Komeda, H., Li, Z., Mano, Y., Saito, D., et al. (2009). Neural basis of individualistic and collectivistic views of self. *Human Brain Mapping, 30*, 2813–2820.

Chiao, J. Y., & Immordino-Yang, M. H. (2013). Modularity and the cultural mind: Contributions of cultural neuroscience to cognitive theory. *Perspectives on Psychological Science, 8*, 56–61.

Choi, I., Koo, M., & Choi, J. A. (2007). Individual differences in analytic versus holistic thinking. *Personality and Social Psychology Bulletin, 33*, 691–705.

Costello, E. J., & Angold, A. (1988). Scales to assess child and adolescent depression: Checklists, screens, and nets. *Journal of the American Academy of Child and Adolescent Psychiatry, 27*, 726–737.

Dadds, M. R., Moul, C., Cauchi, A., Dobson-Stone, C., Hawes, D. J., Brennan, J., et al. (2014). Methylation of the oxytocin receptor gene and oxytocin blood levels in the development of psychopathy. *Development and Psychopathology, 26*, 33–40.

Dadds, M. R., Moul, C., Hawes, D. J., Diaz, A. M., & Brennan, J. (2015). Individual differences in childhood behavior disorders associated with epigenetic modulation of the cortisol receptor gene. *Child Development, 86*, 1311–1320.

Devlin, A. M., Brain, U., Austin, J., & Oberlander, T. F. (2010). Prenatal exposure to maternal depressed mood and the *MTHFR*C677T variant affect *SLC6A4* methylation in infants at birth. *PLoS ONE, 5*, e12201. doi:10.1371/journal.pone.0012201.

Dressler, W. W., Balieiro, M. C., Ribeiro, R. P., & Santos, J. E. D. (2008). Cultural consonance, a 5HT2A receptor polymorphism, and depressive symptoms: A longitudinal study of gene × culture interaction in urban Brazil. *American Journal of Human Biology, 21*, 91–97.

Essex, M. J., Boyce, W. T., Hertzman, C., Lam, L. L., Armstrong, J. M., Neumann, S. M., et al. (2013). Epigenetic vestiges of early developmental adversity: Childhood stress exposure and DNA methylation in adolescence. *Child Development, 84*, 58–75.

Fraga, M. F., Ballestar, E., Paz, M. F., Ropero, S., Setien, F., Ballestar, M. L., et al. (2005). Epigenetic differences arise during the lifetime of monozygotic twins. *Proceedings of the National Academy of Science, 102*, 10604–10609.

Franklin, T. B., Russig, H., Weiss, I. C., Gräff, J., Linder, N., Michalon, A., et al. (2010). Epigenetic transmission of the impact of early stress across generations. *Biological Psychiatry, 68*, 408–415.

Gelfand, M. J., Raver, J. L., Nishii, L., Leslie, L. M., Lun, J., Lim, B. C., et al. (2011). Differences between tight and loose cultures: A 33-nation study. *Science, 332*, 1100–1104.

Gill, M. (2012). Developmental psychopathology: The role of structural variation in the genome. *Development and Psychopathology, 24*, 1319–1334.

Grigorenko, E. L., & Cicchetti, D. (2012). Genomic sciences for developmentalists: The current state of affairs. *Development and Psychopathology, 24*, 1157–1164.

Han, S., & Northoff, G. (2008). Culture-sensitive neural substrates of human cognition: A transcultural

neuroimaging approach. *Nature Review Neuroscience, 9*, 646–654.
Han, S., Northoff, G., Vogeley, K., Wexler, B. E., Kitayama, S., & Varnum, M. E. W. (2013). A cultural neuroscience approach to the biosocial nature of the human brain. *Annual Review of Psychology, 64*, 335–359.
Harden, K. P., Turkheimer, E., & Loehlin, J. C. (2007). Genotype by environment interaction in adolescents' cognitive aptitude. *Behavioral Genetics, 37*, 273–283.
Hicks, B. M., Johnson, W., Durbin, C. E., Blonigen, D. M., Iacono, W. G., & McGue, M. (2013). Gene-environment correlation in the development of adolescent substance abuse: Selection effects of child personality and mediation via contextual risk factors. *Development and Psychopathology, 25*, 119–132.
Ishii, K., Kim, H. S., Sasaki, J. Y., Shinada, M., & Kusumi, I. (2014). Culture modulates sensitivity to the disappearance of facial expressions associated with serotonin transporter polymorphism (5-HTTLPR). *Culture and Brain, 2*, 72–88.
Jaffee, S. R. (2011). Genotype-environment correlations: Definitions, methods of measurement, and implications for research on adolescent psychopathology. In K. S. Kendler, S. R. Jaffee, & D. Romer (Eds.), *The dynamic genome and mental health: The role of genes and environments in youth development* (pp. 79–102). New York: Oxford University Press.
Jaffee, S. R., & Price, T. S. (2012). The implications of genotype environment correlation for establishing causal processes in psychopathology. *Development and Psychopathology, 24*, 1253–1264.
Jaffee, S. R., Price, T. S., & Reyes, T. M. (2013). Behavior genetics: Past, present, future. *Development and Psychopathology, 25*, 1225–1242.
Juang, L., Syed, M., Cookston, J., Wang, Y., & Kim, S. Y. (2012). Everyday and acculturation-based family conflict among Chinese American parents and adolescents. *New Directions in Child and Adolescent Development, 135*, 13–34.
Kabat-Zinn, J. (1982). An outpatient program in behavioral medicine for chronic pain patients based on the practice of mindfulness meditation: Theoretical considerations and preliminary results. *General Hospital Psychiatry, 4*, 33–47.
Kaliman, P., Álvarez-López, M. J., Cosín-Tomás, M., Rosenkranz, M. A., Lutz, A., & Davidson, R. J. (2014). Rapid changes in histone deacetylases and inflammatory gene expression in expert meditators. *Psychoneuroendocrinology, 40*, 96–107.
Kaufman, J., Birmaher, B., Brent, D., Rao, U., Flynn, C., Moreci, P., et al. (1997). Schedule for affective disorders and schizophrenia for school-age children-present and life time version (K-SADS-PL): Initial reliability and validity data. *Journal of the American Academy of Child and Adolescent Psychiatry, 36*, 980–988.
Kim, H. S., & Sasaki, J. Y. (2014). Cultural neuroscience: Biology of the mind in cultural contexts. *Annual Review of Psychology, 65*, 487–514.
Kim, H. S., & Sherman, D. K. (2007). "Express yourself": Culture and the effect of self-expression on choice. *Journal of Personality and Social Psychology, 92*, 1–11.
Kim, H. S., Sherman, D. K., Mojaverian, T., Sasaki, J. Y., Park, J., Suh, E. M., et al. (2011). Gene-culture interaction: Oxytocin receptor polymorphism (OXTR) and emotion regulation. *Social Psychological and Personality Science, 2*, 665–672.
Kim, H. S., Sherman, D. K., Sasaki, J. Y., Xu, J., Chu, T. Q., Ryu, C., et al. (2010). Culture, distress, and oxytocin receptor polymorphism (OXTR) interact to influence emotional support seeking. *Proceedings of the National Academy of Sciences, USA, 107*, 1517–15721.
Kitayama, S., King, A., Yoon, C., Tompson, S., Huff, S., & Liberzon, I. (2014). The dopamine D4 receptor gene (DRD4) moderates cultural difference in independent versus interdependent social orientation. *Psychological Science, 25*, 1169–1177.
Kitayama, S., & Uskul, A. K. (2011). Culture, mind, and the brain: Current evidence and future directions. *Annual Review of Psychology, 62*, 419–449.
Klahr, A. M., Thomas, K. M., Hopwood, C. J., Klump, K. L., & Burt, A. (2013). Evocative gene-environment correlation in the mother-child relationship: A twin study of interpersonal processes. *Development and Psychopathology, 25*, 105–118.
Knafo, A., & Jaffee, S. R. (2013). Gene-environment correlation in developmental psychopathology. *Development and Psychopathology, 25*, 1–6.
Knopik, V. S., Maccani, M. A., Francazio, S., & McGeary, J. E. (2012). The epigenetics of maternal cigarette smoking during pregnancy and effects on child development. *Development and Psychopathology, 24*, 1377–1390.
Koenen, K. C., Uddin, M., Chang, S.-C., Aiello, A. E., Wildman, D. E., & Goldmann, E. (2011). SLC6A4 methylation modifies the effect of the number of traumatic events on risk of posttraumatic stress disorder. *Depression and Anxiety, 28*, 639–647.
Labonté, B., Suderman, M., Maussion, G., Navaro, L., Yerko, V., Mahar, I., et al. (2012). Genome-wide epigenetic regulation by early-life trauma. *Archives of General Psychiatry, 69*, 722–731.
Labonté, B., Yerko, V., Gross, J., Mechawar, N., Meaney, M. J., Szyf, M., et al. (2012). Differential glucocorticoid receptor exon 1(B), 1(C), and 1 (H) expression and methylation in suicide completers with a history of childhood abuse. *Biological Psychiatry, 72*, 41–48.
Marceau, K., Horwitz, B. N., Narusyte, J., Ganiban, J. M., Spotts, E. L., Reiss, D., et al. (2013). Gene-environment correlation underlying the association between parental negativity and adolescent externalizing problems. *Child Development, 84*, 2031–2046.
Martin, G. M. (2005). Epigenetic drift in aging identical twins. *Proceedings of the National Academy of Sciences, USA, 102*, 10413–10414.

McGowan, P. O., & Roth, T. L. (2015). Epigenetic pathways through which experiences become linked with biology. *Development and Psychopathology, 27*, 637–678.

McGowan, P. O., Sasaki, A., D'Alessio, A. C., Dymov, S., Labonté, B., Szyf, M., et al. (2009). Epigenetic regulation of the glucocorticoid receptor in human brain associates with childhood abuse. *Nature Neuroscience, 12*, 342–348.

McGowan, P. O., Suderman, M., Sasaki, A., Huang, T. C., Hallett, M., Meaney, M. J., & Szyf, M. (2011). Broad epigenetic signature of maternal care in the brain of adult rats. *PloS ONE, 6*, e14739. doi:10.1371/journal.pone.0014739.

Meaney, M. J. (2010). Epigenetics and the biological definition of gene × environment interactions. *Child Development, 81*, 41–79.

Mill, J., & Heijmans, B. T. (2013). From promises to practical strategies in epigenetic epidemiology. *Nature Reviews Genetics, 14*, 585–594.

Mills-Koonce, W. R., Propper, C. B., Gariepy, J. L., Blair, C., Garrett-Peters, P., & Cox, M. J. (2007). Bidirectional genetic and environmental influences on mother and child behavior: The family system as the unit of analyses. *Development and Psychopathology, 19*, 1073–1087.

Monk, C., Spicer, J., & Champagne, F. A. (2012). Linking prenatal maternal adversity to developmental outcomes in infants: The role of epigenetic pathways. *Development and Psychopathology, 24*, 1361–1376.

Mrazek, A. J., Chiao, J. Y., Blizinsky, K. D., Lun, J., & Gelfand, M. J. (2013). The role of culture-gene coevolution in morality judgment: Examining the interplay between tightness-looseness and allelic variation of the serotonin transporter gene. *Culture and Brain, 1*, 100–117.

Naples, A., Katz, L., & Grigorenko, E. L. (2012). Lexical decision as an endophenotype for reading comprehension: An exploration of an association. *Development and Psychopathology, 24*, 1345–1360.

Nemeroff, C. B., & Binder, E. (2014). The preeminent role of childhood abuse and neglect in vulnerability to major psychiatric disorders: Toward elucidating the underlying neurobiological mechanisms. *Journal of the American Academy of Child and Adolescent Psychiatry, 53*, 395–397.

Nikolova, Y. S., & Hariri, A. R. (2015). Can we observe epigenetic effects on human brain function? *Trends in Cognitive Science, 19*, 366–373.

Oberlander, T. F., Weinberg, J., Papsdorf, M., Grunau, R., Misri, S., & Devlin, A. M. (2008). Prenatal exposure to maternal depression, neonatal methylation of human glucocorticoid receptor gene (NR3C1) and infant cortisol stress responses. *Epigenetics, 3*, 97–106.

Olsson, C. A., Foley, D. L., Parkinson-Bates, M., Byrnes, G., McKenzie, M., Patton, G. C., et al. (2010). Prospects for epigenetic research within cohort studies of psychological disorder: A pilot investigation of a peripheral cell marker of epigenetic risk for depression. *Biological Psychology, 83*, 159–165.

Ouellet-Morin, L., Wong, C. C., Danese, A., Pariante, C. M., Papadopoulos, A. S., Mill, J., et al. (2013). Increased serotonin transporter gene (SERT) DNA methylation is associated with bullying victimization and blunted cortisol response to stress in childhood: A longitudinal study of discordant monozygotic twins. *Psychological Medicine, 43*, 1813–1823.

Pener-Tessler, R., Avinun, R., Uzefovsky, F., Edelman, S., Ebstein, R. P., & Knafo, A. (2013). Boys' serotonin transporter genotype affects maternal behavior through self-control: A case of evocative gene-environment correlation. *Development and Psychopathology, 25*, 151–162.

Plomin, R., DeFries, J. C., & Loehlin, J. C. (1977). Genotype-environment interaction and correlation in the analysis of human behavior. *Psychological Bulletin, 84*, 309–322.

Powell, N. D., Sloan, E. K., Bailey, M. T., Arevalo, J. M., Miller, G. E., Chen, E., et al. (2013). Social stress up-regulates inflammatory gene expression in the leukocyte transcriptome via beta-adrenergic induction of myelopoiesis. *Proceedings of the National Academy of Sciences, USA, 110*, 16574–16579.

Propper, C. B., Shanahan, M. J., Russo, R., & Mills-Koonce, W. R. (2012). Evocative gene-parenting correlations and academic performance at first grade: An exploratory study. *Development and Psychopathology, 24*, 1265–1282.

Putnam, F. W., Helmers, K., & Trickett, P. K. (1993). Development, reliability, and validity of a child dissociation scale. *Child Abuse & Neglect, 17*, 731–741.

Radtke, K. M., Ruf, M., Gunter, H. M., Dohrmann, K., Schauer, M., & Elbert, T. (2011). Transgenerational impact of intimate partner violence on methylation in the promoter of the glucocorticoid receptor. *Translational Psychiatry, 1*, e21. doi:10.1038/tp.2011.21.

Rosenberg, M. (1965). *Society and the adolescent self-image*. Princeton, NJ: Princeton University Press.

Roth, T. L. (2013). Epigenetic mechanisms in the development of behavior: Advances, challenges, and future promises of a new field. *Development and Psychopathology, 25*, 1279–1291.

Rucker, J. J. H., & McGuffin, P. (2012). Genomic structural variation in psychiatric disorders. *Development and Psychopathology, 24*, 1335–1344.

Sasaki, J. Y. (2013). Promise and challenges surrounding culture-gene coevolution and gene-culture interactions. *Psychological Inquiry, 24*, 64–70.

Sasaki, J. Y., Kim, H. S., Mojaverian, T., Kelley, L. D. S., Park, I. Y., & Janušonis, S. (2013). Religion priming differentially increases prosocial behavior among variants of the dopamine D4 receptor (DRD4) gene. *Social Cognitive and Affective Neuroscience, 8*, 209–215.

Sasaki, J. Y., Kim, H., & Xu, J. (2011). Religion and well-being: An analysis of an oxytocin receptor polymorphism (OXTR) and culture. *Journal of Cross-Cultural Psychology, 42*, 1394–1405.

Schwarzer, R., Mueller, J., & Greenglass, E. (1999). Assessment of perceived general self-efficacy on the

Internet: Data collection in cyberspace. *Anxiety, Stress, & Coping, 12*, 145–161.

Singelis, T. M. (1994). The measurement of independent and interdependent self-construals. *Personality and Social Psychology Bulletin, 20*, 580–891.

Suderman, M., McGowan, P. O., Sasaki, A., Huang, T. C. T., Hallett, M., Meaney, M. J., Turecki, G., & Szyf, M. (2012). Conserved epigenetic sensitivity to early life experience in the rat and human hippocampus. *Proceedings of the National Academy of Science, USA, 109*, 17266–17272.

Sulik, M. J., Blair, C., Berry, D., Mills-Koonce, R., & Greenberg, M. (2015). Early parenting and development of externalizing behavior problems: Longitudinal mediation through children's executive function. *Child Development, 86*, 1588–1603.

Szyf, M., & Bick, J. (2013). DNA methylation: A mechanism for embedding early life experiences in the genome. *Child Development, 84*, 49–57.

Tamis-LeMonda, C. S., Way, N., Hughes, D., Yoshikawa, H., Kalman, R. K., & Niwa, E. Y. (2008). Parents' goals for children: The dynamic coexistence of individualism and collectivism in cultures and individuals. *Social Development, 17*, 183–209.

Tucker-Drob, E. M., Briley, D. A., & Harden, K. P. (2013). Genetic and environmental influences on cognition across development and context. *Current Directions in Psychological Science, 22*, 349–355.

Tyrka, A. R., Parade, S. H., Eslinger, N. M., Marsit, C. J., Lesseur, C., Armstrong, D. A., et al. (2015). Methylation of exons 1D, 1F, 1H of the glucocorticoid receptor gene promoter and exposure to adversity in preschool-aged children. *Development and Psychopathology, 27*, 577–585.

Tyrka, A. R., Price, L. H., Marsit, C., Walters, O. C., & Carpenter, L. L. (2012). Childhood adversity and epigenetic modulation of the leukocyte glucocorticoid receptor. Preliminary findings in healthy adults. *PLoS ONE, 7*, e30148. doi:10.1371/journal.pone.0030148.

Uddin, M., Koenen, K. C., Aiello, A. E., Wildman, D. E., de los Santos, R., & Galea, S. (2011). Epigenetic and inflammatory marker profiles associated with depression in a community-based epidemiologic sample. *Psychological Medicine, 41*, 997–1007.

Unternaehrer, E., Luers, P., Mills, J., Dempster, E., Meyer, A. H., Staehli, S., et al. (2012). Dynamic changes in DNA methylation of stress-associated genes (OXTR, BDNF) after acute psychosocial stress. *Translational Psychiatry, 2*, e150. doi:10.1038/tp.2012.77.

van IJzendoorn, M. H., Bakermans-Kranenburg, M. J., & Ebstein, R. P. (2011). Methylation matters in child development: Toward developmental behavioral epigenetics. *Child Development Perspectives, 5*, 305–310.

van IJzendoorn, M. H., Caspers, K., Bakermans-Kranenburg, M. J., Beach, S. R. H., & Philibert, R. (2010). Methylation matters: Interaction between methylation density and 5HTT genotype predicts unresolved loss or trauma. *Biological Psychiatry, 68*, 405–407.

Vijayendran, M., Beach, S., Plume, J. M., Brody, G., & Philibert, R. (2012). Effects of genotype and child abuse on DNA methylation and gene expression at the serotonin transporter. *Frontiers in Psychiatry, 3*, 55. doi:10.3389/fpsyt.2012.00055.

Vogeley, K., & Roepstorff, A. (2009). Contextualising culture and social cognition. *Trends in Cognitive Sciences, 13*, 511–516.

Wang, E., Ding, Y.-C., Flodman, P., Kidd, J. R., Kidd, K. K., Grady, D. L., et al. (2004). The genetic architecture of selection at the human dopamine receptor D4 (DRD4) gene locus. *American Journal of Human Genetics, 74*, 931–944.

Weder, N., Zhang, H., Jensen, K., Yang, B. Z., Simen, A., Jackowski, A., et al. (2014). Child abuse, depression, and methylation in genes involved with stress, neural plasticity, and brain circuitry. *Journal of the American Academy of Child & Adolescent Psychiatry, 53*, 417–424.

Zovkic, I. B., Meadows, J. P., Kaas, G. A., & Sweatt, J. D. (2013). Interindividual variability in stress susceptibility: A role for epigenetic mechanisms in PTSD. *Frontiers in Psychiatry, 4*, 60. doi:10.3389/fpsyt.2013.00060.

Nature and Nurture: Evolution and Complexities

12

Chapter Introduction

This chapter explores the multiple ways in which Nature and Nurture interact. First, it examines contemporary views of evolution that include a role for development, systems, complexity, emergence, and optimization. Similarly, in niche construction, environment, phenotype, and development interact, and it leaves room for cultural influences. Next, the chapter addresses the changing face of the study of intelligence and its factors, including work on the general *g* factor, implicate environmental influences as much as genetic ones. The concept of *g* has led to the equivalent concept of *p* in psychopathology and emotional disorders. Finally, the chapter reviews the fast-emerging field of social genomics, which explains how the environment "gets under the skin." For example, factors such as perceived social loneliness are found to have long-term implications for the health of individuals. The chapter concludes with discussion of complexity in evolution.

Evolution

Evolution is a cross-cutting paradigm that helps amalgamate the biological and life sciences under one inclusive rubric. It took wing with the work of Darwin over one century ago with his conceptualization of the process of natural selection. The concept of evolution has evolved itself, including in the elaborations presented by Darwin himself (e.g., sexual selection). However, despite its theoretical branches, it remains uncontested as the primary driver of morphology, including of the brain, and also of behavior.

For Bjorklund and Ellis (2014), evolutionary theory represents a metatheory for psychological science. It helps unify psychology with the life sciences. Genes are dynamically expressed in proximal contexts, rather than having predetermined, "innate" effects. Not that the environment is random or has random effects; nor is the environment independent of the total developmental system. Nature by nurture interactions take place in a way that phenotypes' characteristics constitute "emergent" properties relative to the environment and the genes involved.

Developmental systems theories are either "soft" or "hard" in version. The former concerns development of the individual organism and is consistent with evolutionary inclusive fitness theory, but the latter is not because it concerns populations of replicating "organism-environment systems" in lineages rather than in individuals. The approach taken by Bjorklund and Ellis (2014) is consistent with the soft (inclusive fitness) approach to evolution and development.

In this regard, they emphasized developmental plasticity as an advantage in changing or variable environments. Plasticity might be fixed prenatally, though, as in the effects that take place due to exposure to elevated levels of stress hormones

G. Young, *Unifying Causality and Psychology*, DOI 10.1007/978-3-319-24094-7_12

in situations of maternal stress. For example, Rice et al. (2010) found that children's antisocial behavior between 4 and 10 years of age was associated with prenatal maternal stress exposure not only if the mothers were the biological mothers but also if they were the genetically unrelated carriers after in vitro fertilization.

Also, plasticity might be constrained by developing in the context of species-typical environments. Further, species-typical genomes act to bias individuals to seek out or create species-typical environments. That being said, phenotypic traits (e.g., cognitive mechanisms) are expressed probabilistically and in bidirectional interaction. Moreover, the traits often are not monomorphic in structure but are genetically polymorphic and varied according to encountered environment. Individual differences are adaptive, with differential cost-benefit trade-offs for different structures or strategies in different niches, and this varies developmentally.

Individuals express life history strategies, or chains of resource allocation decisions in context. Some decisions increase "embodied" capital, or qualities that increase Darwinian survival and reproduction potential but only later on (as with the advantages of juvenile play). Life history theory includes fast or slow reproductive strategies (which are earlier or delayed, respectively), depending on forecasts based on the quality of earlier environments (e.g., maltreatment) for what might be present in later environments (e.g., a delay in reproduction will not bring its typically found long-term advantages in adverse environments).

In differential susceptibility (Belsky & Pluess, 2009), slow and fast life history strategies are affected by biological sensitivity to context. More reactive children are especially susceptible to both highly stressful and highly nurturing environments (Boyce & Ellis, 2005).

For example, Ellis, Shirtcliff, Boyce, Deardorff, and Essex (2011) found that lower quality preschool-parent relations predicted faster/earlier pubertal measures, but only among children indexing biological sensitivity in a heightened sympathic nervous system or adrenocortical reactivity. Similarly, Manuck, Craig, Flory, Halder, and Ferrell (2011) found a relationship between distant familial interpersonal relations/high conflict levels and early pubertal measures, but only in the presence of certain polymorphisms of the estrogen receptor gene, *ESR1* (homozygous for minor alleles of two polymorphisms). Therefore, differential susceptibility qualifies life history strategies as conditional adaptations.

There are also ontogenetic and deferred adaptations. The former refer to the "potency" of natural selection in the early years and its role throughout the lifespan. The latter refer to prepared adaptations, ones that not only increase adaptation to a juvenile's current niche but also to the ones likely encountered later on as adults.

Shackelford and Liddle (2014) argued that Darwinian evolutionary psychology provides a unifying approach to psychology. It emphasizes the interaction between genes and environment, unlike how it has been portrayed. In this approach, a trait is considered to have evolved according to its ability to maximize inclusive fitness (an individual's own reproductive success with the addition of the effect of the individual's actions on the reproductive success of genetic relatives) in the context of the environment of evolutionary adaptiveness (niche) in which it evolved. In this model, the mind and behavior are massively modular, with each component shaped by evolutionary pressures in terms of their specific advantages for survival and reproduction.

Richerson et al. (2014) elaborated the cultural group selection model to explain human cooperation, which is unique in its extent and inclusion of mostly non-relative actors and recipients. They do not exclude a complementary role for traditional evolutionary processes (e.g., natural selection, kin selection, reciprocity, multi-level selection) in explain human cooperativity, in that they allow for gene-culture co-evolution. However, the traditional models cannot easily explain the institutionalized cooperation at the heart of human society. That is, group beneficial behavior is spread not only by evolutionary processes but also by cultural factors, including related mechanisms of selective imitation of successful groups and selective migration between groups.

Epigenesis

Epigenesis is now being understood as a potential co-mechanism to standard evolutionary forces in the process of evolution (Mendizabal, Keller, Zeng, & Yi, 2014). The literature shows that current levels of DNA methylation are predictable from its evolutionary signatures. DNA methylation patterns appear widely conserved over wide-ranging taxa. Human and closely related nonhuman primate species differ in genomic region methylation pattern related to development (aside from tissue specializations). Therefore, genomic sequence variants over evolution encode and appear to regulate distinctive epigenetic patterns (aside from the wide conservations found).

Mendizabal et al. (2014) noted that epigenesis leaves marks that affect one generation to the next. The research indicates that variation in DNA methylation appears heritable, in part, and subject to natural selection, being determined ultimately by genomic variants. Finally, epigenetic evolutionary divergence from one closely related species to the next is aimed at or targets specific functions. Therefore, epigenomic factors appear to express a constant dynamic interplay between short- and long-term evolutionary time scales.

In order to investigate whether epigenetic changes can accumulate over relative long periods of evolutionary time, Skinner et al. (2014) investigated epigenetic changes in five species of finches related to Darwin's finches. Over the species, epimutations (epigenetic alterations associated with differential DNA methylation regions) proved more common than copy number variant (CNV) mutations (genome-wide alterations in genetic mutations according to copy number variations). Also, the number of epimutations was related monotonically (increasingly) with degree of phylogenetic distance.

Skinner et al. (2014) noted that epigenetic changes might contribute to the molecular basis in the evolution over close phylogenetic distance. Epigenetic changes can increase the heritable phenotypic variation on which natural selection could act (Skinner, 2011). Indeed, epigenetics might play a "pervasive" role in evolution (Klironomos, Berg, & Collins, 2013), providing a major component of genome variation or stability within species found in evolutionary change. To conclude, Skinner et al. (2014) noted that genetic and epigenetic changes underlying phenotypic expression might regulate jointly not only genomic activity and consequent phenotypic expression but also evolution generally.

Systems

Badcock (2012) proposed evolutionary systems theory as a unified meta-theory of psychological science in terms of a hierarchical metamodel. In particular, the model integrates Neo-Darwinian concepts of evolution with concepts from nonlinear dynamic systems theory (NLDST, which he referred to as DST, dynamic systems theory). The model permits organizing into one framework: evolutionary psychology; evolutionary developmental biology; developmental psychobiology—and other aspects of psychology. These four areas deal with, respectively—functional bases for evolved characteristics in species; between group differences that are phylogenetically based; individual differences in ontogeny; and mechanisms explaining real-time phenomena.

By focusing on Darwinian and dynamical systems theory, Badcock integrated the process of general selection in evolution (which includes natural selection) and self-organization in systems. The four areas that are synthesized reflect Tinbergen's (1963) four questions about evolution and behavior—adaptive function, phylogeny, ontogeny, and mechanism. Badcock (2012) reviewed each of the four major areas integrated in his model, and I focus on the first three.

(a) Evolutionary psychology considers psychological mechanisms and behavior as evolutionary adaptations that have evolved according to Darwinian natural selection, or by increasing the probability of survival, reproduction, or both in ancestral contexts or environmental niches (which might not be those facing contemporary humans) (Buss, 1995, 2004).

The model of evolutionary psychology is conducive to considering psychological adaptations as modular, or distinct for the survival and reproductive advantages that they bring specifically (referred to as the massive modularity hypothesis). The model seeks (a) "functional," "why" properties of psychological mechanisms, in the sense of ultimate, adaptive properties and (b) "proximate" or "how" mechanisms, in terms of input and output processes (Scott-Phillips, Dickins, & West, 2011). [Note that other models might consider functional properties as proximate ones.]

A major criticism of evolutionary theory relates to its emphasis on modularity, given that different theories emphasize central general systems. Badcock (2012) attempted to resolve the differences in the approaches to modularity-general features of mind by integrating both into a hierarchical model. In his hierarchically mechanistic mind model, the lower-order level consists of domain-specific, exclusive, isolated, and encapsulated innate psychological mechanisms. They are constrained, automatic, and algorithmic in properties. In contrast, at higher levels of his model, Badcock places more plastic, flexible, executive, general, generative, and inclusive processes and properties, and among them is consciousness.

(b) Evolutionary developmental biology has modified the classic Darwinian perspective of natural selection functioning to promote better adaptiveness of phenotypes due, in part, to random mutation or novel variation in genotype (Ploeger, Van Der Maas, & Raijmakers, 2008; West-Eberhard, 2003). In addition to this genetic process, developing phenotypes might express advantageous traits or characteristics that promote fitness "before natural selection has a chance to operate" (Badcock, p. 12). Developmental processes contribute to evolution by promoting novel morphological, physiological, or behavioral traits through mechanisms that are constructive rather than selective yet become subject to natural selection. This approach values differences at the individual and group level, not only the species level.

Evo-devo is a biological field that involves inherited cellular but epigenetically modified systems (Jablonka & Lamb, 2007). As well, in the broader sense, epigenesis concerns socially-mediated learning and symbol-based transmission of information. Organisms can develop through cellular epigenesis as much as socially- and representationally-based accommodations. If environmental conditions persist over generations in a species, selection will enhance the survival and reproduction of the most adaptive phenotypes for the environment [including of their epigenetic stamps or marks, although the latter might not last more than a few generations]. Therefore, (a) lifetime and transgenerational plasticity and (b) species' evolvability through natural selection are complementary and continuously in interaction (Lamm & Jablonka, 2008). By emphasizing the importance of phenotypic ontogenesis in furnishing evolvable traits, the process becomes more plastic and broader in scope than a strict selection one (Ploeger, 2010; Ploeger et al., 2008), and specific mechanisms involved in natural selection become found in ongoing life changes and in transgenerational time.

Note that, compared to evo-devo, evolutionary developmental psychology has a similar integrative approach to evolution and development (Bjorklund & Pellegrini, 2002; Causey, Gardiner, & Bjorklund, 2008; Geary & Bjorklund, 2000). It shows how evolution by natural selection explains the ontogeny of species-typical traits, and how the environment can influence development to produce variable phenotypes from a genotype system in order to adapt to extant ongoing functional needs.

Workers are integrating NLDST into evolutionary models (Caporael, 2001; Hoelzer, Smith, & Pepper, 2006; Kauffman, 1993; Kenrick et al., 2002; Ploeger, 2010; Ploeger et al., 2008). According to Lewis (2000, 2005) and others (Smith & Thelen, 2003; Witherington, 2007), triggered microscopic perturbations and coordinations or recursive interactions in a system among the lower-order elements/components involved might lead to the spontaneous emergence of coherent, higher-order patterns through spontaneous self-organization. The different levels of the system themselves are coordinated in circular causality, so that they are subject to developing increased complexity, or global reorganizations, including in their nested hierarchies and functionality, especially at phase transition or bifurcation points at which there is increased turbulence or variability. Negative feedback loops in the system facilitate stability while positive ones facilitate change through sensitivity to environmental conditions. Attractor patterns appear in the state space trajectories through which system states gravitate over time.

It is worth exploring Kauffman's (1993) seminal ideas on how evolution and self-organizational principles can co-exist in an integrated model. In his model, self-organization influences population trajectories of possible genotypes and phenotypes through their state spaces, and populations express differential fitness in the spaces. As the systems self-organize, they tend to move to the "edge of chaos," or a zone that maximizes change. Indeed, natural selection favors systems that reside in this zone, because it promotes evolvability. Similarly, Hoelzer et al. (2006) referred to natural selection as any "emergent" process. Nevertheless, evolving systems self-organize in ways that preclude deleterious phase transitions, for example, by minimizing entropy (thermodynamic descent into disorder).

(c) Developmental psychobiology also is becoming increasingly integrative (Lickliter & Honeycutt, 2003). Developmentalists are attempting to integrate biological approaches into unified theories (e.g., Sameroff, 2010). The models are multidirectional, or multicausal, interactive, transactive, and dynamically plastic. Similar integrated models are being developed in personality theory (Sheldon, Cheng, & Hilpert, 2011).

Badcock (2012) integrated these diverse aspects of evolutionary study in and related to psychology into an evolutionary systems theory (see Table 12.1). Evolutionary psychology concerns species × environment fit or interaction. Evolutionary developmental biology focused on group × environment interaction. Developmental psychobiology concerns Gene × Environment (G × E) interaction. Psychology as a whole investigates individual × environment interaction. The timeframes for these disciplines are, respectively, evolutionary, generational, developmental, and real-time.

Badcock (2012) has performed a valuable service in showing how these diverse fields have complementary ways of understanding co-acting evolutionary and developmental processes and also showing how NLDST can help explain the general biological change manifold that together they entail. Further conceptualization is needed, however, to explain multiple, simultaneous interactions among species × group × genes × individual × environment as ontogeny and phylogeny reciprocally interact and unfold.

Other models that integrate evolutionary and dynamic approaches include Hoelzer et al.'s (2006). They argued that both natural selection and self-organization function according to thermodynamic energy principles. Moreover, thermodynamics better approaches explanations of ultimate cause while molecular ones better approach explanations of proximate cause (see Fig. 12.1).

Table 12.1 An evolutionary systems theory of psychology

Paradigm	Problem area and core hypotheses	Research question and temporal domain
Psychological	Individual × Environment Biopsychosocial developmental systems	Mechanism Real-time
Developmental psychobiology DEP (dynamical evolutionary psychology)	Gene × Environment (G × E)	Ontogeny Developmental time
Evolutionary psychology	Species × Environment Natural selection; inclusive fitness; genetic inheritance; massive modularity; multi-level selection	Phylogeny Evolutionary time
Evolutionary developmental biology EDP (evolutionary developmental psychology)	Group × Environment Co-evolution; epigenetic inheritance;	Ontogeny/Phylogeny Generational time

Adapted from Badcock (2012)

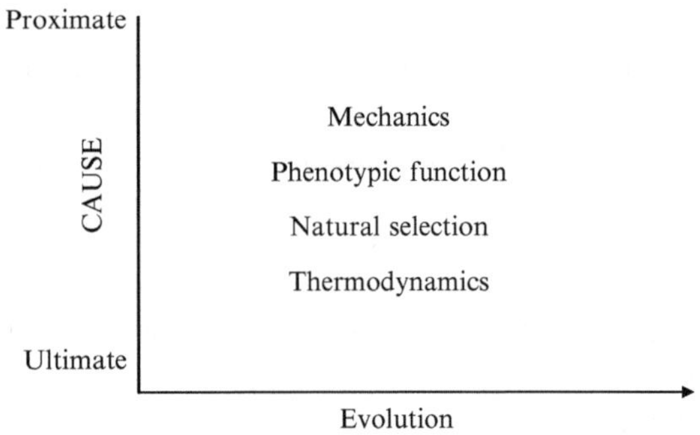

Fig. 12.1 Range spectrum of causal levels (ultimate to proximate). The levels of ultimate and proximate causation (ecology) are indicated as natural selection (NS) and phenotypic function, respectively. Purely mechanical explanations would typically be more proximate in nature than explanations based on phenotypic function, and thermodynamic explanations are more fundamental than those based on NS. *Note*. Relative to the original model presented in Hoelzer et al. (2006). I added an axis for evolution. Adapted from Hoelzer, Smith, and Pepper (2006)

Complexity

Darwin's (1859) stance on complexity in evolution considered that it evolved through adaptive intermediate forms, with each more complex step sculpted by natural selection (Zimmer, 2013). However, biologists are proposing natural selection free processes in evolution of complexity. For example, species change to complexity might reflect the differentiation of parts by "zero-force" evolution that ends up with adaptive advantages (McShea & Brandon, 2010). Or, mutations might arise without intermediate steps, but reach complexity, nevertheless, and without natural selection involved (Lukeš, Archibald, Keeling, Doolittle, & Gray, 2011). In this model, the complexity evolves according to "constructive neutral evolution," as if there were a "ratchet" building the complexity, which then becomes advantageous. Kauffman (1993) had also proposed that complexity can increase in evolution without evolving through natural selection.

Indeed, the implication of these models is that natural selection and complexification are reciprocal dynamic processes. They do not necessarily exclude the traditional base of evolution in randomly occurring adaptive genetic mutations. That being said, if mutations or other processes leading to complexity are less than neutral or deleterious, they could not survive.

Niche Construction

Laland, Sterelny, Odling-Smee, Hoppitt, and Uller (2011) presented an integrated view of proximate (e.g., immediate) and ultimate (e.g., natural selection) causal explanations in biology. According to them, causation is reciprocal between these poles, shaping and responding equally. Developmental processes are the central axis binding them. The phenotypic plasticity in development can "generate" or explain the original evolutionary change, although the developmental phenotype might not be equivalent to the trait ultimately expressed (West-Eberhard, 2003). A cycle of causation between proximate and ultimate causation obtains in cause and effect in biological adaptation. Developmental phenotypes could "bias" phenotypic variants, helping to promote their selection, yet express plasticity allowing for formation of "novelty," too (see Fig. 12.2).

In a combined evolutionary and developmental model, heritable phenotypic traits are not fixed or programmed by genes but are open to environmental effects, which themselves are altered by activities associated with the heritable traits (e.g., in evo-devo, niche construction theory). Feedback prompts reciprocal changes in gene expression, environment, and development. In this sense, development is more than a proximal or immediate mechanism because it induces "additional" causal trajectories deriving from the trait in one generation to the next.

In niche construction, environment-altering, developing phenotypic traits co-evolve with organism-modified factors in the environment, which reciprocally act back, modifying the process of causation by selection. Inheritance is multiply-determined, e.g., as in ecological inheritance, epigenesis, and cultural inheritance or evolution, as well as gene-culture co-evolution (see Fig. 12.3).

In culture-related evolution, a trait is inherited from the prior generation via cultural transmission across generations and from differential cultural selection processes. The behavior is both

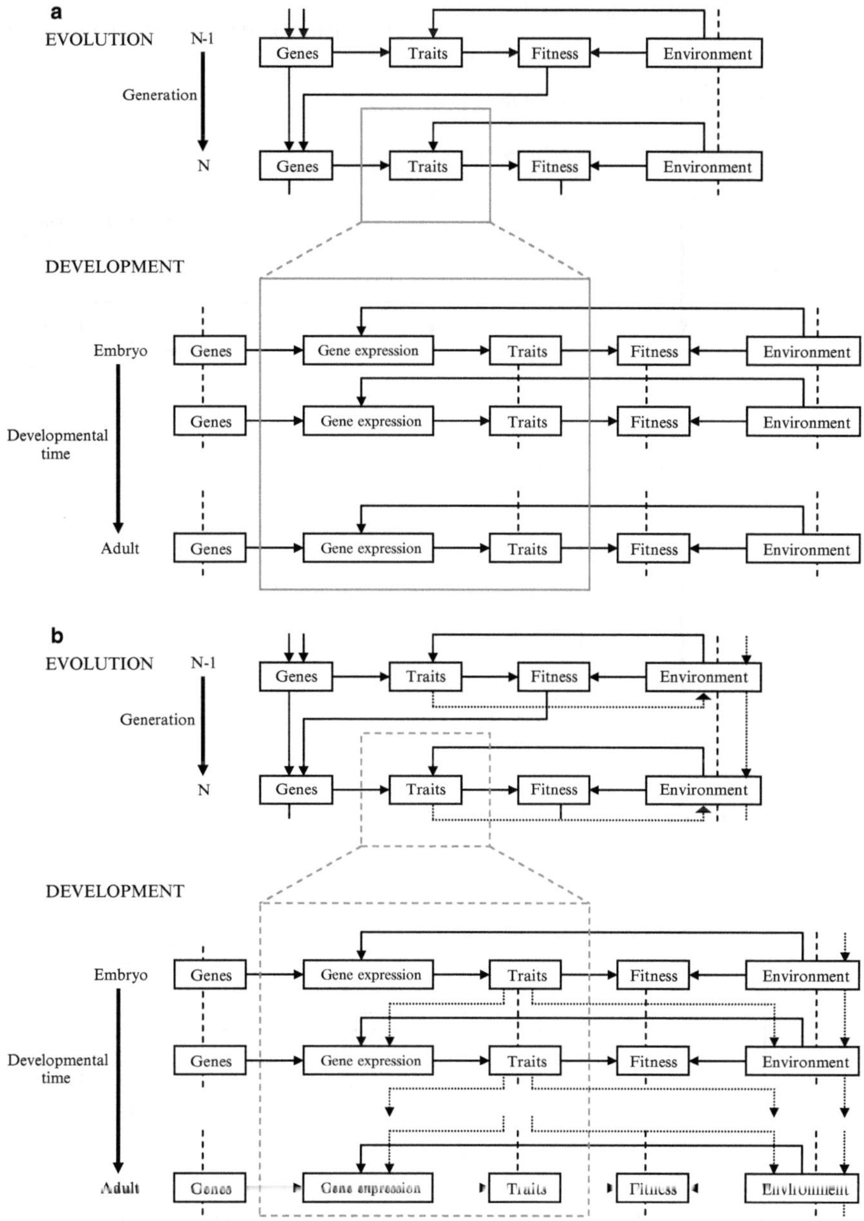

Fig. 12.2 Causal pathways involved in the evolution and development of traits. *Arrows* represent possible causal influences; *dashed lines* represent features that persist over time. (*A*) Classic perspective. In evolution, genes and environment interact to cause the trait, the trait and the environment cause fitness, whereas the genes are determined by the genes carried by the previous generation and the fitness of individuals in that generation. Relative to evolution, the process of development is broken down in a similar manner but on a shorter time scale. The present-day trait is independent of other components in the graph conditional on the present-day genes and environment, so an explanation of the proximate cause of the trait must only account for how genes and environment interact in trait development. The ultimate explanation must then account for how the present-day genes and environment themselves were caused, but, because causation is only in one direction from the environment to the trait, the causes of the environment can be treated as an external system, of little biological interest. The only way in which the trait in one generation causes the trait in the next is through fitness (natural selection), so development can be black-boxed. (*B*) A modern developmental perspective. *Dotted arrows* denote additional causal influences relative to (*A*) recognized by fields such as evo-devo and niche construction theory. During development, features of the trait cause changes in both gene expression and environment, which feed back to the developmental process, resulting in a different trait in the adult and modifications of both developmental and selective environments. Development cannot be considered purely proximately causal because it results in additional causal pathways from the trait in one generation to the trait in future generations. Adopted by permission of AAAS. From Laland, K. N., Sterelny, K., Odling-Smee, J., Hoppitt, W., & Uller, T. (2011). Cause and effect in biology revisited: Is Mayr's proximate-ultimate dichotomy still useful? *Science*, *334*, 1512–1516. Reprinted by permission from AAAS. [Figure 1, Page 1513]

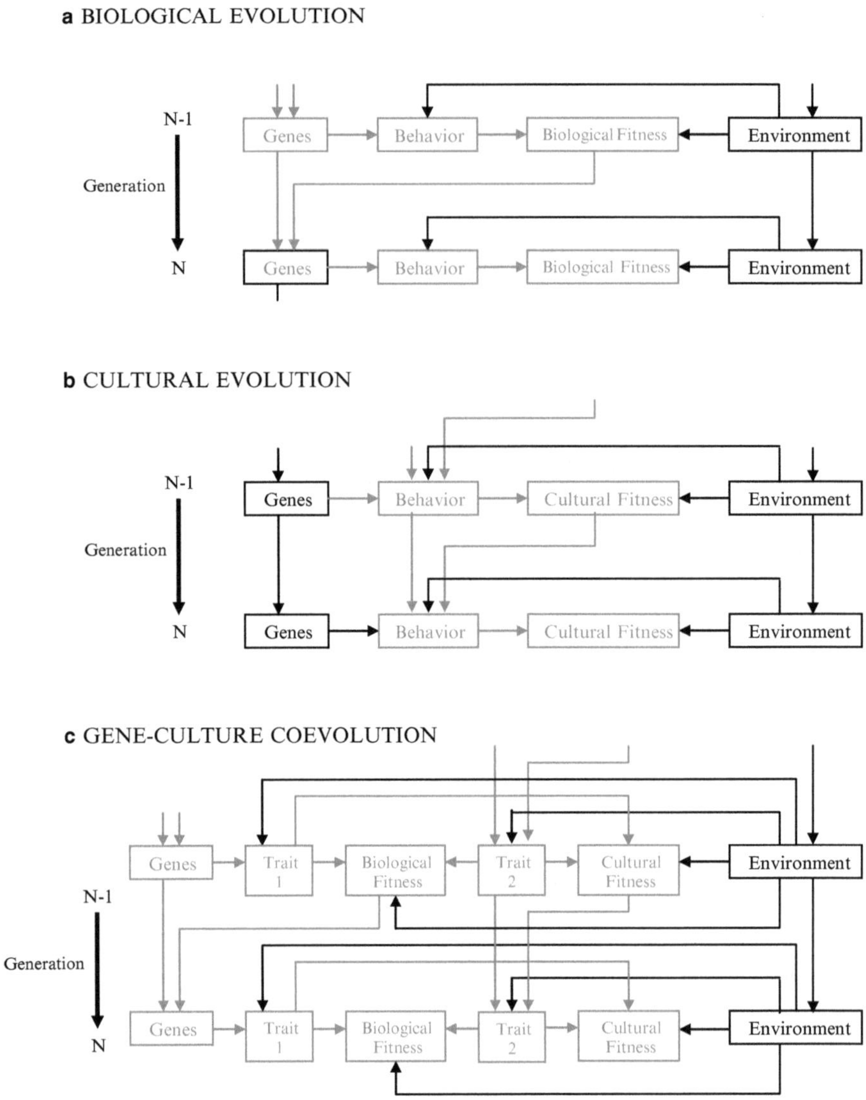

Fig. 12.3 Causal pathways involved in the evolution and development of traits. Alternative evolutionary processes. (*A*) Biological evolution: the ultimate explanation for the behavior lies in its effect on biological fitness. (*B*) Cultural evolution: the behavior can be inherited from the previous generation through intergenerational cultural transmission and differential cultural selection. Here, the ultimate explanation for behavior lies in its effect on cultural fitness. (*C*) Gene-culture co-evolution: genetically and culturally inherited traits co-evolve, with each trait affecting the fitness of the other. [For illustration, trait 1 might be lactose absorption and trait 2 dairy farming or milk use.] Inheritance pathways are shown in *gray*. For any given data set, causal modeling can be used to establish whether a particular causal influence is operating. Adopted by permission of AAAS. From Laland, K. N., Sterelny, K., Odling-Smee, J., Hoppitt, W., & Uller, T. (2011). Cause and effect in biology revisited: Is Mayr's proximate-ultimate dichotomy still useful? *Science*, *334*, 1512–1516. Reprinted by permission from AAAS. [Figure 2, Page 1515]

altered by culture and can alter it; however, genes are not affected intergenerationally. In contrast, in gene-culture co-evolution, traits that are genetically inherited co-evolve with those that are culturally inherited, with the traits in each stream affecting the fitness of the other. For example, recent human cultural agricultural, dairy, and settling practices have favored individuals with adult lactose tolerance alleles, which led rapidly to altering the human genome.

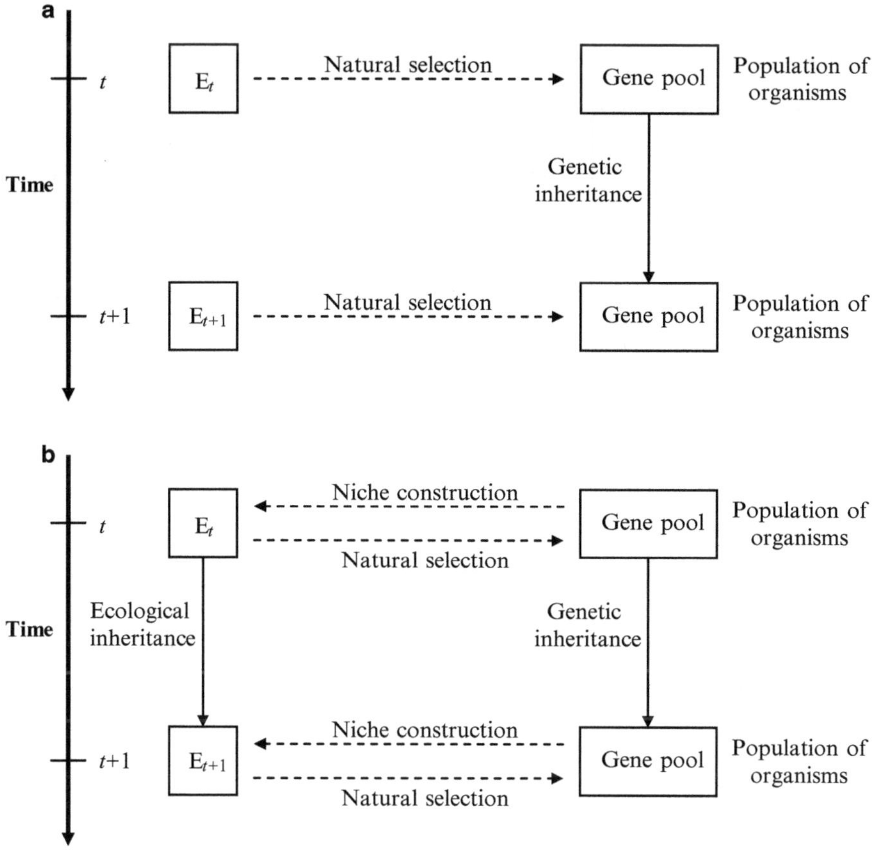

Fig. 12.4 Developmental niche construction. (*a*) A conventional view of the process of adaptation through natural selection. Causation is primarily linear: it starts with selection pressures stemming from the environment and ends with changes in the organism. Reciprocal causation is recognized only in some "special cases" in which the source of selection is biotic (e.g., sexual selection, predator prey co-evolution). (*b*) The niche construction perspective. Niche construction is explicitly recognized as an evolutionary process. The match between organism and environment results from interactions of natural selection pressures in environments and the niche-constructing activities of organisms. Inheritance is expanded to comprise both genetic and ecological components (i.e., legacies of selection pressures previously modified by niche construction). Causation is primarily reciprocal, with selective environments shaping organisms, and organisms shaping selective environments, either relative to themselves or other organisms. Adopted with permission of John Wiley & Sons. Flynn, E. G., Laland, K. N., Kendal, R. L., & Kendal, J. R. (2013). Developmental niche construction. *Developmental Science*, *16*, 296–313. Copyright © 2013 and John Wiley & Sons, Inc. Reproduced with permission of John Wiley & Sons, Inc. [Figure 2, Page 297]

Flynn, Laland, Kendal, and Kendal (2013) elaborated further on developmental niche construction. They defined the term in depth as the modification of both the living and non-living components of the environment through an organism's activities (metabolic, physiological, behavioral) and through its choices. The processes involved are evolutionary ones that modify phenotypes and selection, with environmental modification considered not an effect of but a cause of evolution.

In modifying their environmental niche, organisms co-direct their evolution (see Fig. 12.4). Niche construction and environmental selection interact to affect the gene pool through active shaping or matching of organism and context. Organism and environment engage in reciprocal causality over both developmental and evolutionary time through contingent feedback that might continue to accelerate phylogenetic change after differential selection no longer applies. Organisms, then, are active agents in their evolution.

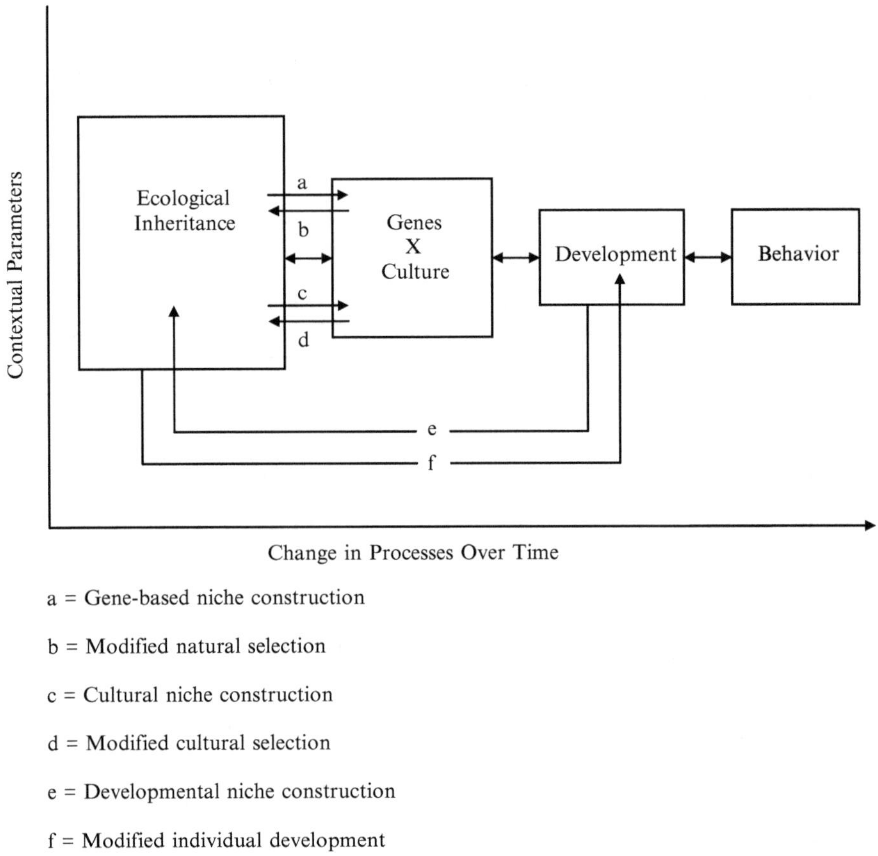

Fig. 12.5 Selective feedback at multiple levels in multiple niche-construction processes. Selective feedback influences niche construction at multiple levels. In this adaptation of the original figure, I placed genetic and cultural influences as interactive factors on development, which then through its own processes produces behavior. Also, in modifying the temporal sequence of process activity, the model avoids the inference that the sequence is from culture first to genes, and then back (including through development) via selective feedback. That being said, culture and environment can act on genes before their expression through inter-generational epigenetic effects. Adapted from Flynn, Laland, Kendal, & Kendal (2013)

Further, niche construction does not have to be a result of genetic variation, for developmental and cultural processes might produce the activity. Cultural, developmental, and gene-based processes engage in reciprocal interaction, with each process affecting ecological inheritance in different ways (see Fig. 12.5). Cultural niche construction modifies cultural selection, and vice versa, in feedback. The same applies to developmental niche construction and modified individual development, as well as to gene-based niche construction and modified natural selection, with each of these levels forming an integrated evolutionary, cultural, and developmental system. In reviewing the literature in support of their position, Flynn et al. (2013) referred to cognitive niche construction and scaffolded learning (Wheeler & Clark, 2008; Fragaszy, 2012; respectively), and also to natural pedagogy and situated learning (Gergely & Csibra, 2013; Sterelny, 2012, respectively). They concluded that a broader evolutionary synthesis appears in the offing.

Laland (2014) argued that classic evolutionary theory focuses on the effect of natural selection on gene frequencies. In his view, development and niche construction work in concert (reciprocally) with evolutionary processes in the causation of behavior and its change in evolution. Developing organisms are not just evolutionary outcomes; in that they are the "causes of evolution." Niche construction considers ecological context in behavior, so that evolution marches in coordination with externally expressed constructed processes (as well as internal ones, development). Developmental plasticity facilitates "subsequent genetic accommodation" and "rapid ecological adjustment."

Developmental processes are not solely the outcome of prior selection ("under-determined"). To conclude, evolution cannot be reduced to natural selection, given the role of development and niche construction.

Development

Frankenhuis, Panchanathan, and Barrett (2013) have presented the best arguments to date that I have encountered on two propositions—that evolution works at the developmental level and that it involves optimization. Typically, evolutionary mechanisms, such as natural selection, are described without much consideration of either the organism's developmental antecedents or the fitness necessity of earlier or developing behaviors (in terms of earlier survival contributing to later survival and reproduction). Moreover, typically, evolution is considered the result of random mutations that, in appropriate ecological niches, confer additive fitness benefits. In this view, there is no optimal adaptive design to which evolution necessarily progresses and that drives the evolutionary process. A third component to the propositions of the authors is that a dynamic systems approach can help integrate the developmental and evolutionary areas.

Frankenhuis et al. (2013) noted that development systems constitute "the central units of evolution." All phenotypes reflect the work of developmental processes. In this sense, evolutionary mechanisms modify phenotypic developmental systems, in particular. Developing phenotypes exist in an external environment separate from them, and natural selection works to maximize the match of developing phenotypic properties with properties of the environments in which they are embedded and related causally. [The concept of niche construction is considered similar to this view (Flynn et al., 2013)].

As for optimization theory in evolution, for Frankenhuis et al. (2013), natural selection works to select from among the options available the best ones that serve to maximize the match between the design properties of phenotypes and the adaptive problems that they confront and need to solve. I would summarize this approach by saying that optimization is not an add-on feature of evolution but the essential driver. Evolutionary fitness in an adaptive sense that promotes survival and reproduction involves fit with the environment in an optimization sense of the behaviors promoted (because their genetic underpinnings are such that natural selection can act on them so that they can confer their adaptive advantage).

Sameroff (2010) also has an inclusive model connecting the biological with systems, in a model referred to as the biopsychosocial ecological system. Li (2003) created an equivalent model, considered a co-constructive, dynamical, biocultural and developmental one (see Fig. 12.6). Li (2013) proposed a development model involving biocultural co-construction. She argued that individual agency is an active driver in development, including in niche construction. Moreover, proximate mechanisms underlie the adaptations involved at the psychological and neuromodulatory levels. Sheldon et al. (2011) and Sheldon (2011) presented a biopsychosocial system model related to personality that included nonbiological as well as biopsychosocial processes (see Table 12.2).

Goldhaber (2012) examined the nature–nurture debate from the perspective of showing the interaction between evolution and development and emphasizing their interdependence (e.g., Bjorklund, 2006). He noted that adaptations might serve immediate survival value in development (ontogenic adaptations) or only be useful in this regard later on (deferred adaptations). Goldhaber (2012) examined the full range of genetic and environment processes impacting development, including epigenetic programs, which are in constant transaction with environment. He supported the importance of developmental systems theory (Gottlieb, 2007). Partridge and Greenberg (2010) emphasized self-organization and developing systems, allowing

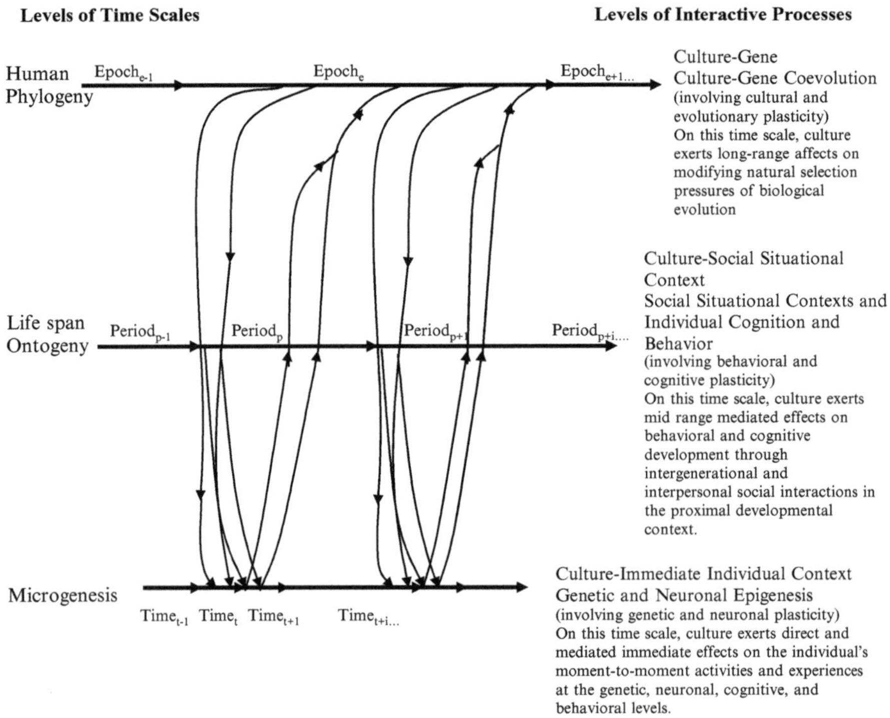

Fig. 12.6 Coconstructive biocultural influences implemented through interactive processes and developmental plasticity across levels. Schematic diagram of the cross-level dynamic biocultural coconstructive framework of development, showing that concerted biocultural influences are implemented through interconnected interactive processes and developmental plasticity across levels and time scales. *Downward arrows* denote culture-individual interaction, culture-situation interaction, and situation-individual interaction; *upward arrows* denote individual-situation interaction and situation-culture-gene interaction. The subscripts *e*, *p*, and *t* represent the current epoch, life period, and moment-to-moment microgenetic time, respectively. The notations of these subscripts $\pm 1 \ldots i$ indicate the sequences before (−) or after (+) the current *e*, *p*, or *t*, where *i* represents an arbitrary number between 1 and infinity (e.g., $p-1$ = the previous life period; $p+1$ = the next life period; $p+i = a$ given number of life periods after the current life period). Adopted with permission of American Psychological Association. Copyright © 2003 by the American Psychological Association. Reprinted with permission. The official citation that should be used in referencing this material is [Li, S.-C. (2003). Biocultural orchestration of developmental plasticity across levels: The interplay of biology and culture in shaping the mind and behavior across the life span. *Psychological Bulletin*, *129*, 171–194.]. The use of APA information does not imply endorsement by APA. [Figure 1, Page 174]

them to be adapted to context. Contemporary models of systems do not find a linear relationship between cause and effect but examine the whole system.

Partridge and Greenberg (2010) referred to "emergent phenomena" in development, and noted that they are real and observable. In addition, they exhibit "radical novelty" or global/macro characteristics that are not within other micro features of the system. Also, emergent phenomena exhibit coherence or a unity over time and are dynamic, being responsive to changes to the system over time.

In terms of early work in the field, Hogan and Bolhuis (1994) edited a book on the causal mechanisms of development. In the book, Hogan (1994) reviewed Tinbergen's four types of questions related to biology: causation, survival value, ontogeny, and evolution. He revised Aristotle's four causal questions (material, efficient, formal, and final) into the language of matter, causation, structure, and consequences, respectively. As for mechanism, Hogan stated that mechanism implies cause. In the different levels of analysis of behavior, one can find behavioral mechanisms, neural mechanisms, and so on, and also functions of

Table 12.2 The biopsychosocial continuum of the self in the social world

Continuum	Process	Component
SOCIAL	Cultural	Social network
	Organizational	
	Group	
PSYCHO	Interpersonal	Self (Traits, goals)
	Personality	
	Cognitive	
BIO	Neuronal	Constitution
	Biological	
	Nonbiological	

Adapted from Sheldon (2011)
Conceptualizing the self as the interface between the person and the social world on the biopsychosocial continuum

behavior. In this regard, Chisholm (1990) presented a life-history perspective on development. For example, early experience has "immediate" effects on development that needs to be analyzed at a Darwinian level for "construction" of alternate developmental pathways to "an adaptive endpoint." Developmental processes affect Darwinian "fitness" through natural selection, and they evolve.

Nature and Nurture (and Ourselves)

In the following, I examine views on two critical higher-order aspects of behavior in terms of the genetic and environmental contributions to their development and expression. The two areas are intelligence and a facet of personality referred to as neuroticism. The literature review in each case emphasizes general factors that are genetically influenced. In both cases, I argue that a proper, integrative model should not only include sociocultural, environmental factors, but also personal, psychological ones. For example, intelligence is influenced by self factors such as motivation and personality is influenced by a multitude of factors, as well.

Intelligence

Introduction Intelligence is a developmental product of genetic and environmental influences. Nevertheless, points of view might support one side of the equation more than the other, although this does not mean that the other side is being diminished.

Environment Although in this chapter we have focused on evolutionary effects in development, in no way have we discounted environmental influences on development. Study of the role of genetics interacting with environment in the development of intelligence continues (e.g., Deary, 2012; Nisbett et al., 2012), but an undeniable strong influence of environmental factors keeps emerging. The role of the environment on long-term development has been made clear in a recent meta-analysis on the Flynn effect, or the finding that over generations, intelligence quotient (IQ) scores have been increasing by several points per generation. For the Flynn effect, Trahan, Stuebing, Fletcher, and Hiscock (2014) showed that the effect is not diminishing and is robust (the observed rise in IQ scores over generations is continuing over time). The research discounted the genetic (heterosis: hybrid vigor) hypothesis.

Sternberg (2014) advocated for an important role of culture in the development of adaptive competence. For example, parents socialize children in view of their own folk conceptions, or implicit theories of intelligence, and not according to standardized test criteria. Also, intelligence is as much practical/social in competencies/knowledge as standard/academic or abstract. Therefore, teachers who understand and use approaches consistent with the former can produce better results in students even on tasks aimed at the latter.

Nisbett et al. (2012) noted that the importance of environmental factors is indicated for IQ by the 12- to 18-point increase in IQ when children in adoption move from working-class to middle-class homes. Also, although early intervention programs might not lead to persisting short-term effects, they do have positive long-term outcomes (e.g., in academic achievement). Further, sex differences in IQ are found to be partly due to environmental factors. And the black–white IQ gap continues to reduce. In addition, reciprocal causation is evident between intellectual functioning and brain morphology. That is, exercise of a particular skill might function to increase the size of a particular brain area (e.g., Haier, Karama, Leyba, & Jung, 2009). On the negative side, aspects of the environment (stress and social class) might act to affect adversely intelligence (e.g., Eccleston, 2011).

Sternberg (2012) noted that the heritability coefficient for intelligence (ratio of genetic to phenotypic variation in the population) varies between 0.4 and 0.8. Despite the evident influence of genetics in intelligence, he also noted that genetics "always" expresses itself "through environment." Moreover, heritability estimates vary according to factors that include socioeconomic status and the range in environment. Further, for racial-group differences, the groups are social "constructed" ones more than biological ones.

Protzko, Aronson, and Blair (2013) added that young children could have their intelligence level raised by environmental interventions that can include reading to children, aside from appropriate nutrition and education. Deary (2012) concluded that intelligence research should be integral in the study of the causes and consequences of human development. He placed it as the center of a wider study of behavior.

Research continues to support a general importance for environmental and not only genetic influences on cognitive and related behavior (e.g., Karmiloff-Smith, Casey, Massand, Tomalski, & Thomas, 2014) and a special G × E (Genetic × Environment) influence on behavior (Tucker-Drob & Briley, 2014). In Karmiloff-Smith et al. (2014), socioeconomic status and stress were considered as factors that affect neurocognitive development, but allelic differences were shown to be important, too. They concluded that phenotypes are emergent rather than predetermined. Tucker-Drob and Briley (2014) examined the continuity of environmental and genetic influences on cognition over the life-span. Their meta-analysis supported Gene × Environment interaction and gene-environment correlation as important in this regard. They found an increasing phenotypic stability in development, which was almost completely mediated by genetic factors. Yet they found the results were most consistent with a transactional model.

Genes Plomin and Deary (2015) described three laws of genetics of complex traits and five special findings related to genetics and intelligence. The former include: (a) all complex traits reveal significant genetic influence; (b) however, no such trait is 100 % inheritable, leaving room for environmental influence; and (c) heritability is the result of multiple genes with each having a small effect.

As for the five findings related to intelligence in these regards, Plomin and Deary (2015) first noted that (a) heritability is relative low in infancy (about 20 %) and increases dramatically into later adulthood (about 80 %). This might occur due to genetic amplification through gene-environment correlation. Also, (b) intelligence relates to diverse cognitive and learning abilities, with the genes involved affecting all of them. There is both pleiotropy (each gene affects multiple traits) and polygenicity (multiple genes affect each of them). Therefore, "generalist" genes are at play in intelligence and have genetic action over diverse cognitive and learning abilities upstream into brain structure and function in a network model. (c) Third, the phenotypic correlation between mating partners in intelligence (assortive mating) is higher than in other traits, which acts to increase additive genetic variance in the case of intelligence. (d) Next, the low- and high-end of the intelligence distribution is subject to different genetic effects, as well as different exposures to deleterious pre- and post-natal trauma. (e) Finally, intelligence, education, and social class might be related for genetic reasons, given that the latter two are correlated with intelligence (and its higher heritability).

The authors called for more research using genome-wide polygenic scores and GCTA (Genome-wide Complex Trait Analysis), without forgetting G, C, T, A (guanine, cytosine, thymine, adenine), and particular genes (DNA variants) that are formed in their base pair sequencing. They appear to be reminding that in the debate over genetics and environment in intelligence, although both apply, the genetic contribution should be given its proper place.

Counterintuitive results have been found in the study of general cognitive ability (*g*, intelligence).

In a longitudinal twin study conducted at ages 7, 9, and 12 years of age, Kovas et al. (2013) studied literacy and numeracy, as well as *g*, in primary school age children. The individual differences found were "significantly" and "substantially" more heritable not for *g* but for literacy/numeracy (ages 7, 9). The results suggest that universal education reduces individual differences in environmental disparity, so that obtained school-related differences in literacy/numeracy are due to genetic differences among the children. Kovas et al. (2013) reminded that the heritability of *g* increases as development proceeds because we increasingly select and create individually appropriate environments that are consistent with our genetic propensities (this is the process of gene-environment correlation, and I add this is the evocative type).

Similarly, Kan, Wicherts, Doland, and van der Maas (2013) analyzed data from 23 twin studies. They obtained results supportive of the counter-intuitive notion that greater heritability coefficients were found on "culture-loaded" compared to "culture-reduced" subtests. Comparable results were found for subtest variance shared with general intelligence—the proportion was a function of cultural load (for children, as well). They concluded that the most heritable abilities are the most culture-dependent ones. The reason relates to a greater contribution of active genotype-environment correlation to culture-loaded compared to culture-reduced cognitive abilities. That is, high achievers, by virtue of a heritable contribution, have actively sought out and had exposure to more stimulating or cognitively-demanding environments (culture), thereby better activating their potential cognitive skill/intelligence.

Bates, Lewis, and Weiss (2013) reported similar results. The higher the SES, the greater the genetic influences on intelligence in adults even though the effect of environmental influences was constant. They concluded that genes serve to "multiply" environmental supports related to intellectual growth. The process of augmenting social resources that act to raise the average of intellectual ability also functions to increase individual differences found in it.

Comment I conclude this section by noting that there is sufficient evidence to support both a genetic and environmental contribution to the development of intelligence and associated cognition. However, in keeping with the general theme of the book, an interactive model of intelligence should be biopsychosocial and consider personal factors as part of the psychological ones, such as those related to motivation, self, coping skills, and even having a belief in and a sense of free will.

Neuroticism

Introduction Most of the present section is about common factors in psychopathology, especially for the personality factor of neuroticism. For continuity in personality development into adulthood, Briley and Tucker-Drob (2014) demonstrated that the trend of increasing phenotypic stability appears to reflect the role of environmental mechanisms rather than genetic ones. Nevertheless, the common factor approach to psychopathology suggests a genetic contribution.

View 1 Barlow, Sauer-Zavala, Carl, Bullis, and Ellard (2014) proposed that the DSM-5 (Diagnostic and Statistical Manual, Fifth edition; American Psychiatric Association, 2013) splits disorders to the point that their differences are trivial. In this regard, they reviewed to the concept of neuroticism (Eysenck, 1947), which is the personality tendency to experience intense and frequent exaggerated negative emotional reactions in response to stressors, along with the evaluation that the external environment is dangerous and constitutes a threat relative to one's inadequate coping skills and lack of control.

The latent temperamental structure of emotional disorders generally supports a two-dimensional view of core dimensions atop a hierarchical structure, and neuroticism emerges at the primary one, with extraversion secondary. Neuroticism has also been referred to as negative affect/emotionality, behavioral inhibition, trait anxiety, and harm avoidance, as well as in terms of internalizing disorders.

Barlow, Ellard, Sauer-Zavala, Bullis, and Carl (2014) presented a triple vulnerability model on the origins of neurotic-type behavior, with general and specific psychological experiences and vulnerabilities channeling earlier biological (heritable) ones to particular expressions of one type of disorder or another. The psychological vulnerabilities involve unpredictability and uncontrollability in the environment leading to the learning of specific maladaptive behaviors, and leading to corresponding alterations in brain function and circuits. According to Barlow, Sauer-Zavala, et al. (2014), neuroticism is malleable, treatable, and even preventable.

Barlow, Sauer-Zavala, et al. (2014) opined that neuroticism is characterized by emotions to the point that it is worthwhile to consider the term of "emotional" disorder instead of neuroticism. In this regard, the authors reported the development of the multidimensional emotional disorder inventory. Its major dimensions include: anxiety/neuroticism; behavioral activation/positive affect; unipolar depression; mania; somatic anxiety; panic and related autonomic surges; intrusive cognitions; social evaluation; past trauma; behavioral/interoceptive avoidance; and cognitive/emotional avoidance.

Barlow, Sauer-Zavala, et al. (2014) noted that therapies that are transdiagnostic might be quite efficacious, given the commonalities in DSM-5 disorders and their common core superordinate dimensions, including neuroticism and extraversion. In this regard, they described their unified protocol for transdiagnostic treatment of emotional disorders (UP) (Barlow et al., 2011). The authors concluded that a broader view of diagnosis, assessment, and treatment might profit from considering the concepts of neuroticism and emotional disorders.

Benke et al. (2014) undertook a genome-wide association meta-analysis of preschool internalizing problems that supported the Barlow, Sauer-Zavala, et al. (2014) approach to mental disorder. They found genome-wide single nucleotide polymorphisms (SNPs) that explained up to 43 % of the total variance in the target behavior, although collectively in a polygenic model. Furthermore, genetic variants influencing preschool internalizing problems overlapped with genetic variants in common child and adult psychiatric disorders (e.g., anxiety, depression, schizophrenia).

In a similar vein, in a meta-analysis of behavior genetic studies, Vukasović and Bratko (2015) showed that the best heritability estimate of personality traits, or genetic contributions to individual differences in personality, is in the order of 40 %. The results were found in studies using different behavior genetic study designs and different personality models. The number of studies involved included 45 primary studies involving more than 100,000 participants, from diverse backgrounds, and varying ages. As with the heritability estimate for intelligence reviewed previously, there is a notable estimate for personality but, nevertheless, the results imply a genetic and environmental contribution to development of the psychological attribute.

View 2 Caspi et al. (2014) have extended the Barlow, Sauer-Zavala, et al. (2014) argument one step further by advocating for a *p* factor, or a general psychopathology factor, in the structure of mental disorders. In their longitudinal study over 20 years (years 18–38), they examined 11 common adult mental disorder types in a representative birth cohort (the Dunedin Multidisciplinary Health and Development Study). They took into account dimensionality, persistence, comorbidity, and sequence. The results showed three core psychopathological dimensions—internalizing, externalizing, and thought-related one—but the best explanation of psychiatric disorder involved a more generalized dimension of General Psychopathology (*p*, akin to *g* in intelligence). The *p* dimension functions to coalesce into one underlying dimension for individual's propensities to develop psychopathology of any nature. It appears associated with early dynamic processes that unfold in the environment, including its adversities, rather than lying in a single unitary cause.

According to Caspi et al. (2014), the disorders in adulthood do not evolve linearly from early disorders because early brief episodes do not necessarily become persistent (see Fig. 12.7). A developmental progression takes place in

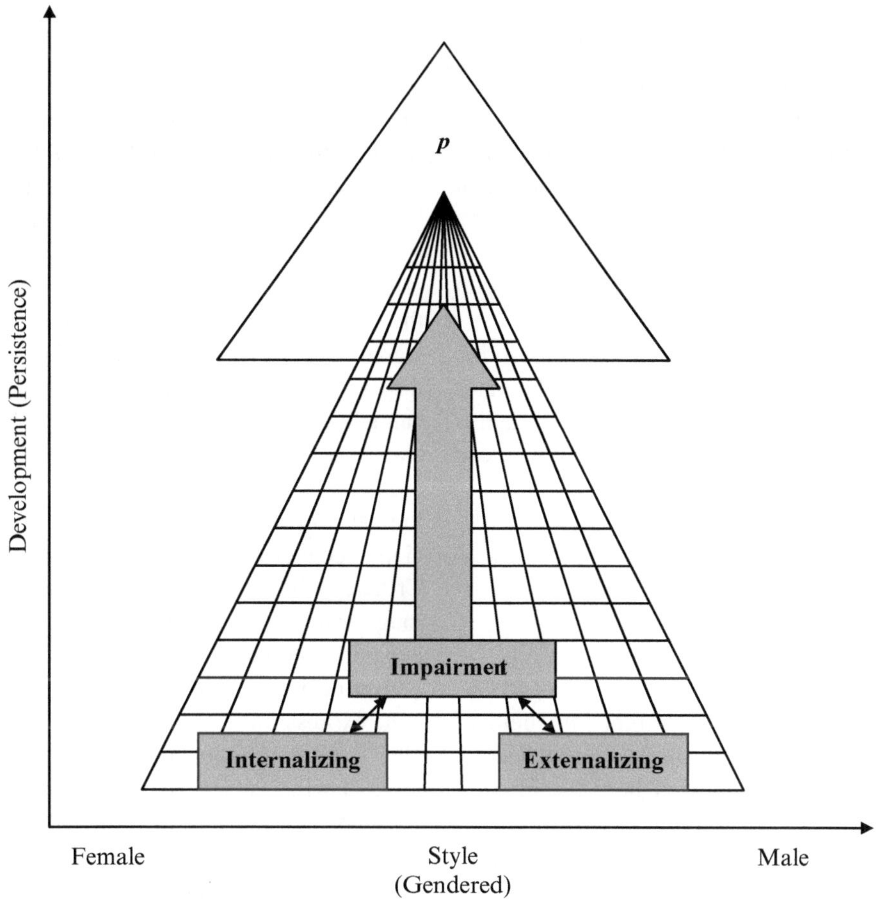

Fig. 12.7 The *p* factor (General Psychopathology). Individuals might briefly manifest an episode of a gendered individual disorder. A subset of these individuals might develop persistent increasingly impairing externalizing and internalizing disorders. Only some individual develop extreme elevation of *p*. Adopted with permission of SAGE publications. Caspi, A., Houts, R. M., Belsky, D. W., Goldman-Mellor, S. J., Harrington, H., Israel, S., Meier, M. H., Ramrakha, S., Shalev, I., Poulton, R., & Moffitt, T. E. (2014). The p factor: One general psychopathology factor in the structure of psychiatric disorders? *Clinical Psychological Science*, *2*, 119–137, Copyright 2014, reprinted with permission of SAGE Publications. [Figure 3, Page 133]

which disorder and impairment become persistent and broad, and often these include thought-related disorder. The genes involved operate pleiotropically to augment risk for "any and all" mental disorders. Caspi et al. (2014) concluded that their *p* factor model implies that it is fruitless to seek causes, biomarkers, consequences, and treatments specific to individual disorders.

In a study with adolescents, Laceulle, Vollebergh, and Ormel (2015) replicated the results found by Caspi et al. (2014) that psychopathology reflects a latent general overall severity *p* factor (as well as smaller internalizing and externalizing factors). The authors concluded that the results speak to the structure of psychopathology, but should not be reified, in that the general factor found could reflect a number of causes, as yet undetermined.

Stochl et al. (2015) also supported the work of Caspi et al. (2014). They found that a bi-factor model with a single, unitary common mental distress factor fit the constellation of symptoms in participants expressing depression, anxiety, and psychotic phenomena.

Comment In later chapters in the book on the DSM-5, my approach to psychopathology is quite similar to that of Barlow, Caspi, and colleagues. The DSM-5 contains too many disorders and it can be simplified, and the disorders have shorter lists of core symptoms than the longer ones that are found at present. Moreover, in my therapeutic work, I adopt a transdiagnostic, componential approach (Young, 2014) that is consistent with the approach of Barlow and colleagues.

In the next section of the chapter, I describe the area of social genomics, which illustrates quite well genes and environment interact, in this case in health, in particular. The environment can indeed get under the skin.

Social Genomics

Model

Cole (2014) described the burgeoning field of human social genomics. His conceptualization and literature review showed how the circumstances of everyday life are capable of influencing gene expression. Humans create complex social systems that have been referred to as "hypersocial," or "meta-organisms." In addition, the social influence on genes indicates the creation of "metagenomes." For Cole, extraorganismic factors in the environment and intraorganismic physiological function stand in reciprocal interrelation in the elucidation of behavior and health.

Cole (2014) continued that the social-environmental conditions that influence genetics in social genomics include not only social isolation but also social threat, low/unstable social status, low SES, and urbanity. When social environments influence gene expression, it takes place through physiochemical processes (e.g., toxins) and psychological ones (e.g., experience of threat/uncertainty). The latter trigger neural and endocrine responses (e.g., activation of the sympathetic nervous system (SNS)). Either way, (physical, psychological) biochemical mediators act to promote receptor system activity that leads to intracellular signal transduction pathways. In turn, these either activate or inhibit relevant transcription factors.

The circuitry described of mapping specific biochemical signals to specific gene expression responses constitutes an evolved, adaptive program in ancestral humans. The question remains whether the mapping that has evolved continues to be adaptive in present social circumstances.

Cole (2011) referred to the genome as "fluid," given the evidence for socioenvironmental effects on gene expression. The social world has the capacity to regulate gene expression. Social signals can influence cell surround microenvironments (e.g., hormones, neurotransmitters), which can end up influencing behavior and health. The classic distinction between environment and organism might not be a clear division in the biological world. Early adversity might be especially deleterious in programming it effects. Critical periods are found and lay the basis for long-term molecular imprints on physiology, behavior, and health.

But even transient events later on could alter gene expression (e.g., loss of one night sleep can alter gene expression profiles related to immunity; Irwin, Wang, Campomayor, Collado-Hidalgo, & Cole, 2006). The ability of even relatively brief socioenvironmental "shocks" to alter gene expression relates to the recursive structure of gene regulation networks. They involve interdigitated feedback mechanisms that might produce nonlinear changes in equilibrium dynamics (Kauffman, 1993; Kim, Shay, O'Shea, & Regev, 2009).

Slavich and Cole (2013) elaborated further on human social genomics, and concluded that we live in a human "metagenome" in which gene expression is determined, in part, by the transcriptomes of other people, generating a system with complex emergent properties (Kauffman, 1993). We are not a fixed molecular (genetic) self but one from among potential biological selves expressed via social-environmental regulation of our genes. The social-environmental factors involved are subjective (e.g., perceived loneliness) more than objective (they are unrelated to social activity/contact), and they influence broad sets of genes (profiles, programs). Therefore, in G×E research, it is not just that the external social world gets "under our skin" it also gets "onto our genome."

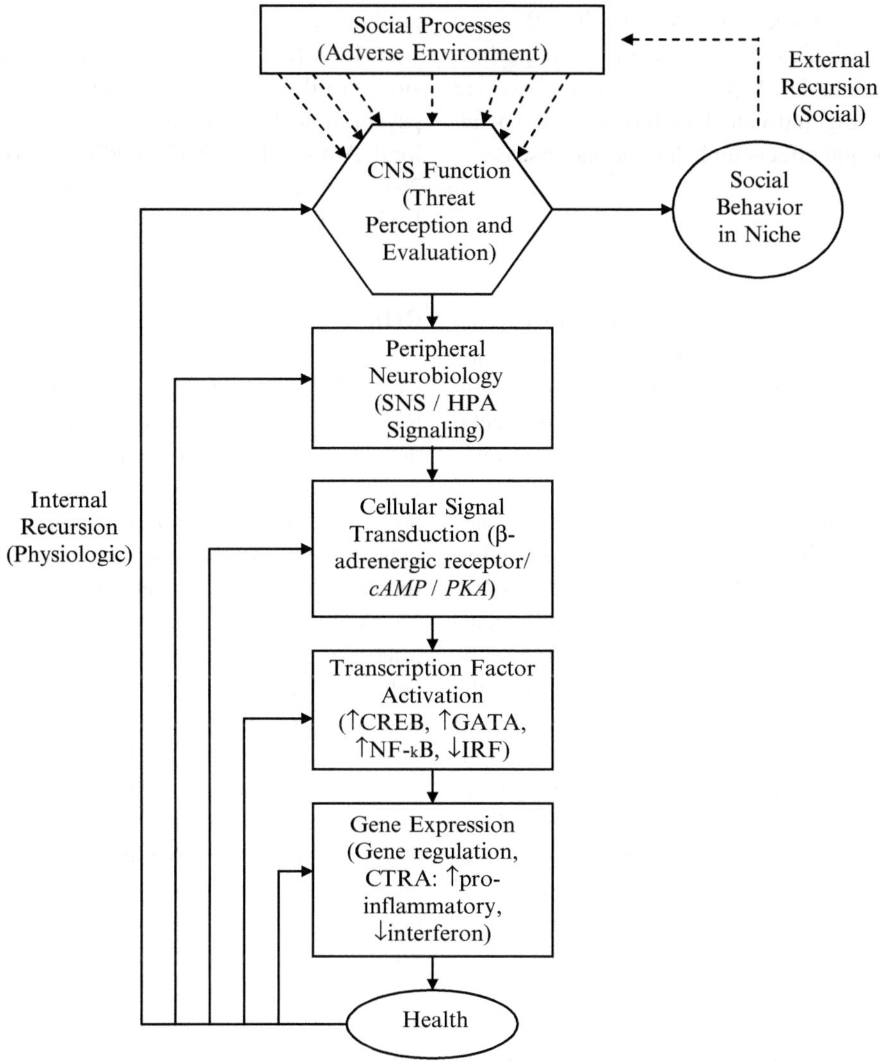

Fig. 12.8 Human social signal transduction and human recursive network genomics. Social experiences become physiologically embedded, first, by *internal physiologic recursion* (the genes targeted by social signal transduction pathways encode the molecules that mediate social signal transduction), which sensitizes signal transduction pathways to the external social environment. Second, *external social recursion* can biologically embed social experience (social signal transduction can modulate genes involved in the regulation of social behavior). The social signal transduction pathway permits mapping of adverse social conditions onto the conserved transcriptional response to adversity (CTRA) in leukocytes. Perceptions of social threat activate the)SNS, causing release of norepinephrine (NE), activation of β-adrenergic receptors, and stimulation/repression of specific transcription factors in response to the cyclic 3′–5′ adenosine monophosphate/protein kinase A (cAMP/PKA) signaling pathway. β-adrenergic-responsive transcription factors induce the CTRA gene expression program by stimulating transcription of genes encoding proinflammatory cytokines and suppressing transcription of genes encoding Type I interferons and IgG antibodies. Adapted from Cole (2014), and Slavich & Cole (2013)

The social environment can affect our genes because proteins are replenished daily (1–2 % are replaced each day), and ongoing physiological processes are stress-responsive. Extracellular signals from the endocrine system (e.g., cortisol) and the SNS (e.g., norepinephrine) impact cell surface receptors. Intracellular transcription factors initiative a metabolic cascade leading to binding of gene promoters by transcription factors, which might dysregulate protein T and, ultimately, behavior and even health. Because there are individual differences in binding affinities related to DNA polymorphisms, there are corresponding individual differences in social/environmental effects on behavior and disease.

CTRA

Slavich and Cole (2013) proceeded to explain how social signals are transduced in hormone and neurotransmitter central nervous system dynamics (see Fig. 12.8). Social-environmental stressors act on the SNS and hypothalamic-pituitary-adrenal (HPA) axis via neurocognitive appraisals, and lead to effects on the genes involved in proinflammatory and)antiviral activity (in *ILIB*, *IL6*, *IL8*, *TNF*; and *IFNA*, *IFNB*, respectively). The effects involved include recursive processes both transcriptionally and socially, which act to affect the sensitivity of and the future activity in the pathways. Other people respond differently to the social changes, amplifying the effects. Given that the neurocognitive appraisals involved are subjective, individual difference factors, such as in personality (e.g., neuroticism), can contribute to the recursions and consequent behavior and health outcomes.

Cole (2014) proceeded to describe that part of the differential expression of gene transcripts related to social adversity includes a common evolutionarily conceived transcriptional response to adversity (CTRA). The CTRA has been found to social conditions involving: low SES (Cole et al., 2010); chronic stress (Miller et al., 2014); bereavement (O'Connor, Schultze-Florey, Irwin, Arevalo, & Cole, 2014); PTSD (posttraumatic stress disorder; O'Donovan et al., 2011); and cancer diagnosis (Cohen et al., 2012). CTRA involves increased expression of proinflammatory genes and also decreased expression of genes in Type I interferon (innate) antiviral responses and IgG antibody synthesis (Cole, 2010)].

Three pathways have been found to up-regulate CTRA gene expression in immune cells due to prolonged social/threat adversity—SNS/β--adrenergic)regulation of transcriptional programs in existing monocytes; de novo monocyte production; and neoinnervation of lymphoid tissues. Cole (2014) noted that CTRA gene expression profiles can be suppressed by physical/psychological interventions (cognitive behavioral, Antoni et al., 2012; meditation, Black et al., 2012; yoga, Bower et al., 2014; and Tai Chi, Irwin et al., 2014).

RNA

Cole (2011, 2014) described a model of how RNA provides a molecular medium of recursive development and can be influenced by social conditions. As the environment influences the body and subsequent behavior and also RNA (or gene expression), the next influence acts on a different body and RNA set (see Fig. 12.9). The micro-level of socioenvironmental impacts has long-term macro-level effects. Regulation of behavior derives not only from genetic characteristics but also from past and current environment, including at the social level.

A self-perpetuating cycle persists well after the originating stimulus has passed. Given the effect on body and RNA in this self-modifying recursive dynamic, gene expression is considered not only a cause but also a consequence of behavior. The model presented is an "environmentally conscious" one of genetics and, moreover, it is a social one, which includes a personal perceptual and meaning component to what is considered social. The "transcriptional memory" that is lain down by adversity suggests that the history of environmental shocks to the person should be detectable or backcasted with current gene expression profiles. Also, molecular forecasting might be possible, e.g., future response to a therapy. Cole (2011) concluded that the social world blows through our bodies like a breeze.

Comment

Cole (2014) discounted epigenesis as a major factor mediating the relationship between social influences and gene expression. Epigenesis has been found as an effect of specific environmental

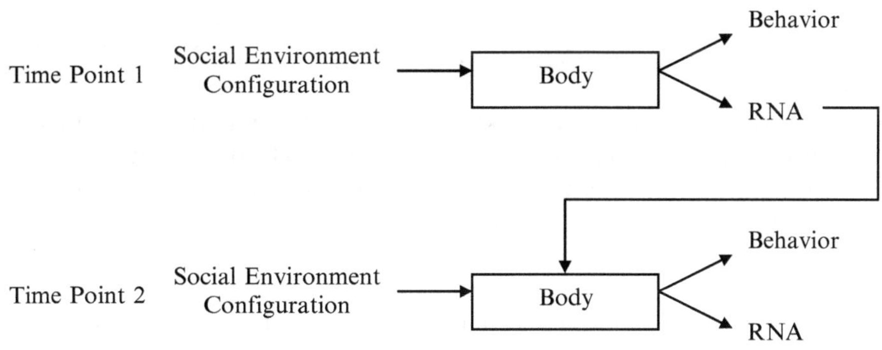

Fig. 12.9 RNA as a molecular medium of recursive development. Social conditions at point one in time (environment) are transduced into changes in behavior and gene expression (RNA) through central nervous system/perceptual processes that trigger neural/endocrine responses (body). The RNA transcriptional dynamics unleashed can alter the molecular characteristics of cells involved in environmental perception/response, yielding a functionally-altered body. This may result in different behavioral and transcriptional responses at time point two, and affect current and future behavior and health. Therefore, RNA appears to serve as the medium for recursive developmental changes that integrate genetic characteristics and historical-environmental regulators. Adapted from Cole (2011), based on Cole (2009)

conditions, but epigenetic profiles are correlated only weakly with differences in immune-cell genetic expression. Cole concluded about epigenesis that even transient environmental conditions can act to produce persistent biological, psychological, and social consequences (e.g., in PTSD) without including any persistent DNA modification, such as through epigenetic stamps.

Evidence

Cole et al. (2007) and Cole, Hawkley, Arevalo, and Cacioppo (2011) showed that people experiencing chronic self-isolation evidenced genome-wide transcriptional profiling of leukocytes, with more than 200 genes that demonstrated greater than 50 % difference in average levels of expression compared to socially-integrated individuals. For the socially isolated individuals, genes that were up-regulated included a set of inflammation-related transcripts (e.g., *ILIB*, *IL8*), and down-regulated ones included a set in the transcription of Type I interferon (innate) antiviral responses (e.g., *ISG*, *IFI*, *MX*) and of antibody production (e.g., *IGL*, *IGH*, *IGJ*, *IGK*).

As described in Slavich and Cole (2013), Cole et al. (2007) found a large change in the expression of two gene profiles within circulating immune cells in chronically socially-isolated individuals relative to integrated ones. They showed both an enhanced expression of proinflammatory immune response genes and down regulation of antiviral immune response genes. Similar effects were found for targeted social rejection (Murphy, Slavich, Rohleder, & Miller, 2013) and PTSD (O'Donovan et al., 2011).

The work of Cole and colleagues on the effect of social loneliness on health is supported by research by Jaremka et al. (2013). They looked at two samples of lonelier adults, one healthy and one post-treatment breast-cancer survivors exposed to acute stress. Compared to less lonely controls, the lonely groups exhibited elevated proinflammatory cytokines (e.g., interleukin-6 (IL6)). The author suggested that lonelier populations express a proinflammatory phenotype.

Health

Genes related to behavior do not only have psychiatric effects but also health ones. Murphy et al. (2013) found that targeted social rejection in adolescents influenced the signaling pathways in inflammation regulation. Over a 2.5-year period, adolescents at risk for major depression who reported targeted rejection had more simultaneous elevations in pro-inflammatory immune response gene activity, nuclear factor-κB (NF-κB), and an inhibitor (I-κB) in leukocyte messenger RNA (mRNA), as well as a lower ratio of NF-κB/I-κB. The same data were not found for low-grade inflammation signals. The results demonstrated an interaction effect, with the findings more evident in participants high in the adolescents' own perceived social standing in their peer group (social status), making them more at risk for long-term illness if targeted rejection should continue, given the upregulation of inflammation gene expression. The authors concluded that the genome is "quite" fluid and quite susceptible to social influence, e.g., adverse social experiences. [Note in the present case, the adolescents of higher perceived social status could have experienced targeted social rejection as more socially adverse because of its signal as a threat to their higher self-perceived social standing.]

Evidence is accumulating in other areas that severe stress can have genetic and psychological consequences and that controlling it by mindfulness promotes healthier states. Epel et al. (2013) examined healthy 50- to 65-year-olds for mind wandering, acceptance, nonattachment, and awareness, as well as depressive symptoms, perceived stress, rumination, and life satisfaction. They measured telomere length as a proxy measure of biological aging and correlate of severe stress. Telomeres protect chromosome termini as DNA-based caps, and their shortness is related to stress, disease,)and mortality. The study examined leukocyte telomere length (LTL) and also, for a portion of the participants, telomere length (TL) in specific types of immune cells, lymphocytes and granulocytes. The sample consisted of highly-educated women with relatively low stress experience.

Relative to measurement of tendency to be present in the moment, measurement of high mind wandering (e.g., feel totally focused vs. not wanting to be there) was associated with shorter telomeres in all cell types, even after controlling for stress level and other confounds. The results suggested that, specifically, less mind wandering, more attentional focus and task-relevant thought and, generally, better executive function and even meditative interventions can promote healthier cell division, control of biological aging, and psychological well-being.

Being present in the moment could lead to a healthier psychology by detracting from trying to avoid unhappy thoughts and adding to the control of chronic arousal. Researchers are finding that the phenomenon of presence and mindful acceptance of negative affect helps reduce clinical symptoms and distress (Bieling et al., 2012). Higher telomerase activity is associated with meditation (Jacobs et al., 2011; Lavretsky et al., 2013). Even social connection has been related to protecting TL, although negative experiential impacts are seen as accumulating even prenatally (Puterman & Epel, 2012).

In this regard, Puterman and Epel (2012) referred to telomere length as capturing the interplay between genetics, life experience, and psychosocial and behavioral factors. They referred to it as a potential marker of multisystem resiliency, depending on the stress and experience involved (or a multisystem vulnerability with increased cellular allostatic load). It is worthwhile noting that healthy lifestyle, in general, can mitigate vulnerability in the telomere-related aging system (Puterman et al., 2010).

Chapter Conclusions

To conclude, I examine in what direction an integrated understanding of the multiple influences of behavior might lead in terms of the new understanding emerging of the evolutionary process. In this regard, complexity might have a bootstrapping effect on evolution and accelerate its natural (selection) speed. More than being a complement to it, complexity might predispose evolution to take place faster. Moreover, complexity might act in evolution through particular developmental phases. For example, according to nonlinear dynamical systems theory and complexity theory (Kauffman, 1993), systems live on the edge of order and disorder because this is the region in their state space that is optimal for change. Indeed, systems that evolve to inhabit this region might be evolutionarily advantaged, even at the population level, through the complexity and diversity that it can foster, just as is the case at the developmental level for which gravitating to the cusp of change is a frequent concept that is encountered.

The theorizing on the relationship between natural selection and complexity has implications for understanding causality. On the one hand, it suggests that, at the biological level, natural selection has a range of forces in its selective power. All things considered, at one extreme, it could be either majorly or uniquely involved in evolution. However, at the other extreme, natural selection in evolution, as well as related evolutionary forces, such as kin selection and reciprocity, might be part of broader evolutionary systems with reciprocal influences from independent processes, such as in complexification, epigenesis, and so on.

Second, complexification would appear to be inherent in the living process at the evolutionary level, just as it is evident at the developmental level. Evolutionarily, there might not be a teleological, grand design toward that end, but it could be inherent in any system that exists because it serves to promote change, which is conducive to adaptation.

Third, causality in systems might become inherently more complex as systems change, including in evolutionary and developmental systems, because of their inherent self-organization toward increasing complexity. The multiplicity of parts, levels, and influences could become increasingly dynamically sophisticated to the point that causality is embedded in a labyrinth of both evident and hidden influences, thus hard to discern.

At the same time, just as systems could manifest hierarchization over macro- and micro-levels, with reduced degrees of freedom in the system by "enslaving" lower-order levels to higher-order ones (Haken, 1983), so could causal influences reflect a hierarchical organizational complexity in order to give more freedom of action. That is, the paradox in losing degrees of freedom through superordinate, top-down enslavement of lower-order, bottom influences is that the system is chunked, which allows more freedom in flexibility of action.

This might be true of free will, for example, or other self factors, which should reside at the apex of causal influences on behavior, at least to some degree, and enslave lower-order influences, such as biological and environmental ones. In this view, genes and environment are not the major influences on behavioral causality, but we are, (ourselves and our selves). We are sources that can promote not only our development as a third force, but even human evolution, for example, by participating in the cultural advances that are at play in gene-cultural co-evolution.

It would seem impossible to separate complexity from either development or evolution, especially because its characteristic of being primed for change is adaptive to both processes. Development and evolution might be hierarchically subsumed to system dynamics, including in complexity. That is, both development and evolution might implicitly involve complexification as a driver of change to some degree, and are processes that have taken advantage of the drive to complexification that are inherent in them. Moreover, complexity itself could hierarchically organize and privilege some factors over others as enslavement ones that are superordinate in causality. Overall, this process might best be termed "causal complexification" (or causal complexity).

To repeat, on the one hand, as systems evolve, they might develop advanced causal complexification such that previously important causal factors lose their causal force or power. On the other hand, relative to the power of prior lower levels, higher-order and emergent levels might take on even more causal importance as the systems complexify, integrating disparate causal mechanisms into superordinate wholes having top-down integrative influences previously not present. That being said, as is implicit in the concept itself of systems, in the proposed causal complexification process, lower-order levels never are subsumed fully as bottom-up influences by higher-order top-down ones. Causality always remains distributed throughout a system despite shifting causal emphasis over time. This reflects the circular causality inherent in the relation between top-down and bottom-up influences of higher-order and lower-order system levels.

The concept of inherent complexification in the evolution of systems, including that of biological evolution, and that causality might be similarly complexified, has implications for the question of determinism versus indeterminism. Prigogine and Stengers (1997) had maintained that demonstration of irreversibility and instability in systems runs counter to determinism. Systems exist "far-from-equilibrium" and, due to "sensitivity to initial conditions," can change dramatically, such as with "emergence," but in a process that is probabilistic or statistical rather than deterministic. Therefore, system properties, such as self-organization, emergence, and complexification, suggest that not only does causality complexify but also, as it does, the systems become increasingly indeterministic. Just as natural selection might express a range in its force or power, from absolute to degrees of relativization with respect to other processes, such as complexity, so might determinism express a range of force or power, from absolute determinism to degrees of relativization with respect to indeterminate processes, including emergence. Therefore, the process that I am describing about system evolution suggests that the term for it that fits best is "deterministic/indeterministic complexification" (or deterministic complexity, for short).

That is, on the one hand, as systems evolve, they might express fully deterministic causal mechanisms. However, on the other hand, as they evolve, they might develop aspects that are consistent with indeterminism, at least in part, as might happen with emergence. Moreover, the deterministic complexity might grow increasingly within the system such that it becomes predominantly indeterministic, and also comes to manifest higher-order enslavement of any deterministic, lower-order levels to flexible, indeterministic higher-order ones. Thus, as systems evolve, previously powerful deterministic levels might lose their deterministic attributes to ascendant, in-process, ones that are higher-order, have indeterministic attributes, and co-opt lower-order deterministic mechanisms. Therefore, nondeterministic influences might dominate in a system, and the intricate combination and dance of deterministic and indeterministic influences might characterize their functioning as complexification proceeds, as if in a dialectical dance.

References

American Psychiatric Association. (2013). *Diagnostic and statistical manual of mental disorders: DSM-V* (5th ed.). Washington, DC: Author.

Antoni, M. H., Lutgendorf, S. K., Blomberg, B., Stagl, J., Carver, C. S., Lechner, S., et al. (2012). Transcriptional modulation of human leukocytes by cognitive-behavioral stress management in women undergoing treatment for breast cancer. *Biological Psychiatry, 71*, 366–372.

Badcock, P. B. (2012). Evolutionary systems theory: A unifying meta-theory of psychological science. *Review of General Psychology, 16*, 10–23.

Barlow, D. H., Ellard, K. K., Fairholme, C., Farchione, T. J., Boisseau, C., Allen, L., et al. (2011). *Unified protocol for the transdiagnostic treatment of emotional disorders*. New York: Oxford University Press.

Barlow, D. H., Ellard, K. K., Sauer-Zavala, S., Bullis, J. R., & Carl, J. R. (2014). The origins of trait neuroticism. *Perspectives on Psychological Science, 9*, 481–496.

Barlow, D. H., Sauer-Zavala, S., Carl, J. R., Bullis, J. R., & Ellard, K. K. (2014). The nature, diagnosis, and treatment of neuroticism: Back to the future. *Clinical Psychological Science, 2*, 344–365.

Bates, T. C., Lewis, G. J., & Weiss, A. (2013). Childhood socioeconomic status amplifies genetic effects on adult intelligence. *Psychological Science, 24*, 2111–2116.

Belsky, J., & Pluess, M. (2009). The nature (and nurture?) of plasticity in early human development. *Perspectives on Psychological Science, 4*, 345–351.

Benke, K. S., Nivard, M. G., Velders, F. P., Walters, R. K., Pappa, I., Scheet, P. A., et al. (2014). A genome-wide association meta-analysis of preschool internalizing problems. *Journal of the American Academy of Child & Adolescent Psychiatry, 53*, 667–676.

Bieling, P. J., Hawley, L. L., Bloch, R. T., Corcoran, K. M., Levitan, R. D., Young, L. T., et al. (2012). Treatment-specific changes in decentering following mindfulness-based cognitive therapy versus antidepressant medication or placebo for prevention of depressive relapse. *Journal of Consulting and Clinical Psychology, 80*, 365–372.

Bjorklund, D. F. (2006). Mother knows best: Epigenetic inheritance, maternal effects, and the evolution of human intelligence. *Developmental Review, 26*, 213–242.

Bjorklund, D. F., & Ellis, B. J. (2014). Children, childhood, and development in evolutionary perspective. *Developmental Review, 34*, 225–264.

Bjorklund, D. F., & Pellegrini, A. D. (2002). *The origins of human nature: Evolutionary developmental psychology*. Washington, DC: American Psychological Association.

Black, D. S., Cole, S. W., Irwin, M. R., Breen, E., St Cyr, N. M., Nazarian, N., et al. (2012). Yogic meditation reverses NF-kappaB and IRF-related transcriptome dynamics in leukocytes of family demential caregivers in a randomized controlled trial. *Psychoneuroendocrinology, 38*, 348–355.

Bower, J. E., Greendale, G., Crosswell, A. D., Garet, D., Sternlieb, B., Ganz, P. A., et al. (2014). Yoga reduces inflammatory signaling in fatigued breast cancer survivors: A randomized controlled trial. *Psychoneuroendocrinology, 43*, 20–29.

Boyce, W. T., & Ellis, B. J. (2005). Biological sensitivity to context: I. An evolutionary-developmental theory of the origins and functions of stress reactivity. *Development and Psychopathology, 17*, 271–301.

Briley, D. A., & Tucker-Drob, E. M. (2014). Genetic and environmental continuity in personality development: A meta-analysis. *Psychological Bulletin, 140*, 1303–1331.

Buss, D. M. (1995). Evolutionary psychology: A new paradigm for psychological science. *Psychological Inquiry, 6*, 1–30.

Buss, D. M. (2004). *Evolutionary psychology: The new science of the mind*. New York: Allyn & Bacon.

Caporael, L. R. (2001). Evolutionary psychology: Toward a unifying theory and a hybrid science. *Annual Review of Psychology, 52*, 607–628.

Caspi, A., Houts, R. M., Belsky, D. W., Goldman-Mellor, S. J., Harrington, H.-L., Israel, S., et al. (2014). The p factor: One general psychopathology factor in the structure of psychiatric disorders? *Clinical Psychological Science, 2*, 119–137.

Causey, K., Gardiner, A., & Bjorklund, D. F. (2008). Evolutionary developmental psychology and the role of plasticity in ontogeny and phylogeny. *Psychological Inquiry, 19*, 27–30.

Chisholm, J. (1990). Life-history perspectives on human development. In G. Butterworth & P. Bryant (Eds.), *Causes of development: Interdisciplinary perspectives* (pp. 238–258). Hertfordshire, UK: Harvester Wheatsheaf.

Cohen, L., Cole, S. W., Sood, A. K., Prinsloo, S., Kirschbaum, C., Arevalo, J. M. G., et al. (2012). Depressive symptoms and cortisol rhythmicity predict survival in patients with renal cell carcinoma: Role of inflammatory signaling. *PLoS ONE, 7*, e42324. doi:10.1371/journal.pone.0042324.

Cole, S. W. (2009). Social regulation of human gene expression. *Current Directions in Psychological Science, 18*, 132–137.

Cole, S. W. (2010). Elevating the perspective on human stress genomics. *Psychoneuroendocrinology, 35*, 955–962.

Cole, S. W. (2011). Socioenvironmental effects on gene expression. In K. S. Kendler, S. R. Jaffee, & D. Romer (Eds.), *The dynamic genome and mental health: The role of genes and environments in youth development* (pp. 195–225). New York: Oxford University Press.

Cole, S. W. (2014). Human social genomics. *PLoS Genetics, 10*, e1004601. doi:10.1371/journal.pgen.1004601.

Cole, S. W., Arevalo, J., Takahashi, R., Sloan, E. K., Lutgendorf, S., Sood, A. K., et al. (2010). Computational identification of gene-social environment interaction at the human IL6 locus. *Proceedings of the National Academy of Sciences, USA, 107*, 5681–5686.

Cole, S. W., Hawkley, L. C., Arevalo, J. M., Sung, C. Y., Rose, R. M., & Cacioppo, J. T. (2007). Social regulation of gene expression in human leukocytes. *Genome Biology, 8*, R189. doi:10.1186/gb-2007-8-9-r189.

Cole, S. W., Hawkley, L. C., Arevalo, J. M., & Cacioppo, J. T. (2011). Transcript origin analysis identifies antigen-presenting cells as primary targets of socially regulated gene expression in leukocytes. *Proceedings of the National Academy of Sciences, USA, 108*, 3080–3085.

Darwin, C. (1859). *On origin of species: By means of natural selection, on the preservation of favored races in the struggle for life*. London: John Murray.

Deary, I. J. (2012). Intelligence. *Annual Review of Psychology, 63*, 453–482.

Eccleston, M. (2011). *In utero exposure to maternal stress: Effects of the September 11th terrorist attacks in New York City on birth and early schooling outcomes*. Cambridge, MA: Harvard University Press.

Ellis, B. J., Shirtcliff, E. A., Boyce, W. T., Deardorff, J., & Essex, M. J. (2011). Quality of early family relationships and the timing and tempo of puberty: Effects depend on biological sensitivity to context. *Development and Psychopathology, 23*, 85–99.

Epel, E. S., Puterman, E., Lin, J., Blackburn, E., Lazaro, A., & Mendes, W. B. (2013). Wandering minds and aging cells. *Clinical Psychological Science, 1*, 75–83.

Eysenck, H. J. (1947). *Dimensions of personality*. Oxford, UK: Kegan Paul.

Flynn, E. G., Laland, K. N., Kendal, R. L., & Kendal, J. R. (2013). Developmental niche construction. *Developmental Science, 16*, 296–313.

Fragaszy, D. (2012). Community resources for learning: How capuchin monkeys construct technical traditions. *Biological Theory, 6*, 231–240.

Frankenhuis, W. E., Panchanathan, K., & Barrett, H. C. (2013). Bridging development systems theory and evolutionary psychology using dynamic optimization. *Developmental Science, 16*, 584–598.

Geary, D. C., & Bjorklund, D. F. (2000). Evolutionary developmental psychology. *Child Development, 71*, 57–65.

Gergely, G., & Csibra, G. (2013). Natural pedagogy. In M. R. Banaji & S. A. Gelman (Eds.), *Navigating the social world: What infants, children, and other species can teach us (social cognition and social neuroscience)* (pp. 127–132). Oxford, UK: Oxford University Press.

Goldhaber, D. (2012). *The nature-nurture debates: Bridging the gap*. New York: Cambridge University Press.

Gottlieb, G. (2007). Probabilistic epigenesis. *Developmental Science, 10*, 1–11.

Haier, R. J., Karama, S., Leyba, L., & Jung, R. E. (2009). MRI assessment of cortical thickness and functional activity changes in adolescent girls following three months of practice on a visual-spatial task. *BMC Research Notes, 2*, 174. doi:10.1186/1756-0500-2-174.

Haken, H. (1983). *Synergetics: An introduction: Nonequilibrium phase transitions and self-organization in physics, chemistry, and biology* (3rd ed.). Berlin, Germany: Springer.

Hoelzer, G. A., Smith, E., & Pepper, J. W. (2006). On the logical relationship between natural selection and self-organization. *Journal of Evolutionary Biology, 19*, 1785–1794.

Hogan, J. A. (1994). The concept of cause in the study of behavior. In J. A. Hogan & J. J. Bolhuis (Eds.), *Causal mechanisms of behavioral development* (pp. 3–15). Cambridge, UK: Cambridge University Press.

Hogan, J. A., & Bolhuis, J. J. (1994). *Causal mechanisms of behavioral development*. Cambridge, UK: Cambridge University Press.

Irwin, M. R., Olmstead, R., Breen, E., Witarama, T., Carrillo, C., Sadeghi, N., et al. (2014). Tai chi reduces cellular and genomic markers of inflammation in breast cancer survivors with insomnia. *Journal of the National Cancer Institute Monographs, 50*, 295–301.

Irwin, M. R., Wang, M., Campomayor, C. O., Collado-Hidalgo, A., & Cole, S. (2006). Sleep deprivation and activation of morning levels of cellular and genomic markers of inflammation. *Archives of Internal Medicine, 166*, 1756–1762.

Jablonka, E., & Lamb, M. J. (2007). Précis of evolution in four dimensions. *Behavioral and Brain Sciences, 30*, 353–392.

Jacobs, T. L., Epel, E. S., Lin, J., Blackburn, E. H., Wolkowitz, O. M., Bridwell, D. A., et al. (2011). Intensive meditation training, immune cell telomerase activity, and psychological mediators. *Psychoneuroendocrinology, 36*, 664–681.

Jaremka, L. M., Fagundes, C. P., Peng, J., Bennett, J. M., Glaser, R., Malarkey, W. B., et al. (2013). Loneliness promotes inflammation during acute stress. *Psychological Science, 24*, 1089–1097.

Kan, K.-J., Wicherts, J. M., Doland, C. V., & van der Maas, H. L. J. (2013). On the nature and nurture of intelligence and specific cognitive abilities: The more heritable, the more culture dependent. *Psychological Science, 24*, 2420–2428.

Karmiloff-Smith, A., Casey, B. J., Massand, E., Tomalski, P., & Thomas, M. S. C. (2014). Environmental and genetic influences on neurocognitive development: The importance of multiple methodologies and time-dependent intervention. *Clinical Psychological Science, 2*, 628–637.

Kauffman, S. (1993). *The origins of order: Self-organization and selection in evolution*. New York: Oxford University Press.

Kenrick, D. T., Maner, J. K., Butner, J., Li, N. P., Becker, D. V., & Schaller, M. (2002). Dynamical evolutionary psychology: Mapping the domains of the new interactionist paradigm. *Personality and Social Psychology Review, 6*, 347–356.

Kim, H. D., Shay, T., O'Shea, E. K., & Regev, A. (2009). Transcriptional regulatory circuits: Predicting numbers from alphabets. *Science, 325*, 429–432.

Klironomos, F. D., Berg, J., & Collins, S. (2013). How epigenetic mutations can affect genetic evolution: Model and mechanism. *Bioessays, 35*, 571–578.

Kovas, Y., Voronin, I., Kaydalov, A., Malykh, S. B., Dale, P. S., & Plomin, R. (2013). Literacy and numeracy are more heritable than intelligence in primary school. *Psychological Science, 24*, 2048–2056.

Laceulle, O. M., Vollebergh, W. A. M., & Ormel, J. (2015). The structure of psychopathology in adolescence: Replication of a general psychopathology factor in the TRAILS study. *Clinical Psychological Science, 3*, 850–860.

Laland, K. (2014). On evolutionary causes and evolutionary processes. *Behavioral Processes*. http://dx.doi.org/10.1016/j.beproc.2014.05.008.

Laland, K. N., Sterelny, K., Odling-Smee, J., Hoppitt, W., & Uller, T. (2011). Cause and effect in biology revisited: Is Mayr's proximate-ultimate dichotomy still useful? *Science, 334*, 1512–1516.

Lamm, E., & Jablonka, E. (2008). The nurture of nature: Hereditary plasticity in evolution. *Philosophical Psychology, 21*, 305–319.

Lavretsky, H., Epel, E. S., Siddarth, P., Nazarian, N., Cyr, N. S., Khalsa, D. S., et al. (2013). A pilot study of yogic meditation for family dementia caregivers with depressive symptoms: Effects on mental health, cognition, and telomerase activity. *International Journal of Geriatric Psychiatry, 28*, 57–65.

Lewis, M. D. (2000). The promise of dynamic systems approaches for an integrated account of human development. *Child Development, 71*, 36–43.

Lewis, M. D. (2005). Bridging emotion theory and neurobiology through dynamic systems modeling. *Behavioral and Brain Sciences, 28*, 169–245.

Li, S.-C. (2003). Biocultural orchestration of development plasticity across levels: The interplay of biology and culture in shaping the mind and behavior across the life span. *Psychological Bulletin, 129*, 171–194.

Li, S.-C. (2013). Lifespan development of neuromodulation of adaptive control and motivation as an ontogenetic mechanism for developmental niche construction. *Developmental Science, 16*, 317–319.

Lickliter, R., & Honeycutt, H. (2003). Developmental dynamics: Toward a biologically plausible evolutionary psychology. *Psychological Bulletin, 129*, 819–835.

Lukeš, J., Archibald, J. M., Keeling, P. J., Doolittle, W. F., & Gray, M. W. (2011). How a neutral evolutionary ratchet can build cellular complexity. *IUBMB Life, 63*, 528–537.

Manuck, S. B., Craig, A. E., Flory, J. D., Halder, I., & Ferrell, R. E. (2011). Reported early family environment covaries with menarcheal age as a function of polymorphic variation in estrogen receptor-a. *Developmental and Psychopathology, 23*, 69–83.

McShea, D. W., & Brandon, R. N. (2010). *Biology's first law: The tendency for diversity and complexity to increase in evolutionary systems*. Chicago, IL: University of Chicago Press.

Mendizabal, I., Keller, T. E., Zeng, J., & Yi, S. V. (2014). Epigenetics and evolution. *Integrative and Comparative Biology, 54*, 31–42.

Miller, G. E., Murphy, M. L. M., Cashman, R., Ma, R., Arevalo, J. M. G., Kobor, M. S., et al. (2014). Greater inflammatory activity and blunted glucocorticoid signaling in monocytes of chronically stressed caregivers. *Brain, Behavior, and Immunity, 41*, 191–199.

Murphy, M. L. M., Slavich, G. M., Rohleder, N., & Miller, G. E. (2013). Targeted rejection triggers differential pro- and anti-inflammatory gene expression in adolescents as a function of social status. *Clinical Psychological Science, 1*, 30–40.

Nisbett, R. E., Aronson, J., Blair, C., Dickens, W., Flynn, J., Halpern, D. F., et al. (2012). Intelligence: New findings and theoretical developments. *American Psychologist, 67*, 130–159.

O'Connor, M. F., Schultze-Florey, C. R., Irwin, M. R., Arevalo, J. M., & Cole, S. W. (2014). Divergent gene expression responses to complicated grief and non-complicated grief. *Brain, Behavior, and Immunity, 37*, 78–83.

O'Donovan, A., Sun, B., Cole, S., Rempel, H., Lenoci, M., Pulliam, L., et al. (2011). Transcriptional control of monocyte gene expression in post-traumatic stress disorder. *Disease Markers, 30*, 123–132.

Partridge, T., & Greenberg, G. (2010). Contemporary ideas in physics and biology in Gottlieb's psychology. In K. E. Hood, C. T. Halpern, G. Greenberg, & R. Lerner (Eds.), *Handbook of developmental science, behavior, and genetics* (pp. 166–202). Malden, MA: Wiley Blackwell.

Ploeger, A. (2010). Evolutionary psychology as a metatheory for the social sciences. *Integral Review, 6*, 164–174.

Ploeger, A., Van Der Maas, H. J. L., & Raijmakers, M. E. J. (2008). Is evolutionary psychology a metatheory for psychology? A discussion of four major issues in psychology from an evolutionary developmental perspective. *Psychological Inquiry, 19*, 1–18.

Plomin, R., & Deary, I. J. (2015). Genetics and intelligence differences: Five special findings. *Molecular Psychiatry, 20*, 98–108.

Prigogine, I., & Stengers, M. (1997). *The end of certainty: Time, chaos, and the new laws of nature*. New York: Free Press.

Protzko, J., Aronson, J., & Blair, C. (2013). How to make a young child smarter: Evidence from the database of raising intelligence. *Perspectives on Psychological Science, 8*, 25–40.

Puterman, E., & Epel, E. (2012). An intricate dance: Life experience, multisystem resiliency, and rate of telomere decline throughout the lifespan. *Social and Personality Psychology Compass, 6*, 807–825.

Puterman, E., Lin, J., Blackburn, E., O'Donovan, A., Adler, N., & Epel, E. (2010). The power of exercise: Buffering the effect of chronic stress on telomere length. *PLoS One, 5*, e10837. doi:10.1371/journal.pone.0010837.

Rice, F., Harold, G. T., Boivin, J., van den Bree, M., Hay, D. F., & Thapar, A. (2010). The links between prenatal stress and offspring development and psychopathology: Disentangling environmental and inherited influences. *Psychological Medicine, 40*, 335–345.

Richerson, P., Baldini, R., Bell, A., Demps, K., Frost, K., Hillis, V., et al. (2014). Cultural group selection plays an essential role in explaining human cooperation: A sketch of the evidence. *Behavioral and Brain Sciences, 28*, 1–71.

Sameroff, A. (2010). A unified theory of development: A dialectic integration of nature and nurture. *Child Development, 81*, 6–22.

Scott-Phillips, T. C., Dickins, T. E., & West, S. A. (2011). Evolutionary theory and the ultimate-proximate distinction of the human behavioral sciences. *Perspectives on Psychological Science, 6*, 38–47.

Shackelford, T. K., & Liddle, J. R. (2014). Understanding the mind from an evolutionary perspective: An overview of evolutionary psychology. *Wiley Interdisciplinary Reviews: Cognitive Science, 5*, 247–260.

Sheldon, K. M. (2011). Consilience within the biopsychosocial system. *Psychological Inquiry, 22*, 52–65.

Sheldon, K. M., Cheng, C., & Hilpert, J. (2011). Understanding well-being and optimal functioning: Applying the multilevel personality in context (MPIC) model. *Psychological Inquiry, 22*, 1–16.

Skinner, M. K. (2011). Environmental epigenetic transgenerational inheritance and somatic epigenetic mitotic stability. *Epigenetics, 6*, 838–842.

Skinner, M. K., Gurerrero-Bosagna, C., Haque, M. M., Nilsson, E. E., Koop, J. A. H., Knutie, S. A., et al. (2014). Epigenetic and the evolution of Darwin's finches. *Genome Biology and Evolution, 6*, 1972–1989.

Slavich, G. M., & Cole, S. W. (2013). The emerging field of human social genomics. *Clinical Psychological Science, 1*, 331–348.

Smith, L. B., & Thelen, E. (2003). Development as a dynamic system. *Trends in Cognitive Science, 7*, 343–348.

Sterelny, K. (2012). *The evolved apprentice*. Cambridge, MA: MIT Press.

Sternberg, R. J. (2012). Intelligence. *Wiley Interdisciplinary Reviews: Cognitive Science, 3*, 501–511.

Sternberg, R. J. (2014). The development of adaptive competence: Why cultural psychology is necessary and not just nice. *Developmental Review, 34*, 208–224.

Stochl, J., Khandaker, G. M., Lewis, G., Perez, J., Goodyer, I. M., Zammit, S., et al. (2015). Mood, anxiety, and psychotic phenomena measure a common psychopathological factor. *Psychological Medicine, 45*, 1483–1493.

Tinbergen, N. (1963). On aims and methods in ethology. *Zeitschrift für Tierpsychologie, 20*, 410–433.

Trahan, L. H., Stuebing, K. K., Fletcher, J. M., & Hiscock, M. (2014). The Flynn effect: A meta-analysis. *Psychological Bulletin, 140*, 1332–1360.

Tucker-Drob, E. M., & Briley, D. A. (2014). Continuity of genetic and environmental influences on cognition across the life span: A meta-analysis of longitudinal twin and adoption studies. *Psychological Bulletin, 140*, 949–979.

Vukasović, T., & Bratko, D. (2015). Heritability of personality: A meta-analysis of behavioral genetic studies. *Psychological Bulletin, 141*, 769–785.

West-Eberhard, M. J. (2003). *Developmental plasticity and evolution*. Oxford, UK: Oxford University Press.

Wheeler, M., & Clark, A. (2008). Culture, embodiment and genes: Unravelling the triple helix. *Philosophical Transactions of the Royal Society B: Biological Sciences, 363*, 3563–3575.

Witherington, D. C. (2007). The dynamic systems approach as metatheory for developmental psychology. *Human Development, 50*, 127–153.

Young, G. (2014). *Malingering, feigning, and response bias in psychiatric/psychological injury: Implications for practice and court*. Dordrecht, Netherlands: Springer Science + Business Media.

Zimmer, C. (2013). The surprising origins of life's complexity: Scientists are exploring how organisms can evolve elaborate structures without Darwinian selection. *Scientific American, 84–89*.

Part III

Normal and Abnormal Development and Free Will: Normal Development and Free Will

13 Differential Susceptibility: Orchids, Dandelions, and the Flowering of Developmental Psychology

Chapter Introduction

Differential susceptibility and related models of development constitute the most integrative and important new frameworks in psychology, combining developmental, genetic, and evolutionary models that have led to impressive empirical research. They argue that certain allelic variations in certain adverse contexts might lead to negative outcomes, as in Gene×Environment (G×E) interaction, but that the genes involved are not only vulnerability ones because, in supportive rather than in adverse environments, the outcomes might be more positive than the norm. The G×E interaction involved leads to positive outcomes more than is the case for related allelic–environmental interactions, i.e., ones involving related alleles without the susceptibility factor. These latter alleles do not lead to the range of positive and negative outcomes depending on the nature of the environment involved; that is, no matter what the extremes are in terms of environmental quality or environmental interactions with the allele at issue, one does not find the extremes in adverse or adaptive outcomes, e.g., more antisocial behavior than otherwise should occur, or less, respectively. The differential susceptibility model has been referred to as the dandelion/orchid hypothesis because those without the susceptibility allele involved will do well enough no matter what is the context, while those with the allele might flower quite well, as the metaphor of the orchid implies, or shrivel without the right support.

The biological sensitivity to context one is a very similar model to the differential susceptibility one. The adaptive calibration model is a variant of the differential susceptibility model. These models contrast with more linear models, such as the diathesis-stress one and the allostatic load one, in which vulnerabilities accumulate, whether biological or environmental, and the outcome is uniquely negative.

These differential susceptibility and related models include a component of environmental monitoring and forecast. Also, they are associated with life history theory. The phenotypic variability that they describe fits an evolutionary adaptive, or fitness, approach to understanding development. The proponents of differential sensitivity/biological sensitivity to context have undertaken research in support of its predictions. The approach carries implications for understanding development, psychopathology, and even education (e.g., more resources for those with more environmentally-sensitive allelic variations).

Differential Susceptibility

Aside from its general advantages for the study of psychological science, evolutionary psychology has been applied to particular psychological domains. For example, it emphasizes that

G. Young, *Unifying Causality and Psychology*, DOI 10.1007/978-3-319-24094-7_13

developmental adaptations evolved for their ability to solve adaptive problems in the periods to which they apply (Bjorklund & Pellegrini, 2002; Buss, 2011; Ellis & Bjorklund, 2012). The following reviews are the most powerful of evolutionary-developmental models.

Model

Introduction The model of differential susceptibility to the environment is an evolutionary one that applies to neurodevelopment and psychopathology, including in risk behavior. It developed out of two research streams [(a) Boyce et al., 1995; Boyce & Ellis, 2005; Ellis, Essex, & Boyce, 2005; Belsky, 1997a, 1997b, 2005; (b) Belsky, Bakermans-Branenburg, & van IJzendoorn, 2007] that have been combined in the work of Ellis and Belsky and colleagues (Belsky, Schlomer, & Ellis, 2012; Ellis, Boyce, Belsky, Bakermans-Kranenburg, & van Iizendoorn, 2011).

The Boyce–Ellis group proposed the biological sensitivity to context theory (BSCT) and the Belsky group the differential susceptibility theory (DST). Together, the models suggest that some individuals express greater susceptibility or disproportionate vulnerability not only to negative environmental conditions that serve to promote risk-taking behavior but also to positive environmental conditions that are development-enhancing. The combined model over the two streams indicates a neurobiological susceptibility in some individuals relative to others in regulating environmental impacts on development, adaptation, and health.

Ellis et al. (2011) presented seven defining features of their model of individual differences in differential susceptibility/vulnerability to the environment. (a) Some individuals but not others exhibit the heightened environmental susceptibility. (b) The sensitivity increases developmental receptivity that promotes sustained behavioral changes. (c) The susceptibilities are genetically underpinned and neurobiologically expressed. (d) The genetic influence is polygenic in origin of variation. The experience involved is developmental. (e) There are both inter- and intra-individual differences in the susceptibility, mediated neurobiologically. (f) The individual differences are evolutionary adaptive, with the susceptibilities having had positive fitness payoffs in evolution. (g) Neurobiological-based differential susceptibilities to the environment constitute regulatory mechanisms of alternate adaptive patterns of human development. To expand this characteristic of the model, even the greater susceptibility to putatively negative outcome in negative environments could be evolutionary advantageous (survival-wise/reproductively).

Ellis et al. (2011) contrasted their susceptibility model to the diathesis-stress/dual risk one of vulnerability, of which G×E interactions is an example. In this latter approach to vulnerability, a synergy between vulnerability genes and environmental stressors leads to psychopathology or poor functioning. The genes involved might include ones such as serotonin-linked polymorphic region [the short allele in *5-HTTLPR* (serotonin transporter gene)]. The vulnerability might be behavioral in nature (e.g., difficult temperament) or physiological (e.g., endophenotypic-heightened biological reactivity to stress). Having less vulnerability means having more resilience. According to Ellis et al. (2011), the diathesis-stress (and any related) model does not consider adequately low susceptibility, positive environments, and favorable/positive developmental enhancement (see Fig. 13.1).

According to Ellis et al. (2011), the notion that evolution has selected the likelihood of positive development to positive environments is consistent with the evolutionary perspective. The more contentious component of their model from an evolutionary standpoint is that negative environments might provoke other survival-reproductive strategies despite apparent disadvantaged, disturbed, or deleterious development and behavior. This latter behavioral outcome also is consistent with the evolutionary perspective, because no matter what might be our opinion of the behavior itself, it would have evolved through natural selection to function to direct or regulate development and behavior that are fit or adapted to the negative environments encountered. For example, Champagne et al. (2008) have shown, for

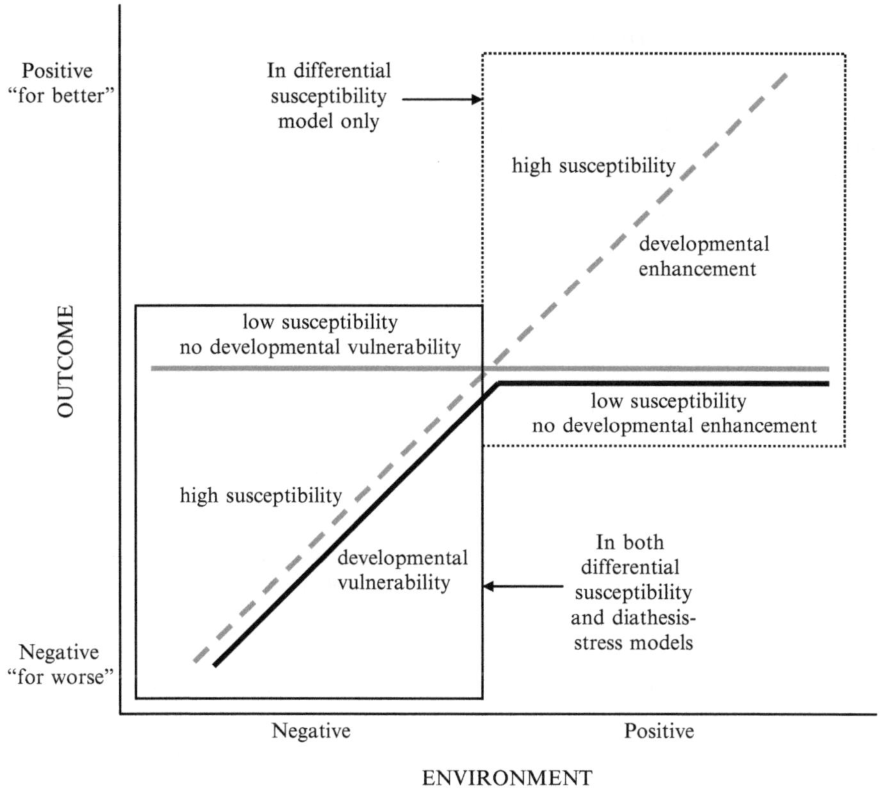

Fig. 13.1 The diathesis-stress/dual risk model and the differential susceptibility model. The differential susceptibility and diathesis-stress models make equivalent predictions for individuals expressing high susceptibility developmental vulnerability. They differ for the context of high susceptibility/development enhancement (the "for better" component of the expression "for better or for worse" that represents metaphorically the model). Generally, negative outcomes are experienced only by individuals displaying high susceptibility/developmental vulnerability. In the differential susceptibility model, more susceptible individuals in positive environments will show more favorable outcomes (i.e., developmental enhancement). To conclude, more susceptible individuals are influenced by both negative and positive environments relative to less susceptible individuals. They are not necessarily "vulnerable," given the positive effects of supportive environments. Adapted from Ellis et al. (2011), based on Bakermans-Kranenburg and van IJzendoorn (2007)

rats, that low levels of maternal licking/grooming (lower quality maternal care for a rat), altered pups' stress and physiology/brain morphology. The effects included higher pup corticosterone levels, shorter length in dendritic branching, and lower spine density in hippocampal neurons. Nevertheless, the pups exhibited enhanced learning and memory processes in stressful conditions. Also, the physiological and brain changes involved mediated the effects of maternal behavior on survival- and reproduction-related behavior in the offspring (e.g., accelerated pubertal development, increased sexual behavior and, later, reduced parenting behavior).

The conclusion offered by Ellis et al. (2011) to this animal model is that, under the circumstances, the maternal care was not poor nor was the pup behavior evolutionarily maladaptive. Rather, the reduced maternal care served to activate alternate behavioral adaptations in the pups that would fit the forecasting that the environment the pups would encounter in the phase of their sexual maturity would be like that of the mother. The development and behavior produced in offspring would make the best of a bad situation, in that the resource-poor or otherwise stressful environment of the mother would be associated with fitness costs on average. The evolutionary mechanism

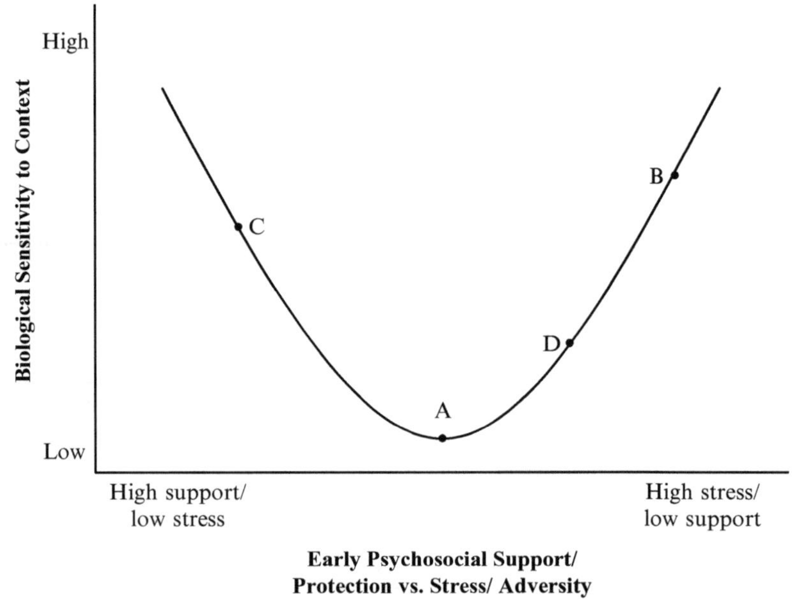

Fig. 13.2 Proposed curvilinear relationship between experiences of psychosocial support/protection compared to stress/adversity in early environments and biological sensitivity to context. The graph illustrates that extremes in support and stress have their effects in contexts of biological sensitivity to context. Adapted from Ellis et al. (2011), based on Boyce and Ellis (2005)

involved has been called "conditional adaptation" (e.g., Boyce & Ellis, 2005), in that there are variations in evolutionary adaptation that are still functional and competent even in stressful, dangerous, and resource-poor environments.

Life History Ellis et al. (2011) proceeded to describe the similarities and differences in the Boyce–Ellis and Belsky and colleagues' approaches to the question of differential susceptibility to the environment. Boyce and Ellis (2005; see Fig. 13.2) modeled the relationship between biological susceptibility to context and degree of psychosocial support/protection against stress/adversity. Only when there is a moderate amount of support/stress does one find low biological sensitivity to context, or a buffering effect (curvilinear relationship).

Belsky (1997a, 1997b, 2000, 2005) advanced a model similar to that of Boyce and Ellis (2005), partly based on an earlier evolutionary model of socialization that he developed with colleagues, that of psychosocial acceleration theory (Belsky, Steinberg, & Draper, 1991). In this model, both conditional and alternative developmental strategies play a role. Conditional adaptive strategies promote in development the ability to "thrive" in a variety of niches, depending on environment encountered and correlated parenting strategies. Alternate adaptive strategies promote less flexibility in development for an offspring, but have other advantages for the family involved.

Ellis and Bjorklund (2012) also discussed the topic of development of life history strategies. Among others, Chisholm (1999) had proposed life history theory based on fitness-related tradeoffs in behavioral "decisions" related to survival and reproduction. Life history strategies could follow slower life histories or faster ones, in which rate of maturation, selection of mates, number of offspring, and parental investment vary (e.g., Ellis, Figueredo, Brumbach, & Schlomer, 2009). Belsky et al.'s (1991) psychosocial acceleration theory applies especially to risky adolescent behavior based on environmental stress (e.g., parental discord, single-parent family, low income), and it is consistent with Chisholm's (1999) life history model.

Others have pointed out that adverse environments might be extrinsic (external sources) or unpredictable (variable; Ellis et al., 2009). Two studies have shown that the latter factor, in particular, especially if experienced in the first 5 years of life, through multiple-step pathways, especially predicts faster life history strategies that develop later on (Belsky et al., 2012;

Simpson, Griskevicius, Kuo, Sung, & Collins, 2012). Other workers have added sexual selection theory to the model. For example, if a teenager is competitively advantaged relative to other peers for mating, riskier behavior is more probable (Dishion, Ha, & Véronneau, 2012; James, Ellis, Schlomer, & Garber, 2012).

Ellis et al. (2011) concluded their comparison of differential environmental susceptibility and other models of psychopathology in development by noting that, in their model, some individuals are more prone to respond to positive and negative life experiences and others less so, which is akin to having a greater or narrower reaction range, respectively (e.g., Manuck, 2010). I made a similar point in Young (2011) about Belsky and Pluess's (2009a, 2009b) version of the DST model.

Also, Ellis et al. (2011) noted that making the best of a bad situation, which might be the way to characterize how differential environmental susceptibilities work in the case of adverse/corrosive/resource-poor environments, is not necessarily evolutionarily maladaptive in the sense of decreasing fitness or survival/reproduction, despite the costs in mental health elicited, as well. That is, it promotes a faster life history strategy, that although is associated with earlier and riskier sexual activity leading to teenage pregnancy, it might be the option that matches best extant negative environmental conditions and similar ones that had been forecasted earlier in development leading to the behavior.

Research Research is increasingly supporting the differential environmental susceptibility model. Biological agents/processes have been found to have bivalent effects that are context-contingent. For example, childhood obesity and insulin resistance appear more common at both ends of the spectrum of birth weight (Gluckman, Hanson, Cooper, & Thornburg, 2008), supporting Ellis' curvilinear model of biological sensitivity to context. The most intriguing supportive research for the models being discussed, though, relate to differential susceptibilities and related genetic susceptibilities, as predicted by Belsky's model.

Bakermans-Kranenburg and van IJzendoorn (2006) found that, in Dutch children, maternal sensitivity at 10 months of age predicted more than 2 years later the children's mother-reported externalizing problems, but only for those children carrying a certain allele (7-repeat dopamine receptor *D4*, *DRD4-7R*). The results followed a differential susceptibility model for these allele carriers—they displayed the most observed externalizing behavior when their mothers were rated insensitive but the least in the case of the mothers who were judged as highly sensitive. Other G × E results supportive of the differential environmental susceptibility model were reported by Sheese, Voelker, Rothbart, and Posner (2007) and Mills-Koonce et al. (2007).

Work continues on finding the endophenotypic variation underlying differential environmental susceptibility. Candidate genes include not only *DRD4* but also the short (*s*) alleles on the *5-HTTLPR*. These genes are involved in variation in the dopaminergic and serotonergic brain circuitry, respectively, which govern response thresholds to reward and punishment. The allelic variations would influence attention, state regulation, and orienting response, as well.

The mechanism that leads genes to express differential sensitivity to context needs exploration. In this regard, epigenetic processes might lead to phenotypic changes in biobehavioral reactivity to adversity via changes in glucocorticoid receptor gene expression (Weaver et al., 2004). These types of changes would alter the reactivity of the stress-responsive hypothalamic–pituitary–adrenal (HPA) axis. van IJzendoorn, Caspers, Bakermans-Kranenburg, Beach, and Philibert (2010) found that higher levels of epigenetic methylation of the *5-HTT* polymorphism were associated with trauma-resolution difficulties in carriers of the allele *5-HTTLPR ll*, which usually functions protectively, thereby altering the set point for traumatic stress reactivity.

As for neural endophenotypes in context sensitivity, the two peripheral neuroendocrine stress response systems seem implicated—the corticotrophin-releasing hormone and the locus coeruleus-norepinephrine (LC-NE) systems.

When these systems are highly reactive, the individuals involved appear to experience either the worst or the best of developmental and health outcomes, depending on the direction of adversity/support exposed to in the immediate social context. For example, Obradović, Bush, Stamperdahl, Adler, and Boyce (2010) studied 5- to 6-year-olds with high vs. low reactivity of the parasympathetic nervous system, which is modulated by LC-NE)system activity. They found that the high-reactive children growing up in heightened environmental adversity were rated as less prosocial. However, if they were growing up in more favorable environments, they were rated as more prosocial. Moreover, children who were highly cortisol-reactive, when compared to children having low cortisol reactivity, were rated as more prosocial in growing up in low adversity contexts and less prosocial in growing up in high adversity contexts.

As for behavioral phenotypes indicative of differential environmental susceptibility, aside from fast and slow life history strategies, the role of earlier-developing difficult vs. easy temperament has been implicated, which seem reflective of general emotional reactivity (e.g., Pluess & Belsky, 2009, 2010). For example, difficult children compared to easy temperamental ones exhibited more behavioral problems in the early school years if they had been exposed in infancy or in early childhood to low-quality child care, but they expressed fewer problems in the context of high quality care (Pluess & Belsky, 2009).

According to Ellis et al. (2011), further research is needed to differentiate the causal origins of differential susceptibility to the environment in terms of where it "resides" in the spectrum of genomic, epigenomic, neural, neuroendocrine, and behavioral mechanisms with which it has been associated. They opted for a hierarchical model in which each of these levels is mechanistically related to the others below and above it in the complex system involved, constituting "true mediating events" of sensitivity to environment.

Fitness Ellis et al. (2011) next turned to the evolutionary fitness advantages of having differential environmental susceptibility passed on to offspring in certain experienced contexts, but not others. In BSCT, the) evolutionary model that makes sense is conditional adaptation. Individual organisms living in heterogeneous contexts need to be able to monitor reliable cues related to survival and reproduction, both external (e.g., predation, resources) and internal (status, e.g., health, capacity to win agonistic mating-related encounters).

The ability to match development to environmental conditions is fitness-adaptive. The fitness advantage of the predominant implemented phenotype in stable conditions and the alternate phenotype in unstable ones depends on successful tracking of environmental conditions and prediction of optimal phenotypic strategy to match them. Natural selection favors primary phenotypes under favorable fitness conditions but provides for secondary ones that, fitness-wise, make the best of bad fitness conditions.

Ellis et al. (2011) noted that the BSCT) evolutionary model applies to ongoing environmental adaptation both at the individual and population levels. Also, the mechanisms evolved in the course of human history because of their fitness adaptiveness at each point in evolutionary time. They noted that in modal (i.e., neither excessively dangerous nor supportive) environments, whether present or past, heightened environmental sensitivity does not promote fitness, and so should not be selected. Also, for environmentally-susceptible individuals, when in adverse environments, there are not just fitness gains in adopting secondary strategies, because there are fitness tradeoffs (e.g., various short-term and long-term costs, including in health). That is, there are short-term reproductive gains in environments that might not promote either long-term survival (a situation that would short circuit any reproduction) or sufficient health to allow for reproduction.

In terms of the DST's evolutionary approach, it has much in common with the BSCT.) The critical concept in its approach is bet-hedging rather than conditional adaptation. Whereas the latter applies to flexibility in ongoing environmental cue reading and developmental in heterogenous environments, the former refers to adaptively diverse optimal offspring phenotypes in heterogeneous environmental conditions. If environments fluctuate unpredictably over evolutionary time, expressing differential susceptibility to environment and its intergenerational transmission is fitness adaptive. Diversity derives from phenotype A being able to match environment A, phenotype B matching environment B, and so on, with intermediate jack-of-all-trade phenotypes also helpful fitness-wise.

There are fitness costs to the strategy (e.g., in intergenerationally stable environments, having the uniphenotypic strategy of propagating phenotypes equivalent to A, assuming A is the one that fits, would be superior in adaptivity compared to a diversity phenotypic strategy in which phenotype A is produced within a multiphenotypic set, in that some of the adaptive edge of the latter variable-environment phenotype A would not develop in the same fine-tuned way as stable-environment uniphenotypic-based phenotype A). That is, "spreading the risk" by increasing phenotypic variation among offspring might increase the probability of achieving some reproductive success in heterogenous environments in any one generation, but such spreading of the risk is accompanied by the fitness cost of limiting adaptive success in stable, good conditions, although the gain in shielding against total survival and reproductive failure in bad ones is a worthwhile fitness tradeoff.

Research in evolutionary biology supports the contention that strongly fluctuating selection pressures can support variation of offspring phenotypes (in a process termed adaptive coin flipping), even when there is "monomorphic" genetic structure. The process is apparently founded in a "stochastic developmental switch" in which the probability of the phenotypic alternatives involved corresponds to the forecast of the probability of the corresponding environmental condition for the offspring made by the parent organism based on extant environmental cues.

Ellis et al. (2011) noted that diversified bet-hedging, or spreading the risk by producing a diversity of "fixed" offspring, would be favored in highly unpredictable environments. Selection should favor offspring with flexible phenotypic options, as in the differential susceptibility to environment model. If environments are predictable, the latter would be disadvantageous and, in contrast, producing more diverse, fixed phenotypes would be advantageous. These differing strategies apply to the familial context, and act to increase or decrease phenotypic variability in offspring depending on degree of early environmental variations encountered. The authors concluded that the degree of unpredictable environments encountered within a generation alters life history strategies, in order to "optimize" growth rates of lineages across generations.

Ellis et al. (2011) related high and low environmental susceptibility genotypes to their expressed phenotypes in terms of a flower metaphor—or as orchid and dandelion phenotypes, respectively. Orchids are phenotypes with an associated high environmental susceptibility that are better at changing niches when their preferred one becomes "overcrowded," whereas dandelions are phenotypes with an associated low environmental susceptibility and a more fixed phenotype. Normally, both types of phenotypes can co-exist in stable equilibrium.

Moreover, it should be possible to show the adaptive advantages of each type of phenotype in microenvironments. For example, Quas, Bauer, and Boyce (2004) found that children expressing high vs. low autonomic reactivity varied in their memory for a highly stressful event in ways consistent with the differential environment susceptibility model.

Conclusion As an overall conclusion to their most stimulating work, Ellis et al. (2011) noted that susceptibility might translate best as a dimensional rather than categorical construct. Also, susceptibilities might differ at different developmental periods for those with the relevant genotype. Finally, more research is needed on mechanism. For example, orchid phenotypes in supportive environments might differentially profit because they better detect potentially positive opportunities and learn to capitalize on them. As for ontogenetic origins of differential environmental susceptibility, Ellis et al. (2011) noted that Pluess and Belsky (2011) reasoned that maternal stress might lead to prenatal programming of a postnatal plasticity, but that there might be genetic bases (G×E interactions) involved in susceptibility to prenatal programming.

Elaborations

Belsky and Colleagues

Belsky and Ellis have continued to publish on aspects of differential susceptibility. For example, Belsky (2012) referred to his earlier model of psychosocial acceleration, or fast tracking in development and reproduction. Ellis, Schlomer, Tilley, and Butler (2012) explored the dynamics in risk-taking in early sexual behavior. In the following, I examine the recent modeling by both Belsky and Ellis and their colleagues.

Acceleration Belsky (2012) described the psychosocial acceleration theory of human reproductive strategies. It is an evolutionary-influenced model of life-history alternatives, in which both alternatives "fit" in one or other of even in quite different available environmental resources, rendering both evolutionarily adaptive, or promoting of reproductive "fitness." Of the two alternatives in the model, the "fast" or earlier trajectory one is riskier (e.g., teen pregnancy) and comes with costs compared to the other trajectory or "slow" one. However, despite the costs, the fast option still fits the context in which it is promoted, for example, because of its different type of preceding experience, differential resources that had been available, and degree of environmental uncertainty in the present.

In terms of mechanisms of influence, Belsky (2012) indicated that the effect on the child early in life of these various factors on attachment security quality (secure, insecure) is a crucial mediator. For example, insecure mother–infant attachment at 15 months of age is associated with early menarche (Belsky, Steinberg, Houts, Halpern-Felsher, & The NICHD Early Child Care Research Network, 2010). At the physiological level, epigenetic stamps related to rearing regulate gene expression, including for rate of sexual maturation (in rat studies; e.g., Cameron et al., 2005).

Belsky, Ruttle, Boyce, Armstrong, and Essex (2015) investigated sexual maturation and poor health in females in relation to early adversity and elevated stress physiology. Path analysis revealed that more exposure to prenatal stress predicted not only more maternal depression and qualitatively negative parenting in infancy, but also elevated basal cortisol at the age of 4.5 years. Moreover, the latter levels predicted accelerated sexual development, which itself predicted 18-year-old physical and health problems.

Belsky and Pluess (2013a) elaborated their model of differential susceptibility to environmental influences (Belsky & Pluess, 2009a, 2009b), and contrasted it to similar models (Ellis et al., 2011). To review, their model is evolutionary in focus. Under the influence of stressful environments, development is not dysregulated but is directed toward evolutionary strategies that had been adaptive biologically in our ancestors. Granted, the direction might not be optimal for fitness compared to other strategies in more conducive environments, but it does "make the best of a bad situation," or mitigate to a degree reduction in fitness.

Belsky and Pluess (2013a) noted that developmental plasticity has become part of our phenotype, although with qualifications. Some individuals possess alleles that confer greater plasticity, while others are more resilient or canalized despite facing environmental variations. Moreover, the plasticity might lead to negative outcomes more than expected or positive ones, depending on whether there are susceptibility alleles involved that bring with them this increased range of reaction.

In contrast to the workings of a differential susceptibility process in development with its negative and positive outcomes as possible, a diathesis-stress model argues that environmental adversity leads especially to negative outcomes in the presence of risk factors, including genetic ones. I would add that the diathesis-stress model refers to diatheses as an accumulation of vulnerabilities biologically or environmentally and it refers to stress as an immediate trigger that brings out the latent vulnerability into the open as a negative outcome. However, in the differential susceptibility model, not only the vulnerability is different than in the diatheses-stress model, so is the stress. That is, in the latter model it might be an immediate trigger that activates a latent, nearly active vulnerability, but in the former model the stress is a cumulative and longer term one that indicates an ongoing presence of a resource-poor (dangerous, unpredictable, etc.) environment, or at least the forecast of one with this profile.

Belsky (2012) referred to the research with polymorphisms that express differential susceptibility, Belsky and Pluess (2009a, 2009b) had shown that certain at-risk alleles could lead to quite positive outcomes in supportive environments. Research since that review has shown the same results for the (a) *5-HTTLPR* and (b) *DRD4* polymorphisms (e.g., respectively, (a) Kochanska, Kim, Barry, & Philibert, 2011; van IJzendoorn, Belsky, & Bakermans-Kranenburg, 2012, and (b) Knafo, Israel, & Ebstein, 2011; Belsky & Pluess, 2013b).

Genes Other research supports "plasticity gene" status for: (c) brain-derived neurotrophic factor gene (*BDNF*; e.g., Chen, Li, & McGue, 2012; Gunnar et al., 2012); (d) oxytocin receptor gene (*OXTR*; Johansson et al., 2012; Poulin, Holman, & Buffone, 2012; Sturge-Apple, Davies, Martin, Cicchetti, & Hentges, 2012); (e) *FICSO6* binding protein S gene (Bevilacqua et al., 2012); and perhaps (f) catechol-*O*-methyl-transferase gene (*COMT*; Laucht et al., 2012), (g) monoamine oxidase A gene (*MAOA*; Enoch, Steer, Newman, Gibson, & Goldman, 2010; Wakschlag et al., 2010); and (h) the neuronal acetylcholine receptor subunit α-4 genotype (*CHRNA4*; Grazioplene, DeYoung, Rogosch, & Cicchetti, 2013). Work is proceeding on combined or multiple (polygenetic) plasticity genes (e.g., Brody, Chen, & Beach, 2013; Simons et al., 2012). This suggests the validity for a "system-level" genetic approach in the area.

Belsky and Pluess (2013b) investigated whether genetic moderation took place in early child-care effects on social behavior. In particular, with respect to parent- and teacher-rated externalizing problem behavior and social skills they asked whether the effects of daycare experience are genetically moderated by the polymorphisms *DRD4* dopamine receptor gene and the serotonin transporter gene *5-HTTLPR*.

They found differential genetic, outcome measure, and age effects. In particular, the *DRD4* polymorphism, but not *5-HTTLPR*, moderated the effect of child-care quality (but not quantity/type) on caregiver-reported externalizing difficulties when the children were 54 months of age and also in kindergarten and teacher-reported social skills in kindergarten and first grade. Only carriers of the 7-repeat allele of *5-HTTLPR* were found susceptible to quality of care effects.

Analysis revealed the results for behavior problems fit the differential susceptibility model but the ones for social skills fit the diathesis-stress model. Not all results were consistent with the literature, e.g., for *5-HTTLPR*.

Pluess, Stevens, and Belsky (2013) noted that differential susceptibility and its phenotypic consequences appear to be a quantitative trait influenced polygenically by plasticity alleles. Depending on the amount involved, they set up a plasticity gradient that varies on a continuum. For example, Sonuga-Barke et al. (2009) found that children with candidate susceptibility alleles related to *DAT1* and also to *5-HTTLPR* were most susceptible to higher negative maternal emotionality in their conduct disorder outcome. Belsky and Deaver (2011) found that adolescent males measured for self-control were more susceptible to quality of parenting the more they had plasticity alleles related to *5-HTTLPR*, *MAOA*, *DRD4*, *DRD2*, and *DAT1*. Genetic plasticity in this area of differential environmental plasticity appears to be cumulative.

Environment Pluess et al. (2013) also addressed the role of the environment, even prenatally, to shape susceptibility factors. Maternal stress in pregnancy can lead to prenatal programming of altered physiological and behavioral responses to stress, with some fetuses possibly being more susceptible to prenatal stress effects due to their genetic make-up (see Fig. 13.3). In this regard, Pluess, Belsky, and Neuman (2009) found that

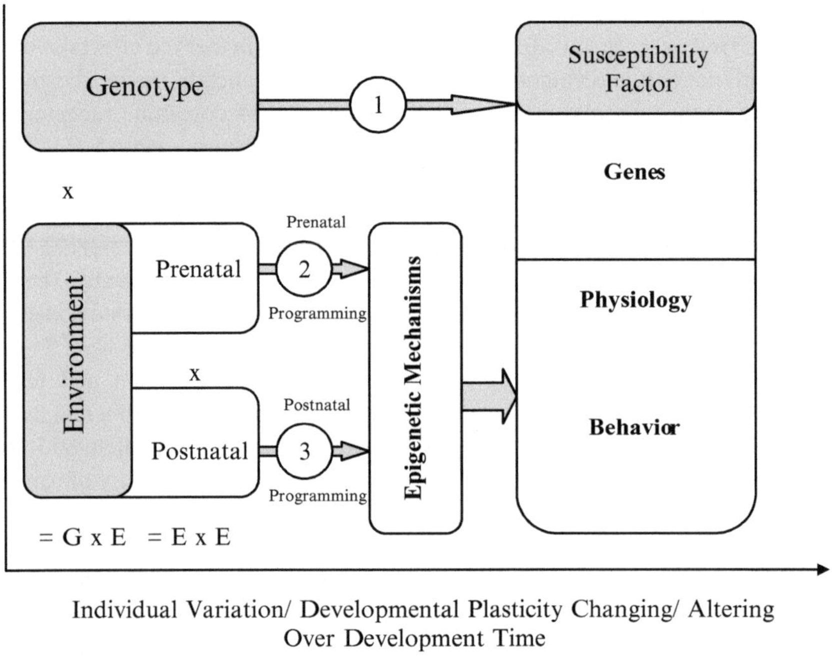

Fig. 13.3 Genes, environment, and differential susceptibility: a process model. The figure indicates that (1) the genetic contribution to general susceptibility is partially mediated by susceptibility factors (nature); (2) the prenatal environment influences susceptibility factors (nurture); (3) postnatal environment also influences susceptibility factors (nurture); also, these variables interact (G×E, E×E; gene–environment interaction, environment–environment interaction, respectively). Adapted from Pluess et al. (2013)

children with the *DRD4-7R* were both the most and least likely to develop attention deficit/hyperactive disorder (ADHD) compared to children carrying other alleles, depending on whether the mothers involved smoked cigarettes during pregnancy, or did not, respectively. Pluess et al. (2011) found that maternal anxiety in pregnancy predicted offspring negative emotionally at 6 months for infants with one or more copies of the short allele (*s*) of *5-HTTLPR*. In contrast, infants homozygous for the long allele (*l*) did not show this outcome. Therefore, certain genotypes in interaction with prenatal stress appear more susceptible to developing postnatal conditions.

Pluess et al. (2013) integrated epigenetic mechanisms in their interactive process model of differential susceptibility and developmental plasticity by referring to research by Oberlander et al. (2008). In that study, depressed maternal mood in pregnancy predicted increased epigenetic methylation of the glucocorticoid receptor gene (*NR3C1*), which itself predicted 3-month cortisol stress reactivity levels.

Pluess et al. (2013) concluded that susceptibility, plasticity, and related terms should be used instead of vulnerability, because differential susceptibility models expound that susceptibilities might lead to not only riskier development in nonsupportive environments but also to enhanced development in supportive environments in cases of carrying certain alleles. Also, resilience should be considered a general immunity to environmental influence in cases of carrying other alleles. In that sense, resilience might be a disadvantage in supportive environments. Clearly, the work in the area of differential environmental susceptibility has profound implications.

Environmental Sensitivity Pluess (2015) developed an integrated model of environmental sensitivity that covers work not only on differential susceptibility (Belsky & Pluess, 2009a) and

Table 13.1 Individual differences in environmental sensitivity vary with sensitivity genes and environmental quality

Environmental quality	Sensitivity gene	Sensitivity type
Supportive	Present	Vantage sensitivity (can profit phenotype more than otherwise)
Adverse	Present	Vulnerability (G × E; diathesis-stress)
Neutral	Absent	General sensitivity (to both negative and positive influences)
Any	Absent	Low sensitivity

Adapted from Pluess (2015)

biological sensitivity to context (Boyce & Ellis, 2005) but also the model of sensory processing sensitivity (Aron, 1996; Aron & Aron, 1997; Aron, Aron, & Jagiellowicz, 2012). He noted that individuals vary in environmental sensitivity, that is, in the way they perceive environmental features and process them (see Table 13.1). Variability in this regard might even reflect a higher-order personality dimension, which would be underwritten by neurobiological sensitivity, or neurosensitivity. High sensitivity in this aspect should characterize about 20–30 % of the population.

Ellis and Colleagues

Risk-Taking Ellis, Schlomer et al. (2012) used a differential sibling exposure design to investigate the role of fathers on risky sexual behavior in daughters. They found that older and younger sisters differed in the effects of quality of fathering on risky sexual behavior (RSB), especially in biologically-disrupted families with a large age gap between sister births (which maximizes differential father exposure to offspring). Low-quality paternal investment appeared causally related to RSB. Variations in the lower end of fathering quality affected RSB the most. Higher quality fathering helped buffer against RSB.

Ellis and Bjorklund (2012) further explored early risk-taking behavior. For example, in dangerous or unpredictable environments, a phenotypic option is to "grow up fast," "live it while you can," etc., which might translate into conduct difficulties, illicit drug use, and teen pregnancy (e.g., Belsky et al., 2012). From an evolutionary standpoint, this risky-behavior phenotypic strategy in adverse environments might be an optimal tradeoff in terms of survival and reproduction, given the probability of a shorter lifespan and uncertain future.

Ellis and Bjorklund (2012) considered maladaptive developmental plasticity in light of their evolutionary stance. Natural selection has favored developmental plasticity and, in turn, it plays a critical role in evolution, being the "creation force" behind evolutionary change. Developmental plasticity allows for extended growth opportunities but, at the same time, is constrained by genetically-influenced reaction norms. Part of developmental plasticity as honed by evolution is that offspring as they develop have been selected for sensitivity to the environment (some differentially so), allowing better adaptation in their environments when the environments reflect ancestral ones, because more likely than not the strategy is based on a reliable prediction and the strategy had been selected in our evolutionary past.

As reviewed by Ellis and Bjorklund (2012), Frankenhuis and Del Giudice (2012) proposed that developmental mechanisms might lead to maladaptive outcomes in three ways: (a) risky behavior that might be adaptively fit in some circumstances could have negative outcomes for some individuals; (b) environments could change in development, rendering previously positive behaviors no longer adaptive; and (c) early developing behaviors that developed due to accurate recognition of environmental cues no longer are matched to the environment because the cue recognition is no longer accurate. Gluckman and Beedle (2012) added that a mismatch between an individual and niche might derive because of environmental changes for an entire species (species-wide environmental novelty) as opposed to individual developmental mismatch.

Physiology Ellis and Bjorklund (2012) moved on to evaluate from a psychological perspective possible mechanisms involved in life history

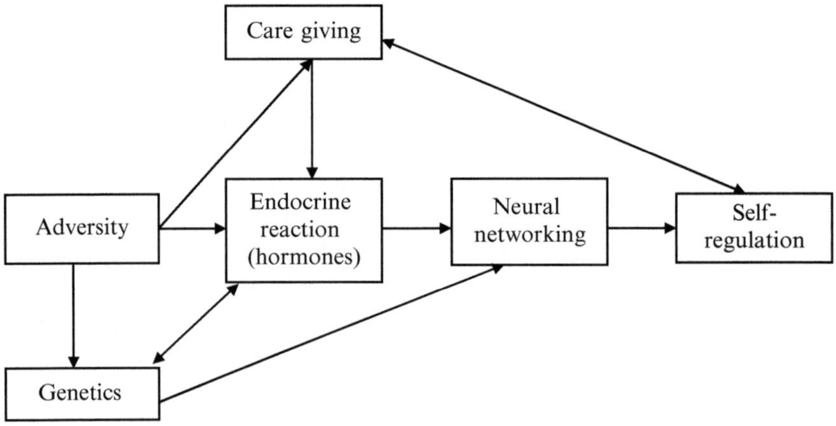

Fig. 13.4 Model of the experiential canalization of self-regulation development. Both distal and proximal influences participate in causal outcome. Adapted from Blair and Raver (2012)

strategy choice. Del Giudice, Ellis, and Shirtcliff (2011) had developed a model of individual differences in stress responsivity from an evolutionary-developmental perspective that linked stress-responsivity individual differences to life history strategy individual differences. In this adaptive calibration model, an individual's stress-responsive physiology is associated or matched with local environmental conditions and, in the early years, danger and unpredictability are the environmental cues to which development of stress reactivity is keyed. Given these individual differences in baseline physiological activities depending on context, life history is primed toward different slower or faster life history strategies. In particular, low compared to high family stress contributes to these differential strategies (Del Giudice, Hinnant, Ellis, & El-Sheikh, 2012). The work of Blair and Raver (2012) related stress-responsive physiology to reactive and reflective regulation and the prefrontal cortex (PFC; see Fig. 13.4).

Conclusions

Ellis and Bjorklund (2012) concluded that their developmental/evolutionary approach is an interactive one that excludes genetic determinism and that, at the same time, includes space for individual differences. They considered their model a metatheory in which natural selection is seen to favor developmental plasticity and that what evolves are developmental systems, in which genes are expressed differentially in different environments. Evolutionary models help understand individual differences in behavior and their prediction. Moreover, they help explain the adaptive value of more proximal mechanisms, such as physiological ones, that undergird the developmental systems and individual differences involved.

Sturge-Apple et al. (2012) presented a comparable model to the differential susceptibility model. As applied to temperament, Hawk-type individuals (e.g., approach, dominance, bold, aggressive, impulsive, risk-prone) raised in harsh (maternal) discipline rearing conditions were found to have a basal physiological activity (e.g., heightened parasympathetic nervous system and cortisol responsivity) primed for fight-flight responses to adversity. In contrast, Dove-type individuals (e.g., avoidance, inhibition, shy, unaggressive, risk adversive) had a basal physiology that appeared to prepare for vigilance, orienting, and inhibitory control. Over time, Hawks developed more externalizing behavior and Doves more internalizing behavior.

Extensions

Ellis and Del Giudice (2014) described further their adaptive calibration model (ACM) of stress-health relations. They contrasted it with the allostatic load (AL) model. ACM (Del Giudice et al., 2011) describes a broad theory of individual differences in stress-related health outcomes based on integration of life history theory (Belsky et al., 1991) and the AL model (McEwen & Stellar, 1993). The ACM mode)l is embedded in the evolutionary perspective, in which adaptation refers to the selective promoting of appropriate matches of phenotype to niche for purposes of Darwinian survival and reproduction, rather than adaptation referring to the public health concept of "desirable" outcome.

In ACM,)development programming takes place in the calibration of the stress response system to local environmental conditions. When the environment is adverse early, it promotes "fast"-track life history strategies (e.g., risky behavior, early reproduction; biological fitness tradeoffs) compared to a more long-term "slow" life history strategy facilitated in less aversive environments. The AL model does not deal with long-term adaptive changes in biobehavioral systems, given its focus on disease outcome, unlike the case for the ACM. In ACM and related models, fast life histories are accompanied by short-term instabilities and also by long-term disadvantages relative to a slow approach, but they make the best of a bad situation.

Ellis and Del Giudice (2014) continued that evolution favors adaptive phenotypic and developmental plasticity in an Organism × Environment structured interaction. This type of interaction permits individuals to better keep track of their environments as they develop and to adjust commensurately their growing phenotypes (West-Ebehard, 2003). Therefore, in the evolutionary-developmental approach, stressful rearing environments, no matter the degree and duration, serve to regulate physiological systems toward set points and patterns of reactivity that have adaptive functions (Ellis et al., 2011; Ellis, Del Giudice, et al., 2012).

As the organism adjusts to reading present environmental conditions, it is also predicting and preparing for future environments, given that, in evolutionary history, encountered environments generally are stable. However, this conditional adaptation might not predict well in some contexts, leading to mismatch and maladaptation. The mismatch might be due either to novel contemporary environments that differ relative to past ones encountered in the evolution of the species or due to the incorrect prediction of future environments from contemporary cues earlier in life. The stress response system serves as the physiological system that receives and embeds the cues sensed earlier in life, and it becomes altered in ways consonant with the cues so sensed and also anticipated.

In terms of set points and reactivity patterns, and their recalibrations, the mediating role of the stress response system in "coordinating" development of alternative fast or slow life history strategies is crucia)l in ACM. Ellis and Del Giudice (2014) explained that heightened stress responsivity in dangerous, unpredictable environments is quite adaptive in the circumstances for purposes of Darwinian adaptation. The health costs of constant stress response system activation are counterbalanced in a tradeoff by an improved detection management of possible danger. The fast-track, reproductive strategy that is entailed optimally counterbalances long-term health risks in the dangerous, unpredictable environment involved. Overreponse to potential danger might be costly but is necessary, and, as with the analogy of smoke detectors, this behavioral regime is not dysregulated or dysfunctional.

For example, in early life maltreatment, children demonstrate an enhanced capacity to detect, to learn, and to remember relevant stimuli (Frankenhuis & de Weerth, 2013). Similarly, the behavioral problem that might result can be interpreted as adaptive in context (e.g., McCullough, Pedersen, Schroder, Tabak, & Carver, 2013).

Rickard, Frankenhuis, and Nettle (2014) modified the psychosocial acceleration or life history model to include an internal state monitoring component. According to the model, in adverse environments, forecasting that the milieu will continue as negative leads to accelerated female maturation rate. However, Rickard et al. (2014) added that the mediating link might relate to monitoring of altered internal states associated with increased risk of morbidity/mortality, rather than any external state, per se, involved in leading to the noted accelerated maturation rate. Belsky (2014) considered this addition to his model as complementary and in the "evo-devo" framework to which he adheres.

Life History Theory

Gibbons et al. (2012) undertook research that combined the differential susceptibility model and psychosocial acceleration theory. They studied longitudinally African American adolescents. They found that higher stress in environments (e.g., low parental investment, racial discrimination) increased the probability of adopting faster life history strategies, with the opposite true for lower stress contexts. However, the results obtained only among study participants who carried more environmentally susceptible alleles. See Fig. 13.5 for a good summary of slow and fast like history strategies (adapted from Ellis, Del Giudice et al., 2012).

Additional research on psychosocial acceleration theory tackled the concept that developing individuals in early childhood are differentially responsive to environment type, and there might be genetic and sex differences involved as well as neurobiological indicators (Eisenberg et al., 2012; Sulik et al., 2012).

White, Li, Griskevicius, Neuberg, and Kenrick (2013) tested life-history strategy theory by examining indices of mortality threat (related to perceived crime), childhood socioeconomic status (SES), and diversification (e.g., in crop planting preferences having different payoffs). For those from low-SES backgrounds, mortality threat augmented bet-hedging diversification strategies (and a biomarker index of it, oxidative stress); but for those from high-SES backgrounds, the effect found was the opposite (diversification reduction, putting eggs in one basket, decreased bet-hedging). The authors concluded that people raised in poor compared to wealthy backgrounds perceive adult mortality threat differentially according to perceived control and predictability.

Research on life history strategies is specifying its drivers and effects. Mittal and Griskevicius (2014) related fast strategies in financially poor populations to exposure to uncertainty and to lower sense of control over the environment in childhood. They did not find equivalent results of the effects of uncertainty/sense of control in individuals from wealthier environments. Among the proxy measures of fast strategies were delay of gratification/impulsivity and persistence. The authors concluded the life history strategy models have had a gap in describing adequate mechanisms that could account for the differential effects of fast and slow strategies, and the ones postulated are plausible drivers in this regard.

Sherman, Figueredo, and Funder (2013) argued that their data on personality differences in slow and fast life history strategies do not implicate that the former is more adaptive than the latter. Each style is adaptive to different environments, with positive and negative personality attributes evident in both. In particular, in their analysis of archival data and also observed behavior, the slow strategy was associated with being considerate, kind, hard-working, and reliable. However, also it was associated with being socially awkward, insecure, and overcontrolling. In contrast, the fast strategy was associated with talkativeness, social skill, dominance, and charm, aside from behavior that is unpredictable, hostile, manipulative, and impulsive.

Sheskin, Chevallier, Lambert, and Baumard (2014) used life history theory to explain the apparent earlier emergence of social evaluation, which can be found in infants (e.g., Hamlin, Ullman, Tenenbaum, Goodman, & Barker, 2013) and the apparent later emergence of moral motivation and behavior, which can be found in 3-year-olds. The former helps in responding to and obtaining appropriate secure caregiving, while the latter helps in the transition to the wide social world. The argument proposed indicates that, in life history theory, each developmental epoch can be analyzed for the adaptive advantages in an evolutionary sense of modal behavior.

FASTER	AREA	SLOWER
	Physiology	
Faster	Development Rates	Slower
Earlier	Puberty Onset	Later
Faster	Aging (Biological)	Slower
	Mating Behavior	
Earlier	Sexual debut	Later
More	Sexual partners	Fewer
Casual	Relationships	Pair bond
	Parenting Behavior	
Earlier	Reproduction Age	Later
Higher	Offspring Number	Fewer
Lower	Offspring Investment	Higher
	Economic Behavior	
Short	Time horizon	Long
Seek	Immediate gratification	Delay
Take	Risk losses for big gains	Avoid

Fig. 13.5 Faster versus slower life history strategies. Like history theory depicts faster and slower life course trajectories, depending of resources and their forecast. In the faster relative to the slower mode, physiology accelerates, mating takes place earlier, parenting is variable, and the psychology of economics is more immediate and riskier. Adapted from Ellis, Del Giudice et al. (2012)

In a G×E (Gene×Environment) study, Beach et al. (2014) investigated the association of the promoter region of the *5-HTTLPR* (solute carrier family C6, member 4 [*SLC6A4*] linked polymorphic region) with epigenetic susceptibility/vulnerability in socioeconomically at-risk African American youth (age 19). In the sample studied, the short allele (that has 12 copies of the long variant compared to 14 of a 22 base pair repeat element for the long allele) in the promoter region of the serotonin transporter genotype was found to moderate the negative effect of early SES adversity on epigenetic methylated change in the CpG sites involved in the depression pathway.

The results supported a differential susceptibility (Belsky & Pluess, 2009a), for better/for worse pattern, compared to a diathesis (for "worse") one of the effects of the allele involved.

Del Giudice (2014a, 2014b) applied life history evolutionary theory to psychopathology. There are fast and slow life history strategies that have been postulated, and they seem associated with "fast" spectrum and "slow" spectrum psychopathology. In supportive environments, risk-aversive, slow strategies are favored (e.g., pair-bonding). In this strategy, resources are allocated in a way consistent with the forecast that a constructive environment (e.g., without physical abuse) will continue. Behavioral inhibition is promoted, facilitating the slow strategies. However, fast life history strategies are promoted in environments that early on are unfavorable for slow strategies and associated resource allocation.

The consequence of fast life history strategies is that they could lead to the development of disorders such as schizophrenia, bipolar disorder, borderline personality disorder, and depression with somatic symptoms. There are dangers for psychopathology when the slow life history strategy leads to too much inhibition, among other vulnerabilities. The disorders that might arise in this regard are autism and depression without somatic symptoms. Del Giudice (2014a, 2014b) concluded that the fast–slow life style distinction might be a better way to classify psychopathology in broad strokes than the internalizing–externalizing one.

Recent Research

Supportive Research

5-HTTLPR Sumner, McLaughlin, Walsh, Sheridan, and Koenen (2015) tested the differential susceptibility model compared to the diathesis-stress model using a theory-driven confirmatory approach. In a study of adolescents, they investigated whether the *5-HTTLPR* genotype moderated the effect of self-reported early maternal care giving (e.g., critical, concerned) on a test of autonomic nervous system (ANS) stress reactivity. A goal of the study was to determine the underlying mechanisms in differential susceptibility—if a genomic allele confers susceptibility in a better or worse fashion (G×E interaction), depending on the quality of the environment—what is the relatively immediate effect physiologically of the allele involved that can effect, in turn, the behavioral differences found?

In the study, the adolescents ($N=113$) were 14.8 years of age. To measure early care giving, the study used the CECA interview (Childhood Experience of Care and Abuse; Bifulco, Brown, & Harris, 1994). To measure ANS reactivity, it used the TSST (Trier Social Stress Test; Kudielka, Hellhammer, & Kirschbaum, 2007). The TSST involves recording ECG (electrocardiogram) and cardiac impedance in each of three 5-minute periods involving speech—preparation, giving the speech, and post-speech mental subtraction in front of evaluators. Blood pressure also was recorded. In the TSST, the SNS (sympathetic nervous system) could activate either with increased cardiac output (CO) and decreased vascular resistance (TPR; total peripheral vascular resistance) or with the opposite (termed the challenge/approach or threat/withdrawal responses, respectively).

The short allele (*s*) of *5-HTTLPR* is a polymorphism in the serotonin transporter gene promoter. Compared to the long allele (*l*), it is associated with reduced serotonergic function (having less serotonin transporter protein available). The differential susceptibility model for this polymorphism lies with having one or more of the *s* alleles (*ss*/*sl*, vs. *ll*).

The confirmatory approach of Belsky, Pluess, and Widaman (2013) was used to test the differential susceptibility model vs. the diathesis-stress model. It involved employing a reparameterized regression model. Depending where the points on the regression lines for the gene groups cross on the care giving variable (X), the G×E interaction would be disordinal or ordinal (supporting the differential susceptibility or diathesis-stress model, respectively). In testing the strong version of the differential susceptibility model, the slope for X for *ll* carriers was constrained to zero. That is, in the strong version of the model, *ll* carriers are not affected anywhere in the range in care giving. In contrast, in the weak model, *ll* carriers can be affected by care giving, but to a lesser extent than carriers with one or more *s* alleles.

The results of the study supported the strong differential susceptibility model, in particular, especially during the speech phase of the TSST. That is *ss/sl* carriers having reported higher-quality early care manifested on the TSST approach-type responsivity during the speech component. In contrast, low-quality care giving for these carriers was associated with withdrawal type responses. Individuals without the susceptibility allele (*ll*) were not affected by care giving.

Sumner et al. (2015) concluded that ANS reactivity might be a plausible intermediate phenotype between variation in *5-HTTLPR* and individual differences in behavior related to it, such as depression. However, the cross-sectional, retrospective nature of the study precluded arriving at firm conclusions about causality.

Li, Berk, and Lee (2013) researched G × E in adolescent depression, finding a differential susceptibility effect (Belsky & Pluess, 2009a). They found that both negative and positive environmental conditions can influence "susceptible" alleles of certain genes associated with problematic behavior. Specifically, they examined longitudinally youth beginning between 12 and 20 years of age in three waves (on average, at ages 15, 16, and 22 years, respectively; $N = 1030$). Indices of depression, suicidality, and family support were based on responses to self-report questionnaires.

In their study, Li et al. (2013) found that the 44-base pair polymorphism in the *5-HTTLPR* was associated with family support in influence on the outcome measures. Specifically, aside from main effects of family support (cohesion, communication, warmth), the study found a G × E interaction effect for boys involving the short (*s*) (vs. long, *l*) allele of *5-HTTLPR*. Having at least one short allele of the gene (in comparison to boys with two *l* alleles), as well as having poor family support, was associated in the boys with more depressive symptoms and a greater risk of suicide attempts. In contrast, high family support in these gene carriers led to the fewest depressive symptoms (but not fewest suicide attempts). Li et al. (2013) concluded that the *s* allele of *5-HTTLPR* confers increased reactivity to family influences, whether positive or negative, in the development of depression in youth. This pattern fits the differential susceptibility model.

South and Krueger (2013) found evidence in support of the differential environment susceptibility model in the relationship between marital satisfaction and physical health. They studied married twin pairs, and variation in self-reported health was greatest for marital satisfaction for both high and low levels (as measured by heritability estimates). They implicated the *5-HTTLPR* polymorphism as the genetic moderator that might be involved in the results.

DRD4 Berry, Deater-Deckard, McCartney, Wang, and Petrill (2013) studied the interaction between the dopamine receptor *DRD4* 7-repeat polymorphism and early maternal sensitivity as predictors of pathways to the development of inattention in middle childhood.

Berry et al. (2013) examined one polymorphism within the *DRD4*, a 48 base pair dopamine receptor gene (bp) variable number tandem repeat (VNTR) in region exon III, because it has been associated with childhood attention difficulties. The 7-repeat variant is one of the major variants in this locus, and dopamine D4 receptors are quite present in the prefrontal cortex, with the 7-repeat marker apparently implicated in reducing D4 receptor expression in the brain region.

The authors investigated the differential environmental susceptibility model in relation to the 7-repeat variant of the 48 bp VNTR polymorphism in the above-mentioned *DRD4* gene (Belsky & Pluess, 2009a; Boyce & Ellis, 2005). Specifically, they posited that adversity in context (e.g., low-quality early child care) affects negatively attention-problem trajectories in children with the *DRD4* 7-repeat polymorphism; however, the inverse obtains for high quality maternal caregiving for those with the *DRD4* 7-repeat. That is, over time, they will manifest better attention and related skills. The time frames examined involved infancy and early childhood, and then the period from pre-kindergarten to grade 5.

Berry et al. (2013) examined longitudinal data gathered in an NICHD study of 711 children and families (National Institute of Child Health and Human Development). The methods were comprehensive. Maternal sensitivity was rated during mother–offspring interactions at 6, 15, 24, and 36 months, and again at the pre-kindergarten and grade 1, 3, and 5 levels. The observations involved a semi-structured play procedure adjusted to developmental level, and a composite score was derived. As for inattention, both observational and questionnaire data were used to create composite scores (e.g., Teacher Report Form, TRF items, Achenbach, 1991). Control variables included those related to maternal prenatal smoking (estimated), maternal personality, and maternal depression.

The results revealed the proposed cross-over effect, in that, in association with early insensitive maternal ratings, the *DRD4* 7-repeat polymorphism was found to be associated with higher levels of childhood inattention. In contrast, the association of sensitive care and the polymorphism involved lower levels of inattention, although less clearly. The results are consistent with the model of differential susceptibility. As for developmental changes, the degree of the absolute genetic effect shown increased with age, in that the developmental inattention trajectories increasingly diverged, and in that early compared to later maternal sensitivity proved partially important for inattention development.

5-HTTLPR & DRD4 For antisocial behavior, Lei, Simons, Edmond, Simons, and Cutrona (2014) found a complex relationship among environmental disadvantage, social network support, and genetic variation in adult African American women. The genetic moderators included the *5-HTT* gene (*5-HTTLPR*) and the *DRD4* involved in the dopaminergic neurotransmitter system. To review, for *5-HTTLPR*, the short allele (*s*) contains 14 repeats of a 20–22 base pair unit in the 5′ promoter region; the long (*l*) one contains 16 repeats. In carriers, the short allele, relative to the long allele, is associated with reduced serotonin transporter expression and antisocial and related behavior, relative to the long allele. For *DRD4*, the gene has a functional polymorphism of a 48 base-pair unit that typically is grouped into a short (2–6 repeats) group and a long (7–9) one. In this case, the long allele is the one that is at-risk, being associated with less efficient transcription and antisocial-related behavior. For both at-risk genes, the polymorphisms do not express direct effects on antisocial behavior because they interact with adverse environmental conditions (e.g., Barnes & Jacobs, 2013). In their methods, Lei et al. (2014) constructed a combined *5-HTTLPR/DRD4* allelic risk score.

Lei et al. (2014) hypothesized that not only environmental diversity but also social support/network ties need to be considered in establishing the possible effects of at-risk alleles for antisocial-related behavior. They studied 397 female respondents in a study of neighborhood and family effects on health and development in the African American population. For the result critical to the present analysis, they found that the effects of neighborhood disadvantage and of social ties on antisocial behavior were moderated by the alleles studied. In particular, the at-risk alleles were associated with higher rates of antisocial behavior in adverse neighborhood circumstances, but lower rates in advantaged neighborhoods, however, only if strong social ties were present, too. The findings are consistent with a differential susceptibility model of G×E interaction, although I would add that the effect found is more like G×G×E×E, although not quite so. Susceptibility genes could lead to positive outcomes compared to other genetic variants in more positive/supportive environments, aside from any findings related to them in adverse environments (Ellis et al., 2011).

COMT Sulik et al. (2015) studied the relationship between variants of *COMT* in relation to parenting quality at 18 months of age and to later inhibitory and attention control (assessed at 42, 54, 72, and 84 months) as well as to internalizing symptoms (at 24, 30, 42, 48, and 54 months) in 146 children (79 male). Of the three variants studied, $Val^{158}Met$ [*rs4680* = $Val^{158}Met$] proved the most informative in explaining outcome variance. Each of the variants was involved in significant three-way interactions, with sex and parenting, especially for inhibitory control and for internalizing symptoms. [The other two variants were intron 1′ [*rs737865*] and 3′-untranslated region [*rs165599*]. *COMT* is involved in neurotransmitter activity, and $Val^{158}Met$ is involved in lower *COMT* efficiency.] The specific results are complex, but supported a differential susceptibility model (Pluess & Belsky, 2013). For example, $Val^{158}Met$ appeared associated with internalizing symptoms in conditions of lack of supportive parenting, but its association with inhibitory control was apparent in conditions of supportive parenting.

The supportive research of differential susceptibility compared to diathesis-stress modeling in G×E interactions shows that the effect works not only for internalizing-related behaviors in children, but also for externalizing ones even for the same genetic polymorphism. In this regard, for *COMT rs4680* and the $Val^{158}Met$ polymorphism, Hygen et al. (2015) showed that this polymorphism reveals a G×E interaction effect for teacher-rated aggression that fits the differential susceptibility model, when it is examined in conjunction with a history of serious life events, as in their study of community-based children of 55 months of age. Specifically, regression analyses showed no main effects for either the *COMT* genotype or serious life events on the aggression variable, but there was a significant interaction effect of the former two variables on the outcome variable. That is, Val/Val homozygotes together with the children have experienced many serious life events was a combination related to more aggression on the measure used compared to the findings for other *COMT* polymorphisms. Also, the polymorphism in conjunction with no history of serious life events was associated with lower aggression scores compared to the findings for the other polymorphisms. In short, the authors noted that the differential susceptibility model is supported more so than a simple vulnerability model to negative life experiences for the *COMT* genotype (Val/Val polymorphism) and its effects on childhood aggression.

GABRA2 The GABRA2 gene codes for the alpha-2 subunit of the receptor of the neurotransmitter GABA-2A, and the receptors are expressed primary in the amygdala and motor areas. Therefore, allelic variants that allow for increased activity in these areas are associated with increased emotional responsiveness/sensitivity to context.

In a prospective study of externalizing behavior trajectories, especially over ages 11–17, Trucco, Villafuerte, Heitzeg, Burmeister, and Zucker (2015) examined genetic variants of GABRA2 (*rs279807*, *rs279826*, *rs279858*) in relation to parental knowledge of adolescents' ($N = 504$) peer group, their whereabouts, and their expectations about time spent outside the home (and the adolescents disclosure of this information to their parents). Externalizing behavior was measured using the YSR (Youth Self-Report; Achenbach & Rescorla, 2001). As for the results of the study, those with the minor (G–G) genotype were affected by the parental monitoring in a better or worse fashion, fitting the differential susceptibility model, unlike those who were A carriers. That is, adolescents with the GG genotype and at low parental knowledge/disclosure (monitoring) were more likely to belong to higher risk externalizing classes, but the opposite was found for GG adolescents at high monitoring. Trucco et al. (2015) concluded that the results do not support a diathesis-stress model but the differential susceptibility one.

Multigenic Boyce and Kobor (2015) related the differential susceptibility effect to the working of epigenesis. In this regard, they referred to "individual variation in epigenetic susceptibility." Research is implicating genetic polymorphisms as "sources" of differential susceptibility.

Although the research cited by Boyce and Kobor (2015) are not directly on epigenesis, the studies speak to the issues, for example, through the early stressors in the life of the participants, which are known to induce epigenetic modifications. In this regard, consider that Bush, Guendelman, Adler, and Boyce (2014) found that the *BDNF* $Val^{66}Met$ polymorphism is related to SES context, with Met-carriers expressing both the highest and lowest cortisol levels, depending on SES level. Babineau et al. (2014) found that children having the *s* and *l*G (an *l* allele variant functioning like *s*) alleles of the gene *5-HTT* in conjunction with exposure to prenatal maternal depression had more behavioral/cognitive dysregulation, in contrast to children without the exposure, who had more such regulatory capacity. Bogdan, Agrawal, Gaffrey, Tillman, and Luby (2014) found a risk allele × stress exposure interaction in a differential manner for depressive symptoms in 3-year-old preschoolers. Children with the risk allele of *5-HTTLPR* had either the most or least depressive symptoms, depending on the degree of exposure to stress. More directly on the question, Beach et al. (2014) found the differential susceptibility pattern for cumulative SES adversity in a sample of African American youth from working poor communities, for the *5-HTT s* allele and for methylation of a group of depression-related genes.

Boyce and Kobor (2015) concluded that epigenetic chromatin modification by environmental conditions, and the marks that they leave that endure, serve as "actual" molecular mechanisms in promoting the differential susceptibility effect. Whether children are more resilient or susceptible to factors such as early adversity might depend not only on the presence of certain susceptibility alleles (for good or for bad outcomes, depending) but also on the epigenetic modifications to which they are susceptible.

Nonsupportive Research

Not all research supports the differential susceptibility. For example, in the development of preschooler disruptive problems, Davies, Cicchetti, and Hentges (2014) reported a G × E interaction involving a genetic composite of *DAT1* susceptibility alleles (*rs27072*, *rs40184*) and unresponsive maternal caregiving. The two alleles are single nucleotide polymorphisms (SNPs) located on exon 15 (*rs27072*) and intron 14 (*rs40184*) locations of the 3′ UTR regions of the *DAT1*. *DAT1* is involved in dopamine regulation especially in the mesolimbic reward circuit. The CC genotype constitutes the susceptibility allele. Uninhibited temperament served as the upstream behavioral mediation in the effect. The results were more consistent with a diathesis-stress model (Beauchaine & Gatzke-Kopp, 2012) rather than a differential susceptibility one (Belsky & Pluess, 2009a) in that the risk allele in conjunction with lack of unresponsive maternal caregiving had no effect on the results.

Conclusion

Note that the diathesis-stress and differential susceptibility models might explain different vulnerabilities to psychopathology, or behavioral disturbance, even in the same study (e.g., Hastings et al., 2014; Nederhof, Belsky, Ormel, & Oldehinkel, 2012). Moreover, the methodologies needed to support one model relative to the other are becoming more rigorous (Bakermans-Kranenburg & van IJzendoorn, 2015). Hastings et al. (2014) concluded that multilevel models are needed to understand the complexity involved. Bakermans-Kranenburg and van IJzendoorn (2015) indicated new paradigms are needed (e.g., G × Ee; the e representing experimental intervention).

van IJzendoorn and Bakermans-Kranenburg (2015) conducted a meta-analysis of differential susceptibility research involving randomized control trials (RCTs). They included studies in the special issue on the topic (Belsky & van IJzendoorn, 2015), only some of which are mentioned individually in the following.

van IJzendoorn and Bakermans-Kranenburg (2015) referred to G × E studies involving RCTs as Gene × Experimental Environment interaction studies (which I simplify to G × Eexp). They referred to the model of differential susceptibility to the environment as the model of genetic differential susceptibility. They noted the advantages of RCTs in this type of study as helping in providing causal evidence.

van IJzendoorn and Bakermans-Kranenburg (2015) found 22 studies with an accumulative *N* of 3257 that compared the effect size of the experimental manipulation (relative to controls) involved. For participants carrying susceptibility alleles (e.g., *DRD4* 7-repeat; short, *s*, variant of *5-HTT*) compared to those without them (*DRD4* 4-repeat; *5-HTT* long, *l*, respectively), they queried whether the results differed according to ethnicity, type of intervention, e.g., nano vs. programmatic, and behavioral outcome (e.g., externalizing, internalizing). The authors noted that limited number of studies in the area do not exclude significant results being found later when the cumulative *N*s involved as the research accumulates permit more statistical power.

The results of the meta-analysis conducted by van IJzendoorn and Bakermans-Kranenburg (2015) on G×Eexp supported the genetic differential susceptibility model in RCT research. The combined effect size of the interventions for the susceptibility genotypes was significant, but it was not for the nonsusceptible ones. This was especially true for the dopamine-related genes (*DRD4*) and not the serotonin ones (*5-HTT*), and for programmatic ("macro") trials.

Generally, the results in the field appear to support a strong version of differential susceptibility (nonsusceptible genotype carriers are not affected by the environmental effect; in the weak version of the model, individuals are affected differentially). van IJzendoorn and Bakermans-Kranenburg (2015) concluded that the vantage sensitivity version of the differential susceptibility model is incomplete in that it only considers the positive susceptibility component of the effects found in the research.

Belsky and van IJzendoorn (2015) dealt with the ethically difficult issue of whether the results in the field indicate that interventions should be reserved only for those with susceptibility genotypes. They noted that nonsusceptible individuals in any one study still might be susceptible to the positive effects of other interventions. This suggests that differential susceptibility might be a question of degree rather than kind or type.

In the special series on G×Eexp, as examples, Brett et al. (2015) conducted a study on *5-HTT*, early care giving, and externalizing behavior at 54 months, and Brody, Yu, and Beach (2015) conducted one on *DRD4*, family risk, and drug use in adolescents. Chen et al. (2015) conducted a study with *BDNF*, maternal anxiety, and neonatal brain volumes, to which I refer because of its lateralization findings (see the study for details—briefly it is consistent with neonatal hemispheric specialization in the adult direction for emotional function, aside from the differential susceptibility findings).

Chapter Conclusions

The work in differential susceptibility and related modeling is relatively new, yet it is gathering much influence and import in the field of developmental psychology and beyond. It is notable for its integration of developmental, evolutionary, physiological, and psychopathological mechanisms. As well, its emphasis of susceptible alleles having multiple phenotypic outcomes depending on environment-related underpinnings is powerful. It allows for optimal and reduced risk in development in the presence of supportive environments for certain critical alleles that otherwise are associated with negative developmental outcomes in nonsupportive or adverse environments. The understanding of the plasticity involved in the behavioral variability described by developmental susceptibility and related models, and the mechanisms underlying them, augurs well for a more nuanced appreciation of individual differences in behavior and their developmental and evolutionary underpinnings. These models help to bloom psychology in important directions, to follow up on the orchid-dandelion metaphor that so well represents them (dandelions can grow anywhere; orchids need supportive contexts).

References

Achenbach, T. M. (1991). *Integrative guide for the 1991 CBCL/4-18, YSR, and TRF profiles*. Burlington, VT: University of Vermont, Department of Psychiatry.

Achenbach, T. M., & Rescorla, L. (2001). *Manual for the ASEBA school-age forms & profiles*. Burlington, VT: University of Vermont, Research Center for Children, Youth, & Families.

Aron, E. N. (1996). *The highly sensitive person: How to thrive when the world overwhelms you*. New York: Broadway Books (Rev. ed).

Aron, E. N., & Aron, A. (1997). Sensory-processing sensitivity and its relation to introversion and emotionality. *Journal of Personality and Social Psychology, 73*, 345–368.

Aron, E. N., Aron, A., & Jagiellowicz, J. (2012). Sensory processing sensitivity: A review in the light of the evolution of biological responsivity. *Personality and Social Psychology Review, 16*, 262–282.

Babineau, V., Gordon Green, C., Jolicoeur-Marineau, A., Minde, K., Sassi, R., St-André, M., et al. (2014). Prenatal depression and 5-HTTLPR interact to predict dysregulation from 3 to 36 months: A differential susceptibility model. *Journal of Child Psychology and Psychiatry, and Allied Disciplines, 56*, 21–29.

Bakermans-Kranenburg, M. J., & van IJzendoorn, M. H. (2006). Gene-environment interaction of the dopamine D4 receptor (DRD4) and observed maternal insensitivity predicting externalizing behavior in preschoolers. *Developmental Psychobiology, 48*, 406–409.

Bakermans-Kranenburg, M., & van IJzendoorn, M. H. (2007). Genetic vulnerability or differential susceptibility in child development: The case of attachment [Research review]. *Journal of Child Psychology and Psychiatry, 48*, 1160–1173.

Bakermans-Kranenburg, M. J., & van IJzendoorn, M. H. (2015). The hidden efficacy of interventions: Gene × environment experiments from a differential susceptibility perspective. *Annual Review of Psychology, 66*, 381–409.

Barnes, J. C., & Jacobs, B. A. (2013). Genetic risk for violent behavior and environmental exposure to disadvantage and violence crime: The case for gene-environment interaction. *Journal of Interpersonal Violence, 18*, 92–120.

Beach, S. R. H., Brody, G. H., Lei, M. K., Kim, S., Cui, J., & Philibert, R. A. (2014). Is serotonin transporter genotype associated with epigenetic susceptibility or vulnerability? Examination of the impact of socioeconomic status risk of African American youth. *Development and Psychopathology, 26*, 289–304.

Beauchaine, T. P., & Gatzke-Kopp, L. M. (2012). Instantiating the multiple levels of analysis perspective in a program of study on externalizing behavior. *Development and Psychopathology, 24*, 1003–1018.

Belsky, J. (1997a). Variation in susceptibility to rearing influences: An evolutionary argument. *Psychological Inquiry, 8*, 182–186.

Belsky, J. (1997b). Theory testing, effect-size evaluation, and differential susceptibility to rearing influence: The case of mothering and attachment. *Child Development, 68*, 598–600.

Belsky, J. (2000). Conditional and alternative reproductive strategies: Individual differences in susceptibility to rearing experience. In J. Rodgers, D. Rowe, & W. Miller (Eds.), *Genetic influences on human fertility and sexuality: Theoretical and empirical contributions from the biological and behavioral sciences* (pp. 127–146). Boston: Kluwer.

Belsky, J. (2005). Differential susceptibility to rearing influences: An evolutionary hypothesis and some evidence. In B. Ellis & D. Bjorklund (Eds.), *Origins of the social mind: Evolutionary psychology and child development* (pp. 139–163). New York: Guilford Press.

Belsky, J. (2012). The development of human reproductive strategies: Progress and prospects. *Current Directions in Psychological Science, 21*, 310–316.

Belsky, J. (2014). Toward an evo-devo theory of reproductive strategy, health, and longevity: Commentary on Rickard et al. (2014). *Perspectives on Psychological Science, 9*, 16–18.

Belsky, J., Bakermans-Branenburg, M. J., & van IJzendoorn, M. H. (2007). For better and for worse: Differential susceptibility to environmental influences. *Current Directions in Psychological Science, 16*, 300–304.

Belsky, J., & Deaver, K. M. (2011). Cumulative-genetic plasticity, parenting and adolescent self-regulation. *Journal of Child Psychology and Psychiatry, 52*, 619–626.

Belsky, J., & Pluess, M. (2009a). Beyond diathesis stress: Differential susceptibility to environmental influences. *Psychological Bulletin, 135*, 885–908.

Belsky, J., & Pluess, M. (2009b). The nature (and nurture?) of plasticity in early human development. *Perspectives on Psychological Science, 4*, 345–351.

Belsky, J., & Pluess, M. (2013a). Beyond risk, resilience and dysregulation: Phenotypic plasticity and human development. *Development and Psychopathology, 25*, 1243–1261.

Belsky, J., & Pluess, M. (2013b). Genetic moderation of early child-care effects on social functioning across childhood: A developmental analysis. *Child Development, 84*, 1209–1225.

Belsky, J., Pluess, M., & Widaman, K. F. (2013). Confirmatory and competitive evaluation of alternative gene-environment interaction hypotheses. *Journal of Child Psychology and Psychiatry, 54*, 1135–1143.

Belsky, J., Ruttle, P. L., Boyce, W. T., Armstrong, J. M., & Essex, M. J. (2015). Early adversity, elevated stress physiology, accelerated sexual maturation, and poor health in females. *Developmental Psychology, 51*, 816–22. doi:10.1037/dev0000017.

Belsky, J., Schlomer, G. L., & Ellis, B. J. (2012). Beyond cumulative risk: Distinguishing harshness and unpredictability as determinants of parenting and early life history strategy. *Developmental Psychology, 48*, 662–673.

Belsky, J., Steinberg, L., & Draper, P. (1991). Childhood experience, interpersonal development, and reproductive strategy: An evolutionary theory of socialization. *Child Development, 62*, 647–670.

Belsky, J., Steinberg, L., Houts, R. M., Halpern-Felsher, B. L., & The NICHD Early Child Care Research Network. (2010). The development of reproductive strategy in females: Early maternal harshness → earlier menarche → increased sexual risk taking. *Developmental Psychology, 46*, 120–128.

Belsky, J., & van IJzendoorn, M. H. (2015). What works for whom? Genetic moderation of intervention efficacy. *Development and Psychopathology, 27*, 1–6.

Berry, D., Deater-Deckard, K., McCartney, K., Wang, Z., & Petrill, S. A. (2013). Gene-environment interaction between dopamine receptor D4 7-repeat polymorphism and early maternal sensitivity predicts inattention trajectories across middle childhood. *Development and Psychopathology, 25*, 291–306.

Bevilacqua, L., Carli, V., Sarchiapone, M., George, D. K., Goldman, D., Roy, A., et al. (2012). Interaction between FKBP5 and childhood trauma and risk of aggressive behavior. *Archives of General Psychiatry, 69*, 62–70.

Bifulco, A., Brown, G. W., & Harris, T. O. (1994). Childhood Experiences of Care and Abuse (CECA): A retrospective interview measure. *Journal of Child Psychology and Psychiatry, 35*, 1419–1435.

Bjorklund, D. F., & Pellegrini, A. D. (2002). *The origins of human nature: Evolutionary developmental psychology*. Washington, DC: American Psychological Association.

Blair, C., & Raver, C. C. (2012). Individual development and evolution: Experiential canalization of self-regulation. *Developmental Psychology, 48*, 647–657.

Bogdan, R., Agrawal, A., Gaffrey, M. S., Tillman, R., & Luby, J. L. (2014). Serotonin transporter-linked polymorphic region (5-HTTLPR) genotype and stressful life events interact to predict preschool-onset depression: A replication and developmental extension. *Journal of Child Psychology and Psychiatry, 55*, 448–457.

Boyce, W. T., Chesney, M., Alkon, A., Tschann, J. M., Adams, S., Chesterman, B., et al. (1995). Psychobiological reactivity to stress and childhood respiratory illnesses: Results of two prospective studies. *Psychosomatic Medicine, 57*, 411–422.

Boyce, W. T., & Ellis, B. J. (2005). Biological sensitivity to context: I. An evolutionary-developmental theory of the origins and functions of stress reactivity. *Development and Psychopathology, 17*, 271–301.

Boyce, W. T., & Kobor, M. S. (2015). Development and the epigenome: The "synapse" of gene-environment interplay. *Developmental Science, 18*, 1–23.

Brett, Z. H., Humphreys, K. L., Smyke, A. T., Gleason, M. M., Nelson, C. A., Zeanah, C. H., et al. (2015). Serotonin transporter linked polymorphic region (5-HTTLPR) genotype moderates the longitudinal impact of early care giving on externalizing behavior. *Development and Psychopathology, 27*, 7–18.

Brody, G. H., Chen, Y., & Beach, S. R. H. (2013). Differential susceptibility to prevention: GABAergic, dopaminergic and multilocus effects. *Journal of Child Psychology and Psychiatry, 54*, 863–871.

Brody, G. H., Yu, T., & Beach, S. R. H. (2015). A differential susceptibility analysis reveals the "who and how" about adolescents' responses to preventive interventions: Tests of first- and second-generation gene-intervention hypotheses. *Development and Psychopathology, 27*, 37–49.

Bush, N., Guendelman, M., Adler, N., & Boyce, W. T. (2014, submitted). BDNF allelic variants moderate social disparities in children's basal cortisol expression.

Buss, D. M. (2011). *Evolutionary psychology: The new science of the mind* (4th ed.). Boston: Allyn & Bacon.

Cameron, N. M., Champagne, F. A., Parent, C., Fish, E. W., Ozaki-Kuroda, K., & Meaney, M. J. (2005). The programming of individual differences in defensive responses and reproductive strategies in the rat through variations in maternal care. *Neuroscience and Biobehavioral Reviews, 29*, 843–865.

Champagne, D. L., Bagot, R. C., van Hasselt, F., Ramakers, G., Meaney, M. J., de Kloet, E. R., et al. (2008). Maternal care and hippocampal plasticity: Evidence for experience-dependent structural plasticity, altered synaptic functioning, and differential responsiveness to glucocorticoids and stress. *Journal of Neuroscience, 28*, 6037–6045.

Chen, J., Li, X., & McGue, M. (2012). Interacting effect of BDNF Val66Met polymorphism and stressful life events on adolescent depression. *Genes, Brain, and Behavior, 54*, 1066–1073.

Chen, L., Pan, H., Tuan, T. A., Teh, A. L., MacIsaac, J. L., Mah, S. M., et al. (2015). Brain-derived neurotrophic factor (BDNF) Val66Met polymorphism influences the association of the methylome with maternal anxiety and neonatal brain volumes. *Development and Psychopathology, 27*, 137–150.

Chisholm, J. (1999). *Death, hope, and sex: Steps to an evolutionary ecology of mind and morality*. New York: Cambridge University Press.

Davies, P. T., Cicchetti, D., & Hentges, R. F. (2014). Maternal unresponsiveness and child disruptive problems: The interplay of uninhibited temperament and dopamine transporter genes. *Child Development, 86*, 63–79.

Del Giudice, M. (2014a). An evolutionary life history framework for psychopathology. *Psychological Inquiry, 25*, 261–300.

Del Giudice, M. (2014b). A tower unto heaven: Toward an expanded framework for psychopathology. *Psychological Inquiry, 25*, 394–413.

Del Giudice, M., Ellis, B. J., & Shirtcliff, E. A. (2011). The adaptive calibration model of stress responsivity. *Neuroscience and Biobehavioral Reviews, 35*, 1562–1592.

Del Giudice, M., Hinnant, J. B., Ellis, B. J., & El-Sheikh, M. (2012). Adaptive patterns of stress responsivity: A preliminary investigation. *Developmental Psychology, 48*, 775–790.

Dishion, T. J., Ha, T., & Véronneau, M.-H. (2012). An ecological analysis of the effects of deviant peer clustering on sexual promiscuity, problem behavior, and childbearing from early adolescence to adulthood: An enhancement of the life history framework. *Developmental Psychology, 48*, 703–717.

Eisenberg, N., Sulik, M. J., Spinrad, T. L., Edwards, A., Eggum, N. D., Liew, J., et al. (2012). Differential susceptibility and the early development of aggression:

Interactive effects of respiratory sinus arrhythmia and environmental quality. *Developmental Psychology, 48*, 755–768.

Ellis, B. J., & Bjorklund, D. F. (2012). Beyond mental health: An evolutionary analysis of develop under risky and supportive environmental conditions: An introduction to the special section. *Developmental Psychology, 48*, 591–597.

Ellis, B. J., Boyce, W. T., Belsky, J., Bakermans-Kranenburg, M. J., & van Iizendoorn, M. H. (2011). Differential susceptibility to the environment: An evolutionary-neurodevelopmental theory. *Development and Psychopathology, 23*, 7–28.

Ellis, B. J., & Del Giudice, M. (2014). Beyond allostatic load: Rethinking the role of stress in regulating human development. *Development and Psychopathology, 26*, 1–20.

Ellis, B. J., Del Giudice, M., Dishion, T. J., Figueredo, A. J., Gray, P., Griskevicius, V., et al. (2012). The evolutionary basis of risky adolescent behavior: Implications for science, policy, and practice. *Developmental Psychology, 48*, 598–623.

Ellis, B. J., Essex, M. J., & Boyce, W. T. (2005). Biological sensitivity to context: II. Empirical explorations of an evolutionary-developmental theory. *Development and Psychopathology, 17*, 183–187.

Ellis, B. J., Figueredo, A. J., Brumbach, B. H., & Schlomer, G. L. (2009). Fundamental dimensions of environmental risk: The impact of harsh versus unpredictable environments on the evolution and development of life history strategies. *Human Nature, 20*, 204–268.

Ellis, B. J., Schlomer, G. L., Tilley, E. H., & Butler, E. A. (2012). Impact of fathers on risky sexual behavior in daughters: A genetically and environmentally controlled sibling study. *Development and Psychopathology, 24*, 317–332.

Enoch, M. A., Steer, C. D., Newman, T. K., Gibson, N., & Goldman, D. (2010). Early life stress, MAOA, and gene-environment interactions predict behavioral disinhibition in children. *Genes, Brain, and Behavior, 9*, 65–74.

Frankenhuis, W. E., & de Weerth, C. (2013). Does early-life exposure to stress shape or impair cognition? *Current Directions in Psychological Science, 22*, 407–412.

Frankenhuis, W. E., & Del Giudice, M. (2012). When do adaptive developmental mechanisms yield maladaptive outcomes? *Developmental Psychology, 48*, 628–642.

Gibbons, F. X., Roberts, M. E., Gerrard, M., Li, Z., Beach, S. R., Simons, R. L., et al. (2012). The impact of stress on the life history strategies of African American adolescents: Cognitions, genetic moderation, and the role of discrimination. *Developmental Psychology, 48*, 643–646.

Gluckman, P. D., & Beedle, A. S. (2012). Match fitness: Development, evolution and behavior: Comment on Frankenhuis and Del Giudice (2012). *Developmental Psychology, 48*, 643–646.

Gluckman, P. D., Hanson, M. A., Cooper, C., & Thornburg, K. L. (2008). Effect of in utero and early-life conditions on adult health and disease. *New England Journal of Medicine, 359*, 61–73.

Grazioplene, R. G., DeYoung, C. G., Rogosch, F. A., & Cicchetti, D. (2013). A novel differential susceptibility gene: CHRNA4 and moderation of the effect of maltreatment on child personality. *Journal of Child Psychology and Psychiatry, 54*, 872–880.

Gunnar, M. R., Wenner, J. A., Thomas, K. M., Glatt, C. E., McKenna, M. C., & Clark, A. G. (2012). The brain-derived neurotrophic factor Val66Met polymorphism moderates early deprivation effects on attention problems. *Development and Psychopathology, 24*, 1215–1223.

Hamlin, J. K., Ullman, T., Tenenbaum, J., Goodman, N., & Barker, C. (2013). The mentalistic basis of core social cognition: Experiments in preverbal infants and a computational model. *Developmental Science, 16*, 209–226.

Hastings, P. D., Helm, J., Mills, R. S. L., Serbin, L. A., Stack, D. M., & Schwartzman, A. E. (2014). Dispositional and environmental predictors of the development of internalizing problems in childhood: Testing a multilevel model. *Journal of Abnormal Child Psychology*. doi:10.1007/s10802-014-9951-0.

Hygen, B. W., Belsky, J., Stenseng, F., Lydersen, S., Guzey, I. C., & Wichstrøm, L. (2015). Child exposure to serious life events, COMT, and aggression: Testing differential susceptibility theory. *Developmental Psychology*. doi:10.1037/dev0000020.

James, J., Ellis, B. J., Schlomer, G. L., & Garber, J. (2012). Sex-specific pathways to early puberty, sexual debut and sexual risk-taking: Tests of an integrated evolutionary-developmental model. *Developmental Psychology, 48*, 687–702.

Johansson, A., Bergman, H., Corander, J., Waldman, I. D., Karrani, N., Salo, B., et al. (2012). Alcohol and aggressive behavior in men – moderating effects of oxytocin receptor gene (OXTR) polymorphisms. *Genes, Brain, and Behavior, 11*, 214–221.

Knafo, A., Israel, S., & Ebstein, R. P. (2011). Heritability of children's prosocial behavior and differential susceptibility to parenting by variation in the dopamine receptor D4 gene. *Development and Psychopathology, 23*, 53–67.

Kochanska, G., Kim, S., Barry, R. A., & Philibert, R. A. (2011). Children's genotypes interact with maternal responsive care in predicting children's competence: Diathesis-stress or differential susceptibility? *Development Psychopathology, 23*, 605–616.

Kudielka, B. M., Hellhammer, D. H., & Kirschbaum, C. (2007). Ten years of research with the Trier Social Stress Test-Revised. In E. Harmon-Jones & P. Winkielman (Eds.), *Social neuroscience: Integrating biological and psychological explanation of social behavior* (pp. 56–83). New York: Guilford Press.

Laucht, M., Blomeyer, D., Buchmann, A. F., Treulein, J., Schmidt, M. H., Esser, G., et al. (2012). Catechol-O-methyltransferase Val158Met genotype, parenting practices and adolescent alcohol use: Testing and differential susceptibility hypothesis. *Journal of Child Psychology and Psychiatry, 53*, 351–359.

Lei, M.-K., Simons, R. L., Edmond, M. B., Simons, L. G., & Cutrona, C. E. (2014). The effect of neighborhood disadvantage, social ties, and genetic variation on the antisocial behavior of African American women: A multilevel analysis. *Development and Psychopathology, 26*, 1113–1128.

Li, J. J., Berk, M. S., & Lee, S. S. (2013). Differential susceptibility in longitudinal models of gene-environment interaction for adolescent depression. *Development and Psychopathology, 25*, 991–1003.

Manuck, S. B. (2010). The reaction norm in gene × environment interaction. *Molecular Psychiatry, 15*, 881–882.

McCullough, M. E., Pedersen, E. J., Schroder, J. M., Tabak, B. A., & Carver, C. S. (2013). Harsh childhood environmental characteristics predict exploitation and retaliation in humans. *Proceedings of the Royal Society B: Biological Science, 280*, 1750. doi:10.1098/rspb.2012.2104.

McEwen, B. S., & Stellar, E. (1993). Stress and the individual. Mechanisms leading to disease. *Archives of Internal Medicine, 153*, 2093–2101.

Mills-Koonce, W. R., Propper, C. B., Gariepy, J. L., Blair, C., Garrett-Peters, P., & Cox, M. J. (2007). Bidirectional genetic and environmental influences on mother and child behavior: The family system as the unit of analyses. *Development and Psychopathology, 19*, 1073–1087.

Mittal, C., & Griskevicius, V. (2014). Sense of control under uncertainty depends on people's childhood environment: A life history theory approach. *Journal of Personality and Social Psychology, 107*, 621–637.

Nederhof, E., Belsky, J., Ormel, J., & Oldehinkel, A. J. (2012). Effects of divorce on Dutch boys' and girls' externalizing behavior in gene × environment perspective: Diathesis stress or differential susceptibility in the Tracking Adolescents' Individual Lives Survey study? *Development and Psychopathology, 24*, 929–939.

Oberlander, T. F., Weinberg, J., Papsdorf, M., Grunau, R., Misri, S., & Devlin, A. M. (2008). Prenatal exposure to maternal depression, neonatal methylation of human glucocorticoid receptor gene (NR3C1) and infant cortisol stress responses. *Epigenetics, 3*, 97–106.

Obradović, J., Bush, N. R., Stamperdahl, J., Adler, N. E., & Boyce, W. T. (2010). Biological sensitivity to context: The interactive effects of stress reactivity and family adversity on socioemotional behavior and school readiness. *Child Development, 81*, 270–289.

Pluess, M. (2015). Individual differences in environmental sensitivity. *Child Development Perspectives, 9*, 138–143.

Pluess, M., & Belsky, J. (2009). Differential susceptibility to rearing experience: The case of childcare. *Journal of Child Psychology and Psychiatry, 50*, 396–404.

Pluess, M., & Belsky, J. (2010). Differential susceptibility to parenting and quality child care. *Developmental Psychology, 46*, 376–390.

Pluess, M., & Belsky, J. (2011). Prenatal programming of postnatal plasticity? *Development and Psychopathology, 23*, 29–38.

Pluess, M., & Belsky, J. (2013). Vantage sensitivity: Individual differences in response to positive experiences. *Psychological Bulletin, 139*, 901–916.

Pluess, M., Belsky, J., & Neuman, R. J. (2009). Prenatal smoking and attention-deficit/hyperactivity disorder: DRD4-7R as a plasticity gene. *Biological Psychiatry, 66*, e5–e6. doi:10.1016/j.biopsych.2009.04.019.

Pluess, M., Stevens, S. E., & Belsky, J. (2013). Differential susceptibility: Developmental and evolutionary mechanisms of gene-environment interactions. In M. Legerstee, D. W. Haley, & M. H. Bornstein (Eds.), *The infant mind: Origins of the social brain* (pp. 77–96). New York: Guilford Press.

Pluess, M., Velders, F. P., Belsky, J., van IJzendoorn, M. H., Bakermans-Kranenburg, M. J., Jaddoe, V. W., et al. (2011). Serotonin transporter polymorphism moderates effects of prenatal maternal anxiety on infant negative emotionality. *Biological Psychiatry, 69*, 520–525.

Poulin, M. J., Holman, E. A., & Buffone, A. (2012). The neurogenetics of nice: Receptor genes for oxytocin and vasopressin interact with threat to predict prosocial behavior. *Psychological Science, 23*, 446–452.

Quas, J. A., Bauer, A., & Boyce, W. T. (2004). Physiological reactivity, social support, and memory in early childhood. *Child Development, 75*, 797–814.

Rickard, I. J., Frankenhuis, W. E., & Nettle, D. (2014). Why are childhood family factors associated with timing of maturation? A role of internal prediction. *Perspectives on Psychological Science, 9*, 3–15.

Sheese, B. E., Voelker, P. M., Rothbart, M. K., & Posner, M. I. (2007). Parenting quality interacts with genetic variation in dopamine receptor D4 to influence temperament in early childhood. *Developmental Psychopathology, 19*, 1039–1046.

Sherman, R. A., Figueredo, A. J., & Funder, D. C. (2013). The behavioral correlates of overall and distinctive life history strategy. *Journal of Personality and Social Psychology, 105*, 873–888.

Sheskin, M., Chevallier, C., Lambert, S., & Baumard, N. (2014). Life-history theory explains childhood moral development. *Trends in Cognitive Sciences, 18*, 613–615.

Simons, R. L., Lie, M. K., Stewart, E. A., Beach, S. R. H., Brody, G. H., Philibert, R. A., et al. (2012). Social adversity, genetic variation, street code, and aggression: A genetically informed model of violent behavior. *Youth Violence and Juvenile Justice, 10*, 3–24.

Simpson, J. A., Griskevicius, V., Kuo, S. I., Sung, S., & Collins, W. A. (2012). Evolution, stress, and sensitive periods: The influence of unpredictability in early versus late childhood on sex and risky behavior. *Developmental Psychology, 48*, 674–686.

Sonuga-Barke, E. J., Oades, R. D., Psychogiou, L., Chen, W., Franke, B., Buitelaar, J., et al. (2009). Dopamine and serotonin transporter genotypes moderate sensitivity to maternal expressed emotion: The case of conduct and emotional problems in attention deficit/hyperactivity disorder. *Journal of Child Psychology and Psychiatry, and Allied Disciplines, 50*, 1052–1063.

South, S. C., & Krueger, R. F. (2013). Marital satisfaction and physical health: Evidence for an orchid effect. *Psychological Science, 24*, 373–378.

Sturge-Apple, M. L., Davies, P. T., Martin, M. J., Cicchetti, D., & Hentges, R. F. (2012). An examination of the impact of harsh parenting contexts on children's adaptation within an evolutionary framework. *Developmental Psychology, 48*, 791–805.

Sulik, M. J., Eisenberg, N., Lemery-Chalfant, K., Spinrad, T. L., Silva, K. M., Eggum, N. D., et al. (2012). Interactions between serotonin transporter gene haplotypes and quality of mothers' parenting predict the development of children's noncompliance. *Developmental Psychology, 48*, 740–754.

Sulik, M. J., Eisenberg, N., Spinrad, T. L., Lemery-Chalfant, K., Swann, G., Silva, K. M., et al. (2015). Interactions among catechol-*O*-methyltransferase genotype, parenting, and sex predict children's internalizing symptoms and inhibitory control: Evidence for differential susceptibility. *Development and Psychopathology, 27*, 709–723.

Sumner, J. A., McLaughlin, K. A., Walsh, K., Sheridan, M. A., & Koenen, K. C. (2015). Care giving and 5-HTTLPR genotype predict adolescent physiological stress reactivity: Confirmatory tests on gene × environment interactions. *Child Development*. doi:10.1111/cdev.12357.

Trucco, E. M., Villafuerte, S., Heitzeg, M. M., Burmeister, M., & Zucker, R. A. (2015). Susceptibility effects of GABA receptor subunit alpha-2 (GABRA2) variants and parental monitoring on externalizing behavior trajectories: Risk and protection conveyed by the minor allele. *Development and Psychopathology*. doi:10.1017/S0954579415000255.

van IJzendoorn, M. H., & Bakermans-Kranenburg, M. J. (2015). Genetic differential susceptibility on trial: Meta-analytic support from randomized controlled experiments. *Development and Psychopathology, 27*, 151–162.

van IJzendoorn, M. H., Belsky, J., & Bakermans-Kranenburg, M. J. (2012). Serotonin transporter genotype 5HTTLPR as a marker of differential susceptibility? A meta-analysis of child and adolescent gene-by-environment studies. *Translational Psychiatry, 7*, e147. doi:10.1038/tp.2012.73.

van IJzendoorn, M. H., Caspers, K., Bakermans-Kranenburg, M. J., Beach, S. R. H., & Philibert, R. (2010). Methylation matters: Interaction between methylation density and 5HTT genotype predicts unresolved loss or trauma. *Biological Psychiatry, 68*, 405–407.

Wakschlag, L. S., Kistner, E. O., Pine, D. S., Biesecker, G., Pickett, K. E., Skol, A. D., et al. (2010). Interaction of prenatal exposure to cigarettes and MAOA genotype in pathways to youth antisocial behavior. *Molecular Psychiatry, 15*, 928–937.

Weaver, I. C., Cervoni, N., Champagne, F. A., D'Alessio, A. C., Sharma, S., Seckl, J. R., et al. (2004). Epigenetic programming by maternal behavior. *Nature Neuroscience, 7*, 847–854.

West-Eberhard, M. J. (2003). *Development plasticity and evolution*. Oxford, UK: Oxford University Press.

White, A. E., Li, Y. J., Griskevicius, V., Neuberg, S. L., & Kenrick, D. T. (2013). Putting all your eggs in one basket: Life-history strategies, bet hedging, and diversification. *Psychological Science, 24*, 715–722.

Young, G. (2011). *Development and causality: Neo-Piagetian perspectives*. New York: Springer Science + Business Media.

Early Adversity, Fetal Programming, and Getting Under the Skin

14

Chapter Introduction

The present chapter examines models and research on early influences on development especially in terms of environmental adversity. The models include the ones of differential susceptibility, adaptive calibration, and allostatic load, which were considered in the prior chapter. However, the chapter also deals with models on: enduring effects; stress generation; stress sensitization, amplification, and inoculation; and Gene × Environment effects. Major environmental influences considered include early abuse, attachment style, and socioeconomic status/poverty. Overall, the work described in the present chapter supports an interactive approach across biology and environment in long-term development, but in a process that includes nuanced effects, such as relating to preconceptual influences and epigenesis on the outcome of behavior. I conclude that a biopsychosocial approach to early adversity could be a fruitful one.

Enduring Effects

Model

Experience early in life might be discounted as relevant environmental influences on later development. However, in the enduring effects model, they are considered important in these regards. Concepts such as early adversity, allostatic load, prenatal programming, and even preconceptual and epigenetic influences speak to this model.

Christian (2015) reviewed the research showing that maternal psychosocial stress during pregnancy has adverse behavioral and health outcomes for offspring. The mediator in the relationship might involve dysregulation of inflammatory processes in the mother. For example, Haeri, Baker, and Ruano (2013) compared depressed pregnant mothers and controls. The former group expressed alterations in immune parameters—higher serum interleukin 6 (IL-6) and tumor necrosis factor alpha (TNF-α).

There are relevant differential factors in fetal programming of physiological stress reactivity. Tibu et al. (2014) found that prenatal risks lead to increased stress reactivity in female infants but decreased reactivity in males. In this regard, they examined vagal reactivity from respiratory sinus arrhythmia during stressful and nonstress procedures.

Quas et al. (2014) examined classes of sympathetic/parasympathetic and HPA (hypothalamic-pituitary-adrenal) axis reactivity over four studies of 4- to 14-year-olds (to laboratory challenges). They found six patterns by latent profile analysis: moderate reactivity (most frequent); parasympathetic reactivity (e.g., withdrawal); anticipatory arousal; multisystem reactivity (exaggerated); HPA reactivity, and underarousal. The findings suggest different avenues of fetal programming, for example, due to maternal prenatal anxiety.

G. Young, *Unifying Causality and Psychology*, DOI 10.1007/978-3-319-24094-7_14

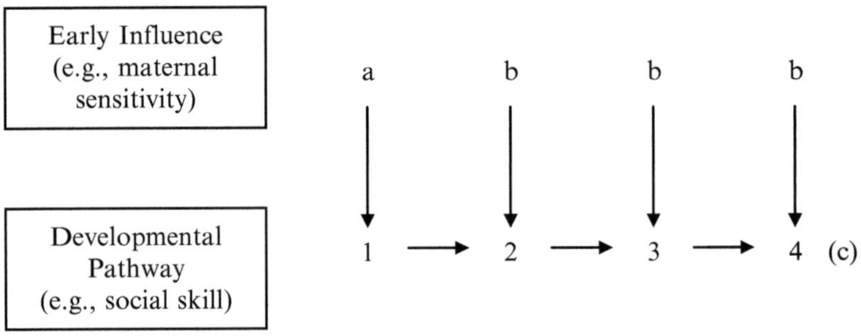

Fig. 14.1 Early influences and developing skills according to revisionist and enduring effects perspectives. A focal developmental experience (e.g., maternal sensitivity) might influence early outcomes (path *a*; such as social skills). Also, the outcomes might have some degree of stability early in life over development (path *c*). In addition, the outcomes could be affected by experiences that are uncorrelated with the particular developmental experience at issue. In addition to these assumptions, the enduring effects model also assumes that the focal experience continues to have an ongoing effect on outcome over development (path *b*), unlike the revisionist model. Adapted from Roisman and Fraley (2013), based on Fraley et al. (2013)

Roisman and Fraley (2013; also Fraley, Roisman, & Haltigan, 2013) have argued that longitudinal developmental research has not been constructed in a rigorous enough fashion to determine developmental mechanisms, and have proposed a methodological solution. Their work calls into question our understanding of whether there are legacy sequelae of early developmental acquisitions in later developing systems. They queried whether the "revisionist" model that early experience shapes development but dissipates in influence (becomes weakly related or unrelated) as development proceeds has enough empirical support to replace traditional models of preserved, sustained effects on development (enduring effects models). They used a path modeling approach (see Fig. 14.1) to show that the critical information needed in traditional longitudinal studies do not provide or are insensitive to the requisite information to distinguish the validity of the two developmental models.

Evidence

Roisman and Fraley (2013) re-analyzed data from a longitudinal study that ran until participants arrived at the age of 15–18, which was on early maternal sensitivity in care giving in relation to later academic performance, social competence, and psychopathology. The results supported the enduring effects model of legacy of childhood experiences. Much of the field could profit from Roisman, Fraley, and colleagues methodological refinement in understanding developmental mechanisms in developmental systems and, indeed, how they might have evolved.

Raby, Roisman, Fraley, and Simpson (2015) investigated whether the enduring effects model provides an adequate fit to the data gathered in a longitudinal study spanning 32 years for an at-risk population. They replicated the results of a comparable study by Fraley et al. (2013), but also extended them. Neither study supported the "revisionist" model, in which early experiences gradually dissipate in their effects over time.

Initially, Fraley et al. (2013) had used data from the NICHD (National Institute of Child Health and Human Development) Study of Early Child Care and Youth Development (SECCYD) in a study of a normative population into mid-adolescence. In their replicating study, Raby et al. (2015) used data from the MLSRA (Minnesota Longitudinal Study of Risk and Adaptation) on pregnant mothers living below the poverty line and receiving prenatal services. About half were teenage mothers ($N=243$).

To measure early maternal sensitivity in Raby et al. (2015), mother–child interactions were videotaped in a home feeding situation. For later observations at 6 months, there were two feedings and one play interaction. For 24 and 42 months, the situations were laboratory ones on problem solving and teaching. For the two younger ages, maternal sensitivity was measured using the scales of Ainsworth, Blehar, Waters, and Wall (1978). For the two older ages, the mother's supportive presence (positive involvement and secure base provision) was evaluated.

A factor analysis indicated the different maternal sensitivity measures could be combined into a composite score. Social competence during childhood and adolescence was measured using teacher rankings (during kindergarten, grades 1–3 and 6, and at age 16). For the adult period, semi-structured interviews were used at 23 and 32 years to determine competence in social relationships. For academic competence, the PIAT (Peabody Individual Achievement Test; Dunn & Markwardt, 1970) was used for grades 1–3 and 6. At age 16, the study used the WJTA (Woodcock–Johnson Tests of Achievement; Woodcock, 1990; Woodcock & Johnson, 1989). For the young adult period, it was evaluated as academic attainment at ages 23, 26, 28, and 32 years. Control variables concerned child gender, child ethnicity, SES (socioeconomic status), and maternal education. These variables were considered covariates in the analyses undertaken.

The results in the Raby et al. (2015) study favored the enduring effects model compared to the revisionist model. Specifically, early maternal sensitivity predicted academic development, in an enduring manner, or without diminishing over age. Moreover, neither the covariates nor the stability of the measures over time (and the transactions that they represented) could account for the results. [Note that the enduring effect model was not supported for the outcome measures used for social competence.]

Comment

Other research is consistent with the enduring effects model. Gliga, Jones, Bedford, Charman, and Johnson (2014) suggested that early neurodevelopmental mechanisms could be brainwide and also long term in effects in conditions such as autism. Cumulative and cascading effects could derive from disturbances in early sensory processing, which, as well, are related downstream to synaptic function impairments that affect biological and psychological functions (e.g., control of attention). In this sense, for the case of autism, the disorder might be more than a reflection of an atypical "social" brain (which in regards to the formulation suggested is too upstream and too localized).

Allostasis and Allostatic Load Model

Model

The concepts of allostasis and allostatic overload (AL) are important in the area of the effects of early adversity on development. It includes description of the physiological mechanisms involved.

For Ramsay and Woods (2014), allostasis concerns more dysregulatory (or disordered) forms of physiological regulation. The greater the allostatic load, the more the pathology. Psychosocial stress is an important source of allostatic system overload. Allostatic mechanisms include overconnected effector responses or persistent and no longer adaptive ones, causing more dysregulated concurrent effector competition.

Juster et al. (2011) expanded the allostatic load model (AL; McEwen & Stellar, 1993; Sterling & Eyer, 1988) to psychopathology across the life span (see Fig. 14.2). For Juster et al. (2011), AL refers to the "wear and tear" experienced by the organism exposed to chronic stress. The model that they developed is transdisciplinary and focuses in an integrative way on chronic stress. Stress is considered a multidimensional construct among biological, psychological, and environmental factors. Specifically, it is considered a real or subjectively perceived threat of a person's physiological or psychological integrity. That leads to biological and behavioral responses likely to increase adaptation. According to AL, the three factors that are involved in stress (biopsychosocial) work in synergy. Stress hormone function is especially altered under chronic stress, leading to system collapse and disease.

The AL index is a quantitative measure that illustrates the factors involved in chronic stress. It comprises variables related to dysregulated neuroendocrine, immune, metabolic, and cardiovascular markers (Seeman, Singer, Rowe, Horwitz, & McEwen, 1997).

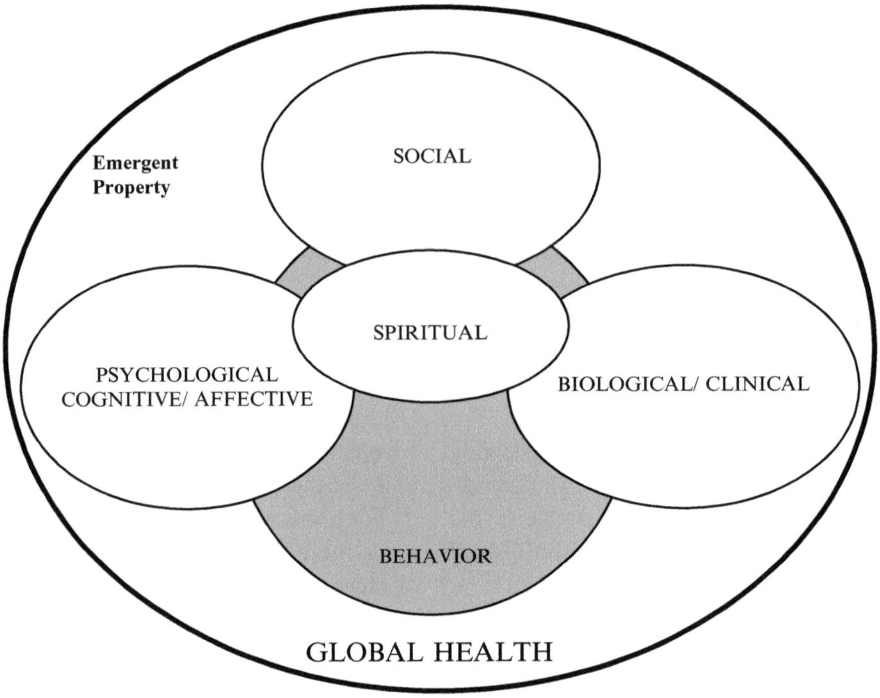

Fig. 14.2 Transdisciplinary, global health framework: an integrated biopsychosocial model. In the 1970s, Jean Piaget coined the term "transdisciplinarity" to describe integrative, multilevel approaches to scientific inquiry. For Kessel and Rosenfield (2008), emergent properties derive from the dynamic interactions among health domains at the biological, psychological, social, behavioral, and spiritual levels, which collectively shape global health. A transdisciplinary approach to health research is consistent with the allostatic load model, in which health/disease is believed to emerge as a totality of life domains that are best understood when studied in synergy. Adapted from Juster et al. (2011), based on Picard, Sabiston, and McNamara (2011)

The antecedents of AL include: (a) early adversity; (b) genetic factors; (c) epigenetic factors; (d) environmental toxins; and (e) interactions among biological and sociocultural factors. Together, these factors contribute probabilistically to health outcomes (not deterministically; Cicchetti & Toth, 2009).

The perception of stress leads to not only immediate (e.g., adrenalin) but also slightly delayed (e.g., cortisol) biological responses. The sympathetic-adrenal-medullary (SAM) axis is involved in the former and the HPA axis in the latter. Other brain areas involved in the stress response include the hippocampus, amygdala, and prefrontal cortex.

SAM and HPA activity provide examples of allostasis, which is meant to maintain equilibrium. Its parameters are multiply-controlled, and so health is a state of responsiveness rather than a simple homeostatic process (Sterling, 2004). The interconnected allostatic system can falter, as primarily indexed by stress hormone dysregulation (McEwen & Stellar, 1993). When the dysregulation becomes chronic, pathophysiological effects are potentiated. The allostatic overload system can mutually affect the psychological and biological in nonlinear ways, with context crucial, as well. Disease develops in allostatic overload, which takes place after system over-activation and nonlinear dynamical interactive imbalances, leading to the breaking point (McEwen, 1998a, 1998b).

McEwen and Wingfield (2003) noted that allostatic overload can occur in two types. In the first variant, energy demands exceed energy inflow, representing a negative energy balance. In the second variant, the energy balance is positive (e.g., obesity). McEwen (2006) added that system factors affect not only metabolism and other disease-potential physical processes but also central nervous system (CNS) functions (e.g., cognition, depression).

Juster et al. (2011) explicated in depth how allostatic overload contributes to developmental and long-term psychopathology. The model was developed for populations but works for the individual level, too. Similarly, I have maintained that chronic stress is the factor that is common to psychological injuries (Young, 2008a) and that somatization is a multifactorial process that can begin early in life (Young, 2008b).

Evans, Li, and Whipple (2013) reviewed the research and methodology on cumulative risk and adverse development impact. Multiple risk factor exposure is considered more deleterious than single adverse impact exposure. The findings are consistent with, among others, the AL model of chronic stress (McEwen, 1998a, 1998b) and developmental evolutionary theory (Ellis, Figueredo, Brumbach, & Schlomer, 2009).

Figure 14.3 presents Ganzel and Morris's (2011) model of modulated allostasis in development, which goes beyond initial gene and environment sets. It indicates that allostatic accommodation and accumulation vary over development according to differential stressor sensitivities and variations in context. Beyond that, the model applies equally to short- and long-term (e.g., stage) developmental periods and their changes. Finally, the changes in any one period reflect particular stress responses and allostatic processes unique to the period and stressors involved, leading to distinct long-term consequences for health for the associated periods, stressors, and contexts involved.

Evidence

Conradt et al. (2014) conducted a prospective longitudinal study of prenatal substance abuse exposure (for $N=860$) and its relationship to 11-year-old outcome, with cortisol reactivity also assessed at the latter age. Adversity was measured using a summary index over prenatal substance abuse exposure and also cumulative risk across early-life stressful events. The exposure index was collapsed over type of substance abuse.

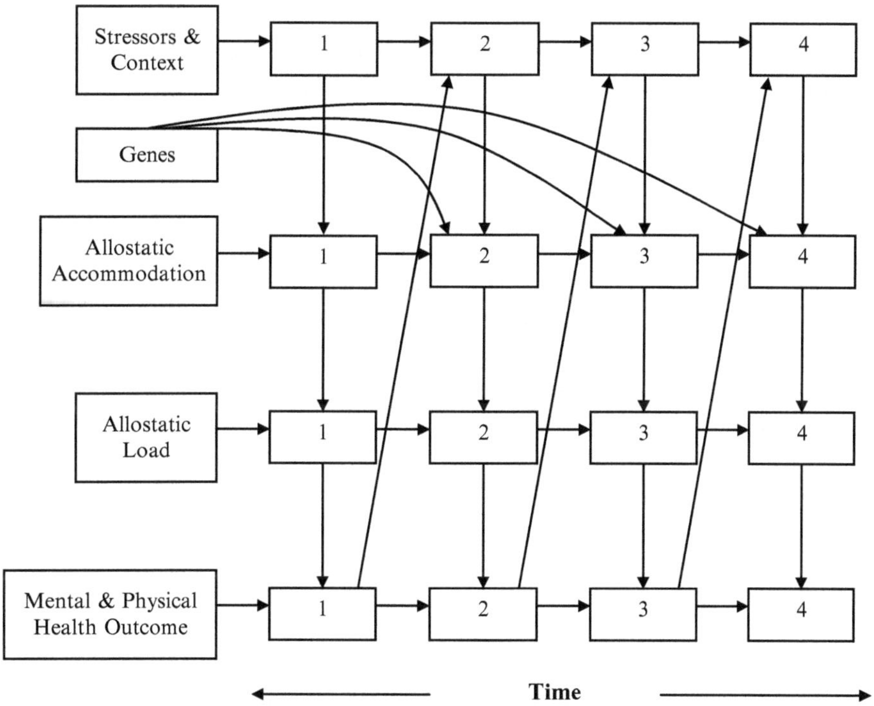

Fig. 14.3 Modulated allostasis. Allostatic accommodation and also accumulation of allostatic load are seen to vary as a function of changing stress sensitivity across time (development). Different patterns might arise at each time period (qualitative and/or quantitative differences), for example, in physiological processes. Adapted from Ganzel and Morris (2011)

Outcome was assessed using the CBCL (Child Behavior Checklist; Achenbach, 1991) and the DISC-IV (Diagnostic Interview Schedule for Children-IV; Shaffer, Fisher, Lucas, Dulcan, & Schwab-Stone, 2000), as well as delinquency scores and a measure of executive function (EF) involving spatial working memory, thinking time, and planning. The sample included African and non-African Americans.

The results showed that, in the first 6 years of life, greater prenatal substance exposure was related to more postnatal adversity. Also, for African Americans, more early adversity exposure related to decreased or attenuated cortisol reactivity, which in turn related to more problematic outcome at age 11 (more externalizing behavior, executive dysfunction, delinquency, and poor student–teacher relations).

The results support the allostatic load model for which early adversity becomes "biological embedded," leading to deleterious consequences in stress reactivity and later psychopathology (e.g., Lester & Padbury, 2009; McEwen, 1998a, 1998b). In these regards, cumulative early adversity also has effects. However, in the research, moderate cortisol reactivity had more positive effects, aiding in alertness, memory, and problem solving during stressful situations.

Comment

Allostatic load is a model that is consistent with a diatheses-stress understanding of health and disease. However, other models do not simply consider the cumulative effects of vulnerabilities related to biology and environment. In particular, the differential susceptibility model examines differential alleles in the workings of vulnerabilities on outcome.

Differential Susceptibility

Model

The last chapter reviewed the differential susceptibility and related models. The model indicates that only in the presence of certain alleles will adversity have deleterious consequences. Moreover, in the presence of supportive environments, the alleles involved could lead to positive outcomes rather than negative outcomes, again more than expected compared to the average and those without the alleles in question. Differential susceptibility informs the area of the effects of early adversity on long-term development. Recent research is consistent with the model in these regards.

Evidence

Oldehinkel, Ormel, Verhulst, and Nederhof (2014) found evidence in support of each of three distinct and apparently contradictory models of the effect of early adversity on adolescent depression. The stress sensitization model argues that childhood adversity reduces the threshold to a recent stressor (e.g., Rudolph & Flynn, 2007). The stress amplification model maintains that only high-stress conditions can interact with early adversity to facilitate depression (e.g., Kendler, Kuhn, & Prescott, 2004). The stress inoculation model indicates that adversity in childhood protects or "steels" the developing person against the effects of stressors later in life (e.g., Rutter, 2006). Oldehinkel et al. (2014) argued that individual differences in the effects of early adversities vary according to regulatory capacity, coping, and resilience for resultant reaction patterns.

The details of their study are complex, but they showed that early adversity in adolescents increases depression risk after exposure and then wanes in this effect. Also, if the onset is later, counter intuitively, depression is facilitated in low-risk rather than high-risk stress conditions. The authors argued that early adversity functions to program resilience for high-stress conditions, but not for low-stress conditions, in cases in which depression does not appear early. They concluded that the results support the "biological sensitivity to context" model (Boyce & Ellis, 2005). In particular, relative to moderate exposure, both low- and high-adversity exposure earlier in life program individuals for sensitivity to the current context.

Mitchell et al. (2014) studied the effect of social disadvantage on children's telomere length (TL), which is a biomarker of stress, in the context of moderation by genetic variants related to serotonin and dopamine pathways that are associated with genetic sensitivity. TL shortening refers to the shortening of the protective repeat sequence at the end of each chromosome (TTAGGG) that takes place with each cycle of chromosomal replication and cellular division; research has shown that it is affected by chronic stress.

Mitchell et al. (2014) studied TL in a sample of Black American 9-year-old boys exposed to disadvantaged environments, and measured by a combine index. Early adversity was associated with TL shortening, but genetic sensitivity scores over the two neurotransmitter pathways moderated the results. That is, the more genetically sensitive participants had the shortest TL, but only if they were exposed to disadvantage. In contrast, they had the longest if they were exposed to advantageous environments.

The study was longitudinal, with the first wave taking place within 2 days of birth. Environment quality was measured using a combined index of family economic conditions, parenting practices, and family structure/stability. The measure was also decomposed to examine each component.

The serotonin-related sensitivity score summed four serotonin markers from two genes (*5-HTT*: *5-HTTLPR*, *STin2*; *TPH2*: *rs4570625*, *rs1386494*). For dopamine, the sums involved *DAT1*, *rs40184*; *DRD4*, third exon variable number tandem repeat (VNTR); *DRD2*, Taq1a polymorphism (*rs1800497*); and catechol-*O*-methyltransferase (*COMT*), *rs4680* (Val158Met). For each neurotransmitter system genetic variants, the authors examined two pathways, involving homozygous genotypes and sensitizing alleles.

Based on these measures and their results, Mitchell et al. (2014) concluded that an individual's genetic architecture related to TL, which is like a mitotic clock of senescence, interacts with exogenous stressors in moderating the magnitude and direction of physiological response to the latter. The gene × social environment interaction found with (dis)advantage and TL is consistent with the differential susceptibility/biological sensitivity to environment context (Belsky, Bakermans-Kranenburg, & van IJzendoorn, 2007; Boyce & Ellis, 2005).

Comment

Differential susceptibility factors influence the effects of early adversity on developmental outcome, but the results in the research are complex. The same is true for a variation of the model, that of adaptive calibration.

Adaptive Calibration Model

The adaptive calibration model has been reviewed in the prior chapter. This chapter reconsiders it in the context of discussing early adversity.

Hostinar and Gunnar (2013) contrasted two models applicable to the developmental effects of stress early in life, one being more evolutionary and the other more contextual. In the allostatic load (AL) model (McEwen, 1998b, 2008; McEwen & Stellar, 1993; McEwen & Wingfield, 2003), stress that is frequent and chronic accumulates in wear-and-tear effects, taking a corporal toll that can lead to physical and mental disease via allostatic overload (see Fig. 14.4).

In the adaptive calibration model (ACM) (Del Giudice, Ellis, & Shirtcliff, 2011), individuals differ in stress reactivity due to evolutionary selection facilitative of phenotypic matching to contextual conditions (see Fig. 14.5). The ACM is related to the work of Ellis and Boyce (2008) and Belsky and Pluess (2009) on biological/differential sensitivity/susceptibility to context/environment. It suggests that differential adversities play a role in life-history strategies (e.g., early childbirth in unpredictable, uncontrollable environments). The AL and ACM models differ in focus, with the former concentrating on proximal (e.g., physiological) rather than distal (evolutionary) mechanisms. The ACM can be applied

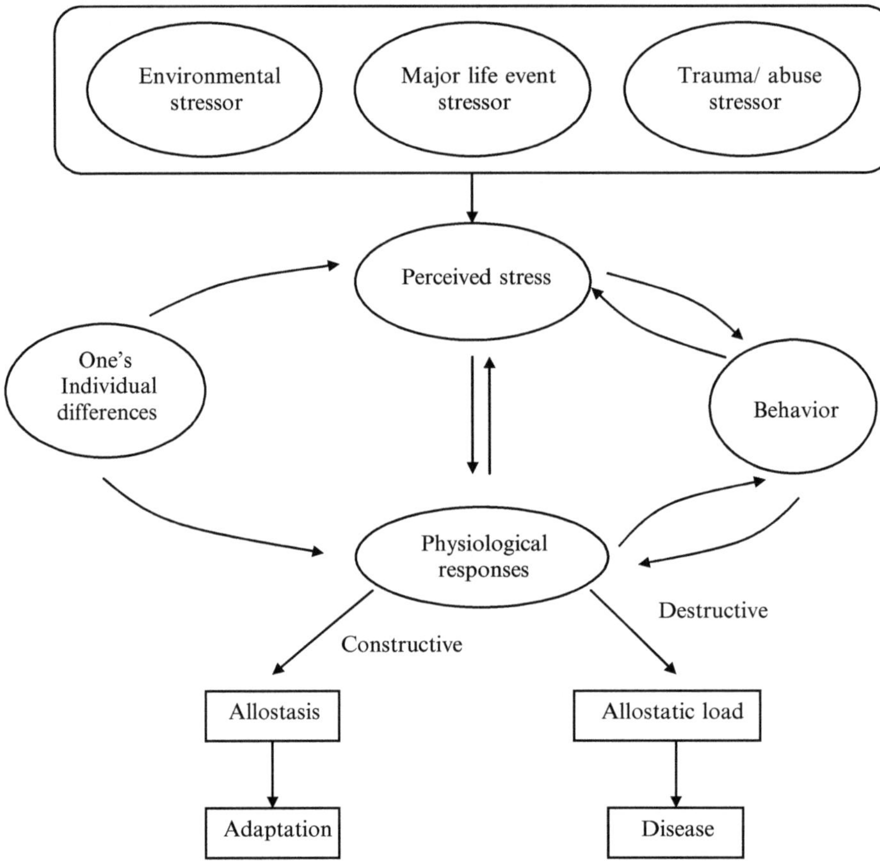

Fig. 14.4 Allostasis and allostatic load model. The perception of stress is influenced by experience, genetics, and behavior. There are individual differences in this regard. I added to the figure feedback loops among perceived stress, and behavior? Physiological response. When stress is perceived, physiological/behavioral responses begin, leading to allostasis/adaptation. However, over time, allostatic load (wear/tear) can accumulate, and can have adverse effects on various organ systems, leading to disease. Adapted from McEwen (1998a)

to development (childhood stressors), and does consider plasticity in development. The authors concluded that both models need further work and that the mechanism of epigenesis could provide a means to integrate better the models.

Frankenhuis and de Weerth (2013) proposed that early psychosocial adversity might not only impair cognition but also improve aspects of it related to danger and survival. The early stressors might promote a here-and-now focus that orients development toward adapting to local environmental conditions. Early-life stress exposure could shape perception to detect and predict threat, leading to hyperattention to threat and danger, and even better reasoning in ecologically-valid tasks. Minds are "adapted" to their environments no matter how their localization or particular attributes had been derived.

Stress Generation

Model

Stress has been implicated in susceptibilities in development, including in genetic-mediated ones. However, stress should not be considered purely an exogenous, environmental event that is acting on a passive organism. Stress might have its effects on development through endogenous

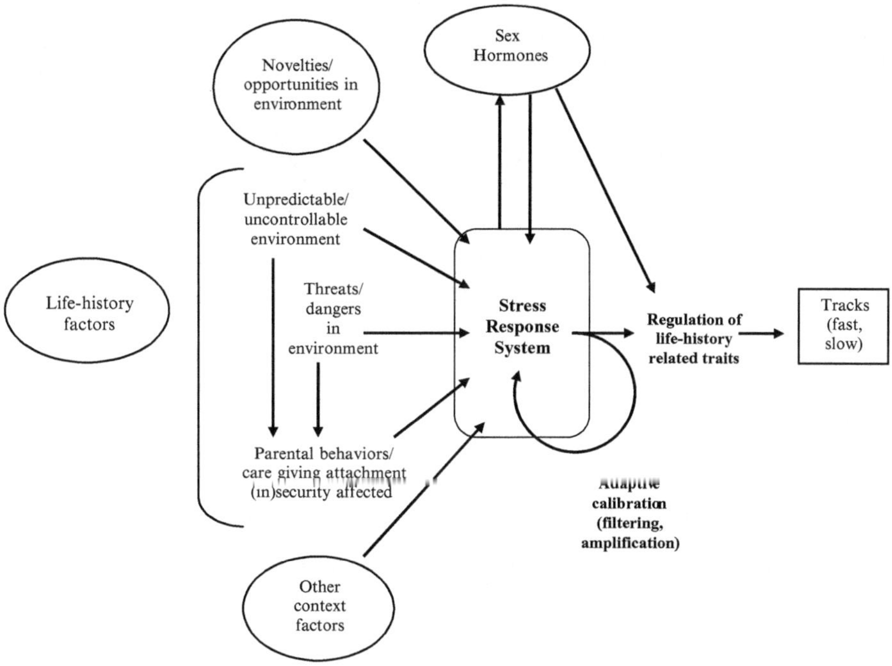

Fig. 14.5 Adaptive calibration model. *Note*. Growth/learning; maturation/fertility; competition/risk-taking; and pair bonding/care giving factors involved in early or later mating and related behavior. Conceptual structure of the adaptive calibration model. It illustrates that life-history trajectories are influenced by evaluating and forecasting unpredictable/uncontrollable environments and threats/dangers. The opportunities and novelties in the environment, as well as parenting and context, in general, also influence the life-history traits and tracks (fast, slow). The mediator in the behavior is the stress response system, which involves an adaptive calibration (filtering, amplification). Adapted from Del Giudice et al. (2011)

and not only exogenous processes. In this regard, the stress generation hypothesis of depression has yielded relevant findings (e.g., the person objectively contributes him- or herself to dissolution of a romantic relationship). However, the stress generation hypothesis of depression not only considers this factor but also others, such as differential susceptibility.

Liu (2013) reviewed the concept of stress generation in relation to depression. The standard model of depression includes the stress-diathesis model (e.g., Morris, Ciesla, & Garber, 2008), in which stress exposure interacts with pre-existing depression-related vulnerabilities. In the stress generation model (Hammen, 1991, 2006), objective, agent-dependent stressors could actively serve to promote depression, in addition to any effect of independent stressors. As depression-related symptoms increase, so does the probability of experiencing more stress, in a reciprocal relationship. The source of dependent stressors relates to factors such as depressogenic cognitions, behaviors, and interpersonal patterns that persist even as the depression might not.

Evidence

Risk factors for stress-related depression generation include not only childhood maltreatment (Liu, Choi, Boland, Mastin, & Alloy, 2013) but also genetic factors. Starr, Hammen, Brennan, and Najman (2012) found that the serotonin transporter gene polymorphism (*5-HTTLPR*) interacted with depression in 15-year-olds to predict dependent stressors at age 20, especially for those with one short (*s*) allele at the gene locus. Starr, Hammen, Brennan, and Najman (2013) found for stress generation that the *5-HTTLPR* genotype interacted with relational security.

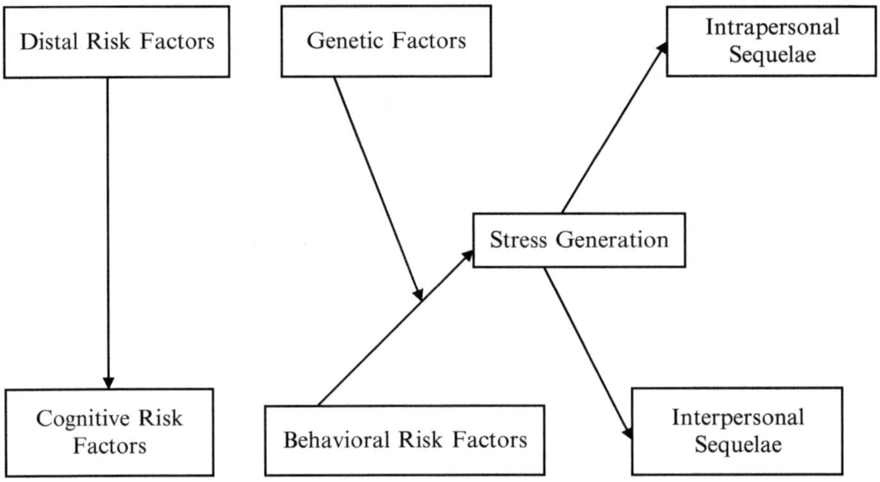

Fig. 14.6 Risk factors and negative outcomes of stress generation in depression. The figure illustrates that depression might be a consequence of stress generation facilitated by an individual's various risk factors, including genetic. Examples of risk factors include those that are: distal-childhood maltreatment; genetic (*5-HTTLPR*); cognitive (negative inferential style); and behavioral (negative attachment style, dependency). Examples of depression-related sequelae include: intrapersonal (depressive recurrence) and interpersonal (depression contagion) ones. Adapted from Liu (2013)

Specifically, the *s* allele was associated with decreased deleterious (dependent) stressors in adolescents with high security but increased stress generation in those with low security.

Liu (2013) presented an integrated model of stress generation that includes distal and proximal risk factors (see Fig. 14.6). The distal risk factors include childhood emotional abuse, which Liu et al. (2013) studied in relation to negative inferential cognitive style and stress generation (i.e., dependent stressors). Cognitive risk factors such as these exert indirect influence in the model relative to direct ones, such as behavioral risk factors (e.g., negative attachment style, dependency). Finally, genetic risk factors (e.g., *5-HTTLPR*) act to moderate the behavioral risk factors.

In this regard, Dix, Meunier, Lusk, and Perfect (2012) found that, for 14- to 27-month-olds, the mother's depressive symptoms influenced their infants' facial emotions. The authors explained that depressed mothers give their infants less support, leading to increased inhibition in their emotional communication. In consequence, the children exhibit flatter affect and less joy but also less sadness and negative emotion. However, infant passivity mediated the relationship between their mother's depressive symptoms and their infrequent emotional displays. Depression, therefore, is considered due to the infant's inhibition, i.e., general withdrawal from the mother, whether or not she is unresponsive.

Comment

Although the stress generation hypothesis of depression has been supported empirically and an interaction effect with genetic substrate has been found, the independent environment still has an important role to play in the development of depression. Charles, Piazza, Mogle, Sliwinski, and Almeida (2013) investigated whether minor daily stressors can after mental health in the long term. Increased levels of self-reported negative affect on nonstressful days were associated with general affective distress and with affective disorder symptoms 10 years later. A critical explanatory variable in the relationship appeared to be heightened affective reactivity to the wear and tear of relatively minor daily stress events.

Another factor to consider in stress research concerns resilience. Rutter (2012) considered resilience as a dynamic construct. He noted that response to stress varies and also that a negative response for some people leads to a "steeling effect," or a resistance in effect. Later responses to major stress or adversity include either decreased sensitivities or strengthening (thus, better overcoming it, yielding better outcomes). Mediators include factors such as a sense of self-efficacy. G × E research has implicated an interaction with the serotonin transporter promoter gene, as well (e.g., Caspi et al., 2003; Caspi, Hariri, Holmes, Uher, & Moffitt, 2010). Cicchetti and Rogosch (2012) found a G × E interaction effect in resilience related to this gene and several others in maltreated and nonmaltreated 6- to 12-year-olds, with genetic variation having a greater impact on resilient functioning among the controls.

Genes and Environments

The environment has an important role to play in long-term development. However, it acts interactively with genetics in many developmental phenomena (see Chap. 11). The following does not deal with G × E interactions, per se, but the effects of genes and environments on early adversity influences.

Asok, Bernard, Roth, Rosen, and Dozier (2013) examined whether parental responsiveness in a semi-structured interaction task moderated the link between early life stress in 4- to 6-year-olds (either high- or low-risk) and reduced telomere length. They explained that telomeres are chromosome-end TTAGGG tag repeats that help protect chromosomal DNA from damage as they replicate. Telomeres naturally reduce with each replication so that they are considered markers of biological aging. Moreover, they shorten due to factors such as oxidative stress, including due to childhood adversity (Price, Kao, Burgers, Carpenter, & Tyrka, 2013).

In their research, Asok et al. (2013) found that high-risk children compared to low-risk ones had shorter telomeres, after controlling for confounding variables. However, parental responsiveness served to moderate the association between risk and length of telomere; parental responsiveness was associated with longer telomeres, but only among high-risk children, indicating its protective or buffering function in stress modulation. The authors concluded that possible mechanisms affecting telomere length due to early-life adversity include dysregulation by the HPA axis and overproduction of proinflammatory cytokines.

Gotlib et al. (2015) found that TL in daughters (10–14 years) of depressed mothers was shorter than daughters of mothers with no history of depression. Also, shorter TL was associated with greater (cortisol) stress reactivity in both daughter groups. Covariates did not alter the results (Tanner stage or Child Depression Inventory (CDI) scores; Kovacs, 1992). The daughters were healthy psychopathologically (according to the Kiddie-Sads-Present and Lifetime (K-SADS-PL); Kaufman, Birmaher, Brent, Ryan, & Rao, 2000). The authors concluded that shortened TL appears to be an antecedent risk factor for possible depression, and also that mediation of the effect could involve HPA axis dysregulation.

Environment

The biological approach to early adversity is compelling, with captivating research findings in its support. Nevertheless, the environmental point of view is equally powerful in these regards. Both influences affect development in the long-term, and this happens in an interactive way.

Support

Hostinar, Sullivan, and Gunnar (2014) reviewed the literature showing the influence of social support, or its lack, on stress response and the HPA axis, as well as its biological mediators in the oxytocinergic system and prefrontal cortical neural networks. The model that they developed is a life span and social buffering one, which begins to function prenatally through programming effects (see Fig. 14.7). In positive circumstances, early relationships are supportive, attachment figures are appraised in a safety framework, and self-esteem and personal control/self-regulation develop. Mediators of the HPA axis are moder-

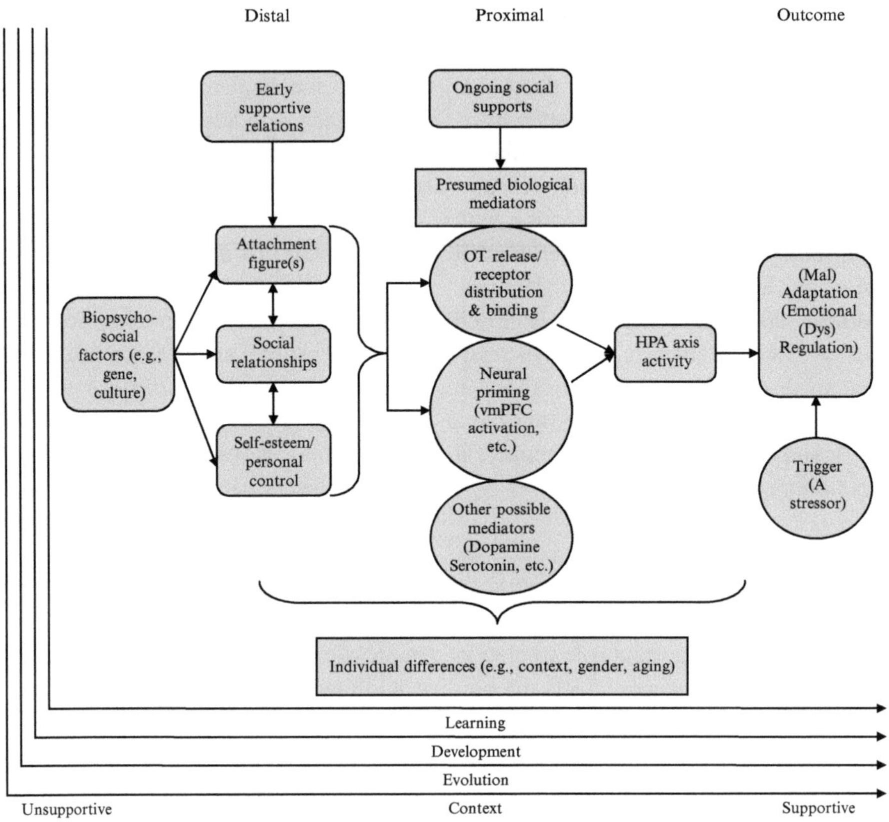

Fig. 14.7 A developmental working model of social buffering of the hypothalamic-pituitary-adrenal (HPA) axis in humans. Both early and ongoing social support can moderate stressful conditions, and function as buffers of any impacts on activation of the HPA axis, which might have deleterious effects when it is not moderated. Early care giving support from attachment figures leads to better self-esteem and behavioral regulation. Mediators in the development of HPA activation involve OT mechanisms and neural priming. The behavioral system described includes crucial individual differences in reactivity. *OT* = oxytocin, *vmPFC* = ventromedial prefrontal cortex, *Epi* = epinephrine, *NE* = norepinephrine. Adapted from Hostinar et al. (2014)

ated by stress buffers early in life, in that care giving experiences influence both social competency and biological reactivity to stressors.

Some of the evidence in support of the model reviewed by Hostinar et al. (2014) included the following: (a) Sensitive, early care giving predicts later positive self-esteem, self-regulation, and social competence, e.g., caregiver quality predicts later positive, attachment-secure representations of partners in young adult romantic relations (Haydon, Collins, Salvatore, Simpson, & Roisman, 2012). (b) Abnormal care giving experience/maltreatment impairs social development, e.g., in insecure attachment patterns in preschoolers (Cicchetti, Rogosch, & Toth, 2006). (c) Social input can tamp HPA axis reactivity, e.g., having much psychosocial resources relates to lower stress response in the HPA (Taylor et al., 2008). (d) Social contact stimulates oxytocin release, e.g., of plasma or urinary oxytocin (e.g., Feldman, Singer, & Zagoory, 2010, for infants). (e) Oxytocin possesses stress-relief properties, e.g., in studies with intranasal administration in males, breastfeeding in females (Heinrichs, Baumgartner, Kirschbaum, & Ehlert, 2003; Heinrichs et al., 2001, respectively). (f) Early social experience is associated with receptor expression and binding of HPA axis biological mediators, e.g., childhood maltreatment is associated with adult women expressing lower oxytocin levels in cerebrospinal fluid (Heim et al., 2009). (g) Abnormal rearing can lead to absent

HPA axis social buffering, e.g., in orphanage children (Wismer Fries, Ziegler, Kurian, Jacoris, & Pollak, 2005). (h) In negative affect regulation, prefrontal cortex activation in stress-buffering takes place, e.g., in pain-related neural activation in women presented images of their romantic partners (Eisenberger et al., 2011). (i) Early care giving experiences appear to shape connections between prefrontal cortical and limbic system areas possessing excitatory input to the HPA axis (e.g., Tottenham et al., 2010).

Biglan, Flay, Embry, and Sandler (2012) emphasized the influence of nurturing environments in developing human well-being and contributing positively to society. The environment could be "toxic" but also could act to promote self-regulatory behavior and psychological flexibility. For toxic effects, the authors cited research that parental conflict in kindergarten children leads to externalizing problems two years later (Davies, Sturge-Apple, Cicchetti, & Cummings, 2007). Parental verbal abuse is associated with white matter tract intensity (Choi, Jeong, Rohan, Polcari, & Teicher, 2009).

Rifkin-Graboi et al. (2015) determined that prenatal maternal anxiety predicted their children's neurodevelopment neonatally and even psychopathology-related behavior at one year of age. Specifically, they measured maternal anxiety using the Spielberger State-Trait Anxiety Inventory (STAI; Spielberger, 1983) at the age of 16 weeks gestation of their offspring. Also, they measured variation in newborn (5–17 days postnatal) neuronal microstructures using diffusion tensor imaging (DTI). Finally, they measured infant socio-emotional behavior at one year of age using the Infant Toddler Socio-Emotional Assessment (ITSEA; Carter & Briggs-Gowan, 2006) instrument.

As for the result of their study, they found that prenatal maternal anxiety predicted variations in fractional anisotropy (FA) of various corticolimbic regions of the brain in the neonate that are known to be associated with cognitive-emotional response to stress, as well as related functions (e.g., the right insula, the right dorsolateral prefrontal cortex, the right middle occipital region, and the right angular gyrus). The results have implications for the cross-generational transmission of the effects of anxiety.

Preconception

Class, Khashan, Lichtenstein, Långström, and D'Onofrio (2013) demonstrated that the preconception environment can influence postnatal development. They studied maternal stress in relation to infant mortality. Preconception was defined as 0–6 months before conception. Maternal stress was indexed by as the death of the mother participants' first-degree relative. Infant mortality was indexed relative to the first year of life. The results showed that preconception stress was associated with increased infant mortality, unlike the case for prenatal stress.

Class et al. (2013) concluded that the bereavement involved could affect the mother's health to the point of having epigenetic effects on the fetus to be conceived. This would act to compromise survivability if it occurred in the sensitive period involved.

The authors described the hypothesized mechanism that could account for the association between preconception maternal stress and post-birth infant mortality. The bereavement could affect the psychological, cognitive, behavioral, endocrine, physiological-somatic, and immune functioning of the mother to be, thereby affecting in turn her nutritional or hormonal systems. The mother's lack of preparedness for pregnancy could affect the fetus's organogenesis in a vulnerable period (e.g., brainstem-based control of autonomic functioning of breathing via serotonergic and noradrenergic neuronal systems).

Socioeconomic Status/Poverty

Tomalski et al. (2013) showed a relationship between SES and functional brain development in early infancy. They investigated resting baseline electroencephalographic (EEG) activity in 6- to 9-month-olds. Infants' SES was classified according to gross family income and parental occupation, which were involved in the results, unlike maternal education. Methodologically, the research recorded absolute power of resting EEG in two gamma frequency ranges (21–30 Hz and 31–45 Hz) in four scalp areas—frontal, left temporal, right temporal, and occipital.

Specifically, the results of the study revealed region-selective differences in early infancy (reduced gamma power over the frontal area) among infants from lower-income families (and at-risk occupation). The authors concluded that the results implicate a relative desynchronization in developing language networks, placing low SES infants at risk for deficits in selective attention and executive control of attention.

As for mechanisms in the effects found, the authors suggested exploration of prenatal factors, epigenetic factors, and various environmental factors. I would add to this list all factors that compromise maternal preparedness for pregnancy.

Evans and Cassells (2013) investigated the relationship between early poverty and 17-year mental health. Externalizing (but not internalizing) and learned helplessness behavior appeared affected by child poverty. However, the results were mediated by age-13 cumulative risk exposure/psychosocial risk factors and also physical risk factors (respectively: violence, family turmoil, family separation; noise, crowding, substandard housing). The authors concluded that early deprivation could have lasting mental health effects into emerging adulthood, with factors in the adolescent period mediating the relationship.

Noble et al. (2015) conducted a cross-sectional study of family income, parental education, and brain structure in participants varying between 3 and 20 years of age. This is the first study of SES factors in relation to brain structure that attempted to control for genetic ancestry; it included as covariates continuously varying measures of genetic ancestry degree.

The results revealed that, for children from lower-income backgrounds, small incremental differences in family income were associated with relative large differences in brain surface area, unlike the case for children from higher income backgrounds. The variable of parental education accounted for offspring variation in brain structural characteristics that were different from those accounted for by parental education. The results on brain structure in this study generally concerned those areas that are associated with language, reading, executive function, and spatial skills in development.

Other Work

To conclude review of early adversity influences on long-term development, the chapter considers other work. For example, there are long-term effects on development due to factors related to attachment, stress, and inflammation.

Attachment

The importance of early infant attachment in later development even into adulthood is illustrated in the following research. Puig, Englund, Simpson, and Collins (2012) conducted a 32-year longitudinal study. Attachment type at 12 and 18 months in the situation of caregiver reunion after separation (Ainsworth et al., 1978) was related to physical condition later on. Specifically, insecure attachment relative to secure attachment in infancy was associated with physical illness (inflammation-based) 30 years later. In another study, this research group found an association between attachment and global adaptive functioning at age 28 (Englund, Kuo, Puig, & Collins, 2011). Puig et al. (2012) had noted that adult attachment style also is associated with physical illness (McWilliams & Baily, 2010).

Esbjørn, Bender, Reinholdt-Dunne, Munck, and Ollendick (2012) presented a model that early attachment style (as well as dysfunctional emotional regulation) influences the development of anxiety disorders into the adolescent period (see Fig. 14.8). Caregivers might not match their behavior to their children's emotional needs. Coupled with other variables, attachment insecurity and consequent emotional regulation and anxiety might develop (e.g., Colonnesi et al., 2011).

Morley and Moran (2011) examined other consequences of early attachment insecurities and their effects, in this case on later depression. The insecure attachment style is associated with helpless attributions and responses to stress, e.g.,

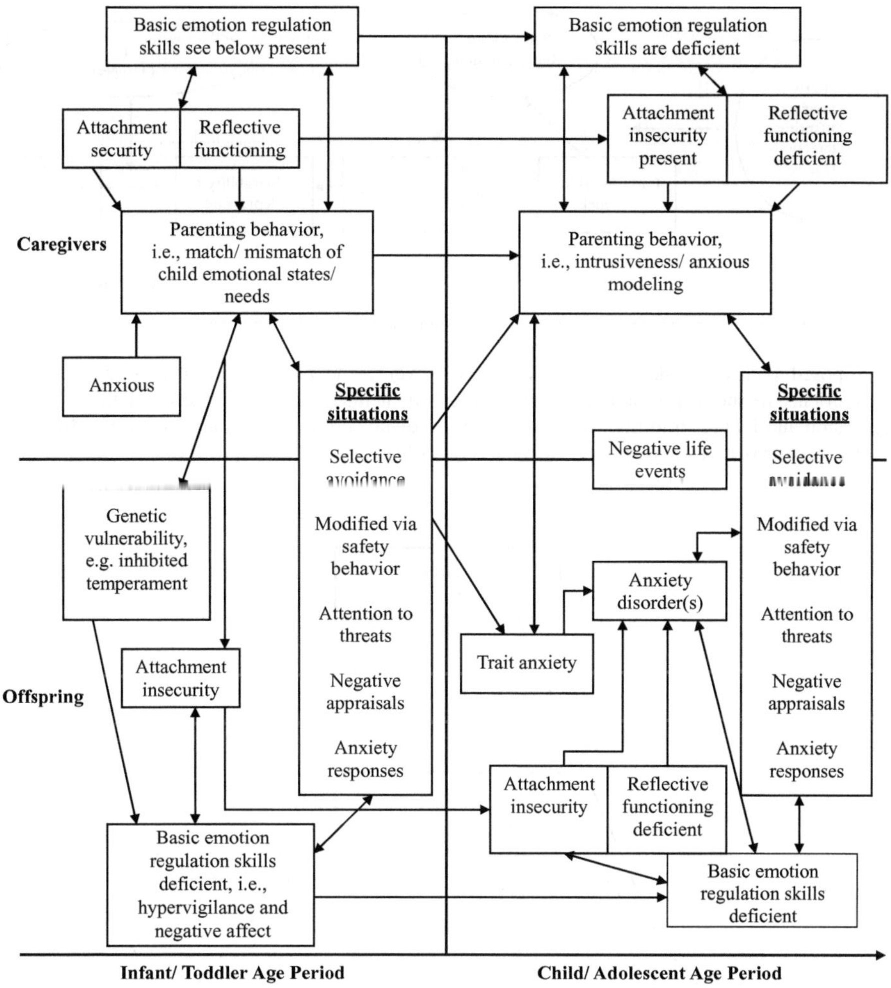

Fig. 14.8 The role of attachment and emotion regulation on the development of childhood anxiety disorders. The figure indicates the complexity of causal models in dyadic (parental) relations. Adapted from Esbjørn et al. (2012)

failure, negative life events, and vulnerability to depression (see Fig. 14.9).

Kochanska and Kim (2012) differentiated the view of attachment as contributory to later disturbances in behavior (see Fig. 14.10). The child brings characteristics, such as anger proneness, that complicate linear causality from early parental behavior to outcomes (e.g., antisociality in early school age). They found that early insecurity in interaction with anger proneness led to power-assertive parenting and, ultimately, antisocial behavior in early school-age children. Secure infants were buffered from this effect.

Booth-LaForce (2014), Booth-LaForce and Roisman (2014), and Roisman, Fraley, and Booth-LaForce (2014) and colleagues questioned the unitary construct underlying adult attachment insecurity, finding relatively independent dismissing and preoccupied states of mind in a study using the Adult Attachment Interview (AAI; Main, Kaplan, & Cassidy, 1985). Moreover, individual differences reflected more of a dimensional than categorical model. This type of reworking of the attachment construct might lead to more nuanced models of how early attachment affects long-term developmental outcome. In this regard, refer to my developmental model of the 25 steps over the life span of attachment-related social self-working schemata (see Chap. 31).

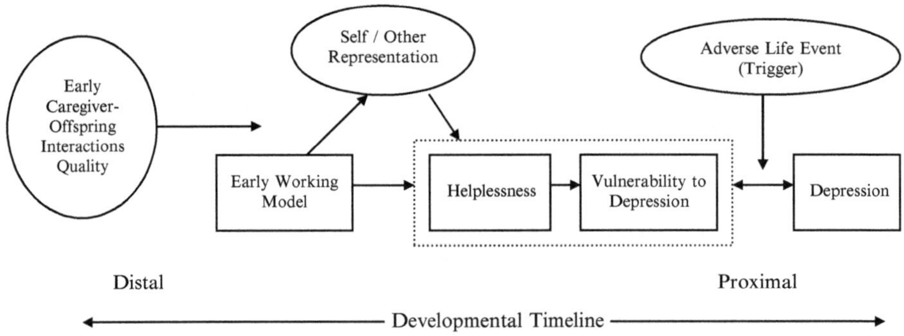

Fig. 14.9 Proposed pathway linking quality of early attachment experience to later depression. In the development of depression and its vulnerability, there are potential lifelong effects of proximal stressors (e.g., adverse life event) and of early negative (parent–offspring) attachment interactions and representations (working models) (distal influence). Adapted from Morley and Moran (2011)

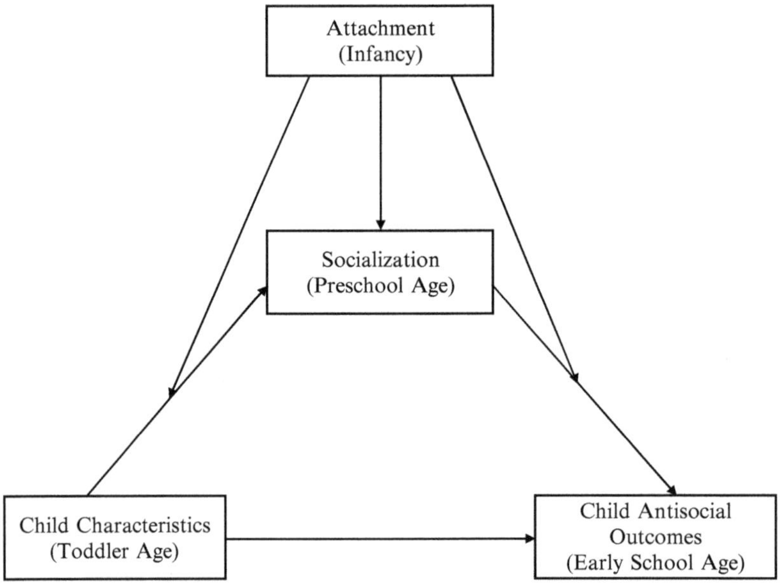

Fig. 14.10 The causal chain from child characteristics to parental socialization to child antisocial outcomes in insecure and secure attachment. Child and parental contributions to attachment and outcome. Attachment develops in infancy (secure, insecure), and has consequences for socialization of the child. Socialization involves control, discipline, and power assertion. Child characteristics include temperament, anger proneness, and difficulty. Child outcomes include poor self-regulation, rule-breaking, opposition, aggression, callousness, and disruptiveness. Adapted from Kochanska and Kim (2012)

Early Adversity

Slopen, Kubzansky, McLaughlin, and Koenen (2013) found that early life adversity increased indices of inflammation even into 15 years of age, having consequences for adulthood health. They measured early adversity by maternal report of five acute adverse events: foster care, being physically hurt, sexual abuse, maternal separation, and paternal separation. Ratings were obtained at seven age points between 1.5 and 8 years, and total scores were derived. The inflammatory markers were interleukin-6 and C-reactive protein (CRP). Cumulative risk also played a role (e.g., in the first 8 years in relation to CRP at age 15).

Romens, McDonald, Svaren, and Pollak (2015) found an association between early life stress (physical maltreatment) and epigenetic methylation changes in a portion of the glucocorticoid receptor gene in 11- to 14-year-olds (within exon 1_F in the *NR3C1* promoter region of the gene; CpG site 3, in particular). The gene is involved in stress regulation, and stress or trauma has been shown to be correlated with higher methylation of the gene in cases of abuse and later psychopathology (e.g., McGowan et al., 2009; Perroud et al., 2014). The results suggested that HPA axis dysregulation serves as a mechanism in stress-related psychopathology in children.

St. Clair et al. (2014) conducted a study delineating early adversity subtypes and links to later adolescent depression. They found that early experiential adversity did have predictive effects, and the effects were not linear. Moreover, the links diminished in boys but not in girls. The normative/optimal parenting subtype was distinguished from three suboptimal ones—aberrant, discordant, and hazardous. The latter two subtypes had wider effects (in both genders).

Inflammation

Fagundes and Way (2014) reviewed that early severe life stress can impact physical health through augmented inflammation. For example, Lam et al. (2012) found that early-life adversity was related to genome-wide methylation (epigenesis) in adulthood. The physical illnesses potentiated in this chain include cardiovascular disease, type 2 diabetes, some cancers, and Alzheimer's disease.

Brain

Bryck and Fisher (2012) reviewed research showing that experience acts to shape the architecture of the brain in development (National Scientific Council on the Developing Child, 2007). Animal research reveals that stressful rearing environments appear to affect critical neural regulatory systems (Levine, 2005). Young children reared in extremely neglectful institutions evidence lasting alterations in the development of the brain (Pollak et al., 2010), with similar results found for maltreated and foster children (Cicchetti, Rogosch, Gunnar, & Toth, 2010; Fisher, Gunnar, Dozier, Bruce, & Pears, 2006, respectively). The adverse effects on brain development might derive from cumulative effects rather than extreme ones (i.e., allostatic load; Shonkoff, Boyce, & McEwen, 2009). Fisher and Gunnar (2010) implicated, in particular, the first 2 years of life in this effect.

Just as the developing brain is plastic to adverse effects, so can it be affected by interventions designed to promote neural plasticity. Generally, enriched environments work best when they include complexity and novelty (Sale, Berardi, & Maffei, 2009). Physical exercise also appears salutatory in this regard (Hillman, Erickson, & Kramer, 2008). Studies on laboratory-based executive training studies with children show positive findings, as well (Bryck & Mayr, 2005; Holmes, Gathercole, & Dunning, 2009; Karbach & Kray, 2009; Mackey, Hill, Stone, & Bunge, 2011; Thorell, Lindqvist, Nutley, Bohlin, & Klingberg, 2009; Tominey & McClelland, 2011). Training now includes ecological components (e.g., Mackey et al., 2011).

Coping

Foland-Ross, Kircanski, and Gotlib (2014) found that 12-year-olds with a depressed mother used more involuntary (e.g., escape, rumination) compared to voluntary (e.g., problem solving, positive thinking) coping strategies in dealing stress, which in turn was associated with exacerbation of HPA axis dysfunction (increasing already high levels of diurnal cortisol levels). The authors noted that different coping strategies are not inherently adaptive or maladaptive; for example, low-risk controls exhibited a more negative association between cortisol level and the use of involuntary coping strategies, indicative of the blunting of cortisol secretion.

Crum, Salovey, and Anchor (2013) demonstrated that stress experience is contingent on belief/mindset. For example, inducing a "stress-is-enhancing" mindset is associated with moderate cortisol reactivity.

Biopsychosocial Findings

The most recent research examined on adversity shows influences on development consistent with a multifactorial biopsychosocial confluence of influences on development in early adversity. The first section of the following review shows genetic and environmental influences in the effect of early adversity on development. The section after that reviews research pointing to the role of personal contributions, or of the person him- or herself, in influencing the effects of early adversity or stress on development.

Genes and Environment Contribution

Strüber, Strüber, and Roth (2014) proposed a double pathway model in the effects of early adversity on glucocorticoid regulation (GR) and later mental disorders. In the first pathway, early stress, acting in conjunction with either high maternal care or with the *s* allele of *5-HTTLPR*, first produces upregulation of hippocampal GR and then produces long-term HPA axis hyperfunction. In turn, this produces downregulation of *5-HT1A* receptors, thereby heightening activity of ventromedial prefrontal cortical (VMPFC) areas. This pathway leads to increase in emotional sensitivity and melancholic depression.

In the second proposed pathway of the effects of early stress on GR and consequent mental disorder, early adversity either in absence of high maternal care or in the presence of the *l* allele of *5-HTTLPR* causes downregulation of hippocampal GR, long-term HPA axis hypofunction, upregulation of *5-HT1A*- receptors, decreased VMPFC activity, reduced emotional sensitivity, and atypical depression/psychopathy.

Ruttle, Armstrong, Klein, and Essex (2014) found that early life stress and cortisol served as independent predictors of the covariation of internalizing symptoms and negative life events. In this longitudinal study, the early life stress served as a sensitizing agent along with later cortisol readings in the participant adolescents. Early life stress was measured through maternal report in infancy; the cortisol was assessed at 11, 13, and 15 years; and life event quality and internalizing symptoms were evaluated at 18 years of age. Specifically, the authors found that early life stress led to a "tighter" covariation between negative life events and internalizing symptoms. Also, among other results, lower afternoon cortisol assays led to the same tighter covariation. The authors concluded that the results address the differential stress sensitization model of early negative stressful experiences.

Gee et al. (2014) demonstrated that maternal buffering affects amygdala-prefrontal circuitry in children, improving affect-related regulation. Also, they found individual differences in this regard, for example, with greater maternal influence on the indicated circuitry in stronger mother–child relationships. The children were 4–10 years of age. The circuitry was established using fMRI (functional magnetic resonance imaging) during examination of the mother's pictured face or one of a matched stranger. Affect regulation was assessed in a go/no-go task. The task was administered once with the mother present and once with a stranger (research assistant) present. In the go/no-go task, the children had to press a button to a target facial expression (go), but not to a distractor one (no-go). At first, a happy face was used for the go condition and a sad one for the no-go one; then, a neutral expression was used for the no-go one. In the third block of tasks, the neutral and happy expressions served as the go and no-go conditions.

The authors found that adolescents did not reveal the same buffering effect, showing that childhood appears a sensitive period for linkage in circuitry of the amygdala and prefrontal cortex. The maternal buffering effect indicates the neurobiological locus of care giving on affect regulation in childhood; the effect may take place through action on the HPA axis.

Crone and Elzinga (2015) examined the literature showing how fMRI can be used to establish longitudinal cognitive and socioaffective growth trajectories and their relationship to the changing brain. For example, Emerson and Cantlon (2014) related left intraparietal sulcus (IPS) change to improvement in performance on a numerical processing task in children followed 2–3 years (to ages 4–9).

Also, in children tested 2–3 times in the age range 6–18 years, unlike for Met/Met, carriers of the VAT/VA1 *COMT* genotype showed during a relatively easy working memory (WM) task an increasing neural activation in ventral lateral PFC and the angular gyrus (Dumontheil et al., 2011). In contrast, for a harder WM task, the Met/Met carriers were the ones who expressed a steeper increase in performance over time.

According to Crone and Elzinga (2015), the results described show that individual differences in genetics could participate in shaping brain development trajectories. Overall, individual characteristics, such as in genetics and temperament/personality, render individuals differentially susceptible to their environment in their development, including in brain growth trajectory.

The Personal Contributions

In a study over 16 years with individuals as young as 16 as starting age, Jeronimus, Riese, Sanderman, and Ormel (2014) showed that neuroticism and life experiences expressed a "reciprocally causal," mutual reinforcing process, to the point that neuroticism appears to function as a regulatory set point. By reciprocal causation, the authors meant that, aside from other aspects of the relationship between neuroticism and experience, individuals seek, shape, and evoke life events consistent with their personality characteristics (Caspi & Shiner, 2011). Experiences did play a role in the results, and also the authors distinguished temporary changes in neuroticism from persistent changes in one's neuroticism set point.

Comment

The most recent research that I examined on the topic of early adversity is increasingly specifying the pathways, predictors, and consequences involved, as well as the genes, neurocircuitry, and neuroendocrinology involved. At the same time, the role in the environment, for example, as buffers, is mentioned, as well as individual differences in development in the multifactorial array that influences it. Early adversity could express long-term consequences, but many factors are involved in long-term outcomes, and a biopsychosocial approach to development and its outcomes appears a fruitful one.

Chapter Conclusions

The area of the effect of early environmental experiences on later development has a long history in psychology. Freud's classic model of psychodynamic development (psychoanalysis), for example, emphasizes the role of the early years in development. The ethologists refer to early critical periods in development. Contemporary understanding of development refers to transactions between organism and environment from conception on, as well as concepts such as developmental windows in which environments are more liable to have an impact. Recent models emphasize the concepts of—prenatal or early programming; epigenesis and its long-term environmental effects on genes, even over generations; and differential susceptibility to the environment [all of these models are central to the present work]. These increasingly complex and variegated developmental models indicate the importance not only of early environmental factors, such as early adversity and parental quality, but also of the genetic substrates on which they act and function to condition them, in turn. The environment does not act independently on the organism, nor do genes. They genuinely interact, and this takes place from the earliest phases of development, if not before, as in epigenetic effects in parents transmitted to offspring. That being said, research is showing direct environmental effects on development from the earliest phases of life. McCrory and Viding (2015) described a similar concept. In their model, childhood maltreatment constitutes a latent vulnerability involving altered threat processing. Also, statistically speaking, in development, one finds both main and interaction effects. However, in the ecology of those interactions in real life, the complexities are of orders of magnitude beyond what we have conceived until recently, and the research is pointing to fast-differentiating concepts that we are just beginning to grasp.

References

Achenbach, T. M. (1991). *Integrative guide for the 1991 CBCL/4-18, YSR, and TRF profiles*. Burlington, VT: University of Vermont, Department of Psychiatry.

Ainsworth, M. D. S., Blehar, M. C., Waters, E., & Wall, S. (1978). *Patterns of attachment: A psychological study of the strange situation*. Hillsdale, NJ: Erlbaum.

Asok, A., Bernard, K., Roth, T. L., Rosen, J. B., & Dozier, M. (2013). Parental responsiveness moderates the association between early-life stress and reduced telomere length. *Developmental and Psychopathology, 25*, 577–585.

Belsky, J., Bakermans-Kranenburg, M. J., & van IJzendoorn, M. H. (2007). For better and for worse: Differential susceptibility to environmental influences. *Current Directions in Psychological Science, 16*, 300–304.

Belsky, J., & Pluess, M. (2009). The nature (and nurture?) of plasticity in early human development. *Perspectives on Psychological Science, 4*, 345–351.

Biglan, A., Flay, B. R., Embry, D. D., & Sandler, I. N. (2012). The critical role of nurturing environments for promotion of human well-being. *American Psychologist, 67*, 257–271.

Booth-LaForce, C. (2014). Abstract. *Monographs of the Society for Research in Child Development, 79*, vii–viii.

Booth-LaForce, C., & Roisman, G. I. (2014). Introduction. *Monographs of the Society for Research in Child Development, 79*, 1–14.

Boyce, W. T., & Ellis, B. J. (2005). Biological sensitivity to context: I. An evolutionary-developmental theory of the origins and functions of stress reactivity. *Development and Psychopathology, 17*, 271–301.

Bryck, R. L., & Fisher, P. A. (2012). Training the brain: Practical applications of neural plasticity from the intersection of cognitive neuroscience, developmental psychology, and prevention science. *American Psychologist, 67*, 87–100.

Bryck, R. L., & Mayr, U. (2005). On the role of verbalization during task set selection: Switching or serial order control? *Memory and Cognition, 33*, 611–623.

Carter, A. S., & Briggs-Gowan, M. (2006). *The Infant-Toddler Social and Emotional Assessment (ITSEA)*. San Antonio, TX: Pearson.

Caspi, A., Hariri, A. R., Holmes, A., Uher, R., & Moffitt, T. E. (2010). Genetic sensitivity to the environment: The case of the serotonin transporter gene and its implications for studying complex diseases and traits. *American Journal of Psychiatry, 167*, 509–527.

Caspi, A., & Shiner, R. (2011). Temperament and personality. In M. Rutter, D. Bishop, D. Pine, S. Scott, J. Stevenson, E. Taylor, & A. Thapar (Eds.), *Rutter's child and adolescent psychiatry* (5th ed., pp. 182–198). Malden, MA: Wiley.

Caspi, A., Sugden, K., Moffitt, T. E., Taylor, A., Craig, I. W., Harrington, H., et al. (2003). Influence of life stress on depression: Moderation by a polymorphism in the 5-HTT gene. *Science, 301*, 386–389.

Charles, S. T., Piazza, J. R., Mogle, J., Sliwinski, M. J., & Almeida, D. M. (2013). The wear and tear of daily stressors on mental health. *Psychological Science, 24*, 733–741.

Choi, J., Jeong, B., Rohan, M. L., Polcari, A. M., & Teicher, M. H. (2009). Preliminary evidence for white matter tract abnormalities in young adults exposed to parental verbal abuse. *Biological Psychiatry, 65*, 227–234.

Christian, L. M. (2015). Stress and immune function during pregnancy: An emerging focus in mind-body medicine. *Current Directions in Psychological Science, 24*, 3–9.

Cicchetti, D., & Rogosch, F. A. (2012). Gene x environment interaction and resilience: Effects of child maltreatment and serotonin, corticotrophin releasing hormone, dopamine, and oxytocin genes. *Development and Psychopathology, 24*, 411–427.

Cicchetti, D., Rogosch, F. A., Gunnar, M. R., & Toth, S. L. (2010). The differential impacts of early physical and sexual abuse and internalizing problems on daytime cortisol rhythm in school-aged children. *Child Development, 81*, 252–269.

Cicchetti, D., Rogosch, F. A., & Toth, S. L. (2006). Fostering secure attachment in infants in maltreating families through preventive interventions. *Development and Psychopathology, 18*, 623–649.

Cicchetti, D., & Toth, S. L. (2009). The past achievements and future promises of developmental psychopathology: The coming of age of a discipline. *Journal of Child Psychology and Psychiatry, 50*, 16–25.

Class, Q. A., Khashan, A. S., Lichtenstein, P., Långström, N., & D'Onofrio, B. M. (2013). Maternal stress and infant mortality: The importance of the preconception period. *Psychological Science, 24*, 1309–1316.

Colonnesi, C., Draijer, E. M., Stams, G. J. J. M., Van der Bruggen, C., Bögels, S., & Noom, M. J. (2011). The relation between insecure attachment and child anxiety: A meta-analytic review. *Journal of Clinical Child and Adolescent Psychology, 40*, 630–645.

Conradt, E., Abar, B., Lester, B. M., LaGasse, L. L., Shankaran, S., Bada, H., et al. (2014). Cortisol reactivity to social stress as a mediator for early adversity on risk and adaptive outcomes. *Child Development, 85*, 2279–2298.

Crone, E. A., & Elzinga, B. M. (2015). Changing brains: How longitudinal functional magnetic resonance imaging studies can inform us about cognitive and social-affective growth trajectories. *Cognitive Science, 6*, 53–63.

Crum, A. J., Salovey, P., & Anchor, S. (2013). Rethinking stress: The role of mindsets in determining the stress response. *Journal of Personality and Social Psychology, 104*, 716–733.

Davies, P. T., Sturge-Apple, M. L., Cicchetti, D., & Cummings, E. M. (2007). The role of child adrenocortical functioning in pathways between forms of interparental conflict and child maladjustment. *Developmental Psychology, 43*, 918–930.

Del Giudice, M., Ellis, B. J., & Shirtcliff, E. A. (2011). The adaptive calibration model of stress responsivity. *Neuroscience & Biobehavioral Reviews, 35*, 1562–1592.

Dix, T., Meunier, L. N., Lusk, K., & Perfect, M. M. (2012). Mothers' depressive symptoms and children's facial emotions: Examining the depression-inhibition hypothesis. *Development and Psychopathology, 24*, 195–210.

Dumontheil, I., Roggeman, C., Ziermans, T., Peyrard-Janvid, M., Matsson, H., Kere, J., et al. (2011). Influence of the COMT genotype on working memory and brain activity changes during development. *Biological Psychiatry, 70*, 222–229.

Dunn, L. M., & Markwardt, F. C., Jr. (1970). *Peabody Individual Achievement Test.* Circle Pines, MN: American Guidance Service.

Eisenberger, N. I., Master, S. L., Inagaki, T. K., Taylor, S. E., Shirinyan, D., Lieberman, M. D., et al. (2011). Attachment figures activate a safety signal-related neural region and reduce pain experience. *Proceedings of the National Academy of Sciences of the United States of America, 108*, 11721–11726.

Ellis, B. J., & Boyce, W. T. (2008). Biological sensitivity to context. *Current Directions in Psychological Science, 17*, 183–187.

Ellis, B. J., Figueredo, A. J., Brumbach, B. H., & Schlomer, G. L. (2009). Fundamental dimensions of environmental risk: The impact of harsh versus unpredictable environments on the evolution and development of life history strategies. *Human Nature, 20*, 204–268.

Emerson, R. W., & Cantlon, J. F. (2014). Continuity and change in children's longitudinal neural responses to numbers. *Developmental Science, 18*, 314–326.

Englund, M. M., Kuo, S. I., Puig, J., & Collins, W. A. (2011). Early roots of adult competence: The significance of close relationships from infancy to early adulthood. *International Journal of Behavioral Development, 35*, 490–496.

Esbjørn, B. H., Bender, P. K., Reinholdt-Dunne, M. L., Munck, L. A., & Ollendick, T. H. (2012). The development of anxiety disorders: Considering the contributions of attachment and emotion regulation. *Clinical Child and Family Psychology Review, 15*, 129–143.

Evans, G. W., & Cassells, R. C. (2013). Childhood poverty, cumulative risk exposure, and mental health in emerging adults. *Clinical Psychological Science, 2*, 287–296.

Evans, G. W., Li, D., & Whipple, S. S. (2013). Cumulative risk and child development. *Psychological Bulletin, 139*, 1342–1396.

Fagundes, C. P., & Way, B. (2014). Early-life stress and adult inflammation. *Current Directions in Psychological Science, 23*, 277–283.

Feldman, R., Singer, M., & Zagoory, O. (2010). Touch attenuates infants' physiological reactivity to stress. *Developmental Science, 13*, 271–278.

Fisher, P. A., & Gunnar, M. R. (2010). Early life stress as a risk factor for disease in adulthood. In E. Vermetten, R. Lanius, & C. Pain (Eds.), *The impact of early life trauma on health and disease* (pp. 133–141). Cambridge, UK: Cambridge University Press.

Fisher, P. A., Gunnar, M. R., Dozier, M., Bruce, J., & Pears, K. C. (2006). Effects of therapeutic intervention for foster children on behavior problems, caregiver attachment, and stress regulatory neural systems. *Annals of the New York Academy of Sciences: Resilience in Children, 1904*, 215–225.

Foland-Ross, L. C., Kircanski, K., & Gotlib, I. H. (2014). Coping with having a depressed mother: The role of stress and coping in hypothalamic-pituitary-adrenal axis dysfunction in girls at familial risk for major depression. *Development and Psychopathology, 26*, 1401–1409.

Fraley, R. C., Roisman, G. I., & Haltigan, J. D. (2013). The legacy of early experiences in development: Formalizing alternative models of how early experiences are carried forward over time. *Developmental Psychology, 49*, 109–126.

Frankenhuis, W. E., & de Weerth, C. (2013). Does early-life exposure to stress shape or impair cognition? *Current Directions in Psychological Science, 22*, 407–412.

Ganzel, B. L., & Morris, P. A. (2011). Allostasis and the developing human brain: Explicit consideration of implicit models. *Development and Psychopathology, 23*, 955–974.

Gee, D. G., Gabard-Durnam, L., Telzer, E. H., Humphreys, K. L., Goff, B., Shapiro, M., et al. (2014). Maternal buffering of human amygdala-prefrontal circuitry during childhood but not during adolescence. *Psychological Science, 25*, 2067–2078.

Gliga, T., Jones, E. J. H., Bedford, R., Charman, T., & Johnson, M. H. (2014). From early markers to neurodevelopmental mechanisms of autism. *Developmental Review, 24*, 189–207.

Gotlib, I. H., LeMoult, J., Colich, N. L., Foland-Ross, L. C., Hallmayer, J., Joormann, J., et al. (2015). Telomere length and cortisol reactivity in children of depressed mothers. *Molecular Psychiatry, 20*, 615–620.

Haeri, S., Baker, A. M., & Ruano, R. (2013). Do pregnant women with depression have a pro-inflammatory profile? *Journal of Obstetrics and Gynaecology Research, 39*, 948–952.

Hammen, C. (1991). Generation of stress in the course of unipolar depression. *Journal of Abnormal Psychology, 100*, 555–561.

Hammen, C. (2006). Stress generation in depression: Reflections on origins, research, and future directions. *Journal of Clinical Psychology, 62*, 1065–1082.

Haydon, K. C., Collins, W. A., Salvatore, J. E., Simpson, J. A., & Roisman, G. I. (2012). Shared and distinctive origins and correlates of adult attachment representations: The developmental organization of romantic functioning. *Child Development, 83*, 1689–1702.

Heim, C., Young, L. J., Newport, D. J., Mletzko, T., Miller, A. H., & Nemeroff, C. B. (2009). Lower CSF oxytocin concentrations in women with a history of childhood abuse. *Molecular Psychiatry, 14*, 954–958.

Heinrichs, M., Baumgartner, T., Kirschbaum, C., & Ehlert, U. (2003). Social support and oxytocin interact to suppress cortisol and subjective responses to psychosocial stress. *Biological Psychiatry, 54*, 1389–1398.

Heinrichs, M., Meinlschmidt, G., Neumann, I., Wagner, S., Kirschbaum, C., Ehlert, U., et al. (2001). Effects of suckling on hypothalamic-pituitary-adrenal axis responses to psychosocial stress in postpartum lactating women. *Journal of Clinical Endocrinology and Metabolism, 86*, 4798–4804.

Hillman, C. H., Erickson, K. I., & Kramer, A. F. (2008). Be smart, exercise your heart: Exercise effects on brain and cognition. *Nature Reviews Neuroscience, 9*, 58–65.

Holmes, J., Gathercole, S. E., & Dunning, D. L. (2009). Adaptive training leads to sustained enhancement of poor working memory in children. *Developmental Science, 12*, F9–F15.

Hostinar, C. E., & Gunnar, M. R. (2013). The developmental effects of early life stress: An overview of current theoretical framework. *Current Directions in Psychological Science, 22*, 400–406.

Hostinar, C. E., Sullivan, R. M., & Gunnar, M. R. (2014). Psychobiological mechanism underlying the social buffering of the hypothalamic-pituitary-adrenocortical axis: A review of animal models and human studies across development. *Psychological Bulletin, 140*, 256–282.

Jeronimus, B. F., Riese, H., Sanderman, R., & Ormel, J. (2014). Mutual reinforcement between neuroticism and life experiences: A five-wave, 16-year study to test reciprocal causation. *Journal of Personality and Social Psychology, 107*, 751–764.

Juster, R.-P., Bizik, G., Picard, M., Arsenault-Lapierre, G., Sindi, S., Trepanier, L., et al. (2011). A transdisciplinary perspective of chronic stress in relation to psychopathology throughout life span development. *Development and Psychopathology, 23*, 725–776.

Karbach, J., & Kray, J. (2009). How useful is executive control training? Age differences in near and far transfer of task-switching training. *Developmental Science, 12*, 978–990.

Kaufman, J., Birmaher, B., Brent, D. A., Ryan, N. D., & Rao, U. (2000). K-SADS-PL. *Journal of American Academy of Child Adolescent Psychiatry, 39*, 1208. doi:10.1097/00004583-200010000-00002.

Kendler, K. S., Kuhn, J. W., & Prescott, C. A. (2004). Childhood sexual abuse, stressful life events and risk for major depression in women. *Psychological Medicine, 34*, 1475–1482.

Kessel, F., & Rosenfield, P. L. (2008). Toward transdisciplinary research: Historical and contemporary perspectives. *American Journal of Preventative Medicine, 35*, S225–S234.

Kochanska, G., & Kim, S. (2012). Toward a new understanding of legacy of early attachments for future antisocial trajectories: Evidence from two longitudinal studies. *Development and Psychopathology, 24*, 783–806.

Kovacs, M. (1992). *The Children's Depression Inventory (CDI)*. Toronto, ON: Multi-Health Systems.

Lam, L. L., Emberly, E., Frazer, B., II, Neumann, S. M., Chen, E., Miller, G. E., et al. (2012). Factors underlying variable DNA methylation in a human community cohort. *Proceedings of the National Academy of Sciences of the United States of America, 109*, 17253–17260.

Lester, B. M., & Padbury, J. F. (2009). Third pathophysiology of prenatal cocaine exposure. *Developmental Neuroscience, 31*, 23–35.

Levine, S. (2005). Stress: An historical perspective. In T. Steckler, N. H. Kalin, & J. M. H. M. Reul (Eds.), *Handbook on stress and the brain* (pp. 3–23). Amsterdam, Netherlands: Elsevier Science.

Liu, R. T. (2013). Stress generation: Future directions and clinical implications. *Clinical Psychology Review, 33*, 406–416.

Liu, R. T., Choi, J. Y., Boland, E. M., Mastin, B. M., & Alloy, L. B. (2013). Childhood abuse and stress generation: The mediational effect of depressogenic cognitive styles. *Psychiatry Research, 206*, 217–222.

Mackey, A. P., Hill, S. S., Stone, S. I., & Bunge, S. A. (2011). Differential effects of reasoning and speed training in children. *Developmental Science, 14*, 582–590.

Main, M., Kaplan, N., & Cassidy, J. (1985). Security in infancy, childhood, and adulthood: A move to the level of representation. In I. Bretherton & E. Waters (Eds.), *Growing points of attachment theory and research: Vol. 50: Monographs of the society for research in child development* (1-2, Serial No. 209, pp. 66–104). Boston, MA: Blackwell.

McCrory, E. J., & Viding, E. (2015). The theory of latent vulnerability: Reconceptualizing the link between childhood maltreatment and psychiatric disorder. *Development and Psychopathology, 27*, 493–505.

McEwen, B. S. (1998a). Stress, adaptation, and disease: Allostasis and allostatic load. *Annals of the New York Academy of Sciences, 840*, 33–44.

McEwen, B. S. (1998b). Protective and damaging effects of stress mediators. *New England Journal of Medicine, 338*, 171–179.

McEwen, B. S. (2006). Protective and damaging effects of stress mediators: Central role of the brain. *Dialogues in Clinical Neuroscience, 8*, 367–381.

McEwen, B. S. (2008). Central effects of stress hormones in health and disease: Understanding the protective and damaging effects of stress and stress mediators. *European Journal of Pharmacology, 583*, 174–185.

McEwen, B. S., & Stellar, E. (1993). Stress and the individual. Mechanisms leading to disease. *Archives of Internal Medicine, 153*, 2093–2101.

McEwen, B. S., & Wingfield, J. C. (2003). The concept of allostasis in biology and biomedicine. *Hormones and Behavior, 43*, 2–15.

McGowan, P. O., Sasaki, A., D'Alessio, A. C., Dymov, S., Labonté, B., Szyf, M., et al. (2009). Epigenetic regulation of the glucocorticoid receptor in human brain associates with childhood abuse. *Nature Neuroscience, 12*, 342–348.

McWilliams, L. A., & Baily, S. J. (2010). Associations between adult attachment ratings and health conditions: Evidence from the national comorbidity survey replication. *Health Psychology, 29*, 446–453.

Mitchell, C., Hobcraft, J., McLanahan, S. S., Siegel, S. R., Berg, A., Brooks-Gunn, J., et al. (2014). Social disadvantage, genetic sensitivity, and children's telomere length. *Proceedings of the National Academy of Sciences of the United States of America, 111*, 5944–5949.

Morley, T. E., & Moran, G. (2011). The origins of cognitive vulnerability in early childhood: Mechanisms linking early attachment to later depression. *Clinical Psychology Review, 31*, 1071–1082.

Morris, M. C., Ciesla, J. A., & Garber, J. (2008). A prospective study of the cognitive-stress model of depressive symptoms in adolescents. *Journal of Abnormal Psychology, 117*, 719–734.

National Scientific Council on the Developing Child. (2007). *The timing and quality of early experiences combine to shape brain architecture* (Working Paper No. 5). Retrieved from http://developingchild.harvard.edu/library/reports_and_working_papers/working_papers/wp5/

Noble, K. G., Houston, S. M., Brito, N. H., Bartsch, H., Kan, E., Kuperman, J. M., et al. (2015). Family income, parental education and brain structure in children and adolescents. *Nature Neuroscience, 18*, 773–778.

Oldehinkel, A. J., Ormel, J., Verhulst, F. C., & Nederhof, E. (2014). Childhood adversities and adolescent depression: A matter of both risk and resilience. *Development and Psychopathology, 26*, 1067–1075.

Perroud, N., Dayer, A., Piguet, C., Nallet, A., Favre, S., Malafosse, A., et al. (2014). Childhood maltreatment and methylation of the glucocorticoid receptor gene *NR3C1* in bipolar disorder. *British Journal of Psychiatry, 204*, 30–35.

Picard, M., Sabiston, C. M., & McNamara, J. K. (2011). The need for a transdisciplinary, global health framework. *Journal of Alternative and Complementary Medicine, 17*, 179–184.

Pollak, S. D., Nelson, C. A., Schlaak, M. F., Roeber, B. J., Wewerka, S. S., Wiik, K. L., et al. (2010). Neurodevelopmental effects of early deprivation in postinstitutionalized children. *Child Development, 81*, 224–236.

Price, L. H., Kao, H. T., Burgers, D. E., Carpenter, L. L., & Tyrka, A. R. (2013). Telomeres and early-life stress: An overview. *Biological Psychiatry, 73*, 15–23.

Puig, J., Englund, M. M., Simpson, J. A., & Collins, W. A. (2012). Predicting adult physical illness from infant attachment: A prospective longitudinal study. *Health Psychology, 32*, 409–417.

Quas, J. A., Yim, I. S., Oberlander, T. F., Nordstokke, D., Essex, M. J., Armstrong, J. M., et al. (2014). The symphonic structure of childhood stress reactivity: Patterns of sympathetic, parasympathetic, and adrenocortical responses to psychological challenge. *Development and Psychopathology, 26*, 963–982.

Raby, K. L., Roisman, G. I., Fraley, R. C., & Simpson, J. A. (2015). The enduring predictive significance of early maternal sensitivity: Social and academic competence through age 32 years. *Child Development, 86*, 695–705.

Ramsay, D. S., & Woods, S. C. (2014). Clarifying the roles of homeostasis and allostasis in physiological regulation. *Psychological Review, 121*, 225–247.

Rifkin-Graboi, A., Meaney, M. J., Chen, H., Bai, J., Hameed, W. B., Tint, M. T., et al. (2015). Antenatal maternal anxiety predicts variations in neural structures implicated in anxiety disorder in newborns. *Journal of the American Academy of Child & Adolescent Psychiatry, 54*, 313–321.

Roisman, G. I., & Fraley, R. C. (2013). Developmental mechanisms underlying the legacy of childhood experiences. *Child Development Perspectives, 7*, 149–154.

Roisman, G. I., Fraley, R. C., & Booth-LaForce, C. (2014). Pulling ourselves up by our bootstraps: A rejoinder to van IJzendoorn and Bakermans-Kranenburg (2014). *Monographs of the Society for Research in Child Development, 79*, 168–173.

Romens, S. E., McDonald, J., Svaren, J., & Pollak, S. D. (2015). Associations between early life stress and gene methylation in children. *Child Development, 86*, 303–309.

Rudolph, K. D., & Flynn, M. (2007). Childhood adversity and youth depression: Influence of gender and pubertal status. *Development and Psychopathology, 19*, 497–521.

Rutter, M. (2006). Implications of resilience concepts for scientific understanding. *Annals of the New York Academy of Sciences, 1094*, 1–12.

Rutter, M. (2012). Resilience as a dynamic concept. *Development and Psychopathology, 24*, 335–344.

Ruttle, P. L., Armstrong, J. M., Klein, M. H., & Essex, M. J. (2014). Adolescent internalizing symptoms and negative life events: The sensitizing effects of earlier life stress and cortisol. *Development and Psychopathology, 26*, 1411–1422.

Sale, A., Berardi, N., & Maffei, L. (2009). Enrich the environment to empower the brain. *Trends in Neurosciences, 32*, 233–239.

Seeman, E., Singer, B. H., Rowe, J., Horwitz, R. I., & McEwen, B. (1997). Price of adaptation – Allostatic load and its health consequences. *Archives of Internal Medicine, 157*, 2259–2268.

Shaffer, D., Fisher, P., Lucas, C. P., Dulcan, M. K., & Schwab-Stone, M. E. (2000). NIMH Diagnostic Interview Schedule for Children Version IV (NIMH DISC-IV): Description, differences from previous versions, and reliability of some common diagnoses. *Journal of the American Academy of Child & Adolescent Psychiatry, 39*, 28–38.

Shonkoff, J. P., Boyce, W. T., & McEwen, B. S. (2009). Neuroscience, molecular biology, and the childhood roots of health disparities: Building a new framework for health promotion and disease prevention. *The Journal of the American Medical Association, 301*, 2252–2259.

Slopen, N., Kubzansky, L. D., McLaughlin, K. A., & Koenen, K. C. (2013). Childhood adversity and inflammatory processes in youth: A prospective study. *Psychoneuroendocrinology, 38*, 188–200.

Spielberger, C. D. (1983). *Manual for the State-Trait Anxiety Inventory, STAI (Form Y) ('Self-Evaluation Questionnaire')*. Palo Alto, CA: Consulting Psychologists Press.

Starr, L. R., Hammen, C., Brennan, P. A., & Najman, J. M. (2012). Serotonin transporter gene as a predictor of stress generation in depression. *Journal of Abnormal Psychology, 121*, 810–818.

Starr, L. R., Hammen, C., Brennan, P. A., & Najman, J. M. (2013). Relational security moderates the effect of serotonin transporter gene polymorphism (5-HTTLPR) on stress generation and depression among adolescents. *Journal of Abnormal Child Psychology, 41*, 379–388.

Sterling, P. (2004). Principles of allostasis: Optimal design, predictive regulation, pathophysiology and rational therapeutics. In J. Schulkin (Ed.), *Allostasis, homeostasis, and the costs of adaptation* (pp. 17–64). Cambridge, UK: Cambridge University Press.

Sterling, P., & Eyer, J. (1988). Allostasis: A new paradigm to explain arousal pathology. In S. Fisher & J. Reason (Eds.), *Handbook of life stress, cognition and health* (pp. 629–649). New York: Wiley.

Strüber, N., Strüber, D., & Roth, G. (2014). Impact of early adversity on glucocorticoid regulation and later mental disorders. *Neuroscience and Biobehavioral Reviews, 38*, 17–37.

St. Clair, M. C., Croudace, T., Dunn, V. J., Jones, P. B., Herbert, J., & Goodyer, I. M. (2014). Childhood adversity subtypes and depressive symptoms in early and late adolescence. *Development and Psychopathology, 24*, 1–15.

Taylor, S. E., Burklund, L. J., Eisenberger, N. I., Lehman, B. J., Hilmert, C. J., & Lieberman, M. D. (2008). Neural bases of moderation of cortisol stress responses by psychosocial resources. *Journal of Personality and Social Psychology, 95*, 197–211.

Thorell, L. B., Lindqvist, S., Nutley, S. B., Bohlin, G., & Klingberg, T. (2009). Training and transfer effects of executive functions in preschool children. *Developmental Science, 12*, 106–113.

Tibu, F., Hill, J., Sharp, H., Marshall, K., Glover, V., & Pickles, A. (2014). Evidence for sex differences in fetal programming of physiological stress reactivity in infancy. *Development and Psychopathology, 26*, 879–888.

Tomalski, P., Moore, D. G., Ribeiro, H., Axelsson, E. L., Murphy, E., Karmiloff-Smith, A., et al. (2013). Socioeconomic status and functional brain development – associations in early infancy. *Developmental Science, 16*, 676–687.

Tominey, S. L. M., & McClelland, M. M. (2011). Red light, purple light: Findings from a randomized trial using circle time games to improve behavioral self-regulation in preschool. *Early Education and Development, 22*, 489–519.

Tottenham, N., Hare, T. A., Quinn, B. T., McCarry, T., Nurse, M., Gilhooly, T., et al. (2010). Prolonged institutional rearing is associated with atypically large amygdala volume and emotion regulation difficulties. *Developmental Science, 113*, 46–61.

Wismer Fries, A. B., Ziegler, T. E., Kurian, J. R., Jacoris, S., & Pollak, S. D. (2005). Early experience in humans is associated with changes in neuropeptides critical for regulating social behavior. *Proceedings of the National Academy of Sciences of the United States of America, 102*, 17237–17240.

Woodcock, R. W. (1990). Theoretical foundations of the WJ-R measures of cognitive ability. *Journal of Psychoeducational Assessment, 8*, 231–258.

Woodcock, R. W., & Johnson, M. B. (1989). *Woodcock-Johnson Psycho-Educational Battery-Revised*. Allen, TX: DLM Teaching Resources.

Young, G. (2008a). Causality and causation in law, medicine, psychiatry, and psychology: Progression or regression? *Psychological Injury and Law, 1*, 161–181.

Young, G. (2008b). Somatization and medically unexplained symptoms in psychological injury: Diagnoses and dynamics. *Psychological Injury and Law, 1*, 224–242.

15 Connecting the Social Dots

Chapter Introduction

Social connection helps distinguish the human species. Moreover, the mechanisms involved range from biological to environmental and to self, as well as other psychological ones. A prominent behavior complex in social connection relates to empathy and prosocial behavior. Models of the development of social behavior, including of the empathic, prosocial type, implicate either (a) innate factors and early onset or (b) more gradual development, with those in the latter camp maintaining that the studies in infancy implicating innate factors are over-interpreted. However, the bulk of the evidence supports the view of a rapid onset of empathic/prosocial behavior early in life. That being said, the degree to which this constitutes core, innate primitives in this regard needs further verification. Moreover, there has been a paucity of research querying whether these acquisitions reflect stage like acquisitions, which would constitute a compromise view to the debate, despite workers relating this area of research to that of Piaget.

Feldman's (2014) work on early biobehavioral synchrony addresses the early precursors to later social behavior. In this regard, she found both biological and parental influences. Other groups are specifying the neural and brain bases for social behavior (e.g., Anderson & Beauchamp, 2012a, 2012b). The embodiment model includes the mirror neuron system, and it is integral to the approach that social behavior of the empathic/prosocial type is biologically mediated. The evolutionary roots of social behavior suggest nonhuman primate origins to the behavior. However, cultural evolution also appears involved. Moreover, developmentally, the evidence indicates that the quality of early morality surpasses that of chimpanzees (Tomasello & Vaish, 2013).

The work of Hamlin (2014a, 2014b) on early helping behavior shows that, in the first few months of life, infants develop context-dependent social evaluations about helpers/givers/nice puppets and about hindering/mean/taking ones. For the second year of life, Waters, West, and Mendes (2014) and Cirelli, Einarson, and Trainor (2014) demonstrated caregiver/parent intersynchrony factors, and Paulus (2014) described various models of prosocial behavior, while opting for a multifaceted view. Govrin's (2014) approach appears similar.

Others have developed models related to intersubjectivity. Legerstee (2013) described an early affective attunement through an affective sharing process. Davidov, Zahn-Waxler, Roth-Hanania, and Knafo (2013) described an early-developing sympathy and social connectedness. Despite these models supporting an early-developing view of infant empathy/prosociality, some have queried the validity of the research and models (e.g., Dahl, 2014; Tafreshi, Thompson, & Racine, 2014).

Work with adults emphasizes the core capacity for positive sociality, such as in social cooperation and politics and the public good.

G. Young, *Unifying Causality and Psychology*, DOI 10.1007/978-3-319-24094-7_15

The narratives in self-development that people create are fundamental to adult identity (McAdams, 2013), and so the stories that we tell about ourselves can come to include the innate goodness early in life that philosophers like Descartes had described. Locke's blank slate may have met its match in contemporary research in that empathy/prosociality might be prepared.

However, the ephemeral degree to which this takes place, that it can be easily derailed by lack of support or its opposite attitude, and the importance of environmental input in sustaining it all speak to the standard biology × environment interaction for understanding early empathy/prosociality. Nevertheless, as with many areas in the present book, the typical Nature and Nurture view of behavioral causality is deemed insufficient to capture the full range of influences on it, which is especially the case for empathy/prosociality. Without the personal choices made to actively engage in the behavior out of free will, it will be continually subject to the passive influences of changing biology and environment instead of being bootstrapped by the powerful active forces in the agency of the person him- or herself.

The chapter concludes by showing that the literature review on changes in empathic and prosocial behavior in infancy fits Piaget's model of six sensorimotor substages in infancy, with minor adjustments. My own Neo-Piagetian model (Young, 2011) is quite similar to Piaget's for the infancy period, so that the empirical findings reviewed closely fit my model, as well.

Biology

Undoubtedly, the environmental contributions to social development and behavior are pervasive, so for balance the chapter starts with elucidation of all things biological in this regard, from brain to evolution. Development, however, is dynamic in its integration of these and other factors, so that emphasis on either biology or environment in the equation that governs social development is bound to be incomplete. The following section on relevant influences on social connection highlights not only the biological and related perspectives (e.g., embodiment) but also integrated ones. The section after the next one is on evolution, which also emphasizes the biological perspective. The section that follows the one on evolution is on culture, which brings back the integrated perspective.

Biobehavioral Synchrony

Mikulincer and Shaver (2014a) traced mechanisms of social behavior from brain to group behavior. Briefly, the neural basis of social bonds lies in the collection of factors of neuropeptide hormones, such as oxytocin, neural circuitry of primary emotions, the mesolimbic dopamine system, the mirror neuron system, and other bases in evolution and neuroscience (Mikulincer & Shaver, 2014b). Developmentally, critical mechanisms include infant attachment, biobehavioral synchrony, and parental factors. These mechanisms extend into romantic and couple relationships in adults and into social groups.

Feldman (2014) reported results linking biobehavioral synchrony to genetics and to the brain. In this regard, higher levels of parent–infant gaze synchrony during parent–infant interactions were associated with higher levels of oxytocin (in plasma) and also with the low-risk *CD38* allele (Feldman et al., 2012). Other research found biobehavioral synchrony in maternal–infant heart rate synchrony. Feldman, Magori-Cohen, Galili, Singer, and Louzoun (2011) found that, in maternal face-to-face interactions with 3-month-olds, the heart rates of mother and infant were synchronized within lags of less than one second. The same synchrony was not found with stranger–infant interactions. Moreover, the synchrony was more evident during epochs of affective and vocal synchrony.

Feldman (2014) concluded that biobehavioral synchrony early in life is fine-turned. The infant's early subjective experiences become transformed into interpersonal dyadic activity that changes the subjective into the intersubjective. The latter extends into intersubjective, shared brain activity and other bodily (e.g., heart rate) processes. For further description of Feldman's work, see

Feldman (2015). In that article, not only does she describe biobehavioral synchrony, but also she relates it to the oxytocin system and critical/sensitive period.

Activation/Inhibition Coordination

Tucker, Poulsen, and Luu (2015) related two models of developmental learning to possible associated later developmental disturbances. Specifically, in externalizing learning, neural representations are highly responsive to environmental influences, and this type of learning might facilitate the development of externalizing behavior, depending on the course involved. The learning is associated with dorsal limbic circuits (cingulate, septal, lateral hypothalamic, hippocampal, ventral striatic), and is regulated partly by locus coeruleus norepinephrine and other projection systems (brain stem raphe nucleus serotonin). The internalizing learning system serves to separate attention and self-regulation from immediate environmental influences, especially if there is avoidance and threat. The learning is associated with ventral limbic circuits (anterior temporal and orbital cortex, extended amygdala, dorsal striatal, mediodorsal thalamic) and is self-regulated in part by ventral tegmental dopamine and forebrain acetylcholine projections. This type of learning might facilitate internalizing behavioral disturbance, depending on developmental course.

Developmentally, the external learning system predominates, at first, and then the internalizing one increasingly balances it, but at the cost of lesser flexibility. Neural stability controls in the learning at issue include the balancing of excitatory and inhibitory processes.

Feldman (2015) concurred that early development involves a balancing of activation and inhibition processes. In critical periods, their transition involves inhibitory mechanisms related to GABAergic processes. Generally, the neurobiological mechanisms in critical/sensitive periods involve change in "balance of excitation" to inhibition.

Brain

Introduction Brain scans such as fMRI (functional magnetic resonance imaging) are helping elucidate the functional activity of brain regions and their circuits that are associated with socially relevant behavior, such as prosocial behavior and empathy, not only in adults but also in children. This research is too preliminary to establish the exact regions and circuits involved, and different workers provide different regions, which vary, as well, with the behaviors examined, the tasks used, the populations studied, their ages, and the particular scan methodology used. Therefore, I refrain from trying to integrate this diverse and preliminary work, but do summarize it in detail.

The Prosocial/Empathic Brain Chakroff and Young (2014) referred to the brain as "prosocial." They related the brain regions involved in social cognition (mind perception); processing conflict and discomfort (unpleasant states in others); and reward processing (reward anticipation) to prosocial behavior (and sentiments), as well. These include, respectively, the temporoparietal junction, precuneus, and medial prefrontal cortex (mPFC); anterior cingulate cortex (ACC) and anterior insula (AI); and the ventral striatum and ventral mPFC.

Some of the research that they cited in support of the circuitry of the prosocial brain that they described included the following. In fMRI studies, Rameson, Morelli, and Liberman (2012) found that both empathy and self-report of helping behavior were associated with greater activity in the mPFC and the ACC. Masten, Morelli, and Eisenberger (2011) related prosocial (e.g., consoling) content of emails to activity in the dorsal mPFC and the right AI. Waytz, Zaki, and Mitchell (2012) found that prosocial behavior (e.g., helping in a tedious task) was related to activity in the dorsal mPFC.

Decety and Howard (2014) described brain responses to someone else being in distress. For the adult, a meta-analysis by Lamm, Decety, and Singer (2011) integrated research on brain imaging while adults are exposed to stimuli about someone else expressing pain or distress. The neural network found associated with when another person is expressing pain or distress included the posterior portion of the insula, the amygdala, and the medial orbitofrontal cortex. For Decety and Howard (2014), frontalization takes place over development in cognitive control and response inhibition related to brain responses in the perception of another's distress (e.g., Decety & Michalska, 2010).

As for brain circuits underlying moral cognition, Decety and Howard (2014) specified associations with the orbitofrontal cortex, anterior cingulate cortex, amygdala, ventromedial prefrontal cortex, medial prefrontal cortex, and posterior superior temporal sulcus. They noted that the circuits involved are not unique to moral cognition. Developmentally, moral thinking depends on an emotional learning system and another one associated with decision-making related to reinforcement expectations (mediated by the amygdala and ventromedial prefrontal cortex, respectively; Blair & Fowler, 2008).

As for the neuroscience of empathy, Singer and Hein (2012) presented a model that differentiated it from compassion, emotional contagion, and theory of mind (see Fig. 15.1). Some of the brain regions involved include the medial prefrontal cortex, the superior temporal sulcus, and the temporoparietal junction (see Table 15.1).

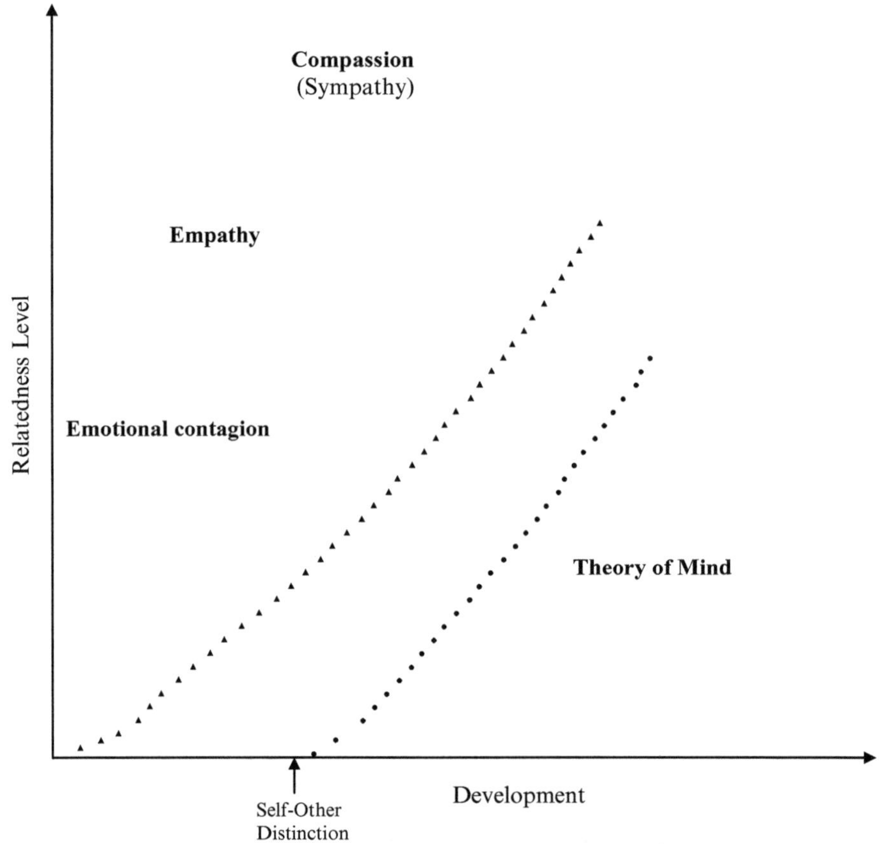

Fig. 15.1 Social relating in evolution: based on emotional contagion, empathy, compassion, and theory of mind. The figure shows the association between relatedness and development as drivers in evolution. Compassion: a feeling of concern for the other and the wish to increase the other's welfare—"Feeling *for* the other." Empathy: emotions of the other are shared; one knows that they are not one's own emotions—"Feeling *as* the other." Emotional contagion: emotions are passed from one person to another; affected individuals are not aware that these emotions originate from others. Theory of mind: (cognitive perspective taking, mentalizing) cognitive inference about the other's mental state. Adapted from Singer and Hein (2012)

Table 15.1 Brain regions associated with understanding others/social relating

Theory of mind	Empathy
Medial prefrontal cortex	Anterior cingulate cortex
Temporal poles	Anterior insula
Superior temporal sulcus	Secondary somatosensory cortex
Temporoparietal junction	–

Adapted from Singer and Hein (2012)

Brain, Cognitive, and Social

Anderson and Beauchamp (2012b) presented a model in developmental neuroscience that helps understand social functioning in childhood (see also Beauchamp & Anderson, 2010). The model is referred to as the sociocognitive integration of abilities model (SOCIAL), and it is a biopsychosocial one that is developmental (see Fig. 15.2).

The model integrates social cognition, communication, and attention/executive function with brain development and internal and external factors toward the development of social skills, such as adjustment, competence, and participation. The neural bases involved relate to the prefrontal and orbitofrontal cortex, in particular.

The model is informed by the somatic marker hypothesis and research on the bilateral ventromedial prefrontal cortex (vmPFC; Taber-Thomas & Tranel, 2012). The former integrates basic motivational, affective, complex reasoning, and action, including in the sociomoral domain (Damasio, 1994, 1995; Damasio, Anderson, & Tranel, 2011; Damasio, Tranel, & Damasio, 1998). The vmPFC is essential for reactivating emotional states that bear on decision-making, e.g., in selecting adaptive behavior, through its interactions with subcortical and cortical structures. In doing so, "somatic markers" are activated as emotional stamps in initial learning associated with rewarding or punishing responses of options chosen. In this sense, somatic markers constitute learned anticipations of emotional experiences associated with future choices (Bechara & Damasio, 2005). In this regard, Thomas, Croft, and Tranel (2011) found that the vmPFC is critical for integrating emotions and sociomoral cognition in cases of ambiguity, uncertainty, and conflict. Greene (2007) has associated the vmPFC with more emotion-based moral judgments and less so with more rational, utilitarian moral judgments. However, Taber-Thomas and Tranel (2012) qualified this dual process model into a more integrative "emotion-reasoning" perspective of moral affect and cognition. Also, they described neural systems theory of mind/face processing and basic motivational/emotional processes.

As for the socialization of social competence in terms of the SOCIAL model, Root, Hastings, and Maxwell (2012) emphasized the parental role (e.g., according to attachment theory, systems theory). For biological influences, among others, they referred to the diathesis-stress model (Beck, 1967, 1983), the Gene × Environment interaction (G × E) model (Caspi et al., 2003), and the differential susceptibility model (e.g., Belsky & Fearon, 2002; Belsky & Pluess, 2009; Ellis & Boyce, 2008; Ellis, Boyce, Belsky, Bakermans-Kranenburg, & van IJzendoorn, 2011; Obradović, Bush, Stamperdahl, Adler, & Boyce, 2010).

About their own research, Root et al. (2012) reported that Hastings and De (2008) conducted a study of emotional socialization and parasympathetic control that supported the diathesis-stress model. Hastings et al. (2008) reported similar results supportive of the differential susceptibility model. Hastings et al. (2011) also found results supportive of this model, this time with salivary cortisol levels to assess adrenocortical functioning.

Yeates et al. (2012) presented a complementary model to the SOCIAL one for social competence in developmental brain disorder (after Yeates et al., 2007; see Fig. 15.3). In their model, the social competence or adjustment outcomes of self-perception and perception of others relate to social information processing, social interaction style, and social environmental factors, aside from the brain insult and abnormalities and risk/resilience that might be involved.

About the brain regions and structures involved in social cognition, Yeates et al. (2012) provided an extensive list (see Table 15.2). They noted that most of the regions/structures are involved in multiple

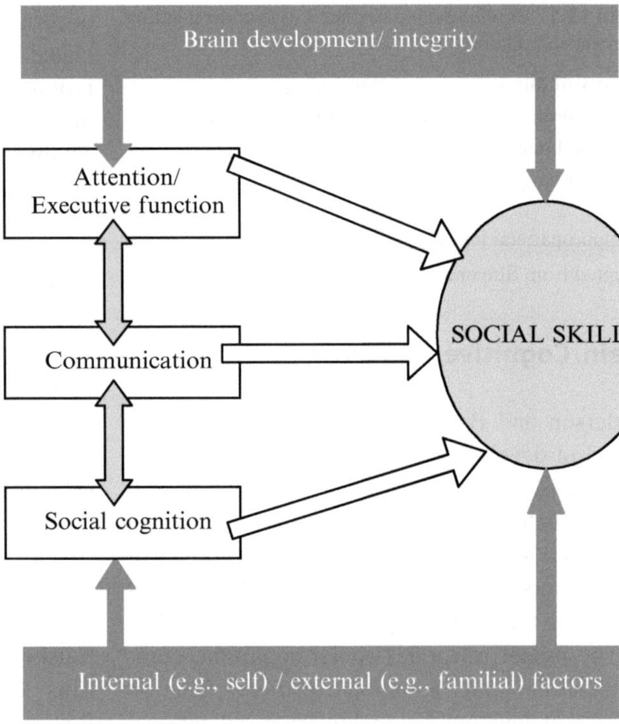

Fig. 15.2 The *So*cio-*co*gnitive *I*ntegration of *A*bilities Mode*l*. The SOCIAL model relates brain, social skills, and other factors in social-cognitive function. Adapted from Anderson and Beauchamp (2012b), based on Beauchamp and Anderson (2010)

social functions, and most specific functions draw on multiple regions/structures. They noted a strong overlap in cognitive/executive and social-cognitive/emotional functioning. They noted the hemispheric asymmetries involved, especially that the left frontal regions are approach-related in function and the right withdrawal-related/disinhibitory (Davidson, 1992; Fox, 1994; Fox et al., 1995; Powell & Voeller, 2004).

Max (2012) also contributed an applied perspective to the SOCIAL model (see Fig. 15.4). In their model, behavioral and psychiatric symptoms are influenced by internal–external factors, attention/executive ones, and social skills/function, with an important mechanism related to approach-avoidance regulation (e.g., Sharp et al., 2011).

Embodiment

Supportive Shai and Fonagy (2014) referred to the parent–infant dance and how parental embodied mentalizing helps orchestrate this interaction. Interactions between parent and infant are implicit and body-based, and not just linguistic. Mentalizing, therefore, is implicit and relies on observable bodily actions. Social cognition is best conceived as embodied (Gallese, 2006), and is adjustable and mutual.

The authors' team developed a parental embodied mentalizing coding system. Using it, they showed that, when measured at 6 months, parental embodied mentalizing predicted infant attachment security at 15 months (Shai & Fonagy, 2014), even after controlling for the more traditional measure of maternal sensitivity. Moreover, it predicted 54-month-old social skills/competence and psychological problems (internalizing and externalizing).

Shai and Fonagy (2014) concluded that parental embodied mentalizing is a meaningful concept and reveals how parent–infant interactions involve the entire body and not just the head or face. For example, their coding system for it includes personal and interpersonal space, kinesthetics in movement quality, and self- and other-regulation of distress and arousal.

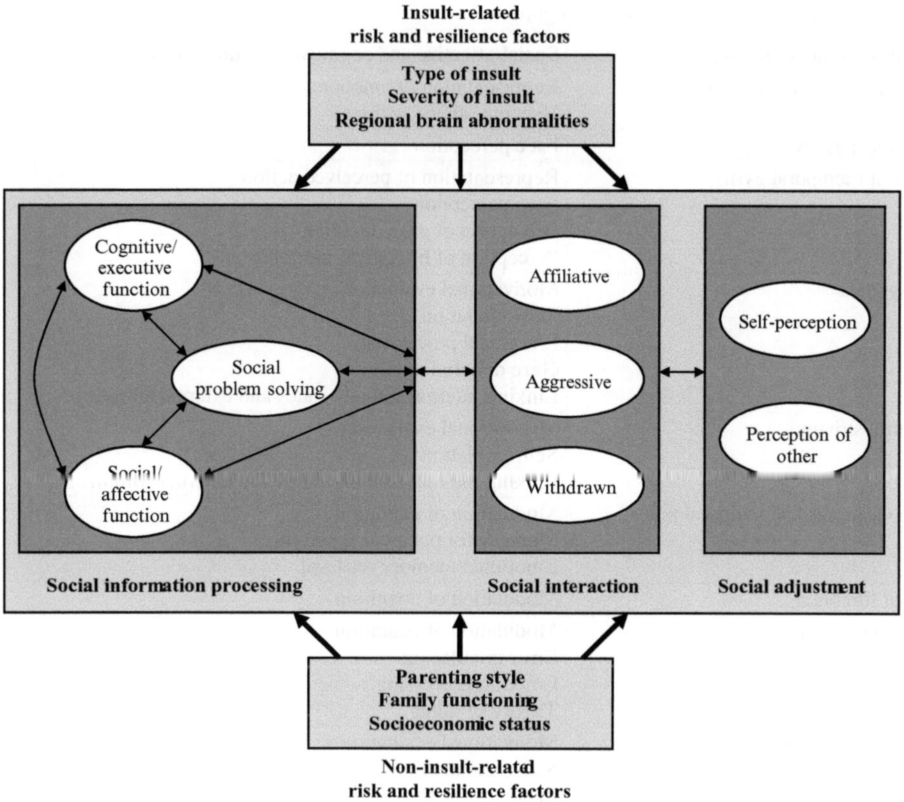

Fig. 15.3 An integrative, heuristic model of social competence in children with brain disorder. The model is based on the SOCIAL one and integrates social information processing/interaction/adjustment with brain insult/abnormalities/disorder and other factors. Adopted with permission of Guilford Press. Theoretical approaches to understanding social function in childhood brain insults: toward the integration of social neuroscience and developmental psychology by Yeates, K. O., Bigler, E. D., Gerhardt, C. A., Rubin, K. H., Stancin, T., Taylor, H. G., & Vannatta, K. in *Developmental social neuroscience and childhood brain insult: Theory and practice* by V. Anderson & M. H. Beauchamp, Copyright 2012, reproduced with permission of Guilford Press. [Figure 10.1, Page 210]

Nonsupportive The demonstration that neonates can imitate has been controversial (Meltzoff & Moore, 1997). The study involved showed that newborns can imitate mouth movements such as tongue protrusion and mouth opening. The authors offered a nativist account of the early imitation, relating it to proprioceptive, kinesthetic feedback mechanisms involving the development of early maps of body movement in relation to supramodal perception. However, the research has not always been replicated and alternative interpretations rely on simpler mechanisms, such as stimulus–response ones related to oral behavior.

Lodder, Rotteveel, and van Elk (2014) cast doubt on claims that neonatal imitation is innate. Their review found that only one behavior (tongue protrusion) might show consistent results in these regards. Moreover, the imitation of this behavior might not reflect neonatal imitation, per se. Therefore, the concept of nativist enactivists, that infants possess non-mentalistic, embodied intersubjective understanding, does not meet the empirical test. More likely, early imitation reflects learning through social interaction and is neither general nor innate. The data support a point of view for this area that involves "empirical enactivism."

Table 15.2 Brain structures and social cognition

Brain structure or region	Social/affective and cognitive/executive functions
Temporoparietal junction	Representation of emotional response Viewing others' actions
Fusiform gyrus	Face perception
Superior temporal gyrus	Representation of perceived action Face perception Perception of gaze direction Perception of biological motion
Amygdala	Motivational evaluation Self-regulation Emotional processing Gaze discrimination Linking internal somatic states and external stimuli
Ventral striatum	Motivational evaluation Self-regulation Linking internal somatic states and external stimuli
Hippocampus and temporal poles	Modulation of cognition Memory for personal experiences Emotional memory retrieval
Basal forebrain	Modulation of cognition
Cingulate cortex	Modulation of cognition Error monitoring Emotion processing Theory of mind
Orbitofrontal cortex	Motivational evaluation Self-regulation Theory of mind
Medial frontal cortex	Theory of mind Action monitoring Emotional regulation Emotional responses to socially relevant stimuli Monitoring of outcomes associated with punishment and reward
Dorsolateral frontal cortex	Cognitive executive functions Working memory

Adopted with permission of Guilford Press. Theoretical approaches to understanding social function in childhood brain insults: Toward the integration of social neuroscience and developmental psychology by Yeates, K. O., Bigler, E. D., Gerhardt, C. A., Rubin, K. H., Stancin, T., Taylor, H. G., & Vannatta, K. in *Developmental social neuroscience and childhood brain insult: Theory and practice* by V. Anderson & M. H. Beauchamp, Copyright 2012, reproduced with permission of Guilford Press. [Table 10.1, Page 215]

Zmyj and Buttelmann (2014) proposed an integrative model of imitation infancy that accommodated the opposing views that it takes place (a) due to the similarity between the infant's and model's body posture and the elicitation of action effects (e.g., Paulus, Hunnius, Vissers, & Bekkering, 2011a, 2011b), or (b) due to a rational evaluation of the observed action (e.g., Gergely, Bekkering, & Király, 2002). In the integrated model of Zmyj and Buttelmann (2014), imitation in infancy is enabled by the perception of motor resonance and, then, is guided by rational evaluation of modeled action. Also, infants are capable of early imitation even if it might not be in the neonatal period (Meltzoff, 2007). Multiple researchers are referring to mirror neurons in this regard.

Mirror Neurons Fogassi and Rizzolatti (2013) described the mirror neuron mechanism as the neurophysiological basis for unifying action perception and action execution. These neurons reside in the parieto-frontal mirror system or network. Originally, they were demonstrated to function in the ventral premotor cortex of the macaque

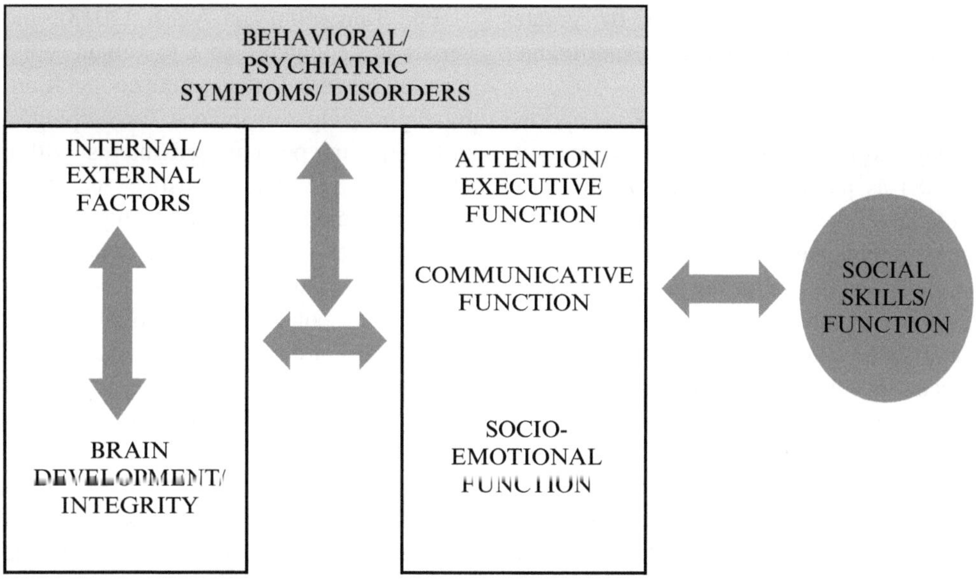

Fig. 15.4 The SOCIAL model applied to mental symptoms/disorders. Behavioral and psychiatric symptoms are contributors and outcomes of the SOCIAL model the other components. Adapted from Max (2012)

monkey. Mirror neurons show congruence between visual and motor responses, matching the goal of an observed motor act and the goal of an executed one. They might respond equally to seeing food grasped and grasping it, for example. Recently, mirror neurons for eye movements have been found in the lateral intraparietal area. Other neurons encode body-directed rather than object-directed motor acts, further cementing "understanding" of others. The mirror system has been found to have other areas associated with it (e.g., middle temporal cortex). The authors showed that the "intention" to realize a particular motor goal is represented "directly" by "dedicated" "chained" neuronal networks in the motor system.

Developmentally, Fogassi and Rizzolatti (2013) described that as soon as a motor sequence is executed, the entire motor chain implicated is activated (Cattaneo et al., 2007). EMG (electromyography) activity of the mylohyoid muscle (MH; involved in mouth opening) was recorded during children's grasping for either eating or placing (in a container) or to observations of the same. Reaching even before contact activated MH activity increase in the condition of reaching for eating, whether self-conducted or observed, but not in the condition of reaching for placement.

Cook, Bird, Catmur, Press, and Heyes (2014) offered an account of mirror neurons that involves associative learning rather than a "richer," more advanced action understanding and sociocognition. Mirror neurons are adapted to encode the multiple correlated sensorimotor experiences that are prevalent in the developmental environment. These experiences derive from "lean" factors, such as self-observation, being imitated (and being rewarded for imitation), and the resulting correlations in kinesthetic and proprioceptive as well as sensory experiences in isomorphic observed and executed movements (per contra, for richer interpretations of mirror neuron function, for example, see Rizzolatti, 2014).

Cannon et al. (2016) found evidence for a neural mirror system in 9-month-olds. They measured in the mu frequency band (6–9 Hz) event-related desynchronization (ERD) from electroencephalogram (EEG) recording during reaching events (scalp electrodes over motor regions). The infants both reached for toys and watched an experimenter reach for toys. Reaching competence was measured for latency to reach, reach errors, hand preshaping, and bimanual reaches. Reaching/grasping competence (especially speed) was associated with ERD. Also, the more the reaching was competent, the greater was the ERD while observing the experimenter reach/grasp.

As for adults, Michael et al. (2014) supported a differentiated model of the mirror neuron system (MNS) as playing a causal role in action understanding (identifying the goals/underlying intentions of movements). They used continuous theta-burst stimulation over the premotor cortex, which serves to inhibit tissue excitability. The stimulation was applied over the subjects' premotor hand or lip areas. Then, the participants completed a pantomime recognition task; half of the trials involved pantomimed hand actions and half mouth ones.

The results were consistent with a model of distinct components of action understanding in the prefrontal motor cortex (PMC), part of the MNS. Hand and lip area stimulation reduced accurate recognition of observed, pantomimed hand and mouth action, respectively. The authors concluded that somatically organized regions of the PMC contribute differentially to the causality of action understanding. The mechanisms for action understanding and action production overlap. [For a recent review of social cognition from the perspective of embodiment and mirror neurons, see Uithol and Gallese (2015). It concerns the emotional component compared to the action one, in particular.]

Evolution

Nonhuman Primates

Model Tomasello and Vaish (2013) explored the origin of cooperation and morality by comparing human evolution, nonhuman primate findings, and human development for these behavioral dimensions. The authors developed a general two-step sequence applicable to human evolution and child development, in particular. First, individuals express sympathy or fairness to specific others in mutualistic, prosocial interaction. Then, they follow and enforce group-wide social norms in the larger world. Respectively, these concepts refer to second-person morality and agent-neutral morality.

For Tomasello and Vaish (2013), morality serves as a counterbalance to human selfishness. Its main function is to promote cooperation either by suppressing self-interest for helping/sharing or by equating personal self-interest with that of others (in reciprocity, justice, equity, norm-following, and norm-enforcement).

Great apes have been found to help and share, but only in situations of low cost or if reciprocity is a realistic outcome. They collaborate, but not with an overarching attitude, except for some groups in some circumstances. To the contrary, they socialize especially in terms of dominance hierarchies.

Showing a different pattern, human society exhibits critical cooperative social organization in at least six major spheres. These include food procurement (subsistence), socially-sanctioned property-ownership, designation, child care, teaching, politics, and norm creation. According to Tomasello and Vaish (2013), these social behaviors evolved in two major steps. First, our ancestors became collaborative foragers. Joint success assured self-interest needs, so that helping others in trouble served self-interest. Controlling cheating in interdependent groups facilitated joint and thus personal success, as well. The morality that evolved, therefore, was "joint." In the second phase of evolution of cooperation and morality in our ancestors, intergroup competition (present when modern humans first evolved) accelerated motivation to collaborate and to participate in group life. Individuals had to conform to a "group mindedness" (e.g., in tribes). Norms that were created (to follow and to control others) were impersonal and agent-neutral. Morality became "collective."

Vaish and Tomasello (2014) further developed their theoretical model on the evolution and early ontogeny of cooperation and morality. They described their model as the "interdependence" hypothesis because, evolutionarily, our human ancestors became interdependent in collaborative foraging or in their mutualistic collaboration (they were "forced" to by ecological change; good cooperators were "advantaged." I would add that they were "selected"). In a second evolutionary step, emerging contemporary humans increased their collaborative skills and motivations related to living in groups, in general. They developed "group mindedness." In this regard, note that I refer to adult though as "collective intelligence" (Young, 2011).

Herrmann, Misch, Hernandez-Lloreda, and Tomasello (2015) demonstrated that the development of self-control from 3 to 6 years of age includes comparable skills not found in chimpanzees at the latter age. They gave six ecologically-valid tasks on self-control to both human and chimpanzee subjects. There were two tasks in each of three categories: reactivity (approach-avoidance in situations of novelty or uncertainty); inhibitory control (inhibit a prepotent response for immediate gratification or for a just-learned behavior when the task demands were changed slightly); and attentional control (focus on a problem having attractive distractions or repeated failures).

The results showed that the 6-year-olds were distinguished both from the 3-year-olds and from chimpanzees in controlling their impulses. For example, they could better resist the impulse for immediate gratification in order to get a later reward; they could better resist the impulse to repeat a previously successful action that had become ineffective; they could better resist attending to distracting noises while engaging in problem-solving; and they could better persist in light of repeated task failure.

The authors concluded that advances in humans' self-control skills take place at an age consistent with the start of formal schooling. I maintain that the results of this study on self- and impulse-control address the question of human exceptionality, for example, in terms of advances in Neo-Piagetian thought into the stage of concrete operations (Young, 2011) and beyond (e.g., adolescent abstract formal and adult collective intelligence thought).

Others Warneken's (2015) review of early prosocial behavior supported a view that it has evolutionary advantages, for example, preparing for participating in family chores as of 3 years of age. Some of the research cited includes studies on 12-month-olds warning not to reach into a container having an aversive object (Knudsen & Liszkowski, 2013; also Knudsen & Liszkowski, 2012a for 18-month-olds). Other research with 18-month-olds showed they could direct people to the correct location of a sought object when the target person had a mistaken belief about its location (Knudsen & Liszkowski, 2012b). At this age, they would fetch an object from the correct location when a target person had a mistaken belief it was in a box and had struggled to open it. At 2 years, children would return an object to a target person who had not ever noticed it had rolled away (Warneken, 2013). At 3 years, children would give a target person a functioning object instead of a nonfunctioning one when the latter had been requested (e.g., in a method using a cup with a hole in it; Martin & Olson, 2013).

Fletcher, Simpson, Campbell, and Overall (2015) proposed that the evolution of human social intelligence and cooperative skills had been facilitated by the prohominin propensity for pair bonding, engaging in romantic love to solidify the pair bonding, and their associated massive investment in child rearing. For example, long term monogamy is associated across species with a larger brain. *Homo erectus* appears to have lived in small groups centered on monogamous pair bonds and cooperative breeding. Our stretched development gives us the large window needed for our complex culture, and romantic love and long term pair-bonding have accelerated evolutionarily this acquisition.

In terms of evolutionary mechanisms influencing human altruism, Kurzban, Burton-Chellew, and West (2015) referred to natural selection, inclusive fitness, kin selection, reciprocity, indirect reciprocity, and the like. They considered group selection in the multilevel selection approach (Wilson, 1975) as a conceptualization of evolutionary dynamics in the same way as kin selection. Both approaches (group, kin selection) find that cooperation is promoted by the behavior resulting in increased group benefits and reduced individual costs.

de Waal (2012), who works with primates, presented a hard-wired model of empathy and imitation. Empathy activates an emotional state through a "perception-action mechanism" (PAM). The "other" in a social exchange shares the "same" PAM, leading to imitation and other social intelligence behavior. The model is presented in

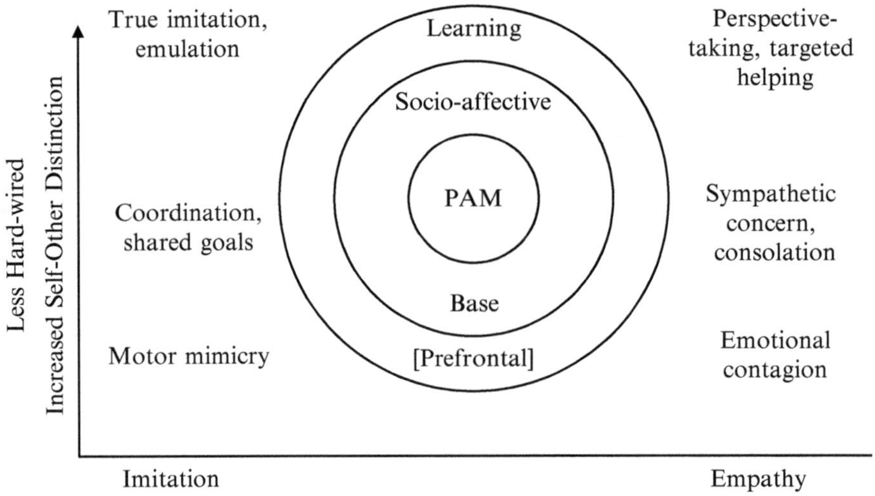

Fig. 15.5 Social relating in evolution: subsumed cores. Empathy (at right) induces an emotional state in the subject similar to that of the object. The perception-action mechanism (PAM) is at its core. The figure's outer layers (e.g., sympathetic concern, perspective taking) build on a hard-wired socio-affective base. As for the left side of the figure (imitation), it starts with motor mimicry, and then coordination, shared goals, imitation, and emulation. The person's more recent evolutionary acquisitions depend both on learning and on prefrontal functioning, but they still are fundamentally linked to the inner core. Adapted from de Waal (2012)

Fig. 15.5. de Waal and Ferrari (2012) argued for a neuroscientific approach to mind in primates. Ferrari and Fogassi (2012) described the evolution of the mirror neuron system.

For an evolutionary perspective on cognition, motivation, and social behavior consult Cosmides and Tooby (2013). Their evolutionary psychology perspective includes discussion of game theory, cooperation, and detection of cheaters. Granted, knowledge of evolution can inform social psychology, but a developmental perspective also is needed, and it should be one that covers the lifespan.

Culture

For examination of the concept of cultural evolution, exclusive of its interaction with biological evolution, see Kemp and Mesoudi (2014). They described the concept of "cultural group selection." In the end, Darwinian theory can explain human culture and serve to synthesize all the social sciences (Mesoudi, 2011).

Smaldino (2014a, 2014b) has developed a model of cultural evolution that considers group-level traits as emergent. For example, a bee colony can solve problems only at the level of the whole. Also, conscious attention reflects a higher-order behavioral entity beyond the activity of the individual neurons involved. Groups are considered in terms of the differentiated roles of individuals. Classic multilevel selection theory (Wilson, 2014) emphasizes less these aspects of cultural group activity. The approach by Smaldino has extended multilevel selection to the point that it is equivalent to the approach of inclusive fitness.

Kesebir (2012) proposed a systems account of human social behavior. He applied the concept of "superorganism" derived from work with bees (Hölldobler & Wilson, 2009) to the human case. Humans appeared to possess all the properties of a superorganism, such as in communication, unity of action, low levels of heritability, egalitarianism, and collective conflict resolution.

Henrich (2011) related the work on cultural learning to gene–culture co-evolutionary theory (Boyd & Richerson, 1985). Cultural learning provides adaptations that constitute a second means of adaptive transmission, because it can alter both the physical and social environments in which reproducing phenotypes function (with their characteristics often underpinned by their genotypes to a degree). He cited the example of how cooked food became a selective force through the physical/physiological changes it permitted, leading to more energy available for "brain building" (Wrangham, 2009). Henrich (2011) proposed that over-imitation might have evolved not only to help acquire information but also to learn social norms, which are crucial to social integration (e.g., rituals, etiquette), and to keeping one's reputation.

Nielsen (2012) supported the role of imitation in cultural evolution, but also, he valued the role of pretend play. Fogarty, Strimling, and Laland (2011) pointed out the parallel importance of teaching and imitation, arguing that the latter is "extremely rare" in other animals. Dean, Kendal, Schapiro, Thierry, and Laland (2012) added that, among the suite of (a) sociocognitive and (b) teaching skills that are unique to humans, are (a) imitation of actual actions made by others and (b) verbal instruction, respectively.

Developmentally, Hopper, Marshall-Pescini, and Whiten (2012) described social learning and culture in children and chimpanzees. Table 15.3 presents four social learning mechanisms active in social learning: imitation, response facilitation, program-level (hierarchical) imitation, and emulation.

Table 15.3 Mechanisms of social learning in evolution

Social learning mechanism	Definition
Imitation	Learning an intrinsic portion of a novel act
Response facilitation	A viewed action increases the probability of doing the same. Only actions already in the repertoire can be facilitated in this process (Byrne, 1994)
Program-level imitation	Combining novel and already existing actions to duplicate a hierarchically-organized sequence
Emulation	Object movement reenactment—the observer replicates the movements of the physical artifact with which the model interacted Goal emulation—achieving but by using their own method to attain it Affordance learning—learning about the physical properties of the environment/relations among objects

Adapted from Hopper et al. (2012)

Development

Models

Nativist

In their edited book, Mikulincer and Shaver (2012) included chapters on the development of moral and related behavior that covered the range of biological, environmental, and cognitive factors as causes. For example, Bloom (2012) examined the nativist approach to the development of morality. He argued that we are born with an "innate and universal" moral evaluation system. As young as 3 months of age, infants prefer to look at prosocial characters (Hamlin, Wynn, & Bloom, 2010).

Jensen, Vaish, and Schmidt (2014) considered that humans are unique in their ability to cooperate with nonkin. Infants appear automatically attuned to others (Geangu, Benga, Stahl, & Striano, 2010). Even in the first year, infants can express empathy (Rochat, 2003). They express concern for distressed victims, as inferred from their nonverbal behavior (Roth-Hanania, Davidov, & Zahn-Waxler, 2011). They can express a sense of fairness (Sommerville, Schmidt, Yun, & Burns, 2013). They are capable of engaging in sharing in the first year (Schmidt & Sommerville, 2011).

Legerstee (2013) argued for innate social developmental or early affective attunement mechanisms. According to her, neoconstructivists consider that the newborn is preadapted for early communication and intersubjective sharing. They connect with the social surround, share affect, and bond socially. The young brain provides a biological basis for social interaction (for example, large neocortices; Dunbar, 2013) and a mirror neuronal system (Gallese & Rochat, 2013).

Legerstee (2013) presented her concept of an "affect sharing device" (AFS) with which infants appear to be born. Its components include the ability to: (a) recognize others as self-similar; (b) express sensitivity to the emotions of others and self; and (c) perceive whether adults are in tune with their needs/emotions. The AFS provides infants with an inborn "sense" of the people around them with whom they can engage in intersubjective experience and social attunement.

People are not only perceived as whether they are "like me" (Meltzoff, 2007) but also whether they are emotionally "with me."

Environment

Janoff-Bulman (2012) related parental practice to moral-type development. Restrictive-type parenting versus more nurturant type behavior should elicit proscriptive vs. prescriptive type responses (sensitive to negative outcomes, based on inhibition; and sensitive to positive outcomes, based on activation, respectively, Gray, 1990). Shaver and Mikulincer (2012) related attachment security/insecurity experiences to empathy and authenticity.

Govrin (2014) described various models of early moral development. The author proposed that moral judgment develops in the first year of life through the internal representations framed in caregiver attachments that develop. Early social interactions facilitate the development of an internal representation of rules system about right/wrong judgments and their construal, understanding, and use.

Govrin (2014) described another model of early prosocial behavior. That is, young children act prosocially in order to facilitate interacting socially, because of the latter's pleasure and social affiliation. The behavior evident is more for reasons of social motivation than an explicit prosocial one.

In the fourth model under discussion, the social-normative one, the social environment is considered as the source of prosocial behavior through its support, fostering, and scaffolding (e.g., Hammond & Carpendale, 2012).

Govrin (2014) continued with goal-alignment models, in which the young child lacks self-other differentiation skills, but still can act prosocially because he/she appropriates the goal of the other as if it were his/her own. The child might feel the same emotion as another in need or distress, and "rely" on the witnessed object-directed behavior and effort to understand the "cause" of the evident need/distress that has developed. In order to "alleviate" the need/distress, the child acts in a manner that appears prosocial but, in actuality, is "nonsympathetic."

Overall, the models that Govrin (2014) described for early morality are experience-based (attachment), social-motivational (pleasureful), and cognitive (goals). For recent work on the importance of the early environment on prosocial (helping) behavior and awareness of the other's mental state, see Dahl (2015) and Kärtner (2015), respectively. The former emphasizes the role of encouragement/thanking/praising and the latter parenting (cultural) beliefs and practices. The next model under discussion was generated in the adult context, but has relevancy to children. It, too, is cognitive-oriented.

Cognitive

Self Control Baumeister (2012) distinguished the root causes and also the proximal causes in expressing behavior that can be considered evil. He referred to: (a) evolution; (b) threatened egotism; (c) idealism; and (d) sadism as root causes and, as proximal causes, he referred to factors such as self-control and its breakdown. In this regard, Baumeister and Graham (2012) related moral behavior to self-control, rational choice, and intentional planning as part of a set of psychological capacities involved in free will. We can consciously imagine multiple alternatives, choose the best ones, resist temptations and antisocial impulses, and we can even select prosocial actions involving the sacrifice of selfish advantage through these capacities, thereby promoting moral judgment and moral action.

Piaget Hammond (2014) took the position that Piaget (1932/1997, 1945/1951, 1976) developed a body of developmental theory that could help explain early prosocial behavior in children. Piaget only briefly mentioned early moral-related behavior. He considered it as involving a practice phase as preparatory to a later representational one. Helping begins at the action level and morality develops further in a developing cognitive base. It is motor and egocentric in nature. In his model, infants should be able to help instrumentally by learning and using their sensory and motor skills.

Piaget's work can reconcile views that infants are natural altruists and unhelpful helpers. For Piaget, children must first engage actively, or practice, morally relevant activity (Carpendale, 2009). The young child acquires some early learning of some aspects of helping, which is "purely motor" and individualized, leading to "ritualized" schemas rather than moral representations (e.g., as in helping by engaging in cleaning with others). Infants can imitate helpful actions, but only instrumentally without moral (empathic) understanding. This view does not presuppose that early helping must involve knowledge of the mind of the other, unlike some contemporary accounts. Hammond (2014) concluded that research is needed on ecologically valid, naturalistic helping behavior.

Comment

The review of the various models on the origins of early morality range from the biological (nativist) to the environmental (parental). There are also various cognitive models. Most likely, all the models contribute to understanding the development of early morality. In origin, it is surely interactively social, motivational, cognitive, environmental, including cultural, and biological.

Developmental Research Review

In the following, I review developmental research and concepts that further specify the origins of early morality. The work involves not only the earliest years but also work with children.

Year 1 and Before

Biobehavioral Synchrony Feldman (2014) has explored extensively biobehavioral synchrony as a basis of social affiliation from early in life onward. It is a process that facilitates social group adhesion and collaborative function. Human mothers engage in synchronous, coordinated temporal correspondences with their infants. Indeed, they create temporal contingencies between their social behavior and infant state right from the first hours post-birth (Feldman & Eidelman, 2007). In this way, infants experience a temporal matching across their state with maternal/social environment responsivity.

At about 3 months, Feldman (2014) continued, infants' behavior in maternal interactions becomes more active. The sequences involve coordinated gaze patterns, co-vocalizations, mutual positive affect expression, and affectionate touch. Next, the 3- to 9-month period constitutes a critical period in biobehavioral synchrony. The degree of synchrony in this period predicts later childhood cognitive and social-emotional acquisitions (Feldman, 2007a, 2007b), as well as extent of optimal social adaptation and depression in adolescence (Feldman, 2010).

Nativism Hamlin (2014a) studied the development of helping behavior in young infants. She showed that, in the first few months of life, infants do not exhibit global social evaluation in context because they lack domain-general rather than domain-specific skills (related to limited memory and processing capacities). However, at 4.5 months of age, infants in the appropriate laboratory task context could indeed prefer (as demonstrated in the behavior of selectively reaching to) those who were "nice" (givers) compared to "mean" (hinderers) in action toward "nice" (helping, prosocial) puppets and those who were mean (not nice) to mean (antisocial) puppets. This demonstrates that, at this age, infants can exhibit context-dependent social evaluation.

Hamlin (2015) showed that 6- to 11-month-olds preferred to reach for animated helpers compared to hinderers. Scarf, Imuta, Colombo, and Hayne (2012) had argued that, rather than reflecting a choice for the social value of helping, the infants were choosing helpers due to confounding influences of uncontrolled lower-order perceptual events in the scenes witnessed. However, Hamlin (2015) controlled for the possible confounds. For example, the climbers in the revised experiment to the original (Hamlin, Wynn, & Bloom, 2007) did not bounce when they arrived at the top of the hill after being helped. Moreover, when the climber's gaze was not consistent with (looking up) to the goal of climbing, the helper was not preferred relative to the hinderer in the test phase.

Hamlin (2015) concluded that infants appear sensitive to the "goal" of the actor involved, and respond to the helpful/hindering actions of agents in terms of their inferred mental states. When goals are facilitated by prosocial behavior, even young infants selectively attend to and reach for prosocial agents relative to antisocial hindering ones.

Hamlin et al. (2007) and Hamlin, Wynn, Bloom, and Mahajan (2011) had shown that infants generally prefer individuals who help others and those who mistreat others who had harmed third parties. Hamlin, Mahajan, Liberman, and Wynn (2013) reported results with 9- and 14-month-old infants that there might be an early preference to like whom one recognizes as similar to oneself and to dislike others who are not. Specifically, they found that, even at 9 months of age, infants preferred individuals who treated well others similar to them and poorly others who were not. Hamlin et al. (2013) noted that infants did not have a blanket liking of helpers, so that the results reflect a liking related to self–target similarity. The authors concluded that the social preferences described might have an innate basis, but research with younger infants is required before any statement about innate origin is testable.

Tafreshi et al. (2014) questioned the face validity of laboratory studies using looking and reaching to infer the nature of infant morality. Dahl (2014) added that morality taken in the broad sense (of judging right/wrong, good/bad, and deserving of reward/punishment) has not been appropriately investigated in the first year of life. There are as yet no studies in this age period on infant evaluating negatively their own transgressions.

Hamlin (2014b) maintained that the evidence does not support these assertions. She argued that some of the terminology of the critics is confused. Moreover, there is sufficient evidence in favor of the "core knowledge" model of the early human mind pertaining to early morality and sociomoral evaluations. For example, Hamlin (2014b) reported that, by 4 ½ months of age, infants prefer those who prevent the goals of those who had engaged in the hindering of others. This shows that infants do not solely prefer helpers. The results suggest that context is taken into account and, at this age, preferences are established based on influences about the mental state(s) of the character(s) involved.

Prenatal Davidov et al. (2013) argued that already in the first year infants can express concern for others, and in their literature review they concentrated on the feeling of concern for others (e.g., sympathy). In this regard, relative to the control condition of loud sounds, newborns already respond to recorded cries of other infants by getting distressed (e.g., Geangu et al., 2010).

For infants, for the self–other differentiation underlying feeling of concern, a simpler implicit type of self-knowledge should suffice (e.g., the subjective pre-reflective knowledge involved when newborns discriminate their own recorded cries and those of another newborn; Dondi, Simion, & Caltran, 1999). Infants do not need the explicit, self-reflective knowledge as found in toddlers (e.g., as demonstrated in their touching of their surreptitiously rouged nose seen in the mirror compared to the nose reflection in the mirror, which is the behavior evident in the year-old, for example).

According to Davidov et al. (2013), Roth-Hanania et al. (2011) demonstrated that moderate levels of affective and cognitive empathy are already present in 8-month-olds responding to maternal distress and to peer distress. Moreover, the degree of empathy predicted prosocial behavior in the second year, indicative of early dispositional individual differences. For Davidov et al. (2013), infants express a fundamental motive for social connectedness.

Further, for twin pairs examined *prenatally*, movements by one co-twin toward the other compared to self-directed movements differed in motion pattern (Castiello et al., 2010). Therefore, for Davidov et al. (2013), the self–other differentiation necessary to support other concern, and so recognize the other relative to the self as hurting, appears to develop even in utero.

Preparation Kuhlmeier, Dunfield, and O'Neill (2014) reviewed models of early prosocial behavior and found the "partner choice" model appropriate. This model involves choosing partners based on prior interactions and inferred characteristics of the characters involved. When reciprocity can be expected from others having prosocial dispositions and "positive valence," early prosocial behavior is promoted. The social evaluation evidenced in the first year of life in this context (e.g., Hamlin & Wynn, 2011) might serve as an "adaptive preparation" for later childhood prosociality.

Social Other researchers are more conservative about any rich interpretation of early prosocial behavior. In this regard, Martin and Olson (2015) maintained that early prosocial behavior is quite selective and is multiply motivated. For the former, for example, generally it is more directed to adults that children. For the latter, it might take place for both internal and external motivations but might be generally social in nature rather than prosocial, per se.

Comment The review of the developmental material on early morality and related behavior that has been undertaken has a decidedly biological flavor, with research addressing prenatal influences, biobehavioral synchrony, nativism, and preparedness. As for the work on the second year of life in the next section, this basic theme is expanded to include embodiment and normative approaches, in particular. The section after the next one for the second year of life is on children and it returns to biological themes in developing morality, along with cognitive ones, but with the experiential/social always included. It would seem that, like many other phenomena in the present book that have been discussed, a biopsychosocial perspective affords an integrating model.

Year 2

Embodiment Waters et al. (2014) studied stress or affect contagion in 12- to 14-month-olds after their mothers were placed in a laboratory situation designed to induce negative or positive social evaluative stress concurrent with their separation from the infants. Sympathetic nervous system activity was monitored by electrocardiography in both participants. The infants were not directly exposed to the maternal stressor.

The study showed that mothers' stress reactions are embodied in the infants in the reunion situation. The infants' heart reactivity mirrored that of the mother's reactivity to the stress exposure. The stress situation induced greater physiological covariation when it was negative, and the effect became more pronounced with time. There were behavioral consequences, as well—social stress in the mothers led to more infant stranger avoidance.

Waters et al. (2014) concluded that stress contagion involves a reciprocal dynamic between mothers and infants. Moreover, maternal stress immediately influences offspring physiological reactivity, indicating that mother and infant engage in a "physiological attunement" in which stress "gets under the skin." Finally, the external social world can affect indirectly the infant physiologically through its effects on the caregiver.

Relative to controls, Cirelli et al. (2014) found that prosocial behavior in 14-month-olds was promoted by having bounced in synchrony to music with the partner. Interpersonal motor synchrony at this age encourages social bonding. The authors concluded that interpersonal motor synchrony helps establish each other as similar to the other, which potentiates affiliative behavior. According to me, this model is consistent with the shared embodiment or enactive (and dynamical) perspective of social origins.

Contagion Paulus (2014) explored models of prosocial behavior in the 1- to 2-year-old period. He described four competing models in the field. He opted for a multifaceted approach in which varied types of motivations underlie different types of prosocial behavior; also, each might have different ontogenies and mechanisms.

In this regard, infants might help comfort and share because of emotional or affect sharing or contagion. In this model, perceiving another in a mode of need or distress triggers an equivalent (isomorphic) emotional state empathically in the infant/toddler. The result is that very young children might try to comfort him/herself, and through this self–other differentiation and feeling sympathy for the other, prosociality (comforting the other) develops.

Strategic Selectivity Martin and Olson (2015) reviewed the evidence for three major theories of early sociality and concluded that infants in the second year of life demonstrate prosocial behavior due to multiple motivations, and are selective in doing so. The research, then, support neither an extrinsic model of reinforcement leading to learning of prosociality nor an intrinsic model of indiscriminate prosociality that becomes more selective with age. Note that selectivity at this age is strategic, for example, recipients receive help from infants so that the infants might achieve another goal. That is, early prosociality is not inherently altruistic. However, this does not mean that the behavior is consciously strategic or expressed for purely selfish reasons.

As for the evidence in support of the model, Martin and Olson (2015) noted that (a) 18-month-olds helped a party to complete a task even if they had to disengage from fun toys (Warneken & Tomasello, 2008); (b) 19-month-olds preferred to reward helpers of third parties over hinderers (Dahl, Schuck, & Campos, 2013); and (c) 21-month-olds gave a desirable object to an adult who had tried to help them (albeit unsuccessfully; control conditions—refusal to help; accidentally help; no intention to help).

Norms Tomasello and Vaish (2013) addressed early collaboration/commitment, sympathy/helping, and equality/sharing. For example, when cooperative activity breaks down, 1-year-olds will try to actively re-engage the other, and this happens even if the partner is not necessary for completion of the task at hand (Warneken, Gräfenhain, & Tomasello, 2012). Also, 1-year-olds express concern and prosocial activity toward a victim of harm even if the victim is not overtly distressed (Vaish, Carpenter, & Tomasello, 2009). Further, they prefer to touch prosocial characters relative to antisocial ones (Hamlin & Wynn, 2011). Finally, they expect fair resource distribution and also prefer fair distributors (respectively, Schmidt & Sommerville, 2011; Geraci & Surian, 2011).

Overall, for Tomasello and Vaish (2013), even infants readily engage in collaboration and they recognize social interdependence. They help others even without personal benefit, and they express social equity. However, they behave from an individual standpoint and not from a norm-based one, unlike the case for toddlers.

According to Tomasello and Vaish (2013), preschoolers enter a second stage of norm-based morality. They are able to enforce social norms, behave appropriately when anticipating that they will be judged, react negatively to a lack of remorse, and, indeed, actively seek to understand and abide by norms.

As for mechanisms that enable the developmental progression in cooperation and morality that has been described, Tomasello and Vaish (2013) referred to social-cognitive developmental and socialization/culture influences. The former changes in development, but not necessarily abruptly.

Vaish and Tomasello (2014) described further research on early individual prosocial tendencies and individual group-minded, normative tendencies. For example, infants participate in joint activities. Preschoolers ensure that a partner receives a reward in a task even after they had received theirs. At this age, cooperation is "inherently joint" and interdependent (Hamann, Warneken, & Tomasello, 2012).

Joint activity is indicated when infants can point to a location known to them for the placement of an object when an adult is searching for it ("informative" pointing, at 12 months of age; Liszkowski, Carpenter, & Tomasello, 2008). Further, as mentioned above, they show concern and prosocial actions when a "victim" is harmed even if the victim does not indicate overt distress (at 18 months of age; Vaish et al., 2009). Also, they prefer equal distributors and equal distributions (at 15 months of age; Geraci & Surian, 2011; Schmidt & Sommerville, 2011).

Children

Cognition Chernyak and Kushnir (2013) investigated whether giving choice to preschoolers plays a causal role in prosocial sharing. In the study, children who made a costly choice of allocating a resource that they could have kept were later more prosocial with a different individual. The results are consistent with a prosocial-construal model, in which rational cognitive processes are promoted in choice that affects subsequent prosocial behavior. It is as if children infer that, in being prosocial, they signal to themselves that they are prosocial and like being prosocial. In this regard, making costly choices might make an important contribution to young children's development of their self-understanding as "moral beings."

Vaish and Tomasello (2014) cited multiple studies indicating that, by 3 years of age, children recognize social norms as "general, agent-neutral, mutual expectations" in the emergence of a "collective intentionality" (e.g., Riedl et al., 2011; Schmidt, Rakoczy, & Tomasello, 2012; Vaish, Missana, & Tomasello, 2011). They contrasted their approach to that of Piaget.

Brain Decety, Michalska, and Kinzler (2012) studied developmental changes in response to morally-related stimuli. The participants were 4–37 years of age. The stimuli were brief, animated scenarios that showed either people or objects being injured/damaged (and either by intentional or unintentional actions). For the scenarios with people who were injured intentionally, according to fMRI scan measurement, the regions of the brain that differentially activated involved the right posterior superior temporal sulcus and other regions associated with the perception, prediction, and interpretation of the intentions of people. In addition, regions associated with processing of affective consequences of these actions were differentially activated (i.e., the temporal poles, insula, amygdala, and ventromedial prefrontal cortex). Other relevant findings underscored the role of the subgenual prefrontal cortex, which is extensively connected to circuits involving emotional behavior and stress response. Decety and Howard (2014) concluded that the ventromedial prefrontal cortex plays a crucial role in integrating bodily response and affective representation related to empathy and moral decision-making.

Heritable Knafo-Noam, Uzefovsky, Israel, Davidov, and Zahn-Waxler (2015) conducted a twin study with 7-year-olds using questionnaire measures filled in by mothers with items related to prosociality. Statistical analysis showed five meaningful clusters that they considered facets of a common single factor concerning a prosociality phenotype. The five facets involved: sharing, social concern, kindness, helping, and empathic concern. Abbreviated examples of the items involved included, respectively, shares readily with others, shows sympathy, kind to younger children, volunteers to help others, and helpful if someone hurts.

Knafo-Noam et al. (2015) estimated a high heritability of 69 % for the common-prosocial factor. Also, each of the facets involved unique genetic and environmental contributions. Overall, the authors concluded that genetics is strongly involved in the common factor trait of prosociality, with the environment additionally involved in the facets.

Comment As a comment, I would add that the social-cognitive development evident in the preschooler continues to grow and, moreover, it should follow the Neo-Piagetian scaffold of stages and substages in cognitive development, as per either of Young's (2011) model or other models. For adults to express the "hypercollaboration" described by Tomasello and Vaish (2013), their cognitive sophistication needs to grow well beyond the preschooler level. There should be more than the two-steps in cooperation and morality described by these authors not only in human development but also in evolution. Young's (2011) model would predict 25 precursor, initiation, and elaboration steps in the former case and multiple underpinning steps in the latter one.

Applications

Public Good

Parks, Joireman, and Van Lange (2013) presented an integrative model of how cooperation, trust, and other variables influence decisions about the public good (see Fig. 15.6). The model is relevant to present purposes because it includes relatively more distal and proximal causes in navigating the social dilemmas involved. The model includes a biological component and cultural influences, as well as common factors and individual differences. Proximally, the self in context is influenced by distal evolutionary forces, such as kin selection and reciprocal altruism, and also by cultural influences, such as individualism/collectivism. Other influences in the model relate to individual factors, such as attachment (in)security developmental history, as well as the major opposition between cooperation and antagonism.

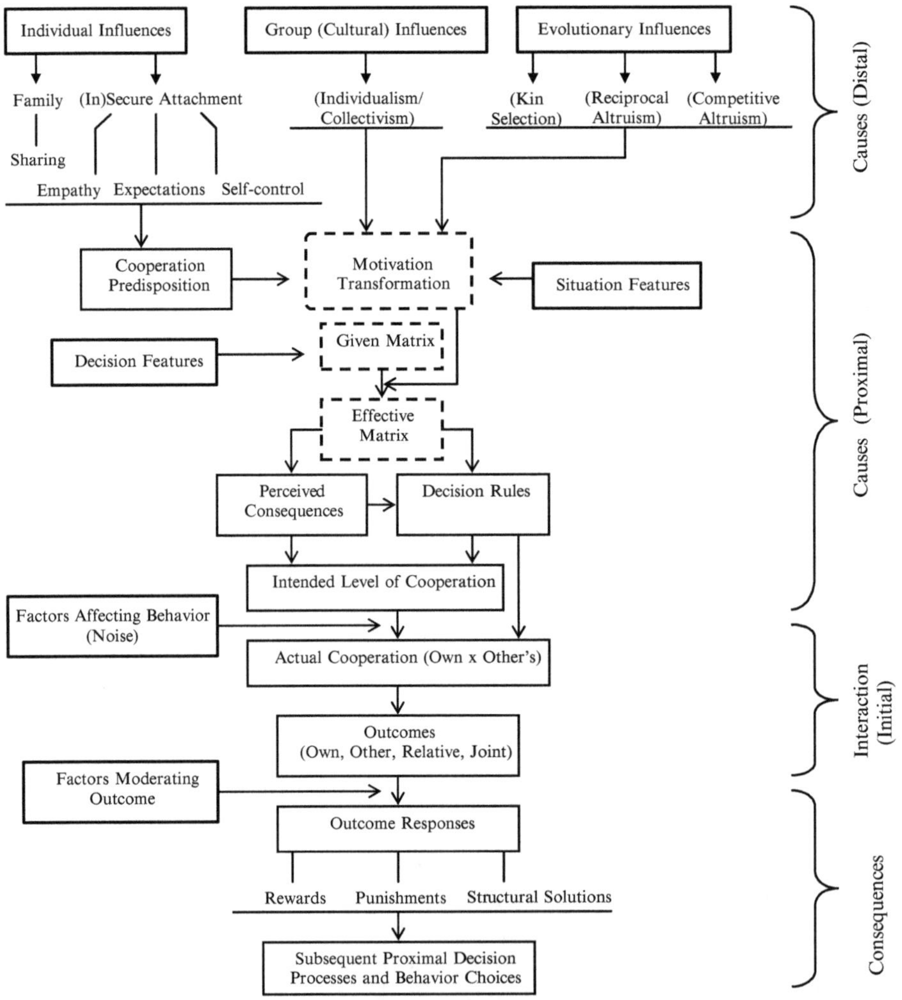

Fig. 15.6 Integrative model of social dilemma decision-making: from influences (distal, proximal) to outcome (interactions, consequences). The figure indicates the multitude of variables involved in decision-making with respect to social dilemmas. The model applies equally to other areas of behavior. There are distal causes involved, such as personal, cultural, and evolutionary (biological). The model is a biopsychosocial one in this regard. In terms of proximal causes, the model mostly concerns personal factors, such as motivation, but also there are more biological (predispositional) and contextual (situational) ones. The personal component includes a cognitive component and appraisals (decision feature, decision rules, perceived consequences). Adapted from Parks et al. (2013)

Politics

Fraley, Griffin, Belsky, and Roisman (2012) examined the relationship between 1-month parenting attitudes and 18-year-old political ideology. They also included temperament at 5 years of age in their longitudinal analysis. Prior research had indicated that preschoolers who had been relatively more anxious, guilt-prone, and indecisive had developed to endorse conservative values at age 23 (Block & Block, 2006).

Participants were taken from a National Institute of Child Health and Human Development (NICHD) longitudinal study (the Study of Early Child Care and Youth Development; SECCYD). Sample sizes ranged from 635 to 708. Parental political attitude was assessed with the Parental Modernity Inventory (PMI; Schaefer & Edgerton, 1985). It gave two composites—authoritarian and egalitarian parenting style (e.g., about obeying the parent vs. the child's point of view being taken into account). Maternal sensitivity was scored from videotaped mother–child interactions at 6, 15, 36, and 54 months of age. At 54 months, the Children's Behavior Questionnaire (CBQ, Rothbart, Ahadi, Hershey, & Fisher, 2001) was administered to assess early temperament. Five factors were extracted in the temperament questionnaire, related to: restlessness/activity, shyness, attentional focusing, passivity, and fear. It was noted that none of the factors resembled the adult's openness to experience in the FFM (Five Factor Model, Costa & McCrae, 1992). Political ideology at 18 years was measured with the Conservatism Scale (Wilson & Patterson, 1968). The covariates that were controlled included: gender, cognitive ability (as measured by Woodcock-Johnson Psychoeducational Battery, Woodcock, 1990; Woodcock & Johnson, 1989), and SES (socioeconomic status).

In terms of results, Fraley et al. (2012) reported that parents who had scored as more authoritarian in parental attitude when their children were 1-month-old had their children develop conservative political ideologies at 18 years, whereas a more egalitarian parenting attitude early on was associated with a later liberal ideology in the offspring.

Although the Fraley et al. (2012) study was longitudinal, the authors maintained that it could not address mechanism. For example, there could be multiple confounders involved related to very early and much later developmental relationships. I would add that the findings were weak. First, the correlations involved were low even if significant. Moreover, the significant level (alpha) was set at 0.05, which risks Type I error. The regression results were in the same order (they were consistent with the correlations, but low and at $p<0.05$).

As for temperament, the associations/predictions were consistent with the literature. Early fearfulness and deficits in attentional control predicted a later conservative attitude. Also, early activity/restlessness predicted a later liberal attitude.

Fraley et al. (2012) posited that conservatives might self-organize psychologically to defend/protect the status quo, whereas liberals might express an under control of ego-related function. These conclusions might go too much beyond the data, especially in typecasting liberals and conservatives. Moreover, there are differences in liberal and conservative attitudes with respect to social and economic issues (see below), making it premature to lump people together into two distinct categories politically.

Nevertheless, at some point in determining differences in some aspect of liberalism vs. conservatism, I conjecture that a common variable in differential political attitude and its underpinnings might relate to degree and type of inhibitory function. That is, everything else being equal, conservatives might deploy inhibitory function toward presenting equilibrium, and liberals might use it to open equilibrium to change at thresholds less than is typical for conservatives.

The research on the relationship between personality traits and political ideology is becoming more nuanced. For example, Osborne, Wootton, and Sibley (2013) found that the politeness component of agreeableness correlated positively with political conservatism but the compassion component evinced the opposite relationship.

McAdams, Hanek, and Dadabo (2013) demonstrated that the narrative approach to personality provided results related to political ideology above and beyond personality traits. Openness to experience did relate to conservatism–liberalism (openness was negatively correlated with conservatism), but political conservatives also emphasized the narrative theme of self-regulation while political liberals emphasized the theme of self-exploration. The results are consistent with Janoff-Bulman's (2009) model that liberals aim to provide and also that they value prescriptive moralities, whereas conservatism is associated with protection and, as well, proscriptive moralities.

There is a debate in the literature whether conservatives compared to liberals are more fearful, defensive, and low in self-esteem. Schlenker, Chambers, and Le (2012) conducted four studies in which political conservatives, compared to liberals, were shown to be happier due to specific attitude and personality differences associated with positive adjustment/mental health. For example, conservatives expressed more personal agency, positive outlook, transcendent moral beliefs, and a generalized fairness belief.

Choma, Hafer, Dywan, Segalowitz, and Busseri (2012) developed a measure of conservative and liberal political ideology in which conservatism and liberalism did not appear to lie on poles of the same continuum but emerged functionally independent, or as separable constructs. In their study, liberalism was associated with a universal orientation and conservatism with dogmatism. Other results related liberalism to tolerance of ambiguity. Findings demonstrated that the two political orientations were moderately correlated. Note that in Choma et al. the measure of political liberalism–conservatism consisted of six items (how (a) conservative/(b) liberal (2 options) do you tend to be—(a) in general, (b) for economical policy, and (c) for social policy [(3 areas), $(2\times3)=6$]), as evaluated on a 9-point Likert scale. The factors that emerged were found by confirmatory factor analysis tested for fit to a bipolar (single dimension) and to a bidimensional model, which proved the superior one.

Similarly, Carney, Jost, Gosling, and Potter (2008) opined that conservatives relative to liberals are more orderly, conventional, and organized, whereas liberals relative to conservatives appear more open, creative, curious, and seeking of novelty.

Pulfrey and Butera (2013) demonstrated that accentuating "neoliberal" (i.e., economically conservative) values ("self-enhancement") predicted actual cheating behavior. Moreover, in promoting their opposite values (universalism, benevolence, self-transcendence), the predictive relationship between self-enhancement and the condoning of cheating no longer was present.

Self

Model

McAdams (2013) presented a developmental model of the self comprised of three components (actor, agent, author) that emerge sequentially in development. The first self is a social actor. As newborns, we are already primed in a rudimentary sense for social performance and, in the first months, we express constitutionally-present differential temperament patterns. By around 18 months, we recognized ourselves in mirrors (e.g., Rochat, 2003).

The social actor self continues to evolve throughout the lifespan, but a second self emerges continuously as a motivated agent by the end of childhood. However, even in the first year, infants express a preliminary appreciation of agency. For example, they prefer to imitate intentional rather random acts (Woodward, 2009). By the age of 4, they develop a theory of mind. By 8 or 9 years, personal goals are established, and children are defining and evaluating themselves by family, peers, school, and cultural experiences and goals. The stage acquisitions described by Erikson (1963, industry vs. inferiority) and Piaget (1970, concrete operational thought) in the age range concerned facilitate these comparisons and constructions proposed for children.

The third self is the autobiographical self, or the self-narrative author, that emerges in adolescence and early adulthood. Preliminary signs of it are evident in early childhood with the development of autobiographical memory (Howe & Courage, 1997), and also the child's capacity to recall recent episodes (Fivush, 2011). As the autobiographic author self emerges, self-stories are amalgamated into narrative identities (McAdams & Pals, 2006). At this stage in self-growth, people use autobiographical reasoning (Habermas & Bluck, 2000). They create organized autobiographical themes. They sequence personal-valued episodes into causal chains that self-explain their development, which facilitates personal growth and mature self-authorship.

McAdam and McLean (2013) argued that aspects of narrative identity help promote mental health, well-being, and psychological maturity. Specifically, narratives with redemptive sequences, or stories with meanings in suffering/adversity (i.e., from "bad" to "good" outcome, e.g., loss of loved one promoting family cohesion), or with themes of personal agency/exploration, serve positive mental health ends. The authors called for research to disentangle which features of life stories actually promote positive psychological adaptation in "causal relations."

McFarland, Brown, and Webb (2013) suggested that identification with all humanity is an important moral concept and psychological construct. I note that this concept could be combined with the concept of narrative identity (McAdam & McLean, 2013) and studied for its components that contribute to positive mental health, if any.

Comment

There is value in examining the primary characteristics of narratives. They need to be cohesive and coherent, to borrow terms from functional linguistics. The former term refers to interlinked chains in discourse and the latter term to overall integration and meaning (Halliday & Hasan, 1976; Young, 2011). Moreover, self-identity narrative stories could be considered as complex networks. In this sense, the networks that they create could be analyzed to include indicators of network cohesion and coherence. In this regard, in terms of the topic of causality, generally, and of narratives, specifically, causality could be specified for cohesion and coherence, too. For example, one could ask whether the causal stories of self-integration are consistent or inconsistent between and across linkages in the stories relative to stories that lack self-integration (cohesion and coherence, respectively). It would appear there is room to integrate network and narrative science.

Moreover, other models of self-development are more elaborate than McAdams (2013). For example, Young (2011) also used Piaget and Erikson as bases in his work, and developed a five stage × five substage model of unitary Piagetian and Eriksonian development that translated into a 25-step (5 stages × 5 substages) model of self-development. The three selves described by McAdams would appear to readily fit Young's model (e.g., actor in sensorimotor development, agent in perioperational development, and author in abstract development).

Chapter Conclusions

Piaget Missing

This chapter has reviewed the multiple factors that influence the development especially of empathic/prosocial behavior. The area is marked by disagreement about the rapidity and biological, innate bases for the development of the behavior. The different points of view on the matter are similar to the ones encountered in other areas of development, and they emphasize the common refrain of disambiguating the influences on development of Nature, Nurture, or both. However, a more inclusive model that would help explain the onset and growth of this behavior would include the self component, as well as related ones, given that Nature and Nurture are passive influences on development and we contribute actively as agents in our own growth. Moreover, in these regards, any causal developmental model should include a Piagetian perspective, given the cognitive underpinnings to prosocial/empathic and related behavior and their consequences for behavior such as this.

In this regard, in the following I attempt to show that the steps in the development of empathic and prosocial behavior described in the literature are consistent with Piaget's six substages in infancy. In my approach to this parallel, I add the influence of mirror neuron processes that apparently allow for empathic and prosocial behavior earlier than Piaget might have predicted.

His model for this age is based on sensorimotor activity, with little hint of representational thought until the last substage, and empathy and prosocial behavior would appear to need some form of primitive representation for the behaviors to manifest. However, the "like me" (Meltzoff, 2007) comparisons that can be integrated into sensorimotor development through early (quasi) imitative and perhaps mirror-system enabled processes might be sufficient to have develop in the sensorimotor period intuitive, action-based, embodied quasi-representational models somewhat removed from objects, events, activities, and people in the environment that allow for a progressively developing early empathic and prosocial behavior.

Research Review

In order to build the model showing the comparability of recent findings on empathy and prosocial behavior in infancy and Piaget's model of substages in infancy, I considered critical findings for the infancy period in the literature review undertaken in the present chapter on empathic and prosocial behavior. In particular, I noted the following from the review already provided.

(a) In the newborn period infants are capable of engaging in biobehavioral synchrony with the mother (Feldman, 2014). They have an implicit type of self-knowledge, a subjective pre-reflective knowledge (Davidov et al., 2013).
(b) At 3 months of age, they show coordinated gaze patterns, co-vocalizations, mutual positive affect expression, and affectionate touch (Feldman, 2014).
(c) At 4 months of age, infants can be nice to puppets that had been nice to other ones (Hamlin, 2014a) and prefer those who prevent the goals of those who had hindered others (Hamlin, 2014b). At 6 months, they seem sensitive to the goals of others and their inferred mental states (Hamlin, 2015).
(d) At 9 months, they appear to like self-similar people (Hamlin et al., 2013).
(e) At 14 months of age, they express interpersonal motor synchrony, e.g., in bouncing to music, which helps each of the actors see the other as like me (Cirelli et al., 2014). Also, at 15 months of age, they prefer equal distributors and equal distributions (Vaish & Tomasello, 2014).
(f) At 18 months of age, they show concern and prosocial actions when a "victim" is harmed even if the victim does not express overtly any distress (Vaish et al., 2009).

Piaget

These results are highly consistent with the six substages in Piaget's sensorimotor period. In the following, I describe the six substages in Piaget's infant sensorimotor series (Young, 2011).

(a) The first substage in the newborn is termed reflex exercise (reflexes concern repeated patterns in behavior rather than reflex-arc controlled ones).
(b) The second one in the 1-month-old involves primary circular reactions, which are accidentally-discovered, liked repetitive behaviors with the body (e.g., thumb sucking).
(c) At 4 months of age, secondary circular reactions develop, which are accidentally-discovered, liked repetitions with objects (e.g., rattle shaking). This step is notable for visually-directed reaching.
(d) In the next step at 8 months, infants engage in coordinated secondary schemas in which the schemas established in the prior step are coordinated toward new ends. For example, reaching can be used in a detour to move a barrier that is hiding a liked object before grasping the object.
(e) At 12 months, infants can experiment to create new means-end combinations using previously acquired relations in this regard, but only accidentally.
(f) Finally, at 18 months, they can invent new means-end relations by mental combinations,

but the behavior is not fully representational for the behavior is still tied to actions (e.g., Piaget's daughter opened her mouth before solving a problem in which she had to open a drawer).

Explaining the Review According to Piaget

By comparing the two sequences, the Piagetian and the experimental, it is clear that the results of the recent studies are consistent with what the Piagetian series in infancy would predict. The comparison undertaken next is in this vein.

(a) In the reflex period, neonates do behave intuitively in creating interpersonal coordination.
(b) In the second one of circular or repetitive reactions involving the body, 3-month-olds manifest various interpersonal coordinations, including of vocalizations, just as would be predicted by knowing the qualities of Piaget's step of secondary (that is, nonbody) circular reactions.
(c) Next, at 4 to 6 months of age, they can differentiate nice and mean puppets and even infer mental states. This type of behavior seems more advanced than what the Piagetian substage sequence would predict, given that it concerns at this age only the ability to engage in secondary circular reactions, or the repetition of liked behaviors, such as shaking rattles. However, by adding in the advances in behavior that Piaget could not have foreseen because of his lack of knowledge of mirror neurons and the system built on them, it is possible to suggest that a less rich and leaner interpretation of the empathic and prosocial type behavior that is being described for the 4- to 6-month period is not that nice and mean behaviors are being differentiated nor that mental state inferences are being made, but that infants at this age are merely acting out of self-similarity recognition in their behavior. In this regard, the behavior at issue is engaging the other party perceived as like oneself. Does the child behave toward the other like he/ she would toward the self? The behavior does appear repetitive, out of interest, and accidentally discovered, though not with intention at the outset.
(d) At 8 months of age, the next Piagetian step develops, and it involves coordination of secondary schemas. Empirically, it has been shown that the infant at this age appears to like self-similar people. This acquisition is dependent on more advanced cognitive abilities than in the prior step, because the infant is coordinating self and other, and cognition and emotion, and in a way that goes beyond just behaving toward the other because the individual is "like me." That is, in this step, first, there is the like me comparison, and, then, as might be predicted from knowing of the coordination of secondary schemas in the Piagetian model, there is a subsequent step feeding back to the other individual of liking him or her.
(e) Next, at one year of age, the infant engages in accidental discoveries according to Piaget, reworking previously acquired means-end relations. In this regard, the empirical finding at this age is that infants are quite engaged with the other, e.g., in motor synchrony and in egalitarian distribution. These are new behaviors that clearly require rearrangement of existing means-ends relations, yet I suggest that they are not preplanned but arise out of accidental variations in behavior that eventually become incorporated into the infant's repertoire.
(f) Finally, the empirical research in the age period of Piaget's sixth sensorimotor substage of mental invention of new behavioral combinations at 18 months of age is quite consistent with the properties of that age period. That is, at this age infants are concerned with victims even if they do not manifest openly their distress. This shows that infants at this age can infer by mental combination the mental state of another person and feel emotions accordingly. However, I maintain that careful analysis of the behavior involved would reveal some vestige of sensorimotor action. It is only at 24 months of age that Piaget's model would allow for

completely action-divorced representation, as in language and pretend play.

Conclusion

The extensive literature review undertaken on the development of empathy and prosocial behavior has allowed for comparison of the research with Piaget's model, but with the model of "like me" (Meltzoff, 2007) used as well. Piaget's model appears to have served as a good scaffold to help understand the changes in empathy and prosocial behavior from one age to the next in the infancy period. Moreover, it stands as a compromise path in the sometimes vociferous debate whether the nativist or gradual acquisition approach to the behaviors involved applies. The model has helped avoid the rich interpretation of the findings in terms of the nativist account, but it is not necessarily a lean one that describes the situation better, given the relatively advanced acquisitions that Piaget's account can help explain even in the earliest substages of infancy.

My Neo-Piagetian model of the stages and substages of development is highly compatible with the Piagetian substage series because I built my model especially by considering them. In this regard, the six substages involved in infancy in my model involve reflex coordination, which I split off from the other five sensorimotor substages, and then the five sensorimotor substages, which I relabeled coordination, hierarchization, systematization, multiplication, and integration. Careful inspection of the empirical findings used in the present section will show that the characteristics of the behaviors that I would predict at each age period in infancy are indeed evident in the empirical findings. In fact, it can be no other way in that the reworking of Piaget's series in my model fits his series and the empirical findings discussed in this chapter have been shown to fit his model, so that, by transposition, the findings involved must fit my model.

To elaborate further my full model, in Young (2011), I presented a Neo-Piagetian model of cognitive development and applied it to multiple areas of social behavior and cognition. Basically, the model describes five stages in development quite consistent with those of Piaget. Essentially, it adds a reflexive stage before the sensorimotor one and a collective intelligence stage after the formal, abstract stage. The perioperational stage consists of Piaget's preoperational and concrete operational stages, a period to which he referred to as representational. There are simplified way of describing the major foci in the stages—for example, from the physical to the spiritual.

In my work, I have extrapolated to what this might mean for the development of empathy and theory of mind. These are conjectures simply to show that (a) the developments involved might have a cognitive stage or substage basis beyond the empirical demonstrations of their changes and (b) that the Neo-Piagetian approach might help hone understanding of the progressions that might be involved.

References

Anderson, V., & Beauchamp, M. H. (Eds.). (2012a). *Developmental social neuroscience and childhood brain insult: Theory and practice*. New York: Guilford Press.

Anderson, V., & Beauchamp, M. H. (2012b). Social: A theoretical model of developmental social neuroscience. In V. Anderson & M. H. Beauchamp (Eds.), *Developmental social neuroscience and childhood brain insult: Theory and practice* (pp. 3–20). New York: Guilford Press.

Baumeister, R. F. (2012). Human evil: The myth of pure evil and the true causes of violence. In M. Mikulincer & P. R. Shaver (Eds.), *The social psychology of morality: Exploring the causes of good and evil* (pp. 367–380). Washington, DC: American Psychological Association.

Baumeister, R. F., & Graham, J. (2012). Good and evil, past and future, laboratory and world. In M. Mikulincer & P. R. Shaver (Eds.), *The social psychology of morality: Exploring the causes of good and evil* (pp. 401–412). Washington, DC: American Psychological Association.

Beauchamp, M., & Anderson, V. (2010). Social: An integrative framework for the development of social skills. *Psychological Bulletin, 136*, 255–260.

Bechara, A., & Damasio, A. R. (2005). The somatic marker hypothesis: A neural theory of economic decision. *Games and Economic Behavior, 52*, 336–372.

Beck, A. T. (1967). *Depression: Clinical, experimental, and theoretical aspects*. New York: Harper & Row.

Beck, A. T. (1983). Cognitive theory of depression: New perspectives. In P. J. Clayton & J. E. Barrett (Eds.), *Treatment of depression: Old controversies and new approaches*. New York: Raven.

Belsky, J., & Fearon, R. M. P. (2002). Early attachment security, subsequent maternal sensitivity, and later child development: Does continuity in development depend on continuity of caregiver? *Attachment and Human Development, 4*, 361–387.

Belsky, J., & Pluess, M. (2009). The nature (and nurture?) of plasticity in early human development. *Perspectives on Psychological Science, 4*, 345–351.

Blair, R. J. R., & Fowler, K. (2008). Moral emotions and moral reasoning from the perspective of affective cognitive neuroscience: A selective review. *European Journal of Developmental Science, 2*, 303–323.

Block, J., & Block, J. H. (2006). Nursery school personality and political orientation two decades later. *Journal of Research in Personality, 40*, 734–749.

Bloom, P. (2012). Moral nativism and moral psychology. In M. Mikulincer & P. R. Shaver (Eds.), *The social psychology of morality: Exploring the causes of good and evil* (pp. 71–89). Washington, DC: American Psychological Association.

Boyd, R., & Richerson, P. J. (1985). *Culture and the evolutionary process*. Chicago, IL: University of Chicago Press.

Byrne, R. W. (1994). The evolution of intelligence. In J. B. Slater & T. R. Halliday (Eds.), Behaviour and evolution (pp. 223-265). Cambridge, UK: Cambridge University Press.

Cannon, E. N., Simpson, E. A., Fox, N. A., Vanderwert, R. E., Woodward, A. L., & Ferrari, P. F. (2016). Relations between infants' emerging reach-grasp competence and event-related desynchronization in EEG. *Developmental Science, 19*, 50–62.

Carney, D. R., Jost, J. T., Gosling, S. D., & Potter, J. (2008). The secret lives of liberals and conservatives: Personality profiles, interaction styles, and the things they leave behind. *Political Psychology, 29*, 807–840.

Carpendale, J. I. M. (2009). Piaget's theory of moral development. In U. Müller, J. I. M. Carpendale, & L. Smith (Eds.), *Cambridge companion to Piaget* (pp. 270–286). New York: Cambridge University Press.

Caspi, A., Sugden, K., Moffitt, T. E., Taylor, A., Craig, I. W., Harrington, H., et al. (2003). Influence of life stress on depression: Moderation by a polymorphism in the 5-HTT gene. *Science, 301*, 386–389.

Castiello, U., Becchio, C., Zoia, S., Nelini, C., Sartori, L., Blason, L., et al. (2010). Wired to be social: The ontogeny of human interaction. *PLoS One, 5*, e13199. doi:10.1371/journal.pone.0013199.

Cattaneo, L., Fabbi-Destro, M., Boria, S., Pieraccini, C., Monti, A., Cossu, G., & Rizzolatti, G. (2007). Impairment of actions chains in autism and its possible role in intention understanding. *Proceedings of the National Academy of Sciences, USA, 104*, 17825–17830.

Chakroff, A., & Young, L. (2014). The prosocial brain: Perceiving others in need and acting on it. In L. M. Padilla-Walker & G. Carlo (Eds.), *Prosocial development: A multidimensional approach* (pp. 90–111). New York: Oxford University Press.

Chernyak, N., & Kushnir, T. (2013). Giving preschoolers choice increases sharing behavior. *Psychological Science, 24*, 1971–1979.

Choma, B. L., Hafer, C. L., Dywan, J., Segalowitz, S. J., & Busseri, M. A. (2012). Political liberalism and political conservatism: Functionally independent? *Personality and Individual Differences, 53*, 431–436.

Cirelli, L. K., Einarson, K. M., & Trainor, L. J. (2014). Interpersonal synchrony increases prosocial behavior in infants. *Developmental Science, 17*, 1003–1011.

Cook, R., Bird, G., Catmur, C., Press, C., & Heyes, C. (2014). Mirror neurons: From origin to function. *Behavioral and Brain Sciences, 37*, 177–241.

Cosmides, L., & Tooby, J. (2013). Evolutionary psychology: New perspectives on cognition and motivation. *Annual Review of Psychology, 64*, 201–229.

Costa, P. T., & McCrae, R. R. (1992). The five-factor model of personality and its relevance to personality disorders. *Journal of Personality Disorders, 6*, 343–359.

Dahl, A. (2014). Definitions and developmental processes in research on infant morality. *Human Development, 57*, 241–249.

Dahl, A. (2015). The developing social context of infant helping in two U.S. samples. *Child Development, 86*, 1080–1093.

Dahl, A., Schuck, R. K., & Campos, J. J. (2013). Do young toddlers act on their social preferences? *Developmental Psychology, 49*, 1964–1970.

Damasio, A. R. (1994). *Descartes' error: Emotion, reason, and the human brain*. New York: Grosset/Putnam.

Damasio, A. R. (1995). Toward a neurobiology of emotion and feeling: Operational concepts and hypotheses. *The Neuroscientist, 1*, 19–25.

Damasio, A. R., Anderson, S. W., & Tranel, D. (2011). The frontal lobes. In K. M. Heilman & E. Valenstein (Eds.), *Clinical neuropsychology* (4th ed., pp. 417–465). New York: Oxford University Press.

Damasio, A. R., Tranel, D., & Damasio, H. (1998). Somatic markers and the guidance of behavior. In J. M. Jenkins, K. Oatley, & N. L. Stein (Eds.), *Human emotions: A reader* (pp. 122–135). Malden, MA: Blackwell.

Davidov, M., Zahn-Waxler, C., Roth-Hanania, R., & Knafo, A. (2013). Concern for others in the first year of life: Theory, evidence, and avenues for research. *Child Development Perspectives, 7*, 126–131.

Davidson, R. J. (1992). Anterior cerebral asymmetry and the nature of emotion. *Brain and Cognition, 20*, 125–151.

de Waal, F. B. M. (2012). A bottom-up view of empathy. In F. B. M. de Waal & P. F. Ferrari (Eds.), *The primate mind: Built to connect with other minds* (pp. 121–138). Cambridge, MA: Harvard University Press.

de Waal, F. B. M., & Ferrari, P. F. (Eds.). (2012). *The primate mind: Built to connect with other minds*. Cambridge, MA: Harvard University Press.

Dean, L. G., Kendal, R. L., Schapiro, S. J., Thierry, B., & Laland, K. N. (2012). Identification of the social and cognitive processes underlying human cumulative culture. *Science, 335*, 1114–1118.

Decety, J., & Howard, L. H. (2014). Emotion, morality, and the developing brain. In M. Mikulincer & P. R. Shaver (Eds.), *Mechanisms of social connection: From brain to group* (pp. 105–122). Washington, DC: American Psychological Association.

Decety, J., & Michalska, K. J. (2010). Neurodevelopmental changes in the circuits underlying empathy and sympathy from childhood to adulthood. *Developmental Science, 13*, 886–899.

Decety, J., Michalska, K. J., & Kinzler, K. D. (2012). The contribution of emotion and cognition to moral sensitivity: A neurodevelopmental study. *Cerebral Cortex, 22*, 209–220.

Dondi, M., Simion, F., & Caltran, G. (1999). Can newborns discriminate between their own cry and the cry of another newborn infant? *Developmental Psychology, 35*, 418–426.

Dunbar, R. I. M. (2013). An evolutionary basis for social cognition. In M. Legerstee, D. W. Haley, & M. H. Bornstein (Eds.), *The infant mind: Origins of the social brain* (pp. 3–19). New York: Guilford Press.

Ellis, B. J., & Boyce, W. T. (2008). Biological sensitivity to context. *Current Directions in Psychological Science, 17*, 183–187.

Ellis, B. J., Boyce, W. T., Belsky, J., Bakermans-Kranenburg, M. J., & van IJzendoorn, M. H. (2011). Differential susceptibility to the environment: An evolutionary-neurodevelopmental theory. *Development and Psychopathology, 23*, 7–28.

Erikson, E. H. (1963). *Childhood and society* (2nd ed.). New York: Norton.

Feldman, R. (2007a). Mother-infant synchrony and the development of moral orientation in childhood and adolescent: Direct and indirect mechanisms of developmental continuity. *American Journal of Orthopsychiatry, 77*, 582–597.

Feldman, R. (2007b). On the origins of background emotions: From affect synchrony to symbolic expression. *Emotion, 7*, 601–611.

Feldman, R. (2010). The relational basis of adolescent adjustment: Trajectories of mother-child interactive behaviors from infancy to adolescence shape adolescent's adaptation. *Attachment & Human Development, 12*, 173–192.

Feldman, R. (2014). Synchrony and the neurobiological basis of social affiliation. In M. Mikulincer & P. R. Shaver (Eds.), *Mechanisms of social cognition: From brain to group* (pp. 145–166). Washington, DC: American Psychological Association.

Feldman, R. (2015). Sensitive periods in human social development: New insights from research on oxytocin, synchrony, and high-risk parenting. *Development and Psychopathology, 27*, 369–395.

Feldman, R., & Eidelman, A. I. (2007). Maternal postpartum behavior and the emergence of infant-mother and infant-father synchrony in preterm and full-term infants: The role of neonatal vagal tone. *Developmental Psychobiology, 49*, 290–302.

Feldman, R., Magori-Cohen, R., Galili, G., Singer, M., & Louzoun, Y. (2011). Mother and infant coordinate heart rhythms through episodes of interaction synchrony. *Infant Behavior & Development, 34*, 569–577.

Feldman, R., Zagoory-Sharon, O., Maoz, R., Weisman, O., Gordon, I., Schneiderman, I., et al. (2012). Sensitive patenting is associated with plasma oxytocin and polymorphisms in the OXTR and CD38 genes. *Biological Psychiatry, 72*, 175–181.

Ferrari, P. F., & Fogassi, L. (2012). The mirror neuron system in monkeys and its implications for social cognitive functions. In F. B. M. de Waal & P. F. Ferrari (Eds.), *The primate mind: Built to connect with other minds* (pp. 13–31). Cambridge, MA: Harvard University Press.

Fivush, R. (2011). The development of autobiographical memory. In S. T. Fiske, D. L. Schacter, & S. E. Taylor (Eds.), *Annual review of psychology* (Vol. 62, pp. 559–582). Palo Alto, CA: Annual Reviews.

Fletcher, G. J. O., Simpson, J. A., Campbell, L., & Overall, N. C. (2015). Pair-bonding, romantic love, and evolution: The curious case of Homo sapiens. *Perspectives on Psychological Science, 10*, 20–36.

Fogarty, L., Strimling, P., & Laland, K. N. (2011). The evolution of teaching. *Evolution, 65*, 2760–2770.

Fogassi, L., & Rizzolatti, G. (2013). The mirror mechanism as neurophysiological basis for action and intention understanding. In A. Suarez & P. Adams (Eds.), *Is science compatible with free will? Exploring free will and consciousness in the light of quantum physics and neuroscience* (pp. 117–134). New York: Springer Science+Business Media.

Fox, N. A. (1994). Dynamic cerebral processes underlying emotion regulation. In N. A. Fox (Ed.), The development of emotion regulation: Biological and behavioral considerations. *Monographs of the Society for Research in Child Development, 59* (2–3, Serial No. 240), 152–166.

Fox, N. A., Rubin, K. H., Calkins, S. D., Marshall, T. R., Coplan, R. J., Porges, S. W., et al. (1995). Frontal activation asymmetry and social competence at four years of age. *Child Development, 66*, 1770–1784.

Fraley, R. C., Griffin, B. N., Belsky, J., & Roisman, G. I. (2012). Developmental antecedents of political ideology: A longitudinal investigation from birth to age 18 years. *Psychological Science, 23*, 1425–1431.

Gallese, V. (2006). Intentional attunement: A neurophysiological perspective on social cognition and its disruption in autism. *Brain Research, 1079*, 15–24.

Gallese, V., & Rochat, M. (2013). The evolution of motor cognition: Its role in the development of social cognition and implications for autism spectrum disorder. In M. Legerstee, D. W. Haley, & M. H. Bornstein (Eds.), *The infant mind: Origins of the social brain* (pp. 19–48). New York: Guilford Press.

Geangu, E., Benga, O., Stahl, D., & Striano, T. (2010). Contagious crying beyond the first days of life. *Infant Behavior & Development, 33*, 279–288.

Geraci, A., & Surian, L. (2011). The developmental roots of fairness: Infants' reactions to equal and unequal distributions of resources. *Developmental Science, 14*, 1012–1020.

Gergely, G., Bekkering, H., & Király, I. (2002). Rational imitation in preverbal infants. *Nature, 415*, 755. doi:10.1038/415755a.

Govrin, A. (2014). The ABC of moral development: An attachment approach to moral judgment. *Frontiers in Psychology, 5*, 1–15.

Gray, J. A. (1990). Brain systems that mediate both emotion and cognition. *Cognition and Emotion, 4*, 269–288.

Greene, J. D. (2007). Why are VMPFC patients more utilitarian? A dual-process theory of moral judgment explains. *Trends in Cognitive Sciences, 11*, 322–323.

Habermas, T., & Bluck, S. (2000). Getting a life: The emergence of the life story in adolescence. *Psychological Bulletin, 126*, 748–769.

Halliday, M. A. K., & Hasan, R. (1976). *Cohesion in English*. London: Longman.

Hamann, K., Warneken, F., & Tomasello, M. (2012). Children's developing commitments to joint goals. *Child Development, 83*, 137–145.

Hamlin, J. K. (2014a). Context-dependent social evaluation in 4.5-month-old human infants: The role of domain-general versus domain-specific processes in the development of social evaluation. *Frontiers in Psychology, 5*, 614. doi:10.3389/fpsyg.2014.00614.

Hamlin, J. K. (2014b). The conceptual and empirical case for social evaluation in infancy. *Human Development, 57*, 250–258.

Hamlin, J. K. (2015). The case of social evaluation in preverbal infants: Gazing toward one's goal drives infants' preferences for helpers over hinderers in the hill paradigm. *Frontiers in Psychology, 5*, 1563. doi:10.3389/fpsyg.2014.01563.

Hamlin, J. K., Mahajan, N., Liberman, Z., & Wynn, K. (2013). Not like me = bad: Infants prefer those who harm dissimilar others. *Psychological Science, 24*, 589–594.

Hamlin, J. K., & Wynn, K. (2011). Young infants prefer prosocial to antisocial others. *Cognitive Development, 26*, 30–39.

Hamlin, J. K., Wynn, K., & Bloom, P. (2007). Social evaluation by preverbal infants. *Nature, 450*, 557–559.

Hamlin, J. K., Wynn, K., & Bloom, P. (2010). 3-month-olds show a negativity bias in their social evaluations. *Developmental Science, 13*, 923–929.

Hamlin, J. K., Wynn, K., Bloom, P., & Mahajan, N. (2011). How infants and toddlers react to antisocial others. *Proceedings of the National Academy of Sciences, USA, 108*, 19931–19936.

Hammond, S. I. (2014). Children's early helping in action: Piagetian developmental theory and early prosocial behavior. *Frontiers in Psychology, 5*, 759. doi:10.3389/fpsyg.2014.00759.

Hammond, S. L., & Carpendale, J. I. M. (2012). *Rethinking children's everyday help: Often active, occasionally unhelpful, and guided by parents*. Poster presented at the biennial meeting of the International Society on Infant Studies, Minneapolis, MN.

Hastings, P. D., & De, I. (2008). Parasympathetic regulation and parental socialization of emotion: Biopsychosocial processes of adjustment in preschoolers. *Social Development, 17*, 211–238.

Hastings, P. D., Ruttle, P. L., Serbin, L. A., Mills, R. S. L., Stack, D. M., & Schwartzman, A. E. (2011). Adrenocortical responses to strangers in preschoolers: Relations with parenting, temperament, and psychopathology. *Developmental Psychobiology, 53*, 694–710.

Hastings, P. D., Sullivan, C., McShane, K. E., Coplan, R. J., Utendale, W. T., & Vyncke, J. D. (2008). Parental socialization, vagal regulation, and preschoolers' anxious difficulties: Direct mothers and moderated fathers. *Child Development, 79*, 45–64.

Henrich, J. (2011). A cultural species: How culture drove human evolution. A multi-disciplinary framework for understanding culture, cognition and behavior. *Psychological Science Agenda*. http://www.apa.org/science/about/psa/2011/11/human-evolution.aspx

Herrmann, E., Misch, A., Hernandez-Lloreda, V., & Tomasello, M. (2015). Uniquely human self-control begins at school age. *Developmental Science, 18*, 979–993.

Hölldobler, B., & Wilson, E. O. (2009). *The superorganism: The beauty, elegance and strangeness of insect societies*. New York: Norton.

Hopper, L. M., Marshall-Pescini, S., & Whiten, A. (2012). Social learning and culture in child and chimpanzee. In F. B. M. de Waal & P. F. Ferrari (Eds.), *The primate mind: Built to connect with other minds* (pp. 99–118). Cambridge, MA: Harvard University Press.

Howe, M. L., & Courage, M. L. (1997). The emergence and early development of autobiographical memory. *Psychological Review, 104*, 499–523.

Janoff-Bulman, R. (2009). To provide or protect: Motivational bases of political liberalism and conservatism. *Psychological Inquiry, 20*, 120–128.

Janoff-Bulman, R. (2012). Conscience: The do's and don'ts of moral regulation. In M. Milkuciner & P. Shaver (Eds.), *The social psychology of morality: Exploring the causes of good and evil* (pp. 131–148). Washington, DC: American Psychological Association.

Jensen, K., Vaish, A., & Schmidt, M. F. H. (2014). The emergence of human prosociality: Aligning with others through feelings, concerns, and norms. *Frontiers in Psychology, 5*, 1–16.

Kärtner, J. (2015). The autonomous developmental pathway: The primacy of subjective mental states for human behavior and experience. *Child Development, 86*, 1298–1309.

Kemp, M., & Mesoudi, A. (2014). Experimental and theoretical models of human cultural evolution. *Wiley Interdisciplinary Reviews: Cognitive Science, 5*, 317–326.

Kesebir, S. (2012). The superorganism account of human sociality: How and when human groups are like beehives. *Personality and Social Psychology Review, 16*, 233–261.

Knafo-Noam, A., Uzefovsky, F., Israel, S., Davidov, M., & Zahn-Waxler, C. (2015). The prosocial personality and its facets: Genetic and environmental architecture of mother-reported behavior of 7-year-old twins. *Frontiers in Psychology, 6*, 112. doi:10.3389/fpsyg.2015.00112.

Knudsen, B., & Liszkowski, U. (2012a). 18-month-olds predict specific action mistakes through attribution of false belief, not ignorance, and intervene accordingly. *Infancy, 17*, 672–691.

Knudsen, B., & Liszkowski, U. (2012b). Eighteen- and 24-month-old infants correct others in anticipation of action mistakes. *Developmental Science, 15*, 113–122.

Knudsen, B., & Liszkowski, U. (2013). One-year-olds warn others about negative action outcomes. *Journal of Cognition and Development, 14*, 424–436.

Kuhlmeier, V. A., Dunfield, K. A., & O'Neill, A. C. (2014). Selectivity in early prosocial behavior. *Frontiers in Psychology, 5*, 1–6.

Kurzban, R., Burton-Chellew, M. N., & West, S. A. (2015). The evolution of altruism in humans. *Annual Review of Psychology, 66*, 575–599.

Lamm, C., Decety, J., & Singer, T. (2011). Meta-analytic evidence for common and distinct neural networks associated with directly experienced pain and empathy for pain. *NeuroImage, 54*, 2492–2502.

Legerstee, M. (2013). The developing social brain: Social connections and social bonds, social loss, and jealousy in infancy. In M. Legerstee, D. W. Haley, & M. H. Bornstein (Eds.), *The infant mind: Origins of the social brain* (pp. 233–248). New York: Guilford Press.

Liszkowski, U., Carpenter, M., & Tomasello, M. (2008). Twelve-month-olds communicate helpfully and appropriately for knowledgeable and ignorant partners. *Cognition, 108*, 732–739.

Lodder, P., Rotteveel, M., & van Elk, M. (2014). Enactivism and neonatal imitation: Conceptual and empirical considerations and clarifications. *Frontiers in Psychology, 5*, 1–11.

Martin, A., & Olson, K. R. (2013). When kids know better: Paternalistic helping in 3-year-old children. *Developmental Psychology, 49*, 2071–2081.

Martin, A., & Olson, K. R. (2015). Beyond good and evil: What motivations underlie children's prosocial behavior? *Perspectives on Psychological Science, 10*, 159–175.

Masten, C. L., Morelli, S. A., & Eisenberger, N. I. (2011). An fMRI investigation of empathy for "social pain" and subsequent prosocial behavior. *Neuroimaging, 55*, 381–388.

Max, J. E. (2012). Pediatric brain-injury-related psychiatric disorders and social function. In V. Anderson & M. H. Beauchamp (Eds.), *Developmental social neuroscience and childhood brain insult: Theory and practice* (pp. 284–298). New York: Guilford Press.

McAdam, D. P., & McLean, K. C. (2013). Narrative identity. *Current Directions in Psychological Science, 22*, 233–238.

McAdams, D. P. (2013). The psychological self as actor, agent, and author. *Perspectives on Psychological Science, 8*, 272–295.

McAdams, D. P., Hanek, K. J., & Dadabo, J. G. (2013). Themes of self-regulation and self-exploration in the life stories of religious American conservatives and liberals. *Political Psychology, 34*, 201–219.

McAdams, D. P., & Pals, J. L. (2006). A new big five: Fundamental principles for an integrative science of personality. *American Psychologist, 61*, 204–217.

McFarland, S., Brown, D., & Webb, M. (2013). Identification with all humanity as a moral concept and psychological construct. *Current Directions in Psychological Science, 22*, 194–198.

Meltzoff, A. N. (2007). "Like me": A foundation for social cognition. *Developmental Science, 10*, 126–134.

Meltzoff, A. N., & Moore, M. K. (1997). Explaining facial imitation: A theoretical model. *Early Development and Parenting, 6*, 179–192.

Mesoudi, A. (2011). *Cultural evolution: How Darwinian theory can explain human culture and synthesize the social sciences*. Chicago, IL: University of Chicago Press.

Michael, J., Sandberg, K., Skewes, J., Wolf, T., Blicher, J., Overgaard, M., et al. (2014). Continuous theta-burst stimulation demonstrates a causal role of premotor homunculus in action understanding. *Psychological Science, 25*, 963–972.

Mikulincer, M., & Shaver, P. R. (2012). *The social psychology of morality: Exploring the causes of good and evil*. Washington, DC: American Psychological Association.

Mikulincer, M., & Shaver, P. R. (2014a). *Mechanisms of social connection: From brain to group*. Washington, DC: American Psychological Association.

Mikulincer, M., & Shaver, P. R. (2014b). Introduction. In M. Mikulincer & P. R. Shaver (Eds.), *Mechanisms of social connection: From brain to group* (pp. 3–12). Washington, DC: American Psychological Association.

Nielsen, M. (2012). Imitation, pretend play, and childhood: Essential elements in the evolution of human culture? *Journal of Comparative Psychology, 126*, 170–181.

Obradović, J., Bush, N. R., Stamperdahl, J., Adler, N. E., & Boyce, W. T. (2010). Biological sensitivity to context: The interactive effects of stress reactivity and family adversity on socioemotional behavior and school readiness. *Child Development, 81*, 270–289.

Osborne, D., Wootton, L. W., & Sibley, C. G. (2013). Are liberals agreeable or not? Politeness and compassion differentially predict political conservatism via distinct ideologies. *Social Psychology, 44*, 354–360.

Parks, C. D., Joireman, J., & Van Lange, P. A. M. (2013). Cooperation, trust, and antagonism: How public goods are promoted. *Psychological Science in the Public Interest, 14*, 119–165.

Paulus, M. (2014). The emergence of prosocial behavior: Why do infants and toddlers help, comfort, and share? *Child Development Perspectives, 8*, 77–81.

Paulus, M., Hunnius, S., Vissers, M., & Bekkering, H. (2011a). Bridging the gap between the other and me: The functional role of motor resonance and action effects in infants' imitation. *Developmental Science, 14*, 901–910.

Paulus, M., Hunnius, S., Vissers, M., & Bekkering, H. (2011b). Imitation in infancy: Rational or motor resonance? *Child Development, 82*, 1047–1057.

Piaget, J. (1932/1997). *The moral judgement of the child.* New York: The Free Press.

Piaget, J. (1945/1951). *Play, dreams, and imitations in childhood.* London: W. Heinemann.

Piaget, J. (1970). Piaget's theory. In P. Mussen (Ed.), *Handbook of child psychology* (Vol. 1, 3rd ed.). New York: Wiley.

Piaget, J. (1976). *The grasp of consciousness*. Cambridge, MA: Harvard University Press.

Powell, K. B., & Voeller, K. S. (2004). Prefrontal executive function syndromes in children. *Journal of Child Neurology, 19*, 785–797.

Pulfrey, C., & Butera, F. (2013). Why neoliberal values of self-enhancement lead to cheating in higher education: A motivational account. *Psychological Science, 24*, 2153–2162.

Rameson, L. T., Morelli, S. A., & Liberman, M. D. (2012). The neural correlates of empathy: Experience, automaticity, and prosocial behavior. *Journal of Cognitive Neuroscience, 24*, 235–245.

Riedl, K., Jensen, K., Call, J., & Tomasello, M. (2011). No third party punishment in chimpanzees. *Proceedings of the National Academy of Sciences, USA, 109*, 14824–14829.

Rizzolatti, G. (2014). Confounding the origin and function of mirror neurons. *Behavior and Brain Sciences, 37*, 218–219.

Rochat, P. (2003). Five levels of self-awareness as they unfold early in life. *Consciousness and Cognition, 12*, 717–731.

Root, A. E., Hastings, P. D., & Maxwell, K. L. (2012). Environmental contribution to the development of social competence: Focus on parents. In V. Anderson & M. H. Beauchamp (Eds.), *Developmental social neuroscience and childhood brain insult: Theory and practice* (pp. 91–115). New York: Guilford Press.

Rothbart, M. K., Ahadi, S. A., Hershey, K. L., & Fisher, P. (2001). Investigations of temperament at 3–7 years: The Children's Behavior Questionnaire. *Child Development, 72*, 1394–1408.

Roth-Hanania, R., Davidov, M., & Zahn-Waxler, C. (2011). Empathy development from 8 to 16 months: Early signs of concern for others. *Infant Behavior and Development, 34*, 447–458.

Scarf, D., Imuta, K., Colombo, M., & Hayne, H. (2012). Golden rule or valence matching? Methodological problems in Hamlin et al. *Proceedings of the National Academy of Sciences, USA, 109*, E1426. doi:10.1073/pnas.1204123109.

Schaefer, E. S., & Edgerton, M. (1985). Parent and child correlates of parental modernity. In I. E. Sigel (Ed.), *Parental belief systems: The psychological consequences for children* (pp. 287–318). Hillsdale, NJ: Erlbaum.

Schlenker, B. R., Chambers, J. R., & Le, B. M. (2012). Conservatives are happier than liberals, but why? Political ideology, personality, and life satisfaction. *Journal of Research in Personality, 46*, 127–146.

Schmidt, M. F. H., Rakoczy, H., & Tomasello, M. (2012). Young children enforce social norms selectively depending on the violator's group affiliation. *Cognition, 124*, 325–333.

Schmidt, M. F. H., & Sommerville, J. A. (2011). Fairness expectations and altruistic sharing in 15-month-old human infants. *PLoS One, 6*, e23223. doi:10.1371/journal.pone.0023223.

Shai, D., & Fonagy, P. (2014). Beyond words: Parental embodied mentalizing and the parent-infant dance. In M. Mikulincer & P. R. Shaver (Eds.), *Mechanisms of social connection: From brain to group* (pp. 185–203). Washington, DC: American Psychological Association.

Sharp, C., Pane, H., Ha, C., Venta, A., Pate, A. B., Sturek, J., Fonagy, P. (2011). Theory of mind and emotion regulation difficulties in adolescents with borderline traits. *Journal of the American Academy of Child and Adolescent Psychiatry, 50*, 563–573.

Shaver, P. R., & Mikulincer, M. (2012). An attachment perspective on morality: Strengthening authentic forms of moral decision making. In M. Mikulincer & P. R. Shaver (Eds.), *The social psychology of morality: Exploring the causes of good and evil* (pp. 257–274). Washington, DC: American Psychological Association.

Singer, T., & Hein, G. (2012). Human empathy through the lens of psychology and social neuroscience. In F. B. M. de Waal & P. F. Ferrari (Eds.), *The primate mind: Built to connect with other minds* (pp. 158–174). Cambridge, MA: Harvard University Press.

Smaldino, P. E. (2014a). The cultural evolution of emergent group-level traits. *Behavioral and Brain Sciences, 37*, 243–254.

Smaldino, P. E. (2014b). Group-level traits emerge. *Behavioral and Brain Sciences, 37*, 281–288.

Sommerville, J. A., Schmidt, M. F. H., Yun, J.-E., & Burns, M. (2013). The development of fairness expectations and prosocial behavior in the second year of life. *Infancy, 18*, 40–66.

Taber-Thomas, B. C., & Tranel, D. (2012). Social and moral functioning: A cognitive neuroscience perspective. In V. Anderson & M. H. Beauchamp (Eds.), *Developmental social neuroscience and childhood brain insult: Theory and practice* (pp. 65–90). New York: Guilford Press.

Tafreshi, D., Thompson, J. J., & Racine, T. P. (2014). An analysis of the conceptual foundations of the infant preferential looking paradigm. *Human Development, 57*, 222–240.

Thomas, B. C., Croft, K. E., & Tranel, D. (2011). Harming kin to save strangers: Further evidence for abnormally utilitarian moral judgments after ventromedial pre-

frontal damage. *Journal of Cognitive Neuroscience, 23*, 2186–2196.
Tomasello, M., & Vaish, A. (2013). Origins of human cooperation and morality. *Annual Review of Psychology, 64*, 231–255.
Tucker, D. M., Poulsen, C., & Luu, P. (2015). Critical periods for the neurodevelopmental processes of externalizing and internalizing. *Development and Psychopathology, 27*, 321–346.
Uithol, S., & Gallese, V. (2015). The role of the body in social cognition. *Wiley Interdisciplinary Reviews: Cognitive Science, 6*, 453–460.
Vaish, A., Carpenter, M., & Tomasello, M. (2009). Sympathy through affective perspective-taking and its relation to prosocial behavior in toddlers. *Developmental Psychology, 45*, 534–543.
Vaish, A., Missana, M., & Tomasello, M. (2011). Three-year-old children intervene in third-party moral transgressions. *British Journal of Developmental Psychology, 29*, 124–130.
Vaish, A., & Tomasello, M. (2014). The early ontogeny of human cooperation and morality. In M. Killen & J. G. Smetana (Eds.), *Handbook of moral development* (2nd ed., pp. 279–298). New York: Psychology Press.
Warneken, F. (2013). Young children proactively remedy unnoticed accidents. *Cognition, 126*, 101–108.
Warneken, F. (2015). Precocious prosociality: Why do young children help? *Child Development Perspectives, 9*, 1–6.
Warneken, F., Gräfenhain, M., & Tomasello, M. (2012). Collaborative partner or social tool? New evidence for young children's understanding of joint intentions in collaborative activities. *Developmental Science, 15*, 54–61.
Warneken, F., & Tomasello, M. (2008). Extrinsic rewards undermine altruistic tendencies in 20-month-olds. *Developmental Psychology, 44*, 1785–1788.
Waters, S. F., West, T. V., & Mendes, W. B. (2014). Stress contagion: Physiological covariation between mothers and infants. *Psychological Science, 25*, 934–942.
Waytz, A., Zaki, J., & Mitchell, J. P. (2012). Response of dorsomedial prefrontal cortex predicts altruistic behavior. *The Journal of Neuroscience, 32*, 7646–7650.
Wilson, D. S. (1975). A theory of group selection. *Proceedings of the National Academy of Sciences, USA, 72*, 143–146.
Wilson, D. S. (2014). Groups as units of functional analysis, individuals as proximate mechanisms. *Behavioral and Brain Sciences, 37*, 279–280.
Wilson, G. D., & Patterson, J. R. (1968). A new measure of conservatism. *British Journal of Social and Clinical Psychology, 7*, 264–269.
Woodcock, R. W. (1990). Theoretical foundations of the Wj-R measures of cognitive ability. *Journal of Psychoeducational Assessment, 8*, 231–258.
Woodcock, R. W., & Johnson, M. B. (1989). *Woodcock-Johnson Psycho-Educational Battery-Revised*. Allen, TX: DLM.
Woodward, A. L. (2009). Infants' grasp of others' intentions. *Current Direction in Psychological Science, 18*, 53–57.
Wrangham, R. W. (2009). *Catching fire: How cooking made us human*. New York: Basic Books.
Yeates, K. O., Bigler, E. D., Dennis, M., Gerhardt, C. A., Rubin, K. H., Stancin, T., et al. (2007). Social outcomes in childhood brain disorder: A heuristic integration of social neuroscience and developmental psychology. *Psychological Bulletin, 133*, 535–556.
Yeates, K. O., Bigler, E. D., Gerhardt, C. A., Rubin, K. H., Stancin, T., Taylor, H. G., et al. (2012). Theoretical approaches to understanding social function in childhood brain insults: Toward the integration of social neuroscience and developmental psychology. In V. Anderson & M. H. Beauchamp (Eds.), *Developmental social neuroscience and childhood brain insult: Theory and practice* (pp. 207–230). New York: Guilford Press.
Young, G. (2011). *Development and causality: Neo-Piagetian perspectives*. New York: Springer Science+Business Media.
Zmyj, N., & Buttelmann, D. (2014). An integrative model of rational imitation in infancy. *Infant Behavior and Development, 37*, 21–28.

Causal Learning: Understanding the World

16

Chapter Introduction

The topic of causal learning is marked both by the common issues that bedevil the field of child development, in general, for example, related to how early it develops and through what processes, and by striking innovations in its own terms in thought and theory as well as in empirical research. Some of the issues on causal learning relate to: whether it begins, at least in primitive form, right from the first months of life; whether it is innately prescribed or gradually learned; and whether it is domain general or specific. Some of the methodological innovations in the field include use of sticky mittens and everted rabbits. The area of causal learning lies in the forefront of modeling in child development related to Bayesian learning, intervention accounts of causality, and rational constructivism. Also, it is integrally related to research on social cognition, theory of mind, and the "theory" theory in these regards.

In terms of theory related to causal learning, I provide discussion of cognitive schemas early in life, and show how a more integrated view of early cognitive schemas affords compatibility with the Piagetian view of cognitive development and other views for the area of causal learning. Moreover, I provide a Neo-Piagetian (sub) stage model of cognitive development that is applicable to causal reasoning.

As for the empirical research, I review the recent literature on causal learning relative to each age period in childhood, in particular, and point to the contrasting perspectives supported by the research, such as in terms of the issues about nativism versus empiricism, which constitutes a debate, in general, in child development. The area is a dynamic, fast-evolving one, because casual reasoning provides a window on cognitive development (and causality), in general.

Bayesian Learning Model

Introduction

Gopnik and Wellman (2012) presented a Bayesian learning model of mechanisms involved in constructing cognitive theories in infancy and childhood. They phrased their model in terms of reconstruction of constructivism, asking how concrete exemplars in the experience of the child could function in the development of abstract structures of knowledge. Extant accounts are either empirical/systemic or nativist/modular.

Unfortunately, the authors dismissed the Piagetian approach at the outset as being theoretically vague and empirically inadequate (Piaget, 1926, 1930). However, I shall show that for the question of development of causality, it is rigorous on both counts and sets the stage for a combined Piagetian–Bayesian account.

G. Young, *Unifying Causality and Psychology*, DOI 10.1007/978-3-319-24094-7_16

The critical bridge to both lies in nonlinear dynamical system theory, which Gopnik and Wellman associated with the empiricist approach, although it is atheoretical with respect to the learning-genetic continuum of the origins of the components of the systems it examines and how they collate into wider, global wholes.

Model

Gopnik and Wellman (2012) referred to their approach to the development of causal models from the Bayesian perspective as "rational" constructivism. Later in their article, they referred to the approach of Goodman, Ullman, and Tenenbaum (2011) on "minimal" nativism in early learning of causal models and theories. Either way, it appears that the infant is endowed with necessary precursors to the ability to engage in model and theory building and these mental structures can be constructed rapidly, including at the rational, abstract level.

Gopnik and Wellman were involved in developing the particular constructivist model of cognitive development that has been labeled the "theory" theory (e.g., Gopnik & Wellman, 1992; Wellman & Gelman, 1992). In this approach, children first develop "intuitive" theories about the world and, then, they revise them to fit new evidence. The children's theories include causal representations about the world and, moreover, the representations might coalesce into more global "framework" theories. Children's theories allow for interpretation, predictions, and wondering how things might be different with the implementation of interventions (counterfactuals). These theories dynamically evolve with new evidence, including into the higher-order frameworks.

Children gather evidence by learning probabilistic, statistical contingencies between events. Moreover, children learn about causal structures by informally experimenting or acting on the world, by playing, or by observing others. As children revise their theories, they do so by revising the probabilities associated with them and alternatives.

One of the areas of children's theorizing concerns the mind of others and the social world. For example, children move (a) from understanding action and intention with respect to others (b) to representations and interpretations (theory of mind). However, there is dispute whether initial perceptual structures and core knowledge constitute intuitive theories or whether they are simply innately-present "nontheoretical" structures. The authors opt for the former stance.

Probabilistic or Bayesian models have been applied to theory-like cognitive development because they can help understand how children build hypotheses, test them, and so on, transforming them into causal generative representations. Bayes' theorem can be represented as $P(H/E)\ \alpha\ [P(E/H)\ P(H)]$, in which P = probability, H = hypothesized structure, E = Evidence, and / = given. $P(H)$ is referred to as the prior, $P(E/H)$ as the likelihood, and $P(H/E)$ as the posterior. The rule, therefore, is that the posterior is a function of the likelihood and of the prior. A hypothesis can be represented by a map, tree, or causal graph.

One type of probabilistic model is termed causal Bayes nets, or causal graphical models (Pearl, 2000; Spirtes, Glymour, & Scheines, 2001). Woodward (2003) developed an interventionist account of causation that "dovetails" with the causal Bayes net approach. In the approach, graphs with just a few nodes can generate multiple predictions about events, and graph "surgery" or altering interventions (e.g., fixing variable values) can be performed on the nodes to alter the causal chains and probabilities involved. Or, one could ask what would happen counterfactually if different variable values were in place.

Research

The empirical research with children has been supporting a Bayesian view of their representational learning about causal structures, and also that even infants can detect complex statistical patterns (for example, Wu, Gopnik, Richardson, & Kirkham, 2011). Also, they can use probability learning to infer causal properties.

Gopnik, Sobel, Schulz, and Glymour (2001) conducted the first study in the area. Children were shown a "blicket" detector, which is an apparatus that lights up and plays music when an appropriate combination of block objects is placed on it. Children who were as young as 2 years of age could infer the causal structure in the apparatus. In the study, children could use what they learned causally to make the apparatus either stop or go.

Gweon and Schulz (2011) found that even 16-month-olds could infer causation from variations in block placement. Sobel, Tenenbaum, and Gopnik (2004) and Sobel and Kirkham (2007) showed that children as young as 18 months of age could make correct causal inferences from more complex statistical patterns. Gopnik et al. (2004) found that children could differentiate the direction of a causal relationship ($A \rightarrow B$, not $B \rightarrow A$).

Schulz, Gopnik, and Glymour (2007) found that 4-year-olds could work with three variables (A, B, C). Kushnir and Gopnik (2005) found that 4-year-olds could make inferences about probabilistic relations. Studies also showed that children can integrate prior knowledge and new evidence (Griffiths, Sobel, Tenenbaum, & Gopnik, 2011; Kushnir & Gopnik, 2007).

Children can make inferences in areas other than physical causation (e.g., psychological causation). Ma and Xu (2011) showed that 16-month-olds used probabilistic sampling in learning that another person's desires could differ from their own. For example, Kushnir, Xu, and Wellman found that 20-month-olds could use statistical Bayesian reasoning in inferring the desires of another person, which is an underlying mental state. Seiver, Gopnik, and Goodman (2013) found that 4-year-olds could infer others' personal traits and use the information to predict behavior patterns. Children can generalize from learned causal relationships to infer more abstract generalizations (Lucas, Gopnik, & Griffiths, 2010; Schulz, Standing, & Bonawitz, 2008). Indeed, children might develop abstract framework theories before detailed specific ones, or computational causal primitives constructed from simpler patterns of evidence.

In the following, I indicate areas of child cognitive development in which Bayesian modeling had been applied. They include theory of mind (ToM), abstractions, generative modeling, and reasoning.

Elaboration

ToM Gopnik and Wellman (2012) have integrated a major, rapidly evolving area in child development. Their work also includes description of the steps that young children go through as they develop insight about mind. Wellman and Liu (2004) created a ToM Scale that uses tasks that inform about the following progression, which has been found in most cultures studied. (a) First, children develop to appreciate diverse desires (having different desires targeting the same thing). (b) Next, they develop diverse beliefs (having different beliefs about the same situation). (c) Third, they develop awareness of knowledge–ignorance (someone might not know something that is true). (d) Older children then develop false belief (someone might believe something different about something true, e.g., the classic Sally/Anne and Smarties box tasks; 4-year-olds but not 3-year-olds realize that if a peer or puppet do not see either displacement of a hidden item or its contents (with the container involved visibly indicating contents different than what is in the container), then the other party will have a false belief on the task because the 4-year-old can take the perspective of the viewer, unlike the case for the 3-year-old). (e) Fifth, in hidden emotions, children learn that people can feel emotionally one way but display their emotions publically in another way. The results fit the Bayesian perspective because development changes as new evidence is experienced. Also, the order of the developmental sequence that is described is found in most societies, but it can be altered in different cultural contexts.

Abstraction Goodman et al. (2011), cited by Gopnik and Wellman (2012), used the Bayesian framework to study the ideal learner, and their work led to inferences for cognitive development. Their hierarchical Bayesian model, and the ideal learning paradigm, showed that learning can take place simultaneously at the specific and abstract levels. In fact, the learning that takes place at the abstract level might be surprisingly fast, a phenomenon referred to as the "blessing" of abstraction. In terms of infant learning, abstractions are acquired quickly, but this could not take place without innate perceptual input "analyzers" (Carey, 2009). These modules perform simple perceptual transformations of input, preparing for further cognitive analysis. The perceptual input analyzers are domain-specific, and make input suitable for domain-general inference.

Goodman et al. (2011) viewed the world as a collection of causal systems that infants can begin to model probabilistically. Then, learning about events leads to full-scale models, which are further generalized into theory. Developmentally, abstractions such as this could serve as scaffolds for later, language-mediated causal understanding.

Generative Models Bonawitz, Denison, Griffiths, and Gopnik (2014) postulated that children appear to cope with multiple possible hypotheses to explain the information before them by sampling hypotheses, rather than by producing the best guess or by naively matching frequency. Children might construct "generative" models (intuitive theories). Moreover, they might revise them through Bayesian inferences, using prior knowledge. In Bayesian terms, Bayes' rule specifies the way to compute a "posterior" distribution that incorporates the information (data) at hand. This is a probabilistic approach to cognitive development, in which children appear to "rationally" update a probability distribution of possible hypotheses in accordance with Bayes' theorem and computations.

It is unlikely children assess all possible hypotheses in dealing with information, and so they appear to use algorithms that maximize finding the most likely hypotheses. The strategy is rational in that it is a compromise between the cost of arriving at inductions that are in error and the cost of entertaining more hypotheses by sampling all the possible ones. Being guided by "priors" (prior knowledge) provides a rational basis for limiting options to those that are more likely.

Denison, Bonawitz, Gopnik, and Griffiths (2014) produced evidence in support of the Bayesian sampling hypothesis in children's cognitive development. Children were exposed to a bin with varying amounts of red and blue chips. The children "guessed" blue or red in the receiving area in proportion to the color distribution in the containing bin. When the experimental parameters were varied, hypothesis selection conformed to the posterior probability or distribution of hypotheses.

Bonawitz et al. (2014) determined that, on these types of tasks, children used a win-stay/lose-shift strategy. They stayed with their original guess until the evidence became too strong that it did not apply. In a trial-by-trial analysis, the authors showed that initial guesses exhibited subsequent patterns of "dependencies" consistent with the win-stay/lose-shift strategy, such that the aggregate responses "approximated the exact analytical Bayesian solution" (p. 500).

For the authors, this research illustrates that Bayesian modeling specifies the nature of generative models that children probabilistically construct and the likelihood functions involved based on priors (formally, prior knowledge is expressed in a distribution of "prior" probabilities over hypotheses; in the ones to be sampled). The precise quantitative predictions that derive in the Bayesian approach to understanding children's probabilistic sampling and learning needs further work in other cognitive domains and tasks, as well as the types of algorithms involved and their possible individual differences.

Gopnik and Bonawitz (2014) explained that in Bayesian learning, cognitive models help generate predictions about data—we create models based on data, and we revise them based on new data, all while using probability estimates of which models might be the most probable. In doing so, we start off with belief about which models might be more probable (the priors). For example, Kushnir, Xu, and Wellman (2010) found that 20-month-olds could infer preferences/desires in terms of nonrandom patterns in choice of objects. [In contrast, for a deterministic account of mental model building, see Khemlani, Barbey, & Jonson-Laird, 2014].

Reasoning Rottman and Hastie (2013) provided a tutorial on Bayesian probabilistic causal networks used in the study of reasoning and in making inferences about causal relationships and networks. Causal cognition, in general, is an area of research that can profit from the particular formalisms of their model. However, the empirical research offers areas in which the model does not apply. Nevertheless, it illustrates the power of Bayesian probability approaches to causal reasoning.

Comment

Generally, research in which Gopnik has been involved continued to support a Bayesian account of causal learning while de-emphasizing Piaget. Although his sensorimotor stage in infancy appears incompatible with the work showing that abstraction and generative models develop in this period, and although his concept of schemas in cognition lacks the Bayesian probabilistic aspect in learning, the Bayesian and Piagetian views are compatible in that infant cognitive structures in the Piagetian sense can be understood as primitively generative and also their creation can be understood as dependent on stochastic processes. That is, one could elaborate a Neo-Piagetian approach to early causal learning that marries the Piagetian emphasis that they develop in fancy as cognitive schemas, and moreover, that they develop through substages via Bayesian learning modalities that facilitate the process of their acquisition.

Toward the development of this integrated Bayesian–Piagetian model of early causal learning, the next section of the chapter reviews Piagetian thought on causal learning. Also, it reviews the literature on causal learning that incorporates Piagetian thought. Finally, I make suggestions related to how my Neo-Piagetian model (Young, 2011) can help elaborate an integrated Bayesian–Piagetian account of early causal learning.

Piagetian Contributions to Understanding Causal Learning

Piaget on Causality

Desrochers, Ricard, and Décarie (1995) have developed a series of tasks to determine the substage of causality understanding in infants according to Piaget's cognitive developmental model. That is, Piaget had elaborated a model of cognitive development in infancy that consisted of six substages, as described at the end of the last chapter. Moreover, he described the acquisitions in causality associated with three substages. In this regard, Desrochers et al. (1995) constructed a sequence of tasks on causality in infancy and the steps within them that are consistent with the Piagetian model. Finally, the results of their study point to a sequential acquisition of the steps in causal learning that fits Piaget's description of the sensorimotor steps involved, as shown by the behavioral steps in the tasks (see Table 16.1).

The work that relates early causal learning to Piaget has not dealt with his developmental substage model in infancy, per se. Rather, as shown next, different points of view point to the value of sensorimotor and action-related influences on early causal learning, as per Piaget.

Rational Construction

Model Sommerville, Upshaw, and Loucks (2013) presented a view of rational constructivism in relation to early causal learning that is quite consistent with the Piagetian tradition (Piaget, 1952) [for an opposing view on the value of Piaget's possible contribution to understanding causal learning, see Xu and Kushnir (2013a, 2013b) below.]. Sommerville et al. (2013) noted that, in some ways, infants not only construct concrete-specific representations but also build abstract representations (e.g., about unseen event outcomes). Representations might be simultaneously concrete and abstract, and are action-based, or built by actions on the world.

The concrete aspects of representation relate to "goal-relevant" features of actions in a way that is either action-specific or event-specific. Moreover, the abstract components of the representations also are action-related. They "support" infant perception of the action of others and also inferences about outcome actions that are not seen. By one year of age, infants use their representations more flexibly, and also language becomes a factor that adds to their abstraction.

Table 16.1 Piagetian causality scale (8 tasks): procedure, stage, and criterion response(s)

Task	Procedure	Stage	Criterion responses(s)
1	A bell is fastened to a wooden board, or a rattle is presented to S within reach	3	Hits the object systematically. *OR* Performs a repetitive motor act during the pause following presentation
2	An object, which produces an interesting show, is activated by E in front of S, and kept out of reach. Once the object stops, E puts his/her hand within S's reach	4	Touches E's hand lightly during the pause and waits
3	E drums on the table or snaps fingers, and stops abruptly, leaving his/her hand within S's reach	4	Touches E's hand lightly during the pause and waits
4	E moves his/her fingers along S's body to amuse S, and stops abruptly, leaving his/her hand within S's reach	4	Touches E's hand lightly during the pause and waits
5	A small mechanical TV toy is turned "on" and "off" by pushing a button in front of S, out of reach. After 2–3 demonstrations, the object is given to S	5	Demands the toy by pointing to it between demonstrations. *OR* Takes the TV and gives it back to E or to mother. *OR* Attempts to activate or succeeds in activating the toy
6	A roly-poly toy in the form of a Mickey Mouse is set in motion by a gentle push. This task is presented in the same way as in task 5	5	Demands the toy by pointing to it between demonstrations. *OR* Takes the object and gives it back to E or to mother when it is given to S
7	Four little wooden chickens are fastened to a board and set in motion by pulling a string. This task is presented in the same way as in task 5	5	Demands the toy by pointing to it between demonstrations. *OR* Acts directly on the string while looking at the toy when it is presented to S
8	From a position behind S, E throws a ball, which rolls close to S	6	Turns head and looks for E. *OR* Picks up the ball and gives it to E

Adopted with permission of Springer Science+Business Media. Young, G. (2011). *Development and causality: Neo-Piagetian perspectives*. New York: Springer Science+Business Media; with kind permission from Springer Science+Business Media B. V. [Table 3.5, Page 66]
S subject, *E* experimenter

According to Sommerville et al. (2013), the evidence supports Piaget's (1952) view that infants build representations of actions on an action-by-action basis. Their understanding of goals seems "embedded" within specific actions. However, at the same time, the abstract aspect of their representations participates in guiding their perception, thereby facilitating inferences about unseen action outcomes, either in their own actions or that of others.

Sommerville et al. (2013) reviewed the literature showing that, despite "impressive" inferential skills (Xu & Garcia, 2008), 1-year-olds still learn highly specific abstractions in certain areas. For example, they learn which heights can be descended one posture at a time (Kretch & Adolph, 2013) and which parts of a tool are meant for holding (Barrett, Davis, & Needham, 2007). Baillargeon, Li, Gertner, and Wu (2010) showed that infants learn in a "category-specific" way instead of learning principles across a range of event outcomes (e.g., for specific properties, such as object height). There might be separate event-related representations rather than global learning (e.g., in learning means–ends sequences; Sommerville, 2007). Infants appear to learn about things in a wide variety of domains that are "object specific" and "action specific" (e.g., containment, occlusion, collision, covering; Baillargeon et al., 2010).

Also, the following indicates the primacy of activity in infant representation. It appears that infants' capacity to undertake goal-directed action "drives" development of their perception of the actions of others. For example, the degree to which they can perform specific actions predicts their skill in identifying goals of these behaviors in the activity of other people. Moreover, when 10-month-olds were given active training in novel tool use to retrieve an object out of reach, they could better recognize another person's use of the tool as goal-directed, relative to a control group that experienced visual familiarity with the tool rather than production of goal-directed behaviors, per se (Sommerville, Blumenthal, Venema, & Braun, 2011). Acting on the world, rather than merely engaging in observation, appears integral to representational construction and reconstruction.

Other research by Sommerville and colleagues illustrates that infants can make quite specific inferences about others' goal-directed actions yet, in this regard, it helps to be advanced motorically. Loucks and Sommerville (2011) found that infants can infer the physical "outcomes" of particular goal-directed actions (dropping actions). Loucks and Sommerville (2012) found that 10-month-olds could use information about how an actor grasped an object (with a precision grasp) in order to make inferences about the outcome of the event. Infants who were relatively skilled in precision grasping, unlike those who were not, could "generate" outcomes for actions involving the grasp made by actors.

In terms of moving from action-specific to more general representations, Gerson and Woodward (2010, 2012) suggested that infants use an "analogy-like" procedure. They appear to use a general cognitive mechanism that creates correspondences between their own familiar actions and ones that are novel that they might witness.

Sommerville et al. (2013) concluded that, at the level of the construction of goal-centered representations of the action of others relative to the more passive observational process, the active experience within which infants typically engage plays a "privileged and/or preferential role." Action is one aspect in the development of representation.

Comment I would add that although more abstract and analogy-driven processes might be involved increasingly with age in infancy, Piaget's emphasis on the "active" and activity-driven nature of early representation development indicates that it should be emphasized for early causal learning even more than in the work of Sommerville et al. (2013). It would appear that there is room for a revised understanding of the nature of sensorimotor schemas and their evolution through Neo-Piagetian substages in infancy that allows for the construction of schemas related to early sensorimotor activity yet the development of representational primitives that move in steps toward increasing complexity, flexibility, and full representation by 2 years of age. That Piaget's work and Bayesian-type approaches can be integrated are illustrated in the following section.

Construction and Computation

Model Sobel and Legare (2014) reviewed the literature and models of how children learn the causal structure of the environment. They ended up supporting an integrated approach involving the computational and constructivist accounts.

From an early age, children have been shown to possess "sophisticated" domain-specific causal reasoning that makes them "remarkable" causal learners (Piaget, 1929). Since Piaget's consideration of the development of causality in early life, research has emphasized that preschoolers can deal with ("recognize the importance," "possess") temporal priority, spatial priority, contingency, prediction, explanation, and counterfactual reasoning (e.g., Legare, Gelman, & Wellman, 2010; Sobel, 2004).

Theories of causal learning are investigating children's domain-general learning and not only their domain-specific learning. The first block of theories in this regard involves associative strength and parameter estimation. Very young children manifest statistical learning capacities and the ability to generalize (Sobel & Kirkham, 2007; Xu & Garcia, 2008). The second block of theories of children's causal learning considers that even early on children learn an abstract causal "model" or map. The models are domain specific, but the ability can represent knowledge in different ("across") domains. Children develop "naïve" theories and the models stand as "computational descriptions" (e.g., Gopnik et al., 2004; Gopnik & Wellman, 2012). For example, 4-year-olds infer that "hidden" causes are present when they are shown probabilistic, stochastic data (Schulz & Sommerville, 2006). This approach to children's causal learning is represented by building causal graph models (following Pearl, 2000, 2009).

According to Sobel and Legare (2014), an integrated account of the two causal learning models in the field—the statistical, probabilistic learning approach and the causal model mapping one—can derive from the approach of Piaget (1952, 1955). In terms of the statistical view, for Piaget, infants in the early sensorimotor stage experience causality only as a form of association of experiences. However, by engaging in activity in the environment, infants can develop recognition of "deeper" relationships over events. As the infants learn that objects themselves can be efficacious in affecting the environment (approximately in substage 4, at 8 months of age), they are capable of abstracting the conditional probability information contained in event associations.

Sobel and Legare (2014) noted, as well, that the Piagetian description of infant causal learning is consistent with the causal graphic modeling approach (which is interventionist in understanding the essence of causality). Contemporary research supports the graph model mapping approach to early causal learning (Muentener & Carey, 2010; Sommerville & Woodward, 2005; Teglas et al., 2011).

Sobel and Legare (2014) noted that the causal graph modeling approach to causal learning in children has limits, though, if considered by itself. The approach is Bayesian, and does not provide algorithms of how children make causal inferences. An integrated approach to the area needs to take account of how children form specific models and more general frameworks.

According to the authors, inconsistency in observed data plays an important role in explanation and hypothesis generation in children's causal reasoning. The child actively participates in constructing causal theories, knowledge, and conceptual change by exploring, and the processes of explanation and exploration interact as causal learning proceeds (Legare, 2012, 2014). Moreover, causal learning is a social construction in that children integrate what they learn from others in this regard with the data that they acquire themselves (Sobel & Kushnir, 2013). As they develop causal explanations, they begin to generate "why?" questions (Wellman & Liu, 2007). This opens a whole new chapter in their causal learning.

Comment Sobel and Legare (2014) have continued the integrative process needed in the area of causal learning over the Bayesian and Piagetian perspectives. However, we still need more work on the mechanism involved in the growth of causal learning through the actions that Piaget described. Sensorimotor growth takes place through internal dynamics, to be sure, but also through external impetus, and among them are the imitations that the environment could foster, as discussed next.

Observation

Introduction The imitation function is not usually associated with transitional steps in the Piagetian model. However, there is no reason why imitation cannot be examined from the framework of the Piagetian model, especially in its modern guises.

Early That infants' cognitive schema might involve matching schemas of own-bodily sensorimotor activity and those related to actions with respect to the other is supported by work on infant mirror system mechanisms. Turati et al. (2013) demonstrated that 6-month-olds watching an agent reaching for, grasping, and then bringing an object toward the body (mouth or head) led to recruitment and selective modulation of the mirror motor system, as indicated by electromyographic (EMG) measurement. EMG activity was recorded from suprahyoid muscles (SM) that are involved in chewing and swallowing, and that are responsible for mouth opening. In mirror mechanisms, the actions of the other are mapped onto the observer's motor representation of the same actions.

For the 6-month-olds studied, SM activity increased especially during observation of the action involving mouth opening in the agent (only in the bringing back phase). This suggests a motor resonance-related, or modulation, effect already present in early infancy, and also that the motor system is recruited in observing relevant agent actions. The authors also found that the modulation of motor activity correlated with overt mouth opening behavior. It appears that the infant's motor system simulates "below threshold" observed action as sensorimotor processing proceeds. Turati et al. (2013) concluded that motor resonance effects might even be present at birth (e.g., Lepage & Théoret, 2007; Meltzoff & Decety, 2003) and disappear at about 3 months, only to reemerge at 6 months.

Later Meltzoff, Waismeyer, and Gopnik (2012) queried how infants and young children learn the causal structure of their world. They focused on 2-year-olds in their research, and they presented an observational causal learning perspective. There have been three other mechanisms that have been proposed for causal learning, which I describe first. I note that two of them involve the Bayesian statistical approach and Piaget's, with the third one on more specific Michottean causal launching learning.

(a) The Michottean causal learning that takes place in infancy involves the learning of launching contingencies by focusing on specific, narrowly-tuned spatiotemporal features and patterns of movement as cues in causal learning (e.g., Scholl & Tremoulet, 2000).
(b) The second approach to mechanism in causal learning focuses on Piaget's (1954) idea that infants might learn causal relations between their "willed" actions and the effects or outcomes of the actions. Also at this age period, they might infer relations such as this in seeing someone act intentionally and directly on an object. However, infants in their cognition at this age are still "precausal" (Piaget, 1930) because they fail to appreciate fully event–event and "downstream" effects.
(c) A third way of learning causality in early life seems to involve "noting" correlations and associations in events, e.g., in patterns of statistical covariation (Rogers & McClelland, 2004) and also in associating some events with others (e.g., Kuhl, 2004). However, Meltzoff et al. (2012) noted that the statistical approach involves more than pattern learning because in order to infer causality in correlation, infants appear to use "interventions," or knowing that their use could be informative (e.g., Gopnik & Schulz, 2007).

About observational causal learning, Meltzoff et al. (2012) suggested that an even more powerful (and ubiquitous) mechanism of causal learning involves observing others engaging in interventionist causally-informative behavior, and inferring the presence of causal relations from the observations. The authors investigated their model by designing a "two-choice" causal procedure. Infants observed an experimenter perform two actions on two objects with equal frequency, but only one of them was followed consistently by an effect. The control condition involved reversing outcome and intervention. Methodological innovations implemented in the study involved control of contaminants: by avoiding infants hearing causal language (by the experimenters); avoiding spatial/temporal conjunction (in the intervention-outcome); and avoiding intentional actions by people (experimenters) in one of the conditions (by using surreptitious magnets). Also, to increase generalizability, the authors varied objects, events, and actions over four studies. Finally, the measures that were used varied (i.e., infant actions, looking).

Meltzoff et al. (2012) concluded that the results of the four experiments indicated that, at 2 years of age, infants are "adept" in observational causal learning. They do more than learn associations or imitate directly actions of people. Rather, in watching events, even without human intervention, they can infer causal links between paired, sequential events. Moreover, they can learn from what they see and intervene appropriately themselves. They can intervene selectively on a cause producing an effect (e.g., to get a marble; lift a cone; move a disc). The various control conditions and control of contaminants instituted by the authors precluded interpretations other than genuine observational causal learning taking place in the 2-year-olds. Infants at this age seem to adhere to the scientific maxim that correlation does not necessarily mean causation [and that intervention can discern it]. The authors concluded that different developmental possibilities are worth considering in causal intervention learning by observation, e.g., in hypothesis construction and constraint.

Yu and Kushnir (2014) showed that, unlike 2-year-olds, 4-year-olds are more likely to over-imitate in different games. One explanation offered was that, unlike toddlers, preschoolers are learning about social and cultural norms, so that over-imitation could be valuable in this regard. Other explanations concerned increased affiliative motivation. The authors added that over-imitation could be important in pedagogical demonstrations (e.g., Csibra & Gergely, 2005, on natural pedagogy).

Comment Observations afford powerful learning opportunities and, further, imitation substantiates them. However, models of observational learning do not generally consider that it is a constructive cognitive activity that improves with the dynamic transitions of infant cognition from one skill level to the next. Observational learning, as much as any phenomenon based on the formation of cognitive schemes in the activity, lends itself to models of its transformation in Piagetian substages in infancy.

For example, in the 4- and 8-month-old, from a Piagetian perspective, infants enter into a sensorimotor substage in which they develop a degree of coordination in schemas, such as in visually-directed reaching, and more intentional ones, such as moving a barrier (screen) to get at a partially hidden object with which it had been playing. Both these types of sensorimotor actions could be ones on which imitation after observation is mapped. Moreover, in the next sensorimotor substage from 8 to 12 months of age, these behaviors become more differentiated, and the reaching can serve removing a barrier in a detour action to get a fully hidden object (object permanence being indicated by the action). This behavior would suggest intent from the beginning of the action to get at the desired object, although there are limits to the behavior (e.g., not being able to shift search to a second hiding place, even when the transfer has been seen), and the intent is guided by perceptual images of the hidden object rather than by abstract representational plans. Nevertheless, imitative learning could map onto the schemas being created in the searching behavior involved, a postulate that illustrates the potential of the Piagetian model to show how observational learning can develop in cognitive complexity even in the first year of life.

Also, according to Bayesian proponents, research with infants in the second year of life consistently shows that infants at this age are capable of making inferences, appreciating intentions, and engaging in higher-order relational cognition (e.g., Walker & Gopnik, 2014). However, as with younger ages, one could ask the extent to which the evolving capacities map onto Piagetian or Neo-Piagetian substages in the sensorimotor stage of infancy. For example, in the 12- and 18-month benchmarks in Piagetian theory, infants are capable of trial and error quasi-mental combinations and invention of new mental combinations, respectively, but with sensorimotor conditionals/constraints involved. Actions and sensorimotor experience still constitute the anchors for the emerging representations in the second year of life, and imitations of them after observation could add to the growing complexity of the schemas involved, but not move them by themselves uniquely into the representational sphere.

Natural pedagogy is related to imitative learning, but carries the learning into a different level by arguing that social learning, in general, is critical to cognitive acquisition. In the next section, I examine this area but, once more, argue that it can only complement and not replace a Piagetian perspective based in action learning.

Natural Pedagogy

Model Gergely and Jacob (2013) presented evidence that infants can make inferences that do not require action support. Moreover, they appear to be at a phase in which they are open to "natural pedagogy," having a facility to profit from social learning (e.g., on the basis of ostensive, nonverbal referential actions/demonstration). For example, infants look longer when an actor/agent chooses relatively less efficient actions compared to other ones toward a goal state (Gergely & Csibra, 2003). Surian, Caldi, and Sperber (2007) found that 1-year-olds look longer at an actor/agent retrieving a preferred food that is hidden from view for the agents but not the infants. Infants can follow an agent's gaze shift to one of two objects (but only if a referential expectation had been set up by ostensive signals, such as eye contact or infant-directed speech; Senju & Csibra, 2008).

As for most studies directly on natural pedagogy, they typically concern older infants, unlike the case for the ones cited above (e.g., Gweon, Tenenbaum, & Schulz, 2010; Ma & Xu, 2011). In all cases, actions were not required of the infants in order to demonstrate social learning based on social-pragmatic cues.

Comment Overall, the research reported by Gergely and Jacob (2013) indicates that a more passive than active learning has a role to play in infant cognitive development and that the social environment contributes to it. However, this does not deny Sommerville et al.'s (2013) conclusion of the primacy of action-based learning and inference. The concept of schema in the Neo-Piagetian tradition should be expanded to include observation and social inputs. However, I note that this does not preclude that a type of analogic process might be involved, but at the action level; e.g., from proprioceptive and kinesthetic feedback mapping on wider intersensory/intermodal schema formations that permit action mapping and prediction (e.g., Meltzoff, 2007).

Integrating Bayes and Piaget

There could be room for integrating the Bayesian approach of infant cognitive development with the Piagetian one. Below, I consider early cognitive development along these lines.

Rational Constructivism

Model The area of cognitive development often is marked by extreme empiricism or extreme nativism. Xu and Kushnir (2013a, 2013b) elaborated the burgeoning middle ground or integrative approach of rational constructivism (already briefly introduced in discussing Gopnik and Wellman (2012) and Sommerville et al. (2013)). Xu and Kushnir (2013b) offered some basic tenets underlying this perspective and described its integrative stance.

In this regard, from one point of view, even developmentally, human learning is especially an active inferential process and is more than just a correlational, associative learning. It generates abstract, novel, and causal processes in learning, conceptualization, representation, and modeling.

However, as well, early learning also might be statistical, computational, probabilistic, partial, or graded and Bayesian. The learner begins with a distribution of prior probabilities related to a set of hypotheses and then computes the hypotheses' prior probabilities in light of the evidence as indicated by Bayesian algorithms. Also, any model generated is open to revision, but with the constraint that whatever has been constructed becomes part of the priors on which revisions can be devised, and their influence in this regard varies with their "strength." The child gradually moves from more general purpose "domains" or mechanisms to more specific ones.

Xu and Kushnir (2013b) contrasted their approach with that of Piaget (1954). First, the rational constructivist point of view does not endorse the concept of stages in development. [This is where their view differs from mine, and I note that this exclusion of Piagetian (sub)stages in the rational constructionist perspective is not part of the approach as discussed by Sommerville et al. (2013).] Second, cognitive development does not begin with sensorimotor "primitives" having no differentiation between child and world. Instead, very early in life, new learning and concepts are driven by rational inferential learning processes.

Comment Once more, as with Gopnik and Wellman (2012), Piaget is not considered relevant to this area of contemporary study of cognitive development. However, other workers (e.g., Sobel & Legare, 2014; Sommerville et al., 2013) consider Piaget's work central to elucidating the nature of early causal learning. Perhaps the exclusion of Piaget in understanding causal and related learning early in life is because workers who support the exclusion do so *grosso modo* about the sensorimotor stage conception, in general, without examining the progression through the six substages involved. That being said, Piaget's conception to causal learning should indeed be complemented by other approaches, as applicable. Moreover, one can ask the extent to which the Piagetian and Bayesian approaches are really exclusive, nonoverlapping alternative explanations of early causal learning.

The following considers whether the rational constructivist and Neo-Piagetian views are indeed in opposition, as maintained by Xu and Kushnir (2013b). In contrast, to their perspective, I elucidate how the rational constructivist view is not antithetical to the Piagetian one. (a) On the one hand, Neo-Piagetians have revised his model to make it more consistent with contemporary research. (b) On the other hand, the cognitive developmental processes that Piaget described early in life are not incompatible with the learning, conceptual, and inferential processes that characterize rational constructivism.

About the former point (a) above, Young (2011), for example, presented a modified Piagetian cognitive developmental stage progression over the lifespan that begins with a reflexive stage prenatally and then with the sensorimotor stage at 1 month of age, which then consists of the remaining five sensorimotor substages in Piaget's substage model of the sensorimotor period. Removal of Piaget's first sensorimotor substage of Reflex Exercise from his sensorimotor substage sequence and expanding it into its own stage, as I have done, might help modify some of the criticisms associated with his version of the sensorimotor period as being "primitive" and being neither able to permit separation of person and world and unable to support some sort of inferential activity. In this regard, Schulz (2013) noted that Piaget's (1937) concept of the child as an active learner includes in early life "systematic attempts" to try to understand the workings of the world.

About the latter point (b) above, sensorimotor schemas as described by Piaget are environmentally-responsive yet also constraining in their conservative tendency to resist change (accommodation and assimilation, respectively). There is no reason to exclude that they function in the Bayesian manner suggested in the rational constructivist approach. In this regard, assimilation, by definition, is based on prior constructions framing present sampling of the environment statistically. Similarly, accommodation, by definition, constitutes revision of extant schemes according to probability estimates of what might work better in context.

There might have to be theoretical compromise by both parties (accommodations!) to properly assimilate the point of view of the other in each of their perspectives. For example, Piagetian schemas should be understood as experience-dependent models that have probabilistic components. Nothing that Piaget has written would deny this reworked understanding of schema. Similarly, the rational constructivist approach should acknowledge that its abstractions are activity-based and sensorially-based. Even if they have domain-general components, either they are innately prescribed or they are readily activated by experience. Also, they exist adaptively as means to further promote differentiation toward the specific that affords better reality-based activity. Further in this regard, although they are channeled through that sensory-based activity beyond their original domain-general status, they do not become isolated abstract models that are separate from the actions that help differentiating them.

In short, to rephrase Piaget in more contemporary terms, the concept of schema as described by Piaget is an embodied one that is activity- and world-contact dependent. It describes a participatory regime in early learning and abstraction that demands and encourages engagement by the child in a unified body–mind–brain activity. It is a feedback and feedforward anticipatory mechanism that permits abstractions that facilitate adaptation. However, the abstractions are reality-dependent even if they are constructed. They are probabilistic, empirical, rational, and "afforded," as well as constructed, abstracted, and inferred. They are primitive relative to later abstractions, quite intuitive, and kinesthetic- and proprioceptive-driven through their action base, forming integrated cross-modal body mapping that gives them their generic, action-distant properties, to the degree that the process permits, which is only minimal. They are social, observational, and imitative as much as personally driven by active construction and curiosity. In the end, they are the essence of what is demanded in a rational constructivist approach with respect to the cognitive constructions formulated by the child early in life. That is, they build on the stochastic process, but on an internal scaffold of cognitive schemas pregnant with a growth program in the way indicated, moreover, one that includes bursts of change through generic substages that can bootstrap them forward to a degree.

Moreover, by understanding the concept of schema in cognitive development as highly compatible with the rational constructive approach, a logical model is available to understand how the child's abstracted modeling of the world both begins and is carried forward and altered in cognitive development. Neo-Piagetian conceptualizations of stages in cognitive development include substages, dynamic evolution, and relations to discoveries in developmental neuroscience that make them not only quite consistent with the Piagetian approach but also quite consistent with the recent literature (Young, 2011).

As much as cognitive development is individualized, there are also universal features to consider. Not that the latter reflect innate, unchanging mechanisms. Rather, the Neo-Piagetian stages and substages that I have described reflect individualized and contextualized acquisitions above all, but ones having universal features. This obtains because they represent common dynamical solutions in the developmental process, ones that elegantly emerge in the constant rational construction of the child's mind in the environment's world. The program is not a prearranged one that passively appears but an inevitable one through comparable molding by each individual as individuals confront the world.

If Piaget would be available to reflect on rational constructivism, he would applaud its inroads. However, he might argue, as I have done, that being a Piagetian (or Neo-Piagetian) is not contradictory with being a rational constructivist. Moreover, there is nothing in the term itself that runs counter to Neo-Piagetian tenets. The only concern that I have in this regard is the statements by Xu and Kushnir (2013b) that the rational constructivist and Piagetian approaches are in opposition. As I hope I have shown, there could be nothing further from the rational, constructed truth.

In this regard, early causal learning would appear especially based on action sequence learning in an associative way, but on that would typically involve social sequencing and the inherent intersubjectivity in the process right from early in life. As the causal learning expands through the Neo-Piagetian cognitive substages in the sensorimotor substage sequence that bootstraps it along with the social participation that marks early life, it takes on the cognitive attributes of the substages involved, as described in Desrochers et al. (1995) as much as by Piaget and Young. Primitive sensorimotor action and activity-based abstractions do become possible. The last section of the book deals extensively with the present Neo-Piagetian stage model of development and its extrapolations.

Changes by Age in Causal Learning

This section of the chapter examines the empirical research on early causal learning from the newborn period onward. It illustrates the dynamic tension between the nativist and learning points of view. The Piagetian approach that I promote could be one way of integrating the diverse points of view on early causal learning by providing a scaffold on which the earliest primitives can develop in complexity in association with generalized, step-by-step cognitive advances in the sensorimotor period.

Newborns

Neonates Mascalzoni, Regolin, Vallortigara, and Simion (2013) tested the origin of causal perception at birth. Newborns (only a few hours old) demonstrated sensitivity (by looking longer) to some visual spatiotemporal cues (temporal continuity, continuity of trajectory, order appropriate) of a launching event. The newborns preferred a direct physical launching compared to delayed or noncausal relations. The authors concluded that innate or early developing appreciation of physical causality is a type of "jumpstart" to the development of causal reasoning.

One-Month-Olds Rakison and Krogh (2012) examined causal learning in 1-month-olds. The methodology used by Rakison and Krogh (2012) was quite innovative. There was an action phase and then a habitation one in each of two experiments. In the first experiment, in one condition, the 1-month-olds interacted with green balls while wearing red Velcro sticky mittens. The mittens enabled them to contact and pick up the balls by swiping or batting. In the second condition, the mittens were nonsticky. After the first phase, the sticky-mitten condition was followed by the infants having access to Velcro-covered balls. For the nonsticky condition, the balls were glued to their tray. The situations lasted 3 min.

The habituation phase involved animated events shown on a computer screen. In the habituation event, a launching event took place with two balls, with a "ding" noise heard on contact once the first ball struck the second and before the second took over in moving. Once habituation took place (<50 % of the looks), three test events followed. In the familiar condition, direction was switched to right to left instead of left to right. In the causal switch test, the colors of the balls were switched (from red → green to green → red). In the noncausal switch condition, the first ball stopped just before contact, but there was still a "ding" and subsequent movement by the second ball. The test event order was essentially counterbalanced across the participants in each condition.

In the first experiment, in the test phase, for the sticky-mitten condition, infants increased looking especially for the causal switch and noncausal switch events (i.e., unfamiliar). However, for the nonsticky-mitten condition, only the noncausal switch condition led to more looking. In the second experiment, the infants did not perceive causality in the test phase, when their causal action experience was not matched perceptually to the causal launching events viewed during the habituation phase.

The authors concluded that 1-month-olds are capable of early causal learning. Also, other putative milestones in perception and cognition (beyond causality) might be found to occur earlier, should appropriate real-world type experiences be used in the experiments.

Comment

The empirical research on the origin of causal knowledge right from birth is striking both in its methodological sophistication and its theoretical import. Mascalzoni et al.'s (2013) research supports the view that Michottian physical launching is perceived causally in the newborn period, setting the stage for more advanced causal learning. Rakison and Krogh (2012) demonstrated that 1-month-olds are capable of perceiving differences in causal switching conditions, especially if they had participated previous to the test phase with sticky mittens that allowed them to pick up colored balls. To conclude, physical launching sensitivity might be innate if the right cues are present. Moreover, more advanced causal perceptions are facilitated by participation in relevant actions, as Piaget might predict.

Young Infants

Six-Month-Olds Schlottmann, Ray, and Surian (2012) found that 6-month-olds demonstrated understanding of causal reaction events, with 6 months also being the time period in which they demonstrate understanding of causal launching events. For example, in causal reaction events, A (a shape) moves toward B, which moves before contact. Then, both move simultaneously until A arrives at its final resting position.

In a causal launching study, Kim, Feldman, and Singh (2013) found evidence that causally coherent interpretations can influence basic perceptual processes. This conclusion does not deny that perceiving causality in launches is the end result of a chain of visual analyses involving specialized neural populations (Rolfs, Dambacher, & Cavanagh, 2013).

Gerson and Woodward (2012) found that 7-month-olds could compare a familiar and novel action, and that this helped understand the goal of a tool-use action. The study used an interesting technique of aligning reaching with a tool claw. The relational analogic learning involved had required active sensorimotor activity (reach aligning, participating).

Sobel and Kirkham (2013) noted the social influences on infant statistical learning. Infants need joint attention to disambiguate multiple simultaneous co-occurrences. Social influences shape cognitive development by helping selective focus and the avoidance of distractions (e.g., Wu and Kirkham (2010); using social cues in a study of 8-month-olds). Social cues also teach about intentionality.

Consistent with Sobel and Kirkham (2013), Buchsbaum, Seiver, Beidgers, and Gopnik (2013) noted that, just as children employ covariation in physical cause–effect relations to learn about the world, so do they use covariation in the actions of people and context to form inferences about causation of behavior. That is, psychological causation and attribution belong to the same causal system as causation in the physical domain.

Brandone (2015) demonstrated that, in 8- to 11-months-olds, maternal report of infant joint attention initiations and of self-locomotion skills were associated with eye-tracking documented ability to predict the outcome of an agent's failed reaching actions. The results suggested to the author that social and motor experiences at this age may serve to "shape" infant comprehension of the other as an intentional agent.

Ten-Month-Olds Hohenberger et al. (2013) performed a study that showed understanding of physical causality in 10-month-olds was associated with maternal sensitivity. They argued that sensitive mothers would give more freedom to explore objects. This study shows that even if understanding of physical causality might happen quite early for some tasks, the (maternal) environment still has a supportive role in promoting it.

Denison, Trikutam, and Xu (2014) demonstrated that 11-month-old infants could reason about the probability of different outcomes after they had learned about physical constraints on objects. The infants reasoned by applying physical rules to adjust population base rates in estimating by inference the probabilities involved. They eschewed reasoning by perceptual similarity. The authors concluded that infants can learn stochastic, variable physical constraints by powerful statistical learning mechanisms, they can do so rapidly, and they can integrate them to predict outcomes of future events.

Recent research on false belief does not support the precocious view of infant cognition. Carlson, Koenig, and Harms (2013) argued that infants demonstrate System I understanding of false beliefs (fast, implicit, inflexible), which precedes development of a second system that is slower, explicit, and flexible. Therefore, early cognition might be preconceptual, rudimentary, and implicit (Apperly & Butterfill, 2009; Low, 2010; Onishi & Baillargeon, 2005). That is, the role of abstraction in false belief development appears to emerge in later infancy at the earliest.

However, Hamlin (2013) has shown that, for another aspect of social cognition, young infants appear quite preconscious. Specifically, she proposed that some aspects of moral sense might be built in early in life. In her research, as early as 3 months, infants appreciated the distinction between hinderers and helpers (Hamlin & Wynn, 2011). By 6 months, they evaluated positively helpers and also negatively hinderers (e.g., in a task with a puppet either opening or slamming shut a box with a toy in it).

Also, 10-month-olds appear to evaluate mental states. In Hamlin, Ullman, Tenenbaum, Goodman, and Baker (2013), infants preferred helpers to hinderers in a task that required lifting for both agents. They appeared to evaluate others as good or bad on a mentalistic level. Good agents are actors who "knowingly and intentionally" help another person. Finally, strikingly, Hamlin (2013) found that even 5-month-olds preferred "antisocial" agents who appropriately had harmed hinderers relative to "prosocial" ones who inappropriately had helped hinderers. Hamlin (2013) concluded that infants can engage in some morally relevant "evaluations" from early in life onward, and these mentalistic facilities are innate.

Comment

Research on causal understanding in the 6-month period has studied launching events, tool use, and physical causality, action-based causality, but also the social context, maternal sensitivity, and so on. It has queried the degree to which young infants use statistical estimations/covariations, and the extent to which the understanding is in any way abstract. For example, Carlson et al. (2013) considered that infants show System I understanding of false beliefs, which is implicit rather than abstract. However, elsewhere in the present work I have argued that System I vs. II thinking applies best to preschool vs. school-age thought, as in Piaget's preoperational vs. concrete operational stage. The primitive type of thought in early sensorimotor development is not implicit in the sense of System I thought, which is an automatic, unconscious, fast type of thought compared to System II's deliberative, conscious, slow one (see Chap. 19). Rather, for early infancy, intuitive thought best refers to moving from a straight associative thought process that is solely action-based to one with primitive guiding images, even if accidentally discovered and linked to sensorimotor activity. This type of understanding of early sensorimotor causal understanding does not conflict with the work of Hamlin (2013) on early appreciation of helping versus hindering. However, I would predict that, in the studies that she has conducted, analysis of concomitant sensorimotor activity in the helping mode will reveal patterns that distinguish the types of evaluations claimed.

That is, I predict that we will be able to specify (a) an early intuitive, primitive, still quite action-based intuitive thought in early sensorimotor activity vs. (b) a later intuitive thought, still representational to a degree even if automatic, i.e., System I related, in the preoperational sense of Piaget; with an intermediate phase between these two types of intuitive thought involving transitional passage through various sensorimotor substages. For example, early intuitive cognition will be governed by action-based sensorimotor schemas that involve primitive cognitive modules prepared evolutionarily that, nevertheless, are susceptible to development through experience. They would concern reflexive patterning based on supramodal models formed through kinesthetic and proprioceptive feedback deriving from actions. They would have mirror system properties that allow for early imitations, which would accentuate their development. They would evolve to include action repetitions of accidentally-discovered behavior that are interesting, first with the body and after with objects. Then, as intuitive thought of this type develops, the substages involved would include various increasing coordinations, such as Piaget described, e.g., for the object permanence and for the causality series. By the end of the series, toddlers will act with representational ability, but still tied to vestigial sensorimotor activity, before developing independent representations by 2 years of age, but only of the System I preoperational intuitive type, that is, lacking reversibility, dimensionality, and so on.

One- to Two-Year-Olds

One-Year-Olds Xu and Kushnir (2013a) elaborated that, in cognitive development, "rational constructivism" applies to causal learning and reasoning. It blends nativism and empiricism. As we have seen, in this view, early learning is considered as rational, statistical, and inferential and the learner as constructivist. Further, innate/core concepts/knowledge are combined with associative learning. Rational learners integrate prior belief/knowledge/bias with new evidence gathered, generating posterior probabilities of the hypotheses involved (Perfors, Tenenbaum, Griffiths, & Xu, 2011).

One-year-olds are sensitive to probabilistic relations in making inferences (Denison, Reed, & Xu, 2013). When given prior constraints, they make statistical computations, including integrating them (Xu & Denison, 2009). They use probability sensitivity to predict and to guide action (Denison & Xu, 2010a). They consider statistics in input as they evaluate multiple possible hypotheses (Gerken, 2006).

As for constructivism, infants at this age engage in hypothesis testing (Gerken, 2010). Older ones notice anomalous data (Kushnir et al., 2010) and statistical evidence is a driver in concept acquisition (Ma & Xu, 2011). One-year-olds can form hypotheses at multiple levels (over-hypotheses) involving perceptual input (Dewar & Xu, 2010). Infants are indeed active learners (Piaget, 1954), as the research by Denison and Xu (2010b) revealed. The authors concluded that infants engage in active, inductive, inferential constructivist, and rational statistical learning across multiple domains (domain general), including causal learning.

Rakison and Krogh (2012) conducted informative research on causal action and perception using the sticky-mitten paradigm in a habituation study with 12-month-olds. Piaget (1954) had proposed that infants of this age are already sensitive to their own actions. However, research had failed to demonstrate understanding at this age of Michottian launching events. Therefore, the authors created an experimental situation involving events more consistent with real-world experience.

The results showed that engaging even briefly in causal action facilitated causal perception. The mechanism permitting the perception appears related to attention/encoding. The mental representation formed can generalize somewhat to different contexts (objects), but not to significantly different ones.

Cesana-Arlotti, Téglás, and Bonatti (2013) argued that 1-year-olds have an "intuitive" notion or representation of probability. They can even use these for single events that they had never experienced, predicting what might happen next (e.g., Xu & Garcia, 2008). They can entertain future possibilities because they can represent them logically and consistently in a "surprisingly sophisticated reasoning" ability. The intuitive view of early cognition, in which modal representations are found that help "reasoning" about the probability of a single, future event, contrasts with the frequentist view, which is that infants possess simpler frequency detection mechanisms that track relevant distributions. Cesana-Arlotti et al. (2013) concluded that infants are like "little logicians." They can create logical representations and use them rationally.

Denison and Xu (2013) were more circumspect in how they describe infants' emerging cognition. They argued that infants can make "rudimentary" probabilistic inferences and are like "intuitive statisticians." Their "intuitive probabilities" notions do not appear available to awareness and reflection. Their "intuitive abstractions" are inductively formulated, allowing their rapid creation from "sparse" data. Their "guesses" are revisable, educated, probabilistic, Bayesian ones. Nevertheless, they integrate "substantive domain" knowledge when arriving at judgments. The authors concluded that the capacity to make probabilistic inferences might be an "innate" mechanism in learning from which later learning can build.

Fourteen-Month-Olds Chen and Waxman (2013) followed up on evidence indicating that infants go beyond observing to infer underlying goals that other might have (Brandone & Wellman, 2009). Infants selectively re-enact behavior inferred as intentional (Southgate, Chevallier, & Csibra, 2009). Gergely, Bekkering, and Kiraly (2002) had 14-month-olds observe an adult experimenter produce a novel, unconventional action (head touching with the forehead to turn on a light). The infants duplicated the behavior when the adult's hands were freed rather than being occupied, implying that infants had understood that there had been a choice not to use a hand and an intention to use the forehead.

Chen and Waxman (2013) extended this type of research on infant intentionality comprehension by incorporating that infants "appreciate" that a word could signal an adult's underlying intention (Martin, Vouloumanos, & Onishi, 2012). In the head-tapping condition, in which 14-month-olds were tested by Chen and Waxman, the adult experimenter commented that (a) she would "blick" the light on or, (b) she announced "Look"/"Watch" (novel word and neutral language control condition, respectively). As with the hands-free compared to the hands-occupied condition undertaken in the first part of the study, the novel word (blicket) condition compared to the control condition prompted imitation. Chen and Waxman (2013) concluded that understanding another's intentions at 14 months of age can be framed or clarified by language. Infants at this age appear to assess goals and intentions of the other and arrive at "principled-decisions" about whether or not to they should imitate (novel) actions observed. [For a neural network view of how events in the world are learned for causal dependency, as in the blicket experiments, see Fernando (2013).]

Cacchione, Schaub, and Rakoczy (2013) used an ingenious procedure to show that 14-month-olds take cognizance of causality properties in dealing with objects. Half the participants saw how a stuffed animal (pig) could be transformed (everted) into a different object (a ball) by a simple mechanism. In the test phase, both aware and unaware infants viewed a stuffed rabbit hidden in a box. It could be everted into a carrot. In half of the trials of the study, the rabbit was everted surreptitiously (switched).

Only infants who viewed the causal mechanism previously searched equally in both conditions (i.e., they expected two objects to be involved in the event). In contrast, the naïve infants reacted differently to the two situations—they expected to find a rabbit in the box and searched longer when it was a carrot. The authors concluded that infants at this age treat the causal features of objects as more important than non-causal surface ones, even if nonobvious.

Sixteen-Month-Olds Scott and Baillargeon (2013) tested whether 16-month-olds expect agents to act rationally. Unlike in prior research on the question, they did not use agents expressing infrequent or odd actions (e.g., Csibra, Bíró, Koós, & Gergely, 2003), but used scenarios involving typical, everyday situations. They found that the infants generally and robustly expected agents to pursue efficiently their goals, with little excess effort expended. Specifically, infants expected agents to choose the objects that were more accessible, whether physical or mental.

Howe and Otgaar (2013) proposed that early memories are developmentally invariant because of their adaptiveness/fitness in evolution. The memory principles involved concern item-specific and relational processing, self-referential processing, elaboration, and distinctiveness processing. These principles allow better preservation of memory traces that are important for survival (and reproduction). Once more, for core cognitive processes, early infant skills are posited.

Eighteen-Month-Olds Walker and Gopnik (2014) demonstrated that 18-month-olds can infer higher-order relational causal principles and use the inference to guide subsequent behavior. Moreover, achieving such causal mastery appears unique to humans. Humans might be uniquely adapted for "higher-order relational cognition" (Penn, Holyoak, & Povinelli, 2008) or a general "causal cognition" (Heyes & Frith, 2012).

Comment

The research related to causal learning in the second year of life has expanded in scope, using sophisticated methodologies and nuanced concepts. For the former, the techniques include use of sticky mittens and even everted rabbits. For the latter, the infants have been posited to possess constructed, intuitive representations, rudimentary probabilistic inferences, capacity to understand the intention of others, giving importance to the causal features of objects, and higher-order relational causal principles. As for the Bayesian and statistical approach to their learning, these computational mechanisms are still championed as being integral.

It is worth noting that the types of advances in causal learning in the second year of life appear to be qualitatively different in the second half of the year compared to the first. Indeed in this regard, Walker and Gopnik (2014) referred to the presence of higher-order relational cognition at 18 months of age, and qualified it in terms of human exceptionalism. This is consistent with my view that humans should be called *Homo Causa*. However, on the one hand, there is enough evidence to indicate that higher nonhuman primates express not only 18-month-old Piagetian cognition but also the ensuing one of the preoperational period (see Chap. 33). In this regard, human exceptionalism at the causal level might be found in the concrete operational guidance of causal thought in the older child. Moreover, on the other hand, the higher-order relational cognition attributed by Walker and Gopnik to the 18-month-old should reveal sensorimotor vestiges according to Piagetian thought (he referred to invented mental combinations at this age, but one still sensorimotorically-informed), so might be best to conceive of a higher-order relational cognition at this age in less than a purely representational form.

Children

Three-Year-Olds Kuhn (2012) presented a framework for understanding the development of causal reasoning, and also individual differences therein, in terms of how the inference rules needed in the process develop. Kuhn (2012) organized her framework based on a distinction between causal inference and causal prediction (the more important).

For understanding the launching event as causal (as in A strikes B), Michotte (1946) had suggested that an innate mechanism is involved. Recent work continues with this perspective, or similar models of early causal understanding (Carey, 2009; Cohen, Chaput, & Cashon, 2002; Sobel & Kirkham, 2007).

However, even if developed early, the mechanism for perceiving a causal connection between two events needs addition of more specific and complex inference rules. For example, early on, infants develop expectations about the physical environment and its event-related causal relations, a capacity that is revealed by surprise reactions upon expectation violation (Baillargeon et al., 2010).

Kuhn (2012) continued that causal modeling by infants affects understanding of the nature of the events and categories involved (e.g., Sobel & Buchanan, 2009). Causal understanding becomes “a source of concept formation,” or a “conceptual glue” bringing concepts beyond their set of features (Lombrozo, 2009). This has been demonstrated in preschoolers who were able to construct representation of causal relations that included data and mechanism (Schulz & Gopnik, 2004). Wellman and Liu (2007) had presented results that supported that prediction is secondary in causal learning to reasoning from an event about its cause. Kuhn and Dean (2004) showed that preschoolers update their beliefs (expectations) in light of new evidence (but outside of awareness/control).

Kuhn, Pease, and Wirkala (2009) specified some of the inference rules needed for better causal reasoning. For example, attributing causality from co-occurrence needs to move toward comparison. Kuhn (2010) showed that preschoolers can reason from outcome to cause (backwards, diagnostic reasoning) and also from cause to expected outcome (predictive reasoning), with explanatory causal model building central to learning.

Booth (2014) had shown that 3-year-olds remember novel labels better when the reference involved concerns causal properties rather than causally-irrelevant ones. Alvarez and Booth (2015) further studied 3-year-olds, who in the research observed two puppets describing properties of items that were either causal ones or matched noncausal ones. The children significantly preferred hearing causal descriptions on test trials after familiarization ones.

Alvarez and Booth (2015) noted that the results support Piaget (1952), who had argued that children function as “little scientists” in their quest for knowledge. The authors concluded that preschoolers are highly motivated to learn about the causal structure of their world and to seek out in an active way and to use learned information regarding novel causal properties.

Four-Year-Olds Seiver et al. (2013) showed that, as in making physical causal inferences, children

(4- to 6-year-olds) use both covariational evidence and prior knowledge to make social causal inferences or hypotheses. The results fit the general findings in the field that even preschoolers are constructing more abstract causal schemes or "framework theories" (also, see Goodman et al., 2011), which in the social arena are akin to social schemata (Kelley, 1967). I would add that these schemata are liable to development within the Piagetian cognitive developmental model, as per Young's (2011) Neo-Piagetian elaboration of social schemata (see Chap. 31).

Banerjee and Bloom (2015) studied children's beliefs about purpose in life events. Their three experiments showed that children favor purpose-based teleological explanations. This could reflect a general bias in children to reason teleologically (e.g., about social behavior). Teleological explanations appear helpful to children in understanding why significant life events had occurred. Children seem to believe that events occur to teach lessons, for example. At first, they do this indiscriminately (e.g., age 5), but then develop a more discerning approach to what is relevant.

Young, Alibali, and Kalish (2012) studied causal learning in 5- to 6-year-olds and 9- to 10-year-olds. They focused on disagreements—do others' (agents, puppets) hypotheses affect the children's evaluations. When agents had disagreed with the children's hypotheses, for later conditions without direct observation, children drew stronger causal inferences in response to disagreements. Older children were especially sensitive to disagreement with ambiguous evidence.

Sobel and Kushnir (2013) showed the parallels between children's causal learning and their social learning from social information. Children generally rationally evaluate their observational and action-related evidence in relation to their existing conceptual knowledge in order to ascertain the relevance and informativeness of the evidence. At the social level, select social learning takes place and involves selective trust of another's evidence or "testimony." For both experiential and social evidence selection, children are active selectors compared to passive knowledge recipients.

The authors concluded that causal learning and social information search are both active processes in children. They related their model to the contention of Boyd, Richerson, and Henrich (2011) that humans are unique not only in their causal reasoning capacities but also, and even more so, because of our ability to learn from others. Boyd et al. (2011) also noted that experts might acquire a causal understanding of adaptive tools and techniques by cultural learning, including overcopying; the causal understanding improves in micro-steps.

Atance, Metcalf, Martin-Ordas, and Walker (2014) examined children's causal explanations in terms of whether alterations in post-action information can alter their causal attributions. They found that 3- to 6-year-olds could not grasp that actions need to be related only to pre-action information, and not at all to post-action information. Specifically, the participants were shown a dog, and then asked to obtain some cheese to feed it. Upon return, they found a mouse present rather than a dog. Until the age of 7, the children claimed that they obtained the cheese in order to give it to the mouse. The results stand in contrast to earlier 3-year-old understanding of physical causality (e.g., a marble makes a puppet jump before being impacted by it rather than after). The authors concluded that the delay in reasoning about the psychological world relative to the physical world in terms of causality (in identifying the causes of their own actions) is based on deficits in theory of mind, inhibition, and executive function, as well as the play of hindsight bias, at least for 3-year-olds. In 4- to 6-year-olds, the delay might be caused by associative knowledge (use of scripts, gists).

Hoerl, McCormack, and Beck (2011) underscored that each of McCormack, Frosch, and Burns (2011), Beck, Riggs, and Burns (2011), and Perner and Rafetseder (2011) noted that counterfactual thought is a sophisticated cognitive acquisition that does not fully develop until 10–12 years of age. Younger children might have their counterfactual reasoning masked, however (Sobel, 2011). They might lack sufficient knowledge of a domain to apply their counterfactual reasoning. Nevertheless, at this age, they lack a proper grasp of the functional role of knowledge.

Comment

The research on children related to causal learning has especially focused on causal reasoning and its limits. The research with older children has moved into the area of counterfactual reasoning. Once more, there might be parallels between the findings with preschoolers and school-age children in terms of Piaget's model in that, at this age, there is a transition from preoperational to concrete operational thought. Please understand that I am not arguing that the Piagetian model can explain all the results in the field of causal learning in children. However, it might provide a scaffold to help better integrate the diverse data and explain the qualitative differences from one age period to the next. In this regard, I note that my Neo-Piagetian version of Piaget's work contains substages in the preoperational/concrete operational period, and they might help explain differences in causal learning in 2-year-olds compared to 4-, 6-, 8-, and 10-year-olds, the approximate ages associated with the substages involved.

Adults

Causal Reality Recent modeling of causal reasoning in adults has illustrated the diversity in approaches in this area. Sloman and Lagnado (2015) considered causal knowledge as crucial to thought. The cognitive system is constructed to help determine the causality of the unfolding of events. Causal notions constitute the infrastructure of human thought.

Kahneman and Tversky (1982a, 1982b) had found that people substitute causal inferences for other types of judgments that had been requested. Waldmann and Holyoak (1992) and Cheng (1997) had argued that people judge in a manner that is tuned tightly to belief about causal structure and its strength. Bechlivanidis and Lagnado (2013) found that causal beliefs can have people reorder events so that they are consistent with the temporality in the belief (even if the belief is trained by an intervention). Chater and Oaksford (2013) maintained that causal notions are critical to learning, perception, reasoning, and aspects of language. Sloman, Fernbach, and Ewing (2009) considered causal structure as serving the infrastructure for moral judgments.

For Sloman and Lagnado (2015), these types of findings indicate that causal thought cannot be accounted for by a strict Bayesian, probabilistic approach (e.g., Pearl, 2000). The latter approach does not consider sufficiently mechanisms. Moreover, in causal thinking, people think in narratives and by mental simulation, which is not accounted for by dependency modeling of probabilistic knowledge. The authors concluded that mechanisms, narratives, and mental simulation together constitute the hallmark of causal reasoning.

Güss and Robinson (2014) maintained that causality is central to the decision-making process. Decision makers need to predict the consequences of their decisions in the process of arriving at them. Normally, one considers the predicted effects of each option in the planned actions that fit the particular contexts. This approach to predicted causality is a constructivist one, in that the agents' predictions are personally-derived. Moreover, culture constitutes another factor influencing the decision-making process. For example, a cultural environment might not be conducive to long-term predictions. The authors concluded that all decisions are embedded within specific eco-cultural historical circumstances. In this sense, all decisions are cultural ones (I would add: as much as personal ones).

Reuter, Kirfel, van Riel, and Barlassina (2014) showed how the cognitive process of causal selection in adults is influenced by both temporal factors and moral judgment. In causal selection, one or more aspects of a causal structure that is complex are attributed causality for an index effect. Typically, later actions are attributed as causal relative to early ones. However, the effect is moderated by judgments of norm violation, for example.

Soto, Gershman, and Niv (2014) proposed a statistical, Bayesian model to explain compound generalization (e.g., learning from one situation to the next when they are similar) in associative and causal learning. The person appears to use rational principles of dimensional generalization, and the model expands the scope of latent cause theories in this regard.

Meder, Mayrhofer, and Waldmann (2014) examined diagnostic reasoning from single effects to single causes. They argued that the beliefs of the person reasoning about the existence and strength between cause and effect in linkages are involved in diagnostic judgments, which then are not only based on using empirical probabilities of causes given effects. People go beyond the information available and infer using the unobserved causal level and not just the observed data level.

Flores, Cobos, López, and Godoy (2014) showed that even expert adults engage in fast causal reasoning processes when dealing online (in an ongoing way) with cases in their discipline. Specifically, clinicians use idiosyncratic casual theories, structures, or scripts in dealing with hypothetical clinical reports for common DSM-IV-TR (Diagnostic and Statistical Manual of Mental Disorders, Fourth Edition, Text Revision; American Psychiatric Association, 2000) disorders. This type of finding represents a "causal bias" and it comes into play early in dealing with cases. The causal reasoning process is akin to the intuitive, automatic thinking described in Evans and Stanovich (2013) and Kahneman (2011; Type I and System I, respectively). Of course, clinicians also use slow, deliberative, logical reasoning (e.g., when there are inconsistencies, Type II and System II, respectively).

Widlok (2014) reviewed concepts of agency in the ethnography in causality. One finds narratives on natural causes and superhuman agents, including witchcraft, powers, and gods. For example, the Dinka considers ultra-human powers as part of the natural world. Similarly, Kronenfeld (2014) queried the meaning of "causal cognition." He referred to "collective" action, knowledge, and cognition in this regard. These anthropological concepts add to the biopsychosocial understanding of behavior and its causality, with one aspect of behavior in this regard being causal understanding and the influence on it of culture.

Haidle (2014) argued that humans are unique in the "drive" to seek and to generalize "causal explanations." We excel relative to other primates in inferring causal mechanisms relating covariations in cause and effect, which is inferential causal reasoning. Also, we excel in the ability to recognize that causal mechanisms underpin events that are analogous causally, which is analogical causal reasoning (Vaesen, 2012). She applied this model to cultural performances, including tool use. She concluded that the same model can apply to "performances" in the cognitive sphere, I note that her model of cultural/cognitive performances is quite biopsychosocial in nature (see Fig. 16.1).

Böhm and Pfister (2015) specified layperson causal theories of behavior. The model includes seven categories in the "what" of causal explanation: goals; dispositions; temporary states, e.g., emotions; intentional actions; outcomes; events; and attributes of stimuli. The seven categories of lay explanations of causality appear to work according to inference rules. Finally, the process of causal explanation in adults appears to incorporate knowledge-based aspects or contents.

Gilbert, Tenney, Holland, and Spellman (2015) found evidence in support of a model of causal attributions based on the primacy of actors having knowledge relevant to a potential outcome (even without having an intent for the action at issue or a motive to immorality). In addition, the causal attributions were mediated by counterfactual thinking (imagining how the outcome at issue could have been prevented by different controllable actions that could be implemented).

Causal analysis has been applied to trait differences and their conjunctions within people by using causal trait theory. Critcher, Dunning, and Rom (2015) noted that causal trait theories are used to explain why an individual's status on one trait relates to his or her status on other ones ("causes or is caused by"). People use models such as these not only about the self but also about others, as they create implicit theories of their personality.

Lefèvre, Lepresle, and Chariot (2015) applied Bayesian causal network analysis to determine

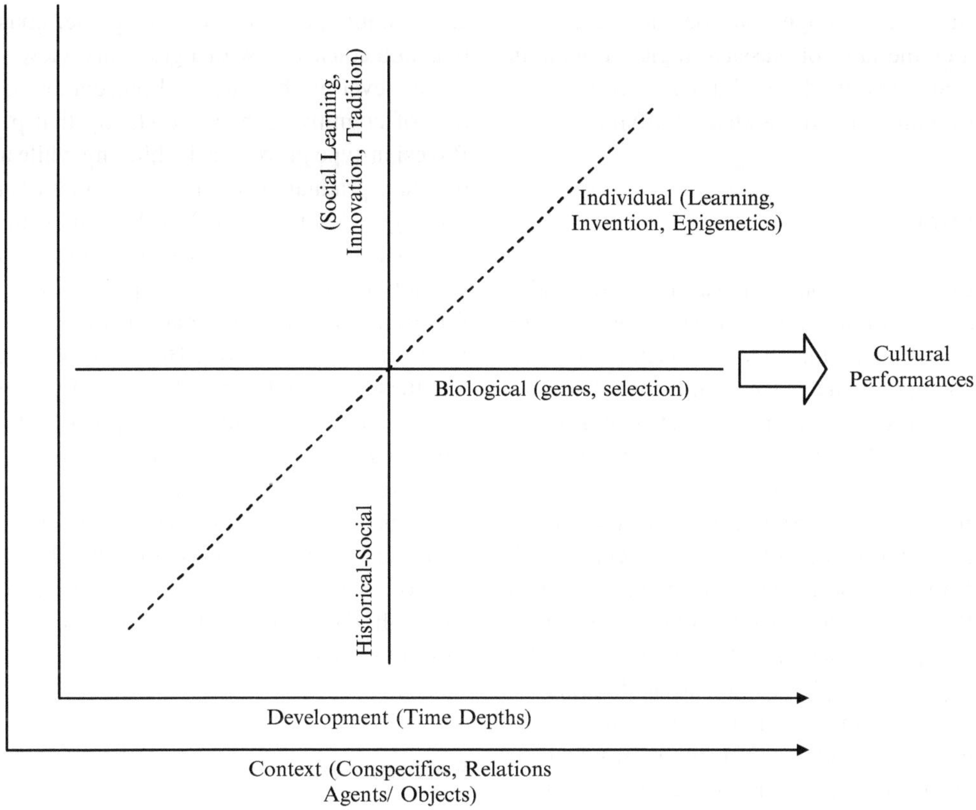

Fig. 16.1 A dimensional model of cultural performances. The three dimensions of cultural performances are embedded in/interdependent with the particular environmental context. Adapted from Haidle (2014)

factors in total incapacity to work in assault survivors. The results complemented those of traditional analyses.

Causal Irreality Trueblood and Busemeyer (2014; also see Trueblood & Busemeyer, 2011) developed a quantum probability model of causal reasoning. It is beyond the scope of the present work to present the advanced mathematics involved, but the authors presented four factors in support of their approach.

According to Trueblood and Busemeyer (2011), a quantum approach to human judgment making is viable because of the following four reasons:

(a) When humans arrive at judgments, they construct them from the question in context; judgments are not merely read-outs from a pre-existing, recorded state. Belief state is not determined before measurement; measurement "forces a resolution" of the pre-existing indeterminacy.
(b) Preceding the process of measurement, cognition functions more like a wave than a particle; this allows people to experience simultaneously ambiguities about different belief states. Consistent with quantum probability modeling, the beliefs that one might have remain in a superimposed (simultaneous) state until the final judgment is made. This resolves the uncertainty in the process, resulting in collapse of the cognitive wave into a particle having a specific position.
(c) Each judgment that is made disturbs and generates uncertainty about another in a process of incompatibility, e.g., any one judgment can affect context and, therefore, later judgments.

(d) The logic of cognition does not necessarily obey the laws of classical logic. A quantum probability model of human reasoning can accommodate to this state of affairs.

Comment

Children are well on their way to causal understanding, learning, and reasoning by the preschool period. Piaget's preoperational and concrete operational stages in this regard are similar to the proposed distinction between System I and System II thinking, and therefore might inform the progression on these matters in the childhood period. Similarly, Piaget's formal, abstract period that develops in adolescence could be informative for that age period. Neo-Piagetian models that construe a postformal stage in the adult age period might also be beneficial in understanding the complexity of causal thinking the adult. For example, in my model (Young, 2011), the postformal adult stage is referred to as Collective Intelligence. It would appear that not only the higher-order thinking in adults might be characterized especially by causal reasoning at a superordinate abstract level but also the collective or group cognition that we create culturally might be marked by the causality imperative being discussed as part of human exceptionalism.

Chapter Conclusions

The study of causal learning in childhood has even considered how neonates might express antecedents of abstract thoughts in "primitives" that are implicitly inferential and abstract. The young infant might rationally construct causal cognitions both at the physical launching level and at more complex levels, including the understanding of perceived events and action-supported activities. The notion that these more advanced cognitive skills could take place so early on has been attributed to Bayesian, probabilistic learning mechanisms even early in life. As usual in work in development, other points of view about early acquisitions are more sanguine, conservative, and consistent with a gradualist view.

However, in the chapter, I present an elaboration of cognitive schema modeling that permits Bayesian-type probabilistic thinking while allowing their gradual development through cognitive substages, such as in Neo-Piagetian models. The social and practical experience in sensorimotor activity might lead to rapid, sophisticated Bayesian-type estimates that consolidate in inferences or their precursors. However, perspectives like these need to be complemented by cognitive models that allow the development of more advanced abstractions on which the hypothesis-generation process maps, so to speak. Nevertheless, this type of hybrid modeling needs to respect the limits imposed by the characteristics of the sensorimotor substages involved, although these are evolving in Neo-Piagetian work (e.g., Young, 2011).

References

Alvarez, A. L., & Booth, A. E. (2015). Preschoolers prefer to learn causal information. *Frontiers in Psychology, 6*, 60. doi:10.3389/fpsyg.2015.00060.

American Psychiatric Association. (2000). *Diagnostic and statistical manual of mental disorders: DSM-IV-TR* (4th ed., text rev.). Washington, DC: Author.

Apperly, I. A., & Butterfill, S. A. (2009). Do humans have two systems to track beliefs and belief-like states? *Psychological Review, 116*, 953–970.

Atance, C. M., Metcalf, J. L., Martin-Ordas, G., & Walker, C. L. (2014). Young children's causal explanations are biased by post-action associative information. *Developmental Psychology, 50*, 2675–2685.

Baillargeon, R., Li, J., Gertner, Y., & Wu, D. (2010). How do infants reason about physical events? In U. Goswami (Ed.), *Handbook of childhood cognitive development* (2nd ed., pp. 11–48). Oxford, UK: Blackwell.

Banerjee, K., & Bloom, P. (2015). "Everything happens for a reason": Children's beliefs about purpose in life events. *Child Development, 86*, 503–518.

Barrett, T., Davis, E. F., & Needham, A. (2007). Learning to use a tool in infancy. *Developmental Psychology, 43*, 352–368.

Bechlivanidis, C., & Lagnado, D. A. (2013). Does the "why" tell us the "when"? *Psychological Science, 20*, 1221–1228.

Beck, S. R., Riggs, K. J., & Burns, P. (2011). Multiple developments in counterfactual thinking. In C. Hoerl, T. McCormack, & S. R. Beck (Eds.), *Understanding counterfactual, understanding causation: Issues in philosophy and psychology* (pp. 110–122). New York: Oxford University Press.
Böhm, G., & Pfister, H.-R. (2015). How people explain their own and others' behavior: A theory of lay causal explanation. *Frontiers in Psychology, 6*, 139. doi:10.3389/fpsyg.2015.00139.
Bonawitz, E., Denison, S., Griffiths, T. L., & Gopnik, A. (2014). Probabilistic models, learning algorithms, and response variability: Sampling in cognitive development. *Trends in Cognitive Sciences, 18*, 497–500.
Booth, A. E. (2014). Effects of causal information on early world learning: Efficiency and longevity. *Cognitive Development, 33*, 99–107.
Boyd, R., Richerson, P. J., & Henrich, J. (2011). The cultural niche: Why social learning is essential for human adaptation. *Proceedings of the National Academy of Sciences, USA, 108*, 10918–10925.
Brandone, A. C. (2015). Infants' social and motor experience and the emerging understanding of intentional actions. *Developmental Psychology, 51*, 512–523.
Brandone, A., & Wellman, H. M. (2009). You can't always get what you want: Infants understand failed goal-directed actions. *Psychological Science, 20*, 85–91.
Buchsbaum, D., Seiver, E., Beidgers, S., & Gopnik, A. (2013). Learning about causes from people and about people as causes: Probabilistic models and social causal reasoning. In F. Xu & T. Kushnir (Eds.), *Advances in child development and behavior: Rational constructivism in cognitive development* (Vol. 43, pp. 125–160). Waltham, MA: Academic.
Cacchione, T., Schaub, S., & Rakoczy, H. (2013). Fourteen-month-old infants infer the continuous identity of objects on the basis of nonvisible causal properties. *Developmental Psychology, 49*, 1325–1329.
Carey, S. (2009). *The origins of concepts*. New York: Oxford University Press.
Carlson, S. M., Koenig, M. A., & Harms, M. B. (2013). Theory of mind. *Wiley Interdisciplinary Reviews: Cognitive Science, 4*, 391–402.
Cesana-Arlotti, N., Téglás, E., & Bonatti, L. L. (2013). The probable and the possible at 12 months: Intuitive reasoning about the uncertain future. In F. Xu & T. Kushnir (Eds.), *Advances in child development and behavior: Rational constructivism in cognitive development* (Vol. 43, pp. 1–25). Waltham, MA: Academic.
Chater, N., & Oaksford, M. (2013). Programs as causal models: Speculations on mental programs and mental representation. *Cognitive Science, 37*, 1171–1191.
Chen, M. L., & Waxman, S. R. (2013). "Shall we blick?": Novel words highlight actors' underlying intentions for 14-month-old infants. *Developmental Psychology, 49*, 426–431.
Cheng, P. (1997). From covariation to causation: A causal power theory. *Psychological Review, 104*, 367–405.
Cohen, L., Chaput, H., & Cashon, C. (2002). A constructivist model of infant cognition. *Cognitive Development, 17*, 1323–1343.
Critcher, C. R., Dunning, D., & Rom, S. C. (2015). Causal trait theories: A new form of person knowledge that explains egocentric pattern projection. *Journal of Personality and Social Psychology, 108*, 400–416.
Csibra, G., Bíró, S., Koós, O., & Gergely, G. (2003). One-year-old infants use teleological representations of actions productively. *Cognitive Science, 27*, 111–133.
Csibra, G., & Gergely, G. (2005). Social learning and social cognition: The case for pedagogy. In Y. Munakata & M. H. Johnson (Eds.), *Process of change in brain and cognitive development. Attention and Performance XXI* (pp. 249–274). Oxford, UK: Oxford University Press.
Denison, S., Bonawitz, E., Gopnik, A., & Griffiths, T. L. (2014). Rational variability in children's causal inferences: The sampling hypothesis. *Cognition, 126*, 285–300.
Denison, S., Reed, C., & Xu, F. (2013). The emergence of probabilistic reasoning in very young infants: Evidence from 4.5- and 6-month-old infants. *Developmental Psychology, 49*, 243–249.
Denison, S., Trikutam, P., & Xu, F. (2014). Probability versus representativeness in infancy: Can infants use naïve physics to adjust population base rates in probabilistic inference? *Developmental Review, 50*, 2009–2019.
Denison, S., & Xu, F. (2010a). Integrating physical constraints in statistical inference by 11-month-old infants. *Cognitive Science, 34*, 885–908.
Denison, S., & Xu, F. (2010b). Twelve- to 14-month-old infants can predict single-event probability with large set sizes. *Developmental Science, 13*, 798–803.
Denison, S., & Xu, F. (2013). Probabilistic inference in human infants. In F. Xu & T. Kushnir (Eds.), *Advances in child development and behavior: Rational constructivism in cognitive development* (Vol. 43, pp. 27–58). Waltham, MA: Academic.
Desrochers, S., Ricard, M., & Décarie, T. G. (1995). Understanding causality in infancy: A reassessment of Piaget's theory. *Cahiers de Psychologie Cognitive, 14*, 255–268.
Dewar, K. M., & Xu, F. (2010). Induction, overhypothesis, and the origin of abstract knowledge. *Psychological Science, 21*, 1871–1877.
Evans, J., & Stanovich, K. (2013). Dual-process theories of higher cognition: Advancing the debate. *Perspectives on Psychological Science, 8*, 223–241.
Fernando, C. (2013). From blickets to synapses: Inferring temporal causal networks by observation. *Cognitive Science, 37*, 1426–1470.
Flores, A., Cobos, P. L., López, F. J., & Godoy, A. (2014). The influence of causal connections between symptoms on the diagnosis of mental disorders: Evidence from online and offline measures. *Journal of Experimental Psychology: Applied, 20*, 175–190.
Gergely, G., Bekkering, H., & Kiraly, I. (2002). Rational imitation in preverbal infants. *Nature, 415*, 755. doi:10.1038/415755a.

Gergely, G., & Csibra, G. (2003). Teleological reasoning about actions: The Naïve theory of rational actions. *Trends in Cognitive Sciences, 7*, 287–292.

Gergely, G., & Jacob, P. (2013). Reasoning about instrumental and communicative agency in human infancy. In F. Xu & T. Kushnir (Eds.), *Advances in child development and behavior: Rational constructivism in cognitive development* (Vol. 43, pp. 59–94). Waltham, MA: Academic.

Gerken, L. (2006). Decisions, decisions, decisions: Infant language learning when multiple generalizations are possible. *Cognition, 98*, B67–B74.

Gerken, L. (2010). Infants use rational decision criteria for choosing among models of their input. *Cognition, 115*, 362–366.

Gerson, S., & Woodward, A. L. (2010). Building intentional action knowledge with one's hands. In S. P. Johnson (Ed.), *Neo-constructivism* (pp. 295–313). Oxford, UK: Oxford University Press.

Gerson, S. A., & Woodward, A. L. (2012). A claw is like my hand: Comparison supports goal analysis in infants. *Cognition, 122*, 181–192.

Gilbert, E. A., Tenney, E. R., Holland, C. R., & Spellman, B. A. (2015). Counterfactuals, control, and causation: Why knowledgeable people get blamed more. *Personality and Social Psychology Bulletin*. doi:10.1177/0146167215572137.

Goodman, N. D., Ullman, T. D., & Tenenbaum, J. B. (2011). Learning a theory of causality. *Psychological Review, 118*, 110–119.

Gopnik, A., & Bonawitz, E. (2014). Bayesian models of child development. *Cognitive Science, 6*, 75–86.

Gopnik, A., Glymour, C., Sobel, D. M., Schulz, L. E., Kushnir, T., & Danks, D. (2004). A theory of causal learning in children: Causal maps and Bayes nets. *Psychological Review, 111*, 3–32.

Gopnik, A., & Schulz, L. (2007). Introduction. In A. Gopnik & L. Schulz (Eds.), *Causal learning: Psychology, philosophy, and computation* (pp. 1–15). New York: Oxford University Press.

Gopnik, A., Sobel, D. M., Schulz, L., & Glymour, C. (2001). Causal learning mechanisms in very young children: Two-, three-, and four-year-olds infer causal relations from patterns of variation and covariation. *Developmental Psychology, 37*, 620–629.

Gopnik, A., & Wellman, H. M. (1992). Why the child's theory of mind really is a theory. *Mind & Language, 7*, 145–171.

Gopnik, A., & Wellman, H. M. (2012). Reconstructing constructivism: Causal models, Bayesian learning mechanisms, and the theory. *Psychological Bulletin, 138*, 1085–1108.

Griffiths, T. L., Sobel, D. M., Tenenbaum, J. B., & Gopnik, A. (2011). Bayes and blickets: Effects of knowledge on causal induction in children and adults. *Cognitive Science, 35*, 1407–1455.

Güss, C. D., & Robinson, B. (2014). Predicted causality in decision making: The role of culture. *Frontiers in Psychology, 5*, 479. doi:10.3389/fpsyg.2014.00739.

Gweon, H., & Schulz, L. (2011). 16-month-olds rationally infer causes of failed actions. *Science, 332*, 1524. doi:10.1126/science.1204493.

Gweon, H., Tenenbaum, J. B., & Schulz, L. E. (2010). Infants consider both the sample and the sampling process in inductive generalization. *Proceedings of the National Academy of Sciences, USA, 107*, 9066–9071.

Haidle, M. N. (2014). Building a bridge – An archeologist's perspective on the evolution of causal cognition. *Frontiers in Psychology, 5*, 1472. doi:10.3389/fpsyg.2014.01472.

Hamlin, J. K. (2013). Moral judgment and action in preverbal infants and toddlers: Evidence for an innate moral core. *Current Directions in Psychological Science, 23*, 186–193.

Hamlin, J. K., Ullman, T., Tenenbaum, J. B., Goodman, N., & Baker, C. (2013). The mentalistic basis of core social cognition: Experiments in preverbal infants and a computational model. *Developmental Science, 16*, 209–226.

Hamlin, J. K., & Wynn, K. (2011). Young infants prefer prosocial to antisocial others. *Cognitive Development, 26*, 30–39.

Heyes, C., & Frith, U. (2012). New thinking: The evolution of human cognition. *Philosophical Transactions of the Royal Society B: Biological Science, 367*, 2091–2096.

Hoerl, C., McCormack, T., & Beck, S. R. (2011). *Understanding counterfactual, understanding causation: Issues in philosophy and psychology*. New York: Oxford University Press.

Hohenberger, A., Elsabbagh, M., Serres, J., de Schoenen, S., Karmiloff-Smith, A., & Ascherslenben, G. (2013). Understanding goal-directed human actions and physical causality: The role of mother-infant interaction. *Infant Behavior and Development, 35*, 898–911.

Howe, M. L., & Otgaar, H. (2013). Proximate mechanisms and the development of adaptive memory. *Current Directions in Psychological Science, 22*, 16–22.

Kahneman, D. (2011). *Thinking, fast and slow*. New York: Farrar, Strauss, Giroux.

Kahneman, D., & Tversky, A. (1982a). The simulation heuristic. In D. Kahneman, P. Slovic, & A. Tversky (Eds.), *Judgment under uncertainty: Heuristics and biases* (pp. 201–208). Cambridge, UK: Cambridge University Press.

Kahneman, D., & Tversky, A. (1982b). Variants of uncertainty. *Cognition, 11*, 143–157.

Kelley, H. H. (1967). Attribution theory in social psychology. In D. Levine (Ed.), *Nebraska symposium on motivation* (Vol. 15, pp. 192–238). Lincoln, NB: University of Nebraska Press.

Khemlani, S. S., Barbey, A. K., & Jonson-Laird, P. N. (2014). Causal reasoning with mental models. *Frontiers in Human Neuroscience, 8*, 849.

Kim, S. H., Feldman, J., & Singh, M. (2013). Perceived causality can alter the perceived trajectory of apparent motion. *Psychological Science, 24*, 575–582.

Kretch, K. S., & Adolph, K. E. (2013). Cliff or step? Posture-specific learning at the edge of a drop-off. *Child Development, 84*, 226–240.

Kronenfeld, D. B. (2014). What "causal cognition" might mean. *Frontiers in Psychology, 5*, 1204. doi:10.3389/fpsyg.2014.01204.

Kuhl, P. K. (2004). Early language acquisition: Cracking the speech code. *Nature Reviews Neuroscience, 5*, 831–843.

Kuhn, D. (2010). What is scientific thinking and how does it develop? In U. Goswami (Ed.), *Handbook of childhood cognitive development* (2nd ed., pp. 497–523). Oxford, UK: Blackwell.

Kuhn, D. (2012). The development of causal reasoning. *Wiley Interdisciplinary Reviews: Cognitive Science, 3*, 327–335.

Kuhn, D., & Dean, D. (2004). Connecting scientific reasoning and causal inference. *Journal of Cognitive Development, 5*, 261–288.

Kuhn, D., Pease, M., & Wirkala, C. (2009). Coordinating effects of multiple variables: A skill fundamental to causal and scientific reasoning. *Journal of Experimental Child Psychology, 103*, 268–284.

Kushnir, T., & Gopnik, A. (2005). Young children infer causal strength from probabilities and interventions. *Psychological Science, 16*, 678–683.

Kushnir, T., & Gopnik, A. (2007). Conditional probability versus spatial contiguity in causal learning: Preschoolers use new contingency evidence to overcome prior spatial assumptions. *Developmental Psychology, 43*, 186–196.

Kushnir, T., Xu, F., & Wellman, H. M. (2010). Young children use statistical sampling to infer the preferences of other people. *Psychological Science, 21*, 1134–1140.

Lefèvre, T., Lepresle, A., & Chariot, P. (2015). Detangling complex relationships in forensic data: Principles and use of causal networks and their application to clinical forensic science. *International Journal of Legal Medicine, 129*, 1163–1172.

Legare, C. H. (2012). Exploring explanation: Explaining inconsistent evidence informs exploratory, hypothesis-testing behavior in young children. *Child Development, 83*, 173–185.

Legare, C. H. (2014). The contributions of explanation and exploration to children's scientific reasoning. *Child Development Perspectives, 8*, 101–106.

Legare, C. H., Gelman, S. A., & Wellman, H. W. (2010). Inconsistency with prior knowledge triggers children's causal explanatory reasoning. *Child Development, 81*, 929–944.

Lepage, J. F., & Théoret, H. (2007). The mirror neuron system: Grasping others' actions from birth? *Developmental Science, 10*, 513–523.

Lombrozo, T. (2009). Explanation and categorization: How "why?" informs "what?". *Cognition, 110*, 248–253.

Loucks, J., & Sommerville, J. A. (2011, October). *Adult and infant attention during action perception in context dependent*. Poster presented at the biennial meeting of the Cognitive Development Society, Philadelphia, PA.

Loucks, J., & Sommerville, J. A. (2012). The role of motor experience in understanding action function: The case of the precision grasp. *Child Development, 83*, 801–809.

Low, J. (2010). Preschoolers' implicit and explicit false-belief understanding: Relations with complex syntactical mastery. *Child Development, 81*, 597–615.

Lucas, C. G., Gopnik, A., & Griffiths, T. L. (2010). Developmental differences in learning the forms of causal relationships. In R. Camtrabone & S. Ohlsson (Eds.), *Proceedings of the 32nd Annual Conference of the Cognitive Science Society* (pp. 2852–2857). Austin, TX: Cognitive Science Society.

Ma, L., & Xu, F. (2011). Young children's use of statistical sampling evidence to infer the subjectivity of preferences. *Cognition, 120*, 403–411.

Martin, A., Vouloumanos, A., & Onishi, K. (2012). Understanding the abstract role of speech in communication at 12 months. *Cognition, 123*, 50–60.

Mascalzoni, E., Regolin, L., Vallortigara, G., & Simion, F. (2013). The cradle of causal reasoning: Newborns' preference for physical causality. *Developmental Science, 16*, 327–335.

McCormack, T., Frosch, C., & Burns, P. (2011). The relationship between children's causal and counterfactual judgements. In C. Hoerl, T. McCormack, & S. R. Beck (Eds.), *Understanding counterfactual, understanding causation: Issues in philosophy and psychology* (pp. 54–74). New York: Oxford University Press.

Meder, B., Mayrhofer, R., & Waldmann, M. R. (2014). Structure induction in diagnostic causal reasoning. *Psychological Review, 121*, 277–301.

Meltzoff, A. N. (2007). "Like me": A foundation for social cognition. *Developmental Science, 10*, 126–134.

Meltzoff, A. N., & Decety, J. (2003). What imitation tells us about social cognition: A rapprochement between developmental psychology and cognitive science. *Philosophical Transaction of the Royal Society London B, Biological Sciences, 358*, 491–500.

Meltzoff, A. N., Waismeyer, A., & Gopnik, A. (2012). Learning about causes from people: Observational causal learning in 24-month-old infants. *Developmental Psychology, 48*, 1215–1228.

Michotte, A. E. (1946/1963). *The perception of causality*. New York: Basic Books.

Muentener, P., & Carey, S. (2010). Infants' causal representations of state change events. *Cognition Psychology, 61*, 63–86.

Onishi, K. H., & Baillargeon, R. (2005). Do 15-month-old infants understand false beliefs? *Science, 308*, 255–258.

Pearl, J. (2000). *Causality: Models, reasoning, and inference*. Cambridge, MA: Cambridge University Press.

Pearl, J. (2009). *Causality: Models, reasoning, and inference* (2nd ed.). New York: Cambridge University Press.

Penn, D. C., Holyoak, K. J., & Povinelli, D. J. (2008). Darwin's mistake: Explaining the discontinuity between human and nonhuman minds. *Behavioral and Brain Sciences, 31*, 109–178.

Perfors, A., Tenenbaum, J. B., Griffiths, T. L., & Xu, F. (2011). A tutorial introduction to Bayesian models of cognitive development. *Cognition, 120*, 302–321.

Perner, J., & Rafetseder, E. (2011). Counterfactual and other forms of conditional reasoning: Children lost in the nearest possible world. In C. Hoerl, T. McCormack, & S. R. Beck (Eds.), *Understanding counterfactual, understanding causation: Issues in philosophy and psychology* (pp. 90–109). New York: Oxford University Press.

Piaget, J. (1926). *The language and thought of the child.* London, UK: Kegan Paul, Trench, Trubner, & Co. (Original work *Le langage et la pensée chez l'enfant* published 1923).

Piaget, J. (1929). *The child's conception of the world.* London, UK: Routledge and Kegan Paul.

Piaget, J. (1930). *The child's conception of physical causality*. New York: Harcourt Brace.

Piaget, J. (1937). *La construction du reel chez l'enfant [The construction of reality in the child]*. Neuchatel, Switzerland: Delachaux et Niestle.

Piaget, J. (1952). *The origins of intelligence in children.* Oxford, UK: International Universities Press.

Piaget, J. (1954). *The construction of reality in the child* (M. Cook, Trans.). New York: Basic Books.

Piaget, J. (1955). *The child's conception of the world.* London: Routledge & Kegan Paul.

Rakison, D. H., & Krogh, L. (2012). Does causal action facilitate causal perception in infants younger than 6 months of age? *Developmental Science, 15*, 43–53.

Reuter, K., Kirfel, L., van Riel, R., & Barlassina, L. (2014). The good, the bad, and the timely: How temporal order and moral judgment influence casual selection. *Frontiers in Psychology, 5*, 1336. doi:10.3389/fpsyg.2014.01336.

Rogers, T. T., & McClelland, J. L. (2004). *Semantic cognition: A parallel distributed processing approach.* Cambridge, MA: MIT Press.

Rolfs, M., Dambacher, M., & Cavanagh, P. (2013). Visual adaptation of the perception of causality. *Current Biology, 23*, 250–254.

Rottman, B. M., & Hastie, R. (2013). Reasoning about causal relationships: Inferences on causal networks. *Psychological Bulletin, 140*, 109–139.

Schlottmann, A., Ray, E. D., & Surian, L. (2012). Emerging perception of causality in action-and-reaction sequences from 4 to 6 months of age: Is it domain-specific? *Journal of Experimental Child Psychology, 112*, 208–230.

Scholl, B. J., & Tremoulet, P. D. (2000). Perceptual causality and animacy. *Trends in Cognitive Science, 4*, 299–309.

Schulz, L. (2013). Finding new facts; thinking new thoughts. In F. Xu & T. Kushnir (Eds.), *Advances in child development and behavior: Rational constructivism in cognitive development* (Vol. 43, pp. 269–294). Waltham, MA: Academic.

Schulz, L. E., & Gopnik, A. (2004). Causal learning across domains. *Developmental Psychology, 40*, 162–176.

Schulz, L. E., Gopnik, A., & Glymour, C. (2007). Preschool children learn about causal structure from conditional interventions. *Developmental Psychology, 43*, 1045–1050.

Schulz, L. E., & Sommerville, J. (2006). God does not play dice: Causal determinism and children's inferences about unobserved causes. *Child Development, 77*, 427–442.

Schulz, L. E., Standing, H. R., & Bonawitz, E. B. (2008). Word, thought, and deed: The role of object categories in children's inductive inferences and exploratory play. *Developmental Psychology, 44*, 1266–1276.

Scott, R. M., & Baillargeon, R. (2013). Do infants really expect agents to act efficiently? A critical test of the rationality principle. *Psychological Science, 24*, 466–474.

Seiver, E., Gopnik, A., & Goodman, N. (2013). Did she jump because she was the big sister or because the trampoline was safe? Causal inference and the development of social attribution. *Child Development, 84*, 443–454.

Senju, A., & Csibra, G. (2008). Gaze following in human infants depends on communicative signals. *Current Biology, 18*, 668–671.

Sloman, S. A., Fernbach, P. M., & Ewing, S. (2009). Causal models: The representational infrastructure for moral judgment. In D. M. Bartels, C. W. Bauman, L. J. Skitka, & D. L. Medin (Eds.), *Psychological of learning and motivation* (Moral judgment and decision making, Vol. 50, pp. 1–26). San Diego, CA: Academic.

Sloman, S. A., & Lagnado, D. (2015). Causality in thought. *Annual Review of Psychology, 66*, 223–247.

Sobel, D. M. (2004). Exploring the coherence of young children's explanatory abilities: Evidence from generating counterfactuals. *British Journal of Developmental Psychology, 22*, 37–58.

Sobel, D. M. (2011). Domain-specific causal knowledge and children's reasoning about possibility. In C. Hoerl, T. McCormack, & S. R. Beck (Eds.), *Understanding counterfactual, understanding causation: Issues in philosophy and psychology* (pp. 123–146). New York: Oxford University Press.

Sobel, D., & Buchanan, D. (2009). Bridging the gap: Causality-at-a-distance in children's categorization and inferences about internal properties. *Cognitive Development, 24*, 274–283.

Sobel, D. M., & Kirkham, N. Z. (2007). Bayes nets and babies: Infants' developing statistical reasoning abilities and their representation of causal knowledge. *Developmental Science, 10*, 298–306.

Sobel, D. M., & Kirkham, N. Z. (2013). The influence of social information of children's statistical and causal inferences. In F. Xu & T. Kushnir (Eds.), *Advances in child development and behavior: Rational constructivism in cognitive development* (Vol. 43, pp. 321–350). Waltham, MA: Academic.

Sobel, D. M., & Kushnir, T. (2013). Knowledge matters: How children evaluate the reliability of testimony as a process of rational inference. *Psychological Review, 120*, 779–797.

Sobel, D. M., & Legare, C. H. (2014). Causal learning in children. *Cognitive Science, 5*, 413–427.

Sobel, D. M., Tenenbaum, J. B., & Gopnik, A. (2004). Children's causal inferences from indirect evidence: Backwards blocking and Bayesian reasoning in preschoolers. *Cognitive Science, 28*, 303–333.

Sommerville, J. A. (2007). *From ends to means: Infants' developing tool use representations*. Invited talk at Department of Psychology colloquium series, Duke University, Raleigh-Durham, NC.

Sommerville, J. A., Blumenthal, E. J., Venema, K., & Braun, K. (2011). The body in action: The impact of self-produced action on infants' action perception and understanding. In V. Slaughter & C. Brownwell (Eds.), *Early development of body representations* (pp. 247–266). Cambridge, UK: Cambridge University Press.

Sommerville, J. A., Upshaw, M. B., & Loucks, J. (2013). The nature of goal-directed action representations in infancy. In F. Xu & T. Kushnir (Eds.), *Advances in child development and behavior: Rational constructivism in cognitive development* (Vol. 43, pp. 351–387). Waltham, MA: Academic.

Sommerville, J. A., & Woodward, A. L. (2005). Pulling out the intentional structure of action: The relation between action processing and action production in infancy. *Cognition, 95*, 1–30.

Soto, F. A., Gershman, S. J., & Niv, Y. (2014). Explaining compound generalization in associative and causal learning through rational principles of dimensional generalization. *Psychological Review, 121*, 526–558.

Southgate, V., Chevallier, C., & Csibra, G. (2009). Sensitivity to communicative relevance tells young children what to imitate. *Developmental Science, 12*, 1013–1019.

Spirtes, P., Glymour, C., & Scheines, R. (2001). *Causation, prediction, and search*. Cambridge, MA: MIT Press.

Surian, L., Caldi, S., & Sperber, D. (2007). Attribution of beliefs to 13-month-old infants. *Psychological Science, 18*, 580–586.

Teglas, E., Vul, E., Girotto, V., Gonzalez, M., Tenenbaum, J. B., & Bonatti, L. L. (2011). Pure reasoning in 12-month-old infants as probabilistic inference. *Science, 332*, 1054–1059.

Trueblood, J. S., & Busemeyer, J. R. (2011). A quantum probability account of order effects in inference. *Cognitive Science, 35*, 1518–1552.

Trueblood, J. S., & Busemeyer, J. R. (2014). A quantum probability model of causal reasoning. *Frontiers in Psychology, 3*, 1–13. doi:10.3389/fpsyg.2012.00138.

Turati, C., Natale, E., Bolognini, N., Seena, I., Picozzi, M., Longhi, E., et al. (2013). The early development of human mirror mechanisms: Evidence from electromyographic recordings at 3 and 6 months. *Developmental Science, 16*, 793–800.

Vaesen, K. (2012). The cognitive bases of human tool use. *Behavioral and Brain Sciences, 35*, 203–218.

Waldmann, M. R., & Holyoak, K. J. (1992). Predictive and diagnostic learning within causal models: Asymmetries in cue competition. *Journal of Experimental Psychology: General, 121*, 222–236.

Walker, C. M., & Gopnik, A. (2014). Toddlers infer higher-order relational principles in causal learning. *Psychological Science, 25*, 161–169.

Wellman, H. M., & Gelman, S. A. (1992). Cognitive development: Foundational theories of core domains. *Annual Review of Psychology, 43*, 337–375.

Wellman, H. M., & Liu, D. (2004). Scaling of theory-of-mind tasks. *Child Development, 75*, 523–541.

Wellman, H., & Liu, D. (2007). Causal reasoning as informed by the early development of explanations. In A. Gopnik & L. Schulz (Eds.), *Causal learning: Psychology, philosophy, and computation* (pp. 261–279). New York: Oxford University Press.

Widlok, T. (2014). Agency, time, and causality. *Frontiers in Psychology, 5*, 1264. doi:10.3389/fpsyg.2014.01264.

Woodward, J. (2003). *Making things happen: A theory of causal explanation*. New York: Oxford University Press.

Wu, R., Gopnik, A., Richardson, D. C., & Kirkham, N. Z. (2011). Infants learn about objects from statistics and people. *Developmental Psychology, 47*, 1220–1229.

Wu, R., & Kirkham, N. Z. (2010). No two cues are alike: Depth of learning during infancy is dependent on what orients attention. *Journal of Experimental Child Psychology, 107*, 118–136.

Xu, F., & Denison, S. (2009). Statistical inference and sensitivity to sampling in 11-month-old infants. *Cognition, 112*, 97–104.

Xu, F., & Garcia, V. (2008). Intuitive statistics by 8-month-old infants. *Proceedings of the National Academy of Sciences, USA, 105*, 5012–5015.

Xu, F., & Kushnir, T. (2013a). *Advances in child development and behavior: Rational constructivism in cognitive development* (Vol. 43). Waltham, MA: Academic.

Xu, F., & Kushnir, T. (2013b). Preface. In F. Xu & T. Kushnir (Eds.), *Advances in child development and behavior: Rational constructivism in cognitive development* (Vol. 43, pp. xi–xiv). Waltham, MA: Academic.

Young, A. G., Alibali, M. W., & Kalish, C. W. (2012). Disagreement and causal learning: Others' hypotheses affect children's evaluations of evidence. *Developmental Psychology, 48*, 1242–1253.

Young, G. (2011). *Development and causality: Neo-Piagetian perspectives*. New York: Springer Science+Business Media.

Yu, Y., & Kushnir, T. (2014). Social context effects in 2- and 4-year-olds' selective versus faithful imitation. *Developmental Psychology, 50*, 922–933.

Developing the Mind, Minding Development

17

Chapter Introduction

The first part of the present chapter reviews two areas of child development that relate to growing self-control and awareness of others. The areas are theory of mind/false belief and executive function/inhibition. Both areas show a transition to increased skills around 3–4 years of age. However, to a degree in both cases, the skills appear evident earlier and keep developing after it.

The chapter shifts gears in its second part, because it is the last one on development, so that I return to major models discussed in the book, but this time, from a developmental perspective. Most of the chapter consists of presenting three major models described at the outset of the book for their developmental component. The three models are the biopsychosocial, embodiment, and systems perspectives. These models are similar in that they are broad and potentially unifying, as well as emphasizing that development is about being grounded in relational participation and interaction with the world. However, none of the three models include a stage component to development, unlike my own (Young, 2011). In this regard, there is room for a fruitful integration of their views with mine.

Major Acquisitions of Mind

Theory of Mind in Early Childhood

Introduction

For the area theory of mind in early childhood, including infancy, Low and Perner (2012) described the nativist, modular view (e.g., Surian & Geraci, 2012). That is, infants either possess innately, or through preparation, critical domain-specific acquisitions, and the environment serves to offer facilitatory prompts in their emergence and refinement from their innate base.

This nativist, modular account contrasts with the associativist, empirical one of gradual conceptual gains in new principles discovered as development proceeds. There might be core knowledge components, but external constraints, in particular, limit the full use of early knowledge (e.g., in memory capacity, adequate inhibition).

Low (2010; and Low & Perner, 2012) advocated for the latter model for the earliest ages, by suggesting a stepwise progression. First, there is an early-developing implicit, unconscious cognitive system that develops piecemeal. Second, as development proceeds, one finds a later-developing explicit, conscious cognitive system.

G. Young, *Unifying Causality and Psychology*, DOI 10.1007/978-3-319-24094-7_17

Rakoczy (2012) supported Low's (2010) perspective by indicating that early cognitive abilities do not necessarily indicate even an early "implicit" theory of mind. Simpler psychological states alone might be involved. That is, the earliest acquisitions are neither complex/core nor innate/prepared, or nativist. Their simpler start leads to later more complex acquisitions.

In the following, I elaborate further these two opposing models in the development of early cognition, especially for the area of theory of mind. As with the prior developmental chapters, I show how Piaget's model can help moderate the differences in the various accounts of early development, and I add aspects that enrich the approach, as well.

Gradual View

Ruffman (2014) provided a conservative view of early infant social understanding. Focusing on false belief, he contended that radical interpretations attributing intentionality and the like to early cognitive activity in such tasks are too "rich" and premature. In the second year, at best, infants might reflect on or represent another's behavior rather than the person's mental state. Infants do not understand false belief (per contra, Carruthers, 2013), nor is it innate or very early developing (per contra, Scott & Baillargeon, 2009).

Only simpler capacities are innate in the infant—related to statistical learning (e.g., Gopnik & Wellman, 2012) and domain-specific biases for faces, eyes, motion, and people. With the help of environmental social factors, such as parental verbal behavior to describe agent behavior, an implicit (striatum-based) understanding of behavior develops (e.g., by perceptual access and pattern recognition), which only later develops into an explicit understanding of mental states (frontal cortex based).

Heyes (2014a) argued that the putative false belief and theory of mind understanding in infancy could be interpreted at a simpler level. These acquisitions reflect domain-general processes and reaction to "low-level novelty." They include focus on colors, shapes, and movements in the typical procedures used. According to Heyes, the research to date has yet to show that infants possess even an "implicit" theory of mind.

Scott and Baillargeon (2014) attempted to refute Heyes (2014a) reasoning. However, Heyes (2014b) countered their argument that infants use more advanced lab-demonstrated cognitive capacities in false-belief tasks.

Research by Kovács, Télglás, and Endress (2010) has given fodder to debate. In their novel procedure, 7-month-olds observed a false-belief scene using "Smurfs." A Smurf left the scene after which a ball was moved, so it held the false belief that a ball was behind a barrier, as it had perceived before leaving. When the Smurf returned, the barrier involved was lowered and the Smurf expressed surprise at the result. However, the infant watching what transpired did not express surprise. There was also a control condition (true belief) in which the Smurf saw what happened to the ball, not leaving the scene.

The modular approach adherents maintain that the infants in the Kovács et al. (2010) study are "computing" online the Smurf's beliefs, or, they have a theory of mind. However, Ruffman, Taumoepeau, and Perkins (2012) noted that a simpler (less "rich") explanation is that the infants in that study "register" differing perceptions in the situations. They could be "representing" the ball's location "as much as" the Smurf's belief about it.

For Ruffman et al. (2012), as infants engage in reasoning, they use experiences of behavior sequences rather than mental states (supported by statistical learning skills). They use situation–action rules to derive an implicit sensitivity to actions without directly representing "mental intermediates" or "intervening mental states" in the causal link to action from situation.

Yott and Poulin-Dubois (2012) and Thoermer, Sodian, Vuori, Perst, and Kristen (2012) also resisted a "rich" interpretation of their findings with 18-month-olds for the cognitive advances shown in their particular studies. They preferred to use behavior-based (situation-action) explanations.

From a usage-based perspective, Liszkowski (2013) went so far as to attribute a preliminary theory of mind to infants. Infants appear to use flexible action expectations to communicate with and interact socially with others, including prosocially, depending on the situation and person. For example, a 12-month-old, who is asked ambiguously about several objects, considers the object with which the adult has not yet interacted (Moll & Tomasello, 2007). Infants of this age also initiate interactions flexibly depending on expectations of the others' reactions (Liszkowski, Carpenter, Henning, Striano, & Tomasello, 2004).

Also at this age, Knudsen and Liszkowski (2013) found that infants could even intervene in a proactive way by anticipating a mistake by another person. They would warn an adult before she reached for an "oversize" object that had been put back in its original place by a second confederate adult while she had left the scene. (Control conditions: object not oversized; replacement observed by first adult).

The usage-based account of theory of mind presented by Liszkowski (2013) argues that theory of mind is not only used in interaction but also that interactional experiences, including those related to it, "drive" development of prediction of actions. In this sense, competence drives performance so that the model is not nativist, even if the competence arises early in development. As early as 2–3 months of age, infants participate in dyadic face-to-face interaction that incorporates contingency detection (Gergely & Watson, 1999).

Low and Perner (2012) supported the view that the development of a coherent theory of mind awaits a later age. Further developments in language skills assist in this acquisition (e.g., San Juan & Astington, 2012). [In this regard, see other work on the role of language framing in children's causal interpretations (by Muentener and Schulz (2012), and Butler and Markman (2012), as well as Legare (2012) and Cimpian and Erickson (2012)).]

Rapid View

Others have rejected the approach that infants have only an implicit understanding of the other. They reject the minimalist view of the development of theory of mind (ToM) based on statistical learning and pattern recognition. They prefer a view that is richer in conceptualization of these early capacities (e.g., Scott, 2014). The latter view is that infants can mentally attribute goals, intentions, and beliefs to agents (Baillargeon et al., 2014). Infants can use mental-state reasoning and infer aspects of the mind of the other, rather than simply using behavioral rules to interpret and predict the intentional actions of others. When infants are tested on appropriate tasks (that do not trigger a prepotent bias to respond based on reality or demand inhibitory skills to suppress inappropriate prepotent responses), their rich ToM capacities can be ascertained.

In a study with puppets, Choi and Luo (2015) demonstrated that infants of 13 months of age possess an emergent theory of mind. After puppets A and B interacted positively by hopping, clapping, facing each other, and having a laugh (mouth open) face, the infants who watched the puppets behaved as if they expected them to continue interacting this way. But, if one puppet hit another and a third one saw it, the observer infants expected the watching puppet not to continue the interaction, unless the hit was by accident. The study demonstrated that one-year-olds take into account agent intentions in interpreting actions and formulating how agents should act socially. Additionally, the research demonstrated that one-year-olds understand the false belief of others.

Piaget's View

Dice and Dove (2011) related the early developing social cognitive act of joint attention at about 1 year of age to Piaget's sensorimotor stages in infancy. In the social cognitive view, young infants can engage in this behavior because either they intend to share information or they understand the intent of others to share information. This happens because infants can become aware of another's subjective attention/experience, having a theory of mind, or mindedness.

In Piaget's (1950, 1952, 1960) cognitive developmental model, infants are not yet able to think about another's mental state, being cognitively "egocentric." In the infants' sensorimotor world, someone looking at what they are looking at sees it as they see it.

At 12 months of age, infants are well into Piaget's stage of coordination of secondary circular reactions, which is focused heavily on goal-directed behavior, including in detours. In this sense, joint attention can be conceived of as goal-directed coordination of action in reference to an (desired) object. That is, the referential behaviors/gestures in this activity suggest that they are "motor signifiers," or outward manifestations of internal thought (albeit action-based). Further, the actions indicate that the thought involved, or schema, includes the other person as a vicarious agent or source of causality, in a precursor step to theory of mind and transition to the next sensorimotor substage of tertiary circular reactions. In this Piagetian account of referencing/joint attention, the social cognitive concept of joining another person does not apply.

Comment

The rich point of view of the early theory of mind of the infant and its related capacities emphasizes that early on infants can infer about the other, mentally attribute about the other, and understand beliefs that the other might hold. They can reason mentally about the other, use flexible expectations in action, anticipate mistakes by the other, and take into account the intention of the other in interpreting their actions and understanding how the other should act. Even at the age of one year, infants can understand the other's false beliefs.

In contrast, the minimalist nativist point of view considers pattern recognition and action-based rule construction as better ways to understand the behavior evident in the research at issue. Infants use statistical learning unconsciously or implicitly in a low-level, associative way, and domain-specific and general processes that are independent of any cognitive modeling or schemas.

A Piagetian account might help explain the findings better. For example, joint attention in the 1-year-old might involve goal-directed coordination of activity in relation to a wanted object, as suggested by translating the behavior into the language of Piaget's fourth sensorimotor substage of coordination of secondary circular reactions. I return below to further presentation of the Piagetian approach to the development of theory of mind.

In the following, I review some of the evidence with older children and adults on theory of mind. There is no reason to doubt that it develops like other cognitive acquisitions in terms of complexity and abstractness into adulthood.

Beyond Infancy

Children

Devine and Hughes (2014) conducted a meta-analysis of prior research on the question of the temporal relation between false belief understanding and early childhood executive function (EF). Their analysis revealed that early individual differences in executive function predict later variation in understanding of false belief. The relationship was not bidirectional; variation in early false belief understanding did not predict later executive function differences (Hughes, 1998).

The meta-analysis conducted by Devine and Hughes (2014) involved 102 articles and data sets. The results of the meta-analysis were moderately significant. The cumulative sample numbered almost 10,000 3- to 6-year-olds, who were typically developing. Among the studies reviewed, 10 were longitudinal, like that of Hughes (1998). The effects shown were "clearly" consistent with Hughes, 1998 findings.

Devine and Hughes (2014) concluded that the theory that best explains the data is the emergence-expression one (Russell, 1996). Executive function includes factors such as working memory and inhibition, which help young children to "attend to and reflect upon" the mental states of themselves and others, thereby facilitating later understanding of false belief (as in the classic Sally-Anne task).

Adults

Dunbar (2014) presented a model of the social brain that related social group size in evolution to neocortical volume. The model applies to individual differences in social networking, as well. Lewis, Rezaie, Browne, Roberts, and Dunbar (2011) and Powell, Lewis, Roberts, García-Fiñana, and Dunbar (2012) found that, in neuroimaging research, the size of face-to-face social networks correlates with prefrontal cortex size measures. Kanai, Bahrami, Roylance, and Rees (2012) reported similar results for Facebook friends. Path analysis suggested that size of medial prefrontal cortical regions, which are associated with mentalizing belief states in others (theory of mind), mediates the former results. The social brain effect appears influenced by evolution, genetics, and learning.

Comment

The select research examined for children and adults on social sensitivity indicates that individual differences are important. Moreover, the behavior is so primary that the brain is referred to as a social organ. Finally, specific areas of the brain might mediate the activity. Executive function seems critical, as per the following section, as well.

Executive Function

Infants

Diamond (2013) reviewed the development of executive function (EF). It is considered top-down, and its cognitive control processes develop to control automatic instinctual or intuitive ones that are "ill-advised, insufficient, or impossible." EF use requires "effort." Consensus has noted three core EFs: inhibition, working memory, and cognitive flexibility.

Inhibition involves the control of attention, behavior, emotions, thoughts, or any of their combination in order to "override" either an internal predisposition or an external enticement. It includes self-control (behavioral inhibition) and interference control (selective attention and cognitive inhibition). Self-control concerns resisting temptations, controlling impulses, and delaying, as required. Developmentally, Diamond (1990, 1991) found that shielding a perceptual "pull" helps even 6-month-olds inhibit an incorrect prepotent response.

Working memory involves holding information in mind and using it mentally (e.g., in problem solving). It refers to our mental scratch pad. Developmentally, Diamond (1985) found that 10- to 12-month-olds could find an object at Place B even 5 s after having seen it hidden in Place A (also see Bell & Cuevas, 2012).

Cognitive flexibility involves changing approach or perspective to a problem, and adjusting contextually to new demands, rules, or priorities. An example is found in task-switching or shifting set. It includes creative thinking. Developmentally, cognitive flexibility builds on the other two core EFs and develops later than them (e.g., at 2 ½ to 3 years). All three EFs continue to develop over the lifespan.

EF is implicated both as an important source of long-term development and an important outcome that is dependent on early infancy variables. Cuevas and Bell (2013) found that, in early infancy, infants who were efficient information processors at 5 months of age, as indexed by looking time, exhibited higher EF skills from 2 to 4 years of age ("short lookers" were compared to "long lookers"). Looking at 5 months was measured toward glove puppets adorned with facial features. EF was measured using a composite score over multiple age-appropriate tasks, including a variant of the game Simon Says. The authors concluded that, already at 5 months of age, individual differences in the maturation of the frontal cortex, its connectivity, or both could underlie the findings.

Rose, Feldman, and Jankowski (2012) showed an association between infant (7, 12 months) and toddler (24, 36 months) EF (in attention, processing speed, memory) and 11-year-old EF (in working memory, inhibition, shifting). Also, the results revealed a path from early speed and memory to later working memory, and another from speed to shifting. Rose et al. (2012) reported another study showing an association in self-restraint as early as 14 months and EFs as late as 17 years (Friedman, Miyake, Robinson, & Hewitt, 2011).

Children

The three basic core EFs themselves help contribute to the development of higher-order EF, which concerns relational reasoning, logical reasoning, or fluid intelligence. Diamond (2013) presented a model showing the relationship between the core EF and higher-level EF (see Fig. 17.1). The figure illustrates that the core EF of inhibitory control is embedded in self-regulatory processes (response inhibition, attention inhibition, and maintaining optimal arousal levels).

Diamond (2012, 2013) concluded that EF could be trained in children, e.g., by training in task switching (Karbach & Kray, 2009), through martial arts (Lakes & Hoyt, 2004), and in school curricula (Raver et al., 2011). According to Diamond, even infants can profit in EF training (also see Kray & Ferdinand, 2013).

Chevalier, Martis, Curran, and Munakata (2015) found that 5-year-old compared to 10-year-old children engage in reactive compared to proactive (advance preparation) executive control because of deficits in metacognitive processes (metacognitive decisions when they engage it proactive control), rather than due to fundamental constraints in cognitive capacities. When the experimenters made the task of reactive control in response to events more difficult (on three tasks involving task switching), this type of control was not favored by the younger children, as was the case with the older children.

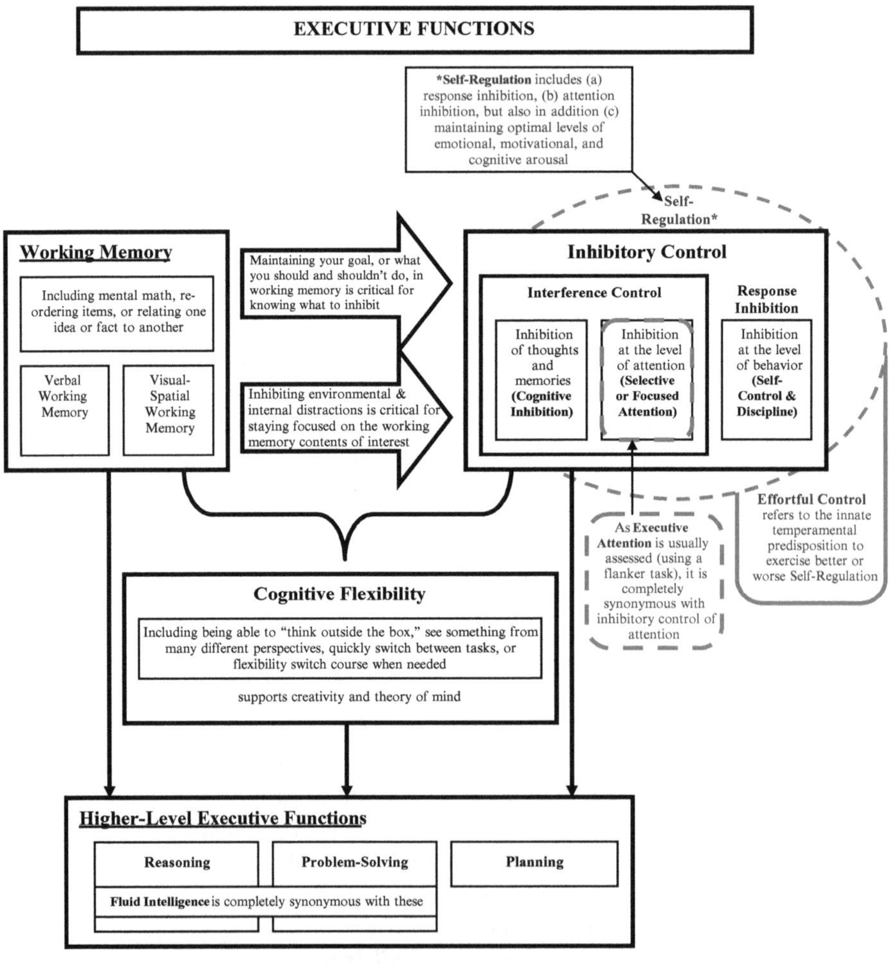

Fig. 17.1 Executive functions and related terms. The figure shows the three major executive functions: their attributes, relations, and superordinate functions are shown. Adopted with permission of Annual Reviews. Republished with permission of Annual Reviews, from Diamond, A. (2013). Executive functions. *Annual Review of Psychology*, *64*, 135–168; © by Annual Reviews, http://www.annualreviews.org. [Figure 4, Page 152]

Lee, Bull, and Ho (2013) investigated core EFs in 6- to 15-year-olds, and found a shift to the predominant three-factor model from an earlier two-factor one. This is consistent with Diamond's emphasis on only the core EFs of inhibition and working memory being present in infancy. Richland and Burchinal (2013) found a relationship between early elementary school EF and 15-year-old verbal analogy performance.

The approach taken by Engelhardt, Briley, Mann, Harden, and Tucker-Drob (2015) for middle childhood is that there are four core executive functions, with the three core ones already mentioned complemented by a fourth one of updating, defined as monitoring of incoming stimuli leading to replacement of stored information with information that is new. In their twin study, Engelhardt et al. (2015) found a common EF factor that can be extracted from the four core ones, and that it is 100 % heritable. In contrast, variance related to the four EF domains could be explained by both genetic and environmental influences. They concluded that general EF could function as an early genetic marker for later psychopathologies. Their study extended the similar work of Friedman et al. (2008) on adults.

Adults

Gross and Jazaieri (2014) defined emotional regulation in terms of activating a goal to influence the emotion-generating process, either implicitly or explicitly. It can take place by regulating one's own emotions (intrinsic, intrapersonal) or those of others (extrinsic, interpersonal). The process model of emotion regulation involves five sequentially cycled active families of processes: situation selection, situation modification, attention, appraisal, and response (modulation; see Fig. 17.2). Emotion regulation strategies can be adaptive or maladaptive. Gross (2015a, 2015b) further elaborated his model. In particular, he described that emotional regulation involves cycles of valuations, including emotionally. Diaz and Eisenberg (2015) added that, developmentally, parenting affects individual differences in emotional regulation.

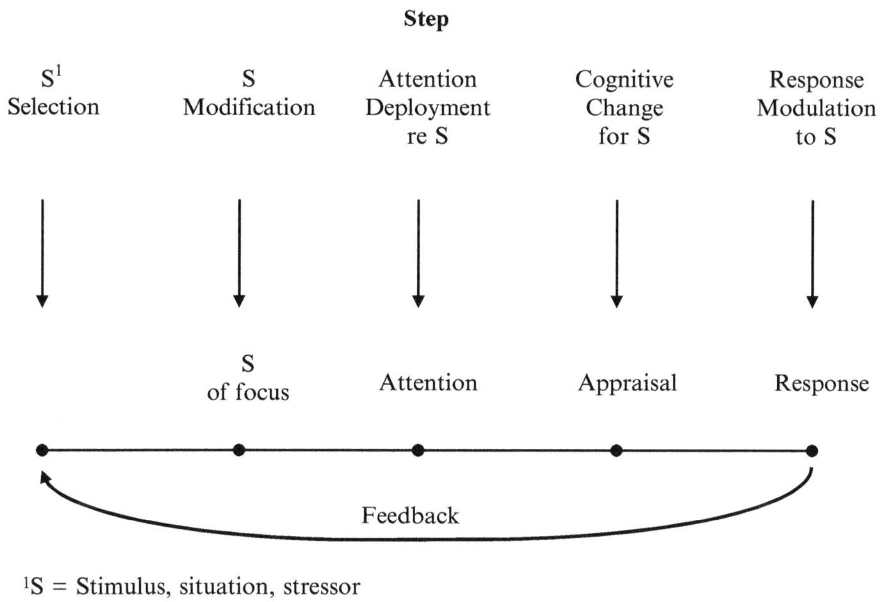

Fig. 17.2 The process model of emotion regulation. The five steps in processing in emotional regulation moves from stimulus/situation/stressor selection/modification to attention/cognition and then response. *Note.* I added a circular interactive component to depiction of the model between S presentation/selection and its modification. Adapted from Gross and Thompson (2007)

Bickel, Quisenberry, Moody, and Wilson (2014) considered addiction as the result of a strong impulsive decision system due to deficits in the executive control system. They referred to their model as a dual model of self-control failure (competing neurobehavioral decision system). The model applies transdiagnostically, e.g., also to risky sexual behavior. As well, for them, appropriate self-control involves choosing more adaptive delayed rewards over immediate ones and the process becomes dysfunctional with faulty learning or short-term depletion (Baumeister, Vohs, & Tice, 2007). Immediate stimuli associated with short-term wants and needs are overvalued relative to those associated with longer-term rewards (e.g., drug usage versus working for money).

Peña-Sarrionandia, Mikolajczak, and Gross (2015) showed that Gross's (2013) model of emotional regulation informs work in emotional intelligence (EI). For example, those high in EI regulate their emotions flexibly.

Comment

EF is instrumental in developing self-control. Already in infancy, its components of inhibition and working memory are developing. Its third primary aspect of cognitive flexibility develops later. Skills in EF predict better outcomes, and also skills related to it (e.g., with respect to information processing) predict its better development. Self-control is at once cognitive and emotional. When it goes awry, difficulties might ensue, such as in addictions. In addition, I would add that difficulties in having an adequate theory of mind of the other could be compromised by EF deficits.

Inhibition

Early

Gandolfi, Viterbori, Traverso, and Usai (2014) noted that, for the area of inhibition in EF, there are unitary, dual, and tripartite models (e.g., Wiebe et al., 2011; Usai, Viterbori, Traverso, & De Franchis, 2014; Diamond, 2013, respectively). The authors used the two-factor model of Bunge, Dudukovic, Thomason, Vaidya, and Gabrieli (2002) to structure a study with 24- to 32-month-olds and 36- to 48-month-olds. Response inhibition was measured with tasks such as finger circle drawing (regular speed, slowly) and a central target (fish) pointing task (with distractor stimuli present).

The results according to confirmatory factor analysis showed a single undifferentiated inhibition structure at the younger age and a two-factor structure in the older children. The latter appeared to involve response inhibition (e.g., inhibition of an impulsive/inappropriate dominant response, as per the circle task) and interference suppression (e.g., cognitive inhibition/suppression of interfering/prepotent/irrelevant information/ mental representation, as per the fish task). The authors concluded that a sequential developmental model from a unifactor to a bifactor structure in inhibitory control can help explain early EF development.

Blackwell and Munakata (2014) demonstrated that cognitive control in the child develops from a reactive form to a proactive one. Nevertheless, context determines when the latter form is advantageous rather than disadvantageous (i.e., maintaining task-relevant information in anticipation of needing it rather than merely retrieving task-relevant information when it is needed).

Cuevas et al. (2014) demonstrated that maternal EF even more so than care giving quality in some analyses was associated with early child EF (without minimizing the importance of early negative quality caregiving). Maternal EF provides unique information about child EF relative to negative quality caregiving. Maternal EF is important for self-regulation and regulation of the infant.

Moriguchi (2014) related the development of EF to social interaction; they work reciprocally in development. In this regard, he referred to the quality of social interaction involved as supportive/scaffolding vs. negative/controlling parenting. As well, he noted that EF development relates to the aspect of social development concerned with moral development. He added a biological dimension, relating performance on an EF task (switching dimensional categorization of cards from one dimension, e.g., color, to another, e.g., shape) to activation in the lateral prefrontal areas of the brain.

Children

Wiebe, Morton, Buss, and Spencer (2014) presented a developmental model of EF that is grounded in an activation/inhibition dynamic. The model incorporates a role for Hebbian or neural cell assembly learning. Also, see Arsalidou, Pascual Leone, Johnson, Morris, and Taylor (2013) for a model of activation and deactivation balancing in brain pattern activity under cognitive load.

Castellano and Tannock (2002) had suggested that inhibitory control could constitute an "endophenotype" for attention deficit hyperactivity disorder (ADHD), as per Barkley's model (1997) of inhibitory deficits underlying ADHD. Berger, Alyagon, Hadaya, Atzaba-Poria, and Auerbach (2013) investigated further the question by a stop-signal reaction time task in 5-year-old boys. Parental characteristics predicted aspects of task performance. Also, for a subset of the children, higher hyperactivity, in particular, was related to less activity in left frontotemporal brain areas, which are associated with inhibition.

Howard, Johnson, and Pascual-Leone (2015) differentiated inhibitory control into automatic and effortful types in the context of attention. In research with 7- to 12-year-olds, they found that the 7-year-olds arrive at adult levels for automatic inhibition, but even 12-year-olds had not yet attained these levels for effortful inhibition.

Piaget

Houdé and Borst (2014) related inhibitory control to cognitive development. In particular, advances in cognitive development according to Piagetian stages are correlated with inhibitory function in domain-general executive ability, and is associated with prefrontal cortical activity. Specifically, inhibition damps less advanced solutions in various cognitive domains associated with earlier developing Piagetian stages or, to use another language, associated with heuristic, System I thinking compared to more advanced logical System II thinking (Houdé, 2015).

Joliot et al. (2009) had participants resolve a Piagetian numerical conservation-type task requiring inhibition of the stratagem of "length equals number," while gathering simultaneously combined ERP (event-related potential) and MEG (magnetoencephalography) data. Among their complex results, inhibitory processes appeared evident in the late components of the electromagnetic brain activity (a right side P 2 related frontal orbital activation, in particular). The authors concluded that a top-down executive control for switching might be involved. Leroux et al. (2009) noted that the task used in this type of research is spatial and consistent with a right-hemisphere advantage, aside from its executive function demands.

Adults

Duque, Olivier, and Rushworth (2013) related inhibitory control to the pre-supplementary motor area (pre-SMA) in the medial prefrontal cortex for tasks involving unwanted motor responses in competition or conflict. This inhibitory process facilitates appropriate response selection. The study leading to these conclusions was conducted with adults using "virtual surgery" by repetitive transcranial magnetic stimulation (TMS) over the pre-SMA, in particular. The authors concluded that in their study a top-down inhibitory control by TMS exerted effects in action selection in the reaction time visuomotor task used.

The importance of self-regulation (and of metacognition) also are implicated in research on learning and on personality (Bjork, Dunlosky, & Kornell, 2013; Denissen, van Aken, Penke, & Wood, 2013, respectively). In both cases, inhibitory function seems integral to the models developed (metamemory framework and five regulatory mechanisms, respectively).

Comment

Inhibitory control appears to develop from a reactive, unifactorial process to a proactive, bifactorial process, with better coordination with activation. It is facilitated in development by appropriate parenting (and parental EF, as well) and it is associated with different brain regions, especially frontally. Inhibition is related to Piagetian development, and surely is involved in the development of theory of mind and related acquisitions, as well.

The next section of the chapter shifts gears into general models of development that are applicable across diverse developmental topics. For example, in the following, I describe the biopsychosocial model and its application to understanding gender differences in development. Next, the model of embodiment in development is rapidly expanding in its reach, and has applications in multiple developmental areas, e.g., learning/education. Finally, the systems model is a primary one found in this present work, and it has been applied widely to both behavioral and brain development.

Major Developmental Models Related to Mind

Biopsychosocial Model

Model

Figure 17.3 presents an integrated biopsychosocial model that I have developed. The model is also evolutionary, developmental, ecological, relational, and includes system/network outcomes that are adaptive or maladaptive. The model allows for understanding of both individualizing and communalizing processes in mental disorder (i.e., ideographic and nomothetic, respectively). It emphasizes that the person can exert self-control in an active way (e.g., think having a belief in free will and its benefits, Baumeister, 2008), aside from the usual more passive controls affecting the person (biology,

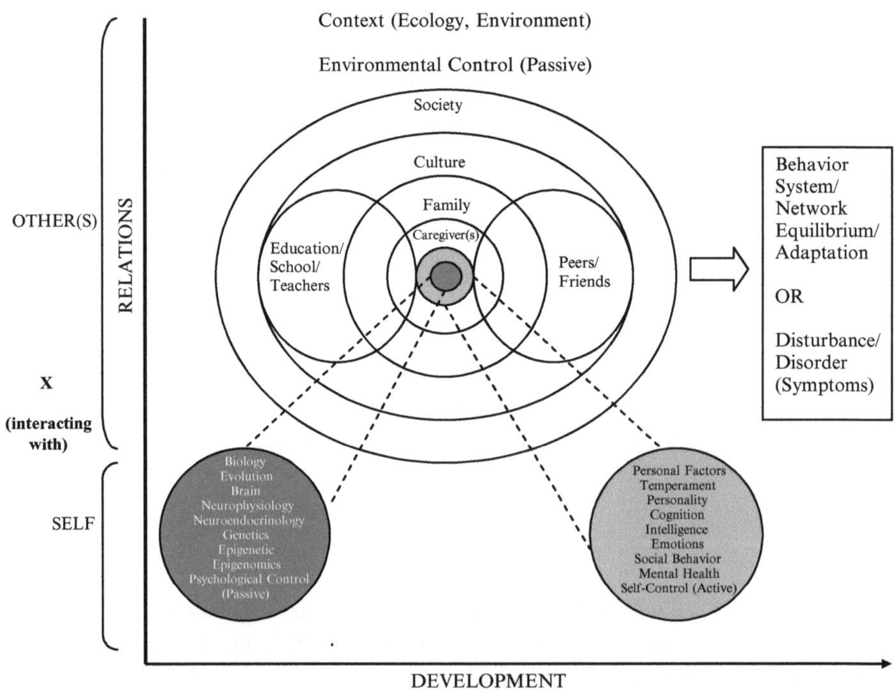

Fig. 17.3 Biopsychosocial/ecological model. The figure represents an integrated biopsychosocial and ecological model of development, including the developmental (personal change), context, and self-regulation models. Adapted from Sameroff (2010), modified

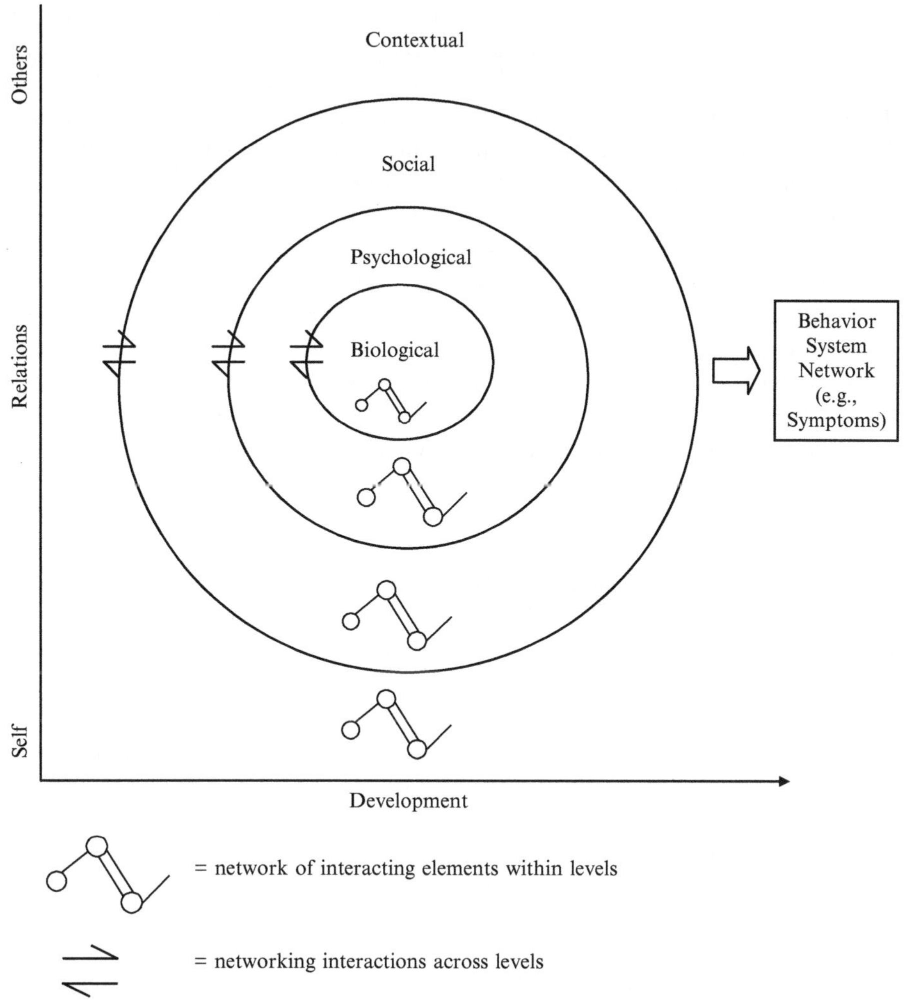

Fig. 17.4 Developmental, systemic (networking) biopsychosocial psychiatric model. This figure is a simplified integrated biopsychosocial and ecological model of development, including the developmental (personal change), context, and self-regulation models

environment). In this sense, the model is as much as "biopersonalsocial" one as much as it is a biopsychosocial one (Young, 2011). Figure 17.4 offers a simplified version of the integrated model that illustrates the network component.

Some of the factors in the model include the following. Epigenesis indicates the complexity in etiology in current biological study. Epigenesis concerns gene silencing due to DNA methylation induced by the environment (e.g., adversity, Szyf, 2013). It indicates that genes and environment are not considered anymore as distinct entities of influence on phenotypes. Phenotypic expression is a product of multiple biological and environmental influences, including genetic and epigenetic ones.

Applied to Gender Differences

That nature and nurture collaborate in development is a truism. However, Eagly and Wood (2013) noted that, in the area of gender differences and similarities, researchers rarely integrate these two causal sources. For example, to explain the sex difference favoring male children and adults in spatial ability (e.g., mental rotation of three-dimensional objects), some workers emphasize biological causes and others sociocultural ones.

For the biological influence on spatial ability, Courvoisier et al. (2013) related the observed sex difference in spatial ability to hormonal cycles, whereas Chou, Cheng, Chen, Lin, and Chu (2011) related the spatial skill sex difference to brain structure differences. As for sociocultural explanations of the spatial sex difference, Estes and Felker (2012) referred to self-confidence as a differentiating factor and Moè (2012) referred to gender stereotyping and other external causes.

Eagly and Wood (2013) adopted an interactionist position on the roles of nature and nurture in sex-related differences, referring, in this regard, to a balance, as in the balance of Yin and Yang. For them, the area of socialization, in general, would do well to adopt an interactionist perspective. Granted, sociocultural factors are important in socialization (e.g., Leaper, 2013), but so are biological ones (e.g., Campbell, 2012). Even for the topic of mate preferences, emerging mating theories integrate hormonal and social influences (e.g., Wood & Eagly, 2013).

In this vein, Eagly and Wood (2013) proceeded to build an integrated nature–nurture perspective on sex differences in behavior. For example, they noted that genetic influences depend on social environmental ones. In this regard, Lickliter and Honeycutt (2003) argued that genes participate in networks that are modulated by environmental influences in order to construct and maintain an adaptive brain. About female sexual maturation, James, Ellis, Schlomer, and Garber (2012) found that, for girls (and not boys), lower family quality accelerated signs of pubertal maturation. The intermediate mechanism in this developmental acceleration could involve stress hormone release that acts on pubertal development (cortisol, epinephrine in the hypothalamic-pituitary-adrenal (HPA) axis → adrenal androgens → pubertal effects).

For Eagly and Wood (2013), biology and environment interact in the development of sex differences in a "biosocial constructionist" manner. Biological sex differences are moderated by the social environment even in cases of division of labor of biologically-mediated labor in societies. The activities constituting the division of labor reflect differential, evolved physical capacities (women: reproductive activities; men: size, strength). Social psychological processes help to create gender-role beliefs that help self-regulate the division of labor, which is tailored to each culture's contemporary conditions.

Wood and Eagly (2013) continued that an interactive biosocial construction model of human sex differences allows for explanation of variation in sex differences across culture and historical epoch. Evolutionarily, humans adopted not to particular environmental features, but to their variation (Richerson & Boyd, 2005). In this view, human mind and cognition are not modular but are "general purpose." This view contrasts in the extreme with the modular one of Shackelford and Liddle (2014).

Comment
Note that Eagly and Wood (2013) are describing a biopsychosocial model of sex differences/similarities as much as a biosociocultural one (although they did not use directly the biopsychosocial label). For example, they refer to agency, assertiveness, and power emerging in women, which are psychological processes that bootstrap, catalyze, and build on biological and cultural-contextual ones.

The biopsychosocial model is an integrative one because, by definition, it covers a full range of influences on behavior. However, it lacks specific change mechanisms, unlike the systems model that is presented later on in the chapter.

Embodiment

Introduction

Embodiment represents a quickly evolving, unifying construct in psychology that is especially relevant for development. In the following, I review the model, how the Piagetian approach is consistent with it and informs it, and studies on developmental embodiment. The research in the infancy period suggests that embodiment is crucial right from birth if not prenatally. The work on the mirror neuron system supports a place for embodiment early in development. As for young children, among others, the work on force dynamics and speech-gesture mismatches reveals the value of the embodiment approach to development.

Embodiment and Relational Development

Model Marshall (2013) discussed embodiment in terms of relational developmental systems (Overton, 2013). Embodiment includes brain–body–environment coupling (Kiverstein, 2012). Actions modify the environment, which affects actions, in turn. Brain function involves a feedback loop as it guides and coordinates action (Clark, 2013). Embodiment enables enaction for making sense of the world (Thompson, 2007). Living systems act to create the boundary conditions for the creation and maintenance of their self-organization (Witherington, 2011).

Overton (2013) situated embodiment within a relational developmental perspective, which is also a biopsychosocial one, and related it to causality. Relationism constitutes a worldview superordinate to developmental relationism. It decreases the separation of basics, such as brain and mind, arguing for their nondecomposable, indissociable, unified, inclusive complementarity. In this approach, causality is a reciprocal, coactive, fused, bidirectional, interpretative, and circular process among co-equal constitutives. Behavioral systems are holistic, synthesized, and biological/personal/cultural.

This worldview allows for individual differences and universals to co-exist in a biopsychosocial network that is co-constructed and co-evolves toward increasing complexity. Living systems are active and self-organizing, with novelty emerging from their activity.

In this model, embodiment is manifested in the interdigitating relations of biology, person, and culture. We are active, contextualized agents mediating constitutively the world with our bodies through which our brain and mind develop. The body is a reflection of lived, actively-engaged experience. It references our biology, psychology, and culture in a bridged, joined, unified whole.

Marshall (2014) suggested a cross-theoretical integration is needed to better understand development. He emphasized the importance of the points of view of embodiment, relational developmental systems, and dynamical systems theory. In embodiment, the organism and environment are dynamically coupled. In relational developmental systems, conceptual opposites, in effect, are complementarities. In dynamical systems theory, top-down and bottom-up influences are reciprocally in tension. Marshall (2014) concluded that a fruitful integrative approach for psychology resides in the area of radical embodied cognitive science (Chemero, 2009). He maintained that developmental theory should be person-centered. Also, Mascolo (2013) referred to the "extended" person-environment system. Intentionality continues to grow into adulthood, and the evidence indicates that the embodied human mind exhibits a unified mind–body that is both enacted and sustained via neuromotor physiology. Similarly, Ho (2013) referred to the "fluid genome" because there are no specific "intelligence genes." Behavior is a multifactorial causal product in which the process of embodiment could be central.

Comment Embodiment, by definition, is an interactive model. It relates body, brain, person, development, and cultural context. Therefore, it is a natural ally to other positions related to it, such as the biopsychosocial model and systems theory. When the embodiment approach is considered with these other models, developmental behavioral causality is not only biological/body-centric and linked to the physical, it is also active, predictive, proactive, and anticipatory, being fluid, extended, and all-inclusive dynamically of the multiple and emerging co-acting personal and social influences upon it.

Piaget

Model Witherington (2015) considered that embodiment is consistent Piaget's concept of constructivism. In this regard, Needham and Libertus (2011) maintained that Piaget's cognitive developmental model provides one framework supporting the concept. In the model, infants are seen to construct understanding of the world via their own actions upon it and engagement with it.

Using the sticky mittens paradigm, Needham and colleagues demonstrated that young infants develop an increased interest in objects through the experience of reaching for them (e.g., increased looking at, mouthing them), as well as an earlier ability to interpret another person's reaches as goal-directed (e.g., Needham, Barrett, & Peterman, 2002; Sommerville, Woodward, & Needham, 2005).

Gerson and Woodward (2014) studied 3-month-old infants in situations of self-produced and observational action experience and the differential effects of the experiences on action understanding. The authors used the sticky mitten paradigm in the training of the infants, and concluded that, even at this age, active, agentic experience helps recognize the goals of other agents. By acting on the world, or self-producing actions (Piaget, 1953), young infants change, among others, their knowledge, goals, social perceptions, behavior, and development.

Wellsby and Pexman (2014) noted that early development is especially about embedded cognition, as per Piaget (1952). Further, sensorimotor experience continues to influence development throughout the lifespan, albeit in a more refined or flexible way (Antonucci & Alt, 2011). Sensorimotor experiences continually influence and shape learning, perception, action, language, and conceptual representation (e.g., Thelen, 2008).

Bornstein, Hahn, and Suwalsky (2013) illustrated the importance of early embodied cognition to later cognition in their study. They measured 5-month motor-exploratory competence (motor maturity, active exploration, in particular) and found that it related longitudinally to 14-year academic achievement. Specifically, the more motorically mature infants were at 5 months of age and the more active exploration takes place, the higher was their academic levels at 14 years of age. The authors considered the findings consistent with Piaget's (1970/1988) emphasis that infant motor actions/exploration are "foundational" in development. They described a developmental cascade within a systems framework as providing a good explanatory model. Another one would be embodied cognition.

Comment The research on self-produced actions and their effects in infancy are consistent not only with the embodiment model but also with that of Piaget's. Experience is partly self-generated and this component of it is essential for understanding cognition, as Piaget (1953, 1954) had maintained.

The Piagetian model includes the sensorimotor period as the first stage and, by definition, this stage is an embodied one. The ones after it are representational, but analyses of child and adult cognition, and not only infant cognition, reveal the pertinence of sensorimotor experience in cognition. This might imply that the Piagetian program does not apply to embodied cognition after infancy. However, Piaget had maintained that each new stage in his model builds on prior stages. Moreover, in Young (2011), I had argued that prior stages might still be active as new ones function, and even complement them in cognitive activity. That is, in my Neo-Piagetian understanding of cognition, sensorimotor intelligence is continually available to us, although transformed by its interactions with higher-order intelligences. In this regard, I developed the concept of yoking of earlier developed stages to later ones in cognitive activity, as the context requires, including even of the infant sensorimotor one in adults who engage in more advanced thought and activities, such as problem-solving. In this sense, the Piagetian project is exquisitely an embodied one throughout all phases of the lifespan.

Moreover, the work showing a role in behavior of early mirror neuron activity is consistent with both the Piagetian and embodied view, and these neurons, too, are available throughout the lifespan. They provide one biological register of the embodiment process and constitute one ground for the changing cognitive activity throughout the lifespan.

That being said, an integration of the embodied and Piagetian view would show how passage through the sensorimotor substages that he describes in infancy modify and add to the embodiment driver in behavioral causality. The Piagetian model might provide an axis to show how qualitative transitions in cognition in infancy lead to qualitative changes in embodied cognition. In the following, I examine the behavior of reaching as it passes through the sensorimotor substages in infancy that Piaget described. He described that a new sensorimotor substage appeared every few months on average, so that in the first few years of life, the infant manifests six of them. Examination of reaching in infancy affords both a good introduction to Piaget and also reveals how he respected the embodiment process and how the cognitive changes in the sensorimotor period alter that process—embodiment and cognitive development are mutually interactive in this model, as they should be.

Reaching for the Mind

Neonate In this regard, at first, in the neonatal period, and consistent with Piaget referring to this age period of one involving reflex exercise, it is ballistic when triggered by a target, so that, as a body-focused activity, it derives mostly from the body, and with only a prompt from the environment.

One Month Next, in the 1-month-old, reaching is better coordinated with the object, and successful reaches obtain, even with coordinated hand opening and grasping involved. Piaget referred to primary circular reactions at this age, so that the coordinations in the behavior improve, but the objects are apparently discovered accidentally as interesting, or without intention preceding the action. Moreover, the repetitions involved in the behavior are body-focused more than object-focused. In this regard, at one month of age, infants might be engaging more in spatial exploration around them as they flail and only when ready do they engage in object-directed reaching (Young, 2011).

Four Months Next, for Piaget, the infant engages in visually-directed reaching, so that the object becomes primary in the activity. Moreover, he referred to this age as involving secondary circular reactions, so that the accidentally-discovered interesting behavior revolves around objects more so than the body, which evidently still is involved.

Eight Months At this age, Piaget referred to the coordination of secondary schemas, for example, in reaching to get around a detour in order to get a hidden object that had been interesting before being hidden. In this step, embodiment is beginning to serve cognition as much as the inverse. The behavior is still body-centered and sensorimotor, but the cognition provides an image to guide the behavior from its start. That being said, the cognition is not yet representational; as well, the guiding image is rudimentary and can be a poor one when there are constraints on the behavior, such as shifting the object involved in sight to a second screen. There is still room for active reaching in the form of groping around and exploration in an effort to find these secondarily displaced objects, but errors abound.

Twelve Months For Piaget, the 1-year-old begins a process of differentiating already learned means–end combinations, but by accidental exploration rather than by a preconceived purely mental plan. In this regard, they engage in the behavior, that as parents we know all to well, of trying out new behaviors in different ways; for example, reaching might be used to knock over a bowl and the infant gets to see our reactions, instead of the infant engaging in reaching for the spoon in the bowl and eating. In this sense, the reaching is even further removed from the original body source and even the simple object that it usually seeks. Rather, it becomes intertwined in cognition to the point that it allows for new cognitions after the result of its behavior becomes known. Reaching becomes not only a means to a new end but also a means to a new cognition.

Eighteen Months Piaget referred to the toddler as developing the possibility of mental combinations to discover new means–end relationships, but he still linked the behavior involved to associated action-based sensorimotor activity. For example, the toddler might covertly or even overtly open the mouth before reaching to a drawer to open it in order to remove something from it. Only at 2 years of age, after the sensorimotor period of infancy, can behavior be guided in full by representations without sensorimotor concomitants. In terms of the relationships among reaching, cognition, and embodiment, this example shows that cognition has taken the upper hand in the relationships and guides the behavior from the start mentally, although still with an embodied component. Reaching is subsumed to wider goals, and it leads to predicted cognitive outcomes after internal planning rather than ones that are discovered post-behavior, as found in the prior substage. The representation at this step is not quite divorced from action and the body, but is working toward that step.

That being said, contemporary research shows that representation never becomes divorced in full from the body, and indeed that the two are co-constitutive. To repeat, this conjecture is consistent with my model that, as adults, we yoke sensorimotor behavior to our more advanced thought processes, as needed. This is not to say that we reach for bowls and examine others for consequences that we could not foresee, or, perhaps on the other hand, we do in our moments of comedy, in ways that might be real or imagined.

Mirror Neurons

Model About the mirror neurons that seem involved in early embodied cognition, Needham and Libertus (2011) noted that they are localized in the premotor cortex and parietal lobe in macaque monkeys (di Pellegrino, Fadiga, Fogassi, Gallese, & Rizzolatti, 1992; Gallese, Fadiga, Fogassi, & Rizzolatti, 2002), and that they have been found in humans (Iacoboni, 2008; Rizzolatti & Craighero, 2004), including developmentally (Lepage & Theoret, 2007; Nystrom, 2008; Shimada & Hiraki, 2006). As we observe actions, the mirror system matches the observation with the motor system, providing a "sense" of action (Gallese, Rochat, Cossu, & Sinigaglia, 2009; Shapiro, 2009). Also, it is activated selectively by actions within our repertoire and also it is modifiable by experience (Buccino et al., 2004; Tai, Scherfler, Brooks, Sawamoto, & Castiello, 2004).

Evidence Saby, Meltzoff, and Marshall (2013) found that 14-month-olds exhibit somatotopic neural responses to viewing human actions. The results speak to the early origins of embodied cognition and its shared nature. Adults have been shown to demonstrate "neural somatotopy," in which viewing another person that is using a specific body part, such as a hand or foot, is associated with the corresponding activation in the viewer's brain of the matched brain area of the sensory strip, motor strip, or both.

To verify whether infants exhibit the phenomenon, Saby, Meltzoff, and Marshall (2013) had 14-month-olds watch an adult reach toward/touch an object (musical, spinning, colorful) using either the hand or foot (condition randomly assigned) in 2 s trials, with inter-trial intervals of 5.5 s. The investigators recorded electroencephalogram (EEG) scalp signals; event-related changes were analyzed in the EEG's sensorimotor mu rhythm. The results showed more mu rhythm desynchronization over sensorimotor cortex hand areas during hand action observation (vs. foot areas), and the reverse for foot action observation.

Saby et al. (2013) concluded that the simple act of watching someone's use of actions with a particular body part activates the infant observer's corresponding sensorimotor cortical areas. According to the authors, this developing somatotopic organization through intercorporal or self-other mapping, "supports" observational and rapid cultural learning in infancy.

The mu suppression response in EEG activity has been related to infants' observations of real and mimicked goal-directed actions. Mu suppression is a measure of the action observation/action execution matching system, commonly referred to as the mirror system. Warreyn et al. (2013) observed 18- to 30-month-olds during the aforementioned actions while recording EEG power data from frontal, central, and parietal sites. The central sites provided the strongest evidence of mirror system activity. Also, mu suppression correlated with imitation quality.

Comment Mirror neurons form a mirror neuron system that includes an integrated circuitry involving motor, cognitive, social, and related networks. They constitute a quintessential embodying mechanism. However, the biology of embodiment does not reside in this unique neural system. Surely, individual differences will be found related to genes, brain regions and their connectivity, and other aspects of the central and sympathetic nervous systems.

Embodiment by Age Period

In the following, I review points of view on embodiment that are specific to developmental periods. Embodiment has been related to the prenatal period right through to the adult one.

Prenatal

The research that has been undertaken in the prenatal and neonatal periods indicates the importance of early embodied experience in development. The results relate especially to motor planning and behavior but also to visual and visuomotor coordination.

Delafield-Butt and Gangopadhyay (2013) reviewed research indicating the validity of sensorimotor intentionality, or goal-directedness, even prenatally. At this age, intentionality is primary, prereflective, and preconceptual. Movements are guided, even prenatally, by prospection, or anticipation of future events. Cognition reflects an embodied agent in action even in this developmental phase; that is, there is a "proximal" prospectivity that anticipates the later development of a more complex, serial, distal (goal)-oriented one. The authors concluded that the origin of sensorimotor intentionality, even prenatally, in prospective agent action indicates the origins of intentionality "driving" development and learning.

According to Delafield-Butt and Gangopadhyay (2013), at 10- to 14-weeks gestation, actions express goal direction toward the body (Piontelli, 2010) and, at 14 weeks, motor planning is evident (Castiello et al., 2010). Prospective control is evident as fetuses reach to touch a twin (Piontelli, 2010).

Neonatal

As development proceeds, other findings suggest that there is continuity in early and later enaction. For example, neonates will engage in arm movements in order to achieve specific sensory effects (e.g., van der Meer & van der Weel, 2011).

Schilbach et al. (2013) claimed that social engagement is facilitated by the "mentalizing" network (Firth & Firth, 2008) and also by the "mirror" neuron system (Rizzolatti & Sinigaglia, 2010). The nonlinear dynamics characterizing the relational interactions, at times, even "constitute our awareness" of the minds of others. Developmentally, the system involved might even be present neonatally.

Lewis and Stack (2013) took issue with Schilbach et al.'s (2013) nativist approach to embodied cognition and presented a relation, action-based account. They conducted work in which they proposed that, after direct social interaction, the social representation that is developed persists at the "bifurcation point" of reduced social activity.

Wilkinson, Paikan, Gredebäck, Rea, and Metta (2014) proposed an embodied model of neonatal facial preference. Rather than considering it innate and reflective of monocular stimulus properties, they suggested it derived from system level, binocular-driven integration, or embodiment.

First 6 Months

Introduction The research on embodiment early in life underscores the intimate link between sensorimotor experience, brain, mirror neurons, and behavior. The work refers to embodiment processes as drivers of behavior, and it involved in anticipation, intention, and contextually-appropriate execution of behavior.

Glenberg (2010) made the broad claim that body-based processes influence all psychological processes, including those involving body morphology, sensory systems, motor systems, and emotions. For example, already in infants, physical development and associated changes in action function to "drive" cognitive and social development. Mirror neurons are involved in the latter (Gallese & Lakoff, 2005). Moore and Paulus (2013) emphasized the role of joint attention and joint goal-directed action in developing understanding of self and other as intentional agents.

Evidence Research has shown the intercoordinated nature of reaching by the arm with other bodily systems, as well as cognition. In this regard, at 4 ½ to 5 months of age, hand orientation coordinates with reaching to accommodate to different objects (Wentworth, Benson, & Haith, 2000).

The embodied intersubjectivity in caregiver–infant interactions includes word learning. Seidl, Tincoff, Baker, and Cristia (2015) found that experimenter touch facilitated word-finding in 4-month-olds during continuous speech. They proposed that direct caregiver–infant interactions are essential in "body part" word lexical acquisition (and also that acoustic emphasis helps in learning object words). They found that the touch cues facilitated specification of word boundaries related to body part words in the 4-month-olds.

6–12 Months

Perception de Klerk, Johnson, Heyes, and Southgate (2015) found that the development of perceptual-motor couplings in the brain in infancy is related to associative learning rather than an intrinsic connection between perception and action. Instead of experience merely shaping or refining existing perceptual-motor couplings from birth (e.g., Marshall, Young, & Meltzoff, 2011), it plays a critical role in their generation through correlated sensorimotor experience (e.g., Cook, Bird, Catmur, Press, & Heyes, 2014).

de Klerk et al. (2015) studied the stepping movements of pre-walking 7- to 9-month-olds. The infants were placed on a treadmill while they either contingently observed their own real-time leg movements or, for a control group, those of another infant. Another control group received visual experience only with stepping actions. Sensorimotor alpha suppression originates in the primary somatosensory cortex and, as measured by EEG, it is an index of sensorimotor cortex activation (having downstream modulation of the sensorimotor cortex by mirror neuron regions in the parietal and frontal cortices).

The results showed that, for the contingency group participants (during the training period), sensorimotor alpha suppression (cortical activation) at post-test was related to (as predicted by) a stronger contingency between visual-motor observed and performed stepping experiences. The authors concluded that, although other aspects of their results were not significant, the mechanism of perceptual-motor coupling in the infant brain is generation by experience of a correlated visuomotor nature.

A study by Corbetta, Friedman, and Bell (2014) demonstrated the embodied sensorimotor nature of infant cognition. They found that 12-month-old infants align their look to where they reach to search, at least for certain objects, rather than vice versa. They learn to map visual attention onto bodily-focused experience, in which they first spatially direct their movement using self-produced proprioceptive and haptic feedback, in a process of visuo-motor mapping. This leads to visual-elicited, prospective control of movement. The learning involved is not a top-down but a bottom-up process that involves coordinating reaching, proprioception, intrinsic arm movement dynamics, and the goal of the reaching in space. To conclude, the authors noted that intentions and arm movement mapping develops through sensorimotor experiences, in a "deeply embodied" process.

Cognition Rivière (2014) elaborated that, in embodied cognition, mind is embedded in the body through bodily interaction of the organism with the environment. This can take place without the requirement for modeling of the environment and other advanced cognitive processes, such as planning and decision-making but, instead, cannot be achieved without participatory engagement of the perceptual-motor system in action. The adaptive task is not to represent the environment but to continuously engage the body with it in order to achieve adaptive, coordinated behavior patterns.

For Rivière (2014), this enactive model of cognition applies quite readily to development. For example, Piaget described the A-not-B error that takes place in the latter half of the first year. As the infant attempts to solve more complex object permanence tasks, she or he can perseverate in seeking hidden objects under a first location (A, already successfully understood as the hiding spot of the object in question), after it is transferred to (B), at least when there is a delay of a few seconds before the search for the transferred object (from A to B) is permitted to take place.

Standard explanations of the A not B error invoke inhibitory limitations, insufficient working memory, and motor memory (the effect of prior reaches). Rivière (2014) proposed that automatic hand movements that are triggered by sensory signals are involved. The infants develop strong, entrenched motor habits/routines that impede performance rather than their failing due to representational constraints. The process of retrieving sensorimotor information mediates subsequent action. Rivière's model is consistent with that of Cisek (2012), in which decisions emerge as a multilevel, distributed consensus of various representations, some of which might be involved in sensorimotor control and others of which might relate to more abstract portions of behavior.

Social de Barbaro, Johnson, and Deák (2013) studied the development of "triadic" (child, mother, object) attention or play at 12 months of age, and its relationship to earlier mother–infant coordination. They found that, for the five infants studied longitudinally, changes in dyadic activity, as well as internal cognitive shifts, appeared reciprocally related to each other and built over sessions, in an approach that they considered reflective of embodied cognition.

Comment In the second 6 months of life, embodiment has been shown to involve perceptual, cognitive, and social consequences. Embodiment in infancy extends beyond the motor and visual of early life into relations with language development, as well, and even long-term academic development. The results emphasize not only the theoretical significance of early embodiment for development but also its long-term practical effects. Embodiment seems the participatory medium in which development takes place.

Year 2

Social Yu and Smith (2013) demonstrated that parents and infants coordinate object visual attention using eye–hand coordination, but without the traditional pathway of gaze following. They studied the moment-to-moment tracking of eye gaze in parents and in 13-month-olds as they played with toys.

The results revealed coordinated joint switches in visual attention, including looking simultaneously at the held toys. This goal-directed action did not involve gaze following. Instead, over the pairs, an eye–hand coupling pathway appeared predominant. Neither social partner dominated the joint attention. Hand actions of one or the other had direct effects on the other's looking, leading to rapid online coordination in visual attention.

Yu and Smith (2013) concluded that finding attention and sensitivity to hand actions in 1-year-olds is consistent with other research. Studies have shown that infants at this age have the ability to interpret the "causal" implications of gestures and movements (Olofson & Baldwin, 2011).

Adamson, Bakeman, Deckner, and Nelson (2014) showed the importance of joint engagement in early childhood. They studied social interaction in infancy, and the longitudinal results showed a relation to preschool conversational symbol-infused joint engagement (e.g., verbally expressed/mediated), and also with caregiver support.

Language Levy and McNeill (2013) argued that, already in the 1½-year-old, in narrative development, gestures help create simple referential functional constructions. In their study, imagistic gestures embodied discourse themes that had recurred, cementing narrative cohesion, or inter-utterance linkage (Halliday & Hasan, 1976). The authors concluded that speech is inseparable from the imagery embodied in gestures at this age, which constitutes the beginning of the shift to intralinguistic cohesion.

Comment Research in 1-year-olds related to embodiment emphasizes behavioral effects on brain activity. Visual activities alone reflect embodied processes and they are active in social embodiment, as well. There are language and social factors to consider, as well.

Children

Causality Göksun, George, Hirsh-Pasek, and Golinkoff (2013) examined whether preschoolers could understand not just simple but also interacting dual forces as they impact the movement of objects. In an ingenious methodology, a foam ball exiting a slanted tube (cause) could be either facilitated or impeded in its motion by the "wind" of a hairdryer (enabled, prevented, respectively). After practice trials, in the test phase of the "board" game that had been set up, the children had to predict the end point of the ball.

The experiment was based on "force dynamics" theory (Wolff, 2007), which has been applied to language, in particular. The findings revealed that preschool children mostly understood the force interactions behind each type of causal situation; and this could happen even at a developmental period that preceded acquisition of the capacity for verbal representations of the forces/causes. Also, in their judgments of ball direction and end point in the board game, the older preschool children understood better the integration of two forces.

Therefore, young children seem to understand causal events that are more complex than Michottian collisions. They realize that causal agents can coordinate. That children at this age can focus on two causal dimensions simultaneously suggests that Piaget's (1955) concept of egocentrism, or the one-dimensional focusing found in preschoolers, does not apply to this type of task. Children's representations of causality at this age suggest the steps toward development of understanding complex causal events.

In addition, I note that the findings by Göksun et al. (2013) are consistent with the point of view of embodied cognition. The causes understood early in life reflect the forces impacting children and the ones that they can affect themselves.

Language/Gesture For children, physical manipulation of toys that were represented in stories improved children's comprehension of the stories. The same occurred with imagined manipulation (Glenberg, Goldberg, & Zhu, 2011; Glenberg, Gutierrez, Levin, Japuntich, & Kaschak, 2004).

Berk (2013) reviewed an aspect of cognitive development related to embodiment. Speech-gesture mismatches occur when gestures reveal more than verbal statements as children try to solve problems. Goldin-Meadow (2003, 2006) showed that children who received instruction following a speech-gesture mismatch were more likely than others to learn match problems. This assumes that children who produce speech-gesture mismatches are in a transitional state. Children in this state seem to have strategies that are accessible to gesture but not to verbal acts (Goldin-Meadow, 2002), facilitating awareness of conflicting ideas. Parents and teachers can help children use gestures. Adults who gesture while teaching help children to use their hands as they learn, which leads to improved performance (Goldin-Meadow, Cook, & Mitchell, 2009). Goldin-Meadow (2005) noted that adults would teach more problem-solving strategies to children who expressed mismatches compared to children who did not (Goldin-Meadow & Singer, 2003). The mechanism imputed to explain how working with speech-gesture mismatches in transition states involves the facilitation of representation of thoughts not yet amenable to verbal representation, which helps in executive (working memory) function (Ping & Goldin-Meadow, 2010). Similarly, Mumford and Kita (2014) found an embodied cognitive effect in 3-year-olds. Iconic gestures helped map novel verbs to specific referents.

Cook, Duffy, and Fenn (2013) conducted a study with second- to fourth-graders that illustrates that embodiment facilitates consolidation and transfer of learning. In mathematical training that involved equations having two sides, it helped to sweep the left hand back and forth under the left half of the equation and the right hand under the right half. The gestural activity helped in this task because they might lead to simulation of motor action, activation of relevant motor regions, facilitation of a "more proceduralized" representation, and creation of a more "enduring" memory.

The embodied account of development has been extended into moral reasoning. Beaudoin-Ryan and Goldin-Meadow (2014) showed that requiring gestures (encouraging to gesture) in fifth-graders during moral reasoning tasks led to more sophisticated problem-solving strategies (more multiple perspectives) and also to profiting from a lesson in more reasoning. The authors concluded that gestures allow (child) learners to spatialize non-spatial ideas, affording the use of spatial learning mechanisms. I note that the technique might help better integrate interhemispheric communication and bihemispheric use in the problem-solving involved.

Comment Embodied processes in the child reflect not only language and cognitive development but also causal understanding. The force dynamics of actions and in the world appear related to the core of developmental processes and products.

For the next section on embodiment in adults, I refer to just a few studies. A full review of this research is beyond the scope of the present work. Moreover, the general model has been presented in Chap. 5.

Adults

Language Zwaan (2014) presented a model of language comprehension that integrates both abstract symbols and grounding involving perception and action. The latter includes sensorimotor experience. The context that permits the pluralist model (it involves five levels of situational embeddedness, with abstract concepts the fifth), concerns narrative, which becomes a chief site of embodied language.

Pulvermuller and Garagnani (2014) suggested that long-term memories are more embodied than elements residing in working memory. Zwaan (2014) suggested that the degree of embodiment in language comprehension depends on the degree of environmental embeddedness involved.

Comment No matter the age, embodiment processes not only appear to complement acquisitions related to perception, cognition, reasoning, problem solving, language, and sociality, but also they facilitate, promote, and even allow for them, creating an integrated field of body, action, feedback, brain, mind, person, and environment. Embodiment processes are not merely tangential to behavior, but *are* behavior.

This section of the chapter on the embodiment model has considered not only the model but also evidence for it over the lifespan. The next section of the chapter considers the systems theory model of behavior. This next section completes examination of three major models that have been presented in the book for their developmental roots.

System Theory

General Model

Recent Griffiths and Tabery (2013) explained that a systems view of development includes hierarchical levels. Therefore, superordinate ones can exert top-down influence or causation through inter-level relations and their action on inter-level ones (Craver & Bechtel, 2007). The larger causal mechanisms produce changes in its parts. Bechtel and Abrahamsen (2010) also noted that dynamic explanations at the mechanistic level involve decomposition and re-composition. Greenberg, Callina, and Mueller (2013) similarly underscored the importance in development of dynamical systems concepts, including self-organization and emergence in an integrated biopsychosocial model.

Richardson (2013) elaborated that, in dynamical systems, states hover in the region of far-from-equilibrium, criticality, or the edge of chaos. This transition region permits the states to engage in maximum information exchange, novel adaptiveness, and readiness to shift basins of attraction (attractors). This permits harmonious, coordinated, system-wide response to perturbation across multiple nonlinear relations. In this regard, systems evidence global reorganization akin to a ballet, symphony, or orchestra, yet with no conductor present, for example, as found in bacteria (e.g., Buescher et al., 2012). Even slime moulds are being described as having "learning and memory," and also unicellular prokaryotes as having knowledge, intelligence, "thinking," and cognitive resources (e.g., del Moral, González, Navarro, & Marijuán, 2011).

As for our senses, they are active, having a structure-search and abstraction function. Signals are transformed early in transmission into patterns or neural connections and correlates rather than remaining independent and static. The relational patterns that are abstracted serve to function as attractor basins in nested hierarchies of attractor landscapes. The resulting networks are optimized to detect and interpret novel data, yet allow for multiple "expressions" for feeding forward. The brain then can elaborate actions that are more adaptive because the seemingly disordered world that has been forwarded to it is more predictable. Nevertheless, the brain at this level is flexible or experience-responsive, creating a "dynamical brain" that operates robustly (Tschacher & Haken, 2007).For Richardson (2013), cognitive function expresses an emergent activity. It can generate more complex, powerful intelligence from its own activity. He draws a comparison with this concept to Piaget's (1970/1988) concept of "reflective abstraction." Either way, the organism can "transcend immediate experience," which I take to mean that the organism is not simply passively buffeted by the environment.

Richardson (2013) continued that individuals coordinate in ways analogous to neurons. They form "epicognitive" patterns that are emergent from their joint activity. At a further superordinate level, culture is created.

Richardson (2013) concluded that experience with cultural tools or procedures can change brain networks (e.g., May, 2011). Finally, "epicognitive regulations" among individuals can serve to "greatly expand" the collective intelligence or "cognomen."

I would add that culture can be described as a collective attractor landscape replete with multiple, coordinated levels across groups and individuals that render it highly adaptive and ever changing, and also novelty seeking, in order to better promote and increase its "intelligence complexity" and power of its activity. In this regard, in Young (2011), I referred to adult intelligence as a collective intelligence (both for the individual as the person creates superordinate abstract structures and for the group intelligence that individuals create, e.g., in brainstorming).

Witherington and Heying (2013) considered the holistic, inter-level coordinative nature of systems, advocating for causal explanations that include both parts-to-whole and whole-to-parts aspects. The organizational whole can exert a top-down influence not because it acts on lower levels but because it is a unitary structure of which its constituent elements are constitutively influenced by it, so that it is both subject and object. The whole gives meaningful context to bottom-up, real-time, local dynamics of the parts.

Huys, Perdikis, and Jirsa (2014) presented a dynamical model of sensorimotor behavior. They contrasted their approach with each of the computational, equilibrium point, free energy/active influence, and ecological models. The latter two views, in particular, are consistent with, or informative of, the dynamic approach (e.g., Adams, Shipp, & Friston, 2013; Friston, 2011; Gibson, 1966; Warren, 2006, respectively).

The dynamical approach is founded on the concept of self-organized pattern formation (e.g., Haken, 1983) and dynamical systems theory (e.g., Perko, 2006). It describes functional architecture in sequential movements as structured flows on manifolds. Functional modes emerge and bind one after the other. Each of them corresponds to an invariant structure in phase space topology that can be accommodated to task constraints in the quantitative aspects of the flow involved.

Other Spencer, Perone, and Buss (2011) considered the systems view as a meta-approach. Self-organization is essential to this perspective. Developmental structure and organization come "for free," without a master controller. Nonlinear and time-dependent interactions over the multiple levels of high-dimensional systems take place. Systems intrinsically create patterns, including qualitatively different emergent ones (e.g., new attractors) in freely-combined ongoing soft assemblies. Each second, body and brain engage in continual dialogue, even in cognition (Spencer, Perone, & Johnson, 2009). For Spencer et al. (2011), the concept of soft assembly renders it difficult to define (sub)system components, as well as to discern the "cause" of behavior. For the latter, different behavioral outcomes occur because of variations in context and one's history. They concluded that the systems approach needs to integrate development from the ongoing moment to moment time scale to the long-term one (see Fig. 17.5; Smith & Thelen, 2003).

Fogel (2011) continued with the theme of moment and long-term time frames. He contended that change can be found in the stability of real-time, microscopic behavior, and also that this type of developmental change seeds macroscopic ones. System constituents impose self-regulatory constraints on patterns (e.g., attractors). In developmental systems, time scales are embedded. For example, an infant's smile or reach is soft-assembled each time according to context and history (e.g., Fogel & Garvey, 2007). As development proceeds and new regimes self-organize, historical and emerging frames might co-exist by way of "bridging" frames that allow them to experience less stress or trauma in abrupt shifting.

van Geert (2011) described a property of dynamic systems that speaks to the approach's applicability to development. He wrote that dynamic systems are complex, by displaying a combination of orderliness and randomness. Intriguingly, he noted that the microscopic random

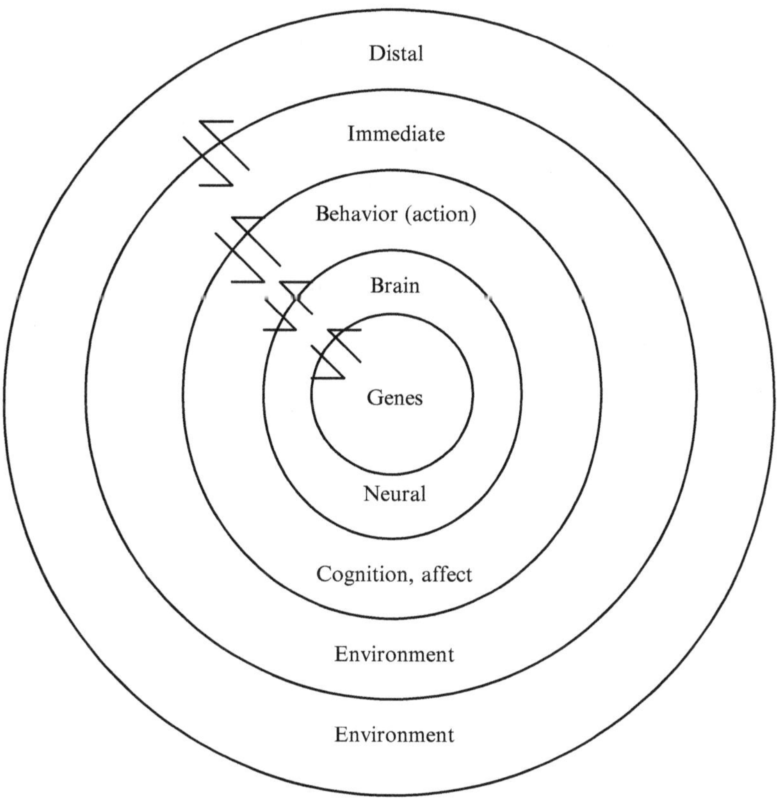

Fig. 17.5 Dynamic systems theory levels needing integration. Dynamic systems theory needs to formally integrate the different reciprocally interacting levels in the biopsychosocial approach. Adapted from Spencer et al. (2011)

erratic behavior of the components of a system directly relates to and maintains its macroscopic orderliness. At the latter level, each state is determined by its history of prior states but, nevertheless, any state can evolve along different pathways, even emergent and novel ones, depending on its evolution rule or "term."

Lewis (2011) discussed developmental trajectories in terms of alternations between turbulent phase transitions and normative stages, as in cognitive development. He noted that Neo-Piagetians began including dynamicist notions in their cognitive developmental models (Case et al., 1996; Fischer & Bidell, 2006).

Witherington and Margett (2011) queried whether the dynamical approach is more consistent with Piaget's constructionist stage approach (Piaget, 1952, 1954) or with Gibson's more empirical approach to development (Gibson, 1979, 1982; Gibson & Pick, 2000). For Piaget, the child and environment are constitutive components that serve to structure each other, and knowledge acquisition depends on this interaction. For Gibson, the environment provides "objective affordances" that the child has to "discover." For Witherington and Margett (2011), both approaches can be considered compatible with a dynamic systems approach because both are "relational" and depend on child "activity."

As for causality in systems, Witherington (2011) described circular causality between micro- and macro-dynamics. However, the bottom-up, local-to-global direction is "privileged" compared to the global-to-local, downward one. Nevertheless, all levels in a system engage in reciprocal interactions. Systems, through their interrelated level interactions, can help explain embodiment in behavior, including cognitively (e.g., Thelen, Schöner, Scheier, & Smith, 2001).

Witherington (2011) elaborated that the dynamical systems approach to causality is pluralistic and allows for emergence through self-organizational circular causality in structure-function cycling. Causality is "irreducible" and cannot be described simply in terms of lower-order levels. Upper levels are just as "causally effective" as lower-order ones. The process is "bidirectional" between lower and upper levels. System causality is integral to the whole system, and cannot be decomposed into part–part relations. The local and the global move together, with neither privileged. Contextualist approaches emphasize local processes; but organismic-contextualist ones do not. The whole system organization is what "imparts meaning" to lower-order components and their relationships as much as the lower-order levels are "generative" of upper levels. The upper levels help create the "boundary conditions" enabling their self-organizational stability, and their ability to head off "dissipative" processes. When systems regulate energy and matter flow this way, they "embody" circular causality. Self-organization establishes stability at "far-from-equilibrium" conditions in a downward causation from upper levels. In this sense, systems express "agency."

Witherington (2011) summarized the position of Deacon (2003, 2006) on first-, second-, and third-order emergence. In first-order emergence, as in thermodynamically basic systems, each emergence is local and does not influence future ones, such as in the successive changes of state of water. In second-order emergence, the prior system state constrains future ones by downward causation. In third-order emergence, the history of prior states has a cumulative effect, as in development.

Neural Model

Perone and Spencer (2013) presented a dynamical systems-based model of infant habituation, referred to as the Dynamic Neural Field (DNF) model. It supports the view that infants learn dynamically as they engage in exploratory looking to and away from a stimulus.

Schöner and Thelen's (2006) DNF model for neural network models of infant behavior in looking tasks consists of coupled excitatory and inhibitory layers. Looking is generated by excitatory layer activation. The excitatory layer activation also generates inhibition (and a decline in looking) by way of suppression of the excitatory layer. This particular DNF model does not include a long-term learning component, which Perone and Spencer (2013) addressed in their modified DNF model.

In Perone and Spencer's (2013) integrated DNF model, layers of neurons are organized by functional topography along continuous dimensions (metrics, e.g., color). These DNF layers consist of neighboring or "similarly tuned" neurons that mutually excite each other while inhibiting neurons tuned dissimilarly. This type of neural interaction is common in the nervous system—local excitatory/lateral inhibitory dynamics (e.g., Fuster, 2003). The DNF layers constitute lower levels of the neural "attractor" states in which they enter (a "higher dimensional space").

Neural attractor states oscillate between resting, self-stabilizing ones during stimulation, and self-sustaining ones after stimulation, e.g., to keep items in working memory (WM). When stimuli reach thresholds (above localized peak activity thresholds), they leave an activation trace in a superordinate neural cell assembly, or Hebbian learning layer of the system, which feeds back into the perceptual field. Connections among previously excited neurons become strengthened, and the neural response to subsequent stimuli of the same order is strengthened. When the DNF excitatory and inhibitory layers engage in stronger interaction (stronger local excitation/lateral inhibition), and this interaction is accompanied by Hebbian learning layer activation, as well, the overall system can enter into a self-sustaining state. For stimuli that are "re-presented," WM becomes more easily self-sustaining and keeps relevant items in memory, which also happens through this process of reaching stable peak activation and its associated effects. As for differences between infant and adult DNFs, the process is more gradual in infants and learning plays a more important role.

DNF has been applied to infant motor behavior (Schöner & Dineave, 2007; Thelen et al., 2001). The DNF is conceived as a distribution of neural activation applicable to a relevant aspect of behavior. Neuronal interactions/recurrences "drive" the systems involved. Localized peaks of activation (governed by a "movement parameter"), for one target or another (e.g., in the case of reaching), are influenced by attention, task, context, and behavioral (prior reaching) history.

In neural dynamics, neural interactions stabilize local excitatory peaks and, in addition, global inhibitory interactions contain competing responses. When the system is unstable, new stable states possibly might emerge. Developmentally, instabilities in neural regimes characterize the developmental state prior to the growth in behavior that emerges after "boosting" of activation levels in interaction-dominated regimes. Different stable solutions might materialize, depending on past and present system configuration. Moreover, the changes might be graded/continuous or abrupt/discontinuous ones.

Comment

In Young (2011), I considered the systems model crucial to understanding the mechanisms that drive behavior. The review of present systems conceptualizations in this regard gives further support to this notion. The biopsychosocial and embodiment perspectives described previously in this chapter are quite integrative. However, they need the process account of change in the systems model as a complement.

Chapter Conclusions

The research in the area of theory of mind/false belief and executive function/inhibition illustrates the burgeoning work in developmental psychology, but also the need for more integrative models. The period of infancy for the study of both theory of mind/false belief and executive function/inhibition has been described as the time for rapid and major, advanced acquisitions, yet others have called for a more conservative interpretation of the data involved. For example, in the conservative approach, for early theory of mind/false-belief research, the more plausible view is that early abstractions are quite limited, at best, if not absent, and that advocating for core, innate modules in these areas is premature, if not misplaced.

One way of understanding the research in the area is to view the development of theory of mind/false belief and executive function/inhibition from the point of view of Neo-Piagetian modeling (Young, 2011). Another is to consider their relation to the other models described in this chapter. For example, taking the perspective of the other appears to involve parallel embodied processes even early in life through the mirror neuron system. Moreover, a broad understanding of any developmental phenomenon should consider the biopsychosocial model. Finally, dynamical system theory can help explicate transition mechanisms. There is much integrative theoretical work needed on the question of early, supposedly sophisticated, and innate or prepared acquisitions, as demonstrated in these three developmental chapters in the present book that have been presented. In this regard, rather than seeking all-or-none modeling solutions one way or another about innate and gradual approaches to early infant acquisitions, Piagetian-type modeling could provide the needed scaffold for an integrative account both through the capacities that its schema-based cognitive development affords and the transitions it describes in infancy from one developmental substage to the next.

References

Adams, R. A., Shipp, S., & Friston, K. J. (2013). Predictions not commands: Active inference in the motor system. *Brain Structure and Function, 218*, 611–643.

Adamson, L. B., Bakeman, R., Deckner, D. F., & Nelson, P. B. (2014). From interactions to conversations: The development of joint engagement during early childhood. *Child Development, 85*, 941–955.

Antonucci, S. M., & Alt, M. (2011). A lifespan perspective on semantic processing of concrete concepts: Does a sensory/motor model have the potential to bridge the gap? *Cognitive, Affective, & Behavioral Neuroscience, 11*, 551–572.

Arsalidou, M., Pascual-Leone, J., Johnson, J., Morris, D., & Taylor, M. J. (2013). A balancing act of the brain: Activations and deactivations driven by cognitive load. *Brain and Behavior, 3*, 273–285.

Baillargeon, R., Scott, R. M., He, Z., Sloane, S., Setoh, P., Jin, K-S., Wu, D., & Bian, L. (2014). Psychological and sociomoral reasoning in infancy. In M. Mikulincer & P. R. Shaver (Eds.), E. Borgida & J. A. Bargh (Assoc. Eds.), *APA handbook of personality and social psychology: Attitudes and social cognition* (Vol. 1, pp. 79–150). Washington, DC: American Psychological Association.

Barkley, R. A. (1997). Behavioral inhibition, sustained attention, and executive functions: Constructing a unifying theory of ADHD. *Psychological Bulletin, 121*, 65–94.

Baumeister, R. F. (2008). Free will in scientific psychology. *Perspectives on Psychological Science, 3*, 14–19.

Baumeister, R. F., Vohs, K. D., & Tice, D. M. (2007). The strength model of self-control. *Current Directions in Psychological Science, 16*, 351–355.

Beaudoin-Ryan, L., & Goldin-Meadow, S. (2014). Teaching moral reasoning through gesture. *Developmental Science, 17*, 984–990.

Bechtel, W., & Abrahamsen, A. (2010). Dynamic mechanistic explanation: Computational modeling of circadian rhythms as an exemplar for cognitive science. *Studies in the History and Philosophy of Science, 41*, 321–333.

Bell, M. A., & Cuevas, K. (2012). Psychobiology of executive function in early development. In J. A. Griffin, L. S. Freund, & P. McCardle (Eds.), *Executive function in preschool age children: Integrating measurement, neurodevelopment and translational research.* Washington: American Psychological Association.

Berger, A., Alyagon, U., Hadaya, H., Atzaba-Poria, N., & Auerbach, J. G. (2013). Response inhibition in preschoolers at familial risk for attention deficit hyperactivity disorder: A behavioral and electrophysiological stop-signal study. *Child Development, 84*, 1616–1632.

Berk, M. (2013). The DSM-5: Hyperbole, hope, or hypothesis? *BioMed Central Medicine, 11*, 128. doi:10.1186/1741-7015-11-128.

Bickel, W. K., Quisenberry, A. J., Moody, L., & Wilson, A. G. (2014). Therapeutic opportunities for self-control repair in addiction and related disorders: Change and the limits of change in trans-disease processes. *Clinical Psychological Science, 3*, 140–153.

Bjork, R. A., Dunlosky, J., & Kornell, N. (2013). Self-regulated learning: Beliefs, techniques, and illusions. *Annual Review of Psychology, 64*, 417–444.

Blackwell, K. A., & Munakata, Y. (2014). Costs and benefits linked to developments in cognitive control. *Developmental Science, 17*, 203–211.

Bornstein, M. H., Hahn, C.-S., & Suwalsky, J. T. D. (2013). Physically developed and exploratory young infants contribute to their own long-term academic achievement. *Psychological Science, 24*, 1906–1917.

Buccino, G., Lui, F., Canessa, N., Patteri, I., Lagravinese, G., Benuzzi, F., et al. (2004). Neural circuits involved in the recognition of actions performed by nonconspecifics: An FMRI study. *Journal of Cognitive Neuroscience, 16*, 114–126.

Buescher, J. M., Leibermeister, W., Jules, M., Uhr, M., Muntel, J., Botella, E., et al. (2012). Global network reorganizing during dynamic adaptations of *Bacillus subtilis* metabolism. *Science, 335*, 1099–1103.

Bunge, S. A., Dudukovic, N. M., Thomason, M. E., Vaidya, C. J., & Gabrieli, J. D. E. (2002). Immature frontal lobe contributions to cognitive control in children: Evidence from fMRI. *Neuron, 33*, 301–311.

Butler, L. P., & Markman, E. M. (2012). Finding the cause: Verbal framing helps children extract causal

evidence embedded in a complex scene. *Journal of Cognition and Development, 13*, 38–66.
Campbell, A. (2012). The study of sex differences: Feminism and biology. *Zeitschrift für Psychologie [Journal of Psychology], 220*, 137–143.
Carruthers, P. (2013). Mindreading in infancy. *Mind and Language, 28*, 141–172.
Case, R., Okamoto, Y., Griffin, S., McKeough, A., Bleiker, C., Henderson, B., & Stephenson, K. M. (1996). The role of central conceptual structures in the development of children's thought. *Monographs of the Society for Research in Child Development, 61*, i+iii-vi+1-295.
Castellano, F. X., & Tannock, R. (2002). Neuroscience of attention-deficit hyperactivity disorder: The search for endophenotypes. *Nature Reviews in Neuroscience, 3*, 617–628.
Castiello, U. B., Cristina Zoia, S., Nelini, C., Sartori, L., Blason, L., D'Ottavio, G., et al. (2010). Wired to be social: The ontogeny of human interaction. *PLoS One, 5*, e13199. doi:10.1371/journal.pone.0013199.
Chemero, A. (2009). *Radical embodied cognitive science*. Cambridge, MA: MIT Press.
Chevalier, N., Martis, S. B., Curran, T., & Munakata, Y. (2015). Metacognitive processes in executive control development: The case of reactive and proactive control. *Journal of Cognitive Neuroscience, 27*, 1125–1136.
Choi, Y.-J., & Luo, Y. (2015). 13-month-olds' understanding of social interaction. *Psychological Science, 26*, 274–283.
Chou, K.-H., Cheng, Y., Chen, I.-Y., Lin, C.-P., & Chu, W.-C. (2011). Sex-linked white matter microstructure of the social and analytic brain. *NeuroImage, 54*, 725–733.
Cimpian, A., & Erickson, L. C. (2012). The effect of generic statements on children's causal attributions: Questions of mechanism. *Developmental Psychology, 48*, 159–170.
Cisek, P. (2012). Making decisions through a distributed consensus. *Current Opinion in Neurobiology, 22*, 927–935.
Clark, A. (2013). Whatever next? Predictive brains, situated agents, and the future of cognitive science. *Behavioral and Brain Sciences, 36*, 1–24.
Cook, R., Bird, G., Catmur, C., Press, C., & Heyes, C. (2014). Mirror neurons: From origin to function. *Behavioral and Brain Sciences, 37*, 177–192.
Cook, S. W., Duffy, R. G., & Fenn, K. M. (2013). Consolidation and transfer of learning after observing hand gesture. *Child Development, 84*, 1863–1871.
Corbetta, D., Friedman, D. R., & Bell, M. A. (2014). Brain reorganization as a function of walking experience in 12-month-old infants: Implications for the development of manual laterality. *Frontiers in Psychology, 5*, 245. doi:10.3389/fpsyg.2014.00245.
Courvoisier, D. S., Renaud, R., Geiser, C., Paskchke, K., Gaudy, K., & Jordan, K. (2013). Sex hormones and mental rotation: An intensive longitudinal investigation. *Hormones and Behavior, 63*, 345–351.
Craver, C. F., & Bechtel, W. (2007). Top-down causation without top-down causes. *Biology and Philosophy, 22*, 547–563.
Cuevas, K., & Bell, M. A. (2013). Infant attention and early childhood executive function. *Child Development, 85*, 397–404.
Cuevas, K., Deater-Deckard, K., Kim-Spoon, J., Watson, A. J., Morasch, K. C., & Bell, M. A. (2014). What's mom got to do with it? Contributions of maternal executive function and caregiving to the development of executive function across early childhood. *Developmental Science, 17*, 224–238.
de Barbaro, K., Johnson, C. M., & Deák, G. O. (2013). Twelve-month "social revolution" emerges from mother-infant sensorimotor coordination: A longitudinal investigation. *Human Development, 56*, 223–248.
de Klerk, C. C. J. M., Johnson, M. H., Heyes, C. M., & Southgate, V. (2015). Baby steps: Investigating the development of perceptual-motor couplings in infancy. *Developmental Science, 18*, 270–280.
Deacon, T. W. (2003). The hierarchic logic of emergence: Untangling the interdependence of evolution and self-organization. In B. H. Weber & D. J. Depew (Eds.), *Evolution and learning: The Baldwin effect reconsidered* (pp. 273–308). Cambridge, MA: MIT Press.
Deacon, T. W. (2006). Emergence: The hole at the well's hub. In P. Clayton & P. Davies (Eds.), *The re-emergence of emergence: The emergentist hypothesis from science to religion* (pp. 11–150). Oxford, UK: Oxford University Press.
Delafield-Butt, J. T., & Gangopadhyay, N. (2013). Sensorimotor intentionality: The origins of intentionality in prospective agent action. *Developmental Review, 33*, 399–425.
del Moral, R., González, M., Navarro, J., & Marijuán, P. C. (2011). From genomics to scientomics: Expanding the bioinformation paradigm. *Information, 2*, 651–671.
Denissen, J. J. A., van Aken, M. A. G., Penke, L., & Wood, D. (2013). Self-regulation underlies temperament and personality: An integrative developmental framework. *Child Development Perspectives, 7*, 255–260.
Devine, R. T., & Hughes, C. (2014). Relations between false belief understanding and executive function in early childhood: A meta-analysis. *Child Development, 85*, 1777–1794.
Diamond, A. (1985). Development of the ability to use recall to guide action, as indicated by infants' performance on A-not-B. *Child Development, 56*, 868–883.
Diamond, A. (1990). Developmental time course in human infants and infant monkeys, and the neural bases, of inhibitory control in reaching. *Annals of the New York Academy of Sciences, 608*, 637–676.
Diamond, A. (1991). Neuropsychological insights intro the meaning of object concept development. In S. Carey & R. Gelman (Eds.), *The epigenesis of mind: Essays on biology and cognition* (pp. 67–110). Hillsdale, NJ: Erlbaum.
Diamond, A. (2012). Activities and programs that improve children's executive functions. *Current Directions in Psychological Science, 21*, 335–341.
Diamond, A. (2013). Executive functions. *Annual Review of Psychology, 64*, 135–168.

Diaz, A., & Eisenberg, N. (2015). The process of emotion regulation is different from individual differences in emotion regulation: Conceptual arguments and a focus on individual differences. *Psychological Inquiry, 26*, 37–47.

Dice, J. L., & Dove, M. K. (2011). A Piagetian approach to infant referential behaviors. *Infant Behavior & Development, 34*, 481–486.

di Pellegrino, G., Fadiga, L., Fogassi, L., Gallese, V., & Rizzolatti, G. (1992). Understanding motor events: A neurophysiological study. *Experimental Brain Research, 191*, 176–180.

Dunbar, R. I. M. (2014). The social brain: Psychological underpinnings and implications for the structure of organization. *Current Directions in Psychological Science, 23*, 109–114.

Duque, J., Olivier, E., & Rushworth, M. (2013). Top-down inhibitory control exerted by the medial frontal cortex during action selection under conflict. *Journal of Cognitive Neuroscience, 25*, 1634–1648.

Eagly, A. H., & Wood, W. (2013). The nature-nurture debates: 25 years of challenges in understanding the psychology of gender. *Perspectives on Psychological Science, 8*, 340–357.

Engelhardt, L. E., Briley, D. A., Mann, F. D., Harden, K. P., & Tucker-Drob, E. M. (2015). Genes unite executive functions in childhood. *Psychological Science, 26*, 1151–1163.

Estes, Z., & Felker, S. (2012). Confidence mediates the sex difference in mental rotation performance. *Archives of Sexual Behavior, 4*, 557–570.

Firth, C. D., & Firth, U. (2008). Implicit and explicit processes in social cognition. *Neuron, 60*, 503–510.

Fischer, K. W., & Bidell, T. R. (2006). Dynamic development of action, thought, and emotion. In W. Damon & R. M. Lerner (Eds.), *Theoretical models of human development: Handbook of child psychology* (6th ed., pp. 313–399). New York: Wiley.

Fogel, A. (2011). Theoretical and applied dynamic systems research in developmental science. *Child Development Perspectives, 5*, 267–272.

Fogel, A., & Garvey, A. (2007). Alive communication. *Infant Behavior and Development, 30*, 251–257.

Friedman, N. P., Miyake, A., Robinson, J. L., & Hewitt, J. K. (2011). Developmental trajectories in toddlers' self-restraint predict individual differences in executive functions 14 years later: A behavioral genetic analysis. *Developmental Psychology, 47*, 1410–1430.

Friedman, N. P., Miyake, A., Young, S. E., DeFries, J. C., Corley, R. P., & Hewitt, J. K. (2008). Individual differences in executive functions are almost entirely genetic in origin. *Journal of Experimental Psychology: General, 137*, 201–225.

Friston, K. (2011). What is optimal about motor control? *Neuron, 72*, 488–498.

Fuster, J. M. (2003). *Cortex and mind: Unifying cognition*. New York: Oxford University Press.

Gallese, V., Fadiga, L., Fogassi, L., & Rizzolatti, G. (2002). Action representation and the inferior parietal lobule. In W. Prinz & B. Hommel (Eds.), *Common mechanisms in perception and action: Attention and performance* (Vol. XIX, pp. 334–355). New York: Oxford University Press.

Gallese, V., & Lakoff, G. (2005). The brain's concepts: The role of the sensory-motor system in conceptual knowledge. *Cognitive Neuropsychology, 21*, 1–26.

Gallese, V., Rochat, M., Cossu, G., & Sinigaglia, C. (2009). Motor cognition and its role in the phylogeny and ontogeny of action and understanding. *Developmental Psychology, 45*, 103–113.

Gandolfi, E., Viterbori, P., Traverso, L., & Usai, M. C. (2014). Inhibitory processes in toddlers: A latent-variable approach. *Frontiers in Psychology, 5*, 381. doi:10.3389/fpsyg.2014.00381.

Gergely, G., & Watson, J. S. (1999). Early socio-emotional development: Contingency perception and the social-biofeedback model. In P. Rochat (Ed.), *Early social cognition: Understanding others in first months of life* (pp. 101–136). Mahwah, NJ: Erlbaum.

Gerson, S. A., & Woodward, A. L. (2014). Learning from their own actions: The unique effect of producing actions on infant's action understanding. *Child Development, 85*, 264–277.

Gibson, E. J. (1982). The concept of affordances in development: The renascence of functionalism. In W. A. Collins (Ed.), *The Minnesota Symposia on Child Psychology* (The concept of development, Vol. 15, pp. 55–81). Mahwah, NJ: Erlbaum.

Gibson, E. J., & Pick, A. D. (2000). *An ecological approach to perceptual learning and development*. New York: Oxford University Press.

Gibson, J. J. (1966). *The sense considered as perceptual systems*. Boston, MA: Houghton Mifflin.

Gibson, J. J. (1979). *The ecological approach to visual perception*. Hillsdale, NJ: Erlbaum.

Glenberg, A. M. (2010). Embodiment as a unifying perspective for psychology. *Wiley Interdisciplinary Reviews: Cognitive Science, 1*, 586–596.

Glenberg, A. M., Goldberg, A., & Zhu, X. (2011). Improving early reading comprehension using embodied CAI. *Instructional Science, 39*, 27–39.

Glenberg, A. M., Gutierrez, T., Levin, J. R., Japuntich, S., & Kaschak, M. P. (2004). Activity and imagined activity can enhance young children's reading comprehension. *Journal of Educational Psychology, 96*, 424–436.

Göksun, T., George, N. R., Hirsh-Pasek, K., & Golinkoff, R. M. (2013). Forces and motion: How young children understand causal events. *Child Development, 84*, 1285–1295.

Goldin-Meadow, S. (2002). Constructing communication by hand. *Cognitive Development, 17*, 1385–1405.

Goldin-Meadow, S. (2003). *Hearing gesture: How our hands help us think*. Cambridge, MA: Harvard University Press.

Goldin-Meadow, S. (2005). Gesture in social interactions: A mechanism for cognitive change. In B. D. Homer & C. S. Tamis-LeMonda (Eds.), *The development of social cognition and communication* (pp. 259–283). Mahwah, NJ: Erlbaum.

Goldin-Meadow, S. (2006). Talking and thinking with our hands. *Current Directions in Psychological Science, 15*, 34–39.

Goldin-Meadow, S., Cook, S. W., & Mitchell, Z. A. (2009). Gesturing saves cognitive resources when talking about nonpresent objects. *Cognitive Science, 34*, 602–619.

Goldin-Meadow, S., & Singer, M. A. (2003). From children's hands to adults' ears: Gesture's role in the learning process. *Developmental Psychology, 39*, 509–520.

Gopnik, A., & Wellman, H. M. (2012). Reconstructing constructivism: Causal models, Bayesian learning mechanisms, and the theory. *Psychological Bulletin, 138*, 1085–1108.

Greenberg, G., Callina, K. S., & Mueller, M. K. (2013). Emergence, self-organization and developmental science. In R. M. Lerner & J. B. Benson (Eds.), *Advances in child development and behavior. Embodiment and epigenesis: Theoretical and methodological issues in understanding the role of biology within the relational development system. Part A: Philosophical, theoretical, and biological dimensions* (Vol. 44, pp. 95–126). Waltham, MA: Academic Press.

Griffiths, P. E., & Tabery, J. (2013). Developmental systems theory: What does it explain, and how does it explain it? In R. M. Lerner & J. B. Benson (Eds.), *Advances in child development and behavior. Embodiment and epigenesis: Theoretical and methodological issues in understanding the role of biology within the relational development system. Part A: Philosophical, theoretical, and biological dimensions* (Vol. 44, pp. 65–94). Waltham, MA: Academic Press.

Gross, J. J. (2013). Emotion regulation: Taking stock and moving forward. *Emotion, 13*, 359–365.

Gross, J. J. (2015a). Emotion regulation: Current status and future prospects. *Psychological Inquiry, 26*, 1–26.

Gross, J. J. (2015b). The extended process model of emotion regulation: Elaboration, applications, and future direction. *Psychological Inquiry, 26*, 130–137.

Gross, J. J., & Jazaieri, H. (2014). Emotion, emotion regulation, and psychopathology: An affective science perspective. *Clinical Psychological Science, 2*, 387–401.

Gross, J. J., & Thompson, R. A. (2007). Emotion regulation: Conceptual foundations. In J. J. Gross (Ed.), *Handbook of emotion regulation* (pp. 3–24). New York: Guilford Press.

Haken, H. (1983). *Synergetics: An introduction: Nonequilibrium phase transitions and self-organization in physics, chemistry, and biology*. Berlin, Germany: Springer (3rd rev. ed).

Halliday, M. A. K., & Hasan, R. (1976). *Cohesion in English*. London: Longman.

Heyes, C. (2014a). False belief in infancy: A fresh look. *Developmental Science, 17*, 647–659.

Heyes, C. (2014b). Rich interpretations of infant behaviour are popular, but are they valid? A reply to Scott and Baillargeon. *Developmental Science, 17*, 665–666.

Ho, M.-W. (2013). No genes for intelligence in the fluid genome. In R. M. Lerner & J. B. Benson (Eds.), *Advances in child development and behavior. Embodiment and epigenesis: Theoretical and methodological issues in understanding the role of biology within the relational development system. Part B: Ontogenetic dimensions* (Vol. 45, pp. 67–92). Waltham, MA: Academic Press.

Houdé, O. (2015). Cognitive development during infancy and early childhood across cultures. In J. D. Wright (Ed.), *International encyclopedia of the social and behavioral sciences* (2nd ed.). Oxford, UK: Elsevier Science.

Houdé, O., & Borst, G. (2014). Measuring inhibitory control in children and adults: Brain imaging and mental chronometry. *Frontiers in Psychology, 5*, 616. doi:10.3389/fpsyg.2014.00616.

Howard, S. J., Johnson, J., & Pascual-Leone, J. (2015). Clarifying inhibitory control: Diversity and development of attentional inhibition. *Cognitive Development, 31*, 1–21.

Hughes, C. (1998). Finding your marbles: Does preschoolers' strategic behavior predict later understanding of mind? *Developmental Psychology, 34*, 1326–1339.

Huys, R., Perdikis, D., & Jirsa, V. K. (2014). Functional architectures and structured flows on manifolds: A dynamical framework for motor behavior. *Psychological Review, 121*, 302–336.

Iacoboni, M. (2008). Mesial frontal cortex and super mirror neurons. *Behavioral and Brain Sciences, 31*, 30. doi:10.1017/S0140525X07003214.

James, J., Ellis, B. J., Schlomer, G. L., & Garber, J. (2012). Sex-specific pathways to early puberty, sexual debut, and sexual risk taking: Tests of an integrated evolutionary-developmental model. *Developmental Psychology, 48*, 687–702.

Joliot, M., Leroux, G., Dubal, S., Tzourio-Mazoyer, N., Houdé, O., Mazoyer, B., et al. (2009). Cognitive inhibition of number/length interference in a Piaget-like task: Evidence by combining ERP and MEG. *Clinical Neurophysiology, 120*, 1501–1513.

Kanai, R., Bahrami, B., Roylance, R., & Rees, G. (2012). Online social network size is reflected in human brain structure. *Proceedings of the Royal Society B: Biological Sciences, 279*, 1237–1334.

Karbach, J., & Kray, J. (2009). How useful is executive control training? Age differences in near and far transfer of task-switching training. *Developmental Science, 12*, 978–990.

Kiverstein, J. (2012). The meaning of embodiment. *Topics in Cognitive Science, 4*, 740–758.

Knudsen, B., & Liszkowski, U. (2013). One-year-olds warn others about negative action outcomes. *Journal of Cognition and Development, 14*, 424–436.

Kovács, A. M., Télglás, E., & Endress, A. D. (2010). The social sense: Susceptibility to others' beliefs in human infants and adults. *Science, 330*, 1830–1834.

Kray, J., & Ferdinand, N. K. (2013). How to improve cognitive control in development during childhood: Potentials and limits of cognitive interventions. *Child Development Perspectives, 7*, 121–125.

Lakes, K. D., & Hoyt, W. T. (2004). Promoting self-regulation through school-based martial arts training.

Journal of Applied Developmental Psychology, 25, 283–302.
Leaper, C. (2013). Gender development during childhood. In P. D. Zelazo (Ed.), *Oxford handbook of developmental psychology* (pp. 327–377). New York: Oxford University Press.
Lee, K., Bull, R., & Ho, R. M. H. (2013). Developmental changes in executive functioning. *Child Development, 84*, 1933–1953.
Legare, C. H. (2012). Exploring explanation: Explaining inconsistent evidence informs exploratory, hypothesis-testing behavior in young children. *Child Development, 83*, 173–185.
Lepage, J. F., & Theoret, H. (2007). The mirror neuron system: Grasping others' actions from birth? *Developmental Science, 10*, 513–523.
Leroux, G., Spiess, J., Zago, L., Rossi, S., Lubin, A., Turbelin, M.-R., et al. (2009). Adult brains don't fully overcome biases that lead to incorrect performance during cognitive development: An fMRI study in young adults completing a Piaget-like task. *Developmental Science, 12*, 326–338.
Levy, E. T., & McNeill, D. (2013). Narrative development as symbol formation: Gestures, imagery and the emergence of cohesion. *Culture & Psychology, 19*, 548–569.
Lewis, C., & Stack, J. (2013). A mature second-person neuroscience needs a first-person (plural) developmental foundation. *Behavioral and Brain Sciences, 36*, 428–429.
Lewis, M. D. (2011). Dynamic systems approaches: Cool enough? Hot enough? *Child Development Perspectives, 5*, 279–285.
Lewis, P. A., Rezaie, R., Browne, R., Roberts, N., & Dunbar, R. I. M. (2011). Ventromedial prefrontal volume predicts understandings of others and social network size. *NeuroImage, 57*, 1624–1629.
Lickliter, R., & Honeycutt, H. (2003). Developmental dynamics: Toward a biologically plausible evolutionary psychology. *Psychological Bulletin, 129*, 819–835.
Liszkowski, U. (2013). Using theory of mind. *Child Development Perspectives, 7*, 104–109.
Liszkowski, U., Carpenter, M., Henning, A., Striano, T., & Tomasello, M. (2004). Twelve-month-olds point to share attention and interest. *Developmental Science, 7*, 297–307.
Low, J. (2010). Preschoolers' implicit and explicit false-belief understanding: Relations with complex syntactical mastery. *Child Development, 81*, 579–615.
Low, J., & Perner, J. (2012). Implicit and explicit theory of mind: State of the art. *British Journal of Developmental Psychology, 30*, 1–13.
Marshall, P. J. (2013). Coping with complexity: Developmental systems and multilevel analyses in developmental psychopathology. *Development and Psychopathology, 25*, 1311–1324.
Marshall, P. J. (2014). Beyond different levels: Embodiment and the developmental system. *Frontiers in Psychology, 5*, 929. doi:10.3389/fpsyg.2014.00929.
Marshall, P. J., Young, T., & Meltzoff, A. N. (2011). Neural correlates of action observation and execution in 14-month-old infants: An event-related EEG desynchronization study. *Developmental Science, 14*, 474–480.
Mascolo, M. F. (2013). Developing through relationships: An embodied coactive systems framework. In R. M. Lerner & J. B. Benson (Eds.), *Advances in child development and behavior. Embodiment and epigenesis: Theoretical and methodological issues in understanding the role of biology within the relational development system. Part B: Ontogenetic dimensions* (Vol. 45, pp. 185–226). Waltham, MA: Academic Press.
May, A. (2011). Experience-dependent structural plasticity in the adult human brain. *Trends in Cognitive Sciences, 15*, 475–482.
Moè, A. (2012). Gender difference does not mean genetic difference: Externalizing improves performance in mental rotation. *Learning and Individual Differences, 22*, 20–24.
Moll, H., & Tomasello, M. (2007). How 14- and 18-month-olds know what others have experienced. *Developmental Psychology, 43*, 309–317.
Moore, C., & Paulus, M. (2013). A second-person approach cannot explain intentionality in social understanding. *Behavioral and Brain Sciences, 36*, 430–431.
Moriguchi, Y. (2014). The early development of executive function and its relation to social interaction: A brief review. *Frontiers in Psychology, 5*. doi:10.3389/fpsyg.2014.00388
Muentener, P., & Schulz, L. (2012). What doesn't go without saying: Communication, induction, and exploration. *Language Learning and Development, 8*, 61–85.
Mumford, K. H., & Kita, S. (2014). Children use gesture to interpret novel verb meanings. *Child Development, 85*, 1181–1189.
Needham, A., Barrett, T., & Peterman, K. (2002). A pick-me-up for infants' exploratory skills: Early simulated experiences reaching for objects using 'sticky mittens' enhances young infants' object exploration skills. *Infant Behavior and Development, 25*, 279–295.
Needham, A., & Libertus, K. (2011). Embodiment in early development. *Wiley Interdisciplinary Reviews: Cognitive Science, 2*, 117–123.
Nystrom, P. (2008). The infant mirror neuron system studied with high density EEG. *Social Neuroscience, 3*, 334–347.
Olofson, E. L., & Baldwin, D. (2011). Infants recognize similar goals across dissimilar actions involving object manipulation. *Cognition, 118*, 258–264.
Overton, W. F. (2013). Relationism and relational developmental systems: A paradigm for developmental science in the post-cartesian era. In R. M. Lerner & J. B. Benson (Eds.), *Advances in child development and behavior. Embodiment and epigenesis: Theoretical and methodological issues in understanding the role of biology within the relational developmental system. Part A: Philosophical, theoretical, and biological dimensions* (Vol. 44, pp. 21–64). Oxford, UK: Elsevier.

Peña-Sarrionandia, A., Mikolajczak, M., & Gross, J. J. (2015). Integrating emotion regulation and emotional intelligence traditions: A meta-analysis. *Frontiers in Psychology, 6*, 160. doi:10.3389/fpsyg.2015.00160.

Perko, L. (2006). *Differential equations and dynamical systems* (3rd ed.). Berlin, Germany: Springer.

Perone, S., & Spencer, J. P. (2013). Autonomy in action: Linking the act of looking to memory formation in infancy via dynamic neural fields. *Cognitive Science, 37*, 1–60.

Piaget, J. (1950). *The psychology of intelligence*. London, UK: Routledge & Kegan (Original work published 1947).

Piaget, J. (1952). *The origins of intelligence in children*. New York: International Universities Press.

Piaget, J. (1953). *The origin of intelligence in the child*. London: Routledge & Paul.

Piaget, J. (1954). *The construction of reality in the child*. New York: Basic Books.

Piaget, J. (1955). *The child's conception of the world*. London: Routledge & Kegan Paul.

Piaget, J. (1960). *The child's conception of the world*. Oxford, UK: Littlefield, Adams.

Piaget, J. (1970/1988). Piaget's theory. In P. Mussen (Ed.), *Handbook of child psychology* (Vol. 1, 3rd ed. pp. 703–732). New York: Wiley. Reprinted in K. Richardson & S. Sheldon (Eds.), *Cognitive development to adolescence*. Hove, UK: Lawrence Erlbaum.

Ping, R. M., & Goldin-Meadow, S. (2010). Gesturing saves cognitive resources when talking about nonpresent objects. *Cognitive Science, 34*, 602–619.

Piontelli, A. (2010). *Development of normal fetal movements: The first 25 weeks of gestation*. Milan: Springer.

Powell, J., Lewis, P. A., Roberts, N., García-Fiñana, M., & Dunbar, R. I. M. (2012). Orbital prefrontal cortex volume predicts social network size: An imaging study of individual differences in humans. *Proceedings of the Royal Society B: Biological Sciences, 279*, 2157–2162.

Pulvermuller, F., & Garagnani, M. (2014). From sensorimotor learning to memory cells in prefrontal and temporal association cortex: A neurocomputational study of disembodiment. *Cortex, 57*, 1–21.

Rakoczy, H. (2012). Do infants have a theory of mind? *British Journal of Developmental Psychology, 30*, 59–74.

Raver, C. C., Jones, S. M., Li-Grining, C., Zhai, F., Bub, K., & Pressler, E. (2011). CSRP's impact on low-income preschoolers' preacademic skills: Self-regulation as a mediating mechanism. *Child Development, 82*, 362–378.

Richardson, K. (2013). The evolution of intelligent developmental systems. In R. M. Lerner & J. B. Benson (Eds.), *Advances in child development and behavior. Embodiment and epigenesis: Theoretical and methodological issues in understanding the role of biology within the relational development system. Part A: Philosophical, theoretical, and biological dimensions* (Vol. 44, pp. 127–160). Waltham, MA: Academic Press.

Richerson, P. J., & Boyd, R. (2005). *Not by genes alone: How culture transformed human evolution*. Chicago, IL: University of Chicago Press.

Richland, L. E., & Burchinal, M. R. (2013). Early executive function predicts reasoning development. *Psychological Science, 24*, 87–92.

Rivière, J. (2014). Embodiment in children's choice: Linking bodily constraints with decisional dynamics. *Current Directions in Psychological Science, 23*, 408–413.

Rizzolatti, G., & Craighero, K. (2004). The mirror-neuron system. *Annual Review of Neuroscience, 27*, 169–192.

Rizzolatti, G., & Sinigaglia, C. (2010). The functional role of the parieto-frontal mirror circuit: Interpretations and misinterpretations. *Nature Review Neuroscience, 11*, 264–274.

Rose, S. A., Feldman, J. F., & Jankowski, J. J. (2012). Implications of infant cognition for executive functions at age 11. *Psychological Science, 23*, 1345–1355.

Ruffman, T. (2014). To belief or not belief: Children's theory of mind. *Developmental Review, 34*, 265–293.

Ruffman, T., Taumoepeau, M., & Perkins, C. (2012). Statistical learning as a basis for social understanding in children. *British Journal of Developmental Psychology, 30*, 87–104.

Russell, J. (1996). *Agency: Its role in mental development*. Hove, UK: Taylor & Francis.

Saby, J. N., Meltzoff, A. N., & Marshall, P. J. (2013). Infants' somatotopic neural responses to seeing human actions: I've got you under my skin. *PLoS One, 8*, e77905. doi:10.1371/journal.pone.0077905.

Sameroff, A. (2010). A unified theory of development: A dialectic integration of nature and nurture. *Child Development, 81*, 6–22.

San Juan, V., & Astington, J. W. (2012). Bridging the gap between implicit and explicit understanding: How language development promotes the processing and representation of false belief. *British Journal of Developmental Psychology, 30*, 105–122.

Schilbach, L., Timmermans, B., Reddy, V., Costall, A., Bente, G., Schlicht, T., et al. (2013). Toward a second-person neuroscience. *Behavioral and Brain Sciences, 36*, 393–462.

Schöner, G., & Dineave, E. (2007). Dynamic instabilities as mechanisms for emergence. *Developmental Science, 10*, 69–74.

Schöner, G., & Thelen, E. (2006). Using dynamic field theory to rethink infant habituation. *Psychological Review, 113*, 273–299.

Scott, R. M. (2014). Post hoc versus predictive accounts of children's theory of mind: A reply to Ruffman. *Developmental Review, 34*, 300–304.

Scott, R. M., & Baillargeon, R. (2009). Which penguin is this? Attributing false beliefs about object identity at 18 months. *Child Development, 80*, 1172–1196.

Scott, R. M., & Baillargeon, R. (2014). How fresh a look? A reply to Heyes. *Developmental Science, 17*, 660–664.

Seidl, A., Tincoff, R., Baker, C., & Cristia, A. (2015). Why the body comes first: Effects of experimenter

touch on infants' word finding. *Developmental Science, 18*, 155–164.
Shackelford, T. K., & Liddle, J. R. (2014). Understanding the mind from an evolutionary perspective: An overview of evolutionary psychology. *Wiley Interdisciplinary Reviews: Cognitive Science, 5*, 247–260.
Shapiro, L. (2009). Making sense of mirror neurons. *Syntheses, 167*, 439–456.
Shimada, S., & Hiraki, K. (2006). Infant's brain responses to live and televised action. *NeuroImage, 32*, 930–939.
Smith, L. B., & Thelen, E. (2003). Development as a dynamic system. *Trends in Cognitive Sciences, 7*, 343–348.
Sommerville, J. A., Woodward, A. L., & Needham, A. N. (2005). Action experience alters 3-month-old infants' perception of others' actions. *Cognition, 96*, 1–11.
Spencer, J. P., Perone, S., & Buss, A. T. (2011). Twenty years and going strong: A dynamic systems revolution in motor and cognitive development. *Child Development Perspectives, 5*, 260–266.
Spencer, J. P., Perone, S., & Johnson, J. S. (2009). The dynamic field theory and embodied cognitive dynamics. In J. P. Spencer, M. Thomas, & J. L. McClelland (Eds.), *Toward a unified theory of development: Connectionism and dynamic systems theory reconsidered* (pp. 86–118). New York: Oxford University Press.
Surian, L., & Geraci, A. (2012). Where will the triangle look for it? Attributing false belief to a geometric shape at 17 months. *The British Journal of Developmental Psychology, 30*, 30–44.
Szyf, M. (2013). How do environments talk to genes? *Nature Neuroscience, 16*, 2–4.
Tai, Y. F., Scherfler, C., Brooks, D. J., Sawamoto, N., & Castiello, U. (2004). The human premotor cortex is 'mirror' only for biological actions. *Current Biology, 14*, 117–120.
Thelen, E. (2008). Grounded in the world: Developmental origins of the embodied mind. In W. F. Overton, U. Muller, & J. L. Newman (Eds.), *Developmental perspectives on embodiment and consciousness* (pp. 99–130). New York: Taylor & Francis.
Thelen, E., Schöner, G., Scheier, C., & Smith, L. B. (2001). The dynamics of embodiment: A field study of infant preservative reaching. *Behavior and Brain Sciences, 24*, 1–86.
Thoermer, C., Sodian, B., Vuori, M., Perst, H., & Kristen, S. (2012). Continuity from an implicit to an explicit understanding of false belief from infancy to preschool age. *British Journal of Developmental Psychology, 30*, 172–187.
Tschacher, W., & Haken, H. (2007). Intentionality in non-equilibrium systems? The functional aspects of self-organized pattern formation. *New Ideas in Psychology, 25*, 1–15.
Thompson, E. (2007). *Mind in life: Biology, phenomenology, and the sciences of mind*. Cambridge, MA: Belknap Press/Harvard University Press.
Usai, M. C., Viterbori, P., Traverso, L., & De Franchis, V. (2014). Latent structure of executive function in 5-to and 6-year-old children: A longitudinal study. *European Journal of Developmental Psychology, 11*, 447–462.
van der Meer, A. L. H., & van der Weel, F. R. (2011). Auditory guided arm and whole body movements in young infants. In P. Strumillo (Ed.), *Advances in sound localization*. InTech. http://www.intechopen.com/books/advances-in-sound-localization/auditory-guided-arm-and-whole-body-movements-in-young-infants
van Geert, P. (2011). The contribution of complex dynamic systems to development. *Child Development Perspectives, 5*, 273–278.
Warren, W. H. (2006). The dynamics of perception and action. *Psychological Review, 113*, 358–389.
Warreyn, P., Ruysschaert, L., Wiersema, J. R., Handl, A., Pattyn, G., & Roeyers, H. (2013). Infants' mu suppression during the observation of real and mimicked goal-directed actions. *Developmental Science, 16*, 173–185.
Wellsby, M., & Pexman, P. M. (2014). Developing embodied cognition: Insights from children's concepts and language processing. *Frontiers in Psychology, 5*. doi:10.3389/fpsyg.2014.00506.
Wentworth, N., Benson, J. B., & Haith, M. M. (2000). The development of infants' reaches for stationary and moving targets. *Child Development, 71*, 576–601.
Wiebe, S., Morton, J. B., Buss, A. T., & Spencer, J. P. (2014). The emergent executive: A dynamic field theory of the development of executive function. *Monographs of the Society for Research in Child Development, 79*, 1–132.
Wiebe, S., Sheffield, T., Nelson, J. M., Clark, C. A. A., Chevalier, N., & Espy, K. (2011). The structure of executive function in 3-year-olds. *Journal of Experimental Child Psychology, 108*, 436–452.
Wilkinson, N., Paikan, A., Gredebäck, G., Rea, F., & Metta, G. (2014). Staring us in the face? An embodied theory of innate face preference. *Developmental Science, 17*, 809–825.
Witherington, D. C. (2011). Taking emergence seriously: The centrality of circular causality for dynamic systems approaches to development. *Human Development, 54*, 66–92.
Witherington, D. C. (2015). Dynamic systems. In W. F. Overton, P. C. M. Molenaar, & R. M. Lerner (Eds.), *Handbook of child psychology and developmental science* (7th ed., Vol. 1). New York: Wiley.
Witherington, D. C., & Heying, S. (2013). Embodiment and agency: Toward a holistic synthesis for developmental science. In R. M. Lerner & J. B. Benson (Eds.), *Advances in child development and behavior. Embodiment and epigenesis: Theoretical and methodological issues in understanding the role of biology within the relational development system. Part A: Philosophical, theoretical, and biological dimensions* (Vol. 44, pp. 161–192). Waltham, MA: Academic Press.

Witherington, D. C., & Margett, T. (2011). How conceptually unified is the dynamic systems approach to the study of psychological development? *Child Development Perspectives, 5*, 286–290.

Wolff, P. (2007). Representing causation. *Journal of Experimental Psychology: General, 136*, 82–111.

Wood, W., & Eagly, A. H. (2013). Biology or culture alone cannot account for human sex differences and similarities. *Psychological Inquiry, 24*, 241–247.

Yott, J., & Poulin-Dubois, D. (2012). Breaking the rules: Do infants have a true understanding of false belief? *British Journal of Developmental Psychology, 30*, 156–171.

Young, G. (2011). *Development and causality: Neo-Piagetian perspectives*. New York: Springer Science+Business Media.

Yu, C., & Smith, L. B. (2013). Joint attention without gaze following: Human infants and their parents coordinate visual attention to objects through eye-hand coordination. *PLoS One, 8*, e79659. doi:10.1371/journal.pone.0079659.

Zwaan, R. A. (2014). Embodiment and language comprehension: Reframing the discussion. *Trends in Cognitive Sciences, 18*, 229–234.

Free Will in Behavior: Believing Makes It So

18

Chapter Introduction

Free will is debated endlessly in philosophy, perhaps to little avail, but psychologists study the consequences of believing in it and altering the belief, which indicates its relevance to the daily lives of people. The present chapter considers free will in terms of philosophy, social psychology, neuroscience, developmental psychology, and evolution. Overall, the chapter emphasizes individual differences in free will beliefs and their consequences in multiple areas of psychological function. Its origin lies in biological, environmental, and self (e.g., personality) factors. As for the study of the conscious and unconscious influences on behavior and their relationship to free will, conceptualization and research informs that both are involved in behavior decision-making and unfolding.

Philosophy

The topic of the philosophy of free will has been given more extensive coverage in Chap. 4. In this chapter, I review some philosophical positions why free will cannot be dismissed outright in psychology.

Views

Shields (2014) referred to free will as conscious causation and also as causal efficacy of consciousness. It is the ability to initiate or to control one's thoughts/actions in a conscious, voluntarily way. One's self-controlled conscious choices can contribute significantly to behavior. Events might be entirely determined; however, nonlinear neural mechanisms allow for variable behavior relative to those events, in that consciousness is an emergent property that can modify the events leading to it. Volitional action appears to be the outcome of a complex, rapid decision-making process involving prior decisions and cognitive elements. Individuals appear to be able to consciously control their actions.

Doyle (2013) maintained that we have a Macro mind so that we are creative authors and originators of our ideas. We can evaluate alternatives and, after generating alternatives, fall back to thinking again so that we avoid the fixed past and also behave in ways different from those prescribed by our Micro mind. For Doyle, first, we are "free" and, then, we "will." First, thoughts come "freely" and, then, actions are produced "willfully."

Kane (2013) also adopted a two-stage model in free will. Deliberation happens unpredictably, and its outcomes influence the choices that are

G. Young, *Unifying Causality and Psychology*, DOI 10.1007/978-3-319-24094-7_18

made. Decisions are "torn" rather than being decided deterministically. The brain is described using the language of nonlinear dynamics. Kane argued that far-from-equilibrium brain states render the brain sensitive to "micro-indeterminacies" at the lower neuronal level. This is accompanied by a temporary "screen-off" of deterministic past influences. Kane (2013) concluded that full consciousness allows the "deep" responsibility associated with "genuine" free will.

For Nahmias (2012), generally, free will is considered the set of capacities for choice and for action control that are essential for agents to demonstrate moral responsibility and blame. Moreover, from a psychological point of view, different people will have varying degrees of it, thereby exercising it to different degrees. Because most people believe in free will, and people develop more autonomy and control as they grow, in evaluating other people, we are prone to holding people responsible for their actions, at least to varying degrees. Cognitive science can help determine the cognitive capacities important in free will and to responsible agency, as well as the individual differences therein. For example, consciousness or conscious deliberation would appear to be a requisite for free will, as would intention-formation skills and a capacity for moral reasoning. For those scholarly perspectives that consider free will as an illusion (e.g., Wegner, 2002) or otherwise try to explain it away, the conclusions offered seem to depend on how free will is defined.

Libet (1985, 1999, 2001, 2004) conducted the now classic research arguing that the brain "decides" to prepare to initiate simple motor actions prior to the person reporting subjective awareness of corresponding intention to make the movement. In Libet, the onset of the readiness potential (RP) in scalp EEG (electroencephalogram) occurred 550 ms on average before movement onset, and it also had preceded the participants' reported time of conscious awareness of the movements involved by 350 ms on average. The RP precedes the awareness of "intention, desire, or urge" (RP → awareness 350 ms later → movement another 150 ms later; Nahmias, 2012).

Libet concluded that the initiation of voluntary action begins "unconsciously." In addition, people have a window of conscious veto control or movement inhibition of about 200 ms between awareness of will and action performance. Libet argued that the results refute the common sense notion that free will requires conscious action initiation. Libet argued that the results demonstrate that although we might not have free will in the classic sense, they show that we have "free won't"—that is, free will constituted by the capacity to control actions consciously via vetoes.

However, Nahmias (2012) maintained that (a) the RP onset could correspond to nonconscious "urges" (Pockett & Purdy, 2011) rather than intentions or decisions, or, (b) simply, in the research, the reporting of consciousness is delayed relative to the presence of conscious intention. Nahmias (2012) concluded that conscious intention does not have to take place prior to action (or neural correlates) in order to causally influence actions. Rather, as long as conscious deliberations, plans, and distal intentions (or the neural correlates involved) have a proper effect downstream on actions, conscious causation is taking place. Conscious causation of this type could lead to acting according to consciously-considered reasons. For example, Nahmias (2012) indicated that Baumeister, Masicampo, and Vohs (2011) had provided examples of behaviors being improved by conscious reasoning and conscious attention to action.

In addition, Mele (2013) provided conceptual and methodological criticisms of the research by Libet. For Mele, Libet's data do not warrant the conclusions that conscious decision-making and intention are not involved in generating behavior.

Countering Libet, Schlosser (2012a) proposed that, in motor initiation, the timing of conscious mental events is a secondary consideration to the covariations in intentions, reasons, choices, and actions involved. Every step in a causal chain might have unconscious precursors, but the whole chain might still be reason-responsive. Moreover, our conscious intentions might be among the various causes of our actions. Having said that, the approach taken by Schlosser does not require that the origin or source of choices that are made freely need to lie within the person, or that the person must be a conscious initiator.

Schlosser (2012b) examined another model critical of free will—that of apparent mental causation (Wegner, 2002, 2004, 2005, 2008). In this model, the conscious self is considered spectators or epiphenomena; they do not cause conscious choice, and are not causally efficacious in the initiation and in the guidance of action (see Fig. 18.1). In the apparent causation model, we might experience a sense of having conscious will in the relation between thought and action. However, the genuine precursor to action lies in preceding unconscious causes/thoughts.

In response to Wegner (2002), Schlosser (2012b) posited the "real mental causation" model (see Fig. 18.2). The model distinguishes the subpersonal "realizer" of intentions and the intentions. Moreover, intentions can be subverted for multiple reasons and so desired actions not realized. Therefore, in the model, everything else being equal, conscious intentions at the personal level can be causally efficacious in initiating/guiding relevant basic actions. In support of his model, Schlosser (2012b) cited a meta-analysis by Gollwitzer and Sheeran (2006). They found that the formation of "implementation" intentions (and their changes) affects subsequent performance and goal attainment (and matching changes in behavior).

Comment Suarez and Adams (2013) posed the provocative question whether science is compatible with free will. Much of the book that they wrote deals with quantum physics. Adams and Suarez (2013) maintained that quantum randomness and freedom in behavior are not incompatible. Brain output may exhibit quantum interference effects so that its output might derive from "nonmaterial" or "immaterial" agency. Consciousness might "self-influence" the brain's physiological parameters. Conscious choice, although "causal," could be "unpredictable." Uncertainty rather than determinism in behavior prevails due to "free will." In brief, mental agencies involving consciousness and free will "influence" neurons and "produce" behavior.

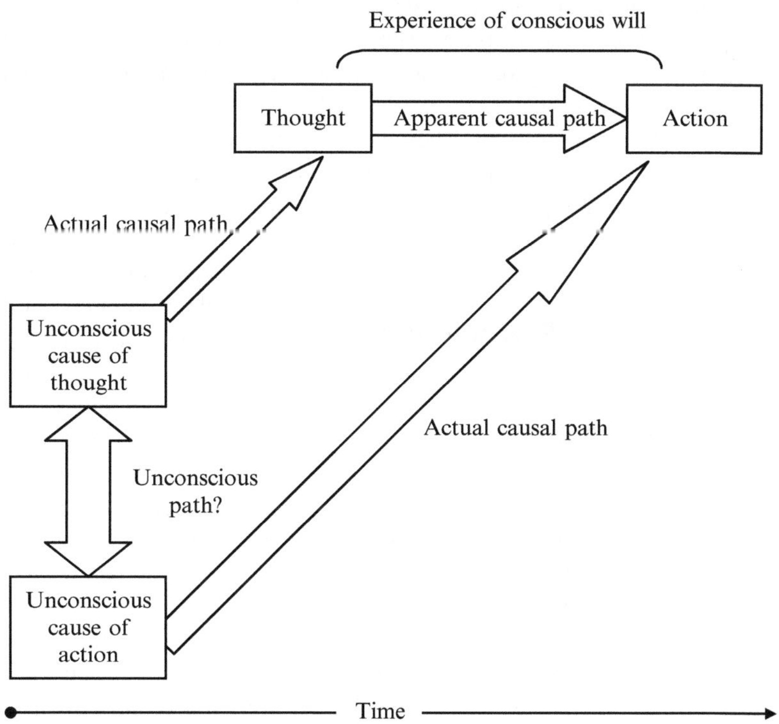

Fig. 18.1 Model of apparent mental causation (AMC). The figure illustrates one model of unconscious determination of motor action. Adapted from Schlosser (2012b), based on Wegner (2002, p. 68) and Wegner and Wheatley (1999, p. 483)

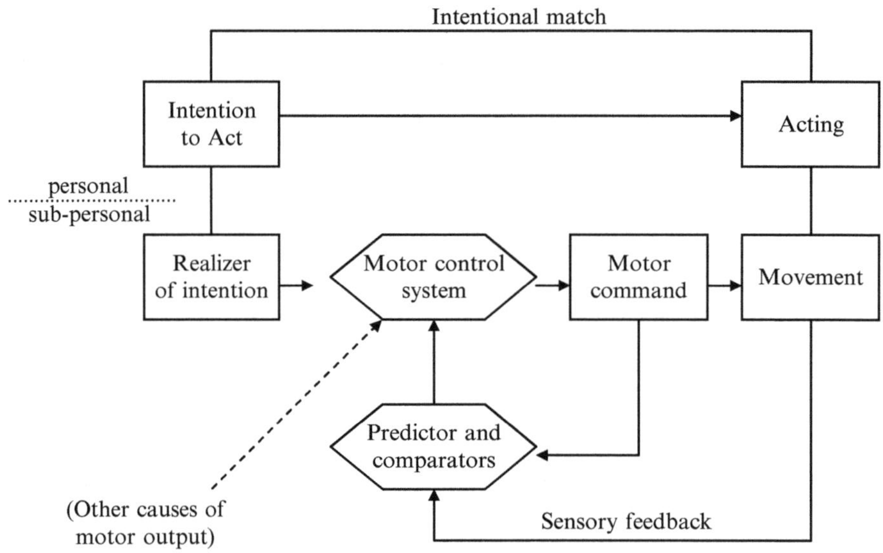

Fig. 18.2 Model of real mental causation (RMC). RMC includes sources of the sense of agency. At the personal level, the mental intention to act leads to action with an intentional matching process involved. There are other components to the action system not necessarily amenable to consciousness. Adapted from Schlosser (2012b)

I conclude that philosophers who support the position that free will exists refer to our capacity for conscious causation and making independent choices. They consider it emergent as the nonlinear dynamical systems approach describes. They relate it to moral responsibility. They view it as involving a two-step process, such as blocking off deterministic influences to be free in thought and then choosing willfully. They deny that the putative research demonstrating that it is inexistent is valid for the question. They describe that individual differences exist in free will.

Free Will from a Psychological Perspective

Free Will Psychology

Introduction Bode et al. (2014) tackled the complex issue of free will from a definitional, philosophical, neuroscientific, and behavioral perspective. They noted that believing in free will is fundamental to our identity and self-concept. Whether it exists has been debated in philosophy but, experimentally, the arguments against its existence do not stand up to scrutiny. Libet, Gleason, Wright, and Pearl (1983) and Libet (1985) had shown that the RP (Bereitschafts potential, BP), as measured by EEG over the pre-supplementary motor cortex (pre-SMA), preceded by several hundred milliseconds not only a voluntary action (moving quickly, in a self-paced mode, finger/wrist flexion, or both) but also the time points that participants had reported having made the conscious decision to act. However, multiple methodological critiques of the Libet studies query whether the participants were truly engaging in arriving at free decisions, for example, the context of the laboratory could have had an influence on the behavior.

In terms of definition, Bode et al. (2014) noted the ambiguities prevalent in the field. Therefore, most workers prefer to use terms such as voluntary action/movement and internal decisions. The approach taken by Bode et al. concerning this imbroglio was to examine the neuroscience underlying research on free (or voluntary) decisions. When participants are asked to self-initiate an action, neuroimaging techniques (fMRI, functional magnetic resonance imaging; EEG) have found an associated network of brain regions, mostly in the medial prefrontal cortex (PFC), including the pre-SMA/SMA and the rostral cingulate zone, the posterior parietal cortex (PPC, especially the lateral regions of the PFC and PPC), and the basal ganglia. The "default mode" network also has been implicated. Using multivariate pattern classification analysis (MVPA) and ultra high-field fMRI, Soon, Brass, Heinze, and Haynes (2008) and Bode et al. (2011) demonstrated that decisions relating to pressing one or two buttons at a time of the participants' choosing could be predicted a full seven seconds before the reported time of consciously deciding according to the activity of the medial prefrontal and medial posterior parietal cortex, with other findings related to the anterior prefrontal cortex. Soon, He, Bode, and Haynes (2013) found similar results in making abstract decisions about adding or subtracting numbers.

The authors concluded that consciousness of all these types of decisions for simple choices happens after their unconscious decision-making. However, this does not mean that it has been demonstrated that more complex decisions cannot include a free, conscious volitional component. Whether simple or complex, all decisions are susceptible to contextual influence. Therefore, decisions at any level might involve a process of "evidence accumulation," or of integrating—the probability of stimuli; external context; internal environment; expectations, or associated factors values; past stimuli and experiences; personal history/past cues, choices, and actions; internal motivation, preferences, and attitudes; and so on. In decision-making, all these factors serve to create an embodied dynamical decision state network. As long as cues are relevant, even if they are weak, unconscious, or unattended, potentially, they can influence decision-making. By arriving at a better understanding "hidden" cognitive systems, a better understanding of the "personal" component of "free" decision-making will emerge.

Comment The model of decision-making in Bode et al. (2014) allows for voluntary action and interval decision-making in movements. All levels of the relevant control system components need to be described, as well as all aspects of the environment that contribute to the dynamical decision-making system. However, the person's past history, values, motivation, etc., also contribute to the system. Because the system is a dynamic network, it can arrive at emergent states that are unpredictable from the collection of components constituting it. It is especially in this sense that decisions might be emergent and free, and reflect the person's free choice as much as or more than any one putative deterministic influence.

The next section of the chapter on free will examines the consequences of believing in it, or not, and most people do believe in it. Moreover, there are individual differences in this regard. These types of statements are based on excellent research, and so they are *not* an illusion.

Belief in Free Will

Model Baumeister et al. (2011) separated the psychological questions about free will and the philosophical ones. First, although research shows that people who believe in free will end up with the belief affecting their behavior, research such as this cannot address the philosophical question of whether free will really exists. That said, even though most people believe in free will, in psychological experiments, the belief can be manipulated (Nahmias, Morris, Nadelhoffer, & Turner, 2005; Vohs & Schooler, 2008).

The research on belief in free will includes experimental studies (Alquist, Ainsworth, & Baumeister, 2013; Baumeister, 2008; Baumeister & Brewer, 2012). For example, in experiments on free will, participants are induced to believe either less or more in free will, and dependent measures are examined for effects of the change in belief, such as being more antisocial or less conforming. There are numerous behavioral effects of believing in free will, in not believing in it, or having the belief manipulated.

Vohs and Schooler (2008) initiated the latter type of research and found that inducing disbelief in free will resulted in participants not only cheating but also lying and stealing! Baumeister, Masicampo, and DeWall (2009) found that it caused aggressive behavior (giving unwelcome hot sauce in food). It reduced volunteer behavior

(Stillman & Baumeister, 2010). It appears that free will belief reduction makes people less inclined to expend effort, affecting their motivation and self-control.

That is, belief in free will has powerful consequences in the daily lives of people, and not believing in it takes away its potential positive effects. In this regard, Nichols (2011) reported that when asked about concrete cases of wrongdoing that were highly affective, people who were manipulated toward believing in determinism still maintained that wrongdoers have agency and are morally culpable. This is a compatibilist response—people believe that we are responsible for our actions of this moral kind even if they believe that the universe is determined.

Miles (2013a, 2013b) criticized the Baumiesterian approach to free will, and Vonasch and Baumeister (2013) ably responded. The exchange is beyond the scope of the present work. Essentially, Vonasch and Baumeister summarized that free will belief is associated with greater empathy, support for social mobility, desire for SES (socioeconomic status) equality, and belief that the working poor's poverty is not a fate.

Several recent papers have related free will belief to retribution for committed transgressions. Shariff et al. (2014) found that reducing free will belief led people to be less retributive in their punishment attitudes. They implied that weakening free will belief lessened belief in moral responsibility and also in seeing "bad" behavior as morally reprehensible. The studies involved functioned to move the participants toward a more mechanistic view of human behavior. Monroe, Dillon, and Malle (2014) found that people's judgment of free will and blame were clearly related to agents' choice capacity.

Comment Relative to correlational research, experiments better ensure that causality can be addressed for an issue. Belief in free will research uses experimental manipulations to show the power of the belief. The belief is strong enough to allow for findings of a compatibilist nature—the universe might be deterministically caused but free will still has a role to play in behavior, especially of the moral responsible kind.

However, in daily life, the complexities of believing in free will lead to various subtle findings that make it difficult to state with sufficient precision its causal role in behavior except that individual differences abound and have pertinent consequences. Before reviewing the research on the latter matter in this regard, I examine the issue of lay beliefs on free will. Do they differ from academic ones? Then, I look at the relationship between free will and conformity. Does the belief lead to more or less conformity?

Lay Belief

Model Laypeople struggle with understanding of free will. Baumeister and Brewer (2012) noted that Monroe and Malle (2010) asked university students open-ended questions on what it means to have free will. Responses especially involved defining free will as having choice, doing things to fulfill personal desires, and not submitting to coercion or external pressure. Stillman, Baumeister, and Mele (2011) studied the question by asking people to describe their actions either done or not done with free will. Analysis of the data revealed that, for the layperson, behaving with free will involved the following themes: reaches goal; achieves positive outcome; works toward long-term/distal goal; decides on basis of conscious, deliberate thought, or reflection; behaves according to moral values; resists external influences/overcomes obstacles; and avoids harming the person's social group.

Most laypeople report believing in free will, but in a naïve compatibilist way, in that they also express some belief in determinism (Nahmias et al., 2005). Sarkissian et al. (2010) also found that the majority believes in free will, including in many different cultures.

Kuhl and Quirin (2011) referred to a model of free will that does not mean freedom "from" causal determination, but to freedom "of" self-determination (e.g., Baumeister, 2008; Pinker, 2008). Volitional freedom lies on a continuum of different psychological systems or functional levels, from habits to global personal goals (self-determined behavior). In this regard, Shepherd (2012) demonstrated that, in folk psychology, appreciating behavior as consciously caused evokes judgments that free will is involved in an agent's actions. Knobe et al. (2012) added that free will is attributed in cases that are more "real and personal" (even when behavior is determined).

Comment Folk psychology appears to have developed concepts similar to those of some in philosophy and psychology. The debate on the existence of free will is hotly contested academically, but, in contrast, the typical layperson acts according to deeply held personal beliefs.

Conformity

Model Believing in free will reduces conforming (Alquist et al., 2013), and it increases job performance and expectations of work success (Stillman et al., 2010; Stillman et al., 2011, respectively). These results are found even after possible confounds are controlled (e.g., in the two studies, controlled, respectively, were—work ethic/life satisfaction, and intelligence/personality traits/locus of control).

Alquist et al. (2013) investigated the relationship between disbelief in free will and social conformity. They used both correlational and experimental research. In their correlational study, Alquist et al. (2013) examined the association between the FAD-Plus's scale of free will (Free Will and Determinism Plus Scale; Paulhus & Carey, 2011) and a conformity scale. The FAD-Plus consists of seven items related to free will (with 21 others on three other factors—scientific determinism, fatalistic determinism, and unpredictability). They found a correlation between the scales such that those individuals who scored higher in free will belief scored lower in conformity. This illustrates that individual differences in the degree of belief in free will influence social behavior, such as conformity.

As for their two experiments, Alquist et al. (2013) assigned participants to a pro-free will condition, an anti-free will condition, or a control condition, with a fourth condition in the second study involving manipulation of "meaning threat." The pro-free will and anti-free will conditions were based on the study by Vohs and Schooler (2008). In the latter study, participants were exposed passively to statements that either supported or denied free will. Alquist et al. (2013) modified this procedure by having the participants actively read the sentences and rewrite them in their own words. An example of a pro-free will statement is "I have free will to control my actions and, ultimately, to control my destiny in life." An example of an anti-free will statement is "Science has demonstrated that free will is an illusion." In these experiments, the conformity measure involved rating art work after having seen different opinions of it that were written by the experimenters independent of the actual quality of the work (and unknown to the participants).

The results showed that participants who were exposed to anti-free will statements conformed significantly more in their artwork ratings compared to participants in the other two conditions (that is, the pro-free will condition and control condition). Similar results were found in the second study, but this time it controlled for "meaning threat" and used a different measure of conformity, that of generating predictable or novel names for products.

Alquist et al. (2013) concluded that believing in free will contributes to resisting pressures and temptations to conform and also it contributes to autonomy and action. People who believe in free will think more for themselves and, also, they will depart more from social pressures and expected norms. In contrast, not believing in free will leads to lower motivation to engage in exertion of mental effort. They noted that, among laypersons, free will is considered to involve making choices based on self-directed thoughts and values rather than based on external forces (Monroe & Malle, 2010).

Comment It is intriguing to note that Alquist et al. (2013) emphasized that free will involves having a sense of making the right choice, but that the seven items in Paulhus and Carey's (2011) scale on free will do not include anything about choice. They include the concepts of control, responsibility, and strength of mind/overcoming, as well as having free will. I return below to the issue of creating a better free will questionnaire.

Believing in free will has consequences for being less conforming in nature and for resisting conformity. At the same time, in manipulating the belief, consequences for conformity in thought and in behavior arise. Of course, some people do not believe in free will and many people cannot deploy effectively their free will belief. I discuss ways of repairing these difficulties in the context of therapy for addictions in Chap. 20.

In the following, I address the consequences of believing in free will according to correlational research seeking individual differences. As with any correlational research, causation cannot be established, but the patterns are consistent with the notion that variations in free will belief lead to variations in consequences.

Individual Differences

Introduction

Disbelief in free will, or the induction of this belief, has a host of consequences, such as engaging in less helping of others and lesser work quality (e.g., Baumeister et al., 2009). Believing in free will varies and the degree of belief in free will is associated with variables such as having self-control.

Model

Baumeister and Brewer (2012) reviewed the literature on individual differences in belief in free will, or its disbelief, in relation to subjective correlates and consequences. They noted that, generally, free will belief shows no or modest correlations with other variables, so that it appears to be a distinct trait. Nevertheless, it correlates positively with a range of variables, such as satisfaction and self-control.

Baumeister and Brewer (2012) concluded their review by indicating that free will belief is associated with a prosocial/procultural attitude. In contrast, its disbelief is associated with disregard of societal norms and rules. Also, it is associated with personal agency, while its disbelief is associated with passivity, indifference, and so on.

Research in judging others demonstrates that greater belief in free will leads to giving lighter prison sentences (Carey & Paulhus, 2011; Shariff et al., 2014). However, high free will belief is associated with low criminal forgiveness, although the opposite seems to apply to forgiving relationship partners (respectively, Shariff et al., 2014; Crescioni, Baumeister, Ainsworth, Ent, & Lambert, 2015). Free will belief is related to holding people responsible for their actions, and manipulating it to be lower leads to more willingness to forgive others (Brewer, 2011).

Another area studied in relation to free will belief is on beliefs, attitudes, and thoughts of the self. Crescioni et al. (2015) found that free will belief correlated with more gratitude, finding life as meaningful and being more satisfied and having less life stress, as well as with perceived self-efficacy and with relationship variables (relationship commitment, and partner forgiveness, but not with all positive variables, e.g., it did not correlate with empathy). Other research implicates belief in free will being associated with ways of avoiding harming others (Alquist, Ainsworth, Baumeister, Daly, & Stillman, 2015), learning lessons from past guilt-inducing actions (Stillman & Baumeister, 2010), and developing long-term goals (Crescioni et al., 2015).

As for other traits, the associations of belief in free will with other personality variables include extraversion and agreeableness (Paulhus & Carey, 2011), as well as conscientiousness, emotional stability, and openness to experience (Stillman et al., 2011). Internal locus of control generally correlates with it (e.g., Paulhus & Carey, 2011; Stillman et al., 2011). Paulhus and Carey (2011) related it to right-wing authoritarianism, Brewer and Baumeister (2010) to self-control, and Crescioni et al. (2015) to self-efficacy.

Research has demonstrated that the induction of a disbelief in free will changes EEG recordings that correlate with preconscious motor preparation (Rigoni, Kühn, Sartori, & Brass, 2011). The readiness potential of the readings at more than one second before participants took the decision consciously to move was reduced in those individuals who had read an excerpt from a book implying that free will is an illusion. Indeed, it is noteworthy for present purposes that the degree of disbelief in free will reported in a questionnaire correlated with the amplitude of the readiness potentials in question in the experimental group.

Alquist et al. (2015) demonstrated that individual differences in (and experimental manipulation of) free will belief were related to counterfactual thinking. They concluded that free will belief relates positively to counterfactual thinking, which allows for multiple possible outcomes and runs counter to deterministic views of the origins of behavior.

Comment

Although most people believe in free will, the variation in the strength of the belief has important consequences, as shown by the growing literature on the question. The research is expanding to study individual differences in free will belief related both to brain activity and to critical concepts related to free will, such as counterfactual thinking. Based on this type of research, we realized that there has been little research on individual differences related to student motivation, and so Yang (2013) conducted the following study.

Motivation

Study For her Bachelor of Arts thesis under my supervision, Yang (2013) conducted a study of free will belief in relation to mastery-approach goal orientation. Undergraduates ($N = 179$, mostly female, of varied cultural background) were administered the FAD-Plus (Paulhus & Carey, 2011) to evaluate whether individual differences in free will belief predicted mastery-approach motivation, as measured by three items on the Achievement Goal Questionnaire (Elliot & McGregor, 2001). Free will was measured using seven items on the free will scale of the FAD-Plus. Control variables included demographics, acculturation, as measured by Tsai, Ying, and Lee's (2000) General Ethnicity Questionnaire (25 items), and an individualism-collectivism scale (13 items), as measured by a scale in Kim and Cho (2011). Questionnaires were administered in a standard order: FAD-Plus, individual-collectivism, acculturation, and motivation.

For purposes of the data analysis, alpha was set at 0.01 because of the multiple analyses involved. The results showed that, in the university students, free will belief predicted degree of master-approach motivation, but only at a trend level ($p < 0.05$).

Specifically, the multiple regression analysis that was conducted was hierarchical and, first, it entered demographic variables, with the individualism/collectivism and acculturation data entered next. Demographic factors did predict mastery-approach, while the cultural variables did not add to the predictive accuracy. Finally, in the last step, free will belief, as measured by the FAD-Plus, was found to predict mastery-approach motivation above and beyond the other factors controlled, but only at the trend level, as indicated.

Comment We can conclude believing in free will might have some consequences for motivation to study in university students, although further research is needed. Aside from replicated this study with larger and different samples, it should be determined whether the variations in free will belief and motivation correspond to variation in course grades.

In the next portion of the chapter, the focus shifts to a topic related to free will, that of consciousness. One would think that we are quite conscious in our behavior, but much of it takes place automatically or unconsciously. Moreover, the two modes of thought work in concert.

Consciousness

Introduction

Baumeister and Bargh are leaders in the field in the study of unconscious, conscious, and their relation to free will. In the following, I discuss their work; each shows that conscious and unconscious processes collaborate in behavioral unfolding.

Baumeister

Model Baumeister and Masicampo (2010) argued that consciousness is best considered a place in which the unconscious acts to construct meaningful sequences of thought. They linked this notion to evidence, for example, that the unconscious functions to process single words but not sentences and paragraphs (e.g., Baars, 2002). Likewise, logical reasoning deteriorates sharply when consciousness is preoccupied and, in contrast, it improves when consciousness is engaged (DeWall, Baumeister, & Masicampo, 2008). Logical reasoning requires putting together complex sequences of ideas while ruling out other possible sequences, and that may too big a task to do effectively without a role for consciousness, as well.

Baumeister et al. (2011) reported key themes from their survey of experimental findings on conscious causation. They included the following: Conscious thoughts integrate across time; that is, conscious thought permits the deliberate combining of past and future into causing present behavior, as well as helping present cognitions to cause future behavior, and probably other combinations.

Conscious thought also appears to help translate abstract principles into specific behaviors, such as abstract moral principles, legal rules, economic calculations, and application of scientific and mathematical principles. The unconscious benefits form abstract principles in guiding behavior.

Baumeister et al. (2011) also found that conscious causation of behavior is typically evident in situations involving multiple possibilities, such as in deliberating multiple possible courses of action. Consciousness enables the person to mentally simulate nonpresent realities, including possible sequences of future events. The research has not established definitely whether the act of choosing is conscious or unconscious—but decisions based on conscious thought should be more effective when considering what each possible action will produce and also whether associated downstream consequences are desirable.

Most important, consciousness is especially useful in communication (Baumeister & Masicampo, 2010), for example, in sharing information and coordinating joint performance. Conscious thinking helps to facilitate talking. In this regard, Baumeister, Masicampo, and Vohs (2015) contended that consciousness serves not only in reflection/reasoning and elaborating sense of self, but also it serves to integrate information, thereby helping to resolve conflict. Consciousness is associated with advanced thinking, and it facilitates social communication, cooperation, and collective planning/learning, as well as even teaching. It allows for thinking and complex sentences and logic instead of the use of simple words and thoughts. It enables thoughts as complex as those associated with laws and causal theories.

Comment The work by Baumeister and colleagues on conscious causation, in particular, constitutes a powerful demonstration of the reality and efficacy of conscious thought because their review of research considered only ones involving experimental manipulations. Conscious and unconscious thought work together toward optimal adaptation. That it has been shown to exist offers support to the notion that free will exists, as well. [For a longer description of this work by Baumeister on conscious causation, see Chap. 20].

In the next portion of the chapter, I examine the work of Bargh and colleagues, who have also shown that conscious and unconscious thought work in concert. In this sense, even the work that emphasizes the role of unconscious processes in thought leaves room for free will as a valid part of behavioral causation.

Bargh

Model Bargh, Schwader, Hailey, Dyer, and Boothby (2012) highlighted the ubiquity of automaticity in social-cognitive processes, especially in childhood. Automaticity in this sense refers to efficient and unintentional social-cognitive processes that operate out of conscious awareness. The authors countered the standard view that conscious and effortful skill acquisition precedes and sets the stage for higher-order conscious processes. In contrast, rather than needing extensive practice and experience to become automatic after their acquisition consciously, they might emerge innately or very early in development as automatic.

Bargh et al. (2012) distinguished between preconscious and postconscious (goal-dependent) automaticity. The former is generated from effortless, triggering sensory/perceptual activity, which might input into/activate conscious mental processes. The latter is dependent on prior or concurrent conscious/intentional/motivated mental activity, including in attention, cognition, and decision-making. These two types or domains of activity work in tandem.

A good example of automaticity research lies in the area of embodiment studies. For instance, holding a warm beverage container activates a sense of social warmth (Williams & Bargh, 2008). Social rejection causes social pain and distress, thereby activating the same brain regions associated with physical pain (Eisenberger, Lieberman, & Williams, 2003). Early sensorimotor experience serves as a foundation for later abstract development (Williams, Huang, & Bargh, 2009; also Piaget, see Young, 2011).

Mechanisms Bargh et al. (2012) described three mechanisms contributing to embodiment effects. (a) Phylogenetically, associative connections evolved due to their adaptive significance and, moreover, they are underlain by anatomical connectivity (e.g., in the insula for physical warmth/coldness and social warmth/coldness; Kang, Williams, Clark, Gray, & Bargh, 2011). (b) Ontogenetically, early sensorimotor experiences contribute, as described above. (c) Also, language affords the semantic acquisition of metaphors that strengthen the associations (e.g., he's a "cold" person).

In the area of moral judgments, even here an innate, hard-wire basis has been proposed, one that includes automatic processes. For example, research has found that manipulations of time constraints and cognitive load, which impair controlled processes but not automatic ones, serve to affect utilitarian (benefit/cost) analysis but not rule-based moral judgments (Greene, Morelli, Lowenberg, Nystrom, & Cohen, 2008; Suter & Hertwig, 2011).

The areas of motivation and goal pursuit also have been fruitful in elucidating a role for unconscious processes. In the latter the same executive function and working memory resources are recruited as needed in their conscious unfolding (e.g., Dijksterhuis & Aarts, 2010). For example, Hassin (2008) and Hassin, Bargh, and Zimerman (2009) found that the nonconscious operation of an achievement goal increased working memory capacity on standard executive function tasks. Marien, Custers, Hassin, and Aarts (2012) found that subliminally priming goals (e.g., academic performance) diverted attentional capacity away from an ongoing conscious task (e.g., proofreading).

Bargh et al. (2012) noted that individuals lacking in awareness of pursuing nonconsciously operating goals could engage in self-deception in describing them. For example, Bargh, Lee-Chai, Barndollar, Gollwitzer, and Trötschel (2001) found that nonconsciously pursuing a cooperative goal did not lead to self-report of how much cooperation had taken place. Bar-Anan, Wilson, and Hassin (2010) found that people misattribute behaviors driven by nonconscious goals to other reasons that were plausible; consciously accessible and erroneous self-understandings such as these could have long-term consequences.

Table 18.1 Automatic processes observed in infancy/early childhood

Domain	Summary of findings
Objects	Infants (i.e., under 12 months) comprehend that objects, but not substances, are solid (i.e., two objects cannot occupy the same space at the same time) and that objects are cohesive (i.e., they persist as single entities; Hespos & van Marle, 2012)
Numbers	Infants appear to possess a core system that represents small quantities as individual objects. They have a second system to represent quantities as approximate numerical values (Feigenson, Dehaene, & Spelke, 2004)
Space	Infants express sensitivity to distance, angles, and direction. They can use both egocentric and allocentric frames of reference to navigate spatial environments (Vasilyeva & Lourenco, 2012)
Agents	Infants organize the actions of agents in terms of the goals of the agents goals (Woodward, 2009)
Social evaluation	Infants prefer prosocial agents to antisocial ones (Hamlin & Wynn, 2011)
False beliefs	Children younger than 4 years do not verbally express knowledge of an agent's false belief, yet infants younger than that show false-belief understanding when tested with looking-time or other implicit measures (Baillargeon, Scott, & He, 2010; Perner & Roessler, 2012)
Priming	Priming can induce social behavior in toddlers and young children. For example, it can induce helping in 18-month-olds (Over & Carpenter, 2009a). Also, it can induce affiliative imitation following social exclusion in 5-year-olds (Over & Carpenter, 2009b)
Implicit attitudes	By 12 months of age, infants can distinguish faces differing by gender and race (Pascalis et al., 2011). By 5 years of age, children show implicit racial attitudes that are identical to those of adults (Dunham, Baron, & Banaji, 2006)

Adapted from Bargh et al. (2012)

Development As for the development of automatic and unconscious psychological processes in infancy and early childhood, Bargh et al. (2012) reviewed the literature on (a) objects/numbers/space, (b) agents/social evaluation/false beliefs, and (c) priming/implicit attitudes (see Table 18.1). For point (a), the research indicates that infants possess early sensitivities, understanding, and core representations. For (b), others' goals are understood, prosocial others are preferred and, eventually, the ability to navigate false-belief tasks develops. For (c), priming can induce helping in toddlers (Over & Carpenter, 2009a, 2009b) and, also, the basis for implicit attitudes is set in early facial discrimination skills.

Unconscious First About the topic of goal-dependent automaticity, Dijksterhuis and Nordgren (2006) proposed the "unconscious thought" theory, which suggests that decisions made unconsciously are superior in quality relative to consciously-made ones. The research by Bargh (2011) supports the theory to a degree, as that does that of Ham and colleagues, in areas such as justice and morality (Ham & van den Bos, 2010; Ham, van den Bos, & van Doorn, 2009).

Both Together Nordgren, Bos, and Dijksterhuis (2011) proposed an integrated model in which both conscious and unconscious thought processes could be involved in complex decision-making, and noted that the decisions are better when this happens. For a similar and more general perspective, see Hassin (2013).

As for Bargh et al. (2012) in this regard, they concluded that unconscious processes can cause conscious ones, which in turn activate unconscious ones (also Baumeister & Bargh, 2014; for a full review of this publication, see the next chapter, Chap. 20). Bargh et al. (2012) agreed with Baumeister and Masicampo (2010) that unconscious processes are the primary causal triggers in social behavior, but with conscious ones important, too. In this regard, Briñol and DeMarree (2012) have demonstrated that the latter can change and redirect the former in interplay.

According to Bargh et al. (2012), free will in philosophy refers to an "original, uncaused cause." However, in psychology, it refers to a causal role for conscious thought. The authors concluded that the evidence supports the existence of conscious thought. They repeated that unconscious and conscious thought work together.

Comment I add that there are some questions that Bargh et al. (2012) have not addressed that seem worth pursuing, especially related to free will. For example, to what degree does free will participate in conscious thought and thereby influence unconscious thought, given their reciprocity? How exactly does it participate moment to moment in the causal chain from stimulus to response, in the steps of stimulus selection, executive work on the stimuli selected, including in planning and decision-making, and response execution and monitoring, given its reciprocity with unconscious thought? Indeed, how does consciousness become conscious?

Bargh and colleagues' work on the unconscious refers to developmental processes, in this regard. One way of addressing the developmental aspect of conscious vs. unconscious thought and their collaboration is to examine their development from early intuitive to later logical thought, for example, in the Neo-Piagetian perspective, as I have done (Young, 2011). In particular, I reworked the concept of different types of thought (Type/System I; conscious, slow, deliberate; Type/System II; unconscious, fast, automatic) into a Neo-Piagetian developmental framework, and the model speaks to the differences in unconscious and conscious thought processes and how they develop (see Chap. 32).

Others

Awareness Pallar and Suzuki (2014) maintained that conscious awareness emanates from the reciprocal exchange of information over multiple brain regions. Consciousness is constituted by the exchange of complex information in this manner. It is richer when it involves more neuronal connections/regions. Self-awareness takes place this way, and it facilitates modeling and predicting not only of our own behavior but also that of others (e.g., of our attention and intention, and also that of others).

Conscious reasoning involves coordinating information associated with multiple brain sources. Unconscious influences on reasoning are those that are separate and parallel instead of integrated. The unconscious mode of reasoning might be more protracted so that, because its influence is not perceived or made aware, we are left with the impression that our conscious reasoning had been instantaneous and free in deciding, when this has not been the case.

Graziano (2013) proposed a theory of consciousness that differs from those of Libet (e.g., Libet, 1985) and others, who deny its capacity to influence behavior. Consciousness refers to both information of which we are aware and the process of awareness of it. Through attention schema, we build not only models of others' attention but also of our own. Awareness is associated with the temporo-parietal junction and the superior temporal sulcus. It allows the brain to construct descriptors of awareness.

The processes of being aware and of attending engage in a positive feedback loop. Although attention is considered an active process, awareness is not but, because of their link, awareness can become an "active controller" in directing, enhancing, suppressing, and guiding each of signals, choices, and actions. Awareness can actually "cause," thus, awareness is a phenomenon that has the capacity to alter its focus, shaping brain processes to control behavior. To conclude, Graziano's (2013) attention schema theory allows consciousness to have control over behavior.

Fingelkurts, Fingelkurts, Bagnato, Boccagni, and Galardi (2012) argued that consciousness does not have to have an isomorphic or reductionist relationship to brain processes (see Fig. 18.3). Instead, consciousness could be an "emergent" phenomenon in which changes in it can take place without corresponding constitutive changes in lower-order neural phenomena.

Comment Neuronally, consciousness has been related to attentional and awareness mechanisms, as well as to emergence. Once more, the ground is laid for free will (as an emergent, aware, attentional process) as part of conscious thought. Keep in mind (no pun intended), however, that unconscious thoughts are still important and positive components of our thought, as per the following.

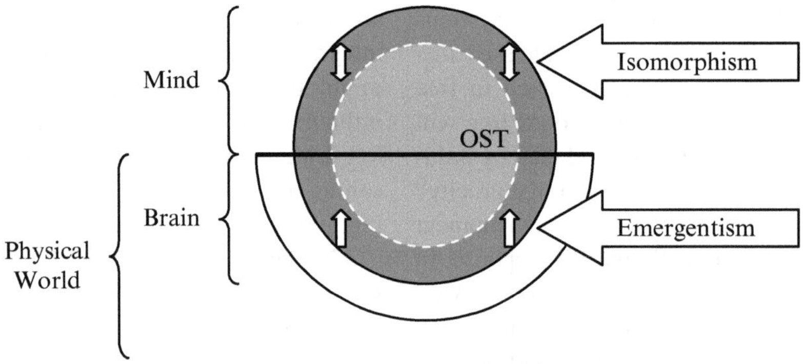

Fig. 18.3 Different levels in brain–mind organization relations. OST indicates the operational space-time of the brain. In this model, the OST level represents a constitutive mechanism of phenomenal consciousness and ties the phenomenal (subjective) and neurophysiological (physical) levels together. Isomorphism might be taken to mean that there cannot be change in the arrangement of higher-order phenomena (phenomenal mind) without changing their underlying microphysical properties (brain operational architectonics). Emergentism, on the other hand, usually allows for changes of higher-order phenomena (brain operational architectonics) that need not possess a one-on-one, direct linkage with changes at any underlying lower-order levels (internal physical space-time of the brain). Adapted from Fingelkurts et al. (2012)

Hidden Kraft and Pressman (2012) demonstrated the influence of a positive psychological frame on stress reactivity, even if it is induced manipulatively and remains out of awareness. They studied 18- to 25-year-old university students. Participants were trained to activate either (a) a sincere, genuine, or broad (Duchenne) smile, by activating the zygomatic major and orbicularis oculi muscles, or (b) a more contained smile (zygomatic major muscle only). There were three conditions (Duchenne smile, standard smile, neutral), with half of the participants for the smile groups told to smile during the instruction period.

The participants were asked to grip chopsticks in their mouths by mimicking the teeth-gripping behavior of a research assistant. In the neutral group, the chopsticks were held downward (vertically). In the standard smile group, the chopsticks were held downward, but also with zygomatic major muscle activation. In the Duchenne group, the chopsticks were held horizontally, and with the two indicated muscle groups activated. Heart rate was measured at base line and during two stress-inducing tasks (star tracing, cold pressor). Changes in positive and negative affect also were measured. The resting period after each stressor lasted 5 min, and they did not include the chopstick holding.

The results showed that mean heart rate during the stress-recovering period was highest in the neutral condition, whether compared to the smile conditions or the aware/nonaware conditions, with the results still significant while controlling covariates such as perceived stress. The Duchenne smile was particularly advantageous in stress recovering. Kraft and Pressman (2012) concluded that "grinning and bearing it" could have advantage in stress regulation. The positive affect generated might have positive effects physiologically as well as psychologically, in addition to its inhibitory effect on negative affect and the latter's potentially deleterious consequences for health.

The study of causation has become more important in psychological and psychiatric approaches to behavioral difficulties. At the same time, the hoped-for progress in understanding etiology of disease in the medical field has not reached the levels aspired to. For example, Axmacher (2013) examined the hidden world of causation in one branch of mental health that is controversial—psychoanalysis. The Freudian account is that psychic material repressed into the unconscious is inaccessible but still an important driver of behavior. Axmacher (2013) argued that unconscious processes can be revealed in therapy partly by offering hypotheses that elicit "surprise" in the patient.

I note that it would seem that the therapist who proposes a psychoanalytic hypothesis is suggesting something akin to a counterfactual–manipulationist intervention. In this sense, even the obscure psychodynamic processes involved in unconscious repression might be amenable to understanding by an interventionist account. Also, neuroscience is helping to understand and even update Freudian metatheory.

Comment The issue of nonconscious processes in the causation of behavior is a critical one (e.g., Bargh et al., 2012). However, the degree to which its contemporary study is investigating the Freudian approach to the unconscious seems minimal. Nevertheless, there would appear to be room for its inclusion in neuroscientific study.

The unconscious might be hidden, but through its automaticity, it allows the chunking needed to deal with the complexity of rapid, online adaptivity. Moreover, even the repression into the unconscious that might take place with "intra-psychic" conflicts might be adaptive, at least in the short term. The unconscious is not merely the seat of the primitive. Rather, it is the workhorse of our thought and needs to work seamlessly with the conscious to causally effect adaptive behavioral outcomes.

The following section of the chapter switches gears back to the topic of free will, but from a developmental perspective. Free will might be a critical focus of human activity and development.

Development of Free Will

Model

Goldman (2012) introduced a novel theory of free will couched in neurogenetics. The latter is a deterministic point of view, but proposes that, nevertheless, the brain is capable of freely choosing. Each of us is not only neurogenetically determined but also neurogenetically individual, including in our brains and personalities, so our DNA entails allowing us freedom. This is not a paradoxical state of affairs—determinism and freedom co-existing—because in the web of causation of genes and environment people are still free to make choices despite constraints and limitations imposed by biology and context.

Neurodevelopment is a lifelong sequential unfolding guided not only by genotype but also by environmental exposures, which might be random and, moreover, which might be ones that we choose. This type of theorizing provides a mechanism for understanding the origins of free will.

We do not need to treat people "as if" they have free will because they do, although we do need to treat children that way. Free will derives from variations in cognitive structure due to neurodevelopmental adaptation. Therefore, free will, paradoxically, is "neurogenetically determined." Brain development unfolds stochastically (in response to randomness) in a way that makes each of us self-determined. The freedom does not originate in the randomness. Rather, our brains capitalize on it and, along with biological parameters, lead us to develop as individual, free selves.

Genes influence us but are in interaction with the environment. Moreover, we can choose to select and alter our environment, accentuating our uniqueness. Unpredictability frames genes in context, so that behavior is an attempt to control unpredictability. But this does not say the same thing as behavior is deterministic. It can vary, for example, according to belief in free will. Believing that people have free will does not deny causality, which is multi-dimensional. But causality in behavior does not deny autonomy, which is real for us, and is a paradoxically emergent phenomenon deriving from our genome-guided neurodevelopmental program.

The brain builds itself, or its multineuronal complex and hierarchical networks, through self-assembly or self-organization. The neurons converse, cross-talk, and self-construct without superordinate guides helping them but, instead, with a constant, nuanced and subtle adjustment, adaptation, refinement, regulation, and feedback looping. As a result, unique circuitry develops in the brain. Moreover, individuality is amplified by the (free) choices that we make, because they act to help shape our brains.

Our brains are plastic as they develop. Neurons are dynamically interconnected, shaped, and being shaped by neighbors, with the same reciprocal shaping applying to superordinate neural networks. In self-organization, minor inputs to the system can lead to chaotic or major changes, as in the so-called butterfly effect. Globally, the system still is determined in this effect, although it appears random at first when we see the small differences in perturbations that lead to the disproportionate cascade. Note that the new and old state of the system can be characterized as attractors, and their basins "tamp" or help control the unpredictability of the system. Nevertheless, "brainbow" images taken of the brain reveal that it has "infinite randomness" even with the presence of the architectural framework that guides, or constrains, the randomness. The blueprint might be "strong," but it does not lead to exact prediction of the details of the map involved.

Comment

Goldman (2012) concluded in his book that "we all share one paradoxical legacy of causality and the stochastic unfolding of the of the brain's developmental program: we were born free." (p. 234) He clarified that free will is an attribute that develops and is reflected in the individuality of our personality and self. Genes are not destiny (nor is environment). "Humans do seem to be able to choose." "Genetic influences are weak and probabilistic." They also interact with the environment and also how we "consciously steer" our lives. Finally, according to Goldman (2012), part of our freedom should be to help people towards ably choosing, too, thereby increasing their freedom.

Goldman (2012) has elucidated a model of the development of free will that includes biological, environmental, and personal components. Biology and environment are passive components among these influences on development of free will. Our ability to develop to choose constitutes the core of the active component of our behavioral causality. Note that, to his credit, much of the major themes of the present book are echoed in the work of Goldman (2012).

Evolution

Model

Baumeister, Crescioni, and Alquist (2011) described that four forms of behavior evolved sequentially to increase the capacity to behave as if we had free will. First, initiative evolved to actively guide motivation and behavior. Then, nascent ability for self-control emerged (overriding a response or impulse in order to act in a different manner). Rational choice followed in evolution (arriving at an intelligent choice by logical reasoning of the best course of action). Fourth, planned behavior evolved (mentally working out and then executing an organized, optimal sequence of actions aimed at a desired result).

Baumeister (2010) related consciousness to planning and simulating possibility. He used the metaphor of making an inner movie that the brain constructs for itself. It helps to decide what actions are performed. Consciousness is linked to free will, because only conscious thought can conceptualize multiple options from which to choose. As with the capacities that permit the perception that one has free will in thought and action, consciousness evolved in steps and humans express the most advanced form.

Comment

Young (2011) had presented a quite similar model of the steps in changes in free will, but instead of proceeding evolutionarily, he organized a model of the development of free will around his model of five stages in development. In this regard, a fifth evolutionary step in the development of free will belief might relate to the step of adult collective intelligence that Young (2011) had described as the final step in cognitive development. To follow through with this idea, free will belief might be conceived as a superordinate abstract construction that evolved in our recent past through gene-culture co-evolution due to the survival and reproductive benefits it adds to cultural practice.

The next part of the chapter considers another biologically-related aspect of free will, on whether brain function even allows it. Reductionists in the field would argue against any biological support possible for the phenomenon of free will in behavior. That said, there are workers who support the counter view that free will is inherent in brain function.

The Brain and Free Will

Model

Callard and Fitzgerald (2014) and Filevich et al. (2013) argued that the subjective experience of behaving voluntarily might be dissociated from brain circuits with action selection. Moreover, having choice might be a constraint more than a reason to feel free. Both Shields (2014) and Navon (2014) argued that conscious control and initiation of behavior do occur and are not byproducts of preconscious brain activity. According to them, the research implying that this cannot happen contains both methodological limitations and conceptual ambiguities. Shields (2014) concluded that volitional action is the outcome of a complex, rapid decision-making process that incorporates cognitive elements and prior decisions. Navon (2014) argued that a wholly physicalistic conception of behavior that denies some role for "mind" could drive to a "dead-end."

In de Jong (2011), a neurological model of perception of free will includes the parietal cortex as well as the prefrontal cortex. The model also gives a place to processing in the (dorsal) premotor cortex (see Fig. 18.4). In Rappaport's model (2011), aside from the prefrontal and parietal area of the brain, as well as relevant motor areas, the insula is considered important toward the perception of having free will (see Fig. 18.5). The insula is involved in taking ownership of the sense of one's body. The neuronal network involved in perceiving free will allows us authorship of and taking responsibilities for our actions. Because having a sense of free will is embedded in our brains, and in a way that is widely distributed in the brain, the argument that makes sense follows. It is not that free will is reducible to brain processes and that there is no individual responsibility; rather, our whole neurological and psychological profile functions toward the development of responsibility within the social context.

Siegel and Douard (2011) emphasized that free will appears a product of inhibitory control and the underlying substrate in the brain. Their model involves the PFC as a site in conditioning neurons (see Fig. 18.6). The PFC is involved in regulating lower-level areas, leading to impulse control. Therefore, even if mediating factors, such as low serotonin, are present, the person can still exert inhibition, control, consciousness, and responsibility.

Pockett (2006) presented a model of willed intentions in relation to the external world leading to movement. The model is among the first contemporary ones to implicate multiple brain regions that are involved in having a sense of free will. She distinguished between willed intentions and sensorimotor ones, which are lower in level and more immediate. The model stresses that consciousness does not necessarily cause simple kinds of behavior nor it is necessarily involved in the correction of ongoing actions. However, for complex decisions and long-term intentions, actions might be initiated consciously. In these cases, the dorsolateral prefrontal cortex (DLPFC) and/or the pre-SMA might be involved in long-term intentions, and the posterior parietal cortex might be involved in more immediate intentions. Moreover, Fig. 18.7 indicates that there is a complex way of processing involved in these conscious intentional actions, including in the frontal cortex.

Keller and Iverson (2013) contended that the voluntary inhibition of reflex behavior underpins free will. Suppressing reflex responses allows selection from among different possible plans of behavior.

Comment

Pierre (2013) reviewed the neuroscience of free will. He introduces the notion that causal explanation of change in psychotherapy (cognitive, behavioral) is based on the assumption that thoughts are subject to conscious change so that behavior can

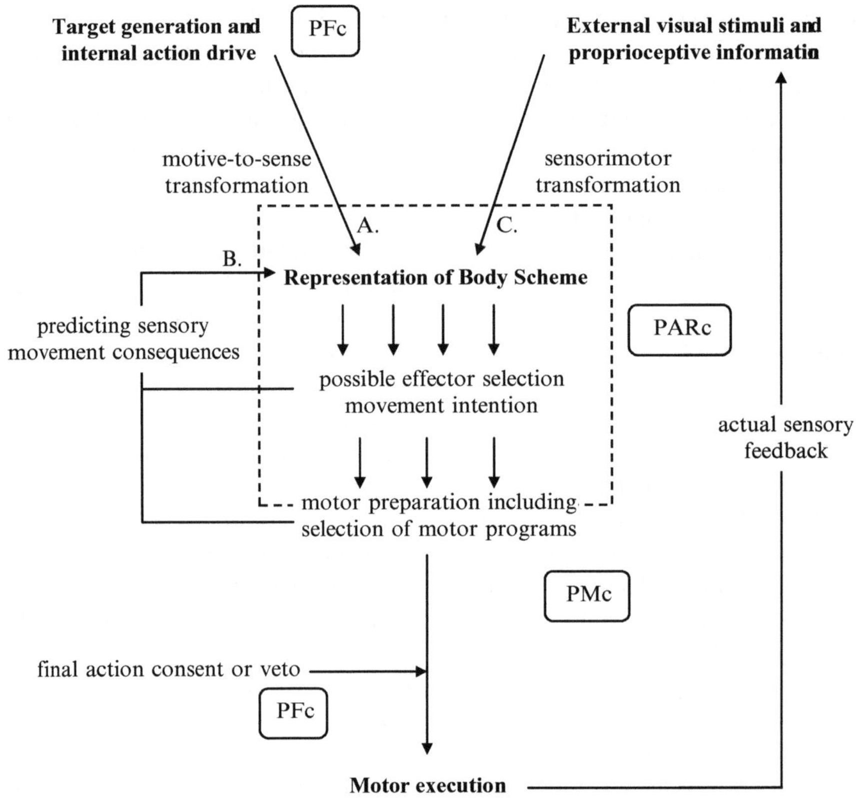

Fig. 18.4 Body-scheme-centered parietal processing associated with free selection. *Abbreviations. PARc* processing in the parietal cortex, *PFc* processing in the prefrontal cortex, *PMc* processing in the (dorsal) premotor cortex. This scheme illustrates the putative sequence of initial target generation, fuelling the motive for action, and the subsequent transformation to the neuronal representation of a body scheme [*A*]. The latter is a prerequisite for the selection between possible action effectors, a basic step of "embodiment" apparently associated with the perception of self-intended movement, i.e., *the perception of free will*. Early-stage selection in the parietal cortex concerns free selection between body parts that may be used for goal-directed movement. This is further elaborated in motor preparation, which includes selection between motor programs within parietal–premotor circuitry. Selection associated with the perception of self-intended movement additionally concerns the distinction of movement "sensations" being either predicted [*B*] or recorded [*C*], thus providing the adequate sense of a causal relation between movement and its effect. Adopted with permission of Elsevier. Reprinted from *Cortex*, Vol. 47, de Jong, B. M., Neurology of widely embedded free will, Pages 1160–1165, Copyright 2011; with kind permission from Elsevier. [Figure 1, Page 1163]

change. He suggested that the construct of free will should be updated by emphasizing, instead, volitional self-control. Volitional control implies the capacity to choose and to decide. However, neuroscientifically, choices are often made unconsciously and "within neural networks."

It is the individual's brain that is clearly "fully" and "always" responsible for the person's behavior (Hallett, 2007). Dualistic conceptions give importance to free will as opposed to volitional control. Even when behavior is unconsciously determined, the self exists (Haggard, 2009). Even a perfectly functioning brain does not have free will, per se. Areas of the brain involved in volitional control and its absence, e.g., in addictions, include the insula cortex, which integrates amygdala and ventromedial prefrontal cortex (VMPC) signals (Verdejo-Garía, 2009; Li, Lu, D'Argembeau, Ng, & Bechara, 2010).

The neuroscience research grapples with the question of free will in multiple ways—some by promoting its possibility and localization, or at least association, with particular brain regions; some by maintaining reductionist models denying its independence (and existence) from neuronal processes; and some by changing the grounds of

Fig. 18.5 A neuroanatomical sketch of willed motion. Agency is an awareness dependent on feedback between the movement that ensures after creation of a sensory model (related to the parietal lobe). Perceiving ownership of the body might be involved (related to the insula). Adapted from Rappaport (2011)

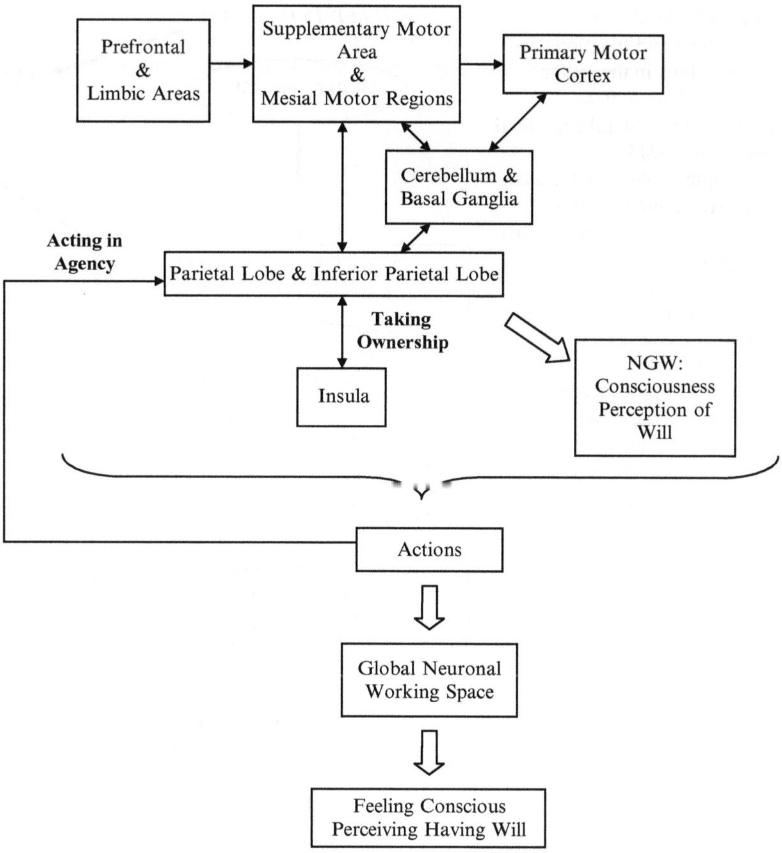

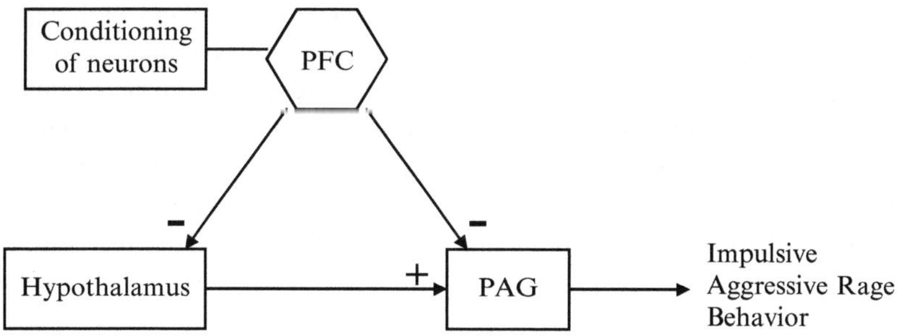

Fig. 18.6 Schematic diagram illustrating the role of the prefrontal cortex (PFC) as a key site in the conditioning process. PFC regulates and controls aggressive impulsive behavior that is mediated by the medial hypothalamus and midbrain periaqueductal gray (PAG). The PFC receives major inputs from sensory regions of cortex and thalamus. These inputs provide the basis by which classical conditioning of neurons in this region takes place and accordingly provide the substrate for cognitive associations to be formed in this region. Activation of these cognitive associations is associated with activation of PFC neurons, which then suppress medial hypothalamic and PAG mechanisms, thus reducing or eliminating the expression of the impulsive rage response. The figure helps understand the neuroscience source of action and its control. Adopted with permission of Elsevier. Reprinted from *International Journal of Law and Psychiatry,* Vol. 34, Siegel, A., & Douard, J., Who's flying the plane: Serotonin levels, aggression and free will, Pages 20–29, Copyright 2011; with kind permission from Elsevier. [Figure 1, Page 27]

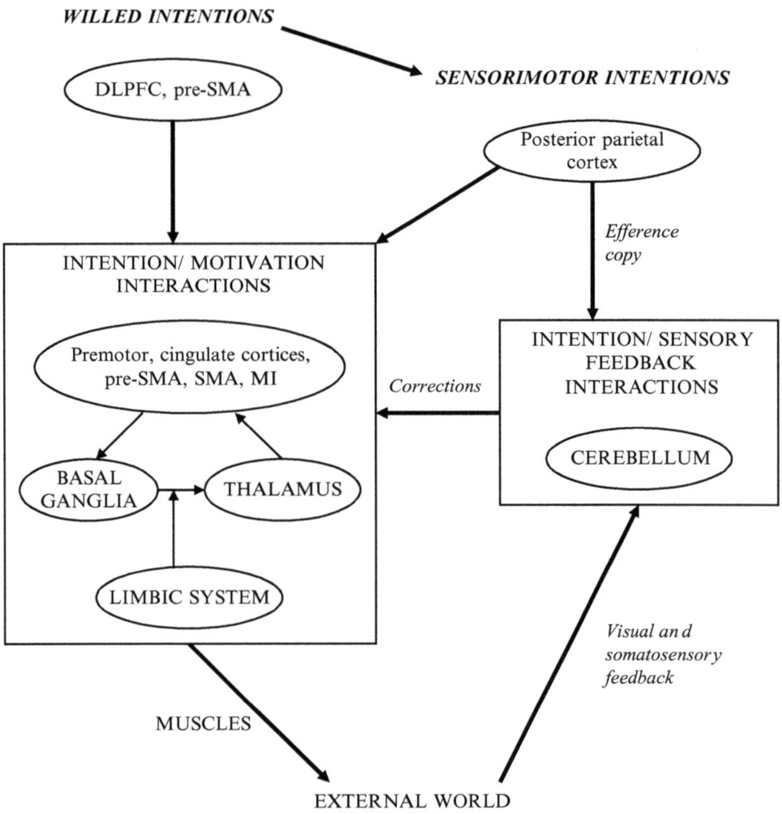

Fig. 18.7 Model of anatomical and functional relationships in the motor system. *Abbreviations. DLPFC* dorsolateral prefrontal cortex, *pre-SMA* presupplementary motor area, *SMA* supplementary motor area, *MI* primary motor cortex. Adopted by permission of The MIT Press. Pockett, Susan, William P. Banks, and Shaun Gallagher, eds., *Does Consciousness Cause Behavior?* Figure 1.2, pp. 11, © 2006 Massachusetts Institute of Technology, by permission of The MIT Press. [Figure 1.2, Page 11]

the debate, and referring to volitional control, intention, and so on. The present perspective is that free will is an emergent and biopsychosocial phenomenon and that it is multiply determined, with brain structure and function involved.

The last part of the present chapter moves from the individual to the group for some topics related to free will, such as in politics. The next chapter includes material on free will, as well, especially in a proposal for a new questionnaire on the topic.

The Politics of Free Will

Model

Hibbing, Smith, and Alford (2014) queried the nature of differences between conservatives (supporters of tradition/stability) and liberals (supporters of innovation/reform). The former tend to experience an increased physiological response to negative (adverse) environments compared to the latter; in addition, conservatives devote more psychological resources to them. The results of the research are more robust for the strength of this negativity bias in conservatives compared to the strength for more distal factors such as genetic differences and for more proximal parental political preferences. Commentators on Hibbing et al. (2014) referred to other aspects of the environment in these regards, as well (e.g., threat sensitivity, arousal), cognitive closure, values, positive aspects of the environment, and economic vs. sociocultural issues. The authors denied a critical role of personality variables (e.g., neuroticism) in differentiating conservatives and liberals.

Carey and Paulhus (2012) investigated the relationship between free will belief and measures related to a conservative worldview. They used the FAD-Plus (Paulhus & Carey, 2011), and found free will belief is associated with "traditional conservative values" as well as "religiosity" and a belief in a "just world." Another study they conducted related it to punitiveness and moralistic standards (in judging self/others). The authors suggested that free will belief promotes "a strong sense" of personal responsibility for one's behavior. They combined the work of Baumeister (2008) and Haidt (2008) to argue that free will belief is associated with the expectation that others will demonstrate self-control of impulses and, also, that they will criticize people for not expressing such self-control. In addition, they expect punishment as a rightful response to misbehavior.

Comment

The politics of the psychology of politics is highly psychological. It needs the correct methodology and instruments. It could be that there are diverse answers to these issues depending on individual's constellation of biopsychosocial factors influencing them.

Chapter Conclusions

There is enough evidence to show that free will is not an illusion. The mind can function emergently and distinctly from passive biological and environmental influences. It can function actively and proactively to facilitate accommodative adjustment and adaptation to the environment, choosing and deciding appropriately toward its optimal goals. The person has much to say in his or her own behavior and in social relations with others. Free will is a property of mind as much as is perception and action. The former is guided by subjective appraisals that are personally constructed and the latter is guided by personally-derived desires, wishes, and goals. The person is a thinking and emotional whole who is not confined to the prescriptions of genetics and the proscriptions of the environment.

Free will is integral to the human psychology, and can help escape the tyranny of determinism. Behavior is unconscious and automatic at lower levels but guided by conscious deliberation at higher levels, being fully present and participatory in the moment rather than fashioned uniquely by the past, whether in terms of prior contexts/environments, psychological states/characteristics, or biological/genetic fixities. Free will is inscribed in the brain and body; genetics and physiology; and behavior and mind as a potential that increasingly activates and dominates in behavioral determination as development proceeds and matures.

Free will is what makes us free as humans, willful as humans, and confident in our ability to adapt potentially in a successful way to any and all contingencies of life. It is the hallmark of our intelligence, our emotivity, and our being. It is our birthright and our life long right. Free will is as much in our reality as reality lies in our free will. It is as real and vibrant as the best that is in us and the best that we can help make the other.

Free will speaks not only to the stream of our daily lives, the long-term goals that we set for ourselves, and the strategies for problems that immediately confront us, but also, free will can be used when things go awry psychologically. In this regard, free will can be used in face of deep issues that beguile us. Further in this regard, when we cannot marshal by ourselves the resources to implement it effectively and psychological difficulties become ingrained and troublesome, free will should be an integral part of psychotherapy. Individual differences in free will have wide-ranging impacts, and seeding its belief and sense can help people in need, such as those suffering from addictions and psychopathologies. It is impossible to understand the causality of behavior without understanding free will. It is the epitome of who we are and the essential driver of what we become.

As for the flip side of free will, the debate that one or the other of consciousness and unconsciousness is primary or even unique in decision-making and action is sterile. Both are entwined in behavioral determination, and free will is related to consciousness, which develops as much as free will. That being said, the research in the area needs careful examination, for example, on the studies that lead to the conclusion that conscious experience follows decision-making rather than preceding it (e.g., Libet, 1985). If free will is the driver of adaptive behavior, consciousness is the ground on which it is permitted to deploy and function.

References

Adams, P., & Suarez, A. (2013). Introduction. In A. Suarez & P. Adams (Eds.), *Is science compatible with free will? Exploring free will and consciousness in the light of quantum physics and neuroscience* (pp. 1–4). New York: Springer Science+Business Media.

Alquist, J. L., Ainsworth, S. E., & Baumeister, R. F. (2013). Determined to conform: Disbelief in free will increases conformity. *Journal of Experimental Social Psychology, 49*, 80–86.

Alquist, J. L., Ainsworth, S., Baumeister, R., Daly, M., & Stillman, T. (2015). The making of might-have-beens: Effects of free will belief on counterfactual thinking. *Personality and Social Psychology Bulletin, 41*, 268–283.

Axmacher, N. (2013). Causation in psychoanalysis. *Frontiers in Psychology, 4*. doi:10.3389/fpsyg.2013.00077.

Baars, B. J. (2002). The conscious access hypothesis: Origins and recent evidence. *Trends in Cognitive Sciences, 6*, 47–52.

Baillargeon, R., Scott, R. M., & He, Z. (2010). False-belief understanding in infants. *Trends in Cognitive Sciences, 14*, 110–118.

Bar-Anan, Y., Wilson, T. D., & Hassin, R. R. (2010). Inaccurate self-knowledge formation as a result of automatic behavior. *Journal of Experimental Social Psychology, 46*, 884–894.

Bargh, J. A. (2011). Unconscious thought theory and its discontents: A critique of the critiques. *Social Cognition, 29*, 629–647.

Bargh, J. A., Lee-Chai, A., Barndollar, K., Gollwitzer, P. M., & Trötschel, R. (2001). The automated will: Nonconscious activation and pursuit of behavioral goals. *Journal of Personality and Social Psychology, 81*, 1014–1027.

Bargh, J. A., Schwader, K. L., Hailey, S. E., Dyer, R. L., & Boothby, E. J. (2012). Automaticity in social-cognitive processes. *Trends in Cognitive Sciences, 16*, 593–605.

Baumeister, R. F. (2008). Free will in scientific psychology. *Perspectives on Psychological Science, 3*, 14–19.

Baumeister, R. F. (2010). Understanding free will and consciousness on the basis of current research findings in psychology. In R. F. Baumeister, A. R. Mele, & K. D. Vohs (Eds.), *Free will and consciousness: How might they work?* (pp. 24–42). New York: Oxford University Press.

Baumeister, R. F., & Bargh, J. A. (2014). Conscious and unconscious: Toward an integrative understanding of human mental life and action. In J. W. Sherman, B. Gawronski, & Y. Trope (Eds.), *Dual-process theories of the social mind* (pp. 35–49). New York: Guilford Press.

Baumeister, R. F., & Brewer, L. E. (2012). Believing versus disbelieving in free will: Correlates and consequences. *Social and Personality Psychology Compass, 6*, 736–745.

Baumeister, R. F., Crescioni, A. W., & Alquist, J. L. (2011). Free will as advanced action control for human social life and culture. *Neuroethics, 4*, 1–11.

Baumeister, R. F., & Masicampo, E. J. (2010). Conscious thought is for facilitating social and cultural interactions: How mental simulations serve the animal-culture interface. *Psychological Review, 117*, 945–971.

Baumeister, R. F., Masicampo, E. J., & DeWall, C. N. (2009). Prosocial benefits of feeling free: Disbelief in free will increases aggression and reduces helpfulness. *Personality and Social Psychology Bulletin, 35*, 260–268.

Baumeister, R. F., Masicampo, E. J., & Vohs, K. D. (2011). Do conscious thoughts cause behavior? *Annual Review of Psychology, 62*, 331–361.

Baumeister, R. F., Masicampo, E. J., & Vohs, K. D. (2015). Conscious thoughts and the causation of behavior. In M. Mikulincer & P. R. Shaver (Eds.), *APA handbook of personality and social psychology* (Attitudes and social cognition, Vol. 1, pp. 231–250). Washington, DC: American Psychological Association.

Bode, S., He, A. H., Soon, C. S., Trampel, R., Turner, R., & Haynes, J. D. (2011). Tracking the unconscious generation of free decisions using ultra-high field fMRI. *PLoS One, 6*, e21612. doi:10.1371/journal.pone.0021612.

Bode, S., Murawski, C., Soon, C. S., Bode, P., Stahl, J., & Smith, P. L. (2014). Demystifying "free will": The role of contextual information and evidence accumulation for predictive brain activity. *Neuroscience and Biobehavioral Reviews, 47*, 636–645.

Brewer, L. E. (2011). *Forging freely: Perceptions of moral responsibility mediate the relationship between belief in free will and willingness to forgive* (Doctoral dissertation). Retrieved from Electronic Theses, Treatises and Dissertations. Paper 3044.

Brewer, L. E., & Baumeister, R. F. (2010). *Relationship between free will belief and self-control*. Tallahassee, FL: Florida State University.

Briñol, P., & DeMarree, K. G. (Eds.). (2012). *Social metacognition*. New York: Psychology Press.

Callard, F., & Fitzgerald, D. (2014). Experimental control: What does it mean for a participant to "feel free?". *Consciousness and Cognition, 27*, 231–232.

Carey, J., & Paulhus, D. L. (2011, January). *The independence of free will and determinism in judgments of moral responsibility*. Poster presented at the 12th Annual meeting of the Society for Personality and Social Psychology, San Antonio, TX.

Carey, J. M., & Paulhus, D. L. (2012). Worldview implications of believing in free will and/or determinism:

Politics, morality and punitiveness. *Journal of Personality, 81*, 130–141.

Crescioni, A. W., Baumeister, R. F., Ainsworth, S. E., Ent, M. R., & Lambert, N. M. (2015). Subjective correlates and consequences of belief in free will. *Philosophical Psychology, 9*, 41–63.

de Jong, B. M. (2011). Neurology of widely embedded free will. *Cortex, 47*, 1160–1165.

DeWall, C. N., Baumeister, R. F., & Masicampo, E. J. (2008). Evidence that logical reasoning depends on conscious processing. *Consciousness and Cognition, 17*, 628–645.

Dijksterhuis, A., & Aarts, H. (2010). Goals, attention, and (un) consciousness. *Annual Review of Psychology, 61*, 467–490.

Dijksterhuis, A., & Nordgren, L. F. (2006). A theory of unconscious thought. *Perspectives on Psychological Science, 1*, 95–109.

Doyle, R. O. (2013). The two-stage model to the problem of free will: How behavioral freedom in lower animals has evolved to become free will in humans and higher animals. In A. Suarez & P. Adams (Eds.), *Is science compatible with free will? Exploring free will and consciousness in the light of quantum physics and neuroscience* (pp. 235–254). New York: Springer Science+Business Media.

Dunham, Y., Baron, A. S., & Banaji, M. R. (2006). From American city to Japanese village: A cross-cultural investigation of implicit race attitudes. *Child Development, 77*, 1268–1281.

Eisenberger, N. I., Lieberman, M. D., & Williams, K. D. (2003). Does rejection hurt? An fMRI study of social exclusion. *Science, 302*, 290–292.

Elliot, A. J., & McGregor, H. A. (2001). A 2×2 achievement goal framework. *Journal of Personality and Social Psychology, 80*, 501–519.

Feigenson, L., Dehaene, S., & Spelke, E. (2004). Core systems of number. *Trends in Cognitive Sciences, 8*, 307–314.

Filevich, E., Vanneste, P., Brass, M., Fias, W., Haggard, P., & Kühn, S. (2013). Brain correlates of subjective freedom of choice. *Consciousness and Cognition, 22*, 1271–1284.

Fingelkurts, A. A., Fingelkurts, A. A., Bagnato, S., Boccagni, C., & Galardi, G. (2012). Toward operational architectonics of consciousness: Basic evidence from patients with severe cerebral injuries. *Cognitive Processing, 13*, 111–131.

Goldman, D. (2012). *Our genes our choices: How genotype and gene interactions affect behavior*. Amsterdam, Netherlands: Elsevier Academic Press.

Gollwitzer, P. M., & Sheeran, P. (2006). Implementation intentions and goal achievement: A meta-analysis of effects and processes. *Advances in Experimental Social Psychology, 38*, 69–119.

Graziano, M. S. A. (2013). *Consciousness and the socials brain*. New York: Oxford University Press.

Greene, J. D., Morelli, S. A., Lowenberg, K., Nystrom, L. E., & Cohen, J. D. (2008). Cognitive load selectively interferes with utilitarian moral judgment. *Cognition, 107*, 1144–1154.

Haggard, P. (2009). The sources of human volition. *Science, 324*, 731–733.

Haidt, J. (2008). Morality. *Perspectives on Psychological Science, 3*, 65–72.

Hallett, M. (2007). Volitional control of movement: The physiology of free will. *Clinical Neurophysiology, 118*, 1179–1192.

Ham, J., & van den Bos, K. (2010). On unconscious morality: The effects of unconscious thinking on moral decision making. *Social Cognition, 28*, 74–83.

Ham, J., van den Bos, K., & van Doorn, E. A. (2009). Lady Justice thinks unconsciously: Unconscious thought can lead to more accurate justice judgments. *Social Cognition, 27*, 509–521.

Hamlin, J. K., & Wynn, K. (2011). Young infants prefer prosocial to antisocial others. *Cognitive Development, 26*, 30–39.

Hassin, R. R. (2008). Being open minded without knowing why: Evidence from nonconscious goal pursuit. *Social Cognition, 26*, 578–592.

Hassin, R. R. (2013). Yes it can: On the functional abilities of the human unconscious. *Perspectives on Psychological Science, 8*, 195–207.

Hassin, R. R., Bargh, J. A., & Zimerman, S. (2009). Automatic and flexible: The case of non-conscious goal pursuit. *Social Cognition, 27*, 20–36.

Hespos, S. J., & van Marle, S. J. (2012). Physics for infants: Characterizing the origins of knowledge about objects, substances, and number. *Wiley Interdisciplinary Reviews: Cognitive Science, 3*, 19–27.

Hibbing, J. R., Smith, K. B., & Alford, J. R. (2014). Differences in negativity bias underlie variations in political ideology. *Behavioral and Brain Sciences, 37*, 297–307.

Kane, R. (2013). Can a traditional libertarian or incompatibilist free will be reconciled with modern science? Steps toward a positive answer. In A. Suarez & P. Adams (Eds.), *Is science compatible with free will? Exploring free will and consciousness in the light of quantum physics and neuroscience* (pp. 255–272). New York: Springer Science+Business Media.

Kang, Y., Williams, L. E., Clark, M. S., Gray, J. R., & Bargh, J. A. (2011). Physical temperature effects on trust behavior: The role of insula. *Social Cognitive and Affective Neuroscience, 6*, 507–515.

Keller, F., & Iverson, J. M. (2013). The role of inhibitory control of reflex mechanisms in voluntary behavior. In A. Suarez & P. Adams (Eds.), *Is science compatible with free will? Exploring free will and consciousness in the light of quantum physics and neuroscience* (pp. 107–116). New York: Springer Science+Business Media.

Kim, K., & Cho, B. (2011). Development of an individualism-collectivism scale revised: A Korean sample. *Psychological Reports, 108*, 393–401.

Knobe, J., Buckwalter, W., Nichols, S., Robbins, P., Sarkissian, H., & Sommers, T. (2012). Experimental philosophy. *Annual Review of Psychology, 63*, 81–99.

Kraft, T. L., & Pressman, S. D. (2012). Grin and bear it: The influence of manipulated facial expression on the stress response. *Psychological Science, 23*, 1372–1378.

Kuhl, J., & Quirin, M. (2011). Seven steps toward freedom and two ways to lose it: Overcoming limitations of intentionality through self-confrontational coping with stress. *Social Psychology, 42*, 74–84.

Li, X., Lu, Z., D'Argembeau, A., Ng, M., & Bechara, A. (2010). The Iowa Gambling Task in fMRI imaging. *Human Brain Mapping, 31*, 410–423.

Libet, B. (1985). Unconscious cerebral initiative and the role of conscious will in voluntary action. *The Behavioral and Brain Sciences, 8*, 529–539.

Libet, B. (1999). Do we have free will? *Journal of Consciousness Studies, 6*, 47–57.

Libet, B. (2001). Consciousness, free action and the brain. *Journal of Consciousness Studies, 8*, 59–65.

Libet, B. (2004). *Mind time*. Cambridge, MA: Harvard University Press.

Libet, B., Gleason, C. A., Wright, E. W., & Pearl, D. K. (1983). Time of conscious intention to act in relation to onset of cerebral activities (readiness-potential): The unconscious initiation of a freely voluntary act. *Brain, 106*, 623–642.

Marien, H., Custers, R., Hassin, R. R., & Aarts, H. (2012). Unconscious goal activation and the hijacking of the executive function. *Journal of Personality and Social Psychology, 103*, 399–415.

Mele, A. R. (2013). Free will and neuroscience: Revisiting Libet's studies. In A. Suarez & P. Adams (Eds.), *Is science compatible with free will? Exploring free will and consciousness in the light of quantum physics and neuroscience* (pp. 195–207). New York: Springer Science+Business Media.

Miles, J. B. (2013a). "Irresponsible and a disservice": The integrity of social psychology turns on the free will dilemma. *British Journal of Social Psychology, 52*, 205–218.

Miles, J. B. (2013b). The integrity of social psychology turns on the free will dilemma: Reply to Baumeister, Vonasch, and Bargh. *British Journal of Social Psychology, 52*, 231–237.

Monroe, A. E., Dillon, K. D., & Malle, B. F. (2014). Bringing free down to earth: People's psychological concept of free will and its role in moral judgment. *Consciousness and Cognition, 27*, 100–108.

Monroe, A. E., & Malle, B. F. (2010). From uncaused will to conscious choice: The need to study, not speculate about people's folk concept of free will. *Review of Philosophy and Psychology, 1*, 211–224.

Nahmias, E. (2012). Free will and responsibility. *Wiley Interdisciplinary Reviews: Cognitive Science, 3*, 439–449.

Nahmias, E., Morris, S., Nadelhoffer, T., & Turner, J. (2005). Surveying freedom: Folk intuitions about free will and moral responsibility. *Philosophical Psychology, 18*, 561–584.

Navon, D. (2014). How plausible is it that conscious control is illusory? *American Journal of Psychology, 127*, 147–155.

Nichols, S. (2011). Experimental philosophy and the problem of free will. *Science, 331*, 1401–1403.

Nordgren, L. F., Bos, M. W., & Dijksterhuis, A. (2011). The best of both worlds: Integrating conscious and unconscious thought best solves complex decisions. *Journal of Experimental Social Psychology, 47*, 509–511.

Over, H., & Carpenter, M. (2009a). Eighteen-month-old infants show increased helping following priming with affiliation. *Psychological Science, 20*, 1189–1193.

Over, H., & Carpenter, M. (2009b). Priming third-party ostracism increases affiliative imitation in children. *Developmental Science, 12*, F1–F8.

Pallar, K. A., & Suzuki, S. (2014). The source of consciousness. *Trends in Cognitive Sciences, 18*, 387–389.

Pascalis, O., de Viviés, X. d. M., Anzures, G., Quinn, P. C., Slater, A. M., Tanaka, J. W., et al. (2011). Development of face processing. *Wiley Interdisciplinary Reviews: Cognitive Science, 2*, 666–675.

Paulhus, D. L., & Carey, J. M. (2011). The FAD-Plus: Measuring lay beliefs regarding free will and related constructs. *Journal of Personality Assessment, 93*, 96–104.

Perner, J., & Roessler, J. (2012). From infants' to children's appreciation of belief. *Trends in Cognitive Sciences, 16*, 519–525.

Pierre, J. M. (2013). The neuroscience of free will: Implications for psychiatry. *Psychological Medicine, 44*, 2465–2474.

Pinker, S. (2008). The fear of determinism. In J. Baer, J. C. Kaufman, & R. F. Baumeister (Eds.), *Are we free? Psychology and free will* (pp. 311-324). New York: Oxford University Press.

Pockett, S. (2006). The neuroscience of movement. In S. Pockett, W. P. Banks, & S. Gallagher (Eds.), *Does consciousness cause behavior?* (pp. 9–24). Cambridge, MA: MIT Press.

Pockett, S., & Purdy, S. (2011). Are voluntary movements initiated preconsciously? The relationships between readiness potentials, urges, and decisions. In W. Sinnott-Armstrong & L. Nadel (Eds.), *Conscious will and responsibility*. New York: Oxford University Press.

Rappaport, Z. H. (2011). The neuroscientific foundations of free will. *Advances and Technical Standards in Neurosurgery, 37*, 3–23.

Rigoni, D., Kühn, S., Sartori, G., & Brass, M. (2011). Inducing disbelief in free will alters brain correlates of preconscious motor preparation: The brain minds whether we believe in free will or not. *Psychological Science, 22*, 613–618.

Sarkissian, H., Chatterjee, A., De Brigard, F., Knobe, J., Nichols, S., & Sirker, S. (2010). Is belief in free will a cultural universal? *Mind & Language, 25*, 346–358.

Schlosser, M. E. (2012a). Free will and the unconscious precursors of choice. *Philosophical Psychology, 25*, 365–384.

Schlosser, M. E. (2012b). Causally efficacious intentions and the sense of agency: In defense of real mental causation. *Journal of Theoretical and Philosophical Psychology, 32*, 135–160.

Shariff, A. F., Greene, J. D., Karremans, J. C., Luguri, J. B., Clark, C. J., Schooler, J. W., et al. (2014). Free will and punishment: A mechanistic view of human nature reduces retribution. *Psychological Science, 25*, 1563–1570.

Shepherd, J. (2012). Free will and consciousness: Experimental studies. *Consciousness and Cognition, 21*, 915–927.

Shields, G. S. (2014). Neuroscience and conscious causation: Has neuroscience shown that we cannot control our own actions? *Review of Philosophy and Psychology, 5*, 565–582.

Siegel, A., & Douard, J. (2011). Who's flying the plane: Serotonin levels, aggression and free will. *International Journal of Law and Psychiatry, 34*, 20–29.

Soon, C. S., Brass, M., Heinze, H. J., & Haynes, J. D. (2008). Unconscious determinants of free decisions in the human brain. *Nature Neuroscience, 11*, 543–545.

Soon, C. S., He, A. H., Bode, S., & Haynes, J. D. (2013). Predicting free choices for abstract intentions. *Proceedings of the National Academy of Sciences, USA, 110*, 5733–5734.

Stillman, T. F., & Baumeister, R. F. (2010). Guilty, free, and wise: Belief in free will facilitates learning from self-conscious emotions. *Journal of Experimental Social Psychology, 46*, 951–960.

Stillman, T. F., Baumeister, R. F., & Mele, A. R. (2011). Free will in everyday life: Autobiographical accounts of free and unfree actions. *Philosophical Psychology, 24*, 381–394.

Stillman, T. F., Baumeister, R. F., Vohs, K. D., Lambert, N. M., Fincham, F. D., & Brewer, L. E. (2010). Personal philosophy and personnel achievement: Belief in free will predicts better job performance. *Social Psychological and Personality Science, 1*, 43–50.

Suarez, A., & Adams, P. (2013). *Is science compatible with free will? Exploring free will and consciousness in the light of quantum physics and neuroscience*. New York: Springer Science+Business Media.

Suter, R. S., & Hertwig, R. (2011). Time and moral judgment. *Cognition, 119*, 454–458.

Tsai, J., Ying, Y.-W., & Lee, P. A. (2000). The meaning of "being Chinese" and "being American." Variation among Chinese American young adults. *Journal of Cross-Cultural Psychology, 31*, 302–332.

Vasilyeva, M., & Lourenco, S. F. (2012). The development of spatial cognition. *Wiley Interdisciplinary Reviews: Cognitive Science, 3*, 349–362.

Verdejo-Garía, A. (2009). A somatic marker theory of addiction. *Neuropharmacology, 56*, 48–62.

Vohs, K. D., & Schooler, J. W. (2008). The value of believing in free will: Encouraging a belief in determinism increases cheating. *Psychological Science, 19*, 49–54.

Vonasch, A. J., & Baumeister, R. F. (2013). Implications of free will beliefs for basic theory and societal benefit: Critique and implications for social psychology. *British Journal of Social Psychology, 52*, 219–227.

Wegner, D. M. (2002). *The illusion of conscious will*. Cambridge, MA: MIT Press.

Wegner, D. M. (2004). Précis of the illusion of conscious will. *Behavioral and Brain Sciences, 27*, 649–692.

Wegner, D. M. (2005). Who is the controller of controlled processes? In R. R. Hassin, J. S. Uleman, & J. A. Bargh (Eds.), *The new unconscious* (pp. 19–36). Oxford, UK: Oxford University Press.

Wegner, D. M. (2008). Self is magic. In J. Baer, J. C. Kaufman, & R. F. Baumeister (Eds.), *Are we free? Psychology and free will* (pp. 226–247). Oxford, UK: Oxford University Press.

Wegner, D. M., & Wheatley, T. P. (1999). Apparent mental causation: Sources of the experience of will. *American Psychologist, 54*, 480–492.

Williams, L. E., & Bargh, J. A. (2008). Experiencing physical warmth promotes interpersonal warmth. *Science, 322*, 606–607.

Williams, L. E., Huang, J. Y., & Bargh, J. A. (2009). The scaffolded mind: Higher mental processes are grounded in early experience of the physical world. *European Journal of Social Psychology, 39*, 1257–1267.

Woodward, A. L. (2009). Infants' grasp of others' intentions. *Current Directions in Psychological Science, 18*, 53–57.

Yang, Y. (2013). *Free will belief predicts master-approach goal orientation among university students*. Unpublished honors thesis. York University, Ontario, Canada.

Young, G. (2011). *Development and causality: Neo-Piagetian perspectives*. New York: Springer Science+Business Media.

An Integrated Model of "Free Will" and New Free Will Questionnaires

19

Chapter Introduction

Free will is a central topic in psychological study, and a fascinating one for the public. We can never be sure it exists, but believing in free will has positive consequences, including for self-control. However, self-control can be derailed by a host of factors. The phenomenon has been referred to as resource or "ego" depletion. A more elaborate term for the model would be limited-resource model of self-regulation and executive function (Vohs et al., 2014). Different models have been proposed to explain it, from the biological to the psychological to the social. After reviewing the literature, I propose an integrative biopsychosocial model of depletion in self-control.

Part of the proposal includes a role in self-control for dual process thinking processes. These have been described as (a) unconscious, fast, and automatic thinking, and (b) conscious, slow, and deliberative thinking. Throughout the chapter, I relate depletion and dual process models to my own work on activation/inhibition coordination as a general mechanism in behavioral causality. Also, I relate depletion and dual process models to my own work on Neo-Piagetian stage modeling for understanding different types of thinking.

The chapter concludes with a section on questionnaires. I review the basic ones in the field on free will, describe my concerns, and develop my own based on them. Not surprisingly, the approach that I take is to consider free will as a biopsychosocial phenomenon. In this regard, the work on free will has emphasized free will belief and its effects. However, I argue that this cognitive component needs to be complemented by a socioaffective one. In the end, I develop an elaborate set of items related to a free will questionnaire that involve five major domains, each with eight subdomains. Also, toward the end of the chapter I propose a more inclusive questionnaire on resource/ego-depletion. To end this chapter, I also consider passion as a component of the personal agency that we bring to behavioral causation. I review the work by Vallerand and colleagues, in particular (e.g., Vallerand, 2010), on the topic, presenting both their definition and questionnaire. At the same time, I develop improved versions for both.

Depletion

Introduction

The field of depletion of self-control is a divided one, with proponents extolling the advantages of various unifactorial models while decrying the disadvantages of the others. Self-control is subject to depletion effects in the laboratory according to one factor or the other, or one or the other is proposed as the mechanism that can account

G. Young, *Unifying Causality and Psychology*, DOI 10.1007/978-3-319-24094-7_19

for it. In the following, I review each of the major areas on conceptualization and research on depletion effects in self-control. Their diversity and the partial support each garners together suggest that they might all play a role in depletion effects, depending on the individual and context involved. Moreover, equally, they would all seem necessary to explain resistance to depletion effects, again, depending on the individual and context.

Glucose

Baumeister and colleagues (e.g., Baumeister, Bratslavesky, Muraven, & Tice, 1998) developed the "ego depletion" model. It is a resource model of self-control in which the overriding of predominant response tendencies affects afterwards a limited resource related to resistance, or "will power," even in apparently unrelated tasks. Belief in free will is subject to depletion in its effects. Baumeister, Masicampo, and Vohs (2011) not only argued that believing in free will has behavioral consequences, but also that engaging in tasks requiring self-regulation leads to impaired performance on ensuing tasks. "Ego-depletion," then, is a term referring to using limited resources that are available to maintain self-control so that, after people have exerted self-control, they do not do as well on ensuing tasks involving self-regulation (Vohs, Baumeister, & Schmeichel, 2012, 2013).

For Baumeister et al. (2011) energy depletion refers to the effect of using cognitive resources associated with a belief in free will on brain activity, which depends on blood level glucose. Therefore, according to them, the resource depletion effect that is involved in self-control activity especially concerns a metabolic-related depletable energetic resource.

The evidence on blood glucose depletion in the study of ego-depletion supports its effects (e.g., Masicampo & Baumeister, 2008). Because the physiological basis of self-control appears to lie in the resources of glucose availability in circulating blood, its depletion can be measured by its levels, as well as those related to heart-rate variability (HRV) and error-related negativity (ERN). The research showing the HRV and ERN could index resource depletion was conducted, respectively, by Segerstrom and Nes (2007) and Inzlicht and Gutsell (2007).

Gailliot et al. (2007) found that a self-regulation condition lowered blood glucose more than a control condition. Moreover, the lowered levels predicted future self-regulation task failure. Finally, a sugary drink countered the ego-depletion, unlike the case for an artificial sweetener.

In short, laboratory tasks with a self-control component acted to deplete blood levels of glucose relative to tasks without the component. Moreover, interventions (receiving lemonade with sugar) that boost blood glucose helped study participants to resist irrational decisions, compared to those who were not similarly boosted (receiving lemonade with diet sweetener).

Baumeister et al. (2011) concluded that there is sufficient basis to support an energy and physiological model of free will. They added that more research is needed to establish the neural concomitants of the phenomenon.

Carter, Kofler, Forster, and McCullough (2015) conducted a series of meta-analysis to test the limited-resource model of the depletion effect. There have been over 200 published studies of the depletion effect and Hagger, Wood, Stiff, and Chatzisarantis (2010) conducted a meta-analysis that supported it. However, Carter et al. (2015) followed that meta-analysis with their own that implemented several methodological improvements. For example, they included results from unpublished studies as well as published ones. Their results showed that the depletion effect research, in general, produced nonsignificant results, at least in terms of the laboratory studies typically used. They concluded that the depletion effect, as mediated by limited resources that affect self-control, is not a valid psychological phenomenon. They encouraged the development of other theories on when and why self-control might be depleted.

Personal Belief/Will Power

In this regard, the phenomenon of ego-depletion has been explained by different models. The limited-resource model maintains that, after exertion of energy or volition in self-control, people perform worse on ensuing following self-regulatory tasks (e.g., Baumeister, Vohs, & Tice, 2007). Vohs et al. (2013) investigated challenges to the model related to personal belief and will power, and found them wanting. That is, when depletion is severe, profound, or extensive, unlike what has been found for mild depletion, they demonstrated that the effects on self-control cannot be washed out or reversed in laboratory studies by either motivation or belief in unlimited will power.

Vohs et al. (2013) elaborated that the subjective or personal belief/motivation model maintains that mindset could render people "immune" from ego-depletion and that depletion is all in the mind. Factors such as pondering personal values, getting incentives, or believing in unlimited will power can offset any (a) resource, (b) energy, or (c) ego-depletion (respectively, Schmeichel & Vohs, 2009; Muraven & Slessareva, 2003; Job, Dweck, & Walton, 2010).

In their test of these latter models of self-control and its depletion, Vohs et al. (2013) varied the amount of self-control tasks administered to participants (0, 2, 4), with examples of the tasks involved including the Stroop task, stifling facial/emotional reactions to a film, and changing set in a cross-out task. Beforehand, a questionnaire was used to manipulate will power belief (e.g., concentrating can be inspiring; or it can be tiring). Dependent measures related to self-control ability (on delayed gratification and a cognitive estimation task). In the second study, the manipulation was of different degrees of motivation.

Vohs et al. (2013) concluded that their results had revealed that both of the ego-depletion model and the personal beliefs/motivational models contribute positively to understanding self-control and its interference. Physiologically-based energy states interact with subjective, psychological factors in determining performance in self-control tasks. The latter can moderate the former in incipient or mild resource depletion, including due to fatigue. However, will power is not objectively unlimited, and extensive ego-depletion results in decline in self-regulatory behavior. Having a belief in unlimited will power cannot genuinely cause unlimited will power.

Embodiment

Ent and Baumeister (2014) related free will belief to embodied influences. They examined it in people (a) who had epilepsy/panic disorder, (b) who were experiencing more physical symptoms (e.g., fatigue), and (c) who were on diets. In all cases, bodily state affected free will belief. In study 1, the authors demonstrated that, relative to controls, people with less control of bodily state (epileptic group, panic disorder group) reported less general free will belief (according to a subscale developed by Rakos, Laurene, Skala, & Slane, 2008). In a second study, the more participants reported feeling sexual desire, fatigue, or the need to urinate, the less were their scores on the "personal free will" subscale in Rakos et al. (2008). In the third study, for non-dieters only, hunger related negatively to belief in personal free will. The authors concluded that even specific low-level bodily cues (sensations, states) could affect people's abstract beliefs, such as philosophical beliefs about free will.

Social

Other social and personality factors are involved in self-control. Ent, Baumeister, and Vonasch (2012) speculated that wielding power can have ego-depletion effects. Gailliot, Gitter, Baker, and Baumeister (2012) conducted research that showed that lower trait self-control can lead to greater violations of social norms and rules that are difficult to follow.

Coan, Brown, and Beckes (2014) contrasted the physical resource/self-control depletion approach in human self-regulation (Gailliot & Baumeister, 2007) to the social baseline model (Coan, 2008). That is, social interaction/contact constitutes a powerful mediator of self-control and its depletion. In the physical resource model, a specific quantity of a metabolic resource (i.e., glucose) is available for self-regulation but, in the latter model, social resources can update the "budget" for self-regulation. Information related to proximity to social resources allows for a cognitive regulation "economizing" of activity (Beckes & Coan, 2011). Physical contact with someone else lowers the activation of threat-responsive areas of the brain (Coan, Schaefer, & Davidson, 2006).

These results are inconsistent with a down-regulation model or inhibitory model of self-regulatory brain areas responsiveness to stress in the absence of social contact. Given the bottom-up regulatory impact of social support on inhibition of threat-responsive brain regions, it appears that social support acts by returning an individual organism to a "default" or baseline state (the "social baseline"). The neuropeptide oxytocin constitutes one possible mechanism that mediates decreased, socially responsive elevations in threat situations.

Brain

Sripada, Kessler, and Jonides (2014) related depletion in regulatory control to the brain's default network. Baumeister et al. (1998) constructed the depletion of regulatory control hypothesis as a strength model. The model indicates that the exercise of sustained regulatory control is limited in capacity and is depletable. Sripada et al. (2014) argued that methylphenidate should be capable of blocking the depletion effect because it serves to increase brain dopamine and norepinephrine levels at the synaptic cleft by functioning as a catecholamine reuptake blocker. They showed that methylphenidate (Ritalin) blocked the depletion that normally takes place.

The study involved 94 participants with complete data. In Phase 1, there were four groups, organized according to drug administration and task (Placebo/Methylphenidate × Control task/Regulation task). Phase 2 involved the test condition for all four groups. The two drug groups received the intervention 60 min before beginning. The letter-e task was used in Phase 1 (Baumeister et al., 1998), and was manipulated to demand effortful regulation of participants. This was accomplished by having them press a button when they viewed the letter "e" in the displayed word, except if the letter was next to, or one letter away from, another vowel. This condition requires suppression of prepotent tendencies, relative to the control condition of pressing the button no matter where the latter e is situated in the displayed word.

The second phase involved a different task (a modified multisource interference task; Bush, Shin, Holmes, Rosen, & Vogt, 2003). Its trials were either congruent or incongruent. In the task, three single-digit numbers are displayed, with the target one different from the other two, which are identical. The digits are between 0 and 3, and presented horizontally. On congruent trials, the value of the target number (e.g., 3) corresponds to its location (e.g., third position, to the far right). Moreover, the font of the target number is larger than for the other two, and the latter is always set as 0. For incongruent trials, this type of matching does not take place, nor is there consistency in which number is larger in font or in having nontarget numbers always set at 0. The dependent measure in Phase 2 was reaction time variability over trials, in particular. Statistics used ex-Gaussian modeling to account for skewed distributions and then Fast Fourier Transform (FFT).

The results showed that the methylphenidate blocked the depletion of regulatory control. The spectral analysis showed that, over trials, the effect took place in the slow-4 frequency band, which is associated with the operation of the resting state default brain network (DFN).

Sripada et al. (2014) concluded that, in their study, methylphenidate affected top-down regulatory processing of a network that concerns attention, i.e., the DFN is associated with mind-wandering and task-irrelevant thought. By boosting the brain regions involved in effortful control (at the synaptic clefts involved), that is, prefrontal circuits including regions of the lateral and dorsal prefrontal cortex and the exterior cingulate, the drug halted the typical compromise in the functioning of these regions by prior regulatory exertion (e.g., by DFN suppression).

Inhibition

In a study using reaction time, Rigoni, Kühn, Gaudino, Sartori, and Brass (2012) addressed the question of which part of information processing changes from weakening or undermining self-control in people to negative consequences, such as antisocial behavior (Baumeister, 2008; Baumeister, Masicampo, & DeWall, 2009). They examined the basic neurocognitive processes underlying intention actions and also their degradation when people are induced not to believe in free will. They found that the mediator in the effect appears to relate to intentional inhibition, or the voluntary inhibition of an intentional response (with perceived self-control mechanisms at play, as well).

A critical mechanism in behavioral and brain organization and output in the present work relates to activation/inhibition coordination (Young, 2011). In this regard, the findings of Rigoni et al. (2012) point to a direction in the type of inhibitions involved in self-control and its deployment and in the latter's undermining.

The notion that inhibition-related mediators are involved in the pathway to self-control degradation because of glucose depletion in prior tasks has been elaborated by Sanders, Shirk, Burgin, and Martin (2012). Molden et al. (2012) had shown that merely rinsing with glucose without swallowing served to negate self-control impairment from one self-control task to another. The results suggest that the activation of motivation is sufficient to interrupt the ego-depletion phenomenon.

Using a somewhat different methodology, Sanders et al. (2012) replicated the primary results of Molden et al. (2012). They suggested that energy resource replenishment is not what maintains self-control. Molden et al. (2012) had suggested that the motivation involved in the process related to reward. However, Sanders et al. (2012) suggested a more specific mechanism. In particular, they reasoned that the anterior cingulate cortex and striatum are activated, which are associated with the "selection and inhibition" of action (Balleine, Delgado, & Hikosaka, 2007; Eagle & Baunez, 2010) and also the detection of errors and response competition (Carter & Van Veen, 2007). These mediators might be the direct operations that underlie successful self-control. Therefore, a critical component implicated in self-control appears to be action selection and inhibition, consistent with my emphasis on activation/inhibition coordination as a general brain–behavior regulator (Young, 2011).

Minda and Rabi (2015) related ego-depletion to effects on inhibitory processes. They related the inhibitory processes involved to self-regulatory ones. For example, in their depletion task, story writing had to be undertaken without using the letters "a" or "n." Also, they found the depletion task worked for affecting learning rule-defined categories (RD) rather than non-rule-defined ones (NRD). They related RD learning to the explicit, verbally-mediated system (prefrontal cortex related) and the implicit associate learning one (related to striatal cortex, tail of the caudate). They related RD and NRD learning to development, with the former harder to learn than the latter (Rabi & Minda, 2014).

I would add that the explicit, verbally-mediated system resembles System/Type II cognitive processes (Evans & Stanovich, 2013; Stanovich, West, & Toplak, 2014) and the implicit one System/Type I cognitive processes. This suggests that ego-depletion effects generally should work on System/Type II higher-order cognitive processes (e.g., conscious, slow, deliberative) compared to lower-order ones (unconscious, fast, intuitive).

Wiecki and Frank (2013) have presented a much more complex model of inhibitory control of behavior in relation to conflicting responses that might be made in a particular situation, in this case, with respect to the ocular motor system. Override or inhibitory mechanisms need to be in place to suppress habitual activity and allow executive control. They emphasized the computational model and the neural network nature of their model (see Fig. 19.1). The areas of the brain involved in the model include the area of frontal cortex (e.g., DLPFC, dorsolateral prefrontal cortex; pre-SMA, presupplementary motor). Inhibitory pathways for the behavior that they addressed include those from the striatum (in the basal ganglia) to the globus pallidus (GP) and then to the substantia nigra pars reticulate (SNr).

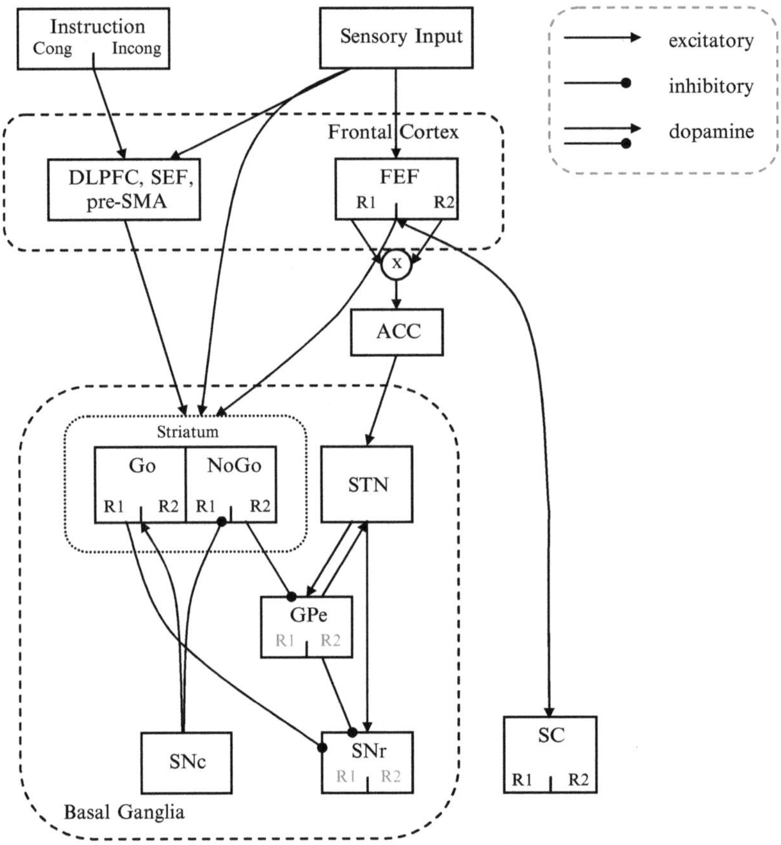

Fig. 19.1 Neural network model. The sensory input layer projects to the frontal eye fields (FEF), striatum, and executive control (i.e., dorsolateral prefrontal cortex [DLPFC], supplementary eye fields [SEF], and presupplementary motor area [pre-SMA]). Via direct projects to FEF (i.e., cortico-cortical pathway), stimulus-responses-mappings can become ingrained (habitualized). FEF has excitatory projections to the superior colliculus (SC) output layer that executes saccades once a threshold is crossed. However, under baseline conditions, SC is inhibited by tonically active substantia nigra pars reticulate (SNr) units. Thus, for SC units to become excited, they have to be disinhibited via striatal direct pathway Go unit activation and subsequent inhibition of corresponding SNr units. Conversely, responses can be selectively suppressed by striatal NoGo activity, via indirect inhibitory projections from striatum to globus pallidus (GP) and then to SNr. Coactivation of mutually incompatible FEF response units leads to dorsal anterior cingulate cortex (dACC) activity (conflict or entropy in choices), which activates the subthalamic nucleus (STN). This STN surge makes it more difficult to gate a response until the conflict is resolved, via excitatory projections to SNr, effectively raising the gating threshold. Striatum is innervated by dopamine (DA) from substantia nigra pars compacta (SNc), which amplifies Go relative to NoGo activity in proportion to reward value and allows the system to learn which actions to gate and which to suppress. The instruction layer represents abstract task cue (e.g., anti-saccade trial). The DLPFC integrates the task cue together with the sensory input (i.e., stimulus location) to initiate a controlled response corresponding to task rules, by activating the appropriate column of units in FEF and striatum. *Cong* = congruent, *Incong* = incongruent, *R1* = response 1, *R2* = response 2, *ACC* = anterior cingulate cortex, *Gpe* = external segment of the globus pallidus. Adopted with permission of American Psychological Association. [Figure 1, Page 333]

The dorsal anterior cingulate cortex (dACC) also is involved when there are incongruent and incompatible activities. The neurotransmitter in this system consists of dopamine. This study does not relate directly to depletion effects in self-control, but it indicates the ubiquity of inhibition in brain–behavior relationships, and the complexities that need to be taken into account in further inhibitory model of self-control depletion.

Motivation

Botvinick and Braver (2015) considered that motivation interacts with cognitive control in behavior. Work in the area should focus on reward in control models, which appears a more fruitful approach than just fixating on resources and its depletion. Exerting control does have intrinsic subjective costs, but they are balanced by benefits in terms of the rewards or incentives in engagement. At the neuroscientific level, the authors' review showed that cognitive effort is associated with the executive control network, which includes the DLPFC, the ACC, and the intraparietal cortex. Other relevant networks in this regard relate to motivation, and include one involving reward value. Affective factors have been found in cognitive decision-making, as well (Lerner, Li, Valdesolo, & Kassam, 2015).

Inzlicht and Schmeichel (2012) also addressed the underlying mechanism in ego-depletion. They implicated an interaction between motivation and attention. According to the authors, the proposed mechanism related to glucose availability is less powerful than that of their own. Specifically, in their model, at first, an initial exertion in self-control shifts motivation toward gratification and away from control. Second, attention to cues shifts from ones for the need for control to ones for indulgence or reward (see Fig. 19.2).

Consistent with my other comments on the matter, I note that it is easy to translate these shifts in terms of inhibition of control and activation of gratification (i.e., to activation/inhibition coordination). Therapeutically, the concept of activation/inhibition coordination being involved in moderating resource/ego-depletion suggests that altering positively the dynamic involved at this level could help people maintain self-control, as in addictions.

The research described by Inzlicht and Schmeichel (2012) supports their model. For

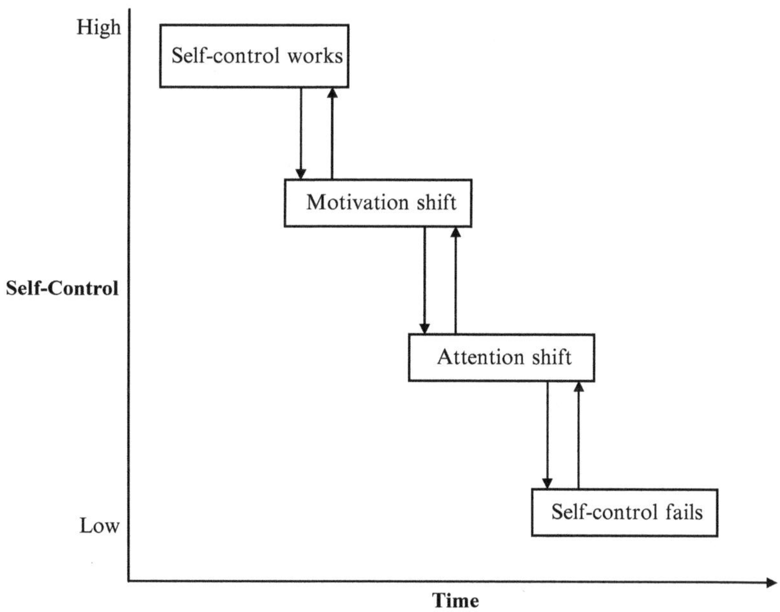

Fig. 19.2 The process model of ego-depletion. Belief in free will leads to behavioral consequences, but it can be depleted, e.g., in loss of "ego" resources. Exertion in self-control leads to self-control failure later on. The mechanism involves shifts in motivation away from self-regulation. This is accompanied by shifts toward self-gratification. Also, there are shifts in attention away from cues signaling the need for control and toward cues signaling reward. Adapted from Inzlicht and Schmeichel (2012)

example, Schmeichel, Harmon-Jones, and Harmon-Jones (2010) showed that self-control exertion leads to stronger approach-related impulses (e.g., low-stake gambles). For attention, Inzlicht and Al-Khindi (2012) found that self-control application "dulls" the attentional system. These core mechanistic processes help promote immediate gratification relative to better self-control. The authors maintained that the model that they have proposed for self-control loss after its exertion avoids metaphorical language such as "ego depletion."

Kurzban, Duckworth, Kable, and Myers (2013a, 2013b) questioned the value of any resource model of reduced self-control with successive cognitive effort. In commentaries to the target article, variations in self-control models in terms of will-power, ego-depletion, or glucose utilization were not supported, nor were they defended to any noticeable degree. Kurzban et al. supported a model that highlighted cost/benefit analyses, computations, and motivation reallocation. The authors defended their model with regard to Inzlicht and Schmeichel's (2012) criticism that it is a cognitive "hyperrational" one.

Cognitive

Vohs et al. (2014) argued that the act of making choices, in particular, is the factor that especially depletes self-control. In this regard, they conducted a series of studies. For example, they found that individuals who had to make choices showed self-control depletion compared to individuals who did not have to make choices. The act of choosing was more depleting of self-control than only thinking about the options from which to choose. In another study, the act of choosing depleted self-control more than the process of putting choices into action. Also, it was more depleting of control than forming a preference while considering the options involved. Vohs et al. (2014) concluded that choosing itself has a special place in self-control depletion. It produces lasting changes in the individual's mental structure by "etching" into it the requirement of what has to be done.

Methodologically, the series of studies by Vohs et al. (2014) was noteworthy by having multiple experiments, manipulations, and measures. For example, the choices involved could be either binding or reversible. They could be either assigned or made spontaneously. They could have either no time limit in the task involved or have one. They could involve either unsolvable puzzles or time taken to try to solve solvable ones. Also, the impairment in self-control found by Vohs et al. (2014) was shown on quite different tasks, for example, physical stamina and tolerance for pain, persisting despite failure, and numerical calculation tasks.

Vohs et al. (2014) considered alternative explanations of self-control depletion for their results and ruled them out. For example, they considered that mood affects choice, that duration affects choosing, that cognitive load could explain the depletion, and that mental effort and mental fatigue could explain it. In all these regards, the model that best explained the phenomenon about self-control depletion was the one that they espoused of limited-resource model of self-regulation and executive function.

Dweck (2012) maintained that believing in depletion is the cause of depletion, and not any metabolically-mediated (e.g., glucose-related) effect. Also, see Job et al. (2010) on the matter.

Combining these ideas with those of Baumeister on personal agency and social underpinnings as well as Inzlicht and Schmeichel (2012) on motivation and attention in depletion control could lead to fruitful avenues in how to bolster self-control.

Self

Hagger (2015) showed that Chen, Westman, and Hobfoll's (2015) updated model of conservation of resources (COR; e.g., Hobfoll, 1989) offers ways to revise the "strength" or limited-resource model of self-control (e.g., Baumeister et al., 2007). In particular, in COR, the individual can use resources from different levels to regulate behavior and manage stress, including in personal traits related to the self (efficacy, esteem).

These resources could help moderate the depletion effect on self-regulatory capacity especially by promoting resilience.

Comment

The review of the various models for ego/resource depletion in self-control has covered the gamut of possible influences. Biologically, glucose, embodiment, and the default brain network have been implicated. As for psychological factors, they concern cognition, belief, attention, motivation, personal belief, and power, as well as inhibition. Socially, a social baseline model has been proposed. In these regards, an integrative model is needed to consider the multiple factors in ego/resource depletion that acknowledge its biopsychosocial complexity.

Moreover, it would attempt to find the underlying common mechanism on which the various influences act. Executive function concerns factors such as working memory, shifting set, and inhibition. The research has shown that inhibition is critical to maintaining self-control, and the all various factors that deplete it might affect inhibitory mechanisms in self-control. I have argued that inhibition by itself is insufficient in the regulation of behavior, because it is embedded in a dynamic of activation/inhibition coordination (Young, 2011) that needs to be considered in brain/behavior relations. Therefore, the algorithm of activation/inhibition coordination might serve as the core nexus to help integrate the various ego/resource depletion factors.

Another possible common factor in both the phenomenon of ego/resource depletion and its possible underlying mechanism resides in dual-process modeling. Specifically, as self-control is depleted, there might be an inability to continue to engage in higher-level deliberative, slow conscious Type/System II thinking relative to lower-level automatic, fast, unconscious, Type/System II thinking. Before reviewing dual model work, I consider the area of self-regulation.

Self-regulation constitutes an area of work that is related to that of self-control and that illustrates the biopsychosocial factors involved. After presentation of work in the area, I present the integrative model of the biological, psychological (personal), and social influences on self-control.

Self-Regulation

Introduction

The book by Sokol, Grouzet, and Müller (2013) illustrates the biopsychosocial nature of self-regulation and self-control in relation to the development of autonomy. For example, Grouzet, Sokol, and Müller (2013) described that self-regulation refers to the regulation of thought, emotion, and action by an inner self that is guided from the perspective of the organism's goals and purposes. Compared to self-regulation, self-control is a narrower concept involving selection of "desired" behavior.

For Deci and Ryan (2013), self-determination involves different types of self-regulation that vary in their degree of external social influence. The self-determination types in their model include—introjected (less autonomous); and those that are more autonomous (identified, intrinsic, integrated). Intrinsic forces might specify what to value as being healthy (organismic valuing processes), although sociocognitive valuing processes interact co-existentially with organismic ones (Grouzet, 2013).

Social

The personal (autonomy) and social (communal) interact in self-growth and its regulation, with the dimension of being active or passive orthogonal to this one (Grouzet et al., 2013). Activity is evidenced in self-organization and self-regulated growth, although they both depend on social support to achieve autonomy and related acquisitions. The acquisition of autonomy also depends on meta-cognitive abilities that facilitate self-authoring and owning.

In short, in self-regulation, one finds a dialectic between organismic and social (and cognitive) processes (e.g., respectively, organismic integration/valuing; emergence and social-cultural demands/metacognition). Parents and teachers need to manifest balance in their support for autonomy and in providing structure.

The child develops self-regulation in the sense of voluntary control of impulses toward the service of personally-valued standards/goals (Duckworth & Carlson, 2013). They develop self-talk explanations to better internalize standard/goals, intentions, and so on, and then transform/reformulate them into personal standards/goals, intentions, etc. (Kinnucan & Kuebli, 2013, after Vygotsky).

Biological

The biological component of self-regulation involves serotonin-mediated impulse-constraint processes (Carver, Johnson, & Joormann, 2013) and dorsal and ventral limbic cortical divisions (Waters & Tucker, 2013). More nuanced models (e.g., Grouzet et al., 2013) have replaced simpler ones, such as that of Baumeister et al. (2007) on energy modulation and resource depletion of self-regulation (control).

Moller, Deci, and Ryan (2006) found that autonomous types of self-regulation (intrinsic, identified) were not associated with energy depletion. Rather, they appear to serve as a locus of "psychological vitality." However, consistent with the ego or energy/resource depletion model of self-control (Baumeister et al., 2007), depletion in control was evident with less autonomous self-regulation types (i.e., more controlled, introjected).

Wagner, Altman, Boswell, Kelley, and Heatherton (2013) presented functional neuroimaging data that implicated neural network alterations in self-regulatory depletion. A reward-associated center appeared enhanced, and connections between it and a center associated with self-control appeared reduced in connectivity. Specifically, chronic dieters were exposed to appetizing or desirable foods, and half of them had completed a self-regulatory depletion task. The depleters showed greater food-cue related activity in the orbito-frontal cortex (OFC). This region is associated with coding reward value/motivation salience/liking aspects of desired food. The depleters also showed less functional activity coupling between the OFC and the inferior frontal gyrus. This region is associated with self-control.

The authors concluded that their data is consistent with the motivational model of Inzlicht and Schmeichel (2012) but, also, the data supports the balance model of self-regulation (Heatherton & Wagner, 2011). In ongoing self-control, normally a balance is struck between brain regions associated with impulse-control and others involved in representing the reward value, desirability, and emotional valence of stimuli (respectively, the lateral/medial areas of the frontal cortex and the OFC and striatum). The frontal portions of the brain are involved in executive control and, in depletion/disruption, an imbalance is set up in the reciprocally-tuned systems. This leads to a loss of inhibition of the system for motivational salience, which serves to free expression of impulses toward temptations and also serves in a loss of self-regulation.

Personal

Nucci (2013) examined self-regulation in the context of personal choice. His model and research place the personal component as a central focus in self-regulation. For Nucci, children develop in a personal domain as well as moral and social ones. They develop preferences and predictions that enhance their sense of identity, personal autonomy, and individuality. The preferences relate to areas in which they can have some authority in their personal zone of privacy, prerogatives, discretion, and own choices and decisions. This manifests in their affirmative, committed noncompliance (resistance to external control). Children begin to show the development of their personal domain in their play and social relations with friends. Personhood in these areas is self-constructed. According to Nucci (2013), this happens in developing people in all cultures, who actively construct and express this zone no matter what mixture of individualistic and collectivistic tendencies that the culture expresses.

Dual-Process Models

Models

Introduction Dual-process theories in social psychology constitute one of its most significant developments (Gawronski, Sherman, & Trope, 2014). They are concerned with mechanisms (algorithms; Marr, 1982) that mediate or translate inputs into outputs. In Marr's system, the computational level concerns input–output relations. The implementation level concerns (neural) underpinnings. Simply, dual-processing theories divide mental processes into automatic and non-automatic ones. The book by Sherman, Gawronski, and Trope (2014) illustrates the range of dual-process theories and the scope of their operational application.

Gawronski et al. (2014) clarified the distinction between what dual-process theories try to explain (empirical explanandum) and the theoretical assumptions behind the explanations (explanans). Events lead to observed behavior, which is a way of depicting causal explanation. However, asking about the "how" of the caused or resultant behavior by the event goes one step further by seeking mechanism (mechanistic explanation).

Mental mechanisms also are called operating principles. They function in operating conditions. If a mental process is automatic, we still might not know the how behind the automaticity. We need to learn each of when there is no conscious awareness, the goal of any automatic activity, the presence of any associated cognitive resource reduction, and if the goal could include altering or stopping the process (Bargh, 1994). However, knowing this still does not give us the how of the automaticity.

Dual-process theories could be either domain-specific or generalized. The latter integrate and seek applicable rules over content (e.g., automaticity is associative rather than rule-based; Sloman, 1996). They are concerned with the basic architecture in information processing (e.g., Smith & DeCoster, 2000).

Dual-process theories focus on functionally distinct mental processes. Dual representation theories emphasize different behavior outcomes linked to functionally distinct mental representations. Other models include both process and representation (dual system theories). The latter theories note the similarities of sets of features (e.g., associative vs. rule-based) and seek domain-independent accounts of the human mind.

Gawronski et al. (2014) concluded that there are not only dual process but also uniprocess and multiprocess models of mind. Nevertheless, the dual-process models are more influential.

Variations In their work on dual processes, Baumeister and Bargh (2014) argued that both conscious and unconscious processes contribute to guiding behavior. The unconscious influences on behavior are known to be powerful (Freud, 1933/1965), and contemporary research supports their influence on behavior (e.g., Bargh, 2005). However, this does not mean that conscious will is an "illusion" (Wegner, 2002).

The authors contended that one way that the two systems could be complementary is that conscious thoughts ultimately are in charge of actions. However, unconscious processes provide input and support. In another integrative view, normally, unconscious processes govern behavior. In addition, conscious ones can intervene occasionally by overriding, regulating, redirecting, and altering the course of behavior, thereby providing a supporting role (Baumeister & Masicampo, 2010). Only consciousness can integrate and manage the different potential response outputs (Morsella, 2005).

Consciousness is like a navigational system that can simulate mentally different possible streams of behavior and their associated probable consequences. The unconscious can work with these mental projections in its decision-making and implementation. However, it cannot construct complex plans itself. Consciousness sets the goals/desired end states, while the unconscious organizes actions toward their completion.

Behavior might begin with unconscious impulses but the conscious is needed to imagine and plan, as well as self-regulate toward the plan's unfolding that the unconscious executes. If there are competing or conflicting motivations, consciousness mediates, especially in allowing the "higher" impulse to predominate. In short, we need the unconscious to plan, reason logically, interpret, communicate, anticipate, and simulate, or otherwise to facilitate adaptive responses.

Others Newell (2015) supported the utility and advantage of conscious higher-order compared to implicit, unconscious cognition in the context of complex perceptual category learning and also multi-attribute decision-making. When higher-order thought "takes over" in these contexts, the outcomes are more "optimal."

Edelman and Tononi (2000) related conscious experience to the activation/deactivation of distributed neuronal populations. They described a higher-order consciousness evolving in humans beyond a basic primary consciousness. It includes concepts of the self, past, future, and of consciousness itself. They related consciousness to a high degree of neural complexity, which is based on information in the neural system.

Sloman (2014) updated his earlier (Sloman, 1996) associative vs. rule-based dual-process model by referring to intuition (e.g., pattern recognition) and deliberation (e.g., thoughtful, reflective) thinking modes. The former is generative and might be capable of sophisticated symbolic causal reasoning. The latter serves to attenuate the former, via gating, which is a modulating inhibitory mechanism, which might be "leaky" or not always successful. The two systems interact, for example, when there is a novel cognitive act that is needed (problem solving, decision-making). The intuitive system is tightly linked to affect, while the deliberate system is amenable to direct control through "force of will." The strong view is that the systems are distinct with their own brain circuitry, yet they are complementary and interactive.

Cushman and Greene (2012) contrasted (a) intuitive attitudes and (b) explicit moral principles or commitments. They indicated that their tug-of-war enables achievement of a "reflective equilibrium." This approach reminds me of the dual-process models of cognition (Stanovich et al., 2014), which also consider intuitive and more advanced models.

Types

Stanovich et al. (2014) referred to their dual-processing theory in terms of Type I and Type II processing. The former type is marked by autonomy and the latter is marked by inhibitory mechanisms, which enables cognitive decoupling of real-world and imaginary representations. Type II processing is subdivided into the algorithmic (fluid intelligence) and the reflective (rational thinking dispositions, including higher-level goal states and epistemic thinking dispositions that regulate behavior at a more general level).

Evans and Stanovich (2013) added that Type I processes constitute the default type, and are qualitatively-different from higher-order reasoning processes (Type II), which are used to intervene on Type I processes, as needed (e.g., for difficulty, novelty) and if not inhibited. Type I and II cognitive processes correspond roughly to intuitive and reflective thought. The latter requires working memory (and controlled attention) and functions with cognitive decoupling (distinguish supposition from belief; run through experiments) and mental stimulation. Typically, Type II processes are slower, serial, conscious, abstract, rule-based, and flexibly controlled, with import for decision-making, hypothetical thinking, and cognitive ability, including fluid intelligence, which is more related to a subcomponent, the algorithmic mind. Also, it can vary in mode, e.g., between holistic and analytic styles (see Fig. 19.3). Evans and Stanovich (2013) noted that the two thinking types have different underlying neural substrates.

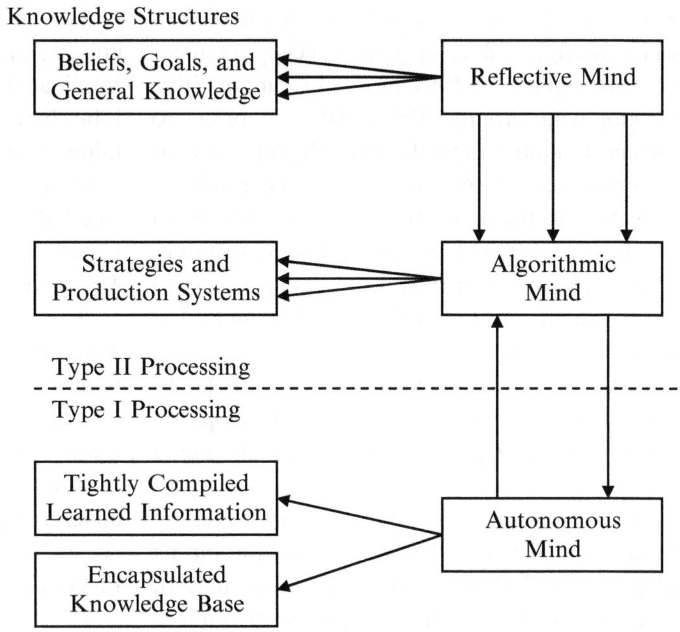

Fig. 19.3 Knowledge structures in the tripartite framework. The figure illustrates the distinction between automatic, intuitive, algorithmic, unconscious thought and reflective, deliberate, autonomous, conscious thought. Adopted with permission of Elsevier. Reprinted from *Developmental Review*, Vol. 31, Stanovich, K. E., West, R. F., & Toplak, M. E., The complexity of developmental predictions from dual process models, Pages 103–118, Copyright 2011; with kind permission from Elsevier. [Figure 1, Page 107]

Brain

Spunt and Lieberman (2013, 2014) related more automatic behavior (identification) to the brain's mirror neuron system (MNS). They related the capacity for making controlled social causal inferences or attributions to the brain's mentalizing system (MZS). The MNS appears to make sense of the body's actions and the MZS uses the information to make sense of what is going on in another person's mind. Participants were asked how a viewed behavior occurred or why (e.g., reaching for phone in order to speak). This study by Spunt and Lieberman (2012) showed that the two brain systems were recruited for the different task goals in the way hypothesized.

Spunt and Lieberman (2014) indicated that the MNS includes the dorsal (dPMC) and ventral (vPMC) regions of the premotor cortex, as well as a region of the parietal cortex in the rostral inferior parietal lobule (IPL) that extends into the intraparietal sulcus (IPS). Mirror neurons translate sensory input about another person's motor actions into representations of the goals of the actions.

The MZS includes the dorsomedial prefrontal cortex (dmPFC), a portion of the medial parietal cortex from the precunius to the posterior cingulate cortex (PC/PCC), the temporoparietal junction at the superior temporal sulcus (TPJ/STS), and the anterior temporal cortex (aTC). The MZS is involved in inferring mental states, traits, social context, and so on. Both brain systems are important in social perception, but they subserve different systems, with one more automatic and the other more mentalizing.

Piaget

Pons, Harris, and de Rosnay (2012) described Piaget's approach to consciousness. In terms of its evolution with cognitive stages of development, Piaget (1974) described three levels, with correspondences to the stages of sensorimotor intelligence, representation (the pre-operational and concrete operational stages), and formal, abstract intelligence.

For Piaget, in the sensorimotor period, consciousness is practical and nonreflective (e.g., consciousness of an activation and its success/failure). In the representational period, consciousness is conceptual (e.g., consciousness of the purpose of actions and the means to achieve them, their organization, and the causative relationship between means–goals). In the formal period, consciousness is reflective (consciousness of one's cognitive functions and the objects of knowledge). I developed the concept of collective intelligence in 1997 in a book on cognitive development (Young, 1997, 2011). It refers to advanced adult logical thought. Higher forms of consciousness (e.g., involving superordinate reflective abstractions) beyond the one related to the abstract, formal period would be related to it, as well. [Note that in 1997, Lévy also published a book using the term of collective intelligence, but to apply to cyberspace (Lévy, 1997).]

Kopp (2011) maintained that a nonverbal consciousness of body and actions develops in infancy. In this regard, as mentioned, she noted that Piaget had developed the concept of a "practical" consciousness in infancy. At this age, the infant is conscious of his or her behavior and its effects, including emotions experienced. According to Kopp, signs of consciousness might even be evident prenatally and in the newborn period (Rochat, 2003; Trevarthen & Aitken, 2001; Zelazo, Hong Gao, & Todd, 2007). For the latter, it would be a general, minimal, multidimensional consciousness. Nelson (2007) placed its onset in the period after birth, later in the first year. For Kopp (2011), the infant's self-owned actions, simple awareness, and phenomenal experience of consciousness are indicators of a palpable body and action consciousness.

Comment

There are similarities in the various dual-process models in terms of having a more basic and a more advanced mode of thought, but more work is needed to integrate differences in simpler and abstract cognitions and simpler and abstract social processing, as well as their brain network underpinnings. It could be that the Piagetian model offers a way of expanding the type/system view of differential processing into a model with more than two options, which is inherent in the Stanovich model anyway, and in other models that are more than bifactorial. However, that said, there is good evidence at the level of the brain that the two systems proposed have differential neuronal underpinnings,

For the Type I–II model, the right prefrontal cortex and the dorsolateral prefrontal cortex seem implicated, for example, as well as the parietal lobe (Evans & Stanovich, 2013). As for the mentalizing system, there are similarities and differences in proposed associations with brain areas (medial frontal and parietal cortices, temporoparietal junction, anterior temporal cortex; Spunt & Lieberman, 2013).

To conclude, creating an integrated model of different processing modes related to cognition both for reasoning and social cognition might be a goal worthy of consideration. In this regard, Young (2011) has related Type I and Type II thought to Piaget's conception of pre-operational/concrete operational and more advanced thought. As well, Young's model of five stages in Neo-Piagetian development (with five substages each) and corresponding socioemotional (Neo-Eriksonian) (sub)stages at each step over the lifespan, might be informative in this regard. They have been related to Piagetian development by Barrouillet (2011), with automatic ones considered pre-operational, and nonautomatic ones considered operational.

Specifically, Barrouillet (2011) reviewed dual-process models of reasoning, as applied to development, and related them to Piaget's cognitive developmental model. The central distinction between the levels in the various dual-process models is that the less advanced one is unconscious, automatic, implicit, contextualized, effortless, emotion-linked, intuitive, heuristic, and probabilistic (System/Type I) and the more advanced one is conscious, deliberative, explicit, decontextualized, non-emotional, reflective, analytic, controlled, effortful, and mental (e.g., representing alternative possibilities, System/Type II). An integrated approach should consider metacognitive processes and conditional reasoning.

These models are mostly based on the work of Stanovich (1999, 2009, 2011; Stanovich, West, & Toplak, 2011) and Evans (2009, 2010, 2011a, 2011b). Nevertheless, Barrouillet (2011) noted that both authors present a possible third System/Type (III). Further, Barrouillet (2011) remarked that System/Type I thought is not necessarily replaced by System/Type II thought, and that

System/Type I thought stands as the default model in cognition.

According to Barrouillet (2011), the distinction in Piaget's model (Piaget & Inhelder, 1941, 1954) between the pre-operational stage and the concrete operational stage parallels to a degree the model of System/Type I and System/Type II thought, respectively, given the association of the two stages with intuitive and rational (albeit concrete) logical thought, respectively. Moreover, to further the analogy, Piaget added a stage after the concrete operational level (formal operations), which is consistent with aspects of System/Type III models (both involve "higher-order" operations).

Barrouillet (2011) concluded that developmental psychology has a long-standing history in construing dual-process thinking, but that by integrating Piaget in the work a more inclusive model could be found. I concur fully with this suggestion, and elsewhere in the present book (see Chap. 32), I describe how the multiple stages and substages in Piaget's theory can function simultaneously, depending on the problem at hand, ending up yoked together toward adaptive ends (Young, 2011).

A Combined Biopsychosocial/Depletion, Dual-Process/Consciousness-Unconsciousness Model in Behavioral Causality

Introduction

The models on self-control to date appear static and they especially focus on one area of study, or changes in a second self-control task after the "depletion" induced by a first one. Moreover, despite their differences, they appear to converge on the importance of cognitive, emotional/motivation, and contextual (e.g., reward) factors in self-control.

Increasingly, workers are integrating diverse factors that influence self-control. Evans, Boggero, and Segerstrom (2015) proposed a multiple input or factor model of self-regulatory fatigue/ego-depletion that incorporates the physiological substrate (glucose) and psychological process (e.g., motivation) accounts. In the model, within a central governor, subconscious computations integrate sensory/physiological and conceptual/motivational influences on resisting loss of self-control, as well as contextual factors (e.g., current workload, available energy, goal value, opportunity costs, anticipated future exertion). This modeling approach by Evans et al. (2015) is consistent with my own.

Model

However, an appropriate model of self-control and self-regulation should allow both for dynamic shifting due to the influence of multiple systemic factors and the development of longer-term capacities (progressively or regressively). In this sense, Fig. 19.4 presents an integrative model of progressive and regressive influences on self-regulation and the bifurcation or shifting point toward progressive or regressive outcomes. The general dynamic appears to be one of activation/inhibition coordination. Finally, the moment-to-moment decision points in self-regulation appear outcomes of both specific cost/benefit analysis and resource availability. Note the latter can be "depleted," but the concept is meant as a broad one and not just related to metabolic/energetic availability, will power, and the like. Rather, it refers to an integration of personal, social, and biological resources at all levels that serve to support self-regulatory decisions and subsequent actions. In addition, by their very nature, systems models do not give primacy to isolated component influences as causal but consider their interactive dynamics as the driver of change and development.

Evidence

Literature supportive of the proposed model includes the following. Inzlicht and Schmeichel (2012, 2013) have gravitated away from a strict resource model of self-control, for example, as represented in the "ego depletion" effect. As already noted, the resource model involves

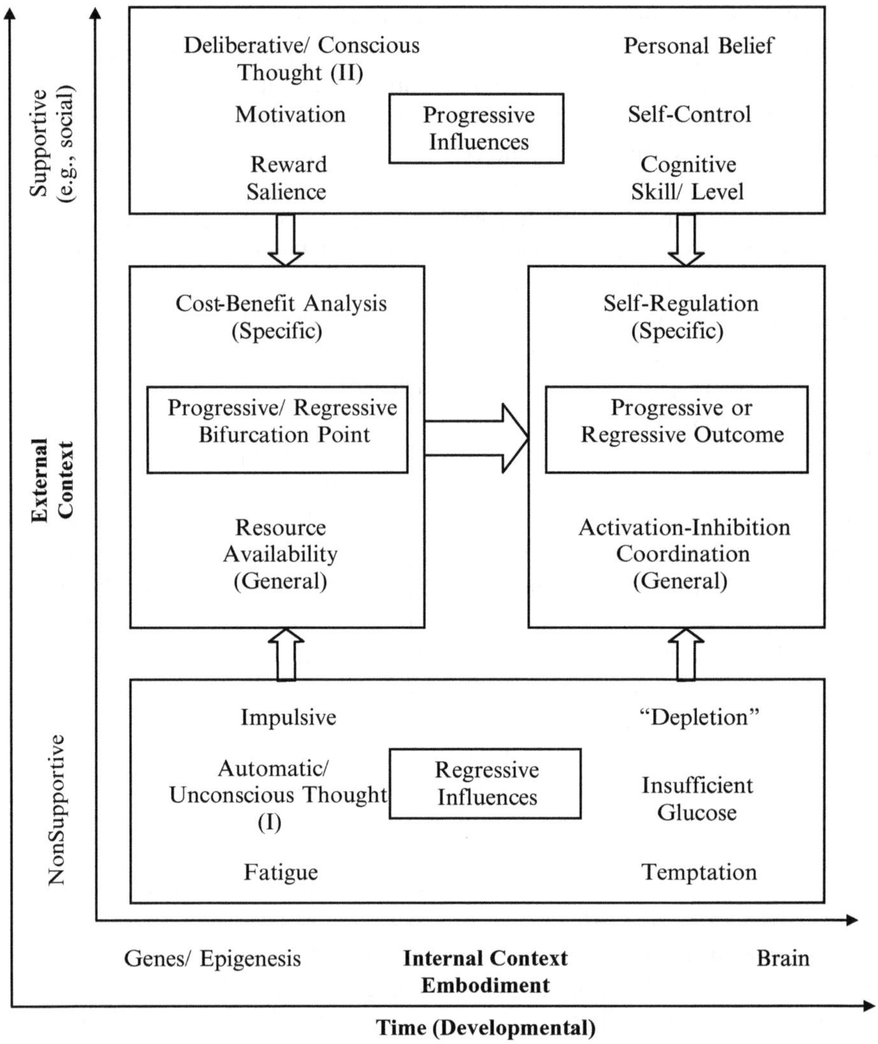

Fig. 19.4 A biopsychosocial model of depletion and dual processing. Depletion and dual process thought need to be considered in the broader context of the biopsychosocial model. The model in the figure considers progressive and regressive changes that are possible in self-regulation. It presents an integrated model of self-control that considers biological/physical factors (e.g., physiology, fatigue, brain), social ones (e.g., support), and personal psychological ones (e.g., cognitive skill level, which includes automatic, conscious (Type/System I) and deliberative, unconscious (Type/System II) thought. It integrates the resource depletion model of Baumeister (2008; Galinsky, Maddux, Gilin, & White, 2008), the motivational emphasis in Inzlicht and Schmeichel (2012, 2013), the cost-benefit model of Kurzban et al. (2013a, 2013b; which includes motivational and other factors), and the balance model of Heatherton (Heatherton & Wagner, 2011; Wagner & Heatherton, 2013). The model is a dynamical systems one that accounts for moment-to-moment changes, which in turn contribute to longer-term changes, and to development. Being a dynamical systems model, it is open to self-organizing, nonlinear, qualitative (emergent) changes in state. The activation/inhibition coordination dynamic is essential in this process. The model includes new conceptualizations (e.g., epigenetic effect of genes, embodiment) that need elucidation of the specific roles that they might play in self-control in the context of the multiple factors in the model

difficulties in self-control after having engaged in a first, different self-control task. Instead of this model, they proposed a process, mechanistic model involving effects on attention and motivation that serve to undermine the self-control for the second task. Motivation and cues associated with self-gratification/immediate reward become favored, facilitating impulsive action.

Other models have been developed to replace the standard ego-depletion model of reduced self-control with sequential cognitive effort. For example, as shown earlier in the chapter, aside from motivational aspects that might contribute in making choices, the general issue of cost-benefit analysis needs to be considered (Kurzban et al., 2013a, 2013b). Particularly, cost-benefit analysis refers to mental representations, and their computational mechanisms related to executive function, which is limited in its ability to be deployed over tasks. In another model (Heatherton & Wagner, 2011), self-control is considered the outcome of competing forces in impulse strength relative to self-control strength.

Comment

To conclude, the present model of self-control, includes the resource depletion paradigm, but is an integrated one. However, its development should continue so that it becomes a genuinely biopsychosocial one.

Self-control constitutes and important driver of behavior and helps the person circumnavigate powerful influences of biology and environment, past and present, and passivity and inertia. In this regard, work on behavioral causality needs the type integrative model proposed.

Free Will and Depletion Questionnaires

Introduction

In the next section of the chapter, I analyze questionnaires on free will, which are quite recent, and then I propose a new one. The extant ones involve few items, but mine is extensive with many items, and it tries to cover free will and related aspects, in a biopsychosocial approach. After, I propose a depletion questionnaire.

Extant Free Will Questionnaires

FAD-Plus Paulhus and Carey (2011) described the development of their questionnaire on free will, which concerned laypersons' beliefs of free will. Overall, the questionnaire consists of 27 items, but for free will itself, only 7 items are involved and an elaborate protocol of factor analysis revealed that the items are organized into four independent dimensions—free will, scientific determinism, fatalistic determinism, and unpredictability (see Table 19.1). Paulhus and Carey (2011) maintained that the factors that emerged are relatively orthogonal and are internally consistent. They found correlations showing that believing in free will is not equivalent to having an internal locus of control, and that, among the Big Five personality traits, it is associated with extroversion and agreeableness.

Free Will Inventory Nadelhoffer, Shepard, Nahmias, Sripada, and Thomson Ross (2014) developed a new measure of free will belief after showing the limitations of extant measures. For example, one such scale is the Free Will and Determinism Scale (Rakos et al., 2008). It places on opposite poles of its scale free will and determinism (as incompatible). However, from a philosophical point of view, it is possible to believe in both constructs (which refers to the approach of compatibilism). Paulhus and Carey (2011) avoided this confusion in constructing orthogonal scales for free will and determinism (see Table 19.2).

However, Nadelhoffer et al. (2014) noted that the fatalistic determinism subscale in Paulhus and Carey (2011) gives scores that correlate with those on their unpredictability subscale. Moreover, Nadelhoffer et al. (2014) noted that scores for fatalistic determinism do not correlate negatively with scores on the free will subscale. Also, among the seven items in the latter scale, three of them involve responsibility and blame, which are not direct representations of free will. Finally, the scientific determinism subscale of the FAD-Plus includes items about genes and environmental influences on behavior rather than the philosophical understanding of determinism (that sufficient causes exist for every event).

The Free Will Inventory that Nadelhoffer et al. (2014) developed after critiquing prior questionnaires is an instrument with 29 items overall, but with only a few related directly to a subscale on free will. In Part I, there are three five-item subscales (on free will, determinism, and dualism/

Table 19.1 FAD-Plus: free will and determinism questionnaire subscales and items

Subscale	Items
Free will	People have complete control over the decisions they make.
	People must take full responsibility for any bad choices they make.
	People can overcome any obstacles if they truly want to.
	Criminals are totally responsible for the bad things they do.
	People have complete free will.
	People are always at fault for their bad behavior.
	Strength of mind can always overcome the body's desires.
Scientific Determinism	People's biological makeup determines their talents and personality.
	Psychologists and psychiatrists will eventually figure out all human behavior.
	Your genes determine your future.
	Science has shown how your past environment created your current intelligence and personality.
	As with other animals, human behavior always follows the laws of nature.
	Parents' character will determine the character of their children.
	Childhood environment will determine your success as an adult.
Fatalistic Determinism	I believe that the future has already been determined by fate.
	No matter how hard you try, you can't change your destiny.
	Fate already has a plan for everyone.
	Whatever will be, will be—there's not much you can do about it.
	Whether people like it or not, mysterious forces seem to move their lives.
Unpredictability	Chance events seem to be the major causes of human history.
	No one can predict what will happen in this world.
	Life seems unpredictable—just like throwing dice or flipping a coin.
	People are unpredictable.
	Life is hard to predict because it is almost totally random.
	Luck plays a big role in people's lives.
	What happens to people is a matter of chance.
	People futures cannot be predicted.

Adopted with permission of Taylor & Francis Ltd. Paulhus, D. L., & Carey, J. M. (2011). The FAD-Plus: Measuring lay beliefs regarding free will and related constructs. *Journal of Personality Assessment*, *93*, 96–104. Reprinted by permission of the publisher (Taylor & Francis Ltd., http://www.tandfonline.com). [Appendix, Page 104]

anti-reductionism). Part II contains 14 items—seven about the nature of free will and seven about moral responsibility.

Part I was developed over four rounds of research using factor analysis. The participants were more representative of the general population compared to those in Paulhus and Carey (2011). The five free will items include statements such as—people always have free will; people ultimately have complete control over their decisions and actions. The determinism scale in Nadelhoffer et al. (2014) includes the item—everything that has ever happened had to happen precisely as it did, given what had happened before. As for an example of dualism, one item is—each person has a non-physical essence that makes that person unique.

Although the three five-item scales in Part I of the Nadelhoffer et al. inventory was subject to confirmatory factor analysis, the 14 items in Part II of the scale were not. They were built in order to explore in more depth associated beliefs and attitudes about free will, determinism, and so on.

Aside from this limitation of the study, there are others to note. First, the validation research did not include use of other measures to examine relevant relationships (e.g., another free will questionnaire, a related concept such as locus of control).

Second, some of the items are complexly written or seem removed from the topic at hand given

Table 19.2 The free will inventory: subscales and items

Subscales	Items
Free will	People always have the ability to do otherwise.
	People always have free will.
	How people's lives unfold is completely up to them.
	People ultimately have complete control over their decisions and their actions.
	People have free will even when their choices are completely limited by external circumstances.
Determinism	Everything that has ever happened had to happen precisely as it did, given what happened before.
	Every event that has ever occurred, including human decisions and actions, was completely determined by prior events.
	People's choices and actions must happen precisely the way they do because of the laws of nature and the way things were in the distant past.
	A supercomputer that could know everything about the way the universe is now could know everything about the way the universe will be in the future.
	Given the way things were at the Big Bang, there is only one way for everything to happen in the universe after that.
Dualism/anti-reductionism	The fact that we have souls that are distinct from our material bodies is what makes humans unique.
	Each person has a non-physical essence that makes that person unique.
	The human mind cannot simply be reduced to the brain.
	The human mind is more than just a complicated biological machine.
	Human action can only be understood in terms of our souls and minds and not just in terms of our brains.

Adopted with permission of Elsevier. Reprinted from *Consciousness and Cognition,* Vol. 25, Nadelhoffer, T., Shepard, J., Nahmias, E., Sripada, C., & Thomson Ross, L., The free will inventory: Measuring beliefs about agency and responsibility, Copyright 2014; with kind permission from Elsevier. [Excerpt of 250 words, Pages 34–35]

their philosophical origin. Examples, respectively, include: (a) people have free will even when their choices are completely limited by external circumstances, and (b) people always have the ability to do otherwise.

For the items in Part II, in this regard, examples, respectively, include: (a) free will is the ability to make different choices even if everything leading up to one's choice (e.g., the past, the situation, and their desire, beliefs, etc.) were exactly the same and (b) free will is the ability to make a choice based on one's beliefs and desires such that if one had different beliefs or desires, one's choice would have been different, as well.

Proposed New Scale on Free Will

Questionnaire Table 19.3 presents possible items for a scale on free will that emphasizes choices and decisions, and covers the full spectrum of categories of items that could be involved in free will (see Table 19.3). In developing items for an improved free will questionnaire, I accommodated to the limitations attributed to extant questionnaires (e.g., Nadelhoffer et al., 2014; Paulhus & Carey, 2011). In particular, I chose/created questions that are both face valid and amenable to tests of construct and related validity.

The tables showing the items on free will that could be used to construct a new questionnaire include items directly on free will, but they are organized into the components of cognitive, socioemotional, self, mental construction, and action components of free will. The placement of the items is driven by psychological constructs rather than empirical factor analysis. Moreover, for each of the five categories that I highlighted as relevant to free will, I described multiple subcategories. This procedure might appear somewhat arbitrary, but it does give an indication of the range of factors involved in free will belief.

Table 19.3 The positive free will belief and related belief questionnaire in five major categories (seven examples each)

Category	Examples
Cognitive	I freely see problems as they are.
	I freely choose to find all the options before continuing.
	I can justify in detail why I do anything.
	I freely choose my way in everything I do.
	I always have the choice to make my decisions my way.
	I know what is right for me.
	I always choose to think for myself.
Social-emotional	I freely choose to help people.
	I freely choose to do what's right for other people.
	Knowing I am free in everything I do lets me take my responsibilities easier.
	I believe that people should pay for the harm they cause others.
	I choose to be moral on my terms and not in the way others tell me.
	The more I believe in freedom in choosing, the more I understand how other people might have problems believing in it.
	The more I believe in freedom in choosing, the more I empathize with people.
Self	I am strong and determined, willful.
	My power lies in me and not in others.
	I can overcome obstacles.
	I am assertive without being offensive.
	I can change myself if I want to or have to.
	I can change things that are not going well.
	When I feel I am being me, people get the best of me.
Mental construction	I make sense of the world my way.
	I explain things and events my way.
	I interpret what happens my way.
	The messages I get from things and events that happen are up to me to make.
	The meanings in things and events come from how I see them.
	Things and events are as important as I let them be.
	What is useful in a situation is for me to decide.
Action	I freely choose to act the way I want.
	I freely choose to live the way I want.
	I can freely choose to act differently than I am acting now.
	I control the series of actions made by me.
	I control the series of actions made by others.
	I keep on track.
	I stop wrong actions.

Note. These questions can be rephrased to construct a general rather than personal free will belief questionnaire. They can stay in the present format, or some items might need to be reversed. The answers can be provided on a 7-point Likert scale (strongly disagree to strongly agree). Factor analytic studies should be constructed to determine their dimensional structure. As per Nadelhoffer et al. (2014), the studies addressing the final organization of the questionnaire should use explanatory factor analysis (principle components, eigenvalues > 1, oblique rotations factor loadings > 0.400) and then confirmatory factor analysis (checking model fit using the Goodness of Fit index, the Comparative Fit Index, and Adjusted Goodness of Fit index, the Root Mean Square Error of Approximation, and, to a lesser degree, the Chi Square test)

Associated Questionnaire The second table of the two that I constructed toward developing a new free will questionnaire borrows from Nadelhoffer et al. (2014) the idea that a second set of items can be used to determine the types of associations and extensions related to free will. In this regard, instead of finding items that allow determination of subtle philosophical questions, as had been the case for Nadelhoffer et al., I adopted a broader psychological perspective on the question, and constructed items that help investigate further each of the five major components of a broad construct of free will that was identified in Table 19.4. Specifically, I examined relevant subcategories for possible items of free will belief related to the cognitive, social–emotional, self, mental construction, and action components in Table 19.4. In each case, I developed the items related to free will belief in terms of eight associated subcategories (three items per set).

Table 19.4 The positive free will belief and related belief questionnaire in subcategories (5 categories, with 8 subcategories; 3 examples each)

Category	Subcategory	Examples
Cognitive	Attention	I have a good ability to pay attention in seeing a problem, thinking, deciding, and acting.
		In doing this, I see all the aspects or things I need to consider in the situation, problem, and so on.
		When I pay attention, I do not leave anything out so I can follow up with free choice in my behavior.
	Selection/detection	Because I pay attention around me, I see what is important to notice.
		I select important things to keep in mind as I deal with a problem.
		I put up front what I select to consider, so that I might act on the information appropriately.
	Choice	Of all the choices I have in a situation, I am the one who can choose the best one.
		No matter what situation I'm in and no matter how many things in it are not of my making, I'm still the one who can choose what to do.
		People tell me what to do, but I choose what to do despite what they say.
	Deciding	I can decide which choices I have in a situation.
		I can decide which choices to choose and act on in a situation, no matter what all the influences in the situation are.
		I have control of my decisions in a situation.
	Reason/logic/thinking	There are valid reasons to everything I do because I always reason what I do.
		I believe that being logical is the only way to be.
		When you think through everything involved, you're really thinking.
	Memory	In solving problems, I keep the problem in mind.
		In solving problems, I remember the possible solutions.
		In solving problems, I keep my mind and memory free by avoiding distractions, losing focus and keeping my mind from wandering.
	Shifting set	When one solution is not working in solving a problem, I can easily try another instead of staying with it.
		I don't get trapped in dead-ends in my thinking.
		I'm flexible in my thinking.
	Inhibition	We have to be able to not only think the right way, but also stop thinking the wrong way.
		When I push away a bad choice, it makes it easier to choose a good one.
		For every situation, I consider the pros and cons, advantages and disadvantages, and what to do and avoid doing.

(continued)

Table 19.4 (continued)

Category	Subcategory	Examples
Social/ emotional	Morality	I am free when I choose the right or moral thing no matter what.
		I believe that when you are truly free, you choose to help others.
		I believe that being free is stopping immorality.
	Responsibility	I choose to be responsible in what I do in my life; it is me.
		I believe that people should be responsible in how they undertake their daily roles and in deal with people.
		I believe that people make good choices when they are responsible in what they do in the home and outside.
	Respect	I respect others in the way I wish others would respect me.
		I respect what other people say and consider the options they give me, but I still choose what to do.
		I respect others' right to have opinions.
	Harm	I like to help other people and not harm them.
		I encourage other people not to be harmful.
		Stopping other people from harming is important.
	Relaxation/emotional regulation	I can think, decide, choose, and act freely because I am always emotionally balanced.
		I can still think, decide, choose, and act freely after I get hyper or stressed out.
		I can think, decide, choose, and act freely, not letting my emotions cloud my judgments.
	Being present	I am always present in the moment.
		I live in the present, instead of being prisoner of the past.
		Living in the present lets me live better in the future.
	Conscious (mindful)	I am aware not only of myself but also of the others.
		Consciousness is not just about me; it is about others, too.
		Being conscious of others and of myself go together.
	Relatedness	Part of how I consider myself socially is that I stay who I am in dealing with, relating to, and being with others.
		I seek to understand who I am in terms of my dealing with, relating to, and being with others.
		I value who I am in terms of my dealing with, relating to, and being with others.
Self	Definition of self	Part of my personal definition of me is that I am myself in my thinking, decisions, and actions.
		I seek to understand who I am in terms of being myself in my thinking, decisions, and actions.
		I value who I am in terms of being myself in my thinking, decisions, and actions.
	Completeness	I feel complete in my definition of self.
		I feel complete in understanding myself.
		I feel complete in valuing myself.
	Autonomy	I am an individual, independent of others.
		I am my own person; I am myself, thinking for myself.
		My behavior is not directed by outside factors, but is self-directed.
	Initiative	I take the initiative needed; I am not passive.
		I am motivated; I do what I have to when I have to.
		I am a go-getter; getting what I want.

(continued)

Table 19.4 (continued)

Category	Subcategory	Examples
	Self-control	I have self-control no matter what.
		I believe that being free does not mean doing what you want no matter what.
		I believe that being free is not just about desire and doing but also is resisting temptation.
	Ownership	I take ownership of my self/my mistakes (decisions, choices, actions, behavior).
		I take ownership of my (choices) errors/mistakes.
		I take ownership of my responsibilities.
	Self-confidence	I believe in myself.
		I have confidence in myself.
		I know how to behave and to be myself.
	Self-deception	I do not like to deceive myself; seeing clearly is better.
		I try not to lie to myself.
		I try to face things as they are.
Mental construction	Memory building	What I remember is not just about what happens or about things; I build memories my way.
		I have a say in how events and things are remembered.
		I build my memories myself; I don't let others do it for me.
	Meaning	I have a say in the meanings that are important to get from events and things.
		I see events and things my way.
		I understand what happens in terms of what is right for me.
	Concepts	I build concepts on what the world is about; these concepts are mine, not from others.
		I build concepts this way also on what I am about.
		I build concepts this way also on what others are about.
	Internal source of control	I control my mind not my brain or body.
		I'm in charge of my brain and body.
		I'm my boss, not my brain or body.
	External source of control	What others think controls how I think.
		What others feel controls how I feel.
		What others do controls how I act.
	Stress	What is stressful is something I decide; it does not come straight from the outside.
		Stress is what I perceive and believe about any situation.
		I can cope with any stress, no matter what it is.
	Culture	Culture (family, country) might tell me what to think, but I am the one who decides what to think.
		Culture (family, country) might tell me what to feel, but I am the one who decides what to feel.
		Culture (family, country) might tell me what to do, but I am the one who decides what to do.
	Causation	I am the cause of my thinking.
		I am the cause of my feelings.
		I am the cause of my actions.

(continued)

Table 19.4 (continued)

Category	Subcategory	Examples
Action	Problem solving	I have good problem-solving skills.
		I break down problems into their manageable parts.
		I juggle (multi-task) well.
	Planning	I make plans, knowing doing so makes life easier.
		I know my priorities.
		I am well organized.
	Goals	Goals are my guides as I live my life.
		Having goals keeps me focused.
		I can stick to my goals.
	Rewards	I can delay getting a reward when it lets me get bigger rewards.
		I believe that sometimes the best rewards are the ones we feel inside.
		Having patience makes me find the right way and get the right reward.
	Monitoring	I believe that the best thinking is when you solve the problem and there is little follow-up needed afterward.
		By seeing the bigger picture, I avoid getting lost in little details.
		Pulling back from a problem helps me go back and solve the problem.
	Feedback	I am a flexible person, always learning from what happens.
		I am a flexible person, always learning from what I do.
		I am a flexible person, always learning from what people tell me.
	Anticipation	When I act, I consider beforehand what might happen.
		My plans and goals take into account the future and not just the present.
		I consider how others might be impacted before I do something.
	Changing things around me	My problem-solving ability, planning, and goal selection include not just adjusting to things around me but also changing them.
		I look forward to changing things around me to make life better.
		I consider how others might need changes in things around them when I try to change what is around me.

For the cognitive component of free will belief in Table 19.4, the relevant categories include: attention, selection/detection, choice, deciding, reasoning/logic/thinking, and three major executive functions (working memory, shifting set, inhibition). The list cannot be exhaustive, but it is representative. The executive function list could be longer. Components of it are elsewhere in the table (e.g., planning). Inhibition is part of the executive function and it could be placed in each of the five subcategories. Recall that a general mechanistic factor that I have proposed for behavior is activation/inhibition coordination (Young, 2011).

For the social–emotional component of the free will belief questionnaire, the relevant categories include the following: morality, responsibility, respect, not harming, relaxing/emotional, regulation, being present, being conscious (mindful), and relatedness. For the self-categories, they number definition, completeness, autonomy, initiative, control, ownership, confidence, and self-deception. For mental construction, the subcategories include memory building, meaning, concepts, internal source of control, external source of control, stress, culture, and causation. For action, the relevant components involve problem solving, planning, goals, rewards, monitoring, feedback, anticipation, and changing the context. Many of these categories would have questionnaires already constructed for them in the literature. However, I have constructed three novel items for each of them so that they are applicable to free will belief and having sense of free will.

Comment Research is needed to organize psychometrically the proposed free will questionnaire items into a coherent whole by establishing their factor structure. As well, it should examine the correlations of the resulting factors with other measures in order to establish the validity of the questionnaire and its full meaning.

Belief in Free Will/Determinism

Nichols and Knobe (2007) conducted an experimental philosophy investigation on moral responsibility and determinism. They asked participants which of two universes is most like ours—one description was determinist and the other was indeterminist (respectively, "Everything that happens is completely caused by whatever happens before it;" "Almost everything that happens is completely caused by whatever happens before it. The one exception is human decision making"). This study led me to create a questionnaire related to belief in free will and determinism that might be useful. In essence, participants should be able to judge on a Likert scale to what degree they believe in each of the two statements on (in) determinism (see Table 19.5).

Table 19.5 Causes in universe questionnaire

Find below three questions describing causes in our universe. For each question, indicate on the 7-point scale how much you agree with the statement. Note. The three answers do not have to total 7; the questions are separate.						
1. Imagine a universe (Universe A) in which everything that happens is completely caused by whatever happened before it. This is true from the very beginning of the universe, so what happened in the beginning of the universe caused what happened next, and so on right up until the present. For example, one day John decided to have French fries at lunch. Like everything else, this decision was completely caused by what happened before it. So, if everything in this universe was exactly the same up until John made his decision, then it had to happen that John would decide to have French fries.						
How much do you think this universe is most like ours?						
Universe A Universe B						
1	2	3	4	5	6	7
Disagree						Strongly Agree
2. Imagine a universe (Universe B) in which almost everything that happens is completely caused by whatever happened before it. The one exception is human decision-making. For example, one day Mary decided to have French fries at lunch. Since a person's decision in this universe is not completely caused by what happened before it, even if everything in the universe is not completely caused by what happened before it, even if everything in the universe was exactly the same up until Mary made her decision, it did not have to happen that Mary would decide to have French fries. She could have decided to have something different.						
How much do you think this universe is most like ours?						
Universe A Universe B						
1	2	3	4	5	6	7
Disagree						Strongly Agree
3. Imagine a universe (Universe B) in which **almost everything** that happens is completely caused by whatever happened before it. The one exception is human decision-making. **Sometimes** these are caused by whatever happens before and **sometimes** not. For example, one day Mary decided to have French fries at lunch. Since a person's decision in this universe is **sometimes** not completely caused by what happened before it, even if everything in the universe is not completely caused by what happened before it, even if everything in the universe was exactly the same up until Mary made her decision, it did not have to happen that Mary would decide to have French fries. She could have decided to have something different.						
How much do you think this universe is most like ours?						
Universe A Universe B						
1	2	3	4	5	6	7
Disagree						Strongly Agree
The key difference, then is, that in Universe A every decision is completely caused by what happened before the decision—given the past, each decision has to happen the way that it does. By contrast, in Universe B, decisions are not completely caused by the past, and each human decision does not have to happen the way that it does.						

(continued)

Table 19.5 (continued)

Choose the best answer for your opinion of how much control we have of our own decisions.
(a) Everything that happens in the universe is completely caused by whatever happened before it and what is happening now. This is true for human decision-making, too. We can *never decide independently* of everything that happened before and is happening now. (b) Everything that happens in the universe is completely caused by whatever happened before it and what is happening now. The one exception is human decision-making, but only sometimes. *We can sometimes decide independently* of everything that happened before and is happening now. (c) Everything that happens in the universe is completely caused by whatever happened before it and what is happening now. The one exception is human decision-making, for which we have total control always. *We can always decide independently* of everything that happened before and is happening now.
This questionnaire is an improvement because it includes the 3 options in one, it adds the present context as important in decision-making, and it removes the example and, instead, restates the case in clear terms.

Table 19.6 Resource/energy/ego-depletion questionnaire

Depletion	Effects
Even if I have	**I still can**
Fatigue/pain/not eaten	Choose right/decide well.
Had to control myself too much already/overexert myself	Think clearly/plan ok/problem-solve
Down feelings/worry/irritability	Stay cool/have self-control
No motivation/get go	Keep perspective/see the big picture and details
Little support/criticism from others	Overcome/keep going on right path, while avoiding errors/wrong path
Nothing to get out of it	Be myself/keep my values/do the right, responsible thing

Note. Arrange each of 36 items on a 5-point Likert scale

Depletion

Questionnaire It would be helpful to the field to have a depletion scale. In this regard, Table 19.6 presents items relevant to six resource/energy/depletion factors that might affect self-control and related behaviors. They include: (1) physical, (2) cognitive, (3) emotional, (4) motivation, (5) social, and (6) incentive-related reasons for resource/energy/ego-depletion. Possible effects of interest of the depletion include: (1) choosing/deciding, (2) thinking/problem solving, (3) staying calm/in control, (4) keeping perspective/seeing the whole, (5) overcoming/keep going, and (6) being oneself/maintaining values/responsibility.

Comment Note that, once established as reliable and valid, both the free will belief and depletion questionnaires can be used therapeutically on an individual basis. For example, the questionnaires can be filled in to monitor cognitive behavioral therapy with people having addictions. The focus could begin with the items choosing/deciding/self-control in each of the questionnaires. For example, the therapist might use them to build up a sense of choosing and deciding better, taking ownership, resisting temptation, and developing a general self-control.

Belief and Passion as Part of Behavioral Causation and Causality Engines

Introduction

As mentioned, I refer to the biopsychosocial model as the biopersonalsocial one (Young, 2011). Aspects of the personal component include the self, free will belief, and coping skills that help give the person a sense of personal agency in her/his own behavioral determination. A primary component to personal agency includes belief, in general, and the associated construct of passion when that belief is powerful, is associated with emotions, and is potentially activating of follow-up associated goals and behaviors.

Belief

The power of belief is illustrated in people making the ultimate sacrifice in the name of a cause (Bélanger, Caouette, Sharvit, & Dugas, 2014). The phenomenon of Martyrdom encompasses a larger range of cognitive, emotional, and behavioral manifestations. In another vein, Thompson, O'Donnell, Stafford, and Nordfjaern (2014) and Sullivan, Yakobov, Scott, and Tait (2014) noted the power of attributions of responsibility/perceived injustice on psychological recovery from trauma. For me, these examples illustrate that belief is a primary "causality engine" in human behavior, especially if extreme in any way. However, beyond these extreme examples, the general beliefs that we hold influence much of our daily activity. It would seem that a biopsychosocial understanding of their origin would apply and be helpful.

Note that the concept of "causality engine" appears general enough so that it might help explain the power of multiple personal psychological processes in the biopsychosocial origins of behavior. The psychological component in the biopsychosocial model is a personal or self one, as noted, and beliefs and passions constitute important subcomponents in this regard. Through them, the person might best demonstrate that he or she should be considered the "third force" in behavioral causality relative to biology and environment. That is, through beliefs and passions, the person individuates in her or his personal or individual psychological standing and characteristics, becoming a special active causal force determining her or his own behavior and, therefore, can take charge of goal establishment and behavioral decision-making and direction (and simultaneously help to put aside the more passive internal (biological) and external (social) forces around us).

Passion

Introduction An example that illustrates the personal nature of the causal factors underlying behavior concerns passion. Vallerand and colleagues have been instrumental in defining it and developing a questionnaire for it (e.g., Vallerand, 2010; Vallerand et al., 2003).

Vallerand and colleagues had defined passion as a strong inclination toward self-defining activities, people, or objects that the person loves, considers important, and is worthy of investment of a significant amount of energy and time. As for the two scales measuring it, the six harmonious items refer to harmony, appreciation, integration, liking, and living. The six items for the obsessive scale involve terms such as obsession, losing control, and "the only thing."

Marsh et al. (2013) confirmed the two-factor structure of the passion scale, harmonious or obsessive passion (each measured using a 6-item inventory; see Table 19.7). Harmonious passion is related to more adaptive outcomes, given its intrinsic base on "loving" as the focus of the passion (Vallerand & Verner-Filion, 2013), while obsessive passion is related to more maladaptive outcomes, partly related to the internal pressures that it creates.

The review by Marsh et al. (2013) showed that passion has been found relevant in the areas of work, education, sport, leisure, and social life, as well as mixed activities. Also, it relates to a measure of life satisfaction (Diener, 1985).

Current research continues to expand the scope of study of passion and its correlates. For example, Fernet, Lavigne, Vallerand, and Austin (2014) and Lavigne, Forest, Fernet, and Crevier-Braud (2014) examined passion in relation to job autonomy and job control, respectively. Stenseng, Forest, and Curran (2015) related it to recreational sports, and Zhang, Shi, Liu, and Miao (2014) to leisure activity. Also, Lafrenière, Vallerand, and Sedikides (2013) and Balon and Rimé (2013) related it to life satisfaction and personality, respectively.

Despite this range of positive findings using the extant definition and measure of passion,

Table 19.7 Items on the two components of the passion scale

Item	Passion scale
Harmonious	
1	This ______ is in harmony with the other ones in my life.
2	The new things that I discover with this ______ allow me to appreciate it even more.
3	This ______reflects the qualities I like about myself.
4	This ______ allows me to live a variety of experiences.
5	My ______ is well integrated in my life.
6	My ______ is in harmony with other things that are part of me.
Obsessive	
1	I have difficulties controlling my urge to do my ______.
2	I have almost an obsessive feeling for this ______.
3	This ______ is the only thing that really turns me on.
4	If I could, I would only do my ______.
5	This ______ is so exciting that I sometimes lose control over it.
6	I have the impression that my ______ controls me.

Adapted from Marsh et al. (2013)
Note. The original scale includes the word "activity" in the blank spaces. One could insert the words activity, object, or person in the blanks, depending on research needs. Also, for items in the harmony scale at the top, I used the word "ones" instead of activities

there is room for improvement in both these regards. In the following, I consider a broader definition of passion and a more inclusive range of items that could be used to measure its harmonious portion.

Comment I noticed that Vallerand and Verner-Filion (2013) had altered the current definition to some extent, reverting to the original definition in Vallerand et al. (2003). Specifically, they referred only to passion involving an activity, and excluded mention of an object or a person as a focus in passion. They indicated the inclination could be a "like" and not only a "love." And they removed the qualifier of "significant" to the investment involved in passion.

I find the last two changes good ones. However, in several senses, the original definition that allows for passion for people or objects as much as for activities should be kept in the current definition. Specifically, passion does extend to these foci. That being said, the items in both the harmonious and obsessive portions of the scale refer to "activities" only, but instead of revising the general definition of passion to fit the scale, the scale should be revised to fit the definition.

New Definition The definition that I have constructed for the concept of passion considers the following. (a) The term inclination is insufficient to capture the emotions involved in passion. (b) It is more than an emotion, though, being a motivator/driver. (c) It involves goals related to the emotion/motivation. And the goals are focused and preferred/favored. (d) The goals involved are more than self-defining; also, they are self-enhancing. (e) The goals could be outward-directed, such as to an activity, object, or person, but also they could be inward-directed, such as improving one's mood or self-worth.

Given these considerations, I have developed a fuller definition of passion, as per below. Note that, as well, it includes the obsessional component that might be involved.

Therefore, toward revising the concept to fit the parameters mentioned, passion should be defined in the following way. It is a "deeply felt (e.g., liking, loving) and motivating/driven inclination or enthusiasm leading to the focused pursuit of positive, personally important, defining or harmonious/integrative self-enhancing, valued goals (which could be outward-directed, such as in investing in an activity, person, or object; accomplishing a task, or learning a preferred skill; or inward-directed, such as in gaining certain positive experiences, feelings, or increments in self-worth) or, rather, passion could lead to difficulties in that process; depending on the nature of the goal, the personality, the context (which includes culture), whether the passion is obsessive, out of control, and so on."

New Questionnaire As for revising the items in the dual-mode passion scale, I focus just on the harmonious component. (a) First, the items should be general and not focus just on activities. (b) Second, they should emphasize goals more than the objects of the goals. (c) Third, they should allow for both inward- and outward-directed focusing. (d) Fourth, they should allow specification if the passion is personally-formulated, externally-driven, or both, and perhaps whether there might be a constitutional (perhaps genetically-based) talent or skill that one is pursuing. That is, the possible causes to the passion at issue might be worth querying.

Given these considerations, I developed a revised passion scale consisting of six parts. The first part specifies the focus of the passion, and whether it has been self-selected for answers or whether it is experimenter-derived. The second part of the questionnaire asks whether the passion is about the sense of accomplishment it brings or the positive internal feelings it brings. The third portion of the revised passion questionnaire is based on the original one, and poses six questions about whether the passion at issue creates harmony, appreciation, self-reflection, living desired experiences, and is an integral part of one's life. The fourth part of the questionnaire asks the respondent to indicate from among a number of adjectives that apply. The adjectives include ones related to the new definition. The fifth portion of the questionnaire also is based on the original, and asks about the negative qualities of passion. Finally, the last part of the questionnaire queries the self-perceived origins of the passion, e.g., following personal talents or not (see Table 19.8).

As with any questionnaire, empirical verification is needed to establish reliability and validity. The items were rationally derived for the most

Table 19.8 Revised passion scale

A. Think of something that is really dear to you, or important (or valued) in what you focus on by your motivation or drive. [Or answer about the focus selected by the person administering the questionnaire.] For this focus, answer the questions that follow:

1. My focus is ___________ ___________.

OR

2. The focus selected for me to consider by the person who gave me the questionnaire is ________ _________.
[Could be filled in for you by the person!]

B. This focus is important for me because of the sense of accomplishment it brings as a reward or, rather, because of positive internal feelings that it brings. In this regard, the focus involved in my answers is about

1. The sense of accomplishment, to the following degree
   0 1 2 3 4 5 6 7
2. The positive internal feeling, to the following degree
   0 1 2 3 4 5 6 7

C. Here are 6 questions about the focus of your answers.
This focus:

1. Is in harmony with the other ones in my life.
   0 1 2 3 4 5 6 7
2. Allows me to discover new things so that I appreciate it even more.
   0 1 2 3 4 5 6 7
3. Reflects the qualities I like about myself.
   0 1 2 3 4 5 6 7
4. Allows me to live a variety of experiences.
   0 1 2 3 4 5 6 7
5. Is well integrated in my life.
   0 1 2 3 4 5 6 7
6. Is in harmony with other things that are part of me.
   0 1 2 3 4 5 6 7

D. For the focus that you are considering, how much does each of the following adjectives apply to it?

Passion	0	1	2	3	4	5	6	7
Love	0	1	2	3	4	5	6	7
Like	0	1	2	3	4	5	6	7

(continued)

Table 19.8 (continued)

Deeply felt	0	1	2	3	4	5	6	7
Motivating	0	1	2	3	4	5	6	7
Driven	0	1	2	3	4	5	6	7
Inclination	0	1	2	3	4	5	6	7
Excitement	0	1	2	3	4	5	6	7
Enthusiasm	0	1	2	3	4	5	6	7
Positive	0	1	2	3	4	5	6	7
Self-defining	0	1	2	3	4	5	6	7
Self-enhancing	0	1	2	3	4	5	6	7
Valued	0	1	2	3	4	5	6	7
Good goal	0	1	2	3	4	5	6	7
Accomplishment	0	1	2	3	4	5	6	7
Internal feeling	0	1	2	3	4	5	6	7
Others TBA								

E. This focus could be very powerful. It could involve:

1. Difficulties controlling my urge to do it.
   0 1 2 3 4 5 6 7
2. Almost an obsessive feeling for it.
   0 1 2 3 4 5 6 7
3. The only thing that really turns me on.
   0 1 2 3 4 5 6 7
4. If I could, it would be my only focus.
   0 1 2 3 4 5 6 7
5. So much excitement that I lose control over it.
   0 1 2 3 4 5 6 7
6. The impression that it controls me.
   0 1 2 3 4 5 6 7

F. Finally, the focus that you are considering might come (a) from inside you, being your choice, or (b) from what was trained or educated in you, or (c) from your innate talents (or all of these). In this regard, my focus is:

1. From inside me, what I have personally chosen.
   0 1 2 3 4 5 6 7
2. From the outside, what I was trained in or taught.
   0 1 2 3 4 5 6 7
3. From my innate talents or skills that I have followed.
   0 1 2 3 4 5 6 7

Note. This scale was developed partly with my university class on emerging adulthood in the winter semester of 2015 (as was part of the definition of passion given in the text that accompanies this table)

part and they need to be empirically tailored. For research on a new questionnaire related to free will, consult Deery, Davis, and Carey (2015a, 2015b). They developed a questionnaire from a philosophical orientation and focuses especially on questions related to ability to do otherwise (ATDO) and sourcehood, considering both relevant freedoms. The factor structure of the questionnaire included items related to compatibilism and incompatibilisim. For the critical ATDO factors, there are five questions for each of them. Relative to the items in my own questionnaire, I found the wordings of their items quite philosophical and complex. Nevertheless, it might give complementary information in empirical research.

Chapter Conclusions

The work in the area of free will, self-control, and depletion is accelerating rapidly. The present chapter has reviewed the areas of depletion and a related one of dual processing. In addition, it presents new questionnaires related to free will and depletion, in particular. Finally, it uses an integrative biopsychosocial model that helps integrate under one umbrella the diverging areas in the study of free will, self-control, depletion, and their measurement.

References

Balon, S., & Rimé, J. L. B. (2013). Passion and personality: Is passionate behaviour a function of personality? *Revue Européenee de Psychologie Appliquée, 63*, 59–65.

Balleine, B. W., Delgado, M. R., & Hikosaka, O. (2007). The role of the dorsal striatum in reward and decision-making. *Journal of Neuroscience, 27*, 8161–8165.

Bargh, J. A. (1994). The four horseman of automaticity: Awareness, intention, efficiency, and control in social cognition. In R. S. Wyer & T. K. Srull (Eds.), *Handbook of social cognition* (pp. 1–40). Hillsdale, NJ: Erlbaum.

Bargh, J. A. (2005). Bypassing the will: Towards demystifying behavioral priming effects. In R. Hassin, J. Uleman, & J. Bargh (Eds.), *The new unconscious* (pp. 37–58). Oxford, UK: Oxford University Press.

Barrouillet, P. (2011). Dual-process theories of reasoning: The test of development. *Developmental Review, 31*, 151–179.

Baumeister, R. F. (2008). Free will in scientific psychology. *Perspectives on Psychological Science, 3*, 14–19.

Baumeister, R. F., & Bargh, J. A. (2014). Conscious and unconscious: Toward an integrative understanding of human mental life and action. In J. W. Sherman, B. Gawronski, & Y. Trope (Eds.), *Dual-process theories of the social mind* (pp. 35–49). New York: Guilford Press.

Baumeister, R. F., Bratslavesky, E., Muraven, M., & Tice, D. M. (1998). Ego depletion: Is the active self a limited resource? *Journal of Personality and Social Psychology, 74*, 1252–1265.

Baumeister, R. F., & Masicampo, E. J. (2010). Conscious thought is for facilitating social and cultural interactions: How mental simulations serve the animal-culture interface. *Psychological Review, 117*, 945–971.

Baumeister, R. F., Masicampo, E. J., & DeWall, C. N. (2009). Prosocial benefits of feeling free: Disbelief in free will increases aggression and reduces helpfulness. *Personality and Social Psychology Bulletin, 35*, 260–268.

Baumeister, R. F., Masicampo, E. J., & Vohs, K. D. (2011). Do conscious thoughts cause behavior? *Annual Review of Psychology, 62*, 331–361.

Baumeister, R. F., Vohs, K. D., & Tice, D. M. (2007). The strength model of self-control. *Current Directions in Psychological Science, 16*, 351–355.

Beckes, L., & Coan, J. A. (2011). Social baseline theory: The role of social proximity in emotion and economy of action. *Social and Personality Psychology Compass, 5*, 976–988.

Bélanger, J. J., Caouette, J., Sharvit, K., & Dugas, M. (2014). The psychology of martyrdom: Making the ultimate sacrifice in the name of a cause. *Journal of Personality and Social Psychology, 107*, 494–515.

Botvinick, M., & Braver, T. (2015). Motivation and cognitive control: From behavior to neural mechanism. *Annual Review of Psychology, 66*, 83–113.

Bush, G., Shin, L. M., Holmes, J., Rosen, D. R., & Vogt, B. A. (2003). The multi-source interference task: Validation study with fMRI in individual subjects. *Molecular Psychiatry, 8*, 60–70.

Carter, C. S., & Van Veen, V. (2007). Anterior cingulate cortex and conflict detection: An update of theory and data. *Cognitive, Affective, & Behavioral Neuroscience, 7*, 367–379.

Carter, E. C., Kofler, L. M., Forster, D. E., & McCullough, M. E. (2015). A series of meta-analytic tests of the depletion effect: Self-control does not seem to rely on a limited resource. *Journal of Experimental Psychology: General, 144*, 796–815.

Carver, C. S., Johnson, S. L., & Joormann, J. (2013). Two-mode models of self-regulation and serotonergic functioning: Divergent manifestations of impulse and constraint. In B. W. Sokol, M. E. Grouzet, & U. Müller (Eds.), *Self-regulation and autonomy: Social and developmental dimensions of human conduct* (pp. 255–278). New York: Cambridge University Press.

Chen, S., Westman, M., & Hobfoll, S. E. (2015). The commerce and crossover of resources: Resource conservation in the service of resilience. *Stress and Health, 31*, 95–105.

Coan, J. A. (2008). Toward a neuroscience of attachment. In J. Cassidy & P. R. Shaver (Eds.), *Handbook of attachment: Theory, research, and clinical applications* (2nd ed., pp. 241–265). New York: Guilford Press.

Coan, J. A., Brown, C. L., & Beckes, L. (2014). Out social baseline: The role of social proximity in economy of action. In M. Mikulincer & P. R. Shaver (Eds.), *Mechanisms of social connection: From brain to group* (pp. 89–104). Washington, DC: American Psychological Association.

Coan, J. A., Schaefer, H. S., & Davidson, R. J. (2006). Lending a hand: Social regulation of the neural response to threat. *Psychological Science, 17*, 1032–1039.

Cushman, F., & Greene, J. D. (2012). Finding faults: How moral dilemmas illuminate cognitive structure. *Social Neuroscience, 7*, 269–279.

Deci, E. L., & Ryan, R. M. (2013). The importance of autonomy for development and well-being. In B. W. Sokol, M. E. Grouzet, & U. Müller (Eds.), *Self-regulation and autonomy: Social and developmental dimensions of human conduct* (pp. 19–46). New York: Cambridge University Press.

Deery, O., Davis, T., & Carey, J. (2015a). The free-will intuition scale and the question of natural compatibilism. *Philosophical Psychology, 28*, 776–801.

Deery, O., Davis, T., & Carey, J. (2015b). Defending the free-will intuitions scale: Reply to Stephen Morris. *Philosophical Psychology, 28*, 808–814.

Diener, E. (1985). *Satisfaction with life scale*. Retrieved from PsycTESTS. doi:10.1037/t01069-000.

Duckworth, A. L., & Carlson, S. M. (2013). Self-regulation and school success. In B. W. Sokol, M. E. Grouzet, & U. Müller (Eds.), *Self-regulation and autonomy: Social and developmental dimensions of human conduct* (pp. 208–230). New York: Cambridge University Press.

Dweck, C. S. (2012). Mindsets and human nature: Promoting change in the Middle East, the schoolyard, the racial divide, and willpower. *American Psychologist, 67*, 614–622.

Eagle, D. M., & Baunez, C. (2010). Is there an inhibitory-response control system in the rat? Evidence from anatomical and pharmacological studies of behavioral inhibition. *Neuroscience & Biobehavioral Review, 34*, 50–72.

Edelman, G. M., & Tononi, G. (2000). *A universe of consciousness: How matter becomes imagination*. New York: Basic Books.

Ent, M. R., & Baumeister, R. F. (2014). Embodied free will beliefs: Some effects of physical states on metaphysical opinions. *Consciousness and Cognition, 27*, 147–154.

Ent, M. R., Baumeister, R. F., & Vonasch, A. J. (2012). Power, leadership, and self-regulation. *Social and Personality Psychology Compass, 6*, 619–630.

Evans, D. R., Boggero, I. A., & Segerstrom, S. C. (2015). The nature of self-regulatory fatigue and "ego depletion": Lessons from physical fatigue. *Personality and Social Psychology Review*, 1–20.

Evans, J. St. B. T. (2009). How many dual-process theories do we need? One, two, or many? In J. St. B. T. Evans & K. Frankish (Eds.), *In two minds: Dual processes and beyond* (pp. 33–54). New York: Oxford University Press.

Evans, J. St. B. T. (2010). Thinking twice: Two minds in one brain. Oxford, UK: Oxford University Press.

Evans, J. St. B. T. (2011a). The psychology of reasoning: Reflections on four decades of research. In K. Manktelow, D. Over, & S. Elquayam (Eds.), *The science of reason* (pp. 423–444). Hove, UK: Psychology Press.

Evans, J. St. B. T. (2011b). Dual process theories of reasoning: Contemporary issues and developmental applications. *Developmental Review, 31*, 86–102.

Evans, J. St. B. T., & Stanovich, K. E. (2013). Dual-process theories of higher cognition: Advancing the debate. *Perspectives on Psychological Science, 8*, 223–241.

Fernet, C., Lavigne, G. L., Vallerand, R. J., & Austin, S. (2014). Fired up with passion: Investigating how job autonomy and passion predict burnout at career start in teachers. *Work & Stress, 28*, 270–288.

Freud, S. (1933/1965). Warum krieg (Why war)? *Standard Edition of the Complete Psychological Works of Sigmund Freud, 22*, 197–224. London: Hogarth Press.

Gailliot, M. T., & Baumeister, R. F. (2007). Self-regulation and sexual restraint: Dispositionally and temporarily poor self-regulatory abilities contribute to failure at restraining sexual behavior. *Personality and Social Psychology Bulletin, 33*, 173–186.

Gailliot, M. T., Baumeister, R. F., DeWall, C., N., Maner, J. K., Plant, E. A., Tice, D. M., et al. J. (2007). Self-control relies on glucose as a limited energy source: Willpower is more than a metaphor. *Journal of Personality and Social Psychology, 92*, 325–336.

Gailliot, M. T., Gitter, S. A., Baker, M. D., & Baumeister, R. F. (2012). Breaking the rules: Low trait or state self-control increases social norm violations. *Psychology, 3*, 1074–1083.

Galinsky, A. D., Maddux, W. W., Gilin, D., & White, J. D. (2008). Why it pays to get inside the head of your opponent: The differential effects of perspective taking and empathy in negotiations. *Psychological Science, 19*, 378–384.

Gawronski, B., Sherman, J. W., & Trope, Y. (2014). Two of what?: A conceptual analysis of dual-process theories. In J. W. Sherman, B. Gawronski, & Y. Trope (Eds.), *Dual-process theories of the social mind* (pp. 3–19). New York: Guilford Press.

Grouzet, M. E. (2013). Self-regulation and autonomy: The dialectic between organismic and sociocognitive valuing processes. In B. W. Sokol, M. E. Grouzet, & U. Müller (Eds.), *Self-regulation and autonomy: Social and developmental dimensions of human conduct* (pp. 47–77). New York: Cambridge University Press.

Grouzet, M. E., Sokol, B. W., & Müller, U. (2013). Self-regulation and autonomy: An introduction. In B. W. Sokol, M. E. Grouzet, & U. Müller (Eds.), *Self-regulation and autonomy: Social and developmental dimensions of human conduct* (pp. 1–16). New York: Cambridge University Press.

Hagger, M. S. (2015). Conservation of resources theory and the "strength" model of self-control: Conceptual overlap and commonalities. *Stress and Health, 31*, 89–94.

Hagger, M. S., Wood, C., Stiff, C., & Chatzisarantis, N. L. (2010). Ego depletion and the strength model of self-control: A meta-analysis. *Psychological Bulletin, 136*, 495–525.

Heatherton, T. F., & Wagner, D. D. (2011). Cognitive neuroscience of self-regulation failure. *Trends in Cognitive Sciences, 15*, 132–139.

Hobfoll, S. E. (1989). Conservation resources: A new attempt at a conceptualizing stress. *American Psychologist, 44*, 513.

Inzlicht, M., & Al-Khindi, T. (2012). ERN and the placebo: A misattribution approach to studying the arousal properties of the error-related negativity. *Journal of Experimental Psychology: General, 141*, 799–807.

Inzlicht, M., & Gutsell, J. N. (2007). Running on empty: Neural signals for self-control failure. *Psychological Science, 18*, 933–937.

Inzlicht, M., & Schmeichel, B. J. (2012). What is ego depletion? Toward a mechanistic revision of the resource model of self-control. *Perspectives on Psychological Science, 7*, 450–463.

Inzlicht, M., & Schmeichel, B. J. (2013). Beyond simple utility in predicting self-control fatigue: A proximate alternative to the opportunity cost model. *Behavioral and Brain Sciences, 36*, 695–696.

Job, V., Dweck, C. S., & Walton, G. M. (2010). Ego depletion – Is it all in your head? Implicit theories about willpower affect self-regulation. *Psychological Science, 21*, 1686–1693.

Kinnucan, C. J. E., & Kuebli, J. E. (2013). Understanding explanatory talk through Vygotsky's theory of self-regulation. In B. W. Sokol, M. E. Grouzet, & U. Müller

(Eds.), *Self-regulation and autonomy: Social and developmental dimensions of human conduct* (pp. 231–252). New York: Cambridge University Press.

Kopp, C. B. (2011). Development in the early years: Socialization, motor development, and consciousness. *Annual Review of Psychology, 62*, 165–187.

Kurzban, R., Duckworth, A., Kable, J. W., & Myers, J. (2013a). An opportunity cost model of subjective effort and task performance. *Behavioral and Brain Sciences, 36*, 661–726.

Kurzban, R., Duckworth, A., Kable, J. W., & Myers, J. (2013b). Cost-benefit models as the next, best option for understanding subjective effort. *Behavioral and Brain Sciences, 36*, 707–726.

Lafrenière, M.-A., Vallerand, R. J., & Sedikides, C. (2013). On the relation between self-enhancement and life satisfaction: The moderating role of passion. *Self and Identity, 12*, 597–609.

Lavigne, G. L., Forest, J., Fernet, C., & Crevier-Braud, L. (2014). Passion at work and workers' evaluations of job demands and resources: A longitudinal study. *Journal of Applied Social Psychology, 44*, 255–265.

Lerner, J. S., Li, Y., Valdesolo, P., & Kassam, K. S. (2015). Emotion and decision making. *Annual Review of Psychology, 66*, 799–823.

Lévy, P. (1997). *Collective intelligence: Mankind's emerging world in cyberspace*. Cambridge, MA: Perseus Books.

Marr, D. (1982). *Vision: A computational investigation into the human representation and processing of visual information*. New York: Freeman.

Marsh, H. W., Lafrenière, M.-A., Carbonneau, N., Bureau, J. S., Guay, F., Vallerand, R. J., et al. (2013). Passion: Does one scale fit all? Construct validity of two-factor passion scale and psychometric invariance over different activities and languages. *Psychological Assessment, 25*, 796–809.

Masicampo, E. J., & Baumeister, R. F. (2008). Toward a physiology of dual-process reasoning and judgment: Lemonade, willpower, and expensive rule-based analysis. *Psychological Science, 19*, 255–260.

Minda, J. P., & Rabi, R. (2015). Ego depletion interferes with rule-defined category learning but not non-rule-defined category learning. *Frontiers in Psychology, 6*, 35. doi:10.3389/fpsyg.2015.00035.

Molden, D. C., Hui, C. M., Noreen, E. E., Meier, B. P., Scholer, A. A., D'Agostino, P. R., et al. (2012). The motivational versus metabolic effects of carbohydrates on self-control. *Psychological Science, 23*, 1130–1137.

Moller, A. C., Deci, E. L., & Ryan, R. M. (2006). Choice and ego depletion: The moderating role of autonomy. *Personality and Social Psychology Bulletin, 32*, 1024–1036.

Morsella, E. (2005). The function of phenomenal states: Supramodular interaction theory. *Psychological Review, 112*, 1000–1021.

Muraven, M., & Slessareva, E. (2003). Mechanisms of self-control failure: Motivation and limited resources. *Personality and Social Psychology Bulletin, 29*, 894–906.

Nadelhoffer, T., Shepard, J., Nahmias, E., Sripada, C., & Thomson Ross, L. (2014). The free will inventory: Measuring beliefs about agency and responsibility. *Consciousness and Cognition, 25*, 27–41.

Nelson, K. (2007). *Young minds in social worlds: Experience, meaning, and memory*. Cambridge, MA: Harvard University Press.

Newell, B. R. (2015). "Wait! Just let me not think about that for a minute": What role do implicit processes play in higher-level cognition? *Current Directions in Psychological Science, 24*, 65–70.

Nichols, S., & Knobe, J. (2007). Moral responsibility and determinism: The cognitive science of folk intuitions. *Noûs, 41*, 663–685.

Nucci, L. (2013). "It's a part of life to do what you what": The role of personal choice in social development. In B. W. Sokol, M. E. Grouzet, & U. Müller (Eds.), *Self-regulation and autonomy: Social and developmental dimensions of human conduct* (pp. 165–188). New York: Cambridge University Press.

Paulhus, D. L., & Carey, J. M. (2011). The FAD-Plus: Measuring lay beliefs regarding free will and related constructs. *Journal of Personality Assessment, 93*, 96–104.

Piaget, J. (1974/1980). *Adaptation and intelligence: Organic selection and phenocopy*. Chicago, IL: University of Chicago Press.

Piaget, J., & Inhelder, B. (1941). *Le développement des quantités physiques chez l'enfant*. Neuchâtel, Switzerland: Delachaux & Niestlé.

Piaget, J., & Inhelder, B. (1954). *La genèse des structures logiques élémentaires*. Neuchâtel, Switzerland: Delachaux & Niestlé.

Pons, F., Harris, P., & de Rosnay, M. (2012). Piaget and consciousness: Retrospect and prospect. In E. Marti & C. Rodriguez (Eds.), *After Piaget* (pp. 95–122). New Brunswick, NJ: Transaction Publishers.

Rabi, R., & Minda, J. P. (2014). Rule-based category learning in children: The role of age and executive functioning. *PLoS One, 9*, e85316. doi:10.1371/journal.pone.0085316.

Rakos, R. F., Laurene, K. R., Skala, S., & Slane, S. (2008). Belief in free will: Measurement and conceptualization innovations. *Behavior and Social Issues, 17*, 20–39.

Rigoni, D., Kühn, S., Gaudino, G., Sartori, G., & Brass, M. (2012). Reducing self-control by weakening belief in free will. *Consciousness and Cognition, 21*, 1482–1490.

Rochat, P. (2003). Five levels of self-awareness as they unfold early in life. *Consciousness and Cognition, 12*, 717–731.

Sanders, M. A., Shirk, S. D., Burgin, C. J., & Martin, L. L. (2012). The gargle effect: Rinsing the mouth with glucose enhances self-control. *Psychological Science, 23*, 1470–1472.

Schmeichel, B. J., Harmon-Jones, C., & Harmon-Jones, E. (2010). Exercising self-control increases approach motivation. *Journal of Personality and Social Psychology, 99*, 162–173.

Schmeichel, B. J., & Vohs, K. D. (2009). Self-affirmation and self-control: Affirming core values counteracts ego depletion. *Journal of Personality and Social Psychology, 96*, 770–782.

Segerstrom, S. C., & Nes, L. S. (2007). Heart rate variability reflects self-regulatory strength, effort, and fatigue. *Science, 18*, 275–281.

Sherman, J. W., Gawronski, B., & Trope, Y. (2014). *Dual-process theories of the social mind*. New York: Guilford Press.

Sloman, S. A. (1996). The empirical case for two systems of reasoning. *Psychological Bulletin, 119*, 3–22.

Sloman, S. A. (2014). Two systems of reasoning: An update. In J. W. Sherman, B. Gawronski, & Y. Trope (Eds.), *Dual-process theories of the social mind* (pp. 69–79). New York: Guilford Press.

Smith, E. R., & DeCoster, J. (2000). Dual-process models in social and cognitive psychology: Conceptual integration and links to underlying memory systems. *Personality and Social Psychology Review, 4*, 108–131.

Sokol, B. W., Grouzet, M. E., & Müller, U. (2013). *Self-regulation and autonomy: Social and developmental dimensions of human conduct*. New York: Cambridge University Press.

Spunt, R. P., & Lieberman, M. D. (2012). An integrative model of the neural systems supporting the comprehension of observed emotional behavior. *NeuroImage, 59*, 3050–3059.

Spunt, R. P., & Lieberman, M. D. (2013). The busy social brain: Evidence for automaticity and control in the neural systems supporting social cognition and action understanding. *Psychological Science, 24*, 80–86.

Spunt, R. P., & Lieberman, M. D. (2014). Automaticity, control, and the social brain. In J. W. Sherman, B. Gawronski, & Y. Trope (Eds.), *Dual-process theories of the social mind* (pp. 279–296). New York: Guilford Press.

Sripada, C., Kessler, D., & Jonides, J. (2014). Methylphenidate blocks effort-induced depletion of regulatory control in healthy volunteers. *Psychological Science, 25*, 1227–1234.

Stanovich, K. E. (1999). *Who is rational? Studies of individual differences in reasoning*. Mahwah, NJ: Erlbaum.

Stanovich, K. E. (2009). Distinguishing the reflective, algorithmic, and autonomous minds: Is it time for a tri-process theory? In J. S. B. T. Evans & K. Frankish (Eds.), *In two minds: Dual processes and beyond* (pp. 55–88). New York: Oxford University Press.

Stanovich, K. E. (2011). *Rationality and the reflective mind*. New York: Oxford University Press.

Stanovich, K. E., West, R. F., & Toplak, M. E. (2011). The complexity of developmental predictions from dual process models. *Developmental Review, 31*, 103–118.

Stanovich, K. E., West, R. F., & Toplak, M. E. (2014). Rationality, intelligence, and the defining features of type 1 and type 2 processing. In J. W. Sherman, B. Gawronski, & Y. Trope (Eds.), *Dual-process theories of the social mind* (pp. 80–91). New York: Guilford Press.

Stenseng, F., Forest, J., & Curran, T. (2015). Positive emotions in recreational sport activities: The role of passion and belongingness. *Journal of Happiness Studies, 16*, 1117–1129.

Sullivan, M. J. L., Yakobov, E., Scott, W., & Tait, R. (2014). Perceived injustice and adverse recovery outcomes. *Psychological Injury and Law, 7*, 325–334.

Thompson, J., O'Donnell, M., Stafford, L., & Nordfjaern, T. (2014). Association between attributions of responsibilities for motor vehicle crashes, depressive symptoms, and return to work. *Rehabilitation Psychology, 59*, 376–385.

Trevarthen, C., & Aitken, K. J. (2001). Infant intersubjectivity: Research, theory, and clinical applications. *Journal of Child Psychology and Psychiatry, 42*, 3–48.

Vallerand, R. J. (2010). On passion for life activities: The dualistic model of passion. In M. P. Zanna (Ed.), *Advances in experimental social psychology* (pp. 97–193). New York: Academic Press.

Vallerand, R. J., Mageau, G. A., Ratelle, C., Léonard, M., Blanchard, C., Koestner, R., et al. (2003). Les passions de l'âme: On obsessive and harmonious passion. *Journal of Personality and Social Psychology, 85*, 756–767.

Vallerand, R. J., & Verner-Filion, J. (2013). Making people's life most worth living: On the importance of passion for positive psychology. *Terapia Psicológica, 31*, 35–48.

Vohs, K. D., Baumeister, R. F., & Schmeichel, B. J. (2012). Motivation, personal beliefs, and limited resources all contribute to self control. *Journal of Experimental Social Psychology, 48*, 943–947.

Vohs, K. D., Baumeister, R. F., & Schmeichel, B. J. (2013). Erratum to "motivation, personal beliefs, and limited resources all contribute to self control.". *Journal of Experimental Social Psychology, 49*, 184–188.

Vohs, K. D., Baumeister, R. F., Schmeichel, B. J., Twenge, J. M., Nelson, N. M., & Tice, D. M. (2014). Making choices impairs subsequent self-control: A limited-resource account of decision making, self-regulation, and active initiative. *Motivation Science, 1*, 19–42.

Wagner, D. D., Altman, M., Boswell, R. G., Kelley, W. M., & Heatherton, T. F. (2013). Self-regulatory depletion enhances neural responses to rewards and impairs top-down control. *Psychological Science, 24*, 2262–2271.

Wagner, D. D., & Heatherton, T. F. (2013). Self-regulatory depletion increases emotional reactivity in the amygdala. *Social Cognitive and Affective Neuroscience, 8*, 410–417.

Waters, A. C., & Tucker, D. M. (2013). Self-regulation of neural development. In B. W. Sokol, M. E. Grouzet, & U. Müller (Eds.), *Self-regulation and autonomy: Social and developmental dimensions of human conduct*. New York: Cambridge University Press.

Wegner, D. M. (2002). *The illusion of conscious will*. Cambridge, MA: MIT Press.

Wiecki, T. V., & Frank, M. J. (2013). A computational model of inhibitory control in frontal cortex and basal ganglia. *Psychological Review, 120*, 329–355.

Young, G. (1997). *Adult development, therapy, and culture: A postmodern synthesis*. New York: Plenum.

Young, G. (2011). *Development and causality: Neo-Piagetian perspectives*. New York: Springer Science+Business Media.

Zelazo, P. D., Hong Gao, H., & Todd, R. (2007). The development of consciousness. In P. D. Zelazo, M. Moscovitch, & E. Thompson (Eds.), *Cambridge handbook of consciousness* (pp. 405–432). New York: Cambridge University Press.

Zhang, S., Shi, R., Liu, X., & Miao, D. (2014). Passion for a leisure activity, presence of meaning, and search of meaning: The mediating role of emotion. *Social Indicators Research, 115*, 1123–1135.

Part IV

Abnormalities in Development and the DSM-5

20 Free Will in Psychotherapy: Helping People Believe

Chapter Introduction

This chapter presents a transdiagnostic psychotherapeutic module related to belief in free will and the change process that could be used to facilitate patients making better choices and also making gains in psychotherapy. The module consists of a series of tables that were made upon reviewing the literature on free will belief, consciousness, self-control, and factors that could interfere with belief in free will (termed resource/ego depletion, e.g., in the research of Baumeister and colleagues). The tables are constructed similarly, with phenomena related to belief in free will, control, consciousness, change, and so on, on the left and corresponding therapeutic questions deriving from them on the right. The module could work well with patients having conditions especially related to self-control in which belief in free will can help. In this regard, one of them concerns the application of the concept to addiction.

Note that this chapter is based on the one in Young (2014), but with the literature cited therein quite elaborated. Also, it includes a new table on the use of the concept of free will in psychotherapy based on Baumeister (2014a, 2014b). Finally, there is overlap with the prior two chapters on free will that is inevitable, but the overlap helps with the module being developed on applications of free will in psychotherapy.

Free Will in Psychotherapy

Introduction

In the edited book of Sinnott-Armstrong (2014a), the philosophical, psychological, and neuroscientific are areas that meld together on the topic of free will. His introductory chapter (2014b) explicated the quandaries in the field, and explains the diverse points of view that are still contested despite the increasing scientific research on the question. Arguments still vary about whether free will exists, but workers are adopting a more limited, nuanced, compatibilistic view (e.g., Nahmias, 2014; Roskies, 2014), or a semi-compatibilistic one (e.g., Gazzaniga, 2014; semi-compatibilism in the sense that even if free will cannot be assumed to exist, we still have freedom from gaining options and are responsible for our actions).

Believing in free will has important consequences related to making appropriate choices, behaving more morally, and otherwise adopting better habits and a more goal-oriented lifestyle (Baumeister, 2008; Baumeister, Masicampo, & Vohs, 2011; Baumeister & Vohs, 2011). Although there is endless debate about the construct philosophically in terms of whether free will exists, adopting the attitude psychologically that it does exist (believing in free will) is relevant in rehabilitation and psychotherapy.

G. Young, *Unifying Causality and Psychology*, DOI 10.1007/978-3-319-24094-7_20

Cognitive behavior therapy is the predominant empirically-supported psychotherapeutic approach in rehabilitation (Young, 2014). However, other approaches, such as the narrative one and positive psychology, can be useful adjuncts toward treating the whole person. Moreover, transdiagnostic approaches are the one being used increasingly (e.g., Barlow et al., 2011). In this regard, in this chapter, I have formulated a transdiagnostic psychotherapeutic module consisting of a series of tables based on belief in free will that psychotherapists could use to facilitate better motivation for change.

Model

The concept of free will belief is applicable throughout the psychotherapeutic process. It can help challenge dysfunctional beliefs and prepare the patient to learn better habits. To illustrate this, I have proposed tables based on cognitive behavior therapy that includes accommodations to incorporate free will belief. In the following, I review the literature that served as the basis for each table as I present them. Before beginning, however, I examine how free will belief fits into a cognitive behavioral approach to psychotherapy.

Figure 20.1 indicates that, as with any behavior, belief in free will is influenced by biological, personal, and environmental factors. Ongoing behavior gives feedback into the model by altering the experiences that can influence its subsequent expression, the person variables that could intervene, the biological and environmental influences on it, and so on.

Behavior takes place in context; but context is influenced by appraisals, perceptions, filters, schemas, and representations. The context

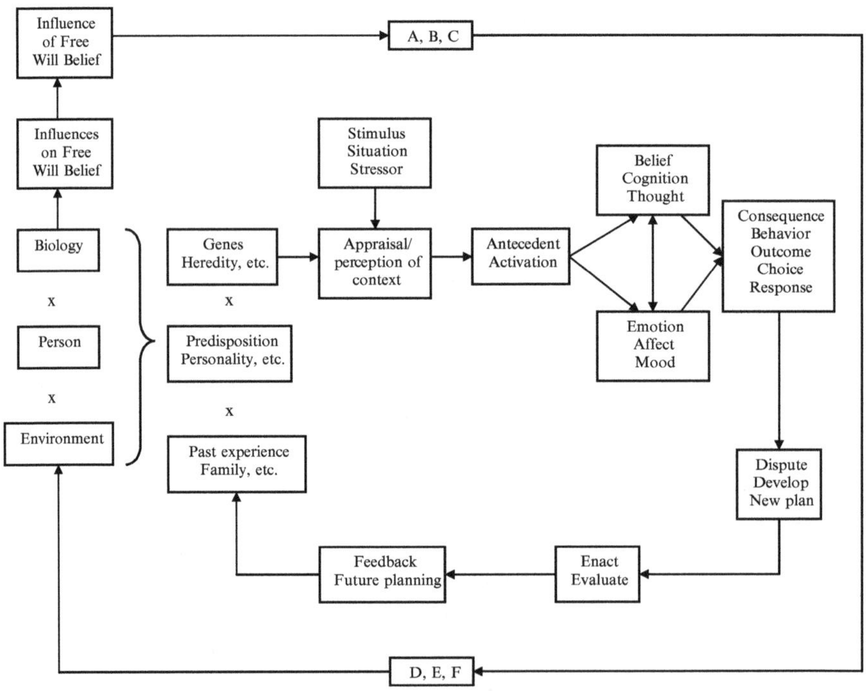

Fig. 20.1 The ABCs of free will in psychotherapy. Belief in free will has positive consequences for behavior (Baumeister, 2008). The present model combines the belief with the cognitive-behavioral approach to psychotherapy. The proposed model is based on the ABC component of the cognitive behavioral approach, and illustrates at what points free will belief can influence behavior and psychotherapy. Behavior is considered as the outcome of biological, personal, and environmental factors, which can influence free will belief. At the same time, free will belief can influence the activators, beliefs, cognitions, emotions, and choices in behavior (*A*, *B*, and *C*), as well as their monitoring and revision (*D*, *E*, and *F*)

provides stimuli, situations, or stressors that serve to activate behavior (or give the antecedents to it, the A part of the ABC model), but they are as much subjective as objective.

The classic ABC model emphasizes beliefs elicited by activators that, in turn, influence consequences. However, a broader view of the sequence would include emotional mediators as much as cognitive ones (or their interactions), although individual differences might favor either the cognitive or emotional pathway. As presented, the model does not give precedence to either emotions or cognition as preludes to behavior.

The ABC sequence that leads to behavior in context might produce adaptive behavior in the behavioral option chosen. However, better choices often could have been made, and this becomes an issue in psychotherapeutic cases. The classic ABC model includes a D (dispute) component, and it can be expanded to include E and F components to allow for new choices and more adaptive outcomes.

Free will belief relates to believing that choice is possible and that best choices can be made in relevant situations. The emergence of behavioral options and the choices made in behavior do not automatically flow deterministically from past influences and present context. The person has a choice partly stemming from personal characteristics that incorporate free will belief as an important mediator in behavior. The psychotherapist can work to facilitate a greater belief in free will, and its application for making better choice in context.

In terms of the model presented, this refers to increasing the range of adaptive appraisals or perceptions of context and, consequently, what become activators of behavior. In addition, automatic, maladaptive associations to the activators, either in terms of cognition or emotion (or their interaction) would become better controlled or countered, freeing openings to consider more adaptive behavioral response to contextual activators. Also, this would encourage less need for dispute of past pattern and also the need for new planning, as well as an increased learning how to use optimally belief in free will.

Helping People Believe

Introduction

The following section of the chapter gives a brief overview of self-control in free will in psychology, preparing the way for presentation of the psychotherapeutic module on free will. It overlaps in content with material in the last two chapters.

Self-Control in Free Will

Alquist and Baumeister (2012) reviewed the role of self-control in behavior. This topic is particularly relevant for a psychotherapy module of free will, which involves self-control deployment. Self-control is defined as the ability to alter one's state or response, including by exerting control over desires, impulses, emotions, and thoughts. Mischel, Shoda, and Peake (1988) and Shoda, Mischel, and Peake (1990) had shown that a young child's ability to resist taking immediately one marshmallow in order to obtain a later choice of two marshmallows predicted their teenage scholastic achievement test scores (SATs) and even their adult interpersonal success. Duckworth and Seligman (2005) found that self-discipline more than IQ predicted grade point average. Having self-control as a child led to less adult arrests and more family stability (i.e., raising one's own children in intact families; Moffitt et al., 2011). The benefits of self-control extend to mental health and relationships (e.g., Tangney, Baumeister, & Boone, 2004; Vohs, Finkenauer, Baumeister, 2011; Walter, Gunstad, & Hobfoll, 2010).

The components of self-regulation include: (a) standards (what goals regulating toward); (b) monitoring/tracking goal progress; and (c) execution (plan implementation, executing toward goal) (Baumeister & Heatherton, 1996). However, good self-control requires effort, but the energetic resources involved are limited, so they need appropriate deployment.

Studies show that the energetic resources involved in self-control can be manipulated.

In this research, participants who engage in self-regulation tasks perform worse on a second unrelated one, as per the resource or ego depletion model. For example, Baumeister, Bratslavesky, Muraven, and Tice (1998) found that resisting cookies led to participants to quit an unsolvable puzzle earlier than those who had to resist (less appetizing) radishes. Moreover, the results are not explainable in terms of factors such as mood, arousal, frustration, or even fatigue. Other research (e.g., Vohs, Glass, Maddox, & Markham, 2011) shows that people conserve resources when the resources are scarcer or when people are anticipating future self-regulation needs (e.g., Muraven, Shmueli, & Burkley, 2006). However, people also can expend limited resources when motivated or given incentives (Muraven & Slessareva, 2003). They can express less self-control if reading about someone who did not exert self-control or even if told they had good self-control (respectively, Ackerman, Goldstein, Shapiro, & Bargh, 2009; Nordgren, van Harreveld, & van der Pligt, 2009). Also, it is worth noting that high self-control relates to attachment security and relationship satisfaction (Tangney et al., 2004; Vohs, Finkenauer, et al., 2011).

After their extensive review of self-control in adults and the variables that impact it, Alquist and Baumeister (2012) concluded that self-control is essential to social life and that it can be managed. At the same time, it is noted that its lack is related to increased mental illness and antisocial behavior and to less success in relationships and work. Research using methods that interfere with people's beliefs has shown that free will belief can be altered. Vohs and Schooler (2008) found that undermining belief in free will even increase the probability of cheating.

Comment

Augmenting belief in free will might facilitate behavioral change in psychotherapy. Patients become less able to think rationally when they are stressed, ill, or hurt. Therefore, increasing belief in free will could help in this regard. Also, consider that the belief in free will is a general undercurrent of focus in all psychotherapy and psychological interventions. If we did not believe that our patients were amenable to change, we would not provide treatment. At the same time, as far as I know, there has not been a specific attempt to integrate free will belief directly as a module into psychotherapeutic work. The tables in this chapter accommodate to that lacunae.

However, there are limits to free will belief. One always confronts psychological constraints, whether developmental or otherwise, that inhibit manifestation for each of us of a totally free and uncontaminated ability to make in every situation constructive positive choice. In this sense, I support an asymptotic paradoxical model of free will. In such a model, we might come closer to an ideal state of effective use of a belief in free will, but none of us can achieve perfectly this summit in personal growth. At the same time, development can proceed fairly well, and even when events happen that are negative, e.g., in Posttraumatic Stress Disorder (PTSD), ameliorative factors, such as posttraumatic growth, might develop (either through personal and social resources or in rehabilitation due to psychotherapeutic interventions, such as the one described in this chapter). Therefore, to conclude, for those in need of them, the tables and figures developed for the free will psychotherapeutic module described in the present chapter might be helpful as part of psychotherapeutic work. Clients for whom augmenting a belief in free will would be beneficial might profit from use of these tables in psychotherapy.

The Transdiagnostic Psychotherapeutic Module on Free Will Belief and Change

Introduction

A fundamental assumption underlying psychotherapy is that patients can learn to make better choices. The next seven tables and two figures specifically present the psychotherapeutic module developed in the present work for promoting free will in psychotherapy, which is aimed at helping patients make better choices.

There are numerous barriers to the development of having a sense of free will, or believing in free will. At the risk of being oversimplicity, they reduce to a formula involving the person, biology, and environment.

Functional Perspective

In the first table of the series, I use the FACCDs (Functional Analytic Clinical Case Diagrams; Haynes, O'Brien, & Kaholokula, 2011) model to stimulate thought on working toward liberating issues related to past, present, and future. As reviewed in Chap. 6, functional analysis involves the identification of important, controllable functional relationships in indexed behaviors of people, whether the behaviors are causal or not. Psychotherapeutically functional analysis allows for dynamic modeling of client symptomology, goals, and social relationships. This approach especially individualizes causality the causes of behavior in relation to psychological difficulties that are being expressed by clients in their immediate contexts.

However, the patterns found in therapy also have roots in the past, so this should be considered in developing a free will belief module for psychotherapy. In order to facilitate their change, Table 20.1 illustrates how past patterns can be reframed. For present ones, I emphasize developing appropriate problem solving. For moving better toward the future, the table emphasizes that patients can increase having a sense of free will.

Deception

Deception of self and others is considered critical to normal functioning (e.g., Mlodinow, 2012; Trivers, 2011). However, deception can become a major focus in psychotherapy (Kottler & Carlson, 2011). According to Trivers (2011), we humans have inherited the capacity to deceive ourselves in order to better deceive others. This capacity is facilitated by a notable unconscious, internal information reorganization. Deception could take the form of overt lying, but it involves much more, including of unconscious active self-deception. Moreover, active other-deception need not be defensive or passive; indeed, often it is conscious and offensive. However, the main

Table 20.1 Facilitating free will in making life choices through psychotherapy from a functional perspective

Strategy[a]	How can you use this knowledge to help yourself?[a]
Free will with respect to past: Reframing functional causal links from perspective of choosing new ways of viewing past	Freeing the past: We are seeking in you when some coping, growth, stress reduction, etc., had taken place in the past; what are lessons that can be learned from the past in this regard
Free will with respect to present: Developing behavioral, cognitive, interpersonal, narrative, and other relevant strategies to work on extant relevant causal links still present from past	Freeing the present: How can you have a better capacity to create effective plans to deal with issues, and better ways of implementing/monitoring them
Free will with respect to future: Developing capacity to choose different options, plans, behaviors, etc., with respect to issues indicated by any causal analysis of problems/predicaments/stresses that might arise in future	Freeing the future: Explaining yourself that you can develop a sense of free will that can help you be yourself and have others be themselves You can create models of yourself that include not only things like self-confidence and sensitivity to others, but also sensing if one has free will and can feel free in even the most difficult of times [and that you can manage constraints that impinge on that growing feeling]

Adopted with permission of Springer Science+Business Media. Young, G. (2014). *Malingering, feigning, and response bias in psychiatric/psychological injury: Implications for Practice and court*. Dordrecht, Netherlands: Springer Science+Business Media; with kind permission from Springer Science+Business Media B. V. [Table 23.1, Page. 595, modified]

[a]Analysis of causal links leading to patient presentation in functional analytic clinical case diagrams (FACCDs; Haynes et al., 2011)

Table 20.2 Self- and other-deception in the growth of free will for topics in psychotherapy

Type	Example
Self-deception, constructive	Over-valuing abilities Are you underestimating challenges This could lead to constructive outcomes if the self-depletion is not extreme, all else being equal
Self-deception, destructive	Self-depletion is extreme For example, we hide or openly lie about personal faults, conflicts, intentions, etc., that need moderation/resolution
Other-deception, constructive	Self-depletion could involve the other, but not extremely so
Other-deception, destructive	But it could be extreme, and we do not see the person clearly, perhaps with very negative consequences
Balance	The more self- and other-deception are toward the constructive side, the more likely the constraints on developing a sense of free will and feeling free are minimized. How can you develop balance in this regard?

Adopted with permission of Springer Science + Business Media. Young, G. (2014). *Malingering, feigning, and response bias in psychiatric/psychological injury: Implications for Practice and court*. Dordrecht, Netherlands: Springer Science + Business Media; with kind permission from Springer Science + Business Media B. V. [Table 23.2, Page. 595, modified]

Note. The table illustrates one barrier to the growth of belief in free will—that of self- and other-deception. The table illustrates how the psychotherapist can work toward balance in these regards

function of self-deception lies in its unconscious origins, which helps make deception more difficult to detect and helps lead one to deny it had been intentional.

Self-deception can be moderated by having constructive compared to destructive directions in this regard, as per Table 20.2. The same applies to other-deception. The therapist who is analyzing and becoming aware of these tendencies in the patient should seek to readdress their imbalance in the way indicated in the table.

The next four tables on free will in psychotherapy are based on the work of Roy Baumeister. In the present tables for the psychotherapeutic module involving belief in free will, I work from the conceptions of Baumeister and colleagues on free will in everyday life and on the cognitive underpinnings to free will and apply them to the psychotherapeutic context.

Daily Life

Table 20.3 focuses on the work of Stillman, Baumeister, and Mele (2011) on the psychology of free will in daily life. The authors conducted a study of autobiographical narratives given by psychology undergraduates. Half of the participants had to write about actions that they considered "free." The other participants had to describe their past behavior when it had not appeared to reflect their own free will.

Stillman et al. (2011) continued that belief in free will might be an evolved human adaptation. It has been selected because it confers advantages in reaching desired states and goals, especially in our complex social and cultural environments (Baumeister, 2005). In addition, from an evolutionary perspective, free will belief contributes to survival and reproduction ("enlightened self-interest") by its promotion of the ability to make informed choices, resist temptation and societal pressure, and achieve greater gain later on. The authors equated free will with free action and also with action undertaken from the agent's "own free will."

As for the results of their investigation, Stillman et al. (2011) found that folk conceptions of free will organized around major themes. They include the adaptive value of free will and also the positive outcomes and goals that having a belief in free will facilitate. Some cognitive concomitants are considered relevant, too, e.g., delay in decision making and making conscious choices. The social-affective aspect is considered, as well, for example, morality and avoiding external control.

Table 20.3 Topics of free will in psychotherapy I: free will in everyday life

Area	Now can you use this knowledge to help yourself?
Free will and adaptation: In our everyday life, having a sense of free will helps us reach positive things we want for ourselves, especially social ones, such as attaining certain states/conditions, goals, or outcomes.	Think of several ways in your daily life that you show you have a sense of free will. Then, think of several ways your sense of free will can be improved, e.g., in helping you reach desired goals and outcomes. How can you help yourself increase your sense of free will in your everyday life? Think of several ways.
Positive outcomes and goal attainment	Here are some specific examples to consider.
Self-interest and time frame: Having a sense of free will can help us delay wanting benefits right away and wait for better ones later on.	For example, having a sense of free will allows us to resist temptations and delay seeking immediate gratification for better results that we could get in waiting. Would developing this skill help you in obtaining positive outcomes and attainment of desired goals? How can you develop the skill? List several ways.
Consciousness and freedom: Having a sense of free will is accompanied by the belief that our behavior is undertaken consciously rather than automatically out of our awareness.	For example, viewing our behavior as a product of conscious thought means that we can improve our awareness of it, which would help in our reasoning, problem analysis, and decision making, so that our choices appear freely chosen rather than not free. How can you increase conscious awareness of your automatic thought so that your sense of having free will increases? List some exercises that you might do in this regard.
Morality and collective benefits: Behaving morally helps the other person and the group, aside from the outcome that it is part of the behavior that enables individuals to fit into the group. However, it also might be part of human nature because it brings benefits to the person acting morally, e.g., respect of others, access to resources related to the actions involved.	Having a sense of free will means behaving toward others with a sense of having chosen freely, and this includes behaving morally, as well as following a set of group standards and prohibitions that might seem to work against our self-interest at first. However, fitting into the group brings benefits to the person, and this might be lacking. How can you improve your sense of free will in terms of the choices that you are making socially, morally, and collectively? List your ideas.
External influence: Having a sense of free will socially also means that external forces, pressures, and authorities can be overcome, resisted, or somehow controlled when their exertion of control over us is too detrimental.	For example, you might have to deal with it directly, such as presenting counter-arguments, negotiating, etc., or doing what you require and knowing how to deal with the consequences. Or, you might have to deal with it indirectly, such as manipulating toward your desired ends, getting allies to argue for you and support you. This all requires much skill, but you might have done some of this in the past. What did you do this way? How can you do more? List the ways.

Adopted with permission of Springer Science+Business Media. Young, G. (2014). *Malingering, feigning, and response bias in psychiatric/psychological injury: Implications for Practice and court.* Dordrecht, Netherlands: Springer Science+Business Media; with kind permission from Springer Science+Business Media B. V. [Table 23.3, Page. 597, modified]

Note. This table and the next four ones use in promoting free will in psychotherapy are based on the work of Baumeister and colleagues for the present table. The left side of the table is adapted from Stillman et al. (2011). Their work describes the role of free will in everyday life. On the right side of the table, I indicate how free will might be promoted on the basis of their understanding of free will in everyday life

As for the psychotherapeutic interventions that can be used to promote free will that are given in the table, they were created partly based on the explanations and text accompanying Stillman et al.'s (2011) explanation of these folk psychological concepts of free will. The psychotherapeutic component of the table guides patients in adapting a more flexible cognitive and social approach to problem solving and daily living.

Self-Regulation

Baumeister and Vohs (2011) reviewed the cognitive capacities needed for effective executive function and self-regulation. Baumeister and Vohs (2011) viewed the self as active, involved, responsive, and intentional, including in changing, altering, or modifying behavior. In this regard, the self manifests self-control, and its

Table 20.4 Topics of free will in psychotherapy II: self-regulation and the executive function of the self

Area	How can you use this knowledge to help yourself?
Delay of gratification	Delay of gratification is important to everyday life. List several benefits in waiting for better choices later on rather than seeking immediate gratification. How can you improve this skill?
Feedback loops	We need to monitor our plans, strategies for reaching them, motivation to follow them, etc. How can you improve these skills?
Trait self-control	Maintaining good habits is a great way of keeping control. How can you work toward developing better habits and controlling bad or interfering ones?
Strengths model of self-regulation	Self-regulation requires good habits related to sleep, nutrition, exercise, etc. How can you plan effectively to reach your goals and work toward not depleting your energy by using ineffective actions toward your goals, following improper lifestyle habits, etc.?
Beyond self-regulation: choice, initiative, and free will	People can improve their sense of having free will and also their current sense of having choices and their initiative by completing brief exercises. These include … How can you apply these exercises to yourself? Can you think of others?

Adopted with permission of Springer Science+Business Media. Young, G. (2014). *Malingering, feigning, and response bias in psychiatric/psychological injury: Implications for Practice and court*. Dordrecht, Netherlands: Springer Science+Business Media; with kind permission from Springer Science+Business Media B. V. [Table 23.4, Page. 598, modified]
Note. Left side of table adapted from Baumeister and Vohs (2011). In this free will psychotherapeutic model, I build on Baumeister and Vohs (2011) work on self-regulation and executive function. The right side of the table proposes statements and questions that can be used with clients in these regards

executive function selects/initiates behavior toward this end. In addition, self-regulation concerns self-directed, volitional behaviors, but it does not have to be consciously initiated.

Baumeister and Vohs (2011) especially reviewed the literature related to self-regulation, and the following summarizes their review of (a) the "strengths model" of self-regulation and (b) patterns of ego depletion. In terms of the strength model, self-regulation is considered to require sufficient psychological energy or resource, and it can be depleted by self-regulatory demands. For example, low levels of blood glucose are linked to various poor behavioral outcomes (Gailliot & Baumeister, 2007) and self-regulatory acts can serve to lower glucose bloodstream levels (Gailliot et al., 2007).

As for overtaxing self-regulatory resources, Baumeister and colleagues referred to the process of "ego depletion." It has been found to influence cognitive processes and even performance on IQ tests (Schmeichel, Vohs, & Baumeister, 2003). It affects resistance to cheating and honesty (Mead, Baumeister, Gino, Schweitzer, & Ariely, 2009). It involves more than being physically tired (Vohs, Glass, et al., 2011). To conclude, the ego depletion section of their review, Baumeister and Vohs (2011) referred to a meta-analysis by Hagger, Wood, Stiff, and Chatzisarantis (2010) on the "medium to large" effect size found for the effect of an ego depletion task on self-control compared to similar tasks not involving ego depletion.

These higher-order cognitive skills relate to self-control, problem solving, planning, working memory deployment, and etc., as presented in Table 20.4. Also, the table presents Baumeister's model of ego depletion (e.g., Baumeister, 2008). As indicated, behaving from a belief in free will requires energy; and research has shown that tasks that deplete/interfere with energy adversely affect free will belief and its attendant advantages. Developing and maintaining a belief in free will requires a healthy lifestyle and also appropriate in thinking and affect.

Consciousness

Baumeister et al. (2011) conceptualized a relationship between free will and consciousness. They argued that consciousness appears especially useful in allowing both "nonpresent" factors and social/cultural information to "shape" behavior and also to deal with multiple, competing options/ impulses. However, in supporting this position, the authors are not disputing the notion that unconscious influences impact "almost every" behavior in people, and that they mix frequently with conscious ones.

To begin their review, Baumeister et al. (2011) asked the provocative question of whether conscious thoughts cause behavior. The behaviorists had considered conscious thought without relevance, an epiphenomenon, at best. Detractors had argued that behavior is almost fully or is fully "automatic," does not "originate" with conscious processes, etc. (e.g., Bargh, 1997; Dijksterhuis, Chartrand, & Aarts, 2007). Others added that it has no causative properties and is post-hoc (Dijksterhuis, Aarts, & Smith, 2005; Jeannerod, 2006). Roediger, Goode, and Zaromb (2008) referred to Libet's (1985) classic research that brain wave activity related to finger movement showed a sharp increase prior to self-reported conscious decision to move. They indicated that Libet's findings deny that conscious "intention" causes action.

Baumeister et al. (2011) moved the debate to another plane by indicating that there are two forms or levels of consciousness—the phenomenal one, e.g., subjective experience, and the uniquely human one of "reflection," reason, and elaborated sense of self. Moreover, they pointed out that even if the origins of a behavior are unconscious, conscious contemplation intervenes in determining the outcome.

To verify their hypothesis of a role in behavior for conscious causation, Baumeister et al. (2011) and Baumeister, Masicampo, and Vohs (2015) restricted their literature review to experimental designs with random assignment. For example, studies of simulation in mental practice or rehearsal have shown that it reliably improves performance in a host of areas (Kosslyn & Moulton, 2009). Also, Masicampo and Baumeister (2011) studied Zeigarnik effect in terms of mental causation. In the effect, goals that are unfulfilled cause intrusive thoughts about the unfulfilled goals even when the individual is attempting to do something else. Masicampo and Baumeister (2011) found that if study participants formed implementation intentions (see next) to undertake the behavior, these types of intrusive thoughts were reduced greatly. Another line of research involves implementation intentions, which were shown to induce behavioral change beyond the effects of simply intending, desiring, goal setting, and valuing (e.g., Gollwitzer & Sheeran, 2006; Papies, Aarts, & de Vries, 2009). Similarly, Watkins (2008) found that repetitive thought helped improve later outcome/performance when it focused on planning.

About replaying, interpreting, and reflecting on events in the past, Baumeister et al. (2011) continued that the research demonstrates that thinking related to past events can alter future behavior/outcomes. For example, Anseel, Lievens, and Schollaert (2009) conducted a study that shows that if a person reflects on an unsuccessful task performance or on feedback related to it, this acts to improve subsequent performance. In another example, Ciarocco, Vohs, and Baumeister (2010) showed that ruminating about how one had erred in a failed task caused significant improvement in subsequent performance. Also, writing or speaking about traumatic events one had experienced causes mental health improvement (Pennebaker & Chung, 2007). In terms of reasoning, deciding, and problem solving, Baumeister et al. (2011) reviewed that unconscious processes might be "superior" for lower-order mental processes but not higher-order ones, such as logical reasoning. For example, DeWall, Baumeister, and Masicampo (2008) showed that telling participants that they would have to explain their results improved performance on logic problems. The meta-analysis by Fox, Ericsson, and Best (2011) reported similar findings and conclusions. Indeed, merely expecting to require an explanation of one's actions appears to stimulate conscious thought and alter behavior (Scholten, van Knippenberg, Nijstad, & De Dreu, 2007).

The evidence in favor of conscious causation includes research on mentally stimulating perspective taking by the other (e.g., Galinsky, Maddux, Gilin, & White, 2008); manipulation of self-regard/self-affirmation (e.g., Schmeichel & Vohs, 2009); mental framing/goal setting (e.g., McGlone & Aronson, 2007); and facilitating intergroup communication (e.g., Halevy, Bornstein, & Sagiv, 2008; Sutter & Strassmair, 2009). Other research affirms that conscious thought can override automatic responses. Westling, Mann, and Ward (2006) demonstrated this in their study. They showed that under low compared to high cognitive load, smokers were less affected by pro-smoking compared to anti-smoking cues.

After this comprehensive review of the literature, Baumeister et al. (2011) concluded that conscious causation exists and is especially shown by "offline and indirect" effects on subsequent downstream behavior compared to direct control. The authors noted that conscious thought functions to "facilitate" social life and culture (Baumeister & Masicampo, 2010).

In the psychotherapeutic approach in Table 20.5, psychotherapists might ask patients to engage in exercises that promote conscious causation compared to automatic, unconscious causation. For example, patients might engage in exercises that help practice, plan, reflect, reason, create, empathize, self-value, reframe, and communicate. In this way, a belief in and sense of free will should be facilitated.

Reasoning and Motivation

Table 20.6 includes work by Baumeister and colleagues on reasoning in free will (Pocheptsova, Amir, Dhar, & Baumeister, 2009). In addition, it includes work by Inzlicht and Schmeichel (2012) on motivation and attention in self-control and on resource or ego depletion. The former emphasizes focus on long term as opposed to short term

Table 20.5 Topics of free will in psychotherapy III: conscious causation

Area	How can you use this knowledge to help yourself?
Mental simulation, mental practice	Mentally rehearsing important activities improves performance and reaching the goals associated with them. Give example
Anticipating, planning, intending	Having specific behaviorally-focused plans helps arrive at goals. Give example
Replaying, interpreting, reflecting on past events	Writing about or talking about past events that need reworking, such as traumas, improves the ability to move forward. Give example
Reasoning, deciding, solving problems	Increasing the conscious motivation to be logical, to explain oneself, etc., improves performance. Give example
Counterproductive, maladaptive effects	Having conscious goals to be creative enhances creativity. Give example
Mentally simulating others' perspectives	Taking the perspective of the other, or seeing their world, view, theory, mind, etc., helps. Give example
Manipulations of self-regard, self-affirmation	Thinking positively about the self, its core, etc., changes behavior positively. Give example
Mental framing and goal setting	Believing that one is part of a high-performing group, e.g., being good in math, helps performance. Give example
Communication and mutual understanding	Being good in group communication enhances the person's and the group's functioning. Give example
Overriding automatic responses	It is easier to override automatic responses and be conscious about choice when our ego or self resources are not overtaxed. Give example

Adopted with permission of Springer Science+Business Media. Young, G. (2014). *Malingering, feigning, and response bias in psychiatric/psychological injury: Implications for Practice and court*. Dordrecht, Netherlands: Springer Science+Business Media; with kind permission from Springer Science+Business Media B. V. [Table 23.5, Page. 598, modified]

Note. Left side adapted from Baumeister et al. (2011). In this table, I provide constructive suggestions and exercises that might help in becoming more conscious about causation and behaving with a belief in free will

Table 20.6 Topics of free will in psychotherapy IV: mechanisms in motivation, attention, and reasoning

Problematic area	Counter example (How can you use this knowledge to help yourself?)
Shifts in motivation: I do not want to control myself	I still can control myself, if I focus and try harder. Even if my motivation lags, I can boost it. The rewards in the end will be worth it. I have the resources to shift back to being motivated.
Shifts in motivation: I want to go with my gut	I might feel that I should act impulsively, but I can get back on target and control that.
Shifts in attention: Do I need to control myself now?	I can focus on things (cues) that get me motivated again instead of on things that get in the way, like shifting to actions that bring short term rewards instead of long term ones that are much better.
Shifts in attention: I see immediate rewards	Instead of paying attention to what is important to beneficial long term goals, attention shifts to paying attention to cues related to immediate rewards that are not as beneficial. However, I can shift back by ignoring these cues and rewards and focusing on cues related to the long term goals. It is not just about the short term pleasures but also about a different kind of pleasure related to having a job well done, and the like.
Shifts in Reasoning: Resource depletion enhances the role of intuitive reasoning by impairing deliberate careful processing	When I get tired or low, I might think less carefully and reason by intuition only instead of using good problem solving skills and seeing the big picture. But because I know that can happen, I can work hard to control it. Better to see all the choices and choose the best one, e.g., which one is best for the long term.

Adopted with permission of Springer Science+Business Media. Young, G. (2014). *Malingering, feigning, and response bias in psychiatric/psychological injury: Implications for Practice and court.* Dordrecht, Netherlands: Springer Science+Business Media; with kind permission from Springer Science+Business Media B. V. [Table 23.6, Page. 599, modified]

Note. Left side adapted from Inzlicht and Schmeichel (2012) for attention and motivation and from Pocheptsova et al. (2009) for reasoning. The table illustrates how knowledge of core psychological processes can lead to therapeutic affirmative self-statements that facilitate belief in free will and constructive actions therefrom

goals. The latter refers to using deliberate reason when there is no depletion compared to using intuition when it is present. Specifically, in exerting self-control, temporary shifts in motivation and attention take place that serve as negative influences on subsequent efforts at self-control. Self-regulation is reduced and self-gratification increased, so that cues related to the need for self-control become less salient, while those related to signals of reward are favored.

The research described by Inzlicht and Schmeichel (2012) supports their model. For example, Schmeichel, Harmon-Jones, and Harmon-Jones (2010) showed that self-control exertion leads to stronger approach related impulses (e.g., low-stake gambles). For attention, Inzlicht and Al-Khindi (2012) found that self-control application "dulls" the attentional system. These core mechanistic processes help promote immediate gratification relative to better control. Note that the model proposed by Inzlicht and Schmeichel (2012) for self-control loss after its exertion avoids metaphorical language such as "ego depletion."

Meaning

Baumeister (2014a) defined free will as the capacity for free action, or that the person could have acted differently in a situation (Haggard, Mele, O'Connor, & Vohs, 2010). Free will is essentially a belief in that we can never know if it really exists. In this sense, as a belief rather than as demonstrated empirical fact, free will is not an illusion. For Baumeister (2014a), free will exists at higher organizational levels, and cannot be reduced to lower-level brain or neural functions, although it is constrained by them. Free will exists on a continuum, rather than being all-or-none. As for the related question of whether actions are all determined by previous actions and context, for Baumeister (2014a), the world is not deterministic in process but it operates probabilistically, including at the psychological level. There are multiple alternate futures that are possible. Randomness to some extent and variability in behavior are adaptive.

Baumeister (2014a) continued that because free will exists at higher self-organized levels, it

Table 20.7 Facilitating free will in psychotherapy by promoting better meaning making

Strategy	How can you use this knowledge to help yourself?
Free will is not an illusion; it exists as a belief.	Whenever you think that free will does not exist for you, how can you bring it back as a part of you?
Free will exists on a continuum, rather than being all-or-none.	Sometimes we have a sense that we have less free will than more of it. How can you increase that you have more free will?
There is room for free will in our lives because the world in our future is probable rather than definite (it is not determined without choice involved).	Because things and events in the future are only probable, how can you guide them to where you want them to go?
Our mind also can think differently and generate choices because it can think of options; it is good that there is some leeway for alternatives.	We do not always think the same way every time; how can we take advantage of that and choose better alternatives?
Free will comes from higher levels of our mind in the self and its organization.	Sometimes we are too tired, stressed, and so on, to function at our highest levels. What could we do to make this better so that we can feel we have more free will?
The meanings that we create about the world are ours; that is a sign of free will.	How can we improve the meaning that we give to things so we choose better in what we think, feel, and do? Sometimes we let other people tell us what a situation means; how can we decide this for ourselves, especially if the other person is off-base?
Because we explain and communicate our choices, this is another sign of free will.	How can we improve our explanation and communication better about our choices? This would help improve our sense of free will.
The meanings that we choose guide our behavior; our behavior is not just caused by the outside.	How can we guide our behavior better from the inside? This will help improve our sense of free will too.
Being free means capitalizing on options (opportunities) out there.	How can we guide our behavior better using things from the outside?
The more we regulate ourselves (and our behavior), the more we behave with free will.	How can we be in control better of our thinking, feeling, and doing, and improve our sense of free will?

Adapted from Baumeister (2014a)
Note. The left side of this table is adapted from Baumeister (2014a). His work describes the role of free will in meaning making. On the right side of the table, I indicate how free will might be promoted on the basis of their understanding of free will in meaning making

reflects the "meanings" incorporated into action control and causation (see Table 20.7). Meaning derives from rational thought/calculation, moral actions, and so on. Meaning exists in a network of possible thoughts and ideas that are tapped differently by different cultures. In this framework, free will lies in explaining choices made to others and in communicating to coordinate with others, which means using meaning. Therefore, freedom is linked to meaningful causation. It is one step removed from physical causation, natural laws, and animal processes. The capacity to guide one's behavior by meaning is what we mean by free will. Meaning use frees the causes of action from being only physical and natural. For an agent to be free, the agent must use meaning as they decide in/deciding how to act. Then, after the decision making, there is top–down causation of action movements. For Baumeister (2014a), by deliberately participating in the process of causation by meaning, free will derives. Free will does not create the probabilistic outcomes possible in choice, but "capitalizes" on their existence.

Baumeister (2014b) added that self-regulation or the control of behavior is the essence of free will. It affords freedom of action so that the person can follow the dictates of rational thought. Further, culture conditions free will. Overall, Baumeister (2014b) referred to his approach to free will as compatible with soft determinism.

Table 20.8 Free will in psychotherapy: promoting logic and free will

Strategy	How can you use this knowledge to help yourself?
Thinking automatically and intuitively helps, but deliberate use of logic and problem solving helps, too.	How have you used automatic thought, intuition, or fast responding without thinking through first, and it helped? When did it not? How could you have handled it differently?
Using the first thing that comes to mind to deal with something can help, but thinking through options can help, too.	How have you used the first thing that comes to mind to deal with something in a way that helped? When did it not? How could you have handled it differently?
People often have less patience than needed. Trying out different pathways in thought can help, but it means thinking through them and having patience.	How have you used patience to control the impulse to act quickly and to allow you to think through different options? When did you not? How could you use it more?
Returning to a starting point of a problem to start again in a different direction could help.	How have you used the idea of returning to a starting point to try something else? Think of a social situation, a work or school one, or a family situation. How could you do this more?
Seeing the big picture always helps. When we focus on just one dimension of a problem we become fixed on it and do not see all the ways to handle it.	Think of times when you have fixed on one aspect of a problem and missed the big picture. How could you learn to focus on more than one aspect or dimension of a problem, or even more? Will it help seeing the big picture and solving problems easier?
Pulling back to think about what is happening always helps. Taking a time out to think can lead to better solutions.	How can you encourage an attitude of stepping back to reflect? Think of times when doing this might have helped.
When we take time to understand the points of view of other people, we might get less trapped in our own views that are not helpful. This does not deny they might be the best option.	How can you increase your understanding of the points of view or perspective of others? When we understand their mind, motivations, and even ways they can help us, things could go better. How can you learn from others yet still keep your point of view in mind while you expand it, leading to the best of all possible worlds, and the best solutions to problems!
Being free to think helps solve a lot of problems.	Think of times when you were either not free to think, or could not think freely and problems only got worse rather than better. How could you have handled it differently? How could you do this more?

Adopted with permission of Springer Science+Business Media. Young, G. (2014). *Malingering, feigning, and response bias in psychiatric/psychological injury: Implications for Practice and court*. Dordrecht, Netherlands: Springer Science+Business Media; with kind permission from Springer Science+Business Media B. V. [Table 23.7, Page. 599, modified]

Note. Piaget's developmental model includes a shift from preschool pre-operational thought to child and adolescent logical thought (concrete and formal operational, respectively). The transition is based on developing decentration, perspective taking, reversibility, etc. Pre-operational thought includes intuitive thought, which can be useful, but it might be used as a matter of course instead of choice, compromising logical thought and free will belief

Change

Tables 20.8 and 20.9 present psychotherapeutic modules related to change in underlying cognition. They are based on Piagetian notions of transition from pre-operational to operational thought, which includes transition from intuitive to logical thought (Ferrari & Vuletic, 2010; Morra, Gobbo, Marini, & Sheese, 2008; Müller, Carpendale, & Smith, 2009; Young, 2011a). The transition is akin to the distinction described for nonconscious, intuitive and conscious, deliberate thought. The central mechanisms of change in Piaget's model in this transition concern centration, egocentrism, animistic thought, irreversibility, a lack in perspective taking, etc. Based on these concepts, I provide simplified explanations on the left side of the table and then probe on the right to facilitate transitions to thinking more logically. Intuitive, automatic thought has an important role to play in behaving and choosing (Kahneman, 2011; Stanovich, West, & Toplak, 2011). However, patients might be too engaged in this type of thinking relative to more logical modes, in relation to certain important issues, or dilemmas, bad habits in need of change, decisions that have to be made, and so on.

Table 20.9 Change process and creating a better sense of having free will

Area	How can you use this knowledge to help yourself?
Change means genuine transformation	Just by thinking about the answers to these questions in the table, you are getting there. The secret is to keep the positive changes in place so that your core thoughts, emotions, and behaviors change toward the positive on a more permanent basis. How can you help that happen?
Change means conflict, in ideas and with people	Change is never easy. Your old and new ideas will conflict and you and others will struggle toward better outcomes, solutions, and situations. How can you manage all that disruption for the better?
Change means constant communication, within the self and with others	Growth happens by exchanging ideas, talking, reflecting on the exchanges and ideas, etc. How can you keep it going so that change for the better continues or is maintained despite ups and downs over time?
Change means placing new ideas in contrast with old ideas and seeing their advantages, and perhaps keeping old ideas around for the times they still might be useful	Change does not mean altering everything you were to develop a totally new you. It means keeping the best of the past as you change for the better. How can you ensure that happens as you change?
Change means having new ideas work their way into other areas of your life and thinking beyond the original use and function for which they developed.	Can you think of new situations and places to which your new ideas can be applied socially, with family, friends, etc., in other situations, e.g., work, school, and most importantly, how you think of life, yourself, and others?
Change means being active in life and adjusting to changing situations	How can you be the source of change, initiating them or the pathways leading to them, rather than being passive all the time and letting change happen around you without your say? How can you adjust constantly to new situations so that the situations reflect you and your ideas as much as anything else, depending on the circumstances?
Having a better sense of free will means having not only better logical thought but also better automatic, intuitive thought working at solutions to problems	This therapeutic exercise is aimed at increasing logical thought in solving problems, but automatic, intuitive thought works with it. So by improving use of logical thought we are not letting go the automatic, intuitive thought. Rather, we are making available both forms of thought so they can work together. Think of some situations in your life where this would be true (e.g., for social problem, a work or school one, a family problem).

Adopted with permission of Springer Science+Business Media. Young, G. (2014). *Malingering, feigning, and response bias in psychiatric/psychological injury: Implications for Practice and court*. Dordrecht, Netherlands: Springer Science+Business Media; with kind permission from Springer Science+Business Media B. V. [Table 23.8, Page. 600, modified]

Note. In this table, I continue using Piagetian concepts of change, but ones that are more generic. For Piaget, cognitive development refers to qualitative change in thought from one stage to the next. It is facilitated by cognitive conflict among and communication about ideas, whether internally or socially-derived, but only when the person is in a transition state. As new cognitive capacities develop and spread in the cognitive structure of the person, they might be contrasted with prior ones, which still might be activated (e.g., automatic thought still can be effective). The developing person is actively involved in self-growth, through openness, curiosity, will, etc. Psychotherapy could focus on this change model to promote better logical thought and free will belief

Stage

Table 32.10 in Chap. 32 presents a stage model of the development of intuitive and logical thought based on my Neo-Piagetian stage model (Young, 2011a). The latter model is quite consistent with Piaget's, in that his four major stages are included (sensorimotor, pre-operational, concrete operational, formal). However, in my model, I have added a beginning reflexive stage and an adult postformal or collective intelligence stage. Also, instead of referring to the combined pre-operational/concrete operational period as representational, I use the term of peri-operational.

Using this five-stage Neo-Piagetian model, and focusing on the distinction between intuitive (pre-operational) and logical thought (rational thought, concrete operational onward), I have reworked the distinction between Kahneman's (2011) and Stanovich et al.'s (2011) Type/System I thought and Type/System II thought in terms of the stages in development indicated.

Therefore, belief in free will and having a sense of free will should be viewed as underwritten by an increasing cognitive sophistication in terms of improving rational, logical (and Neo-Piagetian cognitive stage) acquisitions. However, involving such as illness, injury, and stress, as well as other ego depletion factors, might serve to undermine use of more logical thought processes.

Table 31.7 in Chap. 31 illustrates how Piagetian stages that develop could co-exist in thought, and how even lower-order ones, such as pre-operational thought and its intuitive component, might be hierarchically predominant in cognitive deployment. The table also indicates that patients might resort to lower-order thought processes even when they are disadvantageous, e.g., due to stress, illness, or injury. Being aware of the possibility of yoked automatic and rational thought in patients might help psychotherapists in their effort to promote more effective, rational thought, at least when it is needed, and (a return to) belief in free will.

Addictions

A major problem in psychotherapeutic work concerns substance dependence and abuse, such as alcohol addiction. The concept of belief in free will and a therapeutic module aimed at promoting it could be quite beneficial to these patients. In this regard, I developed a table based on current understanding of addiction (Köpetz, Lejuez, Wiers, & Kruglanski, 2013; see Table 20.10). It can be modified to apply to other problems in self-control, in which an increased belief in free will can help, such as obsessive–compulsive disorder. Köpetz et al. (2013) emphasized the general nature of motivational and self-regulation problems in addiction. For example, in their view,

Table 20.10 Freeing the will to believe in free will in addictions

Strategy	How can you use this knowledge to help yourself?
Addiction is not a brain disease, but a whole-person psychological problem that can be helped	Belief that addiction can be controlled begins with the belief that it is a condition for which such control is possible; it is not only medical and biological but also psychological and social
Addiction might have a biological basis, but it is learned and can be controlled through learning	By believing that learning can help toward the control of addiction, the person is taking another important step
Addiction is a motivated behavior that becomes an end in itself. Whatever purpose the addiction was serving becomes secondary to the addiction	Behaviors underlying addictions might first function to serve goals, such as keeping friends, feeling better about yourself. But then the addiction starts and gets out of hand and becomes the goal. Seeing this "gateway" pattern helps
Addictions become easily triggered, and even spontaneously.	Addictions become so powerful that simple triggers that could not lead to its behavior at first become good triggers. But the triggers have nothing special about them and can be controlled
Addictions are not about feeling good but about the consequences it brings, e.g., feeling accepted by fellow addicts	There are other ways to obtain the consequences that addictive behaviors had brought at first, such as social acceptance. What are some of these?
Those who are most vulnerable to addiction do not have other means of getting the desired consequences, e.g., socialization, sports	You are free to think of better ways to avoid the consequences that addictions first helped to get. How can you bring out these other ways, i.e., learn of them and choose them?
Addictive behavior can be activated involuntarily, or without conscious awareness or control. Also, it can be activated by triggers/contexts that are selectively attended to	You will be pulled to the addictions despite your new efforts at being free from them. How can you increase your resistance?

(continued)

Table 20.10 (continued)

Strategy	How can you use this knowledge to help yourself?
Addictions take over and there is less energy and will (resources) for other more constructive things	How can you inhibit the addictions, e.g., by freely choosing your new ways? How can you give yourself better effort, energy, resources, social connections, new activities, etc., to do so?
Resisting addictions takes effort cognitively and motivationally	You are on your way. Your new belief in free will is helping you. But the effort needs to be continual. How can you encourage that?
Replacing addictions by constructive activities takes effort cognitively and motivationally	In the end, your new way of living that you are freely choosing, now that you believe in free will, is an immense help. It is bringing you a more satisfying life that reflects self-control. You are harming less yourself and others. Indeed, you are helping more yourself and others. How can you keep doing that?
Addictions can be controlled by growth in belief in free will. The belief in free will starts as a small idea and can grow into an all-encompassing one	How could your belief in free will become a stronger belief, a belief that applies to many parts of your life, and a belief that even makes better your values, morals, and ways of living?

Adopted with permission of Springer Science + Business Media. Young, G. (2014). *Malingering, feigning, and response bias in psychiatric/psychological injury: Implications for Practice and court*. Dordrecht, Netherlands: Springer Science + Business Media; with kind permission from Springer Science + Business Media B. V. [Table 23.11, Page. 607, modified]

Note. Left side of the table adapted from Köpetz et al. (2013). The last entry refers to Table 24.6 in Chap. 24

drug use is perpetuated by automatic goal activation and pursuit. In addition, the transition to addiction from casual use relates to general principles of emotional transfer, accessibility, interconnectedness, and limited resources involving goal adoption, activation, and pursuit, in general.

Köpetz et al. (2013) noted that potential solutions to addiction substance use include: (a) increasing processing resources and (b) reducing the saliency of the drug-use goal. For example, increase in working memory capacity by training has been shown effective (Houben, Wiers, & Jansen, 2011). Also, Houben, Nederkoorn, Wiers, and Jansen (2011) provided evidence that associating pictures of glasses of beer with No-Go signals compared to Go ones reduced weekly alcohol intake.

Bickel, Quisenberry, Moody, and Wilson (2015) considered self-control failure as a transdisorder process. They related it to the inability to forgo immediate rewards for delayed ones. In addictions, the drug "commandeers" normal learning mechanisms, leading to dysfunctional reward processing. This causes, in turn, aberrant decision making. In self-control difficulty, the limbic and paralimbic systems neural network is associated with impulsive decision making and becomes dysregulated relative to its normal balance with the executive decision making system in the frontal and parietal cortices. To help with addiction, the authors proposed interventions related to bolstering the executive system, such as working memory training and episodic future thinking (mind wandering, projecting oneself into a plausible scenario in the future). These transdiagnostic therapeutic processes are consistent with the present approach for control of addictions and related self-dyscontrol behavior by augmenting free will belief.

Comment

This completes presentation of the present transdiagnostic module on the use of free will in psychotherapy. The chapter concludes with a transdiagnostic examination of growth.

Growth

Post-Trauma

Figure 20.2 presents a graphical depiction that I use with patients to help them understand and profit from the concept of posttraumatic growth (e.g., Bonanno, 2004). It applies readily to the

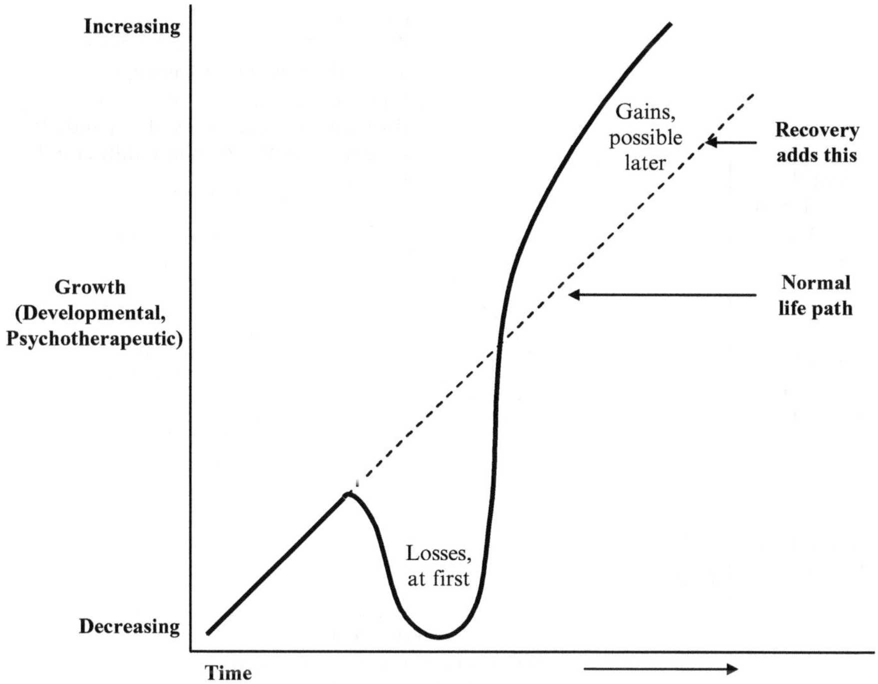

Fig. 20.2 Growing in rehabilitation. The figure emphasizes that recovery from stress, illness, or injury can bring gains that would not have been achieved without the stress, illness, or injury. Recovery in any one area can be more than partial, and it need not return only to the point where it would have been had the stress, illness, or injury not occurred. The concept of posttraumatic growth indicates that we can grow with stress, illness, or injury, that we can learn from them to the point that we are psychologically stronger, and that our life course could change for the better from having experienced them. Adapted with permission of Rejoining Joy Publishing. Young, G. (2011b). *Rejoining Joy: Vol. 2. Destressing*. Toronto: Rejoining Joy Publishing. Reprinted by permission of the Rejoining Joy Publishing. [Figure 10-7, Page. 211]. Adopted with permission of Springer Science+Business Media. Young, G. (2014). *Malingering, feigning, and response bias in psychiatric/psychological injury: Implications for Practice and court*. Dordrecht, Netherlands: Springer Science+Business Media; with kind permission from Springer Science+Business Media B. V. [Figure 23.2, Page. 608]

problems in the growth of belief in free will and difficulties. One functional goal of therapists relates to helping the patient achieve optimal functioning. For example, in the physically injured, the growth of the person qua person should be part of the goal (e.g., quality of life, sense of well-being). Helping in this way includes helping in the growth of belief in free will, which can provide reciprocal feedback into growth, in general.

For another transdiagnostic therapeutic model, refer to Einstein (2014), who described intervention strategies based on reducing intolerance of uncertainty. The model is an extension of perceptual control theory (Mansell, 2005). It applies to internalizing disorders (anxiety, depression) and eating disorders, in particular. It spans strategies used in both cognitive behavior therapy (CBT) and acceptance and commitment therapy (ACT). Dimensions that are targeted include desire for predictability and inhibitory anxiety.

My Model

Figure 20.3 illustrates the growth of belief in free will and feeling free that takes place in development. A similar growth can take place in psychotherapy. Piaget described cognitive schemas at the basis of developing sensorimotor, preoperational, and operational thought. Similarly, attachment theory describes internal working models; and other theoretical work in information processing describes working memory (see Young, 2011a).

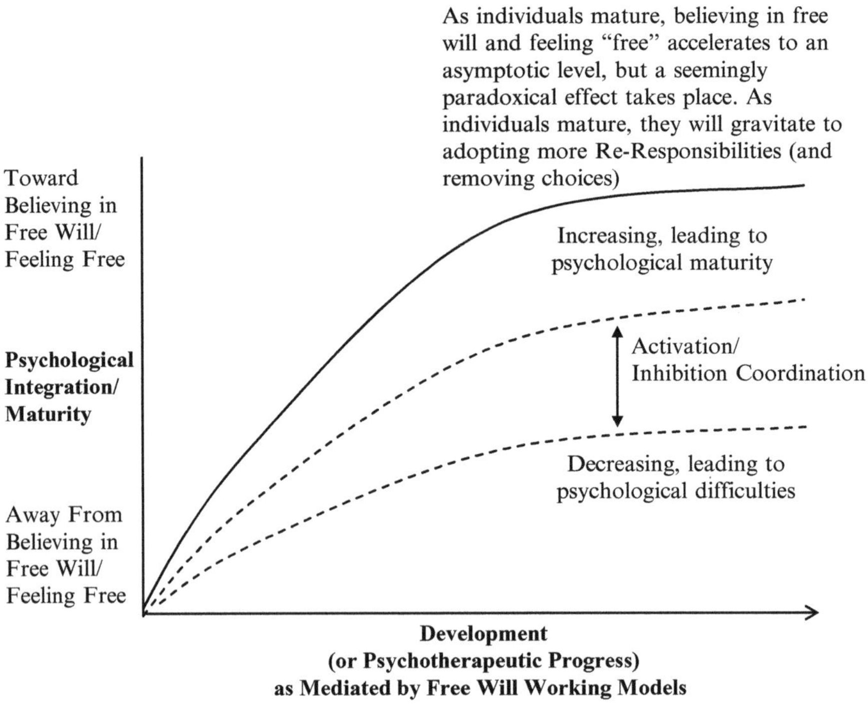

Fig. 20.3 Growth in belief in free will and sense of being free. *Note*. Integration/maturity in free will working models (mindset, mode) and also in free will facilitations/activations and inhibitions/constraints, and their coordinations. The concept of free will working models harkens to the concept of working memory. It is like a scratchpad in which we bring to the fore all that is needed to use extant free will capacities and associated cognitive and emotional underpinnings to help arrive at freely chosen plans and their successful implementation. There are both facilitators and constraints in its development and use, and a good balance in activations and inhibition skills can minimize interference with and successful activation of free will use and growth, and having a sense of feeling free. Free will (feeling free) constitutes a sense that can grow in development and in psychotherapy. As these feelings genuinely manifest, we are more likely than not to choose to undertake responsibilities that, in effect, limit our freedom as defined in other ways. The synthetic model of free will suggests that as we develop a sense of feeling free in the psychologically mature sense, we will choose to undertake responsibilities that, by their demands on us, diminish our sense of having choices. Given that we do not ever attain ultimate psychological maturity, we keep striving for it, and so the model is asymptotic as well as paradoxical. One of the issues confronting individuals as they develop in psychological maturity, and as they feel more free, and believe more in free will, is that they must navigate the tension between individualism and collectivism, which varies over family and culture. There are other factors, such as the effects of developmental impacts, stressors, illness, and injury. Adopted with permission of Springer Science+Business Media. Young, G. (2014). *Malingering, feigning, and response bias in psychiatric/psychological injury: Implications for Practice and court.* Dordrecht, Netherlands: Springer Science+Business Media; with kind permission from Springer Science+Business Media B. V. [Figure 23.1, Page. 605]

I have adopted these concepts to create the concept of "free will working models." They concern the components in thought and affect that we pull together in situations related to belief in free will. They mediate growth in free will in the ways described. That is, as cognitive development proceeds and more logical thought develops, free will working models differentiate.

In optimal human development, growth toward penultimate adult psychological maturity in cognition, affect, sociality, and morality leads to psychological attributes related to Erikson's construct of generativity. The person increases the scope of responsibilities oriented to and worked for (family, society, etc.). In Young (2012), I proposed a Neo-Eriksonian model that parallels the Neo-Piagetian one that I developed.

In terms of free will, this developmental model indicates that as we undertake more responsibilities, we should have less room for less responsible ways of living. Philosophically, Lévinas (1985) considered a critical human characteristic as striving to undertake Responsibility (Morgan, 2011). In that I consider this motive a constant daily re-dedication and a motive of being that takes place in the multiple, I refer to it as Re-Responsibilities. In this regard, we are left with a paradox—the more we mature psychologically, the less we have free will for less responsible action. In this sense, the developmental model that I propose is a paradoxical one about free will; that is, the more we have free will to use because of optimal development and less constraints, the more we choose life options (responsibilities) that limit freedom of action. The free will model presented in the figure is also an asymptotic one. Because we all have constraints in development and it is never fully optimal, we never approach the ideal state of having a full sense of free will and an unfettered free will belief.

Some of the constraints on people, as they develop, concern cultural variations. One factor in this regard that might impact the cognitive constructs underlying development of a sense of free will and belief in free will is the dimension of individualism/collectivism. There are many more related to family, e.g., abuse.

One way of appreciating the change dynamic is to consider it as an activation/inhibition coordination (Young, 2011a). The psychotherapist could work toward activating appropriate free will components in the person's free will working model and inhibiting other maladaptive ones.

Chapter Conclusions

The transdiagnostic psychotherapeutic module on free will belief and change that has been presented in this chapter can be used with patients experiencing stress, illness, injury, mood disorder, or any other relevant diagnosis, syndrome, or condition in which encouragement of proper decision making and positive change is needed, such as addiction. The tables in the module should be used flexibly, depending on the individual profile of the patient. Certain portions might apply to one patient but other portions to another. An analogy would be using worksheets and units involving maladaptive cognitions for which only a portion of the types of distorted thought might apply to any one patient.

The free will belief psychotherapeutic module that is presented deals with a variety of perspectives that cut across schools of psychotherapy, differing patient statuses, and different cognitive components underlying free will belief. In these senses, it could serve as a useful adjunct in psychotherapy for many relevant psychiatric conditions, including those prominent in psychological injury, such as PTSD, pain, and mTBI (mild traumatic brain injury). In addition, because free will belief might be especially relevant for psychotherapeutic populations involving difficulties in self-control, such as in addictions, the module could help facilitate change in many patients with comparable disorders, such as ones related to obsessions and compulsions.

References

Ackerman, J. M., Goldstein, N. J., Shapiro, J. R., & Bargh, J. A. (2009). You wear me out: The vicarious depletion of self-control. *Psychological Science, 20*, 326–332.

Alquist, J., & Baumeister, R. F. (2012). Self-control: Limited resources and extensive benefits. *Wiley Interdisciplinary Reviews: Cognitive Science, 3*, 419–423.

Anseel, F., Lievens, F., & Schollaert, E. (2009). Reflection as a strategy to enhance task performance after feedback. *Organizational Behavior and Human Decision Processes, 110*, 23–35.

Bargh, J. A. (1997). Reply to the commentaries. In R. W. Wyer (Ed.), *The automaticity of everyday life: Advances in social cognition* (Vol. 10, pp. 231–246). Mahwah, NJ: Erlbaum.

Barlow, D. H., Farchione, T. J., Fairholme, C. P., Ellard, K. K., Boisseau, C. L., Allen, L. B., et al. (2011). *Unified protocol for transdiagnostic treatment of emotional disorders*. New York: Oxford University Press.

Baumeister, R. F. (2005). *The cultural animal: Human nature, meaning, and social life*. New York: Oxford University Press.

Baumeister, R. F. (2008). Free will in scientific psychology. *Perspectives on Psychological Science, 3*, 14–19.

Baumeister, R. F. (2014a). Constructing a scientific theory of free will. In W. Sinnott-Armstrong (Ed.), *Moral psychology: Free will and moral responsibility* (Vol. 4, pp. 235–255). Cambridge, MA: MIT Press.

Baumeister, R. F. (2014b). Grateful responses to thoughtful comments by Holton, Paynes, and Cameron. In W. Sinnott-Armstrong (Ed.), *Moral psychology: Free will and moral responsibility* (Vol. 4, pp. 271–277). Cambridge, MA: MIT Press.

Baumeister, R. F., Bratslavesky, E., Muraven, M., & Tice, D. M. (1998). Ego depletion: Is the active self a limited resource? *Journal of Personality and Social Psychology, 74*, 1252–1265.

Baumeister, R. F., & Heatherton, T. F. (1996). Self-regulation failure: An overview. *Psychological Inquiry, 7*, 1–15.

Baumeister, R. F., & Masicampo, E. J. (2010). Conscious thought is for facilitating social and cultural interactions: How mental simulations serve the animal-culture interface. *Psychological Review, 117*, 945–971.

Baumeister, R. F., Masicampo, E. J., & Vohs, K. D. (2011). Do conscious thoughts cause behavior? *Annual Review of Psychology, 62*, 331–361.

Baumeister, R. F., Masicampo, E. J., & Vohs, K. D. (2015). Conscious thoughts and the causation of behavior. In M. Mikulincer & P. R. Shaver (Eds.), *APA handbook of personality and social psychology* (Attitudes and social cognition, Vol. 1, pp. 231–250). Washington, DC: American Psychological Association.

Baumeister, R. F., & Vohs, K. D. (2011). Self-regulation and the executive function of the self. In M. R. Leary & J. P. Tangney (Eds.), *Handbook of self and identity* (2nd ed., pp. 180–197). New York: Guilford Press.

Bickel, W. K., Quisenberry, A. J., Moody, L., & Wilson, A. G. (2015). Therapeutic opportunities for self-control repair in addiction and related disorders: Changes and the limits of change in trans-disease processes. *Clinical Psychological Science, 3*, 140–153.

Bonanno, G. A. (2004). Loss, trauma, and human resilience: Have we underestimated the human capacity to thrive after extremely aversive events? *American Psychologist, 59*, 20–28.

Ciarocco, N. J., Vohs, K. D., & Baumeister, R. F. (2010). Some good news about rumination: Task-focused thinking after failure facilitates performance improvement. *Journal of Social and Clinical Psychology, 29*, 1057–1073.

DeWall, C. N., Baumeister, R. F., & Masicampo, E. J. (2008). Evidence that logical reasoning depends on conscious processing. *Consciousness and Cognition, 17*, 628–645.

Dijksterhuis, A., Aarts, H., & Smith, P. K. (2005). The power of the subliminal: Subliminal perception and possible applications. In R. Hassin, J. Uleman, & J. A. Bargh (Eds.), *The new unconscious* (pp. 77–106). New York: Oxford University Press.

Dijksterhuis, A., Chartrand, T. L., & Aarts, H. (2007). Effects of priming and perception on social behavior and goal pursuit. In J. A. Bargh (Ed.), *Social psychology and the unconscious: The Automaticity of higher mental processes* (pp. 51–132). Philadelphia, PA: Psychology Press.

Duckworth, A. L., & Seligman, M. E. P. (2005). Self-discipline outdoes IQ in predicting academic performance of adolescents. *Psychological Science, 16*, 939–944.

Einstein, D. A. (2014). Extension of the transdiagnostic model to focus on intolerance of uncertainty: A review of the literature and implications for treatment. *Clinical Psychology: Science and Practice, 21*, 280–300.

Ferrari, M., & Vuletic, L. (2010). *The developmental relations among mind, brain and education: Essays in honor of Robbie Case*. New York: Springer Science+Business Media.

Fox, M. C., Ericsson, K. A., & Best, R. (2011). Do procedures for verbal reporting of thinking have to be reactive? A meta-analysis and recommendations for best reporting methods. *Psychological Bulletin, 137*, 316–344.

Gailliot, M. T., & Baumeister, R. F. (2007). Self-regulation and sexual restraint: Dispositionally and temporarily poor self-regulatory abilities contribute to failure at restraining sexual behavior. *Personality and Social Psychology Bulletin, 33*, 173–186.

Gailliot, M. T., Baumeister, R. F., DeWall, C. N., Maner, J. K., Plant, E. A., Tice, D. M., et al. (2007). Self-control relies on glucose as a limited energy source: Willpower is more than a metaphor. *Journal of Personality and Social Psychology, 92*, 325–336.

Galinsky, A. D., Maddux, W. W., Gilin, D., & White, J. B. (2008). Why it pays to get inside the head of your opponent: The differential effects of perspective taking and empathy in negotiations. *Psychological Science, 19*, 378–384.

Gazzaniga, M. S. (2014). Mental life and responsibility in real time with a determined brain. In W. Sinnott-Armstrong (Ed.), *Moral psychology: Free will and moral responsibility* (Vol. 4, pp. 59–74). Cambridge, MA: MIT Press.

Gollwitzer, P. W., & Sheeran, P. (2006). Implementation intentions and goal achievement: A meta-analysis of effects and processes. *Advances in Experimental Social Psychology, 38*, 69–119.

Haggard, P., Mele, A., O'Connor, T., & Vohs, K. (2010). *Lexicon of key terms. Big questions in free will project*. Published online at http://www.freewillandscience.com/wp/?page_id=63

Hagger, M. S., Wood, C., Stiff, C., & Chatzisarantis, N. L. D. (2010). Ego depletion and the strength model of self-control: A meta-analysis. *Psychological Bulletin, 136*, 495–525.

Halevy, N., Bornstein, G., & Sagiv, L. (2008). In-group love and out-group hate as motives for individual participation in intergroup conflict: A new game paradigm. *Psychological Science, 19*, 405–411.

Haynes, S. N., O'Brien, W. H., & Kaholokula, J. K. (2011). *Behavioral assessment and case formulation*. Hoboken, NJ: Wiley.

Houben, K., Nederkoorn, C., Wiers, R. W., & Jansen, A. (2011). Resisting temptation: Decreasing alcohol-related affect and drinking behavior by training response inhibition. *Drug and Alcohol Dependence, 116*, 132–136.

Houben, K., Wiers, R. W., & Jansen, A. (2011). Getting a grip on drinking behavior: Training working memory to reduce alcohol abuse. *Psychological Science, 22*, 968–975.

Inzlicht, M., & Al-Khindi, T. (2012). ERN and the placebo: A misattribution approach to studying the arousal properties of the error-related negativity. *Journal of Experimental Psychology: General, 141*, 799–807.

Inzlicht, M., & Schmeichel, B. J. (2012). What is ego depletion? Toward a mechanistic revision of the resource model of self-control. *Perspectives on Psychological Science, 7*, 450–463.

Jeannerod, M. (2006). Consciousness of action as an embodied consciousness. In S. Pockett, W. P. Banks, & S. Gallagher (Eds.), *Does consciousness cause behavior* (pp. 25–38). Cambridge, MA: MIT Press.

Kahneman, D. (2011). *Thinking fast and slow*. New York: Farrar, Straus, and Giroux.

Köpetz, C. E., Lejuez, C. W., Wiers, R. W., & Kruglanski, A. W. (2013). Motivation and self-regulation in addiction: A call for convergence. *Perspectives on Psychological Science, 8*, 3–24.

Kosslyn, S. M., & Moulton, S. T. (2009). Mental imagery and implicit memory. In K. D. Markham, W. M. P. Klein, & J. A. Suhr (Eds.), *Handbook of imagination and mental stimulation* (pp. 35–51). New York: Psychology Press.

Kottler, J., & Carlson, J. (Eds.). (2011). *Duped: Lies and deception in psychotherapy*. New York: Routledge/ Taylor & Francis.

Lévinas, E. (1985). *Ethics and infinity*. Pittsburgh, PA: Duquesne University Press.

Libet, B. (1985). Unconscious cerebral initiative and the role of conscious will in voluntary action. *Behavior and Brain Sciences, 8*, 529–566.

Mansell, W. (2005). Control theory and psychopathology: An integrative approach. *Psychology and Psychotherapy: Theory, Research and Practice, 78*, 141–178.

Masicampo, E. J., & Baumeister, R. F. (2011). Consider it done! Plan making can eliminate the cognitive effects of unfulfilled goals. *Journal of Personality and Social Psychology, 101*, 667–683.

McGlone, M. S., & Aronson, J. (2007). Forewarning and forearming stereotype-threatened students. *Communication Education, 56*, 119–133.

Mead, N. L., Baumeister, R. F., Gino, F., Schweitzer, M. E., & Ariely, D. (2009). Too tired to tell the truth: Self-control resource depletion and dishonesty. *Journal of Experimental Social Psychology, 45*, 594–597.

Mischel, W., Shoda, Y., & Peake, P. K. (1988). The nature of adolescent competencies predicted by preschool delay of gratification. *Journal of Personality and Social Psychology, 54*, 687–696.

Mlodinow, L. (2012). *Subliminal: How your unconscious mind rules your behavior*. New York: Pantheon Books.

Moffitt, T. E., Arseneault, L., Belsky, D., Dickson, N., Hancox, R. J., Harrington, H., et al. (2011). A gradient of childhood self-control predicts health, wealth, and public safety. *Proceedings of the National Academy of Sciences, USA, 108*, 2693–2698.

Morgan, M. L. (2011). *The Cambridge introduction to Emmanuel Lévinas*. Cambridge, MA: Cambridge University Press.

Morra, S., Gobbo, C., Marini, Z., & Sheese, R. (2008). *Cognitive development: Neo-Piagetian perspectives*. New York: Erlbaum.

Muraven, M., Shmueli, D., & Burkley, E. (2006). Conserving self-control strength. *Journal of Personality and Social Psychology, 91*, 524–537.

Muraven, M., & Slessareva, E. (2003). Mechanisms of self-control failure: Motivation and limited resources. *Personality and Social Psychology Bulletin, 29*, 894–906.

Müller, U., Carpendale, J. I. M., & Smith, L. (2009). *The Cambridge companion to Piaget*. New York: Cambridge University Press.

Nahmias, E. (2014). Is free will an illusion? Confronting challenges from the modern mind sciences. In W. Sinnott-Armstrong (Ed.), *Moral psychology: Free will and moral responsibility* (Vol. 4, pp. 1–25). Cambridge, MA: MIT Press.

Nordgren, L. F., van Harreveld, F., & van der Pligt, J. (2009). The restraint bias: How the illusion of self-restraint promotes impulsive behavior. *Psychological Science, 20*, 1523–1528.

Papies, E. K., Aarts, H., & de Vries, N. K. (2009). Planning is for doing: Implementation intentions go beyond the mere creation of goal-directed associations. *Journal of Experimental Social Psychology, 45*, 1148–1151.

Pennebaker, J. W., & Chung, C. K. (2007). Expressive writing, emotional upheavals, and health. In H. Friedman & R. Silver (Eds.), *Handbook of health psychology* (pp. 263–294). New York: Oxford University Press.

Pocheptsova, A., Amir, O., Dhar, R., & Baumeister, R. F. (2009). Deciding without resources: Resource depletion and choice in context. *Journal of Marketing Research, 46*, 344–355.

Roediger, H. L., Goode, M. K., & Zaromb, F. M. (2008). Free will and the control of action. In J. Baer, J. Kaufman, & R. Baumeister (Eds.), *Are we free? Psychology and free will* (pp. 205–225). New York: Oxford University Press.

Roskies, A. L. (2014). Can neuroscience resolve issues about free will? In W. Sinnott-Armstrong (Ed.), *Moral psychology: Free will and moral responsibility* (Vol. 4, pp. 103–126). Cambridge, MA: MIT Press.

Schmeichel, B. J., Harmon-Jones, C., & Harmon-Jones, E. (2010). Exercising self-control increases approach motivation. *Journal of Personality and Social Psychology, 99*, 162–173.

Schmeichel, B. J., & Vohs, K. D. (2009). Self-affirmation and self-control: Affirming core values counteracts ego depletion. *Journal of Personality and Social Psychology, 96*, 770–782.

Schmeichel, B. J., Vohs, K. D., & Baumeister, R. F. (2003). Intellectual performance and ego depletion: Role of the self in logical reasoning and other information processing. *Journal of Personality and Social Psychology, 85*, 33–46.

Scholten, L., van Knippenberg, D., Nijstad, B. A., & De Dreu, C. K. W. (2007). Motivated information processing and group decision-making: Effects of process accountability on information processing and decision quality. *Journal of Experimental Social Psychology, 43*, 539–552.

Shoda, Y., Mischel, W., & Peake, P. K. (1990). Predicting adolescent cognitive and self-regulatory competencies from preschool delay of gratification: Identifying diagnostic conditions. *Developmental Psychology, 26*, 978–986.

Sinnott-Armstrong, W. (2014a). *Moral psychology: Free will and moral responsibility* (Vol. 4). Cambridge, MA: The MIT Press.

Sinnott-Armstrong, W. (2014b). Introduction. In W. Sinnott-Armstrong (Ed.), *Moral psychology: Free will and moral responsibility* (Vol. 4, pp. xiii–xvii). Cambridge, MA: MIT Press.

Stanovich, K. E., West, R. F., & Toplak, M. E. (2011). The complexity of developmental predictions from dual process models. *Developmental Review, 31*, 103–118.

Stillman, T. F., Baumeister, R. F., & Mele, A. R. (2011). Free will in everyday life: Autobiographical accounts of free and unfree actions. *Philosophical Psychology, 24*, 381–394.

Sutter, M., & Strassmair, C. (2009). Communication, cooperation and collusion in team tournaments – An experimental study. *Games Economic Behavior, 66*, 506–525.

Tangney, J. P., Baumeister, R. F., & Boone, A. L. (2004). High self-control predicts good adjustment, less pathology, better grades, and interpersonal success. *Journal of Personality, 72*, 271–324.

Trivers, R. (2011). *The folly of fools: The logic of deceit and self-deception in human life*. New York: Basic Books.

Vohs, K. D., Finkenauer, C., & Baumeister, R. F. (2011). The sum of friends' and lovers' self-control scores predicts relationship quality. *Social Psychological and Personality Science, 2*, 138–145.

Vohs, K. D., Glass, B. D., Maddox, W. T., & Markham, A. B. (2011). Ego depletion is not just fatigue: Evidence from a total sleep deprivation experiment. *Social Psychological and Personality Science, 2*, 166–173.

Vohs, K. D., & Schooler, J. (2008). The value of believing in free will: Encouraging a belief in determinism increases cheating. *Psychological Science, 19*, 49–54.

Walter, K. H., Gunstad, J., & Hobfoll, S. (2010). Self-control predicts later symptoms of posttraumatic stress disorder. *Psychological Trauma, 2*, 97–101.

Watkins, E. R. (2008). Constructive and unconstructive repetitive thought. *Psychological Bulletin, 134*, 163–206.

Westling, E., Mann, T., & Ward, A. (2006). Self-control of smoking: When does narrow attention help? *Journal of Applied Social Psychology, 36*, 2115–2133.

Young, G. (2011a). *Development and causality: Neo-Piagetian perspectives*. New York: Springer Science + Business Media.

Young, G. (2011b). *Rejoining Joy: Vol. 2. Destressing*. Toronto, Canada: Rejoining Joy Publishing.

Young, G. (2012). A unitary Neo-Piagetian/Neo-Eriksonian model of development: Fundamental assumptions and meta-issues. *New Ideas in Psychology, 30*, 241–249.

Young, G. (2014). *Malingering, feigning, and response bias in psychiatric/psychological injury: Implications for practice and court*. Dordrecht, Netherlands: Springer Science + Business Media.

21 PTSD: Traumatic Causation

Chapter Introduction

The search for endophenotypes that stand between genetics and disease has been applied to the diagnostic entity of posttraumatic stress disorder (PTSD). Advances are being made in understanding the pathway to disorder in PTSD in terms of brain regions, neuronal networks, stress-related systems (e.g., the hypothalamic pituitary adrenal (HPA) axis), and their underlying genetic and neurogenetic bases. Gene × Environmental interactions (G×E) and epigenetic effects (e.g., gene silencing due to DNA methylation of gene promoter regions) affect the latter and, as well, the environment and context reciprocally interrelate with them.

The present chapter concentrates especially on several major directions in the search for biological markers of PTSD. The areas of the review covered also include the diverse topics of PTSD models, allostasis, pathways, and the five-factor model. It especially includes the most recent research. Note that the material reviewed does not fit clearly into the particular categories indicated, in that sometimes some overlap is evident over them in the literature examined.

The research on the genetic basis of PTSD serves as a starting point of the review of the literature. As mentioned, endophenotypes constitute transition pathways from genetics to disease or to disorder, and the goal of endophenotypic research on PTSD is to narrow the search for its genetic pathways to disease/disorder. Thus, the chapter examines multiple areas of study that might be involved in endophenotypes, starting with brain and neuronal network ones. The chapter concludes that, despite the burgeoning research on the topic, we have a long way to go in understanding the multiple influences in PTSD and their relationship to the genetic substrate. Moreover, from a forensic perspective, there are even more advances needed before the population-level research findings are reliable and valid enough, as well as specific to individual and group differences, to help the court and related venues in individual cases.

Note. This contains material from Young, G. (2014). PTSD, endophenotypes, the RDoC, and the DSM-5. *Psychological Injury and Law, 7*, 75–91.

Introduction

PTSD is not only highly researched but also highly controversial (Young, 2014). It is part of a disability epidemic, and its entry criteria, symptoms, and their clusters are all hotly contested. Its testing also is not straightforward, and needs to consider possible malingering, among other negative response biases, that confound cases.

DSM-5

Friedman, Resick, and Keane (2014) described that, in the DSM-5 relative to the DSM-IV-TR

G. Young, *Unifying Causality and Psychology*, DOI 10.1007/978-3-319-24094-7_21

(Diagnostic and Statistical Manual of Mental Disorders, Fourth Edition, Text Revised; American Psychiatric Association, 2000), the number of symptoms of PTSD has increased from 17 to 20 of them, and its clusters from three to four of them; and as well, its entry criteria have changed. On both conceptual and empirical grounds, Friedman et al. defended the validity of the approach taken by the DSM-5 work group on PTSD.

Friedman et al. (2014) described extant criticism of the PTSD construct and replied to it. (a) They denied that the diagnosis of PTSD needlessly pathologizes people exposed to traumatic stress. Granted, the epidemiological research shows that most people exposed to trauma do not develop PTSD, but exposure to traumatic events is quite prevalent in our society. Moreover, not all reactions to trauma exposure lie within the bounds of normality, even though extreme normal reactions are expected and generally nonpathological. (b) Also, PTSD is not a Western construct that is applicable only to European Americans. It has been documented throughout the world. (c) In addition, the research has shown that traumatic memories mostly represent the events that had taken place, despite some memory difficulties and alterations. It has not been supported that traumatic memories are not valid. (d) Similarly, verbal reports are more or less valid (Dohrenwend et al., 2006), so the epidemiology of (and validity of) the posttraumatic reactions to events as determined by these instruments, generally, are valid. (e) Finally, it is unfair to criticize the PTSD construct in terms of opening the floodgates to litigation because it is meant to be primarily clinical rather than forensic, in general, like the DSM-5 in which it is listed. The DSM-5 has "tightened" the definition of a traumatic event applicable to PTSD, but it is beyond its parameters that the diagnosis might be used frivolously, dubiously, and for monetary gain, for example, in court. The best remedy in this regard for professionals using the DSM-5 for PTSD diagnosis is to assess carefully. One day, biomarkers will help in assessment but, to date, they still lack the requisite sensitivity and specificity needed for court purposes.

Friedman and Resick (2014) noted that the DSM-5 placed PTSD in a cluster of "trauma and stressor-related" disorders. They noted that it fits with this category, along with the others (e.g., acute stress disorder, adjustment disorder), because of its broad heterogeneous nature and range of individual differences, including subtypes related to fear, dysphoria/anhedonia, aggression/substance abuse, guilt/shame, and dissociation. They argued that the DSM-5 approach includes the elements of complex PTSD found in the ICD (International Statistical Classification of Diseases and Related Health Problems; Maercker et al., 2013), so it does not have to be separated out. They noted the difference in the DSM-5 approach of listing 20 symptoms subdivided into four clusters with the approach of the ICD-11 (11th Revision; Maercker et al., 2013) of listing only three "core" elements (nightmares/flashbacks, avoidance, hypervigilance/startle), and with the rest as "associated" symptoms.

Epidemiology

Only a minority of individuals exposed to traumatic events sufficient to an entry criteria to diagnose PTSD go on to develop it (Kessler, Sonnega, Bromet, Hughes, & Nelson, 1995; 25 % of those exposed to severe trauma). In their review, Norris and Slone (2014) updated the epidemiology of trauma and PTSD. Most adults will experience a traumatic event in their lifetime, but only about 7 % will develop PTSD in their lifetime. At any given time, only 1–3 % (2 %) of the civilian population will be active cases (the rate is higher in the military). The proportion of those expressing PTSD symptoms is "much larger." Although 2 % seems a small percentage, it translates to over six million of the US population presumably needing treatment for being active PTSD cases at any one time. Nevertheless, there is much resilience in those exposed to trauma.

Pathways

Vogt, King, and King (2014) explored psychosocial risk pathways to PTSD. The most pertinent ones are variable risk factors, which exclude fixed markers (such as demographics). Risk factors might be independent, overlap, be a proxy for another, mediate, or moderate. Observational studies might be all that are possible in the study of the relationship of risk and outcome. Although the manipulation inherent in experimental studies is excluded from observational data, statistical techniques can still tease out, to a degree, causal associations (e.g., by using structural equation modeling, SEM). Nevertheless, the limitations of this type of research suggest using "probable" in conclusions about risk–outcome relationships. The authors concluded that the methodology in the PTSD "risk" research has been limited. PTSD most likely has "multiple causal pathways." Also, resilience needs to be considered.

Modeling

Major Models

Gillihan, Cahill, and Foa (2014) reviewed the major psychological theories of PTSD. Conditioning theories emphasize that it develops through a two-factor learning model. First, classical conditioning leads to associations of the traumatic event and neutral stimuli. Then, operant conditioning leads to avoidance behavior to escape the distress, etc. Keane and Barlow (2002) extended the model to include two generalized vulnerabilities—biological/genetic and acquired, with trauma exposure being a third vulnerability/elicitor. Other learning models emphasize failure to extinguish a learned fear response.

Emotional processing theories revolve around pathological emotions in PTSD. Memories are inappropriately emotion-laden, and they express relations across harmless stimuli and inappropriate or maladaptive emotions. The cognitions that derive are negative (e.g., "The world is dangerous"; "I am incompetent").

In cognitive theory, PTSD results from appraisals related to threat (Ehlers & Clark, 2000). For example, cognitive variables found in motor vehicle accident (MVA) survivors emerged better predictors of PTSD compared to other established predictors (Ehring, Ehlers, & Glucksman, 2008).

Schema theories refer to core assumptions or beliefs that guide the perception and interpretation of traumatic stressors. In PTSD, they become negative and troublesome. The person might either fail to accommodate to or over-accommodate to trauma-relevant information.

Multiple representation structural models build on the concept of distinct representational systems in memory that operate in parallel. For example, in PTSD, one might be more verbal/propositional and the other more sensory and difficult to communicate (Brewin, Gregory, Lipton, & Burgess, 2010). This serves to prolong their effects.

Gillihan et al. (2014) concluded that it is possible to integrate the theories to a degree under the guise of the mechanisms underlying PTSD. In this regard, the formation of associations seems critical. Second, discrepancies arise between existing schemas and current knowledge. Third, cognitive appraisals are involved. For PTSD, the DSM-5 has been revised to take into account negative cognitions and negative emotions. Also, theories of PTSD might need to be revised to account for inclusion in the DSM-5 of a greater amount of symptoms and clusters, and how they are arranged, as well as changes to its entry criterion, especially because the need to have experienced "fear, helpless, or horror" has been removed.

Fear Model

Model Wilker and Kolassa (2013) and Kolassa, Illek, Wilker, Karabatsiakis, and Elbert (2015) examined the multifactorial nature of causality in PTSD. They related PTSD symptoms to the formation of an associative neural fear network. The fear network model helps explain how a trauma-associated stimulus can activate the complete fear memory structure through its associative nature, thereby eliciting sensory, emotional, behavioral, cognitive, and physiological effects. In addition, they related the development and maintenance of autobiographical fear memories and representations as central to the neural fear network. Moreover, they related a brain neurocircuitry network as central to fear learning or conditioning (also see Brewin et al., 2010; Nijdam &

Wittmann, 2015; Schnyder & Cloitre, 2015; on sensory-near/bound memories vs. relative to contextual/verbal representations, as per the work of Brewin et al. (2010) that was mentioned above.).

As for PTSD's core feature, Wilker and Kolassa (2013) referred to pathological or "strong but defragmented traumatic" memories. Moreover, Brewin (2011) referred to pathological memory structure as the "cause of PTSD." The pathological memory has emotional, sensory, perceptual, and cognitive components.

In the following, I review the neurocircuitry of fear. As mentioned, fear conditioning provides the beginning of a model to explain pathological fear memory formation (Brewin, 2008). Beyond this, the learning involved is supported by a neuronal circuitry associated with fear conditioning (e.g., Johnson, McGuire, Lazarus, & Palmer, 2012; see Fig. 21.1). Stimuli reaching the lateral amygdala lead to new associative connections. Once the fear memory is consolidated, repeated associations and accompanying reconsolidations (Nadel, Hupbach, Gomez, & Newman-Smith, 2012) expand the network, while decontextualizing it (e.g., Kolassa & Elbert, 2007). Other components of the neural fear network include the amygdala, medial prefrontal cortex, and hippocampus. Also, it is impacted by the HPA axis and the locus coeruleus noradrenergic systems, which are two major stress pathways.

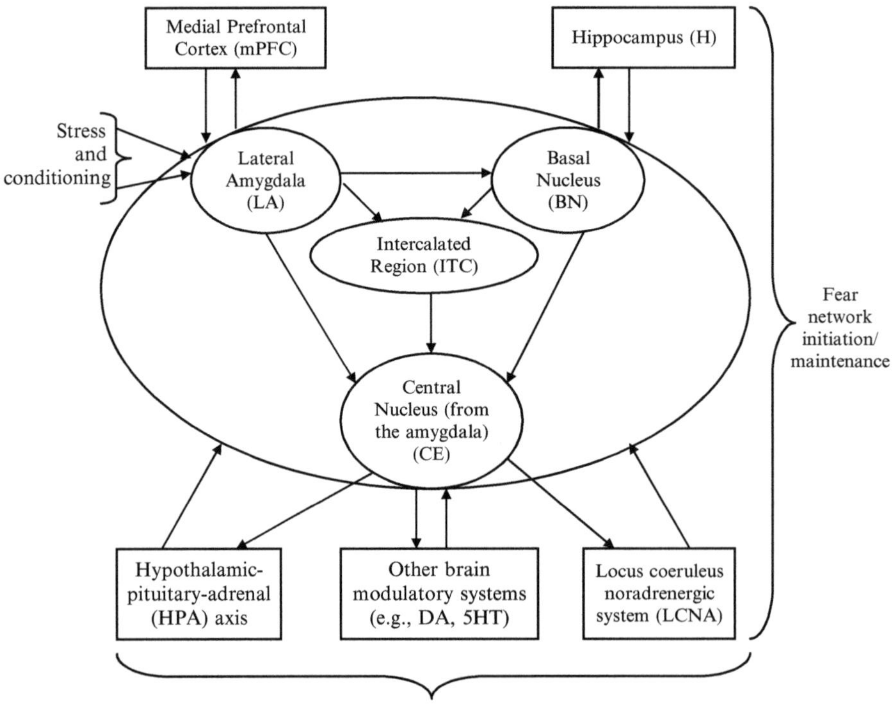

Fig. 21.1 Brain neurocircuitry involved in fear learning. The amygdala is central to fear conditioning. Information about the conditioned stimulus and the unconditioned stimulus converge in the lateral amygdala (LA) during fear acquisition. The latter area projects to the central nucleus (CE) of the amygdala. It controls the initiation responses to a stressor, including by way of the hypothalamic pituitary adrenal (HPA) axis and the locus coeruleus noradrenergic (LCNA) system, in particular. The system includes feedback mechanisms. Context information of fearful situations is transmitted to the amygdala by the hippocampus (H). The medial prefrontal cortex (mPFC) regulates fear expression by projecting to the multiple sites indicated. In fear extinction learning, increased mPFC firing to the basal nucleus (BN) stimulates GABAergic intercalated region (ITC) neurons to inhibit fear response emanating from the CE. Adapted from Johnson et al. (2012); who also referred to Rodrigues, LeDoux, and Sapolsky (2009)

Johnson et al. (2012) considered classical fear conditioning central to PTSD. It is involved in individual differences in the acquisition, consolidation, and extinction of fear memories in PTSD. Pavlovian memory circuits differentiate phenotypes related to PTSD. Memory strength in PTSD is an underlying factor in PTSD that interacts with it; memory has qualitative (emotional, narrative components) and stability (organization) attributes. In PTSD, the emotional quality might be overly "vivid" but lack access to narrative expression, as per the work of Brewin. The stability of the memory might be marked by disorganization.

To conclude, the fear model of PTSD considers it a deficit in fear conditioning, habituation, and extinction (cognitive control to negative valence stimuli), with influence from hyperactivation in the amygdala and inadequate top-down regulation by the mPFC and the hippocampus (e.g., Rauch, Shin, & Phelps, 2006).

Evidence Naim et al. (2014) also implicated a cognitive mechanism in PTSD. They measured threat-related attentional bias in MVA patients admitted to the hospital in the day of their accidents, and they followed up with PTSD assessment at 3 months. The patients' physical injuries were minor. PTSD was assessed using the CAPS (Clinician-Administered PTSD Scale; Blake et al., 1995). Threat bias was evaluated using a dot probe task involving pairings of general threat words (e.g., scared) and neutral words (e.g., carpets).

The results showed that threat attentional bias accounted for variance in PTSD beyond dissociation, as also measured initially in the hospital. The authors concluded that measure of threat bias could serve to index the risk for PTSD. Also, the mechanism involved appears to center on enhanced low-level attention to threat, after the initial trauma, leading to greater memory consolidation of trauma-related elements.

Berntsen and Rubin (2014) showed that emotional arousal at the time of a traumatic event function not only to enhance involuntary memory access but also voluntary ones. Further, the emotional intensity of the trauma predicts well how frequently the events are recalled. According to the authors, memory access is not hampered by a fragmented poorly integrated traumatic memory of an event at issue. [The findings address the inconsistency in the DSM-5 PTSD criteria that PTSD is accompanied by both intrusive recollections yet by difficulty remembering important parts of the event.]

Catarino, Küpper, Werner-Seidler, Dalgleish, and Anderson (2015) related PTSD to deficits in inhibitory suppression of salient memories (episodic retrieval). Not only was retrieval suppression compromised in research using the think/no-think paradigm (using aversive scenes cued by naturalistic reminders) in patients with PTSD compared to trauma-exposed control participants, but also PTSD patients having the largest deficits in "suppression induced forgetting" expressed the most severe PTSD symptomatology.

Other According to Wilker and Kolassa (2013), the limbic frontal neurocircuitry of fear is influenced by several neuromodulatory systems, including those involving serotonin and dopamine. The amygdala expresses an elevated responsivity in the fear of PTSD and, as well, it manifests an insufficient inhibition by the medial prefrontal cortex. Also, PTSD involves impaired memory-related hippocampal functioning. Similarly, Mahan and Ressler (2012) posited that the neural circuitry related to PTSD involves the fear neural circuit, which acts to promote fear conditioning (a function in the amygdala). Other research showed that genetic variations associated with memory increase the risk of PTSD or its fear memory consolidation (e.g., de Quervain et al., 2007).

Comment

With this introduction to PTSD, the chapter moves to tracing its endophenotypic pathway. The search for the latter is hampered by complications in arriving at consensus in its symptoms, clusters, entry criteria, epidemiology, models, assessment, and diagnosis. As well, one can query whether in the research individuals who have grossly exaggerating their PTSD or malingered have been successfully screened out. This confound further renders more difficult the search for PTSD's endophenotypic base.

Endophenotypes

Introduction

The major portion of the chapter relates to presentation of the concept of endophenotype and how it relates to PTSD. I review multiple aspects related to PTSD that might be involved in the pathway from genes to outcome. However, establishing any exact links from gene to disease/disorder is in a nascent stage, with the first major review on the topic having been published in 2011.

Model

Gottesman and Gould (2003) elaborated the concept of endophenotype, which had been developed by Gottesman and Shields (1972, 1973). Gottesman and Gould noted that the concept of endophenotype refers to measurable aspects in the pathway between genotype to disease. For neuropsychiatric diseases, endophenotypes might be found in the areas of neurophysiology, neuroanatomy, neuropsychology, cognition, biochemistry, or endocrinology, and might even include possible self-report data from testing. [A more elaborate presentation of endophenotype is offered below.]

According to Segman, Shalev, and Gelernter (2007), endophenotypes constitute lower levels of analysis of the substrates involved in a disorder, so that they might be closer or more proximal to genetic activity. The ultimate goal of PTSD endophenotype research has been to locate "causative genes" that mediate heritable vulnerability, susceptibility, or risk for PTSD. By seeking proximal candidate endophenotypes (e.g., hippocampal volume), the hope is to narrow the search for causative genes, but the ones targeted so far have had limited diagnostic specificity.

Comment

Part of the difficulty in seeking candidate endophenotypes indicative of causative genes for PTSD is that it does not fit neatly into the psychiatric/medical model for a disease entity. In the standard medical model, a diagnostic category should have one etiology for the disorder and one consequent intervention or cure, especially if the one etiological factor suggested is genetic. However, PTSD is a complex phenotype that is etiologically heterogeneous, including with polygenic underpinnings. It has low penetrance genetically, a finding that is consistent with the resilience to trauma found in the majority of the population. Therefore, given the difficulty in isolating the genetic contributions to PTSD and the limited amount of variance any one gene involved or even a set of genes might have in directly "explaining" PTSD (in main effects), research has focused on Gene × Environmental interactions (G × E) in PTSD vulnerability, onset, and maintenance, as well. Typically, as conditions such as PTSD develop (or are averted), multiple genes and environmental events interact in concert or in parallel with each other and across its course or stream over time. In this regard, candidate PTSD-related genes should include those not only related to brain region and circuit-related precursors in the causal chain but also to related physiology, such as the neurotransmitters serotonin and dopamine, as well as the interactive effects of genes, environment, and the neurobiology involved. I would add that genetic susceptibility to environmental influence, which might vary in different alleles of the genes involved, and the quantification of such effects, should be taken into consideration in the search for PTSD endophenotypes.

Genes

The next section of the chapter reviews the genetic research on PTSD in terms of candidate gene studies and GWAS (genome-wide association study). The field has yet to map a clear genetic basis to PTSD, but there are tantalizing findings in this regard. Kolassa et al. (2015) noted that the most commonly studied genetic polymorphisms are SNPs (single nucleotide polymorphisms; variation in a single DNA base pair) and VNTRs (variable number of tandem repeats; which alters the length of a repetitive region of the genome).

Candidate Genes

Introduction In terms of genetic factors associated with PTSD, in the first comprehensive paper on endophenotypes for PTSD, Sherin and Nemeroff (2011) found that specific polymorphisms are implicated. Further, Pitman et al. (2012) identified 22 candidate genes in PTSD. The following highlights the major polymorphisms involved in PTSD according to recent surveys (Kolassa et al., 2015; Sherin & Nemeroff, 2011; Wilker & Kolassa, 2013). In particular, the research highlights that, rather than having a direct main effect, these critical polymorphisms have an interactive effect with environmental contingencies typically related to trauma. Moreover, one way or another, the polymorphisms typically involve neurotransmitters.

5-HTTLPR According to Wilker and Kolassa (2013) and Kolassa et al. (2015), genetic evidence suggests that there is reduced serotonin transporter binding in the amygdala in PTSD (Murrough et al., 2011), due to a polymorphism in *5-HTTLPR* (serotonin transporter linked polymorphic region; the *s* (short) allele; Lonsdorf et al., 2009). This allele, compared to the *l* (long) one, is associated with lower gene transcription, resulting in less serotonin transporter activity and serotonin clearance from the synaptic cleft (Kolassa et al., 2015). This allows for greater amygdala reactivity to an emotional stimulus and, therefore, an enhanced fear conditioning.

In particular, over six studies have found an association of PTSD risk with both the *5-HTTLPR* genotype and environmental stress level (G×E interactions; Grabe et al., 2009; Kilpatrick et al., 2007; Koenen et al., 2009; Kolassa, Ertl, et al., 2010; Mercer et al., 2012; Pietrzak, Galea, Southwick, & Gelernter, 2013; Xie et al., 2009; Xie, Kranzler, Farrer, & Gelernter, 2012). These studies that are cited found an increase of risk for PTSD when it occurs in association with environmental stress and in conjunction with the *s* variant of *5-HTTLPR*, which, as described, reduces transporter activity, leading to greater fear learning.

SLC6A39 However, according to Wilker and Kolassa (2013) and Kolassa et al. (2015), for dopamine, the results have been inconsistent (e.g., for dopamine receptor D2 (*DRD2*) TaqIA), although Sherin and Nemeroff (2011) reported results related to the dopamine transporter gene (*SLC6A39*).

COMT Other work supports a role for the Val^{158}Met polymorphism in the gene encoding catechol-*O*-methyltransferase (*COMT*; e.g., Kolassa, Kolassa, Ertl, Papassotiropoulos, & de Quervain, 2010; dopaminergic system). The Met polymorphism in the gene encoding COMT functions to enzymatically inactivate catecholamines, thereby lowering catecholamine activity, and leading to higher extra-cellular dopamine and impaired fear extinction learning. According to the research, the Met allele is associated with constant higher PTSD risk in homozygous individuals, but the Val^{158}Met one is more protective of PTSD. That is, in cases of traumatic load, individuals with the allele exhibit a dose-dependent risk association for PTSD (Boscarino, Erlich, Hoffman, & Zhang, 2012; Kolassa, Kolassa et al., 2010).

FKBP5 Other systems that reveal molecular G×E effects in PTSD include the *FKBP5* glucocorticoid receptor (cochaperone *FK506* binding protein 5) *rs9470080* (affecting the HPA axis; e.g., see Binder et al., 2008; Boscarino et al., 2012). Kolassa et al. (2015) noted that the gene encoding *FKBP5* regulates cortisol-binding affinity of the glucocorticoid receptor, decreasing it, and causing a prolonged stress reaction, which is more marked in conjunction with trauma.

Other Skelton, Ressler, Norrholm, Jovanovic, and Bradley-Davino (2012) also mentioned as involved in PTSD the regulator of G-protein signaling 2 (*RGS2*), which is related to the limbic-frontal system (the CC polymorphism). This effect takes place especially in conjunction with the presence of low social support (Amstadter et al., 2009).

Conclusion Sherin and Nemeroff (2011) concluded that there is sufficient evidence for a neurobiological model of PTSD, one that includes genetic and other predisposing factors. Koenen et al. (2014) reviewed the comorbidities in genetics of PTSD. Other risk factors for PTSD include epigenetic factors (gene silencing due to environmental factors). In addition, PTSD risk factors involve female gender, prenatal stress, early childhood stress, physical trauma, and traumatic brain injury (TBI). As for the molecular mechanisms associated with the fear learning in PTSD, for Mahan and Ressler (2012), they concern *BDNF*-tyrosine kinase B (*TrkB*), GABAergic, and glutamatergic ligand receptor systems. In this regard, Kolassa et al. (2015) referred to various immune system factors in disease outcomes associated with PTSD.

Heritability

Evidence

Heritability is a behavioral genetic construct that does not concern finding the genes and alleles related to the phenomenon at issue, but the amount of variance that the genetic factors might help explain, in general. Wilker and Kolassa (2013) queried whether PTSD is heritable (citing Sartor et al., 2011) or whether, simply, its risk is heritable due to gene–environment correlation (i.e., the risk of PTSD and trauma exposure are both heritable in terms of the same gene(s); as per Stein, Jang, Taylor, Vernon, and Livesley (2002)). According to Logue et al. (2012), twin studies give heritability estimates that genetic factors explain up to 70 % of variation in PTSD risk (e.g., Bramsen, Dirkzwager, & van der Ploeg, 2000). Also, Wilker and Kolassa (2013) noted that if there are genetic risk factors for PTSD, the risk appears general for its frequent comorbidities (e.g., depression; Koenen et al., 2008).

Johnson et al. (2012) maintained that the strength of fear memory "is heritable." Their figure 3 lists 21 regulating genes in PTSD, and they include *5-HTTLPR* and *BDNF*. The former is part of a class in which increased gene expression enhances fear memory and the latter in which decreased expression enhanced it.

Comment

According to Logue et al. (2012), candidate gene studies have provided inconsistent results in specifying which genetic loci and alleles might be involved (citing Cornelis, Nugent, Amstadter, & Koenen, 2010). The heritability research related to PTSD suggests that there might be common genetic underpinnings to PTSD and its comorbidities, such as depression, which further leads to questions about its status as an independent diagnostic entity in need of a search for an underlying endophenotype. Moreover, the role of any one candidate gene that could explain the heritability of PTSD would be minimal, and a more polygenic approach is needed. Further, the heritability construct does not account for the complexity of gene–environment interactions and related phenomena, such as epigenetics, which complicate the search for the genetic bases of PTSD.

Overall, the genetic research holds some promise for finding the genetic and gene-interactive bases for PTSD, but to trace them will require their better delineation, although GWAS findings might one day help in this regard, when conducted with the rigor needed. But has the research been promising to date?

GWAS

Evidence

Logue et al. (2012) conducted the first GWAS of PTSD. Logue et al. (2012) examined male and female white non-Hispanic military veterans and their intimate partners. They used two instruments—to measure PTSD, the CAPS, and for traumatic life events, the Traumatic Life Events Questionnaire (TLEQ; Kubany et al., 2000). The sample size was modest (195 cases and 196 controls).

According to Logue et al. (2012), the retinoid-related orphan receptor alpha *(RORA)* gene belongs to the *NR1* subfamily of nuclear hormone receptors. The AA allelic variation reduces the capacity of neurons to respond appropriately to the biological stressors associated with traumatic stress (e.g., oxidative stress, inflammation). With neuroprotective function reduced, the effect is to promote neuronal apoptosis. Overall, the AA allele acts to confer susceptibility to the development of PTSD.

In support of their model, the results showed that the SNP *rs8042149* located in the *RORA* attained significance at the genome-wide level. Further, participants with relatively low trauma exposure according to the TLEQ but with the high-risk (GG) genotype had just as much chance of developing PTSD as participants with high exposure and the low-risk genotype (AA). These results did not replicate with an African American sample.

The authors concluded that, for other results in their study, gene associations involving dopamine and serotonin metabolism were not found as PTSD genetic risk factors, in contrast to the results related to them in prior candidate gene research. Other research has implicated the *RORA* in PTSD (Amstadter et al., 2013). Wilker and Kolassa (2013) also noted GWAS research has shown that the gene encoding for the retinoid-related orphan receptor alpha (*RORA*) appears implicated in PTSD.

Xie et al. (2013) conducted a GWAS with European (EA) and African Americans (AA) diagnosed with PTSD in a larger study on drug dependence/alcoholism. The interview that they used addressed 12 types of traumatic events; also, the PTSD diagnosis was based on the DSM-IV (Diagnostic and Statistical Manual of Mental Disorders, Fourth Edition; American Psychiatric Association, 1994). The SNP that emerged most clearly significant involved *rs406001* on chromosome 7012. The Logue et al. (2012) findings reported above were not replicated.

GWAS are investigating more than 300 genes (Solovieff et al., 2014). In their research, Solovieff et al. (2014) implicated single nucleotide polymorphisms (e.g., the solute carrier family 18 member, *SLC18A2*) in relation to PTSD.

Comment

The GWAS studies in relation to PTSD might be better methodologically than that of candidate gene research, but the results of the studies are in their infancy and are not necessarily being replicated, as has been found in the case of candidate gene research. Nevertheless, genetic polymorphisms related to neurotransmitters do seem to hold promise as influences on PTSD and also on its risks. That being said, the complexities of gene influences on behavior warrant care in search for simple answers toward finding the starting point in the search for endophenotypes in PTSD. This is illustrated by the phenomenon of epigenesis in PTSD, which generally is turning genetic research on its head.

Epigenesis

Introduction

To some extent, genetic explanations of PTSD have had difficulties finding candidate genes and replicating the findings in GWAS. Part of the difficulty in establishing the genetic origins and pathways to PTSD is that genetic explanations now include factors such as Gene × Environment interactions and epigenesis. The latter, in particular, has been studied in depth in relation to PTSD, and it illustrates the complicated relationship between genes and environment in PTSD, which adds to the difficulties in finding simplified endophenotypic PTSD models. DNA methylation (modification) is the most commonly studied epigenetic process; it involves the methylation of cytosine in cytosine-guanine dinucleotides (CpGs; 5meC).

Ptak and Petronis (2010) noted the following about epigenesis. (a) The epigenetic status of an organism is much more dynamic than the status of its DNA sequence. (b) Certain epigenetic marks could be inherited transgenerationally with the DNA sequence that has been altered. (c) Proper genomic function requires epigenetic regulation, e.g., in gene activity regulation, inactivation of "parasitic" DNA elements, and chromosomal segregation. (d) Epigenetic factors might even lead to non-deleterious genes becoming harmful by blocking their timely expression at the required level. (e) Epigenetic regulation is essential for proper neural/neurological function, and its dysregulation contributes to etiopathogenesis. (f) Together, these postulates allow for an integrated understanding of the epidemiological, genetic (DNA sequence), epigenetic, environmental, clinical, and molecular features or mechanisms of complex psychiatric diseases. (g) The epigenetic model of complex disease also assumes that pre-epimutations increase an organism's risk of becoming ill. Pre-epimutations are primary epigenetic disruptions that are insufficient to cause outright disease until a threshold is reached, which might take decades and involve multiple minor dysregulations.

Further, epigenetics forms part of a complex regulatory system in which the environment can affect extant epigenetic marks. The effects might even be reversible by appropriate environmental support or intervention. The focus of future work should be on susceptible "epialleles" and identification of "epigenetic biomarkers" of disease.

Model

Sipahi et al. (2014) found evidence of epigenetic DNA methylation (DNAm) increases within DNA methyltransferase loci for PTSD cases following trauma relative to controls. The sample was small ($N=30$ exposed with PTSD and 30 matched controls). The results mostly involved *DNMT1* and *DNMT3B*, and DNAm varied in pre–post and case–resilience comparisons. The authors concluded that epigenetic variation is involved in regulation of PTSD risk/etiology. According to Koenen et al. (2014), cutting-edge research is implicating environmental epigenetic moderation of genetic effects in PTSD. These involve the serotonin transporter gene (*SLC6A4*), *5-HTTLPR*(s), the glucocorticoid receptor gene (*NR3C1*), and *FK506* binding protein 5 cochaperone (*FKBP5*). Immune system genes also appear involved. Finally, G×E interactions are involved (e.g., for the risk genotype, *rs2267735*).

Fear

Maddox, Schafe, and Ressler (2013) examined epigenetic regulation of fear learning and fear regulation in relation to PTSD. They emphasized epigenetics impact on the *BDNF* pathway and *FKBP5* regulation of glucocorticoid receptor (GR) function. The former gene site and its polymorphisms have been implicated in PTSD by Rakofsky, Ressler, and Dunlop (2012) and Smith et al. (2011). The latter gene site has been implicated in research by Klengel et al. (2013), Mehta et al. (2011), and Xie et al. (2010).

Similarly, Wilker and Kolassa (2013) noted that the dose-dependent effect of traumatic load on PTSD risk appears affected by the epigenetic methylation pattern of the DNA of the serotonin transporter gene (Koenen et al., 2011). Another study found an interaction of the low-function risk allele and higher methylation at the dopamine transporter gene locus in the highest PTSD risk (Chang et al., 2012). To conclude, Wilker and Kolassa (2013) noted that there is interplay of genetic and epigenetic (and so environmental) factors involved in the formation and modification of the fear network in PTSD.

Abuse

Szyf (2013) referred to epigenetics as the way environments "talk" to genes. He described and commented upon the article by Klengel et al. (2013). The authors found an *FKBP5* gene × child abuse interaction in that the haplotype *rs1360780* moderated the risk of developing PTSD after early trauma. The mechanism involved includes *rs1360780* affecting *FKBP5* chromatin shape and transcription. The findings represent a molecular mechanism in PTSD expression; the latter relates to the risk allele of *FKBP5*, which is a stress response regulator active in the hippocampus response regulator. The allele is preferentially demethylated in children exposed to trauma; the effects persist as an enhanced expression of *FKBP5* into adulthood, potentiating PTSD development.

The article by Klengel et al. (2013) is difficult to read for the novice, but Szyf (2013) explicated it well. Normally *FKBP5* participates in a sequence that suppresses the stress response. In its regulation of the stress response, *FKBP5* functions as a proximal negative feedback mechanism of the glucocorticoid receptor. The gene is expressed by activation via the glucocorticoid receptor in reaction to elevated glucocorticoid (a primary stress hormone) levels. *FKBP5* activity downstream promotes resistance to glucocorticoids.

As for the risk allele involved, demethylation of intron 7 in carriers who had been exposed to early-life trauma has an effect on gene expression despite its linear displacement from another intron involved and the promoter (gene silencing site in demethylation) involved. The demethylation can take place, nevertheless, because of three-dimensional molecular activity, through the binding of RNA polymerase II (Pol II), at least when the variant and early-life stressors are present in interaction. The molecular effects on the stress response system in variant carriers appear to affect multiple tissues, including peripheral blood cells from which the samples in the study were taken, thereby indicating the potential in carriers for carrying stress and health effect of early adversity coupled with later PTSD.

Additional research on epigenetic regulation has been conducted on the gene encoding the GR *NR3C1*, and its polymorphism *Bcl1* in stress, anxiety, and fear, and the results suggest that increased *NR3C1* promoter methylation levels in PTSD patients correlate with the severity of their childhood abuse (Perroud et al., 2011). The findings in the field also relate risk and protective factors for PTSD in epigenetic modifications of genetic polymorphisms related to neurotransmitter dopaminergic and serotinergic function (respectively, *SLC6A3*, *SLC6A4*; Chang et al., 2012; Koenen et al., 2011), as well as genes associated with inflammation (Uddin, Aiello, et al., 2010; Uddin, Galea, et al., 2011). Raabe and Spengler (2013) referred to epigenetic programming during early sensitive windows of the HPA axis in response to early-life stress as a risk factor for PTSD.

Stress

Zovkic, Meadows, Kaas, and Sweatt (2013) analyzed epigenesis in PTSD and interindividual variability in stress susceptibility. Epigenetic mechanisms are no longer considered stable in the changes that they effect but dynamic in doing so. Moreover, individuals harbor particular "epigenetic landscapes" on which epigenetic changes are written, for example, due to traumatic events; and the variations involved express individual-specific outcomes, as in vulnerability and resilience to PTSD risk factors and trauma.

PTSD involves deregulation of endocrine stress systems and associated neurotransmitters and neuromodulators (Baker, Nievergelt, & O'Connor, 2012). Epigenetic modifications constitute one set of drivers that serve to dysregulate these PTSD bioregulators through their role in mediating genetic expression of the endocrine system and related neural and neurohormonal elements (e.g., molecules, transcription factors). In a bidirectional fashion, downstream epigenetic modifications themselves are regulated by upstream biofunctions.

In discussing PTSD and the HPA axis, Zovkic, Meadows et al. (2013) indicated the latter's central role in adaptation to stress and the source of individual differences in risk and resilience to stress. Stressful situations lead to the release of corticotrophin releasing hormone (CRH) from the hypothalamus into the pituitary gland, which stimulates the release of adrenocorticotropin hormone (ACTH) and activates the release of glucocorticoids (GCs, cortisol). Receptors for glucocorticoids (GRs) are situated throughout the brain, but are especially prevalent in the hippocampus, thereby influencing memory/cognitive formation/function and also initiating negative feedback to return cortisol to baseline levels after acute stress (Novak, Hamel, Kelly, Dettmer, & Meyer, 2013). PTSD patients generally manifest reduced levels in their cortisol, as well as increased negative feedback, abnormal expression of GR, and more CRH, relative to controls without trauma (e.g., Yehuda, Halligan, & Bierer, 2002). The blunting of the GC cortisol response to stress appears a critical risk factor for PTSD (Yehuda & LeDoux, 2007); it appears epigenetically regulated; and the HPA axis seems an important mediator between genes and expression in PTSD (Yehuda et al., 2009).

Stress exposure regulates epigenetic modification by way of GC action on GRs. The GR gene promoter region is liable to much individual variation in DNA methylation. There are developmental differences (sensitive periods) in epigenetic modification effectiveness. Epigenetic programming could lean toward risk or resilience, depending on the confluence of genes (e.g., polymorphisms), environment (e.g., stressors), developmental period (e.g., sensitive epochs), and stress system function. For example, compared to what might happen at other stages, some stress experiences at certain developmental stages are more likely to lead to resilience to PTSD in adults, by a "stress inoculation" (Ricon, Toth, Leshem, Braun, & Richter-Levin, 2012).

Authors are now referring to Gene × Environment × Epigenome interactions. The environment and epigenetic modifications appear quite salient during early life in affecting behavior, altering the expression of multiple genes (Sundermann, Hauschildt, & Ehlers, 2013; Sundermann, Onwumere, Bebbington, & Kuipers, 2012). The early environment and epigenetic modification have been implicated in potentiating PTSD by their effects on genes associated with the HPA axis (e.g., *FKBP5*; Klengel et al., 2013; *PAC1R*, a receptor for *PACAP* (pituitary adenylate cyclase-activating peptide); Dias & Ressler, 2013; Ressler et al., 2011).

Aside from the HPA axis, Gene × Environment × Epigenetic interactions (G × E × E) relevant to PTSD have been found for neuromodulators, neurotransmitters, and other biochemicals related to synaptic function/plasticity (Boulle et al., 2012; Russo, Murrough, Han, Charney, & Nestler, 2012; Skelton et al., 2012; Wu et al., 2013).

Epigenetic modifications can mediate the effects of serious trauma even independently of a predisposing factor (Chang et al., 2012). Even after controlling for genotype, distinct methylation profiles of the serotonin transporter gene differentially relate to risk and resilience (Koenen et al., 2011). Epigenetic modifications can influence risk/resilience beyond the influence of genetic factors (Ouellet-Morin et al., 2012). The critical developmental window for having stress act to effect long-lasting changes extends even into the teen years (Dudley, Li, Kobor, Kippin, & Bredy, 2011). Finally, epigenetic "writers" can also influence risk/resilience (e.g., by affecting the balance in epigenetic activators/repressors; Zovkic, Guzman-Karlsson, & Sweatt, 2013).

Zovkic, Meadows et al. (2013) provided a summary table of epigenetic modifications applicable to PTSD. They grouped the research by candidate gene studies and genome wide/large scale studies, as well as others. The genes involved and the major findings in the research on them are given in Table 21.1.

Skelton et al. (2012) adopted an approach quite similar to that of Zovkic and colleagues. They argued that stress can lower cortisol level through epigenetic modifications, but only in the context of low maternal care levels in early developmental windows (e.g., Meaney & Szyf, 2005; Seckl & Meaney, 2006; Weaver, 2007). Similarly, epigenetic-mediated changes in HPA axis reactivity might be associated with greater susceptibility to PTSD. The mechanism involved might be an over-cascade in noradrenergic neurotransmission, producing over-consolidation of fear memories and also increased arousal/distress subsequent to trauma, as well as early set-point alterations contributing to the effect early in life (Yehuda et al., 2010).

Table 21.1 A summary of epigenetic modifications in human research of PTSD

Gene (s) of interest	Major findings	Reference
Candidate-gene studies		
ADCYAP1, *ADCYAP1R1*	PTSD symptoms correlated with *Adcyap1r1* locus (in women)	Ressler et al. (2011)
SLC6A4	Controlling for genotype, *SLC6A4* methylation (m) modified the effect of PTEs on PTSD: ↓ *SLC6A4* promoter m associated with ↑ PTSD risk; ↑ *SLC6A4* promoter m protective against PTSD	Koenen et al. (2011)
SLC6A3	↑ *SLC6A3* promoter m associated with ↑ risk of lifetime PTSD in 9R allele carriers	Chang et al. (2012)
COMT	*COMT* Met/Met genotype interacted with CpG m in mediation of impaired fear inhibition in PTSD patients	Norrholm et al. (2013)
FKBP5	GC exposure associated with ↑ *FKBP5* GRE demethylation and ↑ *FKBP5* expression in carriers of the risk allele compared with the protective one	Klengel et al. (2013)
Genome-wide/large scale studies		
Genes involved in immunity, neurogenesis, the startle response, *DNMT3B*, *DNMT3L*, imprinted genes: *NDN*, *MAGEL2*, *ATP10A*	PTSD associated with: (a) ↑ m of *DNMT3B*, ↓ m of *DNMT3L*; (b) deregulated m of genes involved in Prader–Willi and Angelman syndromes; (c) m profiles of other genes	Uddin et al. (2010)
TPR, *CLEC9A*, *APC5*, *ANXA2*, *TLR8*, *BDNF*, *CXCL1*, immune-related genes	PTSD associated with: (a) ↓ m of *TPR* and *ANXA2* and ↑ m of *CLEC9A*, *APC5*, *TLR8* in PTSD; (b) ↑ m of *BDNF* and *CXCL1*; (c) some other differentially methylated immune-related genes	Smith et al. (2011)
Other		
33 loci previously associated with PTSD	↑ *MAN2C1* m interacted with PTE in PTSD risk	Uddin, Galea et al. (2011)
Repetitive elements: *LINE-1*, *Alu*	In post-deployed US military service members, *LINE-1* was hypomethylated in PTSD cases (vs. control). Pre-deployment, *Alu* was hypermethylated in PTSD cases (vs. control)	Rusiecki et al. (2012)

Note. PTE potentially traumatic event, *ADCYAP1* adenylate cyclase activating polypeptide 1 (pituitary), *ADCYAP1R1* adenylate cyclase-activating polypeptide 1 (pituitary) receptor type 1, *BDNF* brain-derived neurotrophic factor, *SLC6A4* solute carrier family 6 (neurotransmitter transporter, serotonin), member, *SLC6A3* solute carrier family 6 (neurotransmitter transporter, dopamine), member, *COMT* catechol-*O*-methyltransferase, *FKBP5 FK506* binding protein 5, *DNMT3B* DNA methyltransferases-3B, *DNMT3L* DNA methyltransferases-3L, *NDN* necdin, melanoma antigen (MAGE) family member, *MAGEL2* MAGE-like 2, *ATP10A* ATPase, class V, type 10A, *TPR* translocated promoter region, *CLEC9A* C-type lectin domain family 9, member A, *APC5* acid phosphatase 5, tartrate resistant, *ANXA2* annexin A2, *TLR8* toll-like receptor 8, *CXCL1* chemokine (C-X-C motif) ligand 1, *MAN2C1* mannosidase, alpha, class 2c, member 1. Adopted with permission of Elsevier. Reprinted from *Frontiers in Psychiatry,* Vol. 4, Zovkic, I. B., Meadows, J. P., Kaas, G. A., & Sweatt, J. D., Interindividual variability in stress susceptibility: A role for epigenetic mechanisms in PTSD, Copyright 2013; with kind permission from the author (J. David Sweatt). [Table 2, Page 14]

Programming

As a risk factor for PTSD, McGowan (2013) explored the possible biological embedding, via gene-altering (silencing) regulatory epigenetic mechanisms, of early adversity into altered HPA axis function. McGowan et al. (2009) had found that suicide completers with a history of child abuse/severe neglect, compared to those without it (and compared to controls), showed higher levels of DNA methylation of the promoter region of the GR gene (*GR1F*), which is involved in HPA function regulation, in a brain area that mediates anxiety and the HPA (i.e., the hippocampus). Labonte et al. (2012) replicated the study. Follow-up research (Suderman et al., 2012) determined that a proto cadherin (*PCDH*) gene cluster of cell-adhesion molecules showed the largest changes in DNA modification within the GR locus. The authors concluded that epigenetic regulation plays a role in programming gene function in response to early life adversity, and might be indexed even by peripheral markers.

Karsten and Baram (2013) posited that neuronal modulation in epigenesis due to early life adversity takes place by early postnatal reprogramming in a "critical window." Early life experiences affect CRH gene expression in the hypothalamus, thereby "rewiring" synaptic connectivity (e.g., reducing excitatory synaptic input onto stress-sensitive neurons). The epigenetic-induced CRH alteration could be life long and might play a role in PTSD.

Applications

Yehuda et al. (2013) found that epigenetic markers could predict symptom amelioration to psychotherapy in American military veterans expressing PTSD. The veterans ($N=16$) received exposure therapy, with half responding and no longer expressing PTSD (as evaluated by the CAPS; Blake et al., 1995). Pre-treatment level of methylation of the GR gene (*NR3C1*) exon 1F in the promoter region predicted treatment outcome, while methylation of the *FKBP5* gene exon 1 promoter region (*FKBP51*) predicted in recovery.

Yehuda et al. (2015) found an epigenetic effect that could differentiate combat veterans with and without PTSD. They examined epigenetic methylation of GR gene promoter 1F (lower *NR3CI*-1F promoter methylation), and the degree was lower in cases of combat PTSD. The methylation was also associated positively with measures of glucocorticoid activity that have been related to combat PTSD and negatively with markers and symptoms of PTSD. The authors concluded that PTSD is associated with enhanced GR sensitivity, and that *NR3CI-1F* promoter methylation could be used as a more sensitive measure of PTSD compared to more downstream endocrine measures.

Conclusion

The construct of epigenesis illustrates the difficulty in treating biology, environment, and organismic factors as isolated in the development of psychopathology. The organism might have allelic variants that are susceptible to environmental silencing via DNA methylation and other processes, which takes place without actually changing the DNA. Moreover, the silencing can be transmitted to subsequent generations. Epigenesis is adaptive in a Darwinian sense in that it facilitates contextual adaptation in the organism experiencing it and also the transmission of the altered genetic activity to offspring, so that the experiences encountered in one generation are stored and passed on to the next, thereby promoting in the offspring a more rapid adaptation to the environment that presumably has the same characteristics that had led to the epigenesis in the first place. The downside of this adaptive process is that offspring might be more susceptible to psychiatric disorder without even experiencing environmental trauma/adversity. Epigenetic stamps might then serve as "biomarkers" of psychiatric disorders, including PTSD. The task is to establish exactly how this works in the case of PTSD and to determine the exact endophenotypic candidate in these regards. For example, epigenetic-mediated changes in brain structure and function (e.g., networks) and in HPA axis reactivity might be associated with greater susceptibility to PTSD and its developmental cascade.

Brain

Introduction

Disease research is moving toward candidate pathway and network levels of analysis beyond the candidate gene approach. The chapter shifts from the genetic/epigenetic bases of PTSD to more downstream portions that might be involved in the endophenotypic pathway. This shift in focus begins with the role of the brain and related factors in PTSD. The conceptual and empirical task that is just beginning and remains extremely daunting is to trace effectively the upstream genetic/epigenetic base of PTSD, the downstream behaviors involved and the mediation between them in brain, neurocircuitry, neuroendocrine function, and so on. In the prior sections of the chapter, the role of the HPA axis, in particular, has been mentioned in this regard, as well as regions of the brain such as the hippocampus and amygdala. Neurocircuitry research does more than simply list the brain regions and their functions involved in PTSD in that it considers pathways, feedback mechanisms, and so on, and it decomposes the functions to steps, such as in learning and extinction.

Imaging

Sherin and Nemeroff (2011) discussed the typical changes in brain structure, circuitry, and function in PTSD found using brain-imaging methods. The regions implicated in PTSD focus on the hippocampus (involved in memory, for example), the amygdala (involved in emotional reactivity), and cortical regions, including the anterior cingulate, insula, and orbitofrontal region (Rauch et al., 2006). Although reduced hippocampal volume might precede the development of PTSD, thereby functioning as a precursor neuroendophenotypic vulnerability (Pitman et al., 2002), in contrast, reduced anterior cingulate cortex volume (ACC, part of the medial prefrontal cortex, mPFC) appears to be a consequence of the development of PTSD (Kasai et al., 2008). The mPFC, in general, is involved in inhibition of reactive stress responses/emotionality and also in the extinction of conditioned fears.

Kolassa et al. (2015) gave a very similar picture of the brain regions involved in the fear network underlying PTSD. They referred to it as the limbic-frontal neurocircuitry.

Neurocircuitry

Nash, Galatzer-Levy, Krystal, Duman, and Neumeister (2014) described the functional neurocircuitry of fear and anxiety. The major afferent pathways involve the "exteroreceptive" sensory systems (auditory, visual, somatosensory). Auditorially and visually, the relevant sensory information is transmitted from peripheral receptor cells to the relay station of the dorsal thalamus (the olfactory and visceral pathways are different). The thalamus relays sensory information to primary cortical sensory receptive regions, which then project to cortical association areas. The latter connect to other brain areas, including the amygdala, entorhinal cortex, orbitofrontal cortex, and cingulate gyrus. The hippocampus is a major relay endpoint, receiving convergent, integrated inputs from all sensory systems. In addition, the thalamus connects to the amygdala both for auditory and visual sensory information. In turn, it interacts neuronally with the orbitofrontal cortex.

As for efferent pathways of the anxiety-fear circuit, it includes the amygdala, locus coeruleus, hypothalamus, periaqueductal gray (PAG), and striatum. The autonomic changes in PTSD are mediated by the sympathetic and parasympathetic nervous systems (e.g., the hypothalamus and its innervations/connections).

The skeletal muscle system is activated in PTSD (e.g., fight, flight) through cortical association areas, the motor cortex, striatum, and amygdala. The amygdala integrates the central nervous system activity in the expression of fear and anxiety. This includes regions associated with sensorimotor, autonomic/endocrine, and affective motivational responses. The brain is integrated in the response, and it involves activity cortically, subcortically, and peripherally, and their interconnections. The mPFC and amygdala form a regulatory connection. Reduction in inhibition of amygdala activity by the PFC has been related to PTSD.

Admon, Milad, and Hendler (2013) developed a causal model of PTSD that disentangled acquired neural abnormalities from predisposing ones. They highlighted that abnormalities within the brain regions of the amygdala (Amy) and the dorsal anterior cingulate cortex (dACC) constitute PTSD pre-exposure vulnerabilities, and that post-exposure consequences of PTSD are found in dysfunctional interactions involving the hippocampus (HC) and ventromedial prefrontal cortex (vmPFC).

The amygdala and dACC appear to be mediators of fear generation and expression (see Fig. 21.2). The areas of the hippocampus and vmPFC involved in PTSD acquisition post-trauma appear to involve the ability to extinguish or inhibit fear. Admon et al. (2013) proposed an interaction of the predisposing and acquired neural abnormalities in PTSD manifestation. The vulnerabilities involved might accentuate one of the three major components of PTSD—the hyperarousal component. In contrast, the acquired dysfunctions might accentuate the re-experiencing and numbing components of PTSD.

Similarly, Johnson et al. (2012) maintained that the amygdala is central to fear conditioning, e.g., in the lateral amygdala during fear acquisition. The latter region projects to the central nucleus of the amygdala. It controls the initiation responses to a stressor including by way of the HPA axis and the locus coeruleus noradrenergic system, in particular. The system includes feedback mechanisms. Context information of fearful situations is

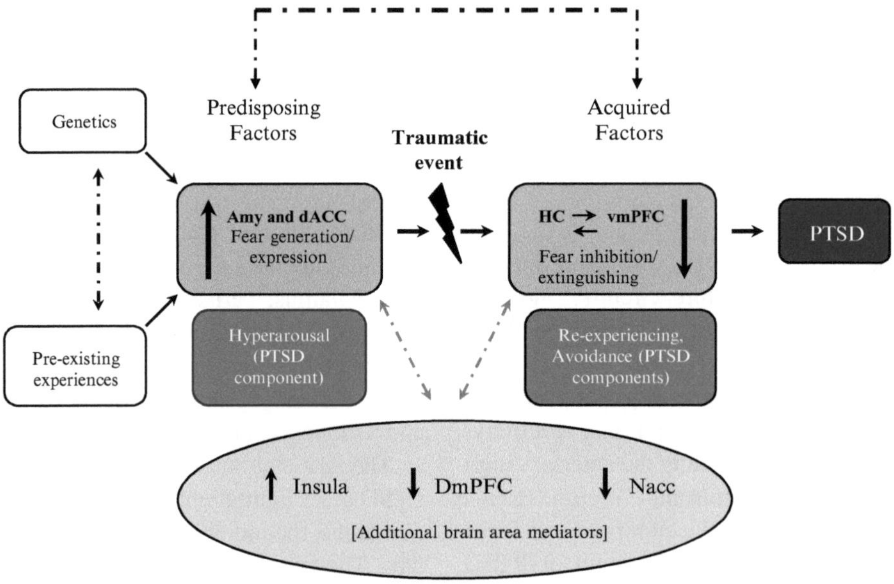

Fig. 21.2 A causal model of influences of neural abnormalities in posttraumatic stress disorder (PTSD): predisposing and acquired factors. The model of neural abnormalities in PTSD includes genetic and environmental factors, as well as their interaction (*broken black line*). The factors might lead some individuals pre-trauma to display abnormal structure/hyperfunction of the amygdala (Amy) and of the dorsal anterior cingulate cortex (dACC). Their predispositions make them susceptible to express heightened fear, expressed as PTSD hyperarousal symptoms. Following the exposure to the traumatic event, a subset of these vulnerable people is prone to acquire additional neural abnormalities in terms of reduced ventromedial prefrontal cortex (vmPFC) volume, and its connectivity with the hippocampus (HC). These acquired abnormalities influence negatively fear inhibition, thereby promoting PTSD symptoms of avoidance and re-experiencing. The described areas of the brain, as well as of their potential interactions (*broken curved line*), could result in all three major DSM IV-TR components of PTSD being expressed. Other brain regions are potential mediators (*broken grey lines*) (nucleus accumbens (Nacc), dorsomedial prefrontal cortex (dmPFC), insula) through their suggested roles in reward processing, emotional regulation, and interoception, respectively. Adopted with permission of Elsevier. Reprinted from *Trends in Cognitive Sciences,* Vol. 17, Admon, R., Milad, M. R., & Hendler, T., A causal model of post-traumatic stress disorder: Disentangling predisposed from acquired neural abnormalities, Copyright 2013; with kind permission from Elsevier. [Figure 4, Page 343]

transmitted to the amygdala by the hippocampus. The medial prefrontal cortex regulates fear expression by projecting to the multiple sites indicated. In fear extinction learning, increased medial prefrontal cortex firing to the basal nucleus stimulates GABAergic intercalated region neurons, to inhibit fear response emanating from the central nucleus.

Networks

Determining brain networks that underscore a behavior involves more than establishing the neurocircuitry involved. For example, in a prior chapter (Chap. 6), McNally et al. (2015) had shown that PTSD symptomology can be mapped for network characteristics, such as centrality. Dysfunctional neural networks have been implicated in PTSD (Bluhm et al., 2009).

Sadeh, Spielberg, Warren, Miller, and Heller (2014) examined neural connectivity during emotional processing in 35 adults, a majority of whom were women, who had experienced a traumatic event, but only a minority of whom (5) met the full criteria for PTSD. Emotional processing was measured on an emotion word Stroop task (pushing buttons on signal to the ink color of words, the different emotional valence of which served as differential distractors). fMRI was used to assess aberrant neural connectivity.

In their study, Sadeh et al. (2014) attempted to identify relationships between the major symptom clusters in PTSD and neural connectivity patterns toward understanding better the "etiological heterogeneity" of PTSD. The study found that PTSD symptom severity served to moderate amygdala-mPFC area coupling (especially for the hyperarousal symptoms of PTSD), during the processing of unpleasant distractor words on the Stroop task (e.g., suicide, war, victim), compared to pleasant (e.g., laughter) and neutral (e.g., carpet) words. Also, the moderation was correlated positively with participant functional impairment (indexed by the DSM-IV Global Assessment of Functioning (GAF) scale) and with amygdala reactivity. Another PTSD cluster showed related results in aberrant neural connectivity—the severity of re-experiencing symptoms moderated hippocampal-insula coupling for Stroop words (pleasant or unpleasant).

Sadeh et al. (2014) concluded that PTSD symptoms differentially moderate functional neural coupling during emotional interference. The neural connectivity patterns may be aberrant in different ways and function as separable indices of dysfunctional inhibitory control during affective processing in PTSD. That overall PTSD severity moderated right amygdala-mPFC coupling is consistent with other research that the right hemisphere is associated with negative emotions or withdrawal (Berntson, Norman, & Cacioppo, 2011; Grimshaw & Carmel, 2014; Harmon-Jones, 2003). In this regard, the authors remarked that PTSD symptom severity can serve as an index of disrupted top-down mPFC regulation of the amygdala. Generally, the results support the cognitive control deficit of PTSD in relation to dysregulation of amygdala by the mPFC.

According to Daniels, Bluhm, and Lanius (2013) the default mode network (DMN; Raichle et al., 2001) appears to be a core network integrating input from other resting networks, such as the one for dorsal attention (Fox, Corbetta, Snyder, Vincent, & Raichle, 2006) and the fronto-parietal control one (Vincent, Kahn, Snyder, Raichle, & Buckner, 2008). The regions that it spans include midline frontal and parietal structures, medial and lateral temporal lobes, the lateral parietal region, the inferior-parietal lobule, and the insula and thalamus. Moreover, the network is active not only just during resting state but also in autobiographical memory recall, theory of mind tasks, and prospection (Spreng, Mar, & Kim, 2009).

According to Daniels et al. (2013), networks of this type might be involved in PTSD. The neural network approach to modeling is appealing for PTSD because it involves networks in interactive dynamics, critical branching, inhibitory control related to volitional action, conflicting habitual response, and override mechanisms that implicate frontal regions, in particular. Also, it has been linked to specific processes involved in mental disorders, and might be a locus in which psychotropic medications have their ameliorative effects. Finally, research might establish that aspects of DMN activity constitute a risk factor in some individuals.

Comment

A candidate neuroendophenotype for PTSD lies in the DMN, which integrates input from other resting networks, such as the ones for dorsal attention and fronto-parietal control. The neural network approach has much to offer the search for PTSD endophenotypes because it is burgeoning and includes cross-region interactive dynamics. However, this simplicity is accompanied by a neuronal mapping complexity that might be difficult to associate with specific genomics, unless regulatory and other top-down allelic variants are found in conjunction with their activity and also with neuronal plasticity due to environmental impacts at different epochs in development.

Neuroendocrine

Nash et al. (2014) reviewed the research on multiple neuroendocrinological and related neurochemical factors in PTSD. They included: prefrontal cortex alpha 2c (PFC α 2c); alpha, noradrenergic (noradrenergic α); dopamine type 1 (*DA1*); serotonin type 2 receptor (*5HT2R*); dehydroepiandrosterone, or its sulfated derivative (*DHEA* (S)); cannabinoid type 1 receptor (*CB1R*); alpha 2c noradrenergic receptor polymorphism (α2cDel1322-325); gamma-aminobutyric acid (GABA); (allo)pregnanolone (ALLO); and neuropeptide Y (NPY).

Rasmusson and Shalev (2014) reviewed neuroendocrinological studies on the role in PTSD of each of catecholamines, serotonin, cortisol, corticotrophin-releasing factor (CRF), NPY, dehydroepiandrostorone, (allo)pregnalolone, and immune factors. They concluded that the study of pathophysiological processes in PTSD could lead to translational therapeutic interventions.

Neuropsychology

Scott et al. (2015) undertook an analysis of the literature with respect to neurocognitive dysfunction in PTSD, involving 60 studies. Their review found moderate effects for verbal learning (i.e., immediate memory), delayed memory, complex speed of information processing, attention/working memory, and verbal memory, in particular, as well as executive function. These results are consistent with a frontal cortex/limbic system circuitry dysregulation in PTSD. However, the analysis could not differentiate whether the neurocognitive deficits related pre-existing factors or post-trauma ones (to the disorder). Nor did most of them include symptom and performance validity testing to check the reliability of the results. Also, they rarely screened using urine toxicology/breathalyzer methods. Nevertheless, the results support a view of PTSD as involving dysregulation of frontolimbic circuitry.

Neurogenesis

Synapses

Nash et al. (2014) also described that, at the synaptic level, plasticity of excitatory glutamatergic mechanisms have been implicated in fear learning, and the mechanisms, particularly, are found in the amygdala and hippocampus. Glutamate receptors are important in this regard (e.g., AMPA, alpha-amino-3-hydroxy-5-methyl-4-isox-azolepropionic acid; and NMDA, *N*-methyl-D-aspartate, and its subtypes, e.g., *GluN2A*, *GluN2B*, the metabotrophic glutamate receptor *mGluR*). Reduced hippocampal polyamine concentrations (SPM, spermine; SPD, spermidine) are the starting point of the chain leading to reduced *mGluR* receptor activity and consequent generalized fear acquisition.

Nash et al. (2014) also described that dissociation in the trauma response might reflect NMDA receptor hypofunction. The endocannabinoid system also might be involved in the pathophysiology in fear extinction of PTSD, and, as well, *BDNF* in neuronal growth and differentiation, or problems therein.

Rasmusson and Shalev (2014) presented an integrated view of neuroendocrinology, neurochemistry, and neuroimmunology of PTSD. Like Nash et al. (2014), they addressed the comorbidities and commonalities with other conditions, such as chronic pain and depression.

Neurogenesis

Research is exploring PTSD endophenotypes not only in brain circuitry, such as involving the hippocampus and prefrontal cortex, but also in the particular neurogenetic processes associated with them. The work could lead to targeted therapies for PTSD.

Kheirbek, Klemenhagen, Sahay, and Hen (2012) reviewed the role of adult hippocampal neurogenesis in relation to PTSD and panic disorder. In their model, pattern completion/separation is modulated by adult neurogenesis in the hippocampus. Under stress, neurogenesis is slowed, leading to poorer event discrimination and overgeneralization, which has consequent emotional effects. The authors concluded that PTSD therapy might target neurogenesis or young neurons in the hippocampus.

Blum et al. (2012) focused their therapeutic proposal for PTSD on natural dopaminergic activation, which is related to the "reward" circuitry and underlying "reward" genes. Hypodominergic function in the brain's reward circuitry is promoted by certain gene polymorphisms, so that dopaminergic intervention affecting gene expression and upregulation via messenger RNA might counteract this deficiency. The authors advocated for a safe product, *KB220Z*, in this regard.

Comment

Adult hippocampal neurogenesis might be a proper neuroendophenotypic candidate in relation to PTSD. Neurons in this area are involved in pattern separation that prepares representations in the hippocampal dentate gyrus. Impairments or deficits in the process might lead to overgeneralization of fear memory, as found in PTSD. Other research has focused on natural dopaminergic activation, which is related to the "reward" circuitry and underlying "reward" genes. The determination of specific and multiple G×E interactions involving neurotransmitters that function in PTSD, as well as others involving neurocircuits and stress-related systems, augurs well for establishing valid PTSD endophenotypes that would help predict either PTSD development or resilience in reaction to traumatic stressors. However, the genome is a complex system itself, and in the field generally G×E interactions are complemented G×G interactions (epistatis), G×E×D (development) ones, and other nuances (e.g., Young, 2011) that render any search for candidate endophenotypes at an integrative genomics level problematic.

HPA Axis

Research

According to Sherin and Nemeroff (2011), the HPA axis constitutes a primary locus of the body's stress-response system. When exposed to stress, the hypothalamus (its paraventricular nucleus, PVN) secretes CRH, which then binds to anterior pituitary cell receptors. This leads to production/release of adrenocorticotropin (ACTH), which is transported to the adrenal gland. In this cascade, cortisol and other adrenal hormones are produced/released. Cortisol acts in pathway (activate the locus coeruleus norepinephrine system, LCNE). Negative feedback results for both the hypothalamus and the pituitary gland, which leads to a lack of moderation of the stress response. Normally, the hippocampus and PFC act to inhibit CRH neurons in the PVN, whereas amygdalar and aminergic brainstem neurons stimulate them. However, in PTSD, the negative feedback is compromised, producing dysregulatory effects.

In PTSD, it appears that the presence of low cortisol levels at the time of the traumatic exposure might predict its development (Yehuda, McFarlane, & Shalev, 1998). The consequence would be to promote abnormal stress reactivity and perhaps abnormalities in general fear processing. According to Sherin and Nemeroff (2011), the catecholamines also constitute potential accurate endophenotypes of PTSD, as do other neurotransmitters/neurochemicals. The changes associated with PTSD in these regards include increased dopamine levels, increased norepinephrine levels, decreased activity levels of the *5HTT* gene involved in serotonin regulation, decreased GABA activity (involved in inhibition), increased glutamate (for activation), and decreased stress-buffering NPY.

Mehta and Binder (2012) concentrated especially on the HPA axis in their model of G×E vulnerability factors in PTSD. They presented a programming-reprogramming-disease model. In the model, genetic susceptibility factors, such as those related to *FKBP5* polymorphisms, especially interact with each other to influence HPA axis reactivity, along with early adversity (e.g., child abuse) and epigenetic modifications. The confluence of these variables sets a baseline, predisposing HPA axis (e.g., in GR supersensitivity) to later exposure to traumatic events (of variable characteristics). In turn, this might lead to HPA axis disease developments, such as PTSD. Moreover, each person might exhibit individual, distinct HPA axis dysregulation and other pathophysiological disturbance in these regards. Higher GR sensitivity/expression in set-point at baseline could be a pre-existing vulnerability, and one that is even set epigenetically in utero (e.g., Yehuda, 2002, 2009).

The authors concluded with more details on their HPA axis reactivity (re)programming model of disease. They emphasized that epigenetic modifications might serve as a mediator of G×E interactions in PTSD development. For example, *FKBP5* might involve alleles conferring an "ultrashort" negative feedback loop on GR activity, as modified epigenetically by early stressors, leading to slower recovery to set-point in cortisol level and also more anxiety symptoms. Prolonged exposure to glucocorticoids (cortisol) thereby would result, which would lead to epigenetic changes in the *FKBP5* locus, and possibly others related to GR-regulation, and so producing cascade effects that facilitate PTSD reactions to trauma.

Comment

Mehta and Binder (2012) have presented an important model of PTSD that integrates many of the factors mentioned in the field. They included HPA axis reactivity, G×E vulnerability, (re)programming, polymorphisms, early adversity (e.g., child abuse), and epigenetic modifications. Their research has shown that G×E interactions involving child abuse and four polymorphisms within the *FKBP5* gene predict adult PTSD symptoms (in African Americans). Other research has examined functional polymorphisms in genes related to serotonin (*5-HTTLPR* on the *SLC6A4* gene). *FKBP5* might involve alleles producing cascade effects that facilitate PTSD reactions to trauma. However, once more, I note that much empirical research is needed on even more complex and integrative models before candidate endophenotypes of PTSD can be determined with rigor. Moreover, the ultimate model of PTSD needs to be a comprehensive biopsychosocial one, which seems implicated in the work of Mehta and Binder (2012), rather than one focused on genes as the starting point toward endophenotypic development in PTSD. The work of this research group is highlighted in the next section of the chapter, as well.

Pathways

Evidence

Mehta et al. (2013) found evidence of distinct, nonoverlapping, biological profiles in PTSD for patients who had experienced childhood maltreatment compared to non-abused patients. Controls had trauma history without any PTSD. The specific biological measure involved epigenetic DNA methylation in peripheral immune-system related blood cells, and the gene expression in the CNS (central nervous system) involved mostly pertained to the prefrontal cortex. The results indicated that different trajectories and outcomes pathophysiologically might accompany PTSD, depending on childhood abuse history. The gene-expression changes were associated with and probably mediated by changes in epigenetic processes, suggesting that the differential profiles for abuse and non-abuse participants include differential epigenetic marks in those with traumatic history, and these marks confer lifelong susceptibility to disease.

Pietrzak,, Feder, Singh, et al. (2014) followed World Trade Center surviving responders over 8 years. Police relative to non-traditional responders demonstrated four PTSD trajectories: resistant/resilient, recovering, delayed onset, and chronic. Aside from these four profiles, the latter chronic group also showed a split in degree of chronicity (moderate, severe) and a "subsyndromal increasing" profile. The groups varied in percentages within each pathway, as well. Further, predictors of PTSD included: prior psychiatric history; Hispanic ethnicity; trauma exposure severity; and trauma incident medical conditions. Protective factors included education and support (family, work). The authors concluded that the limited amount of PTSD trajectories that they found is consistent with other research (Bonanno et al., 2012; Bowler et al., 2010; Hobfoll, Mancini, Hall, Canetti, & Bonanno, 2011).

Gerson and Rappaport (2013) presented evidence for critical developmental windows for impact of traumatic stress at the neurobiological level. They referred to an interaction of risk/resilience, vulnerability, and trauma factors in childhood affecting developmental trajectory. From infancy onward, moments of "burst" of myelination, synapse formation, pruning, and neural networking are susceptible to disruption by stress hormones. For example, cortisol can lead to suppression of glial cell division, dendritic branching, synaptogenesis, and neuronal loss. The effects are compounded by corollary epigenesis (e.g., Heim, Shugart, Craighead, & Nemeroff, 2010). Brain regions affected might include multiple ones involved in stress and trauma mediation (e.g., hippocampus, amygdala, cerebral cortex). Each is related to different symptoms in trauma outcomes. Vulnerabilities include genetic differences (Jovanovic & Ressler, 2010). Sex and age differences play a role in the vulnerabilities. Finally, the lasting effects of these neurobiological impacts early in life include later physical health effects (Yehuda, 2002).

Gong et al. (2014) used structural magnetic resonance imaging (sMRI) in earthquake trauma survivors who were with and without PTSD to determine whether the groups could be distinguished at a case level. They found that those expressing PTSD were discriminated by a highly spatially-distributed neural network involving prefrontal, temporal, parietal, and occipital grey matter regions as well as subcortical structure. The evidence suggested that post-event neuroplastic changes were involved, rather than pre-existing differences, in causing the group differences, making the technique potentially useful forensically.

Comment

Research is showing that different trajectories and outcomes pathophysiologically might accompany PTSD, depending on childhood abuse history, and the research is also revealing that epigenetic marks due to traumatic history appear involved, serving to augment disease susceptibility. Trajectories include not only a resilience course but also different degrees of PTSD severity, with differential predictors involved. The research is also focusing on differential neural networks in those who express PTSD to traumatic stressors relative to those who do not. For example, Gong et al. (2014) found a neural network in such cases among earthquake survivors involving prefrontal, temporal, parietal, and occipital grey matter regions as well as subcortical structure. Pathway analysis might prove more effective in establishing individual differences in PTSD development, relative to the static approach of using DSM-5 symptom criteria. Although neural networks represent the best central candidate of PTSD endophenotype, much work remains to establish which and how many networks are involved, and their variations over groups, such as differences across ages, in the sexes, over cultures and racial groupings, in SES (socioeconomic status), and so on. Only when the massive amount of research is undertaken at this level can we begin to query how to address neuronal network profile and trajectory differences in individual cases. To carry that research enterprise one step further into the realm of forensics, in which the candidate endophenotype so derived can add incremental validity to other measures in assessments, or even replace (some of) them, remains a daunting and long-term task.

Allostasis

Research

Zhou et al. (2014) found that PTSD is associated with dysregulation in microribonucleic acid (miR) expression. The PTSD was expressed in military veterans; also, healthy controls were tested. The PTSD patients had increased pro-inflammatory Th1 and Th17 cytokine cells and decreased regulatory T cells (Tregs). Pathway analysis suggested immunological changes. The authors concluded that the results may help lead to identification of biomarkers of PTSD.

Juster et al. (2011) expanded the allostatic load model (AL; McEwen & Stellar, 1993; Sterling & Eyer, 1988) to psychopathology across the lifespan. According to the allostatic load model, the three factors that are involved in stress (biopsychosocial) work in synergy.

The antecedents of AL model include: (a) early adversity; (b) genetic factors; (c) epigenetic factors; (d) environmental toxins; and (e) interactions among biological and sociocultural factors. Together, these factors contribute probabilistically to health outcomes (not deterministically; Cicchetti & Toth, 2009). Disease develops in allostatic overload, which takes place after system over-activation and also nonlinear dynamical interactive imbalances, leading to the breaking point (McEwen, 1998).

Juster et al. (2011) explicated in depth how allostatic overload contributes to developmental and long-term psychopathology. The model was developed for populations but works for the individual level, too. Similarly, I have maintained that chronic stress is the factor that is common to psychological injuries (Young, 2008a) and that somatization is a multifactorial process that can begin early in life (Young, 2008b). Ganzel and Morris (2011) also extended the AL model to development. For example, the changes in any one period reflect particular stress responses and allostatic processes unique to the period and stressors involved, leading to distinct long-term consequences for health for the associated periods, stressors, and contexts implicated.

Comment

Allostatic overload refers to the overtaxing of the "wear and tear" process experienced by the organism, and it is associated with disease in conditions of chronic stress and the dysregulation of the stress system. The allostatic overload system is a developmental and nonlinear one, in which pathophysiological processes related to disease reflect cumulative system activity but not in a one-to-one reductionistic manner. Disease can emerge in a self-organized and inflationary fashion relative to any stressor, including in PTSD, depending on prior vulnerabilities and history, as well as on the system organization (and its stability and disequilibrium forces at play) at the time of the experiencing of a traumatic stressor. The dynamical nature in the instigation, exacerbation, and maintenance of PTSD in this regard needs to be considered in the task of searching for optimal endophenotypic candidates.

Five Factor Model

Research

The research by Pietrzak, Galea et al. (2013) is indicating new directions in understanding the PTSD endophenotype. Pietrzak, Galea et al. (2013) examined 149 participants in a representative sample of adults who had experienced Hurricane Ike in 2008. The participants were given an interview 2–5 months after the disaster. They were divided into low exposure and high exposure groups according to a summary index based on nine questions; as well, PTSD was assessed with the PCL (The PTSD Checklist; Weathers, Litz, Herman, Huska, & Keane, 1993) and with additional questions. The PCL is keyed to the DSM-IV-TR symptom list. The 17 items of the list as measured on the PCL were subject to Confirmatory Factor Analysis (CFA).

The results supported Elhai et al.'s (2011) five-factor model. In this model, relative to the DSM-IV-TR, avoidance is split into symptoms for avoidance and numbing, and hyperarousal is split into symptoms of dysphoric arousal and anxious arousal. The results showed good-to-excellent reliability for each of the five clusters in terms of Cronbach's alpha ($\alpha = 0.96$).

Pietrzak, Galea et al. (2013) related the *5-HTTLPR* genotype to their results. They found that respondents having the low-expression allele variant (at least one short, *s*, allele) of the *5-HTTLPR* polymorphism, relative to those homozygous for the long (*l*) allele, reported greater PTSD severity, but only if they had been highly exposed to the hurricane. Also, they reported a higher incidence of screening for

PTSD. In terms of the five-factor structure for PTSD, this *5-HTTLPR s* allele genotype × trauma exposure interaction was significant for two of the five clusters—anxious arousal and re-experiencing.

The *5-HTTLPR s* allele has been associated with greater amygdala hyperactivity and reduced coupling of the amygdala-cingulate neurocircuitry (respectively, Hariri et al., 2002; Pezawas et al., 2005). The allele is also associated with attentional vigilance toward negatively-valenced stimuli and difficulty in disengaging from negative stimuli (respectively, Pergamin-Hight, Bakermans-Kranenburg, van IJzendoorn, & Bar-Haim, 2012; Beevers, Wells, Ellis, & McGeary, 2009). These findings help explain the psychological mechanisms behind the mentioned allele × trauma interaction. Finally, Pietrzak, Galea et al. (2013) concluded that the nature of results support the validity of the five-factor model of PTSD (in particular, the separation of anxious arousal and dysphoric arousal.) [For another genetic study in relation to PTSD by the Pietrzak research group, see Pietrzak, Henry, Southwick, Krystal, & Neumeister, 2013.]

Horn, Pietrzak, Corsi-Travali, and Neumeister (2014) noted that there has been a dozen CFA studies on a broad range of sample types that have confirmed the five-factor model as better fitting compared to the DSM-IV-TR and alternative four-factor models (Armour, Carragher, & Elhai, 2013; Pietrzak, Tsai, Harpaz-Rotem, Whealin, & Southwick, 2012).

Horn et al. (2014) conducted a study linking morning plasma cortisol levels to severity of emotional numbing in this five-factor model. They studied drug-free civilian adults having PTSD and the controls of trauma-exposed adults and non-trauma-exposed healthy individuals.

Horn et al. (2014) concluded that basal cortisol does not constitute a biomarker of PTSD in the sense that it did not distinguish trauma survivors with and without PTSD. Nevertheless, its association with emotional numbing suggests that it mediates a key symptom cluster among the five in the new five-factor model of PTSD—that of emotional numbing/restricted affect.

Pietrzak, Feder, Schechter, et al. (2014) investigated the symptom cluster structure in PTSD among World Trade Center 9/11 responders in a longitudinal study spanning 8 years. They used CFA and auto-regressive cross-lagged panel regressions to show that neither the DSM-IV three-dimensional structure (avoidance, hyperarousal, re-experiencing) nor the DSM-5 four-dimensional structure (avoidance split into numbing, as well, aside from other symptoms added), nor another commonly found four-factor model (some hypervigilance symptoms added to the numbing ones, with the factor called dysphoria; Simms, Watson, & Doebbeling, 2002) fit the dimensional structure of PTSD symptoms as effectively as a five-factor model (Elhai & Palmieri, 2011). In the latter, hyperarousal is split into two components—anxious arousal (e.g., exaggerated startle) and dysphoric arousal (e.g., sleep disturbance, concentration difficulties). The authors concluded that the former type of arousal appears to drive, over time, re-experiencing, and the latter appears to drive emotional numbing symptoms.

Comment

The research on a new five-factor model of PTSD constitutes one of the most important developments toward understanding PTSD and its (neuro)endophenotypic intermediaries in the pathways to its development. Young, Lareau, and Pierre (2014) provided a table summarizing how the 17 PTSD symptoms in the DSM-IV-TR are split into the five factors; see Table 21.2.

The value of the five-factor PTSD model for better understanding the pathway from polygenic contributions to phenotypic expression and the individual differences therein in PTSD also is indicated by its efforts to determine which one of the five factors stands out as a core one in PTSD, but the answers to the question vary.

Chapter Conclusions

This chapter on PTSD undertakes a comprehensive review of the recent literature in the areas of endophenotypes, neurogenetics, epigenetics, neural networks, HPA axis, neuronal networks,

Table 21.2 Item mappings of DSM-IV-TR and structural models of PTSD symptom clusters

DSM-IV-TR PTSD symptom	Item mappings		
	DSM-IV-TR	Elhai et al. (2011)	Pietrzak, Galea et al. (2013) Factor loadings
B1. Intrusive thoughts of trauma	R	R	.849
B2. Recurrent dreams of trauma	R	R	.718
B3. Flashbacks	R	R	.693
B4. Emotional reactivity to trauma cues	R	R	.803
B5. Physiological reactivity to trauma cues	R	R	.844
C1. Avoiding thoughts of trauma	A	A	.867
C2. Avoiding reminders of trauma	A	A	.917
C3. Inability to recall aspects of trauma	A	N	.674
C4. Loss of interest	A	N	.782
C5. Detachment	A	N	.824
C6. Restricted affect	A	N	.810
C7. Sense of foreshortened future	A	N	.719
D1. Sleep disturbance	H	DA	.853
D2. Irritability	H	DA	.745
D3. Difficulty concentrating	H	DA	.854
D4. Hypervigilance	H	AA	.825
D5. Exaggerated startle response	H	AA	.833

Adopted with permission of Springer Science+Business Media. Young, G., Lareau, C., & Pierre, B. (2014). One quintillion ways to have PTSD comorbidity: Recommendations for the disordered DSM-5. *Psychological Injury and Law, 7*, 61–74; with kind permission from Springer Science+Business Media B. V. [Table 1, Page 67]

pathways, the five-factor and related PTSD models (the DSM-5 moved from a three-factor model to a four-factor model), and allostasis; then, it returns to the topic of endophenotypes. Neuronal networks constitute one integrating area that could help in arriving at an appropriate model of PTSD endophenotype. Pathway analysis provides a rich field for discerning individual differences in PTSD development, more so than the static approach of using DSM-5 symptom criteria lists. Finally, about implications for the DSM-5, for practice, and for court—it would be premature to seek individual biomarkers of PTSD, given the current state of knowledge in the field, even if it is burgeoning.

References

Admon, R., Milad, M. R., & Hendler, T. (2013). A causal model of post-traumatic stress disorder: Disentangling predisposed from acquired neural abnormalities. *Trends in Cognitive Sciences, 17*, 337–347.

American Psychiatric Association. (1994). *Diagnostic and statistical manual of mental disorders* (4th ed.). Washington, DC: Author.

American Psychiatric Association. (2000). *Diagnostic and statistical manual of mental disorders: DSM-IV-TR* (4th ed., text rev.). Washington, DC: Author.

Amstadter, A. B., Koenen, K. C., Ruggiero, K. J., Acierno, R., Galea, S., Kilpatrick, D. G., et al. (2009). Variant in RGS2 moderates posttraumatic stress symptoms following potentially traumatic event exposure. *Journal of Anxiety Disorders, 23*, 369–373.

Amstadter, A. B., Sumner, J. A., Acierno, R., Ruggiero, K. J., Koenen, K. C., Kilpatrick, D. G., et al. (2013). Support for association of RORA variant and post traumatic stress symptoms in a population-based study of hurricane exposed adults. *Molecular Psychiatry, 18*, 1148–1149.

Armour, C., Carragher, N., & Elhai, J. D. (2013). Assessing the fit of the dysphoric arousal model across two nationally representative epidemiological surveys: The Australian NSMHWB and the United States NESARC. *Journal of Anxiety Disorders, 27*, 109–115.

Baker, D. G., Nievergelt, C. M., & O'Connor, D. T. (2012). Biomarkers of PTSD: Neuropeptides and immune signaling. *Neuropharmacology, 62*, 663–673.

Beevers, C. G., Wells, T. T., Ellis, A. J., & McGeary, J. E. (2009). Association of the serotonin transporter gene promoter region (5-HTTLPR) polymorphism with biased attention for emotional stimuli. *Journal of Abnormal Psychology, 118*, 670–681.

Berntsen, D., & Rubin, D. C. (2014). Involuntary memories and dissociative amnesia: Assessing key assumptions in posttraumatic stress disorder research. *Clinical Psychological Science, 2*, 174–186.

Berntson, G. G., Norman, G. J., & Cacioppo, J. T. (2011). Laterality and evaluation bivalence: A neuroevolutionary perspective. *Emotion Review, 3*, 344–346.

Binder, E. B., Bradley, R. G., Liu, W., Epstein, M. P., Deveau, T. C., Mercer, K. B., et al. (2008). Association of FKBP5 polymorphisms and childhood abuse with risk of posttraumatic stress disorder symptoms in adults. *Journal of the American Medical Association, 299*, 1291–1305.

Blake, D. D., Weathers, F. W., Nagy, L. M., Kaloupek, D. G., Gusman, F. D., Charney, D. S., et al. (1995). The development of a clinician-administered PTSD scale. *Journal of Traumatic Stress, 8*, 75–90.

Bluhm, R. L., Williamson, P. C., Osuch, E. A., Frewen, P. A., Stevens, T. K., Boksman, K., et al. (2009). Alterations in default network connectivity in posttraumatic stress disorder related to early-life trauma. *Journal of Psychiatry & Neuroscience, 34*, 187–194.

Blum, K., Giordano, J., Oscar-Berman, M., Bowirrat, A., Simpatico, T., & Barh, D. (2012). Diagnosis and healing in veterans suspected of suffering from posttraumatic stress disorder (PTSD) using reward gene testing and reward circuitry natural dopaminergic activation. *Journal of Genetic Syndrome & Gene Therapy, 3*, 1000116. doi:10.4172/2157-7412.1000116.

Bonanno, G. A., Mancini, A. D., Horton, J. L., Powell, T. M., Leardmann, C. A., Boyko, E. J., et al. (2012). Trajectories of trauma symptoms and resilience in deployed U.S. military service members: Perspective cohort study. *British Journal of Psychiatry, 200*, 317–323.

Boscarino, J., Erlich, P. M., Hoffman, S. N., & Zhang, X. (2012). Higher FKBP5, COMT, CHRNA5, and CRHR1 allele burdens are associated with PTSD and interact with trauma exposure: Implications for neuropsychiatric research and treatment. *Neuropsychiatric Disease and Treatment, 8*, 131–139.

Boulle, F., Van Den Hove, D. L., Jakob, S. B., Rutten, B. P., Hamon, M., Van Os, J., et al. (2012). Epigenetic regulation of the BDNF gene: Implications for psychiatric disorders. *Molecular Psychiatry, 17*, 584–596.

Bowler, R. M., Han, H., Gocheva, V., Nakagawa, S., Alper, H., DiGrande, L., et al. (2010). Gender differences in probable posttraumatic stress disorder among police responders to the 2001 World Trade Center terrorist attack. *American Journal of Industrial Medicine, 53*, 1186–1196.

Bramsen, I., Dirkzwager, A. J., & van der Ploeg, H. M. (2000). Predeployment personality traits and exposure to trauma as predictor of posttraumatic stress symptoms: A prospective study of former peacekeepers. *American Journal of Psychiatry, 157*, 1115–1119.

Brewin, C. R. (2008). What is it that a neurobiological model of PTSD must explain? *Progress in Brain Research, 167*, 217–228.

Brewin, C. R. (2011). The nature and significance of memory disturbance in posttraumatic stress disorder. *Annual Review of Clinical Psychology, 7*, 203–227.

Brewin, C. R., Gregory, J. D., Lipton, M., & Burgess, N. (2010). Intrusive images in psychological disorders: Characteristics, neural mechanisms, and treatment implications. *Psychological Review, 117*, 210–232.

Catarino, A., Küpper, C. S., Werner-Seidler, A., Dalgleish, T., & Anderson, M. C. (2015). Failing to forget: Inhibitory-control deficits compromise memory suppression in posttraumatic stress disorder. *Psychological Science, 26*, 604–616.

Chang, S.-C., Koenen, K. C., Galea, S., Aiello, A. E., Soliven, R., Wildman, D. E., et al. (2012). Molecular variation at the SLC6A3 locus predicts lifetime risk of PTSD in the Detroit Neighborhood Health Study. *PLoS One, 7*, e39184.

Cicchetti, D., & Toth, S. L. (2009). The past achievements and future promises of developmental psychopathology: The coming of age of a discipline. *Journal of Child Psychology and Psychiatry, 50*, 16–25.

Cornelis, M. C., Nugent, N. R., Amstadter, A. B., & Koenen, K. C. (2010). Genetics of post-traumatic stress disorder: Review and recommendations for genome-wide association studies. *Current Psychiatry Reports, 12*, 313–326.

Daniels, J. K., Bluhm, R. L., & Lanius, R. A. (2013). Intrinsic network abnormalities in posttraumatic stress disorder: Research directions for the next decade. *Psychological Trauma: Theory, Research, Practice, and Policy, 5*, 142–148.

de Quervain, D. J.-F., Kolassa, I.-T., Ertl, V., Onyut, P. L., Neuner, F., Elbert, T., et al. (2007). A deletion variant of the alpha2b-adrenoceptor is related to emotional memory in Europeans and Africans. *Nature Neuroscience, 10*, 1137–1139.

Dias, B. G., & Ressler, K. J. (2013). PACAP and the PACI receptor in post-traumatic stress disorder. *Neuropsychopharmacology, 38*, 245–246.

Dohrenwend, B. P., Turner, J. B., Turse, N. A., Adams, B. G., Koenen, K. C., & Marshall, R. (2006). The psychological risks of Vietnam for U.S. veterans: A revisit with new data and methods. *Science, 313*, 979–982.

Dudley, K. J., Li, X., Kobor, M. S., Kippin, T. E., & Bredy, T. W. (2011). Epigenetic mechanisms mediating vulnerability and resilience to psychiatric disorders. *Neuroscience and Biobehavioral Review, 35*, 1544–1551.

Ehlers, A., & Clark, D. M. (2000). A cognitive model of posttraumatic stress disorder. *Behaviour Research and Therapy, 38*, 319–345.

Ehring, T., Ehlers, A., & Glucksman, E. (2008). Do cognitive models help in predicting the severity of posttraumatic stress disorder, phobia, and depression after motor vehicle accidents?: A prospective longitudinal study. *Journal of Consulting and Clinical Psychology, 76*, 219–230.

Elhai, J. D., Biehn, T. L., Armour, C., Klopper, J. J., Frueh, B. C., & Palmieri, P. A. (2011). Evidence for a unique PTSD construct represented by PTSD's D1-D3 symptoms. *Journal of Anxiety Disorders, 25*, 340–345.

Elhai, J. D., & Palmieri, P. A. (2011). The factor structure of posttraumatic stress disorder: A literature update, critique of methodology, and agenda for future research. *Journal of Anxiety Disorders, 25*, 849–854.

Fox, M. D., Corbetta, M., Snyder, A. Z., Vincent, J. L., & Raichle, M. E. (2006). Spontaneous neuronal activity distinguishes human dorsal and ventral attention systems. *The National Academy of Sciences, 103*, 10046–10051.

Friedman, M. J., & Resick, P. A. (2014). DSM-5 criteria for PTSD. In M. J. Friedman, T. M. Keane, & P. A. Resick (Eds.), *Handbook of PTSD: Science and practice* (2nd ed., pp. 21–37). New York: Guilford Press.

Friedman, M. J., Resick, P. A., & Keane, T. M. (2014). PTSD from DSM-III to DSM-5: Progress and challenges. In M. J. Friedman, T. M. Keane, & P. A. Resick (Eds.), *Handbook of PTSD: Science and practice* (2nd ed., pp. 3–20). New York: Guilford Press.

Ganzel, B. L., & Morris, P. A. (2011). Allostasis and the developing human brain: Explicit consideration of implicit models. *Development and Psychopathology, 23*, 955–974.

Gerson, R., & Rappaport, N. (2013). Traumatic stress and posttraumatic stress disorders in youth: Recent research findings on clinical impact, assessment, and treatment. *Journal of Adolescent Health, 52*, 137–143.

Gillihan, S. J., Cahill, S. P., & Foa, E. B. (2014). Psychological theories of PTSD. In M. J. Friedman, T. M. Keane, & P. A. Resick (Eds.), *Handbook of PTSD: Science and practice* (2nd ed., pp. 166–184). New York: Guilford Press.

Gong, Q., Li, L., Tognin, S., Wu, Q., Pettersson-Yeo, W., Lui, S., et al. (2014). Using structural neuroanatomy to identify trauma survivors with and without posttraumatic stress disorder at the individual level. *Psychological Medicine, 44*, 195–203.

Gottesman, I. I., & Gould, T. D. (2003). The endophenotype concept in psychiatry: Etymology and strategic intentions. *American Journal of Psychiatry, 160*, 636–645.

Gottesman, I. I., & Shields, J. (1972). *Schizophrenia and genetics: A twin study vantage point*. New York: Academic.

Gottesman, I. I., & Shields, J. (1973). Genetic theorizing and schizophrenia. *British Journal of Psychiatry, 122*, 15–30.

Grabe, H. J., Spitzer, C., Schwahn, C., Marcinek, A., Frahnow, A., Barnow, S., et al. (2009). Serotonin transporter gene (*SLC6A4*) promoter polymorphisms and the susceptibility to posttraumatic stress disorder in general population. *American Journal of Psychiatry, 166*, 926–933.

Grimshaw, G. M., & Carmel, D. (2014). An asymmetric inhibition model of hemispheric differences in emotional processing. *Frontiers in Psychology, 5*, 489. doi:10.3389/fpsyg.2014.00489.

Hariri, A. R., Mattay, V. S., Tessitore, A., Kolachana, B., Fera, F., Goldman, D., et al. (2002). Serotonin transporter genetic variation and the response of the human amygdala. *Science, 297*, 400–403.

Harmon-Jones, E. (2003). Clarifying the emotive functions of asymmetrical frontal cortical activity. *Psychophysiology, 40*, 838–848.

Heim, C., Shugart, M., Craighead, W. E., & Nemeroff, C. B. (2010). Neurobiological and psychiatric consequences of child abuse and neglect. *Developmental Psychobiology, 52*, 671–690.

Hobfoll, S. E., Mancini, A. D., Hall, B. J., Canetti, D., & Bonanno, G. A. (2011). The limits of resilience: Distress following chronic political violence among Palestinians. *Social Science and Medicine, 72*, 1400–1408.

Horn, C. A. C., Pietrzak, R. H., Corsi-Travali, S., & Neumeister, A. (2014). Linking plasma cortisol levels to phenotypic heterogeneity of posttraumatic stress symptomatology. *Psychoneuroendocrinology, 39*, 88–93.

Johnson, L. R., McGuire, J., Lazarus, R., & Palmer, A. A. (2012). Pavlovian fear memory circuits and phenotype models of PTSD. *Neuropharmacology, 62*, 638–646.

Jovanovic, T., & Ressler, K. J. (2010). How the neurocircuitry and genetics of fear inhibition may inform our understanding of PTSD. *American Journal of Psychiatry, 167*, 648–662.

Juster, R.-P., Bizik, G., Picard, M., Arsenault-Lapierre, G., Sindi, S., Trepanier, L., et al. (2011). A transdisciplinary perspective of chronic stress in relation to psychopathology throughout life span development. *Development and Psychopathology, 23*, 725–776.

Karsten, C. A., & Baram, T. Z. (2013). How does a neuron "know" to modulate its epigenetic machinery in response to early-life environment/experience? *Frontiers in Psychiatry, 4*, 89. doi:10.3389/fpsyt.2013.00089.

Kasai, K., Yamasue, H., Gilbertson, M. W., Shenton, M. E., Rauch, S. L., & Pitman, R. K. (2008). Evidence for acquired pregenual anterior cingulate gray matter loss from a twin study of combat-related posttraumatic stress disorder. *Biological Psychiatry, 63*, 550–556.

Keane, T. M., & Barlow, D. H. (2002). Posttraumatic stress disorder. In D. H. Barlow (Ed.), *Anxiety and its disorders* (2nd ed., pp. 418–453). New York: Guilford Press.

Kessler, R. C., Sonnega, A., Bromet, E., Hughes, M., & Nelson, C. B. (1995). Posttraumatic stress disorder in the National Comorbidity Survey. *Archives of General Psychiatry, 52*, 1048–1060.

Kheirbek, M. A., Klemenhagen, C., Sahay, A., & Hen, R. (2012). Neurogenesis and generalization: A new approach to stratify and treat anxiety disorders. *Nature Neuroscience, 15*, 1613–1620.

Kilpatrick, D. G., Koenen, K. C., Ruggiero, K. J., Acierno, R., Galea, S., Resnick, H. S., et al. (2007). The serotonin transporter genotype and social support and moderation of posttraumatic stress disorder and depression in hurricane-exposed adults. *American Journal of Psychiatry, 164*, 1693–1699.

Klengel, T., Mehta, D., Anacker, C., Rex-Haffner, M., Pruessner, J. C., Pariante, C. M., et al. (2013). Allele-specific *FKBP5* DNA demethylation mediates gene-childhood trauma interactions. *Nature Neuroscience, 16*, 33–44.

Koenen, K. C., Aiello, A. E., Bakshis, E., Amstadter, A. B., Ruggiero, K. J., Acierno, R., et al. (2009). Modification of the association between serotonin transporter genotype and risk of posttraumatic stress disorder in adults by county-level social environment. *American Journal of Epidemiology, 169*, 704–711.

Koenen, K. C., Fu, Q. J., Ertel, K., Lyons, M. J., Eisen, S. A., True, W., et al. (2008). Common genetic liability to major depression and posttraumatic stress disorder in men. *Journal of Affective Disorders, 105*, 109–115.

Koenen, K. C., Guffanti, G., Yan, L., Haloossim, M., Uddin, M., Nugent, N. R., et al. (2014). Genetics of PTSD. In M. J. Friedman, T. M. Keane, & P. A. Resick (Eds.), *Handbook of PTSD: Science and practice* (2nd ed., pp. 300–312). New York: Guilford Press.

Koenen, K. C., Uddin, M., Chang, S.-C., Aiello, A. E., Wildman, D. E., Goldmann, E., et al. (2011). *SLC6A4* methylation modifies the effect of the number of traumatic events on risk for posttraumatic stress disorder. *Depression and Anxiety, 28*, 639–647.

Kolassa, I.-T., & Elbert, T. (2007). Structural and functional neuroplasticity in relation to traumatic stress. *Current Directions in Psychological Science, 16*, 321–325.

Kolassa, I.-T., Ertl, V., Eckart, C., Glöckner, F., Kolassa, S., Papassotiropoulos, A., et al. (2010). Association study of trauma load and SLC6A4 promoter polymorphism in posttraumatic stress disorder: Evidence from survivors of the Rwandan genocide. *Journal of Clinical Psychiatry, 71*, 543–547.

Kolassa, I.-T., Illek, S., Wilker, S., Karabatsiakis, A., & Elbert, T. (2015). Neurobiological findings in posttraumatic stress disorder. In U. Schnyder & M. Cloitre (Eds.), *Evidence based treatments for trauma-related psychological disorders: A practical guide for clinicians* (pp. 63–86). New York: Springer Science + Business Media.

Kolassa, I.-T., Kolassa, S., Ertl, V., Papassotiropoulos, A., & de Quervain, D. J. (2010). The risk of posttraumatic stress disorder after trauma depends on traumatic load and the catechol-o-methyltransferase Val(158)Met polymorphism. *Biological Psychiatry, 67*, 304–308.

Kubany, E. S., Haynes, S. N., Leisen, M. B., Owens, J. A., Kaplan, A. S., Watson, S. B., et al. (2000). Development and preliminary validation of a brief broad-spectrum measure of traumatic exposure: The Traumatic Life Events Questionnaire. *Psychological Assessment, 12*, 210–224.

Labonte, B., Yerko, V., Gross, J., Mechawar, N., Meaney, M. J., Szyf, M., et al. (2012). Differential glucocorticoid receptor exon 1(B), 1(C), and 1 (H) expression and methylation in suicide completers with a history of childhood abuse. *Biological Psychiatry, 72*, 41–48.

Logue, M. W., Baldwin, C., Guffanti, G., Melista, E., Wolf, E. J., Reardon, A. F., et al. (2012). A genome-wide association study of post-traumatic stress disorder identifies the retinoid-related orphan reception alpha (RORA) gene as a significant risk locus. *Molecular Psychiatry, 18*, 937–942.

Lonsdorf, T. B., Weike, A. I., Nikamo, P., Schalling, M., Hamm, A. O., & Ohman, A. (2009). Genetic gating of human fear learning and extinction: Possible implications for gene-environment interaction in anxiety disorder. *Psychological Science, 20*, 198–206.

Maddox, S. A., Schafe, G. E., & Ressler, K. J. (2013). Exploring epigenetic regulation of fear memory and biomarkers associated with post-traumatic stress disorder. *Frontiers in Psychiatry, 4*, 62. doi:10.3389/fpsyt.2013.00062.

Maercker, A., Brewin, C. R., Bryant, R. A., Cloitre, M., Reed, G. M., van Ommeren, M., et al. (2013). Proposals for mental disorders specifically associated with stress in the International Classification of Diseases-11. *The Lancet, 381*, 1683–1685.

Mahan, A. L., & Ressler, K. J. (2012). Fear conditioning, synaptic plasticity and the amygdala: Implications for posttraumatic stress disorder. *Trends in Neurosciences, 35*, 24–35.

McEwen, B. S. (1998). Stress, adaptation, and disease: Allostasis and allostatic load. *Annals of the New York Academy of Sciences, 840*, 33–44.

McEwen, B. S., & Stellar, E. (1993). Stress and the individual. Mechanisms leading to disease. *Archives of Internal Medicine, 153*, 2093–2101.

McGowan, P. O. (2013). Epigenomic mechanisms of early adversity and HPA dysfunction: Considerations for PTSD research. *Frontiers in Psychiatry, 4*, 110. doi:10.3389/fpsyt.2013.00110.

McGowan, P. O., Sasaki, A., D'Alessio, A. C., Dymov, S., Labonté, B., Szyf, M., et al. (2009). Epigenetic regulation of the glucocorticoid receptor in human brain associates with childhood abuse. *Nature Neuroscience, 12*, 342–348.

McNally, R. J., Robinaugh, D. J., Wu, G. W. Y., Wang, L., Deserno, M. K., & Borsboom, D. (2015). Mental disorders as causal systems: A network approach to posttraumatic stress disorder. *Clinical Psychological Science, 3*, 836–849.

Meaney, M. J., & Szyf, M. (2005). Maternal care as a model for experience-dependent chromatin plasticity? *Trends in Neurosciences, 28*, 456–463.

Mehta, D., & Binder, E. B. (2012). Gene × environment vulnerability factors for PTSD: The HPA-axis. *Neuropharmacology, 62*, 654–662.

Mehta, D., Gonik, M., Klengel, T., Rex-Haffner, M., Menke, A., Rubel, J., et al. (2011). Using polymorphisms in FKBP5 to define biologically distinct subtypes of posttraumatic stress disorder: Evidence from endocrine and gene expression studies. *Archives of General Psychiatry, 68*, 901–910.

Mehta, D., Klengel, T., Conneely, K. N., Smith, A. K., Altmann, A., Pace, T. W., et al. (2013). Childhood maltreatment is associated with distinct genomic and epigenetic profiles in posttraumatic stress disorder. *Proceedings of the National Academy of Sciences, USA, 110*, 8302–8307.

Mercer, K. B., Orchutt, H. K., Quinn, J. F., Fitzgerald, C. A., Conneely, K. N., Barfield, R. T., et al. (2012). Acute and posttraumatic stress symptoms in a prospective gene × environment study of a university campus shooting. *Archives of General Psychiatry, 69*, 89–97.

Murrough, J. W., Huang, Y., Hu, J., Henry, S., Williams, W., Gallezot, J.-D., et al. (2011). Reduced amygdala serotonin transporter binding in posttraumatic stress disorder. *Biological Psychiatry, 70*, 1033–1038.

Nadel, L., Hupbach, A., Gomez, R., & Newman-Smith, K. (2012). Memory formation, consolidation and transformation. *Neuroscience and Biobehavioral Reviews, 36*, 1640–1645.

Naim, R., Wald, I., Lior, A., Pine, D. S., Fox, N. A., Sheppes, G., et al. (2014). Perturbed threat monitoring following a traumatic event predicts risk for posttraumatic stress disorder. *Psychological Medicine, 44*, 2077–2084.

Nash, M., Galatzer-Levy, I., Krystal, J. H., Duman, R., & Neumeister, A. (2014). Neurocircuitry and neuroplasticity in PTSD. In M. J. Friedman, T. M. Keane, & P. A. Resick (Eds.), *Handbook of PTSD: Science and practice* (2nd ed., pp. 251–274). New York: Guilford Press.

Nijdam, M. J., & Wittmann, L. (2015). Psychological and social theories of PTSD. In U. Schnyder & M. Cloitre (Eds.), *Evidence based treatments for trauma-related psychological disorders: A practical guide for clinicians* (pp. 41–61). New York: Springer Science + Business Media.

Norrholm, S. D., Jovanovic, T., Smith, A. K., Binder, E., Klengel, T., Conneely, K., et al. (2013). Differential genetic and epigenetic regulation of catechol-O-methyltransferase is associated with impaired fear inhibition in posttraumatic stress disorder. *Frontiers in Behavioral Neuroscience, 7*, 30. doi:10.3389/fnbeh.2013.00030.

Norris, F. H., & Slone, L. B. (2014). Epidemiology of trauma and PTSD. In M. J. Friedman, T. M. Keane, & P. A. Resick (Eds.), *Handbook of PTSD: Science and practice* (2nd ed., pp. 100–120). New York: Guilford Press.

Novak, M. A., Hamel, A. F., Kelly, B. J., Dettmer, A. M., & Meyer, J. S. (2013). Stress, the HPA axis, and non-human primate well-being: A review. *Applied Animal Behaviour Science, 143*, 135–149.

Ouellet-Morin, I., Wong, C. C., Danesee, A., Pariante, C. M., Papadopoulos, A. S., Mill, J., et al. (2012). Increased serotonin transporter gene (SERT) DNA methylation is associated with bullying victimization and blunted cortisol response to stress in childhood: A longitudinal study of discordant monozygotic twins. *Psychological Medicine, 10*, 1–11.

Pergamin-Hight, L., Bakermans-Kranenburg, M. J., van IJzendoorn, M. H., & Bar-Haim, Y. (2012). Variations in the promoter region of the serotonin transporter gene and biased attention for emotional information: A meta-analysis. *Biological Psychiatry, 71*, 373–379.

Perroud, N., Paoloni-Giacobino, A., Prada, P., Olie, E., Salzmann, A., Nicastro, R., et al. (2011). Increased methylation of glucocorticoid receptor gene (NR3C1) in adults with a history of childhood maltreatment: A link with the severity and type of trauma. *Translational Psychiatry, 1*, e59. doi:10.1038/tp.2011.60.

Pezawas, L., Meyer-Lidenberg, A., Drabant, E. M., Verchinski, B. A., Munoz, K. E., Kolachana, B. S., et al. (2005). 5-HTTLPR polymorphism impacts human cingulate-amygdala interactions: A genetic susceptibility mechanism for depression. *Natural Neuroscience, 8*, 828–834.

Pietrzak, R. H., Feder, A., Schechter, C. B., Singh, R., Cancelmo, L., Bromet, E. J., et al. (2014). Dimensional structure and course of post-traumatic stress symptomatology in World Trade Center responders. *Psychological Medicine, 44*, 2085–2098.

Pietrzak, R. H., Feder, A., Singh, R., Schechter, C. B., Bromet, E. J., Katz, C. L., et al. (2014). Trajectories of PTSD risk and resilience in World Trade Center responders: An 8-year prospective cohort study. *Psychological Medicine, 44*, 205–219.

Pietrzak, R. H., Galea, S., Southwick, S. M., & Gelernter, J. (2013). Examining the relation between the serotonin transporter 5-HTTPLR genotype × trauma exposure interaction on a contemporary phenotypic model of posttraumatic stress symptomatology: A pilot study. *Journal of Affective Disorders, 148*, 123–128.

Pietrzak, R. H., Henry, S., Southwick, S. M., Krystal, J. H., & Neumeister, A. (2013). Linking in vivo brain serotonin type 1B receptor density to phenotypic heterogeneity of posttraumatic stress symptomatology. *Molecular Psychiatry, 18*, 399–401.

Pietrzak, R. H., Tsai, J., Harpaz-Rotem, I., Whealin, J. M., & Southwick, S. M. (2012). Support for a novel five-factor model posttraumatic stress symptoms in three independent samples of Iraq/Afghanistan veterans: A confirmatory factor analytic study. *Journal of Psychiatric Research, 46*, 317–322.

Pitman, R. K., Rasmusson, A. M., Koenen, K. C., Shin, L. M., Orr, S. P., Gilbertson, M. W., et al. (2012). Biological studies of posttraumatic stress disorder. *Nature Reviews Neuroscience, 13*, 769–787.

Pitman, R. K., Sanders, K. M., Zusman, R. M., Healy, A. R., Cheema, F., Lasko, N. B., et al. (2002). Pilot study of secondary prevention of posttraumatic stress disorder with propranolol. *Biological Psychiatry, 51*, 189–192.

Ptak, C., & Petronis, A. (2010). Epigenetic approaches to psychiatric disorders. *Dialogues in Clinical Neuroscience, 12*, 25–35.

Raabe, F. J., & Spengler, D. (2013). Epigenetic risk factors in PTSD and depression. *Frontiers in Psychiatry, 4*, 80. doi:10.3389/fpsyt.2013.00080.

Raichle, M. E., MacLeod, A. M., Snyder, A. Z., Powers, W. J., Gusnard, D. A., & Shulman, G. L. (2001). A default mode of brain function. *Proceedings of the National Academy of Sciences, USA, 98*, 676–682.

Rakofsky, J. J., Ressler, K. J., & Dunlop, B. W. (2012). BDNF function as a potential mediator of bipolar disorder and post-traumatic stress disorder comorbidity. *Molecular Psychiatry, 17*, 22–35.

Rasmusson, A. M., & Shalev, A. Y. (2014). Integrating the neuroendocrinology, neurochemistry, and neuroimmunology of PTSD to date and the challenges ahead. In M. J. Friedman, T. M. Keane, & P. A. Resick (Eds.), *Handbook of PTSD: Science and practice* (2nd ed., pp. 275–299). New York: Guilford Press.

Rauch, S. L., Shin, L. M., & Phelps, E. A. (2006). Neurocircuitry models of posttraumatic stress disorder and extinction: Human neuroimaging research—Past, present, and future. *Biological Psychiatry, 60*, 376–382.

Ressler, K. J., Mercer, K. B., Bradley, B., Jovanovic, T., Mahan, A., Kerley, K., et al. (2011). Post-traumatic stress disorder is associated with PACAP and the PAC1 receptor. *Nature, 470*, 492–497.

Ricon, T., Toth, E., Leshem, M., Braun, K., & Richter-Levin, G. (2012). Unpredictable chronic stress in juvenile or adult rats has opposite effects, respectively, promoting and impairing resilience. *Stress, 15*, 11–20.

Rodrigues, S. M., LeDoux, J. E., & Sapolsky, R. M. (2009). The influence of stress hormones on fear circuitry. *Annual Review of Neuroscience, 32*, 289–313.

Rusiecki, J. A., Chen, L., Srikantan, V., Zhang, L., Yan, L., Polin, M. L., et al. (2012). DNA methylation in repetitive elements and post-traumatic stress disorder: A case–control study of US military service members. *Epigenomics, 4*, 29–40.

Russo, S. J., Murrough, J. W., Han, M. H., Charney, D. S., & Nestler, E. J. (2012). Neurobiology of resilience. *Nature Neuroscience, 15*, 1475–1484.

Sadeh, N., Spielberg, J. M., Warren, S. L., Miller, G. A., & Heller, W. (2014). Aberrant neural connectivity during emotional processing associated with posttraumatic stress. *Clinical Psychological Science, 2*, 748–755.

Sartor, C. E., McCutcheon, V. V., Pommer, N. E., Nelson, E. C., Grant, J. D., Duncan, A. E., et al. (2011). Common genetic and environmental contributions to post-traumatic stress disorder and alcohol dependence in young women. *Psychological Medicine, 41*, 1497–1505.

Schnyder, U., & Cloitre, M. (2015). *Evidence based treatment for trauma-related psychological disorders: A practical guide for clinicians*. New York: Springer Science+Business Media.

Scott, J. C., Matt, G. E., Wrocklage, K. M., Crnich, C., Jordan, J., Southwick, S. M., et al. (2015). A quantitative meta-analysis of neurocognitive functioning in posttraumatic stress disorder. *Psychological Bulletin, 141*, 105–140.

Seckl, J. R., & Meaney, M. J. (2006). Glucocorticoid "programming" and PTSD risk. *Annals of the New York Academy of Sciences, 1071*, 351–378.

Segman, R., Shalev, A. Y., & Gelernter, J. (2007). Gene-environment interactions: Twin studies and gene research in the context of PTSD. In M. J. Friedman, T. M. Keane, & P. A. Resick (Eds.), *Handbook of PTSD: Science and Practice* (pp. 190–206). New York: Guilford Press.

Sherin, J. E., & Nemeroff, C. B. (2011). Post-traumatic stress disorder: The neurobiological impact of psychological trauma. *Dialogues in Clinical Neuroscience, 13*, 263–278.

Simms, L. J., Watson, D., & Doebbeling, B. N. (2002). Confirmatory factor analyses of posttraumatic stress symptoms in deployed and nondeployed veterans of the gulf war. *Journal of Abnormal Psychology, 111*, 637–647.

Sipahi, L., Wildman, D. E., Aiello, A. E., Koenen, K. C., Galea, S., Abbas, A., et al. (2014). Longitudinal epigenetic variation of DNA methyltransferases genes is associated with vulnerability to post-traumatic stress disorder. *Psychological Medicine, 44*, 3165–3179.

Skelton, K., Ressler, K. J., Norrholm, S. D., Jovanovic, T., & Bradley-Davino, B. (2012). PTSD and gene variants: New pathways and new thinking. *Neuropharmacology, 62*, 628–637.

Smith, A. K., Conneely, K. N., Kilaru, V., Mercer, K. B., Weiss, T. E., Bradley, B., et al. (2011). Differential immune system DNA methylation and cytokine regulation in post-traumatic stress disorder. *American Journal of Medical Genetics Part B: Neuropsychiatric Genetics, 156B*, 700–708.

Solovieff, N., Roberts, A. L., Ratanatharathorn, A., Haloosim, M., De Vivo, I., King, A., et al. (2014). Genetic association analysis of post-traumatic stress disorder in over 300 genes among trauma-exposed women from the Nurses' Health Study II. *Neuropsychopharmacology, 39*, 1872–1879.

Spreng, R. N., Mar, R. A., & Kim, A. S. (2009). The common neural basis of autobiographical memory, prospection, navigation, theory of mind, and the default mode: A quantitative meta-analysis. *Journal of Cognitive Neuroscience, 21*, 489–510.

Stein, M. B., Jang, K. L., Taylor, S., Vernon, P. A., & Livesley, W. J. (2002). Genetic and environmental influences on trauma exposure and posttraumatic stress disorder symptoms: A twin study. *American Journal of Psychiatry, 159*, 1675–1681.

Sterling, P., & Eyer, J. (1988). Allostasis: A new paradigm to explain arousal pathology. In S. Fisher & J. Reason (Eds.), *Handbook of life stress, cognition and health* (pp. 629–649). New York: Wiley.

Suderman, M., McGowan, P. O., Sasaki, A., Huang, T. C. T., Hallett, M., Meaney, M. J., et al. (2012). Conserved epigenetic sensitivity to early life experience in the rat and human hippocampus. *Proceedings of the National Academy of Science, USA, 109*, 17266–17272.

Sundermann, O., Hauschildt, M., & Ehlers, A. (2013). Perceptual processing during trauma, priming and the development of intrusive memories. *Journal of Behavior Therapy and Experimental Psychiatry, 44*, 213–220.

Sundermann, O., Onwumere, J., Bebbington, P., & Kuipers, E. (2012). Social networks and support in early psychosis: Potential mechanisms. *Epidemiology and Psychiatric Sciences, 22*, 147–150.

Szyf, M. (2013). How do environments talk to genes? *Nature Neuroscience, 16*, 2–4.

Uddin, M., Aiello, A. E., Wildman, D. E., Koenen, K. C., Pawelec, G., de Los Santos, R. et al., (2010). Epigenetic and immune function profiles associated with posttraumatic stress disorder. *Proceedings of the National Academy of Sciences, USA, 107*, 9470–9475.

Uddin, M., Galea, S., Chang, S. C., Aiello, A. E., Wildman, D. E., de los Santos, R., et al. (2011). Gene expression and methylation signatures of MAN2C1 are associated with PTSD. *Disease Markers, 30*, 111–121.

Vincent, J. L., Kahn, I., Snyder, A. Z., Raichle, M. E., & Buckner, R. L. (2008). Evidence for a frontoparietal control system revealed by intrinsic functional connectivity. *Journal of Neurophysiology, 100*, 3328–3342.

Vogt, D. S., King, D. W., & King, L. A. (2014). Risk pathways for PTSD: Making sense of the literature. In M. J. Friedman, T. M. Keane, & P. A. Resick (Eds.), *Handbook of PTSD: Science and practice* (2nd ed., pp. 146–165). New York: Guilford Press.

Weathers, F., Litz, B., Herman, D., Huska, J., & Keane, T. (1993). *The PTSD checklist (PLC): Reliability, validity, and diagnostic utility. Paper presented at a meeting of the International Society of Traumatic Stress Studies*, San Antonio, TX.

Weaver, I. C. (2007). Epigenetic programming by maternal behavior and pharmacological intervention. Nature versus nurture: Let's call the whole thing off. *Epigenetics, 2*, 22–28.

Wilker, S., & Kolassa, I.-T. (2013). The formation of a neural fear network in posttraumatic stress disorder: Insights from molecular genetics. *Clinical Psychological Science, 1*, 452–469.

Wu, G., Feder, A., Cohen, H., Kim, J. J., Calderon, S., Charney, D. S., et al. (2013). Understanding resilience. *Frontiers in Behavioral Neuroscience, 7*, 10. doi:10.3389/fnbeh.2013.00010.

Xie, P., Kranzler, H. R., Farrer, L., & Gelernter, J. (2012). Serotonin transporter 5-HTTLPR genotype moderates the effects of childhood adversity on posttraumatic stress disorder risk: A replication study. *American Journal of Medical Genetics Part B: Neuropsychiatric Genetics, 159*, 644–652.

Xie, P., Kranzler, H. R., Poling, J., Stein, M. B., Anton, R. F., Brady, K., et al. (2009). Interactive effect of stressful life events and the serotonin transporter 5-HTTLPR genotype on posttraumatic stress disorder diagnosis in 2 independent populations. *Archives of General Psychiatry, 66*, 1201–1209.

Xie, P., Kranzler, H. R., Poling, J., Stein, M. B., Anton, R. F., Farrer, L. A., et al. (2010). Interaction of FKBP5 with childhood adversity on risk for post-traumatic stress disorder. *Neuropsychopharmacology, 35*, 1684–1692.

Xie, P., Kranzler, H. R., Yang, C., Zhao, H., Farrer, L. A., & Gelernter, J. (2013). Genome-wide association study identifies new susceptibility loci for posttraumatic stress disorder. *Biological Psychiatry, 74*, 656–663.

Yehuda, R. (2002). Post-traumatic stress disorder. *The New England Journal of Medicine, 346*, 108–114.

Yehuda, R. (2009). Status of glucocorticoid alterations in post-traumatic stress disorder. *Annals of the New York Academy of Sciences, 1179*, 56–69.

Yehuda, R., Bierer, L. M., Sarapas, C., Makotkine, I., Andrew, R., & Seckl, J. R. (2009). Cortisol metabolic predictors of response to psychotherapy for symptoms of PTSD in survivors of the World Trade Center attacks on September 11, 2001. *Psychoneuroendocrinology, 34*, 1304–1313.

Yehuda, R., Daskalakis, N. P., Desarnaud, F., Makotkine, L., Lehrner, A. L., Koch, E., et al. (2013). Epigenetic biomarkers as predictors and correlates of symptom improvement following psychotherapy in combat veterans with PTSD. *Frontiers in Psychiatry, 4*, 118. doi:10.3389/fpsyt.2013.00118.

Yehuda, R., Flory, J. D., Bierer, L. M., Henn-Haase, C., Lehrner, A., Desarnaud, F., et al. (2015). Lower methylation of glucocorticoid receptor gene promoter 1F in peripheral blood of veterans with posttraumatic stress disorder. *Biological Psychiatry, 77*, 356–364.

Yehuda, R., Flory, J. D., Pratchell, L. C., Buxbaum, J., Ising, M., & Holsboer, F. (2010). Putative biological mechanisms for the association between early life adversity and the subsequent development of PTSD. *Psychopharmacology, 212*, 405–417.

Yehuda, R., Halligan, S. L., & Bierer, L. M. (2002). Cortisol levels in adult offspring of Holocaust survivors: Relation to PTSD symptom severity in the parent and child. *Psychoneuroendocrinology, 27*, 171–180.

Yehuda, R., & LeDoux, J. (2007). Response variation following trauma: A translational neuroscience approach to understanding PTSD. *Neuron, 56*, 19–32.

Yehuda, R., McFarlane, A. C., & Shalev, A. Y. (1998). Predicting the development of posttraumatic stress disorder from the acute response to a traumatic event. *Biological Psychiatry, 44*, 1305–1313.

Young, G. (2008a). Causality and causation in law, medicine, psychiatry, and psychology: Progression or regression? *Psychological Injury and Law, 1*, 161–181.

Young, G. (2008b). Psychological injury and law: An integrative model. *Psychological Injury and Law, 1*, 150–160.

Young, G. (2011). *Development and causality: Neo-Piagetian perspectives*. New York: Springer Science + Business Media.

Young, G. (2014). *Malingering, feigning, and response bias in psychiatric/psychological injury: Implications for practice and court*. Dordrecht, Netherlands: Springer Science + Business Media.

Young, G., Lareau, C., & Pierre, B. (2014). One quintillion ways to have PTSD comorbidity: Recommendations for the disordered DSM-5. *Psychological Injury and Law, 7*, 61–74.

Zhou, J., Nagarkatti, P., Zhong, Y., Ginsberg, J. P., Singh, N. P., Zhang, J., et al. (2014). Dysregulation in microRNA expression is associated with alterations in immune functions in combat veterans with posttraumatic stress disorder. *PLoS One, 9*, e94075.

Zovkic, I. B., Guzman-Karlsson, M. C., & Sweatt, J. D. (2013). Epigenetic regulation of memory formation and maintenance. *Learning & Memory, 20*, 61–74.

Zovkic, I. B., Meadows, J. P., Kaas, G. A., & Sweatt, J. D. (2013). Interindividual variability in stress susceptibility: A role for epigenetic mechanisms in PTSD. *Frontiers in Psychiatry, 4*, 60. doi:10.3389/fpsyt.2013.00060.

DSM-5: Basics and Critics

22

Chapter Introduction

The present chapter is part of a series of chapters that addresses the newest-version of the American psychiatric diagnostic manual, the DSM-5 (Diagnostic and Statistical Manual of Mental Disorder, Fifth Edition; American Psychiatric Association, 2013a, 2013b). The approach of the present work is multiple but, primarily, it takes a scientific approach to understanding both the positive contributions and negative pitfalls found in the DSM-5. (a) In this regard, the chapter begins with an overview of the DSM-5. What are its major changes relative to the DSM-IV-TR (Diagnostic and Statistical Manual of Mental Disorders, Fourth Edition, Text Revision; American Psychiatric Association, 2000)? Is the DSM-5 reliable and valid? (b) Then, voice is given to its multiple critics. Is it clinically useful? I avoid the surface criticisms and hyperbolic rhetoric found in the public media and press. (c) The next two chapters after this one analyze carefully several of the major diagnostic categories in the DSM-5, especially those concerning the area of psychological injury and law (e.g., tort cases involving Posttraumatic Stress Disorder (PTSD), chronic pain, and Traumatic Brain Injury, TBI). The second of the chapters includes discussion of the RDoC (Research Domain Criteria) project, which will help in the revision of the DSM-5, but it, itself, is not without its critics. (d) Finally, in the last chapter of the four on the DSM-5, I examine more general issues, such as etiology in psychiatric disorder and the recommendations that I make for revising the DSM. Practitioners from multiple disciplines will find the present work on the DSM-5 quite informative, whether clinicians, forensic workers, or otherwise and, indeed, so will any stakeholder interested in the DSM-5.

The present chapter specifically adds to the field by emphasizing the need for a biopsychosocial approach for the DSMs. Also, it suggests a new definition to mental disorder. Finally, it suggests that one outcome of dealing with the DSM-5 might be DSM-5 Confusion Disorder!

Introduction

The DSMs constitute a series of psychiatric manuals developed by the American Psychiatric Association (APA) that is used throughout the world for mental illness diagnosis. The fifth edition was released in May 2013, and it is called The Diagnostic and Statistical Manual of Mental Disorder, Fifth Edition (DSM-5; American Psychiatric Association, 2013a). The DSMs usually are published with a series of auxiliary books, and some of these are in development for the DSM-5. The present work highlights the central difficulties in the literature on the DSM-5 and also analyzes some crucial disorders.

G. Young, *Unifying Causality and Psychology*, DOI 10.1007/978-3-319-24094-7_22

The DSM-5 was published after rancorous criticism of the procedures used in developing it, the draft versions, and the final product, with equally vigorous defense at all these levels. A useful psychiatric diagnostic manual should reflect practitioner utility requirements and also scientific reliability and validity requirements. However, on both these grounds, the DSM-5 has been attacked. Moreover, unlike the case for the working groups for the prior version, the DSM-IV (Diagnostic and Statistical Manual of Mental Disorders, Fourth Edition; American Psychiatric Association, 1994; DSM-IV-TR, Text Revised; American Psychiatric Association, 2000), the procedure in constructing the manual was not open and there were accusations of conflicts of interest, for instance, with pharmaceutical companies. Finally, in a point important for the present work, the manual has been criticized for its lack of careful vetting for forensic purposes. This illustrates that much of the criticisms of the DSM-5 involve process as much as product, or how the APA and the DSM editors and working groups proceeded in this present iteration of the manual.

The direction and tenor of the criticisms of the contents of the DSM-5 include not only general criticisms about process and procedure but also specific criticisms about disorders, such as the following. Some of the new categories proposed might not have been carefully thought through, while others were kept intact, and might reflect the same. Some categories lower the bar in diagnosing disorder, while others raise it. Children appear unduly targeted, with a purported ease in diagnosing some disorders and the consequent specter that is raised of overmedicating them.

Only careful analysis of the contents of the DSM-5 (generally; in addition to the categories) and of the literature in the field in psychopathology and its etiology can determine the degree of difficulties contained in the manual and the direction needed in future iterations. Therefore, the goal of the first part of the present section of the present work on the DSM-5 (that is, the present chapter) is to adopt this careful scientific approach in analyzing the validity and value of the DSM-5. In the second portion of the present work on the DSM-5, which consists of the two middle chapters of the four in the series on it, I analyze in depth disorders that are central to the area of psychological injury and law. Two disorders in the DSM-5 of special concern to forensic psychologists (e.g., in disability and related evaluations) are PTSD (posttraumatic stress disorder) and pain disorder. The changes instituted for these two categories will be reviewed carefully and the implications of the changes will be discussed, for example, for what the changes mean for PTSD tests and for what they mean in giving a diagnosis that makes sense for pain patients. Another category of concern is neurocognitive disorder, e.g., in TBI (traumatic brain injury). The changes in it will be discussed, as well.

In the last chapter of the present four-chapter series on the DSM-5, I describe some recent research on psychopathology and nosology (e.g., systems, endophenotypes) that go beyond even the contention that the DSM should be more dimensional than categorical. Then, I move to recommendations for the field, which focus on the appropriate models to use and the broader assessment process, rather than on specific diagnoses and on diagnosing, per se. The DSM should become a manual under constant scrutiny and revision according to state-of-the-art science in the field. To conclude this last chapter in the present book on the DSM-5, for court use, I contend that some of the changes in the DSM-5 could open psychologists to criticisms by both plaintiff and defense attorneys, and even arbitrators/judges. The best manner in hedging these criticisms is to adopt a functional approach in evaluations, in particular, and not to rely especially on specific diagnostic labels as primary factors in conclusions to reports or testimony, which should be the normative approach, in general, in good practice in the field.

Goals

Although the aim of the DSM-5 (and psychiatry, in general) is to associate specific etiologies with each disorder, it is well-known that knowledge of causal factors of psychiatric disorders is limited. Even when causal factors are specified in the

DSM-5 manual for a disorder, the literature supporting these types of statements is not cited (and no sourcebooks are planned, unlike the case of the DSM-IV).

According to its critics, in terms of problems with categories of disorder in the DSM-5, they lack (a) the reliability and validity needed for efficacious use of diagnostic categories; (b) and, therefore, their utility to clinicians is compromised. (c) In addition, they lack grounding in clear etiology; (d) they are not really distinct entities "carved at the joints"; (e) and, therefore, unlike the case for various medical diseases, they are not amenable to efficacious treatment (read: psychopharmacological medication). To conclude, the aspirational goals of the DSM-5 are laudable, but it has yet to achieve them in a consistent way for many of its disorders (Frances, 2013a; Paris, 2013a).

Assumptions

Science and Utility

The fundamental assumptions governing the direction needed with respect to the DSM-5, specifically, and psychiatry, generally, are that a scientifically-informed approach should underlie every step in creation of a psychiatric diagnostic manual and also its use in the clinical context. This will help ensure that the manual is constructed ethically and also used ethically. A subtext is that these manuals are important in the forensic context so that care needs to be taken in these regards both in its construction and use.

Note that by scientifically-informed, I do not mean that the manual must be only or must be especially a research document. Rather, it means that (a) its conceptual basis is scientifically adequate; (b) the research it uses and cites clearly supports both the manual's conceptual or assumptional base and the specific disorders formulated (in terms of constructs and also empirical findings); and (c) also, it means that its users adopt a scientific approach, in terms of both: (1) scrutiny of the literature, so that they arrive at their own opinions on past literature, and revise them as new literature appears and (2) in using the scientific method or reasoning in patient assessment strategies and also in diagnostic hypothesis formation and attribution.

Psychiatric manuals work best in the clinical context when they adopt, to the degree possible, a research approach and also that they respect the clinical needs of practitioners. An approach such as this can help ensure that psychiatric manuals respect the research and scientific process and, also, are responsive to feedback from clinicians on what works for them, which should always be from an informed scientific perspective, as described.

Developers of psychiatric manuals should be open to changing the scientific roots and scientific integrity of their manuals, partly because scientific content changes so rapidly. Similarly, clinicians should be open to scientific learning, for example, through educational workshops and literature review articles for practitioners.

In the end, a balance is needed in the construction of psychiatric manuals in terms of clinical usefulness and research basis. Additionally, as they are revised, balance is needed in research input and clinical input.

Etiology

Wakefield (2013) noted that most diagnostic categories in the DSM do not express "construct validity," which he defined as each disorder representing one condition and having a "distinctive etiology." Instead, he noted that the DSM-5 categories are only "syndromes" and, moreover, they "encompass" multiple etiologies. Ideally, psychiatric disorders should have a specific cause (etiology) and specific pathway to illness (pathogenesis; Paris, 2013a). I would add that any category found to be unreliable and not valid, by definition, cannot represent genuine disorders and, therefore, cannot have "distinct" etiologies.

Given that the starting point of conceptualizing psychiatric diagnostic categories begins with having a clear etiological source for each, the present work reviews recent concepts and research in the field of psychopathology related to causality. It raises issues about the standard medical or psychiatric model of mental disorder, and suggests ways that psychiatric manual might evolve, for example, with hybrid models of distinct diagnostic categories and dimensional constructs of mental health framed from an etiological perspective and the biopsychosocial approach.

Biopsychosocial

Of all the assumptions underpinning the present work on the DSM-5, the one most essential is that psychopathology is best considered from the point of view of the biopsychosocial model or its equivalent. The definition of mental disorder in the DSM-IV-TR and the DSM-5 does not mention this term, nor do their introductory materials.

Nevertheless, it is partially implicit in the DSM approach to mental disorder and its diagnosis, despite the origins of the psychiatric profession in the more biological medical model and in the psychoanalytic model. In the present work, I call for the explicit recognition of the biopsychosocial model or its equivalent as a keystone for psychiatry in understanding etiology, classification, and intervention/treatment (also see McEwen & Getz, 2013).

Part of the reason the DSM enterprise should endorse the biopsychosocial approach is the systems perspective that it offers in understanding psychiatric illness. Another reason is that it suggests a full range of intervention and treatment options, and not just those overly focused on psychopharmacology. Granted, the DSM-5 advises to be aware of indiscriminate prescription of medication and the availability of nonmedicinal intervention/treatment options. But if the DSM openly adopts a biopsychosocial model, patients will be afforded the full range of psychiatric and psychological help that might prove beneficial to them.

It is worth noting my understanding of the role of the biological component in the biopsychosocial formulation of mental illness. On the one hand, biological causation or expression in mental disorder does not have to be found in every case. Any one case might be purely psychosocial in origin and demanding of psychosocial treatments only. However, as a precaution, it is acknowledged that appropriate screening of medical condition should take place in every psychiatric clinical presentation. Moreover, even if not causally pertinent, biological factors still could be at play in any case, for example, worry leading to anxious bodily reactions. Conversely, psychosocial factors might positively affect the dysfunctional biological status of any individual diagnosed with mental disorder.

Another important consideration essential to the present work is its emphasis on multifactorial causality. This approach constitutes an extension of the biopsychosocial model. For example, some of the refined concepts emerging in psychiatric causation include genome-wide association studies (GWAS), Gene × Environment interactions (G × E), gene–environment correlations (rGE), epigenetics, (neuro)endophenotypes, neural circuitry and intrinsic neural networks, differential environmental susceptibility/biological context, prenatal programming, and developmental plasticity. These concepts are not necessarily uniquely genetic or biological, and most of them ascribe at least some role for the environment in psychiatric mental health.

The approach that I have described on the importance of the biopsychosocial model for psychiatry would appear to stand in contrast to the work of Kendler (2012). However, our approaches are quite similar. Kendler (2012) rejected the dualist framework that has governed understanding of the mind/brain system. He argued for a multiple etiological approach involving causal risk factors ("difference makers"), which can range from the genetic and the biological to the psychosocial. However, he maintained that the biopsychosocial approach itself is not critical enough and does not guide sufficiently well the research in psychiatry. Nevertheless, I maintain that it provides a useful heuristic for juxtaposing the more restricted and standard medical model and also psychiatric models with the more open and pluralistic, broader typical psychological approach. Moreover, in its contemporary systemic guises (e.g., nonlinear dynamical system theory, Young,

2011), by definition, the biopsychosocial model does not reflect just an addition of biological, psychological, and social influences on behavior and its psychopathology. This is the case because it gives direction on how the factors interact, how symptoms reflect that interaction, and how treatment should consider the interaction.

In this regard, Kendler supports the equivalent of biopsychosocial formulations for the understanding of psychiatric illness (e.g., Kendler, 2008). Kendler's (2012) approach to etiology of psychiatric illness is strikingly advanced. He attempted to find "causal signatures" for three archetypal psychiatric disorders—schizophrenia, major depression, and alcohol dependence. He considered three superordinate categories of causal risks—biological, psychological, and "higher-order." Biological risks included molecular genetic, molecular neuroscientific, systems neuroscientific, aggregate genetic, and miscellaneous risks. The psychological risks included neuropsychological, personality/cognitive/attitudinal, and trauma exposure risks. The higher-order risks were social, political, and cultural. For each of the three disorders mentioned, he reviewed the empirical research for each of the causal risk factors.

He found interesting results in his review. First, the risks for the disorders included all three major domains (biological, psychological, and higher-order). Also, there was no evidence of duality (separability) in risk, in terms of either genetic/biological or psychosocial factors. Second, aggregate genetic effects made the largest contributions to the causality of the disorders. Third, there were different patterns of risk in the three disorders, with schizophrenia being the most biological, major depression being the most psychological, and alcohol dependence being the most sociocultural.

He noted that despite the separation of the three major domains for purposes of the analysis, they really interact and mediate and moderate each other's effects. They are actively intertwined with each other in multilevel, complex causal webs or etiological pathways, and so the disorders are multifactorial in the causal landscape. He rejected the reductionist argument that the psychological and social can be reduced to brain mechanisms, citing examples with respect to his own research (e.g., the importance of psychological factors, such as meaning, in the recovery of women exposed to severe sexual abuse).

Kendler (2012) concluded that because psychiatric disorders derive from multiple etiological processes, classificatory systems based on etiological considerations are "deeply problematic." I would add that in classificatory systems that are categorical or disorder-based, diagnoses will always have their place. Therefore, their etiological bases should be elucidated to the degree possible, or else this approach to classification will suffer. We should not throw out the baby with the bathwater, that is, we should still attempt to ascertain and use etiological sources of valid diagnostic psychiatric systems. However, to what degree can we find them?

Given this overview of fundamental assumptions guiding the present work, we are ready to explore in detail the DSM-5. After presenting relevant explanatory material, the DSM-5 considers the thorny issue of the definition of a mental disorder. Before considering it, however, I address the preliminary material in the manual.

The DSM in Detail

Preface

Relative to the DSM-IV-TR, the DSM-5 added a preface in which the stated goal in the first sentence is to arrive at reliable diagnosis of disorders. However, it acknowledges in the third sentence that full elucidation of the "underlying pathological processes" is not yet available for most mental disorders. The contrast in these two sentences at the beginning of the DSM-5 illustrates the dominant tension in the field of psychiatric, mental health classification—between research and etiology and the need for a clinically-useful classificatory system.

The preface proceeds to describe the DSM-5 as a "practical, functional, and flexible guide." However, then it suggests that it is also an "official nomenclature." This opposition indicates another tension in the field—the manual and its disorders function like a "bible" in psychiatry, given its official stamp of the APA yet, at the other extreme, it appears as a mixture of disorders and criteria fabricated in committee that lacks reliability. Considering that the reality of the DSM-5 lies somewhere between these poles, it should be used with caution and care.

Next, the preface lists the different "orientations" to which the manual could be useful. These include workers using the biological, psychodynamic, cognitive, behavioral, interpersonal, and family/systems approaches. As for the type of workers, mental health care practitioners who will find it useful include not only psychiatrists and other physicians, but also psychologists and other specialists. The broad range in these listings of approaches and users to which the manual is addressed justify my call to make explicit statements of its biopsychosocial underpinnings.

The preface continues that the listed symptoms of disorders are concise, explicit, and facilitative of objective assessment. Disorders might reflect common underlying vulnerabilities. Moreover, even diagnostic groups might be related in genetic linkage, having common neurocircuitry, genetic indicators, physiological risks, and environmental exposures.

Introduction

Moving on from the preface, the introduction to the DSM-5 adds that many mental disorder categories appear "fluid" in nature, having symptom overlap with other ones. Therefore, nosological symptoms should accommodate dimensional approaches that cut across categories.

I note that the logic expressed in the above is a non-sequitor. If the problem in diagnosis concerns symptom overlap over categories, the direct solution is to have: (a) only distinct marker symptoms for each category; (b) with the more overlapping symptoms removed from specific disorders. That being said, the DSM-5's approach is well taken—categorical and dimensional approaches can co-exist in a hybrid psychiatric nosological system. However, I query whether the DSM-5 has approached in the best way possible this hybrid concept of mental disorder. If one aligns several categories along a dimension of severity, does this equate with leaving aside categories and examining symptoms for their organization and severity along dimensions, for example, ones that are constructed statistically as in factor analysis? I address this question below.

Note that by category-identifying markers, I do not necessarily refer to biomarkers or endophenotypes related to genetic markers. In this regard, marker symptoms could be characteristic expressions of a disorder without having a bio- or genetic origin, or they could be environmentally-related ones (e.g., due to marital conflict, child abuse, adversity, and work stress). This approach to marker symptoms is consistent with the biopsychosocial approach.

The introduction to the DSM-5 continues that diagnosing a categorical disorder implies that it can be isolated or differentiated from "normal life variation" and also from transient stress responses, although the borders in these regards might be "porous." According to the introduction, the categorical approach in prior editions of the DSM included "structural problems," due to "narrow" diagnostic categories that lent to diagnosis of comorbidities, use of the "not otherwise specified" categories, and so on. In this vein, there is too much symptom heterogeneity within disorders and also symptom overlap across them for efforts to continue to seek categories with distinct and homogeneous populations.

Similarly, in Young and Yehuda (2006), and then in Young, Lareau, and Pierre (2014), I had calculated that PTSD could be expressed in over thousands of different ways! The polythetic approach to organizing and scoring criteria in the DSM is the reason for heterogeneity in symptom expression for its disorders. Presumably, some of its other disorders also would reveal large numbers of individual ways of expressing them.

In this regard, I note that the polythetic approach that characterizes the DSM-IV-TR and the DSM-5 should be changed. It is noteworthy that the constellation of potential symptom expression variations in cases of comorbid diagnosis of disorders using the DSM-5 approach reaches into the millions or more (Young et al., 2014).

As for the characteristic of the primary dimensional differentiation to which the introduction to the DSM-5 referred, it concerns internalization and externalization. This polarity is a common dimensional differentiating factor in psychological tests, such as the Child Behavior Checklist (CBCL, Achenbach, 1991; Achenbach & Rescorla, 2001).

The DSM-5 manual indicates that despite its recognition of the dimensional component to psychiatric disorder, it is "premature" to alter extant categorical definitions for most disorders listed in the DSM. Therefore, the DSM-5 remains highly categorical, and without much change from the DSM-IV-TR. Nevertheless, the ultimate goal of the DSM project is to become increasingly dimensional.

I note that this logic constitutes another nonsequitor. By organizing categories into spectra, groups, or dimensions of severity, no matter how defined, the categories still exist. Even by defining each of their aspects dimensionally, they still exist. In this regard, consider how psychological tests, such as the CBCL, treat dimensions. Questionnaire responses are factor-analyzed and each factor constitutes a dimensional construct on which low and high scores can be compared to normative distributions. With this and other information at hand, the clinician is free to assign relevant diagnostic categories, but only if desired or required. This approach is quite unlike the dimensional approach advocated in the DSM-5.

The introduction to the DSM-5 goes on to discuss its developmental, cultural, and gender foci. It ends with an explanation of how its multiaxial system has been replaced with the one using specifiers for psychosocialcontextual factors and disability, aside from having moved personality disorders from Axis II to Section 2. In addition, Axis V on disability was dropped because the Global Assessment of Functioning (GAF) Scale on which it was based had a "conceptual lack of clarity" and "questionable psychometrics." Instead, the DSM-5 uses codes from the ICD (International Statistical Classification of Diseases and Related Health Problems) classification system, as developed by the WHO (World Health Organization). In addition, for disability, the WHO's Disability Assessment Schedule is included in Section 3 as a global measure of disability. Version 2 was tested in the DSM-5 field trials.

Forensics

The introduction to the DSM-5 mentions that it was reviewed extensively in multiple ways. Of interest to the present work, given its forensic component, it is noted that the DSM-5 draft was vetted by members of the APA Council on Psychiatry and Law for its disorders that have forensic application. Either the disorders so vetted appear in forensic environments or have much potential to influence "civil and criminal" courtroom cases. Moreover, DSM-5 workgroups dealing with forensically-related disorders added forensic experts to the groups in order to "advise" them.

A later section of the introductory material in the DSM-5 consists of a "cautionary statement" in using the manual forensically. It is acknowledged that although the DSM-5 may be a "reference" for court, it does not attempt to meet all court needs. This cautionary statement notes that (a) clinically diagnostic and (b) forensic/legal questions do not necessarily "fit" each other (e.g., in criminal responsibility or in civil disability cases). For example, for the former, a disorder does not implicate residual degree of personal control. For the latter, a disorder does not address etiology or cause.

To conclude, for forensic use, the DSM-5 acknowledges that there is an imperfect fit in its application for court because it is clinician-oriented. Moreover, disorders by themselves cannot be used to ascertain: (a) whether legal thresholds have been reached; (b) whether there is a specific level of an impairment or disability; and (c) what level of control a person can have of the symptoms of a disorder. Comparison with the equivalent paragraphs in the DSM-IV-TR reveals almost no change to this page on forensics.

Comment

As a final note to this section of the present work on the introductory material in the DSM-5, I observed that any mention of sourcebooks has been deleted. The DSM-IV had several books published with it within a few years (Widiger, Frances, & Pincus, 1997) that could be used for investigation of its scientific research basis and, if had been needed, for justification of approaches taken by users for court. However, it appears that financial considerations have led to removal of this important aspect of the DSM enterprise. Similarly, it is noted that financial reasons appear to be why the field trials were limited and, moreover, why there was removal of a follow-up testing of the manual after the initial field trials. There had been DSM-5 draft proposals in 2010 that invited response and subsequent modifications, and the final draft proposal appears to be the one field-tested. However, to repeat, the final version of the DSM-5 published in 2013 was not the one that was field-tested. Finally, please note that space limitations have precluded dealing with children's diagnoses in the present work, but the DSM-5 manual deals extensively with developmental considerations.

Specific Changes in the DSM-5 and Their Critique

Changes

Table 22.1 provides the major changes that were instituted in the DSM-5 relative to the DSM-IV-TR. The table indicates the changes that were made according to an appendix in the DSM-5 and in associated web material that is more elaborate (American Psychiatric Association, 2013b). The present work examines closely many of these changes. Moreover, others have presented specific comments and criticisms of the changes, including Frances (2013a, 2013b, 2013c, 2013d, 2013e; see Tables 22.2 and 22.3). In an article in the public media, Sax noted that there are several DSM-5 diagnoses involving the word "unspecified" that could lead to inappropriately diagnosing mental disorders in many people when it is not merited (Sax, 2013). He gave the examples of unspecified schizophrenia spectrum disorder, unspecified attention-deficit/hyperactivity disorder, and unspecified mental disorder. In checking the DSM-IV-TR, he noted that the latter disorder is included there, as well (as "Unspecified Mental Disorder (nonpsychotic)"). Its description states that it can be given when there is not enough information available. The DSM-5 text for the disorder (and for the other two mentioned) indicates that it is used when, based entirely on clinical judgment, a clinician decides "not" to specify why the criteria are not met for a specific mental disorder, and the patient's presentation does not give enough information to allow for a specific diagnosis. Clearly, the category is so open-ended that Sax appears correct about its dangers. This type of concern permeates the commentary by Frances on the DSM-5, as described in Tables 22.2 and 22.3.

After reviewing the scope of the changes in Table 22.1 and these initial concerns by Frances (2013a) in Tables 22.2 and 22.3 on the merits of some of the changes, professionals and stakeholders working in the field should consider the problems I inherent in the DSM-5. Considering (a) the plethora of changes, both minor and major in the DSM-5, and (b) the firestorm around the DSM-5 draft proposals, (c) not to mention the range of criticisms of the final version of the DSM-5, from mild to vociferous, let alone the confusion engendered by the consequent changes to the first set of changes, (d) along with the further changes after the field trials, it is understandable how the DSM-5 has induced quite a state of confusion in professionals and stakeholders.

In this regard, I propose a new diagnostic entity related to the DSM-5 for inclusion in its set of disorders for further study, this one concerning those who try to use it—DSM-5 Confusion Disorder (see Table 22.4). However, I add that there is a rapid cure for any DSM-5 type confusion—careful analysis of the DSM-5 and the literature on it—a goal to which this work is therapeutically dedicated.

Comment

This completes the general introduction to the DSM-5 and my analysis of its introductory material in the preface and introduction. The take-home message is that the DSM-5 might have made several improvements relative to the DSM-IV-TR, but there is still much to do. Its users need

Table 22.1 Notable changes made on the DSM-5 (2013) diagnostic criteria (based on the APA document highlighting changes from DSM-IV-TR to DSM-5 (American Psychiatric Association, 2013b)

Disorder	Change
Neurodevelopmental disorder	
Intellectual disability (Intellectual developmental disorder)	Severity determined by adaptive functioning instead of IQ score.
	The term "mental retardation" is replaced by "intellectual disability."
Communication disorders	Includes language disorder, speech sound disorder, childhood-onset fluency disorder, and social (pragmatic) communication disorder, a new condition.
Autism spectrum disorder	A single disorder, with different levels of severity, is characterized by (a) deficits in social communication and social interaction and (b) restricted repetitive behaviors, interests, and activities (RRBs). Because both components are required for diagnosis of ASD, social communication disorder is diagnosed if no RRBs are present.
Attention-deficit/ hyperactivity disorder	Examples have been added to facilitate application across the life span; the cross-situational requirement has been strengthened to "several" symptoms in each setting; the onset criterion is changed from "present before age 7 years" to "several symptoms present prior to age 12."
Specific learning disorder	Combines reading disorder, mathematics disorder, disorder of written expression, and learning disorder not otherwise specified.
Motor disorder	Motor disorders are included in the neurodevelopmental disorders chapter.
Schizophrenia spectrum and other psychotic disorders	
Schizophrenia	Two Criterion A symptoms are required for diagnosis of schizophrenia. The individual must have at least one of three positive symptoms: delusions, hallucinations, and disorganized speech.
Schizophrenia subtypes	The subtypes (i.e., paranoid, disorganized, catatonic, undifferentiated, and residual types) are eliminated. A dimensional approach to rating severity is provided (which is in proposals for study).
Bipolar and related disorders	
Bipolar disorders	Criterion A includes emphasis on changes in activity/energy as well as mood. Bipolar I disorder, mixed episode, has been removed. For the specifiers, "with mixed features" has been added.
Anxious distress specifier	To identify patients having anxiety symptoms not part of the bipolar diagnostic criteria.
Depressive disorders	A new diagnosis, disruptive mood dysregulation disorder, is now included for patients up to 18 years. Premenstrual dysphoric disorder has been included based on strong scientific evidence. The category of persistent depressive disorder includes both chronic major depressive disorder and the previous dysthymic disorder.
Major depressive disorder	Added the specifier "with mixed features."
Bereavement exclusion	The exclusion criterion for a major depressive episode lasting <2 months is omitted. It is noted that most people experiencing the loss of a loved one experience bereavement without developing a major depressive episode.
Anxiety disorders	
Agoraphobia, specific phobia, and social anxiety disorder (social phobia)	Deletion of the requirement that those over age 18 years must recognize that their anxiety is excessive or unreasonable. The anxiety must be out of proportion to the actual danger or threat in the situation. The 6-month duration is now extended to all ages.
Social anxiety disorder (social phobia)	For social anxiety, the "generalized" specifier has been replaced by a "performance only" specifier.
Specific phobia	The different types of specific phobias are now specifiers.
Obsessive-compulsive and related disorders	The chapter on obsessive-compulsive and related disorders is new in DSM-5. New disorders include hoarding disorder, excoriation (skin-picking) disorder, substance-/medication-induced obsessive-compulsive and related disorder, and obsessive-compulsive and related disorder due to another medical condition.

(continued)

Table 22.1 (continued)

Disorder	Change
Other specified and unspecified obsessive-compulsive and related disorders	Includes obsessional jealousy or nondelusional preoccupation with a partner's perceived infidelity. [Comment: Are there cautions needed here?]
Trauma- and stressor-related disorders	
Acute stress disorder	As with PTSD, Criterion A, the criterion requires being explicit as to whether qualifying traumatic events could be experienced directly, witnessed, or experienced indirectly. The subjective reaction criterion (A2) to the traumatic event has been eliminated. The DSM-IV's emphasis on dissociative symptoms is minimized.
Adjustment disorder	Reconceptualized as syndromes that occur after exposure to a distressing (traumatic or nontraumatic) event, rather than as a residual category from clinically significant distress.
Posttraumatic stress disorder	Now has four symptom clusters: the avoidance/numbing cluster is divided into two. Includes new or reconceptualized symptoms (3 new ones).
Dissociative disorder	Derealization is now included in the diagnosis of depersonalization disorder and is now called depersonalization/derealization disorder.
Somatic symptom and related disorders	Reduces the number of disorders and subcategories. Somatization disorder, hypochondriasis, pain disorder, and undifferentiated somatoform disorder are removed.
Somatic symptom disorder	"Better recognizes the complexity of the interface between psychiatry and medicine" [Comment: Dual thinking?] Positive symptoms added (maladaptive thoughts, feelings, and behaviors), in addition to somatic symptoms.
Medically unexplained symptoms	Qualifier removed. DSM-IV overemphasized the importance of the absence of medical explanation. Medically unexplained symptoms are limited in reliability. The DSM-5 classification defines disorders on the basis of positive symptoms.
Hypochondriasis and illness anxiety disorder	Hypochondriasis is eliminated. Having high health anxiety without somatic symptoms leads to a diagnosis of illness anxiety disorder.
Pain disorder	In DSM-IV, the pain disorder could be due to medical diseases/injuries, psychological, or both. But psychological factors influence all forms of pain, so the disorder has been eliminated. In DSM-5, some individuals with chronic pain might be appropriately diagnosed as having somatic symptom disorder, with predominant pain. In addition, for diagnosis of pain experience, psychological factors affecting other medical conditions or also an adjustment disorder might be appropriate.
Psychological factors affecting other medical conditions and factitious disorder	The first is a new mental disorder. Factitious disorder is included in this DSM chapter because somatic symptoms are predominant.
Conversion disorder (Functional neurological symptom disorder)	Emphasizes the importance of neurological examination. Relevant psychological factors might not be demonstrable in the examination.
Substance-related and addictive disorders	
Gambling disorder	Gambling activates the brain reward system like with drugs of abuse.
Criteria and terminology	Does not separate anymore the diagnoses of substance abuse and dependence.
Neurocognitive disorders	
Major and mild neurocognitive disorder	Dementia and amnestic disorder are subsumed under Major neurocognitive disorder (NCD). Mild NCD is a new disorder. An updated listing of neurocognitive domains is provided. It is stated that the threshold between mild and major NCD is inherently arbitrary.
Etiological subtypes	New separate criteria are presented for major or mild NCD due to frontotemporal NCD, Lewy bodies, TBI, etc.
Personality disorders	The criteria for personality disorders have not changed (Section II). An alternative approach for further study can be found in Section III. It includes core impairments central to personality pathology. It includes characteristic pathological personality traits related to the personality disorders they represent. The section provides an efficient assessment approach with considerable clinical utility. [Comment: The new diagnostic PD system was moved to the appendix Section III after much criticism]

Note. This table on the DSM-5 highlights does not cover every change

Table 22.2 Cautions in using the DSM-5 (Frances, 2013b)

Diagnostic	Caution
General	Beware of diagnostic inflation.
ADHD	The initial onset is now later than age 12. The symptom requirement for adult ADHD is loosened.
Grief vs. major depressive disorder	Overdiagnosis/overtreatment of major depressive disorder possible in people experiencing grief.
Disruptive mood dysregulation disorder	Inability to distinguish disruptive mood dysregulation disorder (DMDD) from normal temper tantrums in children, or from temper tantrums occurring in other psychotic disorders.
Childhood bipolar disorders	Most children diagnosed with childhood bipolar disorders only have nonepisodic temper outbursts/irritability—not classic bipolar swings. Children who could get diagnosed with ADHD, conduct disorder, ODD, or anxiety disorder, or no diagnosis at all, now could get this one. It suggests a lifetime disorder that will require continuous psychopharmacological treatment.
Generalized anxiety disorder	The criteria are too loose both in the required number of symptoms and in their duration, so the "worried well" will be over diagnosed with a mental disorder.
Posttraumatic stress disorder	The gatekeeper threshold has been lowered too much by allowing the diagnosis in people who have had no direct traumatic exposure, but have simply learned about a violent event that was experienced by a close relative/friend. This creates a "forensic disaster."
Substance abuse and substance dependence	Collapses the previously separate substance abuse and substance dependence (substance use disorder). Starting to abuse clinically is now considered in the same category as people who have end-stage addictions.
Mild neurocognitive disorder	Based totally on extremely unreliable and fallible clinical criteria.
Personality dimensions in DSM-5's section 3	The system is untested, cumbersome, impractical, and unacceptable—serving no useful clinical or research purpose.

Table 22.3 Writing "Mistakes" in the DSM-5

Category	Mistake
Autism spectrum disorder (ASD) Criterion A	Does not indicate exactly how many are required for its three symptoms; ambiguous Permits use of the DSM-IV criterion; confusing
Disruptive mood regulation disorder	Indicates four different age ranges applicable—up to 12 years (p. 155), 6–8 (p. 156), <10 (p. 156), 7–18 (p. 157); inconsistent
Major depressive disorder (MDD) (with the bereavement exclusion removed)	The footnote explaining when it can be diagnosed is "so vaguely written," it does not help differentiate MDD during bereavement from mild reactive depressed symptoms
Unspecified mood disorder	Removed. There is no more a way to diagnose patients expressing not yet clear bipolar I or II disorder
Bipolar and depression sections	Not clear, consistent; imprecise, even impenetrable; e.g., the way to use the "melancholic features" specifier not indicated clearly
Persistent depressive disorder	New category groups relatively mild "dysthymia" with the most severe category of chronic major depression
Intermittent explosive disorder	Does not have exclusion criterion ruling out alternate ways that can explain source of violent behavior
Intellectual disability	Removes IQ requirement; forensically questionable
Somatic symptom disorder	Loosely written; will lead to false diagnosis of people with legitimate concerns for their medical conditions as having a mental disorder. Exclusion criterion should make clear somatic complaints not due to a medical or to other psychiatric conditions. If psychological factors present, they should be "far beyond the expectable"
Paraphilia section	Ambiguous; forensic misuses for sure to come
Brief psychotic disorder	The way it is written has made the 4th item "completely superfluous"
Depressive disorders, mixed feature specifier	"Nearly every day during a majority of days"; "tautological," "inconsistent"
Coding	Mistakes made in a number of them

Adapted from Frances (2013e)

Table 22.4 Proposal: DSM-5 confusion disorder

Criterion	Explanation
A	**Diagnostic confusion**
A1	Among practitioners using the DSM-5, there is cognitive, affective, or behavioral disorientation.
A2	Etiologically-induced by studying, using clinically, and/or applying forensically the portions of the DSM-5 that are not reliable/valid/or clinically useful.
A3	Condition is demonstrated by the following: diagnostic confusion symptoms for the diagnostic categories in DSM-5, and these are of the type 1, 2, and/or 3.
	Type 1: Confusion for a category unchanged from DSM-IV-TR
	Type 2: Confusion for a category modified from DSM-IV-TR, or
	Type 3: Confusion for a category new in DSM-5
B	**Diagnostic binging** (inflation)
B1	Too many disorders consistently diagnosed (co-co-co morbidities)
B2	Too many people consistently diagnosed (prevalent prevalence)
C	**Diagnosis belief**
C1	Strict uncritical compliance with DSM-5
C2	Lack of scientific verification in using it in diagnosis
C3	"Disbelief" problems could arise (e.g., in court), due to C1 or C2
D	The confusion significantly impairs important aspects of vocational, social, or personal functioning (at least until cures attempted, although these might include (in)appropriate beverage or substance (ab)use)
E	Duration lasts longer than attending relevant presentations/workshops, reading the literature, etc.
F	Disorder not accounted for by other conditions (e.g., continuation of DSM-IV-TR Confusion Disorder; being a member of a DSM-5 workgroup)
Specify if	Psychiatrist, psychologist, other mental health professional, other stakeholder, or, most harmfully, patient

to be wary in every step of the way in assessment and diagnosis, especially for the disorders that might be attributed to patients based on its nosology. At the same time, the DSM-5 project continues to try to improve, in that it is considered a "living document" and there will be changes. As users and commentators, we need to be proactive in voicing our concerns (as well as our praise, where merited).

Next, in the present work, after a general acceptance of the DSM-5 by its proponents and then a critique of the DSM-5 in books by Joel Paris, I examine journal publications on the DSM-5 for their perspective on its strengths and weaknesses. The chapter terminates with discussion of what is mental disorder, including my own conceptualization and definition.

Supporting DSM-5

Kupfer, Kuhl, and Regier (2013) and Regier, Kuhl, and Kupfer (2013) announced with much fanfare the publication of the DSM-5 ("the future has arrived"). They noted that it emphasizes clinical care and that it is compatible with the rest of medicine. Therefore, in these regards, it has been constructed to be more dimensional. Also, it is harmonized with the upcoming ICD-11.

Kupfer et al. (2013) continued that the DSM-5 has dropped the cumbersome multiaxial system. However, it has added several new disorders or spectra. For example, the autism spectrum disorder combines autistic disorder, Asperger disorder, childhood disintegrative disorder, and pervasive developmental disorder.

The authors addressed concerns that prevalence estimates based on the DSM-5 will be different compared to that for the DSM-IV. They cited Huerta, Bishop, Duncan, Hus, and Lord (2012) to counter this type of concern [But see Mayes, Black, and Tierney (2013)]. In this regard, the newly added disorder of disruptive mood dysregulation is aimed at reducing the high prevalence of childhood bipolar disorder, by giving an option for diagnosis applicable to nonepisodic irritability.

Kupfer et al. continued that PTSD has been switched to a trauma/stress chapter, and now has four symptom clusters instead of three. For depression, the bereavement exclusion has been removed to allow for care of those in mourning who exhibit clinical depression. For substance use, cases of abuse and dependence are now combined. They continued that the DSM-5 manual is "readily updatable," and Section III contains suggestions for further scrutiny, such as for personality disorder. Overall, Kupfer et al. (2013) concluded that the emphasis in the revision has been to give the manual "greater value" to all of medical practice.

Critiquing DSM-5

General Critique

First (2014) argued that changes to the DSM must be empirically derived. For example, the changes proposed for personality disorder (PD; Krueger, Hopwood, Wright, & Markon, 2014) are innovative and based on research, but they changed over the years of the DSM-5 revision process. The notion that the final version for PD should be accepted because its structure is congruent with the Five Factor Model (FFM) of personality is disputed (Widiger, 2011).

Lilienfeld (2014) also advocated for a scientific foundation for the DSM. He was uncertain whether decisions regarding somatic symptom disorder and dissociative identity disorder met this bar. He decried the sacrifice of scientific evidence to the need for clinical utility in how the DSM is constructed. Yet he acknowledged that many DSM categories will be a hybrid of scientific and practical considerations. He emphasized that the construct of categories of mental illness (natural kinds) in comparison to a dimensional model is itself dubious.

Paris (2013)

Product Paris has written two books in 2013 on the DSM-5 that deserve careful scrutiny. In Paris (2013a), he pointed out both where the DSM generally has weaknesses and some specific problems with its newly minted disorders. The DSM-III (American Psychiatric Association, 1980) had been a significant advance, given its rigor in defining disorders with well-described signs and symptoms so that, relative to the original DSM and the follow-up DSM-II, the reliability related to its disorders increased and also theoretical dogma was removed.

However, Paris (2013a) noted that the mental disorders in the DSM-III were not associated with differentiating causes, given the lack of scientific knowledge at that time. He argued that even for the severest mental disorders, we still lack knowledge of etiology, which needs to be disorder-specific and explanatory. Moreover, rather than reflecting scientific origins, the categories are work products of expert DSM committees. Therefore, the DSM-5 is still struggling to create valid categories that reflect psychiatric realities in nature. Also, researchers are still seeking critical "biological markers" for the categories. Therefore, we should not reify the disorders in the manual. They are not truly distinct from all normal variations in behavior. They do overlap, too.

The consequences in using in psychiatry a diagnostic manual such as the DSM-5 merit concern. The public is diagnosed using a manual that is over-inclusive and pathologizes problems in living. The DSM-5's long term solution to use diagnostic dimensions will not solve its problems, in that this approach runs its own risk of over-inclusiveness. The DSM's problems could affect the public by (a) leading to undeserving medication for normal people, (b) their stigmatization, and (c) unwarranted long term, negative consequences.

For Paris (2013a), psychiatric categories are constellations of signs and symptoms structured into syndromes, rather than being disease entities, despite the DSM's goal to create valid psychiatric disorders. However, clinicians generally do not think in terms of signs and symptom lists. Rather, they typically think in terms of prototypes, or ideal cases, to which they try to match their patients. The ICD-10 (World Health Organization, 2007; and forthcoming ICD-11) diagnostic system uses this approach, and, as well, Frances (2013a) advocated for it. This seems to be a major clashing point in psychiatry, and the one that won't be revolved soon.

Comment However, I add that the research indicates that the reliability of prototype diagnoses might not fare as well as the polythetic (symptom and cluster) approach used in the DSMs. Nevertheless, it could be argued that if valid diagnostic categories can be found closer to valid psychiatric etiology, a prototype approach to describing the categories might be easier to use and more valid than a symptom/cluster polythetic approach. Also, consider that, presently, the psychiatric disorder categories have "fuzzy" edges so that their clear-cut use is not guaranteed (Livesley, 2011). Clearly, this sticking point might be intractable and, as with other ones discussed in the present work, a combined, hybrid approach might ultimately be the best.

Process Paris (2013a) continued by discussing the construction of the DSM-5 in its workgroups. He noted that, aside from failing to prepare a source book on the literature involved in decision-making, as had been the case for the DSM-IV, the drafts were not sent to possible opponents to the proposals, as had been the case for the DSM-IV (First, 2010). Also, the full draft was not presented to independent experts for review, thereby sacrificing the important process of peer review.

Paris noted that the field trials were rushed in order to publish the final version in 2013, because the manual had already been delayed by the vociferous objections to many of its proposed changes once it was made public in 2010. I note that in looking over some of the retractions in the proposals occasioned by the criticisms, some were consistent with the criticisms raised by myself, by Michael First, and by colleagues in the special issue that First and I co-edited in 2010 on the DSM-5 draft in the journal *Psychological Injury and Law* (PIL). However, as shall be shown later, the final version of the DSM-5 still contains difficulties for the area of psychological injury and law.

Paris (2013a) noted that the DSM-5 field trials were conducted under a tight deadline with lack of funding, rendering them "inadequate." Moreover, the rigor in the methods used is a far cry from the real world of clinical practice, so that the reliabilities obtained do not reflect what happens in mental health community use. Finally, the levels considered as "acceptable" reliabilities in the DSM-5 (Kraemer, Kupfer, Clarke, Narrow, & Regier, 2012) do not reach the accepted standards in most academic journals.

Paris reflected that, as science progresses, psychiatric diagnosis will become more accurate. Also, it will be shaped by a new initiative that is "unproven" to date. The initiative is on "Research Domain Criteria" (RDoC), which do not consider categories in diagnosis (Insel et al., 2010). The RDoC emphasizes five broad spectra—Negative Valence Systems, Positive Valence Systems, Cognitive Systems, Systems for Social Processes, and Arousal/Regulatory Systems—in relation to biology and brain-based data, in particular. Paris (2013a) criticized the RDoC for its biological emphasis. It is fair to say that the type of broad spectra that will result from further work in this regard should also consider factors that are biopsychosocial in nature.

Definition Paris (2013a) elaborated on the definition of mental disorder. His concerns related to the boundaries between disease or illness and subclinical reactions to life stressors. Aside from the problem that the definition should be clear and rigorous enough to avoid overdiagnosis, he noted that any psychiatric definition requires judgment. For example, Wakefield (1992) defined mental disorder in terms of the construct of harmful dysfunction, which cannot be strictly objective, especially for determining what is harmful.

I would add that Wakefield's definition (also see Wakefield, 2013) considers dysfunction perhaps too strictly as evolutionary mechanisms gone awry, and so rendering activities of daily living impaired. From a biopsychosocial perspective, a dysfunction might be causatively linked to a complex that includes biological mechanisms, but these do not have to be evolutionary nor initiatory. Rather, if they are involved, they also could be exacerbatory byproducts of psychosocial aspects, or minor.

Conclusion Paris (2013a) continued that mental processes cannot be reduced to a brain-based agenda. He opined that mental processes can be studied on their own terms, and that "*mind is an emergent property*" (p. 75). The psychological processes of the person constitute a complex system having simpler components from which higher-order components emerge and, moreover, they are "not fully determined" by the lower-order components.

Although not explicitly framing it this way, I note that Paris is describing brain and behavior in terms of nonlinear dynamical systems theory (NLDST; for example, see Young, 2011). Psychiatrists and neuroscientists are becoming aware of the self-organizing properties of the whole in psychological and neuronal processes. However, it is difficult to translate this perspective into a classificatory psychiatric nosology. Nevertheless as shall be suggested below, adopting a systems perspective might facilitate creating a valid hybrid categorical and dimensional understanding of psychopathology, leading the way toward an integrated diagnostic system.

Paris (2013a) concluded his book with cogent points. Among them, the greatest danger of the DSM-5 is its potential to overpathologize. He supported the search for biological markers to help arrive at more valid diagnostic categories and their clinically-meaningful cut-off points. He asked for better psychometrics for assessing psychopathology, which I note is an important point for psychology and the role it can play in evolving a better psychiatric classification approach. At the level of approach to mental disorder, Paris (2013a) argued that psychiatry must function from the biopsychosocial perspective, which is in strong agreement with my own views.

Paris and Phillips (2013)

These authors co-edited a book on the concepts and controversies behind the construction of the DSM-5. In his chapter, Shorter (2013) presented the processes underlying the historical development of the different editions. He emphasized that the process of consensus in workgroups dominated category construction. Sadler (2013) positioned the DSM project in the middle of the "mental health medical industrial complex" (MHMIC; see Table 22.5). Phillips (2013a) added that, aside from the 10 elements of the MHMIC listed by Sadler, another would be the medical model. Sadler (2013) advocated for an "open source" classification of mental disorder, with changes conditional on appropriate testing. Perhaps with tongue in cheek, Paris (2013b) related psychiatry's embrace of neuroscience ideology as "internist envy."

Kinghorn (2013) maintained that the DSM should refrain from defining mental disorder until

Table 22.5 Mental health medical industrial complex

Component	Description
Millions of people mentally ill	Captive, needy market wanting magic bullets
Pharmaceutical industry (products)	Seeks increasing profits, e.g., by supporting expansion of DSMs
Service-industry (for profit)	Health insurance/managed care would rather pay for drugs that are cheaper than psychosocial treatment
Health care system	They are either acting for-profit or trying to reduce public costs, depending on jurisdiction. Mentally ill caught in middle
National politics	Influence-peddling, lobbying, campaign financing, and conflicts of interest all tolerated and also they are common in contrast to lack of voice given to non-pharmaceutical industry and to patients
Advertising/mass media	Marketing directly to consumer, even for pseudo-disorders. Also, marketing to new users of patent-expiring medications. "There are financial incentives for DSM authors to create new disorders"
National mental health organizations	Supports research that ends up a "default" tax-payer subsidy to Big Pharma Grant reviewers have likely Big Pharma and DSM ties
Popular demand	Passive public acceptance of medication-first approach to mental health. Few or no lobbyists for alternate approaches, such as psychotherapy
Academic medical centers	Have become entrepreneurial with "collosal" conflicts of interest, with DSM participation Need Big Pharma money
American Psychiatric Association	DSM a primary source of income, so changes leading to new editions help sales. But still conservative bias

Adapted from Sadler (2013)

more is known neurobiologically and psychologically. Moreover, the concepts of function and dysfunction need to be clearer. Porter (2013) emphasized the biopsychosocial model, in that biological, psychological, and social factors all contribute to illness. He advocated for psychosocial research in nosological science, as well as inclusion of patient perspectives. Whooley and Horwitz (2013) noted that although the DSM-5 is considered a living document, the manner in which its revisions will be undertaken has not been clarified.

Frances (2013b) exhorted the field to be pragmatic and to use clinical common sense. Neither the biological reductionist nor rationalist social constructionist models are adequate to the task of creating a psychiatric classification system. The DSM should work from a utilitarian, instrumental epistemological stance. The concept of mental disorder defies valid definition, and there are so many mental disorders in the DSM-5 (about 300), diagnostic faddism gets in the way.

Pierre (2013) concurred that the DSM-5 promotes overdiagnosis, but also referred to underdiagnosis in critical arenas (e.g., major depression in primary care settings). Diagnostic classification needs to find a balance between "lumpers" and "splitters" (grouping or separating categories, respectively). Also, it needs to balance the tendencies to minimize false negatives in diagnosis while guarding against creating false positives (i.e., improper attribution of normality and disorder, respectively). Mishara and Schwartz (2013) argued that, in psychiatry, the patient's phenomenology has been minimized in relation to clinical and research endeavor.

Phillips (2013b) referred to the need for the field to examine psychiatric conditions from the point of view of complexity theory (e.g., Bechtel & Richardson, 2010; Kendler, 2012). The whole cannot be reduced to its parts nor can each part be analyzed by itself without considering all the parts in the system. Parts lose their independence in an integrated system, so that disease cannot be reduced to the biological. In terms of etiology, a complexity approach considers that systems compose, decompose, and reassemble the wholes involved in the system. Multiple risk factors are involved, both as direct causal agents and mutually-influencing interacting ones. The etiological processes in disease are, therefore, multiple and intertwined (Kendler, 2012, p. 385).

Comment

The general critique of the DSM-5 has raised important issues that cast doubt on the validity both of its process and product. However, the Paris books point to ways that both can be improved. Some of the major criticisms of the DSM-5 include its embedding in the mental health medical industrial complex and the way the working groups functioned. Its reliability as evaluated in the field trials is contested. The categories that comprise it might not even be represented the best way (it is polythetical rather than prototypical). They do not have their etiology explained, nor do they have signature markers. Indeed, its concept of mental disorder is at issue. The DSM-5 is perceived as overpathologizing, not being user-friendly, and not considering the patient perspective. The emphasis given to the biopsychosocial and systems approach in the Paris books is quite consistent with my orientation to how the DSM-5 can be improved, as shown below.

Others

Frances and Widiger (2012) took a sanguine view of the DSM-5, and cite evidence for "diagnostic inflation" (Kessler & Wang, 2008; Moffitt et al., 2010). They likened the situation to a diagnostic epidemic. Because of the danger, diagnostic conservatism is needed. Frances and Widiger noted that the field trials were inadequate, especially for radical new proposals (First, 2011). Any proposal for further revision should be vetted by "severe" critical review in parallel with publication of the proposals, and with risk/benefit analysis considered for each one. The best organization to undertake this task should be independent of the American Psychiatric Association.

Frances (2013c) considered that the prevalence of mental disorder diagnosis would increase due to the changes in the DSM-5. However, its principle chair, David Kupfer, disagreed and argued there even might be a decreased prevalence (Torjesen, 2013).

Some have given the DSM-5 a "fatal diagnosis" for its overreach (Gornall, 2013), but others maintain that its problem relates to its use by stakeholders. That is, clinicians could use it too loosely; but, further, each of regulators, insurers, and attorneys, in particular, could use it too loosely, as well (Berk, 2013). One solution for Berk is for clinicians to conduct comprehensive clinical assessments before arriving at diagnosis, a point that I emphasize below.

Cosgrove and colleagues have queried the colonization of the DSM workgroup/panel members by the pharmaceutical industry and the inherent conflicts of interest that they had not declared (Cosgrove & Krimsky, 2013; Cosgrove & Wheeler, 2013). They maintained that the transparency had been insufficient in the DSM-5's development (e.g., about speaker fees). They queried the hegemony of the biopsychiatric approach in creation of the new disorder of premenstrual dysphoria (PMDD; Cosgrove & Wheeler, 2013). Also, they gave the example of how the pharmaceutical industry repackages patent-expiring drugs to meet new disorders and their impending prescriptions, such as has been the case for one anti-depressant for PMDD.

Gordon and Cosgrove (2013) addressed the ethics of DSM-5. Ethical use of a psychiatric diagnostic manual should assure its acceptable reliability and validity. They queried whether other diagnostic approaches accomplish this better than the DSM-5, given its categorical orientation. Also, they addressed the ethics of the work groups that developed the DSM-5, in that its members did not fully disclose their financial links to pharmaceutical companies. Moreover, the consensus approach in the DSM-5 work groups might have led to categories being included in the DSM-5 because of economical drivers rather than ones related to scientific validity.

Blumenthal-Barby (2013) contended that the DSM-5 has expanded invalidly its nosology, for example, by failing in some cases to distinguish disordered from non-disordered conditions in people requiring help. It leads to overdiagnosis and false positives, and increases the probability of inappropriate pharmacological management. It could medicalize and trivialize mental health. Its decisions on some changes appear value-based and without validating empirical support. It exhibits conceptual confusing on, for example, in its dimensional construct. Science is even left aside, for example, in the decision to keep an 18+ year criterion for antisocial personality disorder, but not other ones.

In general, Blashfield, Keeley, Flanagan, and Miles (2014) noted that the DSM-5 did not attain its goals. Among other recommendations, they called for a reduction in political bias (e.g., in the work groups).

Joober (2013) argued for a combined categorical and dimensional approach to psychiatric classification. Given that the goal of classification is to have it based on etiology so that treatment can be facilitated, there is no evidence that a dimensional approach is superior in this regard. Joober continued that even if a disorder is heterogeneously expressed, it still could have simple causation. For example, the one label of schizophrenia captures better its polygenic (pleiotropic) nature than the multiple intermediate endophenotypes involving it that have been proposed.

There is concern that the symptom clusters of the DSM mental disorders are more heterogenous than homogenous, casting doubt on the validity of the diagnoses involved. Khoury, Langer, and Pagnini (2014) argued that direct descriptions of an individual's set of phenomenological experiences provide better clinical insight for treatment than a nosological category. Fried, Nesse, Zivin, Guille, and Sen (2014) found that nine symptoms of major depressive disorder (MDD) in the DSM-5 were differentially associated with six risk factors, so that symptom summation procedures are "obfuscating."

Wakefield (2013) is given the final word in this section. He not only advocated for his concept of harmful dysfunction in understanding mental disorder but also for understanding the role of context in this regard. Wakefield and First (2012) had shown that context is considered in a majority of DSM diagnostic categories, but it can be improved in this regard. As mentioned, harmful dysfunction refers to evolutionarily important psychological mechanisms and also dysfunction in them according to socially evaluated effects. I note that Wakefield (2013)'s work on context and social considerations together supports a biopsychosocial approach to mental disorder.

Forensic Critique

Thomas (2013) queried whether the DSM-5 has been sufficiently vetted for its forensic-related context. It might lead to unexpected surprises in court. In terms of specific diagnoses, she reviewed problem with the DSM-5's approach to PTSD and NCD (neurocognitive disorder). For PTSD, she argued that removal of the entry criterion of having a subjective emotional response to the event at issue complicates establishing causality in the forensic context. For NCD, Thomas criticized the DSM-5's exclusion of a category for moderate NCD. Also, use of self-report or knowledgeable informants about any cognitive decline, as permitted in the DSM-5, might not be reliable. Finally, the DSM's understanding of impairment is especially clinical, which might be different than that in the forensic context.

Wortzel (2013) argued that, for the DSM-5, there is room for squabbles both about categories and dimensions. There will be effects in both criminal and civil proceedings. The adversarial system uses opposing experts who already have enough reason to disagree. If the experts criticize the DSM-5 changes, they risk being considered practitioners who are outdated. If they support them, they risk criticisms related to using a system that is too novel. The courts will become increasingly skeptical and cynical about mental health testimony.

The solution to this quandary according to Wortzel (2013) is to conduct meticulous and transparent forensic assessments, a point with which I agree. Moreover, diagnosis usually is secondary in forensic cases to the legal question at hand. The expert needs to show that, whether the DSM-IV or DSM-5 is used, the conclusions offered about legally-relevant constructs are not altered. Also, experts "should be prepared to identify and defend against" any use of the DSM-5 in court that is "inappropriate or unjustified" [presumably in the work by the other side].

First (2010) also noted the differences in using the DSM in clinical and legal applications. He explained that the caution in using the DSM-IV in forensic cases was prepared by a committee of forensic experts charged with reducing its potential for misuse. Moreover, the committee reviewed the diagnostic criteria in the DSM-IV especially to avoid implying that those diagnosed have "diminished" behavioral control. First concluded that, at least from the wording in the DSM-5 draft, it was unclear to what extent an equivalent process had been followed.

To conclude, the DSM-5 has its forensic limitations (Willis & Gold, 2014). It was not developed to meet all the "technical needs" of legal systems. It is an imperfect product, the forensic and legal limitations of which might only be discovered through its use in practice (Appelbaum, 2014).

DSM-5 Field Trial Critique

Freedman et al. (2013) reviewed the results of the DSM-5 field trials, and they reported mixed results. Validity cannot be established without reliability, which in this case was determined by two different trained clinicians seeing patients up two week apart, one time each. Category reliability was calculated using the intraclass kappa statistic.

For some major DSM-5 disorders, such as schizophrenia, "good" kappa statistical results for reliability were obtained. But for others, such as major depressive disorder, the results presented an "obvious" problem. For some new additions to the DSM-5, such as "mixed anxiety and depression," the kappa levels were unacceptable, such as for disruptive mood disorder (Freedman et al., 2013). Results were acceptable for others that were modifications of DSM-IV categories (e.g., PTSD, the results being in the higher end). The new autism disorder spectrum fared well. Other disorders relevant to psychological injury (major neurocognitive disorder, complex somatic symptom disorder) were deemed to have "good" reliability.

The DSM-5 field trial results were published in a set of three articles (Clarke et al., 2013; Narrow et al., 2013; Regier, Narrow et al., 2013), Jones (2012) had previously published a critique. In the following, I review these articles.

Clarke et al. (2013) reported that the field trials were conducted over a 7- to 10-month time frame. They did not give the dates, but inspection of their article reveals that the trials started in 2010 and so the clinicians were trained on an earlier draft. There were 11 sites involved that used 279 clinicians and 2246 patients, most of whom were assessed two times.

The study used a stratified random sampling approach related to a minimal set of target diagnoses, with up to seven target diagnoses per site. This means that the study in the academic centers involved was quite unlike the typical clinical setting in which any patient might be expressing any of hundreds of conditions in the DSM. Training of the clinicians was extensive, which also might not to correspond to typical clinical practice.

A priori, the kappa levels for excellent, very good, good, questionable, and unacceptable reliability were set, respectively, at the points >0.8, >0.6, >0.4, >0.2, and <0.2. Reliability for dimensional measures used parametrical intraclass correlation coefficients. It is noted that the kappa levels for the different degrees of reliability for the DSM-5 field trials were less stringent than for the DSM-IV (Jones, 2012).

Regier, Narrow, et al. (2013) provided the details of the DSM-5 field trials. Over the sites that tested adult populations, sufficient data were gathered for 15 separate diagnoses. Aside from the results already presented in Freedman et al. (2013), reviewed above, it is noteworthy that mild TBI obtained questionable reliability (in contrast to major and minor NCD). Mainstays in diagnosis, such as generalized anxiety disorder and antisocial personality disorder, were in the questionable range. Therefore, given the already reported low results for major depressive disorder, the major internalization categories did not fare well. The lack of reliability for antisocial personality disorder has important forensic implications. For the child/adolescent sites, sufficient data were obtained for eight target disorders and only four were not questionable/unacceptable.

Narrow et al. (2013) reported the reliability for a newly-developed cross-cutting symptom measure. The measure was elaborated as part of the goal to broaden the DSM approach beyond narrow categories. Existing measures were used in a second round of self-report assessment by patients. However, the focus of my comments concerns the first instrument (see Table 22.6). [Other assessment devices were related to clinician-evaluated psychosis and suicidality, and these are not discussed here.] The cross-cutting measure contained 23 questions for adults that involved 12 domains. The items were chosen by the DSM-5 workgroups and also by an instrument development study group, usually de novo.

Table 22.6 DSM-5 dimensional cross-cutting symptom assessment for adult patients

Symptom domain	Number of questions	Content examples
Depression	2	Down
Anger	1	Irritated
Mania	2	Sleeping less but still energetic
Anxiety	3	Worried
Somatic distress	2	Unexplained pains
Suicide	1	Thoughts of self-hurting
Psychosis	2	Hearing things other people couldn't
Sleep	1	Sleep quality
Memory	1	In learning new information
Repetitive thoughts	1	Unpleasant ones
Repetitive behaviors	1	Driven
Dissociation	1	Detached/distant from self
Personality	2	Not knowing who really are
Substance use	3	Drinking/smoking/using without a doctor's prescription, in greater amounts or longer than prescribed (e.g., painkillers, cocaine)

The reliability results in Regier, Narrow, et al. (2013) supported use of the self-report cross-cutting measure in DSM-5 diagnostic assessments. However, I am not sure exactly what the measure concerns. I find it surprising that the items simply represent a short list of major psychiatric symptoms, each related to specific disorders, so that they are not cross-cutting in the sense of overlapping multiple disorders. Perhaps it would be best to refer to the instrument as a general psychiatric screening device rather than a cross-cutting one.

Jones (2012) critiqued the DSM-5 field trials by indicating its trial cancelations, its disorganization, its insufficient validity testing, and its procedural lacunae, such as high clinician evaluator attrition rates. A second phase was dropped on any updates or changes to the draft proposals. The population examined did not include milder levels of conditions, which makes the field trials problematic in light of the lowered bar for diagnostic thresholds for some of the disorders.

Defining Mental Disorder in the DSM-5

In the DSM-5 The DSM enterprise and, indeed, the field of psychiatry, in general, have long acknowledged the difficulty if not impossibility of defining mental disorder. Just as natural kinds of disorders are difficult to carve at the joints, so is psychiatric abnormality difficult conceptually to separate from ranges of normality. The various descriptions of the changes to the DSM-5 do not mention change in definition of mental disorder. However, closer inspection of the definition in the DSM-5 compared to that of the DSM-IV-TR (see Table 22.7) reveals a set of minor changes in the definition that serves to tighten and clarify it to a degree.

New Definition That being said, the psychiatric field does not have one integrated acceptable definition (even as acknowledged in the DSM-5). However, in order to improve the DSM definition of mental disorder, in Young (2014), I considered the various terms in the field related to impairment (e.g., disability). Also, I sought a definition grounded in the biopsychosocial model.

The major concern about the existing definition of mental disorder is that it is not adequate and does not capture the essence of mental disorder. It is a definition of convenience that allows for communication about mental disorder, but lacks the scientific rigor needed for its justification. Wakefield (1992, 2013) has provided alternate approaches to defining mental disorder (as harmful dysfunction). However, the ambiguity and circularity in the definition still apply; for example, it still appears a dualist conception, as evidenced by examination of the characteristics that Wakefield ascribes to the two components of the term (social and evolutionary). We need to use a construct that does not separate the components of mental disorder, but considers them systemically. In this regard, I propose that terminology that is consistent with the biopsychosocial model fits the requirement. Moreover, the term is integral to work in mental disorder in disciplines other than psychiatry, such as psychology. Finally, the term applies to not only mental distress but to functionalities impacted by them. Therefore, by specifying better the relationship of symptomatology to impairment and disability, in particular, some of the lacks in the definition of mental disorder in the DSM-5 might be rectified.

In the table in which I present a revised approach to defining mental disorder, generally, I work toward a better definition of mental disorder along the lines just mentioned. Also, I partially integrate Wakefield's (1992, 2013) concept of harmful dysfunction. Specifically, I try to separate in the definition the constructs of distress, disturbance, dysfunction, impairment, handicap, and disability. Further, I acknowledge the role of judgment in deciding upon mental disorder. Necessarily, I emphasize the need to base the decision on relevant, reliable information. Finally, I refer to the domains that might be involved, as well as the processes.

As for related factors, I consider causality and treatment. I underscore the value of clinical utility in diagnosis. Also, the role of factors, such as sex, gender, and age, is given their due. Overall, the definition that I offer for mental disorder reflects a biopsychosocial approach. In the following, I turn to how disability is evaluated according to the DSM-5.

The WHODAS 2.0

The WHODAS-2.0 (World Health Organization Disability Assessment Schedule 2.0, World Health Organization; Üstün et al., 2010) has been recommended for use by the DSM-5.

Table 22.7 Definition of mental disorder in the DSMs (and a proposal)

Source	Definition
DSM-IV-TR	The clinically significant behavioral/psychological syndrome/pattern is associated with distress (e.g., painful symptom)/disability (impairment in important functional area(s)) or with significantly increased risk of death/pain/disability/important loss of freedom. Not simply expectable/culturally-sanctioned response. Whatever its original cause, it is a behavioral/psychological/biological dysfunctional manifestation. Neither deviant behavior (e.g., political, religious, sexual) nor deviance/conflict is disorder, except if it is symptomatic of a dysfunction as described.
DSM-5	Syndrome characterized by a clinically significant dysfunctional disturbance in cognition/emotion regulation/behavior in psychological, biological, or developmental mental processes. Associated with significant distress or disability in activity (social/occupational/other). An expectable/culturally-approved response is not a mental disorder. Socially deviant behavior also is not, unless dysfunctional as described.
Proposal	*Primary Definition.* A mental health disorder is a behavioral syndrome (or pattern or network of symptoms) in context that is characterized as a clinically significant disturbance, distress, or dysfunction potentially evaluated as harmful to the individual, to others, or to both. It is acknowledged that establishing clinical significance requires a judgment of well-informed (and trained) individuals based on the gathering of reliable and relevant evidence. Primary areas of expression of the disturbance or dysfunction include cognition, mood, relations, interactions, self-regulation, and other behavior and its organization. Primary processes that might be involved include the biological, social, and personal (i.e., psychological), as well as the developmental. Primary impairments usually involved are in social, occupational, or other important functional activities. These might be judged to meet thresholds of disability. Note that mental disorder, impairment, and disability are not handicaps; the latter only refers to possible perception by the individual or by others. *Related Factors.* A mental disorder normally should be demarcated for original (and perpetuating) cause, both normatively in the population and individually for the patient. However, when knowledge either of the science or of the person precludes causal understanding, a mental disorder still can be attributed. A mental disorder normally should be amenable to intervention or treatment, and knowing the cause, and also isolating it as a reliable and valid category, would help in this regard. However, once more, knowledge of the science or of the person might limit effective intervention/treatment. • Nevertheless, the ultimate goal of the mental health professional, and/or the society in which they work, is to develop scientifically-informed and clinically useful mental disorder categories, dimensions, and their combinations (e.g., in diagnostic manuals) that help individuals diagnosed with mental disorders to stabilize/recover and have (or return to) a healthy, functional lifestyle. • Mental disorder has both common elements in its definition and language that allows its application differently to individuals, for example, depending on their context, sex (gender), majority/minority status, culture, age, history, developmental level, socioeconomic status, different informants, and societal and political considerations. • Examples that do not necessarily qualify as mental disorders include (a) an expectable or culturally-approved response to a common stressor or to a common loss, such as in the case of the death of a family member, or (b) socially-deviant behavior (e.g., sexual, religious, political) or conflicts that only express discord of the individual in society. • Overall, a mental disorder is a developmental biopsychosocial (biopersonalsocial) expression that has a (developmental) biopsychosocial etiology or causality and also needs a developmental biopsychosocial intervention/treatment.

Instrument

Üstün et al. (2010) developed the WHODAS-2.0 as a standardized cross-cultural measure of adaptive functioning and disability in six major life domains (see Table 22.8). The latter are tied to the International Classification of Functioning, Disability and Health (ICF, World Health Organization, 2001), and they include: (a) cognition; (b) mobility; (c) self-care; (d) getting along (social interaction); (e) life activities (including at work); and (f) participation in society. The schedule includes 36 items and several forms (e.g., self-report, interviewer-administered) as well as a reduced version (12 items). The DSM-5 contains only the 36-item, self-report version. The self-administered version requires 5–10 min to complete. Each item is answered on a 5-point scale from none to extreme. The timeframe for ratings is the "past 30 days," because some respondents have "problems with remembering" dysfunction that occurred more than one month previously. In testing the instrument, respondents reported difficulties with—increased effort, discomfort/pain, slowness, and changes in how

Table 22.8 World Health organization disability assessment schedule 2.0 (WHODAS 2.0)

Category	Question
Question	About your difficulties due to health/mental health conditions. Answer with one of the responses to these questions (none, mild, moderate, severe, extreme, or cannot do).
Understanding and communication	Concentrating for ten minutes?
	Remembering important things?
	Learning new task?
	Generally understanding?
	Starting/maintaining conversation?
Getting around	Standing 30 min or more?
	Standing up?
	Moving inside home?
	Leaving home?
	Walking a long distance (e.g., 1 k)?
Self-care	Washing?
	Dressing?
	Eating?
	Staying alone a few days?
Getting along with people	Dealing with strangers?
	Keeping a friend?
	Getting along with people close to you?
	Making a new friend?
	Sexual activities?
Life activities—Household	Taking care of household responsibilities?
	Doing the most important ones well?
	Getting all of it done that you had to?
	Getting it done on time?
Life activities—School/work	[Answer only if you work (paid, self-employed) or go to school]
	Difficulty in day-to-day work/school?
	In most important tasks well?
	Getting all of it done that you had to?
	Getting it done on time?
Participation in society	Problem in joining in community activities?
	Problem because of barriers or hindrances?
	Problem living with dignity because of the attitudes/actions of others?
	How much time spent on health condition/consequences?
	How much emotionally affected?
	How much drain on financial resources of you/family?
	How much of a problem does family have because of your health?
	How much of a problem did you have in relaxation/pleasureful activities?

Adapted from World Health Organization, 2012. Measuring health and disability: manual for WHO Disability Assessment Schedule (WHODAS 2.0), World Health Organization 2010, Geneva activities are undertaken. Whether by computer or hand, simple scoring (summing answers) is used to obtain total scores, with the six domain scores also possible. The simple method would seem to be the one of choice (DSM-5) for clinicians. However, it does not come with norms.

Results on the WHODAS-2.0 were calculated with the populations tested in 19 countries. In each site, there were four undefined groups labeled as: apparent good health; people with physical disorders; people with mental/emotional ones; and people with alcohol/drug use. The authors reported that the WHODAS-2.0 schedule evidenced adequate reliability and validity (for the observer/rater version scored with the complex method). As for differences among the four groups, they scored differently on items relevant to their condition or group description, indicating adequate face validity for the instrument. Cut-off scores were not calculated, although IRT (Item Response Theory) analysis indicated that a score of 22 corresponded to a population percentile of 80. This level would appear to be the recommended clinically useful cut score. It does make clinical sense, in that the top 20 % of respondents on the instrument could reasonably be termed disabled. Üstün et al. (2010) concluded that the WHODAS-2's limitations involve its lack of consideration of both bodily impairments and environmental factors. However, we add that, although the manual for the WHODAS-2.0 concludes that reading it and doing its exercises constitute sufficient user training, this does not constitute sufficient training.

Critique

Gold (2014) reviewed the characteristics and limitations of the WHODAS-2.0 for use in disability assessments. (a) She noted that although the DSM-5 recommends it in the assessment of global function and impairment instead of the GAF, it is placed in a section on emerging measures only, and not in the text proper. (b) She noted issues with the psychometrics of the schedule for clinician rating, and these issues apply to the proxy version, as well.

Gold (2014, p. 179) pointed out that although the DSM-5 included the self-report version of the WHODAS-2.0, clinicians can alter the ratings given if the evidence supports the change. Also, for the clinician-rated version, the psychometric properties appear not to have been studied. Therefore, there is no data on its "reliability and validity." Consequently, in some forensic-related examinations, in some sense, careful use of the GAF is preferable to using the WHODAS-2.0, especially given that the DSM-IV-TR is not being discarded for use by the DSM-5 (Gold, 2014).

(c) Further, the WHODAS-2.0 might not be reliable for individuals having a high baseline before its need in an assessment. (d) The simple scoring method, the one that the DSM-5 points out would be preferred by clinicians, has no normative values. (e) The WHODAS-2.0 confounds medical and psychiatric impairment by trying to be global and not differentiating them. (f) It does not exclude appropriately environmental context. (g) It lacks internal indices of validity. (g) Finally, the GAF is not going to disappear, because it is still required in many disability assessment venues.

The WHODAS-2.0 also is in the public domain. Psychological tests in medical/legal contexts are generally only available to professionals, such as psychologists, rather than generally to the public. This helps maintain their validity by preventing claimants from studying for tests used in their assessments. Therefore, the WHODAS-2.0's use in the forensic context appears compromised to begin with because of its general availability.

Conclusion

DSM-5 recommends the WHODAS-2.0 to assess disability. It is a cross-culturally validated scale of 36 items split into six domains. However, it has several properties that reduce its value in some forensic assessments. Among them, it confounds psychiatrically-related and physically-related functional limitations. It does not assess respondent validity. Its user qualifications appear not conservative enough.

Chapter Conclusions

The release of the DSM-5 was preceded by years of criticisms and concerns and, surely, they will follow for more years now that the DSM-5 has been published. I have shown general problems with the DSM-5 that have been described in the literature, as well as problems with specific disorders. In order for it to achieve its goals of being clinically useful and based on extant research, e.g., for biomarkers, it needs to be open to input from clinicians, all stakeholders, forensic practitioners, researchers, and patients. This will help in developing a better definition for mental disorder and also including in it better or more valid diagnostic categories. As well, it will move it toward its goal of integrating a dimensional perspective. However, only use of a stringent scientific approach and an open process in its construction can help the DSM project realize its objectives. As new iterations are developed for clinical use, the kinds of difficulties and tensions described in this chapter should be addressed openly.

In the next two chapters of the present work, I examine more closely some of the major psychiatric disorders in the DSM-5 manual. I scrutinize the specific criteria for them. In addition, I conduct a literature review related to them. The chapters include a preview of the ICD-11 for PTSD, and I compare that approach to the one in the DSM-5. Most important, the chapters examine the RDoC project, and the degree to which it can succeed in its stated goal of establishing the neuroscientific bases, in particular, of mental disorders toward creating a better psychiatric diagnostic system.

References

Achenbach, T. M. (1991). *Integrative guide for the 1991 CBCL/4–18, YSR, and TRF profiles*. Burlington, VT: University of Vermont, Department of Psychiatry.

Achenbach, T. M., & Rescorla, L. (2001). *Manual for the ASEBA School-Age Forms & Profiles*. Burlington, VT: University of Vermont, Research Center for Children, Youth, & Families.

American Psychiatric Association. (1980). *Diagnostic and statistical manual of mental disorders* (3rd ed.). Washington, DC: Author.

American Psychiatric Association. (1994). *Diagnostic and statistical manual of mental disorders (DSM-IV)*. Washington, DC: Author.

American Psychiatric Association. (2000). *Diagnostic and statistical manual of mental disorders: DSM-IV-TR* (4th ed., text rev.). Washington, DC: Author.

American Psychiatric Association. (2013a). *Diagnostic and statistical manual of mental disorders: DSM-5* (5th ed.). Washington, DC: Author.

American Psychiatric Association. (2013b). Highlights of changes from DSM-IV-TR-DSM-5. Retrieved from http://www.dsm5.org/Documents/changes%20from%20dsm-iv-tr%20to%20dsm-5.pdf

Appelbaum, P. S. (2014). Commentary: DSM-5 and forensic psychiatry. *The Journal of the American Academy of Psychiatry and the Law, 42*, 136–140.

Bechtel, W., & Richardson, R. C. (2010). *Discovering complexity. Decomposition and localization as strategies in scientific research*. Cambridge, MA: MIT Press.

Berk, M. (2013). The DSM-5: Hyperbole, hope, or hypothesis? *BioMed Central Medicine, 11*, 128. doi:10.1186/1741-7015-11-128.

Blashfield, R. K., Keeley, J. W., Flanagan, E. H., & Miles, S. R. (2014). The cycle of classification: DSM-I through DSM-5. *Annual Review of Clinical Psychology, 10*, 25–51.

Blumenthal-Barby, J. S. (2013). Psychiatry's new manual (DSM-5): Ethical and conceptual dimensions. *Journal of Medical Ethics, 40*, 531–536.

Clarke, D. E., Narrow, W. E., Regier, D. A., Kuramoto, S. J., Kupfer, D. J., Kuhl, E. A., et al. (2013). DSM-5 field trials in the United States and Canada, part I: Study design, sampling strategy, implementation, and analytic approaches. *American Journal of Psychiatry, 170*, 43–58.

Cosgrove, L., & Krimsky, S. (2013). A comparison of DSM-IV and DSM-5 panel member's financial associations with industry: A pernicious problem persists. *PLoS Medicine, 9*, e1001190. doi:10.1371/journal.pmed.1001190.

Cosgrove, L., & Wheeler, E. E. (2013). Industry's colonization of psychiatry: Ethical and practical implications of financial conflicts of interest in the DSM-5. *Feminism & Psychology, 23*, 93–106.

First, M. B. (2010). The PTSD stressor criterion as a barrier to malingering: DSM-5 draft commentaries. *Psychological Injury and Law, 3*, 255–259.

First, M. B. (2011). DSM-5 proposals for mood disorders: A cost-benefit analysis. *Current Opinions in Psychiatry, 24*, 1–9.

First, M. B. (2014). Empirical grounding versus innovation in the DSM-5 revision process: Implications for the future. *Clinical Psychology: Science and Practice, 21*, 262–268.

Frances, A. (2013a). *Essentials of psychiatric diagnosis: Responding to the challenge of DSM-5*. New York: Guilford Press.

Frances, A. (2013b). DSM in philosophyland: Curiouser and curiouser. In J. Paris & J. Phillips (Eds.), *Making the DSM-5: Concepts and controversies* (pp. 95–103). New York: Springer Science+Business Media.

Frances, A. (2013c). The new somatic symptom disorder in DSM-5 risks mislabeling many people as mentally ill. *British Medical Journal, 346*. doi:10.1136/bmj.f1580.

Frances, A. (2013d). DSM-5 somatic symptom disorder. *The Journal of Nervous and Mental Disease, 201*, 530–531.

Frances, A. (2013e, June 11). DSM-5 badly flunks the writing test. *Psychiatric Times*. Retrieved from http://www.psychiatrictimes.com/dsm-5-badly-flunks-writing-test

Frances, A., & Widiger, T. (2012). Psychiatric diagnosis: Lessons from the DSM-IV past and cautions for the DSM-5 future. *Annual Review of Clinical Psychology, 8*, 109–130.

Freedman, R., Lewis, D. A., Michels, R., Pine, D. S., Schultz, S. K., Tamminga, C. A., et al. (2013). The initial field trials of DSM-5: New blooms and old thorns. *American Journal of Psychiatry, 170*, 1–5.

Fried, E. I., Nesse, R. M., Zivin, K., Guille, C., & Sen, S. (2014). Depression in more than the sum score of its parts: Individual DSM symptoms have different risk factors. *Psychological Medicine, 44*, 2067–2076.

Gold, L. H. (2014). DSM-5 and the assessment of functioning: The World Health Organization Disability Assessment Schedule 2.0 (WHODAS 2.0). *The Journal of the American Academy of Psychiatric and the Law, 42*, 173–181.

Gordon, R. M., & Cosgrove, L. (2013). Ethical considerations in the development and application of mental and behavioral nosologies: Lessons from DSM-5. *Psychological Injury and Law, 6*, 330–335.

Gornall, J. (2013). DSM-5: A fatal diagnosis? *British Medicine Journal, 346*. doi:10.1136/bmj.f3256.

Huerta, M., Bishop, S. L., Duncan, A., Hus, V., & Lord, C. (2012). Application of DSM-5 criteria for autism spectrum disorder to three samples of children with DSM-IV diagnoses of pervasive developmental disorder. *American Journal of Psychiatry, 169*, 1056–1064.

Insel, T. R., Cuthbert, B. N., Garvey, M. A., Heinssen, R. K., Pine, D. S., Quinn, K. J., et al. (2010). Research domain criteria (RDoC): Toward a new classification framework for research on mental disorders. *American Journal of Psychiatry, 167*, 748–751.

Jones, K. D. (2012). A critique of the DSM-5 field trials. *The Journal of Nervous and Mental Disease, 200*, 517–519.

Joober, R. (2013). On the simple and the complex in psychiatry, with reference to DSM 5 and research domain criteria. *Journal of Psychiatry and Neuroscience, 38*, 148–151.

Kendler, K. S. (2008). Explanatory models for psychiatric illness. *American Journal of Psychiatry, 165*, 695–702.

Kendler, K. S. (2012). The dappled nature of causes of psychiatric illness: Replacing the organic-functional/hardware-software dichotomy with empirically based pluralism. *Molecular Psychiatry, 17*, 377–388.

Kessler, R. C., & Wang, P. S. (2008). The descriptive epidemiology of commonly occurring mental disorders in the United States. *Annual Review of Public Health, 29*, 115–129.

Khoury, B., Langer, E. J., & Pagnini, F. (2014). The DSM: Mindful science or mindless power? A critical review. *Frontiers in Psychology, 5*, 602. doi:10.3389/fpsyg.2014.00602.

Kinghorn, W. (2013). The biopolitics of defining "mental disorder.". In J. Paris & J. Phillips (Eds.), *Making the DSM-5: Concepts and controversies* (pp. 47–61). New York: Springer Science+Business Media.

Kraemer, H. C., Kupfer, D. J., Clarke, D. E., Narrow, W. E., & Regier, D. A. (2012). DSM-5: How reliable is reliable enough? *American Journal of Psychiatry, 169*, 13–15.

Krueger, R. F., Hopwood, C. J., Wright, A. G. C., & Markon, K. E. (2014). DSM-5 and the path toward empirically based and clinically useful conceptualization of personality and psychopathology. *Clinical Psychology: Science and Practice, 21*, 245–261.

Kupfer, D. J., Kuhl, E. A., & Regier, D. A. (2013). DSM-5 – The future arrived. *Journal of American Medical Association, 309*, 1691–1692.

Lilienfeld, S. O. (2014). DSM-5: Centripetal scientific and centrifugal antiscientific forces. *Clinical Psychology: Science and Practice, 21*, 269–279.

Livesley, W. J. (2011). The current state of personality disorder classification. *Journal of Personality Disorders, 25*, 269–278.

Mayes, S. D., Black, A., & Tierney, C. D. (2013). DSM-5 under-identifies PDDNOS: Diagnostic agreement between the DSM-5, DSM-IV, and checklist for autism spectrum disorder. *Research in Autism Spectrum Disorders, 7*, 298–306.

McEwen, B. S., & Getz, L. (2013). Lifetime experiences, the brain and personalized medicine: An integrative perspective. *Metabolism, Clinical and Experimental, 62*, S20–S26.

Mishara, A. L., & Schwartz, M. A. (2013). What does phenomenology contribute to the debate about DSM-5? In J. Paris & J. Phillips (Eds.), *Making the DSM-5: Concepts and controversies* (pp. 125–142). New York: Springer Science+Business Media.

Moffitt, T. E., Caspi, A., Taylor, A., Kokaua, J., Milne, B. J., Planczyk, G., et al. (2010). How common are common mental disorders? Evidence that lifetime prevalence rates are doubled by prospective versus retrospective ascertainment. *Psychological Medicine, 40*, 899–909.

Narrow, W. E., Clarke, D. E., Kuramoto, S. J., Kraemer, H. C., Kupfer, D. J., Greiner, L., et al. (2013). DSM-5 field trials in the United States and Canada, part III: Development and reliability testing of a cross-cutting symptom assessment for DSM-5. *American Journal of Psychiatry, 170*, 71–82.

Paris, J. (2013a). *The intelligent clinician's guide to the DSM-5*. New York: Oxford University Press.

Paris, J. (2013b). The ideology behind DSM-5. In J. Paris & J. Phillips (Eds.), *Making the DSM-5: Concepts and controversies* (pp. 39–44). New York: Springer Science+Business Media.

Phillips, J. (2013a). The conceptual status of DSM-5 diagnoses. In J. Paris & J. Phillips (Eds.), *Making the DSM-5: Concepts and controversies* (pp. 143–157). New York: Springer Science+Business Media.

Phillips, J. (2013b). Conclusion. In J. Paris & J. Phillips (Eds.), *Making the DSM-5: Concepts and controversies* (pp. 159–175). New York: Springer Science+Business Media.

Pierre, J. M. (2013). Overdiagnosis, underdiagnosis, synthesis: A dialectic for psychiatry and the DSM. In J. Paris & J. Phillips (Eds.), *Making the DSM-5: Concepts and controversies* (pp. 105–124). New York: Springer Science+Business Media.

Porter, D. (2013). Establishing normative validity for scientific psychiatric nosology: The significance of integrating patient perspectives. In J. Paris & J. Phillips (Eds.), *Making the DSM-5: Concepts and controversies* (pp. 63–74). New York: Springer Science+Business Media.

Regier, D. A., Kuhl, E. A., & Kupfer, D. J. (2013). The DSM-5: Classification and criteria change. *World Psychiatry, 12*, 92–98.

Regier, D. A., Narrow, W. E., Clarke, D. E., Kraemer, H. C., Kuramoto, S. J., Kuhl, E. A., et al. (2013). DSM-5 field trials in the United States and Canada, part II: Test-retest reliability of selected categorical diagnoses. *American Journal of Psychiatry, 170*, 59–70.

Sadler, J. Z. (2013). Considering the economy of DSM alternatives. In J. Paris & J. Phillips (Eds.), *Making the DSM-5: Concepts and controversies* (pp. 21–38). New York: Springer Science+Business Media.

Sax, L. (2013, June 26). "Unspecified mental disorder?" That's crazy. Psychiatry's diagnostic bible has broadened the definition of mental illness to absurdity. *Wall Street Journal*. Retrieved from http://online.wsj.com/article/SB10001424127887323844804578529030063800200.html

Shorter, E. (2013). The history of DSM. In J. Paris & J. Phillips (Eds.), *Making the DSM-5: Concepts and controversies* (pp. 3–19). New York: Springer Science+Business Media.

Thomas, L. C. (2013). The DSM-5 and forensic relationship status: It's complicated. *Psychological Injury and Law, 6*, 324–329.

Torjesen, I. (2013). Architect of DSM-5 rejects claims it will lead to labelling of more people as mentally ill. *British Medical Journal, 346*. doi:10.1136/bmj.f3648.

Üstün, T. B., Chatterji, S., Konstanjsek, N., Rehm, J., Kennedy, C., Epping-Jordan, J., et al. (2010). Developing the World Health Organization Disability Assessment Schedule 2.0. *Bulletin of the World Health Organization, 88*, 815–823.

Wakefield, J. C. (1992). Disorder as harmful dysfunction: A conceptual critique of DSM-III-R's definition of mental disorder. *Psychological Review, 99*, 232–247.

Wakefield, J. C. (2013). The DSM-5 debate over the bereavement exclusion: Psychiatric diagnosis and the future of empirically supported treatment. *Clinical Psychology Review, 33*, 825–845.

Wakefield, J. C., & First, M. B. (2012). Validity of the bereavement exclusion to major depression: does the empirical evidence support the proposal to eliminate the exclusion in DSM-5? *World Psychiatry, 11*, 3–10.

Whooley, O., & Horwitz, A. V. (2013). The paradox of professional success: Grand ambition, furious resistance, and the derailment of the DSM-5 revision process. In J. Paris & J. Phillips (Eds.), *Making the DSM-5: Concepts and controversies* (pp. 75–92). New York: Springer Science+Business Media.

Widiger, T. A. (2011). A shaky future for personality disorders. *Personality Disorders: Theory, Research, and Treatment, 2*, 54–67.

Widiger, T. A., Frances, A. J., & Pincus, H. A. (1997). *DSM-IV sourcebook* (Vol. 1–4). Washington, DC: American Psychiatric Association.

Willis, C. D., & Gold, L. H. (2014). Introduction to the special section on DSM-5 and forensic psychiatry. *The Journal of the American Academy of Psychiatry and the Law, 42*, 132–135.

World Health Organization. (2001). *International classification of functioning, disability and health*. Geneva, Switzerland: Author.

World Health Organization. (2007). *International Statistical Classification of Diseases and Related Health Problems 10th Revision*. Retrieved from http://www.who.int/classifications/icd/en/

Wortzel, H. S. (2013). The DSM-5 and forensic psychiatry. *Journal of Psychiatric Practice, 13*, 238–241.

Young, G. (2011). *Development and causality: Neo-Piagetian perspectives*. New York: Springer Science+Business Media.

Young, G. (2014). Psychological injury and law II: Implications for mental health policy and ethics. *Mental Health Law & Policy Journal, 3*, 418–470.

Young, G., Lareau, C., & Pierre, B. (2014). One quintillion ways to have PTSD comorbidity: Recommendations for the disordered DSM-5. *Psychological Injury and Law, 7*, 61–74.

Young, G., & Yehuda, R. (2006). Understanding PTSD: Implications for court. In G. Young, A. W. Kane, & K. Nicholson (Eds.), *Psychological knowledge in court: PTSD, pain, and TBI* (pp. 55–69). New York: Springer Science+Business Media.

The DSM-5 and the RDoC: Grand Designs and Grander Problems

23

Chapter Introduction

This chapter and the next one examine in depth some of the major categories of mental disorder in the DSM-5 (Diagnostic and Statistical Manual of Mental Disorders, Fifth Edition; American Psychiatric Association, 2013), as well as their criticisms. However, before beginning that process, it presents in depth details and criticisms of the RDoC project (Research Domain Criteria; Insel et al., 2010; Insel & Lieberman, 2013). The RDoC is founded on the assumption that mental illness concerns especially "brain function and structure." The RDoC is a project of the US NIMH (National Institute of Mental Health), and it is meant to guide priorities in American federal funding in mental health research. A second goal of the RDoC project is to inform psychiatric nosology in terms of the scientific bases in genetics, neuroscience, and behavioral science for the task of establishing valid psychiatric categories.

The second part of this chapter considers the major psychological injuries related to trauma, which especially involves posttraumatic stress disorder (PTSD). In particular, this part of the chapter considers the criteria for PTSD, as well as for acute stress disorder, specific phobia, and adjustment disorder. The next chapter of the book continues with presentation of the criteria in the DSM-5 for neurocognitive disorder (NCD) and somatic symptom disorder (SDD). As well, it deals with recent research on the personality disorder proposals in the DSM-5. Another focus of the next chapter is on malingering, especially because it was not changed much in the DSM-5, but merits much change. Then, the last chapter of this two-chapter sequence on the DSM-5's changes to its specific disorders concludes with a comparison of the DSM-5's and the ICD-11's (International Statistical Classification of Diseases and Related Health Problems, 11th Revision; World Health Organization, 2017) approaches to PTSD and related stress disorders.

Research Domain Criteria

Introduction

Insel and Lieberman (2013) qualified that the RDoC (Research Domain Criteria) is based on the assumption that mental illness can be understood best as constituting disorders of "brain function and structure" that affect the domains of cognition, emotion, and behavior. The goal of the RDoC project is to create a new type of psychiatric nosology informed by genetics, neuroscience, and behavioral science. Long term, the goal is that its findings will be incorporated in future iterations of the DSM (Diagnostic and Statistical Manual of Mental Disorders).

The structure of the RDoC includes five domains of function: positive valence systems, negative valence systems, cognitive systems,

G. Young, *Unifying Causality and Psychology*, DOI 10.1007/978-3-319-24094-7_23

social process systems, and arousal regulatory systems (e.g., Simmons & Quinn, 2014). Further, each of the five domains consists of constructs and, also, each must map directly onto specific biological systems, such as neural circuits. Moreover, for each construct, there are eight units of analysis that should be considered in research, from genes to behavior to paradigms. The negative valence domain provides a good example of the RDoC proposal. It is constituted by the systems of acute threat (fear), potential threat (anxiety), sustained threat, loss, and frustrative nonreward.

Comment

I remark that the latter two systems are not associated with a basic emotion, but could be, just as the first two are (i.e., depression and irritability, respectively). As for the cognitive and social process systems, they seem to incorrectly exclude social cognition as part of an integrated psychological model.

Endophenotype and the RDoC

Lenzenweger (2013) reinforced the distinction between endophenotype, intermediate phenotype, and biomarker. He considered the concept of endophenotype as the most proximate to the goal of the RDoC project (Insel et al., 2010). The concept of endophenotype (Gottesman & Gould, 2003; Gottesman & McGue, 2015; Gottesman & Shields, 1972; Gould & Gottesman, 2006; Shields & Gottesman, 1973) refers to a measurable component that lies within the pathway to disease, from distal genotype to manifest phenotype. Normally, an endophenotype is unseen. It is not a risk factor in disease but a reflection of an expressed genetic substrate within the disease pathway. It is an internal manifestation of an underlying disease liability. Not only is it measured at the biological level (neurophysiology, endocrinology, neuroanatomical), but also it can be measured at the psychological one (e.g., cognitive, neuropsychological, self-report inventory), at least as long as the measure involved lies along the disease or syndrome pathway beginning with the genetic underpinning at issue.

Gottesman and colleagues elaborated specific criteria for an endophenotypic candidate. (a) It must be associated with disease in a population. (b) It is heritable (unlike a biomarker, which need not be). (c) Ideally, it is state-independent, being expressed even if the disease is not yet active, and it might be developmentally variable. (d) It expresses increased prevalence in ill relatives of diseased probands (subjects of study) compared to well relatives (cosegregation). (e) There are family associations evident. (f) Ideally, it is uniquely associated with the disease at issue.

There are several benefits of adopting the endophenotypic concept. (a) When it is elementary, an endophenotype likely reflects genetic activity (e.g., physiological, synaptic, and other neural mechanisms). (b) The quantitative measurement involved facilitates quantitative trait linkage analysis. (c) By adding brain-imaging research and infrahuman animal model research, candidate genes can be better identified. (d) Endophenotypes could be used directly in animal models.

As for biomarkers (Biomarkers Definition Working Group, 2001), they include any measurable indicator of a disease, whether heritable (genetic) or not, or actually involved in the causal pathway from gene to disease or not. Therefore, a biomarker might even include the impact of an outside environmental agent on the individual (e.g., a molecular reaction to a toxin, a pharmacological response to a therapeutic intervention). Lenzenweger (2013) added that although all endophenotypes constitute biomarkers, all the latter are not necessarily the former.

With respect to intermediate phenotypes, its definition has varied, and more recently includes that is a heritable trait in the pathogenetic pathway from genetic predisposition to psychiatric disease (Rasetti & Weinberger, 2011). This current definition of intermediate phenotype is indistinguishable from that of endophenotype. Prior definitions were imprecise. Moreover, the use of the word "intermediate" in the term renders it ambiguous, and it has been used in a confused way. For Lenzenweger (2013), the term should be reserved for use at its origins in Mendelian genetics.

Lenzenweger (2013) concluded that finding endophenotypes will serve to reduce heterogeneity in psychopathology research. The endophenotypes for the “main processes” (etiological, psychopathological, developmental) involved in the RDoC proposal appear an important starting point.

Development

Beauchaine and McNulty (2013) indicated how difficult it is to elucidate developmental pathways in disease. Their example concerns trait impulsivity, which has different developmental outcomes at different developmental periods. Research needs to consider comorbidities and continuities associated with developmental disorders and their underlying liabilities or trait vulnerabilities. These latter traits, such as impulsivity, lie at a level of analysis important for the RDoC project, but the behavioral syndromes and diseases to which they contribute are the focus of the DSMs. Disease pathways start from genetic vulnerability and expressed neural/hormonal substrates underpinning RDoC foci, but they also include environmental risk mediators at all developmental phases, including prenatally. Moreover, influences are bidirectional, with recursive feedback loops.

Comment

We can conclude that the complexity of developmental psychopathology precludes a predominant biological, neuroscientific, or exclusively distal centration in the RDoC project. Endophenotypes do not exclusively lie at these levels in the causal pathway from genes to disease. The RDoC goal is laudable; however, we need to ask to what extent it considers environmental impacts, including in epigenesis, gene–environment interactions, and other effects on the causal pathway to disease that complexify the process, rendering RDoC foci more heterogenous than anticipated. Moreover, the research is advancing so quickly in the field that the original RDoC foci might be superceded by more current conceptualizations (e.g., neural networks; Sporns, 2011, 2012). Finally, the pathway from genes to disease presumes understanding of the disease at issue. The difficulties confronted by the DSMs in specifying psychiatric nosology (e.g., Young, 2014) speak to the care needed in this regard. The task is not only to move forward from genes to disease in understanding psychiatric causality but also to move backward from an accurate depiction of disease toward their endophenotypic and genetic substrates.

Not Reductionistic

A major advance in the RDoC approach is that it is fully dimensional, placing normal and abnormal behavior on a continuum on which genetic and related findings apply to the full spectrum of phenotypic expression (Cuthbert & Kozak, 2013). Its findings should cut across diagnostic categories (Owen, 2012).

Cuthbert and Kozak (2013) argued that the RDoC project is not reductionistic of psychiatric illness to biology, genes, and brain disorder, a criticism raised by Berenbaum (2013). Rather, valid psychological constructs have been incorporated in the RDoC project.

Comment

However, I note that psychological constructs in the RDoC are subsumed in domains selected for their biological significance as brain basis. Granted, the RDoC project seeks integrated “psychobiological” explanations of psychiatric problems beyond uniquely biological or psychological ones (Cuthbert & Kozak, 2013). However, the underlying model still excludes an integrated “biopsychosocial” model as an integrating one, at least overtly as a fundamental starting point.

Overt acknowledgment of the important role of environment, context, and the social on an equal footing to the biological, as well as the full panoply of psychological processes, such as with self-processes and self-regulation (and the degree that they can become emergent and go beyond biological and social prescriptions and proscriptions) is fundamental in understanding behavior. Granted, the RDoC program eschews a fundamental brain–mind, or biological–behavioral identity or isomorphism, but it still can be perceived as "eliminative reductionistic," despite its defense and arguments to the contrary, because it does not include directly elements that stand in direct contrast to reductionism.

Note that acceptance of a frank biopsychosocial project to the RDoC proposal would not undermine its genetic, heritable, and biological emphasis, because it only would supplement it with valid mediators and moderators of biological effects on behavior. For example, genetic influences work to cause behavior through environmental supports, and the effects of the environment on genetics now is known to include epigenetic (environmentally-mediated) influences of genetic expression (e.g., gene silencing by DNA methylation).

Therefore, the RDoC project needs to be continually open to new developments in the field. Its levels of analysis component permits that, but it should be embedded directly into its domains, constructs and, indeed, in its overarching model. Environment, psychology, self, and the social are intrinsic to psychiatric disorder, and the fundamental assumptions undergirding the nosological RDoC project should be inclusive of terms such as these in the model it espouses as representative of psychiatric processes. Granted, research in these non-biological lines will be supported by funding agencies, but without acknowledging openly these important avenues, their just place in the RDoC project might not be properly promoted.

Epigenesis

The RDoC project seems to be considering these concerns to a degree. For example, Morris, Rumsey, and Cuthbert (2014) referred to the RDoC as providing a "neuroscience-based" or "anchored" nosological framework using advances in "modern neuroscience." However, they also referred to the processes of learning, brain plasticity (although as an "orthogonal" dimension), the environment, and epigenetics. Mental disorders are considered to express dysfunctional neural circuits that can be insidious in their effects, which might precede frank symptomatology by years. Moreover, the circuits might be widely distributed rather than localized.

According to Morris et al. (2014), brains change in response to experience, exposure, and learning. Developmental neuroplasticity reverberates with changes outside of genetic factors, such as epigenetics. Neurogenesis continues in the adult, but is conditioned ("recapitulates") prenatal neurogenetic "interaction" with it, thereby being "impacted" by early experiences. Moreover, neuroplasticity includes environmental (intrinsic, extrinsic) effects on existing neurons and their circuits. In cases of maladaptive behavior, the neuroplasticity might be hyper- or hypo-, or otherwise dysfunctional.

As for epigenesis (Feil, 2008; Meaney, 2010), it can affect long-term neuroplasticity, learning, and memory, in that a majority of the genes that are affected by epigenesis are expressed in brain tissue (Wilkinson, Davies, & Iseles, 2007). The vital role played in the gene-silencing activity in epigenesis is demonstrated by the inheritance of the genetic silencing that is found in offspring, despite not having experienced the environmental impacts that had, in the first place, induced the epigenetic processes.

Epigenesis can help explain the variation in pattern of risk and inheritance within and among mental disorders. As well, it can help elucidate trajectories of remission and relapse and the cross-disorder overlapping genetic variants. According to Morris et al. (2014), these types of findings do not align with traditional psychiatric classification systems.

Comment

Much of the remaining portions of the review of the RDoC project conducted by Morris et al. (2014) focused on intervention research. To their credit, they included evidence-based psychotherapies along with psychopharmacology. However, I note that the goal of their review was based on a small range of treatments and on their neurobiological effects. A more overtly proclaimed biopsychosocial focus on the RDoC project might serve to expand this lens on psychotherapy, and open it better to effective individualized treatment.

This would not deny the essential scientific and practice value of the RDoC project, nor would it work against its ultimate goal. Although I acknowledge that research along these lines could take place outside of the RDoC parameters, by being inclusive in these areas of psychiatric study (more or less at its outset), it might better help in the RDoC's ultimate goal of improving psychiatric nosology and effective treatment for patients diagnosed with the new classification system that will emerge as it informs work on future DSMs.

DSM-5

Morris and Cuthbert (2013) underscored the advantages of the RDoC project relative to extant psychiatric classificatory systems (DSMs, ICDs; International Statistical Classification of Diseases and Related Health Problems). The latter seek diagnostic categories, but their variability or heterogeneity in symptom expression belies their underlying rationale of including in them categorical disorders, or unitary entities, with "normal variance." Therefore, it might be futile to seek "common causes" that account for the heterogeneity in diagnostic categories.

That being said, for Morris and Cuthbert (2013), the extant diagnostic systems have attained a degree of success that constitutes a major obstacle in their consideration of substantive change. For example, the DSMs are "completely integrated" into practice diagnostic codes, insurance payments, and disability determinations, as well as regulatory agency guidelines and a host of research components, such as clinical trials.

Comment

As a final comment to the RDoC project from Morris and Cuthbert (2013), we learn that the "paradigms" described in the RDoC refer to useful "scientific tasks." This definition is quite unlike the standard one for paradigms, and it hints at their emphasis on the biological origins to behavior and psychopathology. However, once more, I note that paradigms should include complementary perspectives to the major neurobiological or neuroscientific one of the RDoC, that is, a fully scientific RDoC should include within its "paradigms" especially the complementary model to its primary emphasis—the biopsychosocial one.

Most Recent Criticisms

The latter conclusion is echoed in the more recent literature on the RDoC. Insel (2014) referred to the RDoC project in terms of "precision medicine" for psychiatry. Lilienfeld (2014) maintained that the RDoC's emphasis on mental disorder "fundamentally" involving brain circuit disorder risks, while de-emphasizing psychosocial and cultural factors. Harkness, Reynolds, and Lilienfeld (2014) asked that the RDoC consider use of measurement operations tied to theory and that are "falsifiable." Moreover, the best measurement of individual differences in systems require "traditional psychological" ones. About development, Sonuga-Barke (2014) did not consider that the RDoC sufficiently "considered" it in its conceptualization.

Whooley (2014) opined that the "brain-centric" focus of the RDoC serves to "decontextualize" mental illness and set aside "social embeddedness" and culture. It demotes or reduces the social and environmental. On the contrary, the biological and social always should be considered interrelated and intertwined in mental distress. Frances (2014) reminded that context and environment are important in the latter.

Maj (2014) considered the RDoC project perhaps "somewhat distant" from clinical phenomena. It is a dehumanizing oversimplification or downgrade of psychopathology/practice. Jablensky and Waters (2014) indicated that patients enter the office with their phenotypes, not with their genotypes or biosignatures. Parnas (2014) added that psychiatrists treat people, not brain circuits. First (2014) continued that the RDoC has to make "clinical sense." Sartorius (2014) agreed that psychopathological components include the biological, psychological, and social. Stein (2014) concurred that psychopathology has multiple components, including the social context. Fulford (2014) opined that the RDoC needs to take symptoms seriously.

Wakefield (2014) worried that the environmental/social construct in the RDoC does not include that human psychological mechanisms are prepared biologically for sensitive response to the social/environmental context. Phillips (2014) worried that it would not address culture and the biopsychosocial because of its "siren call" for biological "fixes." Weinberger and Goldberg (2014) worried about that "validity" of the behavioral, neural genetic, and functional dimensions of the RDoC.

In response, Cuthbert (2014a) maintained that the overall matrix approach of the RDoC allows for environmental, neurodevelopmental, psychological, and behavioral aspects, with the neural system serving an "implementing" function. Cuthbert (2014b) added that the RDoC eventually will be "useful" for clinical work. Neural systems/circuits play preponderant roles in the RDoC, with the social and environment as factors, too. It is "harnessing" genetics and neuroscience toward more "effective" prevention and treatment.

Comment

The RDoC is an emerging critical framework in mental health research and it will inform and channel conceptualization and empirical investigation in the field, including for the DSM-5, generally, and for specific disorders, such as PTSD. However, its neuroscientific focus (even though it offers qualifications on this issue) appears to preclude a wider model of psychopathology and its development in context, such as the biopsychosocial one. Fixation on biological markers of psychiatric disease might retard the search for appropriate markers of disorder. The field needs both a biological approach to narrow heterogeneity in illness expression and a psychosocial and social one to understand the full range of such heterogeneity.

Perhaps symptoms for disorders can be arranged into primary, secondary, and tertiary clusters (e.g., marker, core, and cross-diagnostic ones, with the latter ones less relevant; Young, Lareau, & Pierre, 2014). This approach could help lead to a better understanding of the disorders, and reduce their heterogeneous expression, by focusing especially on primary and secondary symptoms instead of considering them all equal in their differentiating quality. Once disorders are better understood and simplified, it might be easier to find the correct candidate endophenotypes that are involved in the genomic-disease pathway. An approach such as this will make the RDoC "patient-centric" instead of only "brain-centric" and will help toward improving both the DSM-5 and appropriate psychotherapy with patients diagnosed with its disorders.

The DSM-5 and Psychological Injuries

A psychological injury is a psychological "mental harm" causally related to an event at issue that can result in an actionable claim. It has a functional impact, requires treatment, and leads to disability. It is vetted in assessments in order to have malingering ruled out, as well as rule-out by pre-event psychological vulnerabilities or other factors. However, psychological injury cases are complicated, for example, due to the "gray zone." Among other things, in forensic/disability cases, the gray zone refers to the role of exaggeration and other response styles that are not direct malingering, and to feigning, in general, as well as difficulty in diagnosing and dealing with comorbidities.

All of the critical terms in the area of psychological injury and law can be contested, e.g., mental harm, causality, functional impact, disability, malingering, and the major diagnoses involved. The typical diagnoses are PTSD, pain-related conditions, mild traumatic brain injury (TBI), adjustment disorder, depression, or other anxiety disorders (e.g., phobia, generalized anxiety disorder). The field is further in turmoil because, as has been shown, the new version of the premiere diagnostic manual, the DSM-5, is itself contested. But the critical forensic question is how much do these DSM-5 changes matter—generally, in forensic work, the importance in an assessment relates to the functional impact of the injury at hand for the legal question at hand, and not in the particular disorder(s) diagnosed. That being said, the present chapter examines extremely carefully the criteria of the major diagnoses related to psychological injury and law.

PTSD represents the quintessential DSM-5 disorder for the area of psychological injury and law. It is contested for its causation, symptom expression, ease in malingering, and overall validity. Therefore, we need to analyze it especially carefully as presented in the DSM-5 and in research. The following material in this chapter and the next chapter also analyzes in depth other specific DSM-5 disorders that are relevant to psychological injury and law. In particular, I focus not only on PTSD but also on brain injury-related conditions and chronic pain conditions, along with other related disorders.

PTSD in the DSM-5

Description and Concerns

Table 23.1 presents the criteria defining PTSD in the DSM-5. Aside from the causal criterion, there

Table 23.1 DSM-5 criteria for posttraumatic stress disorder (PTSD), slightly adjusted

A. Exposure to one (or more) of these event(s): death/threatened death; actual/threatened serious injury; actual/threatened sexual violation. This happens in the following way(s): 1. Experiencing oneself 2. Personally witnessing it as it occurs to others 3. Learning that it occurred to a close relative/friend; the actual/threatened death is violent/accidental 4. Experiencing personally repeated/extreme exposure to aversive details (e.g., first responders to human body parts; police officers repeatedly to the details of child abuse); excludes exposure through electronic media/television/movies/pictures, except if work-related
B. Intrusion symptoms associated with it that began after it, as shown by the following way(s) (for the diagnosis, one or more of the five symptoms in this cluster need(s) to be present): 1. Recurrent/involuntary/intrusive distressing memories of it 2. Recurrent distressing dreams; their content, affect, or both are related to it 3. Dissociative reactions (e.g., flashbacks); the person feels/acts as if it is recurring (at worst, a complete loss of awareness of present surrounding) 4. Intense/prolonged psychological distress at exposure to internal/external signals that symbolize/resemble an aspect of it 5. Marked physiological reactions to reminders (internal/external signals symbolizing/resembling (aspect of it))
C. Persistent avoidance of stimuli associated with it that began after it, as shown by efforts to avoid in the following way(s) (for the diagnosis, one or both of the two symptoms in this cluster need(s) to be present): 1. (Tries to) avoid distressing internal reminders (thoughts/feelings/memories) about/associated with it 2. (Tries to) avoid external reminders (e.g., people, places, conversations, activities, objects, situations) that induce distress (thoughts/feelings/memories) about/associated with it
D. Negative alterations in cognitions/mood associated with it begins or worsened after it, as shown by the following ways (for the diagnosis, two or more of the seven symptoms in this cluster need to be present): 1. Inability to remember important aspect of it (typically due to dissociative amnesia, not head injury/alcohol/drugs) 2. Persistent/exaggerated negative beliefs/expectations about one's self, others/world (e.g., "I'm bad," "Trust no one now," "The world is totally dangerous") 3. Persistent, distorted thoughts about the cause/consequences of it, leading to self-blame/blame of others 4. Persistent negative emotional state (e.g., fear/horror/anger/guilt/shame) 5. Markedly diminished interest/participation in important life activities 6. Feeling of detachment/estrangement from others 7. Persistent inability to experience emotions that are positive (e.g., happiness/satisfaction/loving feelings)

(continued)

Table 23.1 (continued)

E. Alterations (marked) in arousal/reactivity associated with it, having begun or worsened after it, as shown by the following ways (for the diagnosis, two or more of the six symptoms in this cluster need to be present): 1. Irritability/angry behavior (to little or no provocation), as verbal/physical aggression to people/objects 2. Recklessness/self-destructiveness 3. Hypervigilance behavior 4. Exaggerated startling response 5. Concentration problems 6. Sleep disturbance (e.g., difficulty falling/staying asleep/restless sleep)
F. Duration lasts at least one month
G. The disturbance induces clinically significant distress/impairment in social/occupational/other important functional areas
H. Disturbance not due to physiological effects of a substance (e.g., medication/alcohol) or to another medical condition

Adapted from American Psychiatric Association (2013)
Specify if:
With Delayed Onset: if fully diagnosable only at 6 months or more after it
Specify if:
Dissociative symptoms present (persistent, recurrent)
1. depersonalization (detailed feelings, e.g., outside observer, in a dream, feeling unreal, moving slowly)
2. derealization (unreality in surroundings (also dreamlike/distant/distorted))
Abbreviation DSM-5 = Diagnostic and Statistical Manual of Mental Disorders, Fifth Edition
Note: Applies to individuals 7 years or more in age

are the four clustering ones and others that are qualifiers. The table gives a slightly revised version of the criteria for PTSD.

Table 23.2 summarizes the research on the factor structure of PTSD. The four-factor model has been taken to provide the best fit to the data in the DSM-5. In particular, the King et al. (1998) model was used to structure the DSM-5. It divides the DSM-IV-TR's (Diagnostic and Statistical Manual of Mental Disorders, Fourth Edition, Text Revised; American Psychiatric Association, 2000) numbing-avoidance cluster into two clusters. However, the Simms et al. (2002) model is the four-factor one usually supported in the literature. It encompasses some numbing and hyperarousal items into one cluster, called dysphoria, thereby reducing the extent of the avoidance and hypervigilance clusters. However, is the four-cluster model the one that is supported currently in the literature? The research on PTSD calls into question its four-cluster organization in the DSM-5. Other research presented below suggests that a five-factor model best fits the DSM-5 symptom organization for PTSD.

Table 23.3 indicates which criteria in the 2010 draft proposal for PTSD that was field tested in 2010–2011 were altered in the DSM-5's final version that was published. Given these extensive changes, the reliability reported for PTSD in the field trials do not apply directly to the final version in the DSM-5 manual. One could ask to what extent these changes in the final version of the DSM-5 relative to the draft compromise its use in relation to PTSD. I consider this an open question with no easy answer, but do believe, nonetheless, that the reliability data apply to a good degree. The subtext is that a scientific, skeptical attitude helps in understanding the DSM-5 and its process. An extreme version of this approach might advocate that, in essence, the published criteria of PTSD in the DSM-5 have *never* been adequately tested for reliability.

In this regard, Table 23.4 summarizes the criteria that might be problematic in the final version used in the DSM-5 for PTSD. Collectively, these apparent problems with the DSM-5 PTSD criteria point to the need for careful assessment and diagnosis of PTSD.

Other

The next few tables present the DSM-5 criteria for other diagnoses relevant to psychological injury cases that are related to traumatic events or

Table 23.2 Possible symptom dimensions of PTSD

	Models		
DSM-IV PTSD symptoms	DSM-IV Three-factor	King, Leskin, King, and Weathers (1998) Four-factor	Simms, Watson, and Doebbeling (2002) Four-factor
B1. Intrusive thoughts of trauma	Intrusions	Intrusions	Intrusions
B2. Recurrent dreams of trauma	Intrusions	Intrusions	Intrusions
B3. Flashbacks	Intrusions	Intrusions	Intrusions
B4. Emotional reactivity	Intrusions	Intrusions	Intrusions
B5. Physiological reactivity to trauma cues	Intrusions	Intrusions	Intrusions
C1. Avoiding thoughts of trauma	Avoidance/numbing	Avoidance	Avoidance
C2. Avoiding reminders of trauma	Avoidance/numbing	Avoidance	Avoidance
C3. Inability to recall aspects of trauma	Avoidance/numbing	Numbing	Dysphoria
C4. Loss of interest	Avoidance/numbing	Numbing	Dysphoria
C5. Detachment	Avoidance/numbing	Numbing	Dysphoria
C6. Restricted affect	Avoidance/numbing	Numbing	Dysphoria
C7. Sense of foreshortened future	Avoidance/numbing	Numbing	Dysphoria
D1. Sleep disturbance	Hyperarousal	Hyperarousal	Dysphoria
D2. Irritability	Hyperarousal	Hyperarousal	Dysphoria
D3. Difficulty concentrating	Hyperarousal	Hyperarousal	Dysphoria
D4. Hypervigilance	Hyperarousal	Hyperarousal	Hypervigilance
D5. Exaggerated startle response	Hyperarousal	Hyperarousal	Hypervigilance

Adapted with permission from Springer Science+Business Media. Young (2014); with kind permission from Springer Science+Business Media B.V. [Table 25.7, Page 639]

Table 23.3 Important changes in the DSM-5 criteria for PTSD in the final version relative to the draft proposal that was field-tested

Criterion	Change	Wording
C1	Replacements	"Internal reminders" changed to "distressing" "Physical sensations" changed to "memories" (closely) "Arouse recollections" changed to "associated with"
C2	Replacements	Same as above
D	Reduction	# of polythetic criteria needed for threshold (3 changed to 2)
D2	Added	"Expectations" changed to "beliefs or expectations"
D3	Replacement addition	"Blame of self/others" changed to "cognitions that lead to blame of self/others"
D7	Replacement	"Unable to have loving feelings/psychic numbing" changed to "inability to experience happiness/satisfaction/loving feelings"
E	Addition	"Alteration" changed to "marked alteration"
E	Reduction	In threshold, 3 criteria changed to 2, as above for D
E1	Replacement	"Aggressive behavior" changed to "angry outbursts/with little or no provocation typically expressed as verbal/physical aggression toward people/objects"

to adapting to them. Table 23.5 indicates key features of acute stress disorder (ASD), which is diagnosed early after a traumatic event. My concerns relate to the weakness of criterion A to prevent a flood of exaggerated and false claims, which is similar to my concern in the case of PTSD. Also, the symptom cluster and duration criteria of ASD could use closer examination.

For specific phobia, the major changes in the DSM-5 involve the duration criterion and the

Table 23.4 Problematic criteria in PTSD in the DSM-5

Criterion	Descriptor	Comment
A2	Witnessing event in vivo	Civil floodgates open
A2	As it occurred to other(s) (family member not specified)	They open even further
A2	The individual's response included "intense fear, helplessness, or horror"	This A2 criterion in the DSM-IV has been eliminated. The floodgates open even further
A3	Learning of event re family member or close friend	Witnessing not required Civil floodgates opened
A4	Experiencing repeated/extreme aversive details; could be electronically if work-related	Civil floodgates opened
B3	Dissociative reactions could include complete loss of awareness of present surroundings	Criminal floodgates opened. Could be used in "not guilty" pleadings
E1	Irritability/anger outburst (with little/no provocation, expressed as verbal/physical aggression)	Criminal floodgates opened. Could be used in not guilty pleadings
E2	Reckless/self-destructive behavior	Criminal floodgates opened. Could be used in not guilty pleadings
Specifier	With dissociate symptoms	See B3
Specifier	With delay possible >6 months	See the concerns for the A criterion

Table 23.5 Acute stress disorder in the DSM-5

Criterion	Descriptor	Comment
A	As for PTSD	See PTSD table (Problematic criteria in PTSD in the DSM-5) about concerns about opening the floodgate
B	≥9 of the 14 symptoms	[So why are they placed in 5 categories?] Dissociation had been a primary symptom in the DSM-IV (3 or more of 5 symptoms) and the others involved symptoms related to the 3 PTSD clusters in the DSM-IV. In the DSM-5, dissociation is de-emphasized: there are only 2 dissociation symptoms and none are necessary for the diagnosis. The other four categories appear to reflect the four symptom clusters for PTSD, but will this division been supported empirically as had been the case for PTSD?
C	3 days to 1 month	Why is 3 days enough for consideration as a disorder? (It had been 2 days in the DSM-IV)
D	The usual impairment criterion	For 3 days, too?

requirement for the fear/anxiety experienced to be "out of proportion" to the danger/cultural context associated with the event at issue. My concern is that the latter criterion (D) could be used to deny valid claims of phobia because of the high bar set for the response to the event (see Table 23.6).

In the DSM-IV-TR, adjustment disorder could not be diagnosed simultaneously with PTSD. However, now it is not considered anxiety-related (nor is PTSD), and it stands in its own chapter (independent of PTSD, other stress disorders and other anxiety disorders). When not full blown, in the DSM-5, adjustment disorder can be diagnosed as "adjustment-like" disorder. In this case, the bar might be set too low (see Table 23.7).

Supportive Research

Miller, Wolf, and Keane (2014) defended the decision to create a new trauma chapter in the DSM-5 and place PTSD in it rather than in the anxiety chapter. They supported the notion that

Table 23.6 Changes to specific phobia in the DSM-5

Criterion	DSM-IV	DSM-5
A	Marked and persistent	Marked
	Excessive or unreasonable	–
B	Immediate anxiety response	Immediate fear or anxiety
C	Recognize it as excessive or unreasonable	–
D	Avoided	Actively avoided
	Endured with intense "anxiety or distress"	Fear or anxiety
E	Interferes significantly, or marked distress	Clinically significant distress or impairment
F	For <18 years, duration >6 months	Typically ≥ 6 months (a general guide having some degree of flexibility) (no age restriction)
	–	(New D) The fear/anxiety "out of proportion" to the actual danger and/or cultural context

Table 23.7 Changes to adjustment disorder in the DSM-5

Criterion	DSM-IV	DSM-5
	In its own chapter	Now classified as one of a set of trauma/stress-related conditions
B1	In excess of expectation to stressor exposure	Out of proportion to the severity/intensity of the exposure, considering external context/cultural factors
	Acute (<6 months) or chronic (≥6 months) specifier	–
	–	If either delayed onset (>3 months) or continuation of disorder for 6 months after stressor cessation, diagnose "adjustment-like disorder" under rubric of "other specified trauma – and stressor-related disorder"

trauma reactions are heterogenous and not necessarily anxiety- or fear-related; for example, PTSD has externalization features.

Miller et al. (2014) supported removal of the peri-traumatic emotionality criterion (A2) from the DSM-IV-TR PTSD criterial definition. For example, in this regard, peri-traumatic emotional experiences have been found not to be predictive of who will develop PTSD, nor has its severity, if it should develop (Friedman, Resick, Bryant, & Brewin, 2011).

They noted that the definition allows for traumatic events as well as a unique event as eliciting PTSD. This is consistent with the finding that lifetime trauma exposures cumulatively affect post-trauma psychopathology severity (McLaughlin et al., 2013).

As for revisions of specific PTSD symptoms, Miller et al. (2014) noted that research has shown little change in PTSD prevalence as a result of the changes. In this regard, they cited Carmassi et al. (2013), Kilpatrick et al. (2013), and Miller et al. (2013).

About the arrangement of the symptoms, Miller et al. (2013) had found that the new four-cluster model in the DSM-5 is supported by confirmatory factor analytic research. [However, the best fit was with the Simms et al. (2002) model rather than the one used by the DSM-5. Moreover, factor structure for the DSM-5 model revealed "weak" loadings for two items on the factors to which they belonged (inability to remember an important aspect of the traumatic event(s); the amnesia symptom; and reckless/self-destructive behavior).]

In terms of the dissociative subtype of PTSD, latent profile analytic research has found that derealization and depersonalization are present in 15–30 % of individuals expressing PTSD (e.g., Wolf et al., 2012). Lanius, Brand, Vermetten, Frewen, and Spiegel (2012) suggested that in the dissociative subtype, frontal brain regions are overactivated, thereby actively inhibiting the limbic regions associated with emotional/fear responsivity. In contrast, other individuals with PTSD manifest hypoactivity in frontal brain regions and lack of inhibitory modulation of limbic regions.

Miller et al. (2014) addressed the ICD-11 (International Statistical Classification of Diseases and Related Health Problems, 11th Revision; World Health Organization, 2017) proposal to separate complex PTSD (CPTSD) from PTSD, in general (Cloitre, Garvert, Brewin, Bryant, & Maercker, 2013). Wolf et al. (2014) disputed the empirical basis for distinguishing CPTSD and PTSD as proposed for the ICD-11. Wolf et al. (2014) found that latent class analyses of trauma-exposed community and veteran samples found symptom severity differences among classes but not ones related PTSD-CPTSD in terms of the psychopathology endorsed. Miller et al. (2014) noted that the ICD-11 symptom cluster for CPTSD resembles symptoms in two clusters of the DSM-5 approach (D, E). Therefore, CPTSD might simply be a more severe form of PTSD rather than a distinct entity.

Criticisms

Entry PTSD is a controversial diagnostic category in the DSM-5 for several reasons, aside from issues with its criteria. First, because of its entry criterion of having been a victim or otherwise part to a traumatic event, it is open to bracket creep in its eliciting stressors (McNally, 2003). Zoellner, Bedard-Gilligan, Jun, Marks, and Garcia (2013) also noted that alteration of the A1 entry criterion for PTSD that has taken place in the DSM-5 encourages "bracket creep" (McNally, 2003), in that it permits traumatic stressors to expand beyond "high-magnitude catastrophic events" to "low-magnitude" ones, such as indirect exposure (e.g., loss of one's farm animals, or simply being present at a military base). As with others, Levin, Kleinman, and Adler (2014) take issue with the approach to PTSD in the DSM-5 at the forensic and legal levels because the changes in the criterion A about the trauma involved will increase claims.

Forensics First (2010) was concerned forensically about the change to Criterion A for PTSD. The situations mentioned as qualifying traumatic events broaden the possibilities and will allow for "creative litigation." The danger in these regards is that more individuals will become in a position to malinger PTSD. First's (2010) concerns about the DSM-5 2010 draft apply equally to the final version of the DSM-5, which has radically changed the A criterion for PTSD in a way the opens the gate keeping role of criterion A to spurious and exaggerated claims.

Forensically, PTSD has become the focus diagnosis for an explosion of tort actions (Kane & Dvoskin, 2011). Moreover, its symptom list is readily available on the Internet and attorney websites as well as being straightforward in description, so that it is subject to facility in malingering (Rosen & Grunert, 2012). For Levin et al. (2014), some of the DSM-5's PTSD symptoms allow for increased scope for claims of diminished criminal responsibility, should PTSD be diagnosed before the act at issue.

Testing Wisdom et al. (2014) noted that PTSD is subject to exaggeration of symptoms for secondary gain. They recommended the use of performance validity testing, noting that this is not common in the VA (Veterans Administration) system. In this regard, the Fp-r scale of the MMPI-2-RF appears to provide valid results differentiating genuine and over-reported PTSD symptoms (Wolf & Miller, 2014; also Arbisi, Polusny, Erbes, Thuras, & Reddy, 2011; Goodwin, Sellbom, & Arbisi, 2013; Marion, Sellbom, & Bagby, 2011; Mason et al., 2013). Generally, the inference is that the DSM-5 diagnostic categories being discussed need improvement in their symptom specification and organization. Also, their verification by testing is difficult and, often, disability systems dealing with them do not even require confirmation by testing of claims made.

In forensic cases, assessors need to administer adequate psychometric testing (Larrabee, 2012), including measures with respondent validity indicators that meet court requirements (e.g.,

MMPI-2-RF, Minnesota Multiphasic Personality Inventory-2 Restructured Form; Ben-Porath & Tellegen, 2008/2011). Nevertheless, even in the most rigorous research, psychometric tests have imperfect sensitivity and specificity (Young, 2014). Therefore, the search for (bio)markers of PTSD that might be able to reliably differentiate valid from invalid cases of PTSD has become an important avenue of research and possible application for court purposes (Lareau, 2011).

Symptoms Weathers, Marx, Friedman, and Schnurr (2014) noted that the DSM-5 kept a broad approach to symptom inclusion in PTSD (20 symptoms) because this facilitates evaluation and treatment. The narrowing approach (e.g., Brewin, 2013; Maercker et al., 2013) refers to using a reduced criterion set in order to facilitate diagnosis, reduce comorbidity, and so on. At the same time, when applied to cases, the new DSM-5 symptom list and structure excludes about 25 % of individuals who would meet the DSM-IV criteria for the disorder (Kilpatrick et al., 2013). This jeopardizes patients who will be assessed with the DSM-5 for benefits.

As for the new symptoms added to the PTSD diagnosis, Zoellner et al. (2013) noted that not only do they serve to increase the heterogeneity of symptom expression in an already diversely presented disorder but also they are the ones that overlap with depression (being about negative beliefs, guilt, persistent negative affect) so that increased comorbidity in diagnosis is promoted.

Zoellner et al. (2013) aptly critiqued the retention of the psychogenic amnesia symptom and the addition of the qualifier of reckless/self-destructive behavior to the DSM-5 PTSD item list. The former occurs much less frequently than other symptoms of PTSD, especially in the severe range and, also, it loads poorly relative to other items in factor analytic studies (Miller et al., 2013). Moreover, retention of the psychogenic amnesia item gives fuel to the debate about whether a trauma survivor can really forget strong emotional events and its relevant details (e.g., Lynn, Lilienfeld, Merckelbach, Giesbrecht, & van der Kloet, 2012; McNally, 2009). As for including risky/self-destructive behavior in the DSM-5 PTSD criteria, the evidence suggests that its association with PTSD might be more due to either depression or borderline personality disorder, which are frequently comorbid with it (e.g., Panagioti, Gooding, Taylor, & Tarrier, 2013; Rytwinski, Scur, Feeny, & Youngstrom, 2013; Zlotnick et al., 2003).

Zoellner, Pruitt, Farach, and Jun (2014) underscored that the heterogeneity of symptoms in PTSD obscures its core characteristics and accentuates its secondary characteristics. Also, in comorbid PTSD and depression, there might be an underlying negative affect factor (Post, Zoellner, Youngstrom, & Feeny, 2011). Zoellner et al. (2014) concluded that because of PTSD's heterogeneity in symptoms in the DSM-5, it is possible for an individual to be attributed the diagnosis of PTSD without even expressing specific fear symptoms. Levin et al. (2014) noted that some particular PTSD symptoms in the DSM-5 are ambiguous or might be hard to differentiate as trauma ones (e.g., reckless behavior).

Young (2013) reviewed the articles in the special issue on the DSM-5 in the journal *Psychological Injury and Law* (Issue 6 (4)). Among his concerns was that the polythetic approach to categorical diagnosis in the DSM-5 leads to symptom heterogeneity in presentation through the extensive symptom combinations allowed. He considered this problem compounded in cases of comorbidity.

Evidence Hoge, Riviere, Wilk, Herrell, and Weathers (2014) and McFarlane (2014) noted that soldiers meeting the DSM-IV-TR criteria for PTSD often did not meet those of the DSM-5, with the percentage involved being 30 %. They attributed the lack of correspondence in the criteria over the two editions of the DSM to the separation of the numbing and avoidance symptoms in the DSM-5 into their own clusters. Soldiers learn to overcome their avoidance tendencies, and so do not meet the DSM-5 criteria as often as those for the DSM-IV-TR. Moreover, the numbing criteria reformulation presents its own issues.

Miller et al. (2013) conducted internet-based surveys on PTSD with two populations—a large nationally representative (American) community sample and a clinical sample of trauma-exposed American military veterans expressing a high prevalence of the disorder. They developed an instrument that included DSM-5 draft PTSD symptoms.

The prevalence results showed that the PTSD draft proposal criteria should be revised by relaxing the polythetic threshold for D and E symptoms (from 3 to 2 in each case). Factor analysis confirmed the four-factor structure of the 20 symptoms for PTSD, but the best one was for a model not used in the DSM-5, that of Simms et al. (2002). The DSM-5 model simply split the avoidance and numbing symptoms that were combined in the DSM-IV (Diagnostic and Statistical Manual of Mental Disorders, Fourth Edition; American Psychiatric Association, 1994), whereas the Simms et al. (2002) results suggested that the best option is a rejuggling of the symptoms in terms of a primary dysphoria factor. Other results questioned inclusion of the "psychogenic amnesia" and the "reckless/destructive behavior" symptoms in any of the factors or clusters.

The authors concluded that the final revision of the DSM-5 should use the relaxed thresholds indicated, which was done. They argued that results about the contested factor structure of the symptoms do not necessitate changing their cluster organization in the DSM-5 because "obtaining a pure diagnostic construct was not the primary object of the DSM-5 PTSD workgroup" (p. 11).

However, I note that the draft proposal made explicit reference to validating the cluster structure in PTSD, but this was deleted in the rationale for the final version. Finally, Miller et al. (2013) stated that future research needs to clarify the placement of the two symptoms that do not fit clearly the DSM-5 factor structure. They recommended that the first of the two perhaps should be a specifier and the second an associated feature. I noted that this recommendation was not adopted for the final version of PTSD in the DSM-5.

Elhai et al. (2012) administered a web survey to college students, using an adapted version of the DSM draft PTSD symptoms. As in Miller et al. (2013), factor analysis and (also Bayesian information criterion (BIC) calculation) revealed that the dysphoria model (Yufik & Simms, 2010) fit the data as robustly or better than the DSM-5 model. However, after considering all the data in their study, the authors ended up concluding that the DSM-5 cluster model is a "best fit" of the data. They added that the changes in PTSD in the DSM-5 relative to the DSM-IV-TR are "modest" improvements and relatively minor and, therefore, are unlikely to have any meaningful impact (e.g., for treatment, forensic application).

Elhai et al. (2012) conducted research indicating that the three-factor structure of the DSM-IV-TR symptoms expresses five factors. In essence, in their model, the avoidance cluster is divided into avoidance and numbing clusters, and the hyperarousal cluster is divided into dysphoric arousal and anxious arousal.

Biehn, Elhai, Seligman, Tamburrino, and Forbes (2013) examined the relationship between the DSM-5 diagnostic categories of PTSD items and depression, in a questionnaire study of participants with trauma history. They noted the high comorbidity between the two disorders (e.g., Elhai, Franklin, & Gray, 2008; Kessler, Sonnega, Bromet, Hughes, & Nelson, 1995). Aside from obtaining evidence supporting the DSM-5 factor structure, they found that PTSD's avoidance and negative alterations in arousal factors were more strongly associated with depression's somatic factor rather than its non-somatic one.

Galatzer-Levy, Nickerson, Litz, and Marmar (2013) examined lifetime PTSD comorbidity patterns using Latent Class Analysis (LCA). The authors applied the technique to a subsample of individuals from the National Comorbidity Study-Replication (NCS-R; Kessler et al., 1995) who had been diagnosed by interview as having PTSD.

The study revealed a best-fitting three-class solution of discrete patterns of lifetime comorbidity. The classes involved a low comorbidity one, a depressed-anxious one, and a substance dependence one. The authors concluded that the amount of PTSD comorbid clusters is relatively small and, moreover, each should be associated with different risks, etiology, and effective therapy. In their study, Müller et al. (2014) replicated these results, but they added that the results held for partial PTSD as much as full PTSD.

Comment Frueh, Elhai, and Acierno (2010) concluded about the degree of change in PTSD in the DSM-5 and their impact, that the changes were not major. However, careful review of both the criteria and research on PTSD in the DSM-5 casts at least some doubt on this type of conclusion.

The literature surveyed on PTSD comorbidity underscores the difficulties presented by the comorbidity construct embedded in the DSMs; however, it also points to promising research directions and solutions. Conceptually, in psychiatric classification, dimensional approaches generally are placed in opposition to categorical ones, and some of the suggestions in these regards have been incorporated into the DSM-5. However, the problem presented by heterogeneity in symptom expression within any one disorder would not be resolved by applying uniformly a dimensional approach, e.g., placing categories on a spectrum. Moreover, comorbidities across spectra would still obtain in a system such as this, with all the problems inherent in this approach still being evident.

Granted, seeking higher-order dimensions over disorders could help reduce the classification complexity in psychiatric classification. However, the clinical utility afforded by disorders such as PTSD might be compromised.

Another simplification procedure with respect to PTSD and its comorbid disorders concerns the search for discrete classes over the lifetime. PTSD and associated disorders might reduce to a few pathways that have clinical utility as well as research compatibility. However, given the amount of possible comorbid conditions in relation to PTSD, this type of approach remains challenging and is still in its infancy.

One promising avenue to reduce the symptom combination problem in PTSD is to consider reducing its diagnosis to core symptoms. For example, Brewin, Lanius, Novac, Schnyder, and Galea (2009) indicated that 6 of the 17 DSM-IV-TR symptoms might be sufficient to index it. Zoellner et al. (2014) focused on its core attribute, related it to fear (e.g., difficulty extinguishing it). This approach to simplifying the symptom list complexity in PTSD is compatible with the research showing that the disorder might be divided into a five-factor or symptom cluster presentation (e.g., Elhai et al., 2012; Horn, Pietrzak, Corsi-Travali, & Neumeister, 2014; Pietrzak, Galea, Southwick, & Gelernter, 2013; it had been comprised of three factors in the DSM-IV-TR and four in the DSM-5). That is, by better understanding the factor structure for PTSD, future iterations of the DSM-5 might better identify its primary, core symptoms.

Galatzer-Levy and Bryant (2013) had determined that in PTSD there are 636,120 possible symptom combinations, and they concluded that this symptom heterogeneity is "astounding" and renders the PTSD category "amorphous." Table 23.8 provides the staggering calculations involving comorbid PTSD presentations (Young et al., 2014). For example, PTSD and MDD (Major Depressive Disorder) could be expressed in as many as 270,351,000 ways. When pain is involved, the amount extends to 1.89 billion. If one includes mild TBI, the amount of symptom combinations is 1.79 trillion. By adding in alcohol use disorder, the total escalates to 3.64 quadrillion. Finally, when all six conditions are involved, i.e., when BPD (Borderline Personality Disorder) is added, the total of possible symptom combinations in cases of polytrauma with PTSD as a focus arrives at inconceivable amount of 1.39 quintillion. One could argue that the DSM-5 is fortunate that the total is several orders of magnitude less than the number of stars in the universe; however, by a several orders of magnitude, the total is more than the number of stars in the Milky Way.

Table 23.8 Total combination calculations of posttraumatic stress disorder and comorbid psychological injuries[a]

Disorder	Combination calculations	Total combinations
Posttraumatic Stress Disorder (PTSD)	B (31) × C (3) × D (120) × E (57)	636,120
Major Depressive Disorder (MDD)	B (425)	425
Somatic Symptom Disorder (SSD)	A (1) × B (7)	7
Mild Neurocognitive Disorder with Traumatic Brain Injury (MND-TBI)	A (63) × B (15)	945
Alcohol Use Disorder (AUD)	A (2036)	2036
Borderline Personality Disorder (BPD)	A (382)	382
PTSD × MDD	PTSD (636,120) × MDD (425)	270,351,000 (270 million or 2.7×10^{10})
PTSD × MDD × SSD	PTSD (636,120) × MDD (425) × SSD (7)	1,892,457,000 (1.89 billion or 1.89×10^{9})
PTSD × MDD × SSD × MND-TBI	PTSD (636,120) × MDD (425) × SSD (7) × MCD-TBI (945)	1,788,371,865,000 (1.79 trillion or 1.79×10^{12})
PTSD × MDD × SSD × MND-TBI × AUD	PTSD (636,120) × MDD (425) × SSD (7) × MCD-TBI (945) × AUD (2036)	3,641,125,117,140,000 (3.64 quadrillion or 3.64×10^{15})
PTSD × MDD × SSD × MND-TBI × AUD × BPD	PTSD (636,120) × MDD (425) × SSD (7) × MCD-TBI (945) × AUD (2036) × BPD (382)	1,390,909,794,747,480,000 (1.39 quintillion or 1.39×10^{18})

Adopted with permission of Springer Science + Business Media. Young, G., Lareau, C., & Pierre, B. (2014). One quintillion ways to have PTSD comorbidity: Recommendations for the disordered DSM-5. *Psychological Injury and Law, 7*, 61–74; with kind permission from Springer Science + Business Media B. V. [Table 5, Page 68]

Note: The total number of possible combinations for each disorder is calculated by multiplying the possible combinations of each disorder's symptom criteria clusters. For example, the total number of possible combinations of MND-TBI was calculated by multiplying the combinations of Criteria A (63) by Criteria B (15), a procedure that gave a total of 925 possible expressions

Possible combinations of comorbid disorders are calculated by multiplying the number of possible combinations for each of the disorders involved in the comorbidity. For example, a diagnosis of PTSD comorbidly with MDD would have [B(31) × C(3) × D(120) × E(57)] × [A(425)] or 270,351,000 possible symptom combinations. By including criteria A of PTSD in this calculation, given that there are 4 types of trauma involved, the total symptom/stressor combination would be approximately 4 billion combinations. However, the table focuses on symptom combinations alone and does not add different stressors for PTSD that could cause them

[a]For comparison purposes, the estimated amount of stars in the Milky Way is 300 billion (3×10^{11}) and in the universe is 1 septillion (1×10^{24}) (Cain 2013; van Dokkum & Conroy, 2010; respectively)

Chapter Conclusions

A useful psychiatric diagnostic manual should reflect practitioner utility requirements in addition to scientific reliability and validity requirements. However, on both these grounds, the DSM-5 has been attacked. Also, the manual has been criticized for its lack of careful vetting for forensic purposes. This illustrates that many of the criticisms of the DSM-5 involve process as much as product, or how the APA and the DSM editors and working groups proceeded in the present iteration of the manual.

One major effort to improve the research base in mental illness has been formulated in the RDoC project. However, review of its criticisms, as presented in this chapter, indicates that, despite its protestations to the contrary, it is especially biological/brain-centric/neuroscientific and, therefore, devalues the biopsychosocial understanding of mental illness. In the end, the RDoC could end up helping the field of psychiatry and psychology in diagnosis and dealing with patients. However, it has to broaden its scope. When the research in the field seeks to understand mental illness from the integrative framework of the biopsychosocial perspective, it will be easier to apply toward revising the DSM-5.

In addition to discussing the RDoC and the DSM-5, in general, the present chapter analyzes carefully the categories of PTSD in the DSM-5. It shows that, as presently conceived, there are problems with both its reliability and validity. There have been improvements in the construction of the PTSD in the DSM-5 relative to the DSM-IV-TR. However, with respect to the DSM-5, analyses show that there is even more potential than had been the case in the DSM-IV-TR for difficulties in forensic assessment and application. For example, in using the DSM-5 approach to PTSD, and considering difficulties with the DSM-5, itself, there is still room for a potential epidemic of unwarranted PTSD litigation in court and related venues.

The concept of endophenotype has been presented in depth in the chapter on PTSD causation. Briefly, it concerns the pathway from genes to disease, and the indices of the pathway and its upstream components that can stand as proxies for the downstream genes involved. However, as with the DSM-5 and the RDoC projects, the search for endophenotypes of psychiatric disorder appears to ignore the biopsychosocial, multifactorial causality of behavior (etiology). The work on PTSD in this chapter speaks to the complexity of describing sufficiently well the mental disorders, the lack of which in the field, in general, stands as an impediment to grasping the nature of mechanisms underlying behavioral dysfunctionality. Therefore, the search for endophenotypes in psychiatry cannot be made simplistic. The field needs to adopt a broad perspective in seeking to understand the complex pathway from gene to any disorder. In this regard, the biopsychosocial perspective serves as one viable model that might be able to contribute to the task.

PTSD is quite understood as biopsychosocial in nature, as is its treatment. In this sense, it could be at the vanguard in revising effectively the DSM-5 once its kinks are worked out and it is protected from forensic disasters. The recommendations to reduce it to its primary, core, and related symptoms, while casting aside as important the common ones it shares with other disorders could be relevant in this regard.

References

American Psychiatric Association. (1994). *Diagnostic and statistical manual of mental disorders* (4th ed.). Washington, DC: Author.

American Psychiatric Association. (2000). *Diagnostic and statistical manual of mental disorders: DSM-IV-TR* (4th ed., text rev.). Washington, DC: Author.

American Psychiatric Association. (2013). *Diagnostic and statistical manual of mental disorders: DSM-V* (5th ed.). Washington, DC: Author.

Arbisi, P. A., Polusny, M. A., Erbes, C. R., Thuras, P. R., & Reddy, M. (2011). The Minnesota Multiphasic Personality Inventory-2 restructured form in National Guard soldiers screening positive for posttraumatic stress disorder and mild traumatic brain injury. *Psychological Assessment, 23*, 203–214.

Beauchaine, T. P., & McNulty, T. (2013). Comorbidities and continuities as ontogenetic processes: Toward a developmental spectrum model of externalizing psychopathology. *Development and Psychopathology, 25*, 1505–1528.

Ben-Porath, Y. S., & Tellegen, A. (2008/2011). *The Minnesota Multiphasic Personality Inventory-2 Restructured Form (MMPI-2-RF): Manual for administration, scoring, and interpretation*. Minnesota, MN: University of Minnesota Press.

Berenbaum, H. (2013). Classification and psychopathology research. *Journal of Abnormal Psychology, 122*, 894–901.

Biehn, T. L., Elhai, J. D., Seligman, L. D., Tamburrino, M., & Forbes, D. (2013). Underlying dimensions of DSM-5 posttraumatic stress disorder and major depressive disorder symptoms. *Psychological Injury and Law, 6*, 290–298.

Biomarkers Definitions Working Group. (2001). Biomarkers and surrogate endpoints: Preferred definitions and conceptual framework. *Clinical Pharmacology & Therapeutics, 69*, 89–95.

Brewin, C. R. (2013). "I wouldn't start from here" – An alternative perspective on PTSD from the ICD-11: Comment on Friedman (2013). *Journal of Traumatic Stress, 26*, 557–559.

Brewin, C. R., Lanius, R. A., Novac, A., Schnyder, U., & Galea, S. (2009). Reformulating PTSD for DSM-V:

Life after criterion A. *Journal of Traumatic Stress, 22*, 366–373.

Cain, F. (2013). *How many stars are there in the universe?* Retrieved from http://www.universetoday.com/102630/

Carmassi, C., Akiskal, H. S., Yong, S. S., Stratta, P., Caderani, E., Massimetti, E., et al. (2013). Posttraumatic stress disorder in DSM-5: Estimates of prevalence and criteria comparison versus DSM-IV-TR in a non-clinical sample of earthquake survivors. *Journal of Affective Disorders, 151*, 843–848.

Cloitre, M., Garvert, D. W., Brewin, C. R., Bryant, R. A., & Maercker, A. (2013). Evidence for proposed ICD-11 PTSD and complex PTSD: A latent profile analysis. *European Journal of Psychotraumatology, 4*. doi:10.3402/ejpt.v4i0.20706.

Cuthbert, B. N. (2014a). Response to Lilienfeld. *Behavior Research and Therapy, 62*, 140–142.

Cuthbert, B. N. (2014b). The RDoC framework: Facilitating transition from ICD/DSM to dimensional approaches that integrate neuroscience and psychopathology. *World Psychiatry, 12*, 28–35.

Cuthbert, B. N., & Kozak, M. J. (2013). Constructing constructs for psychopathology: The NIMH research domain criteria. *Journal of Abnormal Psychology, 122*, 928–937.

Elhai, J. D., Franklin, C. L., & Gray, M. J. (2008). The SCID PTSD module's trauma screen: Validity with two samples in detecting trauma history. *Depression and Anxiety, 25*, 737–741.

Elhai, J. D., Miller, M. E., Ford, J. D., Biehn, T. L., Palmieri, P. A., & Frueh, B. C. (2012). Posttraumatic stress disorder in DSM-5: Estimates of prevalence and symptom structure in a nonclinical sample of college students. *Journal of Anxiety Disorder, 26*, 58–64.

Feil, R. (2008). Epigenetics, an emerging discipline with broad implications. *Comptes Rendus Biologies, 331*, 837–843.

First, M. B. (2010). The PTSD stressor criterion as a barrier to malingering: DSM-5 draft commentaries. *Psychological Injury and Law, 3*, 255–259.

First, M. B. (2014). Preserving the clinician-research interface in the age of RDoC: The continuing need for DSM-5/ICD-11 characterization of study populations. *World Psychiatry, 13*, 53–54.

Frances, A. (2014). RDoC is necessary, but very oversold. *World Psychiatry, 13*, 47–49.

Friedman, M. J., Resick, P. A., Bryant, R. A., & Brewin, C. R. (2011). Considering PTSD for DSM-5. *Depression and Anxiety, 28*, 750–769.

Frueh, B. C., Elhai, J. D., & Acierno, R. (2010). The future of posttraumatic stress disorder in the DSM. *Psychological Injury and Law, 3*, 260–270.

Fulford, K. W. M. (2014). RDoC+: Taking translation seriously. *World Psychiatry, 13*, 54–55.

Galatzer-Levy, I. R., & Bryant, R. A. (2013). 636,120 ways to have posttraumatic stress disorder. *Perspectives on Psychological Science, 8*, 651–662.

Galatzer-Levy, I. R., Nickerson, A., Litz, B. T., & Marmar, C. R. (2013). Patterns of lifetime PTSD comorbidity: A latent class analysis. *Depression and Anxiety, 30*, 489–496.

Goodwin, B. E., Sellbom, M., & Arbisi, P. A. (2013). Posttraumatic stress disorder in veterans: The utility of the MMPI-2-RF Validity Scale in detecting overreported symptoms. *Psychological Assessment, 25*, 671–678.

Gottesman, I. I., & Gould, T. D. (2003). The endophenotype concept in psychiatry: Etymology and strategic intentions. *American Journal of Psychiatry, 160*, 636–645.

Gottesman, I. I., & McGue, M. (2015). Endophenotype. In R. L. Cautin & S. O. Lilienfeld (Eds.), *Wiley-Blackwell encyclopedia of clinical psychology*. Hoboken, NJ: Wiley. doi:10.1002/9781118625392.wbecp423.

Gottesman, I. I., & Shields, J. (1972). *Schizophrenia and genetics: A twin study vantage point*. New York: Academic.

Gould, T. D., & Gottesman, I. I. (2006). Psychiatric endophenotypes and the development of valid animal models. *Genes, Brain and Behavior, 5*, 113–119.

Harkness, A. R., Reynolds, S. M., & Lilienfeld, S. O. (2014). A review of systems for psychology and psychiatry: Adaptive systems, personality psychopathology five (PSY-5) and the DSM-5. *Journal of Personality Assessment, 96*, 121–139.

Hoge, C. W., Riviere, L. A., Wilk, J. E., Herrell, R. K., & Weathers, F. W. (2014). The prevalence of posttraumatic stress disorder (PTSD) in US combat soldiers: A head-to-head comparison of DSM-5 versus DSM-IV-TR symptom criteria with the PTSD checklist. *Lancet Psychiatry, 1*, 269–277.

Horn, C. A. C., Pietrzak, R. H., Corsi-Travali, S., & Neumeister, A. (2014). Linking plasma cortisol levels to phenotypic heterogeneity of posttraumatic stress symptomatology. *Psychoneuroendocrinology, 39*, 88–93.

Insel, T. R. (2014). The NIMH research domain criteria (RDoC) project: Precision medicine for psychiatry. *American Journal of Psychiatry, 171*, 395–397.

Insel, T. R., Cuthbert, B. N., Garvey, M. A., Heinssen, R. K., Pine, D. S., Quinn, K. J., et al. (2010). Research domain criteria (RDoC): Toward a new classification framework for research on mental disorders. *American Journal of Psychiatry, 167*, 748–751.

Insel, T. R., & Lieberman, J. A. (2013). DSM-5 and RDoC: Shared interests. *The National Institute of Mental Health*. Retrieved from http://www.nimh.nih.gov/news/science-news/2013/dsm-5-and-rdoc-shared--interests.shtml

Jablensky, A., & Waters, F. (2014). RDoC: A roadmap to pathogenesis? *World Psychiatry, 13*, 43–44.

Kane, A. W., & Dvoskin, J. A. (2011). *Evaluation for personal injury claims*. New York: Oxford University Press.

Kessler, R. C., Sonnega, A., Bromet, E., Hughes, M., & Nelson, C. B. (1995). Posttraumatic stress disorder in the National Comorbidity Survey. *Archives of General Psychiatry, 52*, 1048–1060.

Kilpatrick, D. G., Resnick, H. S., Milanak, M. E., Miller, M. W., Keyes, K. M., & Friedman, M. J. (2013). National estimates of exposure to traumatic events and PTSD prevalence using *DSM-IV* and *DSM-5* criteria. *Journal of Traumatic Stress, 26*, 537–547.

King, D. W., Leskin, G. A., King, L. A., & Weathers, F. W. (1998). Confirmatory factor analysis of the clinician-administered PTSD scale: Evidence for the dimensionality of posttraumatic stress disorder. *Psychological Assessment, 10*, 90–96.

Lanius, R. A., Brand, B., Vermetten, E., Frewen, P. A., & Spiegel, D. (2012). The dissociative subtype of post-traumatic stress disorder: Rationale, clinical and neurobiological evidence, and implications. *Depression and Anxiety, 29*, 701–708.

Lareau, C. R. (2011). Posttraumatic stress disorder and acute stress disorder. In D. Faust (Ed.), *Coping with psychiatric and psychological testimony* (6th ed., pp. 610–635). New York: Oxford University Press.

Larrabee, G. J. (Ed.). (2012). *Forensic neuropsychology: A scientific approach* (2nd ed.). New York: Oxford University Press.

Lenzenweger, M. F. (2013). Thinking clearly about the endophenotype-intermediate phenotype-biomarker distinctions in developmental psychopathology research. *Development and Psychopathology, 25*, 1347–1357.

Levin, A. P., Kleinman, S. B., & Adler, J. S. (2014). DSM-5 and posttraumatic stress disorder. *Journal of the American Academy of Psychiatry and the Law, 42*, 146–158.

Lilienfeld, S. O. (2014). The research domain criteria (RDoC): An analysis of methodological and conceptual challenges. *Behaviour Research and Therapy, 62*, 129–139.

Lynn, S. J., Lilienfeld, S. O., Merckelbach, H., Giesbrecht, T., & van der Kloet, D. (2012). Dissociation and dissociative disorders: Challenging conventional wisdom. *Current Directions in Psychological Science, 21*, 48–53.

Maercker, A., Brewin, C. R., Bryant, R. A., Cloitre, M., Reed, G. M., van Ommeren, M., et al. (2013). Proposals for mental disorders specifically associated with stress in the International Classification of Diseases-11. *The Lancet, 381*, 1683–1685.

Maj, M. (2014). Keeping an open attitude toward the RDoC project. *World Psychiatry, 13*, 1–3.

Marion, B. E., Sellbom, M., & Bagby, R. M. (2011). The detection of feigned psychiatric disorders using the MMPI-2-RF overreporting validity scales: An analog investigation. *Psychological Injury and Law, 4*, 1–12.

Mason, L. H., Shandera-Ochsner, A. L., Williamson, K. D., Harp, J. P., Edmundson, M., Berry, D. T., et al. (2013). Accuracy of MMPI-2-RF validity scales for identifying feigned PTSD symptoms, random responding, and genuine PTSD. *Journal of Personality Assessment, 95*, 585–593.

McFarlane, A. C. (2014). PTSD and DSM-5: Unintended consequences of change. *Lancet Psychiatry, 1*, 246–247.

McLaughlin, K. A., Koenen, K. C., Hill, E. D., Petukhova, M., Sampson, N. A., Zaslavsky, A. M., et al. (2013). Trauma exposure and posttraumatic stress disorder in a national sample of adolescents. *Journal of the American Academy of Child and Adolescent Psychiatry, 52*, 815–830.

McNally, R. J. (2003). Progress and controversy in the study of posttraumatic stress disorder. *Annual Review of Psychology, 54*, 229–252.

McNally, R. J. (2009). Can we fix PTSD in DSMV? *Depression and Anxiety, 26*, 597–600.

Meaney, M. J. (2010). Epigenetics and the biological definition of gene x environment interactions. *Child Development, 81*, 41–79.

Miller, M. W., Wolf, E. J., & Keane, T. M. (2014). Posttraumatic stress disorder in DSM-5: New criteria and controversies. *Clinical Psychology: Science and Practice, 21*, 208–220.

Miller, M. W., Wolf, E. J., Kilpatrick, D., Resnick, H., Marx, B. P., Holowka, D. W., et al. (2013). The prevalence and latent structure of proposed DSM-5 post-traumatic stress disorder symptoms in U.S. national and veteran samples. *Psychological Trauma: Theory, Research, Practice, and Policy, 5*, 501–512.

Morris, S. E., & Cuthbert, B. N. (2013). Research domain criteria: Cognitive systems, neural circuits, and dimensions of behavior. *Dialogues in Clinical Neuroscience, 14*, 29–37.

Morris, S. E., Rumsey, J. M., & Cuthbert, B. N. (2014). Rethinking mental disorders: The role of learning and brain plasticity. *Restorative Neurology and Neuroscience, 32*, 5–23.

Müller, M., Vandeleur, C., Rodgers, S., Rössler, W., Castelao, E., Preisig, M., et al. (2014). Factors associated with comorbidity patterns in full and partial PTSD: Findings from the PsyCoLaus study. *Comprehensive Psychiatry, 55*, 837–848.

Owen, M. J. (2012). Implications of genetic findings for understanding schizophrenia. *Schizophrenia Bulletin, 38*, 904–907.

Panagioti, M., Gooding, P., Taylor, P. T., & Tarrier, N. (2013). A model of suicidal behavior in posttraumatic stress disorder (PTSD): The mediating role of defeat and entrapment. *Psychiatric Research, 209*, 55–59.

Parnas, J. (2014). The RDoC program: Psychiatry without psyche? *World Psychiatry, 13*, 46–47.

Phillips, M. R. (2014). Will RDoC hasten the decline of America's global leadership role in mental health? *World Psychiatry, 13*, 40–41.

Pietrzak, R. H., Galea, S., Southwick, S. M., & Gelernter, J. (2013). Examining the relation between serotonin transporter 5-HTTLPR genotype x trauma exposure interaction on a contemporary phenotypic model of

posttraumatic stress symptomatology: A pilot study. *Journal of Affective Disorders, 148*, 123–128.
Post, L. M., Zoellner, L. A., Youngstrom, E., & Feeny, N. C. (2011). Understanding the relationship between co-occurring PTSD and MDD: Symptom severity and affect. *Journal of Anxiety Disorders, 25*, 1123–1130.
Rasetti, R., & Weinberger, D. R. (2011). Intermediate phenotypes in psychiatric disorders. *Current Opinions in Genetics & Development, 21*, 340–348.
Rosen, G. M., & Grunert, B. K. (2012). Posttraumatic stress disorder in the workplace. In S. S. Bush & G. L. Iverson (Eds.), *Neuropsychological assessment of work-related injuries* (pp. 163–186). New York: Guilford Press.
Rytwinski, N. K., Scur, M. D., Feeny, N. C., & Youngstrom, E. A. (2013). The co-occurrence of major depressive disorder among individuals with posttraumatic stress disorder: A meta-analysis. *Journal of Traumatic Stress, 26*, 299–309.
Sartorius, N. (2014). The only one or one of many? A comment on the RDoC project. *World Psychiatry, 13*, 50–51.
Shields, J., & Gottesman, I. I. (1973). Genetic studies of schizophrenia as signposts to biochemistry. In L. L. Iverson & S. Rose (Eds.), *Biochemistry and mental illness (Biochemistry Society Special Publication)* (Vol. 1, pp. 165–174). London: Biochemical Society.
Simmons, J. M., & Quinn, K. J. (2014). The NIMH Research Domain Criteria (RDoC) project: Implications for genetics research. *Mammalian Genome, 25*, 23–31.
Simms, L. J., Watson, D., & Doebbeling, B. N. (2002). Confirmatory factor analyses of posttraumatic stress symptoms in deployed and nondeployed veterans of the gulf war. *Journal of Abnormal Psychology, 111*, 637–647.
Sonuga-Barke, E. J. S. (2014). Editorial: 'What's up, (R) DoC?' – can identifying core dimensions of early functioning help us understand, and then reduce, developmental risk for mental disorders? *Journal of Child Psychology and Psychiatry, 55*, 849–851.
Sporns, O. (2011). *Networks of the brain*. Cambridge, MA: MIT Press.
Sporns, O. (2012). *Discovering the human connectome*. Cambridge, MA: MIT Press.
Stein, D. J. (2014). An integrative approach to psychiatric diagnosis and research. *World Psychiatry, 13*, 51–53.
van Dokkum, P., & Conroy, C. (2010). A substantial population of low-mass stars in luminous elliptical galaxies. *Nature, 468*, 940–942.
Wakefield, J. C. (2014). Wittgenstein's nightmare: Why the RDoC grid needs a conceptual dimension. *World Psychiatry, 13*, 38–39.
Weathers, F., Marx, B. P., Friedman, M. J., & Schnurr, P. P. (2014). Posttraumatic stress disorder in the DSM-5: New criteria, new measures, and implications for assessment. *Psychological Injury and Law, 7*, 93–107.
Weinberger, D. R., & Goldberg, T. E. (2014). RDoCs redux. *World Psychiatry, 13*, 36–37.
Whooley, O. (2014). Nosological reflections: The failure of DSM-5, the emergence of RDoC, and the decontextualization of mental distress. *Society and Mental Health, 4*, 92–110.
Wilkinson, L. S., Davies, W., & Iseles, A. R. (2007). Genomic imprinting effects on brain development and function. *Nature Reviews of Neuroscience, 8*, 832–843.
Wisdom, N. M., Pastorek, N. J., Miller, B. I., Booth, J. E., Romesser, J. M., Linck, J. F., et al. (2014). PTSD and cognitive functioning: Importance of including performance validity test. *The Clinical Neuropsychologist, 28*, 128–145.
Wolf, E. J., & Miller, M. W. (2014). The Minnesota Multiphasic Personality Inventory-2 Restructured Form and posttraumatic stress disorder: Forensic applications and considerations. *Psychological Injury and Law, 7*, 143–152.
Wolf, E. J., Miller, M. W., Kilpatrick, D., Resnick, H. S., Badour, C. L., Marx, B. P., et al. (2014). ICD-11 complex PTSD in U.S. national and veteran samples: Prevalence and structural associations with PTSD. *Clinical Psychological Science, 3*, 215–229.
Wolf, E. J., Miller, M. W., Reardon, A. F., Ryabchenko, K. A., Castillo, D., & Freund, R. (2012). A latent class analysis of dissociation and posttraumatic stress disorder: Evidence for a dissociative subtype. *Archives of General Psychiatry, 69*, 698–705.
World Health Organization. (2017). *International Classification of Disease, 11th Revision*.
Young, G. (2013). Breaking bad: DSM-5 description, criticism, and recommendations. *Psychological Injury and Law, 6*, 345–348.
Young, G. (2014). *Malingering, feigning, and response bias in psychiatric/psychological injury: Implications for practice and court*. Dordrecht, Netherlands: Springer Science+Business Media.
Young, G., Lareau, C., & Pierre, B. (2014). One quintillion ways to have PTSD comorbidity: Recommendations for the Disordered DSM-5. *Psychological Injury and Law, 7*, 61–74.
Yufik, T., & Simms, L. J. (2010). A meta-analytic investigation of the structure of posttraumatic stress disorder symptoms. *Journal of Abnormal Psychology, 119*, 764–776.
Zlotnick, C., Johnson, D. M., Yen, S., Battle, C. L., Sanislow, C. A., Skodol, A. E., et al. (2003). Clinical features and impairment in women with borderline personality disorder (BPD) with posttraumatic stress disorder (PTSD), BPD without PTSD, and other personality disorders with PTSD. *Journal of Nervous and Mental Disorders, 191*, 706–714.
Zoellner, L. A., Bedard-Gilligan, M. A., Jun, J. J., Marks, L. H., & Garcia, N. M. (2013). The evolving construct of posttraumatic stress disorder (PTSD): DSM-5 criteria changes and legal implications. *Psychological Injury and Law, 6*, 277–289.
Zoellner, L. A., Pruitt, L. D., Farach, F. J., & Jun, J. J. (2014). Understanding heterogeneity in PTSD: Fear, dysphoria, and distress. *Depression and Anxiety, 31*, 97–106.

The Disordered DSM-5 Disorders

24

Chapter Introduction

This chapter is the second of two chapters on specific categories in the DSM-5 (Diagnostic and Statistical Manual of Mental Disorders, Fifth Edition; American Psychiatric Association, 2013) related to psychological injury. In particular, the chapter deals with Neurocognitive Disorder (NCD) and Somatic Symptom Disorder (SSD). The last chapter had shown that Posttraumatic Stress Disorder (PTSD), as presented in the DSM-5, is open to much criticism and also much uncertainty, and even to potential abuse in court and related venues. The present chapter finds the same for NCD and SSD but, unfortunately, even to a greater degree than for PTSD. For both of the disorders of focus in the present chapter (NCD and SSD), it compares and contrasts the approaches taken in the DSM-IV-TR (Diagnostic and Statistical Manual of Mental Disorders, Fourth Edition; Text Revision American Psychiatric Association, 2000) and in the DSM-5. The chapter critically reviews the changes from one edition to the next in these disorders. Also, it makes recommendations to improve both disorders in the next version of the DSM (DSM-5.1). In particular, for NCD, it recommends that the exclusion of a moderate NCD in the DSM-5 is unwarranted and needs to be corrected. As for SSD, it proposes a quite revised approach to its criteria so that it respects better the category of pain disorder that had been in the DSM-IV-TR and removed in the DSM-5. The chapter also deals with other aspects of the DSM-5, such as personality disorder and malingering, while proposing an improved definition of the latter, as well. By way of introducing a nosological approach different from the one that underwrites the DSM project, the chapter concludes by examining the approach of the ICD-11 (International Classification of Disorders, 11th Edition, World Health Organization, 2017) to PTSD.

Neurocognitive Disorder

Table 24.1 indicates that the DSM-5 (Diagnostic and Statistical Manual for Mental Disorders, Fifth Edition; American Psychiatric Association, 2013) diagnosis of Mild Neurocognitive Disorder (NCD) leaves it open to much criticism and diagnostic uncertainty. It is juxtaposed to Major NCD, with no intermediate Moderate level. The type of neuropsychological or equivalent testing needed to be undertaken for its diagnosis is not clearly specified, leaving it open to different approaches that might lead to opposite conclusions in forensic cases.

Blazer (2013) cautioned that distinguishing between Mild and Major NCD has been challenged as subjective and artificial. There is no marker available for the distinction. It risks being misused.

Schultz (2010) had commented on NCD in the draft version of the DSM-5. She noted significant

G. Young, *Unifying Causality and Psychology*, DOI 10.1007/978-3-319-24094-7_24

Table 24.1 Mild neurocognitive disorder (TBI-related) in DSM-5

Criterion	Descriptor	Comment
A	"Modest" cognitive decline	Does "modest" mean mild or moderate? It is acknowledged in this regard that "precise thresholds difficult to determine" (p. 608)
A1	Mild decline	–
A2	Modest impairment	Mild or moderate?
	Presumably documented	Presumably?
	Standardized neuropsychological testing or an equivalent quantified clinical assessment, including "bedside" examination (in Table 1, p. 593).	Can any other assessment be equivalent?
B	Does not interfere with ADLs, but greater effort/ compensation/accommodation possible	However, it is acknowledged there is "subtle" interference. Moreover, is this criterion B not more than a "subtle interference?"
Neuropsychological testing thresholds (diagnostic feature)	Major: ≥ 2 SD (i.e., ≤ 3rd percentile) Minor: 1–2 SD (i.e., 3rd–16th percentile)	Too conservative? Moderate?
Specifier	Behavioral disturbance possible (e.g., clinically significant psychotic, mood, agitation, apathy symptoms)	If attributed to mild case, is it still mild?
TBI specifiers	In giving a diagnosis, the disorder is rated mild or moderate; the TBI is not rated	Room for confusion?
Functional (re TBI)	Reported depressive symptoms could amplify cognitive and functional effects	Still mild?

questions on conceptual, evidentiary, psychometric, assessment, and practical bases. Moreover, forensically, she noted room for loophole diagnoses related to traumatic brain injury (TBI). She reasoned that omission of a level of moderate NCD will lead to incorrect classification of people at this level into the less severe minor category. She queried the legitimacy of the threshold for the minor category at 1 standard deviation (SD) below the mean (or the 16th percentile level) in neuropsychological testing, which is typically considered low-average in (residual) ability and, therefore, not an impairment. Moreover, Schultz (2010) wondered to what the percentile ratings actually refer (e.g., single or multiple testing, one-session or multiple visits, comparison to population norms or pre-injury baseline). Forensically, Schultz (2010) concluded that the NCD diagnosis as presented does not adequately consider traumatic brain injury and the complexities of forensic practice.

Schultz (2013) updated her 2010 (Schultz, 2010) evaluation of NCD in the DSM-5. The most notable deficit for forensic principles in the 2013 final version of the diagnostic category of NCD remains omission of the level of moderate NCD. Therefore, cases of acquired TBI at this level of cognitive disorder likely will be assigned a mild rather than a major category [the mild case had been referred to as minor in the draft version.] This greatly increases the risks under-representing TBI at the moderate level. Moreover, the mild level of NCD is defined ambiguously enough to over-represent nonproblematic concussion cases within its range. Relative to the draft of the DSM-5 available in 2010, the final 2013 version now only prefers rather than prescribes neuropsychological assessment or quantification. Nevertheless, according to Schultz (2013), the manner in which the criterion involved is phrased will further push moderately injured TBI evaluees into the mild category. Other issues that had been raised by Schultz (2013) included lack of guidelines for neuropsychological assessment and overreliance on effects on ADLs (activities of daily living) relative to other roles (e.g., work effects). To conclude, the category of mild NCD due to a traumatic brain injury is presented in a way that could prevent successful claims when apparently warranted (Simpson, 2014).

Somatic Symptom Disorder[1]

Chronic Pain in the DSM-IV-TR

From a psychological perspective, in the DSM-IV-TR (Diagnostic and Statistical Manual of Mental Disorders, Fourth Edition, Text Revised; American Psychiatric Association, 2000), chronic pain could be diagnosed as a separate disorder in the category of general somatoform disorders; the label used was of pain disorder. The critical feature of pain disorder in the DSM-IV-TR is that pain experience presents as the predominant clinical focus and at a sufficient intensity level to warrant clinical attention. Another major aspect of pain disorder in the DSM-IV-TR is that the pain is at the origin of either (a) a distress that reaches clinical significance or (b) an impairment in important areas (or area) of function (social/occupational). The DSM-IV-TR requires specifying the chronicity of pain disorder (acute or chronic). Importantly, pain disorder in the DSM-IV-TR could be qualified as involving a general medical condition, psychological factors, or both (with the first option not considered a psychological disorder itself). The DSM-IV-TR conceptualization of pain disorder had been criticized as categorical and dualistic because its options include separation of psychological factors and medical ones (Melzack & Katz, 2006).

Chronic Pain in the DSM-5

Perhaps consistent with these criticisms, in the DSM-5, pain disorder has not been included as a separate disorder. Instead, in particular, in diagnosing chronic pain from a psychological perspective, it has been considered a specifier of Somatic Symptom Disorder (SSD). In the DSM-5, somatoform disorders are now referred to as somatic symptom and related disorders, and SSD is one of them. The classification reduces the number of these disorders and subcategories to avoid problematic overlap that was present in the DSM-IV-TR. Specifically, in the DSM-5, aside from not including pain disorder, the diagnoses of somatization disorder, hypochondriasis, and undifferentiated somatoform disorder have been removed.

Table 24.2 indicates that, in the DSM-5, SSD can be used to specify pain as a predominant complaint. However, there is no place for a diagnosis involving pain itself. In this regard, the difficulties with the new superordinate diagnosis of SSD in the DSM-5 could present considerable complications for pain patients, especially in the forensic or disability context. How would a plaintiff's legitimate pain complaints from a psychological perspective be received in court if there is no accompanying pain disorder diagnosis? Moreover, the new SSD was supposed to remove the subtle negative attribution associated with pain complaints that it is "all in the head." However, although the criteria appear to exclude "medically unexplained symptoms" as a factor, this type of stigmatizing language still appears. Overall, in the DSM-5, the option of pain-based diagnosis in terms of SSD only gives much room to deny valid claims in court-type cases.

The developers of the DSM-5 purported that it takes a different approach to the clinical realm of individuals with pain because there are multiple avenues to consider its psychological effects. In the DSM-5, individuals with chronic pain could be diagnosed not only as having somatic SSD with predominant pain but also as exhibiting either psychological factors affecting other medical conditions or an adjustment disorder. As will be discussed later, this conceptualization is not without controversy. First, I examine SSD in more depth and make suggestions to improve its diagnostic criteria.

[1] This section is based on Young (2013).

Table 24.2 Somatic symptom disorder in DSM-5

Criterion	Descriptor	Comment
Exclusion	Cannot be given in cases in which only a "medical cause" has not been demonstrated	Good
Inclusion	Positive psychological symptoms required (cognitive, affective, physical, behavioral)	Good
Expression	Personal suffering in sociocultural context	Draft had referred directly to "biopsychosocial"
A	"distressing" somatic symptoms(s) or "significant disruption in daily life"	Ambiguous: why not use the usual "clinically significant impairment in social, occupational, and other important functional areas"
B	Positive symptoms: Excessive (a) thoughts, (b) anxiety, (c) time/energy devotion	One or more required
C	Persistent (typically, > 6 months), not necessarily continuous	Ambiguous: can it really come and go?
Specifier	Somatic complaints "with predominant pain" involve pain mostly	Can this really capture the appropriate diagnosis of an individual experiencing psychologically-mediated chronic pain?
Specifier	"Persistent": severe symptoms, marked impairment, and long duration (>6 months)	Confusion with C; moreover, this is more than persistent, as "severe" mentioned
Specifier	Severity: mild = 1 symptom from B; moderate = 2; severe = 2 symptoms, and also either (a) multiple somatic complaints or (b) one very severe one	Confusion with "persistence" severity based on either number or intensity of positive symptoms or somatic complaints, which is also confusing
Feature	The person's "suffering" is "authentic," whether or not it is medically explained	So "medically unexplained symptoms" seem implicit in this diagnosis; not good
Feature	Concurrent medical condition frequently co-occurs	Good

Somatic Symptom Disorder in the DSM-5

Major Criteria There are three major criteria (A, B, C) for SSD in the DSM-5, coded as 300.82 (and as F45.1 in the ICD; International Classification of Diseases system). Also, there are three specifiers, one of which is whether the somatic symptoms involved especially ("predominantly") concern pain.

The first diagnostic criterion (A) for SSD is whether there is at least one somatic symptom that is "distressing" to the patient, or that results in "significant disruption" in daily living. The second diagnostic criterion (B) concerns whether there are thoughts/feelings/behaviors about either the somatic symptom(s) or "associated health concerns" that are "excessive." This criterion is indexed by at least one of the following: "disproportionate/persistent thinking about the symptom(s)' "seriousness;" persistent anxiety at a "high" level about the symptom(s)/health involved; and "excessive" time/energy devoted to the symptom(s)/health. Criterion C specifies that the duration must be more than 6 months. The other two specifiers relate to persistence (present, absent) and severity (mild, moderate, severe).

It is instructive to note that the DSM-5 draft's recommendations to measure severity using certain recommended tests were not implemented in the final version. This decision to abandon severity evaluation in the final version of the DSM-5 appears to have happened in multiple places.

Criticism The DSM-5 proposal for SSD has met with telling criticism. Sykes (2012) queried whether the construct of medically unexplained physical symptoms, which have been overtly removed from consideration in diagnosing the disorder, is still implicitly present. The category is considered weak, without a unifying principle, and it leaves room for ambiguity. He queried why a patient with a serious medical condition and who shows concern for it should receive a mental disorder diagnosis. At the same time, he queried whether there are sufficient psychological criteria in the diagnosis.

Frances and Chapman (2013) argued that the diagnostic thresholds for SSD are loose and will lead to false positive diagnoses. In diagnosing patients, instead of using SSD, they suggested use of adjustment disorder for cases of medical illness with psychological features. Frances (2013a) indicated that SSD could be used to mislabel "a sizeable proportion of the population as mentally ill" (because of its over-inclusive formulation). For example, Dimsdale (2012) found it has a false positive rate of 7 % of healthy people in the general population. Frances (2013b) added that its set of criteria seems subjective, unreliable, and easy to meet. He considered it a "fatally flawed" "pseudodiagnosis" that will harm people. Rief, Mewes, Martin, Glaesmer, and Brähler (2011) found the criteria for SSD "restrictive." Sirri and Fava (2013) maintained that the diagnosis appears to neglect "important clinical phenomena," such as "illness denial."

Wollburg, Voigt, Braukhaus, Herzog, and Löwe (2013) recommended that criterion B should be split. Instead of one criterion on expressing disproportionate and persistent thoughts about the seriousness of symptoms experienced, there should be separate criteria of a self-concept of bodily weakness and of somatic illness attribution.

Frances (2013b) offered a revised version of the clinical diagnostic criteria that included having all three B symptoms rather than just one as necessary for the diagnosis. He added that the criterion found for other disorders—of a significant disruption/impairment—needs to be added to SSD. He recommended that when a medical condition is certified as present, a criterion should be added that the B symptoms should be "grossly in excess" of expectations. Moreover, a criterion is needed such that if no medical condition is present, medical work-ups at suitable intervals should be conducted to see if they become ruled in. Also, he added the need for the typical exclusionary clause about the disorder not being diagnosed if better explained by a medical disorder. In short, the SSD diagnosis should be offered only if it is maladaptive, extreme, intrusive, impairing, grossly in excess, and so on, in relation to diagnosed medical illnesses.

Rief and Martin (2014) criticized the decision in the DSM-5 to abolish the distinction in Somatic Symptom and Related Disorders of medically explained and medically unexplained somatic symptoms. They suggested splitting somatic symptom disorder into medically unexplained ones that are either mono- or poly-symptomatic, and also including a type that is with a recognized biomedical condition. In addition, they advocated for the separation of pain disorder as a distinct classification (as well as illness anxiety disorder).

Young (2010) addressed the decision in the DSM-5 of placing pain symptoms solely as a specifier of SSD. His main concerns with this diagnostic approach, given SSD's de-emphasis of pain as primarily psychological, were that patients with valid pain disorders would have their treatment needs questioned and their forensic cases complicated. Moreover, the pejorative (or stigmatizing) connotations associated with the label would still exist, given the stigmatizing properties of SSD, and given the frequent lack of medical evidence of an injury and the frequent lack of one-to-one correspondence in a dose–response relationship to physical injury and pain experience (Young, Kane, & Nicholson, 2007).

At the forensic level, in contested cases, which are typical for pain patients, one side or the other will claim that the evidence is not as clear as stated by the other side (i.e., for or against, as the case may be). When dealing with pain patients, this has been the case for diagnoses involving the DSM-IV-TR, and the situation will be worse with the DSM-5. It has implemented major changes in how chronic pain is considered diagnostically, and they will function to increase confusion, legal contests, and quagmires in court.

My Specific Concerns for SSD

Table 24.3 examines critically some of the major points of contention in the SSD criteria.

Table 24.3 Comments on somatic symptom disorder in DSM-5 (American Psychiatric Association, 2013)

Criterion	Descriptor	Article Author's Comment
Exclusion	"Inappropriate" to diagnose in cases in which a "medical cause" has not been "demonstrated"	Strong criterion
Inclusion	Positive psychological symptoms required (cognitive, affective, physical, behavioral)	Strong criterion
Expression	Personal suffering in sociocultural context	Draft had referred directly to "biopsychosocial"
A	"distressing" somatic symptoms(s) or "significant disruption in daily life"	Ambiguous: why not use the usual "clinically significant impairment in social, occupational, and other important functional areas"
B	Positive symptoms: Excessive (a) thoughts, (b) anxiety, (c) time/energy devotion	One or more
C	Persistent (typically, > 6 months), not necessarily continuous	Ambiguous: can it really come and go?
Specifier	Somatic complaints "with predominant pain" involve pain mostly	Can this really capture the appropriate diagnosis of an individual experiencing psychologically-mediated chronic pain?
Specifier	"Persistent": severe symptoms, marked impairment, and long duration (>6 months)	Confusion with C; moreover, this is more than persistent, as "severe" mentioned
Specifier	Severity: mild = 1 symptom from B; moderate = 2; severe = 2 symptoms, and also either (a) multiple somatic complaints or (b) one very severe one	Confusion with "persistence" Severity based on either number or intensity of positive symptoms or somatic complaints, which is also confusing
Feature	The person's "suffering" is "authentic," whether or not it is medically explained	So "medically unexplained symptoms" seem implicit in this diagnosis; not appropriate
Feature	Concurrent medical condition frequently co-occurs	Good point

Some of the components in SSD are quite positive, for example, it includes both positive and negative symptoms, which is a good distinction to make in defining any psychologically-based somatic disorder. Moreover, it includes cognitive, affective, behavioral, and physical symptoms, which is a good idea for the same reason. However, some of the terms in the diagnostic criteria of SSD are ambiguous, such as the case for the terms of distress, disruption of daily life, persistence, and severity. Moreover, SDD implicates the need for a medical analysis, which might be difficult to ascertain.

One of the goals in revising SSD criteria was to exclude "medically unexplained symptoms" as a factor, as mentioned. However, as noted it could be argued that this type of stigmatizing language still appears. Overall, it can be concluded that, not all the problems associated with the DSM-IV-TR's conceptualization of the diagnosis of pain disorder have been resolved in the DSM-5 by its replacement with the category of SSD involving pain as a specifier.

Alternative Diagnoses Involving Pain in the DSM-5

Adjustment Disorder Note that the DSM-5 recommends alternative diagnoses to SDD (and the pain specifier) for patients in pain. One option is to diagnose an adjustment disorder, and another one is psychological factors affecting other medical conditions. From a psychological perspective, neither of these options appears fully adequate to describe the predominant pain complaints that characterize pain patients. For example, the DSM-5 text for adjustment disorder does not mention pain as an identifiable stressor that could be involved in causing its psychological symptoms. That being said, the text in the DSM-5 for adjustment disorder does mention that a medical condition or illness can be considered sufficient as an identifiable stressor (p. 289, p. 323). Moreover, it might be argued that adjustment to chronic disability, disease/condition, or illness is implicit in attributing the disorder. Nevertheless, without the option of the DSM-IV-TR's pain disorder and only having SSD available as a diagnosis, or perhaps adjustment disorder, as in the DSM-5, one could argue that mental health assessors in the contentious area of psychological injuries who are conducting psychological assessments will be incapable of establishing a valid diagnosable medical disease/condition or disability directly related to the psychological difficulties associated with pain experience.

Psychological Factors Affecting Other Medical Conditions As for psychological factors affecting other medical conditions, its use in the DSM-5 does apply to "idiopathic" medical symptoms, including pain (p. 322), as well as pain-related functional syndromes (e.g., migraines). Once more, the mention of medical pain and headache symptoms presents problems to mental health assessors, who not being qualified as medical doctors, might have difficulty establishing that these conditions are actually in the file and that the disorder can be attributed to the patient. Moreover, my concern is that in contested cases, which are typical for pain patients, one side or the other will claim that the evidence for or against the pain-related medical condition is not as clear as stated (i.e., for or against as the case may be).

Recommendations for the DSM-5.1

Understanding Chronic Pain

The failure to consider chronic pain as the possible basis for a psychological disorder, as has occurred by elimination of pain disorder in the DSM-5, is not consistent with current understanding of its nature. Further in this regard, although a biopsychosocial model seems appropriate in understanding and diagnosing pain conditions (e.g., Gatchel, Peng, Peters, Fuchs, & Turk, 2007), this term does not appear anywhere in the DSM-5, let alone in the pain section. [That being said, the manual does refer to early trauma, learning, cultural and social factors in the contributions to the genetic and biological vulnerabilities in somatic symptom and related disorders.] Indeed, the term biopsychosocial was removed from inclusion in the 2010 draft of the DSM-5 for the 2013 version.

The biopsychosocial nature of pain is illustrated by studies on the effects of loneliness on its experience (Jaremka et al., 2014; Wolf & Davis, 2014). Also, goal-related behavior influences it (Ewart, Elder, Laird, Shelby, & Walker, 2014; Karoly, Okun, Enders, & Tennen, 2014). In this regard, that cognitive-behavior therapy can help is noteworthy, as well (Kerns et al., 2014). The complexity of pain experience is illustrated by the mutual maintenance influences on it and on comorbid conditions (Ruiz-Párraga & López-Martínez, 2014).

In attempting to diagnose patients with pain conditions, there is a frequent lack of one-to-one correspondence, or a dose–response relationship, involving physical injury and pain experience (Gatchel et al., 2007; Melzack & Katz, 2012). Psychological and social factors appear important contributors in understanding chronic pain. Given the problems elucidated in the DSM-5's approach to chronic pain, in the following, I offer an alternative diagnosis to SSD, termed Chronic Pain Complications Disorder. Not only does it consider the biopsychosocial model, but also it preserves the advantages found in SSD, as per Table 24.3, while avoiding its disadvantages.

Chronic Pain Complications Disorder

In part, the present proposal on Chronic Pain Complications Disorder builds on Frances's (2013b) proposal for a revised SSD. For example, rather than referring to excessive and persistent preoccupations with somatic symptoms, as in the DSM-5, in his proposal in how to revise it, he referred also to maladaptive, clearly disproportionate, intrusive, and extreme ones. Note that I did not follow fully Frances's (2013b) suggestion to have all three of cognitive, emotional, and behavioral symptoms necessarily present to receive a SSD diagnosis instead of only one or the other of them, as found in the DSM-5. Rather, I opted for the intermediate position of having any two of these three symptoms present in the patient/evaluee to meet the threshold for the cluster. This decision represents a balanced approach.

Table 24.4 gives criteria for the proposed diagnosis of Chronic Pain Complications Disorder. This replacement condition of SSD can be used in the next iteration of the DSM-5. The proposed pain category would help avoid some of the difficulties associated with SSD in the DSM-5 and the lack of a separate diagnostic entity from a psychological perspective in the DSM-5 for chronic pain.

My proposal for a new DSM category of Chronic Pain Complications Disorder involves five major criteria. (a) First, the patient/evaluee presents with pain in one or more anatomical

Table 24.4 Proposal for DSM 5.1: chronic pain complications disorder (diagnostic criteria)

Criterion	Explanation		
I. Apparent Authentic Biopsychosocial Presentation/Causation			
A.	Pain in one or more anatomical sites is distressing and is the predominant focus of the clinical presentation		
B.	The pain causes clinically significant impairment in social, occupational, or other important areas of functioning (post-pain onset complications)		
C.	Psychological factors are judged to have an important role in the onset, severity, exacerbation, or maintenance of the pain (excessive, persistent, maladaptive thoughts, feelings, or behaviors), as manifested by at least two of the following: (a) thoughts about the symptom seriousness; (b) anxiety about the experienced pain and its perceived consequences; (c) time and energy expended about them		
D.	The symptom or deficit is not intentionally produced or feigned (as in Factitious Disorder or Malingering)		
E.	The pain is not better accounted for by another disorder		
Specifier Duration:	Acute: < 6 months Chronic: ≥ 6 months		
Specifier			
Severity:	<u>Mild</u>	<u>Moderate</u>	<u>Severe</u>
	Consider not diagnosing SSD as clinical, given its manageability at this level	Consider diagnosing SSD as a feature or subsyndromally, although this level is hard to manage	This level is definitely SSD
Pain reported	☐	☐	☐
Distress reported	☐	☐	☐
Impairment reported	☐	☐	☐
II. If Confusing or Complicated Presentation/Causation			
Specify Degree of Feigning, if any			
☐ Minor exaggeration	☐ Gross exaggeration	☐ Outright malingering	
Specify Source of Confusion, if any			
☐ Can be fully explained by pre-existing factors (e.g., psychopathology)			
☐ Pre-existing factors exacerbate the pain			
☐ Post-onset factors exacerbate the pain (e.g., family, work, litigation, distress)			
Specify Certainty of These Ratings			
☐ Unsure	☐ Some data	☐ Clear data	

Note. All terms and qualifiers that could be ambiguous or contentious must be attributed only if clearly evidenced and documented and go beyond the minimal/mild and, if applicable, the moderate range, as the case may be, for example: (a) Excessive and persistent psychological factors in the pain experience; (b) Severe pain/distress/impairment; (c) Gross exaggeration/malingering; and (d) Pre-existing and post-onset factors, as well as any extraneous factors (e.g., an unrelated death of a loved one) sites, and the pain is distressing and predominant in focus. (b) Second, the pain disrupts in the person important activities of daily life (social, occupational, etc.); this criterion constitutes the focus in diagnosing clinical complications due to the pain experience. (c) Third, psychological factors are involved in the onset, severity, exacerbation, or maintenance of the pain experience, or any combination of these factors. In this regard, for the pain symptoms presented by the person, there are excessive thoughts (re seriousness), feelings (e.g., anxiety), or behaviors (time/energy spent). (d) Fourth, the person does not express feigning, dissimulation, or malingering, and the like. (e) Fifth, the person's symptoms cannot be accounted for by another DSM-5 disorder. Further, specifiers relate to chronicity (chronic at 6 months or more), severity (re pain, distress, impairment), patient/evaluee validity (credibility), and causality.

There are several notable advantages to the present proposal for criteria of a new DSM category of Chronic Pain Complications Disorder. I enumerate the following.

(a) First, the proposal addresses the issue of diagnostic inflation by tightening the amount of subcriteria necessary for the diagnosis (in the polythetic Criterion C). It is conservative enough to exclude milder or ambiguous cases.

(b) Second, the proposal includes qualifiers that the assessor needs to arrive at conclusions with documented evidence when considering terms such as: excessive; severe; distress; preexisting factors; and malingering. Given the difficulties and ambiguities associated with these terms, much work is needed on any accompanying text for the proposal so that it is clinically useful and scientifically valid.

(c) Third, the proposal avoids dualistic notions of pain. It refers to anatomically located pain, without anatomically-located a medical or tissue damage origin. Also, it allows for a "role" of psychological factors without denying the relevance of associated tissue damage or medical condition. The proposal is implicitly biopsychosocial in conceptualization rather than either medical, psychological, or both (to use the language of the dualistic DSM-IV-TR). Simply, pain might have a physiological origin and constitute expression of a disease, but psychological and social contributions could make it more for the patient than simply a medical disease.

(d) Fourth, the proposal is detailed and clear enough to help explain the diagnosis to patients/evaluees when it is attributed. Moreover, the table presenting it refers to the need for evidence and documentation so that the patient ends up more assured that than otherwise would be the case about the validity of the diagnosis and, more important, the validity of their pain experience (it is not simply "all in their head").

(e) Finally, by using more precise criteria that need documentation before attribution, and also by acknowledging the issue that the patient's pain could be influenced by biopsychosocial factors, it becomes easier for the clinician/evaluator to recommend psychosocial intervention or psychotherapy, aside from whatever pharmaceutical medications might be prescribed. The current point indicates that the present proposal might make it easier to avoid undue influence of pharmaceutical companies on clinical practice and, as well, serve to moderate the role that they might have had in influencing the DSM-5 construction process, while advocating for non-medicinal (psychological and related) solutions to patients' pain experience.

The disorder proposed contains clauses that consider whether the diagnosis is valid in terms of the need to rule out feigning, dissimulation, gross exaggeration, malingering, etc., thereby making it useful forensically. Of course, similar clauses can be appended to any of the psychological injuries (e.g., PTSD, TBI, and major depression or any depressive disorder or anxiety disorder when it develops after an event at issue). However, these other disorders already are described in the DSM-5. In contrast, for pain patients, work is needed for a dedicated pain-related diagnosis in the DSM-5.1 that respects its complications, including those related to the person's validity in presentation.

It is beyond the scope of the present paper to deal with the issue of the reliability and validity of effectively ruling in or ruling out malingering, and the reader is referred to Young (2014a) about this issue. As per Young (2014a), evaluators who undertake evaluations dealing with pain-centered clinical presentations in the forensic disability and related context need to adopt rigorous procedures in the assessment.

Further, in the way the disorder is phrased in the table, the functional impacts of the pain experienced by the patient need to be addressed (e.g., social, occupational role effects; constituting clinical complications). In the forensic context, the value of identifying functional effects and disabilities of the event at issue (and their relation to symptoms, impairments, and disorders) remains crucial.

Moreover, for chronic pain, if a psychological diagnosis is called for and the assessor considers it validly expressed, he or she should evaluate sources of complications related to causality. The criteria proposed for chronic pain complications disorder includes this factor.

Finally, by referring to chronic pain conditions as a complications disorder, the disorder is somewhat destigmatized. For example, in cases of chronic pain evaluated as valid, the clinician/assessor could explain to the patient/evaluee that the diagnostic issue is not that the pain is "all in the head" but that it is understood as authentic and the complications for the person constitute the main problems being addressed.

Painful Conclusions

Assessment in the area of psychological injury and law often involves pain patients, and the DSM-5 changes to diagnosing chronic pain both reduce its relevance and increase potential harm to patients and evaluees. The category of SSD allows for pain as a specifier, but this is insufficient to capture the psychological state of genuine pain patients/evaluees. In this regard, I have offered an alternative formulation for chronic pain that is partly based on SSD (referred to as Chronic Pain Complications Disorder).

The difficulties presented pertaining to the assessment and diagnosis of chronic pain in the DSM-5 might be confusing not only to assessors working with it in diagnosing patients but also to other users of the manual. For example, when various stakeholders consider the evaluations of mental health assessors, such as adjusters/examiners, arbitrators/workers in legal venues, and triers of fact (judges, juries) in court, will they query whether any of the clinician's/assessor's conclusions are valid? More likely than not, the confusions generated by the diagnostic approach to chronic pain in the DSM-5 will be a source of difficulty not only for mental health assessors but also for those determining whether psychotherapy is appropriate or adjudicating cases. This might serve to aggravate the adversarial divide involving pain patients and plaintiffs in court and related venues.

Other DSM-5 Considerations

Personality Disorder

The personality disorder (PD) DSM-5 draft proposal for change to PD diagnosis elicited a firestorm of criticism, and the new system was relegated for further study. The DSM-5 draft proposal had extensively revised the personality disorder section but, due to criticism, the DSM-IV-TR version was retained. The latter was placed in Sect. 2 of the DSM-5, and the proposal was placed in Appendix for consideration in the next DSM version. Table 24.5 provides the criteria for the proposed Antisocial Personality Disorder.

Given the lack of reliability of personality disorder in the field trials, the whole area needs reconceptualization. However, it is not clear that the proposed alternative will fare better or be clinically usable. Moreover, in the DSM-5, antisocial personality disorder is considered one of the indicators of possible malingering. The difficulty in diagnosing it adds one more barrier in considering the DSM-5 approach to malingering as valid and useful.

The PD section of the manual continues to spark criticism on both scientific and utility grounds (Livesley, 2013; Mullins-Sweatt, Bernstein, & Widiger, 2012; Verheul, 2012). Nevertheless, empirical research does present some findings in their favor (e.g., Morey & Skodol, 2013). Hopwood and Sellbom (2013)

Table 24.5 Proposed antisocial personality disorder for consideration in the next version of the DSM

Criterion	Explanation
A	Definitional impairment in personality functioning in at least one of the following areas: e.g., failure to conform to lawful/ethical behavior; an egocentric, callous lack of concern for others; also deceitfulness, irresponsibility, manipulativeness, and/or risk taking
A1	Identity. Egocentrism; self-esteem from personal gain, power, pleasure
A2	Self-direction. Goal setting based on personal gratification; absence of prosocial internal standards, could include failure to conform to lawful/culturally normative ethical behavior
A3	Empathy. Lack of concern for feelings, needs, suffering of others; lack of remorse after hurting/mistreating someone
A4	Intimacy. Incapacity for mutually intimate relationships, exploitation is primary means of relating, including deceit, coercion; use of dominance, intimidation to control people
B	Six or more of the following seven pathological personality traits
B1	Manipulativeness. An aspect of antagonism
B2	Callousness. An aspect of antagonism
B3	Deceitfulness. An aspect of antagonism
B4	Hostility. An aspect of antagonism
B5	Risk taking. An aspect of disinhibition
B6	Impulsivity. An aspect of disinhibition
B7	Irresponsibility. An aspect of disinhibition
Specifier	At least 18 years of age

reviewed the evidence in favor of the new formulation, which is based on dimensionally-described personality traits.

Quilty, Ayearst, Chmielewski, Pollock, and Bagby (2013) found evidence supporting the psychometric properties of the PID-5 (Personality Inventory for DSM-5), which was developed by the Personality and Personality Disorders workgroup of the DSM-5 project (Krueger, Derringer, Markon, Watson, & Skodol, 2012). In the clinical setting used in the Quilty et al. study, the results generally indicated adequate internal consistency, factor structure, and convergent validity of most PID-5 domains and facets.

Wygant and Sellbom (2012) noted that the PSY-5 (Personality Psychopathology Five; Harkness & McNulty, 1994), part of the MMPI-2 (The Minnesota Multiphasic Personality Inventory-2; Butcher et al., 2001)/MMPI-2-RF (The Minnesota Multiphasic Personality Inventory-2 Restructured Form; Ben-Porath & Tellegen, 2008/2011), corresponds well to the domains of the DSM-5. In particular, (a) DSM-5 Antagonism is akin to PSY-5 Aggressiveness; (b) Schizotypy (psychoticism) to Psychoticism; (c) Disinhibition to Disconstraint; (d) Negative Emotionality (affectivity) to Neuroticism/Negative Emotionality; and (e) Detachment to Introversion/Low Positive Emotionality. Anderson et al. (2012) conducted a study using undergraduates, and administered the PID-5 and the MMPI-2-RF, from which the PSY-5 scales can be scored. They found data in support of the parallel between the PID-5 and PSY-5, except for a slight variation for Antagonism.

A measure of the classic Five Factor Model (FFM) of personality (FFM Rating Form, Mullins-Sweatt, Jamerson, Samuel, Olson, & Widiger, 2006) has been shown to correspond to the PID-5, giving an opening for normative trait research in personality disorder classification (Thomas et al., 2013). Other research has supported using the PAI (Personality Assessment Inventory; Morey, 2007) in DSM-5 PD assessment, because of its "broad" convergence with the DSM-5 traits (Hopwood et al., 2013). Markon, Quilty, Bagby, and Krueger (2013) developed an informant version of the PID-5.

Depression

Gotlib and LeMoult (2014) summarized the changes in depression-related disorders in the

DSM-5 relative to the DSM-IV-TR. They noted that the essential symptoms of the critical disorder of major depression have not changed. The changes to the depression-related disorders and their organization include various additions, deletions, and movement from and to appendices. They noted the controversies in the area and the as-yet unexplored consequences of various changes. Overall, they suggested that the changes have served the goal of coming closer to better reliability and validity on the treatment of depression-related disorders in the DSM-5.

However, Gotlib and LeMoult (2014) appeared to support inclusion of premenstrual dysphoric disorder in the DSM-5, as well as removal of the bereavement exclusion from major depressive disorder. They acknowledged criticism of these decisions (e.g., diagnostic inflation, pathologizing normal responses, stigmatization), but essentially took the pragmatic view that these disorders will enable insurance coverage for affected individuals.

Malingering

Definition Young (2014a) noted that, in the psychiatric approach, malingering involves the "intentional production of false or grossly exaggerated physical or psychological symptoms" that derives from "motivation by external incentives," for example, for obtaining financial compensation (in the DSM-IV-TR).

The DSM-IV-TR specifies that any combination of the following four factors strongly suggests possible malingering: (a) the referral context is medicolegal; (b) the objective findings are "markedly" different from the evaluee's claimed "stress or disability"; (c) the evaluee is not cooperative with the assessment procedure or with suggested treatments; and (d) the evaluee is diagnosed with antisocial personality disorder.

However, the first of the four mentioned factors automatically and erroneously brands each evaluee in forensic disability examinations as a possible malingerer; the second and third factors might reflect the confrontational nature of these types of examinations; and the fourth factor expresses the inclusion fallacy mentioned for the first factor. Given these concerns, Boone (2011) and others have indicated that the DSM-IV-TR does not appear sufficiently accurate with respect to malingering.

Note that Table 24.6 shows that there are some "minor" changes to the definition of malingering in the DSM-5 relative to the approach in the DSM-IV-TR. However, some of the ones included might not be minor in that they appear to lower somewhat the bar for its attribution. [Then again, excluding the term from the subject index, as happened in the DSM-5 manual, seems to raise it out of existence!]

In Young (2014a, 2014b), I noted that the DSM-IV-TR approach to the definition malingering can be qualified by the separation of its two major components. That is, the definition implies the presence of either (a) overt, outright, frank, and conscious, intentional fabrication, feigning, or dissimulation of symptoms, disorders disabilities, or functional impairments for external incentives, such as financial gain, and for which there is incontrovertible, indisputable, or compelling evidence, or (b) conscious, intentional gross exaggerations of symptoms, disorders, disabilities, or functional impairments that clearly are greater than the moderate level, for the same external incentives, and for which there is incontrovertible or compelling evidence.

Young (2014a, 2014b) further qualified that, in malingering, unlike what is specified in the DSM definition, the intention is not to "produce" false or exaggerated symptoms but to clinically present with them. For example, symptoms that are self-reported are not "produced" per se; they are merely presented in description to the evaluator as part of the presenting problem. There might be no symptoms produced, per se. Second, even if there were symptoms produced, the process of somatization could be in play. Moreover, even in the case of somatization, the symptoms produced might be on purpose for financial gain, or malingering, rather than being unconscious. For example, one could firmly wish that one has been injured (although one has not) and the stress, lack of sleep, anger against the insurance process, etc., all conspire to produce pain and related

Table 24.6 Changes to malingering in DSM-5

Criterion	Descriptor	Change
Superordinate category	Nonadherence to medical treatment	In the DSM-IV, had been under "Additional conditions" for clinical focus
Criteria	"Any combination" of the four criteria leads to "strong suspicion"	Same (i.e., 2 or more of the 4)
Criterion 1	Referral to an attorney, but also could be self-referral to the attorney	Had been only referral to an attorney. This lowers the bar
Criterion 2	Marked discrepancy between claims and "objective findings and observations"	Had been only objective findings. This lowers the bar
Criterion 3	Lack of cooperation/compliance	Same
Criterion 4	Antisocial personality disorder	Same
Elaboration	"Definite" evidence of "feigning" "suggests" malingering if the "apparent" goal is to obtain an incentive, such as financial ("money")	Added
	Definite feigning evidence = "clear evidence" of "loss of function" in examination but not at home	Added; but how are home observations obtained? Are they always needed?
	"Symptom relief" could be obtained by "suggestion" or "hypnosis"	Deleted; good idea
Section placement	Other conditions that may be focus of clinical attention	However, it is entered after a subheading nonadherence to medical treatment, which is confusing because malingering might involve overly zealous adherence to medical treatment.
Index entry	–	Removed [Has malingering really ceased to exist?] Solution: put it back

claimable symptoms. That is, a conscious process of presenting with symptoms might serve to actually produce them. Further, the conscious, fabricated origin of the symptoms no longer might be recalled. In this regard, the putative claimable symptoms become seemingly genuine only after intentional exaggeration or malingering produces them. One way or another, symptoms are produced by an otherwise false belief, and the origin of the intent is suppressed or is forgotten, conveniently or otherwise.

Aside from these considerations about somatization, a revised approach to malingering should add a qualifier that the malingering could be partial rather than full, and also mild rather than moderate or severe, but no less in need of detection. That is, once malingering is concluded to have taken place, it should be specified for certain relevant attributes, such as the extent of its range and its degree of intensity.

Note that inclusion of partial and mild malingering in the definition should not obscure that some malingering had taken place. In addition, note that, in cases of partial malingering, there still might be valid aspects of the evaluee's presentation and performance that require regular assessment for diagnosis, functional deficit and disability, treatment recommendations, and conclusions on prognosis.

Finally, note that a definition of malingering that includes the requirement of specification of degree to the point that it might be mild should not be conflated with equating mild or minimal exaggeration to genuine malingering. That is, mild exaggeration should be excluded as part of the definition of malingering and should not be included as an example of mild malingering.

In short, an improved definition of malingering would involve the following:

> Malingering is the intentional *presentation with* false or grossly exaggerated symptoms [physical, mental health, or both; full or partial; mild, moderate, or severe], for purposes of obtaining an external incentive, such as monetary compensation for an injury and/or avoiding/evading work, military duty, or criminal prosecution.

Other advantages of the proposed definition to note is that the use of the word "presentation" instead of "production" more clearly covers negative symptoms as well as positive ones, such as failing to present capable of work when that is not the case. Moreover, other changes that I made to the definition: (a) allow for combined physical and psychological symptoms, (b) value all mental health perspectives, and (c) allow for both trying to obtain financial compensation and also avoiding work.

Detection Systems Slick, Sherman, and Iverson (1999) developed criteria for Malingered Neurocognitive Dysfunction (MND). The latter represented a major advance in the field because it systematized the existing conceptualization and research on malingered disability and related response biases in neurocognitive and related disability assessments. There is another system for detecting malingering, one for pain-related presentations (the MPRD, Malingered Pain-Related Disability; Bianchini, Greve, & Glynn, 2005). Also, Rubenzer (2009) recommended tests for detecting malingered PTSD. But there has not been a malingering detection system, per se, for PTSD. Based on the work of these leaders, I developed such a system in Young (2014a, 2015). Moreover, it was created so that, with minor changes, it is also applicable to MND and MPRD cases.

Slick and Sherman (2012, 2013) revised their 1999 MND model for the detection of malingering, especially by broadening the criteria. However, for each of their changes to the MND model [(a) broadening compelling inconsistencies, (b) using likelihood ratio chaining and positive predictive power, and (c) removing the exclusion criterion], the decisions taken were either not entirely clear or were insufficient. For example, (a) for the case of the inconsistencies, I have developed a much more elaborate scheme in my revised MND model. (b) For the Larrabee, Greiffenstein, Greve, and Bianchini (2007) LR (likelihood ratio chaining) and PPP (positive predictive power) technique, Slick and Sherman (2012, 2013) had indicated that their use would be premature but, nevertheless, they added the procedure to their model (however, in a seemingly inconsistent way). (c) For the exclusionary criterion, they reported it as dropped from their revised system but, in actuality, they kept it (however, in a revised way that did not broaden but constrained use of the model).

The original 1999 MND model has an important place in the history of the field, and still can be considered a model that has the potential to become the gold standard in the field of malingering detection. However, the specific form of the model that might reach that status might relate more to my revision of it more than the revision of the original authors.

Bianchini, Curtis, and Greve (2013) indicated that the MPRD could be used with other conditions, such as PTSD, because it concerns exaggeration and malingering, in general. However, they failed to consider that inspection of their system reveals that it includes quite pain-specific criteria.

Comment

This concludes presentation of major DSM-5 categories and also commentary on their criticisms and limitations. Generally, the DSM-5 psychiatric categories need further work to meet acceptable reliability standards. Their exact wording should be vetted and then their reliability determined. In further versions of the DSM-5, different approaches to classification should be examined. For example, to end the chapter, I look at the ICD-11.

The ICD-11

Complex PTSD

Maercker et al. (2013) described how the International Classification of Diseases-11 (ICD-11, due in 2017) is dealing with categories of mental disorders that are associated with stress. Like for the DSM-5, they are separating stress disorders from other mental disorders. However, many of their decisions take a different direction than in the DSM-5.

They noted that in the ICD-11 draft, for each disorder due to stress, the stressor is a "necessary not sufficient" causal factor. The stressors include those that are within the normal range of human experience (e.g., for adjustment disorder) and those that are "exceptionally severe" (e.g., for PTSD). In defining the disorders, the ICD-11 adopts a clinical utility focus. In this regard, for PTSD, they simplified it only to disorder-specific symptoms and they excluded non-specific symptoms that are also part of other disorders (e.g., Brewin, Lanius, Novac, Schnyder, & Galea, 2009). Moreover, they used only three symptom clusters—(a) re-experiencing the traumatic event; (b) avoidance of reminders; (c) and perceiving heightened current threats as evidenced by arousal (Forbes et al., 2011). They qualified that the event at issue must be "extremely threatening or horrific." They noted that, to differentiate PTSD from normal reactions to extreme stressors, the person must express a functional impairment as well as symptoms of a particular duration.

The other mental disorders involving stress in the ICD-11 include complex PTSD (CPTSD). The stressors in such cases involve ones that are severe and prolonged, and they usually include several or repeated adverse events, such as in sexual abuse (Cloitre et al., 2009; Weiss, 2012). The disorder is also accompanied by "enduring disturbances" in the areas of self, affect, and interpersonal relations. The inclusion of complex PTSD in the ICD-11 contrasts with its exclusion in the DSM-5.

A notable addition to the stress disorders is the inclusion of prolonged grief disorder, which is distinct from depression. In contrast, the DSM-5 allows for a brief grief reaction to be considered as an expression of major depressive disorder. Therefore, the DSM-5 approach differs from the ICD-11 approach in two ways—first, in the DSM-5, the grief reaction can be brief yet still disordered. Second, it is not considered separate from depression, unlike in the ICD-11 proposal.

In the latter proposal, adjustment disorder is a mental condition or a maladaptive reaction arising from a significant life event. Relative to the ICD-10, its definition has been tightened. It is more than a non-clinical acute stress reaction that lasts for only days. The authors concluded that the proposed ICD-11 system will be user-friendly, including for low-resource and humanitarian populations.

Evidence

Wolf et al. (2015) queried the validity of proposing that CPTSD should be split from PTSD, as being proposed for the ICD-11. In each of community and military samples, factor modeling indicated two classes, but they were related to disorder severity and not the PTSD-CPTSD distinction.

To illustrate the difficulties presented by the DSM-5 approach to diagnosis for PTSD, consider the following. O'Donnell et al. (2014) demonstrated that the prevalence rate of PTSD for the DSM-5 and the ICD-11 criteria differs markedly in the two diagnostic systems. They found that, for injury patients, PTSD was diagnosed twice as much using the DSM-5 criteria compared to those of the ICD-11 (6.7 % vs. 3.3 %, respectively). In the DSM-5, 20 criteria symptoms are listed, although only a handful of them for any one patient are needed for the diagnosis. In the ICD-11, as mentioned, only a few core symptoms are required for diagnosis (Maercker et al., 2013). Perhaps reducing PTSD diagnostic symptoms especially to core ones will constrain its diagnosis, a process that should help reduce its prevalence not only in using the ICD-11 but also could help in the next versions of the DSM-5, should they go that route.

Conclusions

The present chapter on specific DSM-5 disorders leaves as much doubt about them as the general criticisms of the DSM-5 reviewed in the prior chapter. The disorders reviewed reveal multiple minor and some major difficulties, and should be revised accordingly. Even the disorders touted as quite reliable, such as the one of PTSD, suffer on close inspection of their criteria and the research related to them. The area of psychological injury and law deals with PTSD, pain, and TBI, in particular, and for all three areas, the present chapter (and the companion one before it) pinpoint considerable concern. The same applies to entities in the DSM-5 that have not changed relative to the DSM-IV-TR, such as malingering. In the present chapter, I end up making specific proposals how chronic pain and malingering can be redefined in the next iteration of the DSM-5. Review of the ICD-11 proposal for stress disorders, as presented by Maercker et al. (2013), leaves much room to ponder the approach taken for these disorders in the DSM-5. For example, for PTSD, they emphasize disorder-specific symptoms and also group them into three clusters. They allow for CPTSD. As for bereavement, they consider it separate from depression and, moreover, it must be prolonged. These and other decisions for the ICD-11 will only serve to accentuate the debate about the utility and validity of aspects of the DSM-5.

Chapter Conclusions

This chapter and the prior one have critically examined both the RDoC (Insel et al., 2010; Insel & Lieberman, 2013) project and the DSM-5. I have showed that both are vast projects that need to be respected for their scope, but both suffer from the same disorder or disease. That is, both do not respect enough or include enough the biopsychosocial approach to mental illness. For both these grand projects, I end up making pertinent suggestions for their improvement in these regards.

In the following chapter of the present work, I move from dealing with psychiatric classification and diagnosis, as in the DSM-5, to broader considerations. These include discussion of causality and etiology, in particular. Then, I suggest recommendations for psychiatry and classification. Finally, I present conclusions related to practice.

References

American Psychiatric Association. (2013). *Diagnostic and statistical manual of mental disorders: DSM-5* (5th ed.). Washington, DC: Author.

American Psychiatric Association. (2000). *Diagnostic and statistical manual of mental disorders: DSM-IV-TR* (4th ed., text rev.). Washington, DC: Author.

Anderson, J. L., Sellbom, M., Bagby, R. M., Quilty, L. C., Veltri, C. O. C., Markon, K. E., et al. (2012). On the convergence between PSY-5 domains and PID-5 domains and facets: Implications for assessment of DSM-5 personality traits. *Assessment, 20*, 286–294.

Ben-Porath, Y. S., & Tellegen, A. (2008/2011). *The Minnesota Multiphasic Personality Inventory-2 Restructured Form (MMPI-2-RF): Manual for administration, scoring, and interpretation*. Minnesota, MN: University of Minnesota Press.

Bianchini, K. J., Curtis, K. L., & Greve, K. W. (2013). Cognitive performance validity assessment in mild traumatic brain injury, physical pain, and posttraumatic stress. In D. A. Carone & S. S. Bush (Eds.), *Mild traumatic brain injury: System validity assessment and malingering* (pp. 323–346). New York: Springer.

Bianchini, K. J., Greve, K. W., & Glynn, G. (2005). On the diagnosis of malingered pain-related disability: Lessons from cognitive malingering research. *The Spine Journal, 5*, 404–417.

Blazer, D. (2013). Neurocognitive disorders in DSM-5. *American Journal of Psychiatry, 170*, 585–587.

Boone, K. B. (2011). Clarification or confusion? A review of Rogers, Bender, and Johnson's a critical analysis of the MND criteria for feigned cognitive impairment: Implications for forensic practice and research. *Psychological Injury and Law, 4*, 157–162.

Brewin, C. R., Lanius, R. A., Novac, A., Schnyder, U., & Galea, S. (2009). Reformulating PTSD for DSM-V: Life after criterion A. *Journal of Traumatic Stress, 22*, 366–373.

Butcher, J. N., Graham, J. R., Ben-Porath, Y. S., Tellegen, A., Dahlstrom, W. G., & Kaemmer, B. (2001). *MMPI-2: Manual for administration, scoring, and interpretation*. Minneapolis, MN: University of Minnesota Press (Rev. ed).

Cloitre, M., Stolbach, B. C., Herman, J. L., van der Kolk, B., Pynoos, R., Wang, J., et al. (2009). A developmental approach to complex PTSD: Childhood and adult cumulative trauma as predictors of symptom complexity. *Journal of Traumatic Stress, 22*, 399–408.

Dimsdale, J. E. (2012, May). *DSM-5 proposals for somatic symptom disorders*. Paper presented at the 165th annual meeting of American Psychiatric Association, Philadelphia, PA.

Ewart, C. K., Elder, G. J., Laird, K. T., Shelby, G. D., & Walker, L. S. (2014). Can agonistic striving lead to unexplained illness? Implicit goals, pain tolerance, and somatic symptoms in adolescents and adults. *Health Psychology, 33*, 977–985.

Forbes, D., Lockwood, E., Elhai, J. D., Creamer, M., O'Donnell, M., Bryant, R., et al. (2011). An examination of the structure of posttraumatic stress disorder in relation to the anxiety and depressive disorders. *Journal of Affective Disorders, 132*, 165–172.

Frances, A. (2013a). *Essentials of psychiatric diagnosis: Responding to the challenge of DSM-5*. New York: Guilford Press.

Frances, A. (2013b). DSM in philosophyland: Curiouser and curiouser. In J. Paris & J. Phillips (Eds.), *Making the DSM-5: Concepts and controversies* (pp. 95–103). New York: Springer.

Frances, A., & Chapman, S. (2013). DSM-5 somatic symptom disorder mislabels medical illness as mental disorder. *Australian and New Zealand Journal of Psychiatry, 47*, 483–489.

Gatchel, R. J., Peng, Y. B., Peters, M. L., Fuchs, P. N., & Turk, D. C. (2007). The biopsychosocial approach to chronic pain: Scientific advances and future directions. *Psychological Bulletin, 133*, 581–624.

Gotlib, I. H., & LeMoult, J. (2014). The "ins" and "outs" of the depressive disorders section of DSM-5. *Clinical Psychology: Science and Practice, 21*, 193–207.

Harkness, A. R., & McNulty, J. L. (1994). The personality psychopathology five (PSY-5): Issues from the pages of a diagnostic manual instead of a dictionary. In S. Stephen & L. Maurice (Eds.), *Differentiating normal and abnormal personality* (pp. 291–315). New York: Springer.

Hopwood, C. J., & Sellbom, M. (2013). Implications of DSM-5 personality traits for forensic psychology. *Psychological Injury and Law, 6*, 314–323.

Hopwood, C. J., Wright, A. G. C., Krueger, R. F., Schade, N., Markon, K. E., & Morey, L. C. (2013). DSM-5 pathological personality traits and the personality assessment inventory. *Assessment, 20*, 269–285.

Insel, T. R., Cuthbert, B. N., Garvey, M. A., Heinssen, R. K., Pine, D. S., Quinn, K. J., et al. (2010). Research domain criteria (RDoC): Toward a new classification framework for research on mental disorders. *American Journal of Psychiatry, 167*, 748–751.

Insel, T. R., & Lieberman, J. A. (2013). DSM-5 and RDoC: Shared interests. *The National Institute of Mental Health*. Retrieved from http://www.nimh.nih.gov/news/science-news/2013/dsm-5-and-rdoc-shared--interests.shtml

Jaremka, L. M., Andridge, R. R., Fagundes, C. P., Alfano, C. M., Povoski, S. P., Lipari, A. M., et al. (2014). Pain, depression, and fatigue: Loneliness as a longitudinal risk factor. *Health Psychology, 33*, 948–957.

Karoly, P., Okun, M. A., Enders, C., & Tennen, H. (2014). Effects of pain intensity on goal schemas and goal pursuit: A daily diary study. *Health Psychology, 33*, 968–976.

Kerns, R. D., Burns, J. W., Shulman, M., Jensen, M. P., Nielson, W. R., Czlapinski, R., et al. (2014). Can we improve cognitive-behavioral therapy for chronic back pain treatment engagement and adherence? A controlled trial of tailored versus standard therapy. *Health Psychology, 33*, 938–947.

Krueger, R. F., Derringer, J., Markon, K. E., Watson, D., & Skodol, A. E. (2012). Initial construction of a maladaptive personality trait model and inventory for DSM-5. *Psychological Medicine, 42*, 1879–1890.

Larrabee, G. J., Greiffenstein, M. F., Greve, K. W., & Bianchini, K. J. (2007). Refining diagnostic criteria for malingering. In G. J. Larrabee (Ed.), *Evaluation of malingering in the neuropsychological examination* (pp. 334–371). New York: Oxford University Press.

Livesley, W. J. (2013). The DSM-5 personality disorder proposal and future directions in the diagnostic classification of personality disorder. *Psychopathology, 46*, 207–216.

Maercker, A., Brewin, C. R., Bryant, R. A., Cloitre, M., Reed, G. M., van Ommeren, M., et al. (2013). Proposals for mental disorders specifically associated with stress in the International Classification of Diseases-11. *The Lancet, 381*, 1683–1685.

Markon, K. E., Quilty, L. C., Bagby, R. M., & Krueger, R. (2013). The developmental and psychometric properties of an informant-report form of the personality inventory for DSM-5 (PID-5). *Assessment, 20*, 370–383.

Melzack, R., & Katz, J. (2006). Pain in the 21st century: The neuromatrix and beyond. In G. Young, A. W. Kane, & K. Nicholson (Eds.), *Psychological knowledge in court: PTSD, pain, and TBI* (pp. 129–148). New York: Springer Science + Business Media.

Melzack, R., & Katz, J. (2012). Pain. *Wiley Interdisciplinary Reviews: Cognitive Science, 4*, 1–15.

Morey, L. C. (2007). *Professional manual for the personality assessment inventory*. Odessa, FL: Psychological Assessment Resources.

Morey, L. C., & Skodol, A. E. (2013). Convergence between DSM-IV-TR and DSM-5 diagnostic models for personality disorder: Evaluation of strategies for establishing diagnostic thresholds. *Journal of Psychiatric Practice, 19*, 179–193.

Mullins-Sweatt, S. N., Bernstein, D. P., & Widiger, T. A. (2012). Retention or deletion of personality disorder diagnoses for DSM-5: An expert consensus approach. *Journal of Personality Disorders, 26*, 689–703.

Mullins-Sweatt, S. N., Jamerson, J. E., Samuel, D. B., Olson, D. R., & Widiger, T. A. (2006). Psychometric properties of an abbreviated instrument of the five-factor model. *Assessment, 13*, 119–137.

O'Donnell, M. L., Alkemade, N., Nickerson, A., Creamer, M., McFarlane, A. C., Silove, D., et al. (2014). Impact of the diagnostic changes to post-traumatic stress disorder for DSM-5 and the proposed changes to ICD-11. *British Journal of Psychiatry, 205*, 230–235.

Quilty, L. C., Ayearst, L., Chmielewski, M., Pollock, B. G., & Bagby, R. M. (2013). The psychometric properties of the personality inventory for DSM-5 in an APA DSM-5 field trial sample. *Assessment, 20*, 362–369.

Rief, W., & Martin, A. (2014). How to use the new DSM-5 somatic symptom disorder diagnosis in research and practice: A critical evaluation and a proposal for modification. *Annual Review of Clinical Psychology, 10*, 339–367.

Rief, W., Mewes, R., Martin, A., Glaesmer, H., & Brähler, E. (2011). Evaluating new proposals for the psychiatric classification of patients with multiple somatic symptoms. *Psychosomatic Medicine, 73*, 760–768.

Rubenzer, S. (2009). Posttraumatic stress disorder: Assessing response style and malingering. *Psychological Injury and Law, 2*, 114–142.

Ruiz-Párraga, G. T., & López-Martínez, A. E. (2014). The contribution of posttraumatic stress symptoms to

chronic pain adjustment. *Health Psychology, 33*, 968–976.
Schultz, I. Z. (2010). Neurocognitive disorders in DSM-V: Forensic perspective. *Psychological Injury and Law, 3*, 271–288.
Schultz, I. Z. (2013). DSM-5 neurocognitive disorders: Validity, reliability, fairness, and utility in forensic applications. *Psychological Injury and Law, 6*, 299–306.
Simpson, J. R. (2014). DSM-5 and neurocognitive disorders. *The Journal of the American Academy of Psychiatry and the Law, 42*, 159–164.
Sirri, L., & Fava, G. A. (2013). Diagnostic criteria for psychosomatic research and somatic symptom disorders. *International Review of Psychiatry, 25*, 19–30.
Slick, D. J., & Sherman, E. M. S. (2012). Differential diagnosis of malingering and related clinical presentations. In E. M. S. Sherman & B. L. Brooks (Eds.), *Pediatric forensic neuropsychology* (pp. 113–135). New York: Oxford University Press.
Slick, D. J., & Sherman, E. M. S. (2013). Differential diagnosis of malingering. In D. A. Carone & S. S. Bush (Eds.), *Mild traumatic brain injury: System validity assessment and malingering* (pp. 57–72). New York: Springer.
Slick, D. J., Sherman, E. M., & Iverson, G. L. (1999). Diagnostic criteria for malingered neurocognitive dysfunction: Proposed standards for clinical practice and research. *The Clinical Neuropsychologist, 13*, 545–561.
Sykes, R. (2012). The DSM 5 website proposals for somatic symptom disorder: Three central problems. *Psychosomatics, 53*, 524–531.
Thomas, K. M., Yalch, M. M., Krueger, R. F., Wright, A. G. C., Markon, K. E., & Hopwood, C. J. (2013). The convergent structure of DSM-5 personality trait facets and five factor model trait domains. *Assessment, 20*, 308–311.
Verheul, R. (2012). Personality disorder proposal for DSM-5: A heroic and innovative but nevertheless fundamentally flawed attempt to improve DSM-IV. *Clinical Psychology and Psychotherapy, 19*, 369–371.
Weiss, D. S. (2012). Introduction to the special feature on complex PTSD. *Journal of Traumatic Stress, 25*, 239–240.
Wolf, E. J., Miller, M. W., Kilpatrick, D., Resnick, H. S., Badour, C. L., Marx, B. P., et al. (2015). ICD-11 complex PTSD in U.S. national and veteran samples: Prevalence and structural associations with PTSD. *Clinical Psychological Science, 3*, 215–229.
Wolf, L. D., & Davis, M. C. (2014). Loneliness, daily pain, and perceptions of interpersonal events in adults with fibromyalgia. *Health Psychology, 33*, 929–937.
Wollburg, E., Voigt, K., Braukhaus, C., Herzog, A., & Löwe, B. (2013). Construct validity and descriptive validity of somatoform disorder in light of proposed changes for the DSM-5. *Journal of Psychosomatic Research, 74*, 18–24.
World Health Organization. (2017). *International Classification of Disease, 11th Revision.*
Wygant, D. B., & Sellbom, M. (2012). Viewing psychopathy from the perspective of the personality psychopathology five model: Implications for DSM-5. *Journal of Personality Disorders, 26*, 717–726.
Young, G. (2010). Chronic pain in the DSM-IV and the DSM-5 draft: The pain of it all. *Psychological Injury and Law, 3*, 289–294.
Young, G. (2013). Ill-treatment of pain in the DSM-5. *Psychological Injury and Law, 6*, 307–313.
Young, G. (2014a). *Malingering, feigning, and response bias in psychiatric/psychological injury: Implications for practice and court.* Dordrecht, Netherlands: Springer Science + Business Media.
Young, G. (2014b). Psychological injury and law II: A critique of psychological injury and law: Implications for mental health policy and ethics. *Mental Health Law and Policy Journal, 3*, 417–470.
Young, G. (2015). Detection system for malingered PTSD and related response biases. *Psychological Injury and Law, 8*, 169–183.
Young, G., Kane, A. W., & Nicholson, K. (2007). (Eds.). *Causality of psychological injury: Presenting evidence in court.* New York: Springer Science + Business Media.

DSM-5: Recommendations 25

Chapter Introduction

Given the comments, concerns, criticisms, and possible harm related to the DSM-5 (Diagnostic and Statistical Manual of Mental Disorders, Fifth Edition; American Psychiatric Association, 2013), it needs revision to become more clinically useful, reliable, and valid. The present chapter emphasizes that this should begin with better conceptualization, including of etiology and of an overarching model. In this regard, it examines an extended biopsychosocial model. The chapter considers new ways of conceiving endophenotypes in terms of the biopsychosocial model. The chapter presents an integrative model of etiology involving combined top-down and bottom-up processes (related to mental disorder and symptoms, respectively). Also, a critical way of improving the reliability in diagnosis involves improving the assessment process. In this regard, I make recommendations related to structuring areas in assessments.

Finally, I deal with practical and court matters, as well as ethics. It should be noted that mental health practitioners of all stripes should consider these practical issues that I raise. For example, I recommend not using uniquely the DSM-5, DSM-IV-TR (Diagnostic and Statistical Manual of Mental Disorders, Fourth Edition, Text Revised; American Psychiatric Association, 2000), or the ICD 10 or 11 (International Classification of Diseases, 10th Revision or 11th Revision; World Health Organization, 2007, 2017) but, instead, I recommend using the manual that is best for any disorder at hand, no matter which one might be involved.

Causality and Etiology in Psychology and Psychiatry

The present book is especially about the causes of behavior, both normal and psychopathological. Behavioral causation in psychopathology is referred to as etiology. In the medical model, specific diseases have specific etiologies and specific cures/treatments. However, the etiology of psychiatric mental disorder is not that straightforward.

Coghill (2014) editorialized that the complexity and heterogeneity of causality in childhood disorder should be acknowledged. Generally, disorders are multicausal and nonspecific or nonlinear in causality (Coghill, Seth, & Matthews, 2014). Moreover, the concept of psychiatric disorder, itself, is not straightforward. Disorders as presently defined often share more similarities than differences (Karalunas, Geurts, Konrad, Bender, & Nigg, 2014). The field needs to consider that, just as etiology is multicausal, mental illness is multifactorial in the sense that it does not compartmentalize easily into distinct, separate disorders. Moreover, the problems in these regards might relate to the way disorders are represented—that is, as a set of possible symptoms with many possible combinations, and, also,

G. Young, *Unifying Causality and Psychology*, DOI 10.1007/978-3-319-24094-7_25

among the symptoms are those that might be common to multiple disorders. Perhaps there is an efficient solution to the dilemma of organizing better the multiple symptoms in psychopathology, the multiple disorders involved, and the large amount of comorbidities and common symptoms therein. Perhaps it is best to focus on what makes each disorder distinct from others and, in doing so, this might serve to reduce their amount, simplify the search for their causal factors, and help in finding efficacious treatment. In this regard, the concept of having separate core, primary and non-core, common symptoms in disorder has a place in psychiatry, but with especially only the former being important diagnostically, etiologically, and therapeutically.

In the following, I examine other concepts relevant to the search for etiological sources to mental disorders, concentrating on the work of Kendler. His work has inspired my own, which ends up quite consistent with his concepts.

Concepts

Kendler (2015) argued for an approach of "limited" realism for psychiatric nosology. Psychiatry needs a less ambitious framework for its truth seeking than outright (scientific) realism, given its limitations. The contrasting position to realism is instrumentalism, which is about establishing useful concepts rather than ones with more absolute truth. "Pessimistic induction" supports an instrumental as opposed to a realism approach to psychiatric nosology. Coherence theory is consistent with the latter view of truth. In this regard, as long as a proposed diagnostic category "fits well" with other aspects of which we know about confidently related to the diagnostic category at issue, it contributes to nosology in psychiatry. Instrumentalism has a certain place in nosology in that categories that work for psychiatry instrumentally help predict and manipulate the world. The overall psychiatric classificatory project reflects realism, thought, and Kendler refers to it as a "type" one. However, in psychiatric nosology, the specific categories reflect a humbler approach to truth, which is consistent with the juvenile or beginning level of their scientific investigation.

Kendler (2008) adopted a systems view of etiology of psychiatric illness. He indicated that the factors involved include biological, psychological, and sociocultural perspectives. He contrasted this approach with hard "reductionism," which is more biological, and, also, he contrasted this approach with hard "emergentism," which is more mental or social in mechanism. In Kendler's multilevel approach, the mechanisms are complex, nonadditive, nondecomposable, nonsubstitutable, interrelational, intricate, pluralistic, multilevel, context-dependent, and both within and outside the individual. The mechanisms allow an easy flow for integration of biological, psychological, and social elements into causal processes. The parts of the system are organized into higher levels within contexts, and they exhibit part-whole or component-system synergistic relations. The process involves feedback, or causal-loop recursive relationships, that are both top-down and bottom-up. Kendler (2008) concluded that causal networks underlying psychiatric disorder contain multiple, nonlinear interactions and causal loops.

Kendler, Zachar, and Craver (2011) contrasted (a) the essentialist, (b) socially-constructed, and (c) practical approaches to understanding psychiatric disorders, leading to their approach of (d) mechanistic property clusters (MPCs). The essentialist model argues that a causal essence is directly responsible for the critical features that characterize a disorder (see Fig. 25.1). The socially-constructed model maintains that disorders are understood as social and cultural constructions. The practical model views disorders from an instrumentalist, pragmatic perspective; as long as the disorder is clinically useful, it is not irrelevant even if it is not genuine.

In the MPC approach, the authors account for the fact that psychiatric disorders are multifactorial and "fuzzy" sets. They are complex, mutually-reinforcing networks related to causal structures or mechanisms. The model facilitates psychiatry developing a more causally-based classification system. MPC allows for individual differences in psychiatric disorder manifestation, in that it

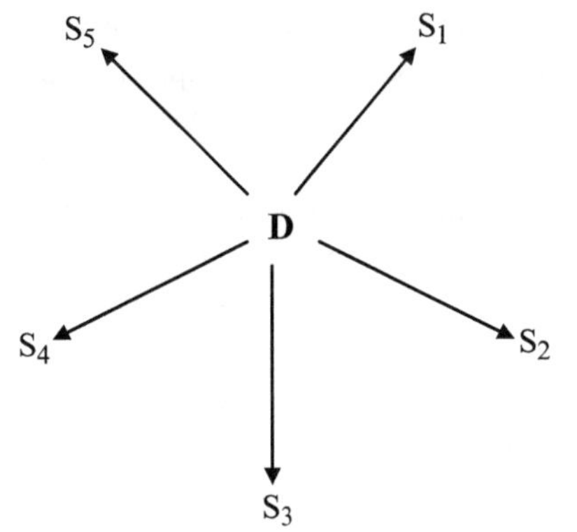

Fig. 25.1 An essentialist model of symptoms/signs (S) and clusters. In an essentialist model of a psychiatric disorder (D), an essence is responsible directly and causally for its critical signs and symptoms (S). Adapted from Kendler et al. (2011)

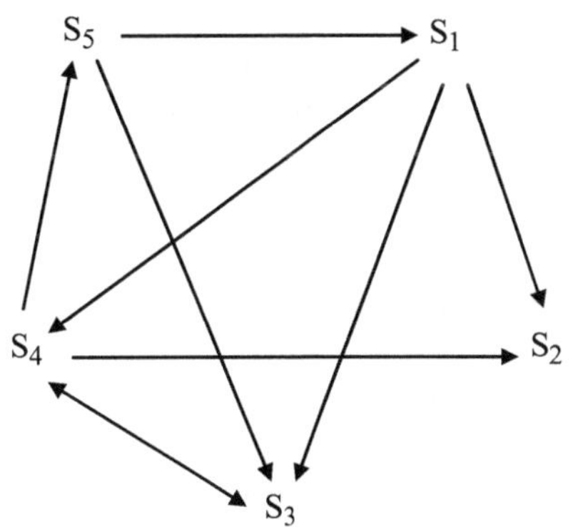

Fig. 25.2 A nonessentialist model of symptoms/signs (S) and clusters. The individual clinical features are causally interrelated to one another but not to a putative latent, organizing universally-labeled disorder that is responsible for them. The clusters could organize such that one symptom (set) causes (an)other(s). Adapted from Kendler et al. (2011)

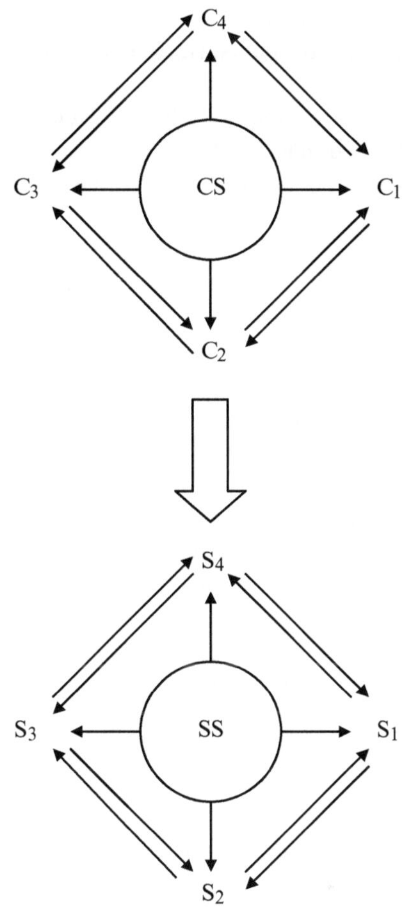

Fig. 25.3 A mixed model of multifactorial causes and symptom clusters of psychiatric disorder. In this mixed model of psychiatric disorder, a series of multifactorial causes (C_1 to C_4) in a causal system (CS) interact with each other to produce an underlying system state (SS) that, in turn, leads to the individual symptoms/signs (S_1 to S_4), which, in their turn, could causally interact amongst themselves. Adapted from Kendler et al. (2011)

considers that there is no single set of traits for disorders. Rather, the traits involved cluster near one or another in a "feature space." There is no one deterministic symptom cluster, nor is there one cause for disorder. That is, cause is considered "messy" and, also, clusters are considered imperfect or heterogeneous. However, this fuzziness does not mean that there is instability in a disorder. There are common co-occurrences of features because of the way causal mechanisms work, as shown in Fig. 25.2. Individual symptoms or signs interact so that they mutually sustain or reinforce each other and appear more or less stable.

Another way to understand the MPC model is shown in Fig. 25.3. A series of causes interact to produce a latent underlying state that influences symptom expression over time. There is no single causal mechanism, but multiple ones. Despite some stability, the relevant causal features express a probabilistic relationship with the clusters of symptoms and signs. Causes are not deterministic, but act to change the degree of probability that symptoms (or their sets) will be manifested. Because there are numerous overlapping mechanisms, linear relationships between cause and effect, or between mechanism and diagnoses, are illusory. Kendler et al. (2011) noted that Borsboom (2008) presented a similar model, which he termed the causal system approach.

Kendler et al. (2011) concluded that sets of symptoms are connected through sets of causal relationships. Moreover, they believed that their approach is consistent with a prototypical perspective on psychiatric disorder. In this approach, exemplar cases rather than lists of symptoms are used to operationalize disorders, and so the approach allows for variation in individual cases and symptom expression. This is the consistent with the notion that boundaries of "kinds" of psychiatric illness are fuzzier than proposed in the essentialist approach. The authors argued that disorders should be defined at the level of property clusters that are underpinned by dysfunctional, yet self-sustaining mechanisms.

Kendler (2012) added further to his etiological approach to nosology. He argued for fuzzy, cross-level mechanisms as sources of psychiatric disorder. Etiology is multiple and higher-order rather than simplistic and singly caused. Cross-level mechanisms are "fuzzy sets" over etiological levels that lead to individual variations in manifestation of a psychiatric disorder.

Genes constitute important etiological sources in psychiatric illness. But, as Kendler has emphasized, psychiatric etiology is multifactorial. Moreover, genes themselves are part of a larger genomic system in which the environment can affect their workings through epigenesis.

Epigenetics

Diwadkar, Bustamante, Rai, and Uddin (2014) argued that epigenetics could affect gene expression levels that mediate the stress response in at-risk individuals for schizophrenia. The functional consequences would lie in impaired cognitive consequences dependent on or subserved by affected brain networks. Thus, epigenetics stands as the proximate mediator in the pathway to schizophrenia. Specifically, a disordered stress response might serve to decouple frontal-striatal and frontal-limbic neuronal networks in at-risk youth.

In relation to underlying epigenetic factors acting in conjunction with genetic, environmental, and neuronal network ones, epigenetic effects might impact progressively gene expression in critical networks during successive developmental epochs (Millan, 2013). The effects on the growing person could relate to increased stress sensitivity as stress-sensitive genes relating to the hypothalamic pituitary adrenal (HPA) axis are impacted. For example, Fillman, Sinclair, Fung, Webster, and Shannon Weickert (2014) found differences in gene expression in stress-related genes as per post-mortem brain tissue analysis in schizophrenics (relative to individuals with other psychiatric disorders and controls). Once more, the authors invoked the hope for finding biological signatures of psychiatric disease in early and progressive epigenetic effects.

Other Considerations

Networks Arguello and Gogos (2012) noted the extensive etiological and pathophysiological heterogeneity and overlap related to psychiatric disorder. They suggested that the temporal dynamics of synaptic plasticity in specific neural circuits could play a role in phenotypic expression of clinical disorders. This might be the case even more so than genetic and environmental causes. Factors to consider in this regard include alterations in synaptic growth and maintenance, synaptogenesis, and axonal guidance, and their developmental changes and trajectories neurodynamically and as they assemble and communicate within neural circuits.

van Os, Delespaul, Wigman, Myin-Germeys, and Wichers (2013) also adopted a system-based approach to psychiatric classification. They argued for a contextual precision diagnosis approach across stages of psychopathology that respects the need for more individualized considerations. That is, diagnoses need to include (a) precision, (b) context, and (c) stages, in which (a) causal influences in system networks are recognized, (b) symptoms are understood as responses to context, and (c) they are understood to develop over time.

In terms of a contextual precision diagnosis, van Os et al. (2013) maintained that disorders are manifested heterogeneously and so should be subject to personalized diagnosis based on patterns of symptom expression in context. They indicated that symptoms are manifested in interacting circuits, combinations, or sets (including in feedback both within and over levels and in interactions at the micro-moment and over time) that are connected through systems of causal relations, thereby allowing for individualized co-occurrence of different symptoms (Borsboom, Cramer, Schmittmann, Epskamp, & Waldorp, 2011; Kendler et al., 2011).

van Os et al. (2013) concluded that contextual precision diagnosis can capture well individualized, idiopathic symptom expression and so replace nomothetic approaches to classification (McGorry & van Os, 2013). Figure 25.4 presents in detail their contextual precision diagnostic model (also see Wigman, Collip, et al., 2013; Wigman, van Os, et al., 2013). They noted that, along with their individualized approach, their nosological recommendations could include common syndromal groupings that are higher-order and more severe.

The approach of Borsboom and colleagues is quite compatible with the psychiatric approach involving systems of symptoms and their causal underpinnings. Borsboom (2008) explained rendition of the difference between the traditional latent variable model of a disorder and a networked causal model. In the former one, underlying constructs are considered sources of symptom expression. In the latter networked model, symptoms can possess linkages independent of any underlying source (see Chap. 6).

The network construct is applied to how personality test items are organized. The traditional reflective model places a latent construct at the epicenter of item loadings, explaining their individual expression via common linkage to it. The formative model runs in the reverse direction, with items contributing to the composite variable representing them. The network model avoids altogether central representations and seeks to represent item linkages and their strengths in a nodal network with edges (links) (see Chap. 7).

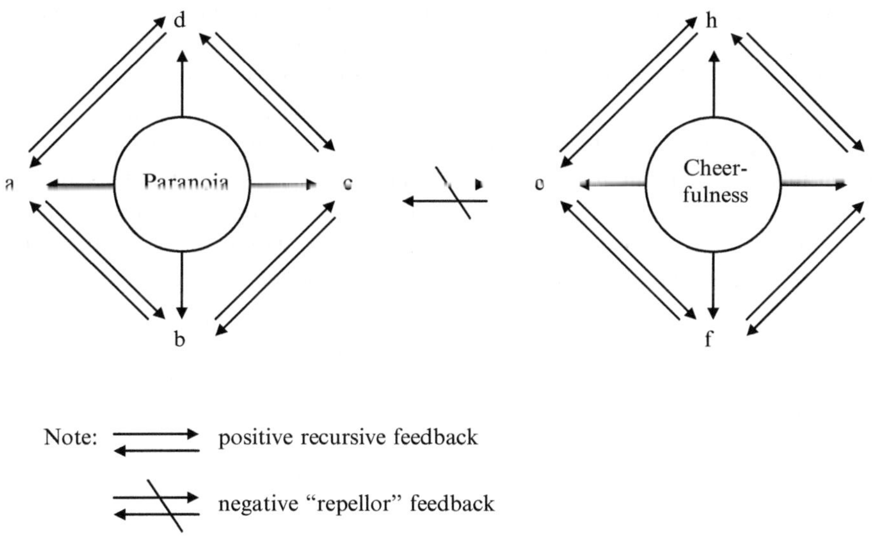

Fig. 25.4 Contextual precision diagnosis. Symptom links can vary in strength of associations. Symptoms form circuit patterns of mental state, resulting in a causal circuit. A strong positive feedback loop exists between similar symptoms and a negative one across opposite ones. For example, stress leads to paranoia, low mood, and anxiety, and also decreased cheerfulness. Both have a strong tendency to persist over time, allowing for stable symptoms. Adapted from van Os et al. (2013), originally from Wigman, Collip et al. (2013); Wigman, van Os et al. (2013)

Brains Goodkind et al. (2015) conducted two studies, one with patients and one with healthy controls. In the patient study, they supported a transdiagnostic perspective of mental illness by finding a common gray matter loss in three brain regions in participant groups having diagnoses as diverse as schizophrenia, bipolar disorder, depression, addiction, obsessive-compulsive disorder, and anxiety. For the first of their two studies, they conducted a meta-analysis of 193 research studies involving almost 16,000 individuals. Also, in a second data gathering undertaking, they studied three independent sets of healthy participants for the interconnections of the three index regions with other regions with gray matter loss in the diagnostic groups mentioned.

To delve further into their two studies, for the first patient one, Goodkind et al. (2015) examined patient/control differences in regional brain volume from whole-brain structural neuroimaging data (in studies reporting coordinates in a defined stereotaxic space), referred to as voxel-based morphometry (VBM). The common gray matter loss regions across the diverse diagnoses involved the anterior insula (left and right) and the dorsal anterior cingulate (dACC). These regions are associated with executive function. There were some between-diagnosis gray matter volume differences, especially involving schizophrenia.

The second parallel study with healthy individuals showed that these regions formed a network both during task performance (mostly on executive function) and also at rest. Indeed, the more the controls in this study evidenced gray matter loss in this network, the lower was their executive function performance.

Generally, the results speak to a shared neurobiological structural substrate or endophenotype across psychopathology, even if a diverse set of etiologies might be involved. The authors concluded that the results are consistent with the goals of the RDoC project (Research Domain of Criteria; Insel et al., 2010) on the dimensional biological underpinnings to psychopathology, which stands in contrast to the DSM-5 categorical approach.

Poldrack et al. (2011) took a very broad view of where cognition fits into the relation between neural systems and syndromes (see Fig. 25.5). They included in their model the DLPFC (dorsal lateral prefrontal cortex), executive processes (e.g., working memory updating), and response inhibition. The signaling pathways include the neurotransmitter dopamine. The model adds genetic covariations, including catechol-*O*-methyltransferase (*COMT*) and dopamine receptor D2 (*DRD2*) genetic variants for dopamine.

A Combined Top-Down/Bottom-Up Integrated Causal (Etiological) Model of Mental Disorder

There are both top-down and bottom-up models of the relationship between mental disorder and symptoms. Whether in terms of full disorder or a cluster in a disorder, a top-down model understands the relationship between disorder and symptom in terms of an underlying psychological construct that represents, integrates, or allows for (or causes) the symptoms expressive of it (Borsboom, 2008; McNally et al., 2015; Schmittmann et al., 2013). This type of modeling is standard in the field (e.g., for psychiatric diagnostic manuals, for psychological tests). In the bottom-up approach to relating mental disorder and symptoms, the latter rather than the former have causal primacy, and their interrelationship represents, informs, and defines the link between disorder and symptom (whether in a full disorder or a cluster within one). Wigman et al. (2015) have elaborated a combined approach to top-down and bottom-up modeling of the relationship of symptoms to mental disorder. However, in their approach, top-down statistical approaches were applied to networked connections (and not the states/symptoms involved themselves).

In the present integrative model of mental disorder (see Fig. 25.6), causation is deemed to lie in both top-down and bottom-up processes that reciprocally interact. The underlying emergent, higher-order psychological phenomenon, such as PTSD, should influence symptom expression in context, but the array and dynamic interaction of

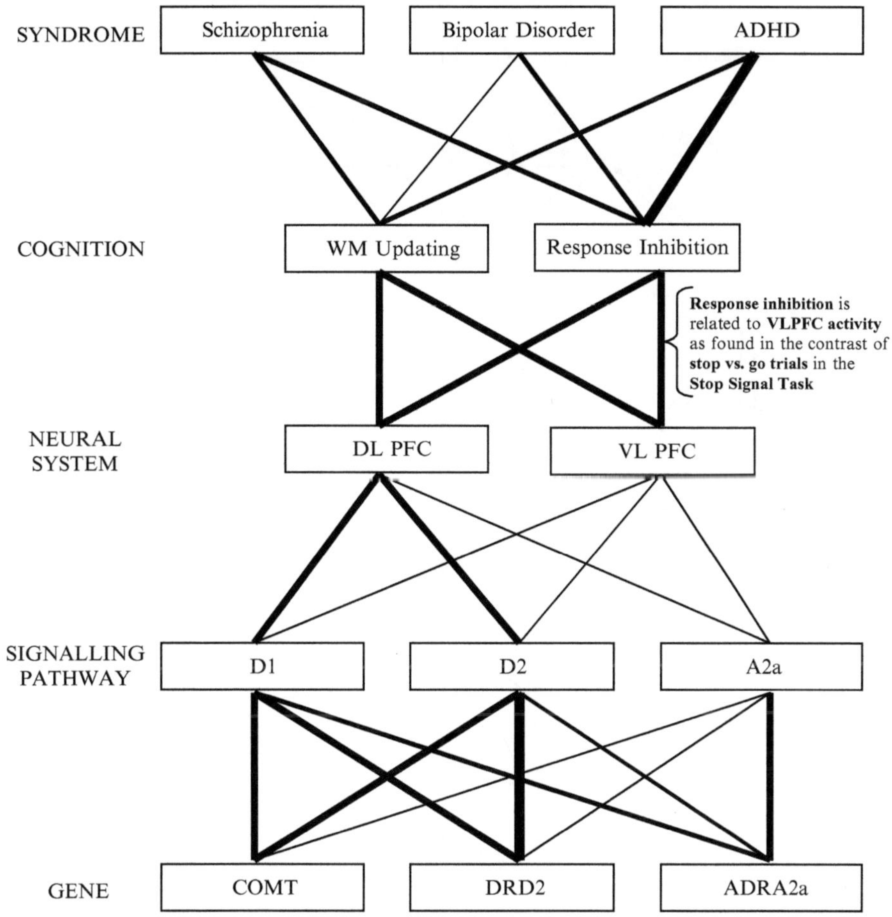

Fig. 25.5 Relating biological functions and processes to psychiatric symptoms and syndromes. *Abbreviations. ADHD*=attention deficit hyperactivity disorder, *WM*= working memory, *DL PFC*=dorsolateral prefrontal cortex, *VL PFC*=ventrolateral prefrontal cortex, *D*= dopamine, *A*=adrenergic, *COMT*=catechol-*O*-methyltransferase, *DRD2*=dopamine receptor D2, *ADRA2a*= alpha-2-adrenergic receptor. The links between the different levels reflect possible empirical relations; the strength of the links (indexed by their width) is proportional to the strength of the scientific literature findings involving them. Each link can be specified for empirical results in the literature, as noted for one of them. Adapted from Poldrack et al. (2011)

the symptoms involved should influence the nature of the higher-order construct, as well. The different levels of the disorder in these regards, its symptoms, and any associated comorbidities and their symptoms constitute dynamic states, their changes, and the transitions between them (which sometimes should lead to newly emergent states in disorder and symptom trajectory). Figure 25.7 further elaborates the relationship between top-down and bottom-up processes in the causal relationship between symptoms and mental health. It incorporates the model of emergent circular causality in Young (2011) and applies it to each of the bottom-up and top-down components of the model. I elaborated this model in order to accommodate the different views of bottom-up and top-down processes in causality over symptoms and mental health as found in McNally et al. (2015) and Wigman et al. (2015).

Endophenotypes

Concept

One criticism of the biomarker approach to psychopathology and psychiatric disorder is that the disorders are polygenetic and little progress has

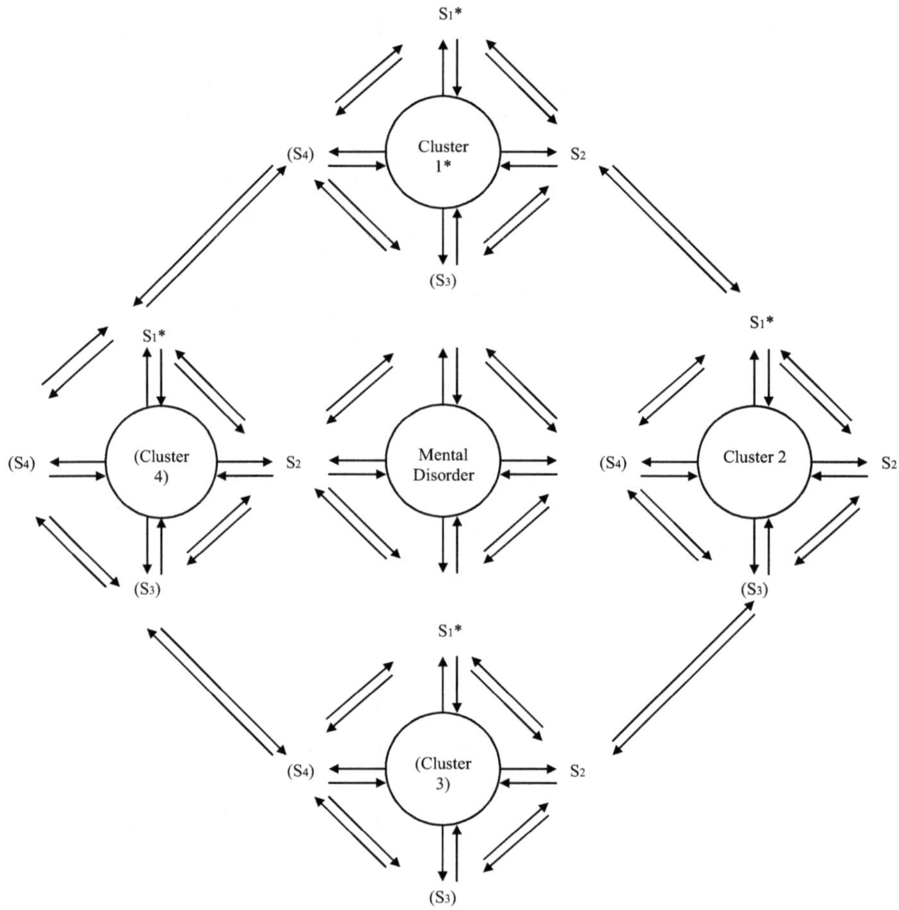

Fig. 25.6 Integrated causal model of mental disorders (bottom up, top down). The figure depicts the relationship between symptoms and mental disorder (or a symptom cluster of one) as dynamically reciprocal in causation. The mental disorder constitutes an underlying, higher-order level in the patient's mental state symptoms, while the symptoms interact at lower-levels of the system, with both the top-down and bottom-up influences dynamically influencing each other in context and over time. *Note*. The *parentheses* indicate that mental disorders might have only 2 clusters, and a cluster might have only 2 symptoms. Of course, either might have more items (i.e., clusters or symptoms, respectively). Of the clusters in any mental disorder, for the symptoms, it would be beneficial to specify which ones are core/primary. For the model presented in the figure, these could be the first clusters or symptoms that are specified by the asterisks

been made in relating genes to global syndromes or disorders, such as schizophrenia. Gottesman (e.g., Gottesman & Gould, 2003) developed the concept of endophenotypes to improve the search for gene-disorder relations. Endophenotypes especially are considered biological, in that they are intermediate expressions of a disorder between genes and global outcome, for example, measures involving brain activity or lobes of the brain (see Fig. 25.8).

In Gottesman's model, gene regions might help specify endophenotypes (such as cell abnormalities or brain function) that interact with environment and susceptibility factors to produce schizophrenia. Research seeks the best candidate endophenotypes in its search for relations in gene loci-disorder outcome. Usually, they are biological and often neuroendophenotypic. For example, Sherin and Nemeroff (2011) described the candidate endophenotypes for

a Emergent Bottom-Up Circular Causality

Superordinate level
(constructed from lower-order levels/ sublevels; distinct from them)

↑

Emergent new levels
(constructed from system elements; distinct from them; also, their interactions might create new lower-order levels/ sublevels)

↑

System elements
(e.g., symptoms; also, their interaction influences/ creates their elements) [1]

b Emergent Top-Down Circular Causality

Superordinate level
(influences/ creates lower (sub)levels/ elements)

↓

Lower-order levels/ sublevels
(influence/ create their elements)

↓

System elements in each level/ sublevel
(as elements change, potential for bottom-up emergent circular causality begins a new) [2]

Note. [1] Configuration/ pattern changes possible, too, within and between (sub) levels.
[2] Bottom-up and top-down causal processes work together reciprocally in system causality

Fig. 25.7 The interaction of top-down and bottom-up emergent circular causality. The figure illustrates the dynamic interaction of bottom-up and top-down processes both within and across levels in a system, including the possibility of emergence of new symptoms, levels, and sublevels. It also indicates the change of patterning or configuration possible within and between levels in the system dynamics involved. Briefly, as system elements (e.g., symptoms) or levels/sublevels interact, they might influence/create their configuration/patterning, expression, or even denovo emergence. This process may occur both through movement from lower to higher levels in the level hierarchy involved (bottom-up), or from higher to lower levels (top-down), or reciprocally in both ways. In essence, the figure clarifies that bottom-up processes work both within and between levels, as do top-down processes, in system function. Adapted from Young (2015)

posttraumatic stress disorder (PTSD; see Table 25.1). Chapter 21 expands that description to contemporary findings.

Miller and Rockstroh (2013) provided an expansive and nuanced view of endophenotypes in psychopathology. They contrasted the traditional approach to understanding psychopathology with an endophenotypic approach, but noted conceptual, methodological, and empirical cautions as they proceeded.

In the traditional view, psychopathology results from a linear causal chain, with earlier links considered as primary ones [genes → (other biology) → psychology = diathesis and stress (environment) → psychopathology]. In more recent views, causality in psychopathology resides in a nomological network organized among relevant factors rather than their causal linking in a sequential manner. The networks are complex patterns of regularities, and they constitute an indefinite set of reciprocal, mutually-influencing, recursive relationships. In this conception, genes do not set the stage, with environment merely combining additively or incrementally with them to create fixed

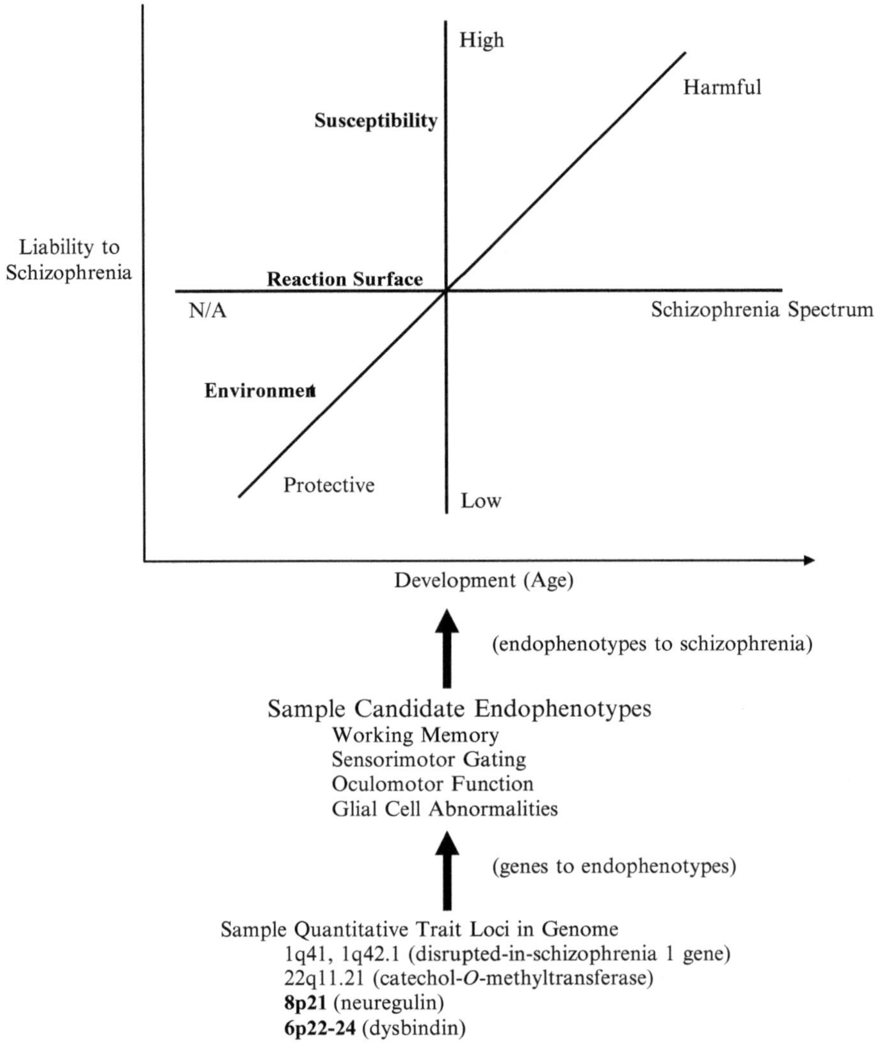

Fig. 25.8 Sample gene regions, genes, and possible endophenotypes implicated in schizophrenia. Dynamic developmental interplay among genetic, environmental, and epigenetic factors produces cumulative liability to expressing schizophrenia. Gene regions with more consistent linkage findings are in bold. Adapted from Gottesman and Gould (2003)

outcomes. Similarly, endophenotypes, which can be conceived as mid-system, midlevel, or downstream (e.g., neuronal) phenotypes, including behavioral ones that might be closer to their presumed genetic/biological associations, should not be construed in a linear model and simply inserted in the chain from gene to behavior (Gottesman & Gould, 2003).

Miller and Rockstroh (2013) addressed the appropriate granularity in defining relevant endophenotypes that might be implicated in psychopathology. For example, in schizophrenia, multiple brain regions have been implicated for multiple executive function deficits, but should they be considered as separate or as integrated circuits in endophenotypic conceptualizations related to the disorder? Moreover, are the circuits and their associated genetic facilitators a function of additive or interactive functions? The authors proposed something more than these options—that both the psychological and neural levels involved might be emergent, whole, dynamical, webbed, superordinate, multilevel networks. The network concept constitutes the best way to

Table 25.1 Summary of neurobiological features with identified abnormalities and functional implications in patients with posttraumatic stress disorder

Feature	Change
	A. Neuroendocrine
HPA	Hypocortisolism
	Augmented level of CRH
HPT	Abnormal T3:T4 ratio
	B. Neurochemical
Catecholamines	Augmented dopamine, norepinephrine levels/activity
Serotonin	Less concentrations of 5HT in dorsal, median, dorsal/median raphe
Amino acids	Less GABA activity
	Augmented glutamate
Peptides	Less plasma NPY
	Augmented CSF β-endorphine
Hippocampus	Less volume/activity
Amygdala	Augmented activity
Cortex	Less prefrontal, anterior cingulate volume
	Less medial prefrontal activity

Adapted from Sherin and Nemeroff (2011)
Abbreviations. HPA=hypothalamic pituitary adrenal axis, *HPT*=hypothalamic pituitary thyroid axis, *CRH*=corticotrophin-releasing hormone, *5-HT*=serotonin, *GABA*=γ-aminobutyric acid, *NPY*=neuropeptide Y, *CSF*=cerebrospinal fluid

approach causation of any associated psychiatric abnormalities, because the ones at issue when they might express deficiencies in executive control. Given their large-scale focus, most likely, some of the networks at work psychiatrically should be transdiagnostic, and inform traditional psychiatric manual-based comorbidities. The network concept in psychiatry is not compatible with a linear model that genes are the beginning of development toward psychopathology in a causal chain. To conclude, Miller and Rockstroh (2013) noted that there is no serial causality in psychopathology but a rich causal cascade.

Goldstein and Klein (2014) used the Gottesman and Gould criteria (Chan & Gottesman, 2008; Gottesman & Gould, 2003; Gould & Gottesman, 2006) for determining when a construct could be considered an endophenotype. They determined that, for depression, several candidate endophenotypes met the criteria to a sufficient degree. The criteria involved the potential endophenotype (a) being associated with the illness at issue; (b) demonstrating heritability; (c) generally evidencing detectability independent of the target illness's current expression; (d) co-segregating within families of probands having the illness; (e) being more common in healthy family members of probands than in the general population; and (f) being measured reliably.

According to these criteria, the results of the literature review on selected candidate endophenotypes for depression indicated some strong support—for neuroticism, in particular; as well as for elevated morning cortisol level and the cortisol awakening response; asymmetry of cortical electrical activity (normally the left side is associated with approach behavior/positive affect and the right with withdrawal/negative affect); deficits in reward learning; and memory/attention biases.

Interim Conclusion

The field of psychiatry can profit from these novel ideas on etiology by addressing the following issues. It should develop (a) an integrated biopsychosocial model that includes systems and networks, (b) an integration of categorical and dimensional approaches to classification that reflects the integrated biopsychosocial model, and (c) a way of systematizing the clinical assessment that could give more credence to any diagnostic conclusion, no matter which diagnostic classification system is used. In the next part of the chapter, I offer a suite of recommendations consistent with these ideas that suggests ways the DSM enterprise can evolve in a dynamically evolving discipline of psychiatry, being part of its growth and contributing to it.

Network approaches, by definition, emphasize which symptoms in a set are core compared to secondary or less important, which will help reduce the fuzziness of psychiatric categories that emerge by their use without sacrificing the notion of probabilistic, fuzzy boundaries characterizing them. Network concepts address individual differences in symptom expression and understanding, which will facilitate precision and personalized medicine/treatment. The suite of recommendations that I propose for psychiatric nosology derives from the scientific domain, but they are meant to be clinical useful (or instrumental). The recommendations begin with a biopsychosocial model of endophenotypes, which prepares the way for other recommendations related to the biopsychosocial model.

Recommendations

Psychiatry needs an integrative model that respects the multiple, individuated symptom expressions encountered in patients and also the multiple intervention/treatment options available in the field, including auxiliary ones such as in psychology. Moreover, the integrative model should be informed by the biopsychosocial model. Finally, it can serve the field if it is linked to contemporary advances in understanding etiology as systems, such as nonlinear dynamics and network modeling.

An Endophenotypic Model

The search for endophenotypes in relation to psychiatric disorder should take a broader view than the standard one. If psychiatric illness is related to biopsychosocial factors, then candidate endophenotypes for any specific disorder could include variables other than biological ones. Also, they might be represented by specific networks of symptoms in the sense described by Borsboom and colleagues (e.g., Borsboom, 2008). In this regard, Table 25.2 presents an expansive model of endophenotypes that includes functions and behavior/test items, including in networked ways, as well as environment, development, and therapeutic agents.

In Table 25.2, I organized candidate endophenotypes according to complexity and degree to which they are distal from genotype. The model is general and applicable to any mental disorder, although, for environment, I included abuse and trauma. I put at the end of the table Gottesman and Gould's (2003) listing of environment and development in their work on endophenotypes.

Table 25.2 Candidate endophenotypes: a vertical and horizontal model

	Level	
Area	Vertical	Horizontal
Genome	Transcriptome Epigenome	Protein Marks
Neurome (neuroendophenotype)	Nervous system Neurons Neurotransmitters	Peripheral/central Dendrites/synapses Dopamine/serotonin, etc.
Brain	Neurons Astrocytes Region Lobe	Network Network Network Network
Function	Control	Executive reflective/automatic habitual
	Activation/inhibition	Coordination/discoordination
Behavior	Single Set	Symptom Syndrome/disorder
Assessment	Test Battery	Above cut score Multiple results
Environment	Pre-existing Differential susceptibility Trauma	Adversity, chronic abuse Perceptual, allelic Exposure, horrific
Development	Age Learning	Younger, older Coping/resilience, catastrophize
Therapy	Pharmacological Psychological	Multiple Multiple

The table includes an area between the areas of brain and behavior that concerns of function, emphasizing control and inhibition. In addition, for each area of possible endophenotype, I give examples both vertically in terms of complexity, or other qualifications, and horizontally in terms of subareas.

For the genome level, I added epigenetics. For neuroendophenotypes, I gave the full range of areas in the neurome. For the brain, I emphasized networks as much as individual components. Further, behaviors can be single or collections, as can be test measures.

The environment and developmental levels of the model stand as relevant contextual modifiers in understanding endophenotypes. Therapeutic agents can act at any area and level of the model, and indicate endophenotypic interactions, as could the environmental and developmental levels.

The table illustrates that the association of genetic loci to disease by way of endophenotypes needs to consider the complex array of candidates at multiple levels of analysis. It queries the efficacy of considering gene-disorder linkages at the macro-level in terms of diagnostic categories, such as found in the DSM-5 (Diagnostic and Statistical Manual of Mental Disorders, Fifth Edition; American Psychiatric Association, 2013) and the upcoming ICD-11 (International Classification of Diseases, 11th Revision; World Health Organization, 2017).

Critique

Although the work in the area of endophenotypes (Gottesman & Gould, 2003) and genetics (Wilker & Kolassa, 2013) might be construed as highly biological in focus, the interactions of the environment with the genome, for example, through allostatic load (McEwen, 2006) and long-lasting and transmittable epigenetic stamps (Meaney, 2010; Szyf, 2013), illustrate that individual pathways either toward the development of disorder or toward resilience are not only biologically-determined. The construct of neural networks (Sporns, 2012) cuts across these areas of study and has emerged important in the literature. Their widely distributed modality would make them harder to detect individually but their integrated nature would make the detection closer to the actual manner in which the brain functions. A science of individual differences of disorder that is based on biological markers (biomarkers), yet includes a role for environment (context), development, and the person's individual pathways and proclivities (e.g., personality, coping), would frame the model as a biopsychosocial one. Young, Lareau, and Pierre (2014) have highlighted the relevance of the latter for PTSD.

The neuroscientifically-based RDoC criteria (Insel & Lieberman, 2013) might emphasize the biological substrate of disorders at the expense of multifactorial influences, as found in the biopsychosocial model. In this regard, I have presented a model for study of endophenotypes that respects multiple influences on etiology of psychiatric disorder, including the psychosocial, without sacrificing the goal of finding causal links from genes to behavior. The DSM-5 has been widely criticized (e.g., Young, 2013; Young et al., 2014), but if it takes the premature step of adhering especially to standard endophenotypic and RDoC models in its revisions, it risks further alienating multiple stakeholders and users.

The field is far from establishing a reliable and valid detection system of disorder that can apply effectively in individual cases based on physiological and neuronal parameters. Nevertheless, sufficient progress has been made such that biological measures related to disorder could one day add incremental validity and complement traditional assessment procedures in increasing the probability of certainty in assessment and diagnostic conclusions. However, at present and in the near future, it would be premature to seek individual biomarkers of disorder for such purposes, given the current state of knowledge in the field, even if it is burgeoning. Nevertheless, workers in the area should keep up to date on the literature for breakthroughs in these regards. For example, the research on the five-factor model of PTSD (Elhai et al., 2011) and its relation to Gene × Environment (G × E) interactions (e.g., Pietrzak et al., 2014) constitutes an important thrust in the search for valid endophenotypes in PTSD and the search for individual-case primary, core (bio)markers.

Modeling

Table 25.3 summarizes the argument that the extended biopsychosocial model supported in the present work can serve as an adequate basis for elaborating a scientifically-informed and clinically useful psychiatric diagnostic classification system. It looks at the questions of mental disorder, diagnoses, etiology, and underlying model in terms of the traditional categorical and dimensional approaches to nosology as well as of the biopsychosocial approach being advocated.

In this representation of the categorical approach to psychiatric classification, mental disorder is considered an all-or-none medical disease with each disorder (operationalized by criteria, including polythetic ones for the symptoms), such that each disorder is a natural kind carved at the joints, with clear etiology (biological in nature), uniform symptom expression, and corresponding unifocal (read; psychopharmaceutical) intervention and treatment direction. As for the dimensional approach, it denies separate categories of disorder, viewing mental illness as ranging on continua that are quantifiable. Statistically, the model might include comparison of individuals to norms, or otherwise estimate their relative placement or deviation with respect to the population at issue. Diagnoses might involve the placement of an individual on relevant collective continua. The model is a probabilistic, statistical one.

In contrast to the traditional categorical and dimensional models, the biopsychosocial model being proposed is a systemic, dynamic, and integrated one that considers: (a) the multifactorial causes in illness expression; (b) the individual ways that its symptoms are manifested in networked patterns; and (c) the individualized medicine or intervention/treatment approaches that would be consistent with the patterns. An extended biopsychosocial model considers the possibility of nonlinear dynamical transitions in mental health, or from one attractor (health) to another (dysfunction; Young, 2011). The patterns in the system are both micro- or local and macro- or global across different levels. Mind is self-organizing and emergent from biological and brain processes, and its pattern could reflect the assembly of categorical states, dimensions, and their combinations. Patterns are constantly constructed in the person, and psychiatric approaches to disorder should be individualized to fit this individualizing symptom reality.

Figure 25.9 presents another way of distinguishing the standard approaches to psychiatry and an integrated biopsychosocial one. In the standard approach, effort is expended to find distinctive mental disorder. Workers then seek out their causes, especially genetically and physiologically as biomarkers, e.g., in the brain. The

Table 25.3 Approaches to psychiatric classification

	Approach		
Issue	Categorical	Dimensional	Biopsychosocial
Mental disorder	All-or-none disease presence	Threshold on normal curve or other estimated or normative distribution	Dysfunctional (network) pattern for context
Diagnoses	Entities with specific symptom arrays, and corresponding causes and treatments (natural kinds, but polythetic)	Degree of difficulty on relevant continua (normative)	Local and global (attractor) system patterns (focus: individual, population) (variables: categorical, dimensional)
Etiology (causation)	Biological (genetic, physiological)	Probabilistic	Systemic, dynamic
Underlying model	Medical/disease	Statistical/deviation	Integrated/illness
Treatment	Of the disease, common	Of the disease, common	Of the person, individual

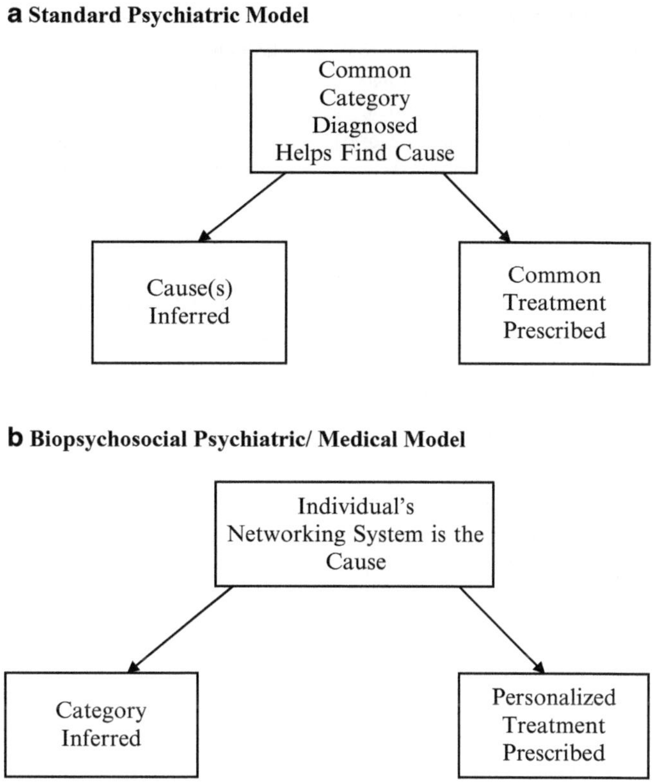

Fig. 25.9 Revised model of causation in psychiatry. Instead of inferring cause from the diagnosis, representing the constellation of symptoms, the latter are analyzed for networks, which themselves are causal. This process allows for personalized treatment and consideration of diagnosis as secondary in importance

categories are associated with one-size-fit-all intervention/treatment.

In contrast, in the proposed extended biopsychosocial model, the symptom complex of the patient is cardinal, as is its linkages in individualized patterns. The network of nodes, edges (relations), and context gives a workable understanding of the patient. The clinician might then find that the case description matches a diagnostic categorical one, e.g., being close to a prototype or close to a polythetic category (and perhaps even a dimensional construction of disorder). Etiology does not lie in an external source that impacts the system, but in the organization of the symptom complex of the individual in relation to the multifactorial proximal and distal (close and far, e.g., genetic) causes. With clear perspective on person and causation, individualized medicine approaches to intervention and treatment are facilitated, including of the psychosocial and not only the biological or psychopharmacological type.

Practice

Table 25.4 reviews the manner in which a combined categorical, dimensional, and biopsychosocial approach to psychiatry can help the field in assessment, diagnosis, and treatment. Categories and dimensions are considered "fuzzy" concepts with no clear boundaries, such that each can be conceived as the other if defined and organized appropriately. The work in this regard must start with assessment. This process, too, concerns both categorical and dimensional constructs; and if these constructs can be simplified into a clinically-friendly and usable framework, the assessments will be quasi-standardized to allow for simplified effective diagnosis.

In this regard, in the next portion of the present work, I provide a coherent yet accessible approach to assessment that prepares the way for a more reliable diagnosis process. In this sense, just as the categories are the dimensions and the dimensions are the categories so, too, is the

Table 25.4 Hybrid categorical/dimensional systems approach to psychiatry

System	Explanation
The categories are the dimensions (dimensionalize the categories)	Evaluate patients dimensionally on multiple relevant categories (0, 1, 2)
The dimensions are the categories (categorize the dimensions)	These ratings give the basis for finding the closest (hopefully accurate) diagnostic categories needed from diagnostic manual
The dimensions and categories for a (hybrid) biopsychosocial system	The categories and dimensions form the individual's network of causal symptom/dysfunction/disorder/impairment/disability and treatment complex

assessment the diagnosis and the diagnosis the assessment.

This interweaving of psychiatric constructs that are fuzzy into dialectical relations that are reciprocal speaks to the proposed extended biopsychosocial model's system and network characteristics, in which the symptom patterns are also causes. Further, there is no pathway from cause to symptoms to treatment that is linear in this model.

In the end, psychiatry distinguishes itself from other medical specialties by its emphasis on the whole person. Mental state is embedded in multiple physiological and brain states that are in interaction, and psychiatry can stand at the forefront in adapting a systemic approach, such as the one being presented.

With an approach such as this, the undue importance given to diagnosis will lose some of its edge, and it will become only one point of an equilibrated psychiatric process. Diagnosis does not constitute the final arbiter of the nature of the patient's dysfunction, but it is simply an ongoing statement that summarizes the most important aspect of the patient, that is, the network of symptoms involved in the biopsychosocial context. By taking an approach such as this, psychiatry would address its problem with clinical utility in diagnosis and intervention/treatment.

To conclude, I offer a tentative structure or template for an organized psychiatric assessment procedure that includes ratings that are amenable to reliability research. Table 25.5 constitutes an introductory table that presents the five major areas or categories of psychiatric assessment that should be accounted for with each patient, as well as a ratings table. The five core psychiatric areas in assessment concern: (a) major; (b) secondary; (c) auxiliary; (d) "dimensional," and (e) complicating categories. Their subcategories or dimensions give precision and detail on their nature and they should constitute the focus in assessment. In the ensuing six tables, for each of the psychiatric areas of assessment in the proposed system, I present their subcategories of the core areas are presented in the ensuing six tables (see Tables 25.6, 25.7, 25.8, 25.9, 25.10, and 25.11).

Table 25.5 Proposed psychiatric assessment dimensions

Grouping	Dimensions
Major	Communication/language
	Mood
	Thought
	Activity/energy
	Function
Secondary	Environment/context
	Relations (e.g., family, partner)
	Social skills
	Coping
	Self/personality
Auxiliary	Age (stage, development)
	Gender
	Culture/minority
	Socioeconomic status
	Medical/physical/neurovegetative
"Dimensional"	Spectrum location
	Frequency
	Duration
	Temporal
	Intensity/severity
Complicating	Self-control
	Substance (ab)use
	Self-deception
	Other-deception
	Aberrant/inappropriate
Rating	0
	(1/2)
	1
	(1 ½)
	2
	NA/TBA

Table 25.6 Proposed major psychiatric assessment dimensions

Dimension	Explanation
Communication/language	Ability to listen and express oneself, verbally and nonverbally; pragmatic, social use of language
Mood	A primary manifestation of psychological distress relates to maladaptive emotional or affective experience and expression. There are four major negative moods: depression, anxiety, anger–aggression, and fear, as well as others (specify); also suicidality
Thought	Thoughts are psychiatrically relevant as thought disorders, cognitive disorders, memory/concentration disturbance, maladaptive thinking, intelligence, insight, judgment, and dissociation
Activity/energy	Activity ranges from inertia and withdrawal to mania. It also includes motivation/interest and also repetitions
Function	Impairments in work, school, care giving and other roles, and in ADLs (activities of daily living)

Table 25.7 Proposed secondary psychiatric assessment dimensions

Dimension	Explanation
Environment/context	Stressors, trauma, court case, triggers, buffers
Relations (e.g., family, partner)	Significant others, social network, leisure activities
Social skills	In dyads, groups; competition, cooperation; helping, hurting others
Coping	Vulnerabilities or resilience and growth; emotion vs. problem-focused
Self/personality	Primary characteristics, traits, self-esteem, assertiveness, five-factor model/Psy-5 model

Table 25.8 Proposed auxiliary psychiatric assessment dimensions

Dimension	Explanation
Age (stage, development)	Chronologically; in relation to developmental level, or perhaps stage (e.g., Erikson, or related models)
Gender	Sex, orientation, roles
Culture/minority	Country, racism/persecution, group norms
Socioeconomic status	Poverty, opportunities
Medical/physical/neurovegetative	Health, body, sleep, eating, pain, self-injury, exercise, etc.

Table 25.9 Proposed "dimensional" dimensions in psychiatric assessment

Dimension	Explanation
Spectrum location	E.g., autism
Frequency	Intermittent/infrequent Often/constant
Duration	In minutes (0), days (1), weeks (2), months (3), years (4)
Temporal	(In)stability Course Sequentially (interruptions, organization)
Intensity/severity	Mild to serious

Table 25.10 Proposed complicating dimensions in psychiatric assessment

Dimension	Explanation
Self-control	Goals/planning, inhibition, flexibility
Substance (Ab)use	Use, dependence, abuse, in withdrawal
Self-deception	Unconscious, naïve, repression, unrealistic
Other-deception	Conscious, lying/manipulation, malingering, criminal activity
Aberrant/inappropriate	Not quantitatively different, but qualitatively different

As for diagnosis, if the assessment is comprehensive in this way, or, another equivalent one, it will be much easier for the clinician to refer to the various diagnostic manuals (DSM-IV-TR, DSM-5, ICD-10, 11) and to find the best diagnostic match for the assessment findings. If diagnosis stems from a comprehensive assessment, and the diagnostic categories available, the nosological system used have some of the fuzzy properties mentioned, the clinician would be adopting a

Table 25.11 Rating scale for each psychiatric dimension

Level	Explanation
0	Absent
(1/2)	Rarely a problem
1	Sometimes a problem
(1 ½)	Often a problem
2	Always (or almost always) a problem
NA/TBA	Insufficient evidence to judge

Note. Where several types of problems exist for a dimension, rate the most important one(s)
Note. ½—points are optional, for research purposes

process that would circumvent possible criticisms of the diagnoses offered, especially if they are derived from a scientific reasoning process.

One or the other of the major psychiatric diagnostic manuals might become obligatory in a clinician's jurisdiction, and used without qualms in this regard. However, the clinician should be sufficiently informed to justify any critique in the field of any manual. In this regard, the prudent clinician might decide to consider the alternate assessment process offered in the present chapter, with its comprehensive assessment approach, because it would facilitate use of a scientific reasoning process in the diagnoses offered.

Ethics

Figure 25.10 brings an important perspective to the present work. It underscores that a proper ethical stance is needed in all aspects of our training, education, and work. By constantly evaluating each aspect of our work from a meta-ethical framework, and not just from the point of view of professional principle and codes, any dilemma related to using one psychiatric manual or the other will be obviated. The best judge of how to use the DSM-5 and scrutinize it for its problems reside in each of the professionals using it. In this regard, in this present work, I have provided a general guide to the DSM-5 that could be useful to the reader. However, the responsibility for how it is used lies directly in the laps of the reader. Then, its disposition and critique should inform each professional using it, but in a dispassionate and critical way.

Chapter Conclusions

For DSM-5 and Etiology

The DSM-5 is the most recent iteration of the DSM enterprise, and it is both strongly defended and roundly criticized. It needs to be clinically useful yet scientifically-informed and validated, so that the work groups involved in creating its different versions often strike compromises. The DSM-5 will change in the DSM versions to follow, and the present chapter has made multiple recommendations in this regard. Perhaps the most salient refers to the new model of etiology that I have proposed. That is, I describe a new model for the causality (or etiology) of mental disorder in terms of the dynamic, reciprocally interactive nature that it has with symptoms. In this regard, the model is a top-down/bottom-up integrative one that considers a role in the etiology of mental disorders both of higher-order psychological constructs, such as PTSD, and of the symptoms (and clusters) that express the disorders.

For Assessment

In the following, I turn to practical considerations for forensic/disability assessment of psychological injury cases. This sets the stage for conclusions on how to deal with diagnoses in court.

In assessing psychological injury, assessors ask: (a) to what extent the event at claim has contributed to the presenting condition of the complainant; (b) what diagnoses and disabilities do the symptoms are represent, if any; (c) how can factors such as possible malingering be ruled out, e.g., which tests to use; and (d) are there functional impacts that can be causally linked to the event (e.g., in work, child care, studies).

A combined biopsychosocial/forensic model should inform/guide assessments, whether for tort, disability claims, requesting treatment plans, etc. A comprehensive, scientifically-informed, and impartial approach is needed in all work in psychological injury cases. Assessments should use the most reliable, valid, and accurate tests,

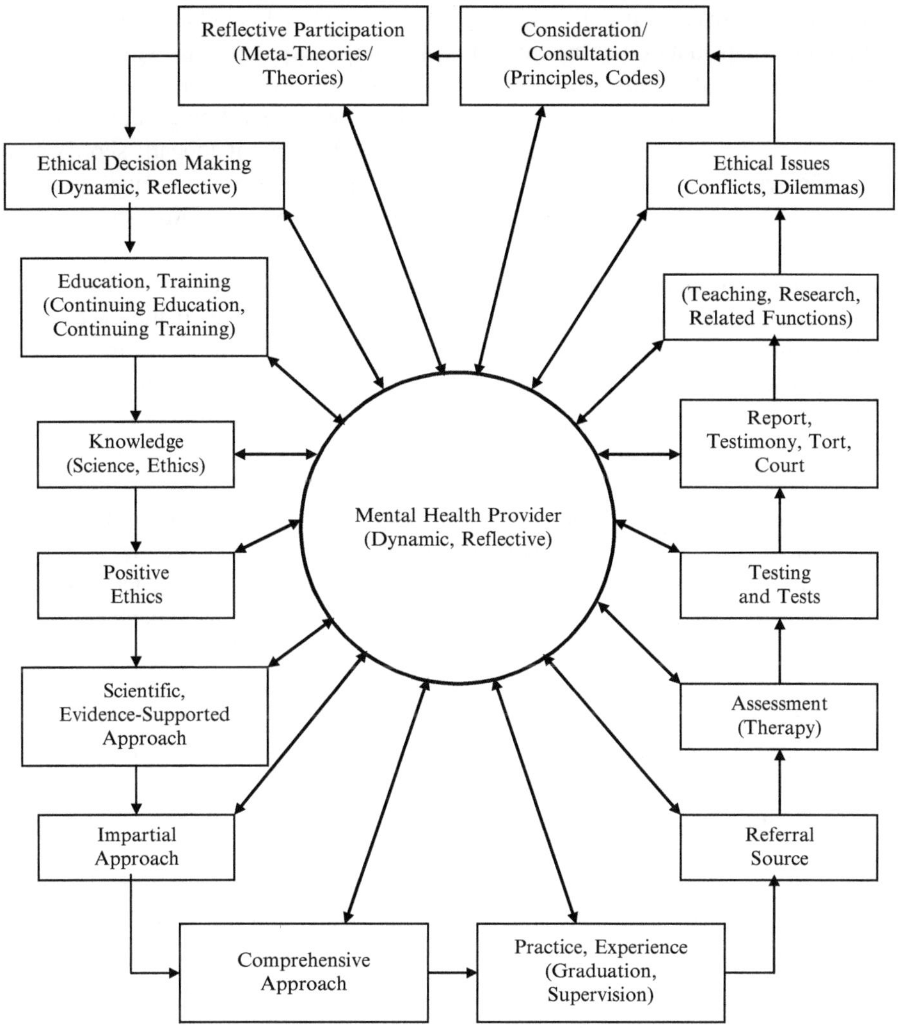

Fig. 25.10 Broad ethics in psychological injury and law. The figure outlines a broad ethical model for practice in psychological injury and law. It describes the typical steps in education and practice, and emphasizes a scientific and ethical approach to the work that is impartial and comprehensive. This way, any ethical dilemma should be resolvable by referring to ethical rules, principles, and theories. Adopted with permission of Springer Science+Business Media. Young, G. (2014). *Malingering, feigning, and response bias in psychiatric/psychological injury: Implications for Practice and court.* Dordrecht, Netherlands: Springer Science+Business Media; with kind permission from Springer Science+Business Media B. V. [Figure 22.4, Page 588]

aside from conducting interviews and accessing collateral information.

Workers in the area need to adopt a multitrait-multimethod testing approach having acceptable sensitivity and specificity (to deal with false positives and negatives). They need to use reliable and valid instruments for the question at hand, such as the MMPI-2 (The Minnesota Multiphasic Personality Inventory-2; Butcher et al., 2001) and, more recently, the MMPI-2-RF (The Minnesota Multiphasic Personality Inventory-2 Restructured Form; Ben-Porath & Tellegen, 2008/2011). When evidence for possible malingering is found, the assessor needs to examine the array of multiple reliable data gathered on the individual (from testing, interview, collateral sources) in order to rule out alternative explanations before arriving at a conclusion that malingering is a reasonable possibility. However, there are ways of describing problematic presentations that do not have direct, incontrovertible evidence of malingering.

For Reports/Court

The DSM-5 presents quandaries for use in reports and in court due to its numerous criticisms and limitations. For court purposes, it is always best to conduct comprehensive interviews and consultation of records to get a functional perspective of the person, and use the diagnoses as supplements, and this might be especially true after the controversy about the DSM-5.

Perhaps for court, workers should specify each disorder attributed in the evaluation both in terms of the DSM-IV-TR and DSM-5 and should indicate which one is primary for the case at hand. When the criteria for a disorder have changed in the DSM-5 relative to the DSM-IV-TR, knowledge of the scientific validity of the disorder(s) at issue in the literature would help justify the choice of using as primary the DSM-IV-TR or DSM-5. Similarly, in diagnosing new disorders in the DSM-5 that were not in the DSM-IV-TR, knowledge of the literature will help determine their validity. Finally, some of the disorders in the DSM-IV-TR can be contested on a scientific basis even if they had not been changed in the DSM-5, so they, too, can also be questioned for their validity.

Of course, an evaluator might find that no diagnosis, impairment, or disorder fits a particular case because of malingering or gross exaggeration. The definition of malingering has not changed in DSM-5, but it, too, has been shown to be problematic. Use of a good battery of tests could help with that imbroglio, but these, themselves, are subject to controversy in some quarters.

As the years progress, we might find that insurers, worker's compensation, veteran's administration, the court, state associations, or even the literature will make strong recommendations on using the DSM-IV-TR or the DSM-5. Unfortunately, the field is in flux about diagnosis because of the process in making the DSM-5 and the product that resulted. However, its goals were fine and future iterations will be an improvement. Perhaps the best statement for court is that the DSM-5 will be followed not by the DSM-6 in 10–15 years, but, it appears, shortly by the 5.1, so that conclusions for any one case in using the DSM-IV-TR or the DSM-5 should be seen in that light.

If the case is civil, the evidential bar is "more likely than not," but, if the case is for criminal court, the bar is the more stringent one of "beyond a reasonable doubt." These different criteria might impact the certainty statements evaluators need to offer about their diagnoses using the DSM-IV-TR or DSM-5.

Aside from all the general issues about the DSM-5 (e.g., overpathologizing, ethics of workgroups), the specific disorders, too, can be criticized from a forensic perspective. About the DSM-5 PTSD criteria relative to those of the DSM-IV-TR, there are some changes to consider forensically. For example, the A2 criterion is removed, which will open the floodgates to more forensic cases. Not only are there three more symptoms in the DSM-5 relative to the DSM-IV-TR, they are arranged into four clusters of the symptoms, not three as before, so that all PTSD-related psychometric tests will have to be redone, which will also complicate forensic cases.

From a forensic perspective, I checked in detail the fourth PTSD DSM-5 symptom cluster. It is on arousal/reactivity. There are now six symptoms in it, not five. The new one is reckless or self-destructive behavior, which will complicate things forensically. The irritability/anger outburst criterion now includes the qualifier "with little or no provocation" and, also, it adds the words "verbal/physical aggression toward people," which will complicate things forensically. There is a new specifier (dissociative symptoms, depersonalization/derealization), which too will complicate things forensically. Other forensic complications include the criterion of a 6-month delay allowed before making the diagnosis. Because of these and other matters raised in the present work, please consult my proposal presented elsewhere on a new diagnostic entry to the DSM 5.1—DSM 5 Confusion Disorder.

Finally, for recent work on causal etiology, and testing models of psychopathology please consult Vaidyanathan, Vrieze, and Iacono (2015) and commentaries, e.g., Lilienfeld and Pinto (2015), Regier (2015), Widiger, Crego, and Oltmanns (2015). Essentially, the authors call for better theory, better method, and better nosology as it applies to psychopathology, its development in the DSM-5, and the RDoC, as well as public policy. I strongly endorse all of these goals while proposing in this chapter specific recommendations aimed at them.

References

American Psychiatric Association. (2013). *Diagnostic and statistical manual of mental disorders: DSM-5* (5th ed.). Washington, DC: Author.

American Psychiatric Association. (2000). *Diagnostic and statistical manual of mental disorders* (4th ed., text rev.). Washington, DC: Author.

Arguello, P. A., & Gogos, J. A. (2012). Genetic and cognitive windows into circuit mechanisms of psychiatric disease. *Trends in Neurosciences, 35*, 3–13.

Ben-Porath, Y. S., & Tellegen, A. (2008/2011). *The Minnesota Multiphasic Personality Inventory-2 Restructured Form (MMPI-2-RF): Manual for administration, scoring, and interpretation*. Minnesota, MN: University of Minnesota Press.

Borsboom, D. (2008). Psychometric perspectives on diagnostic systems. *Journal of Clinical Psychology, 64*, 1089–1108.

Borsboom, D., Cramer, A. O., Schmittmann, V. D., Epskamp, S., & Waldorp, L. J. (2011). The small world of psychopathology. *PLoS One, 6*, e27407. doi:10.1371/journal.pone.0027407.

Butcher, J. N., Graham, J. R., Ben-Porath, Y. S., Tellegen, A., Dahlstrom, W. G., & Kaemmer, B. (2001). *MMPI-2: Manual for administration, scoring, and interpretation* (Revth ed.). Minneapolis, MN: University of Minnesota Press.

Chan, R. C. K., & Gottesman, I. I. (2008). Neurological soft signs as candidate endophenotypes for schizophrenia: A shooting star or a Northern star? *Neuroscience & Biobehavioral Reviews, 32*, 957–971.

Coghill, D. (2014). Editorial: Acknowledging complexity and heterogeneity in causality – Implications of recent insights into neuropsychology of childhood disorders for clinical practice. *Journal of Child Psychology and Psychiatry, 55*, 737–740.

Coghill, D., Seth, S., & Matthews, K. (2014). The neuropsychological effects of chronic methylphenidate on drug-native boys with attention-deficit/hyperactivity disorder. *Biological Psychiatry, 62*, 954–962.

Diwadkar, V. A., Bustamante, A., Rai, H., & Uddin, M. (2014). Epigenetics, stress and their potential impact on brain network function: A focus on the schizophrenia diatheses. *Frontiers in Psychiatry, 5*, 71. doi:10.3389/fpsyt.2014.00071.

Elhai, J. D., Biehn, T. L., Armour, C., Klopper, J. J., Frueh, B. C., & Palmieri, P. A. (2011). Evidence of a unique PTSD construct represented by PTSD's D1-D3 symptoms. *Journal of Anxiety Disorders, 25*, 340–345.

Fillman, S. G., Sinclair, D., Fung, S. J., Webster, M. J., & Shannon Weickert, C. (2014). Markers of inflammation and stress distinguish subsets of individuals with schizophrenia and bipolar disorder. *Translational Psychiatry, 4*, e365. doi:10.1038/tp.2014.8.

Goldstein, B. L., & Klein, D. N. (2014). A review of selected candidate endophenotypes for depression. *Clinical Psychology Review, 34*, 417–427.

Goodkind, M., Eickhoff, S. B., Oathes, D. J., Jiang, Y., Chang, A., Jones-Hagata, L. B., et al. (2015). Identification of a common neurobiological substrate for mental illness. *The Journal of American Medial Association: Psychiatry, 72*, 305–315.

Gottesman, I. I., & Gould, T. D. (2003). The endophenotype concept in psychiatry: Etymology and strategic intentions. *American Journal of Psychiatry, 160*, 636–645.

Gould, T. D., & Gottesman, I. I. (2006). Psychiatric endophenotypes and the development of valid animal models. *Genes, Brain and Behavior, 5*, 113–119.

Insel, T., Cuthbert, B., Garvey, M., Heinssen, R., Pine, D. S., Quinn, K., et al. (2010). Research domain criteria (RDoC): Toward a new classification framework for reach on mental disorders. *The American Journal of Psychiatry, 167*, 748–751.

Insel, T. R., & Lieberman, J. A. (2013). DSM-5 and RDoC: Shared interests. *The National Institute of Mental Health*. Retrieved from http://www.nimh.nih.gov/news/science-news/2013/dsm-5-and-rdoc-shared--interests.shtml

Karalunas, S. L., Geurts, H. M., Konrad, K., Bender, S., & Nigg, J. T. (2014). Annual research review: Reaction time variability in ADHD and autism spectrum disorders: Measurement and mechanisms of a proposed trans-diagnostic phenotype. *Journal of Child Psychology and Psychiatry, 55*, 685–710.

Kendler, K. S. (2008). Explanatory models for psychiatric illness. *American Journal of Psychiatry, 165*, 695–702.

Kendler, K. S. (2012). The dappled nature of causes of psychiatric illness: Replacing the organic-functional/hardware-software dichotomy with empirically based pluralism. *Molecular Psychiatry, 17*, 377–388.

Kendler, K. S. (2015). Toward a limited realism for psychiatric nosology based on the coherence theory of truth. *Psychological Medicine, 45*, 1115–1118.

Kendler, K. S., Zachar, P., & Craver, C. (2011). What kinds of things are psychiatric disorders? *Psychological Medicine, 41*, 1143–1150.

Lilienfeld, S. O., & Pinto, M. D. (2015). Risky tests of etiological models in psychopathology research: The need for meta-methodology. *Psychological Inquiry, 26*, 253–258.

McEwen, B. S. (2006). Protective and damaging effects of stress mediators: Central role of the brain. *Dialogues in Clinical Neuroscience, 8*, 367–381.

McGorry, P., & van Os, J. (2013). Redeeming diagnosis in psychiatry: Timing versus specificity. *Lancet, 381*, 343–345.

McNally, R. J., Robinaugh, D. J., Wu, G. W. Y., Wang, L., Deserno, M. K., & Borsboom, D. (2015). Mental disorders as causal systems: A network approach to posttraumatic stress disorder. *Clinical Psychological Science, 3*, 836–849.

Meaney, M. J. (2010). Epigenetics and the biological definition of gene x environment interactions. *Child Development, 81*, 41–79.

Millan, M. J. (2013). An epigenetic framework for neurodevelopmental disorders: From pathogenesis to potential therapy. *Neuropharmacology, 68*, 2–82.

Miller, G. A., & Rockstroh, B. (2013). Endophenotypes in psychopathology research: Where do we stand? *Annual Review of Clinical Psychology, 9*, 177–213.

Pietrzak, R. H., Feder, A., Schechter, C. B., Singh, R., Cancelmo, L., Bromet, E. J., et al. (2014). Dimensional structure and course of post-traumatic stress symptomatology in World Trade Center responders. *Psychological Medicine, 44*, 2085–2098.

Poldrack, R. A., Kittur, A., Kalar, D., Miller, E., Seppa, C., Gil, Y., et al. (2011). The cognitive atlas: Towards a knowledge foundation for cognitive neuroscience. *Frontiers in Neuroinformatics, 5*, 17. doi:10.3389/fninf.2011.00017.

Regier, D. A. (2015). Potential DSM-5 and RDoC synergy for mental health research, treatment, and health policy advances. *Psychological Inquiry, 26*, 268–271.

Schmittmann, V. D., Cramer, A. O. J., Waldorp, L. J., Epskamp, S., Kievit, R. A., & Borsboom, D. (2013). Deconstructing the construct: A network perspective on psychological phenomena. *New Ideas in Psychology, 31*, 43–53.

Sherin, J. E., & Nemeroff, C. B. (2011). Post-traumatic stress disorder: The neurobiological impact of psychological trauma. *Dialogues in Clinical Neuroscience, 13*, 263–278.

Sporns, O. (2012). *Discovering the human connectome*. Cambridge, MA: MIT Press.

Szyf, M. (2013). How do environments talk to genes? *Nature Neuroscience, 16*, 2–4.

Vaidyanathan, U., Vrieze, S. I., & Iacono, W. G. (2015). The power of theory, research design, and transdisciplinary integration in moving psychopathology forward. *Psychological Inquiry, 26*, 209–230.

van Os, J., Delespaul, P., Wigman, J., Myin-Germeys, I., & Wichers, M. (2013). Psychiatry beyond labels: Introducing contextual precision diagnosis across stages of psychopathology. *Psychological Medicine, 43*, 1563–1567.

Widiger, T. A., Crego, C., & Oltmanns, J. R. (2015). The validation of a classification of psychopathology. *Psychological Inquiry, 26*, 272–278.

Wigman, J. T., Collip, D., Wichers, M., Delespaul, P., Derom, C., Thiery, E., et al. (2013). Altered transfer of momentary mental states (ATOMS) as the basic unit of psychosis liability in interaction with environment and emotions. *PLoS One, 8*, e54653. doi:10.1371/journal.pone.0054653.

Wigman, J. T., van Os, J., Borsboom, D., Wardenaar, K. J., Epskamp, S., Klippel, A., et al. (2015). Exploring the underlying structure of mental disorders: Cross-diagnostic differences and similarities from a network perspective using both a top-down and a bottom-up approach. *Psychological Medicine, 45*, 2375–2387.

Wigman, J. T., van Os, J., Thiery, E., Derom, C., Collip, D., Jacobs, N., et al. (2013). Psychiatric diagnosis revisited: Towards a system of staging and profiling combining nomothetic and idiographic parameters of momentary mental states. *PLoS One, 8*, e59559. doi:10.1371/journal.pone.0059559.

Wilker, S., & Kolassa, I.-T. (2013). The formation of a neural fear network in posttraumatic stress disorder: Insights from molecular genetics. *Clinical Psychological Science, 1*, 452–469.

World Health Organization. (2007). *International Statistical Classification of Diseases and Related Health Problems 10th Revision*. Retrieved from http://www.who.int/classifications/icd/en/

World Health Organization. (2017). *International Classification of Disease, 11th Revision.*

Young, G. (2011). *Development and causality: Neo-Piagetian perspectives*. New York: Springer Science+Business Media.

Young, G. (2013). Breaking bad: DSM-5 description, criticism, and recommendations. *Psychological Injury and Law, 6*, 345–348.

Young, G. (2015). Causality in psychiatry: On nosology, etiology, and networks. *Frontiers in Psychiatry, 6*.

Young, G., Lareau, C., & Pierre, B. (2014). One quintillion ways to have PTSD comorbidity: Recommendations for the disordered DSM-5. *Psychological Injury and Law, 7*, 61–74.

Part V

Personal Contributions to the Study of Causality in Behavior: New Models

26 Causality in Psychological Injury and Law: Basics and Critics

Chapter Introduction

The present chapter includes the description of the criminal forensic approach to causality and the excusing conditions of criminal culpability. This enables a comparison with the civil, tort, and related disability approaches to causation. Outside of the differential legal issues of criminal responsibility and criminal negligence that are involved, respectively, for criminal conduct and for negligence, such as in motor vehicle accidents (MVAs), I maintain that the biopsychosocial model applies equally to both types of cases. On the one hand, in the criminal context, one could ask to what extent the perpetrator's behavior had been caused by any of the biopsychosocial factors that might have been involved, or their interaction. Note that, in the criminal context, the presence of these factors does not automatically lead to exoneration for the crime at issue. The insanity defense, for example, sets a high bar or threshold for disculpability due to psychological factors. As for the negligence in tort and related venues in court in disability cases undertaken by forensic evaluators, one needs to establish whether the survivor involved has a compensable functional- (or role-) related disability (with the presence of a disorder or condition constituting a secondary factor). Further, in this regard, one needs to establish whether the disability might be understood or explained psychologically by biopsychosocial factors (e.g., chronic pain and its limiting effects). Note that the latter biopsychosocial factors might involve pre-existing factors sufficiently severe enough to excuse the negligent action at issue or perhaps just a minor exacerbating factor in the outcome at hand. In such cases, the event at issue is not even material or contributory to the post-event psychological condition/disorder(s), and to their course and functional impacts.

The chapter concludes with provision of new terms that might help disambiguate the legal terms used in causal analysis (cause in fact, proximate cause). In this regard, I propose use of the superordinate, general term of proximate causation for both of these latter terms, as well as use in their stead of the specific terms of legal causes in fact and liable cause, respectively. In addition, the term of "biopsychosocial causation" could be used in either the criminal or civil (e.g., tort) context to help understand the behavior at issue (respectively, criminal conduct versus survivor psychological condition, after a tortious negligent event, for example).

Introduction

The law constitutes a bulwark in our society that helps keep us civil and safe. It is constructed differently in different countries and, in our case, reflects the highest ideals of human nature, trying to balance individual rights with the common good. Laws need to be equitable, fair, and just. At

G. Young, *Unifying Causality and Psychology*, DOI 10.1007/978-3-319-24094-7_26

the same time, they are not made without consultation with multiple stakeholders, including medical doctors, public policy experts, insurers, and mental health professionals.

Moreover, many cases that are brought to court need experts to help resolve disputes, such as in tort claims after personal injury. Psychologists, psychiatrists, and others in the mental health field need proper education and training for their roles in such cases, or else their reports and testimony will not be deemed admissible, or worse, their qualifications will not be considered to have met the accepted bar of competence. For example, they need to understand the legal terms that are involved, how to translate them into psychological practice, and so on. They need to use the best psychometric tests in their assessments and arrive at scientifically-informed, impartial conclusions. They need to know how to deal with court and with testifying on the stand. They need to know how to address ultimate issues, such as relating to disability and its causality. Cases in the field of psychological injury often especially hinge on the latter evaluation.

Causality and Causation Terms in Law

Law

According to Young and Drogin (2014), Young and Kane (2007) pointed out that a tort is a private or civil wrong or injury, such as in a negligent or intentionally tortious act, for which a trier of fact evaluates whether it deserves an award of compensation or damages (McLearen, Pietz, & Denney, 2004). The process of proving that tortious conduct had taken place in court depends on meeting four criteria, which have been referred to as the "4 Ds": duty; dereliction; direct causation; and damages (also see Piechowski, 2014).

If dereliction of duty by the negligent party, such as in a motor vehicle accident (MVA) is established in the case at issue, then the causal question must be satisfied—is there direct causation, that is, is the dereliction of duty, or its lack, the "proximate cause" of the injury at issue; in other words, does the tortious act factually and logically precede the harm incurred by the event in question? For the bar of direct causation, the reasonable person test is applied—normally, would another person in the same situation as the defendant have reasonably predicted that the act (or its lack) would have caused the harm at issue?

Citing Daller (2000), McLearen et al. (2004) noted that "proximate" cause is not defined the same way in different jurisdictions. In this regard, legal standards vary by case law in indicating which harms that have been incurred involve a legally protected right or interest that can be pursued for legal damages.

Young and Drogin (2014) further noted that Foote and Lareau (2013) maintained that in court, the plaintiff must establish that the defendant had been derelict and breached a duty sufficiently to cause a harm, which for psychiatric/psychological harm, involves "negligent infliction of emotional distress," or NIED. In emotional claims in court, the zone-of danger rule allows for emotional claims without a concomitant physical injury, and it has broadened such that bystanders can claim damages just by witnessing a horrific trauma to a family member, although there are limits imposed on the rule (e.g., *Thing v. La Chusa*, 1989).

Causality represents a difficult issue to analyze among the four D's even though it is pertinent to every tort and related forensic disability case. Piechowski (2014) noted that, in the forensic context, psychological damages are impairment- rather than diagnosis-related (e.g., Greenberg, Otto, & Long, 2003). That is, functional impacts are the focus of legal action rather than anything like the diagnosis; disorder, per se. Psychological condition in terms of diagnosis or disorder does not confer in and of themselves impairment or disability without considering match with the environment, (for example, jobs/their demands) and the functional impact that result if there is a sufficient mismatch in these regards. Further, in a causal determination for the tort or related case to have any weight, the impairments and functional impacts for the evaluee in question need to be demonstrated as causally related to the event at issue.

Causality and Causation

Young and Drogin (2014) described that Young (2008) had noted that the definition of causality varies across disciplines and, as per Young and Shore (2007), even within law, there is no consensus on its definition and conceptualization. Moreover, the confusion about causality extends into other disciplines. For example, in philosophy, Russell represents the philosophers who *deny* that causality can be determined, so that the concept of causality is confused and confusing (e.g., Lucy, 2007).

Young (2008) continued that, in law, the "but-for" test cannot cover all contingencies, especially dual or preemptive, duplicative, joint, serial, or severing causality. Therefore, other causality tests have been applied to cases such as these (especially, the material contributions test: as long as the event at issue has contributed more than a minor degree to the liability at issue, it is considered responsible at least in part). Wright (2007) had argued that the NESS test of causality (necessary element of a sufficient set, "a particular condition is a cause of or contributes to a specific consequence if and only if it is a necessary element of a set of antecedent actual conditions that had been sufficient for the occurrence of the consequence") could help in this regard. However, Lucy (2007) maintained that the NESS test also has limits, such as difficulty in differentiating primary cause in circumstances with multiple causes.

Garner (2009) wrote that for causation in the legal context, the causative event needs to be the proximate, dominant, responsible, or essential one, or at least contributory, substantive, or material; it needs to be more than tangential or "de minimus." Material cause is the term most often used and it refers either to the sole legal or legitimate cause of an event at claim or a factor that is part of it (a contribution that is necessary and sufficient). The "substantial" contributions test in causality is recognized in the American Law Institute (ALI) tort statement (American Law Institute, 2000; Piechowski, 2014).

The issue of causation was discussed in the SCOTUS case, 571 US (No. 12-7515) (2014). The court noted that causation has been long considered a "hybrid concept" (Hart & Honoré, 1959). The court referred to the "but-for" test of causality and that terms such as "results from," "because of," "based on," and "by reason of" are consistent with the "but-for" test.

The less demanding standards of causality, such as being a "substantial" or "contributing" factor, is more "permissive" and potentially allows any act or omission, no matter how "small," to serve as a contributing factor in causality determination in any case. The court could not determine any means of differentiating "too insubstantial" and "substantial" causation in the criminal context.

However, for the US Supreme Court, in the indexed case, in tort law "material" or "substantial" factors could constitute "a cause" of an event at issue (Keeton, Dobbs, Keeton, & Owen, 1984); in the civil context it is acceptable to have a more lax burden of proof that makes a material contribution to an event at issue sufficient to render it liable.

Young and Drogin (2014) concluded that in the civil arena, generally, and the one of psychological injury, particularly, the material or substantial contribution test of causality constitutes an adequate basis for apportioning causality in the typical multifactorial causality case involved in tortious and otherwise liable events at issue. Overall, with respect to causality in the psychological injury context, in the law involved, the but for test is consonant with the material contributions test, but events at claim are embedded in a broad multifactorial causal complex that includes: (a) pre-event psychological vulnerabilities if not psychopathologies; (b) complexities in the event at claim, including the perceived, subjective individualized element of participants; (c) extraneous factors, such as unanticipated job loss or the death of a family member incidentally to the event at issue that could complicate psychological course and outcome; and (d) post-event developments in terms of course and outcome, (which might be normative, or consistent with the average in clinical and non-litigating populations, or rather, exacerbated by the insurance process, litigation distress, iatrogenesis, and the adversarial divide, among other factors unique to the area of psychological injury and law, as per below).

Song (2014) reviewed the tests of causation in insurance contract law. The area is considered incoherent and uncertain, but the proximity threshold of causation is considered the predominant test. The "but for" test that is predominant in tort only has an occasional influence in insurance law. Causation is "central" to both types of liabilities. Proximity does not refer to the most recent, immediate, or most remote, distant element of a causal chain. Rather, the liable cause is the "fire-starter," the peril in the efficient chain that constitutes "profoundly" the effective starting point of the loss at issue, unless there is (also) an intervening, outstanding causal addition to the chain.

Hodgson (2011) differentiated the concept of an all-inclusive, deterministic "cone of causation" stretching back from the relevant antecedent event in time to the law's need to select legally-relevant necessary conditions in causality. Intervening events could break the chain of causation and emerge as primary legally. The complexity of such cases explains why in the law of torts, more than for any other topic, causation has "plagued" both scholars and the court (Fleming, 1998).

Goldberg (2011a, 2011b, 2011c) had noted that the central problem in tort law is that of establishing causation. Hoffmann (2011) suggested that instead of referring to proof of causation, law would best use the terminology of "causal requirements." Similarly, Bagshaw (2011) noted that Stapleton (2009) referred to causation as "involvement" (involving, one thing bringing about another).

Dawid (2011) considered that general causation based on population experiments differs from individual causation, and even the best experimental evidence does not clearly apply to particular cases at hand. Rather, at best, it has implications for the range of probability that might apply in individual causation. Goldberg (2011d) argued that an absence of findings on general causation should automatically exclude consideration of possible individual causation. Wright (2011) added that the statistical probability at the basis of general causation research is insufficient to establish individual causation. Concrete, particular evidence relevant to the case at hand also is necessary. Hogg (2011) and Cranor (2011) supported Wright's NESS model of causation (necessary element in a sufficient set) and that it can apply to individual cases; in this regard, it need not apply fully in such cases. It has the advantage of being broader than the traditional "but-for" test and, also, it can help parse joint causation. However, Spector (2011) found that the NESS model is lacking. Bagshaw (2011) referred to "causal contributions," "operative mechanisms," and "the natural process" in causality. He also referred to "causal potency."

Barth, Kertay, and Steinberg (2014) reviewed causation in mental illness. They noted that attributing a diagnosis does not carry with it any implications for causal analysis. Overdiagnosis is producing "fake epidemics." Diagnostic manuals are not meant to serve forensic needs. They conducted a literature review of 41 diagnoses, and could not find one having credible scientific support for legal standards of causation for mental illness. In general, there is no scientific justification for the legal level for any claim of causation for any mental illness. There is also the issue of malingering in such claims.

New Terms

In Young (2010), I described that Golding and Edmundson (2005) had reviewed the epistemological framework of law. In their view, the two main perspectives on the construction of law are (a) the legal positivist-legal realistic one and (b) the contrasting one of natural (moral) law. Young (2008) argued that, at the epistemological level, the law should establish an integrative, middle ground in its approach to causality and causation. That is, the epistemological approach of law to causal factors should not be based solely on either the principled (natural, moral) or pragmatic (positivism, realism) perspectives; rather, an integrative middle ground should be constructed with respect to the said issue having both together, through a synthetic integration. Specifically, on the one hand, a synthetic legal perspective on causality and causation should be established on the basis of fundamental legal principles, for example, related to rights and justice. Also, on the other hand, laws related to causality and causation should have leeway for flexible and pragmatic adaptation to social and other issues.

In Young (2010), I queried the confusion inherent in legal terminology related to causality and causation. *Proximate cause* refers to actionable *causes in fact* that reach thresholds of liability, or which reach sufficient degree in damages incurred as determined legally in the jurisdiction at issue; such level of damages incurred permits opening the case involved to legal (and financial) action for appropriate compensation for the outcome at issue. *Causes in fact* set the stage for considering an act of negligence as actionable for compensation; causes in fact refer to causes established in law as responsible for damages incurred and, therefore, as potentially actionable, irrespective of whether or not they meet the required degree of liability thresholds. Garner (2004) stated that this type of cause is a "but-for" one, in that it refers to the cause without which the event at issue would not have taken place. Alternate terms for causes in fact include factual causes.

Of concern, the term "proximate cause" in the legal field is not defined clearly enough according to the leading law dictionary (Garner, 2004). It usually refers to the liability component of a "cause in fact," but also can refer to a *cause in fact*, itself, or even to both! Moreover, Moore (2009) had noted that the term is a misnomer. Therefore, in an effort to bring structure to the confusion evident in the critical terms in the field of civil law related to causal factors, Young (2010) argued that, the law should create a superordinate term for causes in fact and proximate cause, such as use of the term of *proximate causation* as a combined term; conceptually, this new term indicates events that are together both causally contributory and potentially actionable and liable legally. Young (2010) further suggested new names for the terms of cause in fact and proximate cause. Specifically, the term of "causes in fact," which are also called legal causes, should be called *legal causes in fact*. Also, the term of *liable cause* should replace the one of proximate cause.

Negligence and Law

Green (2014) noted that the concept of causation and its application in negligence cases, such as tort, is "complicated, convoluted, and confused." She developed a pragmatic, practical test of causation, referred to as the Necessary Breach Analysis (NBA). It does not try to define causation nor give an abstract, academic, philosophical, pronouncement of what it means for a cause to exist. Rather, it is a forensic means for dealing robustly with causation on a case-by-case basis.

In the NBA,)the first stage establishes whether or not a breach of duty changed the normal course of events resulting in damage that would not have otherwise happened. In the second stage, the determination for each defendant involved is whether her or his breach was "operative" when the damage occurred.

The NBA)algorithm keeps the classic but-for test as the best one for establishing causation due to negligence. It can account for overdetermined cause, i.e., two or more causes each sufficient by itself to produce the damage. It obviates the need to consider pre-emption, i.e., causes that never become operative (hypotheticals). The NBA initially aggregates all potential causal factors, but then proceeds to rule in or out on a factual basis which ones are relevant to the case at hand.

Green (2014) noted that the facts in the case must be established with certainty. However, in contrast, for meeting the legal test in these types of cases, it is established according to the standard of balance of probabilities/preponderance of the evidence. The factual elements of the case should not be determined according to this less demanding standard.

A breach might be material (relevant, or a part of the cause that surpasses the minimal range), in a larger multifactorial causal array. In this sense, it needs to be shown that the material contributor is at least either a part-cause or had caused a part of an injury. This criterion still demands the but-for test for determination. Green (2014) concluded that although the more-likely-than-not standard is a probability estimate, legally, decisions involve a certainty in an all-or-none fashion.

In short, Green (2014) has shown that, for court in negligence/tort type cases—facts have to be definitive; yet meeting the legal test at issue needs to be only established at the level of more than probable; also causes might be legally acceptable as part causes; and despite all this, in legal decisions, any uncertainty or hedges leading to them do not detract from the ultimate necessity to state that what had taken place either happened absolutely or not, with all the attendant consequences to the decision involved being determined thusly. No wonder court is confusing to the uninitiated in mental health practice.

Psychological Injury and Law

According to Young and Drogin (2014), psychological injury and law is an emerging field in mental health law and assessment. It deals with tort, worker compensation, disability insurance, and related cases that involve psychological impairment and disability, for issues such as posttraumatic stress disorder (PTSD), mild traumatic brain injury (TBI), and chronic pain. The major areas in the field of psychological injury and law, as presented in the masthead of the journal *Psychological Injury and Law* (springer.com), involve: law, forensics, assessment, malingering and symptom validity tests (SVTs, also referred to as PVTs, performance validity tests), disability and return to work, practice affairs, PTSD, (chronic) pain, TBI, rehabilitation, discrimination and harassment, ethics, and general interest and controversies. Malingering is an essential axis for all these topics, as are fabricating/feigning, and even exaggerating, in general, including for purposes of monetary gain, or response biases and threats to validity, in general.

Tables 26.1 and 26.2 present the major terms and concepts used in the present chapter, with each considered an important source of influence and biases on psychological injury. Young (2014) described that "litigation distress" refers to iatrogenic or stressful factors in the insurance and legal process; they add to patient stresses, thereby complicating recovery. Young noted that the psychological injuries of complainants have been referred to as a "compensation neurosis" (litigation resolution cures the complaints at source). However, although this might be true at an individual level for a case at hand, there is insufficient evidence to support this claim at the general population level. For example, complainant psychological injuries generally do not heal "magically" after having received their financial settlements (see Call, 2003).

That being said, the iatrogenic effects in psychological injury cases might be quite palpable, and in different ways depending on the extent of injuries and the extent of feigning involved, if any. In this regard, the evaluee might be quite influenced by the litigation process and by iatrogenic factors. I should point out that this state of affairs could work toward favoring the defense as well as the plaintiff. On the plaintiff side, complainants original psychological injuries might be valid, with no or very little exaggeration, and the injuries worsen due to undue insurance and defense pressures, for instance, in repeated denials of the validity of their claims and of their needed treatments and repeated stressful and confrontational assessments. In contrast, on the insurer and defense side, complainants might have minor injuries, exaggerate or even malinger, and get stresses only because the repeated treatment denials and assessments implicate that they will not get any monetary compensation. For example, evaluees might be stressed by insurance examinations and defense medicolegal examinations because they are anxious about their malingering, fabrication, and deception being exposed.

Young (2008) examined systemic issues in causality assessment. He pointed to the types of stresses associated with the insurance process. With respect to the patient side of the equation in the insurance process, Young (2014) especially dealt with the issue of malingering. For example,

Table 26.1 Major terms in psychological injury and law

Term	Explanation
Compensation neurosis	A complainant is "cured" of psychological symptoms once litigation ends
Conversion disorder	Unconsciously motivated feigning of sensory/motor deficits
Cry for help	Symptom exaggeration/engaging in dramatization behavior in order for complaints to be heard "by the evaluator"
Exaggeration	Conscious or unconscious; the evaluee presents her/his genuine symptoms or impairments caused by an injury as much worse than their actual case
Factitious disorder	Internally motivated and intentional symptom production is high; the intentional production of symptoms for purposes of adopting the sick role rather than for receiving external incentives
Feigning	Deliberate fabrication/gross exaggeration of psychological/physical symptoms (Rogers, 2008)
Gray zone	A possible/probable, indeterminate, ambiguous presentation/performance
Malingering	The intentional feigning of physical/psychological symptoms that is motivated by external incentives or to acquire external outcomes (e.g., financial gain, avoiding to return to work; American Psychiatric Association, 2013)
Somatization disorder	The promotion of somatic symptoms/impairment by one's significant distress via nonconscious processes

Adapted from Young (2014)

Table 26.2 Factors contributing to difficulties in evaluations: litigation/iatrogenic

Type	Examples
Adversarial divide	Plaintiff-defense
	Any legal adversarial process
Iatrogenic (stress/psychological reaction at any point)	Multiple assessments (treatment providers)
	Multiple treatments
	Multiple assessments (plaintiff)
	Multiple assessments (defense)
Insurance process (stress/psychological reaction at any point)	Claims initiated
	Multiple letters/forms
	Claims denied (e.g., for treatments/supports)
	Third party attitude
Litigation distress (stress/psychological reaction at any point)	Potential litigation events
	Engaging attorneys
	Litigation steps begin
	Courts (or related venues)

Adapted with permission of Springer Science+Business Media. Young (2014); with kind permission from Springer Science+Business Media B. V. [Table 14.10, p. 373]

early after the onset of the pain at issue, a patient might not score in the range on respondent validity scales that indicates feigning to any degree, but might reach that level months or years later. The interpretation of these results could indicate the pain patient being assessed is demonstrating increasing pain and desperation, but another possible interpretation is that the said evaluee has attained notable elevations on subsequent respondent validity scales, after a lack of elevations in these regards previously, because the later assessments coincide with the decision to sue for damages due to the original injuries, even if they had been healing, and with resultant consultation of a plaintiff attorney.

Another issue in this regard could involve the complainant obtaining different test results at a similar point in time by assessors working for plaintiff and defense. For example, if the test results show greater pain experience exaggeration with the defense attorney assessor relative to the plaintiff one, a possible interpretation might be that the patient appraises that the defense examination is confrontational (and, indeed, it might be), leading to the greater exaggeration in this context, either in order to reflect a desire to be heard or out of exasperation at the confrontation. That is, it could be that litigation distress is an issue to consider in differing simultaneous outcomes associated with plaintiff vs. defense assessments due to the adversarial pressure on the assessors stemming form the divide and the influence of this factor on evaluees.

To be fair, opposite simultaneous defense and plaintiff results might obtain because the plaintiff assessors put the evaluee at ease knowing that they will be leaning toward them in their conclusions, and the evaluees are aware of this to begin, at any rate. Therefore, in these regards, it is the insurer and defense assessors who handle best the required neutral stance in the assessment. That is, there is anti-litigation distress in the plaintiff examinations compared to regular and not unseemly stress in the insurer–defense ones, which makes the insurer–defense ones seem the more stressful ones on comparison!

Moreover, the adversarial divide could act directly on other parties in the system. For example, in attorney coaching, legal representatives either advise complainants how to present and perform in evaluations, or they provide material to the complainants to learn how to do this (the material might even be posted on a firm's website!). On the other side of the coin, rather than complainants, defense attorneys might "train" or entrain third parties, e.g., claims adjusters/adjudicators, in how to handle cases to their advantage; also, senior third party executives might train or entrain not only these administrators how to handle cases in this way to their advantage but also independent medical examination (IME) evaluators in these regards.

In general, Young (2014) noted that the system in which a person with psychological injuries functions might be filled with bias. Typically, this refers to evaluee bias, such as negative response bias in testing, including to the point of malingering, but also it could refer to the adversarial divide in which workers in the system other than complainants must navigate. In the narrow sense, the adversarial divide refers to the plaintiff and defense opposition in tort and related cases and, in the broader sense, also it refers to the related agents and institutions that function within it, such as insurers and professional evaluators, including mental health ones, who might be aligned with one side or the other. Therefore, the divide captures within its net evaluators, including mental health ones, given the specific types of biases that might influence them, such as confirmatory bias (defined as evaluators giving more weight to information consistent with their belief relative to other opinions; Kane & Dvoskin, 2011).

The multiple factors involved in psychological injury cases render them complex, controversial, and "gray zone," rather than clearly black or white. Young (2014) referred to the difficulty in assessing complainants manifesting problematic presentations and performances, or ones residing in the so-called gray zone. Many of them will present and perform in an ambiguous, mixed, or uncertain way, being indeterminate in their presentation and performance. Gray-zone refers not only to complainant status in presentation and performance but also to the difficulty in interpretation of their presentation and performance. Young (2014) added that, in cases that fit the gray zone, the conclusion on evaluee credibility might be in dispute in the two sides involved in evaluating the examinee, and that the uncertainty either way leads to the types of disagreements that are prevalent in the adversarial divide in the field.

Young (2014) continued that an adequate model of evaluee validity in presentation and performance in evaluations should accommodate the ambiguities presented by many evaluees, that is, when their evidence is not clear-cut either way. For example, in the gray zone, evaluees might exaggerate moderately, or inconsistencies/discrepancies might be found in the file that are moderate, yet the evaluee could still judged to be expressing credible symptoms. In this regard, there might be a cry for help at work. Further, even gross exaggerations could reflect a cry for help (e.g., in the case of desperate patients being consistently and unjustly denied treatments); however, any assessment that leads to this type of conclusion should be well-justified. In another example, as noted above, at the other extreme, even a mild or minimal exaggeration could be totally consciously fabricated for financial gain. In all these cases, evaluees appear to fit the gray zone, and explanations why they fall one way or the other on the credibility continuum should be offered. Young (2014) concluded that the best way to minimize the uncertainty in cases of psychological injury about examinee credibility is to proceed from a scientific perspective—that is, (a) know well the scientific literature, assuming that it has been undertaken in a way that is applicable to the case at hand; (b) use scientifically-informed methods and procedures; and (c) use scientific reasoning in arriving at interpretations and conclusions.

Medical Injury and Law

Melhorn, Talmage, Ackerman, and Hyman (2014) presented the medical view of causation in disease and injury, including at the psychiatric level. The book, on occupational medicine, is meant to accompany the AMA Guides to the evaluation of permanent impairment (American Medical Association Guides, Sixth Edition; Rondinelli et al., 2008), which has important legal implications, given the latter's widespread use in disability and related determinations.

Melhorn, Talmage, et al. (2014) indicated that the definition of causation is "elusive" in some situations. Yet, it is crucial in establishing liability in medical cases. Moreover, scientific and legal approaches often "are in conflict." Causation in occupational medicine must consider all interactive and biopsychosocial factors, including those that are pre-existing. Other factors to consider in this regard involve, on the one hand, fraud (including by the insurer, employer, and physician) and, on the other hand, malingering by the claimant.

Melhorn, Ackerman, Glass, Deitz, and Babitsky (2014) explained that there is a chasm in medical and legal concepts of causation. In law, "cause in fact" is the event that "brings about" another. A direct causal association refers to the necessary and sufficient requirement for the cause at issue. An indirect one indicates other contributing factors need to be present. Proximate cause refers to causes in fact having legal liability. Often, it is established by counterfactual or "but-for" arguments. They noted that different jurisdictions have particular standards of legal liability.

Hegmann, Thiese, Oostema, and Melhorn (2014) noted that population-level research on causation could help address whether an "exposure" contributes significantly to the development, aggravation, or maintenance of a condition. The 1965 Hill criteria provide a useful framework in this regard. The most important ones are temporality, strength of association, dose–response relationship, and consistency.

Brooks and Melhorn (2014) addressed apportionment in causation. Medical causation is typically multifactorial, and there is no simple way to isolate the degree of contribution of the legally relevant factors. Indeed, the task might be impossible in some situations.

Fries, Melhorn, Hyman, and Talmage (2014) focused on the medical examination in terms of establishing causality. Much of the chapter presents medical ways of detecting symptom magnification or disease fabrication.

Talmage, Freeman, Melhorn, and Hyman (2014) described how to present conclusions in reports, including on causality. For example, it must be proved that the negligence at issue actually caused the injury at issue. Discussion of the proximate cause should include not only consideration of the but-for argument but also have a reasonableness component (the injury should have been reasonably anticipated or foreseen as a normal outcome of the negligence at issue).

Talmage, Melhorn, Ackerman, and Barth (2014) argued that, generally, musculoskeletal disorders are conditions of uncertain pathophysiology. They are influenced by psychological and social (e.g., work) factors. For example, pessimism about the return to work could be involved. Moreover, complainants might not be fully forthcoming of past pain complaints or of psychosocial confounders.

DePaolo and Rassp (2014) elaborated the legal approach to causation. They noted that, whether from the plaintiff or defense side, attorneys focus on the "facts." Legal causation involves responsibility for the negligence. Liability can be divided according to apportionment of cause, if applicable. There might be intervening causes, but proximate causation can take them into account by establishing the chain of causation.

Moore (2014) contributed that, legally, causation is established on the basis of factual evidence, so that it is case-by-case and not absolute. Causation determination is neither art nor science, but fact-based, so that it must rely on evidence that is relevant to the case at hand (the evidence must not be immaterial). The evidence must be substantial, probative (helpful), reasonable, credible, and so on, and it must meet the court's standard of proof (e.g., more likely than not).

Deitz (2014) added that basis for claims needs to be "clear." Sometimes percentages are used to define clarity (Overpeck, Krohn, Rabine, & Lovan, 2014).

Overall, the medical approach to causation in the civil context is consistent with the psychological one. There are legal thresholds and concepts to consider but, generally, the causation must be material even if it is part of a multifactorial or biopsychosocial nexus. Population-level research is important to consider, as well as is case law. Malingering is always a concern. Assessment needs to be fact-based and comprehensive.

In the following, I move from the civil to the criminal context in terms of the topic of causality in psychological assessment. I find some basic similarities in the two areas, despite evident differences.

Table 26.3 Definition of key terms related to causality

Term	Definition
Causal test	In tort and related law, the "but-for" test is primary—causation is evident when the outcome at issue would not have transpired absent or without the occurrence of the event at claim or action of the responsible party. Other tests have been proposed, but the material or substantial contribution test allows for attribution of liable causation without the event at issue necessarily being primary.
Causality	Relation between cause and effect; process more than product. Used interchangeably with the term causation.
Causation	Production of effect(s) by cause(s); product more than process.
General causation	Refers to causation in the general population—at the statistical or normative level is the issue at hand or at claim (e.g., toxic exposure, MVA) an inducing factor in individuals of the outcome that ensued (e.g., illness, injury).
Specific causation	In cases in which general causation applies, does the event at issue lead to liable results (illness, injury) to the point that damages can be pursued?

Note. The terms in this table were defined based on Garner (2004), Mish (2003), and Young and Shore (2007). Adopted with permission of Elsevier. Reprinted from *International Journal of Law and Psychiatry,* Vol. 32, Young, G., Causes in the construction of causal law: A psycho-ecological model, Pages 73–83, Copyright 2010; with kind permission from Elsevier. [Table 1, Page 75]

Psychological Causality in Criminal Cases

Introduction

Young (2015) noted that causality (or causation) is central to every legal case, yet its underlying philosophical, legal, and psychological definitions and conceptions vary (see Tables 26.3 and 26.4). The definitional distinction between causation and causality is ambiguous (Young & Shore, 2007), and the terms are used interchangeably. In the criminal context, on the one hand, causality refers to establishing the alleged perpetrator's responsibility for the criminal act at issue in terms of the person's mental state (*mens rea*) and, on the other hand, if the person is found to have committed the act, whether the insanity defense absolves guilt.

To remind, for comparison purposes, in the forensic disability and related context, causality refers to whether the index event is a material or contributing cause in the multifactorial array that had led to the psychological condition at issue. There is no question of guilt to consider in civil cases; simply, does the victim (survivor) express a compensable psychological condition? There is

Table 26.4 Key terms related to causation and causality

Term = Meaning (simplified)
Key terms related to causality and causation in law:
Concurrent = Joint; Contributing = Secondary; Immediate [a] = Most recent; Intervening = Added; Joint = Multiple; Material = Part of joint; Proximate = Dominant (direct); Remote [b] = Initial, too far removed; Superseding = Replacing dominant
Key terms related to causality and causation in medicine:
Component = Part of multiple; Exacerbating = Worsening; Exciting = Direct; Immediate [a] = Beginning, initial; Predisposing = Susceptible; Primary = Principle; Remote [b] = Predisposing, secondary; Secondary = Not principle; Ultimate = Remote
Key terms related to causality and causation in psychology:
Catalytic = Facilitative; Latent = Delayed; Maintaining = Current; Mediating = Intervening; Multiple = Multifactorial; Original = Remote, initial; Remote = Initial; Triggering = Immediate[a]
Key terms related to causality and causation in philosophy:
First = Remote[b]; Immediate[a] = Last; Principle = Primary

Adapted from Young (2008)

Note. The footnoted terms indicate the confusions in their use in law, psychiatry/psychology, and philosophy. The difficulty in translating legal terms to the mental health field, and vice versa is compounded when the terms have different meanings in the various disciplines involved. For example, the footnoted term "immediate" (a) might mean either most recent or last part of a causal chain, which surely seeds immediate confusion to the unwary. A remote component of a causal chain might be involved, nevertheless, as a predisposing factor. In translating between law and mental health, another term that is confusing concerns "reliability," which means "validity" in law as understood in psychology (it refers to replicability in psychology, which is of less relevance than validity). In short, addressing the reliability of a causal argument could evoke different associations in attorneys, judges, psychiatrists, and psychologists

no evaluation of the perpetrator (i.e., the negligent party); simply, once more, only the survivor's condition is at issue. Nevertheless, there are commonalities across the two contexts to consider.

In both the criminal and tort or disability contexts, the legal test is a counterfactual one. (a) On the one hand, for the criminal context, the counterfactual, but-for argument refers to whether the outcome involved (e.g., death) would have resulted absent the act (e.g., who is responsible when the case involves firing the weapon at issue in conjunction and there is also another potentially lethal action by someone else). That is, for the example given, in cases of apparently simultaneous criminal lethal action, which one of the two involved is the "but-for" responsible one? (b) On the other hand, for the disability context, it concerns whether the claimed psychological condition would be present only because of the negligent incident at issue. Normally, the latter negligent event at issue is distinguished from the criminal one by its negligence compared to the voluntary intent behind it in the criminal case, yet both involve the same counterfactual argument in establishing causality.

Biopsychosocial Model

In the literature, in general, the nature of causation in forensic psychiatry and psychology is viewed as deriving from a "multiplicity of causes" (Silva, 2009), and the causal factors can be referred to as a "biopsychosociocultural" nexus (Bernston, 2006). For example, dysfunction or insult to the brain might lead to influence on or more directly affect behavior, but this biological factor must be seen in context of the whole interconnected causes that are involved.

Steinert and Whittington (2013) adopted a similar approach to understanding the origins of violence. In their "bio-psycho-social" approach, individual dispositions relate to an interrelation of: (a) biological factors, such as prefrontal brain structure functioning and genetics; (b) psychological and neuropsychological ones, such as mental illness and impulsivity; and (c) social factors, such as poverty and peer group influence. According to Steinert and Whittington, the situation that triggers the violence at issue is complex, as well, and can include experienced or imagined provocation or threat. Moreover, the violent act is committed in relation to the facilitating and inhibiting factors that might be at play, which include substance misuse and fear of punishment, respectively.

As much as is the situation in the civil context, such as tort or related disability cases, the psychological state of the perpetrator of criminal conduct can be analyzed from a biopsychosocial perspective. In this vein, in the civil case, such as in tort, forensic disability, and related assessments, the evaluator needs to consider preexisting, precipitating, and perpetuating causal factors, with personal and social resilience and protective factors considered, as well. In the criminal context, the same biopsychosocial model with all these variables applies, but with the evaluation of mental competence and voluntariness added as a critical factor. In this regard, evaluators need to be wary of simplistic models; for example, the growth in neurolaw has led to use of neuroscience in court, but it risks reducing the complexity of criminal cases to unifactorial, biological models.

Mens Rea

In the following, I analyze in depth the approach to causality in the criminal context. Zapf, Golding, Roesch, and Pirelli (2014) underscored the tension in law between strict, objective liability and subjective liability as it applies to establishing criminal responsibility and to working from a sense of "fairness" or "justice" in court. Briefly, criminal guilt in committing a proscribed behavior (*actus reus*) requires meeting an appropriate threshold in both degree of and type of mental capacity and intentionality (*mens rea*) before the guilt can be related to "culpable ownership" of the act. Zapf et al. (2014) noted that, outside of any debate about its scientific validity, the issue of *mens rea* (for an *actus reus*) is integral to the fabric of criminal law.

Causality in the criminal forensic context centers on the concept of responsibility. In criminal cases, such as lethal actions, Goldstein, Morse, and Packer (2013) emphasized that causal responsibility and moral responsibility need to be distinguished. For example, the victim might be aggressed by a perpetrator who cannot be conceived as a morally responsible agent even if the actions involved had caused the outcome at issue. Culpability in the legal sense of the word depends on evaluating the actor's mental state at the time of the criminal act at issue. Mental state assessments need to evaluate and to retrospectively reconstruct the alleged perpetrator's cognition, volition, or both at the time of the offense at issue. According to the authors, "mens rea" refers to the intent, purpose, or knowledge component of the mental state of the perpetrator at the time of the conduct involved in the prohibited act ("actus reus").

Goldstein et al. (2013) continued that even when the perpetrator of a crime meets the required standard of proof of guilt of "beyond a reasonable doubt," an "affirmative" defense could be launched. That is, the defense attorneys could have the defendant exonerated on the basis of either a valid justification or an excuse. The latter includes satisfying the criteria for "legal insanity;" in this defense, if the perpetrator is "irrational" to the degree needed, then he/she will be judged not guilty and considered a "nonresponsible agent."

Goldstein et al. (2013) added that the criminal conduct at issue has to be a "voluntary" act according to legal definition. That is, the act in question had to be intentional and undertaken during a state in which the defendant had been of reasonably integrated consciousness. Otherwise, as obtains in significant dissociation, the behavior at issue is judged as being the product of an "automatism."

Goldstein et al. (2013) further noted that a legal insanity claim typically involves a "defect" of cognition, but also it could involve maintaining a defect of "control capacity"; that is, the person at the time of the improper act had a lack of ability to control his/her conduct. However, the latter volitional "prong" in an excusing defense has been criticized as not being independent of the cognitive one. Nevertheless, the control incapacity argument as an excusing condition in a defense against criminal charges is still proffered to court.

Goldstein et al. (2013) tackled the issue of whether having "free will" should be part of the elements to consider in a crime and whether its absence can be used as an excusing condition. According to them, arguments related to free will are irrelevant to the question of criminal guilt. The concept of free will is a distracting confusion in law; it is more the province of philosophy than law, and the issue of free will itself cannot decide its legitimacy. Even though, philosophically, we live in a deterministic world (although I add that there are compatibilist arguments in philosophy), legally, in that world, offenders still can express valid *mens rea* and they are morally responsible for their crimes. Similarly, even if all phenomena in the world are fully caused, deterministic concepts of causality such as this cannot be used as an excuse to deny moral culpability for a crime. Moreover, the presence of mental abnormality cannot be considered, *pro forma*, the cause of a crime, nor a reason why one was compelled to commit it; therefore, its presence cannot be used to exonerate criminal guilt (except in cases in which its presence created a threshold lack of either comprehension of the nature of the act involved or sufficient self-control in relation to it).

Continuing with the question of free will in behavior, Winters, Globokar, and Roberson (2014) introduced models of crime and causation of criminal behavior. They contrasted the approaches of classicalism and positivism. The core assumption of the former view is that human behavior is shaped by the rational use of free will. For the latter view, in contrast, behavior is shaped, deterministically, by biological, psychological, and social forces. Although implicit in their formulation, the authors did not explicitly refer to a biopsychosocial view.

Biological approaches include genetics, neurophysiology, biochemical, and evolutionary approaches. For example, the six genes to date that have been associated with violence, aggression, or conduct disorder include: Dopamine transporter gene 1 (*DAT1*), Dopamine D2 receptor gene (*DRD2*), Dopamine D4 receptor gene (*DRD4*), Serotonin transporter gene (*5-HTTLPR*), catechol-*O*-methyltransferase gene (*COMT*), and Monoamine oxidase A gene (*MAOA*).

Appelbaum and Scurich (2014) reviewed the literature on genetic influence on criminal activity. Genetic factors appear to account for 40–50 % of the variance in its transmission. Heritabilities have been found up to 57 % for aggressive behavior and 67 % for antisocial behavior (Tuvblad, Narusyte, Grann, Sarnecki, & Lichtenstein, 2011). The genes involved include *MAOA* (Caspi et al., 2002), *COMT*, *DAT1*, *DRD2*, *DRD4*, and *5-HTTLPR* (Ferguson & Beaver, 2009).

Wallace (2014) argued that the basis for legal responsibility is not physical but mental and behavioral. The person has to conduct him- or herself reasonably; it is not the brain behaving, nor can the brain explain away any lack in this regard. The law's approach to causality is based on the person as agent, not on the brain nor any mechanism. Conscious states (including intentions, knowledge, comprehension, rationality, and control of compulsion) cause behavior. The brain does not include circuits or pathways of responsibility (e.g., Morse, 2006).

Sadoff and Dattilio (2011) described that the insanity defense has roots in texts written back thousands of years. Perlin (1989) had noted that its modern roots extend back 700 years. The classic case in which the matter was raised in a contemporary way is *R. V. McNaughten*. Sadoff and Dattilio (2011) clarified that the *McNaughten* test does not concern whether the criminal defendant had known the difference between right and wrong. Rather, the legal test involved is whether the alleged perpetrator had known what she or he had been doing in the middle of doing the criminal act at issue and whether she or he had known that the particular act at issue had been wrong. Therefore, the *McNaughten* test of criminal act and *mens rea* is specific both in time and to event.

Frederick (2012) described that different jurisdictions vary widely in the laws concerning insanity. Nevertheless, there are also commonalities over jurisdictions in how insanity is legally defined. For example, jurisdictions agree that the mental impairment at issue in legal insanity arguments needs to be serious in nature in order to constitute a sufficient basis for arriving at a judgment of legal insanity. In this regard, factors such as personality disorder and repetitive criminal activity do not qualify for a valid defense of legal insanity. Instead, the most common disorders/conditions associated with the insanity defense involve attributions of psychosis, brain disorder, mental retardation, bipolar disorder, and dissociative disorder. Each of these disorders/conditions could very well lead to disruptions in thought and in self-awareness that impact negatively the perpetrator's capacity to appreciate the nature of the criminal actions that had been undertaken at the time of their commission. In this regard, mental health assessors need to evaluate defendants carefully about their capacities for "knowing" and "appreciating" not in general but at the time of the alleged act.

Similarly, Melton, Petrila, Poythress, and Slobogin (2007) related that the mental "disease or defect" at issue involved in an insanity defense for a criminal act must "cause" either the criminal act itself or the excusing condition for it. If the mental abnormality in question in the case at hand cannot be shown to have affected the perpetrator's alleged actions, then, at the legal level, it will be considered "irrelevant."

Melton et al. (2007) continued, and referred to the "but-for" causality test. In this regard—it must be shown that without the presence of the mental disorder at issue, the alleged criminal act would not have been committed. However, the but-for test is not easily satisfied. For example, the mental disorder in question might have led to unconscious factors or it might have involved biological (e.g., genetic) ones, but criminal responsibility is not absolved merely by its presence. Antecedent factors such as these must reach legal thresholds, or else they remain, simply, relevant to understanding causation, in general, but not criminal responsibility, in particular.

As for the legal threshold at issue, Melton et al. (2007) informed that establishing criminal responsibility depends especially on establishing rationality in the reasons for the act in question. In the purview of the law, responsibility for one's actions always exists, and also criminal responsibility will not be exonerated, unless the irrationality required for an insanity determination in the case at hand can be clearly established for the timeframe of the harm incurred at issue.

Finally, the concepts involved in establishing criminal responsibility need to be fixed in law, but it appears that they are continually being challenged and changing. Moreover, forensic evaluators do not necessarily agree on the insanity defense, which contributes to the uncertainty in the area.

In this regard, Gowensmith, Murrie, and Boccaccini (2013) investigated the reliability of forensic evaluations of legal insanity in an American state that requires multiple, independent evaluations of the issue (Hawaii). The researchers had an N of 165 criminal cases that included 483 forensic evaluation reports for verification of inter-evaluator agreement. The results showed that full agreement on insanity or its absence, which typically involved three evaluators, was found in 55.1 % of the cases (on the presence of sanity, 38.2 %; on insanity, 17.0 %). As for disagreements related to sanity, a majority of them were about the presence or absence of insanity, per se (30 %), with the remainder of the disagreements about whether the sanity opinion can be given (14.5 %). The researchers reported that both psychotic disorder and psychiatric hospitalization shortly before the offense at hand led to greater agreement about insanity among the conclusions of evaluators.

Neurolaw

In the following, I return to the question of the causes of criminal conduct in terms of voluntariness, but add to it the discussion of biopsychosocial causation. Silva (2009) formulated an argument countering the biological point of view as being the sole causative factor in criminal conduct. He argued that the law is concerned with the responsibility (voluntariness) of the criminal act at issue, and it presumes that voluntariness is always present unless proven otherwise to the required standard of proof. Neuroscience is not able to find an association involving criminal responsibility and neuronal or brain factors because human responsibility lies in considering humans *in toto* and not in their brains considered in isolation (Gazzaniga & Steven, 2004). As Silva (2009) noted, people are held responsible for their actions, and it is not legally defensible to hold that their brains alone are responsible for their actions (Morse, 2006).

Schleim (2012) supported a similar position on the inappropriate focus on the brain in the context of recent pushes in neurolaw. He maintained that there is neither a "seat of morality" nor of appropriate behavior within the brain. The associations found in the literature across the brain and behaviors are not consistent and, moreover, they cannot explain, diagnose, or predict behavior. Brain factors, and even more remote putative causes of behavior, do not provide biomarkers of psychiatric disorder or legally relevant psychiatric conditions. The danger of the data with respect to neurolaw for a case at hand is that they are misused in court.

Moriarty, Langleben, and Provenzale (2013) adopted a similar position on the limited value of brain scan data in forensic criminal cases. Testimony that such data can be used as evidence of brain trauma for a case at hand does not sufficiently analyze the "reliability and validity" of the scan data, and also it can be "potentially misleading."

Meltzer et al. (2013) noted that Consensus medical "statements" support the limited relevance of neuroimaging data in court. Also, Meltzer et al. (2013) addressed the difficulty of inferring human behavior or motivation from neuroimaging data. The state of the brain scanning field does not yet allow the specification of causal relationships in brain findings and mental states related to criminal responsibility or its excusing. Meltzer et al. (2013) called for "more searching judicial analysis" of brain scan evidence in court.

Morse (2011a) couched his call for a need for caution on bringing neurolaw to court in catchy phrases yet cogent analysis. He called for the abandonment of "neuroexuberance," while asking for a better use of appropriate "translation" of neuroscience to law with the goal of attaining "neuromodesty" and of avoiding "brain overclaim syndrome." Morse qualified the law's approach to criminal responsibility and competence in trials for a criminal act as "behavioral," unlike the case for neuroscientific understanding of behavior, which is "mechanistic." Although "brain causation" might be part of the causation for a behavior, understanding causation in any way, including in terms of brain causation, does not help mitigate or excuse a criminal act at issue (believing that it does constitutes the "fundamental psychological error").

Brain causation by itself does not mean that we are non-agentic, compelled automatons in behavior. Moreover, brain activity, such as measured in a brain scanner, cannot be shown to constitute a "necessary, sufficient, or predisposing" causal factor for the behavior involved in a particular study, let alone in the real world of a particular case at hand to which its laboratory results might be generalized, for example, to a particular criminal act at issue.

Morse (2011b) added that in court the question is not whether behavior is caused (because all behavior is caused) but whether the legal criteria of criminal conduct have been satisfied. No matter what are the cause(s) of a behavior at issue (and even if they are known to reside in biological, psychological, or social factors, or in their combination, or even if the cause(s) of a behavior are unknown), the legal test of responsibility for an alleged criminal act does not include causality factors underlying the behavior; exoneration of moral culpability for criminal conduct takes place only in light of an excusing condition. Morse (2011b) continued that "causal knowledge" could be "sufficiently precise" to contribute to the determination of "whether or the likelihood" that the legal threshold involved for the criminal offense in question had been "satisfied," although an excusing condition still might be involved even if its cause is unknown. Finally, causal knowledge might help explain why a perpetrator's rationality might have been fully or partly impaired at the time of a criminal act; however, the excusing condition lies not in the causation of the impairment of the rationality at issue but in the impairment of the rationality itself at the time of the event. For these and other reasons, the data that neuroimaging of the brain can provide to court are modest, at best, and, generally, the causation implied does not bear on the central question of responsibility or its exoneration.

That being said, many authors give some leeway in the use of neuroimaging data in court, for instance, in the mitigation of sentencing. For example, Casartelli and Chiamulera (2013) considered that it is "necessary" although not sufficient to use neuroscientific data in forensic psychiatric evaluations. Also, Meynen (2013) reasoned that neuroscientific data can inform of the nature of the decision-making process of accused perpetrators of prohibited criminal acts in question during psychiatric assessments of their criminal responsibility. Further, Penney (2012) opined that, in some cases, neuroscientific data might be useful in establishing the validity of the attempted excusing argument of total incapacity to have impulse control associated with the act in question.

The insanity defense is accompanied by various nuances. For example, Claydon (2012) noted that there are cultural and jurisdictional differences in neuroscientific defenses related to mental condition, as well as racial ones. [With respect to the latter, consult the research by Korn, Johnson, and Chun (2012) and Perry, Neltner, and Allen (2013)]. Moreover, there is a range of other issues, from folk psychology considerations (conceptions of the average person) to philosophical/jurisprudence issues (conceptions of legal scholars), such as the deterrent value of being conservative about insanity defenses (Aggarwal & Ford, 2013). Together, these further considerations indicate that the issues of criminal responsibility, the insanity defense, and the causation that might underlie them are as much cultural and social constructions as legal and psychiatric/psychological ones. Nevertheless, the evidentiary standards required of good science (Kaufmann, 2013) call for a "cautious" approach to this area of forensics (Morse, 2011a).

To summarize this section of the chapter on neurolaw, Satel and Lilienfeld (2013) have written an accessible book, entitled "Brainwashed," that dispels some of the incorrect logic in the use of the new neuroscientific procedures in court. In the end, the authors maintained that the brain does not make people behave; rather, people themselves do that. Therefore, in this regard, the brain is not the responsible agent for people's (potential) control of their behavior. Granted, the brain constitutes an important substrate underlying behavior, but it does not stand as the unique determinant of behavior. To think otherwise constitutes "neurocentrism." For Satel and Lilienfeld (2013), there is no "neurosignature" of guilt, even though the scientific level might reduce people to their brain function. Satel and Lilienfeld (2013) concluded that people are agentic selves who do the deciding of their behavior after weighing the outcomes of possible decisions in this regard. The brain might "afford" this agency but does not cause it alone.

Human agency needs to be considered from a multi-faceted, pluralistic perspective. In this vein, Martin (2012) adopted a model that is quite biopsychosocial and one that is quite consistent with my own view on the causality of behavior. He referred to the developmental emergence of self-determination (agency) within an evolutionary, biophysical/sociocultural context. For Martin (2012), people can be simultaneously "determined" and self-determinate as complex causal agents. [Note. I had referred to my equivalent biopsychosocial model as one that is developmental, evolutionary, and "biopersonalsocial."]

New Term

Beyond the issue of causality in the sense of responsibility, voluntariness, and cognitive control in the criminal act at issue, or their lack as in the excusing insanity defense, and beyond the issue that free will and determinism are irrelevant to the question, the field of forensic criminal psychology and psychiatry also is addressing the causation of the criminal act in order to obtain possible mitigation of sentencing, in particular. That being said, although criminal responsibility can be exonerated for reasons such as reaching the bar of legally-defined insanity, in many cases, the causation that presumably underlies psychiatric/psychological states at the time of an alleged criminal act cannot be scientifically established with sufficient precision in order to address the matter unequivocally. Moreover, there is usually more than one cause involved in the causation of a criminal act, in the sense that it is best conceived from the biopsychosocial framework, even if individually and collectively the factors involved do not qualify for the insanity defense.

Considering that, in any endeavor to understand human behavior, the biopsychosocial approach provides a plausible model, a more general term on causality that integrates this term could prove useful. As it exists, the term biopsychosocial helps integrate the various physical/psychological, personal (coping, personality, etc.), and sociocultural (family, neighborhood. society) factors applicable to understanding the origins of behavior in a legal case at hand. In this sense, as has been argued above, the model applies to both the criminal and tort contexts. Further, it helps us understand the limits of neurolaw in court. Neurosciences afford only one avenue in understanding causation of behavior and it clearly risks excluding psychosocial factors that complement biological ones in this regard.

In this sense, for understanding behavior in either the criminal or civil (e.g., tort) context, the medical, mental health, and legal fields might want to investigate the value of referring to "biopsychosocial causality" in order to specify its multifactorial components and interactions and to address the common issues that these fields have about causality of behavior (e.g., in criminal conduct by a perpetrator and in survivor psychological condition after a negligent act, respectively). Unifying causality understanding in criminal and civil contexts might help unify forensic psychology, too, which often shows disjoint between the criminal and civil (e.g., tort) sides.

To conclude, I propose a concept that might help disambiguate the legal terms used in causal analysis. The term "biopsychosocial" causation might be used profitably to address causality both in the criminal and civil (e.g., tort) context (e.g., criminal conduct and survivor psychological condition after a tortious event, respectively). The term would give sufficient leeway for understanding the multifactorial nature of behavioral causality in the legal context, and unify the approach to causality of behavior in the law with related disciplines in mental health.

In the following, I propose other terms that might help legally in understanding causation. This time, my suggestions concern legal language itself. First, I review causality and causation in civil law.

Chapter Conclusions

This sojourn in this chapter into the causality of psychological injuries in relation to law has not been a secondary exercise because, in general, the concepts in this field for causality are consistent with and informative for the discipline of psychology and of related ones. Psychological injuries involve biological, personal, and social factors. They involve pre-existing, precipitating, and propagating factors. Their discernment relies on "but-for" argumentation, or the counterfactual. In the end, it seeks the necessary and sufficient, material cause to the injury in the event at claim, as well as other factors that might be involved. These types of considerations in causality determination in legal cases are complementary to those in other areas of mental health practice. However, the legal bars set, such as for reaching thresholds of actionable negligence and tort, or catastrophic impairment, are not typically encountered in other areas of mental health practice or of psychology, in general.

Moreover, this area of causality study involves types of influences not typically encountered in the field, such as iatrogenesis, or how the system can harm complainants, and also the biased nature of the system in which complainants find themselves. The chapter also deals with differences between causality in psychological injury cases and in criminal cases. It does find some commonalities in this regard, such as the importance of factors that speak to the biopsychosocial model. Nevertheless, in the criminal context, the accused needs to meet the bar of having knowingly committed a wrong, and so is responsible for his or her transgressions (and this without the presence of mitigating factors). Overall, this chapter and the next one indicate that the area of the psychological injury and law has much to contribute to the study of causality, in general. Causality is central to most every case in law, and what we learn about it in the area of psychological injury and law should be central to its understanding in psychology, in general.

References

Aggarwal, N. K., & Ford, E. (2013). The neuroethics and neurolaw of brain injury. *Behavioral Sciences and the Law, 31*, 789–802.

American Law Institute. (2000). *A concise restatement of torts*. St. Paul, MN: Author.

American Psychiatric Association. (2013). *Diagnostic and statistical manual of mental disorders: DSM-V* (5th ed.). Washington: American Psychiatric Association.

Appelbaum, P. S., & Scurich, N. (2014). Impact of behavioral genetic evidence on the adjudication of criminal behavior. *The Journal of the American Academy of Psychiatry and the Law, 42*, 91–100.

Bagshaw, R. (2011). Causing the behaviour of others and other causal mixtures. In R. Goldberg (Ed.), *Perspectives on causation* (pp. 361–381). Oxford, UK: Hart.

Barth, R. J., Kertay, L., & Steinberg, J. S. (2014). Mental illness. In J. M. Melhorn, J. B. Talmage, W. E. Ackerman III, & M. H. Hyman (Eds.), *AMA guides to the evaluation of disease and injury causation* (2nd ed., pp. 485–523). Chicago, IL: American Medical Association.

Bernston, G. (2006). Reasoning about brains. In J. Cacioppo, P. Visser, & C. Pickett (Eds.), *Social neuroscience: People thinking about thinking people* (pp. 1–11). Cambridge, MA: MIT Press.

Brooks, C. N., & Melhorn, J. M. (2014). Apportionment. In J. M. Melhorn, J. B. Talmage, W. E. Ackerman III, & M. H. Hyman (Eds.), *AMA guides to the evaluation of disease and injury causation* (2nd ed., pp. 139–148). Chicago, IL: American Medical Association.

Call, J. A. (2003). Liability for psychological injury: History of the concept. In I. Z. Schultz & D. O. Brady (Eds.), *Psychological injuries at trial* (pp. 40–64). Chicago, IL: American Bar Association.

Casartelli, L., & Chiamulera, C. (2013). Which future for neuroscience in forensic psychiatry: Theoretical hurdles and empirical chances. *Frontiers in Psychiatry, 4*, 74. doi:10.3389/fpsyt.2013.00074.

Caspi, A., McClay, J., Moffitt, T. E., Mill, J., Martin, J., Craig, I. W., et al. (2002). Role of genotype in the cycle of violence in maltreated children. *Science, 297*, 851–854.

Claydon, L. (2012). Are there lessons to be learned from a more scientific approach to mental condition defences? *International Journal of Law and Psychiatry, 35*, 88–98.

Cranor, C. F. (2011). The challenge of developing science for the law of torts. In R. Goldberg (Ed.), *Perspectives on causation* (pp. 261–281). Oxford, UK: Hart.

Daller, M. F. (2000). *Tort law desk reference: A fifty state compendium*. New York: Aspen Law and Business.

Dawid, A. P. (2011). The role of scientific and statistical evidence in assessing causality. In R. Goldberg (Ed.), *Perspectives on causation* (pp. 133–147). Oxford, UK: Hart.

Deitz, D. C. (2014). Causation: The insurer's (payer's) perspective. In J. M. Melhorn, J. B. Talmage, W. E. Ackerman III, & M. H. Hyman (Eds.), *AMA guides to the evaluation of disease and injury causation* (2nd ed., pp. 657–666). Chicago, IL: American Medical Association.

DePaolo, D. J., & Rassp, R. G. (2014). Causation: The attorney's perspective. In J. M. Melhorn, J. B. Talmage, W. E. Ackerman III, & M. H. Hyman (Eds.), *AMA guides to the evaluation of disease and injury causation* (2nd ed., pp. 615–626). Chicago, IL: American Medical Association.

Ferguson, C. J., & Beaver, K. M. (2009). Natural born killers: The genetic origins of extreme violence. *Aggression and Violent Behavior, 14*, 286–294.

Fleming, J. G. (1998). *The law of torts* (9th ed.). Sydney, Australia: Thomson Professional Publishing.

Foote, W. E., & Lareau, C. R. (2013). Psychological evaluation of emotional damages in tort cases. In R. K. Otto & I. B. Weiner (Eds.), *Handbook of psychology: Vol. 11. Forensic psychology* (2nd ed., pp. 172–200). Hoboken, NJ: Wiley.

Frederick, R. I. (2012). Insanity defense, diminished capacity, mitigation. In D. Faust (Ed.), *Coping with psychiatric and psychological testimony* (6th ed., pp. 535–541). New York: Oxford University Press.

Fries, I. B., Melhorn, J. M., Hyman, M. H., & Talmage, J. B. (2014). The causality examination. In J. M. Melhorn, J. B. Talmage, W. E. Ackerman III, & M. H. Hyman (Eds.), *AMA guides to the evaluation of disease and injury causation* (2nd ed., pp. 149–173). Chicago, IL: American Medical Association.

Garner, B. A. (Ed.). (2004). *Black's law dictionary* (8th ed.). St. Paul, MN: West.

Garner, B. A. (Ed.). (2009). *Black's law dictionary* (9th ed.). St. Paul, MN: West.

Gazzaniga, M. S., & Steven, M. S. (2004). Free will in twenty-first century: A discussion of neuroscience and the law. In B. Garland & M. S. Frankel (Eds.), *Neuroscience and the law: Brain, mind, and the scales of justice* (pp. 51–70). New York: Dana Press.

Goldberg, R. (2011a). *Perspectives on causation*. Oxford, UK: Hart.

Goldberg, R. (2011b). Preface. In R. Goldberg (Ed.), *Perspectives on causation*. Oxford, UK: Hart.

Goldberg, R. (2011c). Introduction. In R. Goldberg (Ed.), *Perspectives on causation* (pp. xix–xxx). Oxford, UK: Hart.

Goldberg, R. (2011d). Using scientific evidence to resolve causation problems in product liability: UK, US and French experiences. In R. Goldberg (Ed.), *Perspectives on causation* (pp. 149–178). Oxford, UK: Hart.

Golding, M., & Edmundson, W. (Eds.). (2005). *The Blackwell guide to the philosophy of law and legal theory*. Oxford, UK: Blackwell.

Goldstein, A. L., Morse, S. J., & Packer, I. K. (2013). Evaluation in criminal responsibility. In R. K. Otto & I. B. Weiner (Eds.), *Handbook of psychology. Vol. 11: Forensic psychology* (2nd ed., pp. 440–472). Hoboken, NJ: Wiley.

Gowensmith, W. N., Murrie, D. C., & Boccaccini, M. T. (2013). How reliable are forensic evaluations of legal sanity? *Law and Human Behavior, 37*, 98–106.

Green, S. (2014). *Causation in negligence*. Oxford, UK: Hart.

Greenberg, S. A., Otto, R. K., & Long, A. C. (2003). The utility of psychological testing in assessing emotional damages in personal injury litigation. *Assessment, 10*, 411–419.

Hart, H. L. A., & Honoré, T. (1959). *Causation in the law* (2nd ed.). Oxford, UK: Clarendon.

Hegmann, K. T., Thiese, M. S., Oostema, S. J., & Melhorn, J. M. (2014). Causal associations and determination of work-relatedness. In J. M. Melhorn, J. B. Talmage, W. E. Ackerman III, & M. H. Hyman (Eds.), *AMA guides to the evaluation of disease and injury causation* (2nd ed., pp. 105–114). Chicago, IL: American Medical Association.

Hodgson, D. (2011). *Intervening causation law: Common law, civil law and comparative law perspectives*. Saarbrücken, Germany: Lambert Academic.

Hoffmann, R. T. H. L. (2011). Causation. In R. Goldberg (Ed.), *Perspectives on causation* (pp. 3–10). Oxford, UK: Hart.

Hogg, M. (2011). Developing causal doctrine. In R. Goldberg (Ed.), *Perspectives on causation* (pp. 41–56). Oxford, UK: Hart.

Kane, A. W., & Dvoskin, J. A. (2011). *Evaluation for personal injury claims*. New York: Oxford University Press.

Kaufmann, P. M. (2013). Neuropsychologist experts and neurolaw: Cases, controversies, and admissibility challenges. *Behavioral Sciences and the Law, 31*, 739–755.

Keeton, W., Dobbs, D., Keeton, R., & Owen, D. (1984). Causation in fact. In W. L. Prosser & P. Keeton (Eds.), *Prosser and Keeton on torts* (5th ed., pp. 263–271). St. Paul, MN: West.

Korn, H. A., Johnson, M. A., & Chun, M. M. (2012). Neurolaw: Differential brain activity for Black and White faces predicts damage awards in hypothetical employment discrimination cases. *Social Neuroscience, 7*, 398–409.

Lucy, W. (2007). *Philosophy of private law*. Oxford, UK: Oxford University Press.

Martin, J. (2012). Agent causation and compatibilism reconsidered: The evolutionary and developmental emergence of self-determining persons. *Journal of Consciousness Studies, 19*, 161–175.

McLearen, A. M., Pietz, C. A., & Denney, R. L. (2004). Evaluation of psychological damages. In W. O'Donohue & E. R. Levensky (Eds.), *Handbook of forensic psychology: Resource for mental health and legal processionals* (pp. 267–299). San Diego, CA: Elsevier Academic Press.

Melhorn, J. M., Ackerman, W. E., III, Glass, L. S., Deitz, D. C., & Babitsky, S. (2014). Understanding work-relatedness. In J. M. Melhorn, J. B. Talmage, W. E. Ackerman III, & M. H. Hyman (Eds.), *AMA guides to the evaluation of disease and injury causation* (2nd ed., pp. 15–104). Chicago, IL: American Medical Association.

Melhorn, J. M., Talmage, J. B., Ackerman, W. E., III, & Hyman, M. H. (2014). *AMA guides to the evaluation of disease and injury causation* (2nd ed.). Chicago, IL: American Medical Association.

Melton, G. D., Petrila, J., Poythress, N. G., & Slobogin, C. (2007). A closer look at the insanity defense. In G. D. Melton, J. Petrila, N. G. Poythress, & C. Slobogin (Eds.), *Psychological evaluations for the courts: A handbook for mental health professionals and lawyers* (3rd ed., pp. 209–217). New York: Guilford Press.

Meltzer, C., Sze, G., Rommelfanger, K., Kinlaw, K., Banja, J., & Wolpe, P. (2013). Guidelines for the ethical use of NeuroImages in medical testimony: Report of a multi-disciplinary consensus conference. *American Journal of Neuroradiology, 35*, 632–637.

Meynen, G. (2013). A neurolaw perspective on psychiatric assessments of criminal responsibility: Decision-making, mental disorder, and the brain. *International Journal of Law & Psychiatry, 36*, 93–99.

Mish, F. C. (Ed.). (2003). *Merriam-Webster's collegiate dictionary* (11th ed.). Springfield, MA: Merriam-Webster.

Moore, B. E. (2014). Causation: A judge's perspective. In J. M. Melhorn, J. B. Talmage, W. E. Ackerman III, & M. H. Hyman (Eds.), *AMA guides to the evaluation of disease and injury causation* (2nd ed., pp. 627–644). Chicago, IL: American Medical Association.

Moore, M. S. (2009). *Causation and responsibility: An essay in law, morals, and metaphysics*. New York: Oxford University Press.

Moriarty, J. C., Langleben, D. D., & Provenzale, J. M. (2013). Brain trauma, PET scans and forensic complexity. *Behavioral Sciences & the Law, 31*, 702–720.

Morse, S. J. (2006). Brain overclaim syndrome and criminal responsibility: A diagnostic note. *Ohio State Journal of Criminal Law, 3*, 397–412.

Morse, S. J. (2011a). The status of neurolaw: A plea for current modesty and future cautious optimism. *Journal of Psychiatry & Law, 39*, 595–626.

Morse, S. J. (2011b). Gene-environment interactions, criminal responsibility, and sentencing. In K. A. Dodge & M. Rutter (Eds.), *Gene-environment interactions in developmental psychopathology* (pp. 207–234). New York: Guilford Press.

Overpeck, D. L., Krohn, M., Rabine, M., & Lovan, D. T. (2014). Causation: The workers' compensation commission perspective. In J. M. Melhorn, J. B. Talmage, W. E. Ackerman III, & M. H. Hyman (Eds.), *AMA guides to the evaluation of disease and injury causation* (2nd ed., pp. 665–671). Chicago, IL: American Medical Association.

Penney, S. (2012). Impulse control and criminal responsibility: Lessons from neuroscience. *International Journal of Law and Psychiatry, 35*, 99–103.

Perlin, J. (1989). *A forest journey: The role of wood in the development of civilization*. Cambridge, MA: Harvard University Press.

Perry, B. L., Neltner, M., & Allen, T. (2013). A paradox of bias: Racial differences in forensic psychiatric

diagnosis and determinations of criminal responsibility. *Race and Social Problems, 5*, 239–249.
Piechowski, L. D. (2014). Conducting personal injury evaluations. In I. B. Weiner & R. K. Otto (Eds.), *The handbook of forensic psychology* (4th ed., pp. 171–196). Hoboken, NJ: Wiley.
Rogers, R. (2008). An introduction to response styles. In R. Rogers (Ed.), *Clinical assessment of malingering and deception* (3rd ed., pp. 3–13). New York: Guilford Press.
R. V. McNaughten, 8 Eng. Rep. 718 (1843).
Rondinelli, R. D., Genovese, E., Katz, R. T., Mayer, T. G., Müller, K. L., Ranavaya, M. L., et al. (2008). *Guides to the evaluation of permanent impairment* (6th ed.). Chicago, IL: American Medical Association.
Sadoff, R. L., & Dattilio, F. M. (2011). Criminal responsibility. In E. Y. Drogin, F. M. Dattilio, R. L. Sadoff, & T. G. Gutheil (Eds.), *Handbook of forensic assessment: Psychological and psychiatric perspectives* (pp. 121–144). Hoboken, NJ: Wiley.
Satel, S., & Lilienfeld, S. O. (2013). *Brainwashed: The seductive appeal of mindless neuroscience*. New York: Basic Books.
Schleim, S. (2012). Brains in context in the neurolaw debate: The examples of free will and "dangerous" brains. *International Journal of Law and Psychiatry, 35*, 104–111.
Silva, J. A. (2009). Forensic psychiatry, neuroscience, and the law. *Journal of American Academy Psychiatry and the Law, 37*, 489–502.
Song, M. (2014). *Causation in insurance contract law*. New York: Routledge.
Spector, H. (2011). The MMTS analysis of causation. In R. Goldberg (Ed.), *Perspectives on causation* (pp. 339–359). Oxford, UK: Hart.
Stapleton, J. (2009). Causation in the law. In H. Beebee, C. Hitchcock, & P. Menzies (Eds.), *The Oxford handbook of causation* (pp. 744–769). New York: Oxford University Press.
Steinert, T., & Whittington, R. (2013). A bio-psycho-social model of violence related to mental health problems. *International Journal of Law and Psychiatry, 36*, 168–175.
Talmage, J. B., Freeman, G. C., Melhorn, J. M., & Hyman, M. H. (2014). Report writing. In J. M. Melhorn, J. B. Talmage, W. E. Ackerman III, & M. H. Hyman (Eds.), *AMA guides to the evaluation of disease and injury causation* (2nd ed., pp. 175–241). Chicago, IL: American Medical Association.
Talmage, J. B., Melhorn, J. M., Ackerman, W. E., III, & Barth, R. J. (2014). Musculoskeletal disorders: Conditions of uncertain pathophysiology – Acute and chronic pain. In J. M. Melhorn, J. B. Talmage, W. E. Ackerman III, & M. H. Hyman (Eds.), *AMA guides to the evaluation of disease and injury causation* (2nd ed., pp. 389–410). Chicago, IL: American Medical Association.
Thing v. La Chusa, 771 P.2d 814 (Cal. 1989).
Tuvblad, C., Narusyte, J., Grann, M., Sarnecki, J., & Lichtenstein, P. (2011). The genetic and environmental etiology of antisocial behavior from childhood to emerging adulthood. *Behavior Genetics, 41*, 629–640.
Wallace, D. L. (2014). Addiction postulates and legal causation, or who's in charge, person or brain? *The Journal of the American Academy of Psychiatry and the Law, 41*, 92–97.
Winters, R. C., Globokar, J. L., & Roberson, C. (2014). *An introduction to crime and crime causation*. Boca Raton, FL: CRC Press, Taylor & Francis Group.
Wright, R. W. (2007). Acts and omissions as positive and negative causes. In J. W. Neyers, E. Chambers, & S. J. Pitel (Eds.), *Emerging issues in tort law* (pp. 287–307). Oxford/Portland, OR: Hart.
Wright, R. W. (2011). The NESS account of natural causation: A response to criticisms. In R. Goldberg (Ed.), *Perspectives on causation* (pp. 195–220). Oxford, UK: Hart.
Young, G. (2008). Causality and causation in law, medicine, psychiatry, and psychology: Progression or regression? *Psychological Injury and Law, 1*, 161–181.
Young, G. (2010). Causes in the construction of causal law: A psycho-ecological model. *International Journal of Law and Psychiatry, 32*, 73–83.
Young, G. (2014). *Malingering, feigning, and response bias in psychiatric/psychological injury: Implications for practice and court*. Dordrecht, Netherlands: Springer Science+Business Media.
Young, G. (2015). Causality in criminal forensic and in civil disability cases: Legal and psychological comparison. *International Journal of Law and Psychiatry, 42–43*, 114–120.
Young, G., & Drogin, E. (2014). Psychological injury and law I: Causality, malingering, and PTSD. *Mental Health Law & Policy Journal, 3*, 373–417.
Young, G., & Kane, A. W. (2007). Causality in psychology and law. In G. Young, A. W. Kane, & K. Nicholson (Eds.), *Causality of psychological injury: Presenting evidence in court* (pp. 13–47). New York: Springer Science+Business Media.
Young, G., & Shore, R. (2007). Dictionary of terms related to causality, causation, law, and psychology. In G. Young, A. W. Kane, & K. Nicholson (Eds.), *Causality of psychological injury: Presenting evidence in court* (pp. 87–135). New York: Springer Science Business+Media.
Zapf, P. A., Golding, S. L., Roesch, R., & Pirelli, G. (2014). Assessing criminal responsibility. In I. B. Weiner & R. K. Otto (Eds.), *The handbook of forensic psychology* (4th ed., pp. 315–351). Hoboken, NJ: Wiley.

Causality in Psychological Injury and Law: Models

27

Chapter Introduction

As reviewed in the preceding chapter, psychological injuries refer to psychological conditions that eventuate after negligent actions and that cause mental harm and disability sufficient from a legal standpoint to activate claims against the liable party, e.g., conditions such as posttraumatic stress disorder (PTSD), chronic pain, and mild traumatic brain injury (TBI). The said conditions and functional impairments result from events at claim such as motor vehicle accidents (MVAs) and work injuries, which lead to corresponding legal actions in the venues at issue, such as in tort and worker compensation claims, respectively.

Psychological injury and law is best conceived as an area that integrates the biopsychosocial and forensic perspectives. The latter is involved both through the careful assessment procedures requires in the typical psychological injury case and in the possibility that malingering and related negative response biases mark a case. However, possible biases in psychological injury cases are not limited to the examinee. That is, the psychological injury case might be marked not only by possible biases expressed by complainants/evaluees, but also it could involve biases implicit or explicit in evaluators, as well as any third parties involved. Finally, in terms of understanding all the impacts that can complicate cases of psychological injury, participation in the medical, insurance, and legal processes in these types of cases can be iatrogenic for complainants/evaluees.

Given this preamble on the field psychological injury and law, the first part of the chapter focuses on extant models related to psychological injury and law and to causality in the field. In this regard, the chapter works toward proposing an inclusive model that incorporates iatrogenesis, which is critical in the field of psychological injury and law, but which, generally, is given less importance in psychology relative to medicine.

Specifically, the chapter presents models using dimensions related to intention and deception. That is, it examines models involving the intersection of dimensional spaces that can include both valid psychological conditions and processes, such as somatization, that might derive due to negligence, and also the category of negative response biases, including of malingering (which negates any possibility of having a valid psychological condition). This prepares the way for my own model on the matter, which is novel in how it creates a central space for more ambiguous, gray-zone cases. Also, it is novel in the placement in one of the four quadrants of the two-dimensional space of the model a construct related to a cry for help, termed a desperation cry. This term captures the nature of the cry in legitimate complainants in psychological injury cases who feel that they are not being heard and are being subject to undue pressures. A major goal in constructing this model had been to show how iatrogenesis fits into the system that acts on the

G. Young, *Unifying Causality and Psychology*, DOI 10.1007/978-3-319-24094-7_27

genuinely injured (or malingering) complainant/evaluee.

In conclusion, the role of the adversarial (plaintiff-defense) divide is ubiquitous in this area of practice, and recommendations are made for dealing with it and also with other ways in which effective and ethical practice might be compromised. Overall, one can conclude that much of the causality of psychological injuries that are attributed to an event at issue in a claim might be subject to legal dispute and, therefore, needs careful vetting.

Iatrogenesis in Psychological Injury

This chapter deals with a construct that is relatively poorly discussed in the psychological literature—that of iatrogenesis. The first part of the section deals with the term itself and then moves to related ones in the psychological injury and law context, such as litigation distress and the insurance process. The next part of the section reviews the relevant literature, focusing on iatrogenesis in the case of the major psychological injuries (PTSD, TBI, and chronic pain (and somatization)). Also, in this regard, it considers the concept of compensation neurosis.

Iatrogenesis is a concept commonly encountered in medicine, in general. However, it is less prevalent in psychiatry and psychology. In the area of psychological injury and law, iatrogenesis is encountered when treating professionals and disability examiners unjustly dismiss valid claims. Also, the converse of unjustly promoting invalid claims takes place. Iatrogenesis should be considered as part of a larger system in which there is litigation distress, stress from the insurance process, and so on, impacting the complainant or evaluee. At the same time, individuals might unduly exaggerate or even malinger about their symptoms, impairments, and disabilities, or have their attorneys encourage and coach the same. It remains difficult to tease out the effect of iatrogenesis on the development of psychological injuries, such as the major ones of chronic pain, PTSD, and propagation of mild TBI into a persistent post-concussive syndrome (PPCS). These conditions, and related ones that might develop after an event, such as in a worker compensation case or a tort one involving a MVA, reflect multifactorial causality. A biopsychosocial model combined with a forensic one is the best way to approach the causation, assessment and diagnosis, and treatment of psychological injuries. Iatrogenesis can fit nicely as one factor in this type of model.

Terms

Iatrogenesis in psychology refers to the process in which mental health workers generate a mental health condition or disorder through their demeanor, assessment, diagnosis, advice, comment, or treatment or other intervention. Iatrogenesis is commonly considered in the medical field, in general, but is rarely considered in psychology. However, in the area of psychological injury and law, iatrogenesis is considered one part of the multifactorial causality of patients' psychiatric/psychological condition. These causal factors not only include those that are pre-event, event, and post-event related, but also systemic ones, such as iatrogenesis, litigation distress, the insurance process, and the adversarial (plaintiff-defense) divide.

Iatrogenesis is a term that originated in medicine but is quite applicable to psychology. However, it is not as prevalent in the research on and even the lexicon in psychology compared to medicine. For purposes of making this point, I entered the term of iatrogenesis in PubMed, a medical literature search engine, and the number of articles tagged with the term approached 30,000. As for PsychInfo, the search engine for psychology (acknowledging that PubMed and PsychInfo cannot be so clearly divided in their contents), the number of tagged articles barely surpassed the 100 mark. Rees (2012) noted that the prevention for iatrogenic psychological harm is just as important as preventing physical harm, so that the goal of the present piece to bring to the fore this issue in the psychological literature is timely.

From the point of view of medicine, the term iatrogenesis concerns a harm induced by medical advice or treatment given to patients by medical doctors. Causally, the harm would not have arisen but for the intervention or advice involved (Wikipedia, 2014). For the discipline of psychology, Melton, Petrila, Poythress, and Slobogin (2007) provided a definition of iatrogenesis concerning a disorder that is precipitated, induced, or exacerbated by a mental health worker's attitude, evaluation, comment, or intervention. The definition could be more global by including iatrogenesis related to diagnostic issues. In this regard, I would add that giving a psychological diagnosis also could be iatrogenic, for example, if it is incorrect, or if there is no diagnosis at all that is applicable but one is made anyway. Also, missing a relevant diagnosis could be quite devastating to mental health and, therefore, constitute an iatrogenic factor.

In all these regards, from a psychological perspective, an integrated approach to iatrogenesis is that it consists of a product and a process. First, at the level of process, it generates an iatrogenic illness, disease, disorder, or condition through its harmful process. Second, at the level of product, the iatrogenic process consists of the interaction of the patient and the mental health worker (e.g., psychologist, psychiatrist) such that, together, the demeanor, assessment, diagnosis, advice, comment, and/or treatment/intervention of the latter adversely impact the psychological condition of the former.

About iatrogenesis and particular psychological injuries, Schatman (2011) commented on an article by Perret and Rosen (2011). Perret and Rosen addressed pain physicians' overreliance upon opioid analgesics in primary treatment, despite chronic opioid therapy's lack of sufficient evidence bases. Schatman noted the problems of potential safety issues involved and also the iatrogenetic effects that could result. These negative effects could impact both particular individuals and society, in general. The concerns of Perret and Rosen (2011) and Schatman (2011) echo those of Illich (1974). Aside from describing clinical iatrogenesis, Illich also described social iatrogenesis and cultural iatrogenesis.

Andrikopoulos and Greiffenstein (2012) referred to iatrogenesis in the diagnosis of PTSD. They presented two cases in which apparently well-intentioned treatment providers diagnosed PTSD inappropriately, causing unnecessary complications.

As for mild TBI/PPCS, several workers have referred to iatrogenetic effects, as well, for this psychological injury (e.g., Bender & Matusewicz, 2013). For example, the diagnosis of PPCS can be a self-propagating factor independent of any other factors, such as the short-lived effect of the original concussion, which might be associated with it.

Context

When they are valid, the psychological injuries involved in actionable claims are multifactorial in their causality (e.g., Young, 2007, 2008a, 2008b, 2008c, 2010, 2011, 2014a; Young & Yehuda, 2006). However, as noted, aside from biological (e.g., pathophysiological), psychological (e.g., poor coping, personality), and social (e.g., poor support) factors, part of the causal nexus might include iatrogenic effects. Moreover, because of the legal context in which these types of injuries are considered, one finds causal factors unique to these injuries. That is, in psychological injury cases, there are multiple possible factors extraneous to the typical biopsychosocial network in mental health causality. For example, they concern how complainants are perceived (e.g., honest or not) by those named in legal actions (e.g., the presumed negligent party and insurers (and their legal representatives)).

Moreover, the adversarial insurance and defense side against plaintiff actions have their own biases. Therefore, iatrogenesis stands as but one complicating causal factor among the many in the system impacting the complainant, and together they should be viewed as constituting a powerful system that impacts the complainant. Because the full system picture in causality of psychological injuries includes factors impacting the person beyond the usual psychological considerations, they detract from the person's sense of control and can have impacts that affect their recovery from their psychological injuries.

Furthermore, patients might experience not only iatrogenic pressures and also litigation distress, they might have vulnerable histories, personalities, or psychopathologies that can explain either in part or in full. When the latter is the case, their present psychological condition might not relate at all to the negligent event at issue, and so their claims for post-event psychological injuries should be deemed invalid.

Returning to the question of their honesty, they might be unconsciously or consciously exaggerating or even feigning their symptoms, impairments, disorders, and disabilities (e.g., malingering). Note that symptom fabrication/feigning/exaggeration for unconscious reasons is not the same as malingering and, moreover, this process can take place even consciously (as a cry for help).

Historically in the field of psychological injury and law, Schultz (2003) put together the first monograph on the topic, and Young followed suit (Young, Kane, & Nicholson, 2006, 2007; also see Koch, Douglas, Nichols, & O'Neill, 2006; Schultz, 2008; Schultz & Stewart, 2008; Young, 2008a, 2008b, 2008c). Schultz and colleagues recognized iatrogenesis as one causal factor in psychological injuries, including it as part of a biopsychosocial and forensic model. As well, her model included recognition of other factors that I have mentioned, such litigation factors.

Also in this regard, in Schultz (2003), Call (2003) discussed the stressful nature of the legal process on psychological injury claims. He noted that the evidence does not support the contention that psychological symptoms improve once the litigation process comes to an end. Similarly, Bryant and Harvey (2003) found that litigation status had little effect on the maintenance of PTSD, return to work, and so on. Tellingly, Call (2003) argued that litigation can contribute to and maintain psychological trauma. When this happens, he referred to it being "jurisogenic" or "critogenic"—terms that are akin to iatrogenic. Young and Kane (2007) concurred, but added that the whole insurance process (from starting a claim and treatment, to going to multiple medical and other assessments, to passing through tort action and court) might be iatrogenic. In this regard, one could label the effect of the insurance process on psychological injury claimants as "insurogenic" or the like (with the effect being worrisome in different ways for exaggerating and non-exaggerating complainants).

Young and Kane (2007; also Young, 2014b) presented a multifactorial framework in the causality of psychological injury. Part of the context involved the factor of iatrogenic psychotherapy. The overall model included pre-existing, causal event, and post-event outcome factors. The effect of iatrogenic therapy and litigation distress might even begin at the time of the event (think—inappropriate critical incident counseling and ambulance chasers, respectively). Therefore, iatrogenesis not only affects the particular individuals involved but also has pernicious effects on society, in general.

The next part of the present chapter reviews recent publications on the multiple systemic factors that affect particular psychological conditions, impairments, and disabilities in psychological injury cases. They illustrate the problems in dealing with these types of cases, including in terms of iatrogenesis.

How Systemic Factors Influence Outcome in Psychological Injury

Posttraumatic Stress Disorder

Bootzin and Bailey (2005) examined three specific psychological treatments that had been intended to produce positive therapeutic effect; however, to the contrary, negative outcomes occurred (i.e., critical incident stress debriefing for PTSD; group therapy for adolescents with conduct disorders; and psychotherapy for dissociative disorder). The authors noted that, in the case of all three treatments, there was a dynamic interaction between specific and nonspecific mechanisms, which in some cases maximized the negative effects of therapeutic interventions. Iatrogenic effect emerges when intended and unintended diagnosis or treatment interacts to produce negative outcomes for the individual.

Bootzin and Bailey (2005) suggested that further research is needed to examine the interaction of specific and nonspecific mechanisms in order to minimize iatrogenic effects.

Traumatic Brain Injury

Iverson and Lange (2012) showed that the complications in assessment include expectation effects, which, in this case, means that injured individuals believe that certain symptoms will develop inevitably as a result of their injury. In this regard, just by itself, for injured patients, having received a diagnosis is sufficient to affect their presentation and performance. Further, in iatrogenesis, treating professionals might provide diagnoses that are incorrect and, consequently, the patients engage in behavior that facilitates a "self-fulfilling prophecy." Iverson and Lange (2012) added that, in the "good-old-days" bias, evaluees over-report how well they had been doing prior to the event at issue. In the nocebo effect, expectations also are involved (see next).

Vanderploeg, Belanger, and Kaufmann (2014) described the concept of nocebo effect in psychological injury (in the case of mild TBI leading to PPCS). Nocebo effects refer to the mere expectation that treatment or intervention will harm, which leads to the creation of or increase in symptoms. The nocebo is harmless or inert but, to the contrary, the outcome is harmful or negative. Further, inappropriate expectations or beliefs can be conveyed and lead to iatrogenic processes. Moreover, in the litigation context, treating professionals, attorneys, and plaintiff experts might excessively focus on the event at issue as the sole cause of the outcome involved (e.g., negative expectations for recovery). Hahn (1999) referred to nocebo as "expectations of sickness," which goes hand in hand with iatrogenesis.

Figure 27.1 presents a graphic depiction of the multiple factors to consider in one type of psychological injury—mild TBI (after Iverson, 2011, 2012). The figure includes a role for iatrogenesis. It places iatrogenesis in the full spectrum of factors that could influence evaluee outcome. These include pre-injury factors, injury factors, and post-injury factors. The pre-injury ones might be sufficient to explain any and all adverse outcomes, such as PPCS. The post-injury factors include ones unrelated to the event at claim, and these might, as well, fully explain any PPCS. The negative response bias ones include malingering, which would nullify any attribution of PPCS.

Bender and Matusewicz (2013) examined the area of post-concussive syndrome (PCS) and factors that could explain the persistence of PCS, such as malingering. They queried the validity of PCS—it lacks specificity, its diagnostic utility is questionable, and the dividing line between it and genuine symptomatology due to mild TBI is not specifiable. Furthermore, it is subject to extraneous factors, such as iatrogenic and "jurisogenic" ones, which complicate its explanation in terms of malingering. Also, "compensation neurosis" might lead to exaggeration of symptoms, which would then be "mostly internally-generated motivation." In addition, there are psychological factors that develop post-injury that might interfere with recovery (e.g., depression, poor coping). Moreover, illness perceptions in patients might lead to adoption of the sick role. The authors added that expectations of what the symptoms might mean influence patient presentation (called "expectation as etiology," "diagnostic threat"). Finally, evaluees might minimize pre-injury factors, which could influence (or even "create") their presentation and performance.

Pain

In somatoform and dissociative disorders, Merten and Merckelbach (2013) argued that SVT (symptom validity test) failure and negative response bias in evaluees especially indicate their uncooperativeness, lack of genuine presentation, and lack of face value in presented life history and symptoms. Further, neither psychological problems (such as unconscious conflicts and depression) nor context (e.g., a cry for help) could explain evaluee negative response bias in terms other than malingering. Finally, evaluees in non-litigating contexts might have "hidden agendas"

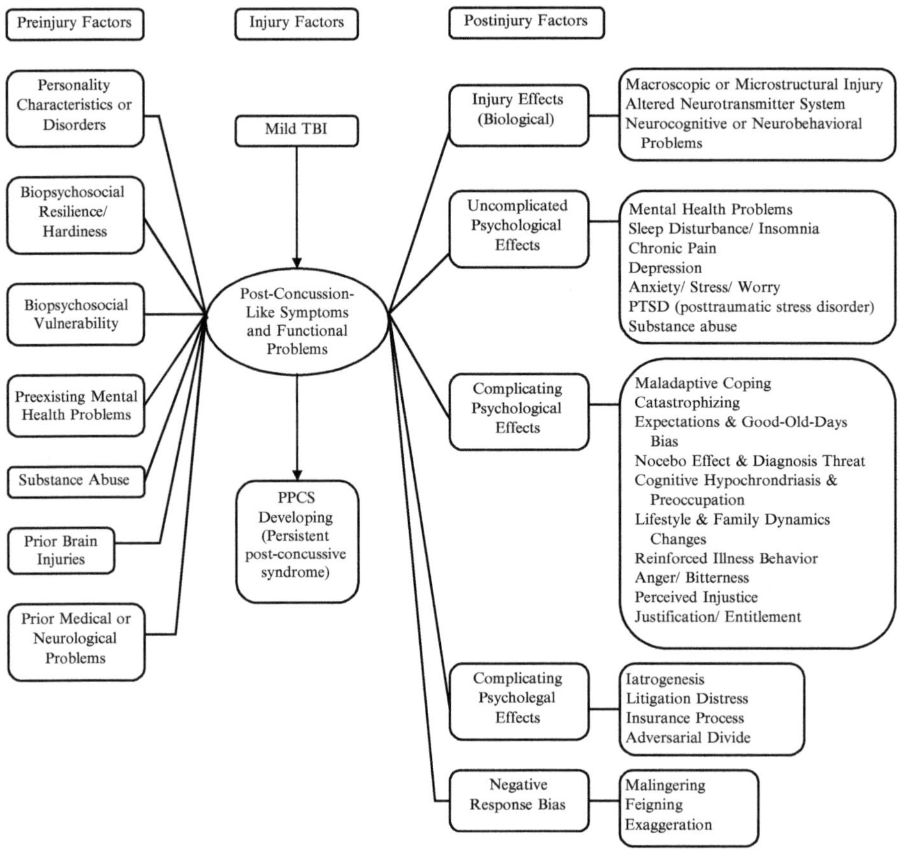

Fig. 27.1 A biopsychosocial conceptual model of poor outcome after mild traumatic brain injury. *Note*. The original figure of their model of poor outcome from mild traumatic brain disorder (TBI) did not mention malingering, feigning, and exaggeration (negative response bias), nor did it include separately complicating legal effects (such as the role of litigation distress, iatrogenesis, the insurance process, and the adversarial (plaintiff-defense) divide). The original figure has been altered to put distal pre-injury factors to the left, injury factors medially, and the post-injury factor to the right. Adapted from Iverson (2011, 2012)

about the outcome of litigation factors (e.g., seeking benefits).

Young (2008b) referred to Deary, Chalder, and Sharpe (2007), who presented a cognitive-behavioral model of medically unexplained symptoms (MUS). In a somatization process, symptom generation takes place because of three factors—predisposing, precipitating, and perpetuating ones. Overall, chronic pain needs to be understood in a systems perspective that examines the whole, including iatrogenic effects due to medical uncertainty and lack of medical explanation/guidance. Moreover, a systems model usually specifies sources of individual differences.

Young (2008b) further pointed to the work of Johnson (2008), who described chronic stress in relation to the HPA (hypothalamic–pituitary–adrenal) axis in MUS. In the normal process, an initial increase in cortisol in reaction to stress decreases through feedback mechanisms. When the system is disturbed, the cycle is interrupted. Hypercortisolism is perpetuated by chronic or multiple stressors that produce, at first, hypercortisolism but, with chronicity, both exhaustion and hypocortisolism develop. Specifically, when stress becomes chronic, the HPA axis is pushed toward hypocortisolism instead of hypercortisolism. Moreover, there are individual differences in hypocortisolism, including those related to decrease in free cortisol, cortisol resistance, and reduced biosynthesis of cortisol; indeed, for some individuals, the development of hypocortisolism does not take place. The allostatic load model is a related one to that of somatization; it explains how chronic stress creates the conditions for decline in health (McEwen & Lasley, 2003). All these models are biopsychosocial in nature.

Compensation Neurosis

Hall and Hall (2012) proposed that the concept of "compensation neurosis" (Kennedy, 1946; Miller, 1961a, 1961b) still should be current in the field. Compensation neurosis concerns symptom exaggeration related to not only the prospect of secondary gain in a case but also to internal motivations (e.g., stress from the case; stress from treatment issues; effects on somatization; aspects of personality, such as dependence). The difference between compensation neurosis and malingering is that in the former the presence of internal motivations is much more than the external incentives but, for the latter, the presence of external incentives is the sole motivator.

According to Hall and Hall (2012), compensation neurosis does not refer to symptom absence, in that there are physical symptoms involved. Rather, it refers to the causes for the symptoms, which do not involve "real" injuries related to the event at hand; instead, they are seen to reflect psychosomatic processes. Moreover, because of their personality structure, those reacting this way might be individuals who are prone to react to in this manner and develop symptoms beyond those expected by the events at claim (and so manifesting compensation neurosis as presently defined). About the stress of the case at hand, Hall and Hall (2012) concluded that it includes conscious and unconscious pressures that influence the complainant not to improve. In all these senses, it easy to understand how the legal and disability arena can be considered iatrogenic.

To conclude the presentation of the paper by Hall and Hall (2012), in Young (2014a), I noted that the iatrogenic potential in the insurance process might derive not only from patients' conscious and unconscious motivations for unfair financial compensation but also from undue pressures brought to bear by insurers or in Insurer Examinations (IEs) and the subsequent unjust denial of claims. Moreover, the notion of compensation neurosis might be difficult to diagnose with any reliability, given its inclusion of conscious and unconscious motivations, internal and external incentives, and so on. However, that being said, to their credit, Hall and Hall (2012) have acknowledged the complexity involved in the process of symptom hardening in patients, and underscored that it might exclude the event at claim as any part of the causes involved.

Disability claims and disability evaluations take place in an adversarial procedure, which serves to increase the psychological costs for the complainant (more anger, wanting revenge, loss aversion). Furthermore, in order to make clear their claim to evaluators, the stress of the compensation/insurance/litigation process might lead evaluees to try too hard rather than less hard. Therefore, when suboptimal effort or symptom magnification is evident in disability assessment, this may occur for reasons other than conscious processes and malingering. That being said, the insurance process might be stressful or effortful not only because of trying harder but also because of efforts to falsely present or produce symptoms, as in malingering.

Overall, the biopsychosocial approach stands as an inclusive one, but it needs to incorporate a systemic or forensic component for better applicability in the area of psychological injury and law. In the present context, the systemic/forensic aspect refers not only to possible malingering by the examinee but also to the host of iatrogenic factors in the insurance process and in medicolegal proceedings that deal with the examinee. Also, it refers to the effect on psychological injury complainants of potential monetary and related compensation (from legal actions). For example, to present a balanced view, rather than just noting the possible deleterious effect of the legal and related system on individual complainants when they have their legitimate injuries denied, potential financial and other benefits that are claimed by the individual or plaintiff (and contested by the third payor/defendant) might function to activate unconscious somatization processes in ways totally independent of the legitimate effects of the event at issue. And, these unconscious somatization processes, consequently, would act to exacerbate injury-related symptoms, with the worsened symptoms so caused presented as event-related and thus meriting compensation, aside from any question of conscious malingering that might further lead to claims of worsening symptoms. Kirmayer and Taillefer (1997) also had integrated forensic components into their model of somatoform symptoms. Their category of social responses includes the effects of treatment providers, work conditions and, of note, the disability insurance and compensation systems.

Conclusion

So far, somatization and malingering, the former being an unconscious process, and the latter a conscious one, have been discussed mostly as two independent pathways to symptom exaggeration. However, there might be ways in which the two processes combine to the point of creating disability. For example, an initial injury might be relatively mild but is exacerbated by conscious wishes for monetary gain that eventually becomes unconscious. In such cases, the process of entertaining unconscious wishes to obtain compensation, at a level beyond what might be indicated by the nature of the genuine injuries involved, propagates post-event symptoms to the point that they attain thresholds of impairment and disability. For example, the patient ends up firmly believing that he/she has been injured seriously (although that had not been the case), and aside from the stress, lack of sleep, anger against the insurance process, and so on, that might act to worsen symptoms, most of the symptom worsening, if not all of it, is due to conscious wishes for monetary gain in legal actions that transforms to unconscious wishes that conspire to produce the serious pain involved and all related symptoms.

The individual, therefore, might facilitate in an unconscious way the development, amplification, magnification, or exacerbation of symptoms, even to the level of being serious, for initial conscious reasons of financial gain or secondary gain that are either conveniently forgotten or unconsciously suppressed to justify the legal actions undertaken for the gain. The unconsciously driven, centrally-mediated sensitization processes that take place for financial ends might even balance out or counter times when the evaluee had initially engaged in good effort to mitigate the losses involved, both physically and psychologically. That is, internally-generated physiological and stress responses might, for financial gain, serve to undermine any improvements made post-injury, with the reasons ultimately being the conscious search for financial profit that only later slips into unconscious processes. Moreover, the individual might become increasingly adamant that the event at claim is responsible for all the effects of the event involved, believing this very strongly and without recall of the original conscious motivation to exaggerate for financial gain.

Therefore, given the somatization that is activated in this scenario, the evaluator should consider that the symptoms presented/produced in a scenario like it should be interpreted as being related to a desire for financial gain, or malingered. The somatization-malingering model being presented excludes from its organization solely conscious malingering for financial gain, given that somatization, per se, would not taking place when malingering alone is at issue.

Of course, there is very little way to prove step by step the model presented in any one case. However, by presenting it, I am alerting assessors to the complex processes that might be involved in malingering. Others refer to partial compared to full malingering, which is only somewhat equivalent to my argument. In the end, only careful, comprehensive assessment with multiple testing can differentiate full, partial, and related malingering, and other negative response biases, as well as feigning and non-credible presentation and performance, in general.

To summarize the various scenarios just offered for the types of evaluee psychological processes that might be involved in psychological injuries, the process involved is the following. First, a conscious incentive for financial gain develops and interrupts legitimate recovery from injuries in an event at claim after a genuine conscious effort to mitigate loss, and involving, at most, a relatively minor injury at that. Then, the person slips into an unconscious mode in which the originally consciously exacerbated/created symptoms in the person take on an unconscious life of their own, and the person might become increasingly strident and feeling entitled despite an absence originally of any genuine serious injury.

Young (2014b) developed several models related to the causation of psychological injury and the manner in which causality is conceived and constructed in the legal system. In the following, I review these models, and present a model that I have developed to integrate them, a model that includes iatrogenesis. The model is forensic in focus, as well. Therefore, it can accommodate complex evaluee scenarios in the gray zone.

New Model of Causation in Psychological Injury, Including Iatrogenesis

Introduction

In the following, I review various models applicable to the field of psychological injury and law. The first one considered is a biopsychosocial and forensic model of coping in psychological injury that I had developed (Young, 2008c). It includes mention of iatrogenesis and so is pertinent to the present discussion of theory in psychological injury and law. However, iatrogenesis must be seen in the broader multifactorial causal complex of psychological injuries, and so modeling in the area should take a broad, systemic approach of not only factors affecting the individual evaluee but also factors affecting the evaluators of evaluees and the whole system, too. Therefore, it helps to see broad causal models not only applicable to these injuries specifically but also to how the field functions generally. The field of psychological injury and law is a young one and, at the outset, in helping to coalesce it, I was concerned in developing integrative models (e.g., for chronic pain, see Young & Chapman, 2007).

Coping

Introduction In Young (2008c), I had created an integrated biopsychosocial and forensic model of coping applicable to the field of psychological injury and law. The model is illustrated in the table accompanying the text; it gives its basic parameters and dimensions (see Table 27.1). Note that the model includes litigation factors and, also, it points to factors compatible with iatrogenesis, although this term is not used explicitly.

After further discussion of this model in what follows, I present a more generalized psychological model of legal causality, as originally described in Young (2010). Finally, this section of the chapter reviews a balanced model that I have recently developed of bias in the system in which psychological injuries are considered (Young, 2014a). It examines not only patient biases but also broader systemic ones. These various models that I have developed have prepared the way for the integrated one on the various strands in the present chapter, as they apply to the relationship of malingering, somatization, psychiatric disorder, iatrogenesis, and related constructs. Before arriving at this final step in the chapter on an integrated model of biases in the field, I review others models that attempt to integrate the influences in these regards in the field. These other models that have been created have oriented me in my modeling endeavors.

Model As mentioned, the biopsychosocial forensic model of coping presented in Young (2008c) does not include iatrogenesis, per se, although it considers other related factors that impact psychological injuries, such as coping with the medico/psycholegal context and the insurance process. In terms of the biopsychosocial influences on coping, as indicated in Table 27.1, biological factors

Table 27.1 Components of a biopsychosocial forensic model of coping

Biological factors	Psychological factors	Sociocultural factors	Forensic factors
Health condition	Coping strategies	Socioeconomics	Medico/psycholegal context
Symptoms	Behavior	Work, school	Apparent effort, malingering
Severity	Appraisals, cognition	Family, spouse	Forensic appraisals, cognitions
Chronicity	Affect	Friends	Pre-existing coping quality
Disability	Role strain	Community	Barriers to good coping
Genetics, congenital	Resilience, resistance	Social support	Impacts on coping skills
Gender, sex	Personality	Family doctor	New techniques learned
Age	Intellectual abilities	Health care, caregivers	Openness to learning
Medications, treatments	Social skills	Insurance	Adherence to learning, mitigation
Stress responses	Coping history	Legal support	Coping with service providers
Addictions	Resilience history	Culture	Coping with insurance
Medical history	Psychological history	Ecology	Coping with court, law

Adopted with permission of Springer Science + Business Media. Young, G. (2008c). Coping in psychological injury: A biopsychosocial and forensic perspective. *Psychological Injury and Law, 1*, 276–286; with kind permission from Springer Science + Business Media B. V. [Table 1, Page 283]

include effects of genetics, stress responses, and addictions. Psychological factors include roles for coping skills, cognitive appraisals, and personality. Sociocultural factors include influences from work, insurance, and health care provider support. Forensic factors include consequences of mitigation of loss, coping with court/law, and malingering.

Young (2008c) noted that therapy should address the *forensic appraisals*, or cognitive evaluations and perceptions that are related to the legal context, which might get in the way of effective coping. These forensic appraisals refer to the cognitions that complainants might develop in the context of their psychological injuries and the pursuit of their case in court. Although the filter of attempting to feign for monetary gain, as in malingering, represents an obvious if not notorious forensic appraisal that might influence complainants in their claims to court, there are others that complicate the forensic assessment process and also the understanding by the courts and related venues of psychological injuries. Moreover, these other forensic appraisals, which are more likely to be present, could discourage optimal recovery, even if they are unrelated to intentions to deceive for monetary gain.

In this regard, individuals with psychological injuries might appraise that the compounding stresses of iatrogenic, insurance, and legal-related matters are taxing beyond acceptable thresholds of their coping capacities. Or, they might believe that their monthly financial benefits are capped too low in their insurance policy (or perhaps inappropriately by the adjudicator involved) and, as a result, they and their family are suffering for reasons beyond their control. These types of forensic appraisals in psychological injury cases, or potentially destructive thought processes, would act to compound the stresses that survivors with psychological injuries making legal claims for their injuries are experiencing from their legitimate injuries.

Or, other forensic appraisals might be formed that serve to undermine any recovery taking place for their psychological injuries. For example, individuals might believe that their treatment providers do not understand their injuries and, therefore, these patients resort to constantly seeking medical cures, even though psychological ones should be targeted. Also, they might appraise that their insurer is denying access to needed therapies without good medical reason and, as a result, the patients feel an increased stress, which functions to aggravate their injuries.

Psycho-Ecological Model

Introduction Young (2010) described another model in the field of psychological injury and law that is related to iatrogenesis, the psycho-ecological model of legal causality. The model in Young (2010) is not just on causality in law but how laws related to causality and related matters get constructed. In this regard, the model consists of five concentric circles that represent the series of increasing distal interacting influences on the construction of law as one gravitates away from the inner circle. Therefore, the model is depicted as a series of concentric circles, for example, with the person in a case represented in the middle and the impacts of increasingly distal influences on the person represented by the concentric circles, but with the influences in the circles mutually influencing each other.

By the term the construction of law, I am not referring to the procedures in drafting laws but to the wider dynamics involved. We need a complex model of legal causality and its construction because legal terms and tests are not as clear as they need to be. Also, the dynamics involved in the creation of causal tests and thresholds in the legal system are influenced by factors that go beyond the law, per se.

Model The model specifies the layers of influence not only tests of causality in the legal arena but also those that influence the psychological injuries of complainants. In this regard, the circle that is closer to any case at hand functions as a direct impact on the person—that is, as represented in the circle, the adversarial divide serves as an immediate influence that exerts pressure on the person, on the one hand, but also on the court system in terms, on the other hand, in terms of the pressures that it exerts on other actors in the system, including attorneys and insurers. In this regard, not only might the person be influenced to exaggerate symptoms or even malinger, but also assessors might feel influenced by the divide, for example, to engage in biased and incomplete assessments for the benefit of either the plaintiff or defense side. Further in this regard, the evidence gathered in an assessment might be insufficiently reliable and valid to meet admissibility standards of good compared to poor or junk science, and not function to help the court according to extant criteria of good science for court purposes, as elucidated in *Daubert v. Merrell Dow Pharmaceuticals, Inc*. (1993), in particular, and subsequent rulings in the *Daubert* trilogy.

These latter rulings require that evidence presented to court should be more probative than prejudicial relative to a case at hand, and fit it relevantly. Also, many other factors could adversely impact and mitigate against impartial assessments, such as use of biased research. The latter might involve conflicts of interest and litigation science, which involves science targeting legal questions without the expected parameters of independent science. When presenting evidence to court in a case at hand, the scientific process followed should be neutral throughout, from assessment and testing, to diagnosis and ruling in or out of malingering and related negative response biases, to conclusions proffered, or else the evidence could be considered impartial and not meeting the criteria of good science as spelled out in the field, in general.

For Young (2010), in order to better grasp the causality of psychological injuries and the construction of laws related to them, models need to consider the psychology of all actors and agents in the system, and not just that of complainants. Granted, the post-incident mental health of a complainant might be malingered or might be compromised by pre-existing mental health difficulties (e.g., personality disorder, psychopathology; and not only by whether the person is engaging in anything like malingering), so that the causality of the psychological injuries at issue might be difficult to ascertain. That being said, beyond this consideration, other aspects of the system could influence outcome of cases outside of the psychology of the complainant. For example, judges' dispositions might impact their reactions and preferences in admissibility hearings. Most important, as mentioned, attorneys argue their case from the adversarial divide, which has profound effects on legal proceedings right from the first contact with complainants. Also, experts who are evaluating complainants might be influenced by the legal referral source within the divide, especially because of their own self-interest and gratifications (e.g., monetary; Young et al., 2007). Finally, there are wider sociocultural and historicopolitical considerations impacting the construction of laws related to psychological injuries in court and related venues, not the least of which might be inordinate pressures on government agencies by the insurance industry.

Comment To conclude, in Young (2010), I noted that the insurance industry in the legal arena acts as a pressure on impartiality. Also, industry stakeholders generally bring pressure on the government to enact laws favorable to their interests.

In this regard, Haack (2008) has revisited the testimony proffered by experts in *Daubert v. Merrell Dow Pharmaceuticals, Inc.* (1993), through the parallel case of *Blum v. Merrell Dow Pharmaceuticals* (764 A.2d 1, 2000) in the US state of Pennsylvania. In this revealing case, Judge Bernstein exposed the lack of forthrightness in the testimony that had been offered in *Daubert*.

For example, a senior executive in the drug company involved in *Daubert* admitted to picking and choosing information over a 30-year period. One scientist after another who had participated in *Daubert* admitted to their lack of scientific rigor under Judge Bernstein's "devastating scrutiny" in Blum. For instance, one expert acknowledged that the biomedical company involved had consistently "underreported" the adverse effects of the medication at issue, and another expert testified that the company had supported research out of its legal defense funds.

Young (2010) noted that his psycho-ecological model of law construction also considers mental health at this level because the general approach of a society toward its members, its minorities, the wronged, those seeking justice, and its most vulnerable are important. Moreover, societal attitudes in this regard play an indirect role in legal construction. They could very well influence parties seeking to influence the process of law construction for their own interests. In short, the influences that affect how laws are constructed, ultimately, include all of us as a society. For the legal context of psychological injury and law, some of the shortcomings found in relevant laws, and in their ultimate disposition and effects, might reflect our own shortsightedness.

To summarize, the psycho-ecological model of causality as developed by Young (2010) is an integrated one for court purposes that incorporates process (e.g., good law) and product (e.g., good mental health evaluation). I use the label of "psycho-ecological" to emphasize the role of context in constructing law and also the role of psychological factors in all major actors and agents involved in the system in which complainants find themselves. These influences range from the individual complainants involved, to the professionals involved, including attorneys and mental health evaluators, to institutions, such as that of the insurance industry, and to the wider society, which means all of us in our attitudes.

Biases

Introduction In Young (2014a), I developed a model that extended my work in Young (2010) on the widespread biases that can influence complainants, evaluators, and parts of the system in psychological injury cases. In that book, I presented a model of the dimensions underlying systemic influences on evaluees claiming psychological injuries and their assessment.

Model The integrated model that I developed on influences on all actors and agents in the psychological injury and law context includes a role for conscious influences for financial gain, in particular, not only for complainants but also for other systemic actors in the tort and disability context (see Fig. 27.2). For example, the top part of the

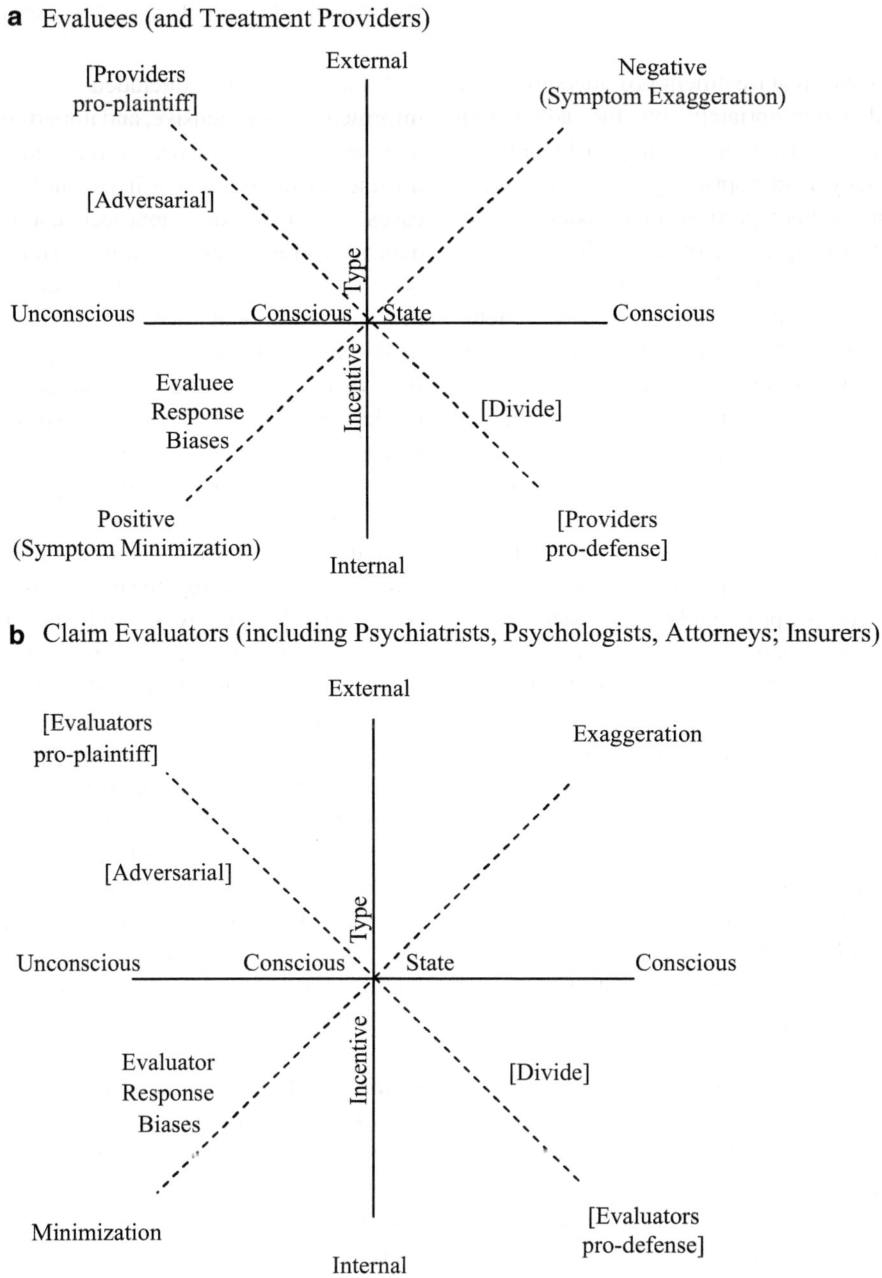

Fig. 27.2 Financial and psychological pressures influencing evaluees/clients and evaluators/treatment providers. (**a**) The figure illustrates the potential of evaluees to malinger or engage in self-unfavorable, non-credible presentations. They might act consciously for external rewards/financial gains by expressing negative response bias or excessive symptom exaggeration, for example. Other types of symptom exaggeration might be unconscious and for internal incentives, for example, as might be found in factitious disorder. Evaluees might express symptom minimization in a positive response bias. The adversarial divide refers to whether evaluators fall on the plaintiff or defense side of the case at hand, but even treatment providers might be unduly influenced by it, e.g., with respect to either their patients' attorneys or their insurers. (**b**) The second part of the figure indicates that the same pressures apply to the full range of evaluating professionals on a case, including mental health professionals, and not only insurers and attorneys. Valid claims might be denied because of undue influence stemming from the adversarial divide, or invalid claims might be supported. Adopted with permission of Springer Science + Business Media. Young, G. (2014). *Malingering, feigning, and response bias in psychiatric/psychological injury: Implications for Practice and court*. Dordrecht, Netherlands: Springer Science + Business Media; with kind permission from Springer Science + Business Media B. V. [Figure 5.1, Page 112]

figure indicates that treatment providers might be influenced inappropriately by the adversarial divide and, therefore, either support inappropriately or deny inappropriately a patient's treatment plan. In this regard, in this model, as with others in this chapter, I emphasize that the influence of bias on actors and agents in psychological injury cases and related disability systems might not be limited just to its effect on complainants (e.g., as in malingering).

The bottom part of the figure specifies a dimension in psychological injury work showing that more than complainants and plaintiffs might engage in behavior for financial gain, whether for reasons that are conscious or unconscious. In this regard, as mentioned previously, insurers might also behave inappropriately, for example, by denying valid treatment plans. Also, plaintiff attorneys might inappropriately coach plaintiffs how to cheat the system (or simply have information on their websites, e.g., about the symptoms of PTSD, that indirectly do the same). To conclude, the range of influences on the individual at the center of a psychological injury case might be extensive, going well beyond anything like having a motivation to malinger.

That being said, Young (2014a) noted that, in cases of psychological injury, malingerers cost the system immensely. Therefore, the best malingering detection methods and systems need to be used, in order to arrive at accuracy in malingering detection and attribution. At the same time, evaluees might express exaggeration and biases for reasons that might be more unconsciously than consciously motivated (i.e., exaggerating for reasons that do not involve financial gain). Factors other than malingering might explain their exaggerations, and these might be legitimate (e.g., crying out for help, catastrophizing). Or, a patient might persist in seeking compensation despite symptom amelioration, in the mistaken belief that the negligent party should pay for the transgression at issue consistent with the level of the original injury and no matter what had been the ultimate outcome of their injuries, e.g., full or great improvement.

Young (2014a) concluded that a science-informed, comprehensive, and impartial approach to assessments can provide some balance to these diverse biasing influences in psychological injury cases. A science-first approach applies to how data are gathered reliably, how the data are interpreted, and how they are presented to court. In this way, additional sources of bias, such as evident in iatrogenesis, the insurance process, litigation distress, and the adversarial divide, are minimized, countered, and reduced to a level at which they cannot do harm, whether this approach applies to the injured party or to the system as a whole (e.g., the insurer).

In this way, additional sources of bias, such as found in each of iatrogenesis, the insurance process, litigation distress, and the adversarial divide, are minimized, countered, and do less or no harm. Mental health assessors have an important equilibrating role to play in this imbalanced system when they adopt this up-front scientific attitude; biases would be diminished, both in terms of dealing with the injured and being part of the system (e.g., the insurer). For example, in a balanced approach to assessment of complainants, appropriate screening for negative response bias would benefit insurers. And, not overinterpreting cases as malingered ones would benefit complainants.

Comment Greiffenstein and Kaufmann (2012) addressed one component of the biases in the legal side of the system in which psychological injury is involved, and their work is consistent with my approach. The authors described legal proceedings that take place in adversarial settings, and they noted that attorneys are "zealous" advocates in this regard. That is, the goal for attorneys in psychological injury cases is to "win" in the proceedings, a goal that is considered more important than functioning with accuracy and objectivity. Moreover, from the point of view of attorneys, justice is considered more important than truth itself. This does not mean that in their ethics and training, and later practice, attorneys are given license to lie. Nevertheless, the legal agenda in psychological injury cases does allow attorneys to exclude expert or other reports if they are not supportive of the goal of advocating successfully for their clients. That is, from the perspective of an attorney, no matter what the side, an accurate, comprehensive, and balanced report might not be helpful or might even be harmful to the case at hand.

Young (2014a) concluded that working in the area of psychological injury is challenging not only because of the need for an integrated biopsychosocial and functional perspective, but also because of the difficulties presented by the additional stresses that accompany the forensic, insurance, and legal contexts. For example, injured parties might have to deal with (a) anger about the insurance process, (b) anxiety about medical examinations, (c) anxiety about insurance examinations, (d) the stress of cross-examinations, (e) the losses due to their inability to work, or (f) stress from having physical therapies terminated prematurely in valid cases or, conversely, stress from being detected in not giving adequate effort in physical therapies and also continuously exaggerating symptoms, even to the point of malingering. Given the forensic and legal aspects of psychological injury cases, mental health professionals should carefully keep track of their patients' apparent effort/motivation, compliance/adherence to treatment, cooperation in completing therapeutic homework assignments, and, in general, their attempts to mitigate loss. Functioning in this manner would ensure that workers in the field obtain valid determinations of patient symptoms, impairments, disorders, and disabilities, or conversely, that the role of exaggeration, response bias, and possible malingering in patient performance and presentation is addressed adequately.

Iatrogenesis

Introduction

Several models have been constructed that represent the relationships among intentionality and deception in behavior to the psychological conditions and categories of malingering, factitious disorder, and other related psychiatric disorders. The said models include psychological conditions that might be problematic in court, such as conversion disorder or somatoform disorder. Among these models, one finds my own (Young, 2014a). All of these models take a dimensional approach, with aspects such as intention ranging from clear to minimal or no overt motivation. After this section, as presented in Young (2014a), I propose a new integrated model along these lines, and include the concepts of iatrogenesis, insurance process, litigation distress, and the adversarial divide. But, first, consider the following related models that have influenced the construction of my own integrated one.

Other Models

(a) Ruff and Jamora (2009) modeled the relationship of malingering, factitious disorder, and exaggeration/reduced effort in the space created by juxtaposing two dimensions, as well. For them, the two dimensions involved those of: (a) incentive (which can be either internal or external) and (b) consciousness (which can be either conscious or unconscious). Ruff and Jamora added the sociocultural context as an encompassing background to their dimensional model (see Fig. 27.3).

(b) Boone (2011) developed a unidimensional model of malingering and psychiatric disorder involving deception. She placed malingering on the "other deception" end of the deception continuum, and somatoform disorder, or adopting the sick role, on the "self-deception one" (see Fig. 27.4).

(c) Bass and Halligan (2007) used a two-dimensional model to represent malingering and related negative response biases. Their model consisted of the dimensions of (a) choice: which can be either intentional or non-intentional; and (b) responsibility: which can be either exculpated or in deception. The two dimensions, when aligned on the vertical

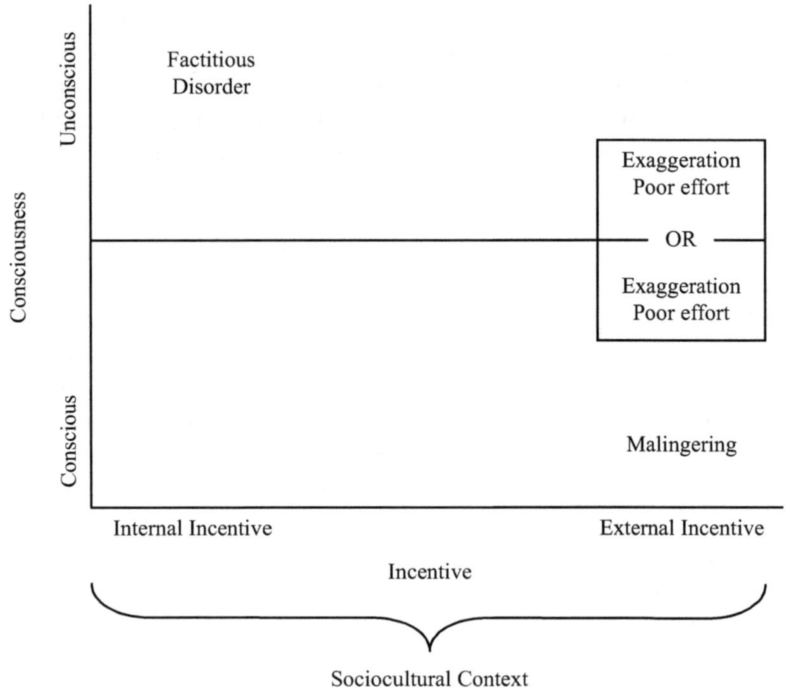

Fig. 27.3 The relationship between conscious/unconscious and incentive in understanding factitious disorder and malingering. Symptom invalidity is difficult to differentiate from malingering, poor effort, and exaggeration. Moreover, the latter two might take place for either conscious or unconscious reasons. Adapted from Ruff and Jamora (2009)

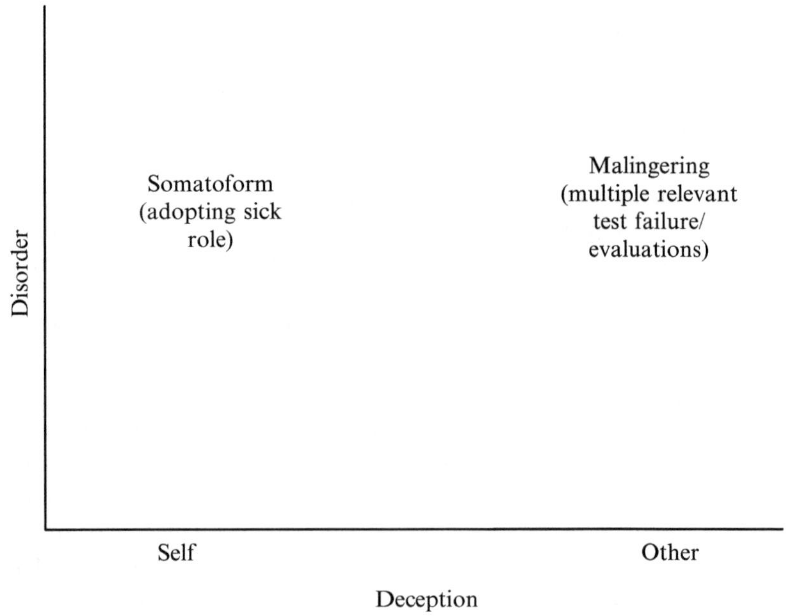

Fig. 27.4 The relationship between disorder and deception in understanding in somatoform presentation and malingering presentation. Malingering is related to deceiving others, somatoform disorder to deceiving oneself. Psychological testing can help differentiate them (e.g., using the MMPI-2-RF). Adapted from Boone (2011)

and horizontal axes, create a space in which both disorders and complicating factors can be situated (see Fig. 27.5). In this regard, the space created by the two dimensions involved allows one to place malingering/exaggeration and related states, as well more genuine psychiatric/psychosocial disorders.

(d) Similarly, Hall and Hall (2012) used a two-dimensional model to represent the various negative response biases and disorders in

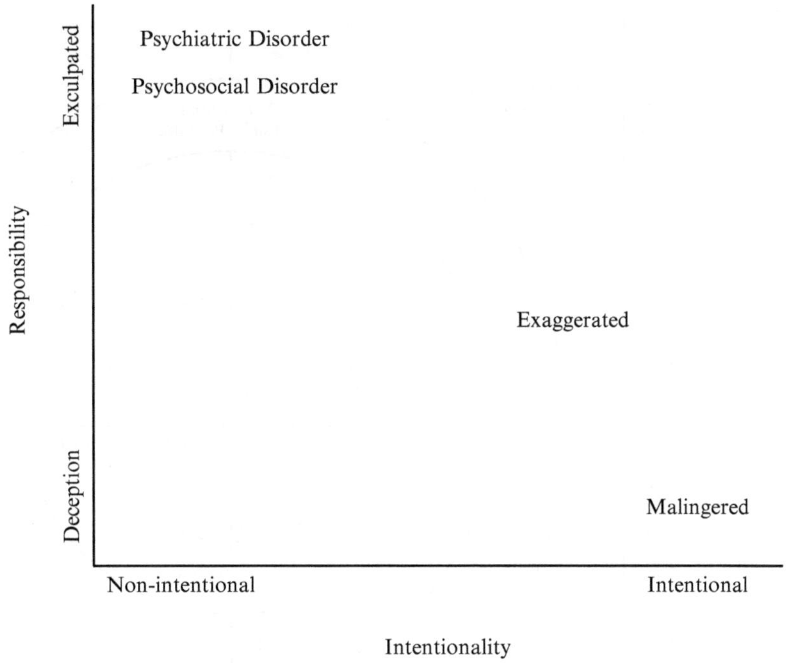

Fig. 27.5 The relationship between responsibility and intention in the generation of malingering. Diagnosis of disorder (and attribution of malingering) depends on where the evaluee stands with respect to two dimensions, involving intention and responsibility, in particular. The assessor does not consider just the choice of assigning disorder or some form of deception (e.g., malingering). Exaggeration might also be a valid option to consider. Adapted from Bass and Halligan (2007)

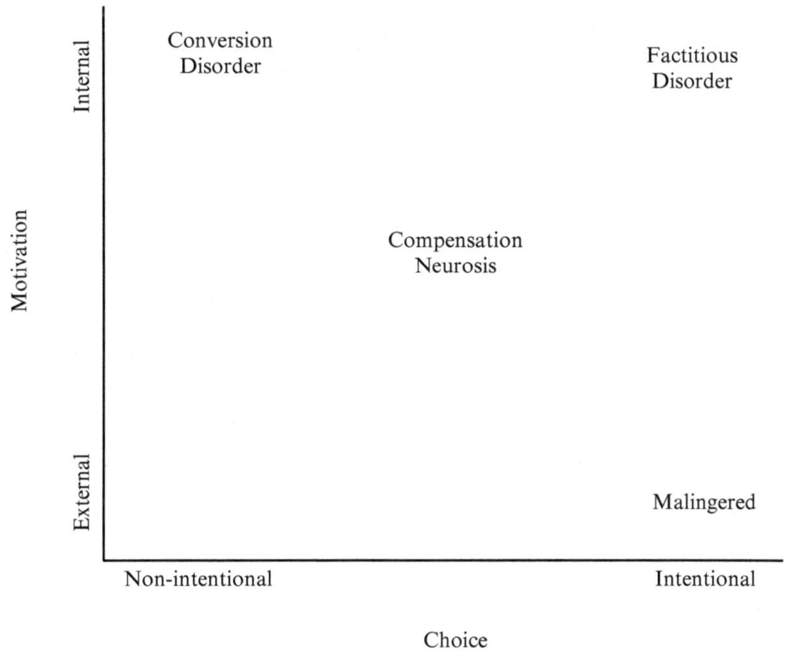

Fig. 27.6 The relationship between motivation and choice in the generation of malingering. Diagnosis of disorder (and attribution of malingering) depends on where the evaluee stands with respect to two dimensions, involving intention and choice, in particular. The assessor does not just consider the choice of assigning disorder or some form of deception (e.g., malingering). Compensation neurosis might also be a valid option to consider. Adapted from Hall and Hall (2012)

psychological injury cases. The dimensions concern the level of (a) choice (intentional, non-intentional) and (b) motivation (internal, external). They allow one to place in the space created malingering, factitious disorder, conversion disorder, and compensation neurosis (see Fig. 27.6).

My Integrated Model of Causality in Psychological Injury and Complicating Factors, Including Iatrogenesis

Model In the following, I present a model that is based on the prior models that are outlined above. The focus of the present model relates to a

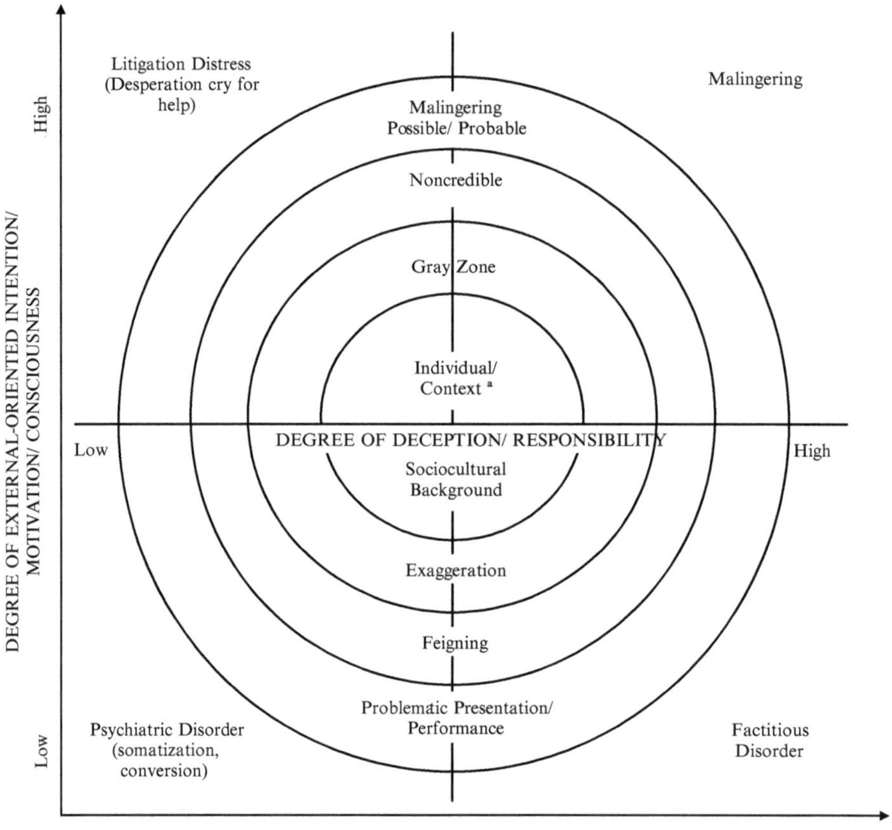

Fig. 27.7 Model of intention and deception in forensic and related disability evaluations and claims. Behavior in forensic and related contexts of disability evaluations and claims is influenced by multiple factors other than the event at claim and any subsequent injuries, physical or psychological. This behavior appears to vary along two major dimensions, relating to intentionality and deception. Developmental age and sociocultural context also are important to consider. Intention might be external, conscious (e.g., for financial gain) or internal, unconscious (e.g., in illness behavior that promotes overly solicitous behavior). The central part of the figure indicates that there is a gray zone in evaluee presentation and performance that makes it difficult to attribute a diagnosis or to infer malingering. Evaluee behavior that elicits doubt can be described as feigning, non-credible, and so on. If the evidence is clear for a disorder or syndrome, however, a diagnosis such as posttraumatic stress disorder (PTSD), pain disorder, or mild traumatic brain injury (TBI) can be given. However, the diagnosis might be one involving a disorder or condition less clearly related to the event at claim, such as conversion disorder. Also, factors such as litigation distress and the insurance process might be responsible for a cry for help, including unconsciously and out of desperation, rather than it reflecting anything like malingering.

As for the four quadrants of the model, they help define and differentiate four crucial conditions in the psychological injury and law context. Assessors might diagnose a psychiatric disorder when there appears to be absent or low conscious intentionality in behavior, presentation, and performance related to externally-oriented motivations. These would include the complicating diagnoses in psychological injuries related to somatization and conversion diagnoses (i.e., in the DSM-5 (Diagnostic and Statistical Manual of Mental Disorders, Fifth Edition; American Psychiatric Association, 2013), these refer to conversion (functional) disorder and complex somatic symptom disorder, respectively). When there is absent to low externally-oriented intention/motivation/ conscious state, but the degree of deception is high, the appropriate diagnosis might be factitious disorder. As for the high end of intentionality related to externally driven incentives, for upper-end levels of deception, malingering is an appropriate inference. As for absent to low levels of deception at this level of intentionality, a desperate cry for help can be attributed (related to litigation distress, for example). *Note.* [a]Context: (1) Degree to which deception is an adaptation that is acceptable and/or is coached. (2) Degree system exacerbates symptoms (iatrogenesis; insurance process; litigation distress; adversarial divide, etc.). (3) Culture, race, etc.

continuum of credible/non-credible presentation/performances in terms of two dimensions—related to (a) whether the individual is expressing deception or responsibility and (b) whether the nature of their expression is intentional or not (see Fig. 27.7). In contrast to the prior models, I indicate that determination of either valid psychological conditions or of malingering and related negative response biases is difficult because many cases in the area involve uncertainty, ambiguity, indecision, and imprecision in diagnosis and ruling in or out complicating factors such as malingering. That is, even though my model resembles the others by using the dimensions of deception/responsibility and intention, the middle area involving the so-called gray zone takes prominence.

That is, by considering these two dimensions of deception/responsibility and degree of intentionality simultaneously, my model places many psychological injury cases, which usually do not present or perform unambiguously, as often lying in the intermediate gray zone. The latter could include the exaggerations mentioned in the model of Bass and Halligan (2007), which they separated from malingering, which is an approach consistent with my own. However, even exaggeration presents difficulties in determining their intent, and they could constitute malingering, depending on what is found in the whole examinee file, including on testing. In this regard, in Young (2014a), I acknowledged the complications and difficulties in discerning the status of the validity of psychological injury claims, and noted that, because of the multiple factors involved in cases, (a) even mild exaggerations could be non-credible and (b) gross exaggerations could be credible. [Note. Aside from the major axes of intention and deception/responsibility and the consideration of context, a third dimension of the model could include developmental level or age.]

Factors Aside from incorporating the approaches and issues inherent in prior models of the relationship of intent and deception with respect to malingering or nonconscious-derived disorders, the combined model that I am proposing presently in this chapter on malingering and related presentations/performances considers the following three factors. These factors concern: (a) context; (b) how the dimensions involved intersect; and (c) the manner of placement in the dimensional space involved those presentations and performances that are not problematic, and not clearly disorder at one extreme nor malingered at the other. The following section of the chapter presents material related to these factors involved in the model currently being discussed.

(a) The context is important in psychological injury cases. In such cases, evaluee behavior is influenced by the complete system in which the evaluation takes place. The evaluee might demonstrate incentive for monetary gain and attempt to consciously fabricate and deceive. At the same time, the evaluee might be subject to systematic pressures to deny valid injury claims; moreover, in this process, even treating professionals might play a role, for example, by denying valid claims themselves (one aspect of iatrogenesis). Therefore, on the one hand, the evaluee might express a culture of entitlement/acceptance of deception as an adaptation, or even be influenced toward this attitude by its coaching (e.g., by the plaintiff attorney in the adversarial divide). These factors stand out as possible important ones in what has been called the disability epidemic (e.g., Bass & Halligan, 2014; Bass, Halligan, & Oakley, 2003). Moreover, treating professionals might contribute to this epidemic in an unwitting fashion, for example, by promoting false or exaggerated claims as involving disability or by administering inappropriate or even harmful therapy or intervention (which is another aspect of iatrogenesis). Conversely, in psychological injury cases, there might be systemic factors minimizing claims (and iatrogenically harming patients) through factors such as the insurance process, litigation distress, and the behavior and actions defense attorneys in the adversarial divide.

(b) The two dimensions typically considered in extant models relating malingering, factitious disorder, and so on, as reviewed above, appear to represent (1) degree of externally-oriented intention/motivation/conscious awareness, and (2) degree of deception/responsibility. These dimensions are continual rather than categorical, in the sense they are not all or none in nature, but they represent different degrees of the behavior involved, i.e., intent and deception/responsibility. Their intersection creates a 2×2 axis model that allows for different degrees of intent and deception/responsibility in psychological injury cases, at least in the sense of how these dimensions are defined. Moreover, the two-dimensional space created by the juxtaposition of the axes allow for the placement of relevant categories and conditions in the psychological injury and law context, including all of those mentioned in the prior models reviewed above. That is, the intersection of the dimensions of intent and deception/responsibility affords the location in the space created of the categories and conditions of malingering, factitious disorder, and so on.In the model that I developed, given the central importance given to gray-zone cases and the placement of these gray-zone cases in the middle of the model in the figure, I positioned these other major constructs being considered (e.g., malingering, genuine psychological disorders) at the outer edges in the two-dimensional space created by juxtaposing the two axes involved, that is, in the extreme outer portions of the four quadrants created by their orthogonal alignment. That is, because the more definite conditions and categories are more extreme in terms of their standing with respect to the continual dimensions of intent and deception/responsibility relative to gray-zone cases that form the heart of the present model, these conditions/categories have been placed at the outer edges of the model.Therefore, less controversial performances and presentations of psychological injury cases, such as those cases that involve only mild exaggeration, are placed in the central portions in the model, and not the outer edges. To remind in this regard, mild exaggeration does not constitute malingering (Bass & Halligan, 2007, 2014; Young, 2014a). That is, presentations and performances of these types in psychological injury cases should not be considered as belonging to an outer end of any quadrant in the proposed model, that is, as clear signs of malingering.

(c) The upshot of the prior explanation of the present model on the nature of presentation and performance of psychological injury complainants in terms of the dimensions of deception/responsibility and intent is that the center of the two-dimensional space that is created by juxtaposing the dimensions should be reserved for the ambiguous, indeterminate gray-zone cases, which are problematic for assessors because they do not clearly indicate either outright malingering at one extreme or genuine disorder at the other extreme. Aspects of behavior in these cases related to mild exaggeration might fit best in this central location of the model, which is reserved for ambiguous or less clear cases, or for those not clearly disordered nor malingered, for example.

Given these considerations, Fig. 27.7 constitutes an integrated model of the relationship among malingering, factitious disorder, and other disorders, as they fit into the dimensions of degree of external/internal-oriented intentionality and degree of deception/responsibility. Further, prior models had not considered the unique combination of overt externally-oriented intentionality in the motivation of complainants coupled with an absence deception for purposes of monetary gain. In this regard, it makes sense to refer to this particular combination in the psychology of psychological injury complainants as litigation distress or a cry for help. The latter term might be used when the evidence points to any degree of exaggeration in patient presentation and performance, perhaps along with mitigating complicating factors, such as psychopathology, yet malingering does not seem apparent. Therefore, the assessor must seek other explanations for the behavior without using the explanation of malingering. It is surprising that the prior models discussed do not mention this common opposition of malingering and a cry for help, but I have rectified the lack in my equivalent model, which suggests alternative interpretations possible for exaggeration that exclude noncredibility or malingering.

However, that being said, cries for help can derive from both conscious and unconscious influences, and it is important to differentiate these motivations in the gray zone. In this sense, I suggest a new term for conscious intentional externally-oriented motivation without deception, per se, in the cries for help of psychological injury complainants, that of "desperation cry." It distinguishes from unconscious cries for help that take place because one is overwhelmed and is reaching out for help in a way that is out of awareness. An advantage of this term of desperation cry is that it reflects the typical meaning of the term of a cry for help in psychological injury cases (i.e., a conscious pleading for help in desperation).

Conclusion As for conclusions that should be offered in these types of assessments of psychological injury cases, professionals dealing with problematic presentations and performances, but without clear evidence of malingering, per se, should refer to feigning or dissimulation, in general, or even to noncredibility or possible/probable malingering. Further, the astute assessor who has enough valid evidence to indicate that gray-zone cases are quite non-credible will find the language needed in the conclusions proffered to discredit enough the examinee, yet without using the term of malingering.

To conclude, I have created a model that integrates the major themes of the chapter, both in terms of conditions that might arise to complicate a clear understanding of the psychological outcome of an event at claim, and in terms of complicating factors in establishing causality, from iatrogenesis to malingering. This model could help disambiguate complex cases in the areas of psychological injury and law, leading to better assessments, interpretations of the reliable data gathered in them, and the ruling in or out of complications, including that of malingering. The model includes important factors in its dimensions, which concern intention and deception for the most part, and it adds a component not considered in prior models, related to a cry for help. This addition helps fill the four quadrants of the model created by the juxtaposition of its two major axes or dimensions. Also, the model excludes for the most part from consideration at the crucial outer areas of the four quadrants involved aspects of cases and their assessment that might be minor considerations, such as mild exaggeration. In this regard, also, it considers gray zone, ambiguous cases in which psychological injury cases are difficult to disambiguate as being part of the central area of the model. Evaluators in this area of practice of psychological injury and law need to function from a scientifically-informed approach in their evaluations, which need to be comprehensive and impartial, as well, so that the present model might help in this regard by helping seeing the relationship of the major complications in the area, such as malingering, exaggeration, iatrogenesis, litigation distress, and the insurance process.

In the development of psychological injuries, such as the major ones of chronic pain, PTSD, and propagation of mild TBI into PPCS, it remains difficult to tease out the effect of iatrogenesis, and apportioning its role in the multifactorial causality involved. These major psychological injury conditions, and related ones that might develop after an event at claim, such as in a worker compensation case or in a tort case involving a MVA, reflect a multifactorial causality that has biopsychosocial origins. However, given the legal side of psychological injury cases, they need careful scrutiny for the validity of the conditions claimed. In this regard, a biopsychosocial model combined with a forensic one is the best way to understand the causation of claimed conditions, the actual conditions involved, and the best treatment for the psychological injuries involved. Iatrogenesis fits nicely as one factor in this type of model. It can exacerbate or even create psychological conditions, so that it should be part of the causal evaluative process in these types of cases. In my own work in the area, when litigation or insurance distress appears to be a causative factor among others, for example, I will indicate this in my conclusions to the assessment. Needless to say, the presence of iatrogenesis and related complications in causal analyses of psychological injury claims renders the cases forensically challenging. Nevertheless, in the complex scenarios of complainants filing legal claims for damages, assessors need to determine whether the event at issue contributed more than minimally (substantially, materially) to the psychological condition that might have developed post-event, and considering iatrogenesis and related complications should be part of the comprehensive assessments undertaken.

Chapter Conclusions

Summary

The present chapter and the last one have considered causality in the field of psychological injury and law. The first one reviewed concepts of causality that are applicable to forensic psychology both in the criminal and civil contexts, including of psychological injury and law. Also, it emphasized the value of the biopsychosocial model in this regard, both for understanding the actions of criminal perpetrators and the psychological effects (psychological injuries, e.g., PTSD) of survivors in civil negligence cases, such as in tort. The present chapter takes a broader view of causality in the civil context of psychological injuries by exploring both models that attempt to integrate the biopsychosocial and forensic aspects of such cases and other models related to bias, malingering, intent, deception, and possible psychological disorder in claimants. In this regard, I focus on the relatively neglected area in psychology of iatrogenesis, which is a prevalent one in medicine, and I develop a model inclusive of it in understanding the full causal system in psychological injury claims.

Specifically in this chapter, I underscore the value of a combined biopsychosocial and forensic approach in psychological injury cases. Also, I propose an integrative model that considers the relationship among malingering, litigation distress, and psychiatric disorders, including factitious disorder, and processes that affect presentation and performance in these types of cases, such as somatization, deception, and conscious motivation for financial gain. This new model includes placement of iatrogenesis among the multiple influences on psychological injury presentations. In addition, it places a new concept that I developed among the possible complications in psychological injury cases, or that of a conscious desperation cry for help. Also, the chapter analyzes the role of biasing effects of other actors and agents in the system, such as treatment providers, insurers, and attorneys.

Recommendations

Psychological injury and law is a burgeoning area of study and practice that asks for an appropriate ethical stance to resist its pulls and pushes. Often, these are implicit, and by becoming familiar with how it functions systematically, the professional is better protected. Also, mental health workers need to be aware of their ethical obligations to function with integrity, impartiality, and fairness (see Table 27.2).

The field of psychological injury and law can develop further if it were taught in graduate programs. Young (2014a) argued that graduate education programs need to consider the appropriate fundamentals for practice in the area of psychological injury and law. Students need to be made aware of: (a) the scientific foundations and controversies that are inherent in the area; (b) the nature of the adversarial divide in tort and other court venues; (c) the best evidence available on assessment tests and procedures; and (d) also the best empirical support for therapeutic intervention practice. Their practical experience should emphasize: (a) state-of-the-art scientific knowledge in the area; (b) the effect of bias in the field, with examination of both sides of debates that

Table 27.2 American Psychological Association forensic practice guidelines: responsibilities

Principle	Explanation
Impartiality and fairness	When providing expert testimony, providing therapeutic services, and so on, forensic workers strive to be accurate, impartial, fair, and independent (Ethical Principles of Psychologists and Code of Conduct Standard 2.01, American Psychological Association, 2002). They appreciate the adversarial nature in legal systems and aim to treat all participants with impartiality, and they also strive to weigh all data, opinions, and rival hypotheses impartially. When conducting forensic evaluations, forensic practitioners aim for an unbiased and impartial assessment, and they aim to avoid partisan presentation of evidence that is unrepresentative, incomplete, or inaccurate, which might mislead fact finders. This guideline does not preclude an assertive presentation of the data gathered and the reasoning used in arriving at any conclusion or professional product based on that data.

Adopted with permission of Springer Science + Business Media. Young, G. (2014). *Malingering, feigning, and response bias in psychiatric/psychological injury: Implications for Practice and court*. Dordrecht, Netherlands: Springer Science + Business Media; with kind permission from Springer Science + Business Media B. V. [Table 22.1, Page 469]

take place in the literature, and (c) training in and use of tests having forensically-acceptable psychometric properties (reliability, validity, etc.) for relevant populations. Continuing education opportunities also should emphasize these major themes for ethical and effective practice.

Researchers need to tackle the controversial, contentious, and divisive issues in the field, including the role of iatrogenesis, litigation distress, and so on. Young (2014a) maintained that it appears that no research deals with: (a) known patients who cry for help/catastrophize/somaticize, or express litigation distress, etc., (b) in comparison to known or presumably known malingerers and the usual control groups, e.g., healthy ones. I would broaden this suggestion to investigate all manners of cases that reside in the gray zone in this area relative to the other types of cases (e.g., known malingering, healthy). Until this type of research is undertaken, the research on putative known malingerers relative to other control groups would seem to be missing critical groups that would enable more accurate interpretations of the results in this type of research.

As for recommendations in dealing with iatrogenesis in the context of psychological injuries, all parties in the system should be aware of its potential presence and pernicious effects. Psychological iatrogenesis has been given little consideration in the literature compared to medical iatrogenesis. But its effects could be just as harmful. Iatrogenesis is part of a multifactorial complex system that patients have to learn about and deal with. However, treatment providers and others in the system dealing with patients have to be equally aware of it and related factors. The mental health of patients deserves nothing less. Patients require best ethical practices in dealing with them from all parties in the system involved (Young, 2014a).

To conclude the chapter, I contend that use of the models in the present chapter, including my penultimate one, in understanding psychological injury complainants and arriving at valid interpretations and conclusions about them is consistent with the scientifically-informed, comprehensive, and impartial approach needed in assessments in the area. This approach is expected both by professional practice standards and ethics and by court and related venues, and is the best one to guarantee fruitful career longevity.

References

American Psychiatric Association. (2013). *Diagnostic and statistical manual of mental disorders: DSM-5* (5th ed.). Washington, DC: Author.

American Psychological Association. (2002). Ethical principles of psychologists and code of conduct. *American Psychologist, 57*, 1060–1073.

Andrikopoulos, J., & Greiffenstein, M. F. (2012). Something to talk about? The status of post-traumatic stress disorder in clinical neuropsychology. In G. J. Larrabee (Ed.), *Forensic neuropsychology: A scientific approach* (2nd ed., pp. 365–400). New York: Oxford University Press.

Bass, C., & Halligan, P. W. (2007). Illness related deception: Social or psychiatric problem? *Journal of the Royal Society of Medicine, 100*, 81–84.

Bass, C., & Halligan, P. W. (2014). Factitious disorders and malingering: Challenges for clinical assessment and management. *The Lancet, 383*, 1422–1432.

Bass, C., Halligan, P. W., & Oakley, D. A. (2003). *Malingering and illness deception*. Oxford, UK: Oxford University Press.

Bender, S. D., & Matusewicz, M. (2013). PCS, iatrogenic symptoms, and malingering following concussion. *Psychological Injury and Law, 6*, 113–121.

Blum v. Merrell Dow Pharmaceuticals, Inc., 764 A.2d 1 (2000).

Boone, K. (2011). Somatoform disorders, factitious disorder, and malingering. In M. R. Schoenberg & J. G. Scott (Eds.), *The little black book of neuropsychology: A syndrome-based approach* (pp. 551–565). New York: Springer Science + Business Media.

Bootzin, R. R., & Bailey, E. T. (2005). Understanding placebo, nocebo, and iatrogenic treatment effects. *Journal of Clinical Psychology, 61*, 871–880.

Bryant, R. A., & Harvey, A. G. (2003). The influence of litigation on maintenance of posttraumatic stress disorder. *The Journal of Nervous and Mental Disease, 191*, 191–193.

Call, J. A. (2003). Liability for psychological injury: History of the concept. In I. Z. Schultz & D. O. Brady (Eds.), *Psychological injuries at trial* (pp. 40–64). Chicago, IL: American Bar Association.

Daubert v. Merrell Dow Pharmaceuticals, Inc., 509 U.S. 579, 113 S. Ct. 2786 (1993).

Deary, V., Chalder, T., & Sharpe, M. (2007). The cognitive behavioral model of medically unexplained symptoms: A theoretical and empirical review. *Clinical Psychology Review, 27*, 781–797.

Greiffenstein, M. F., & Kaufmann, P. M. (2012). Neuropsychology and the law: Principles of productive attorney-neuropsychologist relations. In G. J. Larrabee (Ed.), *Forensic neuropsychology: A scientific approach* (2nd ed., pp. 23–69). New York: Oxford University Press.

Haack, S. (2008). The whole truth and nothing but the truth. *Midwest Studies in Philosophy, 32*, 20–35.

Hahn, R. A. (1999). Expectations of sickness: Concept and evidence of the nocebo phenomenon. In I. Kirsch (Ed.), *How expectancies shape experience* (pp. 333–356). Washington, DC: American Psychological Association.

Hall, R. C. W., & Hall, R. C. W. (2012). Compensation neurosis: A too quickly forgotten concept? *Journal of the American Academy of Psychiatry and the Law, 40*, 390–398.

Iatrogenesis. (n.d.). In *Wikipedia*. Retrieved April 17, 2014, from http://en.wikipedia.org/wiki/Iatrogenesis

Illich, I. (1974). *Medical nemesis: The expropriation of health*. London: Calder & Boyars.

Iverson, G. L. (2011). Evidence-based neuropsychological assessment of sport-related concussion. In F. M. Webbe (Ed.), *Handbook of sport neuropsychology* (pp. 131–154). New York: Springer.

Iverson, G. L. (2012). A biopsychosocial conceptualization of poor outcome from mild traumatic brain injury. In J. J. Vasterling, R. A. Bryant, & T. M. Keane (Eds.), *PTSD and mild traumatic brain injury* (pp. 37–60). New York: Guilford Press.

Iverson, G. L., & Lange, R. T. (2012). Traumatic brain injury in the workplace. In S. S. Bush & G. L. Iverson (Eds.), *Neuropsychological assessment of work-related injuries* (pp. 9–67). New York: Guilford Press.

Johnson, S. K. (2008). *Medically unexplained illness: Gender and biopsychosocial implications*. Washington, DC: American Psychological Association.

Kennedy, F. (1946). The mind of the injured worker: Its effects on disability periods. *Compensation Medicine, 1*, 19–21.

Kirmayer, L. J., & Taillefer, S. (1997). Somatoform disorders. In S. M. Turner & M. Hersen (Eds.), *Adult psychopathology and diagnosis* (pp. 410–472). New York: Wiley.

Koch, W. J., Douglas, K. S., Nichols, T. L., & O'Neill, M. L. (2006). *Psychological injuries: Forensic assessment, treatment, and law*. New York: Oxford University Press.

McEwen, B., & Lasley, E. N. (2003). Allostatic load: When protection gives way to damage. *Advances in Mind-Body Medicine, 19*, 29–44.

Melton, G. D., Petrila, J., Poythress, N. G., & Slobogin, C. (2007). A closer look at the insanity defense. In G. D. Melton, J. Petrila, N. G. Poythress, & C. Slobogin (Eds.), *Psychological evaluations for the courts: A handbook for mental health professionals and lawyers* (3rd ed., pp. 209–217). New York: Guilford Press.

Merten, T., & Merckelbach, H. (2013). Symptom validity testing in somatoform and dissociative disorders: A critical review. *Psychological Injury and Law, 6*, 122–137.

Miller, H. (1961a). Accident neurosis. *British Medical Journal, 1*, 919–925.

Miller, H. (1961b). Accident neurosis II. *British Medical Journal, 1*, 992–998.

Perret, D., & Rosen, C. A. (2011). A physician driven solution – the Association for Medical Ethics, the Physician payment Sunshine Act, and ethical challenges in pain medicine. *Pain Medicine, 12*, 1361–1375.

Rees, C. (2012). Iatrogenic psychological harm. *Archives of Disease in Childhood, 97*, 440–446.

Ruff, R. M., & Jamora, C. W. (2009). Myths and mild traumatic brain injury. *Psychology Injury and Law, 2*, 34–42.

Schatman, M. E. (2011). Editorial: The suppression of evidence-basis in pain medicine and the physician-driven quest to re-establish it. *Pain Medicine, 12*, 1358–1360.

Schultz, I. Z. (2003). Psychological causality determination in personal injury and workers' compensation contexts. In I. Z. Schultz & D. O. Brady (Eds.), *Psychological injuries at trial* (pp. 102–125). Chicago, IL: American Bar Association.

Schultz, I. Z. (2008). Disentangling disability quagmire in psychological injury and law. Part I. Disability and return to work: Theories, methods and application. *Psychological Injury and Law, 1*, 94–102.

Schultz, I. Z., & Stewart, A. M. (2008). Disentangling disability quagmire in psychological injury and law. Part II. Evolution of disability models: Conceptual, methodological and forensic issues. *Psychological Injury and Law, 1*, 103–121.

Vanderploeg, R., Belanger, H. G., & Kaufmann, P. M. (2014). Nocebo effects and mild traumatic brain injury: Legal implications. *Psychological Injury and Law, 7*, 245–254.

Young, G. (2007). Causality: Concepts, issues, and recommendations. In G. Young, A. W. Kane, & K. Nicholson (Eds.), *Causality of psychological injury: Presenting evidence in court* (pp. 49–86). New York: Springer Science + Business Media.

Young, G. (2008a). Causality and causation in law, medicine, psychiatry, and psychology: Progression or regression? *Psychological Injury and Law, 1*, 161–181.

Young, G. (2008b). Somatization and medically unexplained symptoms in psychological injury: Diagnoses and dynamics. *Psychological Injury and Law, 1*, 224–242.

Young, G. (2008c). Coping in psychological injury: A biopsychosocial and forensic perspective. *Psychological Injury and Law, 1*, 276–286.

Young, G. (2010). Causes in the construction of causal law: A psycho-ecological model. *International Journal of Law and Psychiatry, 33*, 73–83.

Young, G. (2011). Erratum to: Trends in psychological/psychiatric injury and law: Continuing education, practice comments, recommendations. *Psycho logical Injury and Law, 4*, 56–87. [Originally published in 2010 in *Psychological Injury and Law, 3*, 323–355.]

Young, G. (2014a). *Malingering, feigning, and response bias in psychiatric/psychological injury: Implications for practice and court*. Dordrecht, Netherlands: Springer Science + Business Media.

Young, G. (2014b). Psychological injury and law II: Implications for mental health policy and ethics. *Mental Health Law & Policy Journal, 3*, 418–470.

Young, G., & Chapman, C. R. (2007). Pain, affect, nonlinear dynamical systems, and chronic pain: Bringing order to disorder. In G. Young, A. W. Kane, & K. Nicholson (Eds.), *Causality of psychological injury: Presenting evidence in court* (pp. 197–241). New York: Springer Science + Business Media.

Young, G., & Kane, A. W. (2007). Causality in psychology and law. In G. Young, A. W. Kane, & K. Nicholson (Eds.), *Causality of psychological injury: Presenting evidence in court* (pp. 13–47). New York: Springer Science + Business Media.

Young, G., Kane, A. W., & Nicholson, K. (Eds.). (2006). *Psychological knowledge in court: PTSD, pain, and TBI*. New York: Springer Science + Business Media.

Young, G., Kane, W., & Nicholson, K. (2007). *Causality of psychological injury: Presenting evidence in court*. New York: Springer Science + Business Media.

Young, G., & Yehuda, R. (2006). Understanding PTSD: Implications for court. In G. Young, A. W. Kane, & K. Nicholson (Eds.), *Psychological knowledge in court: PTSD, pain, and TBI* (pp. 55–69). New York: Springer Science + Business Media.

28 Stimulus–Organism–Response Model: SORing to New Heights

Chapter Introduction

Workers have suggested inverting the causal order involving behavior by placing organism factors before stimulus ones. Moreover, contemporary brain theory (Friston, 2010) has referred to hidden states involving the environment, as well as probabilistic and generative Bayesian constructs behind sensation and perception, and so on. The fuzzy nature of each of the stimulus, the organism (or its brain), and even the response calls for a more inclusive S–O–R (Stimulus–Organism–Response) model. The chapter reviews the literature on the issues related to fuzzy stimulus, organism, and response, leading to presentation of the S–O–R Brain/Agent/Mind/Person (BAMP) model. Behavior is the reflection of a dynamical, self organized, emergent, and hierarchical process in which (a) the structure of the environment does not stand outside the organism and (b) the response of the organism is conditioned by factors such as motivation, anticipation, and personality. (c) Moreover, the responses are complex and conditional, without a necessary determinism.

History

Originally, Woodworth (e.g., 1918) developed the S–O–R (Stimulus–Organism–Response) model, and it reflected a functionalist approach differentiated from strictly a behaviorist S–R (Stimulus–Response) one. The model indicates that stimuli might elicit different responses depending on the state of the organism; that is, the organism mediates the relationship between a stimulus and a response. It is interesting to note that Woodworth (1918) entitled his book, *Dynamic Psychology*, anticipating some 100 years ago contemporary developments in the field.

Another founder of the discipline of psychology also queried the validity of stimulus–response psychology. Thurstone (1923) developed a model striking in its use of contemporary terminology. First, he indicated that, in the traditional model, mind mediates between stimuli and response. Then, he presented his model in which the person is diagrammatically represented to the left, or before the stimulus rather than after it, leading to response. He said that "the causal sequence [starts] with the person himself" (p. 355). That is, the causal sequence starts with "the dynamic living self" and the stimulus is considered "causally intermediate." The person not only utilizes incoming stimuli but also "hunts" for stimuli relevant to one's ongoing personal mental life, including of motives. Therefore, in his model, an external energy source, which in other models might be labeled the stimulus, leads to an internal stimulus and an internal hunt for an external stimulus, thereby producing the desired external stimulus, and so leading to a response.

Note that the S–O–R model is still being used in consumer psychology (see Jacoby, 2002, for a revised version). It is interesting to note that, in

G. Young, *Unifying Causality and Psychology*, DOI 10.1007/978-3-319-24094-7_28

this contemporary S–O–R model, organismic factors precede stimulus ones, leading to a response. The organismic factors and stimulus ones are termed drives and cues, respectively, and the response is differentiated into hierarchies and tendencies.

Contemporary Theory

Fuzziness

Theories in psychology that are more contemporary also refer to the ambiguity or probability of psychological phenomena. For example, Reyna and Brainerd (1995, 2011) proposed fuzzy-trace theory especially for memory and other cognitive phenomena, including cognitive development. Their model is a dual-process one in which the individual forms mental representation evidence through either specific verbatim traces or gist traces, the latter of which are fuzzier representations of past events than the former.

Friston (2010) has proposed a unified, global brain theory that presents a contemporary approach to understanding the "hidden states" of the environment and dynamical systems theory. He proposed that a "free energy" principle underlies behavioral (action, perception, learning) and brain activity. Under the free-energy principle, behavior and brain work according to "optimization," which concerns either value (e.g., expected reward or utility), or its complement, that of "surprise" (prediction error, expected cost).

Comment

Just as the philosophical and epistemological stances that one could adopt in psychology are subject to debate, and might be considered "messy," the same appears to apply to the fundamental notions in psychology of stimulus, person, and response. Is the stimulus an external energy impingement that the person faithfully apperceives and processes into matched adaptive response, with the three components in this behavioral formula distinct? Recent research is questioning the separation of environment and person and also the nature of behavior as response entity, or output. In the following, I elaborate further the concepts of "fuzzy" stimulus, "fuzzy" organism, and "fuzzy" response.

What Is a Fuzzy Stimulus?

Precursors

Gibson (1966, 1979/1986) developed an ecological model of affordances in the environment to counter the mechanistic view. Affordances allow action possibilities, in the same sense as stairs allow stair climbing. The concept implicates the environment as meaningful, or of value in and of itself. Information in the environment specifies affordances. Organisms can perceive directly affordances so that meaning does not originate mentally or internally. Rather than being a collection of stimulus causes of responses, the environment is not directly causal. Instead, it is a manifold of action possibilities.

The organism is an agent of action, rather than a passive puppet. Agents have properties, as does the environment, and their relations define affordances. The same object might have different affordances for different organisms, or even for one organism at different developmental epochs. That being said, affordances do not change as the needs of the organism change. They are ecological properties of the environment, not reflections of mind. They are extracted or obtained information, and they do not impose or cause behavior; as agent, the organism exhibits constraint over behavior, or control of it (in the sense of regulation).

Reed (1982, 1985, 1993, 1996) developed further Gibson's ecological model in terms of agency. He contended that an organism is in charge of its own actions, having self-control. Intentions are patterns of action organization.

According to Withagen, de Poel, Araújo, and Pepping (2012), the mechanistic perspective of behavior dominated psychology until more ecological ones developed. In the mechanistic worldview, mind and behavior are understood as chains of causes and effects, e.g., stimuli in the environment cause responses.

Model

Perception Clark (2013a) has presented a potentially unified science of action and mind. It is based on a hierarchical generative model, or hierarchical prediction approach, to the brain as machine unifying perception and action. In order to minimize prediction error, the brain is a predictive machine in the sense of constantly trying to match incoming sensory inputs with top-down predictions or expectations, in a delicate balance with bottom-up processes.

The world presents as perturbing signal sources that higher-level brain systems model perceptually in order to predict their "hidden" causal structure based on created multiple, linked perceptual models. As predictive errors arise, the models are revised. The models are probabilistic, signal-based, and construct-driven inferences. The body receives and reacts to the signals and, in perception, the causes for the effects are inferred, but as part of multiple probability distributions. That is, even for a single effect, multiple causes are possible. Models of distal causes are not just constructed from accumulated bottom-up data, because the brain acts top-down to create models with best fit to the data.

It is in this sense that the perceptual models created by the brain are considered generative. Generative models attempt to capture, in the statistical structure of stimulus arrays in schemata, the "causal matrix" responsible for the structure. The models are hierarchical (multilevel, bidirectional) in that the causal web that is created balances in an ongoing fashion lower-level top-down tracks or trains of constructed data. Sensory data become selected, sculpted, predictive codes, or "virtual" renditions. Perception is not a map of signals and inner state; rather, it is a constructed state that, at its base, is probabilistic, predictive, and inferential.

Prediction Prediction takes place in multiple levels of the processing hierarchy, which are locked in an integrated "predictive coding regime." The hypothesis that is becoming percept, or driving signal, makes the best predictions, with others relegated out by inhibition. [Note that Friston (e.g., 2010) has developed a hierarchical predictive processing model that includes action. For Friston, both perception and action are probabilistically-based activities, and their linkages extend to cognition.]

Surprisal Another major aspect of Clark's (2013a) Bayesian approach to core human functions concerns situated agents. For example, perception and action work together to reduce "surprisal" ("surprise" in Friston, 2010). Surprisal measures the implausibility of a sensory state in light of a given model of the environment. Perception acts to reduce surprisal by matching input and prior prediction (expectation). Action acts to reduce it by altering the environment (even bodily movement) so that sensory input matches prediction. Therefore, both perception and action selectively sample and actively sculpt the environment, as in situated or embodied cognition. We behave in order to self-structure information flow through our actions, which allows for learning and inference.

Social At the social level, our cognition becomes socially situated so that prediction error construction is mutual, communal, synchronized, shared, and distributed. Also, in order to create the best models of reality, we use culture to refine our predictions, launching them only to have them reenter. The inputs are designed, producing "designer environments" that engineer socially our permeable cognition, allowing its intergenerational transmission on social scaffolds (a concept similar to neuroconstructivism; Mareschal et al., 2007).

Comment The commentaries to the Clark (2013a) article serve to expand its scope. For example, Seth and Critchley (2013) attempted to bridge it with emotion; and Hirsh, Mar, and Peterson (2013) considered adding narrative construction. Clark (2013b) concluded that the action-oriented predictive processing inherent in his model constitutes a mechanism linked to core forms of brain-based processing.

Others

Social Zaki (2013) proposed a common cue integration framework for physical perception and social cognition (e.g., perceiving the mind of others) despite the lower processing level involved in physical perception. Research in the former has indicated that perception involves a "pervasive" multimodal, multisensory unification or integration, which can be modeled by Bayesian probabilities.

In a social process integration perspective on social cues in social cognition, streams are no longer considered separate or isolated, but are integrated and co-activated (e.g., mentalizing and experience sharing), and with shared brain regions associated with them. "Real-world" social cognition involves complex social cues that require difficult, "noisy" task performance, so that cue integration, or interactions between multiple social signals and social information processing streams, is required.

That signals are noisy and probabilistic suggests that Bayesian models can apply to them. Objects and events produce perceptual signals having conditional probabilities [e.g., P (red|engine) refers to the probability of seeing "red" given a "fire engine"]. To form perceptual cues at the level of Bayesian probabilities, the perceiver integrates probabilities such as these with prior knowledge (e.g., P|engine), and the perceptual cues themselves have probabilities associated with them.

The latter probabilities associated with the perceptual inferences are each proportional to the probabilities connecting the inferred perception to the sensory cues encountered in relation to priors (e.g., P(engine|red, siren) × P(red|engine) × P(siren|engine) × P(engine)). Similarly, judging that a gold-medal winner is crying for joy and not happiness is a probabilistic inference that can be represented by P (happy|crying, medal) × P(crying|happy) × P(happy|medal) × P (happy).

Zaki (2013) labeled perceivers as "lay" Bayesians. He concluded that individuals with social impairments might have difficulty with social cue integration. Probabilities that are more neutral than negative might be overinflated (for example, Planger (my example) derives from a neutral stare). Textual cues might be misjudged, and priors might be overestimated (elevated) (e.g., Planger arouses an aggressive response). In the example provided, aggression even could be provoked inappropriately to a disordered or delinquent degree.

Development As for precursors of probability estimation, Frankenhuis, Gergely, and Watson (2013) referred to children using conditional probability estimates of environmental harshness and unpredictability. In "prospective" probability, infants might observe that maternal smiles follow cooing. In "retrospective" probability, the estimate is about the cooing preceding the smiling. Infants not only engage in contingency detection like this in their immediate environment, but also they use it as a guide in long term development. Good prediction facilitates control; however, in compromised environments (harsh, unpredictable), control is variable. Therefore, in terms of evolutionary life-history strategies, early environmental predictions might provide impetus toward adapting fast or slow evolutionary strategies (e.g., early female menarche and reproduction).

Affordances Withagen et al. (2012) added to this rich modeling of the environment in relation to behavior by postulating that affordances do not simply suggest action possibilities but also might invite them or even prompt or urge them, as in immediately drawing the person to them. This suggests that afforded invitations exist in a mutualistic relationship between the organism and the environment, in light of the multidimensional properties of both. In this conception, although affordances are construed as properties of objects, their invitations reflect the relationship between object and organism. Invitations vary with properties of the organism as it develops in context or culture and from its evolutionary history. Invitations can be declined, and so do not constitute causes.

What Is a Fuzzy Organism?

By "fuzzy" organism, I refer to the "messy" processes involved in dealing with incoming information and preparing outgoing response. Clearly, in this regard, there is no one-to-one relationship. For example, the input into the organism is both at least partially constructed by the organism and also enters and alters the processing machinery of the organism. Moreover, the latter machinery is by no means a technologically sophisticated and unchanging smooth-running engine with a primary central command input analyzer and response generator. There are candidate primary components in these regards, such as self-regulation or control and its constituent major tools, including attention and memory (e.g., working memory), inhibition, and other executive skills (such as set shifting). Moreover, the processor has important affective components, too, including affective schemas and filters related to temperamental and experiential influences. Given the potential of the socioaffective/motivational aspect of the organism to affect deployment of other processing components, individual differences in motivation, self-regulation, and related components constitute the quintessential fuzzy component of the organism.

What Is Fuzzy Response?

The model of stimulus in the external world, organism as mediator of its apperception and preparation of the response, and the response itself as a third fuzzy step in behavior rests increasingly on contemporary scientific findings. That is, as with the discussion above of the fuzzy nature of stimulus and organism, response processes are messy themselves, with ongoing online adjustments to situational conditions and planning priorities. In systems and network models, responses are part of behavioral states and cannot be separated from them. They emerge as confluences that might not even be predictable and reflective of ongoing state, but as novel, self-organized entities far-from-equilibrium, and nonetheless (or rather, especially) adaptive.

Marken and Mansell (2013) addressed the fuzziness in psychology in a similar way. They argued that the traditional model of behavior, being caused by events in the environment, does not account for either feedback effects of the behavior or its goal, which is to protect from disturbances (Powers, 1973, 1978). Organisms are considered control systems acting to preserve (goal) states, so that behavior is the control of perception. Causality runs circularly rather than linearly, or in a closed (negative feedback) loop in which sensory input is simultaneously both a cause and an effect of output, the goal of which is to counter or resist disturbance. Causality does not start or end with genes, but with the whole behavioral system.

Michel (2013) proposed a similar model from his work in developmental psychology. Genes carry information and are involved in behavioral causality but neither in a governing nor primarily responsible way. [Yet the power of biological argumentation about behavior is not subsiding. For example, Peterson, Sznycer, Sell, Cosmides, and Tooby (2013) advocated for an evolutionary perspective on the politics of resource distribution.]

Generally, we can conclude that behavior is not simply a linear output after mediation of the effects of external stimuli, but even might be the factor that determines what the incoming stimuli might be. The mechanisms of adaptation do not separate stimulus–organism–response, and models about their relationship should be constructed from that perspective.

What Is a Fuzzy System?

Nonlinear dynamical systems theory (NLDST) provides the answer. NLDST is a theory that is well-suited to the describing and explaining all types of change (Thelen & Smith, 1994). There are variants of the theory, including catastrophe theory, that have been applied to psychological phenomena (e.g., Witkiewitz & Marlatt, 2007). Moreover, NLDST is split into at least two major camps, with the major difference concerning whether states are always soft-assembled de novo bottom-up in an ongoing fashion without, as well, hierarchically more complex levels that work top-down, or whether states can have reciprocally bottom-up and top-down influences. The latter approach is more conducive to the development of increasingly complex states in the system analogous to those of stages in the developing human (e.g., van Geert, 2012). Finally, there are models that are quite similar to NLDST ones, in particular, connectionist models (Tryon, 2012). Both models lead to empirical predictions that have been confirmed developmentally. However, NLDST often is applied to a broader range of areas, even abiotic (but for human case, often it is applied metaphorically rather than mathematically).

Some cardinal features of NLDST include self-organization, hierarchical organization, emergence, attractor formation, far-from-equilibrium, and system perturbation. Systems are wholes in which the whole is greater than the sum of the parts. The wetness of water (H_2O) cannot be predicted by knowing the properties of the component hydrogen and oxygen atoms. As the parts (elements) coalesce into configurations, patterns, or higher-order structures, they do so without a preprogrammed template or central generator governing the assembly. Rather, the elements converge on states that are dynamically open, graceful, and least dissipative of entropy, avoiding disequilibrium and disintegration. The states might have multiple hierarchical levels, also for which the wholes are not predicted from the parts. The self-organization toward unpredictable patterns, states, or other dynamics is referred to as emergence. States might take the form of attractors, or a set range toward which specified variables in the system move at multiple points over time, even if slightly different each time. Attractors tend to stability and resist system perturbations, but when at far-from-equilibrium, they risk variability, transition, and gravitation to new attractor ensembles. As states self-organize this way in systems into attractor formations, there might be more than one to which the system visits, and new ones are generated at bifurcation or other transition points; some might be maladaptive, as in chronic pain states/attractors (Young, 2011).

Revised S–O–R Model

Model

Figure 28.1 presents a revised S–O–R model that maintains the standard sequence of critical components—stimulus–organism–response. However, the model makes clear that stimulus and organism properties are co-active in eliciting response. The model is general enough to apply to humans, animals, and any biological entity, organ, or agent, including the brain or neuron. The model is presented in terms of boundaries between stimulus and organism, but the literature indicates that the boundary is fuzzy, as are stimulus and organism properties, e.g., in the sense of probability models to describe them, and even in their active generation of models as they function or have an impact. In this sense, the response end of the S–O–R model is equally probabilistic; that is, responses are neither definitive nor fixed exclusively by prior events. As in NLDST, likelihoods in state positioning in state response regimes are indeterministic proximally even if they function deterministically according to global attractors.

The proposed revised S–O–R model includes feedback mechanisms that can either amplify or de-amplify stimuli/state patterns that are in progress (positive and negative feedback, respectively). Moreover, feedback mechanisms have feedforward properties when they function, in terms of anticipations or expectations that canalize/filter stimuli toward desired/predicted options. Priors in state are not simply static inputs into a processing system, in that they are colored by feedback mechanisms such as these toward co-active shaping and changing tendencies of the adapting organism/system.

The final general aspect of the revised S–O–R model concerns its adaptive adjustment over context and time. Organisms/organizations/organs (Os) have evolved to optimize adaptation to contingencies in environment, and they do so dynamically as they and it changes over time (changing either developmentally or in terms of altered complexity, depending on the type of "O" involved).

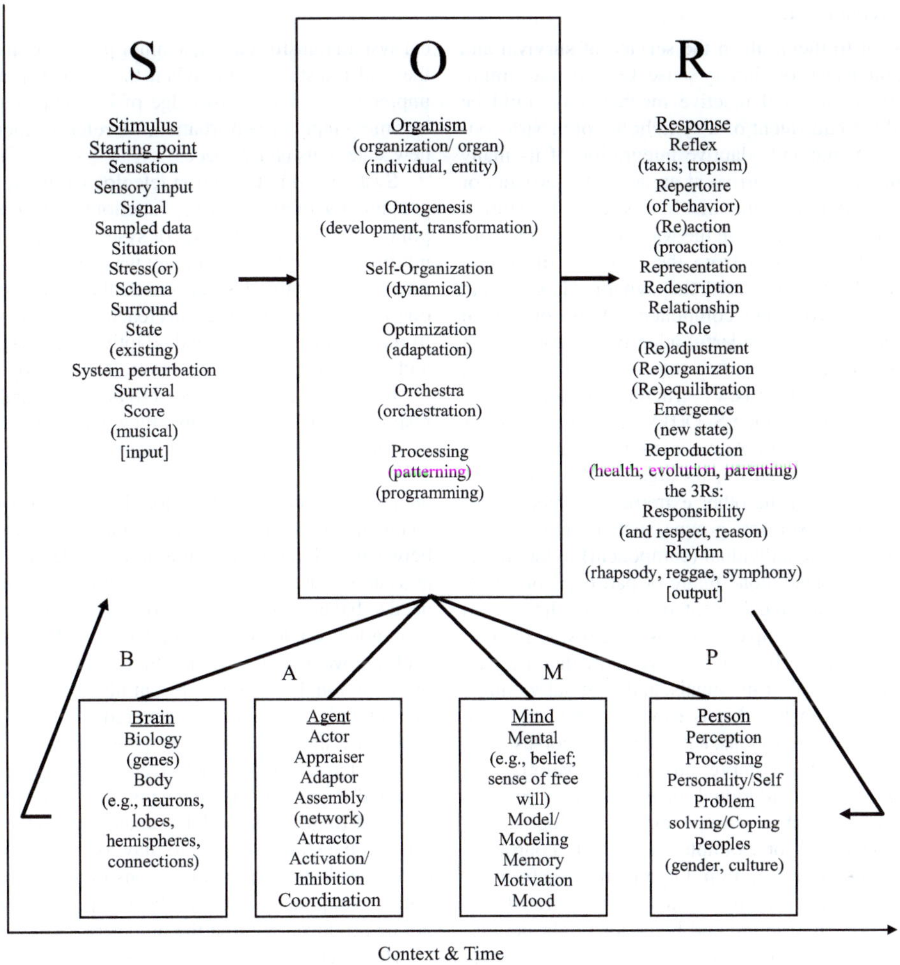

Fig. 28.1 The S–O(BAMP)–R causal psychological model: from stimulus and schema to response and representation. This figure presents an expanded S–R (stimulus–response) model of behavior that includes organismic (person, O) mediational components. The model is referred to as the S–O–R one, with added subcomponents expanding the O portion (BAMP – S–O(BAMP)–R model).

The stimulus component of the model expands the immediate instigator of behavior into a suite of potential initiators. The fundamental starting point might not only be a simple stimulus but also a whole context (situation) or even a complex stressor.

Stimuli, situation, and stressor are never fully objective or empirical, given the important role of perception and cognitive filter in behavior. There might be feed (backward, forward) mechanisms that alter the objective physics or signals in an incoming array. Sensation and sensory input might not reflect, already at this step in behavior and its mediation, the empirical reality of the surround. Sampling of input has beneficial adaptive (evolutionary) advantages in assessing the environment as presently constituted and forecasting future environments in which the organism (person) might live.

The environment provides information to which the organism must adapt in the present to survive and facilitate reproduction (presently or later on, depending on developmental level, if this applies to the organism). The organism builds schemas to represent the environmental information serving as filters in dealing with new incoming information. The schemas might simply be patterns of metabolic activity that have been constructed or entrained by previous environmental conditions and encounters. Or, for more advanced organisms, they could include patterns of neuronal and central or nervous system activity. Together, no matter what their complexity, the schemas of an organism contribute to constructing its current state.

Organisms constitute systems of stimulus sensing, stimulus modulation, and stimulus responsiveness. Their current state both resists reactivity and change to incoming input (system perturbations) and is actively open to their reception, mediation, and potential change, even to new or emergent state and system configurations. Systems function both to adapt to changes in stimuli and to change

Fig. 28.1 (continued)

as they adapt to them, all in the service of survival and reproduction in an evolutionary sense. Organismic stimuli sensing, mediating, and reactive mechanisms could be considered the equivalent of a symphonic orchestra conducting a systemic and adaptive integration of its many components in order to arrive at an aesthetic, artistic, or holistically functioning outcome. In this sense, the stimuli of the environment, at least in the way perceived and constructed by the organism from the empirics of stimuli qualities, could be considered the dynamical score that inputs into the producing component of the orchestral system. Behavior is a wonderful adaptive outcome of an exquisitely evolved "scientific" machine with rhythmic, musical, esthetic, and "artistic" structure and adaptivity.

The O component of the S–O(BAMP)–P model refers to more than an organism. At one extreme, it refers also to components of the organism, its organs (or even organelles), if you will. At the other extreme, it refers also to aggregates of organisms into groups, such as organizations or other entities. The individual (component) in the model could be either a stand-alone figure or part of a collective. Either way, it is the focal agent or actor in the system involved. For more complex species, organisms refer to individual members. They might have individuating psychological attributes. For mammals, and especially human and nonhuman primates, this is especially the case. We then refer to a person, persons, a people, and peoples.

Organisms that are more advanced develop. This could refer both to individual members of a species/group/structure, or their components. Development is termed ontogenesis, for example, when it is contrasted with phylogenesis in evolution. Organisms transform, in general. Even when they resist change, they transform. For example, their structure and behavior might be conservatively strengthened in ongoing configuration after perturbation, which is still a type of transformation.

In their moment-to-moment adaptation, organisms are not static, but they constantly sample the environment, test it and its structure and function, and so on. They achieve equilibrium by constant, ongoing microadaptations, and, if not closed nor inherently static and rigidly fixed, they attune to the constant microchanges in the environment.

Organisms (organs, organization, etc.) that are open systems often function according to nonlinear dynamical system forces. They self-organize without influences of preformed templates or central control mechanisms, but constantly adjust and adapt online. Their state at any moment is not the continuation of a previous state but an ongoing restructuring and configuration of all the internal elements and external impacts involved. If the present state resembles the previous one, it is because the reassembly of the system has arrived at the same optimally adaptive solution as had fit the previous one. That being said, system states might change with time, and radically so. The system could self-organize away from the structure of a prior state, and sometimes this takes place even with minor input change, as in the so-called butterfly effect. If systems are already structured far-from-equilibrium at the point of radical system transformation, a minor perturbation can initiate the said transformation. When the change in a system is unpredictable from knowledge of its components and the incoming input or perturbation, we refer to emergence of a new state in its phase space.

Systems do not function teleologically with a known, presumably more adaptive, functional, or complex endpoint. These latter outcomes of systems transformation are not inscribed in systems in any way. However, as systems gravitate to optimal solutions to their state structure in ongoing context, the solutions reached need to be graceful, fit the context, efficient, and adaptive in an ongoing sense and also in an evolutionary sense, if that is applicable.

In this sense, systems need to be plastic and surround-responsive. At the same time, they need to be able to keep their integrity and coherent adaptive functionality that has worked to date. To help in this regard, systems need to engage in forecasting what should work in upcoming environments. There is a constant balancing of and struggle between seeking equilibrium and also degrees of change as systems enter disequilibrium. Optimization refers to the need to balance well these opposing tendencies, adapt well to ongoing contextual parameters and their change, and find pathways and solutions that are fit for survival and reproduction, both in the present niche and in future ones that might be encountered (and predicted).

To use the music analogy given above, if the behavioral system can be characterized as a symphonic production and its support mechanisms, the organism aspect of the S–O(BAMP)–R model is analogous to the orchestra. It needs the stimulus score to play its music, and the symphony made in consequence constitutes the response or output component of the orchestral process, but it could not be produced without the orchestra.

However, the orchestra in this system does not have a conductor or a chief orchestrator. System control resides in the totality of the system, its components, its levels, its structure, its functionality, and its behavior, as well as the stimuli, context, and surround involved in it. In the human behavioral system, we might think that we ourselves have ultimate authority and decision-making (and follow-through) power. However, we ourselves constitute but one element in the system, albeit perhaps the most important one.

Systems have products as outputs, but they arrive at their outcomes through processes and their mechanisms. These, too, are in constant development and alteration, or at the edge of change, as with brain growth and its change in the human case. The O portion of the S–O(BAMP)–R model is a processor as much as a producer. To use the music analogy, we orchestrate behavior through the orchestration process that manages us and that we manage. The program involved is not inherent to the system, or fixed, but responsive, adaptive, changeable, and liable to growth as much as the production aspect of behavior.

In the end, systems are vibrant wholes greater than the sum of their parts. They create and live patterns that are more than their components, inputs, and outputs. They monitor output, they even change with predictions of out-

Fig. 28.1 (continued)

put, and they are pattern machines nonpareil. In living systems, the patterns achieve a musicality, a rhythm, and even grand symphonies from neural firing patterns to behavioral output designs. It is our responsibility, or at least each of us who are so capable, of having ourselves and also those around us reach these levels, instead of wading in self-indulgence and having the other succumb to the adversities and tragedies of life.

The figure elaborates on the organism component of the S–O–R model by referring to BAMP, or Brain, Agent, Mind (Model/Modeling), and Person. B stands for biology, in general, at least for living systems; for nonliving ones such as organizations, they still have a "basics" through their self-organizing activity. Whether, living or nonliving, organisms have bodies, or a structural morphology and energetic input–output relations to keep them functioning. For an actual brain, the neurons, regions, and their pathways constitute the components or structural architecture. However, the dynamic neural connections or networks that they form are equally important.

The A in the BAMP model component of the S–O–R model refers to the organism as agent. Agents act based on information to produce adaptive outcomes. Rather than functioning passively in this regard, they are active contributors to the process, appraising with filters the input, organizing it (e.g., chunking), and also organizing responses, while using feedback and feedforward mechanisms to help refine the system and anticipate its upcoming needs or likely environment. The agent is the critical adaptor, but is not the sole seat of control, and never discharges its control function without consideration of and participation in context, attuning to it.

Agents in systems could be whole living organisms, organizations of individuals, or parts of either. In models of human behavior, agents are not necessarily individual people. Agents are constituted by networks and they organize networks. Generally, network or pattern assembly is soft, or tuned to the exigencies of the environment, and they are flexible. Assemblies might articulate apparently constant patterns, but they re-assemble at each moment. They might reconfigure in the same way as prior assembly patterns when they are the most adaptive, which often is the case. In NLDST language, systems form attractors, or regions in their state space to which systems flow constantly at the global level even if local or specific changes in system functioning are dynamically flexible and unpredictable directly.

One cohering function that cuts across agent (person), brain, belief (mind), and behavior concerns activation/inhibition coordination. Young (2011) considered this interplay a unifying mechanism in understanding the different levels of functioning within and across brain and behavior. At all levels, activations generate adaptive activity and also inhibitions coordinated with it to control interference. The universal mechanism involved is not about inhibition alone, which is necessary to be sure, but is about the subtle interdigitated links between inhibition and activation as behavior adapts moment-to-moment online (micro) (and even long term (macro) through coordinated executive control (planning) and behavioral processes).

The M portion of the BAMP model in S–O(BAMP)–R model refers to the mind, in particular. Once more, even nonliving systems might have a "mind," e.g., in their organizational function. Mind generates product (models) through process (modeling). Models might be lower-order cognitive or even sensorimotor schemas. They could refer to higher-order outputs, such as representations and even hypotheses, theories, and scientific models. Medium-range models refer to beliefs, thoughts, and so on. Cognition is subserved by memory and propped by motivation and mood. It is a complex output influenced by brain, body, and all aspects mental and related constituents.

The P in the BAMP of S–O(BAMP)–R model refers especially to the person who does the behaving. The person does not respond directly to stimuli but perceives and modulates them as they are processed. Personal factors affect the processing, such as through personality, mood, memory, attentional skills, and problem solving and coping approaches. The individual has varied capacities and temperament, and her or his unique constellation navigates the stimulus perception and related response output function in individual ways, yet with group memberships and considerations influencing and molding the system. These include powerful influences of culture, gender, age, majority/minority, ethnic status, disability status, and so on.

The last component of the S–O–R complex of the present model of stimulus–response connection clarifies the R or response component. Behavior output might be simple in terms of reflexes or related functions but also it might be complex in terms of repertoires of actions or representations (or redescriptions) of action. It might be social in terms of role and relationship behaviors or complex to the point of large organizational output. Behavior is not necessarily a passive response and, indeed, often is active, pro-active, prospective, and engineering of the environment, social relationships, and self toward creative and successful adaptation. We adjust and readjust, organize and reorganize, and equilibrate and re-equilibrate constantly and even collectively. States solidify, modify, or even alter in full, realizing new, emergent qualitative states. We survive (healthily) and reproduce in our behavior. We have evolved this way and develop this way, for example, toward and through parenting.

The 3 R's might be reading, writing, and arithmetic, but they are also giving respect, using reason, and taking responsibility. The challenge to do so is constant and, in this regard, we undertake and rededicate to multiple re-responsibilities (Young, 2011). Whatever our culture, the rhythm of our life becomes a rhapsody to the extent we make it so, everything else being equal. Our R's to S's should always aim for such heights, both for us and others. Partly adapted from Young (2011), Fig. 2.11, p. 43

The overall label that I used to represent the present revised S–O–R model is S–O(BAMP)–R. This acronym represents the multiple types of "S"s involved in the model and the multiple types or "R"s. The Ss and Rs in the model are far removed from the classic stimulus and response formulation in that, in each case, they reflect the multidimensionality and fuzziness that is evident therein. Moreover, I have qualified the O component of the model by BAMP because many of the multiple components involved are readily represented by words beginning with B, A, M, and P.

In terms of the particulars of the revised S–O–R model, in the following I analyze in detail each of the S, O, and R terms. This leads to presentation of the BAMP portion of the model.

Stimuli

According to the Gibsonian perspective, stimuli exist as affordances in the environment and they are not simply constructed de novo by the organism. Stimuli consist of dynamic properties, such as differential arrays, fields, and forces. These are received, sensed, and perceived, depending on the complexity of the organism, organization, or organ involved. They constitute sensory input, signals, or sampled data. They are part of a wider situation, context, or niche. They might be appraised as stressors, including life-threatening or otherwise dangerous ones. The organism or organ transforms the stimulus properties into receptive fields, neuronal or network firings and, ultimately, some form of integration or abstraction, including even in the so-called concept cells or grandmother cells (e.g., to integrate firings related to the hand, Quiroga, 2012). In humans, the first abstractions after reflexes are termed schemas, for example, in the infant's sensorimotor schemas in Piagetian theory.

Organism

Introduction "O" is for organism and related terms, but also for optimization and orchestra. In the following, I review each of these aspects.

Organism/Organ/Organization The mediator between stimuli and response is not a passive receptacle, but a dynamic, active, filtering and constructing one that aims at facilitating adaptive prediction forward in time so that, in consequence, it works backward in dealing with stimuli. The complex just described indicates that the organism and its environmental context constitute a quintessential example of a system.

With respect to dynamical systems theory and other nonlinear models applied to behavior, the individual's behavior and relations to the environment constitute a state in the state space of its trajectories as it transforms in response to system perturbations. The latter might be quite minor, as in the butterfly effect, but still lead to massive, qualitative change, e.g., shifts in state to different or higher-order attractors (basins to which the system's trajectory repeatedly gravitates globally despite minor variations locally; there might be one to several attractors in adapted living systems).

To remind, in this revised S–O–R model, the entity that processes the input to produce an output might be an individual organism, or a collection into a group. Also, it might be a working structure of the individual or group, such as a social (business, political, cultural) organization. Finally, it might be an organ of the entity. In the living case, this would concern especially brains in more complex organisms. Also, it would concern the networks of neurons and other interconnections in the active brain. Organs also refer to neurons themselves, which are no longer understood as passive transmission devices but also as active and integrative responders to incoming signals and tonically active cells. Indeed, they possess thousands of synapses so that their organizational and informational capacities are massive and complexly distributed in parallel, as much as the neuronal networks or cell assemblies of which they might be a part. Further, neurons are actively in communication with glial cells (astrocytes) that not only provide support but also constitute a parallel transmission engine, albeit slower than in the case of neurons. The integration of neurons and astrocytes in coupled arrangements at synapses is referred to as the "tripartite neuron" (De Pittà et al., 2012).

Whatever the entity—organism, organization, or organ—it transforms. In the human and mammalian case, in particular, we refer to the change process as development or ontogenesis. But all living organisms adapt and change as they engage in commerce with the environment or surround. Groups and organizations change, as well. Aside from progressive change, the change could be regressive, or it could involve resistance to change in the solidification of state despite ongoing input, which in a certain sense is a type of change relative to prior state given that, in a system, state is reconfigured constantly and its apparent maintenance in form and characteristics simply is a repetition of the best adaptive pattern or configuration in the present context of the state compared to the prior one.

Optimization Intelligence is defined as involving adaptation to the environment (Sternberg, 2012). Evolution concerns adaptive selection of gene-supported traits of the phenotype that better allow for survival and reproduction. Cognitive behavioral therapy involves working on maladaptive thoughts. However, contemporary concepts of adaptation in any of these spheres have transformed the concept of adaptation to a dynamic, even pro-active one, e.g., intelligence is about altering the environment, and not just passively adapting (Sternberg, 2012); genes involve correlated gene–environment interactions, e.g., active evocative ones (Jaffee, 2011); and psychotherapy involves indirect facilitated change, as in solution-focused therapy (see Young, 1997).

Evolutionary theory has avoided using the term optimization, because adaptation to the environmental niche should not involve one "best," qualitatively superior, or complex way. However, a rejiggling of the concept so that it equates with the traditional understanding of adaptation should be considered. For example, workers have developed dynamical evolutionary models (e.g., Badcock, 2012) and genes in their interactions with the environment often lead to alternate or secondary phenotypes that optimize survival and reproduction in difficult circumstances (life-history theory; Belsky & Pluess, 2009a; Simpson & Belsky, 2008).

The concept of optimization is not found directly in NLDST, but it relates to the one of ongoing search for equilibrium and interference with entropic disorganization. Moreover, the work of Friston (2010) on brain theory (free energy, "surprise," etc.) has presented optimization as the common construct underlying diverse brain theories. To conclude, from an optimization perspective, stimuli, information, bits, sensory input, data, signals, sensations, situations, stressors, and so on, are highly selective and focused toward optimizing adaptation, survival, and reproduction. They compose or reflect patterns, in that the patterns self-organize and emerge in states beyond what can be predicted by the properties of the inputs themselves. The organism/organization/organ together constitutes a supreme creator of patterns (patterner) but without pre-existing programs to guide the way. Novel states arise out of the matrix of elemental interactions, including at higher, more complex levels.

Orchestra As for a good metaphor for the S–O–R mediating mechanism of the system involved, it concerns musical production, which begins with a stimulus score, continues with an orchestra that orchestrates the music; and also the production could constitute a symphony inclusive of its rhythms. This metaphor leads to presentation of details of the response component of the present model.

Response

About the response component of the revised S–O–R model, I have indicated that it includes a range of responses possible, from the most simple (reflex) to the most complex (responsibility, reason, respect; Sternberg, 2012). Out of a vast repertoire of behavior, the entity responds in reaction, action, or proaction. The response might be mediated by a simpler abstraction, such as a schema or network, but more advanced representations (redescriptions) might be involved. Responses could be individual or social (relations, roles) and, ultimately, they need to be mature, generative, and physically or psychologically healthy in order to permit better adaptation and also to facilitate prospering in the long term.

Responses entail new adaptations of the system to the changing stimuli parameters and how they are processed. There is readjustment/reorganization and requilibration and, hopefully, in a constructive way. There is emergence in the confluence of, or engagement with, the environment, entity, and response, leading to new system states. The differentiation and integration of the states involved feed back into the environmental context, stimuli, and flow in which the entity is embedded, streamlining an increased probability of better adaptation and optimization as the (living) process continues.

Further Details

Introduction The bottom portion of Fig. 28.1 provides further details of the entity involved as it engages in the processing and responding to environmental stimuli and their schematic abstractions. In the human case, and for advanced animal forms, the nervous system is the seat of input stimuli processing and of output responding. The body and brain develop because of genes, environment, and their interaction. The interaction might involve Gene × Environment (G × E) interactions in which certain alleles in the context of certain environments produce outcomes different than those deriving from any other genetic–environmental combination (or different from the outcome of either acting primarily alone; main effects).

However, genes have their effects through probabilistic epigenetic processes and through several levels of the developmental manifold, from proteins, to nervous systems, to behavior (Gottlieb, 2007). Moreover, contemporary approaches to epigenesis (Meaney, 2010) are overturning traditional understanding of how genes work, because genes can be "silenced" in their promoter regions by DNA methylation and other processes, e.g., involving histones. Further, epigenetically-silenced genes can transmit their marks or stamps across generations.

Finally, certain alleles (in a process of differential susceptibility) might lead to phenotypic susceptibilities that are not only maladaptive (e.g., increased antisociality in deleterious environments) but also could be quite adaptive (e.g., advantageously developed in supportive environments) because the susceptibilities act to generally increase volatility to the environment or the reaction range (Belsky & Pluess, 2009a, 2009b; independent of any main effect in positive or negative direction that supportive or adverse environments might elicit). This type of G × E interaction illustrates the dynamic interaction of genes, environment, and development. New models have emerged in this regard referred to as G × E × D models.

The brain is an exquisitely complex organ, from neurons and networks, to pathways and lobes, to hemispheres and connections. It has been referred to as being constituted by the "Connectome" (Sporns, 2011, 2012). In a reductionist perspective, behavior can be considered as direct reflection of physiological activity of the body and brain. There is no intermediate engine or homunculus, no self apart from the workings of the material action of neurons, neurotransmitters, and so on, and their interaction. The brain is comprised of quadrillions of connections, and it is a computational workhorse that surpasses any robot or artificial intelligence (AI) program, except in speed and factors related to it. However, the brain is an organ subject to dynamical processes, such as has been described by Friston (2010). Just as emergent phenomena can arise in behavioral system states, similar constructions obtain from brain activity. Barrett (Barrett, 2012; Barrett & Bliss-Moreau, 2009) has referred to "psychological primitives" that constitute the building blocks of behavior (e.g., core affects). They might not be as complex as advanced reasoning and emotional processes, but they are emergent in their way and allow for further emergence of more complex psychological phenomena (e.g., thinking and "affecting").

B In the BAMP component of the Organismic (O) portion of the revised S–O–R model, the "B" portion of the organism refers to the biological (brain, body) base of the behavior. It contributes to producing behavior from the filtered perceptions it schematizes. Physiological processes constitute the body and brain, and the brain integrates stimuli effects in its adaptive preparation for response.

A The "A" key words in the model refer to the agent/actor/appraiser of the stimuli at hand (as well as the responses to be made), in addition to the networked assembly or attractors that define the system. The organism is an integrated perceiver and producer in a poised state that balances stasis, chaos, and change.

M As for the "M" portion, it refers to the mind of the person, the mental life from thought to emotion to willed action. Inputs are (a) stored and moderated in memory (short/long; procedural-implicit/declarative (semantic, episodic), (b) affected by motivation and mood, and (c) processed in working memory and by other executive processes including planning/problem solving.

Baumeister and colleagues have shown that part of mental life includes believing in free will, which has important consequences for behavior (e.g., Baumeister & Brewer, 2012). Having a sense of free will augments self-control but, at the same time, depletion of self-control affects one's sense of free will. There are individual differences in believing in free will and its consequent effects, e.g., related to personality.

P This brings us to the person or "P" component to the revised S–O–R model. Psychology is not only about common laws and principles governing behavior but also about relevant individual and group differences, including those that make each of us unique. Variation in behavior might be noise in some senses but, for the study of individual and group differences, it is the essential focus (which is also the case for NDLST). As the present model applies to humans, a person is involved but, generally, for the model, any entity or agent acting on stimuli toward producing responses could be the processor of input leading to output.

Individual differences are shaped by genes, environment, and genetic–environmental interactions, to be sure, but also by the role of the person him- or herself in development. Piaget referred to the person as the third "(tertium) quid" or force in development. He advocated for the child as an active constructor of her or his cognitive development. Already in terms of individual differences, information processing depends, in part, on the history of environmental presentations to the developing child/person in family, school, neighborhood, community, culture, and country. However, individual differences are accentuated by individualized schemes and representations created by the person; they serve as personally-constructed perceptual and cognitive filters in addressing and functioning adaptively in the environment.

Each of us has a unique complex of resilience, coping; vulnerabilities, risks; strengths, weaknesses; skills, lacunae; problem solving, problem ignoring; adaptive behavior, maladaptive behavior; good habits, bad habits; and so on. Each of us varies in degree of curiosity, exploration, openness; externalization, extroversion; energy, activity, activation; inhibition, internalization, introversion; optimism, pessimism; and so on. Each of us is varied along important dimensions of temperament and personality; degree of security and trust; independence and identity; nurturance and affiliation; and so on. As our temperament and personality and related factors develop and change over time and in context, we become the people we are, contributing to our own growth and that of others.

Reflections

Fuzziness

Research has shown that stimuli do not stand as clear signals that cleanly enter the system but, rather, they are subtle in array, energy, force, and field variations that receptive and perceptual structures of the organism struggle to accurately decipher while otherwise functioning adaptively in context over multiple spheres. Organisms are constantly making probability estimates of what are the stimuli in the environment and what responses are optimally best in light of them, aside from proactively influencing them. Prior states influence present ones, in Bayesian dynamics, but because the internal states themselves are fuzzy, as well as the stimuli in the environment, the links between stimuli-processing and response are not as clear-cut as some models might predict. Indeed, prediction or prospection is a cardinal human attribute (Seligman, Railton, Baumeister, & Sripada, 2013) and it is a probabilistic enterprise that clearly is not deterministic.

It must be recalled that information is defined as the reduction of uncertainty and, of course, absolute certainty can never be ascertained. In considering the putative Heisenberg principle, the principle of entanglement, and other quantum phenomena in the microworld (and perhaps in the more macro world of human activity; think the new field of quantum biology), causation/causality does not lie simply in straightforward linkages of cause and effect, because all components of the equation—stimulus, organism, and response—can be uncertain, probabilistic, fuzzy, and indeterministic.

Philosophy

In the case of human affairs, the philosophical issue of determinism vs. indeterminism cannot be approached as one in which truth one way or the other can be established. Perhaps it is best, like many other aspects of human conceptualization, to accept mystery. One dictum is that God does not play with dice. This presupposes that the universe is determined and our behaviors are its products. But in the new conceptualizations in psychology being discussed, we learn that we intervene in our own behavior and future, and even in our understanding of the past. We have choices available to us, and when we act on them constructively by way of believing in and sensing of our free will, we make better choices. Philosophy might not be satisfied with this practical position, that believing in and sensing free will makes an important difference, because free will, itself, cannot be proved. However, perhaps the notion that we can change our behavior constructively once we believe in and have a sense of free will is the most important truth about our behavior. The belief gives us a power to act positively, morally, responsibly, and in a caring, empathic way. Each such minuscule act of empathy might not seem much, but each functions like a "psychological Higgs Boson," constituting the basic constituent of our higher-order faculties in our personal, familial, group, and wider behavior.

We are adaptive probability modelers engaged in making constant probability estimates. We are implicit computational machines, learning to make at times explicit probability-based decisions, and we follow through on them for our own and others adaptive benefit. This reality of how we function might not prove that we have free will, but it sets the stage for understanding ourselves as the opposite of deterministic beings without a chance of having free will.

Causality

Like some who conjecture about time, perhaps causality doesn't exist (acausalism). Or, perhaps it is the only thing that exists in the physical world, which surely it does, but it is fuzzy in the psychological world. Stimuli and responses are varied, complex components of the behavioral unfolding in humans, but without their causal linkaging, even if that is fuzzy, too, neither would exist. We live as a result of caused behavior and, also, much of our learning is about causation and the question of "why" so that we can better adapt and prosper in our context. Perhaps, at the psychological level, we are complex causal machines, both in how we develop out of the cauldron of gene–environment–personal interactions and how we have effect on others and the world around us.

In summary, the causality of human behavior is not a straight-through sequential process from stimulus, situation, or event to response, act, and outcome. The person is both mediator and moderator in the process, influencing it both directly and indirectly. Stimuli do not just happen before entering as input into the processors of the person in a passive way. Rather, the person actively filters the stimuli, constructs their schemas and representations and, moreover, the person even acts on the environment to shape it to extant adaptive needs, thereby altering stimuli even before they exist. Therefore, stimuli are not absolute but probabilistic, and reflect the optimization involved in response choice, construction, decision-making, enactment, monitoring, and revision. Falling trees do not make sounds if organisms are not around to hear them. Similarly, causation in human behavior involves the person as genuine, active, and proactive participant. As much as are stimuli and responses, causal linkages in behavior are humanly influenced and probabilistic, and they are phenomena on which we ourselves can act to alter putative deterministic outcomes.

In this line of reasoning, there appears to be symmetry across the physical and psychological worlds in terms of space, time, and causality. In the quantum and cosmic reality of the former, that is the physical universe, physical space-time is considered a unified multi-dimension that curves and in which causality is predominant. Similarly, in the latter, that is, at the psychological level, psychological space-time could be considered a unified multi-dimension, one that exists only because it is punctuated by causal stimuli, events, and perceptions and their responses, effects, and outcomes. Given the nonlinearity involved, the causal manifold of living also would appear to be curved, and at times catastrophically so.

Further to this line of reasoning, causality becomes central to the behavioral enterprise and it should become central to its study in psychology. Causality encompasses all things psychological and the relationships in its linkages define equally both the stimuli, situational, and event factors in its sequence and the response, act, and outcome factors after them, as well as, the organism/person/agent factors that mediate, moderate, or otherwise intervene in establishing the linkages.

An important cross-level concept that helps characterize activity in the causal manifold concerns activation–inhibition coordination (Young, 2011). Whether it concerns brain or behavior, or their various levels, activity takes place not only by appropriate activation but also by appropriate inhibition. Think of the infant's finely-tuned reaching hand and then open and grasp movement, and how much successive activations and inhibitions must take place in a coordinated fashion both in behavior and brain for the movement to succeed in its objective. [I have argued, by the way, that the functional specialization involved in left hemisphere "dominance" concerns a superior skill in activation/inhibition coordination (Young, 2011).]

To continue the analogy with the physical world, we can ask to what extent the physical universe exhibits properties related to activation/inhibition coordination, and if the answer is positive, it would help promote the idea that causality is central both to the physical and psychological worlds because of common change mechanisms in both spheres. In this regard, systems theory provides an answer. Systems tend to equilibrium even in a far-from-equilibrium state because they tend to dampen the effects of perturbation, even if major. This obtains until the system is pushed beyond the threshold of change and, then, even a minor perturbation can promote a chaotic response to a new state configuration, aside from the fact that systems might gravitate to the regime in which equilibrium and disequilibrium co-exist at the cusp ready for change. Given this description of systems, it would appear that the dynamic in system activity relates to ongoing coordination of inhibitory (I) and activation (A). Therefore, the mathematical formulae that characterize both physical and psychological systems could involve A/I causal functions.

Dimensions

Figure 28.2 explores dimensions in behavior pertaining to S–O–R modeling of behavior. First, behavior develops, especially in higher-order organisms. Second, mechanisms assure constant, adaptive function, including in feedback and feedforward mechanisms. Third, individuals participate in social activities, and these vary

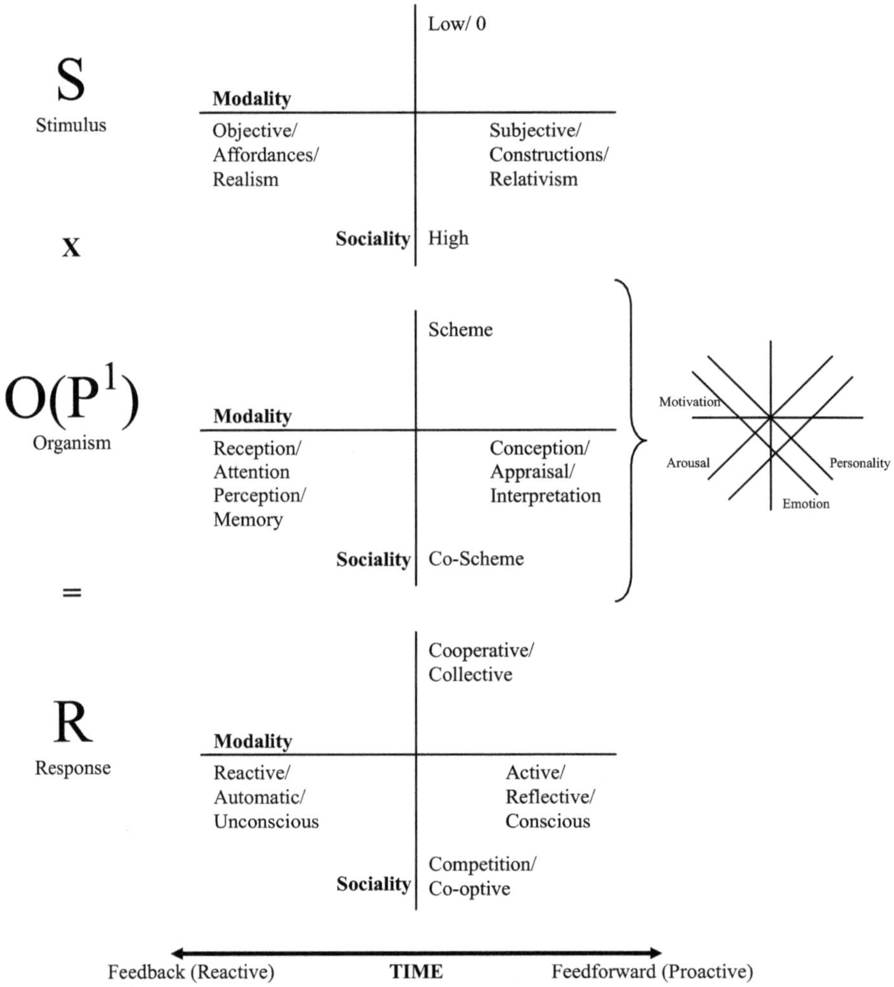

Fig. 28.2 Dimensions of modality and sociality in stimulus–organism–response modeling of developing behavior. [1]In higher-order organisms, especially for humans, the organism (person) increasingly includes effects due to attention, motivation, emotion, and personality, with each dimension varying in degree of being adaptive/maladaptive, equilibrated, positive/negative, intense or not, etc. For each of the components of the stimulus, the processing individual, and the response, there are both modality and sociality dimensions to consider. With increasing psychological complexity, there is greater influence of motivation, attention, emotion, personality [and cognition] to consider, as well as, for each of stimulus, processing, and response

according to whether the S, O, or R component of the model is being examined. For the Stimulus, sociality refers to the degree the S is social. For organism, it refers to whether the appraising of the S is individual or collective (e.g., schemes vs. co-schemes). For Response, it refers to whether cooperative or competitive social dynamics are involved.

As for modality, this dimension also varies over S, O, and R. For S, it refers to the degree to which an S is taken objectively and realistically, for example, is their affordances perceived accurately and do they lead to appropriate action? Or is the S perceived subjectively and relativistically, or is socially constructed? Modality for O refers to the quality of the appraisal of S involved. For example, both lower-order, e.g., attention, and higher-order, e.g., interpretation, factors are involved. These might include complex meaning and meaning-making, as in the narratives that we construct and use as guides in life. Finally, modality for R refers to whether we use deliberative, reflective, slower, conscious thought to guide us or whether we act and react reflexively with reflexes in a manner that is quick, automatic, and unconscious (e.g., Kahneman, 2011; Stanovich, West, & Toplak, 2014). [Note, I have argued that each of these two types or systems of thought can be decomposed into at least two subtypes according to Piagetian/Neo-Piagetian theory, i.e., sensorimotor and pre-operational thought and concrete operational and formal, abstract thought, respectively (Young, 2011).]

As a conclusion to the S–O(BAMP)–R model that I have developed, it is important to note that the individualistic, unique processing, and products involved might go awry or be disturbed to the point of being maladaptive, disequilibrated, majorly negative, and so on. Of course, genes, environment, and their interaction influence how this happens. However, we are agents, selves, whole persons, and adaptive beings who have a role in our own development and behavior, so that our behavior does not have to be deterministically maladaptive even if all the stimuli, situations, stressors, and processing capacities and qualities suggest that this type of outcome is inevitable. In the end, we have a say in "who" we are and "how" we are, to the point that we might say to ourselves and everyone around us that, despite everything involved in the past and present, "I define who I am and how I am."

Chapter Conclusions

In relation to the overriding issue in the present book of causality, the present chapter has considered basic philosophical issues in psychology (especially reductionism, constructivism, determinism, and probabilistic emergence), and basic units in psychology (stimulus input, organismic processing, response output). In both cases, for philosophy and psychology, the issues considered lead to the conclusion that fuzziness best characterizes the conceptual bases involved. For philosophy, this refers to the need for a model of behavior that is less deterministic than some maintain and that affords the possibility of free will, in an all-inclusive model of different points of view that could be seen as co-existential (Young, 1997). For psychology, this refers to the lack of distinct entities and timeframes for each of the components of the stimulus–organism–response input-processing-output sequence.

The present book, in particular, deals with causality and free will in behavior from a systems perspective. Local dynamics might be probabilistic without determinate outcome but, at a global level, in the nonlinear dynamical case, systems inevitably gravitate to deterministic outcomes, as per attractor regimes.

However, in applying this conceptual map to free will in psychology, or at least its belief and having a sense that it exists, I would argue that, even at the global level, the condition of having a belief in and a sense of free will removes the individual out of the deterministic orbit. The person becomes the parameter that can move attractors to new regions of state space, so to speak. The person becomes the effector or agent that can move psychological states even beyond the far-from-equilibrium, cusp-of-change boundary or, if you will, to uncharted attractor regions consistent with the correlated state that one's agency had moved it toward. In "gene–environment correlations" (rGE; see Chap. 11), genes can evoke actively behavior and environmental response consistent with their dynamic. Analogously, in "free will/environment correlations," to coin a term, it is the belief in free will and its effects, as well as having a sense of free will, that help direct behavior this way (see Table 28.1).

Let me continue the analogy that free will is an affordance. It exists in the membrane of possibilities that bind the universe, and it attracts people to its possibilities. However, being an affordance does not mean automatic entry in the

Table 28.1 Local and global determinism and indeterminism in relation to causality

	Local	Global
Causality in universe	Probabilistic fuzzy Indeterminate	Lawful fixed determinate
Free will in psychology	Probabilistic fuzzy Indeterminate	Probabilistic fuzzy Indeterminate

apperceiving or exposed system; rather free will is but an invitation to its possibility and it is ourselves who have to engage it. The beauty of the invitation is that surely we have the capacity to accept free will into our personal system and become it as we cause our own behavior.

References

Badcock, P. B. (2012). Evolutionary systems theory: A unifying meta-theory of psychological science. *Review of General Psychology, 16*, 10–23.

Barrett, L. F. (2012). Emotions are real. *Emotion, 12*, 413–429.

Barrett, L. F., & Bliss-Moreau, E. (2009). Affect as a psychological primitive. *Advances in Experimental Social Psychology, 41*, 167–218.

Baumeister, R. F., & Brewer, L. E. (2012). Believing versus disbelieving in free will: Correlates and consequences. *Social and Personality Psychology Compass, 6*, 736–745.

Belsky, J., & Pluess, M. (2009a). Beyond diathesis stress: Differential susceptibility to environmental influences. *Psychological Bulletin, 135*, 885–908.

Belsky, J., & Pluess, M. (2009b). The nature (and nurture?) of plasticity in early human development. *Perspectives on Psychological Science, 4*, 345–351.

Clark, A. (2013a). Whatever next? Predictive brains, situated agents, and the future of cognitive science. *Behavioral and Brain Sciences, 36*, 1–24.

Clark, A. (2013b). Are we predictive engines? Perils, prospects, and the puzzle of the porous perceiver. *Behavior and Brain Sciences, 36*, 53–64.

De Pittà, M., Volman, V., Berry, H., Parpura, V., Volterra, A., & Ben-Jacob, E. (2012). Computational quest for understanding the role of astrocyte signaling in synaptic transmission and plasticity. *Frontiers in Computational Neuroscience, 6*, 98. doi:10.3389/fncom.2012.00098.

Frankenhuis, W. E., Gergely, G., & Watson, J. S. (2013). Infants may use contingency analysis to estimate environmental states: An evolutionary, life-history perspective. *Child Development Perspectives, 7*, 115–120.

Friston, K. (2010). The free-energy principle: A unified brain theory? *Nature Reviews Neuroscience, 11*, 127–138.

Gibson, J. J. (1966). *The senses considered as perceptual systems*. Boston, MA: Houghton Mifflin.

Gibson, J. J. (1979/1986). *The ecological approach to visual perception*. Boston, MA: Houghton Mifflin.

Gottlieb, G. (2007). Probabilistic epigenesis. *Developmental Science, 10*, 1–11.

Hirsh, J. B., Mar, R. A., & Peterson, J. B. (2013). Personal narratives as the highest level of cognitive integration. *Behavioral and Brain Sciences, 36*, 36–37.

Jacoby, J. (2002). Stimulus-organism-response reconsidered: An evolutionary step in modeling (consumer) behaviour. *Journal of Consumer Psychology, 12*, 51–57.

Jaffee, S. R. (2011). Genotype-environment correlations: Definitions, methods of measurement, and implications for research on adolescent psychopathology. In K. S. Kendler, S. R. Jaffee, & D. Romer (Eds.), *The dynamic genome and mental health: The role of genes and environments in youth development* (pp. 79–102). New York: Oxford University Press.

Kahneman, D. (2011). *Thinking fast and slow*. New York: Farrar, Straus, and Giroux.

Mareschal, D., Johnson, M. H., Siros, S., Spratling, M. W., Thomas, M. S. C., & Westermann, G. (2007). *Neuroconstructivism: How the brain constructs cognition* (Vol. 1). New York: Oxford University Press.

Marken, R. S., & Mansell, W. (2013). Perceptual control as a unifying concept in psychology. *Review of General Psychology, 17*, 190–195.

Meaney, M. J. (2010). Epigenetics and the biological definition of gene x environment interactions. *Child Development, 81*, 41–79.

Michel, G. F. (2013). The role of developmental psychobiology in the unification of psychology. *Review of General Psychology, 17*, 210–215.

Peterson, M. B., Sznycer, D., Sell, A., Cosmides, L., & Tooby, J. (2013). The ancestral logic of politics: Upper-body strength regulates men's assertion of self-interest over economic redistribution. *Psychological Science, 24*, 1098–1103.

Power, W. T. (1973). *Behavior: The control of perception*. Chicago, IL: Aldine.

Power, W. T. (1978). Quantitative analysis of purposive systems: Some spadework at the foundations of scientific psychology. *Psychological Review, 85*, 417–435.

Reed, E. S. (1982). An outline of a theory of action systems. *Journal of Motor Behavior, 14*, 98–134.

Reed, E. S. (1985). An ecological approach to the evolution of behavior. In J. Johnson & A. Pietrewicz (Eds.), *Issues in the ecological study of learning* (pp. 357–383). Hillsdale, NJ: Erlbaum.

Reed, E. S. (1993). The intention to use a specific affordance: A framework for psychology. In R. Wozniak & K. Fischer (Eds.), *Development in context: Acting and thinking in specific environments* (pp. 45–75). Hillsdale, NJ: Erlbaum.

Reed, E. S. (1996). *Encountering the world: Toward an ecological psychology*. New York: Oxford University Press.

Reyna, V. F., & Brainerd, C. J. (1995). Fuzzy-trace theory: An interim synthesis. *Learning and Individual Differences, 7*, 1–75.

Reyna, V. F., & Brainerd, C. J. (2011). Dual processes in decision making and developmental neuroscience: A fuzzy-trace model. *Developmental Review, 31*, 180–206.

Seligman, M. E. P., Railton, P., Baumeister, R. F., & Sripada, C. (2013). Navigating into the future or

driven by the past. *Perspectives on Psychological Science, 8*, 119–141.
Seth, A. K., & Critchley, H. D. (2013). Extending predictive processing to the body: Emotion as interoceptive inference. *Behavioral and Brain Sciences, 36*, 47–48.
Simpson, J. A., & Belsky, J. (2008). Attachment theory within a modern evolutionary framework. In J. Cassidy & P. R. Shaver (Eds.), *Handbook of attachment: Theory, research, and clinical applications* (2nd ed., pp. 131–157). New York: Guilford Press.
Sporns, O. (2011). *Networks of the brain*. Cambridge, MA: MIT Press.
Sporns, O. (2012). *Discovering the human connectome*. Cambridge, MA: MIT Press.
Stanovich, K. E., West, R. F., & Toplak, M. E. (2014). Rationality, intelligence, and the defining features of type 1 and type 2 processing. In J. W. Sherman, B. Gawronski, & Y. Trope (Eds.), *Dual-process theories of the social mind* (pp. 80–91). New York: Guilford Press.
Sternberg, R. J. (2012). Intelligence. *Wiley Interdisciplinary Reviews: Cognitive Science, 3*, 501–511.
Thelen, E., & Smith, L. B. (1994). *A dynamic systems approach to the development of cognition and action*. Cambridge, MA: MIT Press.
Thurstone, L. L. (1923). The stimulus–response fallacy in psychology. *Psychological Review, 30*, 354–369.
Tryon, W. W. (2012). A connectionist network approach to psychological science: Core and corollary principles. *Review of General Psychology, 16*, 305–317.
van Geert, P. (2012). Dynamic systems. In B. Laursen, T. D. Little, & N. A. Card (Eds.), *Handbook of developmental research methods* (pp. 725–741). New York: Guilford Press.
Withagen, R., de Poel, H. J., Araújo, D., & Pepping, G.-J. (2012). Affordances can invite behavior: Reconsidering the relationship between affordances and agency. *New Ideas in Psychology, 30*, 250–258.
Witkiewitz, K., & Marlatt, G. A. (2007). Modeling the complexity of post-treatment drinking: It's a rocky road to relapse. *Clinical Psychology Review, 27*, 724–738.
Woodworth, R. S. (1918). *Dynamic psychology*. New York: Columbia University Press.
Young, G. (1997). *Adult development, therapy, and culture: A postmodern synthesis*. New York: Plenum.
Young, G. (2011). *Development and causality: Neo-Piagetian perspectives*. New York: Springer Science + Business Media.
Zaki, J. (2013). Cue integration: A common framework for social cognition and physical perception. *Perspectives on Psychological Science, 8*, 296–312.

29 Networked Causal Terms

Chapter Introduction

The next two chapters of the book are on novel concepts that I have created related to the subject of causality. In order to promote the importance of the study of the causality of behavior, I have tried to create concepts and terms that bring it to the fore. One integrative way of understanding causality in psychology revolves around the concept of networks. In this regard, I propose an Integrated Cross-Network (ICN) model of psychological causality. In the chapter, I present a table that I developed that includes critical integrative (and sometimes novel) terms related to this construct. Another integrative model that I developed for present purposes concerns the concept of Genes × Environment × Organism × Development × Systems, which attempts to capture a good range of causal influences on behavior. This model also is presented in tabular format. A new model that I created about causality that might have integrative applications for psychology involves Coexistential Intraactive Causality. I created these diverse terms in order to capture the dynamic nature of behavior in the causal nexus, and also to serve as an instigating suite of concepts in the study of psychology and causality.

Terms

Standard

The first table in this chapter on terminology related to causality explains some basic terms in the present work (see Table 29.1). I have undertaken this step in order to avoid any perception of imprecision or use of jargon. First, it gives explanations for critical, common terms, such as genetics, evolution, development, and systems. It includes description of the biopsychosocial and related models. The latter model is an important one in the present work because of its integrative nature. The table also gives supplemental terms, including some complex ones, such as the differential susceptibility model.

Innovation

Landscapes Table 29.1 follows and it presents terms that I innovated about causality related to psychology and psychopathology. First, I describe the concept of the causal landscape. It refers to range of causal influences on behavior, the models of those influences, and the concepts that are developed to understand causality. We

G. Young, *Unifying Causality and Psychology*, DOI 10.1007/978-3-319-24094-7_29

Table 29.1 Causality in psychology: key terms

Term	Explanation
Psychology	Psychology is more than the study of behavior, which is its traditional definition. Among other considerations, it is also the study of its development, and its relationship to the brain–behavior relationships, to evolution, and to causality
Behavior	Refers to the output of psychological systems and to the processes governing them. Takes place at the level of action and its tendencies, and of cognition and emotion, and their constituents and interactions. Behaviors have to be understood at the level of the causal linkages producing them and the causal effects that they have. As an analogy, we could describe clouds and leave it at that, but they are best understood when we can understand their origins and determinants in physical and chemical processes (with biological ones involved, too). For behavior, the analogy applies especially to areas such as development, abnormal development, and psychopathology. The study of behavior independent of causality paints a limited picture and might ellipse background and downstream information not only essential in understanding it but also in even redescribing it more accurately
Development	One definition involves change in behavior and another involves its organization, including steps/phases/stages; but also conserving gains, avoiding regression, if possible
Psychopathology	Disturbances and disorders in behavior
Model	A theory/metatheory that is heuristic, perhaps mathematical, integrative, potentially testable, with operationalized predictions
System	Dynamical, self-organizing, emergent, multiple level, hierarchical, reciprocally, bottom-up and top-down, probabilistic/stochastic
Causal	Proximal and distal influences and mechanisms and their interaction in eliciting/maintaining relevant effecting-effector (determined) relations. They might be conservative/canalyzed/stable or changing/cascading/unstable
Biopsychosocial	A model of behavior and its function/dysfunction related to biological, psychological, and social components. Referred to as biopersonalsocial by Young (2011). Related models are diathesis/stress, person × environment, and risk-resilience
Biopersonalsocial	A model in which behavior is considered the interactive product of biological (e.g., genetic), personal (e.g., personality, coping, curiosity, free will), and social (environmental, contextual) factors with evolutionary and developmental dynamics involved. The biopersonalsocial model is consistent with the biopsychosocial one, in that the component related to the organism (person) is added to the terminology in the model without diminishing the others as psychologically relevant. A term created to counteract the ambiguity in calling referring to the biopsychosocial model as a psychological one—it weakens to a dualistic conception
Generative	Generative refers to part or whole individual/structure or phenotypic (endophenotypic) growth promotion/maintenance. It might also entail negative growth/degeneration/maladaptation
Governing	Steer, direct, influence, guide, control Not in a homuncular, machine-within-the-machine sense, but in a dynamic, self-regulating sense
Gene/genetic/ genotypic/ genomic	The units of, as well as entirety of, an organism's hereditary information, e.g., DNA, including its allelic make-up in the individual. The genotype is an organism's complete hereditary information. The phenotype is its observed properties (morphological, physiological, behavioral). Endophenotypes are intermediary aspects of the phenotype with downstream genetic connections
Genetic	Genes, genome, genetic material, DNA
Epigenetic/ epigenomic	Study of heritable changes in gene expression/phenotype induced by mechanisms beyond changes in underlying DNA sequence (e.g., gene silencing by acting on promoter regions). Collectively, epigenetic changes constitute the epigenome
Evolution	Intergenerational change in inherited characteristics of biological populations, including to the point of speciation

Adaptation (Darwinian)	An evolved (through natural selection) and currently maintained trait contributing to the survival and fitness or reproductive success of an individual. An adaptation might include differential options in phenotypic expression that serves fitness. "Natural selection has also maintained variation (adaptive individual differences)" (Ellis, Boyce, Belsky, Bakermans-Kranenburg, & van IJzendoorn, 2011, p. 7), or differential susceptibilities to environmental variations, even if apparently for worse in a fitness sense in the long term time frame (but not the short term)
Natural selection	A gradual, non-random process that alters the relative frequency of biological traits in a population by way of differential reproduction of individuals possessing the traits
Fitness (survival/ reproduction)	The ability to survive and reproduce. Traits that contribute to survival and reproduction increase their frequency in a population over generations through the process of natural selection
Differential susceptibility (dandelion/ orchid)	More malleable individuals are more susceptible to environmental influences, both for better or worse. For these individuals, development is more positive than the norm in supportive environments but also more adverse in negative ones. Nevertheless, the adverse development in the latter case might bring adaptive advantages in a fitness/evolutionary sense. Therefore, it has been labeled metaphorically as the orchid phenotype (susceptible) compared to an opposing dandelion one (can grow anywhere). The model contrasts with the traditional diathesis-stress model of maladaptive behavior/ psychopathology (vulnerabilities in interaction with stress lead to developmental psychopathology)
Life history theory	Study of how organisms allocate time, energy, and resources to different activities at each phase over the life cycle. Each phase needs to be addressed adaptively
Evolutionary/ Developmental (Evo/Devo)	Origin and alteration of species by natural selection and other evolutionary pressures throughout development
Phylogenetic/ ontogenetic	Ontogeny refers to the developmental, (real or lived) temporal history of an organism, whereas phylogeny refers to its evolution. Development refers to change in behavior or its organization over an organism's lifetime, i.e., it is akin to ontogeny, not phylogeny. Development is ontogenetic stabilization/continuity and change/transformation in product (morphology, physiology, body, brain, behavior, and its organization, including phases/ steps/stages) and process
Ecological niche	The resources/competitors in an organism's/population's context that govern its way of life (responding and altering). Constructed niche refers to changes in the niche created by the organism and its activities
Environment/ ecology	Context/surroundings and their factors/interactions that affect an organism/population, including other organisms and their relations
Sociocultural	Refers to a human individual/population in its ecological context, especially in terms of relations. A wider term would be sociocultural/ historicopolitical, in order to refer to cultural changes over time and how they are embedded in wider societal organizations
Organism/ organismic	Individuals of a species, a living system. Note that the adjective in this context does not refer to holistic, organic approaches in psychology
Organization/ institution	Social structures evolve too. Many of the terms in the model as they apply to individuals can apply equally to societal-type systems
Group	The term is meant to cover different social structures. In the evolutionary sense, it indicates that one focus concerns group selection, distinct from natural selection. In this model, selection can operate on entire groups and lead to group-like traits, even at the sacrifice of individual fitness, at least when constraints mitigating against it do not apply
(Re)Organization	Concerns processes governing behavioral development, which might concern its organization and reorganization, rather than specific behaviors, per se

(continued)

Table 29.1 (continue)

Term	Explanation
Optimization	Evolution considers maximizing survival and reproductive fitness (adaptation), without concern for one optimal strategy and, indeed, from the empirical point of view, none exists in an evolutionary sense. The term optimization is used in the sense of maximizing survival and reproductive fitness for living systems/organisms/individuals and also assuring survival and growth of institutions/organizations/social structures
Dynamical (nonlinear) system	In a system, the whole is greater than the sum of the parts. In dynamical systems, prior states predict present ones (a fixed rule defines the movement of a point in temporally-mediated geometric space). In nonlinear dynamical systems, the local behavior of the system might appear unpredictable or random, but it is still globally deterministic. Nonlinear dynamical systems are marked by self-organized phase transitions in state space leading to emergent reorganizations or attractors that resist disequilibrium from perturbations until they are pushed beyond parameters at bifurcation points or the cusp of change
Quantitative/ qualitative	Development could be continuous, gradual, and without phases, steps, stages, or an increasingly complexity, but also it could be marked by abrupt shifts in organization distinct from prior organizations, as in stages. Feedback (negative, positive) and feedforward mechanisms could speed up or contain cascades in development. Change could be constructive, positive (virtuous) or destructive, negative (vicious)
Stimulus/ response (input/ output)	Behaviorism studies behavior as stimulus–response connections and the mechanisms that change them (e.g., reinforcement), doing so without reference to the organism's black box (e.g., mental, brain). In the information-processing approach, language equivalent to stimulus–response is input–output, as in computers. In this model, attention and motivation are important as mediators. Similarly, in appraising stressors, stimuli might be appraised differentially (e.g., one person's threat is not another's; there are individual differences according to subjective experience). In this regard, different schools of thought vary as to what degree stimuli are "constructed" by the person. Similarly, responses behave differently according to adaptive parameters. For example, they could vary in terms of their automaticity or reflectiveness. The former is fast, intuitive, unconscious and the latter is slow, deliberate, and conscious
Strategic/ strategizing	Strategizing refers to the active mental process in problem solving and directing behavior. In evolution, one discusses strategies in terms of options that genes might help promote in phenotypic adaptation, depending on differential qualities in the environment. The application of evolutionary strategies to humans does not mean the same as conscious strategies in human behavior
Stochastic/ probabilistic	A stochastic system contains non-deterministic states. The successive states of the system are influenced by previous states and probabilistic or random elements. Keeping in mind NLDST, local, in-the-moment states might be probabilistic but global patterns are deterministic or non-random
Deterministic	A system is deterministic when randomness is not a factor in determining its future states. Philosophically, there is debate whether determinism applies universally to events and behavior. Psychologically, belief in free will constitutes an example in which determinism can take a back seat to psychological processes within the person. Systems not functioning deterministically could be termed adeterministic
Emergent	A rearrangement of entities into new patterns that are unpredictable from knowledge of the entities. For example, in H_2O (water), wetness is not predictable from knowledge of the properties of H or O. In children's play, games are unpredictable from knowledge of any one child
Approach/ Withdrawal	Approach and withdrawal concern more than the direction of behavior, because it could refer to tendencies not expressed due to context. Also, approach might be the product of either activation or of release of inhibition. Also, it could refer to negative emotions, such as approaching in anger. Withdrawal could refer to movement away but also to shutting down, although the polar opposite of approach refers to the movement option
Activation/ inhibition coordination	Critical mechanism functioning in multiple levels of behavior, brain, and components/levels, including the genetic

are active seekers and users of causal concepts. Also in this regard, the concept of causal ecological expanses/fields refers to the dynamic causality manifold, for example, in relation to symptom networks.

Embodiism A pair of concepts that are especially important in the present book concerns "embodied causation" and "causal embodiment." Together, these concepts refer to the embodied cognitive origin of causality and its understanding, and also to the essential nature of causality in human behavior. When these concepts are applied to disturbed behavior and psychopathology, they are referred to as embodied etiology and etiological embodiment, respectively.

Homo Causa Collectively, the terms related to causality that I have created, as presented in this chapter, specifically, as well as the contents of the present book, generally, underscore that *Homo Sapiens* should be called *Homo Causa* or (*Homo Humanus Causa*).

Causal Particles In addition, whether we speak of human behavior or of the physical universe, one concept that could unify the importance of causality is that both the behavior and the wider world are constituted by "causal particles," which I refer to as "causicles." I describe in more depth below the concept of causal particles/causicles.

Comment From a scientific point of view, at the psychological and psychiatric levels, the empirical task should be to discover causal relations and their import for normal behavior and also how it (and they) can go awry. In the following, I present an integrated model of causality for psychology and psychiatry based on networks.

Integrated Cross-Network Model

Introduction

Although causality is an important, ubiquitous theme in psychology, it is not dealt with in a coherent manner. I have constructed a preliminary framework that links critical concepts in psychology and causality. Although many of the terms in the framework are ones that are innovative, they are extensions of standard concepts in psychology. Table 29.2 gives the key terms in the framework. I refer to the framework as the ICN framework of psychology and causality because the concept of network is becoming one that is cross-disciplinary. Moreover, in and of itself, it is an integrative term. The table indicates that the ICN model should apply to major areas of psychology and, aside from the ones that listed in it, the areas include social psychology, cognitive psychology, psychopathology, and neuropsychology. Table 29.3 indicates that the essential focus of the framework is on change and behavior and how it takes place. Aside from the processes listed, there are many additions that could be made, including those of genetics/epigenetics and activation/inhibition coordination.

Model

In the following, I briefly address some of the key terms in the ICN framework, as listed in Table 29.2, which include: cross-networks, connectome, yoking, peridynamical, constrained emergence, neoreductioconstructivism, biopersonalsocial, micro–macro hypertransactionalism, causality systematization/systematizing causality, ontophylogenetic/phyloontogenetic, and multicausal systems. These terms give the range of concepts involved in the ICN framework.

Cross-Networks

Cross-networks refer to multiple network interconnections, such as found in neuronal networks and the connectome (Sporns, 2011, 2012). Nonlinear dynamical systems theory (NLDST) includes concepts related to networks, such as patterns, configurations, assembled states, and attractors and, also, one version of complexity theory (Holland, 2012) emphasizes networks.

Table 29.2 Integrated terminology of psychological causality/causation, including an integrated cross-network (ICN) model (behavior, development, psychopathology)

Term	Explanation
Causal landscape	The range of causal factors that influence behavior, as well as the diverse models of how they affect behavior
Causal ecological expanses (fields)	Causality does not lie in an aggregate of direct and indirect factors. Rather, it consists of a field of interacting and emergent constituents from more indirect to direct ones, and related risk factors, moderators, and mediators. The components are not isolated and additive but they form a fluid, metamorphosing manifold that dynamically changes in context and in relation to symptom network expression and plasticity
Causal complexity	The process of establishing the causal network governing a system, and also differentiating causal and acausal influences in a system as it becomes more complex (complexifies) over time, thereby establishing the causal dynamic of the system
Deterministic complexity	The process of differentiating deterministic and adeterministic causal influences in the causal network in a system as it becomes more complex/complexifies (in complexification)
Embodied causation	The acquisition and appreciation of causal understanding through body-focused/body-centric, sensorimotor activity and influence. The concept summarizes a unique, unifying approach to understanding causality in behavior in psychology, etiology in psychopathology in psychiatry. At the level of causation, the term refers to a multifactorial, integrated network, and dynamical approach to understanding causality in behavior, while admitting to limits in present knowledge and science of that understanding. At the level of embodiment, the term refers to the fuzziness in separating environment, organism, and response. Causation does not lie out there independently in the world acting passively on us. Rather, it exists in continual interaction with the adaptive and apperceiving nature of the organism in relationship with the environment through its perceptual and action control mechanisms, and cognitive ones, if they are applicable. Therefore, causality resides in the organism or the person, as the case may be, including the body and mind, and starting with the body in that the individual develops mostly from and initial physical state to an integrated physical and mental one
Causal embodiment	Causality is the context in which behavior lives and is defined. We are active agents of causality search, participation, understanding, and use for Darwinian (selection) survival and reproduction and related processes
Embodied etiology	Embodied causation in the context of disturbed, disordered, dysfunctional (developmental) behavior
Etiological embodiment	Causal embodiment that goes awry in disturbed, disordered, dysfunctional (developmental) behavior
Cross-network (integrated)	Networks concern collections of relational data and their representations. They can exist at multiple levels that form larger networks. Cross-networks refer to connected networks either within a level of a system or over levels. They might be localized or dispersed and distributed
System cohesion and coherence connectivity	Cohesion refers to integration within an element of a system (think; within a sentence) and coherence to integration across them (think, across sentences or even a paragraph), with across-level integrations involving different strata or multiple-level connectivities (think narrative)
Peridynamical	Linear systems are ones that can be mapped for outputs according to inputs and functions such that there might be one-to-one and related slope functions. Nonlinear dynamical systems are ones that can be represented by differential equations such that inputs and outputs are not necessarily linear but can exhibit exponentially different outputs compared to the inputs. The term "peridynamical" refers to systems that might involve dynamical systematization in at least some (if not all) phases of its phase space mapping or trajectory. For example, in human development, trajectories might be especially or uniquely linear, but qualitative jumps in organization, i.e., stages, might be found, as well. Formally, a peridynamical system is one that either includes nonlinear dynamical system components in part or in full, or ones that could transform into them
Constrained emergence	The concept of constrained emergence indicates that system change that leads to novel organizational outputs cannot take any and every form or pattern possible because of the constraints in the characteristics of the constituent elements involved and in the characteristics of their interaction in promoting novel outputs

Circular causal emergence	Circular causality refers to the reciprocal interactions between different levels of a system. Circular causal emergence specifies that the interactions can become constitutive of emergent properties, entities, or levels in the system (within or across the levels) beyond anything predictable from knowledge of the elements involved
Neoreductioconstructivism	There is a tension in psychology and other disciplines about whether reality is positivist, empiricist, and somewhat independent of the observer, or whether it is personally and socially constructed. Reductionism refers to simplifying complex phenomena, including the psychological, to underlying and constituent elements and processes, such as to brain activity and function in the case of psychology. A combined view would acknowledge the objective reality of the external world, in part, while admitting to personal/social constructivist, subjective influence. "Neoreductioconstructivism" refers to not only an integration of reductionism and constructivism into a unified conception but also to a superordinate concept about reality in which the person actively contributes to her/his integration and the person condition others (or the environment) and is conditioned by them
Micro/macro hypertransactionalism	Transactionalism in psychology refers to the moment-to-moment interaction of the person in the environment and how each modifies the other from second to second. "Hypertransactionalism" refers to the rapid, pervasive, multiple-level, and powerful transactions that take place across person and environment. Moreover, it can happen both at the micro- and macro-levels, or extreme micro- (nano) and extreme macro- (giga/mega) levels
Causality systematization/ systemizing causality	Systems are causality machines and also machines that produce causality. They exist only because of causality and through their causality. In their activity, they systematize causality and, as they function in causality, they are systematizing of themselves and their context
Ontophylogenetic/ Phyloontogenetic	Ontogeny and phylogeny are intimately linked not in the sense that the former recapitulates the latter but in the sense that each acquisition of the phenotype at a particular developmental level that is linked to the genotype in some way has evolved because of its immediate adaptive fitness advantage in the age period concerned. Also, the plasticity of the ontogenetic process flexibility enables phenotypic variants to emerge that, if linked to the genotype, could enable better Darwinian survival and eventually reproduction. The term "ontophylogenetic/phyloontogenetic" captures this intimate linkage in a unifying process of ontogeny and phylogeny to the point that neither can exist without the other and each aliments the other
Individualizing/commonalizing	Systems exist in multiple, coordinated opponent, or dialectical relationships. For example, this includes the interrelation of top-down and bottom-up causation or causality. Another example relates to their ongoing, de novo dynamical construction from the array of system components extant at any one moment. This means that a system state is always individualized and novel at each moment of its existence. Nevertheless, the system patterns might give the impression of being universal or standard. However, this appearance is valid only in the sense that the system states resemble each other over a period of time. Thus, although the system states appear to have a common structure and the system appears stable and constant, it is only because the system has reconstituted itself in an adaptive form in a highly similar way or even in an identical way in each minimal time unit of the time period involved. State commonality is a surface although valid appearance that reflects moment-to-moment individualization in the system. Note that because of a system's appearance of communalization, it might not be easy to detect its constant individualization. Overall, individualization is its predominant property relative to communalization, although the latter can serve as a good shorthand in describing it. This description of the individualizing and commonalizing properties of systems is akin to describing them in terms of attractors, which have both local individualized trajectories and global representative patterns in their basins. In general, system communalization can be captured by some sort of mathematical representation, but the formula cannot capture each expression of the system nor its range. At the same time, without commonalizing mathematical representations of a system, its diverse patterns and individual differences, as well as chaotic noise, could become too complex to grasp and discern

(continued)

Table 29.2 (continued)

Term	Explanation
Biopersonalsocial (biopsychosocial)	This refers to the concept developed in Young (2011) about the biopsychosocial model. Young modified the classic term in the way indicated so that is reflects a genuine psychological model, which includes a role for the active self and components of the person's psychology in outputting behavior
Biopsychosocial etiology (symptoms, networks, intervention/therapy)	In the field of medicine and its subfield of psychiatry, causation of disease is referred to as etiology. An appropriate causal or etiological model of psychiatric disorder or illness understands the conditions involved as more than a biological-oriented disease but as expressions of biopsychosocial factors. Similarly, the networks of symptoms expressed are biopsychosocial in nature. Finally, the appropriate interventions/treatments normally should be biopsychosocial
Basics Behavioral Community Model	A variation of the biopsychosocial model that applies equally to nonliving systems. In this regard, the basics refer to (a) the constituents of the systems involved, (b) the behavior and its dynamics involved, and the community in the full context involved. The basics cannot be biological for nonliving systems, the term behavior applies equally to living and nonliving systems, as does the term community
Multicausal biopsychosocial systems	Systems are multifactorial/multicomponential in causality. They have multiple levels, and the levels interact both in defining themselves in their activity and in their causality. In psychology and psychiatry, the multicausal systems are integrally biopsychosocial in nature, as is the system as a whole. Biopsychosocial models now include nonlinear dynamical system properties, and also complexity ones
A∪I: Inter- and Intra-level activation–inhibition coordination cohesion and coherence	The concept of circular causality or circular causal emergence does not specify the mechanism involved in the constitutive emergence of the particular property, entity, or level that coalesces. However, activation–inhibition coordination is a process that might underlie multiple levels of behavior and brain processes, serving to create cohesion, or coherent intrasystem linkages
Fuzzy probabilistics	In a deterministic universe, knowledge of what had happened previously will predict what will happen or, stated differently, given pre-existing conditions, nothing other than what has happened after them could have happened. This concept is based on assumptions that (a) events and conditions can be specified (are separable and identifiable events or conditions). (b) Moreover, the said events and conditions are positivistically and empirically genuine, without subjective, constructed, apperceived impressions about their existence. (c) Finally, they are individually or (sub)collectively associated with definite probabilities both in their initial appearance and their effects. However, all three of these fundamental assumptions can be challenged in the psychological universe. (1) Conditions and events are not distinct, isolatable, objective entities but, rather, they are fuzzy, messy, subjective (person-mediated) constructions that are only partially related to input parameters. (2) Also, they influence each other in systemic interactions, which moreover can create emergent conditions/events, properties, relations, etc., so that they do not have clear probabilities associated with each of them, either in terms of their manifestation in the cause-effect milieu or of the level of certainty of their effects. People might tend more toward establishing cognitive structures with properties more reflective of determinism or stochasticism. However, in these regards, these cognitive structures normally end up as fuzzy or indeterminate hybridizations. Therefore, human determinism tends toward an indeterminate determinism with inchoate partial deterministic mechanisms in place; also, human stochasticism tends toward an exacting probalisticism with the probabilities in the sequential unfolding of events precisely defined. The human mentally normatively gravitates between these thresholds into a zone of fuzzy probabilistics for the most part, with much individual variation in the process. There is room for an inexact admixture of the exact deterministic and in exact probabilistic cognitive structure that make up our cognition

Psychological Co-universe/ Relaverse	The psychological universe is governed neither purely deterministically nor probabilistically, but it is person- or individual-focused and filtered, with feedback from the person into appreciation of the conditions and events about him or her and also feedforward into shaping particular putative cause-outcome conditionals. However, every person is a fuzzy analytic and prediction process mechanism of input and output, so that people live in a constant flux of fuzzy probabilities. The outside world is not a given in reality nor is it directly acted upon. Rather, it is participated in and co-constructed by the participation process, which itself is a reflection of the variegated individuality of person as much as the individualized vicissitudes of the relational matrix involved in the participation. In this sense, there is not simply a person-focused psychological universe, a mental landscape within the person. Rather, there is only a psychological co-universe, which is participatory with multiple, shared relationships. The psychological co-universe in which we live also can be called a psychological "Relaverse." These terms imply a co-actional, relationally constituted psychological world in each of us that emerges from the person through relational activity; and also from which the person emerges (co-constituted by its (the Relaverse's) activity as much as the person's own)
Homo Causa	Homo sapiens can be perceived in terms of a penultimate motivation and ability to search for, participate in, understand, and use causality in behavior because it is part of our evolutionary heritage, facilitating Darwinian survival and reproduction (selection) and related processes
Causal particles (Causicles)	The essence of the physical, chemical, and behavioral universe. Agents and objects exist in light of the causal relations that they seek, participate in, try to understand, and use adaptively
Causal weirdness	The more we learn about causality and causation, the more it becomes apparent that they cannot be explained in standard ways nor does the reality to which they are addressed match standard and logically coherent understandings
Dark causality	Just as in physics, in which there are the concepts of dark matter and dark energy, we should entertain that there are invisible and indeterminate realities about causality in the physical and psychological worlds that defy standard explanations yet that are no less real

Table 29.3 Change processes and related terms in the ICN: integrated cross-network model

Category	Minor	Major
Standard change terms	Stable	Unstable
	Static	Dynamic
	Equilibrium	Disequilibrium
Other change terms	Conservation	Transition
	Linear	Nonlinear
	Instantiation	Transformation
	Reduction	Construction
	Resistance	Revolution
	Merging	Emergence
	Horizontal move	Vertical leap
	Adjust	Cascade
	Refine	Rupture
	Return	Retool
	Quantitative	Qualitative
Other terms	Local	Global
	Micro	Macro
	Deterministic	Stochastic
	Predictable	Unpredictable
	Ordered	Unordered
	Chartable	Unchartable
	Bounded	Unbounded
	Top-down	Bottom-up

Basic Behavioral Community

Note that one way of referring to biopsychosocial/biopersonalsocial model is generically so that it applies to even nonliving systems. That is, all systems have elements of some sort that—link to biological or related physical properties; in one way or another, all systems behave, and; finally, all systems have their elements function in community. In this regard, see Fig. 29.1 that presents a generic, basic behavioral community model of causality in system function.

Intrapersonal, Interpersonal, Interfaced

Cross-networks could exist not only within the brain network (intrapersonal connectome), but also in the social one (interpersonal connectome), linking brain to brain in a certain sense. In addition, the person today is becoming increasingly connected to, or interfaced with, the technological world, and advances in these regards augur

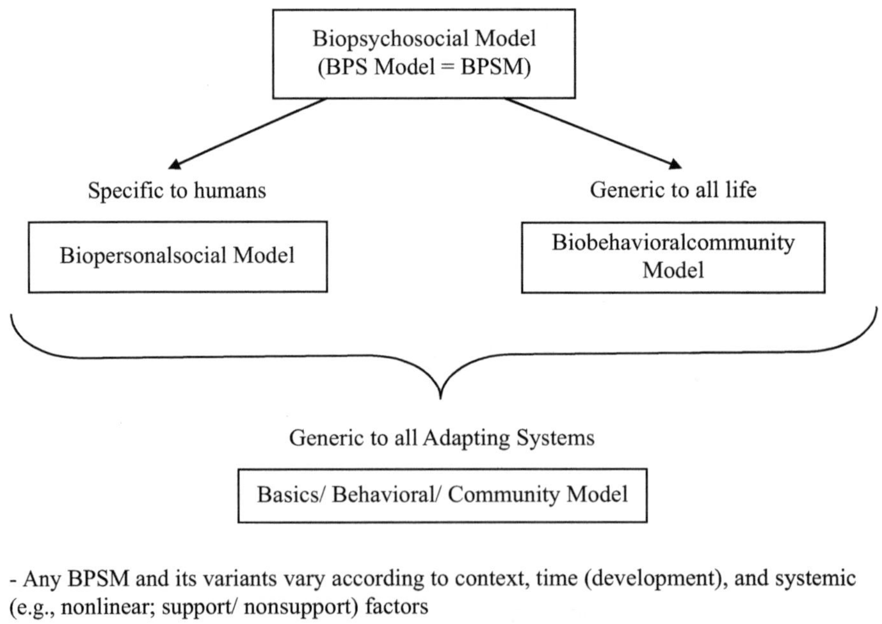

Fig. 29.1 Basic/behavioral/community model of causality

well for spinal cord injury, neurodegenerative diseases, and so on. However, people, in general, have always expressed interconnectivity with the natural and material world (interfaced connectome). These three domains of the cross-network system of the person (intrapersonal, interpersonal, interfaced) constitute a unified tripartite cross-network system.

Yoking

Yoked networks refer to the dynamical nature of network self-assembly to facilitate successful contextual adaptation (e.g., problem discernment and resolution). Just as behaviors coalesce into adaptive patterns from among the elements available in a system, so can underlying and associated neuronal networks. [Also, note that Young (2011) has hypothesized that Neo-Piagetian stages and substages do not disappear as more advanced ones develop but that they remain actively available (perhaps in more evolved forms) for purposes of yoking to higher-order ones in order to decipher and resolve contextual adaptation and problems.]

Peridynamical

Peridynamical is a term constructed to describe systems that might include dynamical processes or systems that could gravitate to a nonlinear dynamical regime. Development provides the classic example, with some aspects residing on the cusp of order and disorder, which facilitates to state transitions in state space due to nonlinear dynamical forces (Young, 2011).

Constrained Emergence

Constrained emergence refers to the property of nonlinear dynamical system to follow trajectories in which system elements coalesce into new patterns, configurations, states, or attractors that are unpredictable from simple knowledge of the constituent elements. Although it is true that the whole is more than the sum of the parts, the concept of constrained emergence acknowledges that the nature of the whole that emerges is somewhat constrained by the nature of the parts.

Neoreductioconstructionism

Neoreductioconstructionism is a term to indicate that both positivist, empirical and personal, social construction components contribute to perceived reality in an interaction that surpasses both. In Young (2011), I described a more elaborate epistemological model of co-existentialism, but essentially it can be conceptualized in these terms.

Biopersonalsocial

In Young (2011), I also modified the term biopsychosocial to biopersonalsocial. A psychological model needs to include all three components of the latter term in interaction in producing behavior. The personal components indicate that behavioral expression is actively influenced by the mediation of ourselves and not just by nature and nurture.

Hypertransactionalism

Micro/macro hypertransactionalism refers to the dynamic, ongoing, continual interaction between person and environment at multiple temporal levels. Both person and environment are intrinsically transformed nano-second by nano-second in their encounter, and their reciprocal interactions over time can lead to transformative (constrained) emergence. Environment enters the person, getting under the skin, even acting on genes through epigenetic mechanisms, such as gene silencing. At the same time, the person acts adaptively on the environment, constructing niches and engaging in correlated behavior to reflect one's genotypic expression. Therefore, just as the person becomes the environment the environment becomes the person.

Causal System

The term "causality systematization/systemizing causality" refers to the causal nature of behavioral systems, both in terms of having diverse influences and producing diverse outcomes from multiple factors. Systems are not only defined by their causal properties but also exist by and through them.

Ontogeny/Phylogeny

The term "ontophylogenetic/phyloontogenetic" refers to the intimate link between ontogeny and phylogeny both in developmental expression and in species' evolution and speciation. Each developmental step exists because of selection for its immediate adaptive fitness and not just what it leads to in the adult. Each phenotypic form is partially the expression of genotype-related successive developmental (evolved) forms.

Multifactorial

Systems are multicausal in origin and determinants, and self-organize into coherent and cohesive forms that gracefully accommodate to their constituents, the characteristics of the latter, and how they interact. System interaction includes bottom-up and top-down forces that exert influence at the multiple levels in the hierarchical arrangement that the system elements form, including emergent ones.

Fuzziness

Systems can be described for the universe, in general, and for the "psychological universe" in particular. In this regard, I refer to the fuzzy probabilistics in the psychological universe, which is consistent with a Bayesian approach to psychological phenomena and a non-deterministic solution to the question of whether we have free will, a capacity to choose for ourselves, and the ability to be part of our own causality.

GEODS Model

Introduction

The genetic study of behavior has differentiated to include Gene–Environmental interactions (G × E). Table 29.4 explains an expanded G × E model that includes organism, development, and systems (O, D, S = GEODS). G × E typically refers to a statistical interaction that narrows genetic effects to the simultaneous present of particular genomic alleles and particular environments. The interaction might even be narrowed further to having its effect in particular developmental periods (G × E × D). The systems get complicated by G × G interactions and by E × E interactions added to the equation, as well as their various combinations.

Model

The present model examines G × E (and G × E × D) interactions more globally in terms of the factors that influence behavior. Although these three types of factors are crucial, they do not act passively in that the person (O; organism, individual) has a role to play in his/her own development, especially at the human level (e.g., personality, motivation, curiosity, coping). Also, the whole system (S) in which behavior takes place needs to be considered. For example, NLDST describes emergent qualitative leaps in behavior and its organization that might take place due to the multifactorial impacts on systems. Genes and environment have their influences on a wider developing system, which might function to either constrain or amplify their interactive influences. The tables illustrate a move from analyzing behavior at the statistical, narrowing level of interaction to the broadening systemic level of interaction.

The table addresses complex issues in NLDST, such as creation of attractors and chaos theory. Genetic and genomic theories are evolving quickly to include epigenetic effects, and -omics, in general, are proliferating. The multiple complications and complexities in behavioral genesis

Table 29.4 Gene × environment × organism × development × systems (GEODS) model

	Variation	
Component	Statistical	Conceptual
Gene × Environment (G × E)	ANOVA (analysis of variance) and multiple regression. Specific levels of main effects differentially involved; they constitute multiplicative or interactive interaction effects (e.g., 2-way, as indicated by X) - to - Advanced techniques (e.g., PCA, principle components analysis; HLM, hierarchical linear modeling) [Complicated by G × G (epistatic) and E × E interactions]	Genes and Environment interact in the sense that both Nature and Nurture contribute in full to behavior (and not only particular alleles in particular environments) - to - Genetic and environmental variations act as differential influences (indirect moderation; direct mediation) on behavior; behavior systems exhibit complexity
Development (add D; G × E × D)	Statistical interactions are 3-way. Outcome (dependent variables) of G × E interactions vary with developmental (D) as another independent variable - to - Advanced techniques	Genes and Environment work their multiplicative interaction in different ways at different developmental periods - to - There might be sensitive periods, or critical windows development in which genes and their interactions have more or exclusive effects. The pattern could include several such phases over the lifespan, with different yet homologous or equivalent outcome measures involved (heterotypic continuity)
Organism (add O; G × E × O × D)	N of studies would have to be high enough to allow for 4-way statistical interactions, either in (M) AN(C)OVAs or multiple regression - to - Aside from variations in factor/main effect levels related to G, E, D, and O, sex or gender as a main effect/fact complicates matters, especially for 4-way statistical interactions in MANANOVs, ANOVAs and multiple regression	Organism (individual, person) variables could concern ones related to attention/motivation, cognition/appraisals, curiosity/appraisals, personality/temperament, coping/resilience, mood/self, majority/minority status (demographics), and so on, as further influences on behavior; the person has a behavioral determination and expression - to - Organism variables might concern correlated genetic ones, such as in evocative or active gene–environment correlation interactions or in niche construction, in which organisms play an active part in changing or eliciting change in their environments - to - Complex factors, such as a belief in free will and unconscious influences, can influence/supercede genetic, environmental, and other factors in their influence on behavior and its choices

(continued)

Table 29.4 (continued)

Component	Variation	
	Statistical	Conceptual
Systems (add S; G×E×O×S)	NLDST is mathematically grounded in approaches quite different from classic parametric approaches in psychology (e.g., differential equations) - to - The variation in the system variables constitutes the foci of attention rather than being considered confounding "noise"	The systems model does not analyze separately each variable of a set of variables one by one and for their main effects and interactive effects on other variables. Rather, a systems approach seeks interactive patterns across all the elements of the system and the manner in which they form patterns, or new superordinate variables. Transformative system change might include those that are self-organized emergent ones, such as in the creation of new attractors, attractor splitting at bifurcation points, major chaotic transitions even with minor perturbations at far-from-equilibrium points, the butterfly effect, etc. - to - In the following, I elaborate each of the terms G, E, O, D, S. (G) generative growth/maintenance promoting, governing gene/genetic/genomic, genotypic/genetic material in concert with epigenetic/epigenomic, and marks/stamps silencing genes × (E) environmental/ecological (constructed) niche, ecological/sociocultural (and historicopolitical) influences × (O) organismic/institutional/group/organization (individual organism/organ) and its (re)organization/optimization (adaptation, susceptibility, diathesis), and differentiation × (D) development (ontogenesis), which is also Darwinian (evolution, phylogenesis, natural selection, survival/reproduction/propagation, fitness) nonlinear, self-organizational (potentially emergent) as well as dialectical/relational and dynamical. It can be quantitative/qualitative, and transformational/plastic. It can include differential susceptibility to environment (e.g., aversive, supportive environments might affect development differentially for certain alleles, not others) × (S) stimulus/response (and organismic) strategic/strategizing system (canalyzed/constrained, yet stochastic/probabilistic, or deterministic) that produces activation/inhibition coordination output in multiple hierarchical levels of the system phenotype (approach/withdrawal, physiology, neuronal, neural, brain, neuropsychological, behavioral, psychological).

(continued)

Table 29.4 (continued)

	Variation	
Component	Statistical	Conceptual
GEODS: G∪E∪O∪D∪S (Gene × Environment × Organism × Development × System interaction)		The standard manner of representing Gene × Environment interaction is G × E. it has been expanded to include G × E × D. These types of interactions are statistical, in the sense that a particular allele in conjunction with a particular environment increases the probability of a particular outcome (perhaps only at a particular developmental time). However, Nature × Nurture is another way of considering biological and experiential (including cultural) interactions. In this conception, the factors are not involved in a statistical interaction, but they reciprocally influence each other, with both contributing to (developmental) outcome. This type of concept can be represented as N∪N, in which ∪ is a union symbol. For the G × E interaction, to indicate how genes and environment might interact generally in a constitutive rather than a statistical way, the representation of G∪E could be used. In this regard, a general model of Gene∪Environment interaction that includes not only development but also the organism and the system as a whole could be represented by G∪E∪O∪D∪S (or simply GEODS).

are being better studied in multiple disciplines. In this regard, only a systems point of view can accommodate to the multivariable and interactive dynamics of behavioral complexity and its development.

Comment

However, the field is far from having sufficiently overarching and fully operationalized (and fully testable) model. New models need to be sufficiently developed and flexible enough to accommodate the ever burgeoning, exponentially growing research and theory that are being published.

Eye-Catching Causal Terms

The Causal Zoo

"Causal weirdness" is the only term that fits the phenomena that are emerging in science about causality for both the microscopic, quantum and macroscopic, cosmic worlds, as explained next. Not being an expert in these disciplines, I refer to popular science magazines to explain these causal findings.

von Baeyer (2013) explained that, in the quantum realm, particles appear to occupy two locations simultaneously, in a process of entanglement or "spooky" action at a distance. The particles, such as electrons, appear to travel at a speed greater than that of light, considered the upper limit of known speed is our known cosmic world. In this view, particles are represented by wave functions. By calculating a particle's wave function over time, probabilities related to its properties, such as their estimated location, can be derived.

According to a new model, Quantum Bayesian Theory (QBism), the problems and paradoxes associated with the standard quantum model concern assuming that a wave function is real. Rather, according to QBism, there is no objective reality. Simply, it is a mathematical formula used to assign one's personal belief. Therefore, the person's own choices and actions affect the quantum system and its calculated properties in a way that is inherently uncertain.

Moreover, different people can have different quantum-related wave functions and, therefore, perceive differently the properties of the quantum system. A collective, coherent worldview of the quantum world emerges from inter-observer communication about observers' private understanding of wave functions. As observers modify suddenly their personal wave functions, and revisit their probability assignments, the wave function "collapses" to a particular value after having "spread out" after prior observation/calculation, so that apparent violations of the principle that particles can only be in one place at a time are more subjective than objective.

According to QBism, the quantum system has not changed, because wave functions are merely probability calculating tools and are subjective and personal rather than objective and real. The only change that takes place with respect to wave functions is in the belief about personally-relevant wave functions, which are individually selected by observers in order to "encapsulate" personal expectations. [Note that this is not to suggest that a person's state of mind brings the world into being.]

The implication of QBism is that reality is shaped actively by ourselves and, moreover, as observers of this reality, our free will participates by setting its measurements. The act of measuring creates the property in question, shaping it "just a little" by its "participation" in a type of "birthing" moment.

If the quantum world, already weird and spooky in its standard formulation, is even stranger so that it reflects collective coordination of personal belief about wave function and quantum particles in action, the causal forces involved in its activity must be inscrutable and intangible, perhaps like Einstein in Wonderland. The only metaphor that comes to mind to explain it is "causal weirdness." In the next paragraphs, I explain another metaphor that captures the unseizeable nature of causality, that of "dark causality."

Powell (2013) described the extent to which our universe is visible and invisible. The visible component consists of light, energy, matter, the Earth, and the infinite number of cosmic particles and bodies in the universe. However, our universe is expanding at a rate that does not fit what we know of the visible universe, so there must be dark matter and energy to account for this and related phenomena.

Scientists are finding not only about dark matter and dark energy but also about their properties, including their dynamic transformative properties. In this regard, dark matter might be able to become visible. Moreover, the ultimate end-point of the logic entailed by this possibility is that there are dark universes in parallel with ours.

In this sense, I propose that just as there is dark matter and dark energy, there must also be "dark causality." Simply, causality is so multifactorial and complex that the algorithms of its emergence and influence might be hidden, ephemeral, ever-changing, and perhaps indecipherable to a degree for at least part of the time.

Causicles

"Causalization" could be the relevant catchphrase to capture the participation of causality in interactive reality, or the extent to which causality defines the universe more than the actions, objects, and sequences involved. Causality could be the "sine quo non" or "nonpareil" variable in defining reality, which might therefore consist uniquely of "causal particles" ("causicles").

To carry the concept enunciated to its logical extreme, the causal co-ordinations between effector (actuator) and effect (linked outcome) constitute the universe, and they need to be considered as a "garden" of entities, both micro- and macroscopic, which defines all things, agents, organisms and, indeed, matter and energy in both the physical and psychological worlds.

One of the hot topics in theology, cosmology, particle physics, and many other disciplines is the topic about why we exist and why the universe exists. For example, the Big Bang might lie at the origin of the universe in its present state, but it does not explain its source or reason. The answers to questions like these await further scientific and conceptual inquiry. However, surely it can be argued that the universe would not exist without causal particles and their underlying stitching together of its constituents and also their stitching of our reality-informed conceptions of it. To conclude, causality constitutes each of the universe, ourselves, and our interactions with it. Without it, there would be neither a universe nor ourselves. We are exquisitely and elegantly honed to live causality and to contribute to it.

Coexistential Causal Intraactivism

Model

Introduction

In reflecting on the integrative theoretical efforts in psychology that are being made involving the biopsychosocial model, dynamical systems theory, and the embodiment model, as well as others, such as those of networks and affordances, it struck me that that I could carry further the notions: (a) that causality is central to understanding behavior; (b) that causality is central to the activity of human behavior; (c) that causality can help cohere the diverse models on human behavior; (d) that causality can help the field of psychology cohere, as well, and it can do the same for related disciplines; (e) that humans are really *Homo Causa* in several ways, such as in their causalization processes and their effective adaptation requiring causal understanding; (f) and that free will is essential to all these aspects of understanding causality and behavior. In all these regards, the unifying model that emerged from my end-of-book reflection is that of "Co-existential Causality" or, more precisely, that of "Co-existential Causal Intraactivism." Let me explain.

Coexistential

The term "co-existential" refers to the dialectical existence of and interaction among diverse components of a topic at issue. I have applied the term to the epistemological stances that have been expressed about realism and constructivism, for example, arguing that an integrated framework would acknowledge the possibility of and even the necessity of having both views integrated into one totality. Just as a photon of light can be viewed as a wave or a particle, depending on the observer and observation process, so can one view among many views on a particular topic reflect aspects of the ontology of the phenomenon even if it apparently in contradiction with others. That is, in the totality of views seen together, each might contribute to the whole even if any two of them seem in opposition.

Intraaction

The term "intraactivism" is quite complementary to the one of co-existentialism. It refers to more than the interaction among components of a phenomenon, whether behavioral, theoretical, or otherwise, because the construct of an interaction among components presupposes that the components can exist independently of the interaction, be dissociated from it and exist otherwise, and exist as separate entities that might conjoin at one moment but not at another. However, the term of intraactivism connotes a reality much more complex and participatory or lived for both the components at issue in a phenomenon and their interaction. That is, the components in an intraactivist system exist because of and through the interactions (of the intraaction type, or simply, "intraactive interaction") involved. Thus, the intraactive interaction in a system at issue is central to the phenomenon more than the components. The components cannot be dissociated or separated from the interactions involved and cannot exist by themselves. They never exist without being in intraactive interaction. They owe their existence to their intraactive interactions and, also, the nature of these intraactive interactions that are involved define their properties.

In this regard, as traditionally defined, interactions do not even exist. The term presupposes that there are components interacting and that interactions relate them. However, in the concept of intraactions, the components are fluid and defined by their interrelations and, also, the constituting interactions involved supercede them. Because they do not exist in and of themselves, their interactions, as traditionally defined, do not exist either. Therefore, the implication is that the intraactions *are* the system rather than the putative system components and their interactions being the system.

If we carry this argument to its extreme, it means that reality is constituted by intraactions and, also, the components of reality are only intraactions. Components do not exist independent of them.

Therefore, it is important that work is undertaken to define intraaction systemics, or what constitutes the nature of intraactions. Network modeling gives us a beginning language in this regard, and so does systems theory. However, I could add that variations in intraaction types might involve—intraactive system stability induction or its alteration; intraactive system component stabilization or their transformation; various reciprocal interactions, feedback looping; growth containment/pruning vs. augmentation/promotion, which includes enhancing adaptive organization vs. regression/dissolution induction; and all with and between different levels of the system to the point that self-organizational emergence can take place even at the intraactive level. In this regard, emergence deriving from intraactive interactions could involve both the nature of the components involved and the nature of the intraactions themselves, with any of these having properties that are defined uniquely by the continual, participatory interdigitation of the components involved in the intraactive interactions.

Note that the term intraactivism is different than the ones of interactionism, interactionalism, interactism, and interactivism (e.g., Bickhard, 2012; Campbell, 2014) because it considers that any term that incorporates the word interactions, by definition, implies that the components in the reciprocally-defining meeting of the components might be independent entities that exist outside the meeting, which is contradictory to how meetings are being defined in the concept of intraactivism. That being said, the concept borrows heavily from the one of interactivism. Finally, note that the term intraactivism is a quite novel one, and for sake of simplicity, I keep using the term interactions in the explication of the concept, but, as indicated already, at the same time, I qualify the interaction as an intraactive one.

Causality

Adding the term of causality (or causal) to the term of intraaction accomplishes several objectives. First, it indicates the centrality of causality for relevant psychological theorizing, as per the various points made about the goals of creating such a term. Second, it allows me to continue emphasizing causality as a cohering theme to the present work, one that goes beyond the focus on any of free will, the biopsychosocial model, evolution or development, including my own model in these regards (Young, 2011), and so on.

Conclusion

Putting together the terms of coexistential, causal, and intraactivism gives a powerful integrative psychological model that demonstrates the following with respect to the five goals in creating the term that were elucidated above. That is, the new Coexistential Causal Intraactivism model that I am creating helps integrate understanding of—human behavior; the activity of human behavior; models in psychology; psychology itself; how humans are *Homo Causa*; and the critical role of free will in all these aspects.

Human Behavior (a) Causality is so central to the understanding behavior that a model that purports to explain behavior in all its complexity needs to include the term in one way or another in its title. Behavior cannot be fully understood without understanding both its "what" and "why," and, indeed, the why takes prominence over the what—the product in behavior derives from a process that shapes it, impregnates it, epitomizes it, and gives it its substance and identity.

Activity (b) Human activity is especially causal in nature in both the means and the ends of behavior. Cognition, emotion, and action are embedded in and focus on causality, and they are an intraactive product of the resonating, intraactivist engagement of the person with the niche as the person undertakes efforts to arrive at contextually adaptive ends, which can be achieved best when the person is the top causal engine in the environment, acting on it toward evolutionary survival and reproduction in one way or another (while respecting it).

Models

Introduction (c) Adopting a coexistential stance to various integrative models in psychology permits seeing each of them as valuable and contributing different aspects to the integration. Adding in causality as central to this theoretical integration enables us to see each of the contributory models in a different light, but also emphasizes that, inevitably, they deal with causality one way or another. Finally, considering the integration of various psychological theories from the point of view of intraactivism indicates how they could be combined themselves through their conceptual interaction. Also, the term of intraactivism indicates that the nature of the integration of psychological theories toward their unification should emphasize the constitutive intraactive interaction that the term implies both for the expression of behavior and also how its causes interact, going beyond each of them in creating the whole and intraactive person.

Biopsychosocial For example, the biopsychosocial model considers the major components to behavioral causality in its formulation, but it is missing a good mechanistic explanation in how they interact. The concept of intraactivism allows for both grasping the manner of component intraactive interaction in behavioral causation among the biological, personal, and social components involved and the nature of the behavior itself. In this regard, I have argued that a mechanism that speaks to the intraactive constitutiveness among the components of the biopsychosocial model involves activation/inhibition coordination, and the nature of the behavioral process reflective of this concept, by definition, is one that expresses perfectly intraactivism.

Systems Examination of systems theory and the model of embodiment lead to the same conclusion—that the notion of Coexistential Causal Intraactivism suggests ways that the models can be extended toward their integration with other models and also toward a model that integrates all of them. For instance, for systems theory, the concept of emergence through self organization is critical in helping explain how behavior can become increasingly complex and differentiated and escape reductionist influences and tendencies. The concept of circular causality has been used to explain the movement out of one level of a system into a more advanced one in its hierarchical arrangement, producing an emergent behavior or a new behavioral organization or level, and I have modified the concept by referring to a circular causal emergence (Young, 2011).

The levels of a system are not separate, though, and, in this regard, they should be subject to the same kind of reciprocal intraactivism that I have explained to apply to linked components of a phenomenon, including for behavior and its causation. That is, in circular causal emergence between levels and components of a system that creates new emergent components or levels, the nature of the constituting interactions that takes place to create the emergence is not the traditional interactive one that has been described but the new intraactive one that is being posited.

Embodiment As for embodiment, this model could profit from considering that the linkages between physical, corporal, bodily, and brain structure and functioning and those involving behavior, action, mind, cognition, and emotion, as well as the linkages between people, are dynamically intraactivist and formative of the components in the intraactive interactions. Body does not meet mind and interact with it, but their intraaction creates both. People are not independent agents who communicate as separate bodies, but they are intraactively created in their intraactive interactions. For example, listening and talking both are constitutively intraactive. In this regard, as I just wrote to my family as they communicated about communication—when you listen, it has to be in an active way in which what you hear genuinely enters and transforms the networks in your thoughts and being, assuming that they have some value. When you talk, it is much the same process. You consider the context, person, and ongoing conversation and speak with new constructions that fit the moment, including novel ones never thought or said. The other is not just a sounding board but also a prism in which your ideas radiate back into yourself in multiple changing forms and lights and also affect the other in the same way.

Comment That said, any of the major extant theories in psychology can be modified in some way to fit the intraactivist concept. For example, in a dynamically growing model of embodiment, theorists should not reject that realism and constructivism can co-exist in one model and that the person can be viewed from the lens of both models.

The same proviso applies to the revised conceptions of the biopsychosocial and systems models that I have presented. For the biopsychosocial model, the three major constituents that interact to create its term also interact to create the person, but in the model as presently constructed, each of its constituent components can stand as independent entities. Each can exist beyond their interaction as direct causal influences on the person.

However, from the perspective of intraactivism, the biopsychosocial model needs some way of realizing that three terms that comprise it are indissociable, mutually constitutive, and serve to create a whole that denies their separability, while, at the same time, defining them. Perhaps the term of the biopersonalsocial model that I created can serve that goal, although it was not constructed for this purpose. That is, the word personal exists in the term, but not as a separate one from the bio and social terms preceding and following it, respectively, so it might fit the bill.

For the systems model, emergence might take place in systems, and that would suggest a kind of intraactivism. However, as shown above in discussing the concept of circular causal emergence, the concept of emergence in systems theory still involves components, or perhaps levels, in interaction, albeit reciprocal. Moreover, emergence is not the only end-point or pathway in systems. There might be minor changes or no changes despite perturbations. In this model, components can exist as independent entities that conjoin in patterns or configurations, as needed, but still keep their properties. Compared to the approach of intraactivism, the interactions that take place in standard systems theory allows for a causality that can be a simple affair instead of emanating from a complexity landscape of intraactions involving the inevitable creation of new properties of components and redefining them.

This example illustrates that: (a) intraactivism is constitutive of phenomena such as reality, and (b) components of phenomena subject to intraactivism are defined by them, and this obtains even in their properties. However, even if at the surface it seems that these are apparently contradictory statements about the nature of things, they reflect a deeper reality—recall that I have argued that apparently contradictory and opposition things might exist simultaneously in the essence of things because they can express a dual nature like do photons of light, being either particle or wave depending on the observer/observation process. In this regard, there is no contradiction in admitting a dialectic between opposite poles of a phenomenon and, as I have argued for the school of relationism itself in Chap. 35, there is no contradiction in having a dialectic between a pole that is dialectical in nature, such as relationism, and one that is not, such as realism, especially if one is seeking a superordinate model that can accommodate both their advantages and disadvantages.

Network The network model has much potential toward the unification of psychology because it resembles the systems model, and even has surpassed it in some ways, for example, through its concepts of centrality, efficiency, betweenness, small worlds, hubs, and so on. Without belaboring the point, it could profit from the presently proposed coexistential, causal, and intraactivist behavioral model by emphasizing that networks involve the constitutiveness inherent in the model. Networks exist not as passive relay stations but as dynamically living and active pathways that are even more important that the localized components or regions involved in the transitioning between them.

Affordances As for the model of affordances, it could be improved by reconfiguring it in terms of intraactivism in the sense that the invitations proffered by salient environmental cues need to be better reinforced as reciprocally-defined intraactive products more than as independently existing environmental properties. Causality inheres in organism–environment relations more than organisms acting on the environment or the environment dictating to the organism how to act.

Comment At this juncture, given that the central argument has been made, I refrain from continuing the exercise of showing how the concepts of co-existentialism, causality, and intraactivism, along with their combination in the model that I have created of Coexistential Causal Intraactivism, can help toward refining other major models in psychology and move them toward an integration that would help unify the field of psychology itself. Instead, in the following, I explore directly the latter proposition in depth.

Psychology

Introduction (d) Psychology is a discipline that is a science. It attempts to understand behavior, its organization, and its causes. It uses scientific methodology to investigate the nature of behavior, and scientific reasoning to explain the outcomes of its investigations. It is a science that is continually evolving in conceptualization, methodology, and aims. It has a practical side, of course, in its clinical applications, in particular. In this regard, it uses the scientific method and experimentation to determine best practices that are evidence-supported. However, there are tens of schools of psychotherapy that have been created, and the research in their support, at times, is criticized for lacking external and ecological validity. Also, the diagnostic manuals of disorders developed in psychiatry have hundreds of categories that they include, and their clinical utility has been questioned. In response, there is a movement to retreat to the medical model and neuroscience as the basis for understanding mental illness and how to best treat it (the RDoC project; Research Domain of Criteria; Insel et al., 2010; Insel & Lieberman, 2013).

However, if psychology (and psychiatry) would attempt to integrate across—experimental work and clinical practice; its major therapeutic schools under one rubric; the disparate disorders into a coherent framework that reduces their overwhelming complexity; and the medical model with ones such as the biopsychosocial one—it might advance beyond the inherent limitations and contradictions that are evident in its present state. The degree to which the presently proposed model of Coexistential Causal Intraactivism can help arrive at these goals is addressed next.

The model being proposed can especially help psychology cohere over its various divisions and splits, and also resolve some of its inconsistencies and contradictions, if not its controversies, because, above all, it offers an integrative model of human behavior. It places at the apex of human activity causally-oriented behavior and the intraactivist nature of behavioral manifestation and its creation, in which intraactive interactions are the constituents of behavior more than the components in these interactions, and also interactions between people define their essence more than their personhood that they bring to the interaction. It depicts the causal mechanisms underlying behavior as multiple, reciprocally interacting, and intraactivist, with emergence a possible outcome through these interactions in the causal web that is greater than the sum of the parts and even defining of the parts.

Application Because of the apogeal understanding of behavior that the Coexistential Causal Intraactivist model permits, the various models that have been proposed to explain behavior can be subsumed under its guise through the types of expansions that I have provided above. The differences among the models can be accommodated by appropriate extensions and modifications to make them more similar to each other and reflective of a broader, superordinate model involving co-existentialism, causality, and intraactivism. Furthermore, this type of thinking can be applied to the schism between experimental and clinical work because people's behavior could be explained using these types of concepts, whether they fall in the normal, adaptive range or the abnormal, disordered one. Also, the diagnostic manuals would be revised to accommodate to the relational, intraactive turn and to fixate less on the internally disordered model of mental illness. This relational stance applies both between the person and the environment and between one symptom and the next. For the former, mental disorder might not lie in a fixed symptom list but in how each symptom relates to and derives from the context as much as from the so-called internally-generated and constitutional factors. For the former, symptom causality might not lie in relation to a latent psychological construct or factor but to the intraactive interactional chains from one symptom to the next and how they relate to context. Finally, treatments would become whole because the person could be understood better as a whole, and the medical model would be complemented by the biopsychosocial and intraactivist one. Etiology would be less of a missed guesswork and more of an appropriately informed scientific enterprise.

That being said, I remind that in the search for the unification of psychology, there can never be one best answer, even the one that I am suggesting as leading toward a better unification. It is better to refer to the process of unifying psychology rather than the state of its unification. Both process and product work together intraactively in systems, and the same would apply to how psychology works, and moreover, the process is continual and the resultant product ever-changing. That is why the present book refers to the *project* of unifying psychology (and of causality). As long as we are on that path, the field can prosper and avoid some of its ingrowing.

Homo Causa (e) This present book has emphasized causality as central to behavior, but it has now shifted to a model in which intraactivism is considered critical to explaining behavior and its causes. In this regard, I still consider humans as causalization machines and the engagement in causal thought and related behavior as the supreme markers of our adaptive efforts. For me, intraactivism as a concept does not override the one of causality in the characterization of our exceptionalism. Causality is the focus of what we do because of its evolutionary advantages, and intraactivism helps explain how we causalize and also what is the nature of the behaviors that we use in doing so. There is no need to call humans *Homo Intraactivus* instead of *Homo Causa* in the present formulation of what especially makes us human. The same applies to the concept of co-existentialism. That being said, the present integrative model of behavior of Coexistential Causal Intraactivism reinforces, by its very nature and label, the importance of causality in human behavior and its essence. In this sense, this addition to the present work adds to the message that causality is central to understanding human behavior.

Free Will (f) Finally, free will is another concept that has been emphasized in the present work, and one needs to ask if my appreciation of its relevance for understanding human behavior and its causes has changed because of the new model that I have created on Coexistential Causal Intraactivism. To the contrary, the grounds for maintaining that free will is an emergent phenomenon and that behavior cannot be reduced to deterministic influences has been reinforced by the concept of intraactivism, as well as the application of the one of co-existentialism to the present question. Intraactivism, by definition, facilitates emergence, and free will cannot exist otherwise.

Conclusions

Coexistential Causal Intraactionism Coexistential Causal Intraactionism is a concept that I created to help summarize the essence of the present book, and a Google search on April 13, 2015, indicated absolutely no entry for the term of intraaction in the listing offered. The term represents a superordinate model of phenomena that includes behavior and its causation. The concept involved is nonlinear in nature, as in systems theory, and it resembles this latter model through its opening to emergence as a possible outcome of the intraactive interaction dynamics that might take place. However, it differs from system theory concepts through the constitutive nature of the interactions that it proposes to take place among the components of the system as it arranges and rearranges its patterns over them. To remind, a system exists through the interaction of its components, which are intraactive interactions, and not in the separate components of the system as they interact. To simplify, pattern (or component configuration) *is* system, and system is not components creating pattern.

This type of conceptualization, when coupled with the concepts of co-existential and causality, can serve as an overarching concept that—integrates the major themes of the book; underscores the centrality of causality both to understanding behavior and in the activity of behavior; points to the centrality of causality to psychology (and related disciplines) and that it can serve as a focus of integration for it; and that free will and related concepts, such as free will belief, having a sense of free will, freedom in being, and free being, are integral to these themes about causality, given their supreme role in behavioral causality. Moreover, the notion of applying together the concepts of coexistentiality, causality, and intraactionality in phenomena would appear to have wider applicability than the topic of the present book.

Broad Intraactive Ethics For example, I have proposed a model of broad ethics (Young, 2014) and it reflects the concept of "broad intraactive ethics" for mental health (Young, 2015). In this regard, ethical behavior should not be considered a component of our professional (or personal) life, but constitutive from it and a product of the multiple, lived intraactive interactions in which we engage. Ethics might rise to the surface as a topic to consider in dilemmas, but their solution can arrive best if we are proactive, positive about it, immersed in it, and informed by it, and living it in each micromoment of our professional lives. Ethics does not reside in the components of the guidelines, standards, and writings on the topic, but in how we are constituted at the ethical level by them as we interact intraactively with them and apply them constitutively in our relationships with patients, colleagues, and society.

Chapter Conclusions

The present chapter defines both basic and critical terms in the field of psychology that help understand causality. Some of the basic terms have been used throughout the present book, but are clarified in this chapter. Some of the terms are new to the present work, and have been created in order to help move the study of causality in psychology more toward center stage, or at least to promote thinking about this critical area. The critical novel models developed in the chapter pertaining to causality in psychology relate to the constructs of networks and intraactivism. The chapter also shows the complexity involved in gene–environment interactions by indicating that development, the organism, and systems also are involved.

References

Bickhard, M. H. (2012). A progress ontology for persons and their development. *New Ideas in Psychology, 30*, 107–119.

Campbell, R. L. (2014). Giving naturalism a chance: Interactivism, emergence, and nonlinearity. *Cosmos and History, 10*, 118–130.

Ellis, B. J., Boyce, W. T., Belsky, J., Bakermans-Kranenburg, M. J., & van IJzendoorn, M. H. (2011). Differential susceptibility to the environment: An evolutionary-neurodevelopmental theory. *Development and Psychopathology, 23*, 7–28.

Holland, J. H. (2012). *Signals and boundaries: Building blocks for complex adaptive systems*. Cambridge, MA: MIT Press.

Insel, T. R., Cuthbert, B. N., Garvey, M. A., Heinssen, R. K., Pine, D. S., Quinn, K. J., et al. (2010). Research domain criteria (RDoC): Toward a new classification framework for research on mental disorders. *American Journal of Psychiatry, 167*, 748–751.

Insel, T. R., & Lieberman, J. A. (2013). DSM-5 and RDoC: Shared interests. *The National Institute of Mental Health*. http://www.nimh.nih.gov/news/science-news/2013/dsm-5-and-rdoc-shared-interests.shtml

Powell, C. (2013). Darklands of the cosmos. *Discover*, 90–93.

Sporns, O. (2011). *Networks of the brain*. Cambridge, MA: MIT Press.

Sporns, O. (2012). *Discovering the human connectome*. Cambridge, MA: MIT Press.

von Baeyer, H. C. (2013). Quantum weirdness? It's all in your mind. *Scientific American, 308*(6), 47–51.

Young, G. (2011). *Development and causality: Neo-Piagetian perspectives*. New York: Springer Science + Business Media.

Young, G. (2014). *Malingering, feigning, and response bias in psychiatric/psychological injury: Implications for practice and court*. Dordrecht, Netherlands: Springer Science + Business Media.

Young, G. (2015, in preparation). A Broad Ethics model. *Ethics, Medicine, and Public Health, 1*.

30 Change Mechanisms

Chapter Introduction

The last chapter on concepts and terms in the field of the psychological study of causality reviewed both basic and new concepts. The latter focused on an integrated network model as well as an intraactive model. The present chapter concentrates on the behavioral change process and its mechanism. In this regard, it describes in depth the activation/inhibition coordination model that I have developed.

First, the chapter expands the network model into the "neurome" (or neuromal network), a term that I created in order to capture the full range of neuronal/central nervous system factors involved in behavior. I explain the construct of the neuromal network and the change mechanisms and processes that affect it.

As with the present book, in general, these change processes and mechanisms are seen to especially relate to nonlinear dynamical systems theory (NLDST), also called chaos theory, and to concept of activation/inhibition coordination. I explore the model from several different perspectives.

In addition, I introduce in much more detail than before my five stages × five substages model of Neo-Piagetian development (Young, 2011) and show how it applies to change processes and also to mechanisms. [Note that this part of the chapter helps to prepare the way for the final part of the book, which explores in much more detail my work on stages and substages in development, and the change processes and mechanisms involved therein.] In this regard, the chapter concludes by presenting models related to readiness for change and dimensions of change. The last part of the chapter expands the concept of intraaction, as well.

Neuromal Network

Introduction

The manner in which systems can self-organize to create emergent phenomena resides in its concept of (a) interactions between components to create amalgams distinct from the components and (b) interactions of components within levels to create superordinate levels. Circular causality derives through these interactions and refers to the reciprocal vertical nested interactions over lower- and higher-order levels of a system (Lewis, 2000a, 2000b, 2005) as well as horizontal within-level interactions or couplings in the system.

Jost, Bertschinger, and Olbrich (2010) presented a model of system emergence based on top levels of a system having higher "scales" or regularities not accessible at lower levels, nor inferable from them. A level of a system that is superordinate to another one gains in resistance to change that would take place at lower levels due to perturbations by the superordinate level

G. Young, *Unifying Causality and Psychology*, DOI 10.1007/978-3-319-24094-7_30

acting to "enslave" variables at lower levels, thereby bringing stability to the system.

In Young (2011), I proposed the concept of "circular emergence" to account for the process of emergence. In this model of emergence, different levels of a system not only are reciprocally coordinated, but also they are reciprocally emergent and bootstrapping, allowing both upper and lower levels of a system to undergo emergent change within themselves beyond creation of any new superordinate levels.

Finally, according to Young (2011), the mechanism that allows the preservation or conservation as well as the escape from far-from-equilibrium of system state concerns activation/inhibition coordination. This union of fundamental system forces might act to help the system resist change or help it facilitate the exploration of novel spaces beyond basic regions (attractor basins) to which a system might typically gravitate or explore, thereby giving it new flexibility to either remain unchanged or to change in its plasticity.

The concepts of system self-assembly, circular causality, circular emergence, and so on, apply generally to any system adapting to its context. When applied to human development, there are specifics to add, including those related to genes (and their biological transcriptions), the environment, neuronally, or of others, such as in parenting, and for the person as a whole.

In the following, I expand these concepts to apply to the neurome, which is a catchword that I created to represent the nervous system and its components from a network and systems perspective. The model is quite developmental, as well.

Model

Table 30.1 presents a model of emergence in behavior that is developmentally-tuned and that allows for development of increasingly complex, advanced, or higher-order stages throughout the lifespan. The crux of the model concerns the developing "neuromal network" complex that can dynamically self-assemble at increasingly sophisticated emergent levels supportive of increasingly sophisticated cognitive capacities related to local and/or domain-specific skills, such as executive function and self-regulation, and to global and/or more advanced steps or even stages, such as in Neo-Piagetian models. By neuromal, I refer to the full range of neurome constituents, from neurons and neurotransmitters, to neuronal and cross-neuronal networks, to cortical lobes and hemispheres.

In this model that I have developed, the neurome is an environmentally-responsive, vital, cue-detecting apparatus that is stochastic or probabilistically-tuned about each of (a) the nature of environmental cues, (b) the perceptual and cognitive systems that deal with them, and (c) the response options and actions that it generates. It is phenotypically plastic, especially given its ongoing developmental modification, even if it is comprised, in part, of genetically-proximal (neuro)endophenotypic constructions. It is adaptive in its function in an evolutionary sense of serving and promoting survival and reproduction, as well as adapting in an ongoing sense in matching organism needs to ongoing environmental exigencies.

The neuromal network is an exquisitely developmental one, both in terms of local, micro-developmental transactive processes online in context and global, macro-developmental, transformative ones over ontogenetic time (e.g., months, years). By development, I refer to change in behavior and its organization that includes not only cognitive ones but also related ones that are social and emotional ones, such that behavioral regulation concerns an executive control at all these levels. Behavior at any one time is a reflection of multiple forces biologically and environmentally, but the person also contributes actively to the probabilistic sampling of behavior, their processing, and the decisions taken on options to follow in action.

Table 30.1 An adapting neuromal network complex—an integrated cross-network (ICN) model: terms

Element	Definition
Probabilistic, plastic	Not fixed, but influenced by pre-existing states; open to experience, sampled; with response options, including anticipatory ones
Adaptive/adapting	Ongoing adjustment and evolutionarily selected
Dynamic, self-organizing	Self-assembling, including with possible major state transitions to different areas of the system's state space, even after minor perturbations if far from equilibrium
Emergent, hierarchical	Systems are multilevel, expressing reciprocal circular causality over top-down and bottom-up levels/influences, allowing for level reorganization and even superordinate level creation
Cognition (dual process)	For cognitive architecture: stages and substages. For self-regulation/executive control: automatic, fast, unconscious; reflective, deliberate, slow, conscious
Activation/inhibition coordination	At each level of a system (and also between them), the dynamic mechanism of adaptation could be described in terms of multiple parameters, including energy flow, information, resources, degrees of freedom, equilibrium, and adaptability. One metric that might be common to these approaches involves activation/inhibition coordination. Whether examining the person at the level of brain, neuron, behavior, personality, or social adaptation, activation/inhibition coordination describes both the process and output
Integrative system	Systems are multilevel hierarchical arrangements that take the form or pattern that best fits its extant components in context. As they accommodate, they become open to further growth toward complexity, as new input/energy, information either arrives or is sought
Neuromal	The collection that is the brain, central nervous system, neurons, neuronal networks, neurotransmitters, etc.
Neuromal networked	The neurome refers to the collection of neuronal and related agents, including neurotransmitters, the various nervous systems, and the brain and its components. They form networks at each level and are networked amongst them

Activation/Inhibition Coordination

Model

I have described previously in the present book the concept of activation/inhibition coordination. In this section, I expand the concept to show how it can promote emergent change in behavior and its organization, in the context of elaborating the concept of the neurome.

The dynamic alteration of extant regimes in a system's state space has been described in terms of (a) reaching critical thresholds of index parameters, (b) the butterfly effect, or major changes in state due to minor perturbations at far-from-equilibrium conditions, (c) accommodating to changing entropic conditions via the metric of free energy, (d) increasing ultimate degrees of freedom in system responsiveness at higher levels, partly by enslaving and reducing degrees of freedom in components at lower levels, and so on.

These explanations of system emergence are not necessarily equivalent and at the same level of explication of system dynamics. Nevertheless, they share common assumptions about nonlinear dynamical system function. (a) Systems are self-organizing and there is no central pattern generator. Systems inherently seek gracefully the best adaptive, online fit of extant components in context in the patterns that they construct. (b) Systems exist in tension or in balance at many levels—locally and globally; probabilistically and deterministically; randomly and predictably; tendency to stability/equilibrium/order and tendency to change/disequilibrium/disorder; familiar, repeating trajectories and novel, transient ones; increasing and decreasing degrees of freedom; and simplicity and complexity.

However, despite the broad understanding of system dynamics in relation to emergence, to my knowledge there has not been one metric proposed related to change toward the novel that is equivalent to the principles underlying the dynamic of atom combination in forming aggregated compounds and molecules. In this regard, I propose that the concept of activation/inhibition coordination holds this potential.

In this regard, activation/inhibition coordination potentially constitutes a common metric over the multiple levels of the neuromal and behavioral system that allows their integration through reciprocal causality both within and across levels. Keep in mind that activation at one level might take place in order to inhibit activity, or vice versa, with the same applying to relations in these functions over levels.

This mechanism has the capacity to temper constant change dynamics in the system with balanced conserving tendencies so that change is environmentally-matched and developmentally constructive. As different system levels (higher, lower, top-down, bottom-up) organize and reorganize in a process of graceful or economic accommodation to the constant input of the environment toward adaptation, change, growth, and complexification, the mechanism of activation/inhibition coordination could be the one that permits the different components and interactions in the system both within and between levels to reciprocally and circularly interrelate, and even to evolve self-assembling and emergent new superordinate levels. Note that the concept of activation/inhibition coordination can be represented by the union function (∪), as in I ∪ A. Also note that I place inhibition before activation in the symbolization of the concept because the inhibitory component of the mechanism is the one that allows the coordination involved to take place smoothly.

Emergence

Figure 30.1 illustrates how the mechanism of activation/inhibition coordination (I ∪ A) could function to create refinements within extant levels of a system that help promote emergent, new superordinate ones. The figure emphasizes the process of circular emergence in the neuromal network leading to corresponding, equivalent developmental and behavioral emergence. In this regard, both neuromal network activity and behavior would seem to be constituted by, and facilitated by, activation/inhibition coordination.

To represent better the activation/inhibition coordination mechanism dynamic, first I indicate how emergence can be represented in a system through the example of water. The classic example of emergence in NLDST concerns how water emerges from the adhering of hydrogen and oxygen (H_2O); its property of wetness is unpredictable from the properties of its constituent atoms. One can represent the process of emergence and maintenance of water in the following way: $H_2O \times E/T \times S = \text{Current State of } H_2O$. That is, water exists in a water cycle managed by energy (E) that circulates in and interacts with the system over time (T) as it governs state system (S) transitions.

To illustrate this argument, as mentioned, activation/inhibition coordination can be represented as I ∪ A, with ∪ representing union, as in set theory. It is important to note that in the model, activation/inhibition coordination refers both to the mechanism of system change (or stability preservation) and to a way of describing the behavior of the system. Activation/inhibition coordination seems to be both a common descriptive device and an actuating mechanism at multiple levels of systems, for example, even in neurons. Therefore, the concept can apply across the full range of behavior, brain, and the neurome.

Figure 30.1 indicates that as "A ∪ I" processes work, allowing for reciprocal system interactions, they form unions themselves, both horizontally within system levels and vertically over levels. This process includes the formation of new, superordinate levels, which then are emergent ones, the nature of which is unpredictable from how the system existed before the emergence.

In this regard, the figure indicates that, as activation/inhibition coordination entities reciprocally interact and lead to superordinate union entities of activation/inhibition coordination, the entities could have properties distinct from the component ones involved in the union in terms of activation/inhibition coordination, per se. Instead

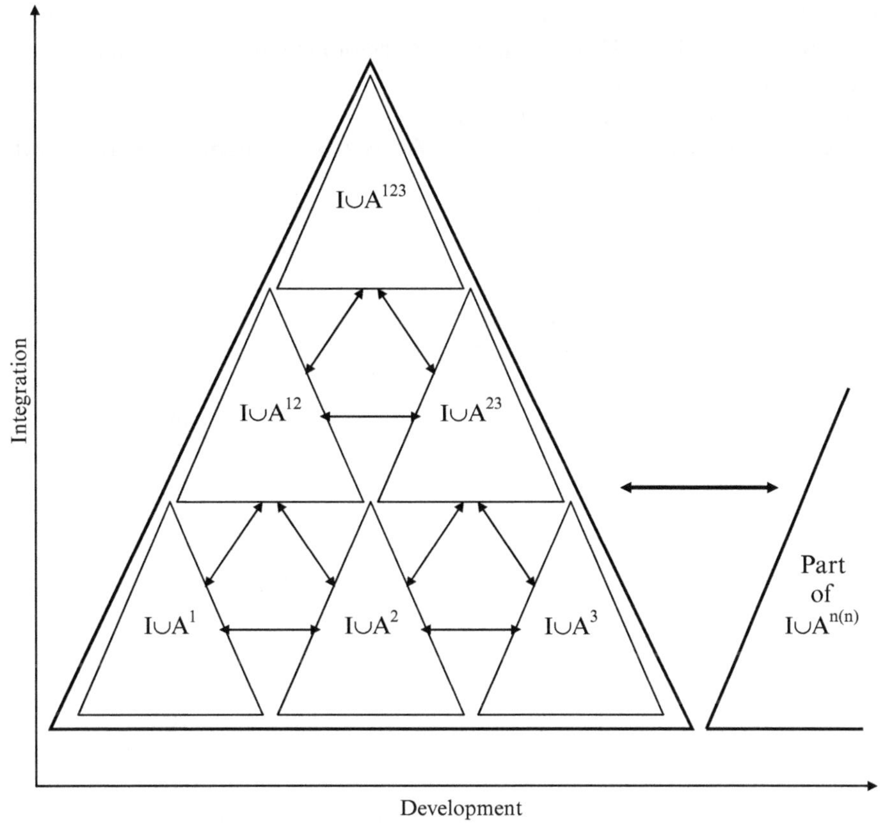

Fig. 30.1 Multilevel, circularly emerging, activation/inhibition coordination neuromal network. *Note.* I = inhibition; A = activation; ∪ = coordination (union); 1, 2, 3 = first-order network; 12, 23 = second-order network; 123 = third-order network; n^n – nth order = n(n); ↗ = reciprocal causality (top-down, bottom-up, including union). Activation/inhibition coordination (I∪A) can be used both to describe behavior and to qualify the process involved in its unfolding. It applies to all levels of the neuronal (neuromal) network and behavior. It is a union or compound function the properties of which are different than those of its components (I, A). As I∪A entities interact and interrelate reciprocally, they form unions themselves, both horizontally within system levels and vertically over levels, including the formation of new, superordinate levels. This process describes how emergence might take place in systems that are neuronal and behavioral in ways analogous to the classic example of how atoms combine to form molecules with properties different from those of the constituents (e.g., wetness in water, H_2O)

of seeing the fields of behavior, brain, and other related entities as distinct and descriptively dissimilar, once can simply state that the parameters in the expression of behavior or output at any level of a system can be described in terms of I∪A and, equivalently, the underpinning mechanisms in body and brain that are associated with the behavioral output of the system involved can be represented by the same formula.

In terms of a formula equivalent to the one for water that I constructed and presented above, it would appear that behavior can be represented in the following way: I∪A (Behavior) × E/T × S = Current State of I∪A (Behavior). That is, behavior can be expressed by an activation/inhibition coordination that exists in a system cycle managed by energy (E) that circulates in and interacts with the system over time (T) as it governs behavioral state system (S) transitions. Note that the formula for brain function is the same: I∪A (Brain function) × E/T × S = Current State of I∪A (Brain function). That is, behavior can be expressed by an activation/inhibition coordination that exists in a system cycle managed by energy (E) that circulates in and interacts with the system over time (T) as it governs behavioral state system (S) transitions: I∪A (Behavior)×E/T×S=Current State of I∪A (Behavior). If one were to construct a general formula over brain and behavior expressed in terms of activation/inhibition coordination, it might look like the following: behavior/brain/neuromal function can be expressed by an activation/inhibition coordination that exists in a system cycle managed by energy (E) that circulates in and interacts with the system over time (T) as it governs behavior/brain/neuromal function state system (S) transitions. Mathematically, the specific formula would be I∪A (behavior/brain/neuromal function)×E/T×S=Current State of I∪A (behavior/brain/neuromal function).

Comment

If the proposal makes sense, more work is needed to marry it to mathematical approaches in NLDST. In the following, I return to the concept of the neurome and its relation to activation/inhibition coordination.

Steps

In the following, I examine how the present five-step model of development and the equivalent one of generic change relate mechanisms that might help move them through the steps involved. First, I show this for activation/inhibition coordination and then I show it for nonlinear dynamical system processes, such as chaotic change in attractor pattern reconfiguration.

Activation/Inhibition Coordination

In Young (2011), I indicated how activation/inhibition coordination could be involved in each step of a generic change model based on my Neo-Piagetian cognitive developmental model. Table 30.2 indicates the extent and type of activation/inhibition coordination associated with the present model of steps in the change process. There are five steps in the present generic change model. Each one appears to witness an increase in the sophistication of activation/inhibition coordination processes, e.g., from fleeting, to flowing, to flexible. The range of application of the activation/inhibition coordination increases, as well, from specific and local to spreading and general. The nature of the activation/inhibition coordination evolves from a short-term simpler variety to a long-term complex variety.

The table illustrates the steps in the process: (a) The column that presents the five steps in the generic sequence indicates an initial coordination of the elements; (b) In the next step, they form a dominant-subordinate hierarchical relationship; (c) Next, the hierarchical relationship evolves into a more systematic relationship; (d) This leads to expansion of the new relationship type throughout the system; (e) Finally, the elements arrive at an integration, which is a step that prepares for a repeat of the cycle.

Table 30.2 Activation/inhibition dynamics within each step of the present generic change model

Step	Activation/inhibition coordination	Range	Type
Coordination	Fleeting	Specific	Short-term simpler
Hierarchization	Fixing	Local	Inhibitory, long damping
Systematization	Flowing, refining	Modular	Short term, complex or long term, simpler
Multiplication	Flexing	Spreading, modifying	Long term, complex
Integration	Flexible	General	Sophisticated, complex
Recursion begins (coordination)	Fleeting	Specific	Short term, simpler

Adopted with permission of Springer Science+Business Media. Young, G. (2011). *Development and causality: Neo-Piagetian perspectives*. New York: Springer Science+Business Media; with kind permission from Springer Science+Business Media B. V. [Table 35.6, Page 829]

The rows of the table indicate the characteristics of each step in terms of activation/inhibition coordination. For example, the systematization row indicates that as new systems within systems form, the activation/coordination dynamic is a short-term but complex one that leads to a modular and internally flowing organization reflective of its new, localized consistency. Note that the last row of the table specifies that should a cyclic recursion of steps take place, it will be based on the new integrated acquisition of the last step in the step cycle. As a new cycle begins with a new coordination, it could involve the integrated systemic structure that had emerged in the prior step coordinating with an equivalent structure in its field or with a different one at its level, or it could involve the new acquisition coordinating or competing with the one of a lower-order level.

Chaos

The present model posits that there are five major stages in development (see Table 30.3). In the table (adapted from Young, 2011), I show how transitions from one stage to the next might involve change in attractor configuration, as specified in chaos theory. The latter specifies that chaotic attractors develop after point ones form cyclical attractors. However, there is little work on how cyclical attractors transform beyond indicating that there might be continual bifurcations. In this regard, especially for living systems, I speculated that the multiple attractors involved might reflect Kauffman's (1993) concept of Complex Adaptive Systems, which in turn could complexify into superordinate ones. Now, these five undergirding steps to change in developmental and any living system might apply to nonliving ones, too.

Therefore, the five-step sequence on change mechanisms that I have described from the point of view of NLDST and complexity theory constitutes a generic model of stages of change. In generic change processes, product and process merge. Just as activation/inhibition coordination seems to constitute a generic change mechanism over brain, behavior, and so on, so might the chaotic processes being described. The five-step model of the processes facilitating change is based on NLDST and complexity theory, but it gives a seamless sequence of transitions that enable the emergence of higher-order levels from lower-level ones. For each stages of the present model, there appears to be an underlying nonlinear dynamical and complexity force that is involved related to attractor reorganization that is exceedingly complex to the point that the system expresses integration over the multiplicities in its manifold. The dynamical evolution described should undergird the processes of change involved not only when sequencing developmental stages, such as the one in the table, but also for ones in nonliving realms, too.

Comment

In this section of the chapter, I have presented two mechanisms of generic change mechanisms, and one could ask if they are equivalent,

Table 30.3 Five-step Neo-Piagetian model of stages of change, with underlying nonlinear dynamical system transition mechanism

Stage of development	Generic stage of change and generic change mechanisms	Nonlinear dynamical system transitions to the stage
Reflexive	Coordination	Point Attractors (2)
Sensorimotor	Hierarchization	Cyclical attractor (over the 2 points)
Perioperational	Systematization	Chaotic attractor
Abstract	Multiplication	Complex adaptive system processes (Inhabiting cusp between order and disorder)
Collective intelligence	Integration	Superordinate complex adaptive system processes

Adopted with permission of Springer Science+Business Media. Young, G. (2011). *Development and causality: Neo-Piagetian perspectives*. New York: Springer Science+Business Media; with kind permission from Springer Science+Business Media B. V. [Table 28.1, Page 647; slightly modified; see Figure 30.4, too] complementary, consistent, and so on. If they are both equally applicable, one could ask which is more general, for example. In this regard, the one of nonlinear dynamical/complexity modeling is the more general, in that its mechanism involves transformation of attractor state configurations, which is a concept that has wide applicability in the sciences, and applies equally to the chaos of nonliving as well as living systems. Nevertheless, attractor configuration and reconfigurations can be seen to involve activation/inhibition coordination, and so the other mechanism discussed in this section appears complementary to the systems one. Moreover, one could argue that the economic adaptation of attractor state reorganization that takes place in systems appears to be one in which the far-from-equilibrium dynamic in which they might be found is accommodated after undue strain on its activation/inhibition coordination properties both within and among the attractors involved.

I wonder to what extent the evolution of the universe toward creation of the planet earth and our presence on it can be captured by a model of attractor reconfiguration into complexity landscapes, such as the one presented, and, if so where do we stand at present in that sequence. Probably, we are in the fourth stage of multiplication before the fifth one integration, which will be a preliminary step to the reverse process of dissolution and extinction, e.g., as our star sun becomes a super nova and the process continues with the universe spreading into a plasma void.

In the next section of the present chapter, I examiner the concept of readiness for change from the point of view of NLDST, and create a new model that depicts the process. Then, I examine new ways of conceiving dimensions of change. In terms of these dimensions, I apply them to my own developmental model. To remind, one model of major qualitative change in development is the Neo-Piagetian one presented in Young (2011), which has five stages: (a) an early reflexive stage; (b) an infant sensorimotor stage; (c) child perioperational (pre-operational, concrete co-operational) stage; (d) a formal, abstract stage; and (e) an adult collective intelligence stage. There are five substages within each stage that cyclically repeat: coordination, hierarchization, systematization, multiplication, and integration. The model consists of five stages with five substages each, or 25 steps in development across the lifespan.

Readiness for Change

Introduction

In the prior section, mechanisms of change were discussed, but not much was said with respect to system readiness for change. For example, one could ask whether a system resides at the transition point to change, how did it get there, and how does it proceed from there. In the following, I elaborate further on readiness for change. In this regard, I use NLDST terminology, such as control parameters that reside at the threshold for change, and collector variables that "collect" the system at issue into variables that represent it and are triggered in the change (Thelen & Smith, 1994).

Developmentally, systems integrate biological, environmental, and organismic (self) readiness-for-change factors in context and also over developmental time. Readiness for change has been discussed at other points in the present book, and typically it has been applied to accepting change and implementing it toward healthier lifestyles and improved subjective well being, as well as in changes needed for dealing with disease or disability, including of mental health.

As applied to systems models, the concept needs to consider what variables represent the critical parameters that reside at the point of change in the system (or the range in critical variable values in this regard), as well as what variable represents the system and is subject to the change. To this point, we have described system change in terms of factors such as attractor configuration and reconfiguration, but underlying these types of change are specific variables that represent the attractor basins involved and the movement in and out of them.

On the one hand, then, attractors change state because the critical variable that acts at the threshold point of change has attained the index levels that promote the change. This process serves to lead the interaction involved to threshold levels that are facilitative of change in the critical variables and the term used to represent them, for example, at system bifurcation points, involves the concept of control or of change in order. Therefore, the variables involved are referred to as control or order parameters. In keeping with the goal of the present chapter to create new terminology related to causality, I refer to these critical parameters of change in systems as "causal" control/order parameters. Also in keeping with the present work, it would appear that the changes involved are especially related to network structure, complexity, and adaptivity.

In terms of the term used for the variables that index a system and alters as it proceeds to change, the one that has been applied is "collector" variables. They incorporate the different degrees of freedom in the system into a master variable representing the degree of freedom relevant to change.

As for specific conceptual specification of the two variables in question—causal control/order parameters/variables and collector variables, in NLDST, the former index potential system change factors should their critical thresholds be traversed and the latter "represent" the system, "compressing" or reducing its lower-level degrees of freedom, opening it to higher-order transition. These variables are akin to independent and dependent variables, respectively.

Model

Introduction We are ready to address directly Fig. 30.2, which is about readiness for change/transition state in causal control (order) parameters and activity in dimensions of change in state collector variables, which function together to leads to local/global networked change in developmental structures/unit and levels. The figure consists of three parts, dealing with the two variables mentioned and the change in state that results from the workings of the factors that they represent. This work includes presentation of a more mathematically-based model of the change process that lies in the control/order and collector variables, or at least the factors in change that they represent.

With respect to the first part of the figure, generally, a system involving changes in state could be indexed by critical variables representing the factors behind the change (e.g., causal collector variables). This happens in context developmentally, at diverse local and global levels.

State/system change could be minor to major either quantitatively or qualitatively, with the latter possibly including novel, emergent change. Systems are not necessarily in state of change or preparatory to it. That is, they resist change and conserve state, even if far-from-equilibrium. However, in a certain sense, even this constitutes change, because the state is preserved despite new inputs into the system from one moment to the next, or despite dissipation in the energy in the system if nothing is added to it.

From a developmental perspective, a good example of system state changes relates to the Piagetian sequence of changes in stage (or substage), as in the infant sensorimotor period. In this regard, Piaget applied NLDST to how changes in stage might take place in development and, in Young (2011), I elaborated further, such as with the concept of transitions in attractor organization and reorganization that might take place in development, as described previously in this chapter. That being said, I consider that further work is needed in this regard, and developed the model in the figure.

Specifically, I reasoned that or the infancy period, whether conceived of as core knowledge, early (quasi)representations, Piagetian schemes, or other cognitive structures or modules, including up to the level of (sub)stages, a general model is needed to indicate how cognitive structures develop, even to the point of qualitative, emergent growth in overall stage structure. Therefore, I worked to develop a model of readiness for change that applies not only to the Piagetian version of the substages of the infancy period but also to other approaches that work toward understanding infant cognition. In this regard, I refer to the general concept of networked change in this model.

Examination of Fig. 30.2 reveals that it consists of three parts, with the first ("a") part of the figure indicating the causal factors in cognitive structure (and in any) development. The second

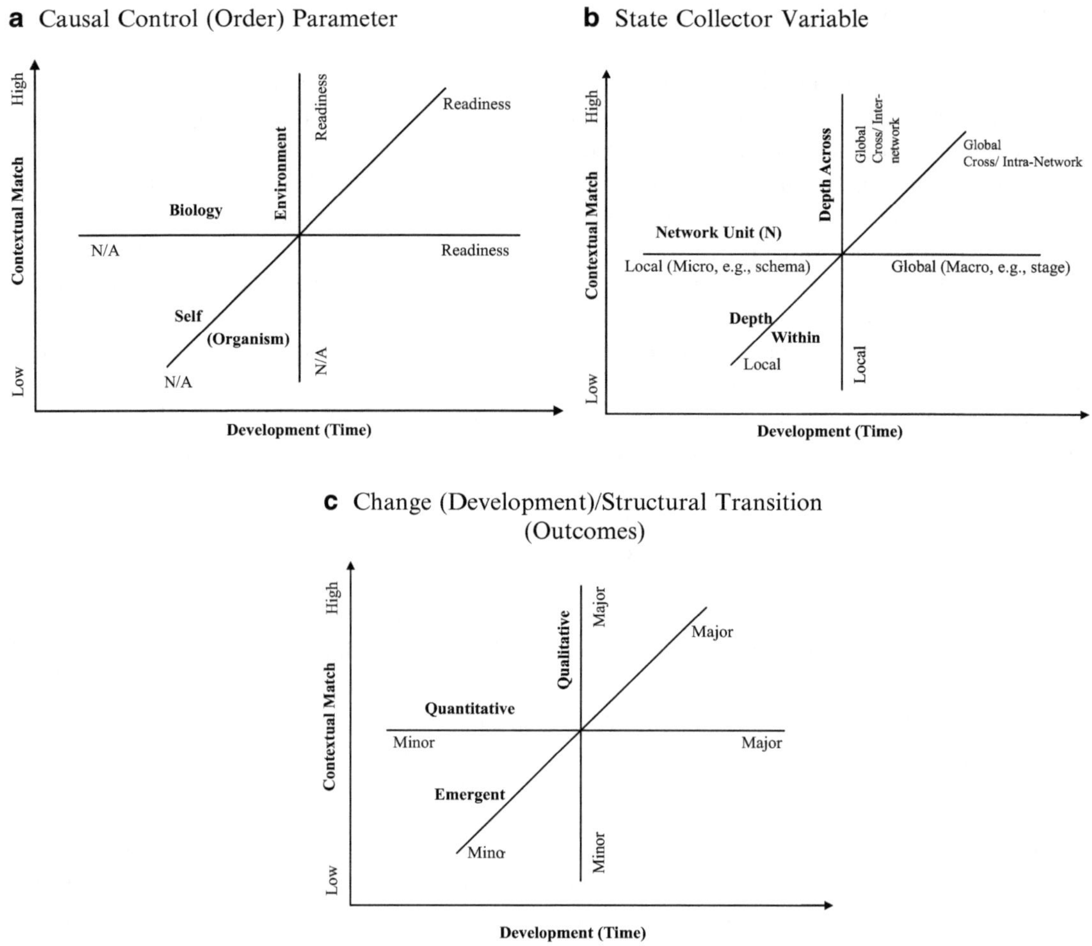

Fig. 30.2 Readiness for change/transition (RC/TR) in causal control (order) parameter(s) (CCP) and state collector variable (SCV) (a) *Note*. CCP = Causal control parameter in generic "readiness for change"/transition of state model. (b) *Note*. SCV = State collector variable; cross-network integration in activity in dimensions of change. Unit refers to local (L), smaller-order schemas up to global (G), larger-order constructs, such as stages. Depth refers to degree of change either within or over levels of the system, e.g., smaller-order (L) or larger-order (G, networked). (c) *Note*. Local (L)/global (G) networked change (N) in developmental structures/unit and level(s). Change (development) [C(D)] is a function (f) of reaching SCV threshold in relation to the nature of system activity structure and associated level(s)).

This figure presents a combined dynamical/network model of developmental change. It uses the language of NLDST—changes in control parameters alter collector variables in systems to the point of threshold for change, which elicits self-organized (and potentially novel/emergent, qualitatively distinct) re-organization of the system. The model also uses the language of networks, in that instead of referring to system states and levels, it includes intra- and inter-level cross-network integrations.

The three portions of the figure (**a**, **b**, **c**) have the constant axes of allowing change over developmental time and needing appropriate contextual organization to facilitate change (referred to as "contextual match"). That is, the same three axes are used to elaborate the central components of the three portions of figure.

In (**a**), the three major axes involve the primary influences on behavior of biology, environment, and person (self, organism). The figure refers to the readiness of change/transition in each of these spheres. Collectively, as the three spheres reach the necessary thresholds for readiness for change/transition, the integrated control parameter that organizes (is organized by) them constitutes a causal impetus for state (system) change.

In the second portion of the figure (**b**), the collector variable of the state (system) can be represented by activity in major aspects of the system. These include the three dimensions of size of unit involved (local, global) and depth of change (within the unit, local to global, intra-network; and across the unit, local to global, inter-network). The proposed state collector variable would vary in the dynamic it covered or represented, depending on the size and depth of the system variables involved.

The three major axes in the third (**c**) portion of the figure indicate that the resultant change in the state/system after the control parameter involved acts on the collector variable involved might be quantitative, qualitative, and even emergent in self organization dynamic ("b") component of the figure indicates the outcome potentials at threshold variables involved in the transitions to change in the system at issue. The third part of the figure ("c") concerns the resultant change in systems according to whether the change is emergent, qualitative, and major, or their opposites. Together, the three components of the model help specify the state of systems that are poised at the point of readiness for change, and what might be the outcome.

Causal Control Parameters In this regard, the model that I have developed integrating the concepts of causal control parameters and collector variables, as well as system state (change) outcome, is referred to as the Readiness for Change or Transition State model because, as systems function in context, their incorporative, assimilative, and accommodatory activity pushes them to the "cusp of change," in which they are more open to change, including of a more radical, qualitative nature. Yet the factors together that promote possible change in the system must reach a certain stretching point that leads to change, and these can be modeled as indicated.

Both the first two parts of the figure consider the situational and developmental (time) factors involved in potential change. The context needs to match with, facilitate, or promote the need for change, whereas the nature and complexity of change might be influenced by developmental epoch. The first part of the figure conceptualizes readiness for change, or being in a state prepared for transition, as involving a synergistic amalgam of biological, environmental, and self-(organismic) constructive variables that coalesce to the cusp of change in the system at hand. The three dimensions vary from lack of readiness for change to full readiness and, collectively, they need to interact to create an inertial impetus causally toward change. This type of interaction does not refer to the statistic G×E type, in which both of specific genetic (allelic) and environmental factors need to be present, but to an additive, multiplicative, cascading interaction of multiple sources toward the cusp of change and its tipping point. In this sense, causal control parameters are conceived of as representations of factors that are more generic or generalized as opposed to being too specific and simplified (and easily quantified).

State Collector Variables The dimensions of the state collector variable in the model that serves as the immediate transition mechanism for change of system state, once readiness for change of state is achieved, is conceptualized as one that is cross-network in integration. It, too, is not a simplified, specific, and readily quantified variable, but an integrative, synergistic one that might lead to state change at any of multiple levels in the system at hand, whether local or global. The structure involved could be local (schematic) or global (macro, e.g., representation, even (sub) stage), and the degree or depth of change within (intra-level) or over (inter-level) levels might be local or global, but either way involving increased cross-network integration at the implicated level.

Network Change Therefore, in the model, as shown in the third part of the figure, development is conceived as an increasing network construction (cross-network) over its elements and levels, to the point that nonlinear dynamic shifts in state might take place as the threshold or cusp of change is traversed. The latter might take place directly and in proportion to input, context variables, or perturbation conditions (quantitative). But, more likely, the system resists equilibrium change until at far-from-equilibrium and then self-organizes into a new regime (qualitative change) that might even have emergent state construction characteristics beyond less complex qualitative state transitions. The types of change can be modeled whether part of a stage model or not, because qualitative shifts in state structure are not limited to stage models.

I illustrate the latter principle by noting the following. The present model is consistent with the microgenetic information processing view, which accentuates a wave pattern in problem solving when performance is analyzed for strategy efficiency. The child generally progresses from use of one less efficient strategy to another, improving speed and accuracy, to arrive at the most efficient strategy (Siegler, 2006, after Berk, 2013). One can apply Young's (2011) Neo-Piagetian model to this micro-developmental process, because that model applies not only to changes over stages and substages but even to micro changes. This eventuates because the model was structured to reflect a fractalization process in which the change process in stages, substages, and micro changes are equivalent in passing through the sequence of the steps of coordination, hierarchization, systematization, multiplication, and integration. Therefore, increased strategy efficiency in problem solving might follow a wave over phases of coordination, hierarchization, systematization, multiplication, and integration. Coincidentally, Siegler's wave model includes five increasingly useful steps in strategy use. [They are not phrased in language that could be transposed into the coordination to integration sequence, but with reworking they might be.]

The upshot of the comparison of my stage model with micro change models is that just as the former is open to the model of readiness for change that has been formulated in the present section so are other models that are nonstage ones. If the former has a structure that opens it to transitioning of the type described in the present model, so too do other models that allow for qualitative change or shifts to more developmentally advanced structure even if not of the stage variety.

Comment

As a conclusion about the model of change presented in Fig. 30.2, note that it can be summarized by the three indicated formula found below. The first concerns causal control parameters, the second concerns system collector variables, and the third concerns change resulting from their dynamic.

The figure indicates a model of behavioral change, as applied to development but applicable to any psychological change. I have formulated the model as a series of equations. In this regard:

(1) CCP f ((B, E, S(O)) [i, c] RC/TR)
 i = individualized (development is about individual differences)
 c = universal generic constant (but development is also about norms and universals)

(2) SCV (RC/TR) f ([i, c] CCP)

(3) C(D) f ((SCV) (N [L, G]))

Environment (E)—e.g., object available for applying sensorimotor scheme; social support facilitating readiness for change

Biology (B)—e.g., maturation of frontal lobes allows necessary organization, inhibitory control

Self (S)/Organism (O)—e.g., self-regulation allows for appropriate self, emotional, and social control/interaction

I have tried to create a specific mathematical formula to represent the developmental process. This attempt to create a viable mathematical formula in this regard focuses on systems theory concepts, but in a way that allows for change either with respect to stages or more generically. They need further work and operationalization.

The following section of the chapters moves from readiness for change to dimensions in change. They carry the impact of the causal change factors impinging on systems.

Dimensions of Change

Dimensions

Introduction Tables 30.4, 30.5, 30.6, 30.7, 30.8, and 30.9 present the most important characteristics evident in change processes in systems, especially from a nonlinear dynamical, complexity, and network point of view. The tables list major and other dimensions/factors, respectively, in general change processes, nonlinear dynamical systems, and networks. This organization might not work for all readers, but it helps serve as an integrative frame for further elaboration. Also, the tables do not include any mathematical work that corresponds to the concepts; therefore, much re-organization, mathematical expression, and gathering of empirical support for the frame should continue.

Evolvability/Developability/Versatility Evolvability concerns the capacity of a system for evolving adaptively. It relates to natural selection not just of an adaptive phenotype with undergirded genotype but also of phenotypes so well-undergirded with the genetic potential for its

Table 30.4 Major dimensions/factors of change processes in systems

Dimension/factor	Examples/poles
Target	Molecule, cell, organism (human), community
Evolvability/ developability	Low, high
Time	Online, ontogenetic, evolutionary
Context/niche	Unconducive/conducive
Conservability	Resistant/fixed, robust/stretchable
Flexibility	Passive/reactive, versatile/active
Dynamic	Linear, nonlinear
Regime	Stable, cusp/edge, unstable

Table 30.5 Other dimensions/factors of change processes in systems

Dimensions/factor	Examples/poles
Turbulence	Prechange, continuous
Flow (energy, resources)	Punctuated, continuous
Change amount	Minor, major
Change quality	Qualitative, quantitative
Change intensity	Burst, bump
Change frequency	Frequent/multiple, intermittent, isolated
Change speed	Fast, slow
Change duration	Long, short

Table 30.6 Major dimensions/factors of dynamic characteristics of systems

Dimension/factor	Examples/poles
Constituents	Elements/states, patterns/space
Openness	Open to input, closed
Order	Ordered, unordered
Perturbation	Far from equilibrium, catastrophe (butterfly effect)
Status	Equilibrium, disequilibrium/far from equilibrium
Threshold	Control parameter/bifurcation; holistic, self-assembly
Self-organization	Lateral, novel/emergence
Emergence	Constrained, unconstrained
Attractors	Point/cyclical, chaotic, multiple

Table 30.7 Other dimensions/factors of dynamic characteristics of systems

Dimension/factor	Examples/poles
Range	Local, global
Predictability	Predictable, unpredictable
Degree	One unit, bi, system-wide
Level	Bottom, top
Direction	Horizontal, vertical
Hierarchy	Strata, nests
Feedback	Negative, positive, forward
Scale repetitions	Attractors, fractals

Table 30.8 Major dimensions/factors of network processes in systems

Dimension/factor	Example/poles
Components	Units/nodes, links/edges
Modifiability	Core (no), peripheral (yes)
Architecture	Hubs/primary, secondary
Scope	Features, form, function
Energy, resources (information)	Incorporation, dissipation, exchange/seeking
Tightness	Loose, cohesion, coherence
Sequencibility	Sequences, simultaneous
Causality	Privileged, distributed

Table 30.9 Other dimensions/factors of network processes in systems

Dimension/factor	Examples/poles
Yoking	Permanent/binding, transient/ non-binding
Autonomy	Maintained, chunked
Locality	Localized, dispersed
Optimization	Increasing, irrelevant
Complexity	Increasing, irrelevant
Control	Increasing, irrelevant
Success	Adaptive, maladaptive
Freedom	In degrees of freedom, in freedom of action, in beliefs of free will

diversity to enable it to continue to evolve (e.g., Colegrave & Collins, 2008; Pigliucci, 2008; Wagner, 2005).

Table 30.4 expands the concept of evolvability to include "developability." This allows inclusion of differential capacity for developmental flexibility in ontogeny as opposed to differential phylogenetic flexibility.

The fundamental assumption underlying the combined differential flexibility in ontogeny and phylogeny presented in the present frame is that of "versatility." Systems evidence change in a dynamic way. This happens to the point that they gravitate to regions in which they are poised for change.

Moreover, in that region, they adaptively seek out and promote new regions reflective of their diversity that can further promote that diversity. The cascading result of their change over the time scale involved is an increasing complex and potentially successfully effort to better challenge, adapt to, control, and even alter their environment for their improved fitness, or their survival and reproduction.

Systems do not just express evolvability; they actively create opportunities for emergence of new features, structures, and functions that can promote it even more. Similarly, in developability, systems actively seek out dynamic contingencies that promote and take advantage of their flexibility.

However, not all systems are equally adept in their evolvability/developability/versatility/flexibility. There are individual differences in this regard even in normative environments. Moreover, in their differential flexibility, systems differ in their capacity to adjust to adverse environments, and this type of difference is evident even in supportive ones.

In child development, for example, the concept that fits the present modeling is differential biological or environmental susceptibility to context (Belsky & Pluess, 2013; Ellis, Boyce, Belsky, Bakermans-Kranenburg, & van IJzendoorn, 2011). In this model, susceptibility genes afford negative outcomes in adverse environments but positive ones in supportive environment, while other related alleles are not susceptible either way.

In the present context, one could generalize the differential flexibility in the latter concepts and term it "differential evolvability susceptibility" or "differential developability susceptibility." A common term that works might be "differential system versatility" or flexibility.

Extensions The remainder of Table 30.4 concerns expansion of the concept of differential flexibility or versatility in systems. The systems being described cover biotic units, from molecules/cells to organisms/communities. With revision, they could readily include abiotic nonliving systems, including galactic and other "Big History" entities. The timelines of system change could be online and rapidly unfolding, as in molecular or micro/nano interactions, or phylogenetically long and even "universally" so. Systems are differentially primed for change not only constitutionally but also contextually. Some environments are more propitious than others for supporting change.

Change takes place out of the balance of two orthogonal tendencies—to conserve stability and to generate change. Conserving systems could be inordinately inflexible or, rather, they could be flexibly stretchable to a degree, with their elasticity being better able to resist perturbations that are more than minor. Systems vary in their flexibility for change, too, as discussed above.

The tension between change and its resistance in systems creates a constant dynamic that interacts with energy and other input and also with context or niche and other considerations, especially in terms of individual differences, to determine change potential and activation. The changes could be linear or dynamically nonlinear, and in the latter, the system could stand at the cusp or edge of change, away from equilibrium (even far from it), ready to escape into more turbulence and instability, which is a risky but probabilistically viable stepping stone to increased adaptability, complexity, and stability.

Energy The next Table 30.5 in the series addresses energy flow and turbulence in the system. If it is open, resources enter the system (energy, information) and are exchanged. Stimuli and related inputs might perturb the system, creating turbulence in structure and opening it to change. Often, turbulence is greater prior to change, and it could be excited during it. Both flow and turbulence could be punctuated, or intermittent. The change that results would vary on the usual dimensions of magnitude, frequency, speed, duration, intensity, and quality, with qualitative change corresponding to new states, stages, and so on.

Dynamics As for the two tables (Tables 30.6 and 30.7) on dynamic characteristics of systems, they concern how element units combine into patterns in state space and also how the systems can change when open, for example, from order to disorder, or vice versa. Stimuli perturb the system, leading to major change when it is far-from-equilibrium, even when the perturbation is minor (the butterfly effect). Systems could change at specific thresholds of control parameters (e.g., at bifurcation points), or also as an action of the whole system in unsustainable disequilibrium.

As system trajectories in state space repeatedly visit the same basin or basins, systems self-organize into attractor regimes, which are locally indeterministic but globally deterministic. The attractors can self-assemble into new regimes at bifurcation points, or in crossing saddle points (e.g., becoming multiple/chaotic instead of simpler point attractors or cyclical attractors). Emergence is a cardinal feature of nonlinear dynamical systems because the form taken might be totally unpredictable from the parts, and also the properties involved might be totally novel compared to those of the parts (priors, constituents). However, to a degree, emergent patterns are still constrained by prior state configuration.

As for other aspects of dynamical systems, they vary in focus/range (local, global), predictability (stochastic/random, deterministic), and extent of action [one unit, bi-unit (e.g., coupling), or multiple-unit (up to system-wide)]. They vary in hierarchization (present, absent, and, if present, type, e.g., strata/layers vs. nests/embeddings). The levels can work bottom-up, top-down, or both (reciprocally). They can work within a level (horizontally) or across them (vertically). Upper levels can regulate or "enslave lower ones," reducing their degrees of freedom (but increasing their own).

The feedback involved in systems can dampen, change, or accentuate them (e.g., negative, positive feedback), or it can alter future activity in a feedforward mechanism. Systems can repeat activity not only in the sense of attractors returning to global basins but also in terms of multiple scale equivalences at different levels (e.g., fractals; think the equivalence in patterns of waves at the beach and in a bay).

Networks As for the two tables (Tables 30.8 and 30.9) on networks, networks are types of systems for which the unit components are termed nodes and their links are termed edges. Some are primary in the sense of being cores or hubs (e.g., with consistency), or multiple nodes and edges. Network architecture also includes descriptors, such as features, form or structure, and function. They include incoming resources (e.g., energy) that are not only used but also sought (because of dissipation). The structure of networks could be loose or less coupled or more cohesive and coherent (in edges, across edges). The nodes could possess sequential relations or simultaneous ones, and, if the former, could express local causality involving them, although causality could be widely distributed in overall system activity.

Networks can express coupling/linkages that are quite bound toward permanency, or they could be more loosely associated. As units coalesce or chunk into higher-order structures, they can possess some degree of autonomy, or not. Chunks can be local or wider. Networks can grow toward increasing optimization or complexity, becoming more adaptive and integrated. They can evidence greater control of the environment and greater adaptive success. They can demonstrate freedom in their degrees of freedom, freedom of action and, for human system entities, belief in and sense of free will.

Comment

Systems can change in so may varied ways that the dimensional change model that I have described in system change stands as a good complement to the readiness for change model described just before it. Together, the two models point to the complexity in change in systems and, therefore, in behavioral causality, as well.

The following section of the chapter examines the developmental change process, in particular. First, it considers the nativist position compared to the empiricist one, and then it attempts an integration using my model as a basis. Note that elsewhere in the present book I have considered the integration of nativist and empiricist positions in development and referred to a combined model as neoreductioconstructivist. In the present approach, I am more specific how this type of combined model would look like in terms of my own.

Infant Development

Introduction

According to Berk (2013), the core knowledge view of infant thought considers that there are innate, specialized knowledge systems that leave the young infant equipped for rapid development of critical modules in cognition (e.g., Spelke & Kinzler, 2007). Two primary core knowledge domains concern physical and numerical knowledge (e.g., about objects and their effects and about keeping track of the amount of objects, respectively). Figures 30.3 and 30.4 present a new way of looking at the issue, with Figure 30.3 on mechanism and Figure 30.4 on content.

Model

Figure 30.4 illustrates that domains can evolve through infant sensorimotor stages conceived generically in the Neo-Piagetian perspective (Young, 2011). The domains might be core, nativist ones or others more open to experiential construction. The classic Piagetian view of domain transitions is limited to certain areas, such as object permanence. In contrast, the Neo-Piagetian model constitutes a generalized change description that can accommodate the perspective of core knowledge acquisitions and other contemporary findings for infancy, including nascent intentionality, theory of mind, and morality.

Biology The figure integrates competing views of early infant cognitive sensorimotor development, which opposes nonstage innate, nativist, and constructionist (sub)stage approaches. Figure 30.4 indicates that domains of development could be generic but also quite specific to core, nativist ones. The latter domain model

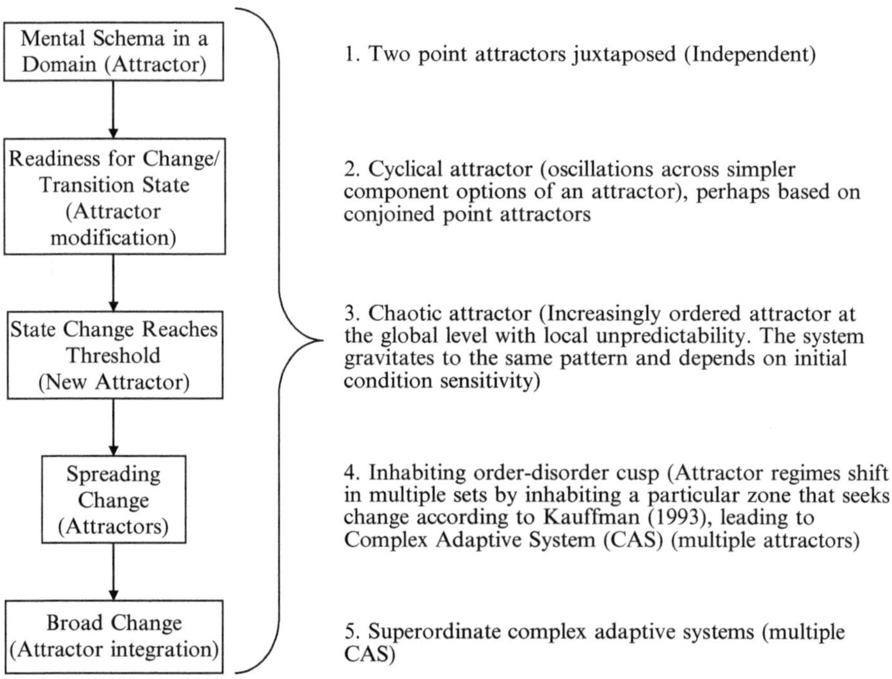

Fig. 30.3 An Attractor Complexity Domain Developmental Model. The figure presents a five-step model of change involving the elaboration of attractors that is consistent with the Neo-Piagetian five-stage model of Young (2011). The five step-change model is a generic one applicable to other change processes. Relative to Young (2011) this version adds a step of two independent attractors (juxtaposed), which coordinate (cyclical attractor) and become "chaotic" (moving to the cusp of change and CAS development)

a Domain Construction/ Scaffolding

Nativist Core Knowledge Domains X Empirical Refinement, Release

"Innate"
e.g., - Numerosity
- Other physical properties
Biologically prepared

Environment minorly contributory

OR

Constructed General Domains X Empirical Induction

- e.g., Piagetian (actively constructed)
- means-end
- object (permanence)
- categories
- space
- time
- causality

- Environmental/ Elaboration
- Support/ Facilitation

b (Sub)Stage Construction/ Scaffolding Outcome

Piagetian (specific to sensorimotor stage)

1. Reflex exercise (0-1 month)
2. Primary circular reactions (1-4)
3. Secondary circular reactions (4-8)
4. Coordination of secondary schemes (8-12)
5. Tertiary circular reactions (12-18)
6. Inventing new means by mental combination (18-24)

OR

Neo-Piagetian (generic, recursive within each stage)

1. Coordination (equivalent of 2nd Piagetian sensorimotor substage)
2. Hierarchization (3rd)
3. Systematization (4th)
4. Multiplication (5th)
5. Integration (6th) [with Reflex exercise shunted to its own stage, beginning prenatally, and also involving five substages]

Fig. 30.4 An Integrative Model of Core Knowledge (Nativist), Piagetian, Neo-Piagetian, and Empiricist Approaches to Infant Cognitive and Sensorimotor Development. The figure presents the opposition of the core knowledge/ nativist approach to early cognitive development and the Piagetian one ending with my Neo-Piagetian model (Young, 2011) appears to stand in opposition to a Neo-Piagetian substage developmental process. This seems the case because Piaget had described a general model of substages in the sensorimotor stage of infancy, but he applied it to specific domains such as object permanence, means-end, and causality. In this regard, the modular and generic are both present in Piaget's model.

Environment The environment plays a fundamental role in any model of cognitive development and, for core knowledge domains that are biologically prepared, the environment functions in a refining, reciprocal interactive modality rather than as one that is more raw inductive, and elaborative. It is not conceived as separate but as reciprocal, mutual, and interactive, or giving scaffolding support. As for the Piagetian perspective, the environment is not considered modular in the sense of the core, nativist one, for which the environment offers specific behaviors to the developing child in support of specific modular domains. Rather, for Piaget, the environment serves a general alimentary function that promotes passage through the generic sequence of substages in the infancy period. Moreover, for Piaget, the environment is less important than the child her- or himself in promoting change.

Self That is, Piaget had emphasized the constructivist nature of the child's cognitive activity and that the child activity pursues that construction. Therefore, the model in the figure allows for an active role of the developing person (infant) in his/her own development through the constructive process in cognition, as had been described by Piaget.

Combined Figure 30.4 presents specific details of Piaget's sensorimotor substage series. There are six substages, and they begin with reflex exercise and end with mental combinations, but still in the sensorimotor modality to a degree. The figure shows how the six substages can be translated into the current Neo-Piagetian (sub)stage model, as described previously in the chapter.

As for the causal factors involved in the substage transitions of my model, it should be clear by now that I support a multifactorial model that is biopsychosocial in nature. At the same time, systems theory provides an avenue for specifying change mechanisms, as per the last portion of the figure.

Mechanism In this regard, for mechanisms of change in my model, Fig. 30.3 presents Young's (2011) translation of his Neo-Piagetian change model into the language of attractors and complex adaptive systems, which I had presented previously in the chapter. As (sub)systems at whatever level of complexity self-organize, over time, they create more adaptive attractors in their state configurations and also their complexity increases, permitting increasing flexibility and adaptivity. [Note that the process of attractor differentiation described in Fig. 30.3 is consistent with that in Young (2011), but is changed slightly in the present version, as indicated in the Figure Caption.]

Comment

The present chapter concerns new terms and models related to causality, and the last portion of it has covered my own developmental model (Young, 2011). Given the value and validity that I see in this model and the arguments made for it (e.g., how it fills gaps in other stage models and how it can better explain experimental data derived from them), my model should take a central place in new conceptions about development and its causality. In the following, I carry this argument one step further by presenting other extensions of my model, this time not just for infancy but also across the age spectrum. Note that beyond what I have given about my model in this latter part of the present chapter, I describe in depth my model (and its extensions) in the next six chapters of the present book.

General Development

Introduction

The next three tables provide further details on the cognitive (mis)perception of the other (by the self) component of Young's (2011) model. They apply to development throughout the lifespan, extending the presentation in the prior section of the chapter on infancy. Specifically, they deal with the nature of child discipline, relationships, and how we treat minorities. They cover development over the lifespan in these areas, as well.

How We Treat Each Other

In Young (2011), I described that management style takes five forms (negate, dominate, relegate, delegate, and integrate), and I related the styles to the present model of five stages in Neo-Piagetian development through the concept of the cognitive (mis)perception of the other. Table 30.10 gives more details of the styles, which is new to the present book. Table 30.11 presents the styles in terms of the model of the cognitive (mis)perception of the other. Table 30.12 relates the styles to the five Neo-Piagetian stages in Young (2011), but includes the Piagetian stages of preoperations and concrete operations.

Specifically for Table 30.10, it indicates the way we treat children, our partners, and minorities resemble each other in terms of five types that range from the most inequitable to the highly equitable. For consistency, I kept the original styles that I created for the management context, but give examples related to different targets (children, partners, minorities). This prepares the way for relating the styles to the cognitive (mis) perception of the other and the present five stages in Neo-Piagetian cognitive development. Their relationship to the latter is more in terms of how the other is perceived rather than the cognitive level in the thinking involved.

Management Style

Table 30.11 presents five management styles that can be considered corresponding offshoots to the five levels of cognitive (mis)perception of the other that Young had derived from the Neo-Piagetian stage model. The styles range from negation to integration. (a) In the management style of negation, the supervisor engages in behavior involving—overloading, treating poorly, rejecting, and denying. (b) In domination, the supervisor acts to—subjugate, repress, oppose, impose, and manipulate. (c) In relegation, the supervisor's behaviors include—neutralize, channel, assimilate, and pacify. (d) Next, in delegation, one might—offer responsibility, show concern, and liberate somewhat. (e) In the

Table 30.10 How we treat children, partners, and minorities

Style	Examples
Negate	The child is abused in neglected, fails to thrive, and is even shaken to death or murdered. The partner is severely beaten, raped, stalked, and even murdered. The minorities are denied basic human rights, tortured, persecuted to death, and subject to genocide.
Dominate	The child is totally controlled, disregarded, and treated harshly as an object worthy of little. The partner is objectified, subsumed to basic/crude desires, overcontrolled, etc. The minorities are considered inferior, persecuted for protests, consigned to poverty, etc.
Relegate	The child is considered as a means to an end, treated with little respect, given little mental space, etc. The partner is treated in the same way. So are minorities.
Delegate	The child is supported in her/ his growth at most levels. There are some issues in giving full freedoms to explore self and other as the child develops into the teen years. A similar pattern applies to partners, but in terms of fully trusting the other. A similar attitude is applied to minorities.
Integrate	From the beginning, the parent wants the child to develop optimally at all levels and promotes the same, giving warmth and appropriate limit setting. Partners are treated with utmost respect and trust, and responds with the same in mutual growth. Majority-minority relations reflect this attitude, as well.

Table 30.11 Five management styles according to Young's Neo-Piagetian stage model

Management style	Description
Negate	Overlord, treat poorly, reject, deny
Dominate	Subjugate, repress, oppose, impose, manipulate
Relegate	Neutralize, channel, assimilate, pacify
Delegate	Offer responsibility, show concern, liberate somewhat
Integrate	Promote individual and collective action, creativity, thought, freedom and awareness; empower, humanize, trust others' wisdom; facilitate emergence of constant adaptation and growth; coparticipate in process

Adopted with permission of Springer Science+Business Media. Young, G. (2011). *Development and causality: Neo-Piagetian perspectives*. New York: Springer Science+Business Media; with kind permission from Springer Science+Business Media B. V. [Table 18.5, Page 428]

penultimate management style in integration, the supervisor works toward—promoting individual and collective action, creativity, thought, freedom, and awareness; empower, humanize, trust others' wisdom; facilitate emergence of constant adaptation and growth, and co-participate in the process.

These five management styles reflect the Neo-Piagetian cognitive levels in Young's (2011) model of reflexive, sensorimotor, perioperational, abstract, and collective intelligence, respectively. The adult might functioning cognitively at the upper level of the model, however, function in management style might not take place at the corresponding level, but a lower one. Therefore, management styles involving abuse or domination are potentiated when the other is perceived as reflexive or not cognitively functional, for example. In contrast, when a manager or a management team is functioning at the highest level of collective intelligence, and the management team perceives the other through this lens, better teamwork in the work environment could be promoted, for example, through brainstorming for the common company (financial) good (and creating a good group harmony, as well).

Because these five management styles reflect how the person might behave in the task of dealing with others, one can qualify the scheme as dealing with the psychology or personal side of the person rather than the biological or environmental side. However, making these types of distinctions for such a complex behavior is more of a heuristic than a natural separation into categories.

Cognitive (Mis)Perception of the Other

In the following, I provide a model of the cognitive (mis)perception of the other as per Young (1997, 2011), but slightly modified (see Table 30.12). In the original, I emphasized how the other can be misperceived according to the perceiver's diminution of the psychological integrity of the perceived. I described the five steps involved, and related them to the five Neo-Piagetian stages of the present model. Moreover, I indicated that the five substages that cyclically recur in the Neo-Piagetian model apply to the cognitive (mis)perception of the other, as well, providing scales to measure the (mis)perception in terms of these substages. In the present rendition of the model, i give only two levels beyond the stages and they are the pre-operational and concrete operational levels from Piaget's model (for the perioperational stage, which he referred to as Representational). I have used this two-level approach for that stage elsewhere in this book.

Essentially, the model indicates that when the person is misperceived as someone to pacify into assimilation, this can happen in first-order (pre-operational) and second-order (concrete operational) ways. In the former, compared to the latter case, the cognitive sophistication attributed to the other is primitively logical and the pacification should be easier.

Comment

The next part of the present chapter returns to a concept described in the last chapter, that of intraaction. In the following, I examine some of the extensions that could be made for this concept.

Table 30.12 The cognitive (mis)perception of the other and individual/group response at each cognitive stage

Stage	Cognitive Misperception of the Other	Individual/ Group Response (A vs. B)
a. Reflexive	Negate (abuse/ reject/ deny)	Obliteration vs. nihilism
b. Sensorimotor	Subjugate (repress, oppose/ compete, impose, manipulate)	Sterilization vs. revolution
c. Perioperational	Pacify/tantalize	Assimilation vs. resistance
Preoperational	First-order	First-order
Concrete operational	Second-order	Second-order
d. Abstract	Limit, partially liberate	Involution vs. evolution
e. Collective intelligence	Humanize	Equalization vs. emancipation

The model of the cognitive (mis)perception of the other indicates that, at the lowest levels of (mis)perception of the other, we treat the person as an infant or young child (levels a-b) of the model). Because of the devaluing nature of these levels, the person is considered as not having much equal rights, which thereby justifies any abuse or suppression undertaken. (c) As for perceiving the other only in terms of the person being akin to an older child, at best, the person engaging in the misperception treats the other as someone who could be canalized or manipulated easily, due to their perceived lack of cognitive sophistication. In the last stages of the model (d-e), the person perceives the other as a teenager or adult, or in the more mature levels of the model. The table also indicates how individuals or groups might respond to the perceiver misattributing maximum cognitive capacity and engaging in mistreatment as a result.
Note. Individuals might be children or partners and the group might be minorities as perceived by majorities. When the misperception is equivalent to the reflexive level, the other will be overpowered and feel obliterated. If there is an effort to avoid obliteration, the only option might be a nihilistic, chaotic behavior, because all others might be not even possible. For the perception of being like a sensorimotor entity at best, the perceived might feel neutralized or sterilized. If there is any fight possible, it will be more overt than nihilism and be overtly a revolutionary one. If the person is perceived equivalent to child-like with some cognitive skills at best, it will foster a more subtle aggressive counter response, should it take place, which we call resistance. The first-order level will be more intuitive/ automatic than logical/ reflective, consistent with the preoperational stage associated with it. If the stage is the concrete operational one, the second-order level of resistance will have logical/ reflective elements, but limited to the physical, tangible environment and options rather than abstract, intangible ones. The latter type will be found is the evolutionary/ emancipation responses of the later responses of the individual group.

The table has presented a model of the cognitive (mis)perception of the other or how individuals perceive the other according to their own predominant developmental socioemotional level. Most likely, each individual simultaneously functions at all five levels of the model (in terms of actual, desired or most mature behavior, etc). Also, the relative proportion of the five levels in any one person should vary according to situation, issue, person being related to, his or her own history, and so on. The same applies to the development in couples and societies; they might also have one major way of (mis)perceiving of the other, but do vary. Adopted with permission of Springer Science+Business Media. Young, G. (1997). *Adult development, therapy, and culture: A postmodern synthesis*. New York: Plenum; with kind permission from Springer Science+Business Media B. V. [Table7.1, Page. 156; slightly modified]

Intraactive Terminology

Introduction

In the last chapter, I presented the concept of intraaction that I developed to indicate, for any phenomenon, the centrality of relations among components relative to the centrality of the components, themselves, along with their interactions in which the components remain separate and unchanged by the interactions in the phenomenon. In this concept, the intraactive interactions among the components of the phenomenon even define the components of the phenomenon so that neither components nor their interactions exist by themselves beyond the whole system they form and that transform them. This concept is so new, even if it is related to other ones, such as interactivism, that a Google search did not find even one entry with this terminology [Most Google searches give hundreds of thousands or millions of listed entries within nano-seconds of data mining.]

Application

The concept of intraactions could have far-reaching implications for specifying and understanding other concepts in psychology, such as many of those in the present book. In this regard, instead of referring to causality alone, given the nature of the concept of intraactivism and its implications for behavior, I suggest that a relevant extension of the concept of causality would be to refer to it as "intraactive causality." This new concept implies that, not only is causality multifactorial and interactive, but also the nature of the causation involved takes precedence over the components and their interactions and, indeed, helps specify, modify, and define the components as well as their interactions.

For example, instead of referring to genes interacting with the environment, and the person contributing to the interaction (e.g., through free will), it would be more exact to say that intraactive genes intraact with the intraactive environment and the intraactive free will belief in the person/self to create a superordinate intraactive causal system of behavior that leads to behavioral causation. That is, the new terminology for genes, environment, and person speak to their intraactive essence, their intraactive interaction, and their intraactive causality. In an intraactive sense, the boundaries of each of the components in behavioral causality are "fuzzy" and "get under the skin" of each other.

Continuing in this vein, the concept of intraaction can be applied to other principle concepts in the present book, leading to their conceptual modification in a way similar to that just described for causality. Therefore, one can speak of intraactive networks, intraactive systems, the intraactive biopsychosocial model, intraactive embodiment, and so on. We can even describe the intraactive person, the intraactive self, the intraactive brain, the intraactive body, and the intraactive mind. The different free will concepts in the book, such as freedom in being and having a sense of free will, could be described in these terms. Other terms that could be so described include freeing the brain and emergence. If behavior is intraactive, then its evolution and development should be described in these terms, too. One could specify each of learning, empathy, theory of mind, executive function, cognition, activation/inhibition coordination, and so on, as intraactive. Similarly, one could refer to intraactive emotions, personality, hierarchical needs, and motivation. At the applied level, it would make sense to refer to intraactive psychotherapy and to define mental disorders and categories in these terms.

Conclusion

Finally, some of the models that I developed could be respecified as intraactive—for example, intraactive stage models, the intraactive Piagetian, Eriksonian, and Maslovian models, and the intraactive stimulus–organism–response model. On the one hand, the concept of intraaction could have very limited scope, and just remain one other way to describe interactions. However, on the other hand, it might help give a superordinate framework, worldview, or metatheory that is applicable not only to integrating work in the area of causality but also work attempting to integrate psychology itself.

Chapter Conclusions

The present chapter has presented novel concepts related to behavioral causality and has integrated many of the themes critical to the present work. One of the most fundamental is that of activation/inhibition coordination, which is considered a primary mechanism in behavioral causality. Note that development involves potential movement toward integration. With respect to the concept at hand of activation/inhibition coordination, integration refers to increasing adaptive flexibility that is entailed in the increasing optimization of activation/inhibition coordination that is found at advanced, higher-order levels of the system. The levels become both more simple through superordinate enslavement of its patterning over lower levels (chunking might be another term), as well as more complex through the increasing scope of control over behavior and adaptation that it allows.

The new terms in the chapter include the one of neuromal networks, which highlights how behavior is developed systemically. Also, it expands the concept of intraactions. The chapter deals extensively with the change processes and mechanisms, readiness for and dimensions of change, and my Neo-Piagetian (sub)stage model (Young, 2011). It re-emphasizes the centrality for the study of causality in behavior of NLDST and the concept of activation/inhibition coordination as a general mechanism. Despite the importance of the study of behavioral causality in psychology, it lacks consistent focus on the topic. Toward unifying both the study of causality and the field of psychology, itself, this chapter and the one before it, which also presents new concepts and terms for the field, could serve as springboards for future thought and research on the topic.

The last part of the book that follows this present chapter comprises six chapters that explain further my Neo-Piagetian stage model and its implications. These include development of a revision of my revised Neo-Maslovian model, as well as a Neo-Kuhnian model of paradigm shift in science and scholarship, which should be innovations worth examining by themselves.

References

Belsky, J., & Pluess, M. (2013). Beyond risk, resilience and dysregulation: Phenotypic plasticity and human development. *Development and Psychopathology, 25*, 1243–1261.

Berk, M. (2013). The DSM-5: Hyperbole, hope, or hypothesis? *BioMed Central Medicine, 11*, 128.

Colegrave, N., & Collins, S. (2008). Experimental evolution: Experimental evolution and evolvability. *Heredity, 100*, 464–470.

Ellis, B. J., Boyce, W. T., Belsky, J., Bakermans-Kranenburg, M. J., & van IJzendoorn, M. H. (2011). Differential susceptibility to the environment: An evolutionary-neurodevelopmental theory. *Development and Psychopathology, 23*, 7–28.

Jost, J., Bertschinger, N., & Olbrich, E. (2010). Emergence. *New Ideas in Psychology, 28*, 265–273.

Kauffman, S. (1993). *The origins of order: Self-organization and selection in evolution*. New York: Oxford University Press.

Lewis, M. D. (2000a). The promise of dynamic systems approaches for an integrated account of human development. *Child Development, 71*, 36–43.

Lewis, M. D. (2000b). Emotional self-organization at three time scales. In M. D. Lewis & I. Granic (Eds.), *Emotion, development, and self-organization: Dynamic systems approaches to emotional development* (pp. 37–69). Cambridge, UK: Cambridge University Press.

Lewis, M. D. (2005). Bridging emotion theory and neurobiology through dynamic systems modeling. *Behavioral and Brain Sciences, 28*, 169–245.

Nowak, M. A., & Highfield, R. (2011). *Supercooperators: Altruism, evolution, and why we need each other to succeed*. New York: Free Press.

Pigliucci, M. (2008). Is evolvability evolvable? *Nature Reviews Genetics, 9*, 75–82.

Siegler, R. S. (2006). Microgenetic analyses of learning. In W. Damon, R. M. Lerner, D. Kuhn, & R. S. Siegler (Eds.), *Handbook of child psychology: Cognition, perception, and language* (6th ed., Vol. 2, pp. 464–510). New York: Wiley.

Spelke, E. S., & Kinzler, K. D. (2007). Core knowledge. *Developmental Science, 10*, 89–96.

Thelen, E., & Smith, L. B. (1994). *A dynamic systems approach to the development of cognition and action*. Cambridge, MA: MIT Press.

Wagner, A. (2005). *Robustness and evolvability in living systems*. Princeton, NJ: Princeton University Press.

Wilson, D. S. (2009). Convergent cultural evolution and multilevel selection: Reply to comments on Janet Landa's 'The bioeconomics of homogenous middleman groups as adaptive units: Theory and empirical evidence viewed from a group selection framework'. *Journal of Bioeconomics, 11*, 185–190.

Young, G. (1997). *Adult development, therapy, and culture: A postmodern synthesis*. New York: Plenum.

Young, G. (2011). *Development and causality: Neo-Piagetian perspectives*. New York: Springer Science + Business Media.

Part VI

The Neo-Piagetian/Neo-Eriksonian Model

A Neo-Piagetian/Neo-Eriksonian 25-Step (Sub)Stage Model

31

Chapter Introduction

The book began with a general view of causality in philosophy and science, in particular. It considered inclusive models, such as the biopsychosocial one, and emphasized the biological bases of behavior (genes, brain), along with their interactions with the environment (Gene × Environment (G × E) interaction, epigenesis, cultural neuroscience, early adversity effects, and so on). It turned to the topic of development, including with respect to evolution and on causal learning. It considered the topic of free will, consistent with my emphasis that we can contribute to our own development as a third force beyond nature and nurture. The book moved to applied chapters, especially on psychopathology and the DSM-5 (Diagnostic and Statistical Manual of Mental Disorders, Fifth Edition; American Psychiatric Association, 2013). Next, it considered innovations in understanding causality, including new terms and my own models.

Up to this point, then, I have concentrated on describing contemporary approaches to causality in psychology, aside from a brief introduction to my model to several points in the book, but especially toward the end of the last chapter (e.g., Young, 2011), and mentioned only briefly at certain points the 25-step (5 stages × 5 substages) Neo-Piagetian cognitive developmental lifespan model at the heart of that book (the model also includes a 25-step Neo-Eriksonian stage model that corresponds to the cognitive one; see Table 31.1).

The next six chapters of the present book especially elaborate from the perspective of causality the model presented in Young (2011), considering that it is developmental, biopsychosocial, and systems in orientation. In this present chapter and the ones to follow in this regard, I describe the original model and innovations for it that further help establish it as an important base in understanding causality in the psychological sciences.

The innovations in understanding causality of behavior in this last series of chapters of the present work are not just based on extensions of my Neo-Piagetian/Neo-Eriksonian developmental model but considers other models related to it, such as Maslow's and Kuhn's. However, it creates new models based on the latter ones, furthering my approach of elaborating innovations related to causality in order to give it a more central role in psychology. Also, this last portion of the book ends with a new integrative model of causality in behavior that is not based on my developmental model, which is intended to spark interest and research in the field.

In this present chapter, I present especially the basics of the cognitive component of the combined Neo-Piagetian/Neo-Eriksonian that I have developed. The first part of the chapter reviews the model, in general, including in terms of the biological, environmental, and personal (psychological) factors involved. This part of the chapter is taken from Young (2011). It includes the concept of yoking (sub)stages. The second part of the chapter gives extensions of the cognitive portion

G. Young, *Unifying Causality and Psychology*, DOI 10.1007/978-3-319-24094-7_31

Table 31.1 A model of 25 steps in Neo-Piagetian cognitive development and Neo-Eriksonian social-affective development

Level	Neo-Piagetian stage	Substage	Age range	Neo-Eriksonian stage	Neo-Eriksonian substage
1	Reflexive	Coordination	Earlier fetal life	Non-participatory reflexive socio-emotions	Distance acts vs. no acts
2		Hierarchization	Quite premature		Nursing vs. rootless acts
3		Systematization	Somewhat premature		Outcome vs. outcast acts
4		Multiplication	Full-term newborn		Care giving vs. careless giving acts
5		Integration	0–1 month		Emotional vs. malemotional acts
6	Sensorimotor	Coordination	1–4 months	Pre-participatory socio-affects	Dyadic vs. dysdyadic acts
7		Hierarchization	4–8 months		Trust vs. mistrust acts
8		Systematization	8–12 months		Sociability vs. unsociability acts
9		Multiplication	12–18 months		Autonomy vs. doubt acts
10		Integration	18–24 months		Interdigitational vs. dedigitational acts
11	Perioperational	Coordination	2–3.5 years	Peri-participatory social cognitions	Superordinate vs. discoordinate acts (quasi-participatory)
12		Hierarchization	3.5–5 years		Initiative vs. guilt acts
13		Systematization	5–7 years		Identification vs. problematic identification acts
14		Multiplication	7–9 years		Industry vs. inferiority acts (participatory)
15		Integration	9–11 years		Role vs. role confusion acts
16	Abstract	Coordination	11–13 years	Hyper-participatory social mutuality	Conscious vs. contraconscious acts
17		Hierarchization	13–16 years		Identity vs. identity diffusion acts
18		Systematization	16–19 years		Nurturing vs. misnurturing acts
19		Multiplication	19–22 years		Intimacy vs. isolation acts
20		Integration	22–25 years		Universal vs. self-singular acts
21	Collective intelligence	Coordination	25–28 years	Superordinate participatory collective sociality	Metacollecting vs. disillusionment acts
22		Hierarchization	28–39 years		Generativity vs. self-absorption acts
23		Systematization	39–50 years		Catalytic vs. midlife crisis acts
24		Multiplication	50–61 years		Ego integrity vs. despair acts
25		Integration	61– years		Cathartic vs. abandonment acts

Adopted from Young (2011, 2012)

of the model into areas such as belief in free will and ethical thought. This part of the chapter is based on Young (2014).

The chapter following this one expands on the socioaffective aspect of the combined Neo-Piagetian/Neo-Eriksonian model. This next chapter is based on Young (2011). It especially deals with my revisions of Erikson's and Maslow's models. The last three chapters of the book are filled with many innovative concepts that could help toward unifying both the study of causality in psychology and the field of psychology itself. Some of these include innovations based on my developmental model or the generic one based on it.

The Present Neo-Piagetian/Neo-Eriksonian Stage and Substage Model

Model

Table 31.1 presents the essentials of the present model of Neo-Piagetian cognitive development throughout the lifespan and its corresponding Neo-Eriksonian levels (Young, 2011 and, as modified in Young, 2012). The model consists of 25 steps in development, comprising five stages and five cyclically recurring substages within each of them. Additionally, given the underlying change process that characterizes the recurring substages, each substage could pass through the same cyclic recursion at its level, in a fractalization process, leading to a model of 125 possible steps in development. [The fractal model is completed by noting that the five major stages in the model themselves can be reworked to describe them as involving the five-step sequence from coordination to integration.]

To introduce, this combined Neo-Piagetian/Neo-Eriksonian model, it constitutes the first lifespan model of corresponding cognitive-affective stages in development. Before describing in full, it is important to note some terminological inconsistencies in comparing the various one developmental models in this section. Piaget had described four major stages in development, but substages only for the first one. [Moreover, he referred to these substages as stages!] Erikson had described eight major stages in developments, but no substages. In these regards, I referred to five major cognitive stages in development, with cyclically referring substages, and applied the same procedure to the Eriksonian series after having added 17 steps to bring it to 25 total steps. Also note that in developing and naming any new stages and substages in the two 25-step series, cognitive Neo-Piagetian and socioaffective Neo-Eriksonian, I considered both the nature of the original reduced series involved (cognitive Piagetian, socioaffective Eriksonian), as well as what was required in terms of being coherent with the cyclically recurring five substages over the five stages.

The cognitive portion of stage names borrows clearly from Piaget. The five-step substage sequence is based on the Piagetian infant sensorimotor substage series (6). However, the first one of the six has been removed and placed as a separate stage (reflexive, and having its own substages), beginning in the prenatal period, something that Piaget had not contemplated. The childhood perioperational stage constitutes a combined stage involving Piaget's preoperational and concrete operational stages. [Piaget had referred to the period of Representation when he referred to these combined stages.] For the adolescent period, often I emphasize its abstract nature although also I use Piaget's label of formal operations. The collective stage refers to the adult ability to create superordinate abstract structures, to brainstorm together, to coordinate affect in cognitive processes, etc.

The series of 25 Neo-Eriksonian stages and substages in the present model corresponds to the cognitive one. The table indicates the placement of the eight original Eriksonian stages within the 25-step Neo-Eriksonian sequence and the overall correspondence of each of the steps in the 25-step Neo-Eriksonian sequence with the equivalent cognitive step in the 25-step cognitive sequence. Within the 25-step Neo-Eriksonian sequence, one finds the names of the 17 new steps that I created needed to add to the original eight-step sequence in order to complete the cognitive-affective correspondence over the 25 steps of the parallel Neo-Piagetian/Neo-Eriksonian model.

In terms of the placement of the original eight Eriksonian steps and their parallel with the cognitive steps that correspond best to them from among the 25 steps of the model, it is noteworthy that the eight original Eriksonian steps appear to emerge in parallel with the second and fourth substages of each of the last four cognitive Neo-Piagetian stages. That is, looking at the major stages that Erikson had described over the lifespan, it appears that he focused on steps in the present more inclusive model that concern elaborations (the hierarchization and multiplication substages; 2, 4) more than major advances (coordination, the first substage; systematization, the third; and integration, the fifth in the series of five substages that recur in each stage). As for naming the new 17 Neo-Eriksonian stages in the present model, I continued the Eriksonian tradition used in labeling the original eight stages in terms of describing them as polarities, but also I included the concept of "acts" in naming them. For the negative poles, I avoided repeating prepositions such as "mis-" or "dis-," choosing a more varied nomenclature.

Note that, the 25-step developmental sequence that I have developed in the present model is a modal one. The model holds that each individual traverses differently the 25-step sequence. For example, although an individual might be at an advanced stage cognitively, on the one hand, that stage might not be used to the fullest in cognitive problem solving. Moreover, the person might not be at all at the corresponding socioaffective stage due to the negative effects of early adversity (e.g., maltreatment) or current conditions (e.g., trauma). The model provides a normative model that covers the lifespan but, more important, it emphasizes the individual differences that take place on its scaffold due to the multiple causal factors influencing development.

The Model as Biopsychosocial

Tables 31.2, 31.3, 31.4, 31.5, and 31.6 elaborates the 25-step Neo-Piagetian cognitive developmental model that I have constructed with details related to biology, environment, and self. The tables' columns are taken from Young (2011). Together, they indicate the biopsychosocial nature of development, as emphasized in Young (2011).

For each step in the developmental model, the second column of the table describes the underlying biology involved at two levels. This second column is from Tables 26.1 to 26.10 in Young (2011). It presents central specializations associated with each (sub)stage of the model and inhibitory function therein. That is, first, it gives the type of central developments taking place in terms of activation/inhibition coordination. In Young (2011), I gave this mechanism cardinal importance in underpinning both brain and behavioral development. Also, the column lists evolutionary origins that might be associated with the steps of the model.

The third column of the table gives the corresponding step in the cognitive (mis)perception of the other that is associated with each of the steps in the model, which is an aspect of the developing person's psychology, as deriving from lived experience in the environment. The third column is from Tables 14.2 to 14.6 in Young (2011). The steps in cognitive (mis)perception of the other refer to how others treat people when they do not perceive and treat them optimally, e.g., as infantile and deserving of abuse. This type of behavior stands as a proxy for an essential component of the environment in development.

The last column in the table gives the label for the step in self-development that corresponds to each of the 25 steps in development. The fourth column is from Table 24.2 to 24.6 in Young (2011). It describes the steps in social self working schemata according to the model. This component of the table represents one important aspect of the "psychology" of the developing individual (the self-concept is core to one's personal representation). This column completes giving some details of my model that illustrates its compatibility with the biopsychosocial approach.

The model of the cognitive (mis)perception of the other, as presented in Young (2011), indicates that, at the lowest levels of (mis)perception of the other, we treat the target person as an infant or young child despite their actual age (levels a–b of

Table 31.2 Neo-Piagetian reflexive stage models in development (in five steps): biology, environment, self (Young, 2011)

(Sub)Stages	Biology	Environment (how parent treats child)	Self
Coordination	At first, reflex centers mature without stimulus sensitive activating mechanisms; nevertheless, they discharge, and this occurs even in pairs through lateral inhibition–activation interplay Evolutionary origin: Reptilian I	The child is seen as an extension of the parent's self so that he or she can negate, abuse, reject, deny, and behave absolutely, with overt insults and rejection toward the child. The intonation is abrasive, negative, and rejecting	No schemata other than reflex pairings
Hierarchization	Fixed order established in reflex pairs by one-way inhibitory suppression of direction in their functional linkage. Also, full stimulus-provoked reflex arcs develop through control by inhibition–disinhibition timing Evolutionary origin: Reptilian II	The child's reasoning or position is attacked, criticized, or rejected. The parent overtly denies the possibility of the child being correct	Reflex pairs coordinate and react to stimuli
Systematization	Above process expands to include other components at second or both phases of movement. This may involve coupling with other reflexes and/or interdigitation with extrareflex neuronal centers primarily sensory-perceptual in nature Evolutionary origin: Reptilian III	The child's reasoning or position is overtly dismissed with no effort to constructively redirect or guide understanding of the other's viewpoint. The child is told that he or she is "wrong," but there is no effort to explain why	Primitive schemata form in visual, auditory, haptic, olfactory, gustatory, and kinesthetic activity/exploration; with intermodal system coordinations
Multiplication	Level 3 units coordinated sequentially in time by inhibition–activation balancing Evolutionary origin: Reptilian IV	Only part of the child's behavior or argument is treated as indicated in the previous substage	Consistencies in care giving lead to the formation of bodily components-of-context associations. Patterned schemata fire mechanically
Integration	Movement becomes partly reflex-free as neuronal clusters incorporate via own inhibition–activation balancing extrareflex neuronal centers involved in control of spatiotemporal changes Evolutionary origin: Reptilian V	Despite such behavior, part of the child's behavior or argument is acknowledged or listened to by the parent. There is a differentiation and reversibility evident in the willingness to acknowledge/listen to the child	Independent schemata that are not reflex controlled allow contextually-adjusted, patterned behavior with emotional integrations

Adopted with permission of Springer Science+Business Media. Young, G. (2011). *Development and causality: Neo-Piagetian perspectives*. New York: Springer Science+Business Media; with kind permission from Springer Science+Business Media B. V. [Second column from Table 26.1, Page 598, its second column, and from Table 26.6, Page 607, its last column; Third column: Table 14.2, Page 318, Fourth column: Table 24.2, Page 565, its second column]

the five-step model). Because of the devaluing nature of these levels, the target is considered as not having much equal rights, which facilitates any abuse or suppression undertaken. As for perceiving the target at the third level of the model, or only in terms of the person being akin to an older child at best, the person engaging in the misperception treats the target as someone who could be canalized or manipulated easily, due to their perceived lack of cognitive sophistication. In the last two stages of the model (d–e), the person perceives the target in a way consistent with their age, that is, as a teenager or adult, or in a more mature way.

Table 31.3 Neo-Piagetian sensorimotor stage models in development (in five steps): biology, environment, self (Young, 2011)

(Sub)Stages	Biology	Environment (how parent treats child)	Self
Coordination	By recruitment process similar to that in step 5, larger neuronal clusters form. They require intracluster inhibition–activation synchrony so that movement sequence is controlled for fine interference by perseverations, and intruding similar movements Evolutionary origin: Paleomammalian I	There is a high degree of parental control, subjugation, repression, authoritarianism, opposition, imposition, manipulation, and dominance in the conversation. It is shaped directly by the parent's ideas or agenda. The child has no independent thought, but waits for the parent to provide direction. The parent uses language to control the child's physical actions and behaviors. An order is given that directs the path in the conversation (e.g., "You don't have to say that," or "You'd better … You have to … You must …")	Working schemata become increasingly coordinative of the socializing self and the other, but only in the sense of partial components of both (e.g., the baby is contented and experiences pleasure)
Hierarchization	Neuronal cluster interdigitation goes one step beyond as pairs form a hierarchy with one subsumed to another by inhibition–activation regulation. The fine interference control described above also applies here Evolutionary origin: Paleomammalian II	The child's reasoning-position is competed with, contradicted, countered, or opposed in an effort to subvert, manipulate, control, or undermine it	As the infant develops a sense of trust, context-activated goals are added to developing schemata, which take on a hierarchical structure (e.g., components of self are interested and delighted in other)
Systematization	Above process expands to permit larger zone-area mobilization. Neuronal cluster hierarchies are synchronized to permit inhibitory control of gross interference at outset and throughout unrelated neuronal clusters Evolutionary origin: Paleomammalian III	The child clearly is directed to speak or act in a particular way with no constructive explanation given as to why (e.g., "No," "Tell me about …," "Why don't you …")	Working schemata include self-defined goals, primitive representations such as images of the caregiver, and the desire for intersubjectivity and proximity and contact. The emotional side of the developing cognitive-affective structure includes feelings of affection and comfort
Multiplication	Widespread expansion into extra zone-area surround is a major step, ensuring that the gross interference control described above comes to include multiple surround neuronal clusters Evolutionary origin: Early prosimian	Only part of the child's discourse is manipulated. Manipulative suggestions are made that flow from that part of the child's previous discourse that seems to have been judged possibly acceptable to the parent	The one-year-old infant acts increasingly autonomous through planned exploratory behavior eagerly implemented, although this does not happen with explicit plans at the behavior's outset (it is "accidental"). The social other is integral to the working schemata being formed, but as an object of sensorimotoric-emotional activity rather than a preconceived representational goal. The primary care-giver who has been sensitive in the first year so that the infant feels "loved" is sought actively in reunion after a brief separation
Integration	The range of interference control now extends cross zone-area, i.e., intrahemispherically to some extend Evolutionary origin: Early monkey	Despite some signs of parental manipulation, etc., suggestions are made in a way that appears to give the child a chance to use them or not (e.g., "You know that you could get what you want if you did it this way.").	Infants at 18 months of age enact symbolically guided, planned activity, but always with a sensori-motoric and affective base. They experience appreciation and pride. Others are understood in terms of the plans, and with consistent participation in them. The infant varies plans involving them on purpose to see the effect

Adopted with permission of Springer Science+Business Media. Young, G. (2011). *Development and causality: Neo-Piagetian perspectives*. New York: Springer Science+Business Media; with kind permission from Springer Science+Business Media B. V. [Second column from Table 26.2, Page 599–600, its second column, and from Table 26.6, Page 607, its last column; Third column: Table 14.3, Page 318, Fourth column: Table 24.3, Page 566, its second column]

Table 31.4 Neo-Piagetian developmental model of the perioperational stage (in five steps): biology, environment, self (Young, 2011)

(Sub)Stages	Biology	Environment (how parent treats child)	Self
Coordination	The process in level 10 radiates across the hemisphere, permitting cross zone-areas to being to form interlinked pairs Evolutionary origin: Early ape	The parent channels/neutralizes/pacifies the child by disrupting/disorganizing/confusing the child (e.g., "You're not thinking right"). The parent gives "I don't know" answers to questions. The child directly attempts to keep the discussion going, but the parent does not participate or give an answer to allow the discussion to proceed. Indiscriminate rewards are used to foster a climate of compliance/assumption	In symbol plan coordinations, the child's plans are more focused on self egocentrically, and the other, while schematized more holistically, needs to adjust. A sense of the other as a loving one grows
Hierarchization	Zone-areas in the same hemisphere form inhibition barriers between them to better control interference during their interrelating and simultaneous functioning Evolutionary origin: *Australopithecus afarensis*	With a younger child, passive listening without comments or encouragement is a type of pacification-channeling, because the child's thought cannot be advanced, coherent, etc., in and of itself. With an older child, a parent can pacify-channel in more indirect ways (e.g., ignore the child's thought, invalidate it; turn to own ideas after child's speaking turn without acknowledgement of listening). The parent is passive with no verbal or nonverbal expressions, direction, or guidance. The parent may acknowledge her or his listening role (e.g., "Hmm hmm"). The parent parrots or paraphrases the child's comments or requests minor restatements. Minor corrections are given by the parent (in vocabulary, pronunciation, grammar), but with no new information. The Parent may make a direct request for information, or may ask a direct question (e.g., "Say that again," "What do you think about …"). The child is rewarded if he or she follows the parent's lead or suggestions, or if the (implicit) promise of such is possible. The result is that the same comments or ideas occur during the discussion. No advances in storytelling or thought are made. An intermediary value of 12.5 is assigned when the parent asks for clarification, e.g., "Is this what you mean?" or corrects constructively, (but still with the limit that channeling, neutralizing, or pacifying is taking place)	The child's symbol plans are more differentiated, with an initiative subordinating the other, who is still responded to with an overriding love, however
Systematization	Interhemispheric communication collaboration (controlled in left hemisphere) by commissural (corpus callosum) inhibition–activation coordination allows brain-wide mobilization. Several phases probably occur, involving intrahemispheric incorporation of emerging anterior areas into the process. The frontal regions, for example, are known for inhibition of action to allow for evaluation Evolutionary origin: Homo habilis for systematization; Homo erectus for multiplication; and Archaic Homo sapiens for integration	The parent points out a position/option that is different from the child's own without constructive explanation (e.g., "Couldn't it be that …", or "Yes, but another way is …"). Or the parent enunciates own thought or position with some explanation	The "I" can take primary perspectives of the self/other through symbol plan systems and Eriksonian "industry," guided by others
Multiplication		Despite some signs of channeling or pacification, a part of the child's discourse is acknowledged/accepted/praised on its own terms. The parent clearly acknowledges the child's answer or comment but without accepting it (e.g., "Yes, I know what you mean," or "I was just going to ask you that."). The parent shows some evidence of warmth and active interest in the child's position, although the conversation is not completely interactive	This ability grows and others are seen to evaluate the self
Integration		A glimmer of possibility is left open for the child's position or argument to emerge as being correct, but in the context of others. The parent points out relationships between the child's position and (an) other(s), their own, etc., integrating the child's view as one differentiated member of a larger perspective (e.g., "You're right, but …")	The child's working schemata include testing of different roles, with others seen as modelers and accepting of this dynamic

Adopted with permission of Springer Science+Business Media. Young, G. (2011). *Development and causality: Neo-Piagetian perspectives*. New York: Springer Science+Business Media; with kind permission from Springer Science+Business Media B. V. [Second column from Table 26.3, Page 600–601, its second column, and from Table 26.6, Page 607, its last column; Third column: Table 14.4, Page 319, Fourth column: Table 24.4, Page 567, its second column]

Table 31.5 Neo-Piagetian abstract stage models in development (in five steps): biology, environment, self (Young, 2011)

(Sub)Stages	Biology	Environment (how parent treats child)	Self
Coordination	The process is level 15 expands to integration of major anterior (frontal) areas. Welsh and Pennington (1988) describe how these may emerge Evolutionary origin: Homo sapiens	The parent indirectly encourages partially independent, novel thought of other possible dimensions to the story/reasoning position, or the way given dimensions may interact (e.g., "Can you think of anything else"; "Why do you say that?"; "What else did he do or say?"; "How does *this* relate to *that*?"). The parent suggests that more may be possible or that there's something important missing (e.g., "Didn't you forget something?"). The parent does not provide information, but hints at a direction so the child can take the lead of the discussion. The parent listens to the child's response and continues the conversation by building on the child's responses or by asking indirect questions	Conscious "I" weighs abstractly
Hierarchization	Interhemispheric integration (controlled in the left hemisphere) occurs by optimal synchronization of inhibition–activation coordination. Several phases may occur, and in the last one the integration may include inhibition of major self-reinforcing systems Evolutionary origin: Cromagnon people for hierarchization; contemporary people for systematization, multiplication, and integration	Part of the child's reasoning is praised, reinforced by the parent directly with a constructive comment (e.g., "That's a really good idea because …"). The parent encourages the child to continue with her on his position/idea/comment. The parent allows the child to control the pace and direction of the discussion	Identity "I" tests and seeks identity
Systematization		The child's whole story/reasoning/position is shown to be valid in a constructive way	Conscientious "I" undertakes adult- (like) functions
Multiplication		The child is prompted to expand on the immediate/proximate implications of her or his story/reason/position	Relativistic "I" delves and debates
Integration		The child is prompted to see how her or his story/reason/position fits into a larger picture and may be harmonious with it	Universal "I" harmonizes

Adopted with permission of Springer Science+Business Media. Young, G. (2011). *Development and causality: Neo-Piagetian perspectives*. New York: Springer Science+Business Media; with kind permission from Springer Science+Business Media B. V. [Second column from Table 26.4, Page 601, its second column, and from Table 26.6, Page 607, its last column; Third column: Table 14.5, Page 320, Fourth column: Table 24.5, Page 567, its second column]

Table 31.6 Neo-Piagetian collective intelligence stage models in development (in five steps): biology, environment, self (Young, 2011)

(Sub)Stages	Biology	Environment (how parent treats child)	Self
Coordination	To this point, I have emphasized macroprocesses in activation–inhibition coordination in the brain relating to increasing intra- and interzone/region integrations. However, throughout the process of hemispheric specialization and of brain growth, in general, microprocesses are taking place related to synaptogenesis, dendritic arborization, synaptic pruning, and sculpting. In a certain sense, circuitry formation and synaptic pruning/reorganization involve neuronal activation and inhibition coordination processes at the microlevel that complement the processes at the macrolevel. To arrive at any of the postformal stages in brain function and specializations, the macro- and microprocesses should be working in a complete, optimal balance Evolutionary origin: Contemporary people for all	The child is prompted to indirectly seek or explore alternative scenarios, stories, perspectives, even ones not espoused by the parent her or himself and which may be discrepant from the parent's own point of view. The parent should be encouraging a "collective" attitude/moral/value in this line of discourse as he or she proceeds (e.g., "Is there another way of seeing …")	The self is collective, fused, and coordinative
Hierarchization		The prompts above given to the child are given in a direct manner, but only for part of, not a full, perspective. The child is encouraged to see where trade-offs, negotiations, bargaining, or give-and-take may apply to certain collective-oriented positions. However, the parent instills in the child the idea that one of them is dominant over the other(s)	The self knows priorities, is multiply complex, and can give multiply, and not for taking
Systematization		The prompts above are direct, and are aimed at eliciting a whole new perspective. The parent encourages the child to consider alternative collective positions as being part of a larger system, and that all are considered equally valid, legitimate, and in a dynamic relationship with each other	At midlife, the self can create and work to transform personal, social, work, and community systems
Multiplication		The parent encourages the child to see the implications of adopting large systems and to compare them. The parent and child discuss together similarities and differences among them. The parent and child together realize that these sometimes conflicting systems can exist simultaneously	The elder self reviews the multiplicity of life and lives
Integration		The parent encourages explicit attempts to put all previous systems into an overarching principle, tempered by contextual pragmatic realities, e.g., living with and growing from conflict	An integrated "I" is really an integrated "We" at life's end

Adopted with permission of Springer Science+Business Media. Young, G. (2011). *Development and causality: Neo-Piagetian perspectives*. New York: Springer Science+Business Media; with kind permission from Springer Science+Business Media B. V. [Second column from Table 26.5, Page 602, its second column, and from Table 26.6, Page 607, its last column; Third column: Table 14.6, Page 320, Fourth column: Table 24.6, Page 567, its second column]

Biology Elaborated in the Model

Activation/Inhibition Coordination

In the following, I elaborate the biological bases corresponding to my 25-step Neo-Piagetian cognitive developmental model (Young, 2011). Inhibitory skills are essential for survival, development, self-regulation, and adaptive behavior. For example, behavior expresses exquisite coordination of activation not only in muscle activation and interference control, but also in one's social synchronization with others. In this regard, I have written

> The concept of inhibition applies fluidly across many levels of psychological analysis … There are biochemical mediators of inhibition. Inhibition is a central characteristic of neuronal network and central nervous system function. Importance is attached to inhibition in overt behavior at multiple levels: motoric, cognitive, social, personality, etc. Even environmental influences … can be conceived in these terms (Young, 1990, p. 119).

As Young (2011) noted, according to Aron (2008), a cardinal hypothesis about the role of the frontal cortex in executive control is that it functions to "inhibit and activate" representations in subcortical or posterior cortical brain regions. As for my particular approach to inhibition in brain–behavior relations, I have maintained that activation/inhibition coordination is critical to left hemispheric function and, as a corollary, other types of less complex inhibition are localized in the right hemisphere (Young, 2011).

As applied to the present 25-step stage model, the concept of activation–inhibition coordination helps understand the increasing complexity of brain organization at each step. As lateralization proceeds through the phases in the 25-step sequence, it is argued that the deployment of an activation–inhibition coordination or balancing helps integrate newly matured zones with previously functional ones. Also, the recent work on dynamic coordinations and networks in the brain (Sporns, 2011, 2012) speaks to the issue of activation–inhibition coordination in the brain throughout the lifespan.

Broad Steps in Evolution

As for other biological underpinnings to the present 25-step developmental model, in Young (2011), I described the evolutionary origins related to the 25-step developmental model. The second column of Tables 31.2, 31.3, 31.4, 31.5, and 31.6 includes these evolutionary correspondences. The sequence is based on work on the evolution of lateralization.

In this regard, MacNeilage, Studdert-Kennedy, and Lindblom (1987, 1988) hypothesized that early prosimians manifested a left hemisphere-controlled whole-body postural organization. The complementary specialization of the right hemisphere in early prosimians concerned left-hand, visually-directed activities (e.g., reaching). Next in evolution, early higher primates evolved to locomote quadrupedally. Thus, the left hemisphere's specialization for whole-body postural control evolved into bimanual foraging in the environment. The left hand evolved to support right-hand manipulation. MacNeilage et al. (1987, 1988) suggested possible paleo-mammalian precursor steps in the evolution of laterality, and they have also suggested possible intermediate nonhuman primate steps involving early monkeys versus apes, in particular.

Corballis (1989, 1991, 1992) depicted a seven-step sequence in the evolution of human laterality and related behavior. First, early ape ancestors evidenced some asymmetries in behavior and brain organization and also in language by manual gesture.

Then, the first hominids, Australopithecus afarensis, emerged about 4–8 million years ago. They showed upright posture, bipedalism, and freeing of the hands. Later australopithecines (gracile, africanus) were quite similar.

Then, Homo habilis evolved, as early as a little over 2 million years ago. This species was characterized by both a larger brain and by a tool culture. The majority of the individuals in the species were right-handers, and apparently possessed in the left hemisphere a larger speech production (Broca's) area as well as probably a larger speech reception (Wernicke's) area.

Then, Homo erectus evolved about 1.5 million years ago. Their tool culture advanced to involve biface hand axes.

The next milestone, about 300,000 years ago, witnessed the evolution of Neandertal and other Archaic homo sapiens. Their cranial size was equivalent to that of contemporary humans.

Homo sapiens sapiens evolved about 150,000–200,000 years ago. They manifested extremely adaptive, rapid speech, and also a flexibility and open-endedness (generativity) in tool-blade manufacture and use.

Finally, Cromagnon people evolved about 37,000 years ago. They exhibited an explosion in culture (e.g., in blade technology, cave art, body ornaments).

By combining the two phylogenetic progressions just presented by MacNeilage et al. and by Corballis, in Young (2011), after eliminating redundancies, I arrived at a sequence in primate and hominid evolution made up of up to 11 steps. The 11 steps include the following landmark points in evolution: paleo-mammalian; early prosimian; ancestral monkey; ancestral ape; Australopithecus afarensis; Homo habilis; Homo erectus; Archaic homo sapiens; Homo sapiens sapiens; Cromagnon people; and contemporary people.

The 25-step ontogenetic sequence presented in my model seems to have correspondences with the phylogenetic emergence of our species, as shown in column 2 of Tables 31.2, 31.3, 31.4, 31.5, and 31.6. There may not be a one-to-one parallel in the development of stages in ontogeny and the evolutionary steps in phylogeny (ancestral ones) because of processes such as neoteny and acceleration (Gould, 1977), which function to alter or affect the former sequence in relation to the latter. [Neoteny concerns a retardation or delay in the appearance or full maturation of a developing behavior relative to the status predicted for it on the basis of prior evolution. Acceleration refers to the inverse of this process.]

Nevertheless, comparison of developmental and evolutionary sequences that have been described can be instructive. In this regard, the best fit of the MacNeilage et al.-Corballis combined 11-step evolutionary sequence and the current 25-step developmental one would place the start of the former at the eighth level of the latter, as shown in Table 31.1.

Mind Evolving

As noted in Young (2011), Donald (2008) and Mithen (2007) have described other sequences in the evolution of behavior, in this case that of the evolution of mind. Donald (2008) hypothesized that there are three major "stages" in the cultural-cognitive evolution of the hominid mind. The stages involve shifting (a) from the marginally symbolic, (b) to the proto-symbolic, and then (c) to the fully symbolic mind. According to Donald (2008), the corresponding age periods in the evolutionary course of these three evolutionary acquisitions, respectively, are about: (a) 2–4 million years ago when the first hominid species appeared, (b) then about 400,000 years ago when the species homo sapiens first appeared, and (c) then when the modern mind emerged in humans. Donald labeled the three stages as (a) mimetic, (b) mythic, and (c) theoretic, respectively. The mimetic stage involved nonverbal action modeling and imitation. The mythic step involved advanced linguistic skills. Finally, the theoretic transition involved extensive use of symbols, formalisms, and external storage of memory. Before these three stages appeared, Donald indicated that the Miocene primates had developed an episodic-type mind. The episodic step involved complex event representation.

Mithen (2007) described five steps in the evolution of the human mind, stretching from 2 million years ago to 50,000 years ago, and he also mentioned changes in the mind that had developed after the Ice Age, 10,000 years ago. In the first step, between 1.5 and 2 million years ago, an advance in brain size allowed our ancestors, *Homo ergaster*, to develop a theory of mind. Next, about 0.5 million years ago, a specialized intelligence evolved to allow for interaction with the social, natural, and technological milieux. Then, about 0.25 million years ago, an advanced holistic communication allowed advanced vocal-gestural communicative abilities, or proto-language. Next, Homo sapiens developed a cognitive fluidity, which concerns cross-modal thought, and this happened about 100,000 years ago. It permitted major cultural advances. In the next step, beginning 50,000 years ago, modern humans developed an "extended" mind. We could extend beyond our brain into the material culture. Finally, 10,000 years ago, with the end of the Ice Age, people began farming by using their intelligence. They developed advanced intellectual skills, such as creating metaphors and analogies.

The work of Donald and Mithen is complementary in their descriptions of the evolution of the human mind. Donald's mythic stage corresponds to Mithen's one of holistic communication about 300,000 years ago (in Neandertals). His theoretic stage corresponds to Mithen's description of the modern mind as extended. Their combined models allow for an eight-step sequence in the evolution of the modern mind. Moreover, the sequence fits nicely into my own model. In particular, the eight steps in the combined Donald–Mithen sequence in the evolution of mind is one that corresponds to the first eight steps of the ten steps in my developmental model that covers the perioperational stage and the abstract stage. It will be recalled that in each of these stages, I describe five substages.

Therefore, by looking further at my model for those steps that have no correspondence with the combined Donald–Mithen sequence on the origins of the modern mind, I would add that after the post-Ice Age acquisitions in the evolution of mind described by Mithen, two more steps in the evolution of the mind took place. First, the abstract systems that had developed beginning about 10,000 years ago entered a phase of multiplication, or spreading out the term used in the present model for the fourth step or substage within the development of each stage. Most probably, this took place about 5000 years ago, happening with the establishment of small non-farming communities. Next, the various abstract systems that had developed became more integrated into coherent abstract structures. This most probably took place within the last 3000 years, as societies became more organized. This proposed step in human evolution of mind reflects the equivalent last step or substage in each stage of my developmental model, which is referred to as integration.

Finally, in my model, I describe the adult as developing a postformal stage of collective intelligence. This would seem to be a very recent acquisition in the evolution of the human mind, and one limited (hopefully only for the moment) in the percentage of people expressing it. As with the other stages in the mode, it passes through a five-step or substage sequence from coordination to integration or, at least should.

Psychology Elaborated in the Model

As a proxy for self-development, the model refers to social self working schemata. This concept is an elaboration of the one of internal working model in the attachment literature (Young, 2011). I have posited that, as with any normative cognitive acquisition, the present Neo-Piagetian cognitive model of 25 steps in development speaks to how social self working schemata evolve throughout the lifespan. The tables give only positive schemata, rather than the equivalents that could derive in aversive, abuse, or otherwise negative environments. The schemata include reference to critical emotions and also to modeling following the work of Erikson.

The first table of the series is on the reflex stage, which is the first in my five-stage Neo-Piagetian development sequence (the others being sensorimotor, perioperational, abstract, and collective intelligence). The table indicates that working schemata in the first month include basic emotional components, and also that the caregiver already could be manifesting sensitive care in an impactful way. The next table on the sensorimotor stage presents the critical period in the first 2 years of life when working schemata are developing their secure or insecure characteristics. For the self, the schemata evolve in this stage from ones concerned with social coordination to those involved in active attachment and feeling loved, to schemata that are more symbolic, even if still sensorimotor. For the other, the schemata move from working models of initial social interactions, trust, and caregivers being security-promoting, to genuine interactions with and constancy in object. In the perioperational stage, working schemata of the self are marked by egocentric conceptions. They move to a better perspective-taking of the other, and to testing different roles. The other evolves from being conceived as being adjustable and to a person having rules and modulating growth, to being capable of evaluating and of modeling roles. In the abstract stage, the working model of the self develops from a conscious being to a conscientious and universalizing one. Symmetrically, ideally, the other acts to raise consciousness, conscientiousness, and universal empathy. In the collective stage, the self moves toward generativity, midlife, and end-of-life concerns. The other is conceived in a mirror way.

Environment Elaborated in the Model

The model of the cognitive (mis)perception of the other has been applied to management style in Young (2011). In the management style of negation, the supervisor engages in behavior involving overloading, treating poorly, rejecting, and denying; in domination, the supervisor engages in behavior involving subjugating, repressing, opposing, imposing, and manipulating; in relegation, the supervisor engages in behavior involving neutralizing, channeling, assimilating, and pacifying; in delegation, the supervisor engages in behavior involving offering responsibility, showing concern, and liberating somewhat; lastly, in integration, the supervisor engages in behavior involving promoting individual and collective action, creativity, thought, freedom, and awareness; empowering, humanizing, trusting others' wisdom; and facilitating emergence of constant adaptation and growth, as well as coparticipating in process. These five management styles reflect the Neo-Piagetian cognitive levels in Young's (2011) model of reflexive, sensorimotor, perioperational, abstract, and collective intelligence, respectively. The adult might be functioning cognitively at the upper level of the model, but might not be functioning in co-management style at the corresponding level (rather, at lower ones). Therefore, management styles involving abuse or domination are potentiated when the other is perceived as reflexive or not cognitively functional (at best). In contrast, when a manager or a management team is functioning at the highest level of collective intelligence, and the management team perceives the other through this lens, better teamwork in the work environment could be promoted, for example, including the emphasis on brainstorming at this stage.

Interim Conclusion

This section of the present work has presented the 25-step stage model of development described in Young (2011, 2012). It elaborated its correspondences with the biopsychosocial model, starting with its biological (central, evolutionary) correspondences, in particular. Also, it presented the cognitive (mis)perceptions of the other that are associated with each step, as a proxy for the environmental impacts of the environment on the developing person. Finally, it turned to the psychological component by examining evolution of social self working schemata that are aspects of self-development.

The three areas of the present model involving biology, environment, and psychology express a consistency with the biopsychosocial model, and illustrate how its 25 steps can flesh out a refined version of the biopsychosocial model.

In the next part of the present work, I present further expansions of the 25-step model as presented in Young (2011). It helps set the stage for presentation of other extensions of my work.

Yoking Further Explained

Introduction

Table 31.7 illustrates how Piagetian stages that develop could co-exist in thought, and how even lower-order ones, such as pre-operational thought

Table 31.7 Yoking in cognitive development: how different Neo-Piagetian stages are combined in thought

	Pre-intuitive		Intuitive	Logical thought	
Cognitive stage	Reflexive	Sensorimotor	Perioperational	Abstract (formal)	Collective intelligence
Reflexive	O	XX	XX	XX	XX
Sensorimotor	XX	O	XX	XX	XX
Perioperational	XX	XX	O	XX	XX
Abstract (formal)	XX	XX	XX	O	XX
Collective intelligence	XX	XX	XX	XX	O

Adopted with permission of Springer Science+Business Media. Young, G. (2011). *Development and causality: Neo-Piagetian perspectives*. New York: Springer Science+Business Media; with kind permission from Springer Science+Business Media B. V. [Table 17.4, Page 408]

Adopted with permission of Springer Science+Business Media. Young, G. (2014). *Malingering, feigning, and response bias in psychiatric/ psychological injury: Implications for Practice and court*. Dordrecht, Netherlands: Springer Science+Business Media; with kind permission from Springer Science+Business Media B. V. [Table 23.10, Page 603]

and its intuitive component, might be hierarchically predominant in cognitive deployment.

Yoking could lead to lower-order cognitive stages becoming predominant in various stage combinations constructed or becoming active in problem solving and thought. There are multiple advantages to use of automatic, intuitive, fast prelogical thought (Barrouillet, 2011; Kahneman, 2011; Stanovich, West, & Toplak, 2011). However, problem solving often requires higher-order thought. Aside from genetic/biological vulnerabilities leading to inappropriate use of or ability to switch to or have logical though lead in cognitive yoking during problem solving, there might be environmental factors at play, as well, such as early childhood abuse or later injury, illness, or environmental insult and stress. When this happens in the rehabilitative context, the therapist needs to understand that ineffective problem solving might result from an inefficient, nonlogical cognitive mode of thought used habitually instead of any inability to problem solving, per se, and appropriate steps can be taken to have the patient increase logical thought processes.

Yoking

The diagonal line represents the development of the five Neo-Piagetian stages of the present model. The stages that are paired by the intersection of the columns and rows and that are not on the diagonal represent the yoking of the paired stages. Developmental stage yoking means that the lower-order stage of any pair is still present in development even as the higher-order one to which it is connected emerges. Moreover, they do not remain in their original form, but both alter in their reciprocal organization through the yoking. For example, perioperational cognitive structures could be coupled with sensorimotor schemes. Of course, yoking could involve more than two stages. Further, it could involve substages rather than stages, making the process quite complex.

Backward–Forward

When the yoking involves a higher-order structure as dominant, the yoking can be qualified as backward. But when the yoking involves the lower-order stage structure as primary, the yoking is considered forward. For example, sensorimotor skills could be yoked to concrete operational ones in the perioperational phase. In the table, the stage couplings under the diagonal represent backward yoking, and those above it represent forward yoking. Normally, backward yoking is the more advanced type of stage structure yoking. However, for adaptive problem-solving forward yoking could be crucial. The context determines the priorities in this regard.

Because of backward and forward yoking, the developing person has more than one set of cognitive repertoires available for problem solving. By taking into account the possibility of triplets and larger aggregates in stage structure formations, it can be shown that the amount of potential stage structure yoking is quite large. Cognitive adaptation has available multiple yoking possibilities. Moreover, socioaffective consideration could interfere in appropriate cognitive yoking and problem solving. In this regard, consider the pull of regressive socioaffective yoking of Neo-Eriksonian step acquisitions as an example.

Multiply Intelligent

This begs the question of how many types of intelligence does the individual call forth in problem solving at any one time, and how they are organized when there are multiples. It also raises the question of the nature of multiple intelligences, because there are myriad patterns of stage structure couplings that could take place in cognitive activity. Note the contrast in this type of conception of multiple intelligences compared to the classic models of Gardner (2011) and Sternberg (2012), which do not concern stages. For example, in my approach to multiple intelligences, one could ask when lower-order stages are primary in yoking, does this mean that the individual is functioning at a lower level cognitively? Perhaps not, because it is the nature of the combination in context that must be taken into account, e.g., the primary stage might be absolutely essential even if lower-order. Moreover, the secondary, higher-order one might still have a role in determining the overall level of the couplings and work to modify the activity of the lower-order one involved. As development proceeds, these lower-order coupled stages could continue to improve in capacity, scope, automaticity, recruitment, refinement, and extension when called forth in similar circumstances to the first time that they were yoked to higher-order ones, but without affecting greatly the chief characteristics of the higher-order level.

Dual Track Stages

The implication is that each stage in cognitive development follows two tracks. First, it lays the seeds for the development of the stage that emerges from it as the next step in the qualitatively advancing series of steps in cognitive development. Second, it continues to develop for what it is at an increasing level of complexity through the stages that follow it in development. For example, sensorimotor intelligence never leaves us, and serves us in good stead throughout our lives. However, this happens as part of the adaptive strategies that we use to accomplish daily tasks, solve daily difficulties and problems, and develop expertise in areas related to it.

Multiple Intelligences

In terms of concept of multiple intelligences, it appears that the present model can accommodate the concept. For example, the sequence of five stages in development could be used to represent five types of multiple intelligences. Because each stage persists even after others have developed having more complexity, at any one time in development after the infancy period, the developing person can draw upon, as required, at least two of the stages.

Moreover, when yoking is involved, the dual structures imply a second or combined tier of multiple intelligences. Therefore, cognitive stage structure yoking is a concept that could help explain that any of lower level types of multiple intelligences represented by the first few of the five stages of the present model might function more or less at upper level in cognitive activity when they are coupled with those levels.

Chapter Conclusions

The present chapter presents the essentials of Young's (2011) model of 25 parallel steps (5 stages × 5 substages) in cognitive (Neo-Piagetian) and socioaffective (Neo-Eriksonian) development. It reviews the steps in the model and its organization into stages and substages. It shows how it treats biological, psychological, and environmental aspects, thereby making it consistent with a developmental biopsychosocial model.

The chapter includes the concept of yoking, which means that the person functioning cognitively not only might use the most advanced cognitive acquisitions for the issue at hand but also hinge to it other lower-order acquisitions. Moreover, unlike in some views of stage models, the present version allows for the parallel existence of lower-order and higher-order ones because the former are not totally subsumed in the latter, but remain available for use, albeit developing all along. Through the concept of yoking, the present model addresses the concept of multiple intelligences in the following way. That is, rather than a model of multiple intelligence involving independent acquisitions, in terms of the present 25-step developmental model, multiple intelligences concern the yoking of primary, more advanced stages and secondary, lower-order ones stages (or their substages) that might help for an issue at hand. Therefore, the different intelligences in my approach to the question relate to the stages in the model presented and, moreover, they can be yoked in context as the situation requires. [Note that the concept of cognitive Neo-Piagetian yoking also can apply to yoking of socioaffective Neo-Eriksonian developmental steps, as in the example of possible regression to a previously mastered lower-order step, perhaps while it is still coupled to others, including the current, most advanced yet less central one to ongoing functioning.]

References

American Psychiatric Association. (2013). *Diagnostic and statistical manual of mental disorders: DSM-5* (5th ed.). Washington, DC: Author.

Aron, A. R. (2008). Progress in executive-function research: From tasks to functions to regions networks. *Current Directions in Psychological Science, 17*, 124–129.

Barrouillet, P. (2011). Dual-process theories of reasoning: The test of development. *Developmental Review, 31*, 151–179.

Corballis, M. C. (1989). Laterality and human evolution. *Psychological Review, 96*, 492–505.

Corballis, M. C. (1991). *The lop-sided ape: Evolution of the generative mind*. New York: Oxford University Press.

Corballis, M. C. (1992). On the evolution of language and generativity. *Cognition, 44*, 197–226.

Donald, M. (2008). How culture and brain mechanisms interact in decision-making. In C. Engel & W. Singer (Eds.), *Better than conscious? Decision-making, the human mind, and implications for institutions* (pp. 191–225). Cambridge, MA: MIT Press.

Gardner, H. E. (2011). *Frames of mind: The theory of multiple intelligence*. Philadelphia, PA: Basic Books.

Gould, S. J. (1977). *Ontogeny and phylogeny*. Cambridge, MA: Belknap.

Kahneman, D. (2011). *Thinking fast and slow*. New York: Farrar, Straus, and Giroux.

MacNeilage, P. F., Studdert-Kennedy, M. G., & Lindblom, B. (1987). Primate handedness reconsidered. *Behavioral and Brain Sciences, 10*, 247–263.

MacNeilage, P. F., Studdert-Kennedy, M. G., & Lindblom, B. (1988). Primate handedness: A foot in the door. *Behavioral and Brain Sciences, 11*, 737–746.

Mithen, S. (2007). Key changes in the evolution of human psychology. In S. W. Gangestad & J. A. Simpson (Eds.), *The evolution of mind: Fundamental questions and controversies* (pp. 256–266). New York: Guilford Press.

Sporns, O. (2011). *Networks of the brain*. Cambridge, MA: MIT Press.

Sporns, O. (2012). *Discovering the human connectome*. Cambridge, MA: MIT Press.

Stanovich, K. E., West, R. F., & Toplak, M. E. (2011). The complexity of developmental predictions from dual process models. *Developmental Review, 31*, 103–118.

Sternberg, R. J. (2012). Intelligence. *Wiley Interdisciplinary Reviews: Cognitive Science, 3*, 501–511.

Welsh, M., & Pennington, B. (1988). Assessing frontal lobe functioning in children: Views from developmental psychology. *Developmental Psychology, 4*, 199–230.

Young, G. (1990). Early neuropsychological development: Lateralization of functions - hemispheric specialization. In C. A. Hauert (Ed.), *Developmental psychology: Cognitive, perceptuo-motor and neuropsychological perspectives* (pp. 113–181). Amsterdam, Netherlands: North Holland.

Young, G. (2011). *Development and causality: Neo-Piagetian perspectives*. New York: Springer Science+Business Media.

Young, G. (2012). A unitary Neo-Piagetian/Neo-Eriksonian model of development: Fundamental assumptions and meta-issues. *New Ideas in Psychology, 30*, 241–249.

Young, G. (2014). *Malingering, feigning, and response bias in psychiatric/psychological injury: Implications for practice and court*. Dordrecht, Netherlands: Springer Science+Business Media.

32 Further Expansions of the Present Stage Models

Chapter Introduction

The present chapter especially elaborates the socioaffective (Neo-Eriksonian and Neo-Maslovian) side of my combined cognitive/socioaffective (sub)stage model of development, as presented in Young (2011). It includes examination not only of the revised Eriksonian and Maslovian models but also extensions, including in revisions of dual process thinking, free will development, and ethical thought, as well as how re-responsibilities might develop (a Neo-Lévinasian concept). Finally, I show how the present model applies to the development of the communal cognitive enterprise of science building. In particular, I apply the present model to the evolution of developmental psychology as a discipline and also to evolution of evolution itself.

Neo-Piagetian

Introduction

After having constructed the 25-step model of development in Young (2011), I sought ways it could be expanded to deal with some of the critical issues in development. This section of the present chapter reviews some of these extensions of my model found in Young (2011).

To begin, it is worth reminding that the present model is unique in proposing, for the full lifespan, parallel Neo-Piagetian and Neo-Eriksonian stages and substages ($5 \times 5 = 25$ steps). Moreover, the present model lends itself to discovering the uniqueness of the human species.

Human Exceptionalism

On the one hand, we are the only species that develops out of the preoperational stage of Piaget, aside perhaps for a few isolated cognitive skills that might be found in other species. Second, our capacity to develop cognitively to such an advanced degree is facilitated not only by biological factors (e.g., a lengthier developmental period) but also by environmental ones (e.g., our better educational procedures and processes). Among others, Young (2011) pointed out that Meltzoff, Kuhl, Movellan, and Sejnowski (2009) and Tomasello and Carpenter (2007) considered enhanced or instructed learning as constitutive of our human uniqueness. Also, both emphasized the importance of early inter-subjectivity and mentalization in human development. The joint attention, empathic understanding, cooperative communication, and social collaboration together undoubtedly contribute to our capacity both to be educated from an early age and also to educate children (a process to which I refer as "co-education").

G. Young, *Unifying Causality and Psychology*, DOI 10.1007/978-3-319-24094-7_32

Social-Emotional

Theory of Mind Social cognition might be seen to develop from the perspective of the present 25-step model (see Table 32.1). (a) In this regard (and consistent with the literature review in Chap. 17), the model specifies that the neonate develops a reflexive inter-subjectivity, as in neonatal imitation, that is facilitated by intramodal visual-kinesthetic processes. (b) Next, the infant in the first 2 years develops an embodied mentalization, facilitated by sensorimotor developmental processes. (c) Then, the preschooler acquires representational capacities that lead to perspective-taking of the other, or the so-called theory of mind. This appears to happen in two steps—a first-order theory of mind, as revealed in the classic false belief task, and a second-order theory of mind, for example, in the Eyes task. This two-step acquisition in theory of mind would seem to correspond to the development of Piagetian preoperational and initial concrete operational thought, respectively. Also, there are precursors in the sensorimotor period that develop related to theory of mind. (d, e) Next, the teenager develops more advanced perceptions and also taking the perspective of the other, in terms of the transition of these capacities according to the development of abstract thought (which leads to postformal equivalents in the adult). [In the table, I list the stages of the model, but it can be expanded to include the model's component of cyclically recurring substages.]

Cognition-Emotion-Body of the Other The table describes a revised model of theory of mind, and how it might develop through the stages of the present developmental model. For several reasons, the concept that I have developed for theory of mind is referred to as "cognition-emotion-body of the other." First, perspective-taking about the other, or the development of relevant precursors in this ability, can happen at any age. Therefore, the concept of a "theory" of mind is one that is too cognitive and limited. Similarly, the component of the term that refers to "mind" is too limited and limiting. As we develop perspective of the other, it is not only about mind, but also about affective and corporal manifestations and processes. Finally, by including all three components of the term (cognition-emotion-body) in the term, we acknowledge the embodied nature of theory of mind, how it can begin developing in the earlier, more physical stages (reflexive, sensorimotor), and how it is relational, participatory, and coconstructed. Compared to the term theory of mind, the one of cognition-emotion-body of the other is a holistic concept and, as such, includes a contextual ground in its unfolding.

Coeducation In terms of the concept of coeducation, I developed it from the concept of coappropriation (Young, 1997), which itself was developed from the concept of appropriation. Developing individuals learn of and internalize the world into coschemes and co-operations, in a shared, relational participation with the world.

Table 32.1 Stages in construction of the cognitive-emotion-body of the other and in coeducation

Stage	Cognition-emotion-body of the other	Coeducation
Reflexive	Nascent intersubjectivity	Scaffolded holding
Sensorimotor	Embodied intentionality	Exploration promoting
Perioperational	Theory of mind	Instructional, teaching
Preoperational	First-order	Informal
Concrete operational	Second-order	Formal
Abstract	Third-order theory of mind	Real-world, transitional
Collective intelligence	Postformal theory of mind	School of life, mentoring

Similarly, as individuals develop, they are instructed, taught, or educated in a shared, relational participation with the world, as promoted by parents, peers, and other significant adults, as well as by associated technological and institutional tools or procedures. In their turn, children act on the enhanced educational contexts that are provided to them, thereby altering to a degree the educational contents and mechanisms received.

The particular advances in the cognition-emotion-body of the other in the early stages of life refer to (a) reflexive, nascent intersubjectivity and (b) sensorimotor, embodied intentionality. The corresponding coeducational functions that can serve to both buffer and to optimize their development refer to a scaffolded holding frame and exploration promotion, respectively. (c) As the child enters the preschool and school-age years, an explicit theory of mind develops (first order, then second order), as described in the literature. These acquisitions could be related, in part, to Piagetian stage acquisitions. (d, e) The teenager and adult become more differentiated in their theories of mind according to their increasing cognitive skills. For the child, coeducation takes the form of informal and formal modeling, instruction, teaching, and education. For the teenager and adult, coeducation is about preparing for and engaging in the real world, whether at school or in work.

Empathy The next table (Table 32.2) expands further the present developmental model by reframing the five major stages of the model in terms of the core characteristic of each, and then extending the revised theory of mind sequence in the prior table to a corresponding sequence for empathy.

First, the five cognitive stages of the present model can be reworked to reflect a transition in development through five steps moving from the physical to the spiritual. For example, the reflex period is especially a physical one, while the adult one potentially is quite spiritual. In between these stages, development moves through an emotional, cognitive, and consciousness sequence. Granted, in infancy, cognition and emotions are developing jointly, in that both are involved intimately in all the stage. However, the core infant characteristic would seem more emotional than cognitive, and for the older child it develops toward the reverse. For the adolescent, modally, consciousness develops in the sense of becoming aware of the self, and of one's own development and past, and in reflecting on and perhaps trying to change the self, or one's identity.

As for extending the revised theory of mind model associated with the present developmental model, as presented in Table 32.2, for the levels of empathy in the model, I refer to quasi-logical and (concrete) logical steps in development of cognitive empathy. These are terms that parallel Piaget's pre-operational and concrete operational stages. They are borrowed from Baldwin (see Young, 2011).

Note that in the table, I refer to the development of empathy in the reflexive period as "somatic

Table 32.2 Neo-Piagetian cognitive, empathy, and theory of mind development

Neo-Piagetian stage	Major focus	Empathy level	Theory of mind level
Reflexive	Physical	Somatic empathy	Preparation (nascent intersubjectivity)
Sensorimotor	Emotional	Emotional empathy	Sensorimotor representation (embodied intentionality)
Perioperational (representation) – Preoperational – Concrete operational	Cognitive	Cognitive empathy – Quasi-logical – Logical	"Theory" theory – First-order – Second-order
Abstract	Conscious	Conscious empathy	Third-order
Collective intelligence	Spiritual	Spiritual empathy	Postformal

Adopted with permission of Springer Science + Business Media. Young, G. (2011). *Development and causality: Neo-Piagetian perspectives*. New York: Springer Science + Business Media; with kind permission from Springer Science + Business Media B. V. [Second column: Table 35.7, Page 832; Fourth column: Table 15.1, Page 350] empathy." As far as I know, this is a term new to the field of psychology, and by this, I mean that the bases for further development of empathy after the neonatal period are present in preliminary fashion already at this age, being "prepared" and embodied in the early cognitive and socioaffective development of the child (Hamlin, 2014).

Free Will

Model Table 32.3 presents a philosophical and psychological model of higher-order human motivations and aspirations. In this regard, Baumeister (2008) noted that functioning as if one has free will involves self-control and deciding things rationally. Free will becomes evident by acting responsibly, deliberating consciously, behaving agentically and autonomously, and comporting in a civilized manner.

According to me, having a sense of free will develops in the context of a psychology imbued with a sense of responsibility in the Lévinasian sense of facing and feeling responsible for the disadvantaged other. Responsibility is not just about discharging daily tasks; more important, it is about growing to be and about constantly desiring to become, in the Heideggerian sense, of "being in the world."

Table 32.3 indicates that having a sense of free will develops as part of a complex involving self-control, consciousness, and taking responsibility. In the following, I examine each of these components from the perspective of the present model.

Consciousness Freud had proposed that the unconscious especially develops in the preschool years, as part of a process of repression of parentally-unacceptable libidinally-promoted desires. Another understanding of consciousness considers it as becoming aware of life and the self, for example, in the teen years when abstract thought develops. Carrying this concept one step further, one way of labeling adult consciousness would be to call it "supra-consciousness." Before the unconscious develops, prior steps in its emergence could be labeled proto- and non-consciousness.

Free Will In terms of corresponding steps in the development of free will, according to the model, it moves from the expression of will in the infancy period to the child gaining more control of it in childhood. It manifests as the traditional understanding of the term in adolescence (having choice, deliberating, etc.), and only in the adult period can it arrive at the advanced and nuanced level described above.

Responsibility Table 32.3 indicates how the sense of responsibility grows with developmental stage.

(a) In terms of responsibility, or its lack, in the first stage of the present model, the reflexive period involves the fetus being responsive but not initiatory. There is no inkling of responsibility.
(b) In the sensorimotor stage, the infant is more active and agentic, as well as voluntary and selective to some degree. In this sense, the infant can be considered "response-able."

Table 32.3 A philosophy of Re-Responsibilities and of freedom from will

Neo-Piagetian stage	Level of self-control	Level of consciousness	Level of free will	Level of responsibility
Reflexive	Involuntary	Non-conscious	–	Responsive
Sensorimotor	Voluntary	Pre-conscious	Will	Response-able
Perioperational	Social-cognitive	Unconscious	Will free	Responsibility
Abstract	Formal-identity	Conscious	Free will	Re-Responsibility
Collective intelligence	Collective	Supra-conscious	Free	Re-Responsibilities

Adopted with permission of Springer Science + Business Media. Young, G. (2011). *Development and causality: Neo-Piagetian perspectives*. New York: Springer Science + Business Media; with kind permission from Springer Science + Business Media B. V. [Table 35.2, Page 813]

(c) As for the child, logic in the Piagetian sense develops. The child is capable of undertaking responsibility, but at first, is limited by the concrete (nonconserving) nature of his/her logic, which changes as the concrete period develops.
(d) The adolescent is capable of rededication to responsibility. In this regard, I refer to the process as involving Re-Responsibility.
(e) Finally, the adult arrives at the level of advanced psychological maturity that can accompany the stage of collective intelligence. Therefore, the adult can have the sense of Re-Responsibility become multiple and varied, in a process that I characterize as involving Re-Responsibilities.

Neo-Eriksonian

Model

Tables 32.4, 32.5, 32.6, 32.7, and 32.8 present in depth the Neo-Eriksonian model that was described in Young (2011, 2012). Erikson characterized each stage in his eight-step model as a crisis, danger, challenge, or issue that needs to be navigated in mutuality with the environment. Each step is a psychosocial one, and is described in terms of specific positive and negative poles (e.g., trust vs. mistrust). As described at the outset of the chapter, I elaborated Erikson's eight-step developmental sequence into a 25-step Neo-Eriksonian one (being consistent with the parallel 25-step Neo-Piagetian sequence).

The tables present only the negative poles in the present 25-step Neo-Eriksonian model. They include descriptions of the emotions that are important at each step. They describe the type of dysregulation in social interaction and support that promotes movement to the negative side of each polarity.

The tables help clarify the 17 steps that I added to Erikson's original 8-step sequence in order to arrive at a 25-step model corresponding to the 25-step Neo-Piagetian one. For example, in the sensorimotor stage, I suggest that Erikson's trust can develop only after some degree of social interaction, as in the proposed dyadic step hypothesized to precede the stage of trust. In the perioperational stage, I suggest that the preschooler does not pass directly from Erikson's

Table 32.4 Dangers in development in the reflex substages

Level	Danger and opposition in substage
1. Distance acts vs. No stance	Distance regulation to target is irregular, too forward, or rarely "near." Without a primary base, behavior is undifferentiated.
2. Nursing vs. Rootless acts	Basic reflexive survival mechanisms are awry, e.g., in reacting to stimuli or in nursing. Given an absence of physical alimentation, behavior is without orientation or stability.
3. Outcome vs. Outcast acts	Target-related appetitive behavior is contextually inappropriate, over- or underenergized, too negative (e.g., avoidance, crying), etc. Because of this foundation, behavior may promote rejection.
4. Care giving vs. Careless giving acts	The caregiver system is not activated appropriately (e.g., newborn too passive or tests caregivers' limits, e.g., too much crying, colicky behavior). Caregivers bring their own agenda, and this may be maladaptive (e.g., indifference, postpartum depression, abuse). The will to live may be compromised by long term, ineffective, nonoptimal, or emotionally absent care giving due to problems with infants, caregivers, or their match.
5. Emotional vs. Malemotional acts	Evaluations along emotion-related dimensions (e.g., whether goals being interfered with) are inaccurate. Component emotional reactions are problematic. In short, emotional scripts are not functioning normatively (e.g., too damped, too negative). For example, infants manifest distress in unpredictable ways, are not soothed in normal manner, are too fussy, and are never engaged by sensorily interesting spectacles/objects. The same extremes may be evident in other emotions as they emerge in the succeeding substages. As in prior substage [and in all subsequent substages], caregivers may contribute to these difficulties.

Adopted with permission of Springer Science + Business Media. Young, G. (2011). *Development and causality: Neo-Piagetian perspectives*. New York: Springer Science + Business Media; with kind permission from Springer Science + Business Media B. V. [Table 20.11, Page 476]

Table 32.5 Dangers in development in the sensorimotor substages

Level	Danger and opposition in substage
6. Dyadic vs. Dysdyadic acts	Social dialogue is marked by poor synchrony with partner, incorrect reading of partner, misplaced actions, variable reactions, too demanding bids, excessive turning off, deficient learning skill, etc. The pleasure and joy typically inherent in a dyadic interaction with caregivers may be replaced by much frustration, gaze aversion, and disinterest instead.
7. Trust vs. Mistrust acts	A sense of mistrust in oneself and the social world takes hold, for care giving is unreliable, intermittent, or otherwise negative (e.g., rejecting, overintrusive smothering). Infants cannot create a normal, mutually-regulated, hierarchical integration with the caregiver where at times infants are dominant and at times subordinate in a reciprocal balance of play. Emotions that emerge involve fear, sadness, crankiness, etc.
8. Sociability vs. Unsociability acts	A lack of sociability pervades social intercourse with the caregiver, family, and strangers. Insecurity in the attachment relationship solidifies in either an anxious avoidant or anxious ambivalent-resistant (mixed) fashion. Infants do not share with caregivers sitting as a secure base, fail to adapt to their departure, ignore them, or are ambivalent on their return, and are not optimally interactive or are negative with strangers. Thus, we see emotions such as worry, dislike, aggressive displacement, and displacement escape.
9. Autonomy vs. Doubt acts	A sense of autonomy is stifled, for toddlers develop pervading, overly-dependent behavior, doubt, hesitation, inertia, or lack of self confidence. Deliberate trial-and-error exploring becomes chaotic, trying, erroneous, imploring (dependency), flat in affect, or with exaggerated fear. Dependent behavior brings with it emotions such as jealousy, greed, and defiance.
10. Interdigitational vs. Dedigitational acts	Mutuality in play is impossible, for young children cannot partake in prolonged, reciprocal, peaceful exchanges, have no facility in smoothly entering such social relations, and are either too. Overpowering/possessive or too submissive/subjugated when participating in them. Thus, give and take social behavior may be avoided. Children evaluate others with contempt, not appreciation, and evaluate themselves with the same and a sense of rejection, not pride

Adopted with permission of Springer Science + Business Media. Young, G. (2011). *Development and causality: Neo-Piagetian perspectives*. New York: Springer Science + Business Media; with kind permission from Springer Science + Business Media B. V. [Table 20.12, Page 476]

Table 32.6 Dangers in development in the perioperational substages

Level	Danger and opposition in substage
11. Superordinate vs. Discoordinate acts	Disjointed, inappropriately juxtaposed oppositions in social behavior manifest. Children seem incoherent, fragmented, and without refined social skills. Language does not fit context, actions mismatch intentions, and emotions improperly contrast. This may be evident (in different ways) both over long stretches and neighboring behaviors. The normal egocentrism of children is inappropriate or compromised, for the "ego" is dispersed or fractionated.
12. Initiative vs. Guilt acts	Initiative is damped by (familial) conflict deriving from too intrusive impositions or fantasies. This may even result in the Oedipus conflict (see Chap. 2). The nascent superego is saturated with guilt related to repressed wishes. Adoption of the same-sex parental identity in a nonvolatile manner is jeopardized.
13. Gender vs. Problematic gender acts	Identification with the primary characteristics of the parents is undermined, for the process may be limited to frontal negative attributes (e.g., anger, rejection, confused signals) or dismissed, producing a frontal negativity (aggressivity, avoidance, depression). This attitude may carry over into peer- and school-related activity (e.g., disobeying parental wishes; compensatory over-inclusion of negative peer models in behavior; resistance, underachievement in schooling). Self-devaluation is seeded.

(continued)

Table 32.6 (continued)

Level	Danger and opposition in substage
14. Industry vs. Inferiority acts	The problems above are magnified, resulting in a sense of rebelliousness, inferiority, or inadequacy. Chains of fight and/or flight become linked in children's minds, overwhelming their ego's image of itself. A propensity to over control may develop as a defense mechanism, leading to exploitation, manipulation, deception, etc.
15. Role vs. Role confusion acts	The social roles imagined in the context of family, friends, school, and other institutions are limited and limiting. These roles are restricted ones, overreactions, compensations of lack, etc., befitting the sense of rebelliousness and/or inferiority developed previously. This emotional cauldron may produce a social (external), role-oriented individual trying to mask internal conflicts.

Adopted with permission of Springer Science + Business Media. Young, G. (2011). *Development and causality: Neo-Piagetian perspectives*. New York: Springer Science + Business Media; with kind permission from Springer Science + Business Media B. V. [Table 20.13, Page 477]

Table 32.7 Dangers in development in the abstract substages

Level	Danger and opposition in substage
16. Conscious vs. Contra-conscious acts	Young adolescents can lapse into conscious self depreciation, a closure to freeing repressed thoughts, cynical ridicule of others and their constructive efforts, and "turning off" free thinking altogether. One reaction to this confusion may be to conform excessively, and adopt the role identifications perceived as preferred by parents, peers, teachers, etc.
17. Identity vs. Identity diffusion acts	The search for identity can be subverted, postponed, meander, lead to back alleys, etc., as Erikson described.
18. Nurturing vs. Misnurturing acts	Responsible adult roles cannot be envisioned. Decisions are not subjected to critical, personal standards. Social relations are more undirectional or parallel than reciprocal. Work and school activities are not future-directed and may be demeaned. Any nurturing is superficial and considered superfluous.
19. Intimacy vs. Isolation acts	This pattern continues, but more so, for multiple adult roles may be foisted on the individual by society. Abandonment of any such roles undertaken, or other self- and other-destructive behavior, becomes possible, yielding sentiments of loneliness, isolation, etc. Instead of a relativist, unique, yet mutual self, there is an absolute, desolate one.
20. Universal vs. Self-singular acts	Rather than encouraging others' development, the self implodes in self-indulgent acts, or worse.

Adopted with permission of Springer Science + Business Media. Young, G. (2011). *Development and causality: Neo-Piagetian perspectives*. New York: Springer Science + Business Media; with kind permission from Springer Science + Business Media B. V. [Table 20.14, Page 478]

Table 32.8 Dangers in development in the collective intelligence substages

Level	Danger and opposition in substage
21. Meta-collecting vs. Disillusionment acts	Disillusionment with society, with groups, and with constructive activity can pervade the individual, for the notion of profiting from collective symbiosis is not entertained.
22. Generativity vs. Self-absorption acts	Generative role models with family, at work, and in the community are sacrificed for self-absorption, a sense of emptiness, and stagnation.
23. Catalytic vs. Midlife crisis acts	Midlife crisis develops; for instead of emerging as a force in whatever collective is of concern, the adult pays the price for having skirted the collective. The confusions and changes engendered are unconscious attempts to return to prior levels through misapplied catalytic discoveries, shifts, inversions, etc., in thought.
24. Ego integrity vs. Despair acts	Disappointment with the meaningless felt in life sets in.
25. Cathartic vs. Abandonment acts	The elderly unwisely shut out spiritual experiences, denying any fellowship with humanity, the unknown, and the infinity.

Adopted with permission of Springer Science + Business Media. Young, G. (2011). *Development and causality: Neo-Piagetian perspectives*. New York: Springer Science + Business Media; with kind permission from Springer Science + Business Media B. V. [Table 20.15, Page 479]

initiative to industry, but first develops into an intermediary stage of gender acts. In the abstract stage, I propose that Erikson's famous stage of identity should be preceded by a stage involving the emergence of consciousness. In the collective stage, Eriksonian generativity has been truncated to allow for a midlife stage, which involves midlife crisis when it is negative.

Elaboration

Dunkel and Sefcek (2009) related life history theory to Eriksonian lifespan development (see Fig. 32.1). Dunkel and Sefcek developed a model of developmental psychopathology involving fast and slow life history strategies, and the authors showed how the strategies change as the person passes through each of the original eight Eriksonian stages. Dunkel and Sefcek (2009) argued that each of the slow and fast lifestyles have developmental consequences throughout the lifespan. Their pilot research supported the model that the negative poles of the oppositions in each original Eriksonian stage are associated with fast lifestyles, in particular. Del Giudice (2014) proposed a similar model of psychopathology, but without the Eriksonian component. Rather, he focused on which disorders are associated with slow and fast strategies.

Aside from its possible application to a more detailed elaboration of steps in fast and slow life history strategies, the present 25-step Neo-Eriksonian model of development affords a more nuanced and complete view of developmental psychopathology, in general. From a Neo-Eriksonian

Fig. 32.1 Crises/challenges in Eriksonian life span stages affected by faster (resource-challenged) and slower life history developmental trajectories. Faster life history trajectory includes high environmental stress and/or father absence; fast development/early maturation; early sexual behavior; quantity reproductive strategy; short-term pair bonds; and little parental investment. Slower trajectory has opposite characteristics. Adapted from Dunkel and Sefcek (2009)

point of view, it allows for specification of the specific problems, disturbances, and psychopathologies that might arise at each developmental stage over the lifespan. I am not suggesting that the model permits determination of possible psychiatric diagnostic categories at each developmental phase. Instead, it appears that the model can be used to create a rich description of the developmental difficulties and dysfunctionalities that could arise at each developmental stage.

Yoking

The present model includes the concept of yoking across cognitive stages and substages, which is quite applicable to its parallel socioaffective series. Cognitively, in Young (2011), I had described how, even as the adult functions in the postformal collective intelligence stage in problem solving, when the context determines it, the person can integrate lower-level stages with higher-order ones in the problem solving processes. Similarly, at the socioaffective level, we might function from a combined framework of pertinent or persistent Neo-Eriksonian (sub) stages. It is common in the psychodynamic tradition to refer to fixations, regressions, etc., in active stage functioning in development. In my model, I would underscore yoking over different (sub)stages in these regards. Therefore, in terms of the present model, the clinicians might be able to specify that one particular stage seems to mark current psychiatric function, it is quite a few steps behind what is expected, it is yoked to other steps both before and after it in the normative sequence, and so on.

Comment

To conclude, as has been evident throughout my work, we owe much to Piaget, in that he provided a framework that I could elaborate into a 25-step developmental progression. Moreover, it permitted me to expand it to a parallel Neo-Eriksonian developmental sequence.

Neo-Maslovian Model

Introduction

In Young (2011), not only did I present a revised Neo-Eriksonian model but also a revised one for Maslow's model based on the revised Neo-Eriksonian one. Maslow's model is a classic, and is the most downloaded work related to psychology, so it still has much contemporary currency. In revising Maslow's model in the image of my own, I followed another recent effort that I considered needed reworking itself.

Schaller, Neuberg, Griskevicius, and Kenrick (2010) presented a revised version of Maslow's model based on evolutionary theory. Maslow's (1943, 1970) classic model of hierarchy of needs consists of five levels. They involve: (a) immediate physiological needs; (b) safety; (c) love (affection, belongingness); (d) esteem (respect); and (e) self-actualization (see Fig. 32.2). Maslow considered the needs as having a sequence of priority, depending on the context confronted by the individual. Also, for Maslow, they have developmental priority, in that as people mature, they move from lower to higher levels in the hierarchy. In this sense, self-actualization represents the highest level of psychological maturity. It stands at the apex of his pyramidal model.

Working from evolutionary theory, Schaller et al. (2010) developed a seven-level revised model of Maslow's classic five-level one. In this regard, Kenrick, Griskevicius, Neuberg, and Schaller (2010) questioned the placement of self-actualization at the top of the hierarchy. Also, they queried the validity of placing sexual needs at the bottom of the hierarchy. Further, they criticized using the label of love in the middle of the hierarchy.

However, their revised model might be too biologically-based in evolutionary theory. Moreover, there is no valid reason to consider self-actualization at a lower level than any other concept for the adult not to consider physiological needs as anything but the lowest level of the hierarchy. However, the original model can be reworked to accommodate to the concerns of Kenrick et al. (2010), which is the approach that

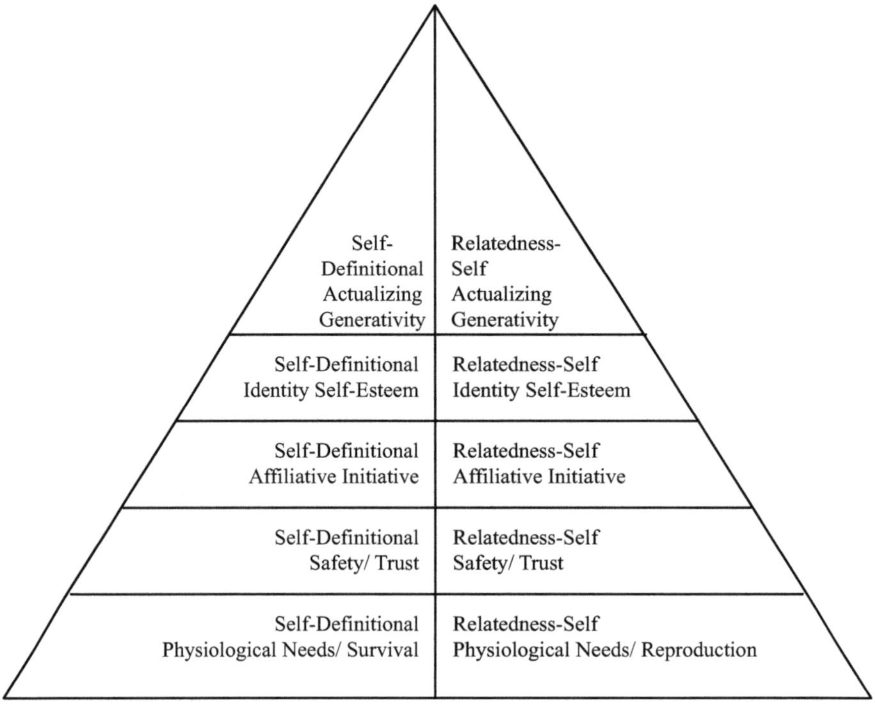

Fig. 32.2 Neo-Maslovian hierarchy of self-definitional and relatedness self needs. Adopted with permission of Springer Science + Business Media. Young, G. (2011). *Development and causality: Neo-Piagetian perspectives.* New York: Springer Science + Business Media; with kind permission from Springer Science + Business Media B. V. [Figure 19.3, Page 452]

I took. Before explaining how I modified Maslow's model in light of Kenrick et al.'s concerns, I describe my approach to the revision of Maslow, because the accommodations made in my work based on Kenrick et al. fit that revision.

Model

Roots I have developed a revised model of Maslow's hierarchy of needs that considers several other theories. In this regard, I included: (a) the Eriksonian perspective; (b) Blatt's (2008) work on the polarities in experience of self-definition and relatedness, so that the model is not just about the self (e.g., as in self-actualization) but also about the role of the other, and even larger collective issues in society; and (c) as per Kenrick et al. (2010), the work of Darwinian on evolutionary processes, but in an approach that includes cultural perspectives (see Fig. 32.2).

Fitting with Blatt (2008), as a starting point in my revision of Maslow's model of five levels in a hierarchy of needs, I developed a model that includes for each of the levels a self-other distinction. The figure that I developed to represent the model adds to the standard five-level hierarchy, as created by Maslow, a perpendicular intersection that divides the triangle in half, one for more direct personal concerns and one for concerns more about the other. To remind, this innovation in the modeling process fits the work of Blatt (2008), who described that there are two basic self- and other-related experiences—self-definition and relatedness.

About the inclusion of the model of Erikson in the revised model, I showed how his description of the stages in development map onto the upper four levels of Maslow's hierarchy of needs, and not just the top level of self-actualization. In particular, I have proposed that, for each of the upper four levels of Maslow's hierarchy, two of Erikson's original eight stages fit the levels involved. Therefore, for example, for the upper level of Maslow's model involving self-actualization, not only have I de-emphasized the self component of the term but also I believe that this level could include the stage in development after the self-actualizing one, or that of ego integrity.

In terms of Maslow's middle level of love, I used Kenrick et al.'s (2010) elaborated term for it (affiliation). However, I showed how Maslow's use of the example of affection in the love category fits Blatt's (2008) concept of self-definition. Also, I showed how Maslow's example of belongingness in love fits Blatt's (2008) concept of relatedness.

Finally, in terms of Darwinian evolutionary underpinnings in the model, I left Maslow's placement of sex as a basic biological need that should go at the bottom of the hierarchy. However, I separated it from hunger and related motivations by placing the latter under self-definitional needs and the former under relatedness needs.

Branches Ultimately, the revisions in my Neo-Maslovian model allow for a correspondence in the five levels of the model and the five stages of the present Neo-Piagetian model. The following explains this Neo-Piagetian/Neo-Maslovian parallel in development.

(a) The lower biological levels involve Maslow's immediate physiological needs and safety needs. However, they have been expanded to include self-related components other-related ones, and they include Darwinian processes in their description. In this regard, in the present model, I separate sex from other basic biological needs by placing it in the component of the model about relatedness. In addition, this allows me to refer to other basic biological processes, such as nursing, as part of the relatedness portion of the model. Once this type of distinction was made, I could relate both types of survival needs to Darwinian processes. Specifically, in terms of the concept of natural selection for purposes of survival and reproduction, one would categorize needs such as nursing as survival-related, and also others related to sexual activity as reproductive-related. Note that this does not imply that sexual activity is active in the neonatal period; only that its precursors relate to that level and, as the person develops and that level grows to include actual sexual activity, it fits the model in the way indicated.

(b) The level of safety in Maslow's model of needs and motivations has been expanded to include the psychological security engendered by positive attachment experiences. The latter develops in a majority of infants, but depends on the quality of care received. Attachment processes are comparable to the ones concerning the development of trust in Eriksonian modeling, and both develop in the first year.

(c) In the next level, Maslow's concept of love as affection and belongingness has been both split and expanded. On the one hand, affection has been placed with the self-definitional component of the model and belongingness with the one of relatedness. On the other hand, the model addresses affiliation rather than love, per se, and it includes education and instruction as part of what affiliation is about.

(d) For Maslow, esteem and respect constitute the next motivational need in the hierarchy. I have elaborated the concept to include self-definitional and relatedness components.

(e) For the penultimate level of self-actualization in Maslow's model, Kenrick et al. (2010) modified it so that it is replaced by family and related needs. However, I have already explained how I handled Kenrick et al.'s insistence that the ultimate Maslovian needs concern Darwinian survival and reproductive needs. Moreover, family relates to Erikson's concept of generativity in the adult period. In generativity, the individual focuses not just on family but also on work, community, and the wider collective. Adults seek meaning in their lives and their context, and they try to obtain for their children optimal educational and instructional experiences. In this regard, adults even form formal educational institutions and other instructional opportunities, with parents contributing either directly or indirectly, thereby helping not only their children but also other children. Overall, by including generativity in the penultimate level of Maslow's model that already includes self-actualization, and by adding to that level a distinction between self and other, my revision of the model to include family on the relatedness part of the model in this penultimate stage makes sense.

Development Outside of Development

Introduction

In Young (2011), I applied the five-step Neo-Piagetian stage model outside of human development. This could happen because it allows for a modeling process that could be used generically to describe stages in development in nonliving systems. For example, its stages have been redescribed in terms of the sequence of the labels for its substages of coordination, hierarchization, systematization, multiplication, and integration. The latter terms can be used to describe changes in nonliving systems, where applicable.

Given these considerations, I applied the present model to two sequences in the growth of science. On the one hand, the model was used to structure the development of developmental psychology itself (see Table 32.9). On the other hand, it applies to the evolution of Darwin's theorizing.

Psychology

The table indicates that the various theories in developmental psychology, and the periods in which they evolved. Moreover, the table relates these theories to the present model of change of coordination, hierarchization, systematization, multiplication, and integration. In this regard, the Freudian psychodynamic model stands as a precoordination one. It elucidated the major influences on development (the biological; id; environmental; superego; and personal/self; ego), but in a way much less refined than is the present case.

In the coordination phase of developmental psychology, before WWII in the last century, the major theories of behaviorism, ethology, and Piaget's stage model emerged. These models allowed for the elaboration of the major influences that Freud had presented in his model.

In the next stage, after WWII, the discipline witnessed the creation of attachment theory, social learning theory, and Erikson's theory. In addition, Neo-Piagetians differentiated the stages in Piaget's theory.

In addition to those theories, new models developed. They concerned the information-processing model, the sociocultural model of Vygotsky, systems theory, and the ecological model.

The modeling process continues in developmental psychology. More recent models in the field include the developmental biopsychosocial model, diathesis-stress models of developmental psychopathology, and interdisciplinary models, e.g., behavior genetics.

The table illustrates clearly how the various theories that have evolved in developmental psychology fit the present model of change. Even though we are not dealing with a living system, the system involved still matches the model.

Evolution

As for how evolution has evolved according to the steps of the present model, consider the following, in which I present a sequence of steps as possible ones in the growth of Darwinian thought. Once more, the steps relate to the present model of coordination, hierarchization, systematization, multiplication, and integration.

(a) First, the concept of natural selection could be construed as the first step of five in the development toward a complex theory of evolution. Specifically, the construction of the concept of natural selection by Darwin involved coordinating the major components of the concept into a coherent theory (e.g., concerning natural variation, competition, etc.).

Table 32.9 Growth of scientific thought in developmental psychology

Stages	Explanation
Precoordination	The Freudian psychodynamic model represents a pre-coordination phase. The major elements involved as influences on the developing human were first elucidated together by Freud (the biological; id; environmental; superego; and personal/self; ego). This prepared the way for their separation in individual theories that deal with them.
Coordination	The first genuine phase in the evolution of developmental psychology took place in the period before WWII in the last century. Three major theories emerged in this period—behaviorism, ethology, and Piaget's stage model. Behaviorism cast its stone against the inherent mentalism of the Freudian model, arguing that behavior can be understood uniquely through the environmental and learning contingencies impinging on and reinforcing the child, for example, through classical conditioning. It focused on the biological bases of behavior by developing more refined models related to imprinting and instincts. He focused on the developing child's contribution to her or his own behavior, through natural activity, active construction of cognitive schemas, and so forth. Thus, the major influences that Freud had presented in his model on the developing person were each elaborated in more refined models, but they focused especially on one or the other of the influences, without attempting more integrative models where the influences were on more of an equal footing.
Hierarchization	Later behavioral models added the learning mechanism of operant conditioning. Instead of classical conditioning, which elaborated by association the stimuli that could instigate responses, operant conditioning elaborated the responses that could be elicited by stimuli through the reinforcement histories to which emitted behavior could be subjected. Ethology added explanations of behavior that emphasized fixed action patterns and innate releasing mechanisms. Piagetians explored the role of environmental effects through décalages, training studies, and simplified tasks. Freudian models explored further the role of the nonlibidinal sources in development (Jung, Adler) and examined further the ego in development.
Systematization	In the next stage in the development of the discipline of developmental psychology, the discipline found its voice and developed models unique to it. The school of ethology influenced the development of attachment theory, in which biological mechanisms related to seeking and maintaining proximity and contact were considered to interact with the quality of care giving received, leading to the development already in the first year of life of either secure or insecure attachments. Social learning theory added observational learning to the behavioral mechanisms in learning, and introduced motivation and attentional mechanisms in learning, as well. Erikson differentiated Freudian theory in several ways that gave more of a role to the person as he or she developed. His innovations included rendering the stages involved more psychosocial than psychosexual in origin. Neo-Piagetians differentiated the stages in Piaget's theory, adding a postformal period, in particular, and positing cyclic recursions in substages.
Multiplication	In addition to those theories that differentiated from the original ones that had developed in the field at the outset, new paradigms in the field of developmental psychology emerged in the 1970s and 1980s. In the information-processing model of development, the computer provides the analogy and guide to how development is conceived. The socio-cultural model built on the work of Vygotsky, whose ideas had been isolated from the West, delaying its impact. He published in the 1930s, but became prominent in the West well after WWII. In systems theory, families are considered as wholes, and the whole system of the family and its members is considered greater than the sum of its parts. In the ecological model, the child is conceived of as an organism with initial characteristics that interact with an environment that can be differentiated into multiple components.
Integration	Subsequent models in the field of developmental psychology have been trying to differentiate further and integrate these diverse theories that had developed in prior stages of the discipline (e.g., the developmental biopsychosocial model, diathesis-stress models of developmental psychopathology, current systems models). Moreover, developmental psychology is becoming increasingly interdisciplinary, borrowing from and integrating both biological and cultural scholarship (e.g., behavior genetics, cultural and minority studies, respectively). Furthermore, a common Piagetian–Eriksonian stage framework is being constructed [and that has been the goal of the present work].

Adopted with permission of Springer Science + Business Media. Young, G. (2011). *Development and causality: Neo-Piagetian perspectives*. New York: Springer Science + Business Media; with kind permission from Springer Science + Business Media B. V. [Excerpt, Pages 718–724]

(b) Darwin's two innovations after he had developed the concept of natural selection (sexual selection; human evolution) could be taken to reflect expansion of his base idea into a hierarchical structure of ideas, with the theory of evolution at the apex, as per the present model. That is, as Darwin expanded the concept of natural selection, the new models were not equivalent in emphasis and scope to natural selection, but devolved from it as part of his movement toward a more encompassing model.
(c) Darwin never arrived at a fully integrated theory of evolution, leaving the task to biologists who followed. It could be argued that the "modern synthesis" that developed in the last century (it incorporated genetics) constituted the first step in that direction. In terms of the present model, that synthesis could be taken to reflect the substage of systematization.
(d) In terms of the present model, the recent development of the "extended synthesis" could reflect the multiplication phase in the evolution of evolution. Evolution now involves epigenetics, evo-devo, gene-cultural co-evolution, multilevel selection, and so on.
(e) In the integrative step of elaborating Darwin's work, new ideas and discoveries keep moving us forward. However, as yet, we have not developed a fully integrated model of evolution.

Comment

I conclude that the tour of past and contemporary theories in the area of developmental psychology and Darwinian thought in terms of the present model had been illuminating. Also, the process that was followed points to the validity of the present model, given the parallel it has with the steps in the evolution of the discipline of developmental psychology and of Darwinian thought. However, until there are overarching models in the discipline of developmental psychology that both respect the theories that have been fundamental in the evolution of the discipline and that also integrate them and their continuing innovations in a comprehensive framework, it can be conjectured that the field of developmental psychology is just beginning the integrative phase of its growth.

Revising Steps

Introduction

In the next section of the chapter, I illustrate how critical concepts that have been discussed in the present work can be extended by explaining how they might develop in terms of the present model. These areas include the ones of dual process thinking, free will, and ethical thought.

Dual Process Revised

Table 32.10 presents a stage model of the development of intuitive and logical thought based on my Neo-Piagetian stage model (Young, 2011). Using this five-stage Neo-Piagetian model, and focusing on the distinction between intuitive (preoperational) and logical thought (rational thought, concrete operational thought onward), I have reworked the distinction between Kahneman's (2011) and Stanovich, West, and Toplak (2011) Type I/System I thought and Type II/System II thought in terms of the stages in development indicated. This approach has led to the construct that the more advanced rational, logical thought compared to intuitive thought in the two type/system modes consists of three qualitatively different and successively more advanced skill sets. These latter three rational thought systems/types are considered: (a) basic rational; (b) advanced rational; and (c) supra-rational skills and their underlying Neo-Piagetian stage acquisitions. Also, the first-developing intuitive thought appears to consist of two successive acquisitions—more reflexive and more sensorimotor. Note that according to the present concept of yoking, the dual process model can have both aspects activated and used simultaneously.

Table 32.10 Multiple processing intuitive and reasoning systems in thought and their development

Neo-Piagetian stage	Thought system/type	
Reflexive	0	Reflexive
Sensorimotor	1	Pre-intuitive
Perioperational	2	Representational
– Preoperational		2a—Intuitive
– Concrete operational		2b—Rational
Abstract	3	Advanced rational
Collective	4	Supra-rational

Adopted with permission of Springer Science + Business Media. Young, G. (2014). *Malingering, feigning, and response bias in psychiatric/psychological injury: Implications for Practice and court*. Dordrecht, Netherlands: Springer Science + Business Media; with kind permission from Springer Science + Business Media B. V. [Table 23.9, Page 602]

Note. The table shows the equivalent of the steps in Young's (2011) Neo-Piagetian model and the concepts of thinking types in the model of dual processing, e.g., Stanovich et al.'s (2011) Type I or System I thinking compared to Type II/System II; or Kahneman's (2011) Intuitive vs. Rational thought. Similarly, more and less refined thought types related to pre-operational, intuitive and concrete/formal (abstract) operational thought are possible according to Piaget (e.g., Barrouillet, 2011). However, Piagetians note that having the potential to think abstractly does not mean it happens, as would any one else. Moreover, even when in the abstract stage, individuals might think at other, less advanced levels. I refer to this as yoking, and explain that the concept multiple intelligences refers to the co-presence of these different Neo-Piagetian modes of thinking, with the more advanced one present not necessarily being the central one yoked to. In short, thinking rationally and abstractly is a complex affair, influencing greatly the capacity to choose freely, see or create options, plan, etc. The more we gravitate to the abstract level compared to the intuitive level, the more we have a sense of freedom, choose appropriately, and feel free. However, factors such as developmental impacts, stress, illness, and injury could complicate the process

Free Will Revised

To illustrate the applicability of my stage model to the psychotherapeutic context, Table 32.11 shows how growth in the belief of free will might take place according to the steps of Young's (2011) stage model. Psychotherapists should be attuned to this growth model and, also, how belief in free will can be lost or degenerate, e.g., due to pain, injury, or illness.

In this regard, according to the steps described in the table, it could be that an emerging belief in free will in the abstract coordination stage becomes subservient, submissive, or controlled by its opposite belief of a lack of free will, leading to its systematic absence. Then, a belief in an absence of free will begins a process of propagation throughout the developing thought of the person, culminating in a pervasive belief or theory that it can never exist. Or, there might be isolated free will beliefs that develop for particular domains or issues in the person, but ones that are never dominant. Next, any effort to create systemic beliefs on the topic fails—to the contrary, the belief of the absence of free will systematically takes hold. Then, the latter absence of belief starts spreading in the general belief system, or at the level of it multiplication in the system involved. Finally, the upshot is that there could be a total, full-scale lack in development of values related to free will, such as in superordinate, morals, altruistic intentions.

Ethical Thought Revised

In Table 32.12, I develop a more general, inclusive, and qualified golden rule by following the steps of the present Neo-Piagetian model within the collective intelligence, or superordinate abstract thought. Generally, ethics evolves in the sequence of considering cases, rules, codes, principles, and theories (see Young, 2014). This sequence matches the steps in the present model in the following way, beginning with the first one of coordination and proceeding through to the fifth one integration.

(a) Coordination In the present model at the level of collective intelligence, abstract thought grows through an initial coordination of abstract ideas. For the present case, a conundrum arises in considering which is primary—the classic golden rule ("do unto others as you would have them do unto you") or the corollary inverse one also used ("do not do unto others as you would not have them do unto you"). Through the cognitive

Table 32.11 Development (and loss) of a belief in having a sense of free will

Stage	Level	Description
Abstract (Piagetian formal stage)	Coordination	The abstract idea that one could have a sense of control and determine one's options, choosing the one best for us in context, emerges. It is juxtaposed to the opposite notion of a lack of control/free will/ability to choose freely, etc.
	Hierarchization	The cognitive dissonance, compare/contrast process/indecisions, etc., created by the juxtaposition of concepts of free will in the prior level begins to resolve, in that the concept of free will becomes the primary belief to which its deterministic opposite becomes subordinated
	Systematization	The evolving concept of free will elaborates, as contingencies and contexts are considered and incorporated into a more systemic concept. The adolescent entertains a strong belief in free will, although its lack might also hold sway, depending on circumstances, manipulation, ego depletion, resource depletion, cognitive load, etc.
	Multiplication	Once systematized, the belief in free will entrenches beyond its initial locus of application (e.g., I can go out with my friends when I want and do what I want), into other areas, perhaps related to parental input (e.g., Sure you can go out, but demonstrate you deserve it, do all your course work first, be responsible and phone in, etc.)
	Integration	The belief in free will becomes a generalized concept that characterizes abstract thought processes and is applied uniformly even if hesitantly to new contingencies and contexts. It facilitates a forward, proactive approach to planning, problem solving, etc.
Collective intelligence (Neo-Piagetian postformal stage)	Coordination	The belief in free will develops into a superordinate abstract structure, beginning integration with other developing abstract structures, such as those related to values and morals. That is, the adult develops a higher-order conception of free will that includes the ability to create one's own value and moral system, one's life path, etc. It is more than a belief that one can have free will in a particular contingency/context but that one can create ways of living imbued throughout with free will even in the most complex choices that one has to make and the most complex situations that one has to confront. This belief is juxtaposed with times when it is not yet apparent, creating conflict, dissonance, etc.
	Hierarchization	The emerging superordinate belief in free will exhibits a dominant–subordinate relationship, with the concept evident about free will that is in place primary over when it is not evident
	Systematization	As contingencies and contexts are considered, the superordinate free will belief refines into a coherent structure
	Multiplication	Once fully matured, the concept spreads out throughout the cognitive architecture of the person, for example, impregnating it with its accompanying higher-order values and morals
	Integration	The superordinate free will belief ends up as an integrated whole that governs cognitive and affective life in its entire vicissitudes. The process is a never-ending struggle to keep it prominent and vigilant

Adopted with permission of Springer Science + Business Media. Young, G. (2014). *Malingering, feigning, and response bias in psychiatric/psychological injury: Implications for Practice and court.* Dordrecht, Netherlands: Springer Science + Business Media; with kind permission from Springer Science + Business Media B. V. [Table 24.6, Page 622]

Table 32.12 Golden rule: growth of ethical thought and practice

Level	Description
Coordination (Cases)	*Do* unto others as you would have them do unto you *Do not* do unto others as you would not have them do unto you Or, Strive to *do* good, benefit, help, and safeguard (Beneficence) *Do no* harm (Nonmaleficence)
Hierarchization (Rules)	Consider positive ethics and, therefore, place the do-strive axis as primary relative to the do-not axis
Systematization (Codes)	Consider that do/striving is an act rather than a whole behavior having thought and feeling. Ethics concerns meeting the other in active, lived participation by the whole person with the whole. This could be called living in a mode of being rather than only living in a mode of doing/acting Consider that being ethical and living wholly in the moment with the other should not expressly involve expectation of return from the other for any good, benefit, safeguarding, or helpful act, although inevitably people behaving ethically might bring it full circle with ample return
Multiplication (Principles)	Consider that the golden rule should be clearly inclusive of others of different ages, conditions (e.g., psychiatric, disability), groups (e.g., gender, race, minority, culture) The golden rule should reflect the individual and group difference of the person living it The person should live it according to not only personal experience but also education, training, and practice, such as in university study or in the helping professions. Knowledge and its application stems from both subjective and objective learning The golden rule could be direct but also indirect (e.g., as a role model; indeed, being a good role model might have the most inspirational influence) When lived and applied, the golden rule should act to promote the same good, beneficial, safeguarding, and helpful attitude in the receiving other person(s) The golden rule should work best when it emanates from a helpful, peaceful, and stimulating attitude or light that is projected and felt The golden rule concerns all others and, moreover, the planet as a whole, as well as beyond There is one proviso: living the golden rule does not mean abrogating one's responsibility to do no harm to one's self/family, etc. That is, applying the golden rule should not be done blindly or naively in a way that the person is taken advantage of
Integration (Theories)	Consider that the optimal golden rule should be dynamically open and responsive to changes and growth in the person, other peoples, times and culture, and ethical understanding and models We should continuously step back reflectively to examine our ethical and moral assumptions and how to live them well Therefore, the integrative golden rule that I am proposing is the following: Be unto others, no matter their age and condition, at the highest level of good and morality as reflects your positive lived participation and positive experience in the world, as well as your academic and personal studies and exploration, while acknowledging that there are personal, familial, cultural, and other group differences, as well as changes and growth over time in people and their daily living and thinking; and, aside from being a superior role model of such for the other, encourage the same superior attitude in the other and in all others, all this being done without expecting anything for yourself nor behaving in any way that is aimed at bringing advantage to yourself (but in a way that checks for being taken advantage of); that is, an appropriate golden rule to guide ways of daily living is to be, to do, and to behave in a way that maximizes a peaceful, stimulating, and helpful attitude in yourself and shown to others, which will inevitably bear positive fruit for each and every one of us and also for the planet and beyond, by the positive light and sense of helpfulness and help that it shows and seeds

Adopted with permission of Springer Science + Business Media. Young, G. (2014). *Malingering, feigning, and response bias in psychiatric/psychological injury: Implications for Practice and court*. Dordrecht, Netherlands: Springer Science + Business Media; with kind permission from Springer Science + Business Media B. V. [Table 24.5, Page 619]
Note. The levels refer to the substages in Young's (2011) model

dissonance created in comparing and contrasting the two dicta, especially in dilemmas found in actual cases that are confronted, the growth of a more refined, integrated golden rule can take place. There is a similar opposition in the ethics of mental health. It has been difficult to decide which is primary—the principle of beneficence ("strive to do good, benefit, help, and safeguard") or nonmaleficence ("do no harm").

(b) Hierarchization In order to clarify the primacy question and elaborate further the golden rule, it can help to examine positive ethics, or being proactive and constructive ethically. In this regard, the positive side of the opposition involving "do unto/do good" compared to "do not do unto/do not harm" should predominate, with the negative aspect subsumed under it in a more inclusive rule. This sets up a hierarchical relationship preparatory to further development of the rule.

(c) Systematization For creating a more systemwide or codified understanding and application of the paired golden rules, with one predominant and positive, and the one phrased negatively but secondary considered and as its inverse (but with both considering all relevant contingencies and contexts), one needs to consider various ethical qualifiers that serve to both differentiate and generalize the golden rule, rendering it more inclusive and nuanced. The qualifiers that I consider important in this regard relate to the following: (a) the act of doing is insufficient as ethical behavior. It should reflect a whole-being perspective; (b) doing/being in order to receive favor, in turn, is less altruistic than genuine and full giving without the expectation of return; and (c) that being said, if all the people involved in behaving by, and receiving the benefits of, the golden rule abide by its moral suasion, reciprocity is inevitable.

(d) Multiplication As for developing higher-order ethical and behavioral moral pathways and guiding models or theories based on principles: (a) they should allow for inclusive doing and being, or giving of the self; (b) they should integrate subjective, experiential learning and objective educational (reading/academic and, if applicable, professional) learning; and (c) they should be modeled appropriately, thereby better facilitating the same attitude in the receiving party or parties. As moral/ethical systems expand and spread into different areas of moral thought, their reach extends in a multiplicative process.

(e) Integration The golden rule or "theory" that develops will not only consider these factors but also will be open to dynamic change as the person or institutions/organizations/peoples living it (in active, shared participation) continuously reflect on the models involved and how they were derived and can still grow, thereby leading to a broad, integrative, changing meta-model. It should be noted that the penultimate golden rule that one constructs in this regard could serve the general meta-reflective process in the construction of personal and professional broad models of therapy and of ethics.

The next table (Table 32.13) illustrates that the sequence in the development of ethical thought in the superordinate collective intelligence stage is preceded by a single-order abstract sequence of steps at the preceding stage of formal thought. In addition, it suggests that the development of cognition about psychotherapy can follow the same single-order abstract formulation through each of the five substages involved.

(a) Specifically, particular cases involving helping or altruistic motives, in general, might provoke *dilemmas* that challenge existing concepts and procedure in ways of dealing with people's problems, difficulties, and issues. The dilemma could be (a) a personal one in the case of a non-professional or (b) a professional one in the case of a practitioner or student (e.g., in placement, in supervision). In this coordination substage, for the professional or student, the dilemma should reflect conflict that is present in past psychotherapeutic modes and in present ones, as well as movement toward their coordination or juxtaposition in thought (therapeutic coordination).
(b) Then in a hierarchization step, a newer model should begin to develop, which at first involves developing a clear hierarchical

Table 32.13 Stages in the development of broad personal and professional ethical perspectives and broad helping motives and professional therapy perspectives

Stage	Substage	Ethical perspective	Mental health perspective
Collective intelligence (Neo-Piagetian postformal stage)	Integration	Superordinate Ethical Theories/Meta-Ethics	Superordinate Therapeutic Theories/ Orientations
	Multiplication	Superordinate Ethical Principles	Superordinate Therapeutic Principles
	Systematization	Superordinate Ethical Codes	Superordinate Therapeutic Guidelines/Codes
	Hierarchization	Superordinate Ethical Rules	Superordinate Therapeutic Rules/ Techniques/Procedures
	Coordination	Particular Superordinate Ethical Cases (Dilemmas)	Particular Superordinate Therapeutic Cases (Dilemmas)
Abstract (Piagetian formal stage)	Integration	Ethical Theory	Therapeutic Theory/Orientation
	Multiplication	Ethical Principle	Therapeutic Principle
	Systematization	Ethical Code	Therapeutic Guideline/Code
	Hierarchization	Ethical Rule	Therapeutic Rule/Technique/Procedure
	Coordination	Particular Ethical Case (Dilemma)	Particular Therapeutic Case (Dilemma)

Adopted with permission of Springer Science + Business Media. Young, G. (2014). *Malingering, feigning, and response bias in psychiatric/psychological injury: Implications for Practice and court.* Dordrecht, Netherlands: Springer Science + Business Media; with kind permission from Springer Science + Business Media B. V. [Table 24.3, Page 615]

structure to which the past model is subsumed under the developing one. This is equivalent to forming a therapeutic rule.

(c) In systematization, a loose collection of rules should develop, leading to creation of an organized structure. As the hierarchization solidifies into a rule, or new system, with other contingencies and contexts incorporated to make it tighter yet flexible, a structured therapeutic system or guideline should develop that, for present purposes, could be considered a therapeutic "code."
(d) Therapeutic systems, once formed, extend into therapeutic practice, creating a loose collection of them involving different domains and therapeutic modules. This fits the step of multiplication in the present model, in which an underlying principle seems evident.
(e) As a therapeutic system is applied to multiple areas, expanding its use and utility, the therapeutic system should grow toward therapeutic theory. A therapeutic theory achieves an integrated, generalized yet individualized model of therapeutic knowledge, theory, and practice that is dynamically flexible.

At each step in the transformative process, once formed, the step is examined from a meta-reflective perspective, in a therapeutic meta-theoretical approach, for example, rendering it open to further dynamical change. In this way, ethical thought potentially is in constant examination and advance.

In the next cycle, the therapeutic model developed in the prior stage transforms at a superordinate level to include second-order abstract structures and processes.

(a) Multiple dilemmas in different domains/ modules are coordinated simultaneously, in a process of coordination.
(b) This leads to the step of hierarchizing superordinate therapeutic rules.
(c) The rules develop into systemic structured guidelines or "codes" (e.g., personal, practitioner or professional, organizational ones).
(d) From the dispersion of codes, therapeutic principles are being distilled.
(e) As they coalesce into superordinate therapeutic theories, the principles gain broad application and flexibility.

There is one more area to which I have applied my step model that I would like to present in this chapter. It concerns how controversies initiate and evolve. This section of the chapter has an applied component, related to therapy, just as the present one on ethics has had.

Controversy

Next, in Table 32.14, I indicate how Young's (2011) stage model can apply to controversies and related oppositions. I show the transformative effect that controversy can have in an area of thought, and, conversely, how it can become entrenched, perhaps to the detriment to the area of thought.

Moreover, the table applies to the internal "controversies" that patients undergoing psychotherapy might express as they react to cognitive dissonance (and how that can be promoted to further their progress, e.g., the belief "I can't get better" juxtaposed with the notion the person can improve). In addition, it applies to controversies and conflicts in groups of more than one person (dyads, couples, families, institutions, societies).

(a) First, the poles of the controversy at hand are juxtaposed. However, the different, outlying approach is denied any adequate space or role, is unjustly criticized, or perhaps is even condemned.
(b) In the second step of hierarchization, even more intensive support is given to pole of the controversy with which one aligns.
(c) Next, in systematization, the side aligned with is totally centralized, and perhaps the other side is treated in a negative, vitriolic, and even illogical, irrational way, with absence of the constructive investigation and conceptualization required to deal with it.
(d) In the fourth step of multiplication, the controversy that has tilted inappropriately to one side might spread to other aspects of thought in the area involved, further damping appropriate investigation and conceptualization.
(e) Finally, in integration, the marked, negative discord in the area becomes permanent to the point that one can refer to the "divide" in the area. To conclude, the application of the present model to the area of controversy indicates its applicability to areas other than development.

Chapter Conclusions

This chapter completes the two describing the current Neo-Piagetian/Neo-Eriksonian model of the steps in development. The steps are descriptive of change in human growth, but they are representative of change processes, in general. They are constituted by five stages that pass through five substages each in a cyclical recursion. The stages and substages in the present model help revise Maslov's model, which has five needs in a hierarchical model, but which is also developmental.

Table 32.14 The transformative effect of controversy (or its entrenchment)

Level	Description
Coordination	Controversy (or, discordant item, issue, dilemma, debate) emerges involving juxtaposition of a standard and a different approach, aspect, empirical finding, etc.
Hierarchization	Investigation and conceptualization leads to one or other component to be considered primary, dominant, e.g., with other criticized, invalidated, e.g., point by point. Of course, proponents of either side have differing opinions of which component is primary, dominant
Systematization	The controversy becomes centralized in the overall thought process, discipline, etc.
Multiplication	Further investigation and conceptualization might lead to (a) it drop out as important; or continue on and (b) remain as is and strident; (c) amplify, become reinforced; (d) transform, taking on new dimensions; or (e) otherwise extend in centralization
Integration	The controversy eventually resolves, with one view predominating and becoming standard. It has extended to the point of informing all or much of the thought process involved

Adopted with permission of Springer Science + Business Media. Young, G. (2014). *Malingering, feigning, and response bias in psychiatric/psychological injury: Implications for Practice and court.* Dordrecht, Netherlands: Springer Science + Business Media; with kind permission from Springer Science + Business Media B. V. [Table 24.7, Page 624]

References

Barrouillet, P. (2011). Dual-process theories of reasoning: The test of development. *Developmental Review, 31*, 151–179.

Baumeister, R. F. (2008). Free will in scientific psychology. *Perspectives on Psychological Science, 3*, 14–19.

Blatt, S. J. (2008). *Polarities of experience: Relatedness and self-definition in personality development, psychopathology, and the therapeutic process*. Washington, DC: American Psychological Association.

Del Giudice, M. (2014). An evolutionary life history framework for psychopathology. *Psychological Inquiry, 25*, 261–300.

Dunkel, C. S., & Sefcek, J. A. (2009). Eriksonian lifespan theory and life history theory: An integration using the example of identity formation. *Review of General Psychology, 13*, 13–23.

Hamlin, J. K. (2014). The conceptual and empirical case for social evaluation in infancy. *Human Development, 57*, 250–258.

Kahneman, D. (2011). *Thinking fast and slow*. New York: Farrar, Straus, and Giroux.

Kenrick, D. T., Griskevicius, V., Neuberg, S. L., & Schaller, M. (2010). Renovating the pyramid of needs: Contemporary extensions built upon ancient foundations. *Perspectives on Psychological Science, 5*, 292–314.

Maslow, A. H. (1943). A theory of human motivation. *Psychological Review, 50*, 370–396.

Maslow, A. H. (1970). *Motivation and personality* (2nd ed.). New York: Harper and Row.

Meltzoff, A. N., Kuhl, P. K., Movellan, J., & Sejnowski, T. J. (2009). Foundations for a new science of learning. *Science, 325*, 284–288.

Schaller, M., Neuberg, S. L., Griskevicius, V., & Kenrick, D. T. (2010). Pyramid power: A reply to commentaries. *Perspectives on Psychological Science, 5*, 335–337.

Stanovich, K. E., West, R. F., & Toplak, M. E. (2011). The complexity of developmental predictions from dual process models. *Developmental Review, 31*, 103–118.

Tomasello, M., & Carpenter, M. (2007). Shared intentionality. *Developmental Science, 10*, 121–125.

Young, G. (1997). *Adult development, therapy, and culture. A postmodern synthesis*. New York: Plenum.

Young, G. (2011). *Development and causality: Neo-Piagetian perspectives*. New York: Springer Science + Business Media.

Young, G. (2012). A unitary Neo-Piagetian/Neo-Eriksonian model of development: Fundamental assumptions and meta-issues. *New Ideas in Psychology, 30*, 241–249.

Young, G. (2014). *Malingering, feigning, and response bias in psychiatric/psychological injury: Implications for practice and court*. Dordrecht, Netherlands: Springer Science + Business Media.

Generic Change Model

33

Chapter Introduction

This chapter examines a generic change model based on the present developmental model, as described in the prior two chapters. Aside from examining its applicability in re-interpreting other models of change in its own terms, I apply it also to change in nonliving systems. A model that resembles mine is the readiness for change model (Maddox, 1995; Prochaska, DiClemente, & Norcross, 1992). In their model, the change process proceeds through the phases of contemplation/preparation to action/maintenance, and to resolution. In Young (2011), I showed how the five steps in their model can be reworked in terms of my own (see Table 33.1).

Most of this present chapter is based on new material not covered in Young (2011, 2014). After an introduction in which the readiness for change model is reworked to fit the present generic change model, it is applied to pain patients. The areas covered also include transformation in discovering learning, dealing with open-ended change, executive function, psychotherapy, evolution, and causality, including in the differentiation of genetic-based models. Some of the work in the chapter addresses my five-stage developmental model rather than the generic change one, but the material fits this chapter better than elsewhere (e.g., on the relationship between evolutionary mechanisms and development).

These various approaches, and that of Prochaska lend themselves to the language of complexity, attractors, and how they can transform. This hearkens to my approach in Young (2011) that the development from attractors to more advanced complexity landscapes undergirds the development of cognitive schemes and operations through the various cognitive stages and substages in the Neo-Piagetian approach that I have modeled.

Generic Change

Model

In Young (2011), I presented a Neo-Piagetian model of stages and substages in development that includes five stages over the lifespan, with each having five cyclically recurring substages. In addition, I showed how it could apply to other areas of psychology. Finally, I showed that it is underpinned by generic change processes based in attractors being altered dynamically, so that it is applicable to general changes, such as might be found in evolution of a discipline or biological evolution. Moreover, it addresses mechanisms, including nonlinear dynamical ones (facilitating transitions), activation/inhibition coordination ones (integrating the brain–behavior axes), and evolutionary ones (associated with the major stages of the model). The common fractal-type pattern across these differing developmental and

G. Young, *Unifying Causality and Psychology*, DOI 10.1007/978-3-319-24094-7_33

Table 33.1 Parallel five-step models of stages of change in therapy and generic model

Stages of change in therapy	Generic stages of change
Contemplation	Coordination
Preparation	Hierarchization
Action	Systematization
Maintenance	Multiplication
Resolution	Integration

Adopted with permission of Springer Science + Business Media. Young, G. (2011). *Development and causality: Neo-Piagetian perspectives*. New York: Springer Science + Business Media; with kind permission from Springer Science + Business Media B. V. [Table 31.3, Page 726]
Note. The stage model of therapy is presented in Prochaska et al. (1994) and Maddox (1995). The stages of change model include a last resolution stage that is mentioned rarely in the literature, nevertheless, but is part of the original conceptualization of the model (e.g., Maddox, 1995; Prochaska et al., 1994)

related transition sequences concerns coordination, hierarchization, systematization, multiplication, and integration.

In developing the recursive substage sequence for my model, I based the work on Piaget's sensorimotor substage series. I found generic descriptions for them reflecting the essence of their characteristics so that they could be applied readily to the successive stages in development right into the adult period. In effect, they can be applied generically to multiple systems (both living and non-living) that change and evolve (see Table 33.1).

Application

As per Young (2011), Table 33.2 indicates the multiple domains in living and nonliving systems that seem to reflect a five-step generic change process. The behavioral domains include not only psychological ones but also economic/political ones, for example. For nonliving ones, five-step models, or their equivalent, even have been found with processes of change in the universe. It might be more than coincidence that a host of domains express five-step change sequences.

Comment

Young (2011) showed that the mechanisms of change undergirding his five-step developmental change sequence could reflect a nonlinear dynamical system evolution involving attractors and complex adaptive systems. If systems gravitate to this change dynamic, with its five steps, then the outcome of the process should be five types of stages in change across the board for nonlinear dynamical systems, whether living or nonliving. Systems that conform to nonlinear dynamical principles should evolve in the sequence indicated because, as they seek far-from-equilibrium conditions that maximize adaptivity, the possibility of change in the direction indicated increases because it offers the best economical and elegant alternative in terms of system tension reduction and flexibility.

Stages of Change in Pain

Introduction

In Young (2011), I described a model of changes in pain experience that is compatible with the present generic change model. Prochaska, Norcross, and DiClemente's (1994) developed a model on stages of change, I have shown that it is compatible with my own, using the example of both progressive and to regressive changes in the pain patient. In the following, I give details of the progressive and regressive steps that pain patients might experience according to my adapted version of their model (see Fig. 33.1 and Table 33.3).

Progressive

(a) Specifically, in terms of the stage of contemplating change, the person appears to be coordinating the phases involving present condition and future possibility. For pain patients in therapy, therefore, the model suggests that, first, they show a readiness for change by coordinating their understanding of their present condition with an understanding of how much they can improve.

Table 33.2 Five stages in system growth in various models of living and nonliving systems

Topic	Source	Stages
Expertise	Sharpless and Barber (2009)	Novice. Advanced beginner. Competence. Proficiency. Expertise.
Leadership	Boyatzis (2008)	Seeing desired future. How acts with others. Developing learning agenda. Experimenting with new habitats. Others helping us.
Business	Zadek (2004)	Denial/defensive. Compliance. Managerial: Managing responsibility. Strategic: Responsible business strategies. Toward civil action.
Economies	Rostow (1990)	Traditional society. Preconditions for take-off. Take-off. Drive to maturity. High mass consumption.
Disciplines	Piaget and Garcia (1989)	Intra-object. Inter-object. Trans-object. [Expanded to five stages in the text.]
Politics	Paxton (1998)	New way. Rooting. Arrival in power. Exercise of power. Dual power.
Non-living/ Systems/ Big Bang	Salthe (2007)	Global microscopic disorder. Local orders, global disorders. Global order. Accelerated expansion. Global symmetry.
Bios/Generic processes	Sabelli (2005)	Flux (continually reversing). Action processes (directed change). Information (co-creation). Structuration (transient stability, expanding). Organization (creating).
Complex systems	Chen and Fang (2008)	Initial. Differentiation. Evolution. Formation. Matured.

Adopted with permission of Springer Science + Business Media. Young, G. (2011). *Development and causality: Neo-Piagetian perspectives*. New York: Springer Science + Business Media; with kind permission from Springer Science + Business Media B. V. [Table 31.1, Page 713]

(b) In the next step of preparing/deciding/determining in transitions in therapy, the person appears to be hierarchically organizing commitment and planning as primary in working toward goals. That is, pain patients appear to hierarchically organize as primary a will to effect change.

(c) In the next stage of deliberate action, systematization seems to characterize psychological organization, given that deliberate action implies a systemic plan of action. In this regard, pain patients appear to engage in deliberate action in order to change, such as participating more effectively in psychotherapy, so that a systematized application is evident in their behavior.

(d) Next in the model, the maintenance phase is consistent with the spreading out or propagation of gains that have been made into wider regions of the system, similar to what I would call multiplication. Thus, pain patients seem to expand their motivated attitude and newly acquired habits into other aspects of their lives.

(e) Finally, the Prochaska et al. step of problem resolution indicates that the system is in dynamic integration, as Young's (2011) model would predict. In this vein, in the last stage of integration, pain patients appear to attain an increasingly healthier lifestyle that is freer of pain, or at least of its limitations.

Regressive

However, conversely, pain patients can sink increasingly toward the chronic state, and this process could be modeled by the same five stages of the present model, but in reverse. (a) In the coordination stage of chronic pain development, the negative effects of acute pain are becoming synchronized with the patient's normal ongoing lifestyle. (b) In the hierarchization stage that develops next, their chronic pain becomes pervasive, and is the primary organizer relative to their prior lifestyle. (c) In the next stage, the patients develop a persistent

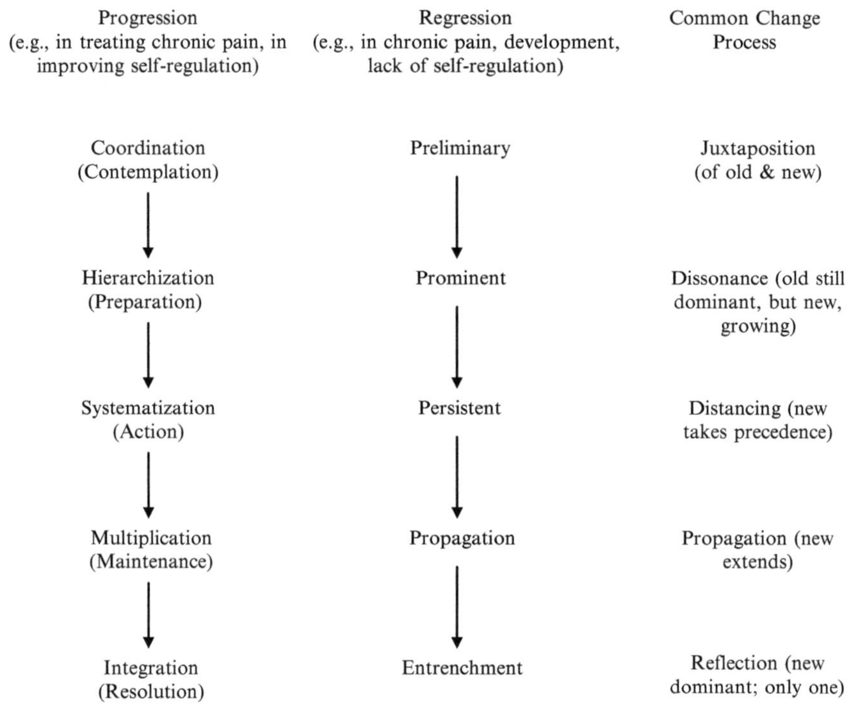

Fig. 33.1 A dynamical model of self-control, system resources, and system depletion. Self-control needs to be considered in the broader context of self-regulation. The model in the figure first considers progressive and regressive changes that are possible in self-regulation according to an equivalent model for chronic pain (steps in treatment, steps toward chronicity, respectively). The second part of the figure presents an integrated model of self-control within a self-regulatory framework. It integrates the resource depletion model of Baumeister (2008; Galinsky, Maddux, Gilin, & White, 2008), the motivational emphasis in Inzlicht and Schmeichel (2012, 2013), the cost-benefit model of Kurzban, Duckworth, Kable, and Myers (2013a, 2013b; which includes motivational and other factors), and the balance model of Heatherton (Heatherton & Wagner, 2011; Wagner & Heatherton, 2013). The model is a dynamical systems one that accounts for moment-to-moment changes, which in turn contribute to longer-term changes, as per part (a) of the figure. Being a dynamical systems model, it is open to self-organizing, nonlinear, qualitative (emergent) changes in state. The activation/inhibition coordination dynamic is essential in this process. The first part of the figure provides a common micro change process that applies to change sequences, whether progressive or regressive. Moreover, it is presented in language that is generic enough to apply to macro change processes. The five steps in change that seem to explain generically the five steps involved in the sequence of coordination, hierarchization, systematization, multiplication, and integration that characterize the present model appears to involve: juxtaposition, dissonance, distancing, propagation, and reflection. For a more elaborate description of the mechanisms underlying the change process, refer to Young (2011)

Table 33.3 Stages of change model

Stage	Explanation
Precontemplation	The person has no intention to change the behavior at issue in the foreseeable future. Most people in this stage are aware or are underaware of their issues.
Contemplation	The person is aware that issues exist. They think seriously thinking about overcoming them, but they have not yet committed to taking action. Contemplators struggle with their conflicts and with the amount of effort, energy, and regression that might be involved in overcoming them.
Preparation	Individuals are intending to take action in the next month and are reporting some small behavioral changes ("baby steps"). Although they have made some improvement in their issues, people in this stage have not yet reached a threshold allowing for effective action.
Action	Individuals behave to modify their issues, experiences, and/or context in order to overcome their difficulties. Actions might be undertaken in overt behavior for timeframe from 1 day to 6 months.

(continued)

Table 33.3 (continued)

Stage	Explanation
Maintenance	The person works to prevent relapse and to consolidate all gains made during the prior stage. This stage extends from 6 months beyond the last one for an indeterminate period. He/she acts to remain free of the issue and/or consistently engages in a new countering behavior for more than 6 months.
Resolution	The person resolves the issues that had been confronted but still needs to control the possibility of incompatible behavior that had been controlled arising again.

Adapted from Norcross, Krebs, and Prochaska (2011)

Note. The stages of change model include a last resolution stage that is mentioned rarely in the literature but is nevertheless part of the original conceptualization of the model (e.g., Maddox, 1995; Prochaska et al., 1994)

chronic pain lifestyle, so that it in this sense it systematizes. (d) Next, chronic pain patients have their pain lifestyle gradually spread throughout all aspects of their lives. (e) Finally, for these patients, the pain has become deeply entrenched, resistant to treatment, and might even characterize an aspect of their personal identity.

Comment

Pain patients are fragile and can slip into healthy or pain state attractor regimes (Young, 2011). Depending on the direction taken, they can gravitate to set points in which pain predominates (regressive) or in which participation in therapy can help (progressive).

Information Processing

Introduction

Young's (2011) Neo-Piagetian (sub)stage model (five substages in each of five stages) applies to online, micro-analytic task problem-solving and not only to macro-developmental stage transitions. At the micro-analytic level, the work of Dodge, Godwin, and The Conduct Problems Prevention Research Group (2013) is consistent with the present proposed change sequence. Dodge et al. (2013) presented an information processing model that takes place in five steps. First, individuals encode situational cues. Next, they interpret the encoded cues. Third, they adopt a goal for the situation. Fourth, they generate possible responses to the encoded cues. Fifth, they engage in decision-making and enact a response.

Model

(a) The first step in Dodge et al.'s (2013) social information processing model is analogous to a coordination process response to the situation. This obtains in that accurate coding is contrasted with possible inaccurate perceptions or hypervigilance to threat cues, which is involved in aggressive behavior (the subject of the Dodge et al. model).

(b) Next, the interpretation involved could have subsumed under inappropriate hostile attributions any accurate perceptions, or vice versa, depending on whether there is an aggression-linked bias. This is consistent with the hierarchization process described in the Neo-Piagetian model.

(c) Next, the adoption of a goal in the Dodge et al. model is consistent with the systematization process in the Young model. Goal adaptation appears a central axis on which adaptation proceeds.

(d) Fourth, generating possible behavioral responses in the former model is akin to the multiplication process in the latter model. As goals lead to possible responses, a multiplication process seems evident.

(e) Finally, decision-making/enacting in social information processing in Dodge et al. reflects the integration process in the cognitive developmental model in Young. Enacting the chosen option is consistent with an integration view of the last step in social information processing.

Discovering Learning

Introduction

In Young (2011), I showed how Boyatzis's (2008) five-step change process in management is consistent with my Neo-Piagetian change model. Boyatzis (2006) also has a corresponding model of self-directed learning that suggests five levels. Dyck and Lovelace (2012) have applied the model to worksite health promotion. The model is an intentional change one. In it, one compares the (a) ideal self and (b) real self to develop a (c) learning agenda, which leads to (d) new behavior and also (e) relationships that can help in this regard. This is not quite a stage model but it is partially consistent with the present Neo-Piagetian one (see Table 33.4).

Model

In Young (2011), the change process is considered to move from a stage of coordination of two possibilities, old and new, to the hierarchization of the new and old. Then, a system develops. In the fourth step, it expands in application in the individual's psychology, leading to a fifth integrative step. The parallel in Boyatzis's and Young's work are evident. In this regard, Boyatzis's step of self-directed learning involves the contrast of an ideal and real self, leading to a self-building agenda (system). Then, through experimentation, akin to multiplication in my model, new psychological acquisitions are realized, leading to an integrative "resonance."

Comment

In this regard, Young (2011) analyzed Harter's (e.g., 2012) model of self processes. He noted that, although it is presented as consistent with the Neo-Piagetian models of Case (1992) and Fischer (1980), it can be reworked to fit Young's model.

Open-Ended Change

Introduction

Wilson, Hayes, Biglan, and Embry (2014) presented a science of intentional change applicable both to individuals (e.g., in therapy) and larger groups. The work of interest to me especially concerned one of the commentaries. Peschl and Fundneider (2014) commented that Scharmer (2007) had developed a model of change (see Table 33.5). I found it quite similar to my own model, especially if one considers theirs a sequence. However, I added an integration step to their model because their suggested result for the fourth stage better fit a new fifth level than simply the output of a fourth level.

Table 33.4 Boyatzis's theory of self-directed learning combined with discoveries, positive and negative emotional attractors, and health promotion applications

Discovery	Name	Explanation	Example of positive and negative health attractors
1.	Ideal self	Who do I want to be?	Personal vision vs. Unarticulated Vision
2.	Real self	Who am I? – Where my ideal and real self are similar – Where my ideal and real self are different	Strengths vs. Gaps
3.	Learning agenda	Building on my strengths while reducing gaps	Seeking knowledge and abilities vs. Complying with authorities
4.	Practice and experimentation	Creating and building new neural pathways through practicing to mastery New behavior, thoughts, and feelings through experimentation	Trying out new lifestyles/ routines vs. Repeating existing ones
5.	Resonant, trusting relationships	Resonant relationships that help, support, and encourage each step in the process	Connecting with others vs. Obtaining constructive feedback

Adapted from Boyatzis (2006) and Dyck and Lovelace (2012)

Table 33.5 Nonexclusive strategies and levels for dealing with (open-ended) change, with last level added to fit current model

Level	Strategy	Question	(Cognitive) Activities
Precoordination	0. Re-acting	Which solutions exist already?	Downloading/applying existing solutions; no change
Coordination	1. Re-structuring	What structures are behind these solutions	Adapting/optimizing structures
Hierarchization	2. Re-designing	What patterns of perception and thinking can help?	Redirecting standpoint; perceptions/ knowledge (owner, others)
Systematization	3. Reframing	What are the bases of my thinking, its deep assumptions?	Reflecting, reframing, questioning and dialogue/leaving behind deep assumptions; new structures of thinking and new assumptions and principles
Multiplication	4. Re-generating	Existential questions concerning the core and its potentialities	Opening up to new uncharted spaces of potential; what wants to emerge?
Integration	5. [Re-Newal]	Integration	Profoundly or presencing new knowledge from the perspective of future possibilities

Adapted from Scharmer (2007) in Wilson et al. (2014)

Model

The description of their strategies is quite consistent with the five-step generic change process in my model. (0) Re-acting in their model involves no change, so is like the pre-coordination level in my model. (1) Re-structuring involves adapting structures behind existing solutions, which might be parallel to what I refer to as coordination. [In coordination, one juxtaposes elements]. (2) Re-designing refers to redirecting, which could be a parallel to hierarchization in my model. [In hierarchization, one places primary elements as dominant to subordinate ones]. (3) Reframing refers to developing new structures, which constitutes a procedure that matches the systematization step in my model. (4) Re-generating involves opening to uncharted spaces, which is quite like my step of multiplication. (5) The result of regenerating, as described in Peschl and Fundneider (2014) and in Scharmer (2007), is "profoundly new" knowledge, which is akin to integration in my own model. Also in this regard, Peschl and Fundneider (2014) emphasized that the output of their change model is "learning from the future as it emerges." Note that this extension of their model is consistent with my own because I created the last step (term) of "Re-Newal."

Executive Function

Introduction

Barkley (2012) has presented a five-step model for the development of executive function (EF) that is consistent with the Young Neo-Piagetian model (see Table 33.6). EF is defined as self-regulation, or self-directed action aimed at goal choosing and what is needed to create, enact, and sustain actions toward the goals. An appropriate definition of EF should consider contextual, personal, and social-cultural factors. EF develops from a pre-executive level to five EF levels.

Model

(a) The pre-executive level involves routine attention, motor, and primary emotional functions, among others. This makes it consistent with the reflexive stage in Young.

(b) The instrumental, self-directed level includes self-directed attention, self-directed sensory-motor action, etc., and appears "early in development," so it is consistent with the Piagetian sensorimotor stage, also found in

Table 33.6 The extended function (EF) phenotype executive

Number	Level
0	Pre-executive
1	Instrumental—self-directed
2	Methodical—self-reliant
3	Tactical—reciprocal
4	Strategic—cooperative
5	Extended—utilitarian

Adapted from Barkley (2012)
The hierarchical arrangement of six phenotypic EF levels involves a bidirectional flow of information between the levels. Information from a lower level flows upward to a higher level, and management of a lower level may be exerted downward by a higher level

Young (2011). However, this level in Barkley also includes verbally-mediated behaviors, so expands into later infancy at least.

(c1) The next EF level to develop is the methodical, self-reliant level. It involves self-directed action, problem solving, social independence, etc., so it is consistent with the pre-operational stage of Piaget, which is the first part of Young's perioperational stage. However, some of the skills at this level could apply to either earlier or later cognitive levels, at least in how they are described.

(c2) Next, tactical-reciprocal EF develops. It includes use of tactics, group living, beginning of economic behavior, etc., so it is consistent with Piaget's concrete operational period, the second part of the perioperational stage.

(d) In the ensuing EF level, strategic cooperative behavior develops. This includes use of strategies and social cohesion, and it could end in principled-mutualistic self-regulation. Clearly, this is consistent with Piagetian formal abstract thought, also found in Young (2011).

(e) The final EF level develops in some individuals (and societies). It refers to the extended utilitarian zone. This involved reflection on the wider culture, one's place in it, and how it can be improved. It involves obtaining relevant feedback in order to improve the "extended" phenotype. In this regard, Young (2011) similarly referred to the postformal Neo-Piagetian stage as a collective intelligence.

Comment

Barkley's developmental model of EF is highly consistent with the present Neo-Piagetian stage model. EF is considered an important mechanistic underpinning to cognitive development (e.g., Zelazo, 2004). Barkley's model could use some refinement to make it more consistent with the present Neo-Piagetian stage model. For example, how does inhibition coordinate with activation at each level and allow increasing sophistication in self-regulation? In Young (2011), I speculated on the centrality of activation/inhibition coordination in development and, in this regard, Barkley (2012) considers inhibition a cardinal EF function. More work is needed in expanding his model to allow for the dynamic control inhibition affords in its coordination with activation over increasing wider domains and more advanced levels in development.

Patients

Introduction

In the following, I show how the present five-step change model (coordination, hierarchization, systematization, multiplication, coordination) can be used to build a better understanding of the patient in psychotherapy and be used to apply psychotherapeutic techniques beyond traditional ways of using them. Note that this effort integrates some of the material in the present work already presented, such as how dysfunctional thoughts or emotions build, or how the five-step model can be used to explain readiness for change.

Model

For example, the stories patients tell themselves about themselves and also about others can be seen from five-step construction process (see Table 33.7). To what extent are the stories (a) coordinated over juxtaposed elements, (b) hierarchized from the axis of a predominant element,

Table 33.7 The stories patients tell: a five-step generic change model of their evolution in psychotherapy

Step	Explanation
Coordination	The patient's narrative is juxtaposed to possibilities presented by the therapist through sensitive guidance.
Hierarchization	The patient begins to place the new story elements in at least one location of his/her narrative as a possible new outlook.
Systematization	The process takes hold and the new story inhabits the narrative landscape of the patient for that issue.
Multiplication	The new story propagates throughout the patient's narrative structure.
Integration	It forms an integrated totality of new habits, both in daily living and in understanding past issues, leading to better optics for the future.

(c) systematized over elements on the basis of the predominant one (or another that has replaced it), (d) extended/expanded/multiplied out into the general narrative of the patient, and (e) even integrated as a coherent theme in that narrative?

Case Formulation

Introduction

Table 33.8 presents a transdiagnostic model of psychotherapy. It considers the patient from a holistic perspective, trying to cover the major components that might be dealt with in psychotherapy. It places the whole person and his or her needs and aspirations as the apex of treatment. Anything like (a) particular diagnoses derived from psychiatric manuals, (b) schools of therapeutic thought, and (c) particular therapeutic techniques are considered subordinate to the needs and goals of the person in psychotherapy. In Young (2014), I presented the model without indicating how it can be applied according to the present five-stage generic change model. In the following, I indicate how such a case formulation process might work (see Table 33.9).

In creating a model of case formulation, I draw a parallel with the scientific process of hypothesis formation and testing. In this regard, the five generic steps of change that I have created, and that I have applied to how science builds itself through these steps (e.g., developmental psychology, see Chap. 31), would seem to represent a generic knowledge building and integration process that could apply to professional knowledge building in case formulation.

Model

Specifically, the five-step model that I have constructed affords differentiation and refinement of extant models of the patient's presenting difficulties as they are explored, tested, and modified in session. Therefore, in applying the five-step model to patient sessions, in the same manner as scientists (or scholars generally) approach their task, the psychotherapist first, engages in (a) knowledge search and (b) hypothesis formulation, and then (c) model testing and (d) elaboration, (e) to the point of acquiring an integrative understanding. In the following, I elaborate further these psychotherapeutic steps, but in combination with my componential psychotherapeutic model that asks that the whole person be treated than adopting any one single approach, school of thought, technique, etc.

(a) In the stage of coordination of case formulation using the present transdiagnostic therapeutic approach, the therapist and patient collaborate to elucidate the primary components that are at issue for the person in need of psychotherapy from among the 10 components of the model. From the basis of the presenting problem as identified by the patient, the therapist and patient gather the relevant psychological issues, symptoms, and presumed facts that govern the presentation, and develop a profile of (juxtaposed) information acquired.

(b) In the stage of hierarchization, the therapist formulates a hypothesis of the primary issues involved in the case at hand, and the implications for treatment. The therapist might refer to the 10-component transdiagnostic model in this regard, and hierarchize the components according to which ones are primary and need treatment

Table 33.8 Componential approach to psychotherapy: the ten major components of the person in psychotherapy

Component	Explanation
1. Psychoeducational, instructional	Much of the feedback functions to alleviate incorrect knowledge about the client's condition, and how therapy can help.
2. Physiological Relaxation techniques	Relaxation techniques allow the individual to moderate initial reactions to stress and emotions, reduce long term stress reactions, learn to maintain equilibrium when confronted with new stresses, and so on.
2a. Physiological Breathing techniques	In my approach, I indicate that any breathing technique itself is secondary to focusing on the rhythms of the breathing, etc.
2b. Physiological Progressive muscle relaxation	Essentially, the client is asked to contract or flex and then stretch or extend zones of the body in a sequential manner.
2c. Physiological Biofeedback	At the core, the person learns to control physiological activity
3. Behavioral General	Reinforcements are administered after a desired behavior so that the frequency of its emission is increased. Also, much behavior is acquired through observational learning, imitation, and so on. This is especially important with children.
3a. Behavioral Additional behavioral techniques for anxiety Systematic desensitization	Systematic desensitization involves exposing the individual to the problematic emotional, arousing, or feared stimulus or situation. However, the exposure is graduated and the arousal is dampened by simultaneous relaxation exercises.
3b. Behavioral Additional behavioral techniques for anxiety Exposure therapy	In exposure therapy, clients safely confront their fears in a systematic way. Relaxation techniques are learned as adjuncts.
3c. Behavioral Additional behavioral techniques for anxiety Interoceptive Awareness/ Sensitization	The goal is to have clients gain mastery in a safe environment of neurovegetative reactions that mimic the ones that they may have experienced during episodes of psychological trauma/distress.
4. Action tendencies, inhibitory control	Learning to better redirect, moderate, inhibit, or otherwise control bad habits that are interfering, disruptive, and so on, is facilitated by techniques that inhibit negative activity, such as using breathing techniques at the first sign of inappropriate or exaggerated emotional upset.
5. Cognitive	Cognitive therapy is a restructuration process that helps clients alter unhelpful, unrealistic, impairing, irrational, dysfunctional, or otherwise inappropriate thoughts.
6. Affective, emotional, intrapersonal	At the emotional level, a common technique is to encourage clients to try to find the meaning behind the emotion being expressed, and to work toward solving the issues raised in this exploration and insight. Constructive affective self-statements include: "Some worry is motivating; too much is not"; "I'm worried because I want to change."
7. Social, relational, interpersonal	The therapist uses the necessary techniques in working with clients to optimize this area of functioning. Interpersonal therapy focuses on these issues, in particular.
8. Self esteem, motivational	The therapist helps the client construct a new, more positive story about the self relative to past stories that have been learned.
9. Coping, problem solving	Optimal coping when confronted by problems or stress of any kind is partly cognitive and partly strategic. Moreover, the therapist guides the client in learning different ways to cope, and, depending on context, ones that are more problem-focused than emotion-focused.
10. Broader cognitive constructions	Although cognitive therapy concerns itself with beliefs that reflect wider concerns in terms of self-confidence, attributions of intentions of others, and so on, there also broader or macro level cognitions that one should consider, such as narratives, life stories, scripts, and existential schemas

Adopted with permission of Springer Science + Business Media. Young, G. (2008). Psychotherapy for psychological injury: A biopsychosocial and forensic perspective. *Psychological Injury and Law, 1*, 287–310; with kind permission from Springer Science + Business Media B. V. [Page 302–306]. The table is adapted, while the text on the right-hand column is adopted

Note. The whole-person, componential approach to therapy is based on understanding the individualized symptom/impairment/disability profile of the person, if any. The profile is established after a scientifically-informed, impartial, and comprehensive assessment. The therapy involves an integrated, individualized therapeutic program based on techniques, principles, and schools/theories that address the components involved

Table 33.9 Case formulation according to the five-step generic change model

Step	Explanation
Coordination	Gather issues, symptoms, "facts" in case (collaboratively).
Hierarchization	Develop initial hypotheses of the primary issue(s) and treatment needs. Revise as new information and responses to implemented therapies/techniques become evident.
Systematization	Arrive at clear understanding of primary issue(s) and treatment need(s).
Multiplication	Determine the degree to which they have affected other aspects of the patient's psychology and those of any significant others that might be involved.
Integration	Proceed to firm up insight in the patient, encourage/monitor techniques that have been effective, and transfer full responsibility for their use (and the person's growth) to the patient.

first. Generally, though, a whole-person perspective is kept in mind. As formulation (and therapy) proceeds, hypotheses might be revised as new information is gathered.

(c) The therapist arrives at a working hypothesis of the patient that potentially can serve toward the development of an integrated framework for understanding and for treatment. As well at this juncture, the therapist might accelerate the process of working toward patient insight. This description of the third step in the proposed five-step psychotherapeutic sequence constitutes the phase of systematization in therapy.

(d) Next, the collaborative patient–therapist relationship enters a new phase of working on the range of issues that bedevil the patient or complicate daily living. Also, it deals with past issues and forward direction (anticipation of issues and planning for them). According to the present five-step change model, this psychotherapeutic step is one involving multiplication.

(e) Finally, in the stage of integration in psychotherapy, the therapist, who has been working on all relevant affected components in the psychology of the patient according to the componential model, arrives at an overarching framework. The therapist works toward the patient acquiring necessary insight along these lines, and prepares for transitioning control to patient of the management of the symptoms, the self, and the present and future, rather than having psychotherapy in control of these issues. Both therapist and patient arrive at a comprehensive understanding of the patient and her/his needs, goals, and appropriate helping mechanisms through their collaborative effort.

Education

Introduction

These examples further illustrate the generalizing nature of the five-step change sequence that I have posited. Other applications follow. For teaching, the goal also is both to understand the learning difficulties being encountered by the child and to deal effectively with the issues encountered. In these regards, the five-step change model that is at the heart of the present section of this work can be used to understand at which step in the change process each student finds him- or herself for each particular domain of learning and study.

Learning

(a) For example, have the students acquired the correct information needed and coordinated it? (b) Have they formed preliminary hierarchical structures of the information? (c) Is a model, concept, theory, hypothesis, or other cognitive frame (e.g., schema, representation), depending on the age and problem at issue, emerging from the coordination and hierarchization process? (d) Does the cognitive structure show signs of spreading into the full cognitive system involved, multiplying in its reach? (e) Finally, has this process led to the construction of a fully integrated new cognitive structure in the student?

Teaching

(a) As for teaching, has the teacher presented to the students information that can be readily coordinated/juxtaposed, and so on? (b) Is the teacher guiding them in creating glimpses of an organization with the kernel of a new idea that can subsume the information coordinated to a beginning and then a more complete degree? (c) Is a teaching process in place to facilitate student acquisition of more coherent systematic cognitive constructs? (d) If so, does the teacher help these generalize? (e) Is the fifth-step of integration of the problem domain by the student enabled by the teaching methods and means used?

Interim Conclusion

These examples illustrate that the five-step change process described in the present work has quite general applications. It could not be too difficult to generalize the model to any instructive or learning situation, such as parenting and the application of discipline, and, for the child, observational learning, imitation, and emulation. These examples, and further ones that can be created, illustrate that the present five-step change model could lead to a paradigmatic change in understanding human behavior and its transformation across a wide spectrum of situations.

The causal nature behind the human condition might lie greatly in the proposed sequence. Causality is not just about Nature × Nurture, or even Nature × Nurture × Self, as I have been suggesting. It is also about the mechanisms of change in the micro-acquisitions in development, learning, and so on, and the factors that promote them. In these regards, the present five-step change model might constitute a cardinal mechanism in human behavior expression and its causal change at all levels.

Evolution

Introduction

In the following, I examine the evolutionary process both in terms of mechanism (e.g., natural selection) and product (stages). For the former, I elaborated the model of Nowak and for the latter I showed how Feist's work is consistent with my own. Then, I turn to Dunbar's work on social drivers in evolution, which, like the other work in this section, is consistent with my own.

Mechanisms

Nowak (2012) explained his model of five mechanisms that could contribute to the evolution of cooperation. They involve: (a) direct reciprocity—these are conditional strategies that depend on previous outcomes with the other individual; (b) indirect reciprocity—conditional strategies are influenced by what is learned about the reputation of the other individual; (c) spatial selection—neighbors are prone to help each other; (d) multi-level selection—includes group selection (everything else being equal, groups of cooperators are evolutionarily advantaged); and (e) kin selection—conditional strategies are based on genetic relatedness (closer relatives are favored; a concept not to be confused with that of inclusive fitness). This model is consistent with Nowak, Tarnita, and Wilson (2010), who maintained that individual level and other evolutionary mechanisms complement group selection processes in the evolution of cooperation. Similarly, Nowak presented this work with colleagues (e.g., Rand & Nowak, 2013).

Young (2011) has shown that the five mechanisms at work in human cooperation according to Nowak are consistent with his developmental model. Moreover, the correspondence proposed across evolutionary mechanism and stage in development occurs in one-to-one way. This illustrates not only the value of my revision of the multilevel model based on the work of Nowak but also the value of my developmental model.

Model

Multilevel selection includes five levels according to the present model (see Table 33.10). The levels are presented on the left side of the table and are reworkings of Nowak's model. He refers

Table 33.10 Five evolutionary mechanisms in a revised model of multilevel selection as applied to the origins of the current developmental stage model

Mechanism	Explanation
Natural selection	For the manner in which individual-level selection influences the expression of cognitive stage acquisitions, the behaviors of the stage facilitated (reflexive) appear directly aimed at resource accrual (surviving the first days, sucking nourishment, etc.). In this regard, they seem to have evolved due to natural selection, and are based on the evolutionary competition among individuals whose phenotypic expressions had included underpinning genotypes involving reflexive cognition. This does not deny that parents provide the opportunities for the reflexive behaviors that are needed to sustain life (and that behavior at this age involves more than this set of behaviors).
Kin selection	In kin selection and its associated cognitive level of sensorimotor intelligence, which begins in the first month, an increased resource networking is facilitated through recruitment of parental or other kin care. Children at this age engage in sensorimotor behavior that facilitates family care giving and kin cooperativity. For example, there is family play, imitation, learning, affection, etc., that takes place with siblings.
Group-for-Individual selection	In the next level in the present model of multilevel selection, group selection is involved, but only in that members of the group (children) have developed behaviors that allow them to take advantage of group-selected traits. In this sense, the range of genetic resources to which the individual has access for survival and reproductive needs expands to members of the group, whether kin or non-kin, who are acting to create social and institutional structures that facilitate obtaining the survival and reproductive advantages. The cognitive level promoted by the level of Group-for-Individual behavior concerns Piagetian representational structures, which allow for symbolic thought, language use, and so on, through pre-operations and concrete operations. The latter, in particular, permit logical thought to be expressed in the physical contexts that the child encounters, such as in the particular school subjects to which school-age children are exposed. Note that in the case of children profiting from learning and educational structures, one cannot speak of immediate reproductive advantages. However, the social and cognitive skills developed in the teaching and learning that takes place in educational and instructional settings, as well as the inter-peer social interactions and links promoted, serve these goals in the long term. That is, the resource networking involved in children attending school and otherwise profiting from learning opportunities created by the group might not be readily apparent, because the information and knowledge-base acquired in the educational learning situations, as well as the social connections, might reveal their adaptive advantages only later in development.
Reciprocity	Next, reciprocal altruism or selection acts to increase the scope of gene pools aiding individual's survival and reproduction by capturing non-kin. In this sense, the formal abstract thought promoted encourages expanded peer and social interaction, mutually beneficial social exchanges, alliances and pacts, the tracking of resource donation and receipt, the monitoring of cooperation and free loading, and so on. This helps enhance resource networking access, acquisition, management, and replenishment, all necessary for survival, reproduction, adaptedness, and fitness.
Individual-for-Group selection	Finally, classical group selection, or Individual-for-Group selection, through the collective intelligence that it facilitates and the social and work groupings that it promotes, acts to increase the array of actors contributing to an individual's fitness, whether kin or non-kin. This acts to increase the extent of resource networking and accrual available to the individual for survival and reproduction. Also, the behavior allows the group to increase its resource access, acquisition, management, and replenishment [think of brainstorming at work], profiting all individuals in the group who are creating the collective product, and others who are indirectly involved [e.g., the profitability of the whole company increases]. Granted, the behavior expressed by the individual may be self-sacrificial, but this need not be the case. Moreover, even if it is, the activity is oriented to increasing group competitiveness, so functions to ensure survival and reproduction of all its members, on the average, whether self or other, or whether kin or non-kin. Other examples for this type of collective intelligence refer to creation of informal and formal educational and learning opportunities.

Adopted with permission of Springer Science + Business Media. Young, G. (2011). *Development and causality: Neo-Piagetian perspectives*. New York: Springer Science + Business Media; with kind permission from Springer Science + Business Media B. V. [Excerpt, Pages 752–753]

to the evolutionary mechanisms of direct and indirect reciprocity, spatial selection, multilevel selection (which includes group selection), and kin selection. I refer to individual or natural selection, kin selection, group for individual selection, reciprocity, and individual-for group-selection (i.e., like group selection). In my model, the levels reflect increasing gene co-opting of the other toward individual survival and reproduction, and I posit that they have been applied sequentially in the evolution of human cooperative behavior. Also, I add a new mechanism of group for individual selection, such as found in educating children. In the following, I show how the five different evolutionary mechanisms in my model relate to the evolution of the five stages in development in my model.

(a) First, in humans, the first cognitive developmental stage of reflexes appears to be the outcome of straightforward natural selection at the individual level. These behaviors seem essential for survival and reproduction at the individual level.

(b) Sensorimotor intelligence is partly a product of kin selection. This obtains because the infant profits in its survival and reproduction by the family links needed, by the behavior of family members co-opted in her or his care, etc.

(c) With perioperational or representational thought, the child can partake in group-created and group-governed education and learning regimens; the impact of Group-for-Individual evolutionary selection pressure and the child's adaptive response to the activity it promotes seems partly involved.

(d) With abstract thought, the teenager can create complex links with peers, including non-kin. This behavior appears partly a product of reciprocal altruism or selection.

(e) With collective intelligence, such as in brainstorming, the group outcome in the cognitive activity helps the group arrive at an adaptive and even competitive outcome. At this stage, the multilevel selection level of Individual-for-Group selection seems to partly apply.

Comment

In keeping with my model in which natural selection is the first evolutionary mechanism in the evolution of cooperation, and indeed, the process of gene co-opting toward the service of the evolutionary needs of the individual can help explain the other mechanisms involved, I note that Hunt (2012) queried whether the evolution of the classic example of eusociality in worker behavior in the social insects did not involve, at first, individual selection, only to progress later to influence through multilevel selection (including of group selection). Indeed, Darwin (1859) had written that the example of tribal-related "sacrifice" for the "common good" could be evolutionarily advantageous and "this would be natural selection" (described in Nowak, 2012).

However, all this does not deny that group selection is empirically-supported and subject to myth (Eldakar & Wilson, 2011; Sober & Wilson, 2011). Group adaptation requires more than group selection, but the latter can be integral to it. Sober and Wilson (2011) concluded that group selection and individual selection are linked.

To conclude, I note that Nowak (2012) referred to humans as "supercooperators." Perhaps the co-cultural/evolutionary model and research on the topic can lead to an integrated model.

Stages

Introduction

Feist (2004, 2006) used Piagetian theory as a basis for a model of cognitive evolution in hominids (see Table 33.11). He identified: (a) a sensory phase; (b) a pre-representational one; (c) a representational one; and (d) a meta-representational one. The phases evolved, respectively, in ancestral monkeys, great apes, and humans, and the last one in modern humans.

Table 33.11 Piagetian stages in hominid cognitive evolution

Phase	Taxon	Piagetian stage
Sensory	Monkeys	ESM LSM
Pre-representational	Great apes *Australopithecus* *Homo habilis–rudolfensis*	ESM LSM EPO *ESM LSM EPO LPO?* *ESM LSM EPO LPO*
Representational	*Homo ergaster–erectus* *Archaic Homo sapiens* *Homo neanderthalensis*	*ESM LSM EPO LPO ECO* *ESM LSM EPO LPO ECO LCO* *ESM LSM EPO LPO ECO LCO*
Meta-representational	Modern humans	ESM LSM EPO LPO ECO LCO FO

Adopted by permission of Yale University Press. Feist, G. J. (2006). *The psychology of science and the origins of the scientific mind.* New Haven, CT: Yale University Press. Reprinted by permission of Yale University Press. [Table 8.2, Page 173]
Abbreviations. E Early, L Late, SM Sensorimotor, PO Preoperational, CO Concrete Operational, FO Formal Operational
Note. Taxa in italics are based on inferences from the archeological record and are hypotheses and conjectures as much as description of fact (cf. Donald, 1991; Mithen, 1996; Parker & McKinney, 1999, p. 279)
Feist's (2006) work is relevant to the present work on two grounds. First, it supports use of Piaget's developmental model in understanding evolutionary changes in thought, which is the same approach taken in Young (2011). Second, the evolutionary sequence that it describes is consistent with the one in Young (2011). Note, however, that Young (2011) has a more elaborate Piagetian model that applies to evolutionary stages both before that of ancestral nonhuman primates and into substages of modern humans

As for the origins of scientific thinking, Feist (2006) presented a model analogous to the four-step hominid cognitive evolution one that he had described. He referred to the (a) preverbal, (b) verbal, (c) applied, and (d) pure phases, respectively (see Table 33.11).

Model

According to Feist (2006), the Piagetian stages associated with these evolutionary stages are the sensorimotor, preoperational, concrete operational, and formal operational, respectively. Feist referred to the research of Parker and McKinney (1999) on nonhuman primates, who, like himself, viewed the correspondence between Piagetian developmental stages and the steps toward the evolution of human behavior as mutually informative. This model speaks to my Neo-Piagetian stage one, in which there are five stages.

For his work on growth in scientific thought, it is interesting that he referred to five core components within each phase that develop sequentially (but not just linearly, also dynamically): (a) observation; (b) categorization; (c) pattern recognition; (d) hypothesis testing; and (e) causal thinking (Table 33.12). There are other components added to each phase. This model speaks to my Neo-Piagetian substage one of five substages cyclically recurring within each stage.

Comment

Feist's (2006) work presaged some of the themes in my own Neo-Piagetian model of development (Young, 2011) and how it can be applied both to (a) understanding evolution and (b) the origins of scientific thought. However, my model is based on five stages with five substages each, whereas he uses the classic Piagetian four-stage sequence, as well as a five-stage component recycling within them. Moreover, I applied my model to science by showing how disciplines such as developmental psychology or evolutionary thought can be modeled to grow according to these stages (and substages; see Chap. 31). Nevertheless, it is heartening to see another worker approaching both the evolution of behavior and the development of scientific thought from a stage frame-

Table 33.12 Phases of scientific thinking and their key components, forms of thought, and age

	Phase			
	Preverbal	Verbal	Applied	Pure
Components	Observation	Observation	Observation	Observation
	Categorization	Categorization	Categorization	Categorization
	Pattern recognition	Pattern recognition	Pattern recognition	Pattern recognition
	Hypothesis testing	Hypothesis testing	Hypothesis testing	Hypothesis testing
	Causal thinking	Causal thinking	Causal thinking	Causal thinking
		Explanation/theory	Explanation/theory	Explanation/theory
		Control (magic)	Control	Control
			Measurement	Measurement
			Incipient math	Developed math
				Controlled experimentation
Forms of thought	Implicit representational	Implicit meta-representational	Implicit–explicit meta-representational	Explicit meta-representational
Age	1.8 million years ago	100 thousand years ago	30 thousand years ago	2.6 thousand years ago

Adopted from Feist (2006)

Note. Feist's (2006) model of evolution in the phases of scientific thought is quite consistent with my development model, which I also applied both to evolution and the growth of scientific thought (e.g., Darwin's theorizing, growth in psychological models since Freud) (see Young, 2011). Feist's repetitive cycle from observation to causal thinking is a five-step one consistent with the five substages of my model. His four-step stage model from ancestral humans to contemporary ones could use another stage mirroring more recent progress in scientific thought. This would render his model comparable to my five-stage developmental one that I applied to growth in scientific thought (which ends in a postformal Neo-Piagetian one beyond the Piagetian abstract, formal stage, which I refer to as a superordinate collective intelligence). However, in successive states Feist does add 12 steps beyond the original five ones, as well, arriving at a total of five more steps by the last pure stage. This renders our two models different, with his involving 10 steps and mine 5 in the penultimate period. Nevertheless, one could argue that the pure stage of scientific thinking in modern humans in Feist's work consists of 10 steps because it reflects the two cognitive stages of adolescent abstract thought and adult collective intelligence in my model, each of which goes through the same five substages, for a total of 10 steps, too. In this regard, the first and sixth stages in Feist's sequence should reflect the substage of coordination in my model, in which entities are juxtaposed. In this regard, one could argue that observation involves juxtaposition of data and then explanation/theory formulation involves juxtaposition of concepts. As for the last steps in each of the five-steps involved in the comparison between Feist and Young, once could argue that both causal thinking and controlled experimentation represent integrations of the preceding four steps involved. Admittedly, the middle three steps in the two five-step recursive cycles involved do not easily match up, so that more conceptual work appears needed work, and one based on Piaget, analogously to the approach that I have taken.

Social Driver

Introduction

Dunbar (2013) presented the social brain hypothesis, which describes an evolutionarily-derived neocortical basis for social cognition. Social life in primate societies is complex and computationally demanding. Primates have large brains because of the evolutionary driver for the need of social bonding, or having deep social ties. Bonding is a dual cognitive and emotional process that is developmentally-rooted. Brain region volume actually causally to determine potential competence in social cognition, and sets the capacity for the extent of an individual's social network.

Model

According to Dunbar (2013), in humans, developmentally, it appears there are transitions in intentionality over five levels. The infant could be considered pre-theory of mind, with the next step at age 4 involving formal theory of mind. Next, levels 3, 4, and 5 in intentionality appear to develop at ages 8, 12, and 18 years, respectively. The levels that are proposed were derived from a study of estimate of mind states of story characters (Henzi et al., 2007; Stiller & Dunbar, 2007). [I note that this model is somewhat consistent with my own five-step developmental stage model.]

Dunbar (2013) related these five developmental levels of intentionality to the person's growing circles of acquaintanceship or social networks. In particular, they correspond approximately to <5, 5, 15, 50, and 150 people, respectively (see Fig. 33.2). He added that, as adulthood proceeds, the network can grow to 500 and, then, 1500 people, which is the upper limit of personal recognition in a circle.

Comment

In my cognitive developmental model, consisting of 25 steps (5 stages × 5 substages over the lifespan, Young, 2011), a basis might be provided for Dunbar's proposed five levels of intentionality in development and social network size. Perhaps Dunbar's five-step model of intentionality and corresponding network size relate somewhat to the sensorimotor, preoperational, concrete operational, and formal operational stages of Piaget, and the postformal adult level. In my model, I add an early reflexive stage and collapse the preoperational and concrete operational ones into a perioperational stage. However, often I keep the separation between these two phases within my combined perioperational stage. Further work is needed on the possible relationship of Neo-Piagetian stage theory, intentionality, network

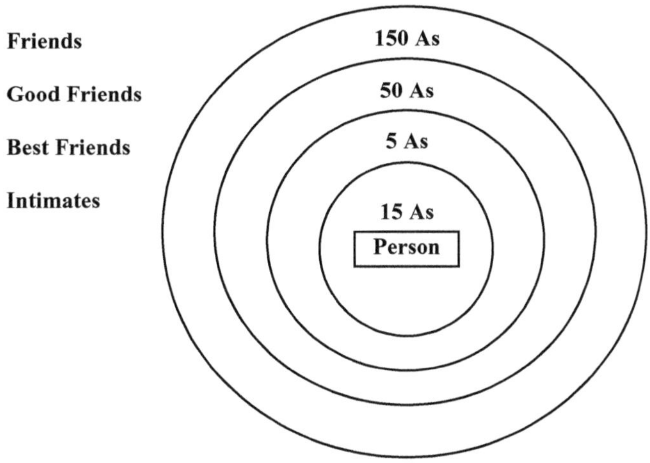

Fig. 33.2 Circles of acquaintances (As): an evolutionary model. The circles of acquaintances refer to the "circles of acquaintanceship." Social networks form series of hierarchically embedded levels of acquaintanceship that organize in a very consistent way (in scales of approximately 5 intimates, 15 best friends, 50 good friends, and 150 friends, with each level inclusive of its inner ones) (Hill & Dunbar, 2003; Roberts & Dunbar, 2011; Zhou, Sornette, Hill, & Dunbar, 2005). Adapted from Dunbar (2013)

size, underpinning brain regions, and the concept of the social brain and its evolution.

Data Driver

Figure 33.3 presents an interesting application of the current five-step generic change step model. I took the work of Sporns on data mining and configured it into a five-step process that is consistent with the current generic change model. I had to add a fifth stage to accomplish this task.

This application of the current model to Sporns' (2011, 2012) work on data driver illustrates two important points. First, the current generic change model is applicable to change processes outside the individual, such as collective search processes including ones driven by computer data mining. Second, the figure that I created on the five steps on data mining illustrates how the present generic change model can help understand work on change processes that are not theoretically informed. That is, I could only add a fifth step to the sequence that I had detected in the work of Sporns on the topic because I applied the current model that I had developed and saw the need for a new step. Finally, this exercise on reinterpreting the steps in data mining according to the current five-step generic change sequence adds to the validation of the five-stage Neo-Piagetian cognitive developmental model on which it is based (Young, 2011).

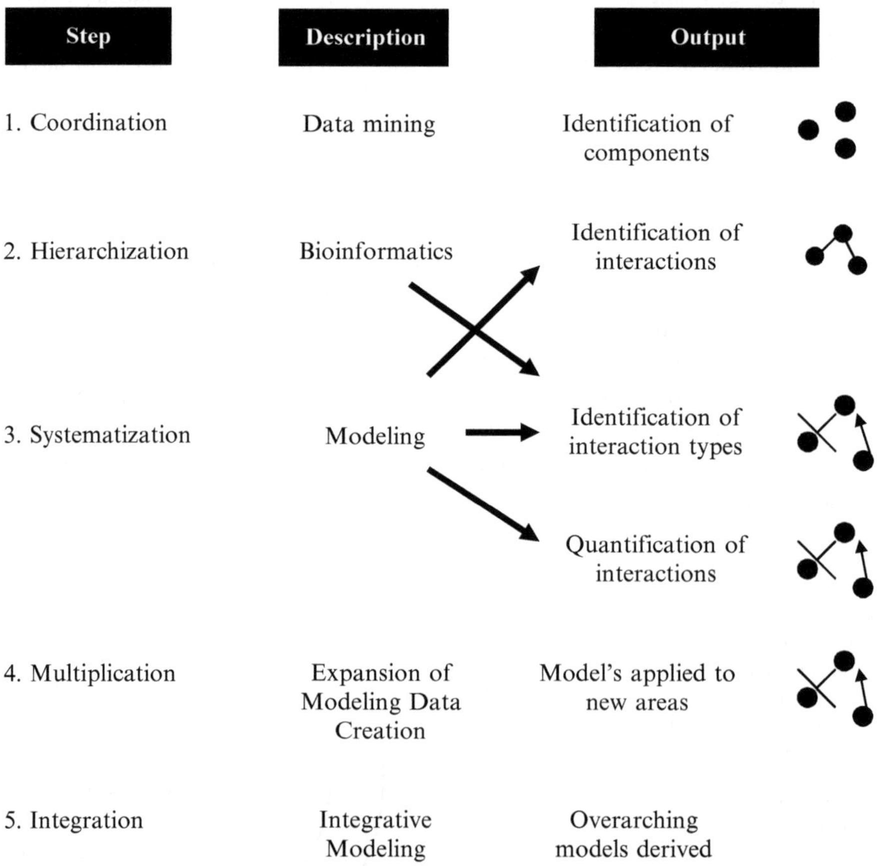

Fig. 33.3 The creation of models from data to integration. The figure illustrates that, according to Sporns (2012), the four steps in the creation of connectome models proceeds from data mining to integration. I have developed a similar sequence for change processes (Young, 2011), as presented in column 1, and to make his model consistent with mine, I added an intermediate step after the third one. Adapted from Sauer, Heinemann, and Zamboni (2007) in Sporns (2012)

Causality

Introduction

The present section illustrates how the generic five-step change model that I have constructed can be used to show how models in the field might evolve from their present state. First, I show how this could happen for the model of G×E (Genetics×Environment). Then, I do the same for causal mapping models. Finally, I take one of my own models and apply to it this logic (on S–O–R; see Chap. 28).

Genes/Epigenesis

For the G×E work, to begin, I present a figure that helps review this area. Figure 33.4 illustrates how the traditional concept of Nature×Nurture interacting in behavior has evolved. The concept of separate genetic and environmental influences on behavior has evolved to allow for their interaction. G×E is a variant that restricts the interaction to certain alleles being present in certain conditions (see Fig. 33.4). But the concept of G×E, itself, has evolved in that genes are now understood to be influenced by environmental-mediated epigenetic (gene-silencing) effects. Also, the environment is not an independent entity relative to genes, in that it responds in a correlated way (passive, evocative, active) to genetic influences.

That is, genes and environment reciprocally influence each other through epigenesis. Also, genes and environment reciprocally influence each other through correlated G×E interactions.

One could modify this model by indicating the distal risk resilience/facilitative factors that individualize the developing person in a complete biopsychosocial interaction. The model could be modified even further by attempting a full-scale integration that includes in it evolution, development, learning, and context.

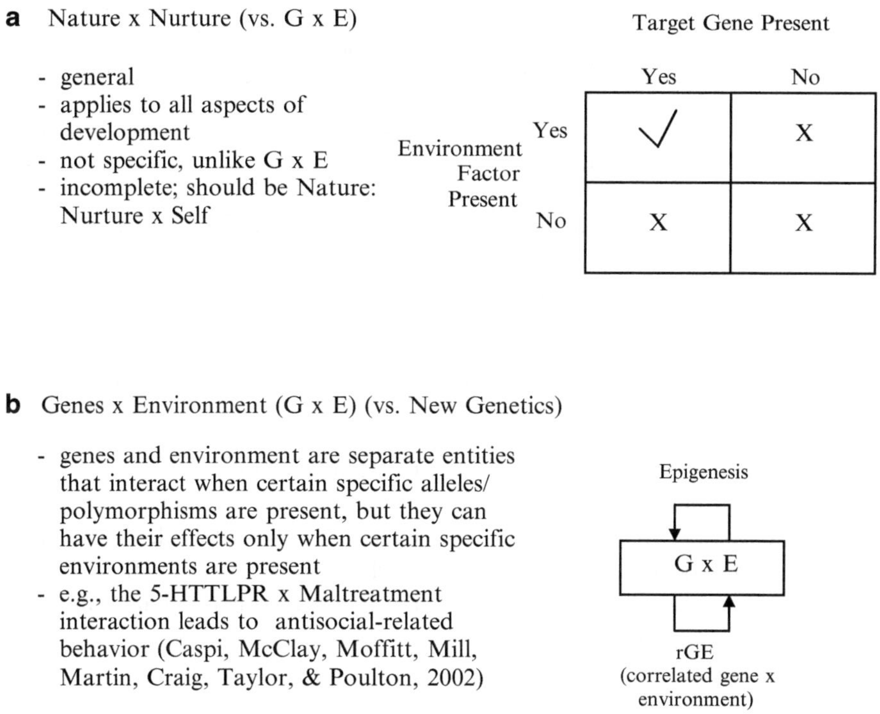

Fig. 33.4 Meanings of Genes×Environment. Nature and nurture are no longer considered separate, additive influences on behavior. They interact, as in Genes×Environment interactions (G×E). G×E is a concept evolving itself, for example, because of epigenesis (e) and correlated G×E (rG×E)

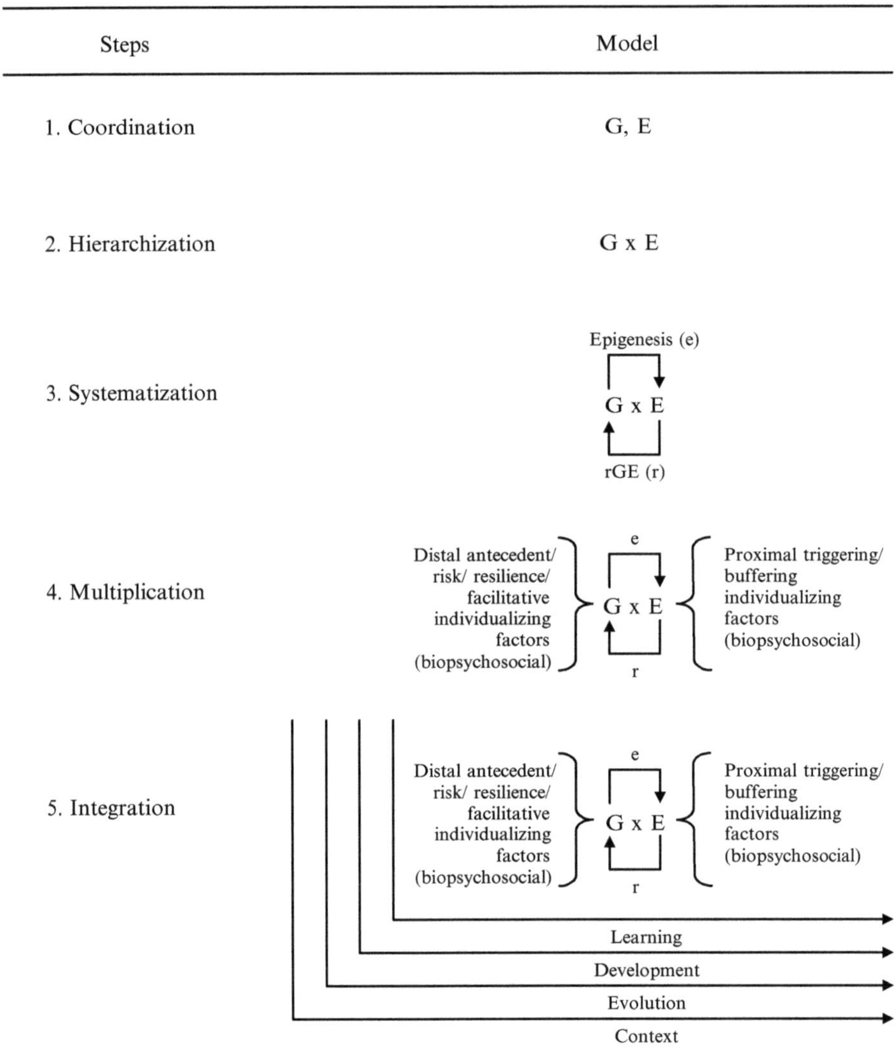

Fig. 33.5 Origins of a comprehensive model of G×E relations. The figure illustrates how the concept of G×E can be modeled to undergo change according to the present five-step change model. This figure presents the concept of G×E influenced by epigenesis (e) and by correlated G×E (rG×E, or r) (step 3). The present modeling effort led me to add steps 4 and 5 in accord with the generic change model described in the present work

These various steps in the evolution toward an integrative genetic/environmental model can be arrayed into the five steps consistent with the present generic change model (see Fig. 33.5). In this regard, (a) in the coordination phase, genes and environment are considered separate influences (are juxtaposed). (b) Next, their interaction can be considered as a hierarchization. (c) Adding epigenetic and correlated G×E effects systematizes G×E. (d) Adding the distal and proximal individualizing components is equivalent to multiplying it out. (e) Finally, the fifth step is a genuinely integrating one.

Causal Graphs

Other causal models described in the present work can be elaborated within the framework of the five-step generic change model that I have constructed. In this regard, Fig. 33.6 presents how graphic representation of cause–effect relations can be shown to have grown from (a) a basic coordinated juxtaposition (A → B), (b) to a hierarchization (e.g., both A, B to C) and, then, (c) to a systematization (reciprocity among A, B, C). (d) A multiplication elaboration of the model would look like the ones in causal mapping

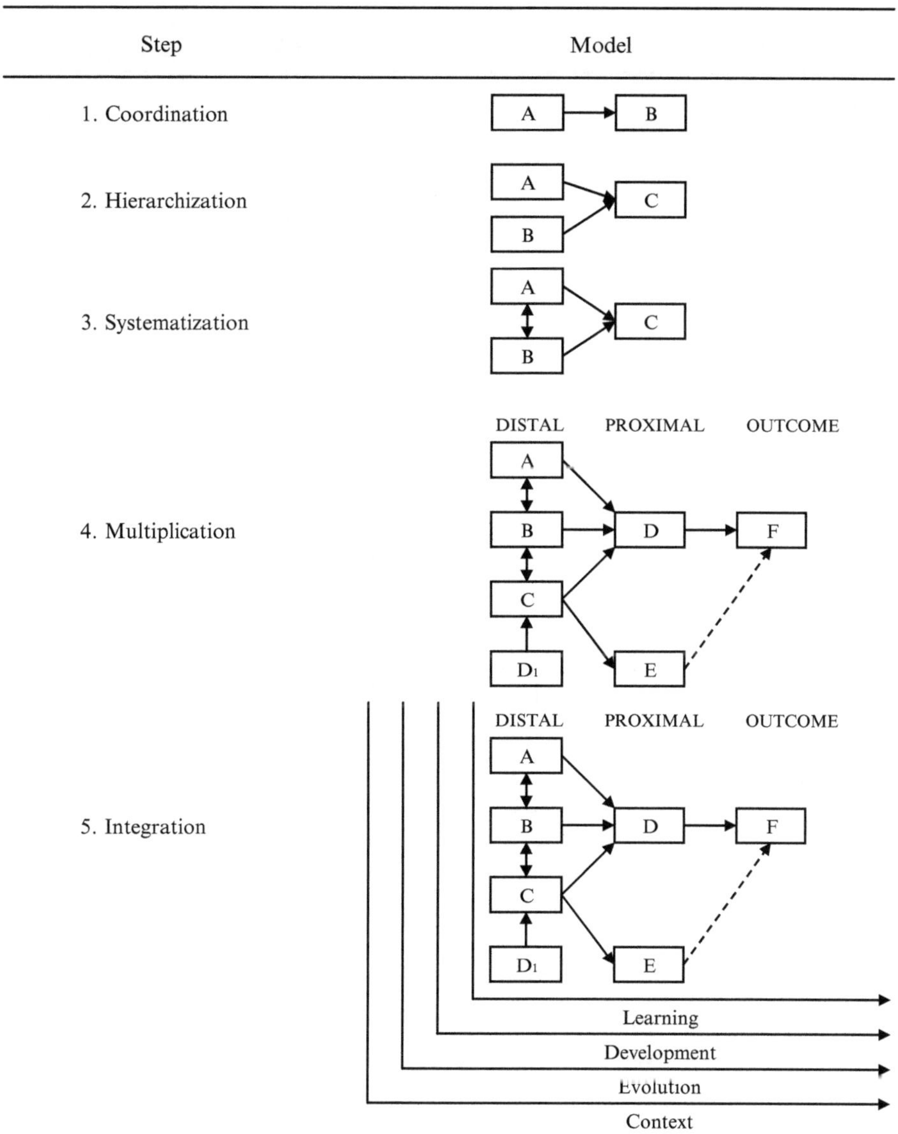

Fig. 33.6 Origins of a comprehensive graph model of distal-proximal outcomes. Using the same logic as in the prior figure, this figure illustrates how graphs representing causal processes can be represented in a five-step change sequence

modeling (e.g., Sloman, 2005). (e) In the integration step, models such as these would add the evolution, development, learning, and contextual component.

Stimulus–Response

The revised S–O–R model that I have developed can be seen to evolve in the same five steps as the revised integrated G×E one in Fig. 33.5 and the revised causal mapping one in Fig. 33.6 (see Fig. 33.7). This figure on the evolution of the S–O–R model begins with (a) the coordinated juxtaposition of S (stimulus) and R (response). (b) Then, the intermediary of the O (organism) is added as a hierarchizing component. (c) The S–O(BAMP)–R model that I created is based on the S–O–R one, and is a systems approach. (d) By adding distal and proximal individualizing components the revised S–O–R model is being multiplied out. (e) Finally, the fifth step adds the evolution, development, learning, and context components to the expanded model, giving it an integrative framework.

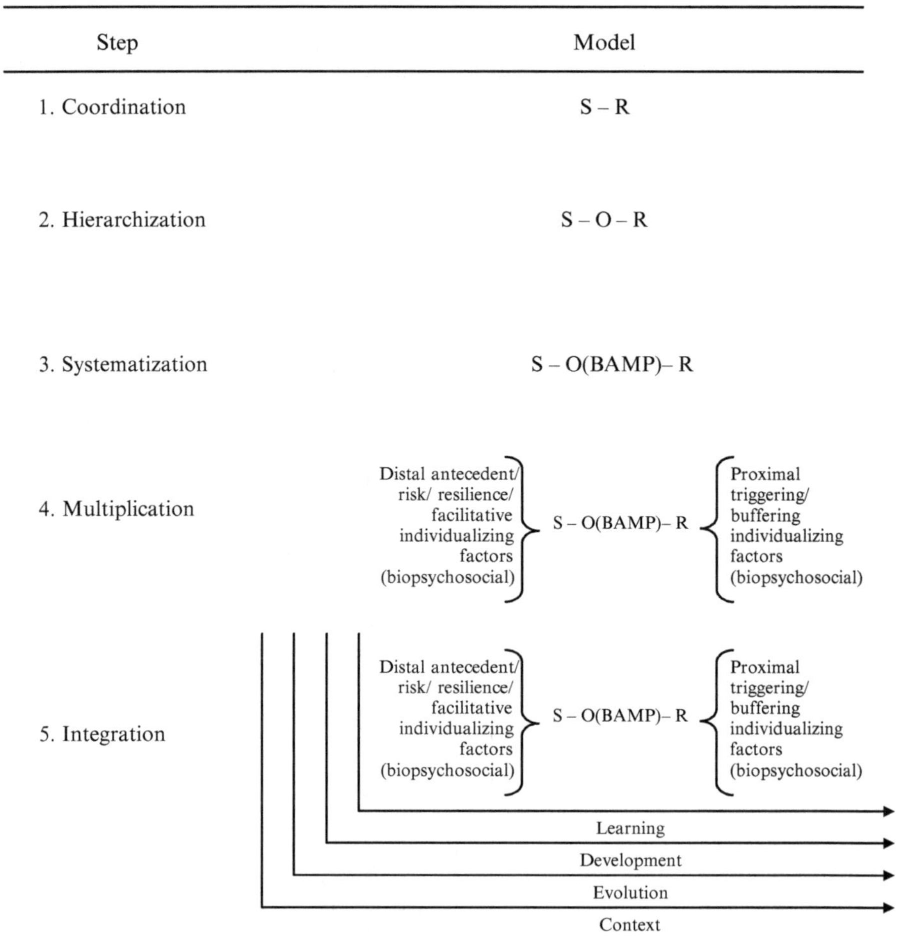

Fig. 33.7 Origins of a comprehensive model of S–R relations. The prior figures illustrated how the concept of G×E and causal mapping can be modeled in a five-step generic change process. In this figure, I indicate how the S–R model (and S–O–R) can be elaborated through five steps consistent with the present five-step generic change model to arrive at a more inclusive, integrated one

Chapter Conclusions

In Young (2011), I had shown that the developmental model that I had created reflects generic change processes. Moreover, I had found similar patterns in other areas of psychology and other disciplines, including the same five-step patterns in non-living systems. In the present chapter, I continue to apply the five-step generic change model to understanding transformation, whether in development or more generally. The proposed generic change model is consistent with other five-step change models, such as the one of readiness for change. It is consistent with other five-step psychological models, such as in information processing and executive functioning. It can help explain both progressive and regressive changes in pain patients. It can help in understanding psychotherapy both in terms of case formulation and the narratives patients tell. It applies to teaching and learning. A large section of the chapter deals with changes evident in and through evolution. Finally, I even apply the model to show how genetics and epigenesis can be perceived through the model, as can other causality-related processes, such as causal graph modeling.

Overall, the present generic change model has both forward and backward ramifications. On the one hand, it should be able to expand its scope of application. On the other hand, it speaks to the validity of the developmental model from which it is derived (my combined Neo-Piagetian/Neo-Eriksonian (sub)stage model, Young, 2011).

Although I have presented a generic change model that has wide applicability and that speaks to the validity of the developmental model from which it is derived, reversing perspectives suggests that had the generic change model been constructed first, it would illustrate that the range of phenomena that it could help explain and place in a unifying light stretches not only from multiple phenomena to the universe itself but also to the child and to development of the child. That is, if the five-step sequence in the generic change model is compatible as a mechanistic explanation of the origins of multiple phenomena that function as open systems subject to nonlinear dynamical change sequences, including the level of the universe, then its applicability to the level of the child is not only not surprising but also quite exemplary of the processes involved.

Carrying this argument one step further, the implication is that the common fractalization process that helps in the elegant, efficient transformation of the disordered nature of dissipative energy flow into increasing order and graceful accommodation reaches from the grandest scales to the minutest, and the change processes in the child is a middle level in the self-similarities over different orders in the fractalization processes in the different micro to macro levels of the universe. That is, the sequence of steps of coordination, hierarchization, systematization, multiplication, and integration, [as underwritten by a parallel sequence of changes in attractor organization (cyclical, chaotic, gravitating to the cusp of change, multiple attractors in a complex adaptive system, superordinate in this regard)] that I found in child development based on analysis of the empirical descriptions made by Piaget of cognitive development in the substages of the sensorimotor stage has served me in constructing a generic model that I applied not only to prior and subsequent stages in the sequence of stages in my Neo-Piagetian cognitive model but also to other systems, including nonliving ones. Also, these systems might have components that go through the same five-step sequence, as I have hypothesized to be the case for the substages of my model, (e.g., microgenetically for particular skills, for particular tasks), or parallel acquisitions that do the same, as I have hypothesized to be the case for Neo-Eriksonian and Neo-Maslovian growth (or blockages and even reversals in these regards, (or in others, such as in the development of chronic pain)).

To conclude, human emergence in the universe might be the inevitable result of a fractalization process governing the management of energy from one level to the next and the process of development within humans might reflect the same dynamic, with my model offering the nature of the fractalization process involved. In this sense, humans are indeed the children of the universe. Moreover, because of this, studying the development of the child offers a window to the origins of the universe.

References

Barkley, R. A. (2012). *Executive functions: What they are, how they work, and why they evolved.* New York: Guilford Press.

Baumeister, R. F. (2008). Free will in scientific psychology. *Perspectives on Psychological Science, 3*, 14–19.

Boyatzis, R. E. (2006). An overview of intentional change from a complexity perspective. *Journal of Management Development, 25*, 607–623.

Boyatzis, R. E. (2008). Leadership development from a complexity perspective. *Consulting Psychology Journal: Practice and Research, 60*, 298–313.

Case, R. (1992). *The mind's staircase.* Hillsdale, NJ: Erlbaum.

Chen, Y., & Fang, M. Q. (2008). A five-stage model for the evolvement of complex system, apocalypse and prospect from research on emergence. *Xitong Gongcheng Lilun Yu Shijian/System Engineering Theory and Practice, 28*, 40–44.

Darwin, C. (1871). *The descent of man, and selection in relation to sex.* London: John Murray.

Dodge, K. A., Godwin, J., & The Conduct Problems Prevention Research Group. (2013). Social-information-processing patterns mediate the impact of preventive intervention on adolescent antisocial behavior. *Psychological Science, 24*, 456–465.

Donald, M. (1991). *Origins of the modern mind: Three stages in the evolution of culture and cognition.* Cambridge, MA: Harvard University Press.

Dunbar, R. I. M. (2013). An evolutionary basis for social cognition. In M. Legerstee, D. W. Haley, & M. H.

Bornstein (Eds.), *The infant mind: Origins of the social brain* (pp. 3–19). New York: Guilford Press.
Dyck, L. R., & Lovelace, K. J. (2012). Finding a fit with fitness: Applying intentional change theory in work-site health promotion programming. *Journal of Workplace Behavioral Health, 27*, 12–31.
Eldakar, M. T., & Wilson, D. S. (2011). Eight criticisms not to make about group selection. *Evolution, 65*, 1523–1526.
Feist, G. J. (2004). Domain-specific creativity in the physical sciences. In J. C. Kaufman & J. Baer (Eds.), *Creativity across domains: Faces of the muse* (pp. 123–137). Mahwah, NJ: Erlbaum.
Feist, G. J. (2006). *The psychology of science and the origins of the scientific mind*. New Haven, CT: Yale University Press.
Fischer, K. W. (1980). A theory of cognitive development: The control and construction of hierarchies of skills. *Psychological Review, 87*, 477–531.
Galinsky, A. D., Maddux, W. W., Gilin, D., & White, J. D. (2008). Why it pays to get inside the head of your opponent: The differential effects of perspective taking and empathy in negotiations. *Psychological Science, 19*, 378–384.
Harter, S. (2012). Emerging self-processes during childhood and adolescence. In M. R. Leary & J. P. Tangney (Eds.), *Handbook of self and identity* (2nd ed., pp. 680–715). New York: Guilford Press.
Heatherton, T. F., & Wagner, D. D. (2011). Cognitive neuroscience of self-regulation failure. *Trends in Cognitive Sciences, 15*, 132–139.
Henzi, P., de Sousa Pereira, L., Hawker-Bond, D., Stiller, J., Dunbar, R. I. M., & Barrett, L. (2007). Look who's talking: Developmental trends in the size of conversational cliques. *Evolution and Human Behavior, 28*, 66–74.
Hill, R. A., & Dunbar, R. I. M. (2003). Social network size in humans. *Human Nature, 14*, 53–72.
Hunt, J. H. (2012). A conceptual model for the origin of worker behaviour and adaptation of eusociality. *Journal of Evolutionary Biology, 25*, 1–19.
Inzlicht, M., & Schmeichel, B. J. (2012). What is ego depletion? Toward a mechanistic revision of the resource model of self-control. *Perspectives on Psychological Science, 7*, 450–463.
Inzlicht, M., & Schmeichel, B. J. (2013). Beyond simple utility in predicting self-control fatigue: A proximate alternative to the opportunity cost model. *Behavioral and Brain Sciences, 36*, 695–696.
Kurzban, R., Duckworth, A., Kable, J. W., & Myers, J. (2013a). An opportunity cost model of subjective effort and task performance. *Behavioral and Brain Sciences, 36*, 661–679.
Kurzban, R., Duckworth, A., Kable, J. W., & Myers, J. (2013b). Cost-benefit models as the next, best option for understanding subjective effort. *Behavioral and Brain Sciences, 36*, 707–726.
Maddox, J. E. (1995). Yes, people can change, but can psychotherapists? *Contemporary Psychology, 40*, 1047–1048.
Mithen, S. (1996). *The prehistory of the mind: The cognitive origins of art and science*. London, UK: Thames and Hudson.
Norcross, J. C., Krebs, P. M., & Prochaska, J. O. (2011). Stages of change. In J. C. Norcross (Ed.), *Psychotherapy relationships that work: Evidence-based responsiveness* (2nd ed., pp. 279–300). New York: Oxford University Press.
Nowak, M. A. (2012). Evolving cooperation. *Journal of Theoretical Biology, 299*, 1–8.
Nowak, M. A., Tarnita, C. E., & Wilson, E. O. (2010). The evolution of eusociality. *Nature, 466*, 1057–1062.
Parker, S. T., & McKinney, M. L. (1999). *Origins of intelligence: The evolution of cognitive development in monkeys, apes, and humans*. Baltimore, MD: Johns Hopkins University Press.
Paxton, R. O. (1998). The five stages of fascism. *The Journal of Modern History, 70*, 1–23.
Peschl, M. F., & Fundneider, T. (2014). Evolving the future by learning from the future (as it emerges)? Toward an epistemology of change. *Behavioral and Brain Sciences, 37*, 433–434.
Piaget, J., & Garcia, R. (1989). *Psychogenesis and the history of science*. New York: Columbia University Press.
Prochaska, J. O., DiClemente, C. C., & Norcross, J. C. (1992). In search of how people change: Applications to addictive behaviors. *American Psychologist, 47*, 1102–1114.
Prochaska, J. O., Norcross, J. C., & DiClemente, C. C. (1994). *Changing for good: The revolutionary program that explains the six stages of change and teaches you how to free yourself from bad habits*. New York: Morrow.
Rand, D. G., & Nowak, M. A. (2013). Human cooperation. *Trends in Cognitive Sciences, 17*, 413–425.
Roberts, S. B. G., & Dunbar, R. I. M. (2011). Communication in social networks: Effects of kinship, network size, and emotional closeness. *Personal Relationships, 18*, 439–452.
Rostow, W. W. (1990). *The stages of economic growth: A non-communist manifesto*. New York: Cambridge University Press.
Sabelli, H. (2005). *Bios: A study of creation*. Singapore: World Scientific.
Salthe, S. N. (2007). The natural philosophy of work. *Entropy, 9*, 83–99.
Sauer, U., Heinemann, M., & Zamboni, N. (2007). Getting closer to the whole picture. *Science, 316*, 593–597.
Scharmer, C. O. (2007). *Theory U. leading from the future as it emerges. The social technology of presencing*. Paper presented at a meeting of the Society for Organization Learning.
Sharpless, B. A., & Barber, J. P. (2009). A conceptual and empirical review of the meaning, measurement, development, and teaching of intervention competence in clinical psychology. *Clinical Psychology Review, 29*, 47–56.
Sloman, S. (2005). *Causal models: How people think about the world and its alternatives*. New York: Oxford University Press.

Sober, E., & Wilson, D. S. (2011). Adaptation and natural selection revisited. *Journal of Evolutionary Biology, 24*, 462–468.

Sporns, O. (2011). *Networks of the brain*. Cambridge, MA: MIT Press.

Sporns, O. (2012). *Discovering the human connectome*. Cambridge, MA: MIT Press.

Stiller, J., & Dunbar, R. (2007). Perspective-taking and social network size in humans. *Social Networks, 29*, 93–104.

Wagner, D. D., & Heatherton, T. F. (2013). Self-regulatory depletion increases emotional reactivity in the amygdala. *Social Cognitive and Affective Neuroscience, 8*, 410–417.

Wilson, D. S., Hayes, S. C., Biglan, A., & Embry, D. D. (2014). Evolving the future: Toward a science of intentional change. *Behavioral and Brain Sciences, 37*, 395–460.

Young, G. (2008). Causality and causation in law, medicine, psychiatry, and psychology: Progression or regression? *Psychological Injury and Law, 1*, 161–181.

Young, G. (2011). *Development and causality: Neo-Piagetian perspectives*. New York: Springer Science + Business Media.

Young, G. (2014). *Malingering, feigning, and response bias in psychiatric/psychological injury: Implications for practice and court*. Dordrecht, Netherlands: Springer Science + Business Media.

Zadek, S. (2004). The path to corporate responsibility. *Harvard Business Review, 82*, 125–132.

Zelazo, P. D. (2004). The development of conscious control in childhood. *Trends in Cognitive Sciences, 8*, 12–17.

Zhou, W.-X., Sornette, D., Hill, R. A., & Dunbar, R. I. M. (2005). Discrete hierarchical organization of social group sizes. *Proceedings of the Royal Society: B. Biological Sciences, 272*, 439–444.

34 Revising Maslow

Chapter Introduction

Maslow's (1943) hierarchical model of needs, motivation, and development is one of the most well-known in psychology. In Young (2011), I modified it so that its five levels correspond to the five stages of my Neo-Piagetian/Neo-Eriksonian model. In the present chapter, once more, I modify this Maslovian approach to needs, motivation, and development by considering, in particular, recent work on moral and foundational motives (Haidt, Janoff-Bulman and colleagues, e.g., Haidt, 2012; Janoff-Bulman & Carnes, 2013) and on motivation (Forbes, 2011). The main difficulties related to these sources concern their lack of developmental factors. Maslow's model itself had a developmental component only as a secondary aspect.

Maslow's model focuses on self-actualization, but in Young (2011), I revised his model by incorporating Blatt's (2008) model of self-definition and relatedness. Motivations and needs would seem to require both a self- and other-focus. In the present revision of this model, I include a third component to needs and motives, that of the material environmental world. This approach is consistent with the work on Deci and Ryan (e.g., 1991), who add a competence factor to their equivalent model.

The present chapter begins by describing Kyselo's (2014) enactive-based self model. This prepares the way for the chapter's conclusions that the revised Neo-Maslovian model that I have created especially is an embodied one.

The beginning of the chapter continues with elaborations by Blatt and colleagues and Ryan and colleagues on their seminal models on self/personality. Blatt (2008) had proposed a duality in experience model and Ryan, Deci, and colleagues' one with tripartite distinctions.

Further, I develop the concepts of "psychological completeness" and "psychological completing" as involved in the apex of human self and personality development. The concepts constitute good complements to those of Maslow and Erikson (self-actualization, generativity, respectively).

In revising the Neo-Maslovian model, I reworked those of Haidt, Janoff-Bulman, and Forbes. In each case, I showed how their models can be revised to fit the current one. In particular, I rework their models from a developmental framework. For example, in this regard, I reworked Haidt's model of moral foundations (which alternatively has been described as being constituted by four, five, or six foundations), to arrive at a five-foundation one, but with variations for the personal, interpersonal, and environmental spheres, and one consistent with the present five-step developmental sequence. Janoff-Bulman and Carnes' (2013) moral motive model also integrates into the present model. When referring to the motivational component of my model, I use the terminology of "foundational moral motives" to indicate the integration that

G. Young, *Unifying Causality and Psychology*, DOI 10.1007/978-3-319-24094-7_34

I undertook of the prior work of Haidt, Janoff-Bulman, and colleagues.

The chapter concludes with presentation of a questionnaire that I developed on political attitudes. It concerns societal control, in general. Moreover, it allows for independent response on a Likert scale for conservative and liberal attitudes, rather than considering them as polar opposites.

Models

Revised Maslow in Young (2011)

Model Young's (2011) Neo-Maslovian model organizes Maslow's hierarchical needs model into a developmental one that shows that it parallels Young's Neo-Piagetian and Neo-Eriksonian models. To review, the cognitive stage portion of my model is Neo-Piagetian, and I describe five cognitive stages (reflexive, sensorimotor, perioperational [pre-operational and concrete operational], formal abstract, and postformal collective intelligence), with each stage having cyclically recurring substages. Moreover, each of the 25 steps in the model (5 stages × 5 substages) witnesses a corresponding development of a Neo-Eriksonian level (also 25, Erikson's 8 and 17 others fitted to the model). As for my Neo-Maslovian model, I showed how Maslow's five hierarchical needs map onto my five Neo-Piagetian stages, therefore, with five developmental steps implicated in the each level of the hierarchical needs model, as well (see Fig. 32.2, in Chap. 32).

Further, in Young (2011), I showed how Maslow's model should include two components related to the self (self-definitional and relatedness, as per Blatt's (2008) concept of polarities of experience). In this regard, for each of the steps in the development of hierarchical needs in Maslow, one should consider the growth that takes place in each of these self components.

Comment In Young (2011), I also developed the concept of yoking, in which earlier developmental levels might stay in function and carry forward (albeit modified) as other levels are deployed or characterize behavior. In this regard, the basic needs level in Maslow would carry forward and still constitute relevant psychological function in a yoking process even as the highest-order levels of the model of self (self-actualization, generativity, etc.) are active in behavior. That is, even the most abstract of behavioral function potentially carries with it the most basic physical (and for cognition, sensorimotor), enactive function.

Re-Revising Maslow in the Present Book

Later in the chapter, I argue that the Neo-Maslovian model that I have developed could be revised even further by adding a third component to the self, that of a competent, material environmental one. We relate not only to ourselves and to others, but also to the environment and objects. As we shall see, this addition to the model is based on the work of Deci, Ryan, Forbes, and others, but stands apart from them, as well.

Enaction

Model Kyselo (2014) presented an enactive model of the self that combines together the social as constitutive, the individual as locus of the self, and the embodied perspective of the body as mediator of a unified self. For Kyselo, the self-identity individuates through the process of self-distinction and also the process of participation with others. Body, self, and sociality are interrelated. We are at once embodied beings and situated social beings; we cannot be reduced from our constitutiveness among these components in our identity to our brain. As we develop, we move from basic sensorimotor cognition to forms that are psychologically and socially mediated. The body and brain change in status as they become both the means and mediator of the self, becoming matrices of an enacted social reality. At the same time, body and brain are the seats of the imprint of the social on the person. The external world is not independent of the self and, reciprocally, selves are not independent of the external word. The body-social split (essentialist) problem is resolved by not only seeing the plurality of self but also by seeing the synthesis of its whole.

Kyselo continued that identity refers to self-generated, self-determined autonomy, a coherent unity co-constituted with interacting others in the social world. The self is embodied in bodily processes (i.e., sensorimotor structure, Gallese, 2014). Also, it is intersubjective, yet supported by the body's mechanisms (e.g., mirror neurons, Gallese, 2013). Identity is constituted by an interconnected network of processes that serves to protect the self from both dissolution and isolation. The body is part of the interface involved in organizing social life. Autonomy is socially enacted, and social enaction participates in the co-construction of an individuating, identifying, embodying self.

The process that promotes this reciprocating mutuality between self and other lies in individuation "through and from the world." It promotes emancipation, but one still predicated on the constraints of bodily, self, and social processes. We are "needful," and social, yet in search of emancipatory freedom. Adaptive regulation involves finding balance in our yearning for distinctiveness and for connection in participation.

Comment This approach taken by Kyselo (2014) on a unifying concept of the self in the "body social" is a coherent one. However, she does not treat much the developmental dimension, although mentioning it briefly. Her work is consistent with mine in several major ways. First, she seeks a unified account of the self that includes the embodied, dynamic perspective. Second, she emphasizes its social nature. Third, she argues for a mutuality in these currents, leading to an integrated whole. Fourth, her concept of distinction and participation as two coordinated poles in her unified perspective of the self is consistent with the work of Blatt (2008), on which I have based my Neo-Maslovian model. Fifth, we would both agree that emancipating toward a sense of freedom is central to psychological growth, but there are constraints, including of needs (which is consistent with Maslow, as well).

Taken together, both Kyselo's unified model of self and also my work that is consistent with it (e.g., in my Neo-Maslovian model of self-development, Young, 2011) afford a more holistic understanding of the self. However, because I have integrated Blatt's (2008) work into my own, I have provided the basis for a developmental account of self-development that fits and elaborates Kyselo's (2014) account. Development is not separate from any behavior, and needs to be understood as the primary constituting force of any behavior. The body-self model elaborated by Kyselo (2014) is complementary to my own, which should be considered a developmental enactive approach to the self and, therefore, a broadening one of Kyselo's (2014) work.

Polarities of Experience

Model Luyten and Blatt (2013) elaborated Blatt's (2008) model of the self on polarities of experience, which involves interpersonal relatedness and self-definition. The duality compares to similar models, such as Bakan's (1966) one of communion and agency and Deci and Ryan's (2013) one of relatedness and autonomy/competence. In their article, Luyten and Blatt (2013) extended the model to disruptions in personality development. They developed a prototype approach to personality disorder related to dependence and self-critical dimensions of personality organization derived from Blatt's (2008) model.

Comment However, other work has extended Blatt and colleagues work beyond a polarity in experience to a tripartite distinction. The model developed in the present chapter is consistent with the latter approach. That being said, I have undertaken this development in a unique way, as shall be shown below.

Self-Determination

Model Weinstein, Przybylski, and Ryan (2013) explored the question of unified self-functioning or personality integration. The concept of the integrative process in self/personality psychology dates to

Freud (1927/1961) and includes Rogers (1963). Ryan and Deci (2000, 2008) have developed self-determination theory (SDT), in which internalization and integration constitute fundamental processes involved (a) in attaining vitality and energy, good health and wellness, and relational benefits and (b) in promoting autonomous, personal-value, and life-goal congruent behavior, leading to a sense of authenticity and full-life engagement.

Weinstein et al. (2013) identified three subprocesses or facets that are involved in unified self/personality integration. They include: (a) awareness (access to self-knowledge; Brown & Ryan, 2003); (b) personal ownership/autonomy (taking responsibility/identifying with one's attitudes/actions or emotions/decisions/thoughts; Weinstein, Deci, & Ryan, 2011); and (c) nondefensive processing (approach-related coping avoidance or defensive blocking of self-knowledge into consciousness; Weinstein, Brown, & Ryan, 2009).

In terms of factors that promote integration in life, early on, unconditional regard is important and, later in life, autonomy-supportive social environments help (Weinstein et al., 2012). As for associations with the brain, research with fMRI (functional magnetic resonance imaging) has linked autonomous activity with the insular cortex (Lee, Reeve, Xue, & Xiong, 2012). Similarly, Legault and Inzlicht (2012) have found that integration-related processes in self-regulation were reflected in electroencephalographic event-related potentials, leading them to discuss the "self-determined brain."

Thagard and Wood (2015) proposed a similar tripartite-self model involving representation, effecting, and changing. The representing self involves self-depicting (to self, to others), such as in their people's self concepts and self-presentation. The effecting self concerns self enhancement/limitation (e.g., self-regulation). The changing self is more long term (about self development, expansions). The authors described the self as a multilevel system.

Comment The work by Deci, Ryan, and colleagues in their SDT model is noteworthy for its emphasis on self and personality unification/integration. It is consistent with the present revised Neo-Maslovian model, but helps add an additional component. As integration takes place in the developing person, a concept that could be used to reflect the integration involved is "psychological completeness." Given that the process is dynamical and ongoing, I also refer to "psychological completing." These terms allow differentiation of the terms: (a) integration in the SDT sense; (b) ego integrity, the last stage in development in Erikson's model; and (c) integration as the last step in development in Young's (2011) model. Approaching/achieving a sense of psychological completing/completeness would constitute a continual, life-long developmental process. It should reach the peak in the sense of being psychologically mature and wise when it is properly promoted in the environment (at least in a biologically-predisposed and healthy individual), which would dynamically lead further to an ingrained health and wellness, as described by Weinstein et al. (2013).

Note that I have not adopted outright Deci and Ryan's approach to self/personality in my own model. It stands as one influence only in this regard. Generally, the new work in Weinstein et al. (2013) is informative, but does not address well Blatt's (2008) emphasis on relatedness to accompany self-definition, which is the theoretical model that is at the basis of my revision of Maslow.

Moral Motives

Model Janoff-Bulman and Carnes (2013) presented a model of moral motives, and they addressed the issue of differences in the motivational base of people judged as liberal or conservative (see Fig. 34.1). They defined morality as a system of rules and behavioral regulation to facilitate and coordinate optimal social living or group living. Traditionally, it is concerned with justice and rights (e.g., Kohlberg, 1981, 1984). Its range is being broadened to include moral foundations or motives (Haidt, 2007, 2008; Haidt & Kesebir, 2010).

Janoff-Bulman and Carnes (2013) presented a model of moral motives based on two axes, one with two levels and one with three of

	Self (Personal)	Other (Interpersonal)	Group (Collective)
Protect/ Inhibition (proscriptive regulation)	Self-restraint/ Moderation	Do not harm	Social order/ Communal solidarity
Provide/ Activation (prescriptive regulation)	Industry	Help be fair	Social justice/ Communal responsibility

Fig. 34.1 Model of moral motives according to mode and target. Janoff-Bulman and colleagues have presented a model of moral motives that focuses on protection/proscription/inhibition vs. provision/prescription/activation in conjunction with the targets of self, other, and group. It is consistent with the present emphasis that activation/inhibition coordination is a common metric organizing brain and behavior (Young, 2011). An activation/inhibition influence is evident in the model of moral motives (in the mode) and the targets of the activation/inhibition balance in the motives might be self, other, or group (focus). Note. The model constitutes one that expands the traditional duality of experience approach (Blatt, 2008) into three targets (personal, interpersonal, collective). Adapted from Janoff-Bulman and Carnes (2013)

them—proscriptive/prescriptive moral regulation and self/other/group focus (personal, interpersonal, collective, respectively; e.g., Brewer & Gardner, 1996; Gilbert, Fiske, & Gardner, 1998; see Fig. 34.1). They considered self-restraint/moderation and industriousness as proscriptive and prescriptive moral motives, respectively. The classic motives of not harming and helping were considered the equivalent interpersonal motives, and the group motives already mentioned, social order and social justice, were considered the equivalent group ones in their model.

A predominant perspective on behavioral self-regulation involves dual regulation by approach/activation vs. avoidance/inhibition (Carver & Scheier, 2008). The behavioral inhibition system is an aversive motivational one based in avoidance and in sensitivity to negative outcomes/punishment. The behavioral activation system is an appetitive motivation one based in approach and in sensitivity to rewards/positive outcomes.

Janoff-Bulman and colleagues applied the difference between the approach/activation and avoidance/inhibition self-regulation systems to the difference between proscriptive and prescriptive morality (Janoff-Bulman, 2012; Janoff-Bulman, Sheikh, & Hepp, 2009). Proscriptive morality is based on avoidance, and it deals with what should not be done, as well as dealing with restraint, overcoming temptation, protecting from harm, and inhibition. Prescriptive morality is based on activation, what should be done, providing for well-being, and helping. This dual system of moral regulation parallels parental behavior in instilling do's and don'ts (e.g., do toy clean up; do not do that, respectively; Aksan & Kochanska, 2005; Kochanska, 2002).

Proscriptive moral regulation is condemnatory and stricter relative to prescriptive moral regulation, which is commendatory. These moral regulatory patterns fit the general negativity bias that is considered important in moving people to behave (Baumeister, Brataslavsky, Finkenauer, & Vohs, 2001); that is, there is greater motivational potency when outcomes are negative compared to positive. In this regard, the difference between prescriptive vs. proscriptive morality reflects the philosophical positions of deontology vs. consequentialism. The former involves strict mandatory rules and is associated with proscriptive morality; whereas the latter focuses on the consequences of moral acts, so is discretionary and utilitarian (the greatest good for the most people), and thus fits the prescriptive approach.

There are two evolutionary views of moral regulation. The traditional view is that altruism is undertaken for selfish reasons (e.g., Hamilton, 1964). More contemporary versions consider that altruism at least partly reflects group selection in a multi-level selection model (e.g., Wilson, 2012). Constraining selfishness involves proscriptive moral regulation. In contrast, tapping altruistic motivation involves prescriptive moral regulation. A proscriptive virtue might be generosity, whereas a proscriptive one might be self-discipline. A proscriptive vice might be greed, and a prescriptive one might be apathy (Carnes & Janoff-Bulman, 2012).

Comment Later in the chapter, I analyze the moral motive approach of Janoff-Bulman and colleagues in relation to development. Just as Maslow's model of hierarchical needs is developmental and can be mapped onto my own developmental model, so can the work on moral motives. In this regard, Janoff-Bulman and Carnes seem to have a developmental movement in their proscriptive/prescriptive axis, with the prospective one emerging first in development.

Moral Foundations

Model Graham and Haidt (2012) listed five foundations of evil based on Haidt and Joseph's (2004) five innate psychological foundations of moral systems (see Table 34.1). The moral foundations involve (a) harm (or its avoidance), (b) fairness, (c) in-group behavior, (d) authority, and (e) purity. The types of corresponding evil involve, respectively, (a) cruelty/violence, (b) racism/oppression, (c) traitors/out-group, (d) anarchists/revolutionaries, and (e) atheists/hedonists. In general in this chapter, I refer to the model as one on foundational motives.

Haidt's moral foundation model lists two individualizing contractual approaches to society—harm/care and fairness/reciprocity (see Table 34.2, Foundations of Intuitive Ethics). As well, it includes three binding foundations about grouping people—in-group/loyalty, authority/respect, and purity/sanctity. Haidt (2012) added Liberty as a moral foundation, which appears individualizing (see Table 34.3, which gives my revision of Haidt's approach to purity/ sanctity). Haidt extended with colleagues this model to moral differences in liberals and conservatives (e.g., Graham et al., 2011). According to them, liberals value the individualizing moral foundations, whereas conservatives value the binding ones. Moreover, provocatively, they argued that liberals rely on only the individualizing ones, unlike conservatives, who value all five foundations.

Janoff-Bulman and Carnes (2013) took issue with Haidt's work at several levels. First, they argued that moral motives include self ones, such as self-restraint, and not just individualizing (or interpersonal) and binding (or group) ones. Second, the motives can be classified according to their proscriptive or prescriptive orientation. Third, the Haidt model excludes a relevant group motive, that of social justice/communal responsibility. Using Janoff-Bulman's terms, the latter is prescriptive, in contrast to another one—social

Table 34.1 Five moral/ethical foundations/sources and associated sacred values and types of evil

	Dimension	
Foundation/source	Sacred value	Type of evil
Harm	Nurturance/care, peace	Cruelty/violence
Fairness	Justice, reciprocity	Racism/oppression
In-group	Loyalty, group self-sacrifice	Treachery/out-group
Authority	Respect/tradition, honor	Anarchism/revolution
Purity	Chastity/piety, self-control	Atheism/hedonism

Adopted from Graham and Haidt (2012)

Note. Variously, Haidt and colleagues have described four, five, and six moral/ethical foundations. The first four in this table appear constant to the different versions. The two poles of sacred values and evil are not the same as in the original formulations, adding to them

Table 34.2 Foundations of intuitive ethics

	Foundations			
Axes	Harm/care	Fairness/reciprocity	In-group/loyalty	Authority/respect
Adaptive challenge	Protect and care for young, vulnerable, or injured kin (e.g., offspring)	Reap benefits of two-way cooperation with non-kin	Reap benefits of group cooperation	Negotiate hierarchy, defer selectively
Proper domain (adaptive triggers)	Suffering, distress, or threat to one's kin (e.g., expressed by an offspring)	Cheating, cooperation, deception	Threat or challenge to group	Signs of dominance and submission
Actual domain (examples of modern triggers)	Newborn seals, attractive cartoon characters	Romantic partner fidelity, vending machines that do not work	Sports teams one roots for, community cohesion	Bosses, respected professionals
Characteristic emotions	Compassion	Anger, gratitude, guilt	Group pride, belongingness; rage at a traitor	Respect, fear
Relevant virtues (and vices)	Caring, kindness (cruelty)	Fairness, justice, honesty, trustworthiness (dishonesty)	Loyalty, patriotism, self-sacrifice (treason, cowardice)	Obedience, deference (disobedience, uppitiness)

Adopted from Haidt and Joseph (2007) and adapted from Haidt (2012). Adopted by permission of Oxford University Press. Haidt, J., & Joseph, C. (2007). The moral mind: How five sets of innate intuitions guide the development of many culture-specific virtues, and perhaps even modules. In P. Carruthers, S. Laurence, & S. Stich (Eds.), *The innate mind: Volume 3: Foundations and the future* (pp. 367–392). New York: Oxford University Press. Reprinted by permission of Oxford University Press, USA. [Table 19.1, Page 382]

Note. In this work on four of the original foundations by Haidt and colleagues, they are described along axes related to adaptation, triggers, and emotions/values. It excludes sanctity/degradation, which later was described as involving purity/sanctity

order/communal solidarity—which is proscriptive. The former is associated with liberalism and the latter with conservatism, whereas both are associated with individualizing and binding moral foundations. In this regard, developmental research is finding parallels in parental attitude early in life and later political ideology (Fraley, Griffin, Belsky, & Roisman, 2012; Janoff-Bulman, Carnes, & Sheikh, 2014).

Comment Although the model by Janoff-Bulman and Carnes (2013) on moral motives addresses some of the concerns presented by Haidt's one, both models are missing some important aspects, especially a developmental framework. In this regard, Haidt might have a developmental component within each of his individualizing and binding foundations, given that they first list, respectively, harm/care and in-group/loyalty compared to more advanced types (e.g., fairness/reciprocity and authority/respect, respectively). The reader should note that both models under discussion have separated interpersonal focus from group/social focus, while Janoff-Bulman and Carnes have added a focus that is on the self.

Integrated Motivations

Model Forbes (2011) constructed a model of motivation built on prior models. Motivation, or the motor/driver of behavior, is an important causal construct of human action, emotion, and thought, and stretches back to the roots of contemporary study of psychology (e.g., Freud, 1933; Maslow, 1943). Forbes viewed motivations as emergent psychological phenomena deriving from a biological substrate (Table 34.3). Forbes (2011) categorized the emotions into a grid of nine blocks that involved two change axes—focus of aspiration (change where) and

Table 34.3 Other foundations of intuitive ethics

	Foundations		
Axes	Purity/sanctity (Haidt & Joseph, 2007)	Purity/sanctity	Liberty (Haidt, 2012)
Adaptive challenge	Avoid microbes and parasites (contaminants)	Participate in spirituality/giving of self for common good without anticipation of reward, but without self-harm, too	Living in small groups where one might encounter domination, bullying/constraint
Proper domain (adaptive triggers)	Waste products, with disease people	Improve lot of other/group; betterment of relationships, social surround, community/culture, etc., which acts to increase sense of psychological maturity, wisdom, flow, presence, etc. [and which in turn acts to increase motive to help others]	Signs of attempted domination/aggressive control
Actual domain (examples of modern triggers)	Taboo ideas (fascism, communism, racism)	More than suffering/distress/threat; rather bootstrap other/group for the better and help them do the same; be inspired/inspire	Rise of a (would-be) dominator/political abuse
Characteristic emotions	Having disgust	Serenity, peace	Righteous/group unifying anger/hatred of oppression
Relevant virtues (and vices)	Showing temperance, chastity, piety, cleanliness (lust, intemperance)	Respect of other/role modeling; allows helping of others to help themselves (a sanctuary) (disrespect)	Freedom fighter/revolution against tyranny

Adopted from Haidt and Joseph (2007) and adapted from Haidt (2012). Adopted by permission of Oxford University Press. Haidt, J., & Joseph, C. (2007). The moral mind: How five sets of innate intuitions guide the development of many culture-specific virtues, and perhaps even modules. In P. Carruthers, S. Laurence, & S. Stich (Eds.), *The innate mind: Volume 3: Foundations and the future* (pp. 367–392). New York: Oxford University Press. Reprinted by permission of Oxford University Press, USA. [Table 19.1, Page 382]

Note. I created the second purity/sanctity foundation. Haidt had described it in terms mixing physical purity needs, and emotions/concepts. In my version, I focused on spirituality/giving/helping, which is a quite different approach

Table 34.4 Framework of human motivations according to focus and level of aspiration

	Focus		
Enhancing in the level	Intrapersonal (self context)	Instrumental (material context)	Interpersonal (social context)
Expectations (being)	Security	Empowering	Belonging
Experiences (doing)	Identity	Engaging	Nurturing
Outcomes (having)	Mastering	Achieving	Esteem

Adopted from Forbes (2011)

Note. The model does not consider development to a sufficient degree, and has been modified accordingly

level of aspiration (type of change). The former included the categories of "intrapsychic" (e.g., sense of self), "instrumental" (e.g., relation to the material world), and interpersonal (e.g., on social relationships; see Table 34.4). Levels of aspiration included: (a) change in potential/expectation; (b) change in process/experience; and (c) change in outcomes/evaluation. Deci and Ryan (1991, 1995) elaborated a triarchic model of innate, universal needs similar to that of Forbes (the need for autonomy, competence, and relatedness).

Comment It should be noted that Forbes (2011) framed his model developmentally as a macro-developmental stage-like movement across the three realms of focus of aspiration—from (a) self to (b) material world to (c) social world. In this regard, he referred to Piaget (1937; Piaget & Inhelder, 1967). However, I will show that it is more likely that the stage-like macro-developmental pathway should concern his axis of level of aspiration, that is, (a) enhanced expectations, (b) experiences, and (c) outcomes (which he considered a micro-developmental sequence rather than a macro-developmental one).

Model As mentioned, Forbes (2011) described his unified motivational model in terms of nine motivational domains formed by the intersection of the axes of focus and level of aspiration. The intrapsychic triad include: (a) security (e.g., Maslow, 1943, 1955, 1967; and also Bowlby, 1969/1999; and Erikson, 1959); (b) identity (e.g., Erikson, 1979); and (c) mastery (e.g., self-actualization; Maslow, 1943). The three instrumental motivations concern: (a) empowerment (e.g., self-efficacy; Bandura, 1977, 1986, 1997; Murray, 1938); (b) engagement (e.g., Murray, 1938); and (c) achievement (e.g., McClelland, 1961). As for the interpersonal motivation triplet, it concerns (a) belonging (e.g., James, 1890/1950; Mead, 1934); (b) nurturance (Bowlby, 1969/1999, 1979); and (c) self-esteem (e.g., Maslow, 1943).

Comment Given my stage model in Young (2011; see Table 31.1 in Chap. 31), and examining directly Erikson's and Maslow's original models, it appears that the movement in Forbes (2011) in the intrapsychic realm for level of aspiration from—security to identity to mastery (e.g., self-actualization)—fits a macro, stage-like developmental progression. Moreover, in this sense, the motivations of Forbes' interpersonal realm complement that progression more than a micro-developmental one. For example, belonging would seem to emerge before identity and nurturing after it, as found in Young (2011), and Forbes' esteem appears analogous to identity.

Also, referring to Maslow (1943), who considered his hierarchical needs model a developmental one, there appears to be missing from Forbes' progression, whether in terms of focus or level of aspiration, a survival-related motivation at the beginning. Moreover, his closing mastering level for the intrapsychic self might be best reserved for his instrumental, material-world progression, with the label of self-actualization used instead of mastery for this intrapsychic level.

Finally, referring to his instrumental progression, in order to arrive at a consistency across the intrapsychic and instrumental domains, it would appear that the survival level should be placed at the beginning of the intrapsychic progression, and also should be matched by an early developing action/approach or exploration/curiosity one in the instrumental progression. Also, note that, macro-developmentally, engagement and empowerment should be switched in position in that engagement should precede empowerment.

In his integrative motivational model, Forbes (2011) contrasted self, social world, and material world motives. This tripartite distinction could help or organize better the prior models on motivations and needs. I note that Janoff-Bulman also had a tripartite distinction in her work. It was related to personal, interpersonal, and group foci, but not environmental ones. A model that more closely resembles that of Forbes is the one of Deci and Ryan (2013) in which autonomy, relatedness, and competence are included. Competence, or mastery, might parallel functioning well in the environment, for example

Revising the Maslow Revision

Introduction

The different models on the self in relation to motivation, morals, and development that have been reviewed have helped me revise my prior revision of Maslow (Young, 2011; see Fig. 34.2). In that model, basically, I had divided the classic Maslovian model of five hierarchical needs into self-definitional and relatedness components. Below, I give the rational for a third component to the revised Neo-Maslovian model. Then, I propose the five foundational moral motives that seem associated with each of the five hierarchical needs, and how they vary over the three components of the model. Before proceeding to these steps in my theorizing, I indicate the assumptions that I used as I developed the revised Neo-Maslovian model.

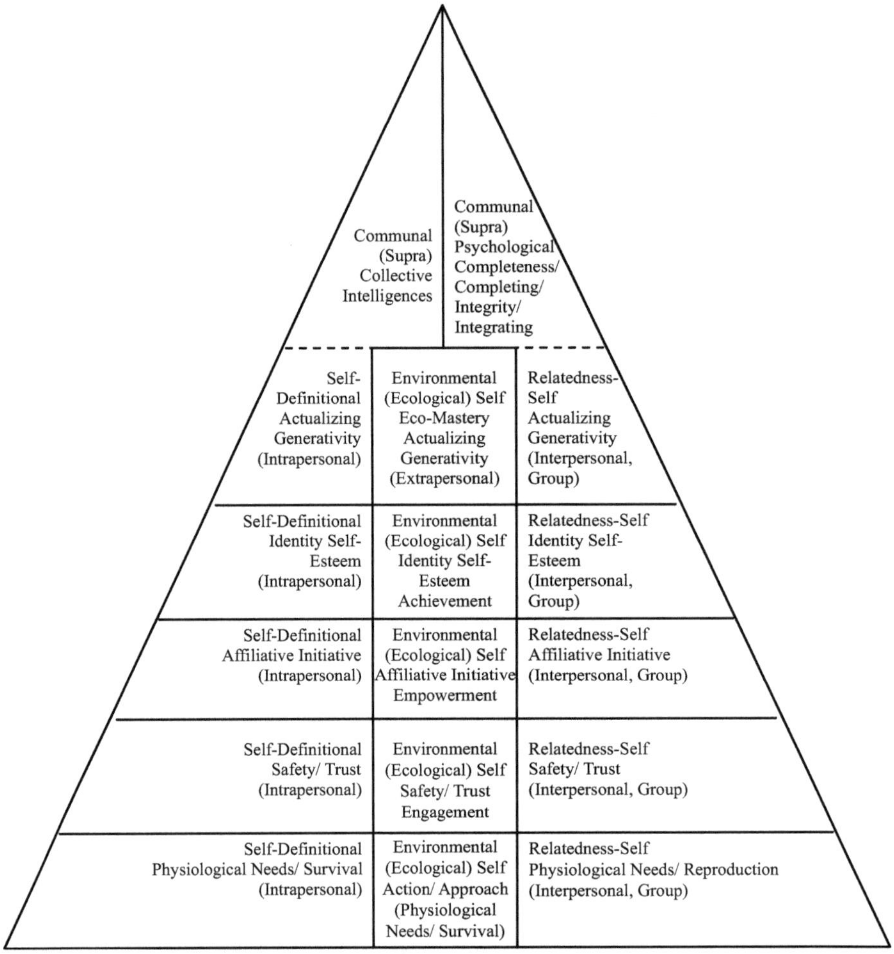

Fig. 34.2 Neo-Maslovian hierarchy of self-definitional, relatedness self, and environmental self needs. The figure gives simplified terms for each of the revised motivational needs in the combined model of Maslow (1943, 1970), Erikson (1980), and Blatt (2008). The major revision entertained of Maslow concerns dividing his different levels of needs in two components, depending on what part of the self is involved. The left-hand column refers to the needs related to the personal self, while the right-hand column refers to the needs of the self in relationship. Blatt referred to polarities of experience in terms of self-definition and relatedness, and I borrowed these terms for this aspect of the model.

In addition, for this version of the Neo-Maslovian model in present book relative to the original revision in Young (2011), I added a middle column related to a third component of the person, or the mastery/competence instrumental/environment aspect of behavior. In particular, this aspect of the model is derived from Forbes (2011), Deci and Ryan (1995), Haidt (2012), and Janoff-Bulman and colleagues (e.g., Janoff-Bulman, 2009).

As for Erikson's model of eight stages in lifespan development, there appear to be two stages in his model that correspond to each of the four more advanced needs of Maslow's model. Therefore, in deriving the labels for the present combined model, I referred to the first of the two Erikson's stages involved in each case. As for the most basic physiological level of needs, I referred to the Darwinian concept of survival and reproduction, using the latter for the personal component and the former for the relatedness component. Note that the terms used to describe the needs also refer to attachment theory for the safety level and affiliation instead of love for the middle level (after Kenrick, Griskevicius, Neuberg, & Schaller, 2010).

The Piagetian component of the model adds an extra level at the peak to account for changes in cognition and behavior that would derive as the person transitions from the formal to the postformal period, which I refer to as the stage of collective intelligence (Young, 2011). Another change made to the original Maslovian revision of the hierarchy of needs model is that I included a superordinate level to the one of self-actualization and related psychological development, such as generativity. This new partial level of the penultimate level in the model concerns "psychological completeness," which is partially akin to Erikson's ego integrity and which corresponds to the stage of collective intelligence cognitively in my own model. Adapted in part with permission from Springer Science + Business Media. Young (2011); with kind permission from Springer Science + Business Media B.V. [Figure 19.3, Page 452]

Assumptions

(a) The model should include a developmental component. Needs, drives, motivations, and other affective processes emerge in development, for example, partly based on underpinning cognitive acquisitions and learning. A developmentally-informed model of motivation does not mean that the motivations involved begin functioning in a mature way at the point of their emergence. Rather, the origins of the motivation are laid in the groundwork of their emergence in the specified levels, and they can continue to develop with growth in cognition and learning and in emotion and sociality.

(b) The motivations in the integrated model should address the three self/social spheres considered in the various models: self, environment, other/group. In my revision of Maslow, I consider the dyadic other and multiple-other group levels together, except where necessary to specify the difference.

(c) Motivations should be described generally, but also they should apply specifically to the moral domain. There is overlap in motivations that apply to the self, social, and material/environmental worlds. Moreover, there is overlap in motivations that are not considered directly moral and those that are considered directly moral. For example, I might strive to obtain liberty for myself, but a corollary motive is that the striving should become applied to the social world, too. Indeed, it can be argued that one cannot really strive for genuine liberty only in one sphere or the other. Also, in this sense, moral/foundational motives apply not only to the social world but also to the material/environmental one (think eco-activism).

Environmental Self

Model

According to these suggestions and the review of the relevant models above, especially of Forbes (2011) emphasis on mastery in motivation, it would appear a third ladder of hierarchical needs or developmental steps can be added to the revised Neo-Maslovian model that I had created in Young (2011), consisting of relations with the material world. That is, Young's (2011) original Neo-Maslovian model is based partially on the work of Blatt (2008) and his conception of two selves, but we now see that there appears to be three instead of two primary components to the self that develops, a self-definitional one and a relatedness one, as per Blatt (2008), but also a material, instrumental self, as per Forbes (2011; see Table 34.5).

Another concept that applies to this instrumental mode is competence or mastery. Note that the concepts involved, such as mastery, have different meanings in different areas of psychology and, in my work here, they are defined especially relative their place in the present model. In this sense, the mastery in the present context could be referred to as "eco-mastery." Eco-activism is an example of such a moral attitude.

Therefore, in this regard, I suggest that an "environmental self" or ecological self develops. [A Google search failed to find any reference to an environmental self, although an ecological self is mentioned in the ecology literature.] Note that an environmental self that acts morally might deal with the biotic as well as abiotic environment, and might include actions toward aspects of the environment relative to groups, such as preserving and improving neighborhoods.

Comment

To review, the prior Neo-Maslovian model that I had created in Young (2011) had split the classic triangular model of Maslow on hierarchy of needs in terms of two half columns (on the self-definitional and relational selves), but the present version has three component columns instead of two, with the third one involving a mastering self. This new conception of how Maslow's model should be revised led me to slightly modify the notion underpinning the two existing columns. Specifically, the relational self is understood to apply to interpersonal or group spheres. In balance, the self-definitional self is referred to as

Table 34.5 Five foundational moral motives in relation to Neo-Maslovian needs and Neo-Piagetian developmental level

	Relation to the self		
Relation to need (Neo-Maslovian)/developmental level (Neo-Piagetian)	Definitional self	Environmental self	Relatedness self (other)/relatedness self (group)
Actualizing generativity/collective intelligence	Liberty, humanizing seeking	Planetary activism (or concern): eco-mastery (striving toward full potential in relation to planetary activism or concern)	Purity/sanctity (other, group)
Identity self-esteem/abstract intelligence	Conscious identifying of values/morality	Achievement (obtaining positive results, feeling proud)	Conscious social application of values/morality (other, group)
Affiliative initiative/perioperational intelligence (preoperational, concrete operational)	Fairness, reciprocity, valuing	Empowerment (being equal to the task, capable, and free to act)	Authority/respect (other, group)
Safety, trust/sensorimotor intelligence	Harm reducing/care promoting	Engagement (productivity involved, absorbed, excited)	Loyalty (other, group)
Physiological survival/reproduction/reflexive intelligence	Life preservation (self)	Action/approach (exploration, curiosity)	Life preservation (other, group)

Note. The first column is based on Young's (2011) model of Neo-Piagetian cognitive development (five stages) and the corresponding reworking of Maslow's (1943) needs hierarchy into a developmental model. The second and fourth columns reflect the original two halves of the Young Neo-Maslovian model as applied to the self-definitional and relational selves (Blatt, 2008). However, they have been reworked in terms of Haidt's (2012) model of five foundational moral motives. Also considered were Janoff-Bulman and Carnes's (2013) model of moral motives. The third column is based on Forbes (2011) work on motives related to the environment, as adjusted to fit the five-stage model described

By examining the various terms/concepts in the columns, the degree of conceptual integration and coherence over the various models that have inspired the present work becomes clear

In the first column, the integration of Maslovian, Eriksonian, and Piagetian terms/concepts is evident in the hierarchical, developmental model proposed to modify/replace the original authors of these seminal models

In the second column, the work of Haidt is emphasized, but this is achieved in concert with the work of Blatt on the definitional self. I added some terms allowing for better paralleling with my model

In the third column on the environmental self, which follows from the work of Forbes (but is also consistent with Deci & Ryan, 1995), I refer to planetary activism/eco-mastery (and related achievement/empowerment/engagement/action). This type of self is an addition to the duality model of Blatt, but adds a wider focus to understanding the self/personality and motives/ethics

The last column puts together Blatt's concept of relatedness with Janoff-Bulman's focus on other/group and Haidt's work on purity/sanctity and other moral motives. Once more, they are reworked to fit the present five-step model

intrapersonal. As for the new column, the development of motives relative to the material world is generalized to refer to the environmental self.

Five Foundational Moral Motives

Introduction

In the following, I re-examine the previously described models of motives that were described by Haidt and by Janoff-Bulman and their colleagues. In particular, I consider them developmentally and in how they have to be revised to fit my own model. Also, I relate them to the self-definitional, individualizing side or sphere of the model and the relational, group side or sphere. This is the first time that I have attempted to expand the two sides of the model, so that the previous analysis of the foundational and moral motives has proven useful for my present theorizing.

The next task, then, is to reorganize the foundational motives so that they fit the present model, which has five levels each with a self and relatedness side to consider (as well as an environmental one, which is not relevant to the present exercise). After this next section of the chapter, I turn to the moral motives for a similar reworking.

Before beginning the elaboration of the five foundational moral motives, it must be kept in mind that the axis on which I constructed them relate to the present revised Neo-Maslovian model, which itself is based on a revised Neo-Piagetian/Neo-Eriksonian model. Therefore, in choosing the final names for the foundational moral motives, I avoided using the terminology of the work on which it was based (on foundational motives and on moral motives). On the one hand, as we shall see, they did not cover the full range of motives required in a complete model that extends from mine. On the other hand, the labels used by the others best serve as exemplars of the more general terms that I created.

Revising Foundational Motives

Revision I tried to place Haidt's foundational moral motives in a developmental sequence that fits the present model. As a general guide, I remind that Maslow's five levels of hierarchically arranged needs include ones related to—physical needs, emotional security, social affiliation, self-esteem, and self-actualization, which I have modified, e.g., referring to safety and trust for the second step. In this regard, the harm/care level in Haidt's model appears to correspond to the level of safety/trust in mine, as does loyalty. Fairness/reciprocity and authority/respect seem to correspond to affiliative initiative. Liberty and purity/sanctity would correspond to self-actualization/generativity. [Note that I use the term purity/sanctity with the highest moral connotations of the term, e.g., spiritually giving of the self with expectation of no return (within the limits of avoiding self-harm).]

Note that I had difficulty aligning the foundational motives with the levels in my model, and had to add ones for the first and fourth levels. In this regard, for the physiological/survival level, I added motives related to life preservation. For the self-esteem/identity level, I added motives related to consciously identifying values/morality. In this regard, given that there are five levels in the Maslovian approach to needs/motives, it would appear that the fourth one of identity/self-esteem level that manifests at the time of the adolescent age period should include moral foundational motives related to consciousness, in the sense of awareness of self and personal growth. As for the earliest level of need/survival, the motive appears to involve survival (e.g., avoid suicide, murder).

Moreover, in developing this model of motives in relation to level of hierarchical needs and their development, I used similar terminology for the three selves associated with the model. Haidt's work especially helped with the self-definitional (individual, personal) and relatedness (other, group) sides of the model. In following up the analysis above in terms of which of the foundational motives aligns with which of the five levels of my model, in the following, I determine which side at any one level (self-definitional or relatedness) they align with best. (a) For safety/trust, I placed Haidt's harm reducing/care promoting on the individualizing, self-definitional level and placed his loyalty on the social, relatedness side. (b) For affiliative/initiative, Haidt's fairness/reciprocity went to the personal side and his authority/respect to the social one. (c) For the self-actualization/generativity, the assignments were for liberty and purity/sanctity on the self-definitional and relatedness sides, respectively.

Next, I justify the placement of the foundational motives at the levels of my Neo-Maslovian model by showing why they do not fit the two levels for which I had to create other motives of this nature to complete alignment of the five levels of my model with five types of foundational motives (and different ones than Haidt had proposed). In this regard, none of Haidt's foundational motives are similar to the first Maslovian level of physical survival needs. The closest might be avoiding harm, but that aligns better with the next level of providing safety or security. Second, fairness/reciprocity aligns with affiliative/initiative, and might be considered as part of the next level upward of identity/self-esteem, as well. However, they would have to evolve from the level of the person behaving with these characteristics in concrete context into more abstract values/morals in order to fit the fourth level better than the third.

Also, note that the foundational motives of liberty, fairness/reciprocity, and the others especially fit into the self-definitional, individualizing side in the present model, but they help qualify the relatedness one, as well. In this regard, we can add to them qualifiers such as seeking, valuing, and promoting (e.g., liberty-seeking, fairness-valuing, care promoting). This makes them consistent with the social/group/other side of the model, in which the motives are more outward than inward, personal, and self-definition related.

Comment Note that my model of the cognitive (mis)perception of the other (Young, 2011), which is developmental, given that it stems from my Neo-Piagetian model of cognitive development, also corresponds to the Maslovian one and the related ones on foundational and moral motives, especially in the way that I have revised them. In this sense, it might serve as a cognitive foundation for understanding the development of the foundational and moral motives.

In the following, I turn to my analysis and revision of the model of moral motives, showing how it can fit my own Neo-Maslovian model. At the same time, I refer to how the former can help explain the development of the relatedness/group side of my model. Therefore, we will see that some of the revision to my model already described in analyzing the model of foundational motives borrowed from the model of moral motives, as well.

Revising Moral Motives

Revision It is helpful to consider how the specific motivations described in the model of moral motives in Janoff-Bulman and Carnes (2013) map onto the present model. I accomplish this task in several steps. I remind that in my model there are five levels related to my revision of Maslow's hierarchy of needs that are related to—physiological/survival, safety/trust, affiliative/initiative, identity/self-esteem, and actualizing/generative. Also, there are three types of selves that are related to each of them—the self-definitional (individual) one, the relatedness (social/group) one, and the material/competent (environmental) one. The present task then is to align the model of moral motives to my model. To remind, that model includes group level moral motives as well as self and other ones, with all three of these types having motives at the prescriptive and proscriptive levels.

Generally, the group motives (social order and social justice) in the moral motive model Janoff-Bulman and Carnes (2013) fit the group or relatedness motives listed in the present model. However, careful inspection of the foundational moral motives in my model reveals only some correspondence between my model and the one of moral motives.

First in this regard, their social order moral motive appears to precede developmentally the social justice one. Second, therefore the two moral motives do not correspond to the same level in my model even if they are placed at the same level in their model. That is, social order aligns with the authority/respect level in my model, and social justice would align with the level above that on conscious social application of values/morality. Fourth, social order includes communal solidarity, which might make this portion of it align best with the loyalty motive in the level before the one where I have indicated it fits. Fifth, their social justice motive also includes communal responsibility, which makes this component of it correspond to the purity/sanctity motive in the upper level of the model, involving spirituality/behaving for the common good.

About the interpersonal motives in the moral motive model in Janoff-Bulman and Carnes (2013) and their relationship to the self-definitional, individual foundational moral motives of my model and their arrangement into five levels in it the interpersonal motives in Janoff-Bulman and Carnes (2013) appear to map onto the present model, but not according to their placement in the interpersonal sphere of their model. (a) That is, they appear to correspond to categories in the definitional self (relatedness, personal) sphere of the present model rather than the interpersonal one. (b) In this regard, for the second category in Janoff-Bulman and Carnes in the interpersonal sphere, the moral motive is helping/fairness. (c) This category can be split, and, in so doing, the fairness component corresponds to Haidt's foundational moral model category of fairness/reciprocity, which lies in the third level of my model. The helping component perhaps fits Haidt's Liberty category, which lies in the fifth level of my model. (d) As for the other interpersonal motive in Janoff-Bulman, the one of not harming corresponds to Haidt's harm/care category, and so is placed in the second level of my model.

About Janoff-Bulman and Carnes (2013) proposed self (personal) moral motives, they do not align very well with the categories in the spheres of the present model. In this sense, self-restraint would appear to be a general self-regulatory skill that applies to motivation in any sphere, personal, social, or group, and industriousness is a higher-order skill that helps in any higher-order category of any sphere, as well.

Comment As shown in a previous section of the chapter, Haidt's foundational motive model included motives that aligned with three of the five levels of the present model, and one of them could be seen as a ready precursor to one more level. As shown in the present section of the chapter, Janoff-Bulman's moral motive model has components that align with four of the levels in my model, but this became clear only after I made the effort to show the parallels between the models using components in the moral motive ones. Overall, both the foundational and the moral motive models have not considered any motives related to the first level of my model, and I had to create them without their work as a guide. However, it was not difficult to do so, given Maslow's description of the needs at this level as physiological, leading me to create a survival-related motive referred to as self preservation.

Creating Environmental Motives

Model Recall that the third component of a revised Neo-Maslovian model related to the self concerned the material, environmental world, and acting with mastery or competence within it. In terms of how the foundational moral motives might pass through a five-step sequence of hierarchical needs, I propose the following; they would involve from lowest to highest level—action/approach (exploration/curiosity), engagement, empowerment, achievement, and mastery. These five levels in hierarchical need development related to the environmental self correspond to the five general levels of the model—respectively, physiological needs/survival, safety/trust, affiliative/initiative, self-esteem/identity, and actualization/generativity.

Comment These five levels, as found with the foundational moral motives that are proposed to arise in correspondence to those for the individual and other/group moral spheres, are differentiated aspects of the five motives for the self at issue, rather than separate ones. Therefore the model of five foundational moral motives that I have developed includes ones that develop sequentially and that apply to three different spheres.

Naming the Five Foundational Moral Motives

Introduction

The best terms to integrate the different types of motives associated with the three spheres of individual, social, and environmental should avoid the exemplars derived from Haidt and Janoff-Bulman and colleagues and, as well, should respect the theoretical origins that drove their creation, which is my revised Neo-Maslovian model. In this regard, the best names for the foundational moral motives should not be ones like loyalty and justice, but ones anchored in Maslovian, Piagetian, and Eriksonian terminology. In this sense, I did not deviate too much from them as I reflected on the present task of naming the foundational moral motives. Moreover, the labels chosen should be general enough to cover the three spheres at each level of individual, social, and environmental. Therefore, for the five levels of the present model, the best labels for the five foundational moral motives involve the following.

Names

(a) The most basic hierarchical need level is concerned with physiological needs and survival, and I have referred to the motive involved at this level as life preservation. In this regard, in order to cover the three spheres involved, I refer to the most primary foundational moral motive as Self/Other/Environment Life Preservation. Although it develops first in life, it carries forward throughout life and, at the moral level, allows for behavior at the highest moral levels, such as great acts of courage in saving people, animals, and even the planet as a whole.

(b) Next, the hierarchical need involved concerns safety/trust, and at this level behavior relates to caring for the self, other, and environment, and not doing them harm. This need (and associated moral motive) develops in infancy and continues throughout the lifespan. It leads to constant vigilance about all those around us, as well as ourselves, therefore, the best label to represent it is Self/Other/Environment Safety/Trust.

(c) Third, the hierarchical need that develops concerns affiliative initiative. It enables activity and moral motivation related to dynamically interdigitating with the self and with the other, as well, in the material world, thereby developing a sense of mastery and competence in these spheres, preparatory to the development of identity and self-esteem. In this phase, we learn to use well our social skills and create social groups, which can act together for moral outcomes, for example. In this regard, the best label for the foundational moral motive involved is Self/Other/Environment Affiliative Initiative.

(d) Next, the foundational moral motive of Self/Other/Environment Identity Self-Esteem develops. Our identities and sense of self grow as we relate well to others, the environment, and our inner workings. We become sure of our moral ideas and outreach, and might apply them with consuming passion. This promotes a sense of (subjective) well being and health that we might transfer to the development of same in others and the environment.

(e) In the penultimate step in the development of hierarchical needs and foundational moral motives, we become concerned with generativity in the widest sense of the word and, in activating moral behavior in this regard, we self-actualize optimally with consequences for the self-actualization of others. There is a self/other actualization that develops or, more precisely for the foundational moral motive involved, a Self/Other/Environment Actualizing Generativity. We are constantly and widely moral at the highest levels in all our responsibilities and endeavors, in what can be referred to as a process of participatory morality.

Poles

Haidt and colleagues had related their model of foundational motives to adaptive challenges, domains, related emotions, and virtues/vices. I have incorporated some of these themes in my description of my version of the motives in the above. However, instead of replicating in much detail his approach to the nature of the foundational motives in describing my own version, I prefer to keep the emphasis on their developmental origins in the models of Maslow, Piaget, and Erikson. In the latter sense, one can present the various foundational moral motives as oppositions, poles, crises, or challenges with which we struggle, for example, just as Erikson did for his eight developmental stages (e.g., trust vs. mistrust).

(a) In this regard, the first foundational moral motive of Self/Other/Environment Life Preservation should be considered as an opposition of Self/Other/Environment Life Preservation vs. Self/Other/Environment Life Destruction. When causes of behavior lead to great difficulties in surmounting this latter challenge, behavior could develop toward the destructive pole of the opposition (for example, which could lead to the development and implementation of evil in behavior).

(b) Next, Self/Other/Environment Safety/Trust should be seen in opposition to Self/Other/Environment Safety Lack/Mistrust. When this crisis is not navigated well, the dangers relate to adopting unsafe behavior and feeling an absence of security. The moral outcome might be wanton disregard for self, other, and environment.

(c) Third, Self/Other/Environment Affiliative Initiative has as its opposite pole Disaffiliative Inertia. The person disengages, retreats, and withdraws morally, and vicious circles might develop in reaction, for example, leading to difficulties in dealing fairly and with authority.

(d) Then, instead of Self/Other/Environment Identity Self-Esteem, the person develops the opposite moral perspective of Self/Other/Environment Identity Self-Esteem Difficulty or Disturbance. This might involve not developing moral values that guide daily life, and the person loses moral concern and compass even when actively participating in life. One's sense of self is compromised, adding to difficulties in establishing a suite of appropriate moral values.

(e) In the highest level in foundational moral motive expression, when it is compromised, it is more like Self/Other/Environment Moral Stagnation in Generativity. The person lives without any moral values, and is just concerned for the most basis needs, even if acting in a presumed generative way, e.g., in family and at work. Perhaps there is perfunctory moral behavior at the surface, but no depth in it (nor rationale or reason for it, if it is present). A moral void exists that the person might try to fill with amoral behavior, along with a constant stream of amoral thought.

Conclusion

I have prepared a table that presents the model of the five foundational moral motives just described (see Table 34.6). In the table, I indicate that a summary label for the issues that have to be navigated for each of the five issues related to the five foundational moral motives relate to the sequence of—physiological needs, emotional security, connection (social, cognitive), conscious abstraction, and participatory morality. I chose these terms because, from a developmental perspective and considering the various steps in Maslow, Piaget, and Erikson in this regard, the five-step passage indicated fits. It might be useful in the psychotherapeutic context, given the problematic behaviors that it describes as possible for each level. In this regard, the therapist would focus on the issues at each of levels of the model that are relevant for the patient at hand, and investigate their developmental underpinnings, where appropriate.

Table 34.6 A model of five foundational moral motives in terms of oppositional poles

	Pole	
Self/other/environment motive origin	Positive	Negative
Physiological survival	Life preservation	Life destruction
Security (emotional)	Safety, trust	Safety lack/mistrust
Connection (cognitive, social)	Affiliative/initiative	Disaffiliative/inertia
Conscious abstraction	Identity/self-esteem	Its difficulty/disturbance
Participatory morality	Actualizing/generativity	Moral stagnation in generativity

Mechanism

The self develops toward unity and integration in terms of its change processes and motivational bases. The transformation involved is dynamical, self-organizational, emergent, constantly de novo, ebbing and flowing with gains and losses, and constantly seeking equilibrium at increasingly more refined levels throughout the diverse levels of its manifold.

Although I have developed a model of foundational moral motives, many factors can hinder their optimal manifestation and application. They present categories and classes that vary on a host of parameters, and perhaps the most important is the degree to which they are inhibited in or activated in their ability to motivate, instigate, or otherwise propulse the person into action. For each motivation, multiple variables might preclude their capacity to be efficient and effective, including adverse life experiences, psychopathology, stressors in context, and self-regulation deficiencies.

That is, although motivations might emerge developmentally at a particular point in time, consistent with their associated cognitive underpinning, they are highly dependent on the type of environment in which the individual is parented, schooled, etc. If the latter is supportive, the motivations take a positive turn; if not, they can manifest negatively (in this regard, Erikson's developmental model of challenges or crises at each stage serves as the classic prototype).

Also for the mechanisms involved, one that I have found important in multiple areas of psychology, brain, and behavior concerns activation/inhibition coordination (Young, 2011). Janoff-Bulman and Carnes (2013) emphasized the activation/approach and inhibition/aversion self-regulation systems as important in moral motivation. I would add that it is the intricate coordination of activation and inhibition that provides the central and behavioral machinery for the unfolding of complex moral cognition, attitudes, motives, and behavior.

Finally, the present model might place a particular motivation at a certain developmental level, but precursors might be evident earlier. Once more, Erikson's model serves as an example; i.e., although identity is considered to emerge in adolescence in his model, he considered that precursors emerge earlier; also, identity factors were judged to be present at each stage after adolescence.

New Questionnaire

Introduction Based on the concept of the cognitive (mis)perception of the other, one could establish the degree to which respondents maintain that the government (conservative option) or people (liberal option) should be (a) controlling people or (b) empowering them. The Neo-Piagetian stage model of development (Young, 2011) consists of five stages, and the five-level model of the cognitive (mis)perception of the other is based on it. Advocating that people need to be controlled (whether by government or people) is consistent with the lower levels of the cognitive (mis)perception model (which means respondents might be cognitively developed to higher stages but misperceive others as reflecting lower levels of development, capacity, merit, etc.). Advocating that people need concern directed toward them and need to be empowered (whether by government or people) is consistent with the higher levels of the model. Irrespective of the level of control preferred, respondents should vary in whether they adapt a conservative or liberal attitude in these regards. Moreover, there might be relevant psychological correlates not only for the level of control advocated but also for their indicated political attitudes.

Janoff-Bulman (2012) offered an account of how conservatives and liberals differ psychologically, as reviewed briefly earlier in the chapter. According to her, liberalism is associated with approach regulation and conservativism with avoidance regulation (e.g., Janoff-Bulman, 2009). Therefore, liberals focus on "prescriptive" moral orientation or "shoulds" and conservatives on "proscriptive" moral orientation or "should nots."

Conservatives wish to protect members of society, whereas liberals wish to provide for their welfare. Conservatives are concerned about societal losses, not gains but, for liberals, it is the opposite. Conservatives seek social order relative to social justice, but it is the reverse for liberals. Conservatives focus on life style issues, unlike liberals, who focus on equity ones. Liberals are concerned with positive obligations, but conservatives focus on prohibition. In short, according to Janoff-Bulman (2012), conservatives aim to "advance" the common "good," whereas liberals aim to prevent the "bad" being inflicted on group members.

Questionnaire Given the issues discussed with respect to conflicts in the literature (a) about conservatives and liberals and their personal attributes and, (b) about how to best measure their political ideology, I developed a scale on the latter that could be used to help elucidate valid differences in the former (see Table 34.7).

The scale is based on several assumptions. First, political ideology concerns the degree to which people should be controlled, in general. Second, both liberals and conservatives will vary in their opinions on the matter, and both are capable of imposing either great or little control on people. Third, respondents filling in the questionnaire might reflect mixed attitudes in these regards, so it should allow for varying mixtures.

Fourth, the questionnaire should be developed from a valid theoretical framework. In this regard, I referred to Young's (2011) developmental model of the cognitive (mis)perception of the other (see Chap. 31). The model examines how people vary in their respect of their children, partner, and minorities based on their developmental level. The model is Neo-Piagetian cognitively and has 25 steps, but also it describes parallel Neo-Eriksonian steps. Therefore, people could vary in the degree of control that they think people need according to the steps of the model;

Table 34.7 Five-point societal control questionnaire (in relation to conservatism–liberalism attitude) [according to Young's (2011) five-stage Neo-Piagetian model of the cognitive (mis)perception of the other]

Instructions					
First, read the <u>five</u> questions, which describe different levels of control of people (from needing total control to deserving the opposite of total empowerment). Then, starting with Question "A," answer the questions. For each question, you decide who should be doing the control—the government (conservative option), and/or the people (liberal option), and also judge how much control should be applied, on a scale from 0 to 5.					
Question A: PEOPLE NEED TO BE TOTALLY CONTROLLED					
People need to be totally controlled and totally restricted.					
<u>Conservative Option:</u> The **government** needs to prevent bad things, so the government should do this, as well as other institutions/groups that they organize (that is, the people themselves should not do this).					
0	1	2	3	4	5
NEVER	RARELY	SOMETIMES	FREQUENTLY	MOSTLY	ALWAYS
<u>Liberal Option:</u> The government needs to promote good things, and the **people** themselves should develop the self-control needed, as well as other institutions/groups that they organize (that is, the government should not do this for the people).					
0	1	2	3	4	5
NEVER	RARELY	SOMETIMES	FREQUENTLY	MOSTLY	ALWAYS
Question B: PEOPLE NEED TO BE CONTROLLED A LOT, NOT TOTALLY					
People should not be treated so poorly as in Question "A," but they still need control, imposition, manipulation, and so on.					
<u>Conservative Option:</u> The **government** needs to prevent bad things, so the government should do this, as well as other institutions/groups that they organize (that is, the people themselves should not do this).					
0	1	2	3	4	5
NEVER	RARELY	SOMETIMES	FREQUENTLY	MOSTLY	ALWAYS
<u>Liberal Option:</u> The government needs to promote good things, and the **people** themselves should develop the self-control needed, as well as other institutions/groups that they organize (that is, the government should not do this for the people).					
0	1	2	3	4	5

(continued)

Table 34.7 (continued)

NEVER	RARELY	SOMETIMES	FREQUENTLY	MOSTLY	ALWAYS
Question C: PEOPLE NEED TO BE CHANNELED MORE THAN CONTROLLED					
People should not be treated this badly (as in Question "B"), but they still need to be channeled, pacified, or neutralized.					
Conservation Option: The **government** needs to prevent bad things, so the government should do this, as well as other institutions/groups that they organize (that is, the people themselves should not do this).					
0	1	2	3	4	5
NEVER	RARELY	SOMETIMES	FREQUENTLY	MOSTLY	ALWAYS
Liberal Option: The government needs to promote good things, and the **people** themselves should develop the self-control needed, as well as other institutions/groups that they organize (that is, the government should not do this for the people).					
0	1	2	3	4	5
NEVER	RARELY	SOMETIMES	FREQUENTLY	MOSTLY	ALWAYS
Question D: PEOPLE NEED OTHERS TO HAVE CONCERN FOR THEIR WELFARE, NOT THEIR CONTROL					
People should be treated with concern for their welfare, offered responsibility, and so on.					
Conservation Option: The **government** needs to prevent bad things, so the government should do this, as well as other institutions/groups that they organize (that is, the people themselves should not do this).					
0	1	2	3	4	5
NEVER	RARELY	SOMETIMES	FREQUENTLY	MOSTLY	ALWAYS
Liberal Option: The government needs to promote good things, and the **people** themselves should develop the self-control needed, as well as other institutions/groups that they organize (that is, the government should not do this for the people).					
0	1	2	3	4	5
NEVER	RARELY	SOMETIMES	FREQUENTLY	MOSTLY	ALWAYS
Question E: PEOPLE NEED FULL EMPOWERMENT, THE OPPOSITE OF CONTROL					
People are capable of helping and trusting each other, and they should be totally empowered to fully grow and also to help others to do the same.					
Conservation Option: The **government** needs to prevent bad things, so the government should do this, as well as other institutions/groups that they organize (that is, the people themselves should not do this).					
0	1	2	3	4	5
NEVER	RARELY	SOMETIMES	FREQUENTLY	MOSTLY	ALWAYS
Liberal Option: The government needs to promote good things, and the **people** themselves should develop the self-control needed, as well as other institutions/groups that they organize (that is, the government should not do this for the people).					
0	1	2	3	4	5
NEVER	RARELY	SOMETIMES	FREQUENTLY	MOSTLY	ALWAYS

however, whether government or the people themselves should do this, and to what degree, would depend on other factors that influence political ideology.

Comment The questionnaire is nuanced, and can give data related to level and extent of belief that people need to be controlled and whether this should take place more conservatively, liberally, or both. After the scale is validated, it could be used in conjunction with other measures of political ideology, personality, and free will to determine the multiple influences on and outcomes of political ideology.

Chapter Conclusions

The revision of Maslow's classic hierarchical needs/motivation model has been an extremely broad-ranging endeavor. On the one hand, it involved better understanding of psychological maturity, which he defined in terms of self-actualization. In the current approach, not only do I integrate the work of Erikson on generativity but also I add the concepts of psychological completeness/psychological completing. As for the basic physiological needs/motivations that carry forward in development and that are consistently present as essential in life, I consider them embodied processes that lead to embodied activities, either by themselves or as incorporated into higher-order needs/motives. We are enactive, participatory beings, and even the simplest of physiological activities are primed and promoted in the social world. In this sense, each step in development (or moving up the hierarchy of needs/motives that corresponds to these steps) is embodied themselves. How they yoke together in the adaptive flux of life reflects not only an internal process of needs and motives but also an external relational adaptation to the social and environmental field in which we navigate, adjust, and adapt, in the balance of self, other, and world.

References

Aksan, N., & Kochanska, G. (2005). Conscience in childhood: Old questions, new answers. *Developmental Psychology, 41*, 506–516.

Bakan, D. (1966). *The duality of human existence: An essay on psychology and religion*. Chicago: Rand McNally.

Bandura, A. (1977). Self-efficacy: Toward a unifying theory of behavioral change. *Psychological Review, 84*, 191–215.

Bandura, A. (1986). *Social foundations of thought and action: A social cognitive theory*. Englewood Cliffs, NJ: Prentice Hall.

Bandura, A. (1997). *Self-efficacy: The exercise of control*. New York: Freeman.

Baumeister, R. F., Brataslavsky, E., Finkenauer, C., & Vohs, K. D. (2001). Bad is stronger than good. *Review of General Psychology, 5*, 323–370.

Blatt, S. J. (2008). *Polarities of experience: Relatedness and self-definition in personality development, psychopathology, and the therapeutic process*. Washington, DC: American Psychological Association.

Bowlby, J. (1969/1999). *Attachment and loss, Vols. 1–3*. New York: Basic Books.

Bowlby, J. (1979). *The making and breaking of affectional bonds*. London, UK: Tavistock.

Brewer, M. D., & Gardner, W. (1996). Who is this "we"? Levels of collective identity and self representations. *Journal of Personality and Social Psychology, 71*, 83–93.

Brown, K. W., & Ryan, R. M. (2003). The benefits of being present: Mindfulness and its role in psychological well-being. *Journal of Personality and Social Psychology, 84*, 822–848.

Carnes, N. C., & Janoff-Bulman, R. (2012). Harm, help, and the nature of (im)moral (in)action. *Psychological Inquiry, 23*, 137–142.

Carver, C. S., & Scheier, M. F. (2008). Feedback processes in the simultaneous regulation of affect and action. In J. Y. Shah & W. L. Gardner (Eds.), *Handbook of motivation science* (pp. 308–324). New York: Guilford Press.

Deci, E. L., & Ryan, R. M. (1991). A motivational approach to self: Integration in personality. In R. Dienstbier (Ed.), *Nebraska Symposium on Motivation: Perspectives on motivation* (Vol. 38, pp. 237–288). Lincoln, NE: University of Nebraska Press.

Deci, E. L., & Ryan, R. M. (1995). Human autonomy: The basis for true self-esteem. In M. H. Kernis (Ed.), *Plenum series in social/clinical psychology. Efficacy, agency, and self-esteem* (pp. 31–49). New York: Plenum.

Deci, E. L., & Ryan, R. M. (2013). The importance of autonomy for development and well-being. In B. W. Sokol, M. E. Grouzet, & U. Müller (Eds.), *Self-regulation and autonomy: Social and developmental dimensions of human conduct* (pp. 19–46). New York: Cambridge University Press.

Erikson, E. (1959). *Identity and the life cycle*. New York: International Universities Press.

Erikson, E. (1979). *Dimensions of a new identity: The Jefferson lectures in the humanities*. New York: Norton.

Erikson, E. H. (1980). *Identity and the life cycle*. New York: Norton.

Forbes, D. L. (2011). Toward a unified model of human motivation. *Review of General Psychology, 15*, 85–98.

Fraley, R. C., Griffin, B. N., Belsky, J., & Roisman, G. I. (2012). Developmental antecedents of political ideology: A longitudinal investigation from birth to age 18 years. *Psychological Science, 23*, 1425–1431.

Freud, S. (1927/1961). The ego and the id. In J. Strachey (Ed.), and J. Riviere (Trans.), *The standard edition of the complete psychological works of Sigmund Freud*. New York: Norton. (Original work published 1927)

Freud, S. (1933). Warum krieg (Why war)? *Standard Edition of the Complete Psychological Works of Sigmund Freud, 22*, 197–224. London: Hogarth Press.

Gallese, V. (2013). Mirror neurons, embodied simulation and a second-person approach to mindreading. *Cortex, 49*, 2954–2956.

Gallese, V. (2014). Bodily selves in relation: Embodied simulation as second-person perspective on intersubjectivity. *Philosophical Transaction of the Royal Society B Biological Sciences, 369*.

Gilbert, D. T., Fiske, S. T., & Gardner, L. (Eds.). (1998). *Handbook of social psychology* (4th ed.). New York: McGraw-Hill.

Graham, J., & Haidt, J. (2012). Sacred values and evil adversaries: A moral foundations approach. In

M. Mikulincer & P. R. Shaver (Eds.), *The social psychology of morality: Exploring the causes of good and evil* (pp. 11–31). Washington, DC: American Psychological Association.
Graham, J., Nosek, B. A., Haidt, J., Iyer, R., Koleva, S., & Ditto, P. H. (2011). Mapping the moral domain. *Journal of Personality and Social Psychology, 96*, 1029–1046.
Haidt, J. (2007). The new synthesis in moral psychology. *Science, 316*, 998–1002.
Haidt, J. (2008). Morality. *Perspectives on Psychological Science, 3*, 65–72.
Haidt, J. (2012). *The righteous mind: Why good people are divided by politics and religion*. New York: Pantheon.
Haidt, J., & Joseph, C. (2004). Intuitive ethics: How innately prepared intuitions generate culturally variable virtues. *Daedalus, 133*, 55–66.
Haidt, J., & Joseph, C. (2007). The moral mind: How five sets of innate intuitions guide the development of many cultural-specific virtues, and perhaps even modules. In P. Carruthers, S. Laurence, & S. Stich (Eds.), *The innate mind: Foundations and the future* (Vol. 3, pp. 367–392). New York: Oxford University Press.
Haidt, J., & Kesebir, S. (2010). Morality. In S. T. Fiske, D. T. Gilbert, & G. Lindzey (Eds.), *Handbook of social psychology* (5th ed., pp. 797–832). Hoboken, NJ: Wiley.
Hamilton, W. (1964). The genetical evolution of social behavior I and II. *Journal of Theoretical Biology, 7*, 1–52.
James, W. (1890/1950). *The principles of psychology*. Mineola, NY: Dover.
Janoff-Bulman, R. (2009). To provide or protect: Motivational bases of political liberalism and conservatism. *Psychological Inquiry, 20*, 120–128.
Janoff-Bulman, R. (2012). Conscience: The do's and don'ts of moral regulation. In M. Milkuciner & P. Shaver (Eds.), *The social psychology of morality: Exploring the causes of good and evil* (pp. 131–148). Washington, DC: American Psychological Association.
Janoff-Bulman, R., & Carnes, N. C. (2013). Surveying the moral landscape: Moral motives and group-based moralities. *Personality and Social Psychology Review, 17*, 219–236.
Janoff-Bulman, R., Carnes, N., & Sheikh, S. (2014). Parenting style and politics: Early bases of distinct moral orientations. *Journal of Social and Political Psychology, 2*. doi:10.5964/jspp.v2i1.243.
Janoff-Bulman, R., Sheikh, S., & Hepp, S. (2009). Proscriptive versus prescriptive morality: Two faces of moral regulation. *Journal of Personality and Social Psychology, 96*, 521–537.
Kenrick, D. T., Griskevicius, V., Neuberg, S. L., & Schaller, M. (2010). Renovating the pyramid of needs: Contemporary extensions built upon ancient foundations. *Perspectives on Psychological Science, 5*, 292–314.
Kochanska, G. (2002). Committed compliance, moral self, and internalization: A mediational model. *Developmental Psychology, 38*, 339–351.
Kohlberg, L. (1981). *The psychology of moral development (Essays on moral development: Volume 1)*. San Francisco, CA: Harper & Row.
Kohlberg, L. (1984). *The psychology of moral development (Essays on moral development: Volume 2)*. San Francisco, CA: Harper & Row.
Kyselo, M. (2014). The body social: An enactive approach to the self. *Frontiers in Psychology, 5*, 986. doi:10.3389/fpsyg.2014.00986.
Lee, W., Reeve, J., Xue, Y., & Xiong, J. (2012). Neural differences between intrinsic reasons for doing versus extrinsic reasons for doing: An fMRI study. *Neuroscience Research, 73*, 68–72.
Legault, L., & Inzlicht, M. (2012). Self-determination, self-regulation, and the brain: Autonomy improves performance by enhancing neuroaffective responsiveness to self-regulation failure. *Journal of Personality and Social Psychology, 105*, 123–138.
Luyten, P., & Blatt, S. J. (2013). Interpersonal relatedness and self-definition in normal and disrupted personality development. *American Psychologist, 68*, 172–183.
Maslow, A. H. (1943). A theory of human motivation. *Psychological Review, 50*, 370–396.
Maslow, A. H. (1955). Deficiency motivation and growth motivation. In M. R. Jones (Ed.), *Nebraska Symposium on Motivation: 1955*. Lincoln, NE: University of Nebraska Press.
Maslow, A. H. (1967). Self-actualization and beyond. In J. F. T. Bugental (Ed.), *Challenges of humanistic psychology*. New York: McGraw-Hill.
McClelland, D. (1961). *The achieving society*. Princeton, NJ: Van Nostrand.
Mead, G. H. (1934). In C. W. Morris (Ed.), *Mind, self, and society*. Chicago: University of Chicago Press.
Murray, H. A. (1938). *Explorations in personality*. Oxford, UK: Oxford University Press.
Piaget, J. (1937). *La construction du réel chez l'enfant [The construction of reality in the child]*. Neuchatel, Switzerland: Delachaux et Niestlé.
Piaget, J., & Inhelder, B. (1967). The child's conception of space. In *The coordination of perspectives, 8* (pp. 209–246). New York: Norton.
Rogers, C. R. (1963). The actualizing tendency in relation to "motives" and to consciousness. In M. R. Jones (Ed.), *Nebraska Symposium on Motivation* (Vol. 11, pp. 1–24). Lincoln, NE: University of Nebraska Press.
Ryan, R. M., & Deci, E. L. (2000). Self-determination theory and the facilitation of intrinsic motivation, social development, and well-being. *American Psychologist, 55*, 68–78.
Ryan, R. M., & Deci, E. L. (2008). From ego-depletion to vitality: Theory and findings concerning the facilitation of energy available to the self. *Social and Personality Psychology Compass, 2*, 702–717.
Thagard, P., & Wood, J. V. (2015). Eighty phenomena about the self: Representation, evaluation, regulation, and change. *Frontiers in Psychology, 6*, 334. doi:10.3389/psyg.2015.00334.
Weinstein, N., Brown, K. W., & Ryan, R. M. (2009). A multi-method examination of the effects of mindful-

ness on stress attribution, coping, and emotional well-being. *Journal of Research in Personality, 43*, 374–385.

Weinstein, N., Deci, E., & Ryan, R. M. (2011). Motivational determinants of integrating positive and negative past identities. *Journal of Personality and Social Psychology, 100*, 527–544.

Weinstein, N., Przybylski, A. K., & Ryan, R. M. (2013). The integrative process: New research and future directions. *Current Directions in Psychological Science, 22*, 69–74.

Weinstein, N., Ryan, W. S., DeHaan, C. R., Przybylski, A. K., Legate, N., & Ryan, R. M. (2012). Parental autonomy support and discrepancies between implicit and explicit sexual identities: Dynamics of self-acceptance and defense. *Journal of Personality and Social Psychology, 102*, 815–832.

Wilson, E. O. (2012). *The social conquest of earth.* New York: Norton.

Young, G. (2011). *Development and causality: Neo-Piagetian perspectives.* New York: Springer Science + Business Media.

35 Staging Revolutions and Paradigms

Chapter Introduction

The present chapter describes a revised approach to Kuhn's (1962, 1970) concept of scientific paradigm and its change (Overton, 2013). Then, it proceeds to modify it, in turn, according to the present five-step model of generic change.

First, the chapter presents Overton's (2013) advance in understanding paradigmatic structure and change relative to the original Kuhn position. Overton's revision of Kuhn's model involves five levels from domain of inquiry to metatheoretical worldview. Then, I present a reworking of this revised Kuhnian model, including use of the concept of "paradigmatic meta-modeling" or a step in the modeling process beyond the ones considered to date for the establishment and change of paradigms.

The remainder of the chapter considers applications and implications of the revised Neo-Kuhnian model. For example, I show how the process that I followed in building my present Neo-Piagetian and parallel Neo-Eriksonian model fits the evolving nature of science as modeled in my Neo-Kuhnian perspective. Then, I consider the crucial issue of whether causality can be considered as a unifying focus in psychology, and indicate how the search for causality can be modeled according to my present five-step generic change model, which is based on the Neo-Piagetian/Neo-Eriksonian one. The chapter continues with examples of application of the present modeling process to the intellectual endeavor of epistemology in philosophy. It concludes by returning to the concept of the causal self that was introduced at the beginning of the book in the first chapter, and shows how the chapters from after that one to the present one includes relevant concepts and research toward establishing the nature of the causal self and the value of the concept for unifying psychology.

Kuhn's Model of Paradigm Change

Model

According to Overton (2013), Kuhn (1962, 1970) had described a broad meaning of paradigm, so that it includes a disciplinary matrix, which involves a network of shared metaphysical beliefs (e.g., analogies, metaphors) and values. In his conception, worldviews are constitutive features of scientific activity. This approach contrasts with that of neopositivism and conventionalism (e.g., Popper, 1959, 1970), for which metaphysical concepts are "purely heuristic." In this latter "scientific realism" perspective, rigid empiricism/objective truth can be established by "hard data" gathered after conjecture in a discovering and justification process, which includes refutable, falsifiable hypotheses that are put to the test. However, by adding a constitutive metaphysical component to scientific activity, Kuhn's new worldview of scientific paradigm

G. Young, *Unifying Causality and Psychology*, DOI 10.1007/978-3-319-24094-7_35

rejected the scientific epistemology of empiricism (although not empirical study itself!). Also, it rejected a scientific ontology of "fixed objectivist foundationalism," which was instrumental for the extant but limited worldview. Therefore, Kuhn's new epistemology was "constructivist" and the ontology involved activity and engagement by scientists as contributory to and influencing of the scientific process and product.

Comment

Others who contributed to the shift in scientific paradigms include Wittgenstein (1958) and Gadamer (1989), and their logic of a "hermeneutical circle." Science accrues knowledge not just by hypothetico-deductive explanation and inductive logic but also by an "abductive" logic that is more inclusive (e.g., of background ideas) and that is relational.

Lakatos (1970, 1978) and Laudan (1977) extended Kuhn's worldview approach to scientific paradigm by more clearly distinguishing the nested conceptual layers involved. Hard core concepts of a "research" paradigm are at the apex of the hierarchy of nested levels, and function like worldviews. Next, positive heuristics are like midlevel metatheories. Then, families of theories constitute a lower level in the nest. Finally, the lowest level involves a "belt of auxiliary hypotheses" that are empirically testable, falsifiable, and refutable.

Revising Kuhn on Paradigm

Relationism

Overton (2013) proposed a nested model of the concept of scientific paradigm (Kuhn, 1962, 1970). In his model, the construct of relationism is placed at its summit. Other aspects of the model include midrange metatheories, theories, hypotheses, and domains at consecutive lower levels (see Fig. 35.1).

Overton (2013) explained that metatheories provide a coherent framework of background concepts, meanings, resources, and guidelines that provide context for the construction of theories. Similarly, metamethods provide a frame for methods (principles that guide empirical inquiry).

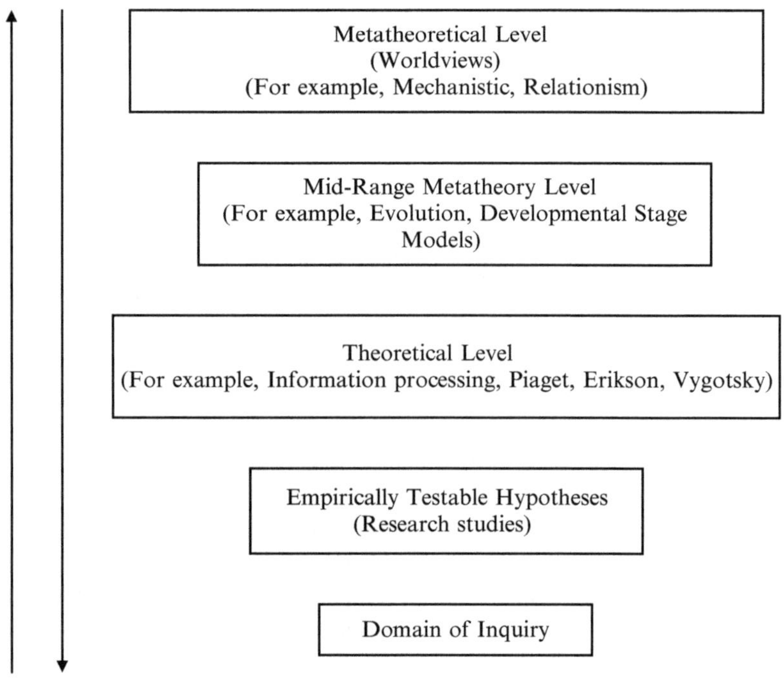

Fig. 35.1 Nested concepts of a scientific paradigm. The figure shows five levels of the nested concepts of a scientific paradigm for a domain. Adapted from Overton (2013, 2015)

Specifically, a metatheory consists of a coherent set of principles and rules (and their narrative) that both describes and delimits the acceptability and meaningfulness of theory or conceptual exploration of a domain and its empirical phenomena. Metamethods describe and delimit the means of inquiry in a discipline.

Overton (2013) referred to scientific disciplines and paradigms, in particular, but I will try to elaborate a paradigmatic frame applicable to any field of scholarship. In this regard, there is little need to change Overton's terminology for the proposed Neo-Kuhnian model. However, for methodology, I refer not only to observation, experimentation, or other rigorous method of data collection, but also to any means of logical analysis of natural phenomena and the product of human activity that helps denote its constituent elements that are helpful for theorizing (which stands in reciprocal relationship to the methods of inquiry in the domain of focus).

Overton (2013) continued that the broadest metatheories in terms of generality and abstractness are worldviews. They consist of a coherent set of principles in epistemology and ontology (issues about the source/justification of knowledge and the fundamental categories of reality, respectively). Worldviews present frameworks about visions of the nature of the world and the nature of how we know it. Midrange metatheories are less broad, general, and abstract than meta-theories, and they are more specific to the domain of inquiry involved. Theories vary in level, too, being either broad or narrow. They align both with the "observational field" of the domain and a superordinate metaview.

Overton (2013) noted that counter evidence to a hypothesis does not literally falsify it in the worldview approach of constructivism. Rather, lack of evidence in support of a hypothesis functions as an anomaly in the problem-solving process associated with the paradigm involved. However, a gathering of sufficient anomalies eventually triggers a scientific crisis that leads to alternative paradigms. The "gestalt switch" in the trigger is pragmatic and heuristic more than realistic.

Comment

In the next section of the chapter, I modify Overton's (2013) Kuhnian model. I show that my version is consistent with the present 25-step Neo-Piagetian/Neo-Eriksonian developmental model. Generally, the compatibility of a revised Kuhnian model of scientific paradigm with my own model gives the latter incremental validity, while giving the former some grounding in a generic model of change.

A Neo-Kuhnian Approach

Model

Overton (2013) has presented a model of paradigm and its change in the sciences that involves five steps (as per Fig. 35.1). However, his model could be expanded by separating into two distinct streams metatheory and theory, and then showing how each develops (e.g., into worldview and integrative theories, respectively). Moreover, a revised Overtonian model of scientific paradigm should show how the two streams of metatheory and theory interact at each level of the nested hierarchy within each stream.

In this regard, in the following, I elaborate a new Kuhnian model of scientific evolution and revolution (as well as the same for rigorous scholarship, in general), using the present five-step model of change. This latter change model underlies the model of steps in cognitive development that I described in Young (2011; 25 steps, having 5 stages × 5 recurrent substages, with 5 steps possible within each of the substages, in a fractalization process).

That is, based on Overton's (2013) five-step Kuhnian model, after its separation into two streams, and also based on my five-step generic change model, I added new components to create two new parallel five-step sequences in each of metatheory and theory building. Then, I determined a common five-step sequence that encompasses both (see Table 35.1).

Table 35.1 The relation of theory, metatheory, and paradigm metamodel in scholarship, in general, and science, in particular

	Area in construction			
Stage	Theory	Metatheory/worldview	Theory creation examples	Paradigmatic metamodel
Coordination	Gathering extent data and concepts in domain of (empirical) inquiry	Gathering extant metaconcepts in domain of reflection	Domain; Development	Coordinated gathering of domain components (facts, constructs)
Hierarchization	Subserving acquired knowledge to testable hypotheses and their (empirical) testing; proof of concept	Subserving acquired knowledge to criticism-resistant metaconcepts impervious to falsification; thought experiments	Stage modeling	Hierarchical arrangement of knowledge and critical analysis
Systematization	Creating mini-theories (leaving the silos), including with further (empirical) inquiry	Creating mini-metatheories	Piagetian series (e.g., infant sensorimotor substage for object permanence); Erikson on steps in identity development	Systematizing mini-metamodels of knowledge base
Multiplication	Expanding broader theories (leaving the silos), including further (empirical) inquiry	Expanding broader metatheories (midrange)	Piagetian stage theory Eriksonian stage theory	Multiplying metamodel scope and application in domain(s)
Integration	Integrating theory in the domain, including with further (empirical) inquiry	Integrating metatheory in the domain	Neo-Piagetian stage theory Neo-Eriksonian stage theory	Integrative metamodeling
Coordination	Five-step process repeats in the multiple		Combined Neo-Piagetian/ Neo-Eriksonian stage theory (Young, 2011, 2012)	Coordinating over domains

In regards to the latter, scientists, scholars, and other deep thinkers move fluidly between theory creation and metatheoretical reflection. The conjoint dialectic between the two modalities leads to creation of an integrated perspective on investigation of the domains(s) at issue and metareflection of their concepts, methods, and data or field of elements. In my model, I refer to this intellectual process that serves toward integrating nature of theory and metatheory as metamodeling. Therefore, I added a column to the table referred to as paradigmatic meta-modeling.

Next, I describe the details of the model in the table, and their relationship to my own models. I start on the left of the table by referring to the five steps in my generic change model, then show how it applies to the change process in paradigms. Specifically, the proposed five steps in change in paradigm relate to the five steps in my generic change model of coordination, hierarchization, systematization, multiplication, and integration. The five-step change model is described generically so that it can apply to any entity in change, within limits, including nonliving systems. In this regard, in Young (2011), I applied it to the development of scientific thought related to developmental psychology and also to Darwinian evolution (see Chap. 12). Therefore, the model is amenable to extension toward explaining paradigm change.

Steps

In this regard, the nested levels of growth in thought about theory, metatheory, and paradigmatic metamodels that I have constructed in a revised Kuhnian/Overtonian model of scientific paradigms and their change consists of five levels, and these are based on the five levels of change in Young's (2011) model of change. Using the same type of logic as used in my extension of my five-step change model to growth in scientific thought in these two latter examples, I formulated five steps in change in each of the columns in Table 35.1 related to the development of theory, metatheory, and paradigmatic metamodel in the growth of scientific paradigm.

In addition, I repeated the coordination level at the end of the five-step series of paradigmatic change in order to indicate that the growth process can continue after passage through the first cycle through more advanced cycles, continuing as each cycle is complete. In the present case, this would refer to coordinating of paradigmatic metamodels and their related metatheories and worldviews. In this regard, I do not maintain that relationism has become the predominant scientific paradigm, nor should it be exclusively so. That is, this should not be the case, given the advantages of the empiricist, neopositivist, and scientific realism approach. The latter worldview is in need of monitoring for its excesses (e.g., reductionism), but it does not require scientific surgery or a full ablation. Rather, it needs coordination with the former, the worldview of relationism. Therefore, it appears to me that we need a productive, constant dialectic between positivism/empiricism and constructivism/relationism in scholarship/science, in general. The table indicates the five steps through which this suggested process might proceed.

The column that is easiest to grasp in the table relates to theory. The five steps involved in theory building relate to: (a) selecting the domain and coordinating the gathering of domain data and concepts. For science, data would refer to outputs of observation, experimentation, and other legitimate means of empirical investigation. The initial impetus for data gathering might be a (testable) hypothesis with an explicit prediction, or the idea involved could be less specific.

(b) Either way, after having gathered (coordinating) the key elements in a domain, the investigator then enters the step of hierarchization and proceeds to develop a hypothesis of the model in which new data are sought in the domain. The investigator subordinates the search for data to some hypothesis or search concept. Methodology proceeds to operationalization and a design that allows appropriate data gathering, and consequent inference, which might end up concluding that either there is a lack of positive, supportive results (toward falsifiability) or, instead, supportive ones of the hypothesis or search concept at issue.

The process described is explicit for science but, for other areas of scholarship, it might apply and be implicit and aspirational, and perhaps having rigorous enough procedures and logical-based criticism and inference, thereby allowing "proof of concept." The data involved in nonscientific scholarship might not be the hard, empirical-type that science seeks but, nevertheless, still these data could be well-defined units of information. Moreover, the relational stance that is part of this integrated model that I have created does not admit to context-free, free-standing scientific bits of information, given their constitutive nature, so that the distinction between scientific and nonscientific data might not be as clear-cut as some presume.

(c) In the third step of theory construction, after the hierarchical phase and the one of coordination, the new data acquired might be organized systematically into a theory, one that can be further tested and one that can help explain the data that has been gathered and allows for new predictions. When new data deriving from hypothesis-testing are relatively narrow in scope, the investigator is working toward creating mini-theories. If the data are inter-, trans-, or otherwise multidisciplinary, or even simply cross-domain within a discipline, the investigator might be leaving the "silo" toward higher-order data and conceptual integration.

(d) This process of theory construction accelerates in the next step in theorizing, in which broader theories are created, perhaps with more synthetic methodologies and data-seeking procedures, as well a process that I refer to as multiplication. The original systemic model is used to traverse a broad range of areas in order to expand its scope and also show its utility in reframing them in its image.

(e) Next, in integrative theory building, investigators build theories that encapsulate much of the data and concepts in a domain, which allows for testable predictions of new supportive data by way of falsifiable hypotheses, and also they permit valid critique of competing theories. The latter might include revealing their empirical and conceptual errors or limitations, explaining their data and concepts in a better way, and so on. [Indeed this type of criticism is part of the scientific or logical reasoning process that should be evident at each stage in theory construction.]

Example

The table gives an example of theory building based on my own work (Young, 2011, 2012) on the present 25-step model of development. The domain concerns my interest in finding parallel cognitive and affective developmental sequences in development over the lifespan based on Piaget's work, in particular. Both Case (e.g., 1992) and Fischer (1980; Fischer & Biddell, 2006) had attempted an integration such as this. In my conceptualization, I juxtaposed their models in a table and compared and contrasted their approaches, leading to my own Neo-Piagetian model of five stages in development. Using Piaget's sensorimotor series of steps in the infancy period, I created generic labels for the steps that could apply to early or later stages, or any change process for that matter, even nonliving (this led to a 5 stage×5 substage model). Then, I created a comparable Neo-Eriksonian sequence, adding 17 steps to his 8-step stage sequence. I assured that within each step of the correspondence between the Neo-Piagetian and the Neo-Eriksonian sequences in the combined 25-step model, the characteristics of any one step in the latter socioaffective sequence matched its pair in the former cognitive one. In short, the theory building process in which I engaged built on Piaget's and Erikson's extant theories to create a superordinate model that expanded both of them so that the new proposed respective pathways are seen to emerge in parallel and match over the lifespan.

In doing this, looking back, I followed the theory building model of five steps described in the table.

(a) That is, first, I coordinated the two major prior Neo-Piagetian stage models in cognitive development. In juxtaposing them, their overlaps and lacunae became evident.

(b) Then, based on the above juxtaposition, I showed what was missing in each. I especially found it useful to show how the missing elements in their models led to incorrect or incomplete understanding of the domain.

(c) This led to the creation of my own model to accommodate to the missing and incorrect elements of the prior models. I showed how it could better explain those inconsistencies and also indicate new ways forward in understanding the field. That I used what I consider Piaget's best empirical work, on the steps in infant sensorimotor development, to elaborate the theory, seemed quite supportive of it. [My elaboration of Erikson's model did not depend on comparison of Neo-Eriksonian models because there have not been any, aside perhaps Marcia's work (1980) on identity, which does not help in revising Erikson's eight-step stage sequence.]

The two integrative models that I created, one cognitive and one socioaffective, not only were built on prior theories and built to parallel each other. That is, in this regard, I had attempted to create a more superordinate level of model building.

Specifically, the Neo-Piagetian and Neo-Eriksonian (sub)stage series that I created allowed the first-ever integrative, cross-domain, lifespan model in the field (Young, 2011, 2012). Therefore, I believe that I have reached the step of systematization in my model building of development and change.

(d–e) Also, the level of theorizing is ready to proceed to the next integrative plane in my model (multiplication), and it is ready for further integration after that. I have begun this process in Young (2014), and it continues in the present work, including with the present model on theory, metatheory, and paradigmatic metamodel relationships in scientific paradigm construction and their own five-step evolution. An integrated theory on development, change mechanisms, causality, and so on, awaits further thought and effort.

This ends presentation of the theory building component of the present model of growth in scientific paradigm, as presented in the table. In the following, I continue to apply the present model to theory building, this time to show how it can help integrate or unify psychology itself.

Unifying Psychology

Modeling

In the following, I review briefly the five steps in the evolution of metatheory or worldview. It moves from a coordinated gathering of relevant material, to a hierarchical arrangement of knowledge, to a presumably inclusive and airtight model (called a metaconcept for present purposes). The process involved might include thought experiments, as in philosophy. In systematization, a mini-metatheory might be established, leading to its multiplicative expansion into a broader, mid-range metatheory, which might then lead to a more integrative one over the domain involved. The process might repeat at a superordinate level, leading to a dialectical fusion of competing or complementary metatheories into a higher-order union, through another cycle of the five steps involved.

In the process of creating paradigmatic metamodels that reciprocally interrelate theory and metatheory at each step of their creation, the same five-step sequence applies. After coordinating information and constructing the theories and metatheories involved, the knowledge acquired would be tentatively arranged hierarchically in what makes first sense for an overarching frame. Critical analysis and reasoning would be used, but, as with all equivalent hierarchical steps in theory and metatheory building, some of the first tentative hierarchical arrangements could be subject to revision or even complete change after further critical analysis. Eventually, a more systematic mini-metamodel would be created, to use the language of the equivalent steps for theory and metatheory at this level. Once achieved, the model could be extended in the domain at issue, or even out of it, or otherwise applied and multiplied. Eventually, an integrated metamodel could be created ready for coordination with others over domains, in a cycle of a paradigmatic growth.

Theories

The present work is based on many critical sources other than those involving Piaget and Erikson (see Fig. 35.2). The bottom portion of the figure gives the names of critical theorists that have influenced my understanding of causality (e.g., Gibson, Bowlby, but especially Darwin, whose evolutionary theory guided me in my doctoral dissertation; Young & Gouin Décarie, 1977). The upper portion of the figure lists areas of study important to the present work, especially those related to genetics and to the brain. There are some areas of study important to psychopathology (e.g., differential susceptibility). Finally, there are some that attempt to be unifying (e.g., embodiment, dynamical systems theory, the biopsychosocial model).

For the middle of the figure, I placed a concept that has not been considered as potentially unifying but it cuts across many areas of brain and behavior and could be an important common unifying behavioral mechanism (activation/inhibition coordination; Young, 2011). However, the central concept of the present work, that of causality, would seem to be the most appropriate unifying construct for psychology and related disciplines. It is central to every area of inquiry on the nature of humans, of nature itself, and of the world and universe. Perhaps because of its centrality and pervasiveness, it has been left

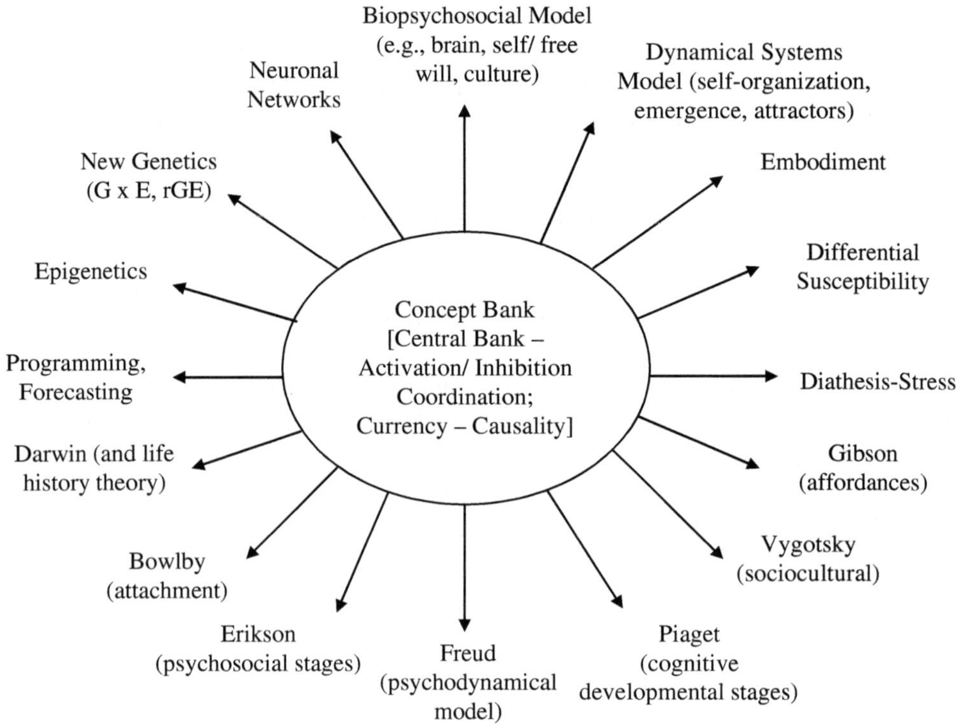

Fig. 35.2 Influential theorizing contributing to the present model of causality as a unifying concept in psychology (and science, scholarship) (noninclusive)

Table 35.2 Stages in scientific (natural, scholarly) exploration

	Question	
Level	What information; observation; data (product)	Why (process)
Coordination	Surface search	Tentative explanation
Hierarchization	Subsurface probe	Causal mapping
Systematization	Deep micro understanding	Mechanistic understanding
Multiplication	Extension/application	System-wide elaboration
Integration	Broad macro understanding	Global causality
Coordination	Five-step process repeats in the multiple	

aside in efforts to unify psychology. However, the present work is dedicated toward filling this conceptual gap.

The Model

Table 35.2 presents my concluding arguments on the centrality of causality for the unification of psychology and of related disciplines (as well as any rigorous study or scholarship on the nature of humans, of nature, and of the world/universe). The table indicates that the cardinal questions in our explorations in these regards concern the "what" (product), or the description of the phenomenon at issue (also other terms in this regard include the "which," the "where") and the "why" (process) of the phenomenon at issue, or the causality (also the "how"). We gather information on a topic of interest, perhaps act to create new information, draw back and reflect toward understanding it, and conjecture about the causes.

Moreover, for each of the two major questions at issue, of what and why, (and I acknowledge they can be subdivided, as with Aristotle's four causes and Tinbergen's (1963) four questions), the answers become more refined as we proceed; moreover, I posit that the evolution of our understanding of the what and why of behavior follow the same five-step sequence as in other growth models in the present work.

In this regard, at the level of the what, the five steps in growth in our inquiry concern surface search (coordination), subsurface probe (hierarchization), forming a deeper understanding, but at the micro level (systematization), extension/application once achieved (multiplication), and then a broad integrative macro-understanding.

For the question of why, the corresponding causal advances move through tentative exploration in coordination, to causal mapping (in hierarchization), and then to the critical level of mechanistic understanding in correspondence with deep micro-understanding. The last two steps refer to elaboration throughout the system involved (multiplication) and, finally, global causality for the macro integration level.

Of course, casual "why" process elucidation could lag behind descriptive "what" product elucidation in the steps involved. At some point, the advances in what and why understanding coalesce into a repeat process of differentiating a broader search and understanding of multiple "whats" and "whys." The human imperative asks for nothing else.

Philosophy

In the following, I provide another way that the present five-step generic change model can be applied to philosophy, and take as a starting point a model developed in Young (2011). Using my models of epistemology and of the change process, I show how epistemological models can be constructed toward increasing integration.

In terms of epistemology, in Young (2011), I presented a flexible, synthetic, overarching stance about the constructed knowledge acquisition process of reality that I referred to as "co-existential." One axis of the model presented considers that some points of view on the matter deny that knowledge acquisition of reality is a social process, while other schools do not. Another axis in the model relates to whether objective reality influences its acquisition, and opinions differ on this issue, too (see Table 35.3).

The combined epistemological view presented, which reflects the integration of the six approaches evident on the matter in the intersection of the two axes of the model, melds the different constructivist and realistic tendencies in epistemological stance. In this regard, the combined or co-existential epistemological model that I created describes a multifactorial, relativistic, and dialectical position on the validity of each of the six perspectives involved in understanding the knowledge acquisition process of reality. On the one hand, objective elements in reality can "inform and dictate" their subjective construction by the individual. Moreover, this might happen in a process of "social co-construction." On the other hand, at the same time, although elements of an individual's reality seem especially constructed socially, there are also objectives/elements in reality that would appear "universally apperceived."

The integrated epistemological model presented might make logical sense, but its manner of construction in each of us needs to go through its own learning process. In this sense, just as I have described how science constructs paradigmatic understanding, and that it appears that each of the apparently contradictory positivistic and relational approaches have their positive attributes that lend themselves to the development of a combined, superordinate science and scholarship construction, each of the schools of thought in epistemology, although apparently contradictory, have their positive attributes that lend themselves to their unification in a superordinate co-existential model. The more realistic or constructivist, schools of thought in epistemology might not be separable at all, and are constituted through their interaction (or intraaction), lending themselves to the creation of a superordinate structure. Therefore, as we navigate these sticky

Table 35.3 Epistemological stances about constructed knowledge acquisition of reality[a]

Is knowledge acquisition of reality social?	Does objective reality influence its acquisition?	
	No	Yes
Not relevant	Reality is constructed (Radical, material constructivism)	Reality informs its gradual construction (Critical, final constructivism)
Not necessarily	Constructing is reality (Existentialism)	Reality dictates its construction (Efficient, objective constructivism)
Yes	Shared constructing is reality (Social, formal constructivism)	Reality informs its social construction (Coconstructivism)

The table summarizes six schools of thought about constructivist epistemology. They are classified according to their perspective on two major issues: (1) Does objective reality influence knowledge acquisition? (2) Is knowledge acquisition always a process of social construction? Three of the six schools of epistemology being considered do not adhere to the view that objective reality can influence very directly the acquisition of knowledge. First, radical constructivism argues that reality does not influence the knowledge acquisition process and that reality is apprehended or invented through mental approximations. In this view, social processes are not necessarily inherently important in knowledge comprehension. Second, existentialism attributes fundamental importance to the social process in knowledge acquisition. Participatory co-beings share cultural meanings. In existentialism, constructing seems crucial in the acquisition of knowledge. Third, social constructivism adds that only through social dialogue could constructs of reality emerge and change. Three of the six epistemological schools under discussion argue that objective reality can directly affect the process of knowledge acquisition. First, critical or alternative constructivism (e.g., Piaget) maintains that humans gradually acquire an increasing accuracy in their representation of reality through interactions with reality. Reality construction is not necessarily a social act, however. Second, efficient constructivism perceives reality's roles as more direct and immediate in fostering its own understanding. Social objects might be involved in the process of knowledge acquisition, but not necessarily so. Third, in co-constructivism, objective reality always co-participates in or informs the social dialogue in which conceptions of reality become formulated. The present approach is to consider each of the schools valid, as none can take precedence or can even exclude the others in all circumstances in thought. Therefore, the model that I am proposing is multifactorial, relativistic, and dialectical, but respects each of the approaches for their contributions to understanding knowledge acquisition and reality. Adopted with permission of Springer Science+Business Media. Young, G. (2011). *Development and causality: Neo-Piagetian perspectives*. New York: Springer Science+Business Media; with kind permission from Springer Science+Business Media B. V. [Table 35.1, Page 810]
[a]Also applies to the epistemology about constructed knowledge acquisition of paradigms

philosophical issues, the present five-step generic change model should apply to how the superordinate structure is created.

Given the presently suggested sequence of coordination, hierarchization, systematization, multiplication, and integration in thought processes within the development of abstract understanding and, then, in the development of superordinate abstract understanding, *grosso modo*, first, at an abstract and then at a superordinate abstract level, it would seem that we might proceed through phases toward the integration of constructive and realist epistemologies. Specifically, in our search for understanding, we might grapple with how to integrate the variants of the extant models within each of these epistemologies by passing through the five-stage sequence described (coordination, hierarchization, systematization, multiplication, integration). For example, for the second stage of constructing superordinate abstract structures, I have traced one integrated solution through these five steps, as presented in Table 35.4.

The general message that follows elaboration of this five-step sequence for epistemological construction is that it might help in most any complex problem solving and logical analysis. The second message is that the integrated epistemological model presented in Table 35.4 can help decipher a more complex model of the creation of paradigmatic thought. It would appear that more than an integration of positivistic and relational perspectives is required, as I had argued previously, in that both views can be further differentiated along the lines of the five steps suggested in the table.

Table 35.4 Epistemological construction according to the present five-step generic change model

Step	Explanation
Abstract coordination	Two models juxtaposed
Abstract hierarchization	One hierarchized as predominant
Abstract systematization	New system subsuming both created
Abstract multiplication	Other extent models reworked into system
Abstract integration	Integrated model developed
Superordinate abstract coordination	Cycle repeats, e.g., for positivism or constructivism, depending on which one had been developed first in the above, or perhaps both develop. Ultimately, both streams might be integrated into an overarching epistemological framework

Causal Self

Introduction

This section of the chapter stands as an overview of the book and its major theme that causality can help in the unification of psychology. I have argued that causality is central to psychology in two major ways. First, it constitutes one part of the task to describe the "what" and the "why" of behavior. Second, causality is central to our thought and behavior. In this regard, I have called our species *Homo Causa*, and argued that the key characteristic of the self is the causal one, leading me to create the term of the "causal self." In the following, I survey some critical concepts in the book that inform the concept of the causal self and also the importance of the causal self for grasping human nature and human exceptionality.

Model

The present work emphasizes the essential role of free will in behavior. It promotes the concept of freedom in being (free will belief and having a sense of free will) as integral to the personal component to the biopsychosocial model of behavioral causality. We ourselves potentially constitute the critical, active axis of the determining forces of our behavior, even surpassing those of the more passive but nevertheless potent forces of biology and environment. This concept helps specify the apex of causal action in the self, in which the freedom of being, belief in free will, and having a sense of free will contribute to the control and direction to our behavior. In this regard, free will exists and helps render us causal selves.

For many models of behavior that we examine, there is room for personal contributions to the causation of our behavior, with clear exceptions found in reductionist views such as radical behaviorism and extreme neuroscience. The self can constitute the third force or tertium quid in behavioral causality. Behavior can be emergent. Psychotherapy is based on the assumption that people can learn to take better control of their lives. Folk psychology admits to a belief in personal control and common sense psychology would agree. The concept of the causal self helps unify these and related conceptions to indicate that the person can be an active agent in determining her or his own behavior and that behavior can emerge from its system beyond what the component pattern in the system at any one time might dictate. We are more than our past and present when we intervene between them and our future.

Causality can be graphed and analyzed statistically in extremis, but in the end it is individually-determined, and created in context from moment to moment rather than reflecting statistical procedures and populations norms. Each moment of our lives can take new directions based on our causality determinations, and components of our behavioral system, such as our self-determining causal axes in thought and behavior, can lead us toward better adaptive ends than our biology and environment might dictate. We are causality engines who function toward adaptive ends that are individually-determined, including in creation of a better functioning causal self that can help free us from those more passive influences on us.

The section on the brain in the book refers to the connectome and the section on genes refers to multiple-omics. However, despite the fast-accelerating work on the biological contributions to biology, as well as on the environmental side (e.g., work on early adversity), behavior is always a reflection of biological and environmental influences acting together. However, even that interaction is compounded by its interaction with each of us as independent, active agents contributing to our own causality. To explain behavior, there is not just Nature or Nurture, or Nature and Nurture, but also Nature, Nurture, and Ourselves (including our Causal Selves).

I have revised Maslow's model of hierarchical needs to integrate a tripartite distinction in the self, which I refer to as the self-definitional self, relatedness self, and environmental or mastery/competent self. Certainly, the concept of the causal self can enrich understanding of the component selves of this model. Moreover, in the model, the selves are considered to develop through five steps, ones related to my developmental model and onto which Maslow's five levels of Maslow's hierarchical needs map quite well. In this regard, the growth of the causal self would seem to follow the same progression. Note that I applied my model to the growth of social self working models, a concept that I developed for attachment theory, and this model might speak to the causal self, as well.

In Table 35.5, I elaborate further these ideas. Essentially, the table indicates that the causal self develops in five stages according to my Neo-Piagetian model. The stages in the development of the causal self are called—(a) reflexive precausal, (b) sensorimotor causal, (c) perioperational causal, (d) abstract causal, and (e) collective intelligence causal. The cognitive logic associated with each of the stages, can be characterized, respectively, as (a) nonlogical, (b) prelogical, (c) perilogical (which refers to quasilogical in the first preoperational part of the stage and logical in the second concrete operational part of the stage), and then (d) hyperlogical, and (e) logical at a collective superordinate level. Therefore, in terms of working models for free will and for the causal self, simply enough, one could describe them as, respectively, free will/causal self—(a) precausal nonlogical models, (b) sensorimotor prelogical causal models, (c) perioperational perilogical (quasilogical and logical) causal models, (d) abstract hyperlogical causal models, and (e) superordinate collective intelligence causal models. Within each of the five stages in the development of these working models, as with other similar models in my work, they should pass through five substages related to coordination, hierarchization, systemization, multiplication, and integration. To see how a model of stages with substages works in presenting cognitive development related to internal working models, refer to Tables 31.2–31.6 in Chap. 31 where social self working models/schemata applied to the development of the social self. These series of tables illustrate well how the models/schemata related to free will/causal self models would change over the lifespan.

Table 35.5 Free will/causal self working models

Stage	Logic	Free will/causal self working models
Reflexive precausal self	Nonlogical	Precausal nonlogical models
Sensorimotor causal self	Prelogical	Sensorimotor prelogical causal models
Perioperational causal self	Perilogical (quasilogical and logical)	Perioperational perilogical (quasilogical and logical) causal models
Abstract causal self	Hyperlogical	Abstract hyperlogical causal models
Collective intelligence causal self	Collective superordinate logical	Superordinate collective intelligence causal models

Adopted with permission of Springer Science+Business Media. Young, G. (2011). *Development and causality: Neo-Piagetian perspectives*. New York: Springer Science+Business Media; with kind permission from Springer Science+Business Media B. V. [Third column: Table 17.1, Page 393]

Conclusion

In the present book I created many more concepts related to causality, such as embodied causality, and together they could help in differentiating the concept of the causal self. Causality would seem to be a central unifying concept in psychology, and the causal self could be helpful toward central unifying concept for both. That being said, the concept of causal self constitutes a heuristic one, and our psychology might not include a single central locus of causality-related personhood. As argued, the concept could help unify the study of causality in behavior, psychology itself, and perhaps even different concepts of the self, but not by itself nor toward considering it the be all and end all in behavioral causality.

Chapter Conclusions

The present chapter is recursive/reflexive one in that it has elucidated how scientific paradigms change, and I applied the model to understanding how the model from which it was derived (Young, 2011; on parallels in Neo-Piagetian and Neo-Eriksonian (sub)stage acquisitions) reflects the structuration and change process described in it. The Neo-Kuhnian model that I have developed has the potential to establish the change process in any type of scholarship, not just science. Moreover, it illustrates, in general, that the generic change model that I have developed based on the Neo-Piagetian/Neo-Eriksonian developmental model that I have created might have extensive applicability.

References

Case, R. (1992). Neo-Piagetian theories of child development. In R. J. Sternberg & C. A. Berg (Eds.), *Intellectual development* (pp. 161–196). New York: Cambridge University Press.

Fischer, K. W. (1980). A theory of cognitive development: The control and construction of hierarchies of skills. *Psychological Review, 87*, 477–531.

Fischer, K. W., & Biddell, T. R. (2006). Dynamic development of action and thought. In W. Damon & R. M. Lerner (Eds.), *Handbook of child psychology: Theoretical models of human development* (Vol. 1, pp. 313–399). New York: Wiley.

Gadamer, H. G. (1989). *Truth and method* (J. Weinsheimer & D. Marshall, Trans.), (2nd ed.). New York: Crossroad. (Original work published 1960).

Kuhn, T. S. (1962). *The structure of scientific revolutions*. Chicago, IL: University of Chicago Press.

Kuhn, T. S. (1970). *The structure of scientific revolutions* (2nd ed.). Chicago, IL: University of Chicago Press.

Lakatos, I. (1970). Falsification and the methodology of scientific research programmes. In I. Lakatos & A. Musgrave (Eds.), *Criticism and the growth of knowledge* (pp. 91–196). New York: Cambridge University Press.

Lakatos, I. (1978). *The methodology of scientific research programmes: Philosophical papers* (Vol. 1). New York: Cambridge University Press.

Laudan, L. (1977). *Progress and its problems: Towards a theory of scientific growth*. Berkeley, CA: University of California Press.

Marcia, J. E. (1980). Identity in adolescence. In J. Adleson (Ed.), *Handbook of adolescent psychology* (pp. 159–187). New York: Wiley.

Overton, W. F. (2013). Relationism and relational developmental systems: A paradigm for developmental science in the post-Cartesian era. In R. M. Lerner & J. B. Benson (Eds.), *Advances in child development and behavior. Embodiment and epigenesis: Theoretical and methodological issues in understanding the role of biology within the relational developmental system. Part A: Philosophical, theoretical, and biological dimensions* (Vol. 44, pp. 21–64). Oxford, UK: Elsevier.

Overton, W. F. (2015). Taking conceptual analyses seriously. *Research in Human Development, 12*, 163–171.

Popper, K. (1959). *The logic of scientific discovery*. London: Hutchinson.

Popper, K. (1970). Normal science and its dangers. In I. Lakatos & A. Musgrave (Eds.), *Criticism and the growth of knowledge* (pp. 51–58). New York; Cambridge University Press.

Tinbergen, N. (1963). On aims and methods in ethology. *Zeitschrift für Tierpsychologie, 20*, 410–433.

Wittgenstein, L. (1958/1953). *Philosophical investigations* (G. E. M. Anscombe, Trans.), (3rd ed.). Englewood Cliffs, NJ: Prentice Hall. (Original work published 1953).

Young, G. (2011). *Development and causality: Neo-Piagetian perspectives*. New York: Springer Science+Business Media.

Young, G. (2012). A unitary Neo-Piagetian/Neo-Eriksonian model of development: Fundamental assumptions and meta-issues. *New Ideas in Psychology, 30*, 241–249.

Young, G. (2014). *Malingering, feigning, and response bias in psychiatric/psychological injury: Implications for practice and court*. Dordrecht, Netherlands: Springer Science+Business Media.

Young, G., & Gouin Décarie, T. (1977). An ethology-based catalogue of facial/vocal behavior in infancy. *Animal Behavior, 25*, 95–107.

New Directions in Psychological Causality

36

Chapter Introduction

In this chapter, I review the models by (a) Barlow, Ellard, Sauer-Zavala, Bullis, and Carl (2014) on neuroticism, (b) Verbruggen, McLaren, and Chambers (2014) on self-control, and (c) Kopala-Sibley and Zuroff (2014) on self-definition and relatedness. In addition, I present modifications of the graphic depictions of their models in light of the generic approach adopted.

Based on their attempts to grasp the causality in these areas, I created an integrated generic graphic model of behavioral causality. The causal model includes distal and proximal influences. The central construct in the former type of influence is the biopsychosocial model. For the latter, it involves an interaction of top-down, macro- and bottom-up micro-processes. For behavior, the outcome includes possible disorder and dysfunction as well as normal behavior. The model involves evolutionary and developmental factors, and includes context. As a type of proof of concept, once the generic model was created, I proceeded to apply it to the area of free will and self-control depletion. Then, I turned to applying it to the area of Posttraumatic Stress Disorder (PTSD). Also, it appeared to help see the larger picture of causality generally.

To close this last chapter of the book (and the book, as well), I return to my five-step generic change model, in particular. I apply it to multiple areas, but focus on free will, one of the primary topics of the book. In addition, I examine changes in worldview with the model, as well as a mechanism in change itself (activation–inhibition coordination). The chapter concludes with brief mention of the limits of my modeling endeavors. Also, it asks to what degree causality can become an integrating construct in psychology and to what degree psychology can be integrated. It ends at the beginning, returning to consider the book's initial goals and the manner in which they were met.

Models of Neuroticism, Self-Control, and Self/Other

Neuroticism

Barlow et al. (2014) postulated that the origins of neuroticism lay in a set of triple vulnerabilities—a general biological one, a general psychological one, and a specific psychological one (see Fig. 36.1). Neuroticism develops when the psychological vulnerability acts on the effects of earlier vulnerabilities.

The general, largely learned psychological vulnerability in the development of neuroticism consists of a heightened sense of unpredictability/uncontrollability, and associated effects resulting from early adverse experience. The specific psychological vulnerability that is involved at the time of the disorder helps channel the neuroticism developed from the general vulnerabilities into specific disorders. The general vulnerabilities

G. Young, *Unifying Causality and Psychology*, DOI 10.1007/978-3-319-24094-7_36

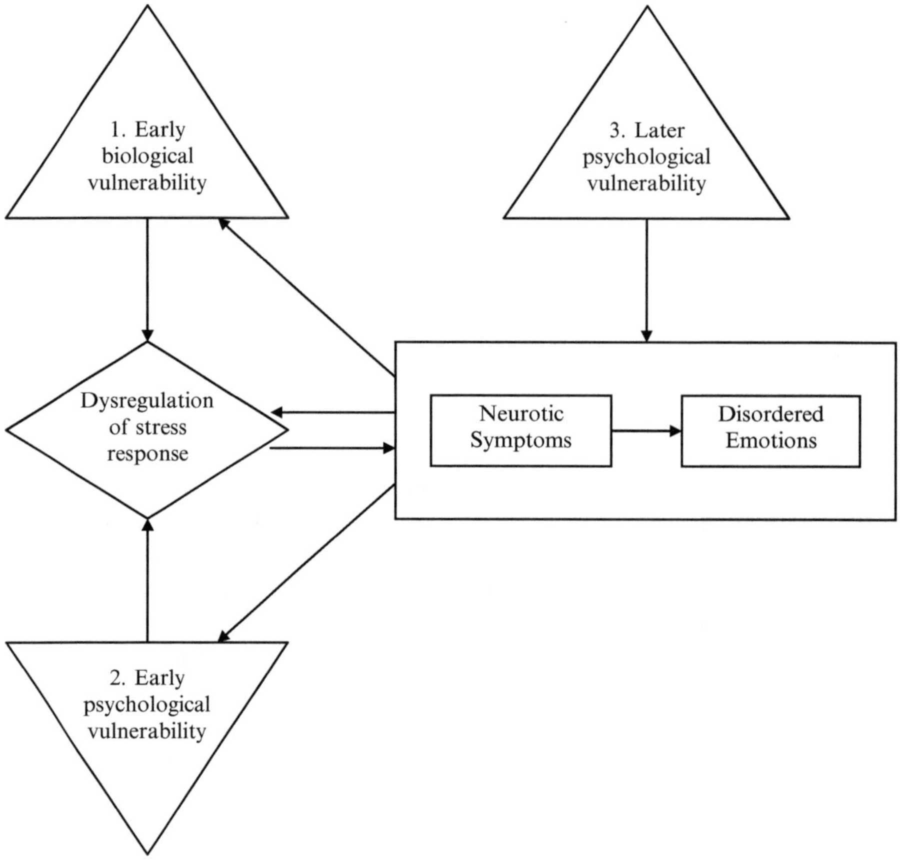

Fig. 36.1 The triple vulnerability model of neuroticism/emotional disorder. Neuroticism/emotionally disordered behavior arises from both early vulnerabilities (biopsychological) and later psychological ones. The mediators include the early effects on the stress response. Adapted from Barlow et al. (2014)

apply earlier on, and they lead to early dysregulation of neural circuits and hormonal functioning associated with heightened response to stress, threat, and fear, e.g., hyperexcitability and exaggerated or inappropriate arousal.

Self-Control

Verbruggen et al. (2014) presented a mechanistic model of self-control involving (at the most basic level) cognitive processes of signal detection, action selection, and action execution (see Fig. 36.2). The authors argued that more general concepts, such as the putative role of inhibition in action control and behavior change, lack sufficient explanatory power.

In their model, Verbruggen et al. (2014) place distal factors to the left. Development and learning constitute factors that influence the more proximal mechanisms in behavioral control. The latter mechanisms include rule construction, predictive control, and outcome monitoring. They are facilitated by cue detection and selection, leading to execution of the behavior involved.

Self/Other

Kopala-Sibley and Zuroff (2014) developed a model of the origins of Blatt's (2008) self-definitional and relatedness domains (see Fig. 36.3). Self-definition refers to the person's habitual patterns of thoughts, feelings, and

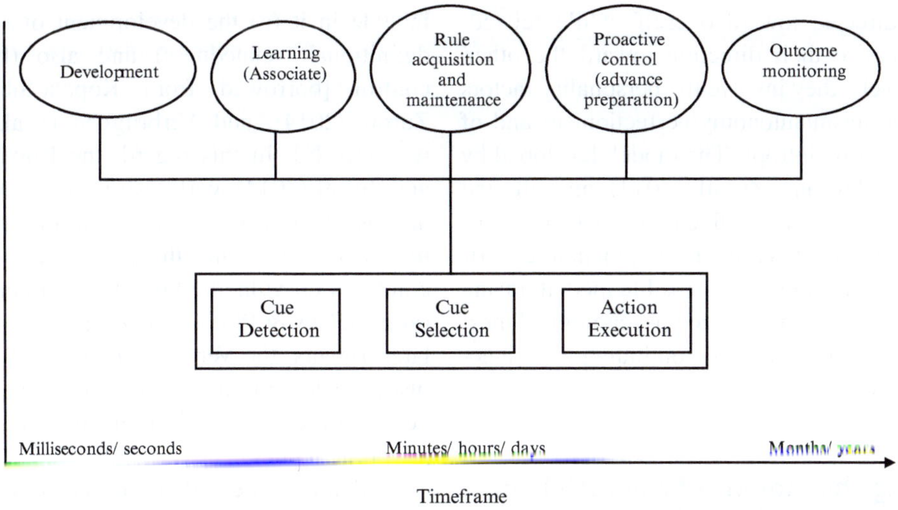

Fig. 36.2 Cues and actions as the basis of behavior. The figure illustrates how rule acquisition/maintenance, proactive control/advance preparation, and outcome monitoring all involve detection/selection and execution in the link between cues and action (over different temporal frames and with influences of learning and development involved). Adapted from Verbruggen et al. (2014)

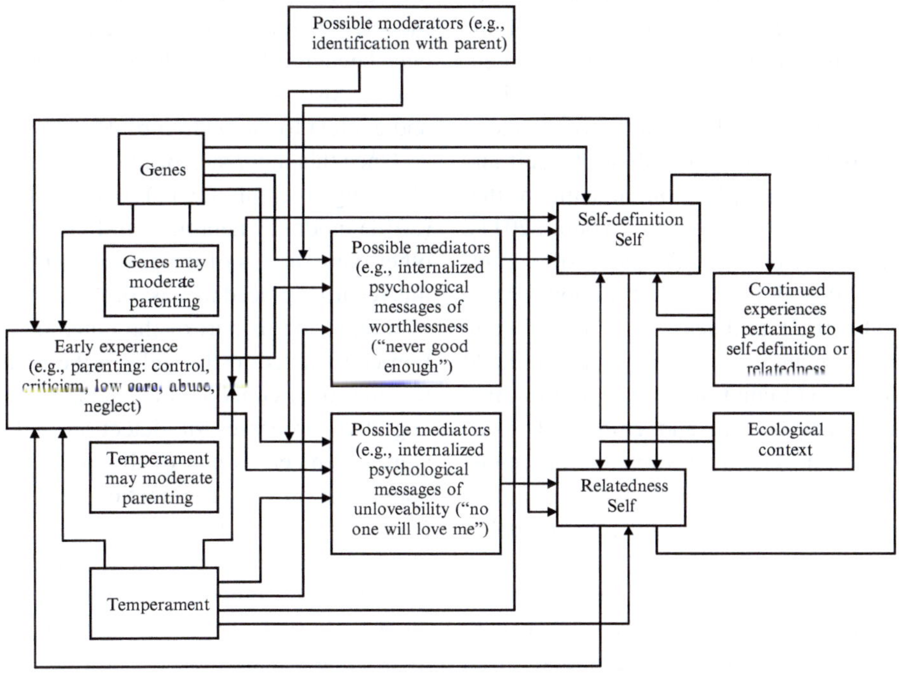

Fig. 36.3 A proposed model of the development of self-definition and relatedness. Based on the work of Blatt (2008) on self-definition and relatedness, Kopala-Sibley and Zuroff (2014) developed a model that illustrates the range of influences on their development. The influences include distal genetic and temporal ones, as well as early experiences. The model includes proximal moderators and mediators, including internalized psychological messages of self-worth and loveability. Relative to the other models in this chapter by Barlow et al. (2014) and Verbruggen et al. (2014), the work of Kopala-Sibley and Zuroff (2014) has provided a more detailed framework for understanding both distal and proximal factors in behavioral outcomes (e.g., genes, early experience, temperament, and mediators and moderators, respectively). Adapted from Kopala-Sibley and Zuroff (2014)

actions directed toward oneself, while relatedness refers to their direction toward the other. Respectively, they involve the personality factors of self-criticism/autonomy/perfectionism and of dependency/sociotropy. The model developed by Kopala-Sibley and Zuroff (2014) on self and other includes distal influences, such as genes and temperament, early developmental experiences (e.g., in parenting), possible mediators and moderators (e.g., internalized psychological messages), and contextual and continuing experiencing factors.

Revising the Models of Neuroticism, Self-Control, and Self/Other

Neuroticism

The figure created by Barlow et al. (2014) to represent their triple-vulnerability model of neuroticism could be altered to include some of the distal risk factors for neuroticism that they mentioned, such as genetics and parenting practices. In addition, one could add proximal risk factors, such as internalized messages about the self and environment (for example, from attachment theory, being loved and loveable; see Young, 2011). Psychological factors include locus of control (Rotter, 1966) and negative attributional style (Alloy et al., 2012), as discussed in Barlow et al. (2014). Also, related to outcome, one could add the behavioral and emotional dysregulation that accompanies neuroticism and emotional disorder. Overall, one could encompass the model within the biopsychosocial framework.

Finally, in constructing an integrated model of the origins of neuroticism in the way indicated, one could borrow from a general framework for graphing behavior origins. The framework should involve the biopsychosocial and distal factors placed to the left, physiological and neural (network) factors in the middle along with other micro- and macro-processes in context, and outcomes (e.g., disorders) to the right, along with monitoring and feedback functions.

Additionally, in developing an integrated theory of neuroticism/emotional disorder, one could include in it (a) the development of self (self-definitional, relatedness) and also (b) action control [borrowed from Kopala-Sibley and Zuroff (2014), and Verbruggen et al. (2014), respectively]. In this regard, the Kopala-Sibley and Zuroff (2014) work justifies the use of internal psychological messages in the integrated model to accompany the Barlow et al. (2014) emphasis on vulnerabilities [and susceptibilities (after Belsky & Pluess, 2009)] as well as specific later triggers; the Verbruggen et al. (2014) work justifies adding to it proximal micro- and macrogenetic processes, such as in the detection and selection of cues.

With this framework, I proceeded to develop a generic model of behavioral causation in graphic format. However, I sought to include the full panoply of possible causal factors in behavior. In this regard, first, I placed development and learning, which are the first two of the five constructs arrayed to the left in the Verbruggen et al. (2014) model, as part of the distal mechanisms that influence behavior. I placed these at the bottom of the figure. Also, I added evolutionary mechanisms and context to the bottom of the figure.

Once this latter step of integrating the work of Verbruggen et al. (2014) into Barlow et al.'s (2014) model of neuroticism, I continued to add other components of their work to the model. In this regard, I placed the last of their five processes of monitoring as part of the outcome configuration constructed to the right in the figure, which includes their concept of triggers. Next, the basic cognitive processes of detection and selection were organized as part of the influences on outcome working in conjunction with triggering. Note that the execution component of the triad of cognitive processes in their model also was moved to the outcome portion of the revised model. [Further work on Verbruggen et al.'s model that I undertook is described in the next section of the chapter.]

Given these parameters and considerations, I developed a revised model of the origins of neuroticism and emotional disorder. It includes not only Barlow et al.'s (2014) model as a starting point (e.g., the triple vulnerabilities), but also adds multiple biopsychosocial factors to the distal

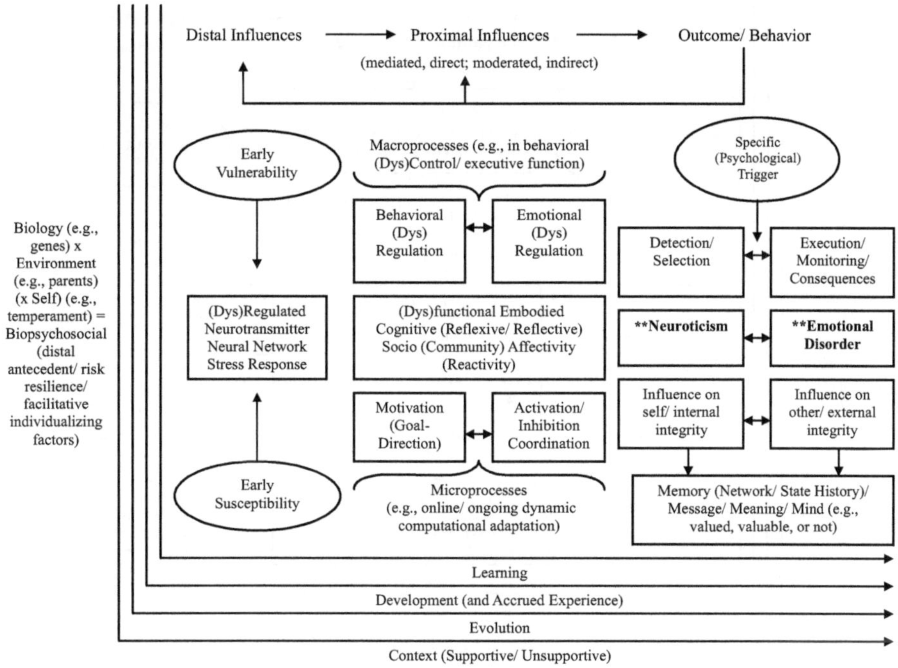

** The stars indicate the unique aspects of the figure relative to the generic model.

Fig. 36.4 A revised model of the development of neuroticism/disordered emotions. The two boxes containing the critical starred concepts of the diagram that are developing and transforming relate to effects that are both internal (e.g., on the self concept) and external (e.g., on concepts of how one should interact with others).

For example, in the present case, one might develop neuroticism, which concerns instability in relations, and this might become a vulnerability factor for a specific mental disorder, but in each case there are effects on self-concept both about the self and the social concept of the other. The figure expands the model of Barlow et al. (2014) by including causal influences under the categories of distal, proximal, and outcome. In the following, I describe the constitution of the model generically, and this description applies to subsequent examples to which the generic model is applied. Behavior is influenced causally by multiple factors, from distal to proximal to concurrent. The distal variables include biological, psychological, and social ones, including self factors. They include early vulnerabilities, as well as susceptibilities (Belsky & Pluess, 2009). They also include influences of evolutionary, developmental, and learning factors, all having their effects in context (supportive, unsupportive). The early vulnerabilities/susceptibilities work to affect behavior not only through an altered stress response but also through effects on central (neural, network), components. The proximal influences include top-down macro-processes in behavior control/executive function and also bottom-up micro—ones, including motivation/goal direction and activation/inhibition coordination (Young, 2011). Micro-processes refer to online, ongoing adaptation (statistical, computational) that is dynamically adaptive. The proximal influences can be summarized as a vital preparatory state of the organism in terms of (dys)function in the multiple arenas of behavior, from the physical (embodied) to the cognitive (reflexive to reflective), to the social (community), to the affective (reactive, as well). The action outcomes of the behavioral process that are executed include triggers that are detected/selected and also monitoring that leads to feedback. The whole system involved retains a memory, which for either simpler organisms or epochs in development could be referred to as state history or network adjustment. For either more advanced organisms or developmental epochs, system memories could involve internal messages with meaning in mind (e.g., I am valued, the world values me)

factors involved. Also, it adds an elaborate, mediating base intermediate between distal factors and outcome (see Fig. 36.4). Also, I added the concept of individualizing factors to the distal influences of the model.

Self-Control

I revised the graph of Verbruggen et al.'s (2014) action/self-control model (see Fig. 36.5) to make it consistent with my revision of Barlow et al.'s

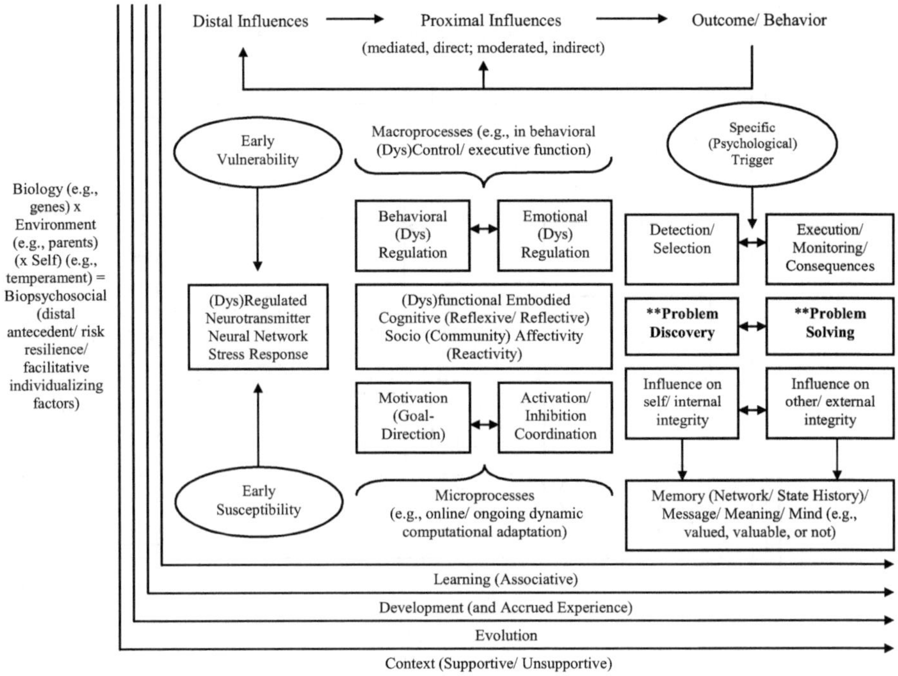

Fig. 36.5 A revised model of action control and behavior change. The figure illustrates how the model of action control in Verbruggen et al. (2014; see Figure 36.2) can be modified according to a generic template of the causality of behavior. For the two boxes in the model that are not generic but that are specific to the area of study, in this case action/self-control, I placed in the boxes the terms Problem Discovering and Problem Solving. This is consistent with the focus of the Verbruggen et al. (2014) article

(2014) model of neuroticism. Notice that I included behavior/emotional (dys)regulation as top-down influences of the micro–macro proximal processes in behavioral determination. In this regard, motivation and activation/inhibition coordination constitute bottom-up microprocesses in ongoing/online dynamic (computational) adaptation. For the central portion in the model of proximal influences on outcome/behavior, I included the concepts of embodiment and cognitive social affectivity. The added terms (reflexive/reflective for cognition; community for social, and reactivity for affectivity) are included to make the model applicable to most species and also to early phases of development of any species. The addition of these constructs to the present generic model of behavioral causality is justified at different junctures of the present work.

Self/Other

In Fig. 36.6, I present a revised model of Kopala-Sibley and Zuroff's (2014) model of the development of self-definition and relatedness. I place distal factors at the left, along with the general label of an inclusive biopsychosocial model. The middle of the diagram includes relevant proximal processes, both micro- and macro-, of which self-regulation (control, behavioral, emotional), generally, constitutes an important one. At the right of the model, I place outcomes, in particular, as related to self-definition and relatedness selves. Also, to the right I place other aspects, such as the internalized psychological messages, as well as action execution and monitoring, which were mentioned in the elaboration of more inclusive models for both neuroticism and action/self-control discussed previously.

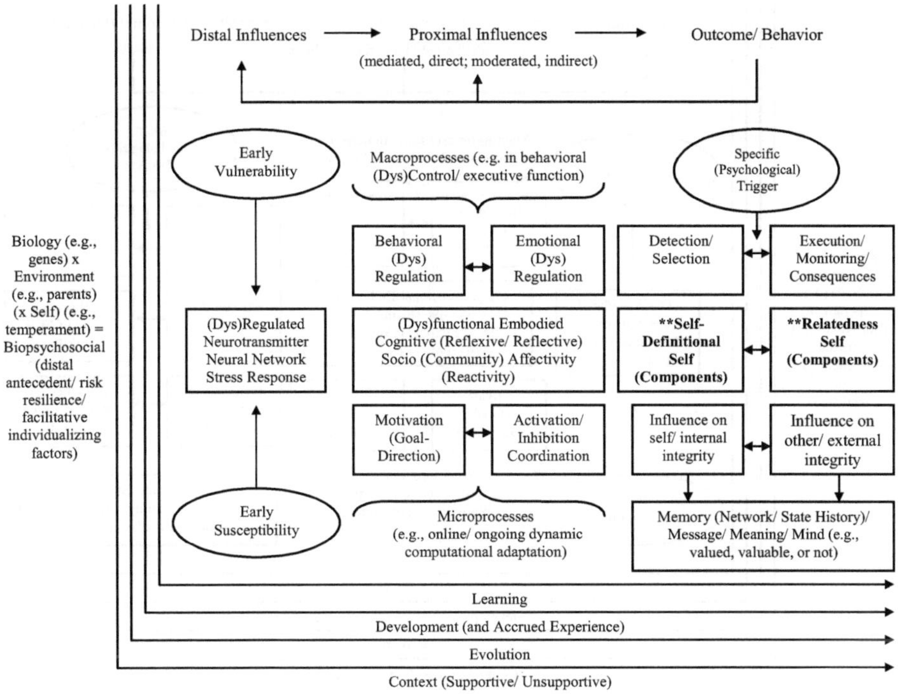

Fig. 36.6 A revised model of the development of self-definition and relatedness. The model in the figure is a variation of the generic one developed on the basis of the ones by Barlow et al. (2014) on neuroticism/emotional disorder, Verbruggen et al. (2014) on action control, and Kopala-Sibley and Zuroff (2014) on self-development. The figure presents a revised model of self-definition and relatedness development. Both of the latter are central to Blatt's (2008) model of polarities of experience. For the two boxes in the model that are not generic but that are specific to the area of study, I placed in the boxes the terms related to self-definition and relatedness

Revising Free Will

Finally, it is worth noting that the present effort to model generically the causality of behavior in graph format has been constructed to the point that it can accommodate most any behavior. All that is needed is to include the behavior of interest in the two starred boxes, as I have done for neuroticism, for example. In this regard, one major focus of the present work is on free will belief. Therefore, a comprehensive model of the construct would place it in the present graphical model of behavioral causality in the way indicated (see Fig. 36.7). In Fig. 36.8, I made a similar graph for ego/resource depletion, which is related to free will and self-control. In both cases, the constructs have been limited in contemporary study in terms of understanding the complexity of their psychology and their origins. However, by adopting a biopsychosocial framework for their multifactorial expression and causality, as being done presently, they are placed more centrally in a generic causal understanding of behavior, including its mechanisms.

For the topic of free will, Fig. 36.7 indicates the relationship of free will belief and having a sense of free will. The former is more cognitive, and the latter is more affective. They express an intimate reciprocity. As for ego/resource depletion, a depleting task in self-control needs to be understood in its broad biopsychosocial context of self-regulation (cognitive/affective). Therefore, although depletion might obtain in the laboratory for a sequence of relevant tasks, the characteristics and origins of ego/resource depletion involve broad factors that complicate any simple understanding of its effects.

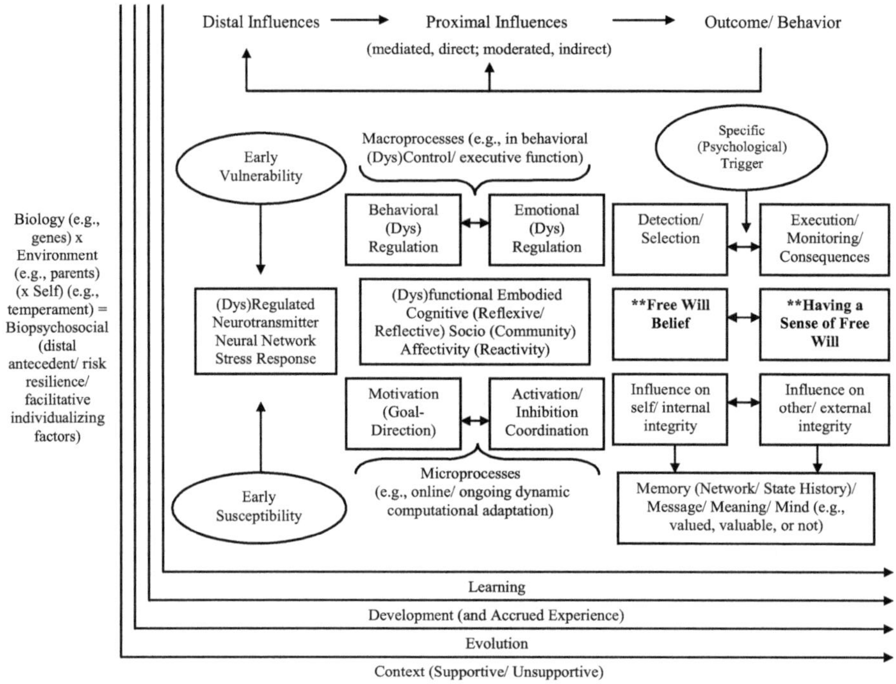

Fig. 36.7 Model of the causality of free will belief and having a sense of free will. This model is consistent with the present generic approach to understanding the causality of behavior in graphic format, including in terms of distal and proximal factors from a biopsychosocial perspective and also with developmental and evolutionary influences taken into consideration, in particular. The model is applicable to the question of individual differences in free will belief and their origins. Free will belief is the cognitive component of a broader concept of free will that I have developed, which includes the affective component of having a sense of free will. These two aspects of the psychology of free will stand in a reciprocal relationship and mutually influence each other, aside from being influenced by a multiple biopsychosocial factors presented in the graph

The power of the present generic model of causality is that it opens up new avenues of investigation to the behavior of interest that might not have been evident beforehand. Also, it suggests that common causal mechanisms and pathways govern the causality of multiple behaviors, and findings in one area could speak to others.

Revising PTSD

In this regard, I have placed the disorder PTSD in the context of the generic model of behavioral causality that I have developed (see Fig. 36.9). It includes an interaction between instability and the expression of the disorder. This parallels the graph for neuroticism, in which this instability stood in interaction with emotional disorder. Also, it is consistent with the literature relating PTSD to general negative affectivity (see Chap. 21).

Further Revising Causality of Behavior

To close the book, I propose other ways the present generic change model can be applied to the major themes of the present work. Also, I focus on the integrative nature of the biopersonalsocial (biopsychosocial) model that I have created, as well as my Neo-Piagetian (sub)stage model. The last portion of the book is presented especially in tabular and figure format, with table notes and figure captions providing much detail. These tables and figures should be considered as proposals for future directions in the synthetic effort constituted by the present work.

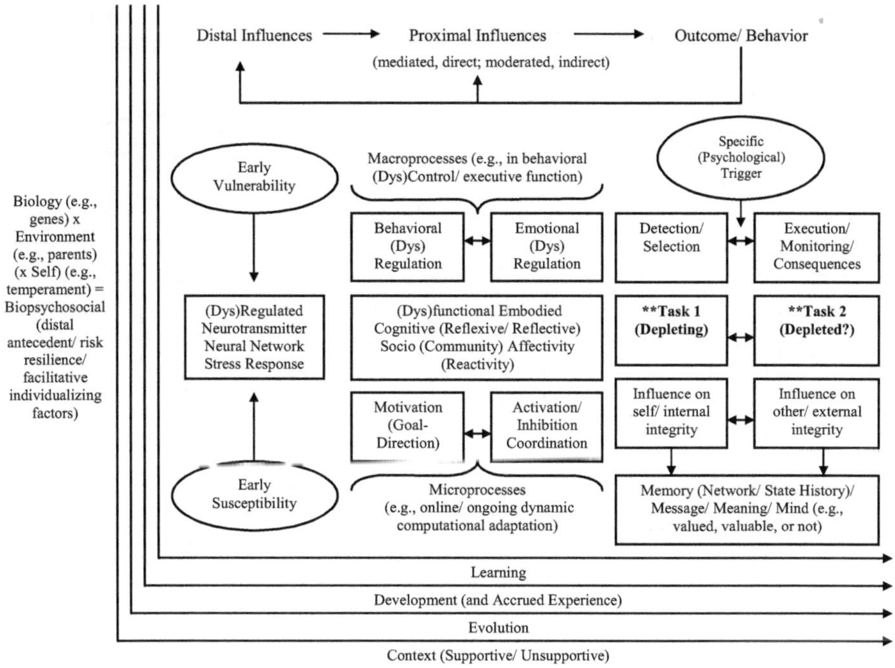

Fig. 36.8 A revised model of the development of ego-depletion. Free will exercise is related to effective option selection and implementation. It requires good executive function. However, the resources in self-control are depletable. Engaging in a demanding task that diminishes one's sense of self-control could affect performance on a similar task afterwards. The ego or resource depletion model is a unidimensional one on force of will being important in depletion effects in self-control. However, I have argued that self-control depletion is multifactorial and involves biological, psychological, and social factors, including motivation.

The generic model of causality that I have developed not only is applicable to free will belief/having a sense of free will, as in Figure 36.7, but also it is applicable to the depletion effect. That is, Tasks 1 and 2 in a depletion study consist of a potentially depleting one and then a possibly depleted one. Given the biopsychosocial nature posited for depletion, the typical depletion tasks might not actually work as indicated in laboratory studies. Moreover, in valid ecological contexts, we engage constantly in potentially self-control depleting tasks but multiple factors might act to inhibit or activate the effects of putatively valid self-control depletion tasks on actual self-control depletion, as in successive maintenance or loss of self-control over a series of potentially self-control depleting tasks (that is, in ecologically valid contexts, there might be more than two depletion tasks involved). Finally, even the anticipation of participating in the first task might already alter self-control in a subsequent one, so the tasks often stand in a reciprocal relationship

Table 36.1 indicates how the present five-step generic change model can apply to a single acquisition, and not just the synchronization of two, as has been emphasized to date. Table 36.2 shows how this might apply to the acquisition of free will belief.

The next two tables relate to the overarching concept of the present work of Freedom in Being (Tables 36.3 and 36.4). The first table of the two shows how its two components of free will belief and having a sense of free will can come to integrate. The second table illustrates how the free decision process that accompanies its development might arise according to the present Neo-Piagetian stage model.

The next graphics relate to the present biopersonalsocial model (Tables 36.5, 36.6, 36.7, and 36.8 and Fig. 36.10). The first shows how it has developed from the biopsychosocial one and can be extended. The second indicates its relation to the worldview of relationism as well as other key models that are described in the present work. The third one indicates its relationship to the basic freedoms in brain, behavior, and being. The next table indicates how the worldview of relationism constitutively incorporates other worldviews and

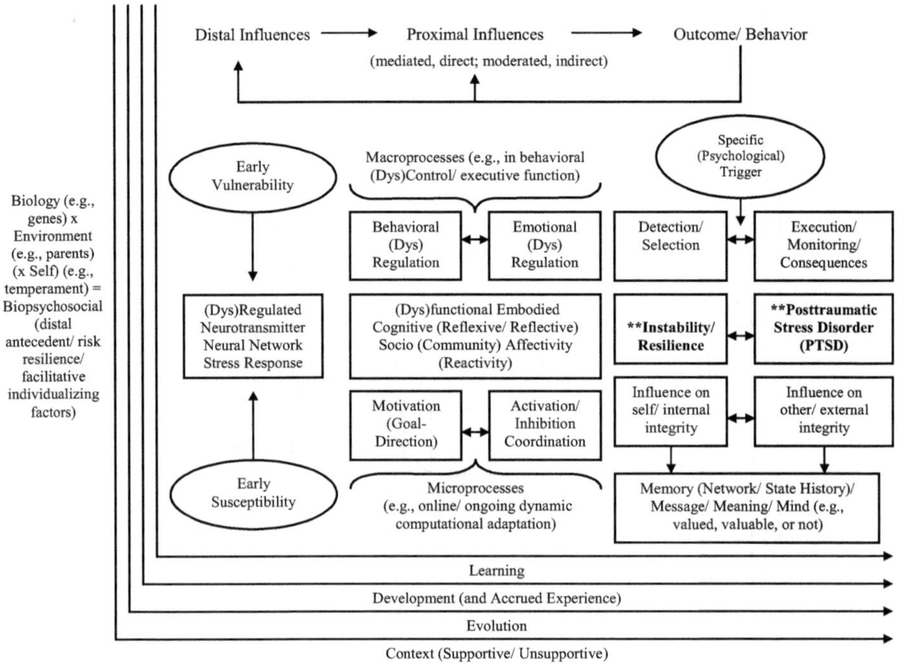

Fig. 36.9 A revised model of the development of posttraumatic stress disorder (PTSD). The generic behavioral causality model can be applied to most any psychiatric disorder. The figure illustrates that it can help explain the multifactorial causal nature of PTSD

should not necessarily deny a place for them. The last table of the present book indicates how the basic change mechanisms presumed to underlie development—that of activation/inhibition coordination—can grow through the present five-step generic change model to become flexibly adaptive in governing brain, behavior, self, and their growth.

Chapter Conclusions

The generic change model of behavioral causality that I have developed integrates the major themes of the present book. As a general framework, I adopted the biopsychosocial model. It afforded me the opportunity to list biological, environmental, and self-factors as part of the causal factors in behavior. The model considers as part of the constellation of forces in the origins of behavior early distal ones, aside from more immediate proximal, triggering ones. Mediators between distal and proximal influences in behavioral causality are important to consider, e.g., motivation. The generic model created also includes room for a role in causation of development and learning as well as evolution, while considering context (e.g., supportive, unsupportive). The model is generic, but it is equally highly individualistic in that the causal nexus that characterizes any one individual for any one outcome of focus applies uniquely to that person.

The generic model of behavioral causality that I have created includes a major section on intermediate, proximal influences that mediate between distal ones and outcome. They include both macro- and micro-processes. The former involve behavior/emotional (dys)control/(dys) regulation, in particular. The latter involve motivation and ongoing processes in adaptation, such as facilitated by activation/inhibition coordination. At the core of micro/macro processes in proximal influences on behavior lie embodied cognitive and socioemotional (re)activity/(dys) functionality. The site of early dysregulation in behavior lies in the stress system. When it is dysregulated, the effects extend beyond the HPA (hypothalamic pituitary adrenal) axis and related

Table 36.1 Two pathways toward system integration

Step	Juxtaposition	Indeterminate presence
Coordination	A, B	A, $\bar{A}$
Hierarchization	A×B	A/$\bar{A}$
Systematization	AB	A
Multiplication	$AB_1 \times AB_2 \times$	$A_1 \times A_2 \times$
Integration	AB_i	A_i

Note. A = phenomenon present; $\bar{A}$ = absent
B = second phenomenon
× = interaction, can also be represented by U; as the interaction solidifies, one or the other component becomes predominant, perhaps variably
To this juncture in my theoretical work on the generic change model and its applications to development, I have considered the first step of coordination as involving the juxtaposition of two components, which then proceed to a hierarchical organization across them, leading to their systematization and, ultimately, to their integration. However, another pathway from coordination to integration in generic/developmental change could involve the juxtaposition of a component transiently or partially present with its absence. Then, as the component grows in presence, it creates a hierarchical arrangement involving its presence primary relative to its absence. This then leads to its systematization as fully present, preparing the way to multiplying it out and then being integrated more fully over the domain in question

stress response components to related neurotransmitters and neuronal networks. In early adversity, fetal or early programming might take place and serve to fix heightened stress reactivity in the long term.

The output portion of the generic model of behavioral causation that I have developed involves a specific trigger being activated, or somehow involved, which leads to detection/selection and then behavioral execution and its consequences. Both the self and other are affected. The message/meaning of the outcome behavior become embedded in memory/mind.

Behavior causality involves much more than this generic overview. At the same time, often workers do not try to see the overall scope of the causality that might be involved in their area of interest, and their models end up narrow in scope. Hopefully, the present generic model of behavioral causality and, as well, the book, in general, helps broaden understanding of behavioral causality.

Table 36.2 Steps in growth of free will (belief, having a sense)

Step	Growth in free will belief[a]	Growth in having a sense of free will[b]
Coordination	FWB, $\overline{FWB}$	SFW, $\overline{SFW}$
Hierarchization	FWB × $\overline{FWB}$	SFW × $\overline{SFW}$
Systematization	FWB	SFW
Multiplication	$FWB_1 \times FWB_2 \times$	$SFW_1 \times SFW_2 \times$
Integration	FWB_i	SFW_i

The figure depicts the steps in the development of components of freedom in being through the five steps of the proposed generic change model:
(a). First, in the step of the coordination, the person develops the component involved, but not in a full manner (only partially in one or some) context(s) or domain(s). The person deals with the juxtaposition of having the component either actively present or not having it, depending on context, state, etc., in a transitional manner.
(b). In the next of hierarchization, the component takes hold and comes to dominate its lack of presence. The person might oscillate between its presence and lack, but its increasing presence resolves the cognitive (and emotional) dissonance of its lack toward its presence.
(c). Eventually, the component is systematized to its full presence in the context(s)/domain(s) at issue.
(d). Then, the component spreads throughout the psychological architecture involved. At each expansion, the dissonance described above manifests and resolves.
(e). Finally, it becomes a generalizable constant presence
Note. [a]Free Will Belief = FWB; not having it is represented by $\overline{FWB}$
[b]Having a Sense of Free Will = SFW; not having it is represented by $\overline{SFW}$

To conclude the chapter (as well as the book), it is important to note the limits of the generic behavioral causality model that I have created. First, although it includes development as part of the causal change process, it does not try to differentiate the role of various developmental models in its working, including the present Neo-Piagetian/Neo-Eriksonian 25-step developmental model. Also, the disadvantage of being a generic model is that it might not apply equally to all behavioral phenomena. In this sense, the limits of the model include both under-reach and over-reach. Future work on the causality of behavior can address these lacunae in the present modeling, not only for the ones in the present chapter but also for all those presented in this book.

Table 36.3 Origins of a comprehensive model of free will

Steps	Model
Coordination	Free will, having a sense of free will
Hierarchization	Free will × having a sense of free will
Systematization	Freedom in Being ↓ Free Will x Having a Sense of Free Will = FOB ↑ Freeing the Brain
Multiplication	$FOB_1 \times FOB_2 \times$
Integration	FOB_i

The figure illustrates the manner in which the components in the growth of freedom in being conjoin into a systematized and integrated psychological entity. Freedom in being appears to be a psychological emergence that relates to the most mature psychological acquisition, along with concepts such as wisdom and Eriksonian generativity:

(a). In the step of coordination, the two components are juxtaposed

(b). Next, they begin to cohere, with the absence of coherence subordinate to its presence

(c). Next, the components form a system, with a cohering entity emerging of freedom in being that encompasses both

(d). Then, the systematization process in the prior stage expands over contexts/domains

(e). Finally, an integrative freedom in being emerges that is generalized across contexts/domains, in a constant way in the person

Book Conclusions

The End

The goal of the present book has been to emphasize the centrality of causality in the study of behavior and to support it as an integrative focus in psychology. These goals are ongoing ones for which I have made some progress and which need further work to arrive at satisfactory ends. Both goals are daunting ones, but the expansive range of the book suggests that both goals are reachable. Both the "what" and the "why" of behavior need to be understood in depth in order to obtain a more complete insight into the nature of behavior and how it can go awry and become disturbed.

Therefore, the goals that I have adopted for the book have not only theoretical importance but also practical relevance. Having an integrated understanding of the "why" of behavior necessarily compliments and guides understanding of the "what" of behavior. Understanding the system of behavior means understanding the product (or outcome), as well as the process (or multiple determining factors). In this regard, the book highlights a model of behavior that is multifactorial, biopsychosocial, and integrative of Nature, Nurture, and the self as major factors in the origins of behavior.

Moreover, the self is not a passive agent in behavioral causality, but an active one. Further, the self is characterized potentially by freedom in being, or grows toward it, depending on the age of the person involved. Freedom in being involves a belief component and a sense of having free will. Both need to develop appropriately, and they are part of our evolutionary heritage because of their adaptive significance. Behavior can be emergent from the full system, which it is embedded both internally and externally in the possibility of an emergence of, and this includes freedom in being.

Paradoxically, as we mature into freedom in being, we choose to limit our freedoms especially to our primary responsibilities, such as self, family, work, and society. I refer to this undertaking of our responsibilities as Re-Responsibilities. Freedom in being means approaching with psychological maturity each of our responsibilities and rededicating ourselves constantly to them.

Therefore, my understanding of the integrated nature of causality and its capacity to help integrate psychology places at its apex the concept of freedom in being and all that it entails for behavior. Asking to place causality as the integrating force in psychology is insufficient without having a model of the ultimate nature of the human condition, which includes a place for free will, and a critical one at that. In this regard, I hope the present book has offered a model of causality that integrates key causal factors.

Table 36.4 Stages in the development of freedom in being

Stage	Substage	Free decision	Growth in free being
Collective intelligence (Neo-Piagetian (adult) postformal stage)	Integration	Superordinate free-decision (sense, being, brain) theories/meta-ethics	Superordinate freeing theories/orientations
	Multiplication	Superordinate free-decision (sense, being, brian) principles	Superordinate freeing principles
	Systematization	Superordinate free-decision (sense, being, brain) codes	Superordinate freeing guidelines/codes
	Hierarchization	Superordinate free-decision (sense, being, brain) rules	Superordinate freeing rules/techniques/procedures
	Coordination	Particular superordinate free-decision (sense, being, brain) cases (dilemmas)	Particular superordinate freeing cases (dilemmas)
Abstract (Piagetian (adolescent) formal stage)	Integration	Free-decision (sense, being, brain) theory	Freeing theory/orientation
	Multiplication	Free-decision (sense, being, brain) principle	Freeing principle
	Systematization	Free-decision (sense, being, brain) code	Freeing guideline/code
	Hierarchization	Free-decision (sense, being, brain) rule	Freeing rule/technique/procedure
	Coordination	Particular free-decision (sense, being, brain) case (dilemma)	Particular freeing case (dilemma)

Adapted from Young (2014), Table 24.3

Note. The two prior figures indicate the manner in which the growth in freedom in being takes place microdevelopmentally, without considering the underlying limitations imposed by the general cognitive development of the person (and associated socioaffective development). Young's (2011) Neo-Piagetian/Neo-Eriksonian model of 25 steps in development (5 stages × 5 substages) considers the last 10 steps to develop according to Piaget's formal, abstract adolescent-initiated stage, and then a postformal Neo-Piagetian one in the adult termed collective intelligence. Young (2014) applied this model to the steps in the growth of ethical thought, showing how it could pass through the sequence of considering cases, rules, codes, principles, and theories first at a uniconstruct level then at a superordinate construct level.

In the table, I have modified the model of development of ethical thought to apply to growth in free being, doing so by proposing a developmental sequence in the thought process of free decision making akin to the ethical one, which then undergirds the corresponding growth in free being. The concept of free being revolves around growth in free will belief and having a sense of free will, which is included in the decision-making column. Also, it mentions the free brain based on Friston's work of the brain adapting to minimizing free energy as it attempts to reduce uncertainty. Finally, consistent with the theme of the table, I refer to the decision-making process in the growth of freedom in being as one of "free decision" making.

As for the growth of free being itself as facilitated by the growth in free decision making capacity, I refer to the sequence from case to theory as "freeing" case(s), rule(s), code(s), principle(s), and theory(ies) passing sequentially through the successive stages of uniconstructs and superordinate ones (in the abstract and collective intelligence stages, respectively).

To conclude, the present model of the growth of freedom in being is based on a Neo-Piagetian/Neo-Eriksonian (sub) stage model. The growth is limited cognitively by the constraints of the corresponding Neo-Piagetian cognitive acquisition. Perhaps more importantly, also it is limited by the difficulties that might arise in the corresponding Neo-Eriksonian socioaffective acquisitions. In this sense, the proposed model of the growth of freedom in being might provide a valuable framework not only in understanding the person but also in working through psychotherapy toward improving freedom in being

The Beginning

This book on causality of behavior constitutes a grand project. In this epilogue, I look back to its roots in the first few chapters, in order to give a survey of how it has addressed some of its primary goals in these regards.

First, it has considered many of the fundamental assumptions behind the book that had been laid out at its beginning, but one that needs further elaboration is the issue of behavioral change. Causality is about changing inertial forces so that change takes place; as well, it refers to arriving at changes that do not simply and always reflect on

Table 36.5 Steps in the development of biopsychosocial understanding

Steps	Model
Coordination	Medical model (biology); Psychosocial factor (PS)
Hierarchization	Biopsychosocial model (BPS) (e.g., in illness, in psychotherapy)
Systematization	Biopersonalsocial model (BPS revised=BPSr)
Multiplication	$BPSr_1 \times BPSr_2 \times$
Integration	$BPSr_i$

Note. The table illustrates the evolution of the biopsychosocial model. It integrates the medical (biological) and psychosocial dualistic notions of illness/disease and how to treat it. In my version of it, I refer to the biopersonalsocial model in order to accentuate that all three components contribute to the psychology of illness. The model can be expanded beyond illness conceptions to areas such as development. Finally, it can grow to represent a comprehensive integrative framework for behavior and causality

a one-to-one, direct basis changes in incoming energy, information, or stimulus parameters. In psychology, this means that behavioral changes are person-mediated as much as biologically- or environmentally-mediated, and that even a minor alteration to input might effect large behavioral change (even a self-organizational, emergent one) or, in contrast, that a major alteration in this regard might effect no change in behavior.

In this regard, the present book presents models of change, including generic and developmental ones, that address these and related issues. For example, based on my cognitive developmental (sub)stage model of development, I expanded it to address socioaffective development (Neo-Eriksonian and Neo-Maslovian models) and analogous generic change in scientific paradigms (a Neo-Kuhnian model).

Second, the book has considered the dimensions that had been posited for causality (in relation to free will). These include: the dimensions of (a) time, (b) the person, as in the biopsychosocial model, (c) self-control, and (d) mechanism. Examples of the dimensions that have been addressed in the present book include, respectively: (a) the proximal and distal timeframes; for example, respectively, immediate stimulus-organism-response dynamics and evolution and life history theory; (b) the brain, genes/epigenetics and differential susceptibility models; cognitive appraisals; and sociocultural and environmental context, including of early adversity; (c) the self, including of free will working models in psychotherapy; and (d) nonlinear dynamical systems models and related ones in the network model.

Third, the book has elaborated many of the areas in Fig. 3.4 in Chap. 3 on the causality landscape, making it genuinely interdisciplinary. For example, aside from its heavy emphasis on major biological fields, such as neuroscience, genetics, evolution, and psychiatry, as well as many areas of development, it examines the philosophy of causality, the view of Big History on causality, the psychiatric approach to psychopathology and its diagnosis in the DSM-5 (Diagnostic and Statistical Manual of Mental Disorders, Fifth Edition; American Psychiatric Association, 2013), causality in law, statistical approaches to causality, and systems and network approaches to causality.

As the area of study of causality in psychology and related disciplines continues to cohere, there will be increasing conceptual refinement, empirical study, and applications to practice and society that will be beneficial and that will lead to causality taking its rightful place as an interdisciplinary lynchpin. The present book has begun with this proposition and is meant to inspire others along this journey.

Humans are the products of an exquisitely complex causality. In this regard, we thrive when we understand causality and use it effectively, whether in the intrapersonal, interpersonal, or material worlds. Also, part of our essence is about causality. In this regard, I have referred to our species as *Homo Causa* and the self as causal. Humans are unique in many ways, and aside from the free will that I have emphasized in this vein, the subject of causality also marks our exceptionalism. It is a privilege to be a sentient human on this planet, which is in so much need of our wisdom. The proper understanding of causality and its implications and applications might constitute one axis to help us to improve we, ourselves, and all those around us, as well as the planet that is so heavily dependent on us.

Table 36.6 Organization of predominant themes in an integrative framework for psychology focusing on the biopsychosocial model

Step	Theme	Example	Cross-step
Integration	Metatheory/worldview	Relationism	Causality Activation–Inhibition coordination Dynamical systems (including emergence) Networks Evolution Embodiment Developmental process Learning Contextual sensitivity Culture/environment
Multiplication	Midrange metatheory	Biopsychosocial (e.g., integrating, respectively, genetics/epigenetics—brain; self/free will belief; family)	
Systematization	Mini-theory	Illness disease modeling (translational psychiatry/psychology)	
Hierarchization	Hypotheses and empirical research in domains	Need to treat all of biological, psychological, social in order to help patients	
		Rigorous multifactorial investigation of multiple illness/disease domains	
Coordination	Domains	Disease/illness categorized/dimensionalized	

Note. The table attempts an integration of the basic themes in the present work. The table describes the steps in the growth of an integrative framework for psychology from domain to metatheory (Overton, 2015), with a focus on the biopsychosocial model. I relate the model to my own five-step generic sequence. The example shows how the biopsychosocial model fits into the sequence from domain study to the worldview of relationism. In order to show how this sequence for a central model of the present work relates to other models described in the book, I list them as cross-step influences for each step of the model

Table 36.7 Steps in the development of world view modeling

Steps	Model
Coordination	Internal reductionistic/external positivistic (Realism); Internal processing/external participation (Relativism) R, R
Hierarchization	R × R
Systematization	+/- ↓ R x R ↑ +/- = relationism (r)
Multiplication	$r_1 \times r_2 \times$
Integration	r_i

The figure illustrates how the metatheoretical view of relationism might reflect the juxtaposition and then systematization and integration of realism and relativism according to the present five-step generic model of change. At the same time, it is worth noting that a fully mature model of relationism in psychology should integrate in a comprehensive systems approach its original components. Both realism and relativism should not be considered as separable components of relationism but as constitutive components still having value because of the strengths of their modeling

Table 36.8 Steps in the differentiation of activation/inhibition coordination

Step	Representation	Explanation
Coordination	A_1, I_1	Activation, Inhibition juxtaposed in one domain
Hierarchization	A_1 X I_1	They coordinate reciprocally, with one or other dominant (not subordinate) but variably
Systematization	+/- ↓ A_1 X I_1 ↑ +/-	They form a system in which they dynamically coordinate, including with activation of inhibition, inhibition of activation, etc., leading to an overall inter-related system
Multiplication	+/- ↓ A_1 X I_1 ↑ +/- X +/- ↓ A_2 X I_2 ↑ +/- X	Activation/inhibition coordination systems spread over domains and interact and coordinate over them
Integration	+/- ↓ A_i X I_i ↑ +/-	A generalized activation–inhibition coordination system manifests

Note. The table indicates how activation/inhibition coordination might develop through the present five-step generic change model. As they coordinate and hierarchize, systematize, multiply and integrate, they include reciprocal feedback and feedforward processes that subserve equilibrium building, flexibility, and adaptation, both within domains and over them, to the point of creating a generic, multiflexible mechanism in organization of brain (biology) behavior and their relationship in context and in the self

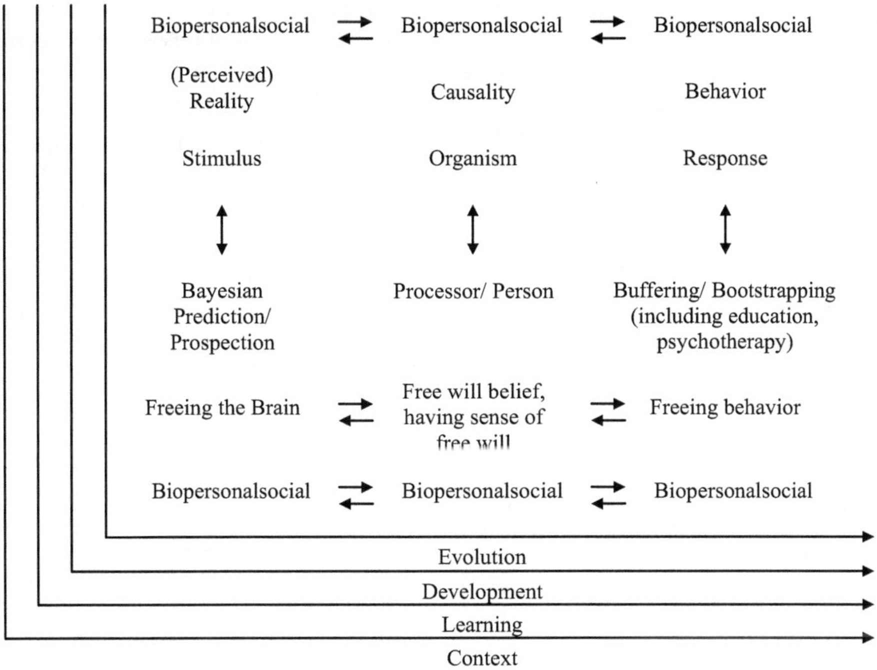

Fig. 36.10 The biopersonalsocial model of the basic freedoms in brain, behavior, and being. The figure attempts another way of integrating the basic themes of the present work, this time in terms of the key terms in its title. It illustrates the reciprocal interaction across stimulus-processor-response, with these components no longer considered as sequential steps in perception and action (Clark, 2013). Causality no longer is considered to reside in the first step in this progression, but emanates, as well, from feedback from the processor (organism, person), for example. Stimuli are not absolute, external entities but probabilistic, Bayesian predictions derived from their affordances, and ones that lead to feedforward predictions/prospection. The environment can buffer impact of stimuli, as well (or accentuate them), with processing mechanisms involved. The brain works to reduce uncertainty, surprise, and free energy, which paradoxically leave degrees of freedom for freer, less constrained response.

Development proceeds toward an integrated maturity of self as freedom in being, composed of free will belief and having a sense of free will. The environment might contribute by acting toward freeing the processor/person in this regard. The brain is one seat of interacting biological, environmental, and self forces in development in the growth to freedom. The latter is not about freedom to choose and act on any whim but to choose and act on responsibility, which paradoxically works against and in control of impulsive, non-responsible promoting whims. Freedom in being is especially about arriving to the point of being able to free the being of others while having this further free one's being (and not self-sacrifice to its detriment or in being taken advantage of)

Finally, I address the title of the book and how successfully the book has treated it. The book's title indicates its focus and concerns "Unifying Causality and Psychology: Being, Brain, and Behavior." As argued at the book's outset, it is impossible to unify psychology in terms of one overarching model, theory, approach, operation, or any one answer or product. However, by taking a process, pathway, or ongoing project view of psychology's integration, the task is facilitated, although it can never be completed. As with any system, psychology should be continually adapting and changing and avoid stasis and stagnation in favor of constructive change and growth.

In terms of the causality project implicated in the title of the present book, I would like to think that the book has advanced the cause, so to speak. It has offered pathways toward integrating behavioral causality itself and toward integrating it in psychology. In this regard, it has helped psychology, itself, move toward the unifying pathway or process called for by the present book. Let the project continue.

References

Alloy, L. B., Black, S. K., Young, M. E., Goldstein, K. E., Shapero, B. G., Stange, J. P., et al. (2012). Cognitive vulnerabilities and depression versus other psychopathology symptoms and diagnoses in early adolescence. *Journal of Clinical Child & Adolescent Psychology, 41*, 539–560.

American Psychiatric Association. (2013). *Diagnostic and statistical manual of mental disorders: DSM-5* (5th ed.). Washington, DC: Author.

Barlow, D. H., Ellard, K. K., Sauer-Zavala, S., Bullis, J. R., & Carl, J. R. (2014). The origins of trait neuroticism. *Perspectives on Psychological Science, 9*, 481–496.

Belsky, J., & Pluess, M. (2009). The nature (and nurture?) of plasticity in early human development. *Perspectives on Psychological Science, 4*, 345–351.

Blatt, S. J. (2008). *Polarities of experience: Relatedness and self-definition in personality development, psychopathology, and the therapeutic process*. Washington, DC: American Psychological Association.

Clark, A. (2013). Whatever next? Predictive brains, situated agents, and the future of cognitive science. *Behavioral and Brain Sciences, 36*, 1–24.

Kopala-Sibley, D. C., & Zuroff, D. C. (2014). The developmental origins of personality factors from the self-definitional and relatedness domains: A review of theory and research. *Review of General Psychology, 18*, 137–155.

Overton, W. F. (2015). Relational developmental systems and developmental science. In R. M. Lerner, W. F. Overton, & P. C. Molenaar (Eds.), *Handbook of child psychology and developmental science, Vol. 1: Theory and method* (7th ed., pp. 9–62). Hoboken, NJ: Wiley.

Rotter, J. B. (1966). Generalized expectancies for internal versus external control of reinforcement. *Psychological Monographs, 80*, 1–28.

Verbruggen, F., McLaren, I. P. L., & Chambers, C. D. (2014). Banishing the control homunculi in studies of action control and behavior change. *Psychological Science, 9*, 497–524.

Young, G. (2011). *Development and causality: Neo-Piagetian perspectives*. New York: Springer Science + Business Media.

Young, G. (2014). *Malingering, feigning, and response bias in psychiatric/psychological injury: Implications for practice and court*. Dordrecht, Netherlands: Springer Science + Business Media.

37 Epilogue

Epilogue Summary

This last portion to the book was added as a final literature review and it led to further conceptualization related to the causality of behavior. After an introduction, it examines recent literature on genes, environment, development, free will, self-control, and posttraumatic stress disorder (PTSD). Next, it looks at recent work on critical models in the field, including the relational, Piagetian/Neo-Piagetian, network (including in neurocircuitry), and nonlinear dynamical systems theory (NLDST), and the ones related to causality (e.g., top-down processes). The epilogue concludes with new models that I created on symptom network-construct relations, the nature of stages, and multiple emotional (socio-affective) intelligences. Conclusions emphasize the individual as the core focus of causal modeling, with normative, population-level research providing an informed basis for understanding individual behavioral causality. I conclude that the study of causality and the unification of psychology are reciprocal processes that constitute ongoing and dynamic projects to which the present book has contributed.

Introduction

Prelude In closing the book, I conducted a final literature review on topics central to it, as well as proposing new models related to the causality of behavior. These research areas reviewed include: (a) genes and environment; (b) development; (c) free will and self-control; and (d) PTSD. Much of the literature review in this section highlights models that inform causality, with certain domains of study highlighted, as well.

Then, the epilogue presents recent work on models critical to the present book: (a) the relational model; (b) the Piagetian model and Neo-Piagetian variants; (c) the network model; and (d) NLDST. Next, the epilogue shifts to review of causal modeling.

The conclusions at this point in the epilogue indicate directions for further modeling related to the causality of behavior. The new models that I have proposed in this epilogue include: (a) an extended hybrid system-construct model (Young, 2015a); (b) a reconceptualization of cognitive stages; and (c) a reconceptualization of emotional intelligence.

Major Points Before reviewing in depth the recent literature, I present its major points. For the area of genes and environment, the review highlights the exquisite interaction between these substrates in development. The field of behavioral genetics has received both praise for the replicability of its major findings and a caution about its limits and misinterpretations. The genetics section also describes recent research on gene–environment interaction and the differential susceptibility model. Then, it considers the burgeoning area of epigenetics, which indicates how

G. Young, *Unifying Causality and Psychology*, DOI 10.1007/978-3-319-24094-7_37

the environment can get "under the skin" and even affect multiple generations. The environment section gives nuanced findings on the effects of the early environment on development and cultural differences related to intelligence.

For development, the research points to critical models in the area, such as the newer biopsychosocial one gaining increasing influence and the classic Eriksonian one. Some of the domains in development mentioned include causal learning, which highlights that children develop a "causal stance."

The area of free will does not constitute just a philosophical one about whether it exists but also a psychological one about the positive effects of believing in free will. Free will belief is one of the factors that guide behavior and allow for self-control. Also, it can be depleted, being a limited resource.

As for PTSD, a central issue relates to its cluster or factor structure. The DSM-5 (Diagnostic and Statistical Manual of Mental Disorders, Fifth Edition; American Psychiatric Association, 2013) has organized PTSD's 20 symptoms into four clusters, and included supplementary ones related to a dissociation subtype. The empirical research supports a dimensional structure for the DSM-5 PTSD symptoms. Confirmatory factor analysis (CFA) indicates up to seven of them and, in Young (2015b, 2016), I proposed an eight cluster/factor model that includes dissociation. PTSD has been shown to have biological bases in genes and the brain, with the HPA (hypothalamic pituitary adrenal) axis one of the mediators in the pathway to its expression. That said, PTSD could be feigned for monetary gain (e.g., Young, 2015c), and the DSM of which it is a part has been criticized, e.g., for its categorical approach and for how it was constructed in working groups.

The most recent work on the relational model shows its value relative to the Cartesian reductionist one that dominates much of psychology, but it now emphasizes "process" instead of causality, per se. However, there is no reason not to see these latter two concepts as complementary and as alternate ways of trying to understand the why of behavior. In my view, the concept of causality includes the dynamic processes behind the construction and development of behavior, and vice versa. It is insufficient to say the system and its functioning constitutes the cause of behavior because elements in the system might have causal priority.

Lourenço (2016) defended the standard Piagetian view of stages, e.g., hierarchical and integrated, but did not defend his four-step stage sequence, per se. I will show that the standard view of stages needs elaboration, as does the standard four-stage sequence of Piaget.

Mascolo and Fischer (2015) presented their Neo-Piagetian five-step model of stages; the model includes the recursive recycling substages. However, I show how their view includes developmental sequences that better fit my own Neo-Piagetian model (five-stage × five-substage lifespan developmental model; Young, 2011). In this section of the epilogue, also I present Case's Neo-Piagetian model of central conceptual structures, even though there is no recent research on it. Case conceived of central conceptual structures as a better way to understand the nature of within-stage organization. This prepares the way for my later presentation of a new way to conceive the nature of stages in development that brings the understanding a long way from Piaget and also other Neo-Piagetians.

The network model considers nodes and edges in their relations, for example, in social networks, neuronal circuitry, symptom networks, and others. Networks are characterized by hubs, their centrality (e.g., betweenness), and so on, and they might even possess "small world" structures (high global connectivity and clustering). In this regard, Sporns and colleagues had described the Connectome in neuronal networks and, in this epilogue, I present his hierarchical modeling of modules and of "modules within modules" at levels superordinate to basic networks. This type of modeling is consistent with NLDST (e.g., intermediate levels to lower-order and superordinate ones) and with my own applications to symptom-construct relations and to within-stage central conceptual structure organization.

NLDST is another model central to the present book. A major point of disagreement in the field is the extent to which systems can possess emergent levels that function top down and in complement to bottom-up lower-order ones. The concept of reciprocal causality affords a bridge between lower level and higher levels in systems, and allows for emergence of the latter in ways that they are irreducible to the former. Attractors are central to NLDST conceptualization. Simply, they refer to regions in the state space of system dynamics to which system trajectories consistently return. In Young (2011), I showed how systems can evolve not only from the standard model of point to oscillatory to chaotic attractors but also to more complex adaptive systems (CAS) with multiple attractors, as in living systems, and even to attractor dynamics superordinate to that. The five-step sequence in attractor evolvability described has been proposed as a generic change model and as underlying the five-stage developmental sequence in my Neo-Piagetian model (Young, 2011). Later in the chapter, I apply the model further to the area of multiple socio-affective intelligences, which is a new concept developed in this last part of the book.

Continuing its review, in the next portion of the epilogue, I consider recent work on the topic of causality. The top-down approach to causality in systems is gaining traction. I show how it is providing a different optic to sciences such as physics and biology. At the level of the brain, it works to influence lower-order levels, e.g., as in frontal neurocircuitry influencing attentional processes. This work reinforces my point of view on hierarchical system modeling, i.e., of a multilevel, hierarchical system approach relevant across multiple areas of science, including in understanding new areas that I develop in this epilogue on the causality of behavior.

New Work The last part of the epilogue before the conclusion examines three models that I have created that inform the causality of behavior. (a) The first model combines network modeling and NLDST; (b) the second model applies the new model just described to a better understanding of stages, especially in terms of its ongoing, dynamic, and individualized nature; and (c) the third model reconfigures emotional intelligence as multiple, yoked, and reflective of the present model of Neo-Eriksonian stages, with the factors in traditional emotional intelligence considered the domains of the new model.

A common structure to these three models relates to a hierarchical multilevel systems view involving reciprocal causality. (a) For example, networks focus on lower-order system structure while NLDST allows for emergence of higher-order levels. Psychological constructs could be conceived of higher-order system levels interacting with lower-order ones in individualized ways for particular people.

(b) When applied to the nature of stages, this type of modeling allows for multiple, interacting levels that are constructed individually in context, with increasing sophistication in higher-order levels as they differentiate into rules, representations, operations, and abstract formulations. The concept of hierarchical, multiple, and interacting, reciprocally-causal levels (and, therefore, emerging ones, too) in a system can help explain both the nature of stages and how they are individualized, as well the mechanisms that propel their evolution through qualitatively distinct organizations (i.e., higher-order stages).

This stage evolution happens, as well, through processes equivalent to the accommodation and assimilation duality in equilibration that Piaget described, in that the schemes so structured within levels keep being applied and generalized and then chunk as they become too complex, and also ready for the next applications horizontal, lateral and vertical, discontinuous generalizations. The child contributes to this process by way of her or his active constructions, curiosity, motivation, metacognition, distancing reflections, and so on.

(c) As for the novel concept of multiple emotional intelligences, it is an extension of the one that I developed for multiple (cognitive) intelligences, in general. For present purposes, I now refer to the latter as multiple cognitive intelligences in order to distinguish it from multiple emotional intelligences. Moreover, I generalize the latter concept by referring to it as involving multiple socio-affective intelligences. In essence, just as multiple cognitive intelligences refer to the yoking of Neo-Piagetian stages and substages (as conceived in my 2011 model, in particular) to resolve tasks and problems confronting the individual, so to are multiple socio-affective intelligences a reflection of my model. That is, for each Neo-Piagetian cognitive (sub)stage that I describe in my model, there is a corresponding Neo-Eriksonian (sub)stage. With respect to conceiving them as multiple socio-affective intelligences, the latter can be combined in individualized ways online to resolve the socio-affective tasks and problems confronting the individual, with the added constraint that past difficulties in navigating the challenges in the (sub) stages involved might make the skills associate with them less than optimally available, or even having the negative poles associated with each (sub)stage predominant relative to the positive one (e.g., as in Trust vs. Mistrust).

To summarize, I had applied the concept of (sub)stage yoking to the multiple cognitive intelligence model, and in the present rendition of the concept, I show how it acts to build individualized hierarchical models of higher-order and lower-order levels in both multiple cognitive and socio-affective intelligences.

Conclusion The conclusion to the epilogue considers the nature of causality of behavior from both a normative and an individualized perspective. I end up giving primacy to the latter, with the former constituting a basis for understanding the latter. The study of causality is relevant in its own right, but its application to better ensuring optimal development, resolving psychopathology, and improving the human condition, in general, accelerates it to the vanguard of the field of behavioral study and mental health broadly considered. It is indeed the coalescing, integrating, unifying axis in this area, and one that is evolving constantly. The epilogue concludes that the study of behavioral causality and the unification of psychology are reciprocal processes and that they constitute ongoing and dynamic projects to which the present book hopes to elevate as central to the field.

Before beginning presentation of the epilogue in depth, I note that there is some overlap with material in prior chapters. On the one hand, this is inevitable given that in the epilogue I review many major areas of the book for new material since the time I had written the prior chapters. On the other hand, I treat material presented previously in new ways. Some of the areas that repeat in the epilogue include those related to my own conceptualizations (e.g., my 25-step stage model), and the attractor/complexity model considered as underlying them. Even here, I present conceptual innovations related to them.

Genes and Environment

The book has considered in depth the genetic basis of behavior, in concert with other influences. The recent literature provides examples related to the areas of behavior genetics, Gene × Environment Interactions (G × E), and differential susceptibility. Recall that, simply, G × E involves the vulnerability of certain alleles and environmental experiences working in concert for risk and psychopathology, while differential susceptibility refers to risk alleles not only conferring vulnerabilities in adverse environments but also positive developmental trajectories in supportive ones. The recent research reviewed does not consider other areas related to genetics that were discussed in the book, e.g., correlated gene–environment interactions, but they, too, indicate the dynamic nature of gene–environment relations and the futile task of considering them separately or statically.

Genes

Behavior Genetics Plomin, DeFries, Knopik, and Neiderhiser (2016) extolled the field of behavioral genetics for the replicability of its major findings. Some of the points raised concerned environment as much as genetics. Also, they had applied implications.

For Plomin et al. (2016), a replicated finding in behavior genetics is that all psychological "traits" show significant, substantial "genetic influence." Traits concern enduring characteristics related to intelligence, personality, and psychopathology (e.g., schizophrenia), in particular. In all three cases, the research points to heritability estimates between 30 and 50 %. It is noted that the estimates are below 100 %, which allows for environmental influence. Also, heritability for a trait is "caused" by multiple genes, each having only a small effect.

When traits are related phenotypically in research, a significant mediation by genetic factors is shown and it is "substantial." Also, heritability increases throughout development (at least for intelligence), which is related to findings of age-to-age stability due to genetics.

The environment can be measured and, further, the results in this research also reveal genetic mediation (e.g., parenting being mediated genetically). Further, the relationship between environmental measures and psychological traits reveals genetic mediation. Genetic research has served to highlight that sibling similarities are not due to growing up in the same family, because genetics "accounts for" these sibling similarities. Finally, environment and genetics both influence psychopathology. Also, genetic research supports a dimensional (quantitative) perspective on psychopathology, which is more accepted in psychology, relative to the categorical (qualitative) approach (psychiatric, DSM).

In response to the article, by Plomin et al. (2016), Turkheimer (2016) criticized the concept of "genetic influence," referring to it as "vague." He considered the concept of "heritability" a "fraught" one. Empirically, he contested the findings in the field of behavior genetics, arguing that "differences in midrange heritabilities do not replicate" (p. 25) and "differences in heritabilities among traits do not replicate" (p. 26). He advised to consider the context as a variable that affects genes and environment.

In the end, Turkheimer (2016) maintained that, "genetic influence is real." However, it must be shown at the level of "strong genetic explanation," or in terms of specific "latent genetic mechanisms" (etiology). Moreover, the traits studied in this regard cannot be operationalized "ambiguously." Finally, the research designs should avoid over-inflated results, as in candidate gene association studies. Even genome wide association studies (GWAS) are nothing more than "*p* hacking," with results significant due to Type I error.

Lee and McGue (2016) were more appreciative of the potential of GWAS, suggesting that, for the study of behavioral traits, the findings are now "highly credible." For example, the results of their study on the genes associated by GWAS for educational attainment (Rietveld et al., 2013) have been replicated in their as-yet unpublished extension and replication study.

Gene × Environment Li et al. (2016) reported a study on the genetic contributions to resilience in children. The level of effortful control (EC) in children at 30, 42, and 54 months of age ($N = 145$) was predicted by an interaction between observed maternal parenting at the child age of 30 months and variants of the dopamine transporter gene, *SLC6A3* (solute carrier family C6, member 3). Specifically, children without the intron 8-A/intron 13-G; intron 8-A3′-UTR (untranslated) VNTR (variable number tandem repeat)-10; or intron 13-G-3′-UTR VNTR-10 haplotypes, which are associated with reduced *SLC6A3* gene expression and so lower dopamine function, had their EC altered according to maternal parental quality. That is, they showed higher EC in conjunction with less supportive maternal parenting.

At first glance, these results seem counterintuitive. However, they suggest that, for the G×E involved, the children exposed to a less supportive environment having the haplotypes noted had, as a result, "decreased" reactivity/sensitivity to the environment, thereby "blocking" its influence, "resisting" the adversity involved, and so demonstrating "resilience," as per their higher EC.

Differential Susceptibility In terms of externalizing behavior trajectories, Trucco, Villafuerte, Heitzeg, Burmeister, and Zucker (2016) found that adolescents with the minor allele (GG) of the *GABA* receptor subunit alpha-2 (*GABRA2* (rs279827, rs27926, rs279858)) were greatly susceptible to either of adverse or adaptive parenting (as measured by an aspect of parental monitoring called parental knowledge). Specifically, the *GABRA2* gene is located on chromosome 4. It codes for the alpha-2 subunit of the receptor of the neurotransmitter *GABA-A*. Alpha 2 *GABA-A* receptors are ones that are expressed especially in the amygdala. *GABRA2* variants seem to heighten activity in this and related brain areas, and are related, then, to heightened emotional responsiveness/sensitivity to social context.

In the Trucco et al. (2016) study, three single nucleotide polymorphisms (SNPs) were examined (rs279827, rs279826, and rs279858), but with rs279827 of focus because the other two demonstrate "high linkage." The subjects were involved in the Michigan longitudinal study, which included high-risk families ($N = 504$), beginning at age 3 and ending at age 17. The YSR (Youth Self-Report; Achenbach & Rescorla,

2001) was used to examine externalizing behavior from age 11 on and the PM-YF (Parent Monitoring-Youth Form; Chilcoat & Anthony, 1996) to assess parental knowledge.

As for the specific results, GG carriers were more likely to be in the group of low-risk externalizing subjects, as determined by growth mixture modeling (GMM), if they reported high parental knowledge but, conversely, they were less likely to belong to this group for reports of low parental knowledge. According to the authors, this pattern of results represents the differential susceptibility model.

Another study examined differential susceptibility in adolescent antisocial behavior (ASB) for the serotonin transporter linked polymorphic region (*5-HTTLPR*) genotype in relation to sensitivity to perceived parental support (Tung & Lee, 2016). The study examined class trajectories and differentiated overt and covert ASB. It was a longitudinal study of a sample of 2558 individuals followed from ages 11 to 26 over three waves. As for differential susceptibility results, the long-long (ll) homozygous allele pair genotype seemed to function like a "plasticity genotype" for the trajectory group of overt ASB that peaked in adolescence, while the short (s) allele carriers (ss, ll) were responsive to quality of perceived parental support in the late onset trajectory group. Specifically, with respect to probability of membership in the adolescent-peak trajectory and in relation to perceived parental support, for s-carriers, the slope increased monotonically while, for ll carriers, the slope decreased. The same pattern was found for probability of membership in the late onset trajectory, respectively, for ll carriers and s-carriers, that is, in a pattern opposite for this class compared to the prior one.

Comment Recall that the metaphor used for this new differential susceptibility model of genes and development is one involving flowers. About one sixth of us have so-called susceptibility alleles, and they allow us to flower into orchids in a supportive environment for the behavior at issue, e.g., the potential for ASD being quite low rather than high. Most other people are more like dandelions than orchids. That is, most of us will fare well enough in any environment, supportive or not, but, metaphorically, we might not reach the level of being a fully blossoming orchid. I note that this version of the flowering metaphor for susceptibility genes in relation to environment quality lacks a flower type for the potential orchid that wilts badly in environments that are non-supportive. Also, it gives dandelions a bad name. In today's culture, dandelions are considered as salad delicacies as well as great sources to make wine. Therefore, the orchid-dandelion model of differential susceptibility needs to be contextualized. In this regard, perhaps we should refer to it as Contextual Orchid-Dandelion Model. Doing so would help account for findings for individuals with susceptibility alleles that adverse or nonsupportive environments might steel processes involved in resilience, e.g., promoting better executive function, instead of merely leading to deleterious developmental consequences.

Epigenetics Lester, Conradt, and Marsit (2016) described the important role of epigenetics in development. It involves mechanisms such as DNA methylation "marking" genes in the promoter region without changing the underlying DNA sequence (of four chemical bases, A, C, T, G; paired as A-T and G-C, with C (cytosine) the most important base in epigenetics). In DNA methylation, a methyl group is added to a chemical base C, and typically this takes place when the C is next to a G (guanine; referred to as a CpG site (p = phosphate)). CpG pairs typically are concentrated in a gene's promoter region. Areas of high CpG site concentration are called CpG islands. They are subject to methylation, and the genes involved negatively have their ability to be read by transcriptional machinery and produce the RNA and proteins for the codes involved affected by methylation. Unlike what is typically believed, methylation does not "silence" genes but only "dims" them, depending on the extent of methylation (or other epigenetic processes).

For example, the gene *NR3C1* encodes genetically the glucocorticoid receptor (GR) and it is involved in cortisol regulation. GR is the receptor site to which cortisol "binds." Methylation of the gene *NR3C1* leads to reduced gene expression, and so a smaller availability in number of GR proteins (and fewer sites for cortical binding), further leading to higher levels of circulating cortisol.

Stroud et al. (2016) showed how early adversity impacts methylation of the *NR3C1*gene. That is, the effect of adversity on behavior is mediated by gene methylation, as with this example. A standard finding in the field is that the environment induces methylation that impacts the brain and behavior. Furthermore, the methylated gene is passed on to the next generation, thereby having intergeneration effects even in the absence of the environmental factors that had first caused the methylation.

Comment Keating (2016) added that the types of adversity that can induce methylation include SES (socioeconomic status); parental sensitivity/acceptance/rejection; child abuse; neonatal intensive care stay; and maternal smoking. The health consequences include ones ranging from; those early in life (e.g., neonatal neurobehavioral integrity); to ones in infancy (temperament; Montirosso et al., 2016); childhood (internalizing symptoms; Parade et al., 2016); adolescence (psychosocial adjustment; Naumova et al., 2016); and young adulthood (psychiatric symptomatology; Smearman et al., 2016). The latter study involved the oxytocin receptor (*OXTR*). Other genes subject to methylation effects and consequent mental health effects include *SLC6A4*, which regulates serotonin exposure (Montirosso et al., 2016). The prior chapters in the book dealing with epigenetics describe multiple genes subject to methylation, including many involved in neurotransmitter regulation.

Environment

Early Life Stress The most recent studies reviewed on early life stress (ELS) and related factors together accentuate the role of the early environment on long-term development especially when the environment is adverse. Moreover, the research traces the physiological effects that result and contribute to the development of developmental psychopathology in a cascade effect. At the same time, as well, recent research points to the influence of and interaction with genetic and more congenital factors in these regards. In the following, I review quite briefly select findings on ELS and related factors.

Grizenko, Fortier, Gaudreau-Simard, Jolicoeur, and Joober (2015) found that maternal stress during pregnancy predicted ADHD (attention deficit hyperactivity disorder) symptomatology, including for internalizing and externalizing behavior as measured by the CBCL (Child Behavior Checklist; Achenbach, 1991). Tearne et al. (2015) found a relationship between known prenatal risk factors and mental health, as measured by the CBCL, up to 14 years of age. Martinez-Torteya, Bogat, Levendosky, and von Eye (2016) showed that prenatal intimate partner violence exposure predicted childhood internalizing and externalizing symptoms (as per the CBCL, among other measures), as well as high cortisol secretion (indicative of HPA axis reactivity).

The predictors in this type of research on effects of early environment on development include birth weight and the findings of vulnerability extended into adulthood (e.g., social trust; Peterson & Aarøe, 2015). The results support different models, including the adaptive calibration one in the latter study and differential susceptibility in Kopala-Sibley et al. (2015). In this regard, Kopala-Sibley et al. (2015) found that better quality parent–child relationship predicted decreased negative emotionality for children with elevated cortisol reactivity but increases in positive emotionality in children with low cortisol reactivity.

As well, ELS has been related to biological effects in the hippocampus, and it is mediated partially by long-term effects on GC (glucocorticoid signaling) pathways, neurotrophin ones, or both (Daskalakis, De Kloet, Yehuda, Malaspina, & Kranz, 2015). Factors in early life adversity also have been related to inflammation at midlife, in results supportive of the stress accumulation model, which, at the same time, does not deny a role for the additive effects of recent stressors (Hostinar, Mroczek, Lachman, Seeman, & Miller, 2015). Adult outcome also includes cortical thickness measures (Sylvester et al., 2016) but, in this case, the predictor involved early childhood inhibition.

Maltreatment Scarpa (2015) qualified that child maladjustment is related to either hypo- or hyperarousal. Jedd et al. (2015) related childhood maltreatment to altered functional connectivity in the amygdala and other effects on frontolimbic circuitry. Peckins, Susman, Negriff, Noll, and Trickett (2015) related child maltreatment to blunted cortisol profiles, with adaptive calibration eventually tempering the difference between maltreated and non-maltreated participants. Hanson, Knodt, Brigidi, and Hariri (2015) found that stress sensitization in child maltreatment participants seemed to affect the uncinate fasciculus connecting the amygdala and ventromedial PFC (prefrontal cortex).

Genetically, Thibodeau, Cicchetti, and Rogosch (2015) found an association of child maltreatment to dopaminergic genes (in African American children; in a complex relationship with impulsivity and ASB). Tyrka et al. (2015) related it to the FK506 binding protein 5 gene (*FKBP5*) in terms of lower levels of methylation (epigenesis) at CpG sites in intron 7. Räikkönen et al. (2015) related placental expression of genes regulating glucocorticoid and serotonin function to infant regulatory behavior, through its mediation of maternal depressive symptoms during pregnancy on infant challenges in regulatory behavior. A twin study (Gagne & Saudino, 2016) also related genetic factors to childhood inhibitory control.

Comment The role of the environment in behavioral causality is indisputable. The field of genetics is rapidly evolving to include topics that reflect environmental influence, such as G×E, differential susceptibility, and epigenetics. Moreover, the work on environmental influence on behavior includes models on ELS, the effects of maltreatment, and stress accumulation. Of course, parenting is critical to behavioral development and will remain the central axis of the ecology involved in behavioral causality, as reviewed, in part, in the following.

Development

Models

Biopsychosocial Model Calkins (2015) has brought the biopsychosocial approach center stage in the study of infant development. She viewed that the spurs to the growth of this approach laid in the work on G×E interactions (e.g., Caspi et al., 2002, 2003) and epigenesis (e.g., Meaney, 2010). Similarly, Leerkes and Parade (2015) referred to the model of differential susceptibility (Belsky, Bakermans-Kranenburg, & van IJzendoorn, 2007). In this regard, Gordon and Feldman (2015) underscored biopsychosocial development through behavioral synchrony with the mother, biological synchrony, and contextual synchrony in adaptive child development. For example, Feldman, Vengrober, and Ebstein (2014) related child PTSD development to genetics, sensitive maternal support, and behavioral withdrawal vs. comfort seeking (the latter being more predictive of better outcome).

Eriksonian Model Malone, Liu, Vaillant, Rentz, and Waldinger (2016) referred to Vaillant and Milofsky's (1980) revised Eriksonian model that inserted a stage of middle adulthood after intimacy/isolation and a stage of old age after generativity/stagnation. These stages were numbered 6a and 7a, respectively, in the Eriksonian sequence. Moreover, they were not given separate "crises," as found in the Eriksonian model for the original eight-step sequence.

Other Models The Piagetian model and its Neo-Piagetian variants are presented below, as is the relational one. The embodied developmental model is implicated in the next section. It is beyond the scope of the epilogue to consider the research on every important developmental model. One that is not discussed is the evolutionary, life history one, for example. The reader is referred to earlier chapters of the book on this model. In the following, I have selected examples of recent developmental research that reveals the precocity of infant development. However, this should not be taken to support a strictly nativist view of development. Early appearing skills might be foundational but not determinant. For example, not only is early experience important in the transactional trajectories that follow from these early skills, but also other models, including my own, refer to the transformations, e.g., through developmental substages, that these early skills negotiate. The review that follows also indicates the primordial role that causal learning and reasoning play in development.

As argued elsewhere in the book, we are indeed *Homo Causa*.

Domains

Motor Libertus, Joh, and Needham (2015) found that motor training at 3 months of age was related to object exploration at 15 months of age. The results showed that new motor skills have developmental cascade effects on ongoing learning opportunities and even the stimulation directed toward the child.

Cognition Baillargeon, Scott, and Bian (2016) defended the view that infants are capable of "psychological reasoning." Infants are capable of making sense of others' actions; for example, infants who observe agents acting in a simple scene appear to infer their mental states and then use them to predict and to interpret their subsequent actions (and to self-guide their own actions vis-à-vis the agent). Baillargeon et al. (2016) added that infants are "born equipped" with this "foundational" system of psychological reasoning.

Causal Learning Recent research on the development of causal learning continues to show the centrality of causality as part of exceptional human attributes. Rakison, Smith, and Ali (2016) showed that 22 month olds expect that the second object in a delayed launching sequence should contain a moving, dynamic component. Alvarez and Booth (2016) described that preschoolers adopt a "causal stance" and that, moreover, its "strength" is related to maternal "explanatory" communication.

Cultural Learning Cultural learning is crucial to human learning, for example, as shown in the research on causal learning just mentioned. Further, Legare and Nielsen (2015) considered the dual engines of cultural learning as imitation and innovation. Heyes (2015) related it to social learning. Grossmann (2015) referred to the social information processing capacity of the infant brain, referring to it as a "social brain." Christensen and Michael (2016) referred to an earlier developing "mind reading" system that employs "simple representations" toward arriving at "fast, resource-efficient" more advanced mind-reading representation processing.

Comment In short, we are a social, developmental, and innovative species that uses simpler and more advanced cognitive processes even in the infancy period. However, I have maintained throughout that the acquisitions that develop in infancy should not be viewed as separate skills but as part of holistic (sub)stages, as indicated by the (Neo-)Piagetian model that I have developed (Young, 2011). Specifically, both psychological reasoning and mind-reading, as well as related cognitive acquisitions, should not be viewed solely in terms of whether they are innate, foundational, and prepared or in terms of whether they are gradually acquired, are simple and non-representational to begin, and so on. Rather, all of these acquisitions should be viewed as subject to a multi-step evolution through many substages in the first year from the reflexive to the sensorimotor to the peri (pre) operational and, therefore, more than acquisitions with only simple two-step transitions from initial to a more elaborate structure and function. That being said, the nature of such a stage model needs the types of revisions descried in this epilogue, as per below.

Free Will and Self-Control

Free Will

Introduction Philosophically, the existence of free will constitutes a topic of interminable debate that is irresolvable. However, psychologically, the belief in free will has many positive consequences. Topics related to free will include the ones of prospection and self-control. Simply, the former involves planning ahead and the latter appropriate behavioral selection and implementation. Self-control can be depleted, e.g., in the second of two demanding tasks.

Baumeister and Monroe (2014) touted "responsible autonomy" as the folk psychological conception of free will. That is, operatively, free will involves "being responsible" and "exercising autonomy." Free will belief "arises" in social structures through the need for self-regulation, choosing appropriately (consciously and without coercion) in acts of commission or omission, and also in the need to regulate others (e.g., moral judgment/punishment).

Belief Feldman, Chandrashekar, and Wong (2016) found that belief in free will predicted better academic performance (course and semester grades) in university students. They maintained that belief in free will facilitates long-term goal pursuit (as well as having social benefits).

Baumeister and Monroe (2014) reviewed the extensive research showing that free will belief has positive consequences. Among the notable consequences, one finds effects on academic motivation and success, even when all other variables that might be at issue are controlled as covariates.

Prospection Baumeister, Vohs, and Oettingen (2016) emphasized the pragmatic aspect of prospective thinking. For them, people think about the future in order to give guidance to their behavior toward actualizing desirable outcomes.

Self-Control

Ego-Depletion Baumeister and Monroe (2014) advocated that the model of "ego-depletion" (or "strength") governs the function of self-regulation, but that it is carefully regulated because it is a limited resource. They advocated for a physiological model, in particular, related to blood glucose availability.

Orquin and Kurzban (2015) held that Baumeister's concept that blood glucose depletion helps explain self-regulation depletion does not apply uniformly to decision-making. In particular, self-control and its depletion varies, with food-related and nonfood related situations having differential effects (e.g., on willingness to play/work).

Kotabe and Hofmann (2015) proposed an integrated model of self-control that included seven major factors: desire; high-order goal; desire-goal conflict; control motivation; control capacity; control effort; and enactment constraints. The moderators in helping determine effort control deployment include: desire strength; perceived skill; and competing goals. The authors concluded that competing models involving "will power" and the like (as in Baumeister's) are vague and lack integration.

Comment In the present causal model of behavior, at the personal level, factors such as curiosity, coping, and free will are as much part of the biopsychosocial, multifactorial influences on behavior as are genetics, physiology, the brain, evolution, and other biological factors, as well as the family, schools, and society and other ecological/environmental factors. In this regard, in this book, I have elaborated a model of self-control that is biopsychosocial and has incorporated motivation and other factors mentioned in this section. Further, I also maintained that, among the personal factors that influence behavior, free will belief stands as the most important. This is reflected in the free will therapeutic approach that I elucidated in one of the chapters in the book.

The following section turns to psychopathology and the DSM-5, through the topic of PTSD. It is a disorder that is biopsychosocial in nature, but work with patients expressing it requires an additional forensic perspective, as in the detection of its feigning for monetary gain. The section begins with discussion of the nature of PTSD; then, it considers factors in its etiology.

Posttraumatic Stress Disorder

Dimensions

The cluster structure of the 20 PTSD symptoms in the DSM-5 has been investigated with CFA. PTSD in the DSM-5 had been built on a four-cluster model, but this four-cluster approach has not been supported in the recent research. For example, Armour et al. (2015) even found a seven-factor solution of how the 20 DSM-5 PTSD symptoms are distributed according to CFA.

This finding has been replicated by the research of Wang et al. (2015).

As for some methodological detail in the research just mentioned, the seven factors in Armour et al. (2015), who studied two trauma-exposed samples, involved: re-experiencing, avoidance, negative affect, anhedonia, externalizing behavior, anxious arousal, and dysphoria arousal. The number of symptoms in each cluster involved, respectively: 5, 2, 4, 3, 2, 2, and 2. Wang et al. (2015) obtained their comparable results with Chinese adolescent earthquake survivors; however, they referred to the first factor as intrusion. In Young (2015b), I had proposed that a composite model of seven clusters in PTSD should refer to re-experiencing/intrusion.

Other research has supported a six-factor model for the 20 DSM-5 PTSD symptoms (Liu et al., 2014; Tsai et al., 2015). More recently, Konecky, Meyer, Kimbrel, and Morissette (2015) found a six-factor in their small sample of military veterans. Zelazany and Simms (2015) also found a six-factor solution, but stated that a larger sample might have given a seven-factor solution.

Based on the seven-factor model, Young (2015b) proposed an eight-cluster one, with the eighth one involving the dissociative subtype. Miller, Wolf, and Keane (2014) cited evidence in support of the addition of the dissociative subtype to the DSM-5. This justifies considering dissociation as the eight PTSD cluster or dimension. Aside from proposing eight clusters/dimensions for PTSD, Young (2015b, 2016) also indicated which symptoms are core for each of them.

Young (2016) concluded that the nature of the dimensional structure of PTSD symptoms depends on: the models tested; whether the DSM-IV-TR (Diagnostic and Statistical Manual of Mental Disorders, Fourth Edition, Text Revised; American Psychiatric Association, 2000) and its 17 symptoms or the DSM-5 and its 20 symptoms had been the basis for the research; the population examined (e.g., civilian or military; external event trauma-exposed or other); and a host of other variables (sample size, their gender, etc.). Perhaps the nature of the PTSD cluster/dimensional structure does not have one solution, e.g., perhaps even cultural differences apply in this regard.

To conclude, the exact cluster/dimensional structure of PTSD still has not been firmly established. That being said, the minimum amount of clusters/dimensions that seem to be involved stands at six, which really is seven if one adds a dissociative subtype, as per Young (2015b, 2016). Moreover, there might be eight such clusters/dimensions (as per Young again). Finally, determining which of the 20 symptoms of PTSD that are core seems essential, perhaps even for better understanding the biological underpinnings to it and also what might be its biomarkers.

Genes and Brain

In this regard, Ashley-Koch et al. (2015) undertook a GWAS of PTSD in Iraq-Afghanistan theater military veterans. PTSD was evaluated using DSM-IV-TR criteria. There were some genes specific to groups (e.g., Black, White), while others emerged in combined analysis. They included protein kinase type 1 alpha cGMP-dependent (*PRKG1*) and DEAD box polypeptide 60-like (*DDX60L*). These genes are not the ones usually associated with PTSD (e.g., *5-HTTLPR*). Goenjian et al. (2015) added that PTSD symptomatology appears related not only to *COMT* but also to *TPH-2* genes (tryptophan hydroxylase 2).

Using fMRI (functional magnetic resonance imaging), Zhang et al. (2015) examined alterations in resting state functional connectivity (FC) in PTSD patients and controls ($N=20$). PTSD was evaluated according to the DSM-IV (Diagnostic and Statistical Manual of Mental Disorders, Fourth Edition; American Psychiatric Association, 1994) using the instrument developed by Blake et al. (1995).

As for the results, relative to controls, PTSD patients evidenced decreased intranetwork FC within the anterior DMN (default mode network), posterior DMN, and the SN (salience network), as well as the sensorimotor network (SMN) and auditory network (AN), but not in the CEN (central executive network). Other results concerned increased FC between posterior DMN and SN.

These sample studies on PTSD reveal the rich biological research being undertaken to round out understanding of PTSD. They speak to the genetic and brain networking associations with PTSD. The mediating pathways from genes to brain to behavior include the stress response system, e.g., the HPA axis and cortisol production. As discussed in the early adversity/maltreatment section of this epilogue, dysregulation of the stress response is critical to mental equilibrium and, in the present case, both hypo- and hypercortisolism due to chronic stressors adds to the vulnerability to and expression of PTSD.

Malingering

As shown in Young (2016), Suhr (2015) advocated for a biopsychosocial approach to assessment, giving importance to the forensic task of assessing for noncredible responding. In this regard, she referred to at least 20 % of PTSD claimants exhibiting noncredible responding (citing Elhai et al., 2004; Frueh et al., 2005).

Moreover, Young (2015c) conducted a literature review, and showed that the frequently cited percentage that malingering takes place in forensic and related disability assessments at the rate of 40 ± 10 % (Larrabee, Millis, & Meyers, 2009) is not supported by the empirical research. Rather, the research shows that malingering in the forensic disability and related assessment context is more toward the rate of 15 ± 15 %, although malingering could be more frequent in cases of PPCS (persistent post-concussive syndrome) after mTBI. In addition, problematic presentations, such as feigning, in general, could be toward 50 % or more. In such cases, there are other ways of suggesting poor evaluee effort or lack of credibility, without using the "M" word.

DSM-5

PTSD is listed in different ways in major nosological systems. For example, the DSM-5 does not include the diagnosis of complex PTSD, which is projected for inclusion in the ICD-11 (International Classification of Disease, 11th Edition; World Health Organization, 2017). Moreover, these nosological systems are not without criticisms. Demazeux and Singy (2015) referred to the theoretical, epistemological, and social weaknesses of the DSM-5. Demazeux (2015) referred to its chaotic revision process, and the absence of the consideration of causality related to the listed mental disorders. Poland (2015) criticized its categories as artificial and its approach as atheoretic (apart from its biocentric approach). Also, it is medical-focused, individual-focused or decontextualized, and symptom-focused. Tsou (2015) advocated for inclusion of a theoretical pluralism in the DSM-5 and inclusion of the causes of its listed disorders, while admitting that the latter goal has to be long term. Kirk, Cohen, and Gomory (2015) even referred to the moral insolvency of the DSM-5, e.g., because of the financial conflicts of interest among the members of its work groups (and one can add the background presence of Big Pharma).

In the next sections, the epilogue turns to critical models in the present book, reviewing ones already mentioned as per the recent literature and adding new conceptual material for consideration. In terms of the latter, I build on my previously presented models and add others.

Modeling

The Relational Model

Overton and Molenaar (2015) have placed on a par the process-relational and relational-developmental-systems view in the paradigm shift that is taking place in developmental science. For example, development derives from multiple coacting influences in a constructive, nonlinear, epigenetic (in the sense of being probabilistic) process over multiple time scales and at multiple levels.

Overton (2015) qualified that viewing nature as "process" stands in opposition to the view of nature as being "substance," which is a Cartesian perspective. For Overton (2015), the relational as opposed to the Cartesian view fits with an approach to explanation of nature that it is best considered "multiple" instead of just the product of "efficient, material" causal factors. Overton (2015) continued that the "process-relational" approach that is embodied in this metatheoretical worldview differs from the mechanistic, Cartesian, reductionist one. He added that the Piagetian developmental model has been aligned with the latter view in some readings, but this is a misunderstanding of Piaget's interdependent, non-dualist, and "non-splittable" stance (for structure and function, for example).

Overton (2015) offered a lifespan stage model of development much like that of Piaget. He referred to the four stages involved as practical (action systems), symbolic (representations), reflective (second-order representations), and "trans-reflective" (third-order representations), with a biological basis/embodiment included at each stage, and with earlier stages still active as higher-order stages appear. His reworking of Piaget's stage concept is interesting, especially the notion that stages can be active simultaneously and are not integrated and no longer functional with the appearance of each new stage [Also see Rochat (2015) below, in this regard].

Overton (2015) argued that the concepts of mechanism and causation have "no place" in the process-relational view. However, he equated mechanism and cause with "external split-off" forces, which are not the sole factors in contemporary understanding of causality (Young, 2011, as well as the present book). That being said, in the present view, the "what" and the "why" of development, or the product and process, are inseparable components of development, as Overton would argue.

Piagetian Modeling

Stages Lourenço (2016) maintained that the Piagetian concept of stages is still valid because its criticisms are based on misunderstandings and also the evidence provided for their existence is supportive. Developmental stages are hierarchical or invariant in order; integrative of prior stages yet with consolidating transitions between them; and characterized as wholes or overarching structures ("structures d'ensemble") that are in equilibration (not easily perturbed). Stages are "descriptive," not "explanatory." Moreover, there is no inconsistency in advocating for stages despite the finding of "décalage" or uneven development within a domain/stage due to task complexity differences. Also, micro-development does appear continuous, which is not evidence against the discontinuity in development that the macro-development of stages represents. In terms of the causality behind development, Lourenço (2016) maintained that Piaget anticipated the dynamic and complexity models that are current today.

Comment Barrouillet (2015) and Carey, Zaitchik, and Bascandziev (2015) also affirmed the value of Piaget's stage model. Bjorklund (2015) provided an evolutionary perspective and Zelazo (2015) emphasized the role of executive function, with Goldin-Meadow (2015) highlighting the action/gestural component in influences on cognitive development. Rochat (2015) presented a stage model of levels of awareness. It is not consistent with Piaget's model nor is it consistent with Neo-Piagetian ones, such as Fischer's (1980). However, it is valuable for its "onion" metaphor of levels in development in which older and newer levels can co-exist and function in parallel.

To conclude, the recent literature on cognitive developmental stages supports the Piagetian approach but does not explicitly refer to the value of Piaget's four-step stage sequence itself. Mascolo and Fischer (2015) presented an alternative to that sequence, in their Neo-Piagetian model, but in the following I indicate some difficulties with it.

Neo-Piagetian Model

Fischer's Model Mascolo and Fischer (2015) reviewed Fischer's (1980) Neo-Piagetian model of development and its implications for social and emotional development, in particular. In Fischer's model, stages are referred to as tiers and substages as levels. There are five stages (reflexes, sensorimotor actions, representations, abstractions, principles), with three cyclic substages recurring in the first four of them (which are referred to as: single, mapping, system).

Generally, my model (Young, 2011) includes five stages, which concern reflexes, sensorimotor actions, representations (perioperations), abstract (formal) thought, and superordinate abstract (collective) intelligence. There are five cyclically recurring substages, which are referred to as coordination, hierarchization, systematization, multiplication, and integration. Thus, my model includes 25 (sub)stages/steps over the lifespan, which is much more than the number in Fischer (and in Case, 1998, too, which is a competing Neo-Piagetian model).

In the following, I review the difference in approach to substages from the 18-month-old period to the next years as found in Mascolo and Fischer (2015), Fischer, 1980 and Young (2011). In my model, the 18–24 month age period is associated with the present sensorimotor substage of integration. Then, at 2 years, the representational stage begins (perioperations), with the first substage being one of coordination. Next, at 3.5 years, the substage of hierarchization begins. These substages in my model are the ones equivalent to those in Mascolo and Fischer's (2015) treatment of the development of emotions, which constituted a good portion of the examples covered in their work. Before criticizing that work, I give my general critique of Fischer's model, as presented in Young (2011).

In Young (2011), I showed that Fischer's model appears to be missing substages at 2, 7, and 9, years, in particular, as well as prenatally and in the adult period, unlike in my own 5-stage × 5-substage lifelong developmental model. Also, I showed how the examples provided by Fischer and colleagues for the development of emotions better fit my model than theirs. For example, in reference to the substage at 18–24 months, the examples provided were as much sensorimotor in nature as purely representation, counter to the Fischerian model that claims that, at this age, representation emerges. Also, in reference to the missing substage at 2 years, Fischer provided for the first (and only) time in his lifetime body of work a substage, which, in contrast, is generally called for in my model. That is, Mascolo and Fischer (2015) had included a substage that is representational in nature, which is consistent with each of the work of Piaget, Case, and myself. Specifically, the missing substage at 2 years had been referred to as "compounded representations/internalized standards" (Mascolo & Fischer, 2007). Moreover, the single representation substage at 18–24 months had been qualified as "evoked and supported," which, to me, indicates its less than pure representational status.

Inexplicably, in Mascolo and Fischer (2015), the new substage used to help explain the development of socio-affective acquisitions in their prior work on emotional development (Mascolo & Fischer, 2007) was not applied to their new work on a related developmental topic, that of moral action in three domains considered. That is, they reverted to Fischer's general model in which a substage at 2 years of age is excluded. Moreover, they did not refer to the 18- to 24-month age period, at least at this point, as being "evoked and supported."

Next, I examine the specific examples provided for moral development in Mascolo and Fischer (2015), which permits me to show their lacunae relative to my own model. In Mascolo and Fischer (2015), the moral action domain of autonomy/rights develops from the substage of single representation of possession ("mine") at the 18- to 24-month age period to that of reciprocity (give me toy, return it) at 3.5–4.5 years. As mentioned, but worthy of repetition, in their description of this development passage, as per the general critique I had presented in Young (2011) of the Fischerian model, there is no substage between the two substages presented that is applicable to 2 years of age. In this regard, I would add to their substage sequence something like their substage found in Mascolo and Fischer (2007), that is, their substage of "compounded representations/internalized standards." In other words, at this age, there should be the substage of representations/internalized standards or an equivalent. Using their examples, it would be captured by the child returning to the scene, after a child has transgressed someone's rights (e.g., inappropriately saying "mine"), in order to say, "Sorry" (as opposed to simply saying "Sorry" without a return component). Of course, another option would be to use my own model in this regard, which refers to coordinated representations at this age (indeed, the example provided fits this terminology, too).

The clearest example of the need to differentiate a 2-year-old level of representation from ones for 18 to 24 months and for 3.5–4.5 years in the work of Mascolo and Fischer (2015) concerns the domain that they presented of developing concern for others. In the examples that they provided for an 18 month old, a child accidentally hurts the mother and says "kiss, kiss" before kissing the mother. The action component to the representation is evident, which I highlight as the reason for considering this age at one still involving sensorimotor actions, as Piaget had maintained (and unlike what they maintained). For an older child (30 months), in the example provided, the concern for others is expressed verbally only ("poor Donna crying"), which, moreover, appears to be a compounded or coordinated representation ("poor" + "crying"), to use their language (or a coordinated representation, to use my language). Clearly, the example reflects a representation without an action component. However, in Mascolo and Fischer (2015), despite the differences that they reflect about representation for the two ages involved, the two examples that they give are both referred to as representational (at the substage of single representations).

Comment To summarize, Fischer's Neo-Piagetian model has fewer substages over the lifespan than my own, and there are striking lacunae in substages that should be present, including at 2 years of age. Moreover, for the same age periods, the description that I give of the substages that make sense are not the same as those in Fischer, e.g., at 18 months of age. To conclude, the value of the Piagetian approach is uncontested, as evidenced in the current literature review. However, the present Neo-Piagetian model might offer new avenues in conceptualization and application relative to others (e.g., Fischer 1980; and Mascolo and Fischer 2015).

A major difficulty with stage models, in general, relates to how causally the abrupt jumps in discontinuous stage-to-stage development take place. Moreover, the nature of stage organization within each stage needs to be clarified better, as well as how they evolve internally (e.g., from initial schema to more complex within-stage structures). Case's concept of central conceptual structures provides fertile ground for new ideas on these matters. I have dealt with these issues in the present book, but explore them further in the following.

Central Conceptual Structures

Model Young (2011) described that Case, Okamoto, Henderson, and McKeough (1993) defined central conceptual structures in terms of organized systems of similar semantic nodes or sets and relations, having both general cross-domain properties and particular domain constraints formed in context. The domains could be numerical, narrative, social, etc. Case (1998) elaborated that they begin as a mental model, then coalesce into sub-dimensions in the domain, and then an explicit rule for modeling inter-dimensional relations. Mental states are inner state schemas that develop from events (e.g., witnessed) and they alternate with actions that they cause, being transformed by them, in turn. As an example, the actions deriving from mental states in narrative conceptual structures could include inferences on mental states, perceived causes, etc.

Case et al. (1993) tested for the presence of conceptual mental structures by administering a broad range of quantitative and social tasks to 5- and 8-year-olds. They found a moderate degree of inter-task correlations within each domain, and less so between them. Further, factor analysis revealed similar results. In terms of cognitive levels in development (a concept similar to substages), 70 % of the participants scored within half of one level on each of the two sets of tasks.

As for related research, McKeough and Griffiths (2010) found similar results for 4- to 12-year-old story telling performance, indicative of conceptual structure development and evolution.

Demetriou, Spanoudis, and Mouyi (2010) conducted research on different domains, elaborating changes every 2 years (or over classes) in the domains of number, causal understanding, space, and verbal skills. Young (2011) concluded that central conceptual structures are "intermediary" structures between "local schemes" and large units, such as (sub)stages.

Comment Although formulated outside of concepts related to systems theory, hierarchies of multiple levels in system dynamics, and so on, the concept of central conceptual structures speaks to concepts such as these. For example, central conceptual structures are comprised of a hierarchy involving more general rules, sub-dimensions, and mental models. In my work below, elaborating the concept of central conceptual structures, I refer to these three different levels in their evolution as developing mental schemas, then specific rules, and then general rules. In terms of the critical aspect of individual differences in development, as systems theory would predict, they allow for differential expression in context, including differences in different domains and a lack of clear correlation of development across domains. In the following, I present other models that speak to similar issues, toward arriving at a new conceptualization of the inner workings of stages that is consistent with systems theory.

The Network Model

Model Dalege, Borsboom, van Harreveld, van den Berg, and Conner (2016) described a model of attitudes that is based on the network model (e.g., Borsboom & Cramer, 2013). It includes interaction of evaluative reactions and their interactions, in turn, which "arise through direct causal influences" and mechanisms. In the network model, relations among components (variables) comprise an ensemble of causally-connected components. "Tight clusters" form across similar components, e.g., evaluative reactions. These component clusters are conceptualized as "nodes," with node links termed "edges." Further, components such as attitudes form network structures. They might be so tight as to conform to the network concept of "small-world structure." Specifically, small-world structures involve "high global connectivity" established through "short-cuts," in conjunction with "high clustering." For example, positive attitudes could exhibit a small-world structure, and one that excludes negative attitudes.

Nodes vary not only in their cluster alignment but also with their "structural importance" (or centrality; with measures of centrality involving "betweenness," "degree," and "closeness"). According to Dalege et al., (2016), this has implications for understanding networks more widely in terms of NLDST. In this regard, the more strongly connected are components, such as attitude networks, the more likely they form a small set of attractors (e.g., positive and negative attitudes). The disadvantage of highly-connected networks is that ambivalence or conflict among elements (e.g., specific attitudes) could arise easier than for cases in which there are weakly connected ones. Finally, it is important to note that networks such as those relating to attitudes are subject to growth over time (Bringmann et al., 2013).

In other work that addresses networks, Sporns and Betzel (2016) described that networks form "communities" or clusters of "dense connected" nodes, which are referred to as "modules." The communities consist of building blocks of subnetworks. For Sporns and Betzel (2016), networks are "strongly coupled" subcomponent networks among nodes and linking edges. Edges can link nodes either within modules or between them. If a node is highly connected, it is called a "hub." Provincial hubs involve node connectivity mostly in the same community, in contrast to connector hubs, which relate nodes belonging to different communities.

For Sporns and Betzel (2016), modules are efficient organizational plans because they allow for adaptability, robustness, evolvability, resilience, stability, buffering, cost reduction, synchronization, and processing efficiency (at least for brain networks, collectively referred to as the Connectome). Hierarchical modularity consists of "modules within modules" over multiple "spatial scales" [One can refer to modules within modules as "sub-modules."]

According to Sporns and Betzel (2016), this type of organization facilitates the attractor dynamic of "criticality" in complex neuronal dynamics (Rubinov, Sporns, Thivierge, & Breakspear, 2011). Criticality (Bak, 1996) constitutes an important concept in systems theory, because it helps predict the thresholds when the system at issue reaches bifurcation points in which attractor regimes are altered (think of trickling sand falling on the top point of a sand pile and releasing an "avalanche").

Comment In this section of their work, Sporns and Betzel (2016) are relating network theory and NLDST. This approach is quite consistent with my own.

Nonlinear Dynamical Systems Theory

Model Specifically, in NLDST, systems gravitate to attractor basins in which their repeated trajectories settle, such as might be evident in systems that remain stable despite perturbation that takes them far-from-equilibrium, or systems that adopt configurations akin to the well-known, chaotic attractor regime, and so on. Attractors are mathematical representations of state space patterning of systems as they change in their phase portraits. Attractors come in multiple types, such as point attractors and oscillatory ones from point to point. As they evolve, they take on more complex patterns, especially of the chaotic variety, which marks a trajectory toward living on the edge of chaos, or on the cusp of change between order and disorder.

Living systems are characterized by inhabiting this latter state space in order to facilitate rapid response to ongoing conditions and changes online; and, also, multiple attractors characterize them. Kauffman (1993) developed the concept of CAS to indicate the complexity of systems beyond attractors, such as might be found in the self-organization inherent in human behavior. In this regard, in Young (2011), I argued that CAS could develop superordinate regimes, just as attractors can create multiple complex solutions.

Therefore, in my model of increasing complexity in attractor organization as systems evolve, especially in the living and human case, but potentially in anything, such as ecological or cosmological systems, there is a natural progression from point and cyclical attractors to chaotic and cusp of change regimes, and then to Complex Adaptive and Superordinate Complex Adaptive regimes. That said, as mentioned below, the direction of the evolution of the contents of the attractors might be negative and not positive, as with entrenchment of disorder rather then their mitigation in therapy.

Witherington (2015) specified that, in attractor dynamics in NLDST, context-general system organization can remain stable despite fluctuation in system content/activity over time/context. The qualitative pattern in attractor dynamics persists globally despite local variation (or micro-development, online behavior). New levels of organization can emerge in a system through its variable micro-level component coactions.

One approach to NLDST views the global higher-order patterns, structures, forms, levels, or organizations as incapable of top-down influence on lower levels because, rather than being independently substantive, they are only epiphenomena of lower-level process dynamics in real time (e.g., Thelen & Smith, 2006), while another view considers that upper levels of a system can be "explanatory" of lower levels (e.g., Lewis, 2005). In this latter view, emergent levels are "causally irreducible." They possess the capacity for downward, "systematic causation" through the "constraints" of their properties. In this view, the various levels of the system—higher-order, top-down and lower-order, bottom-up—stand as "cause and effect for each other."

Lewis's (2005) concepts of reciprocal causality and circular causality within and between levels of a system illustrate the view of system organization as being comprised of levels in which top-down ones can have causal downward effects. For example, an emotional episode might last seconds in micro-development. Over time, these episodes consolidate into moods of up to weeks in duration. Then, in higher-order patterning, personality develops over the years. Further, emotional interpretations (EIs) arise out of emotional "appraisal" and emotion "elements" through coupling and synchronization with each other and in interaction with "emotional feeling states." As EIs stabilize, they can be represented as attractors, and an individual's state space in its behavioral landscape might have "multiple EI attractors." Moods arise in this microdevelopmental context, and then personality follows. In this regard, personality is an emergent level in developmental behavioral system organization that is "hierarchically-nested" and self-organizing" through processes of "assembly" and upward constraints from lower-order (e.g., mood) levels (as much as it imposes downward constraints on lower-order levels).

Comment Notice the three-level hierarchical system structure described by Lewis (2005) for affect—emotions to moods to personality. And notice how it moves from micro-, ongoing feelings to stable, macro- long-term patterns in personality. On the one hand, this work supports the application of a multilevel hierarchical approach to stage development as appears later in the epilogue. On the other hand, it shows how micro-time processes can lead to macro-time stabilities that are included in stage consolidation and transition, also as shown below.

Two further points are worth considering about NLDST, especially as it applies to behavior and development (Young, 2011). First, it allows for the evolution of attractor configurations from the simplest to the most complex, e.g., from point attractors to cyclical and chaotic ones. That is, it concerns the deep level of mechanisms in the change process, including toward attractor configurations that are multiple, as with living systems. My version of this type of modeling adds to the evolution of complexity in single attractors the notion that there can be multiple attractors, e.g., as represented by CAS (and superordinate complex adaptive systems in attractor organization) (Young, 2011).

Second, in Young (2011), not only did I support the view that emergent levels in a system can exert top-down forces on lower-order levels but also that the higher-order levels might be dysfunctional rather than only more functional as they develop. For example, I described how NLDST can help explain shifts in symptoms toward more entrenched or, in contrast, toward less dysfunctional presentations. This type of negative evolution in the content of attractors despite the increasing complexity in their structure also is illustrated in the figure. Later, I refer to this aspect of my model to the development of multiple emotional intelligences.

In the following, I examine the concept of causality, in general, as presented in recent publications. I emphasize the top-down influence of higher-order levels in a system toward developing a generic hybrid model involving, as well, the reciprocal influence of bottom-up lower-order levels.

Causality

Introduction

After considering the models of stress causation and stress generation in the relationship between stress and internalized psychological disorders, Phillips, Carroll, and Der (2015) investigated in adults the different predictions consonant with the models. They found that, for depression, a stress causation concept best modeled the relationship involved (stress in the prior 2 years causes depression), but the inverse causal direction was found for anxiety (stress-generated situations cause anxiety). Moreover, sex differences were involved.

This study illustrates the complexity in dealing with causality and behavior, even for linear models, let alone the nonlinear ones we have been discussing. There is no clear universal pathway for the simplest of relations studied. The question becomes much more complex when vast amounts of variables are considered. Also, when the variables express nonlinear relations, the ability to decipher underlying causes in the data descriptions obtained becomes exponentially more difficult.

Philosophically, there is a school of thought that denies causation (Russell, 1918). Empirically, the same is happening. The movement toward Big Data and our data-driven society that is emerging because of the Internet values, above all, the massive information available and its mining. Chandler (2015) maintained that, in the world of Big Data, the world is becoming one "without causation." Knowledge of causal connection is no longer relevant to the adaptation to real-time challenges and the information provided by Big Data in this adaptation. Chandler (2015) was not enamored of the dynamic of this development, and he called for an accommodation with the world prior to Big Data. In this regard, he referred to the value offered by complexity and emergent causality for animating the critical approach needed toward Big Data.

Areas

Physics Ellis, Noble, and O'Connor (2012) specified that, generally, causation is considered from a bottom-up perspective (e.g., elementary objects exert force on each other) but, throughout the sciences, "solid evidence" supports that top-down causation takes place (e.g., as per attractor science, ecosystem adaptation). They cautioned that systems express hierarchical levels that influence each other and that "interlevel" causation takes place between neighboring levels in a hierarchy.

Ellis et al. (2012) defined top-down causation as involving "higher level features" functioning to exert "irreducible productive" "causal influence" on processes that are lower level. The emergence involved is both "diachronic" (not predictive from a prior state) and "synchronic" (not derivable from laws governing anything at lower levels).

Brain Network theory provides an example of top-down control in brain activity. Marshall, Bergmann, and Jensen (2015) found that "stronger" volume in the medial branch of the superior longitudinal fasciculus (SLF), which is a white matter tract that connects parietal regions to frontal control areas, led to better ability to modulate alpha and gamma band synchronization. In turn, the latter predicted reaction time results, showing downward effects on sensory regions supportive of selective attention. They concluded that frontoparietal structural connectivity mediates in a top-down way the neuronal synchronization associated with selective attention.

Biology Friston, Levin, Sengupta, and Pezzulo (2015) applied a concept from neuroscience to biological regulation. Friston (2010) had developed a "unified brain theory" based on the "free energy principle," which is a variant of the one of thermodynamic regulation. In this application of the principle to biology, with colleagues (Friston et al., 2015), he argued that bottom-up models of molecular protein pathways are insufficient to understand morphogenesis. Specifically, these linear models are insufficient to explain the development of large-scale morphogenetic shapes (e.g., in embryogenesis). However, top-down "constructivist" models can help in this regard, by explaining the dynamics in the emergence of complex patterns and their "remodeling" toward the target anatomy. A dynamical approach allows for "morphogenetic self-organization."

For Friston et al. (2015), the principle "inherent" to system output is "free energy minimization," which involves conceptualizing "the minimization" of thermodynamic free energy in terms of a "variational free energy" (p. 2). The mathematics described is beyond the scope of the present work, but the simulations undertaken in their work involved "generative models" based on "fixed-point" attractors.

Comment

As this review indicates, recent work on causality has emphasized the top-down causation afforded by higher-order levels in systems. This idea has been applied to the areas of physics, biology, and the brain, in particular, in the material that I selected for review. It is a segue into the following model in which bottom-up and top-down causal influences are described for higher-order and lower-order levels of systems, respectively, and that these differing causal influences and associated levels in a system can work in a coordinated way in a hybrid model of system causality.

New Hybrid Symptom Network Construct Model

Model

The next section of the epilogue presents an integrative model of the symptom network and latent variable models concerning symptom-mental disorder relationship (see Fig. 37.1). It avoids some of the pitfalls of prior attempts to do the same (as described in Young, 2015a). Nevertheless, it is an initial conceptualization that itself has limitations, such as not yet being mathematically grounded nor empirically tested.

The lower levels of the model being presented refer to symptoms and their interactions, as per network theory (e.g., PTSD; McNally et al., 2015). The higher levels of the model refer to psychological constructs, such as PTSD or depression, and the clusters of symptoms that might comprise them.

Figure 37.1 shows that, for any one construct or cluster in mental disorder, there is both a top-down influence/creation of symptoms and bottom-up ones, that is, from symptom interactions upward to effects on construct/cluster. Moreover, these top-down and bottom-up effects can function at intermediate levels. Further, the interactions can take place not only horizontally (among symptoms; among levels/sublevels; among their configurations/patterns) but also vertically (upward or downward over (sub)levels).

New to my modeling of symptoms-disorder relations, Fig. 37.2 expands the prior figure by expanding the relationship between symptom and disorder to comorbid condition(s). I arrived at this expansion by considering that if any one disorder and its symptoms can be represented as a system with multiple intra- and inter-level interactions, so can the ensemble of symptoms over comorbid conditions. The figure caption of the model gives its details.

Comment

Therefore, according to the model that I developed integrating bottom-up and top-down causation across levels of a system (Young, 2015a), causality resides in the rich dynamical systemic interactions and reciprocal influences amongst the various levels of a system and their nexus nodes, elements, element (sub)sets, constructs, and other aspects inherent in them, such as symptom and disorder. Specifically, for the topic at issue of symptom networks and constructs such as PTSD, symptoms have causal effects on each other but, reciprocally, constructs have causal effects on them. In this sense, constructs, such as mental disorder, are emergent, irreducible entities that can affect and even initiate the symptoms.

Application

In the following, I apply the hybrid symptom network/construct model that I developed such that an intermediate level in the hierarchy of levels involved is required. Instead of just top-down, higher-order levels and bottom-up, lower-order ones, I add a middle level in the understanding of PTSD that refers to the individual's causal perception of her/his symptoms.

As reviewed in Young (2016), in Frewen, Schmittmann, Bringmann, and Borsboom (2013), university undergraduates (N=288) answered a questionnaire (40 items) related to Major Depressive Episode, PTSD (DSM-IV-TR consistent), symptoms of other anxiety disorders, and other symptoms. Upon statistical analysis, in terms of symptom networks, the two symptoms of flashbacks and avoidance of reminders of the trauma experienced were evident in many feedback loops. Also, anxious worrying, depressed mood, and trauma memory symptoms most influenced other symptoms; and the ones most influenced were about emotions or functional problems (e.g., numbing, work, respectively).

Frewen et al. (2013) added superordinate influences on symptom expression related to the

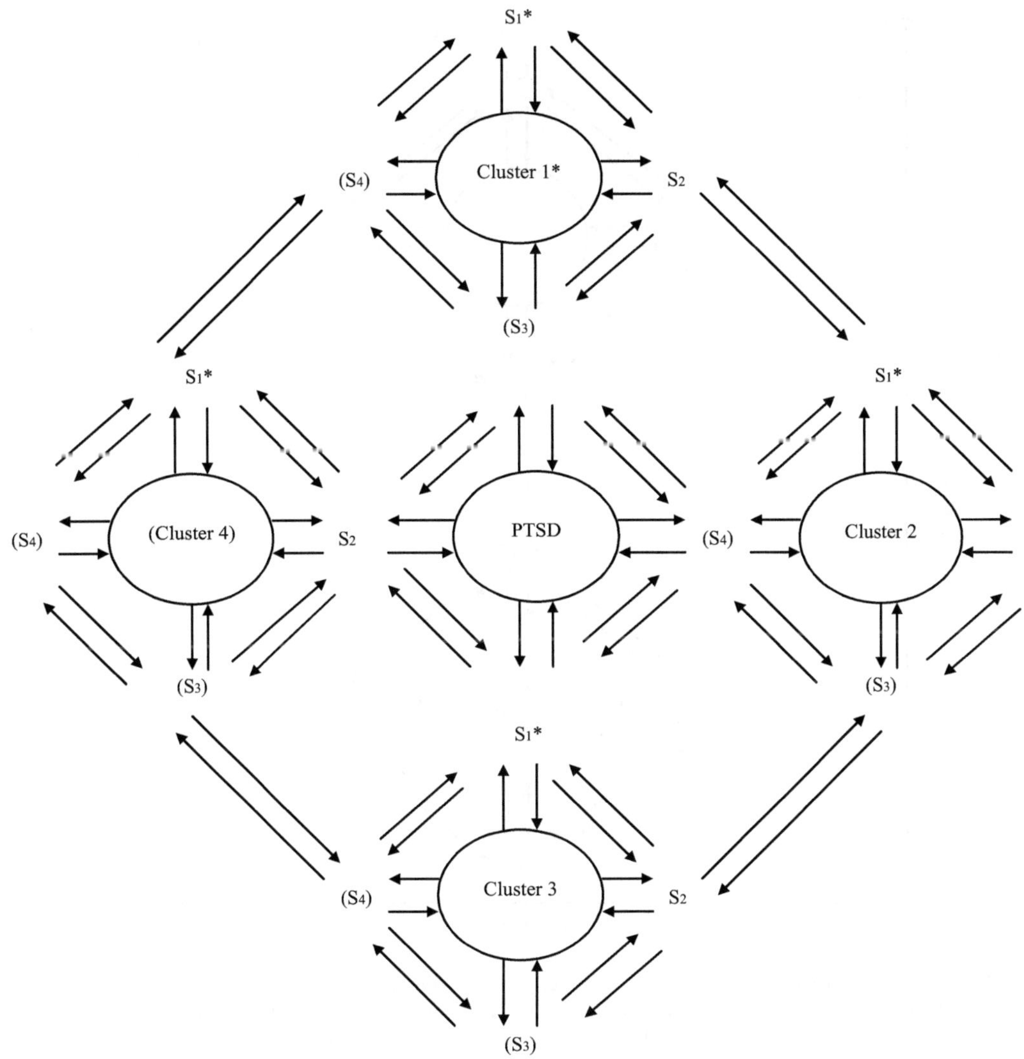

Fig. 37.1 Integrative causal symptom-construct model in mental disorder. The figure depicts the relationship between symptoms and mental disorder (or a symptom cluster of one) as being dynamically reciprocal in causation. The mental disorder constitutes an underlying, higher-order level in the patient's mental state symptoms, while the symptoms interact at lower-levels of the system, with both the top-down and bottom-up influences dynamically influencing each other in context and over time. *Note*: The *parentheses* indicate that PTSD might have only three clusters (as in the DSM-IV), and a cluster might have only two symptoms. Of course, depending on the disorder involved either might have more items (i.e., clusters or symptoms, respectively). Of the clusters in any mental disorder, for their symptoms, it would be beneficial to specify which ones are core/primary. For the model presented in the figure, these could be the first clusters or symptoms that are specified by the *asterisks*. Adopted from Young (2015a)

causal interaction between networked symptoms and the person's higher-order perception of causality. That is, I conclude that the expression of PTSD is not only about symptoms and the construct interacting. Also, it is about the personal appraisal of how an individual's perception of the symptoms as causal of them in individualized ways alters their networking and the nature of the superordinate construct.

In summary, Frewen et al. (2013) have elaborated a level of understanding of PTSD and comorbid symptoms that speaks to the person's

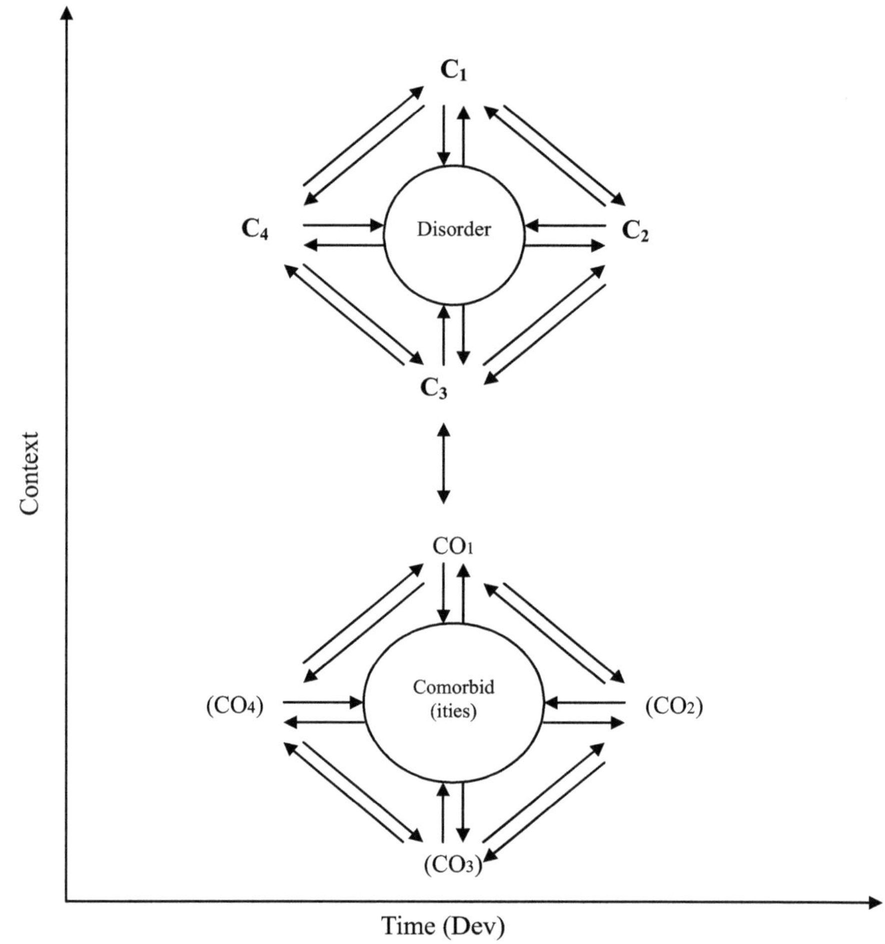

Fig. 37.2 An integrative (bottom-up, top-down) disorder and comorbid(ities). The figure illustrates how a disorder and its comorbidity/comorbidities (CO) might relate to each other in exacerbation, mutual maintenance, or simply in creating a larger symptom complex. It considers disorder and its symptom cluster (C), viewing their relationship as reciprocally causal with the disorder at issue. The same can be said for how symptoms interrelate or network amongst themselves. Therefore, the figure includes the notion that, for any one disorder and its comorbid condition(s), there are both bottom-up (interactive symptom; interactive clusters; interactive comorbidities) and top-down (latent variable) reciprocally-related causal influences on behavior. The figure does not deal with the issue of whether mental disorder can be carved so neatly at its joints into separate and comorbid mental disorders. This figure works for PTSD and its comorbidities.

Finally, the current approach to a hybrid symptom network/mental disorder construct model can be expanded to include intermediate levels outside of symptoms clusters within disorders. In this regard, the patients' perceptions of their symptoms could alter the nature of the symptom experience and how they interact with lower (symptom) and higher (construct) levels. Adopted from Young (2015a)

causal perceptions of the symptomatology involved. In the following, I consider the broader implications of their work. For example, causality is as much a matter of internal perception as external force impact.

Comment

The results in Frewen et al. (2013) speak to my hybrid symptom network-construct model of symptoms, clusters, and the construct of PTSD

(Young, 2015a). In my model, as mentioned, there is a not only a symptom network, bottom-up level but also a construct, top-down level. Furthermore, these levels interact reciprocally. In their case, the top-down level influencing symptom networks is causal perception.

A model that combines their approach and mine would consist of three levels—a higher-order construct one, a lower-order symptom network one, and an intermediate one concerning the causal effect of a person's perception of the symptoms and their networks. These appraisals might be the important components shaping, reciprocally, in a bottom-up way the lower-order symptom networks and, simultaneously, the nature of the higher-order constructs (and clusters) in PTSD. This type of modeling should be transferable to other disorders, their networks, and their personal perceptions.

In Young (2016), I argued exactly for this type of model integration for PTSD that a superordinate integration of the two models of Frewen et al. (2013) and Young (2015a) on the causality of psychopathology (e.g., for PTSD), would place an intermediate level of patient construals of causality as a mediator between symptoms in the lower level of the system involved and latent constructs in the higher level involved (and symptom clusters could be related to both, as well). Moreover, I had maintained that this new level of patient causal perception of the symptoms involved, itself, would be reciprocally related to the lower and higher levels in the symptom configuration through system dynamics.

I would add to this description of a hybrid symptom network-psychological construct model of PTSD that not only could it apply to other disorders but also that it leads to a major conceptual shift of the nature of mental disorder. They are more than DSM symptom lists. They are not uniform expressions of naturally present categories carved by nature at the joints. Rather, they are dynamic entities that are individually expressed yet still exist as superordinate, emergent, higher-order mental conditions or wholes that can influence in a top-down way the symptoms involved (and in individual ways because of their individual configurations).

Conclusion

I have presented a hybrid symptom network/psychological construct model of mental disorder that allows for reciprocal top-down and bottom-up influences. I described the model as one involving systems with multiple interacting levels. The process-relational view (e.g., Witherington, 2015), the network view as applied to attitudes (Dalege et al., 2016), and the network model as applied to modules in the brain (Sporns & Betzel, 2016) all speak to this type of conception of multiple interacting levels in systems (and higher-order levels emergent from activity in the lower-order ones).

In the following, to conclude the book, I propose that this type of modeling can be applied to other areas not only in the cognitive (e.g., development, attitudes) domain, the neuroscientific one (e.g., modules in the Connectome), and the mental disorder one (e.g., to PTSD), but also in other domains. In this regard, I focus on new conceptions of stages of emotional intelligence, in particular.

Specifically, the hierarchical multilevel model implicit in the symptom-perception-construct model of layers in understanding mental disorder (Young, 2015a, 2016) can be applied in a revision of the understanding of stages in development. They have been described as hierarchical, integrative, and so on, and having décalages to account for their uneven development both over and within tasks and domains (Lourenço, 2016). However, below, I criticized the vague nature of hierarchical integration in explaining stages.

In this regard, a hybrid network-construct model with multiple hierarchical levels might be better able to account for individual differences in mastery of tasks and domains in stage-related cognitive development. For example, Case's concept of central conceptual structures in different domains (e.g., quantitative, social, narrative) has been developed to explain better Piaget's concept of "structures d'ensemble." This notion of central conceptual structures could be reworked into systems design, that is, as structures with each of higher-order, intermediate, and lower-order levels that develop in different ways for each individual, depending on biological, environment, and other (e.g., motivational) factors, i.e., according to biopsychosocial factors. In the following, I flesh out this model of an elaboration of central conceptual structures to explain better cognitive stages.

Reconceptualizing Cognitive Stages

Existing Concept

As described previously, according to Lourenço (2016), Piaget considered developmental stages as—hierarchical or invariant in order; integrative of prior stages yet with consolidating transitions between them; and characterized as wholes or overarching "structures d'ensemble" that are in equilibration. They express a "décalage" (uneven development) within a domain/stage due to task complexity differences.

Comment

The concept of stages in the Piagetian tradition is incomplete in at least three levels. (a) First, there is no plausible mechanism that can account for the discontinuous transition from one stage to the next. To say that the stages are integrative speaks neither to their emergence at new levels nor how the integration takes place. (b) Second, there is no plausible understanding of how the uneven and individualized nature of within-stage organization that takes place is structured, aside from saying that there are décalages. (c) Third, there is no plausible explanation of how schemas within a particular stage transform toward higher-order structures, other than indicating that there are transitions involved.

Granted, Piaget and Neo-Piagetians have elaborated concepts in these regards related to information processing, in particular, e.g., memory, executive function, and they have touched upon systems theory (Mascolo & Fischer, 2015). However, the precise details needed about causality for moving from ongoing, continuous micro-developments in one task or the other to discontinuous macro-developments involving stages remain elusive in extant models.

The goal of the next section is to address these issues, especially in terms of applying a hierarchical model of system levels that behave nonlinearly to the second question of within-stage organization and the third of developing schemes within a stage. This model permits extensions into the first question of how the stages move from one to the next, as well.

Reconceptualization

Model In the following, I present through five figures a full model that I have developed to explain better development both within and across levels of a cognitive structure, and even within and across levels of a developmental substage or stage. The figure captions give much of the details of the model and, in the next paragraphs, I give an overview.

Essentially, the model is multifactorial, and explains that multilevel hierarchical models lay at the heart of development. On the one hand, they can represent the development of a conceptual structure related to a set of a few tasks all the way to a set of domains within a stage. Moreover, the structure could advance to a new level of skill that is qualitatively distinct and represents a new (sub)stage.

The first of the figures (Fig. 37.3) presents the way in which a new mental schema that develops for a particular domain in a particular stage for a particular child might grow to a rule over exemplars and then a generalized rule, preparatory to the start of a new stage. This model is based on attractor/complexity/systems theory modeling (after Young, 2011). Then, I expand this work by starting with the simplest of models and works up to the one I have developed involving the differential, temporary yoking of skills from different stages for any immediate task or problem at hand (Fig. 37.4). The next figure deals with individual differences in development, both intra-individual and inter-individual. These differences could be within or across tasks/subdomains/domains within a child or across children in these regards

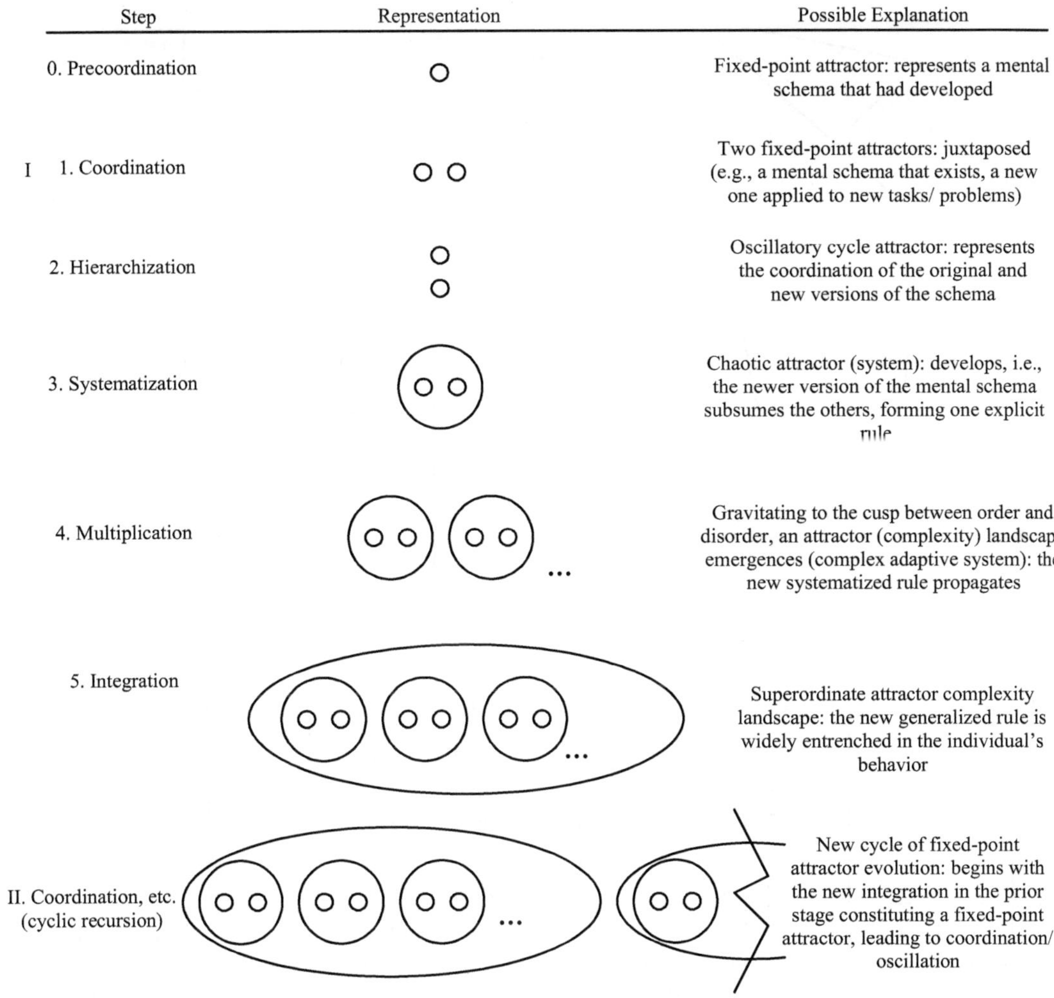

Fig. 37.3 Conceptual control structure development within a domain in terms of attractors/complexity. As mental schemas emerge and spread within a particular domain of a particular stage of cognitive development, they should first be juxtaposed in coordination, then hierarchized with the new one predominant, and then systematized into a new rule. Next, they should spread out or multiply throughout the system, leading to integration of a generalized rule that covers all exemplars within the individual's particular cognitive development for the stage at issue.

This five-step sequence might correspond to changes in attractor-complexity organization. That is, attractors might gravitate from fixed point to oscillatory and chaotic ones and then to more complex architecture involving the cusp of change to CAS and superordinate complex systems. This model has been applied to substage changes in Young's (2011) Neo-Piagetian cognitive developmental model. Also, it might apply to both higher (e.g., stage) and lower (i.e., domain transitions as they move through the phases of coordination (after pre-coordination) hierarchization, systematization, multiplication, and integration, with a cyclic recursion potentially taking place after that.

In another example, the attractor/complexity model can be applied to disorder/disability or competing health trajectories, so that the states of health and disorder/dysfunction/disability involved could be seen to pass through five steps of change from a simpler coordination to a quite stable integration.

Another applied example would be for dealing with the challenges/crises presented by each new Eriksonian/Freudian stage that might develop. Do they begin with a challenge/crisis and their solutions, in a coordination that leads toward resolution and growth, or do they lapse into entrenchment in the crises inherent in the challenges and get worse as development continues, but still toward integration, albeit in a negative mode? This model of attractor evolution can be applied generically to change in both living and nonliving systems, assuming a consistency for the appropriate conditions of nonlinear dynamical system functioning. It can be applied to different levels of a system because of fractal dynamics, e.g., from one developmental stage to the next, within each of the substages involved, within domains within substages, and so on

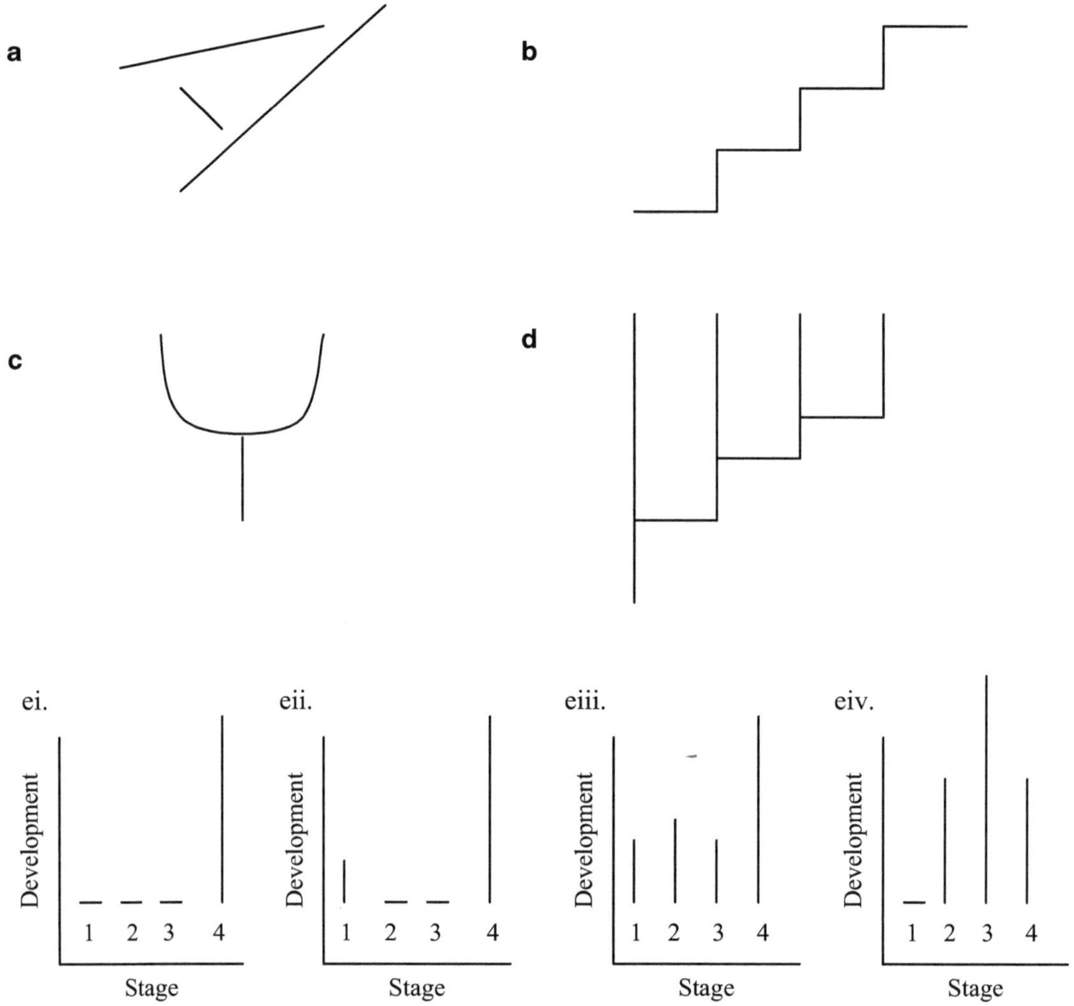

Fig. 37.4 Different conceptions of development. (**a**) Development is linear and can cur in multiple directions over time: for example, it could be progressive (*line slanting upward*), regressive (*downward*), flat, with all pathways possible even in one child, depending on the task and context; development takes place in continuous ways in these various pathways. (**b**) Development is stepwise: with stages, milestones, etc. It takes place in discontinuous ways; e.g., Piagetian cognitive development; Eriksonian socio-affective development. Stages are hierarchical and integrative, with new ones incorporating its prior ones. (**c**) Development reaches bifurcation points or other ways in which it splits, changes, or alters. For example, with respect to bifurcation points, in systems theory, state configuration reaches critical threshold and splits; different state configurations (e.g., attractors) arise. (**d**) Parallel stages develop in that new stages do not incorporate or displace prior ones. Stage development is non-integrative rather than integrative. New stages appear without incorporating prior ones. The prior ones continue to develop even after the ones more complex than them appear. The skills of the prior and new stages can function together, being yoked as needed by the task or problem at hand. (**e**) Different stage (or substage) yokings: (i) only the highest level one is necessary for the task or problem at hand; (ii) a lower one is added; (iii) all are added; (iv) the highest one isn't the primary one needed; not all needed. *Note*: Each of these (sub)stage yoking configurations can be adaptive or maladaptive. Perhaps the highest one isn't the best for a task at hand. Perhaps the ones deployed are used inefficiently, are compromised by brain damage, psychological problems, etc.

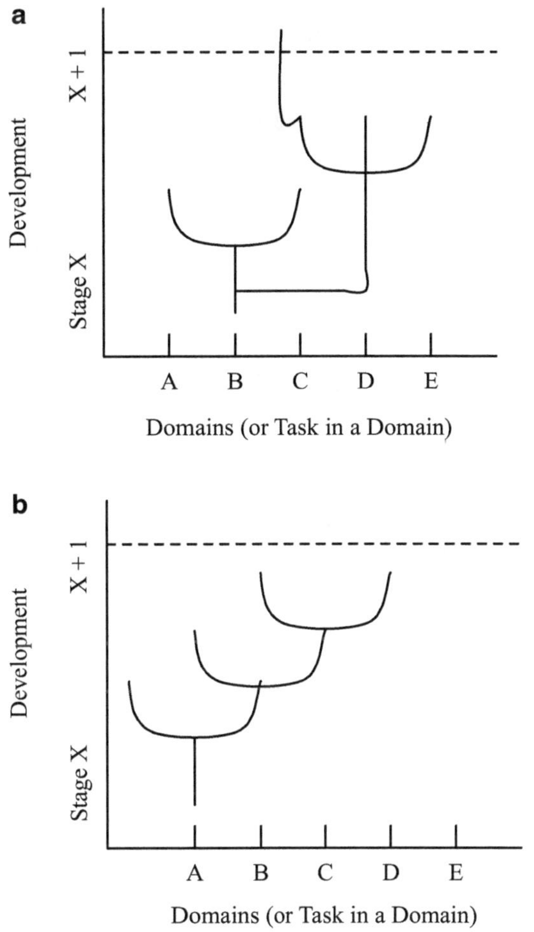

Fig. 37.5 Individual differences in stage development within children and across their within-stage domains (intra-individual) or across children (inter-individual). The figure illustrates development within a stage mostly. It takes place over in different ways for different children, both within a domain or across domains, as per the different trajectories outlined in the first part of the figure compared to the second. For some tasks (domains), development traverses boundaries separating the nature of acquisitions in one stage to the next, as per the second part of the figure. Case (1998) referred to the development of the cognitive schemas in a domain as central conceptual structures. My version of the concept emphasizes the task/domain individual differences involved and that they can develop according to (sub)stages

(Fig. 37.5). The figure after that (Fig. 37.6) is the most complex because it deals with the concept of hierarchical multilevel systems in development. The concept integrates work on: systems theory (NLDST): network theory; my hybrid model of symptom networks and psychological constructs, with intermediate levels between them: and other work, such as the application of NLDST to attitudes (see previously). The figure indicates a smoothed version of the model and a "messier" one that better reflects what real-life cognitive growth would look like.

The next two figures consider mechanisms of change, including the one inherent in NLDST of emergence. This takes place through spontaneous self-organization among system elements when the system configuration is "stretched" beyond carrying capacity and, therefore, more graceful patterns arise. However, I point out that there are limits to the emergence, for example, if the system "machinery" of components included does not support certain higher-order configurations (read as, for example—abstract thought would be impossible at certain ages and in all nonhuman species).

Specifically, Fig. 37.7 illustrates that the mechanisms of change in development involve both lateral, horizontal mechanisms within a level/substage/stage and vertical mechanisms upward to higher-order ones. The process of generalization seems involved in both types. In both cases, better energetic management seems to be involved. The previous discussion of reciprocal causality among levels of a hierarchy also applies here. As for Fig. 37.8, it speaks to the concept of activation/inhibition coordination and another involving energetics, that of vitality and reverberation. The former has been discussed throughout the book, while the latter is new to it.

The vitality/reverberation energetics model indicates that the energy involved in cognitive growth comes from the child through motivation and the like. Energetics is not simply about what "cold" entities within a cognitive system experience as it equilibrates but also about the "hot" energy of curiosity, effort, motivation, a desire to learn, and so on.

This energy reflects a vitality in the child, and one that can be dispersed with multiple reverberations in the child's psychological architecture and cognitive functionality. Many factors can influence it, including the hot energy of proper parental support, school environment, and so on. At the other extreme, many factors can affect it

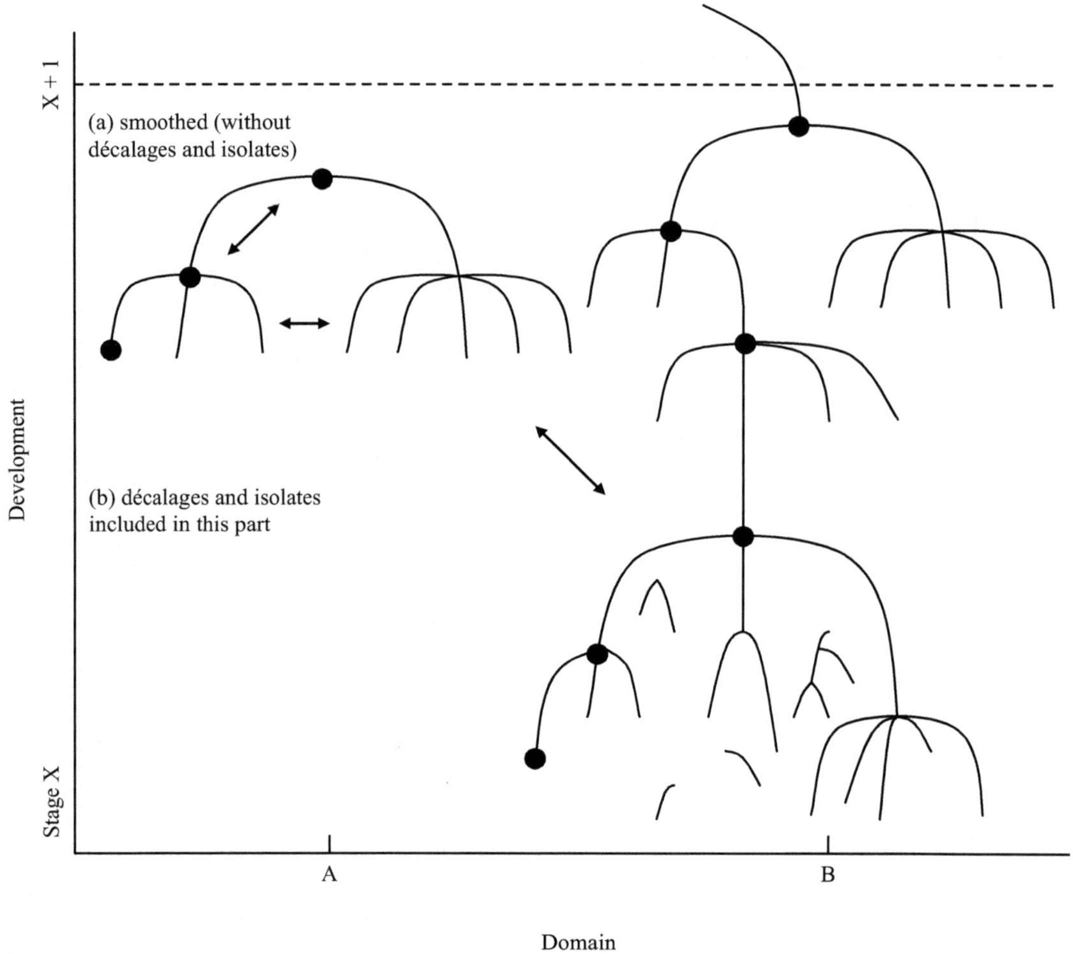

Fig. 37.6 A hierarchical multilevel systems model of across-domain/task organization in development. The figure illustrates how central conceptual structures grow within a stage, or perhaps into a higher-order one, too (in the part of the figure to the *right*, at the *top*). Central conceptual structures apply to particular domains or subdomains (which are task collections; e.g., quantitative, social, narrative). Part (**a**) shows that they might develop from lower-order schemas into second-order consolidations (or more, depending on the complexity involved). They could end with superordinate upper-level integrations, such as mathematical rules, ordered social skill sets, or narrative plot structure knowledge.

Part (**a**) is a smooth rendition, with differential timing of different but equivalent acquisitions shown to emerge at the same time and with all acquisitions related to a central theme. Part (**b**) shows a messier but more probable developmental pathway in these regards. For example, different but related acquisitions emerge at different times (décalages) and some are orphaned isolates not related to others. Moreover, part (**a**) can represent a different domain, subdomain, or lower-order task collection in the same child, indicative of intra-individual differences in domain mastery within a stage. Finally, it indicates that domain development within a stage can traverse the threshold boundary of the nature of skills applicable to one stage compared to the one preceding it. Note that the arrows ↔ indicate interactions between levels, intra-domain acquisitions, and inter-domain acquisitions. The *points* represent critical initial nodes or hubs at which a domain schema or related acquisition develops, leading to its spread

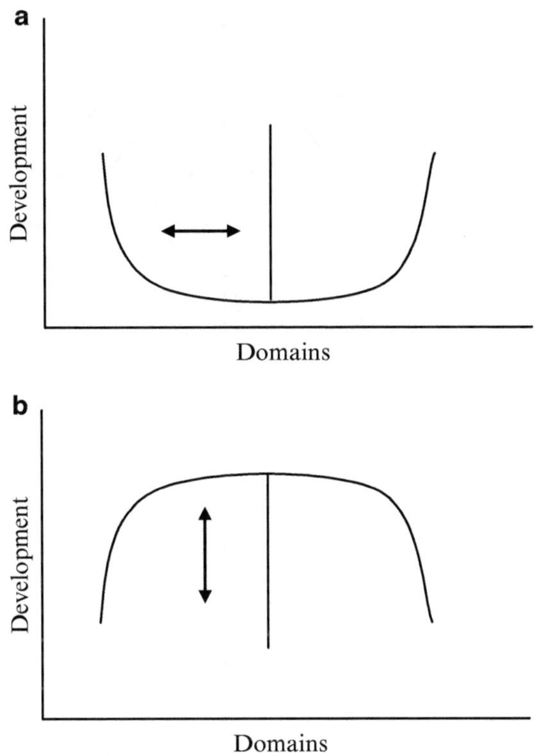

Fig. 37.7 Mechanisms of change in domain/task hierarchical multilevel systems, both within and across stages (intrastage, interstage). Part (**a**) illustrates how change can take place within a stage from the point of view of developmental stages. The development is on-line, local, continuous, task-by-task, strategy-by-strategy. The scheme involved is applied perhaps with minor adjustment. It happens repeatedly, though, creating storage and organization issues. All told, the growth is horizontal rather than vertical. The generalization is lateral rather than emergent to a new level. The horizontal, lateral development within a level is indicated by the *horizontal arrow*.

Part (**b**) illustrates that development could also be toward increasing complexity. For example, a schema becomes broader and flexible in application, and perhaps even reaching threshold for a level that is more representative, like a rule or operation. This takes place because the energetic weight of maintaining a multitude of schematic variations at the same level, as per the process in (**a**), overwhelms the system, or pushes it to the edge of ongoing system configuration dissolution, and over, through the perturbations involved. The child has mastered enough variations of the basic scheme to seek out generalities in the vertical level, or in terms of an increasing generalized skill/rule/thought. This might prepare the way for one or more additional more advanced levels in the system, the latter of which could be the final one for the domain at issue over the tasks involved. In addition, this final one could be either only the most advanced structure within the stage at issue or, also, it could be preparatory to another one that is penultimate, or a qualitatively superior stage. See the text for discussion of the reciprocal causality that might be involved across levels. This is indicated by the *vertical arrow* in the figure.

Note: The developmental change mechanisms being described are complemented by model of transitions in attractor complexity in a process of generic change that I have described. For simplicity, in the figures in this section, I have graphed three-level hierarchical multilevel systems, but alluded to more possible levels. It could be that five levels, as per Fig. 37.1's depiction of a generic attractor-complexity transition sequence, is optimal and applies equally to (sub)domains/task collections within any one stage as they complexify.

I have applied the concept of evolving attractors to cognitive development. However, now that I am showing parallels in multiple cognitive and emotion-related intelligences according to my model, the attractor evolution model might help in understanding the development of multiple emotion-related intelligences.

Also, about change mechanisms in cognitive development, Piaget (1970) referred to the concept of "reflective abstraction" in facilitating cognitive growth, which could be type of reflective distancing or metacognition. According to me, this process illustrates the child's active contribution to her own development. Pulling back to observe, act on, coordinate, unify, etc., demands both understanding and a will to full application, as per Fig. 37.8

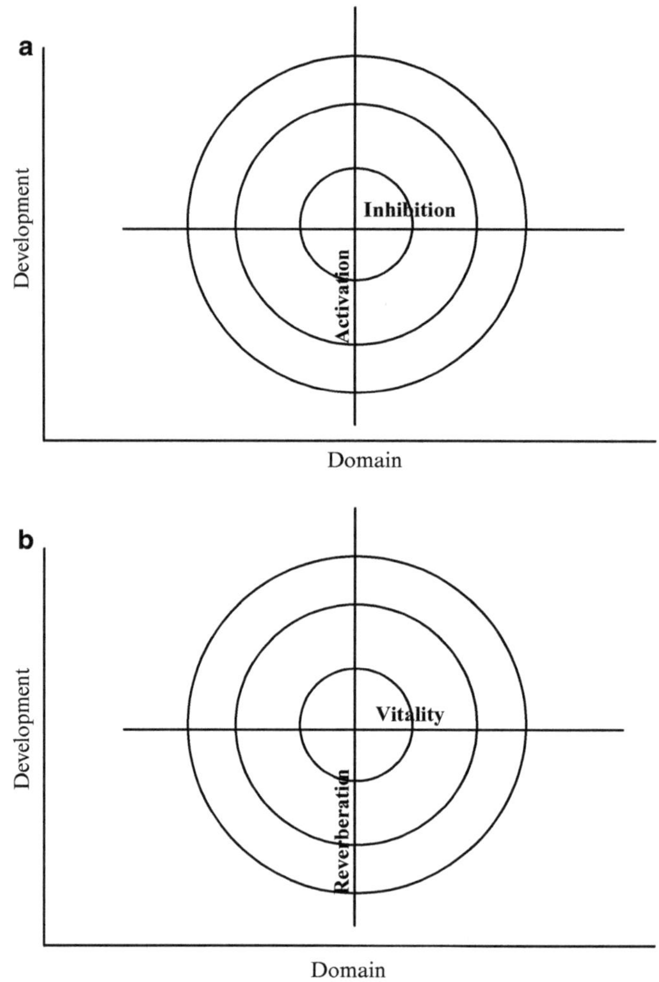

Fig. 37.8 Activation/inhibition coordination and vitality/reverberation in domain/task change. Part (**a**) indicates that development both within a level, or stage grosso modo, takes place through activation/inhibition coordination. The *concentric circles* indicate it can vary in strength. Activation/inhibition coordination applies across the board to developmental and behavioral phenomena, from brain, to behavior, to social interaction, and so on. Activation/inhibition coordination applies to the horizontal, lateral interactions necessary for schema expansion and adjustment that takes place for tasks, subdomains, and domains. Also, it applies vertically to the growth toward more complex levels and even into new stages. That being said, there are limits to upward growth in these regards. The developmental, biological, and behavioral "machinery," or the system composite of elements involved, must be able to support a change to qualitatively distinct levels. Systems have their reaction ranges just as gene complexes might.

Part (**b**) reinforces that development is not machine-like or passive. It involves the individual in active, dynamic participation, including through motivation, giving effort, deploying energy effectively, showing curiosity, paying attention, absorbing or learning, persevering or otherwise coping well, and so on. The *concentric circles* indicate that this active glue in development which we addressing can vary, for example, in the energetic metrics of vitality and reverberation. With the right context, skill, and approach to the task or problem at hand, in conjunction with the right "machinery," emergence to new levels in the domain(s) or (sub)stages at issue is facilitated

detrimentally, including parental abuse, school indifference, and so on. Needless to say, the model could include biological factors that impact child energetics, such as neurodevelopmental difficulties.

Comment In the prior section, I have explained a model of cognitive development that covers mechanisms of change within a level/substage/stage and upward to new ones. I terminated with a model of energetics related to the motivation, curiosity, etc., of the child, and indicated the factors that can affect it, such as parental/school ones. This latter model provides a good segue into the socio-affective realm and how it develops from one level, substage, or stage to the next. My developmental model (Young, 2011) is not only cognitive and Neo-Piagetian but also socio-affective Neo-Eriksonian in its stage conception. In this regard, in the following, I attempt to show how the concept of emotional intelligence can be reworked into a stage model and, moreover, one that is multiple (e.g., with stage yoking), just as I have done with cognitive development.

Before beginning, I review the concept of multiple intelligences and then examine the concept of emotional intelligence. Both areas do not involve stage conceptions. Both areas mention domains and similar concepts. It is not difficult to argue that for each domain involved, they could pass through a stage sequence, and moreover, that the stages could be yoked.

Multiple Emotional Intelligences

Multiple Intelligences

Model The standard model of intelligence is predicated on the assumption that items on the IQ (intelligent quotient) test can give scores that predict academic performance, especially school grades (Berk, 2013; Berk & Meyers, 2016; Ekinici, 2014; Chen & Gardner, 2011; Sternberg, 2015; Young, 2011). Furthermore, it maintains that the aggregate of the scores into a total or intelligence quotient score (IQ) can represent one's general intelligence because it is an integrated adaptive function. That is, in factor analytic research on intelligence testing, a general or *g* factor is found, and others more specific to domains. Further, in this psychometric approach, tests are constructed that are arranged hierarchically such that the full-scale IQ can be decomposed into broad processing scores reflective of factors in empirical studies. For example, the WISC-IV (Wechsler Intelligence Scale for Children, Fourth Edition, 2003) has four broad intellectual factors aside from its IQ score, which are in verbal reasoning, perceptual (or visuospatial) reasoning, working memory, and processing speed. The WISC-IV has 2–3 subtests that contribute to each of the four factor scores (e.g., respectively, vocabulary, block design, digit span, and symbol search).

In order to broaden understanding of intelligence and its testing beyond predictors of academic achievement and because of alternate conceptualizations that do not give primacy to one full-scale score being representative of general intelligence, alternate models of intelligence and its testing have been developed. Gardner and Sternberg have presented the most noteworthy theories on multiple intelligence. Gardner (1983, 1993) and Chen and Gardner (2011) presented a model of independent intelligences that went beyond the traditional domains. Aside from linguistic, logico-mathematical, and spatial intelligence, Gardiner added other intelligences, such as ones that are musical, naturalistic, bodily/kinesthetic, intrapersonal, and interpersonal. As for Sternberg (1985, 2015), the three components of intelligence include not only the standard analytic one but also practical and creative ones. Both Gardner and Sternberg, or their colleagues and those who follow them, have developed tests of their models. For example, Ekinici (2014) determined which of the intelligences in the two models under discussion best predicted academic achievement in Turkish primary school children.

New Model The model of multiple intelligences relates to children but it is still not developmental enough. For example, do all of the intelligences start from birth? How do they grow, simply quantitatively? In order to respond to these types of criticisms, Young (2011) developed a model of multiple intelligences that is based on his Neo-Piagetian model. In particular, the five Neo-Piagetian stages of his model were considered different intelligences. Moreover, in solving tasks and problems, Young posited that they are deployed together as required, in a yoking process. For example, one task might require the highest stage/type of thought available to solve a problem, with the second-highest subsidiary to that one. For another child on a different task, perhaps a lower level stage and its associated thought is best, and there are two higher-order ones that are yoked to it. This modeling is consistent with the onion metaphor of cognitive functioning (Rochat, 2015) and Overton's (2015) Neo-Piagetian approach in which stages persist in development even after new ones are formed.

Young (2011) added that Gardiner's different types of multiple intelligences are simply domains in which the various stages in his model might pass through. As for Sternberg, his three intelligences are complementary adaptive functions in this process. Young noted that the environment determines, too, how intelligence develops (e.g., support vs. abuse), and that personal factors are involved, for example, motivation, curiosity, and socio-affective factors.

Comment In this epilogue, I extend the model that I developed on multiple intelligences to emotional intelligence. The latter is a domain-based approach as much is the case for cognitive intelligence, and factor analytic studies predominate. There is little developmental work on the topic, and none that considers it from the way I would, that is, in terms of passage through developmental stages.

Before presenting my model of multiple emotional intelligences, I note that the stage component of the model to which I refer is not the Neo-Piagetian one but the corresponding Neo-Eriksonian one that I developed (Young, 2011). In this regard, just as the cognitive developmental model that I proposed in revision of Piaget has 25 steps over the lifespan (5 stages × 5 cyclically recurring substages), so does the corresponding Neo-Eriksonian one. In this latter model, I placed Erikson's eight stages in relation to the corresponding step to which they seemed to be in parallel in the Neo-Piagetian steps that I had created, and then added 17 new ones to complete the cycle of 25 steps.

In Young (2012), I gave labels to each set of five Neo-Eriksonian substages that correspond to each set of five Neo-Piagetian substages (the five stages of that model). The five terms are the following (and, as representations of stages, albeit socio-affective in nature and not Piagetian-based, they are posited to develop in sequence over the lifespan): (a) Non-participatory reflexive socio-emotions (up to the first month of life); (b) Pre-participatory socio-affects (the young child); (c) Peri-participatory social cognitions (middle childhood); (d) Hyper-participatory social mutuality (the teenager), and (e) Superordinate participatory collective sociality (the adult).

As can be seen, I organized the definitions of the five sets of Neo-Eriksonian substages according to the concept of "participation" in social relations. Therefore, for the first Neo-Eriksonian stage, or group of five substages, corresponding to the first Reflexive Neo-Piagetian cognitive stage of the present model, I considered them as "non-participatory" and "reflexive." However, I also considered them as socioemotional because the stage ends after birth with the Neo-Eriksonian steps of caregiving acts and emotional acts.

As for the second Neo-Eriksonian stage, it reflects its Neo-Piagetian sensorimotor equivalent stage, and is heavily associated with emotional expressions serving to intercoordinate the baby and the caregiver. Nevertheless, there is a lack of the genuine participation acts in this age period. Therefore, the label for this stage involved the concept of "pre-participatory."

Corresponding to the third cognitive stage under discussion, called perioperational, appears to be a Neo-Eriksonian one in which the child is reaching more genuine participatory socio-affective social coordinations. Therefore, I referred to "peri-participatory" socio-affectivity as the correct Neo-Eriksonian description for this stage. Within it, just as one finds preoperations and concrete operations on the cognitive side, one should find quasi-participatory and full participatory socio-affectivity. In addition, the label for this third Neo-Eriksonian stage includes the concept of socio-cognition because of the extensive development in this age period of aspects of socio-cognition, such as theory of mind and self-regulation.

The fourth and fifth Neo-Eriksonian stages being proposed in the present model reflect socio-affective development that goes beyond basic interactive participations in several ways. First, the socio-affective interchanges of adolescents and emerging adults can be considered "hyper-participatory" in that they include the development of conscious awareness, identity, nurturing, intimacy, and more universal acts. Of course, as with any of the Neo-Eriksonian stages, these tasks might be compromised as the challenges that they present are not met because of difficult circumstances, effects of poor navigation of prior stages, and so on.

The fifth Neo-Eriksonian stage corresponds to the Neo-Piagetian cognitive stage of collective intelligence. The latter is considered to include superordinate abstract systems. Therefore, the label that I have given for this phase of development includes the terms "superordinate participatory" as well as "collective sociality."

These five Neo-Eriksonian substage sets can be considered the equivalent of stages in the Neo-Eriksonian model. It is with these I worked with, rather than the original Eriksonian stages, as I was constructing a model of the components of what constitutes multiple emotional intelligences.

As mentioned, but amplified here, a major difference in the parallel Neo-Eriksonian and Neo-Piagetian steps in development that I have described is that the former relative to the latter are much more sensitive to environmental disruption. By their very nature, they represent challenges that the developing person must confront, and the negative poles of the challenges, if predominant relative to the positive poles because of experience, can lead to delays in development, baggage to work through, fixations, and even regression.

Note that, for terminology, I refer to multiple intelligences as multiple cognitive intelligences and multiple emotional intelligences as multiple socio-affective intelligences. This is consistent with the view that emotions serve social functions, as in social cognition, and also Erikson's emphasis on both the mutuality with the socio-cultural milieu in development, and the nature of his stages (which he referred to as psychosocial rather than psychosexual; Berk, 2013; Berk & Meyers, 2016).

In the next section, I describe emotional intelligence, which prepares the way for presentation of my model of multiple emotional intelligences. After undertaking the latter task, I consider the mechanisms that might underlie its expression in the individual.

Emotional Intelligence

Model Emotional intelligence (EI) is defined as a set of competences that allow people to process emotion-related information toward using the information acquired in guiding thought and behavior (Mayer, Roberts, & Barsade, 2008). The test developed for operationalizing EI (MSCEIT; Mayer-Salovey-Caruso Emotional Intelligence Test; Mayer, Salovey, & Caruso, 2002) includes 141 items that yields an FEI (full scale EI) and two domain scores, each with two branch scores: (a) Experiential EI; and (b) Strategic EI. The former involves tasks on the perception of emotions and others on their use. The latter involves tasks related to understanding emotions and also managing emotions. There are eight tasks on the MSCEIT. Operskalski, Paul, Colom, Barbey, and Grafman (2015) showed, in a factor analytic study with 130 combat veterans having focal penetrating traumatic brain injuries (TBI), that task scores organize into four factors corresponding to the branch scales of the MSCEIT, with two tasks associated with each factor (faces, pictures for perceiving emotions; sensations, facilitation for using emotions; blends, changes for understanding emotions; and emotional management and social management for managing emotions).

Operskalski et al. (2015) conducted a study on the neural networks associated with the four-factor structure of emotional intelligence. They used voxel-based lesion symptom mapping to determine neural substrates of the factors. They found core, domain-general common ones and peripheral, task-specific ones.

The results showed that impairments, as shown by test results, in the ability to perceive emotional information was associated with selective engagement deficits in the medial ventral temporal cortex and the lateral PFC. The association for managing emotions was with the orbitofrontal and parietal cortices. There were no associations for the other two facets of emotional intelligence. As for core, common neural substrates, they concerned the social processing and knowledge networks within the frontal, temporal, and parietal cortices.

The authors concluded that the sub-facets of the two main areas of emotional intelligence (experiential, strategic) represent "separable but related" processing. The results speak to a "networked" brain substrate in emotional intelligence, as opposed to a "modular" one. That being said, the networks involved might not be unique to emotional intelligence functioning, and also they might connect to larger networks not involved particularly in emotional intelligence.

Comment The current concept of emotional intelligence allows for scales that are general and also scales that are specific to functions (areas), such as strategic and experiential. Moreover, the latter have two scales (sub-facets) associated with each of them.

The work on emotional intelligence has focused not only on its factorial structure but also on its possible corresponding brain network underpinnings. Gardner had also attempted to use neuroscientific research to justify his multiple intelligences.

It would appear that there is much similarity with models of intelligence at the cognitive level that are built on finding an overall IQ, and then process scores with several tests under each of them, in a three-level hierarchical model, and the model of the structure of emotional intelligence just described, with its overall score, main areas, and sub-facets. In the following, on the basis of the Neo-Eriksonian stage model that I have developed (Young, 2011), I present an alternative emotional intelligence model that is also hierarchical and consisting of three levels (or more).

Multiple Emotional Intelligences

Model In this section of the epilogue, I present a novel hypothesis about emotional intelligence, which consists of several parts—(a) Emotional intelligence is multiple, as in my model for cognitive intelligence; (b) With respect to stages, it develops like the cognitive aspect of intelligence (as per the Piagetian view); (c) The intelligences involved can be yoked for the socio-affective task at hand, just as with my model of yoked cognitive intelligences; (d) The multiple emotional intelligences can apply to different domains, as argued for the model of multiple cognitive intelligences; (e) The development involved takes place according to the construction of schemas that are similar to those in the more cognitive domains; (f) The mechanisms involved are the same as those driving cognitive development, as presented in the model in this epilogue, e.g., with emergence; multiple, hierarchical levels; horizontal and vertical mechanisms; reciprocal causality; activation/inhibition coordination; vitality/reverberation, so on; (g) The emotional/socio-affective and cognitive realms are not really dissociable—they are separated in the literature either as a matter of convenience or in acknowledgement of the complexity in considering them together, especially in the developmental and lifespan context. In reality, they are mutually interactive realms, feeding each other, engaging in reciprocal feedback, and cascades from one to the other over development; and (h) The development in the emotional/socio-affective realm is not only multiple and parallels the development of the cognitive realm in many ways, but also it is exquisitely individual like in the latter realm, with intra-individual and inter-individual variation the norm.

In the present model, the matrix of multiple emotional intelligences involve the stages of Neo-Eriksonian growth as per the model in Young (2011) and the domains to which they can be applied, as per the work of Mayer and Salovey, in particular. The stages in Neo-Eriksonian growth that I have described above include: (a) Non-participatory reflexive socio-emotions (up to the first month of life); (b) Pre-participatory socio-affects (including Erikson's stages of Trust vs. Mistrust and Autonomy vs. Doubt); (c) Peri-participatory social cognitions (includes Initiative vs. Guilt; Industry vs. Inferiority); (d) Hyper-participatory social mutuality (Identity vs. Identity Diffusion; Intimacy vs. Isolation), and (e) Superordinate participatory collective sociality (Generativity vs. Self-Absorption; Ego Integrity vs. Despair). According to the literature on emotional intelligence, the domains in emotional intelligence include: (a) Experiential emotional intelligence (the perception of emotions and their use); and (b) Strategic emotional intelligence (understanding emotions and managing emotions). Because I have expanded the present model to include the Neo-Eriksonian perspective and not just emotional intelligence, I refer to it as a model of socio-affective multiple intelligences. In this regard, the domains are more numerous than those of Mayer, Salovey, and colleagues. For example, one could add domains related to social interaction information processing and social interaction skills.

As for individual differences in the model presented, the Neo-Eriksonian nature of the model already lends it to allowing for individual differences. Each stage presents challenges or crises to navigate and these are affected by the degree of mutuality with the environment. Also, by adding in my model a yoking component to the multiple intelligences, the particular combination of socio-affective skills that are deployed for any one individual in any one context are innumerable, and the one manifested for any one individual in any one context, most likely, will be unique to him or her. Granted, there might be similar classes of individuals in these regards, but these similarities should not mask the individualized stance each of us takes in our participation in the socio-affective tasks and problems at hand that we face in our daily lives.

Some examples help illustrate the yoking concept as applied to Neo-Eriksonian stages. I give examples related to substages, the development of which is more fine-grained. Moreover, it affords using as examples in the substages in my model the original eight Eriksonian stages, which simplifies the concept for the reader.

A patient might present with Identity issues that are still quite present in the late 20s, or emerging adulthood. Moreover, a primary reason might be relationship issues, perhaps due to questions related to Trust, hearkening back to an unsupportive first year or years of life. The domains that are largely affected in this type of example would be social (information processing, skills).

So far, this example reflects a standard Eriksonian conceptualization of a personal problem. However, even then, there are the advantages inherent in the present yoking concept that can help. In particular, we can consider the following: how the skills in the Neo-Eriksonian stages involved are juxtaposed; which ones are considered primary; which ones yoke to or mask secondary ones; if there is rapid de-yoking in circumstances where the yoking no longer applies to solve the task/problem at hand; and so on. The dynamics described above cognitively in online adaptive yoking would apply to the micro-moments of stages yoking socio-affectively and so the 25 steps in the Neo-Eriksonian stages would not just be functioning as large challenges and crises that dominate the socio-affective life of the individual as a slowly-moving or an unmoveable block. That is, the mechanisms of change as described in the cognitive realm above would apply the same way to this area of development, as micro-changes that at times lead to not only horizontal change but also vertical change in a process of macro-changes, either upward or downward, depending on the factors involved. Of course, a great challenge both in self-promoted growing efforts and in psychotherapy would be to discern these micro-change patterns and understand the conscious and unconscious dynamics that produce them.

A second example of yoking of Eriksonian stages in this new concept being proposed of multiple emotional, or socio-affective, intelligences includes the following. This time, consider a patient who has Initiative and Generativity problems. He has a family but cannot keep a job because of flagging or failing motivation that he does not understand, despite having all the requisite skills and job support. The domains involved are emotional at the base, because he has difficulties with aspects of both experiencing emotions and their strategic use. For example, the perception of emotions is compromised as is their management. Therefore, he does not feel the other, empathize, read the mind from the perspective of the other, etc., nor have good emotional regulation and self-control skills. In the end, he is judged bright but lacking in empathy and emotional control. In terms of his Neo-Eriksonian development, his emotional deficits manifest in his generative tasks, including at work and home. His lack of initiative is tinged with some guilt, but less than might be expected according to the Eriksonian model, because of his emotional deficits.

As for the micro-moment changes that take place as he navigates the day, the more he can mask his difficulties, the less temper he displays, but his energetics take him only so far, and explosions of anger might mar not only his personal life but work life and his ability to keep his family and job. Psychotherapy is addressing his present control problems and past developmental issues, in part by asking for micro-moment awareness along the lines of the parameters of the case conceptualization just enunciated as well as understanding how to change (and foster preparation for change).

Comment This section of the epilogue is the final one, and therefore, it stands as the final one of the book before the last concluding comment. The Neo-Eriksonian multiple socio-affective emotional intelligences model presented appears a promising model because of its implications for psychotherapy, as indicated by the examples provided. As with all new models in the present book, it needs refinement, operationalization, and testing.

The study of causality, in general, requires rigorous study and research in all these ways. As the research is undertaken, the vitality and reverberations that the work might gather could animate further efforts toward unifying psychology with causality as a central component. The book is dedicated to that proposition and the continuing project it entails.

At press time, Harré and Moghaddam (2016) have edited a useful book on causality in social psychology and related social contexts. In Harré (2016) referred to the different "causal formats" and "causal discourses" of disciplines. He considered the concept of causation more specific than the one of causality with the former referring to relations involving "particulars" and the former more generic "processes." The book avoids jargon, and the first part is philosophical in subject matter. The most relevant chapter for present purposes is on mental health.

As a final comment to the book, its major strength is its comprehensive literature review and its conceptual integration. The major limitation of the book is it's broad range, which has to be the case because of its subject matter, and some of the redundancies across chapters, which are inevitable because of its scope.

Epilogue Conclusions

Epilogues are afterthoughts and, in the present case, the thoughts involved complement very well the text of the book that had been written before it was formulated. The book has examined the multiple causal influences on development, from genes to environment to free will and other personal contributions to our behavior. The epilogue has solidified the systems point of view in conceptualizing behavior and its causes. It has reinforced the interaction between top-down and bottom-up influences in systems (and in behavior), and has provided additional ways of conceiving of stages in development and the domains that grow in development. In this regard, free will belief is a critical domain in cognition that can develop in individual ways as per the present modeling exercise. At one point, it could become the superordinate concept in the hierarchy of beliefs related to causality and, therefore, influence self-control, making correct choices, and following through appropriately in our behavior, including at the moral level. Consequently, in this vein, a systems view of behavior allows for the bootstrapping of self-related factors into the gene/biology × environment/social factors that influence behavioral expression.

Even if there are powerful models in behavioral causality, such as the biopsychosocial one, it is important to note that causal modeling in psychology should be more about the individual than the general population to which models in psychology might be typically aimed. Behavior can be described from both a normative and an individualized perspective. However, normative data are averaged over individuals, and the types of modelling being considered, e.g., systems theory, gives primacy to the structure of individual behavior and its function.

The study of causality needs to become central in psychology, both in its own right and for its application to better ensuring optimal development, resolving psychopathology, and improving the human condition, in general. This book has tried to propel its study into the vanguard of the field of psychology and related disciplines. It can become the coalescing, integrating, unifying axis in this area, but it is a topic that is evolving constantly. This epilogue (and the book) concludes that the study of behavioral causality and the process of unifying psychology are reciprocal dynamic projects to which the present book is dedicated.

References

Achenbach, T. M. (1991). *The child behavior checklist/4–18*. Burlington, VT: University of Vermont.

Achenbach, T. M., & Rescorla, L. A. (2001). *Youth self-report for ages 11–18*. Burlington, VT: ASEBA.

Alvarez, A., & Booth, A. E. (2016). Exploring individual differences in preschoolers' causal stance. *Developmental Psychology, 42*, 411–422.

American Psychiatric Association. (1994). *Diagnostic and statistical manual of mental disorders* (4th ed.). Washington, DC: Author.

American Psychiatric Association. (2013). *Diagnostic and statistical manual of mental disorders* (5th ed.). Washington, DC: Author.

American Psychiatric Association. (2000). *Diagnostic and statistical manual of mental disorders* (4th ed., text rev.). Washington, DC: American Psychiatric Association.

Armour, C., Tsai, J., Durham, T. A., Charak, R., Biehn, T. L., Elhai, J. D., et al. (2015). Dimensional structure of DSM-5 posttraumatic stress symptoms: Support for a hybrid anhedonia and externalizing behaviors model. *Journal of Psychiatric Research, 61*, 106–113.

Ashley-Koch, A. E., Garrett, M. E., Gibson, J., Liu, Y., Dennis, M. F., Kimbrel, N. A., Veterans Affairs Mid-Atlantic Mental Illness Research, Education, and Clinical Center Workgroup, Beckham, J. C., & Hauser, M. A. (2015). Genome-wide association study of post-traumatic stress disorder in a cohort of Iraq-Afghanistan era veterans. *Journal of Affective Disorders, 184*, 225–234.

Baillargeon, R., Scott, R. M., & Bian, L. (2016). Psychological reasoning in infancy. *Annual Review of Psychology, 67*, 159–186.

Bak, P. (1996). *How nature works: The science of self-organized criticality*. New York: Springer-Verlag.

Barrouillet, P. (2015). Theories of cognitive development: From Piaget to today. *Developmental Review, 38*, 1–12.

Baumeister, R. F., & Monroe, A. E. (2014). Recent research on free will: Conceptualizations, beliefs, and processes. *Advances in Experimental Social Psychology, 50*, 1–52.

Baumeister, R. F., Vohs, K. D., & Oettingen, G. (2016). Pragmatic prospection: How and why people think about the future. *Review of General Psychology*. http://dx.doi.org/10.1037/gpr0000060

Belsky, J., Bakermans-Kranenburg, M. J., & van IJzendoorn, M. H. (2007). For better and for worse: Differential susceptibility to environmental influences. *Current Directions in Psychological Science, 16*, 300–304.

Berk, L. E. (2013). *Child development* (9th ed.). Boston, MA: Pearson.

Berk, L. E., & Meyers, A. B. (2016). *Infants, children, and adolescents* (8th ed.). Old Tappan, NJ: Pearson Education.

Bjorklund, D. F. (2015). Developing adaptations. *Developmental Review, 38*, 13–35.

Blake, D., Weathers, F., Nagy, L., Kaloupek, D., Gusman, F., Charney, D. S., et al. (1995). Development of a clinician-administered PTSD scale. *Journal of Traumatic Stress, 8*, 75–90.

Borsboom, D., & Cramer, A. O. J. (2013). Network analysis: An integrative approach to the structure of psychopathology. *Annual Review of Clinical Psychology, 9*, 91–121.

Bringmann, L. F., Vissers, N., Wichers, M., Geschwind, N., Kuppens, P., Peeters, F., et al. (2013). A network approach to psychopathology: New insights into clinical longitudinal data. *PLoS One, 8*, e60188.

Calkins, S. D. (2015). *Handbook of infant biopsychosocial development*. New York: Guilford Press.

Carey, S., Zaitchik, D., & Bascandziev, I. (2015). Theories of development: In dialog with Jean Piaget. *Developmental Review, 38*, 36–54.

Case, R. (1998). The development of conceptual structures. In W. Damon, D. Kuhn, & R. S. Siegler (Eds.),

Handbook of child psychology: Vol. 2. Cognition, perception & language (5th ed., pp. 745–800). New York: Wiley.

Case, R., Okamoto, Y., Henderson, B., & McKeough, A. (1993). Individual variability and consistency in cognitive development: New evidence for the existence of central conceptual structures. In R. Case & W. Edelstein (Eds.), *Contributions to human development* (The new structuralism in cognitive development: Theory and research on individual pathways, Vol. 23, pp. 71–100). New York: Karger.

Caspi, A., McClay, J., Moffitt, T., Mill, J., Martin, J., Craig, I. W., et al. (2002). Role of genotype in the cycle of violence in maltreated children. *Science, 297*, 851–854.

Caspi, A., Sugden, K., Moffitt, T. E., Taylor, A., Craig, I. W., Harrington, H., et al. (2003). Influence of life stress on depression: Moderation by a polymorphism in the 5-HTTgene. *Science, 301*, 386–389.

Chandler, D. (2015). A world without causation: Big data and the coming of age posthumanism. *Millennium: Journal of International Studies, 43*, 833–851.

Chen, J., & Gardner, H. (2011). Assessment of intellectual profiles: A perspective from multiple intelligence theory. In D. Flanagan & C. Graham (Eds.), *Contemporary intellectual assessment* (3rd ed., pp. 145–155). New York: Guilford Press.

Chilcoat, H. D., & Anthony, J. C. (1996). Impact of parent monitoring on initiation of drug use through late childhood. *Journal of American Academy of Child & Adolescent Psychiatry, 35*, 91–100.

Christensen, W., & Michael, J. (2016). From two systems to a multi-systems architecture for mindreading. *New Ideas in Psychology, 40*, 48–64.

Dalege, J., Borsboom, D., van Harreveld, F., van den Berg, H., & Conner, M. (2016). Toward a formalized account of attitudes: The causal attitude network (CAN) model. *Psychological Review, 123*, 2–22.

Daskalakis, N. P., De Kloet, E. R., Yehuda, R., Malaspina, D., & Kranz, T. M. (2015). Early life stress effects on glucocorticoid-BDNF interplay in the hippocampus. *Frontiers in Molecular Neuroscience, 8*. doi:10.3389/inmol.2015.00068

Demazeux, S. (2015). The ideal of scientific progress and the DSM. In S. Demazeux & P. Singy (Eds.), *The DSM-5 in perspective: Philosophical reflections on the psychiatric babel* (pp. 3–24). Dordrecht, Netherlands: Springer Science + Business Media.

Demazeux, S., & Singy, P. (2015). *The DSM-5 in perspective: Philosophical reflections on the psychiatric babel*. Dordrecht, Netherlands: Springer Science + Business Media.

Demetriou, A., Spanoudis, G., & Mouyi, A. (2010). A three-level model of the developing mind: Functional and neuronal substantiation and educational implications. In M. Ferrari & L. Vuletic (Eds.), *The developmental relations between mind, brain and education* (pp. 9–48). New York: Springer Science + Business Media.

Ekinici, B. (2014). The relationship among Sternberg's triarchic abilities, Gardner's multiple intelligences, and academic achievement. *Social Behavior and Personality, 42*, 625–634.

Elhai, J. D., Naifeh, J. A., Zucker, I. S., Gold, S. N., Deitsch, S. E., & Frueh, B. C. (2004). Discriminating malingered from genuine civilian posttraumatic stress disorder: A validation of three MMPI-2 Infrequency scales (F, Fp, and Fptsd). *Assessment, 11*, 139–144.

Ellis, G. F. R., Nobel, D., & O'Connor, T. (2012). Top-down causation: An integrating theme within and across the sciences. *Interface Focus, 2*, 1–3.

Feldman, G., Chandrashekar, S. P., & Wong, K. F. E. (2016). The freedom to excel: Belief in free will predicts better academic performance. *Personality and Individual Differences, 90*, 377–383.

Feldman, R., Vengrober, A., & Ebstein, R. P. (2014). Affiliation buffers stress: Cumulative genetic risk in oxytocin-vasopressin genes combines with early caregiving to predict PTSD in war-exposed young children. *Transcultural Psychiatry, 4*, e370.

Fischer, K. W. (1980). A theory of cognitive development: The control and construction of hierarchies of skills. *Psychological Review, 87*, 477–531.

Frewen, P. A., Schmittmann, V. D., Bringmann, L. F., & Borsboom, D. (2013). Perceived causal relations between anxiety, posttraumatic stress and depression: Extension to moderation, mediation, and network analysis. *European Journal of Psychotraumatology, 4*, 1–14.

Friston, K. (2010). The free-energy principle: A unified brain theory? *Nature Reviews: Neuroscience, 11*, 127–138.

Friston, K., Levin, M., Sengupta, B., & Pezzulo, G. (2015). Knowing one's place: A free-energy approach to pattern regulation. *Journal of Royal Society Interface, 12*, 1–12.

Frueh, B. C., Elhai, J. D., Grubaugh, A. L., Monnier, J., Kashdan, T. B., Sauvageot, J. A., et al. (2005). Documented combat exposure of US veterans seeking treatment for combat-related post-traumatic stress disorder. *British Journal of Psychiatry, 186*, 467–472.

Gagne, J. R., & Saudino, K. J. (2016). The development of inhibitory control in early childhood: A twin study from 2–3 years. *Developmental Psychology, 52*, 391–399.

Gardner, H. (1983). *Frames of mind: The theory of multiple intelligences*. New York: Basic Books.

Gardner, H. (1993). *Multiple intelligences: The theory in practice*. New York: Basic Books.

Goenjian, A. K., Noble, E. P., Steinberg, A. M., Walling, D. P., Stepanyan, S. T., Dandekar, S., et al. (2015). Association of COMT and TPH-2 genes with DSM-5 based PTSD symptoms. *Journal of Affective Disorders, 172*, 472–478.

Goldin-Meadow, S. (2015). From action to abstraction: Gesture as a mechanism of change. *Developmental Review, 38*, 167–184.

Gordon, I., & Feldman, R. (2015). A biopsychosocial perspective on synchrony and the development of human parental care. In S. D. Calkins (Ed.), *Handbook of infant biopsychosocial development* (pp. 283–312). New York: Guilford Press.

Grizenko, N., Fortier, M.-È., Gaudreau-Simard, M., Jolicoeur, C., & Joober, R. (2015). The effect of maternal stress during pregnancy on IQ and ADHD symptomatology. *Journal of the Canadian Academy of Child and Adolescent Psychiatry, 24*, 92–99.

Grossmann, T. (2015). The development of social brain functions in infancy. *Psychology Bulletin, 141*, 1266–1287.

Hanson, J. L., Knodt, A. R., Brigidi, B. D., & Hariri, A. R. (2015). Lower structural integrity of the uncinate fasciculus is associated with a history of child maltreatment and future psychological vulnerability to stress. *Development and Psychopathology, 27*, 1611–1619.

Harré, R. (2016). The discourse frame. In R. Harré & F. M. Maghaddam (Eds.), *Questioning causality: Scientific explorations of cause and consequence across social contexts* (pp. 3–20). Santa Barbara, CA: ABC-CLIO, LLC.

Harré, R., & Maghaddam, F. M. (2016). *Questioning causality: Scientific explorations of cause and consequence across social contexts*. Santa Barbara, CA: ABC-CLIO, LLC.

Heyes, C. (2015). When does social learning become cultural learning? *Developmental Science*. doi:10.1111/desc.12350.

Hostinar, C. E., Mroczek, D. K., Lachman, M. E., Seeman, T. E., & Miller, G. E. (2015). Addictive contributions of childhood adversity and recent stressors to inflammation at midlife: Findings from the MIDUS study. *Developmental Psychology, 11*, 1630–1644.

Jedd, K., Hunt, R. H., Cicchetti, D., Hunt, E., Cowell, R. A., Rogosch, F. A., et al. (2015). Long-term consequences of childhood maltreatment: Altered amygdala functional connectivity. *Development and Psychopathology, 27*, 1577–1589.

Kauffman, S. (1993). *The origins of order: Self-organization and selection in evolution*. New York. Oxford University Press.

Keating, D. P. (2016). Transformative role of epigenetics in child development research: Commentary on the special section. *Child Development, 87*, 135–142.

Kirk, S. A., Cohen, D., & Gomory, T. (2015). DSM-5: The delayed demise of descriptive diagnosis. In S. Demazeux & P. Singy (Eds.), *The DSM-5 in perspective: Philosophical reflections on the psychiatric babel* (pp. 63–81). Dordrecht, Netherlands: Springer Science + Business Media.

Konecky, B., Meyer, E. C., Kimbrel, N. A., & Morissette, S. B. (2015). The structure of DSM-5 posttraumatic stress disorder symptoms in war veterans. *Anxiety, Stress, & Coping*. doi:10.1080/10615806.2015.1081178

Kopala-Sibley, D. C., Dougherty, L. R., Dyson, M. W., Laptook, R. S., Olino, T. M., Bufferd, S. J., et al. (2015). Early childhood cortisol reactivity moderates the effects of parent–child relationship quality on the development of children's temperament in early childhood. *Developmental Science*. doi:10.1111/desc.12378.

Kotabe, H. P., & Hofmann, W. (2015). On integrating the components of self-control. *Perspectives on Psychological Science, 10*, 618–638.

Larrabee, G. J., Millis, S. R., & Meyers, J. E. (2009). 40 plus or minus 10, a new magical number: Reply to Russell. *The Clinical Neuropsychologist, 23*, 841–849.

Lee, J. J., & McGue, M. (2016). Why behavioral genetics matters: Comment on Plomin et al. (2016). *Perspectives on Psychological Science, 11*, 29–30.

Leerkes, E. M., & Parade, S. H. (2015). A psychobiological perspective on emotional development within the family context. In S. D. Calkins (Ed.), *Handbook of infant biopsychosocial development* (pp. 206–231). New York: Guilford Press.

Legare, C. H., & Nielsen, M. (2015). Imitation and innovation: The dual engines of cultural learning. *Trends in Cognitive Sciences, 19*, 688–699.

Lester, B. M., Conradt, E., & Marsit, C. (2016). Introduction to the special section on epigenetics. *Child Development, 87*, 29–37.

Lewis, M. D. (2005). Bridging emotion theory and neurobiology through dynamic systems modeling. *Behavioral and Brain Sciences, 28*, 169–245.

Li, Y., Sulik, M. J., Eisenberg, N., Spinrad, T. L., Lemery-Chalfant, K., Stover, D. A., et al. (2016). Predicting childhood effortful control from interactions between early parental quality and children's dopamine transporter gene haplotypes. *Development and Psychopathology, 28*, 199–212.

Libertus, K., Joh, A. S., & Needham, A. W. (2015). Motor training at 3 months affects object exploration 12 months later. *Developmental Science*. doi:10.1111/desc.12370.

Liu, P., Wang, L., Cao, C., Wang, R., Zhang, J., Zhang, B., et al. (2014). The underlying dimensions of DSM-5 posttraumatic stress disorder symptoms in an epidemiological sample of Chinese earthquake survivors. *Journal of Anxiety Disorders, 28*, 345–351.

Lourenço, O. M. (2016). Developmental stages, Piagetian stages in particular: A critical review. *New Ideas in Psychology, 40*, 123–137.

Malone, J. C., Liu, S. R., Vaillant, G. E., Rentz, D. M., & Waldinger, R. J. (2016). Midlife Eriksonian psychosocial development: Setting the stage for late-life cognitive and emotional health. *Developmental Psychology, 52*, 496–508.

Marshall, T. R., Bergmann, T. O., & Jensen, O. (2015). Frontoparietal structural connectivity mediates the top-down control of neuronal synchronization associated with selective attention. *PLoS Biology, 13*, e1002272.

Martinez-Torteya, C., Bogat, G. A., Levendosky, A. A., & von Eye, A. (2016). The influence of prenatal intimate partner violence exposure on hypothalamic-pituitary-adrenal axis reactivity and childhood internalizing and externalizing symptoms. *Development and Psychopathology, 28*, 55–72.

Mascolo, M. F., & Fischer, K. W. (2007). The codevelopment of self and sociomoral emotions during the toddler years. In C. A. Brownell & C. B. Kopp (Eds.), *Socioemotional development in the toddler years: Transitions and transformation* (pp. 66–99). New York: Guilford Press.

Mascolo, M. F., & Fischer, K. W. (2015). Dynamic development of thinking, feeling, and acting. In W. F. Overton & P. C. M. Molenaar (Eds.), *Handbook of child psychology and developmental science. Vol. 1: Theory and method* (7th ed., pp. 240–317). Hoboken, NJ: Wiley.

Mayer, J., Roberts, R., & Barsade, S. (2008). Human abilities: Emotional intelligence. *Annual Review of Psychology, 59*, 507–536.

Mayer, J., Salovey, P., & Caruso, D. (2002). *Mayer-Salovey-Caruso emotional intelligence test (Version 2.0). User's manual*. Toronto, CA: Multi-Health Systems.

McKeough, A., & Griffiths, S. (2010). Adolescent narrative thought: Developmental and neurological evidence in support of central social structures. In M. Ferrari & L. Vuletic (Eds.), *Developmental relations among mind, brain and education* (pp. 213–230). New York: Springer Science + Business Media.

McNally, R. J., Robinaugh, D. J., Wu, G. W. Y., Wang, L., Deserno, M. K., & Borsboom, D. (2015). Mental disorders as causal systems: A network approach to posttraumatic stress disorder. *Clinical Psychological Science, 3*, 836–849.

Meaney, M. (2010). Epigenetics and the biological definition of gene x environment interactions. *Child Development, 81*, 49–71.

Miller, M. W., Wolf, E. J., & Keane, T. M. (2014). Posttraumatic stress disorder in DSM-5: New criteria and controversies. *Clinical Psychology: Science and Practice, 21*, 208–220.

Montirosso, R., Provenzi, L., Fumagalli, M., Sirgiovanni, I., Giorda, R., Pozzoli, U., et al. (2016). Serotonin transporter gene (SLC6A4) methylation associates with NICU stay and 3-month-old temperament in preterm infants. *Child Development, 87*, 38–48.

Naumova, O. Y., Hein, S., Suderman, M., Barbot, B., Lee, M., Raefski, A., et al. (2016). Epigenetic patterns modulate the connection between developmental dynamics of parenting and offspring psychosocial adjustment. *Child Development, 87*, 98–110.

Operskalski, J. T., Paul, E. J., Colom, R., Barbey, A. K., & Grafman, J. (2015). Lesion mapping the four-factor structure of emotional intelligence. *Frontiers in Human Neuroscience, 9*, 649. doi:10.3389/fnhum.2015.00649.

Orquin, J. L., & Kurzban, R. (2015). A meta-analysis of blood glucose effects on human decision making. *Psychological Bulletin*. http://dx.doi.org/10.1037/bul0000035

Overton, W. F. (2015). Processes, relations, and relational-developmental-systems. In W. F. Overton & P. C. M. Molenaar (Eds.), *Handbook of child psychology and developmental science. Vol. 1: Theory and method* (7th ed., pp. 63–157). Hoboken, NJ: Wiley.

Overton, W. F., & Molenaar, P. C. M. (2015). Concepts, theory, and method in developmental science: A view of the issues. In W. F. Overton & P. C. M. Molenaar (Eds.), *Handbook of child psychology and developmental science. Vol. 1: Theory and method* (7th ed., pp. 49–62). Hoboken, NJ: Wiley.

Parade, S. H., Ridout, K. K., Seifer, R., Armstrong, D. A., Marsit, C. J., McWilliams, M. A., et al. (2016). Methylation of the glucocorticoid receptor gene promoter in preschoolers: Links with internalizing behavior problems. *Child Development, 87*, 86–97.

Peckins, M. K., Susman, E. J., Negriff, S., Noll, J., & Trickett, P. K. (2015). Cortisol profiles: A test for adaptive calibration of the stress response system in maltreated and nonmaltreated youth. *Development and Psychopathology, 27*, 1461–1470.

Peterson, M. B., & Aarøe, L. (2015). Birth weight and social trust in adulthood: Evidence for early calibration of social cognition. *Psychological Science, 26*, 1681–1692.

Phillips, A. C., Carroll, D., & Der, G. (2015). Negative life events and symptoms of depression and anxiety: Stress causation and/ or stress generation. *Anxiety, Stress, & Coping, 28*, 357–371.

Piaget, J. (1970). *Structuralism*. (C. Maschler, Trans.). New York: Basic Books (Original work published in 1968).

Plomin, R., DeFries, J. C., Knopik, V. S., & Neiderhiser, J. M. (2016). Top 10 replicated findings from behavioral genetics. *Perspectives on Psychological Science, 11*, 3–23.

Poland, J. (2015). DSM-5 and research concerning mental illness. In S. Demazeux & P. Singy (Eds.), *The DSM-5 in perspective: Philosophical reflections on the psychiatric babel* (pp. 25–42). Dordrecht, Netherlands: Springer Science + Business Media.

Räikkönen, K., Pesonen, A.-K., O'Reilly, J. R., Tuovinen, S., Lahti, M., Kajantie, E., et al. (2015). Maternal depressive symptoms during pregnancy, placental expression of genes regulating glucocorticoid and serotonin function and infant regulatory behaviors. *Psychological Medicine, 45*, 3217–3226.

Rakison, D. H., Smith, G. H., & Ali, A. (2016). Who is the dynamic duo? How infants learn about the identity of objects in a causal chain. *Developmental Psychology, 52*, 355–363.

Rietveld, C. A., Medland, S. F., Derringer, J., Yang, J., Esko, T., Martin, N. W., et al. (2013). GWAS of 126,559 individuals identifies genetic variants associated with educational attainment. *Science, 340*, 1467–1471.

Rochat, P. (2015). Layers of awareness in development. *Developmental Review, 38*, 122–145.

Rubinov, M., Sporns, O., Thivierge, J. P., & Breakspear, M. (2011). Neurobiologically realistic determinants of self-organized criticality in networks of spiking neurons. *PLOS Computational Biology, 7*, e1002038.

Russell, B. (1918). *Mysticism and logic*. London: Allen & Unwin.

Scarpa, A. (2015). Physiological arousal and its dysregulation in child maladjustment. *Current Directions in Psychological Science, 24*, 345–351.

Smearman, E. L., Almli, L. M., Conneely, K. N., Brody, G. H., Sales, J. M., Bradley, B., et al. (2016). Oxytocin

receptor genetic and epigenetic variations: Association with child abuse and psychiatric symptoms. *Child Development, 87*, 122–134.
Sporns, O., & Betzel, R. F. (2016). Modular brain networks. *Annual Review of Psychology, 67*, 613–640.
Sternberg, R. J. (1985). *Beyond IQ: A triarchic theory of human intelligence*. New York: Cambridge University Press.
Sternberg, R. J. (2015). Multiple intelligences in the new age of thinking. In S. Goldstein, D. Princiotta, & J. A. Naglier (Eds.), *Handbook of intelligence: Evolutionary theory, historical perspective, and current concepts* (pp. 229–241). New York: Springer Science Business + Business Media.
Stroud, L. R., Papandonatos, G. D., Salisbury, A. L., Phipps, M. G., Huestis, M. A., Niaura, R., et al. (2016). Epigenetic regulation of placental NR3C1: Mechanism underlying prenatal programming of infant neurobehavior by maternal smoking. *Child Development, 87*, 49–60.
Suhr, J. A. (2015). *Psychological assessment: A problem-solving approach*. New York: Guilford Press.
Sylvester, C. M., Barch, D. M., Harms, M. P., Belden, A. C., Oakberg, T. J., Gold, A. L., et al. (2016). Early childhood behavioral inhibition predicts cortical thickness in adulthood. *Journal of American Academy of Child & Adolescent Psychiatry, 55*, 122–129.
Tearne, J. E., Allen, K. L., Herbison, C. E., Lawrence, D., Whitehouse, A. J. O., Sawyer, M. G., et al. (2015). The association between prenatal environment and children's mental health trajectories from 2 to 14 years. *European Child Adolescent Psychiatry, 24*, 1015–1024.
Thelen, E., & Smith, L. B. (2006). Dynamic systems theories. In R. M. Lerner (Ed.), *Handbook of child psychology. Vol. 1: Theoretical models and human development* (6th ed., pp. 258–312). Hoboken, NJ: Wiley.
Thibodeau, E. L., Cicchetti, D., & Rogosch, F. A. (2015). Child maltreatment, impulsivity, and antisocial behavior in African American children: Moderation effects from a cumulative dopaminergic gene index. *Development and Psychopathology, 27*, 1621–1636.
Trucco, E. M., Villafuerte, S., Heitzeg, M. M., Burmeister, M., & Zucker, R. A. (2016). Susceptibility effects of GABA receptor subunit alpha-2 (GABRA2) variants and parental monitoring on externalizing behavior trajectories: Risk and protection conveyed by the minor allele. *Development and Psychopathology, 28*, 15–26.
Tsai, J., Harpaz-Rotem, I., Armour, C., Southwick, S. M., Krystal, J. H., & Pietrzak, R. H. (2015). Dimensional structure of DSM-5 posttraumatic stress disorder symptoms: Results from the National Health and Resilience in Veterans Study. *Journal of Clinical Psychiatry, 76*, 546–553.
Tsou, J. Y. (2015). DSM-5 and psychiatry's second revolution: Descriptive vs. theoretical approaches to psychiatric classification. In S. Demazeux & P. Singy (Eds.), *The DSM-5 in perspective: Philosophical reflections on the psychiatric babel* (pp. 43–62). Dordrecht, Netherlands: Springer Science + Business Media.
Tung, I., & Lee, S. S. (2016). Latent trajectories of adolescent antisocial behavior: Serotonin transporter linked polymorphic region (*5-HTTLPR*) genotype influences sensitivity to perceived parental support. *Developmental Psychopathology*. doi:10.1017/S0954579416000031.
Turkheimer, E. (2016). Weak genetic explanation 20 years later: Reply to Plomin et al. (2016). *Perspectives on Psychological Science, 11*, 24–28.
Tyrka, A. R., Ridout, K. K., Parade, S. H., Paquette, A., Marsit, C. J., & Seifer, R. (2015). Childhood maltreatment and methylation of FK506 binding protein 5 gene (*FKBP5*). *Development and Psychopathology, 27*, 1637–1645.
Vaillant, G. E., & Milofsky, E. (1980). Natural history of male psychological health: IX. Empirical evidence for Erikson's model of the life cycle. *The American Journal of Psychiatry, 137*, 1348–1359.
Wang, L., Zhang, L., Armour, C., Cao, C., Qing, Y., Zhang, J., et al. (2015). Assessing the underlying dimensionality of DSM-5 PTSD symptoms in Chinese adolescents surviving the 2008 Wenchuan earthquake. *Journal of Anxiety Disorders, 21*, 90–97.
Wechsler, D. (2003). *Wechsler intelligence scale for children* (4th ed.). San Antonio, TX: Psychological Corporation.
Witherington, D. C. (2015). Dynamic systems in developmental science. In W. F. Overton & P. C. M. Molenaar (Eds.), *Handbook of child psychology and developmental science. Vol. 1: Theory and method* (7th ed., pp. 158–239). Hoboken, NJ: Wiley.
World Health Organization. (2017). *International classification of disease,* 11th Revision.
Young, G. (2016). PTSD in court. *International Journal of Law and Psychiatry, 38*.
Young, G. (2011). *Development and causality: Neo-Piagetian perspectives*. New York: Springer Science + Business Media.
Young, G. (2012). A unitary Neo-Piagetian/Neo-Eriksonian model of development: Fundamental assumptions and meta-issues. *New Ideas in Psychology, 30*, 241–249.
Young, G. (2015a). Causality in psychiatry: A hybrid symptom network construct model. *Frontiers in Psychiatry, 6*, 164. doi:10.3389/psyt.2015.00164.
Young, G. (2015b). Dimensions and dissociation in PTSD in the DSM-5: Towards eight core symptoms. *Psychological Injury and Law, 8*, 219–232.
Young, G. (2015c). Malingering in forensic disability-related assessments: Prevalence 15 +/– 15%. *Psychological Injury and Law, 8*, 188–199.
Zelazany, K., & Simms, L. J. (2015). Confirmatory factor analysis of DSM-5 posttraumatic stress disorder symptoms in psychiatric samples differing in Criterion A status. *Journal of Anxiety Disorders, 34*, 15–23.
Zelazo, P. D. (2015). Executive function: Reflection, iterative reprocessing, complexity, and the developing brain. *Developmental Review, 38*, 55–68.
Zhang, Y., Liu, F., Chen, H., Li, M., Duan, X., Xie, B., et al. (2015). Intranetwork and internetwork functional connectivity alterations in post-traumatic stress disorder. *Journal of Affective Disorders, 187*, 114–121.

Index

G. Young, *Unifying Causality and Psychology*, DOI 10.1007/978-3-319-24094-7

D

J

K

L

N

MIX
Papier aus verantwortungsvollen Quellen
Paper from responsible sources
FSC® C105338

If you have any concerns about our products,
you can contact us on
ProductSafety@springernature.com

In case Publisher is established outside the EU,
the EU authorized representative is:
Springer Nature Customer Service Center GmbH
Europaplatz 3, 69115 Heidelberg, Germany

Printed by Libri Plureos GmbH
in Hamburg, Germany